continued on back inside cover

E-commerce

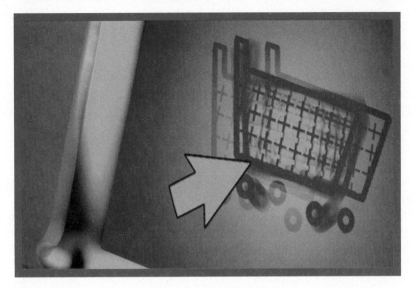

business. technology. society.

SIXTH EDITION

Kenneth C. Laudon
New York University

Carol Guercio Traver
Azimuth Interactive, Inc.

Prentice Hall

Boston   Columbus   Indianapolis   New York   San Francisco   Upper Saddle River
Amsterdam   Cape Town   Dubai   London   Madrid   Milan   Munich   Paris   Montreal   Toronto
Delhi   Mexico City   Sao Paulo   Sydney   Hong Kong   Seoul   Singapore   Taipei   Tokyo

Editorial Director: Sally Yagan
Editor in Chief: Eric Svendsen
Executive Editor: Bob Horan
Editorial Project Manager: Kelly Loftus
Director of Marketing: Patrice Jones
Senior Marketing Manager: Anne Fahlgren
Marketing Assistant: Melinda Jensen
Senior Managing Editor: Judy Leale
Production Project Manager: Karalyn Holland
Senior Operations Supervisor: Arnold Vila
Operations Specialist: Ilene Kahn
Senior Art Director: Janet Slowik

Art Director: Steve Frim
Cover Designer: Jodi Notowitz
Manager, Rights and Permissions: Megan Miller
Media Editor: Denise Vaughn
Media Project Manager: Lisa Rinaldi
Full Service Project Management: Azimuth Interactive, Inc.
Composition: Azimuth Interactive, Inc.
Printer/Binder: Edwards Brothers, Inc.
Cover Printer: Lehigh-Phoenix Color/Hagarstown
Text Font: ITC Veljovic Std. Book, 9.5pt

Credits and acknowledgements borrowed from other sources and reproduced, with permission, in this textbook appear on page C-1.

Microsoft® and Windows® are registered trademarks of the Microsoft Corporation in the U.S.A. and other countries. Screen shots and icons reprinted with permission from the Microsoft Corporation. This book is not sponsored or endorsed by or affiliated with the Microsoft Corporation.

Library of Congress Cataloging-in-Publication Information is Available

10 9 8 7 6 5 4 3

Prentice Hall
is an imprint of

www.pearsonhighered.com

ISBN 10: 0-13-610057-0
ISBN 13: 978-0-13-610057-7

PREFACE

WHAT'S NEW IN THE SIXTH EDITION

Currency

The 6th edition features all new or updated opening, closing and "Insight On" cases. The text, as well as all of the data, figures and tables in the book, have been updated through September 2009 with the latest marketing and business intelligence available from eMarketer, Pew Internet & American Life Project, Forrester Research, Jupiter Research, Gartner and other industry sources.

New Themes and Content

The 6th edition spotlights the following new themes and content:

Business

• Impact of the 2009 recession: Despite the recession, e-commerce continues to thrive.
• Emergence of new e-commerce business opportunities for mobile content (the "4th screen"), software applications, location-based services, shopping on the fly, and mobile payment
• Continued explosive growth in Web 2.0 services such as Twitter and Facebook and expansion of social marketing opportunities
• E-books finally take off
• "Free" and "Freemium" business models for digital content.
• New search engines such as Bing challenge Google
• Music labels, Hollywood and TV producers strike deals for Web distribution
• Google's Chrome enters Microsoft's market, threatens to become a new operating system for netbooks

Technology

• Rapid growth of the mobile digital platform including smartphones, netbooks, and e-book readers, coupled with 3G and 4G cellular network expansion
• Cloud computing provides the computing infrastructure for a massive increase in digital information

- Open source software tools such as Drupal and Hadoop, and declining hardware prices, greatly lower the cost of developing sophisticated Web sites
- Internet security concerns remain high; cyberwarfare incidents increase
- Web 3.0 and the semantic Web continues to inspire technology firms and entrepreneurs
- Net neutrality supporters reconsider differential pricing

Society
- Growth of the mobile, "always on" culture in business and family life
- Intellectual property issues remain a source of conflict; movement toward resolution in some areas, such as Google's deal with publishing industry
- Digital piracy remains prevalent, despite the shutdown of P2P network Pirate's Bay
- Privacy and user control of personal information on social networks conflict with company attempts to monetize investment
- Most new Internet growth in Asia and China; localization of Web increases
- Venture investing in e-commerce drastically falls off, yet entrepreneurial startup firms are as numerous as ever
- Growing government surveillance of Internet users and Web sites

WELCOME TO THE NEW E-COMMERCE

In the 14 years since it began in 1995, electronic commerce has grown in the United States from a standing start to a $228 billion retail business and a $3.4 trillion business-to-business juggernaut, bringing about enormous change in business firms, markets, and consumer behavior. Economies and business firms around the globe, in Europe, Asia, and Latin America, are being similarly affected. During that short time, e-commerce has itself been transformed from its origin as a mechanism for online retail sales in to something much broader. Today, e-commerce has become the platform for new, unique services and capabilities that are just impossible in the physical world. There is no physical world counterpart to Facebook, or Twittter, or Google search, or a host of other recent online innovations. Welcome to the new e-commerce!

Although e-commerce in 2009 has been impacted by the worldwide economic recession, in the next five years, e-commerce in all of its forms is still projected to continue growing at high single-digit rates, becoming the fastest-growing form of commerce in the world. Just as automobiles, airplanes, and electronics defined the twentieth century, so will e-commerce of all kinds define business and society in the twenty-first century. The rapid movement toward an e-commerce economy and society is being led by both established business firms such as Wal-Mart, Ford, IBM, JCPenney, and General Electric, and newer entrepreneurial firms such as Google, Amazon, Facebook, MySpace, Twitter, YouTube, and Photobucket. Students of business and information technology need a thorough grounding in electronic commerce in order to be effective and successful managers in the next decade. This book is written for tomorrow's managers.

While newer Web 2.0 firms such as Facebook, MySpace, YouTube, Twitter, Photobucket, Flickr, and Blinkx have grown explosively in the last two years and grab our attention, the traditional forms of retail e-commerce and services also remain vital and have proven to be more resilient than traditional retail channels in facing the economic recession that has occurred during the past year. The experience of these firms over the last fifteen years is also a focus of this book. The defining characteristic of these firms is that they are profitable, sustainable, efficient, and innovative firms with powerful brand names. Many of these now-experienced retail and service firms, such as eBay, Amazon, E*Trade, Priceline, and Expedia, are survivors of the first era of e-commerce, from 1995 to spring 2000. These surviving firms have evolved their business models, integrated their online and offline operations, and changed their revenue models to become profitable. Students must understand how to build these kinds of e-commerce businesses in order to help the business firms they manage to succeed in the e-commerce era.

It would be foolish to ignore the lessons learned in the early period of e-commerce. Like so many technology revolutions in the past—automobiles, electricity, telephones, television, and biotechnology—there was an explosion of entrepreneurial efforts, followed by consolidation. By 2005, the survivors of the early period were moving to establish profitable businesses while maintaining rapid growth in revenues. In 2010, e-commerce is entering a new period of explosive entrenprenurial activity focusing on social networks, and the mobile digital platform created by smartphones and netbooks. These technologies and social behaviors are bringing about extraordinary changes to markets, industries, individual businesses, and society as a whole. E-commerce is generating thousands of new jobs for young managers in all fields from marketing to management, entrepreneurial studies, and information systems. Today, e-commerce has moved into the mainstream life of established businesses that have the market brands and financial muscle required for the long-term deployment of e-commerce technologies and methods. If you are working in an established business, chances are the firm's e-commerce capabilities and Web presence are important factors for its success. If you want to start a new business, chances are very good that the knowledge you learn in this book will be very helpful.

BUSINESS. TECHNOLOGY. SOCIETY.

We believe that in order for business and technology students to really understand e-commerce, they must understand the relationships among e-commerce business concerns, Internet technology, and the social and legal context of e-commerce. These three themes permeate all aspects of e-commerce, and therefore in each chapter we present material that explores the business, technological, and social aspects of that chapter's main topic.

Given the continued growth and diffusion of e-commerce, all students—regardless of their major discipline—must also understand the basic economic and business forces driving e-commerce. E-commerce has created new electronic markets where prices are more transparent, markets are global, and trading is highly efficient, though not perfect. E-commerce has a direct impact on a firm's relationship with suppliers, customers, competitors, and partners, as well as how firms market products, advertise, and use brands. Whether you are interested in marketing and sales, design, production, finance, information systems, or logistics, you will need to know how e-commerce technologies can be used to reduce supply chain costs, increase production efficiency, and tighten the relationship with customers. This text is written to help you understand the fundamental business issues in e-commerce.

We spend a considerable amount of effort analyzing the business models and strategies of "pure-play" online companies and established businesses now employing "bricks-and-clicks" business models. We explore why many early e-commerce firms failed and the strategic, financial, marketing, and organizational challenges they faced. We also discuss how e-commerce firms learned from the mistakes of early firms, and how established firms are using e-commerce to succeed. Above all, we attempt to bring a strong sense of business realism and sensitivity to the often exaggerated descriptions of e-commerce. As founders of a dot.com company and participants in the e-commerce revolution, we have learned that the "E" in e-commerce does not stand for "easy."

The Web and e-commerce has caused a major revolution in marketing and advertising in the United States. We spend two chapters discussing how marketing and advertising dollars are moving away from traditional media, and towards online media, creating significant growth in search engine marketing, targeted display advertising, online rich media/video ads, and social marketing techniques.

E-commerce is driven by Internet technology. Internet technology, and information technology in general, is perhaps the star of the show. Without the Internet, e-commerce would be virtually nonexistent. Accordingly, we provide three specific chapters on the Internet and e-commerce technology, and in every chapter we provide continuing coverage by illustrating how the topic of the chapter is being shaped by new information technologies. For instance, Internet technology drives developments in security and payment systems, marketing strategies and advertising, financial applications, business-to-business trade, and retail e-commerce. We discuss the rapid growth of the mobile digital platform, the emergence of cloud computing, new open source software tools and applications that enable Web 2.0, and new types of Internet-based information systems that support electronic business-to-business markets.

E-commerce is not only about business and technology, however. The third part of the equation for understanding e-commerce is society. E-commerce and Internet technologies have important social consequences that business leaders can ignore only at their peril. E-commerce has challenged our concepts of privacy, intellectual property, and even our ideas about national sovereignty and governance. Google, Amazon, and assorted advertising networks maintain profiles on millions of U.S. and foreign online shoppers. The proliferation of illegally copied music and videos on the Internet, and the growth of social networking sites often based on displaying copyrighted materials without permission, are challenging the intellectual property rights of record labels, studios, and artists. And many countries—including the United States—are demanding to control the content of Web sites displayed within their borders for political and social reasons. Tax authorities in the United States and Europe are demanding that e-commerce sites pay sales taxes. As a result of these challenges to existing institutions, e-commerce and the Internet are the subject of increasing investigation, litigation, and legislation. Business leaders need to understand these societal developments, and they cannot afford to assume any longer that the Internet is borderless, beyond social control and regulation, or a place where market efficiency is the only consideration. In addition to an entire chapter devoted to the social and legal implications of e-commerce, each chapter contains material highlighting the social implications of e-commerce.

FEATURES AND COVERAGE

Strong Conceptual Foundation We analyze e-commerce, digital markets, and e-business firms just as we would ordinary businesses and markets using concepts from economics, marketing, finance, philosophy, and information systems. We try to avoid ad hoc theorizing of the sort that sprang breathlessly from the pages of many journals in the early years of e-commerce.

Some of the important concepts from economics and marketing that we use to explore e-commerce are transaction cost, network externalities, perfect digital markets, segmentation, price dispersion, targeting, and positioning. Important concepts from the study of information systems and technologies play an important role in the book, including Internet standards and protocols, client/server computing, multi-tier server systems, cloud computing, mobile digital platform and wireless technologies, and public key encryption, among many others. From the literature on ethics and society, we use important concepts such as intellectual property, privacy, information rights and rights management, governance, public health, and welfare.

From the literature on business, we use concepts such as business process design, return on investment, strategic advantage, industry competitive environment, oligopoly, and monopoly. One of the witticisms that emerged from the early years of e-commerce and that still seems apt is the notion that e-commerce changes everything except the rules of business. Businesses still need to make a profit in order to survive in the long term.

Real-World Business Firm Focus From Akamai Technologies, to Google, Microsoft, Apple, and Amazon, to Facebook, Twitter, and Myspace, to Liquidation.com and VWSupplyGroup.com, this book contains well over 100 real-company examples that place coverage in the context of actual dot.com businesses. You'll find these examples in each chapter, as well as in special features such as chapter-opening and chapter-closing cases, and "Insight on" boxes.

In-depth Coverage of B2B E-commerce We devote an entire chapter to an examination of B2B e-commerce. In writing this chapter, we developed a unique and easily understood classification schema to help students understand this complex arena of e-commerce. This chapter covers four types of Net marketplaces (e-distributors, e-procurement companies, exchanges, and industry consortia) as well as the development of private industrial networks and collaborative commerce.

Current and Future Technology Coverage Internet and related information technologies continue to change rapidly. The most important changes for e-commerce include dramatic price reductions in e-commerce infrastructure (making it much less expensive to develop sophisticated Web sites), the explosive growth in the mobile digital platform such as iPhones and netbooks, and expansion in the development of social technologies. What was once a shortage of telecommunications capacity has now turned into a surplus, PC prices have continued to fall, new client-side devices have emerged, Internet high-speed broadband connections are now typical and are continuing to show double-digit growth, and wireless technologies such as Wi-Fi and cellular broadband are playing a larger role in mobile Internet access. While we thoroughly discuss the current Internet environment, we devote considerable attention to describing Web 2.0 and Internet II technologies and applications such as the advanced network infrastructure, fiber optics, wireless Web and 3G and 4G technologies, Wi-Fi, IP multicasting, and future guaranteed service levels.

Up-to-Date Coverage of the Research Literature   This text is well grounded in the e-commerce research literature. We have sought to include, where appropriate, references and analysis of the latest e-commerce research findings, as well as many classic articles, in all of our chapters. We have drawn especially on the disciplines of economics, marketing, and information systems and technologies, as well as law journals and broader social science research journals including sociology and psychology.

Special Attention to the Social and Legal Aspects of E-commerce   We have paid special attention throughout the book to the social and legal context of e-commerce. Chapter 8 is devoted to a thorough exploration of four ethical dimensions of e-commerce: information privacy, intellectual property, governance, and protecting public welfare on the Internet. We have included an analysis of the latest Federal Trade Commission and other regulatory and nonprofit research reports, and their likely impact on the e-commerce environment.

OVERVIEW OF THE BOOK

The book is organized into four parts.

Part 1, "Introduction to E-commerce," provides an introduction to the major themes of the book. Chapter 1 defines e-commerce, distinguishes between e-commerce and e-business, and defines the different types of e-commerce. Chapter 2 introduces and defines the concepts of business model and revenue model, describes the major e-commerce business and revenue models for both B2C and B2B firms, and introduces the basic business concepts required throughout the text for understanding e-commerce firms including industry structure, value chains, and firm strategy.

Part 2, "Technology Infrastructure for E-commerce," focuses on the technology infrastructure that forms the foundation for all e-commerce. Chapter 3 traces the historical development of Internet I—the first Internet—and thoroughly describes how today's Internet works. A major focus of this chapter is Web 2.0 applications, and the emerging Internet II that is now under development and will shape the future of e-commerce. Chapter 4 builds on the Internet chapter by focusing on the steps managers need to follow in order to build a commercial Web site. This e-commerce infrastructure chapter covers the systems analysis and design process that should be followed in building an e-commerce Web site; the major decisions surrounding the decision to outsource site development and/or hosting; and how to choose software, hardware, and other tools that can improve Web site performance. Chapter 5 focuses on Internet security and payments, building on the e-commerce infrastructure discussion of the previous chapter by describing the ways security can be provided over the Internet. This chapter defines digital information security, describes the major threats to security, and then discusses both the technology and policy solutions available to business managers seeking to secure their firm's sites. This chapter concludes with a section on Internet payment systems. We identify the stakeholders in payment systems, the dimensions to consider in creating payment systems, and the various types of online payment systems (credit cards, stored value payment systems such as PayPal, digital wallets such as Google Checkout and others).

Part 3, "Business Concepts and Social Issues," focuses directly on the business concepts and social-legal issues that surround the development of e-commerce. Chapter 6 focuses on e-commerce consumer behavior, the Internet audience, and introduces the student to the basics of online marketing and branding, including online marketing technologies and marketing strategies. Chapter 7 is devoted to online marketing communications, such as online advertising, e-mail marketing, and search-engine marketing. Chapter 8 provides a thorough introduction to the social and legal environment of e-commerce. Here, you will find a description of the ethical and legal dimensions of e-commerce, including a thorough discussion of the latest developments in personal information privacy, intellectual property, Internet governance, jurisdiction, and public health and welfare issues such as pornography, gambling, and health information.

Part 4, "E-commerce in Action," focuses on real-world e-commerce experiences in retail and services, online media, auctions, portals, and social networks, and business-to-business e-commerce. These chapters take a sector approach rather than a conceptual approach as used in the earlier chapters. E-commerce is different in each of these sectors. Chapter 9 takes a close look at the experience of firms in the retail marketplace for both goods and services. Chapter 9 also includes an "E-commerce in Action" case that provides a detailed analysis of the business strategies and financial operating results of Amazon. Additional E-commerce in Action cases will be available online at the authors' Web site for the text, www.azimuth-interactive.com/ecommerce6e. Chapter 10 explores the world of online content and digital media, and examines the enormous changes in online publishing and entertainment industries that have occurred over the last two years. Chapter 11 explores the online world of social networks, auctions, and portals. Chapter 12 explores the world of B2B e-commerce, describing both electronic Net marketplaces and the less-heralded, but very large arena of private industrial networks and the movement toward collaborative commerce.

CHAPTER OUTLINE

Each chapter contains a number of elements designed to make learning easy as well as interesting.

Learning Objectives A list of learning objectives that highlights the key concepts in the chapter guides student study.

Chapter-Opening Cases Each chapter opens with a story about a leading e-commerce company that relates the key objectives of the chapter to a real-life e-commerce business venture.

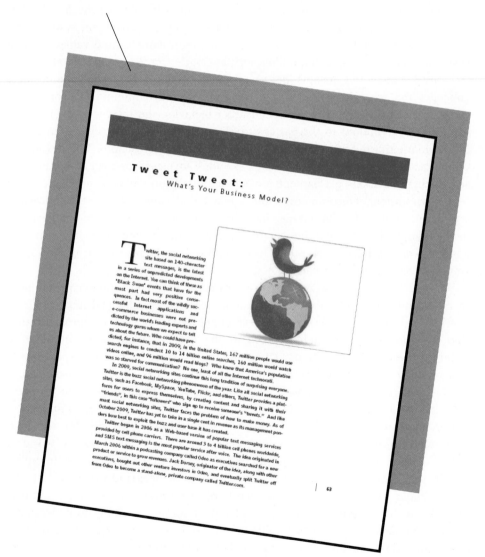

Tweet Tweet:
What's Your Business Model?

"Insight on" Cases Each chapter contains three real-world short cases illustrating the themes of technology, business, and society. These cases create an integrated framework and coverage throughout the book for describing and analyzing the full breadth of the field of e-commerce. The cases probe such issues as the ability of governments to regulate Internet content, how to design Web sites for accessibility, the challenges faced by luxury marketers in online marketing, and the potential anti-competitiveness of Net marketplaces.

Margin Glossary Throughout the text, key terms and their definitions appear in the text margin where they are first introduced.

Real-Company Examples Drawn from actual e-commerce ventures, well over 100 pertinent examples are used throughout the text to illustrate concepts.

Chapter-Closing Case Studies Each chapter concludes with a robust case study based on a real-world organization. These cases help students synthesize chapter concepts and apply this knowledge to concrete problems and scenarios such as evaluating the ethics and legality of advertising spyware, the marketing plans of Liquidation.com, and the business model behind Siemens' Click2procure B2B marketplace.

Chapter-Ending Pedagogy Each chapter contains end-of-chapter materials designed to reinforce the learning objectives of the chapter.

Key Concepts Keyed to the learning objectives, Key Concepts present the key points of the chapter to aid student study.

Review Questions Thought-provoking questions prompt students to demonstrate their comprehension and apply chapter concepts to management problem solving.

Projects At the end of each chapter are a number of projects that encourage students to apply chapter concepts and to use higher level evaluation skills. Many make use of the Internet and require students to present their findings in an oral presentation or written report. For instance, students are asked to evaluate publicly available information about a company's financials at the SEC Web site, assess payment system options for companies across international boundaries, or search for the top ten cookies on their own computer and the sites they are from.

Web Resources A section at the end of the chapter directs students to Web resources available at www.azimuth-interactive.com/ecommerce6e that can extend their knowledge of each chapter with projects and exercises and additional content. The Web site contains the following content provided by the authors:

- E-commerce in Action cases analyze the business strategies and financial operating results public e-commerce companies. For each company, we identify the vision of the company, analyze its financial performance, review its current strategy, and assess the near-term future prospects for the firm. These cases are ideal real-world instructional guides for students interested in understanding the financial foundation of e-commerce firms, their strategic visions and customer value propositions, and their changing strategic objectives. They can also be used as projects where students update the case materials using the most current financial and business news, or provide additional analysis.

- Additional projects, exercises, and tutorials.
- Information on how to build a business plan and revenue models.
- Essays on careers in e-commerce.

SUPPORT PACKAGE

The following supplementary materials are available to qualified instructors through the Online Instructor Resource Center. Contact your Prentice Hall sales representative for information about how to access them.

- **Instructor's Manual with solutions** This comprehensive manual pulls together a wide variety of teaching tools so that instructors can use the text easily and effectively. Each chapter contains an overview of key topics, a recap of the key learning objectives, lecture tips, discussion of the chapter-ending case, and answers to the Case Study Questions, Review Questions, and Student Projects.
- **Test Bank** For quick test preparation, the author-created Test Bank contains multiple-choice, true/false, and short-essay questions that focus both on content and the development of critical/creative thinking about the issues evoked by the chapter. The Test Bank is available in Microsoft Word and TestGen format. The TestGen is also available in WebCT and BlackBoard-ready format. TestGen allows instructors to view, edit, and add questions.
- **PowerPoint lecture presentation slides** These slides illustrate key points, tables, and figures from the text in lecture-note format. The slides can be easily converted to transparencies or viewed electronically in the classroom.

ACKNOWLEDGMENTS

Pearson Education sought the advice of many excellent reviewers, all of whom strongly influenced the organization and substance of this book. The following individuals provided extremely useful evaluations of this and previous editions of the text:

Carrie Andersen, Madison Area Technical College

Dr. Shirley A. Becker, Northern Arizona University

Prasad Bingi, Indiana-Purdue University, Fort Wayne

Christine Barnes, Lakeland Community College

Cliff Butler, North Seattle Community College

Joanna Broder, University of Arizona

James Buchan, College of the Ozarks

Ashley Bush, Florida State University

Andrew Ciganek, Jacksonville State University

Daniel Connolly, University of Denver

Tom Critzer, Miami University

Dursan Delen, Oklahoma State University

Abhijit Deshmukh, University of Massachusetts

Brian L. Dos Santos, University of Louisville

Robert Drevs, University of Notre Dame

Akram El-Tannir, Hariri Canadian University, Lebanon

Kimberly Furumo, University of Hawaii at Hilo

John H. Gerdes, University of California, Riverside

Philip Gordon, University of California at Berkeley

Allan Greenberg, Brooklyn College

Peter Haried, University of Wisconsin-Milwaukee

Sherri Harms, University of Nebraska at Kearney

Sharon Heckel, St. Charles Community College

David Hite, Virgina Intermont College

Ellen Kraft, Georgian Court University

Gilliean Lee, Lander University

Zoonky Lee, University of Nebraska, Lincoln

Andre Lemaylleux, Boston University, Brussels

Haim Levkowitz, University of Massachusetts, Lowell

Yair Levy, Nova Southeastern University

Richard Lucic, Duke University

John Mendonca, Purdue University

Dr. Abdulrahman Mirza, DePaul University

Kent Palmer, MacMurray College

Karen Palumbo, University of St. Francis

Wayne Pauli, Dakota State University

Jamie Pinchot, Theil College

Barry Quinn, University of Ulster, Northern Ireland

Jay Rhee, San Jose State University

Jorge Romero, Towson University

John Sagi, Anne Arundel Community College

Patricia Sendall, Merrimack College

Dr. Carlos Serrao, ISCTE/DCTI, Portugal

Neerja Sethi, Nanyang Business School, Singapore

Amber Settle, DePaul CTI

Vivek Shah, Texas State University-San Marcos

Seung Jae Shin, Mississippi State University

Sumit Sircar, University of Texas at Arlington

Hongjun Song, University of Memphis

Pamela Specht, University of Nebraska at Omaha

Esther Swilley, Kansas State University

Tony Townsend, Iowa State University

Bill Troy, University of New Hampshire

Susan VandeVen, Southern Polytechnic State University

Hiep Van Dong, Madison Area Technical College

Mary Vitrano, Palm Beach Community College

Andrea Wachter, Point Park University

Catherine Wallace, Massey University, New Zealand

Biao Wang, Boston University

Harry Washington, Lincoln University

Rolf Wigand, University of Arkansas at Little Rock

Erin Wilkinson, Johnson & Wales University

Alice Wilson, Cedar Crest College

Dezhi Wu, Southern Utah University

Gene Yelle, SUNY Institute of Technology

David Zolzer, Northwestern State University

5e Reviewers:

Andrew P. Ciganek, Jacksonville State University

Harry J. Foxwell, George Mason University

Jason Little, Franklin Pierce University

Matthew H. Sauber, Eastern Michigan University

Daniel C. Wood, Arizona State University

Kaimei Zheng, University of Massachusetts, Amherst

We would like to thank eMarketer, Inc. and David Iankelevich for their permission to include data and figures from their research reports in our text. eMarketer is one of the leading independent sources for statistics, trend data, and original analysis covering many topics related to the Internet, e-business, and emerging technologies. eMarketer aggregates e-business data from multiple sources worldwide.

In addition, we would like to thank all those at Prentice Hall who have worked so hard to make sure that this book is the very best that it can be. We want to thank Bob Horan, Executive Editor of the Prentice Hall MIS list and Kelly Loftus, Assistant Editor for their editorial support; Judy Leale and Karalyn Holland for overseeing production of this project; and Steve Frim for the outstanding cover design. Very special thanks to Megan Miller and Will Anderson at Azimuth Interactive, Inc., and Ann Cohen, for all their hard work on the production of, and supplements for, this book.

A special thanks also Susan Hartman, Executive Editor for the first and second editions and to Frank Ruggirello, Publisher at Addison-Wesley when we began this project, and now Publisher at Benjamin-Cummings.

Finally, last but not least, we would like to thank our family and friends, without whose support this book would not have been possible.

Kenneth C. Laudon
Carol Guercio Traver

Brief Contents

PART 4 E-commerce in Action

Contents

PART 2 Technology Infrastructure for E-commerce

5   ONLINE SECURITY AND PAYMENT SYSTEMS   262

PART 3 Business Concepts and Social Issues

6	E-COMMERCE MARKETING CONCEPTS	340

7	E-COMMERCE MARKETING COMMUNICATIONS	424

8   ETHICAL, SOCIAL, AND POLITICAL ISSUES IN E-COMMERCE   490

PART 4 E-commerce in Action

9   ONLINE RETAILING AND SERVICES   570

10   ONLINE CONTENT AND MEDIA   648

11   SOCIAL NETWORKS, AUCTIONS, AND PORTALS   716

---

12 B2B E-COMMERCE: SUPPLY CHAIN MANAGEMENT AND COLLABORATIVE COMMERCE   768

Introduction to E-commerce

CHAPTER 1

The Revolution Is Just Beginning

LEARNING OBJECTIVES

After reading this chapter, you will be able to:

- Define e-commerce and describe how it differs from e-business.
- Identify and describe the unique features of e-commerce technology and discuss their business significance.
- Recognize and describe Web 2.0 applications.
- Describe the major types of e-commerce.
- Discuss the origins and growth of e-commerce.
- Understand the evolution of e-commerce from its early years to today.
- Identify the factors that will define the future of e-commerce.
- Describe the major themes underlying the study of e-commerce.
- Identify the major academic disciplines contributing to e-commerce.

Facebook and MySpace:
It's All About You

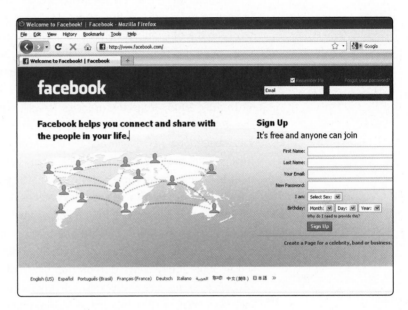

Height ow many people watched the final two-hour episode of America's most popular television series, *American Idol*, in May 2009? Answer: about 26 million (out of a total audience size of 114 million).

Now, how many people in the United States do you think visit Facebook and MySpace, the two most popular social network Web sites, each month? Answer: in August 2009, Facebook had around 92 million unique U.S. visitors, while MySpace had about 64 million. That makes the television audience for *American Idol* seem positively puny in comparison. Worldwide, MySpace and Facebook attract an even bigger audience: over 300 million active users a month for Facebook (with more than 150 million logging on each day), and about 130 million for MySpace. Facebook is growing at more than 100% a year worldwide, although its growth has slowed somewhat in the United States; MySpace is also growing worldwide, although not at the rate of Facebook. Together, Facebook and MySpace make up 90% of the social networking audience. In the space of just a few years, they have created an entirely new media platform, transforming music, television, and Hollywood production and distribution channels.

Facebook and MySpace, along with other "social" sites such as Twitter, YouTube, Bebo, and Photobucket, exemplify the new face of e-commerce in the twenty-first century. When we think of e-commerce we tend to think of selling things online, a retail model based on physical products. While this iconic vision of e-commerce is still very powerful, and online retail remains the fastest growing form of retail in the United States, growing up alongside is a whole new value stream based on providing services to Internet users that allow them to express themselves and network with others.

What are these services and how much are they worth? How can marketers use social media sites to create and sustain brands? How can you make money selling online services and how much can you make? Here, a little background will help.

The founders of MySpace, Tom Anderson and Chris DeWolfe, wanted to create a Web site that would make it possible for people to talk about the things they loved, and do it in a personal way—a sort of bulletin board combined with the capability of building your own Web pages with ease. Their vision was that people would like to talk about themselves, even promote themselves, and find others online to talk with. Anderson and DeWolfe started the business in January 2004, experienced an immediate unparalleled growth spurt, and today, MySpace is consistently among the top five most visited sites on the Internet.

MySpace was not a new vision—other sites such as Friendster preceded it. But MySpace learned from Friendster's limitations. MySpace allowed bands and artists to promote themselves on the site, while Friendster banned self-promoting bands and artists. At MySpace, users could find the bands they liked and share that with their friends, starting a word-of-mouth buzz that promoted the bands but also promoted MySpace as the place to find great music. MySpace sees itself as a "media portal."

In July 2005, Rupert Murdoch's News Corporation bought MySpace for what was thought to be the outrageous price of $580 million. Even more unusual was the buyer. Here was a traditional newspaper and television company buying an Internet venture that at the time was not profitable. In retrospect, many believe the real value of MySpace was in the billions of dollars. In August 2006, MySpace struck a deal with Google for $900 million, allowing Google to display short text ads next to search results generated by MySpace. MySpace generates about $300 million a year from this relationship, although it will end in 2010. In one year, Murdoch had made back his investment and then some. Analysts believe that MySpace had somewhere around $650 million in total revenue for its fiscal year ending in June 2009. News Corporation does not report independent financial results for MySpace, so no one really knows if MySpace is profitable, although the division that includes MySpace (Fox Interactive Media) reported operating income of $7 million for the 2009 fiscal year.

Social media sites typically make money by selling ads to their huge audiences. That's where audience size is critical. Although some companies remain leery of associating their brands with user-generated content they do not control, for many firms, this concern pales when compared to the ability to contact 100 million or more people. MySpace served 31.7 billion display ads in April 2009, second in number only to those served by Yahoo (43 billion), and accounting for almost 50% of the total social network advertising space. In addition to online display advertising, companies are using MySpace to present innovative advertising campaigns. For instance, the luxury jewelry company Cartier created product pages on MySpace for its "Love by Cartier" product line with new music by 12 different artists. Procter & Gamble has used MySpace to launch new products by linking their product pages to the MySpace pages of musicians whose visitors have the right demographics. In 2009, Toyota and MySpace created "Rock the Space," a MySpace page where new bands can compete for a first contract with MySpace Music, an independent record company. Other corporate heavy hitters promoting their brands on MySpace include American Express, Lexus, and Amazon.

MySpace's success has spawned hundreds of focused, niche social networks. There are investor, teen, business, career, family, fishing, music, and travel networks, just to name a few. But its largest rival is Facebook. Founded as thefacebook.com at Harvard by student Mark Zuckerberg, the idea behind Facebook was to create an online digital version of the traditional student class picture or "facebook." It quickly became popular at Harvard, expanded to Yale and Stanford, and then to the nation's 3,000 plus college campuses, creating a social networking phenomenon on campus. About 90% of college students in the United States have a Facebook profile, along with lists of favorites, activities, and accomplishments. Like MySpace, Facebook quickly developed into a general-purpose platform for conducting social life.

Originally restricted to college students, and relying on fixed templates rather than user-designed Web pages, Facebook initially was easily eclipsed by MySpace in terms of sheer numbers of subscribers. In 2006, in an effort to expand its subscriber base, Facebook made itself available to everyone, not just college students, and opened itself up to thousands of widgets—small software programs that make posting of photos, music, and video easy. Facebook even allows users to post ads and make money from their own advertising campaigns. MySpace does not allow user advertising, and does not allow outside vendors to develop software applications to run on its site. Facebook, in contrast, supplies other firms with its source code and encourages them to build applications that run on the Facebook site. Facebook has also attracted users looking for a more structured, defined, and refined environmentthatn that available at MySpace. From May 2008 to May 2009, Facebook grew from 35.6 million monthly U.S. unique visitors to 70 million, a 97% increase, while MySpace's unique visitors decreased by 5%, from 74 million to 70 million. Facebook's online display advertising views has also increased during this period. In April 2009, it served 25 billion online ads, compared to just 3.6 billion in June 2008. In contrast, the number of ads served by MySpace has significantly declined. It served 51 billion ads in June 2008 but only 31.7 billion in April 2009.

Facebook does not release its financial data but admits it is not yet profitable. However, analysts estimate that Facebook will produce somewhere between $300 and $425 million in revenue in 2009. Right now, Facebook is still focusing on growth through international expansion and deepening the online experience for its users, rather than profits. To survive additional years without profit, in May 2009, Facebook sold 2% of its preferred stock to a Russian media giant in a deal that valued Facebook at $10 billion. Earlier in 2007, Facebook sold 1.6% of its stock to Microsoft for $280 million, which valued the company at $15 billion. Currently, Facebook has a bankroll of $500 million to expand its brand worldwide, and seek out a business model that produces profits. For Zuckerberg, still the CEO of Facebook, the goal is to become "the social operating system of the Internet," at the center of users' online lives. This is right up there with the ambitions of Google ("to organize the world's information") and Amazon (becoming the "Earth's Biggest Selection").

In 2009, MySpace, recognizing that it was losing ground to Facebook, fired Chris DeWolfe, MySpace's co-founder, and hired Owen Van Natta (a former Facebook executive) to spruce up MySpace's image, and focus more heavily on the 18–34 year-old demographic, without forgetting the Gen-X audience, or the Baby Boomers (who make up more than half of the MySpace audience). MySpace has developed a new more attractive profile page (similar to Facebook's page), and eliminated dating and weight-loss ads. MySpace also extended its foundation in music by striking deals with major record companies and older artists such as Lionel Richie and Neil Young, placing their entire catalogs of past hits on MySpace for free. Whether these efforts will be enough to reverse the tide in favor of Facebook remains to be seen.

SOURCES: "P&G Collaborates with Google, Facebook, MySpace, and Twitter," by Gaurav Bhalla, Bhalla.com, June 5, 2009; "MySpace Offers Rock and Jazz Classics," by Paul Boutin, New York Times, June 4, 2009; "What Is Facebook Actually Worth?," New York Times, May 27, 2008; "From Russia With Love: Facebook Lands $200 Million," by Spencer Ante, Business Week, May 26, 2009; 'American Idol' Ends on Low Note," by Jill Serjeant, Reuters News Service, May 21, 2009; "MySpace, Toyota launch Rock the Space for Unsigned Artists," by Dennis Bouchand, www.901am.com, May 21, 2009; "Losing a Popularity Contest, MySpace Tries a Makeover," by Brian Stelter and Tim Arango, New York Times, May 4, 2009; "Top 10 US Web Publishers, Ranked by Total Display Ad Views, April 2009" June 1, 2009; eMarketer, Inc. chart based on data from comScore AdMetrix, May 2009; "How Facebook is Taking Over Our Lives," by Jessi Hempel, CNN-Money.com, March 11, 2009; "Social Networks: Five Consumer Trends for 2009," by Debra Aho Williamson,eMarketer,.com, February 2009; "Facebook's Land Grab in the Face of a Downturn," by Spencer Ante, BusinessWeek, November 20, 2008.

I n 1994, e-commerce as we now know it did not exist. In 2009, just 15 years later, around 123 million American consumers are expected to spend about $228 billion, and businesses over $3.36 trillion, purchasing goods and services on the Internet's World Wide Web. And in this short period of time, e-commerce has been reinvented not just once, but twice.

The early years of e-commerce, during the late 1990s, were a period of business vision, inspiration, and experimentation. It soon became apparent, however, that establishing a successful business model based on those visions would not be easy. There followed a period of retrenchment and reevaluation, which led to the stock market crash of 2000–2001, with the value of e-commerce, telecommunications, and other technology stocks plummeting in the space of a year by more than 90%. After the bubble burst, many people were quick to write off e-commerce, predicting that its growth would stagnate, and the Internet audience would plateau. But they were wrong. The surviving firms refined and honed their business models, ultimately leading to models that actually produced profits, and resulting in e-commerce retail growth rates of over 25% per year. during the period from 2002-2008.

Today, as you've learned from the opening case, we are in the middle of yet another transition: a new and vibrant service-based model of e-commerce growing up alongside the more traditional e-commerce retail sales model exemplified by Amazon. Businesses such as Facebook, MySpace, Twitter, YouTube, and Photobucket that enable users to distribute their own content (such as videos, music, photos, personal information, blogs, and software applications) have rocketed to prominence. Never before in the history of media have such large audiences been aggregated and made so accessible. Businesses are grappling with how best to approach this audience from an advertising and marketing perspective. Social networks and user-generated content sites are also technology that is highly disruptive of traditional media firms. The movement of eyeballs towards these sites means fewer viewers of television and Hollywood movies, and fewer readers of newspapers and magazines, and so those industries are also facing a transition. It's probably safe to predict that this will not be the last transition for e-commerce, either.

1.1 E-COMMERCE: THE REVOLUTION IS JUST BEGINNING

In fact, the e-commerce revolution is just beginning. For instance, in 2009:

- Online consumer sales (retail, travel, and online content) lost much less ground than other types of consumer sales, and will remain basically flat, at an estimated $228 billion (eMarketer, Inc., 2009a; AccuStream iMedia Research, 2009).
- The major source of online retail growth is increased spending by existing online buyers rather than new buyers. As trust and consumer confidence build, shoppers are now buying expensive, "high-touch" goods online such as consumer electronics, home furnishings, and apparel.

- The number of individuals of all ages online in the United States increased to about 200 million, up from 193 million in 2008. (The total population of the United States is about 305 million). (eMarketer, Inc., 2009b).

- Of the total 121 million households in the United States, the number online increased to 87 million or about 72% of all households (eMarketer, Inc., 2009c).

- On an average day, around 115 million American adults go online. About 89 million send e-mail, 93 million use a search engine to find information, and 60 million get news. An estimated 30 million use an online social network, 25 million watch an online video, and 16 million read a blog (Pew Internet and American Life Project, 2009).

- The number of people who have purchased something online expanded to about 123 million, with an additional 29 million using the Web to gather information on potential product purchases (eMarketer, Inc., 2009a).

- The demographic profile of online shoppers continued to broaden while at the same time significant generational differences in purchase patterns have emerged (eMarketer, Inc., 2008a).

- B2B e-commerce—the use of the Internet for business-to-business commerce— will total about $3.36 trillion, comprising about 30% of all business-to-business trade (U.S. Census Bureau, 2009; authors' estimates).

- The Internet technology base gained greater depth and power, as around 80.5 million households (about 66.5% of all U.S. households) have broadband cable or DSL access to the Internet and 74 million people access the Internet via mobile devices (eMarketer, Inc., 2009d, e).

These developments signal many of the themes in the new edition of this book (see **Table 1.1**). More and more people and businesses are using the Internet to conduct commerce; smaller, local firms are learning how to take advantage of the Web; the e-commerce channel is deepening as more products and services come online; more industries are being transformed by e-commerce, including all forms of traditional media (movies, television, music, and news), software, education, and finance; Internet technology will continue to drive these changes as broadband telecommunications comes to more households and more people purchase Internet-enabled smartphones. E-commerce business models continue to be refined to achieve higher levels of profitability, while traditional retail brands such as Sears, JCPenney, and Wal-Mart further extend their multi-channel, bricks-and-clicks strategies and retain their dominant retail positions by strengthening their Internet operations. At the societal level, other trends are apparent. The Internet has created a platform for millions of people to create and share content, establish new social bonds, and strengthen existing ones through social networking, blogging, and video posting sites. The major digital copyright owners have increased their pursuit of online file-swapping services with mixed success. States have successfully moved toward taxation of Internet sales, while Internet gaming sites have been severely curtailed through criminal prosecutions in the United States. Sovereign nations have expanded their surveillance of, and control over, Internet communications and content as a part of their anti-terrorist activities and their traditional interest in snooping on citizens. Privacy seems to have lost much of its meaning in an age when millions create public online personal profiles.

TABLE 1.1	MAJOR TRENDS IN E-COMMERCE 2009–2010

BUSINESS

- New business models emerge based on social technologies and consumer-generated content from videos and photos, to blogs and reviews.
- Search engine marketing continues to challenge traditional marketing and advertising media as more consumers switch their eyes to the Web.
- After a flat year due to the recession, retail consumer e-commerce will begin to grow again in 2010, at about a 10% rate.
- Online population growth slows, but the amount of the average purchase expands.
- The online demographics of shoppers continues to broaden with the fastest growth among tweens, teens, and older adults.
- Online businesses continue to strengthen profitability by refining their business models and leveraging the capabilities of the Internet.
- The first wave of e-commerce transformed the business world of music, brokerage, and air travel. Industries facing a similar transformation today include marketing/advertising, telecommunications, entertainment, print media, real estate, hotels, bill payments, and software.
- The breadth of e-commerce offerings grows, especially in entertainment, retail apparel, appliances, and home furnishings.
- Small businesses and entrepreneurs continue to flood into the e-commerce marketplace, often riding on the infrastructures created by industry giants such as Amazon, Google, and eBay.
- Brand extension through the Internet continues to grow as large firms such as Sears, JCPenney, L.L.Bean, and Wal-Mart pursue integrated, multi-channel bricks-and-clicks strategies.
- B2B supply chain transactions and collaborative commerce continue to strengthen and grow beyond the $3.4 trillion mark.

TECHNOLOGY

- Wireless Internet connections (Wi-Fi, WiMax, and 3G telephone) grow rapidly.
- A mobile computing and communications platform based on iPhones, Blackberries, and other smartphones (the "new client") becomes a reality and begins to rival the PC platform.
- iTunes becomes an operating system within Windows for the play of music and video.
- The Internet broadband foundation becomes stronger in households and businesses. Bandwidth prices fall as telecommunications companies re-capitalize their debts.
- Computing and networking component prices continue to fall dramatically.
- Cloud computing and Web services expand B2B opportunities.

TABLE 1.1	**MAJOR TRENDS IN E-COMMERCE 2009–2010 (CONTINUED)**

SOCIETY

- Consumer- and user-generated content, and syndication in the form of social networks, tweets, blogs, wikis, and virtual lives, grow to provide an entirely new self-publishing forum that engages millions of consumers.
- Traditional media such as television, newspapers, and magazines continue to lose subscribers, and adopt online, interactive models.
- Conflicts over copyright management and control continue to grow in significance.
- Explosive growth continues in online viewing of video and television programs.
- Participation by adults in social networks on the Internet increases; Facebook becomes ever more popular in all demographic categories .
- Taxation of Internet sales becomes more widespread and accepted by large online merchants.
- Controversy over content regulation and controls continues to increase.
- Surveillance of Internet communications by repressive regimes and other countries remains an issue.
- Concerns over commercial and governmental privacy invasion increase as firms provide government agencies with access to private personal information.
- Internet fraud, abuse, and identity theft occurrences increase.
- Spam remains a significant problem despite legislation and promised technology fixes.
- Invasion of personal privacy on the Web expands as marketers extend their capabilities to track users.
- China and India Internet populations continue to grow at around 15%–20% annually.

THE FIRST 30 SECONDS

It is important to realize that the rapid growth and change that has occurred in the first 15 years of e-commerce represents just the beginning—what could be called the first 30 seconds of the e-commerce revolution. The same technologies that drove the first decade and a half of e-commerce (described in Chapter 3) continue to evolve at exponential rates. This underlying ferment in the technological groundwork of the Internet and Web presents entrepreneurs with new opportunities to both create new businesses and new business models in traditional industries, and also to destroy old businesses. Business change becomes disruptive, rapid, and even destructive, while offering entrepreneurs new opportunities and resources for investment.

Changes in underlying information technologies and continuing entrepreneurial innovation in business and marketing promise as much change in the next decade as seen in the last decade. The twenty-first century will be the age of a digitally enabled social and commercial life, the outlines of which we can barely perceive at this time. Analysts estimate that by 2013, consumers will be spending about $330 billion and businesses about $4.75 trillion in online transactions. It appears likely that e-commerce will eventually impact nearly all commerce, and that most commerce will be e-commerce by the year 2050.

Is there a terminal point towards which e-commerce is hurtling? Can e-commerce continue to grow indefinitely? It's possible that at some point, e-commerce growth may slow simply as a result of overload: people may just not have the time to watch yet another online video, open another e-mail, or read another blog, tweet or Facebook update However, currently, there is no foreseeable limit to the continued rapid development of Internet and e-commerce technology, or limits on the inventiveness of entrepreneurs to develop new uses for the technology. Therefore, for now at least, it is likely that the disruptive process will continue.

Business fortunes are made—and lost—in periods of extraordinary change such as this. The next five years hold out extraordinary opportunities—as well as risks—for new and traditional businesses to exploit digital technology for market advantage. For society as a whole, the next few decades offer the possibility of extraordinary gains in social wealth as the digital revolution works its way through larger and larger segments of the world's economy, offering the possibility of high rates of productivity and income growth in an inflation-free environment.

As a business or technology student, this book will help you perceive and understand the opportunities and risks that lie ahead. By the time you finish, you will be able to identify the technological, business, and social forces that have shaped the growth of e-commerce and extend that understanding into the years ahead.

WHAT IS E-COMMERCE?

e-commerce

the use of the Internet and the Web to transact business. More formally, digitally enabled commercial transactions between and among organizations and individuals

Our focus in this book is **e-commerce**—the use of the Internet and the World Wide Web (Web) to transact business. (Although the terms Internet and Web are often used interchangeably, they are actually two very different things. The Internet is a worldwide network of computer networks, and the Web is one of the Internet's most popular services, providing access to billions of Web pages. We describe both more fully later in this chapter and in Chapter 3.) More formally, we focus on digitally enabled commercial transactions between and among organizations and individuals. Each of these components of our working definition of e-commerce is important. *Digitally enabled transactions* include all transactions mediated by digital technology. For the most part, this means transactions that occur over the Internet and the Web. *Commercial transactions* involve the exchange of value (e.g., money) across organizational or individual boundaries in return for products and services. Exchange of value is important for understanding the limits of e-commerce. Without an exchange of value, no commerce occurs.

THE DIFFERENCE BETWEEN E-COMMERCE AND E-BUSINESS

There is a debate among consultants and academics about the meaning and limitations of both e-commerce and e-business. Some argue that e-commerce encompasses the entire world of electronically based organizational activities that support a firm's market exchanges—including a firm's entire information system's infrastructure (Rayport and Jaworski, 2003). Others argue, on the other hand, that e-business encompasses the entire world of internal and external electronically based activities, including e-commerce (Kalakota and Robinson, 2003).

We think that it is important to make a working distinction between e-commerce and e-business because we believe they refer to different phenomena. E-commerce is not "anything digital" that a firm does. For purposes of this text, we will use the term **e-business** to refer primarily to the digital enabling of transactions and processes *within* a firm, involving information systems under the control of the firm. For the most part, in our view, e-business does not include commercial transactions involving an exchange of value across organizational boundaries. For example, a company's online inventory control mechanisms are a component of e-business, but such internal processes do not directly generate revenue for the firm from outside businesses or consumers, as e-commerce, by definition, does. It is true, however, that a firm's e-business infrastructure provides support for online e-commerce exchanges; the same infrastructure and skill sets are involved in both e-business and e-commerce. E-commerce and e-business systems blur together at the business firm boundary, at the point where internal business systems link up with suppliers or customers, for instance (see **Figure 1.1**). E-business applications turn into e-commerce precisely when an exchange of value occurs (see Mesenbourg, U.S. Department of Commerce, 2001, for a similar view). We will examine this intersection further in Chapter 12.

e-business
the digital enabling of transactions and processes within a firm, involving information systems under the control of the firm

WHY STUDY E-COMMERCE?

Why are there college courses and textbooks on e-commerce when there are no courses or textbooks on "TV Commerce," "Radio Commerce," "Direct Mail Commerce," "Railroad Commerce," or "Highway Commerce," even though these technologies had profound impacts on commerce in the twentieth century and account for far more commerce than e-commerce? Many colleges, including Massachusetts Institute of Technology (MIT), University of Michigan, Cornell University, University of California at Berkeley, and NSEAD Business School (France), have also developed courses on

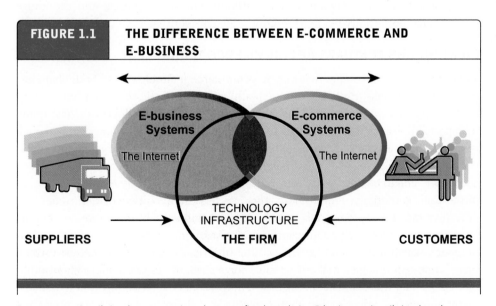

| FIGURE 1.1 | THE DIFFERENCE BETWEEN E-COMMERCE AND E-BUSINESS |

E-commerce primarily involves transactions that cross firm boundaries. E-business primarily involves the application of digital technologies to business processes within the firm.

social interaction technologies and techniques, online social networks, online community development, and consumer-generated media. At least one college offers a YouTube 101 course called "Learning from YouTube."

The reason for the interest specifically in e-commerce is that e-commerce technology (discussed in detail in Chapters 3 and 4) is different and more powerful than any of the other technologies we have seen in the past century. E-commerce technologies—and the digital markets that result—are bringing about some fundamental, unprecedented shifts in commerce. While these other technologies transformed economic life in the twentieth century, the evolving Internet and other information technologies are shaping the twenty-first century.

Prior to the development of e-commerce, the marketing and sale of goods was a mass-marketing and sales force-driven process. Marketers viewed consumers as passive targets of advertising "campaigns" and branding blitzes intended to influence their long-term product perceptions and immediate purchasing behavior. Companies sold their products via well-insulated "channels." Consumers were trapped by geographical and social boundaries, unable to search widely for the best price and quality. Information about prices, costs, and fees could be hidden from the consumer, creating profitable "information asymmetries" for the selling firm. **Information asymmetry** refers to any disparity in relevant market information among parties in a transaction. It was so expensive to change national or regional prices in traditional retailing (what are called *menu costs*) that "one national price" was the norm, and dynamic pricing to the marketplace—changing prices in real time—was unheard of. In this environment, manufacturers prospered by relying on huge production runs of products that could not be customized or personalized. One of the shifts that e-commerce is bringing about is a reduction in information asymmetry among market participants (consumers and merchants). Preventing consumers from learning about costs, price discrimination strategies, and profits from sales becomes more difficult with e-commerce, and the entire marketplace potentially becomes highly price competitive.

information asymmetry
any disparity in relevant market information among parties in a transaction

EIGHT UNIQUE FEATURES OF E-COMMERCE TECHNOLOGY

Table 1.2 lists eight unique features of e-commerce technology that both challenge traditional business thinking and explain why we have so much interest in e-commerce. These unique dimensions of e-commerce technologies suggest many new possibilities for marketing and selling—a powerful set of interactive, personalized, and rich messages are available for delivery to segmented, targeted audiences. E-commerce technologies make it possible for merchants to know much more about consumers and to be able to use this information more effectively than was ever true in the past. Potentially, online merchants can use this new information to develop new information asymmetries, enhance their ability to brand products, charge premium prices for high-quality service, and segment the market into an endless number of subgroups, each receiving a different price. To complicate matters further, these same technologies make it possible for merchants to know more about other merchants than was ever true in the past. This presents the possibility that merchants might collude on prices rather than compete and drive overall average prices up.

TABLE 1.2	EIGHT UNIQUE FEATURES OF E-COMMERCE TECHNOLOGY
E-COMMERCE TECHNOLOGY DIMENSION	**BUSINESS SIGNIFICANCE**
Ubiquity—Internet/Web technology is available everywhere: at work, at home, and elsewhere via mobile devices, anytime.	The marketplace is extended beyond traditional boundaries and is removed from a temporal and geographic location. "Marketspace" is created; shopping can take place anywhere. Customer convenience is enhanced, and shopping costs are reduced.
Global reach—The technology reaches across national boundaries, around the Earth.	Commerce is enabled across cultural and national boundaries seamlessly and without modification. "Marketspace" includes potentially billions of consumers and millions of businesses worldwide.
Universal standards—There is one set of technology standards, namely Internet standards.	There is a common, inexpensive, global, technology foundation for businesses to use.
Richness—Video, audio, and text messages are possible.	Video, audio, and text marketing messages are integrated into a single marketing message and consuming experience.
Interactivity—The technology works through interaction with the user.	Consumers are engaged in a dialog that dynamically adjusts the experience to the individual, and makes the consumer a co-participant in the process of delivering goods to the market.
Information density—The technology reduces information costs and raises quality.	Information processing, storage, and communication costs drop dramatically, while currency, accuracy, and timeliness improve greatly. Information becomes plentiful, cheap, and accurate.
Personalization/Customization—The technology allows personalized messages to be delivered to individuals as well as groups.	Personalization of marketing messages and customization of products and services are based on individual characteristics.
Social technology—User content generation and social networking.	New Internet social and business models enable user content creation and distribution, and support social networks.

This strategy works especially well when there are just a few suppliers (Varian, 2000b). We examine these different visions of e-commerce further in Section 1.2 and throughout the book.

Each of the dimensions of e-commerce technology and their business significance listed in Table 1.2 deserves a brief exploration, as well as a comparison to both traditional commerce and other forms of technology-enabled commerce.

Ubiquity

marketplace
physical space you visit in order to transact

In traditional commerce, a **marketplace** is a physical place you visit in order to transact. For example, television and radio typically motivate the consumer to go some place to make a purchase. E-commerce, in contrast, is characterized by its **ubiquity**: it is available just about everywhere, at all times. It liberates the market from being restricted to a physical space and makes it possible to shop from your desktop, at home, at work, or even from your car, using mobile commerce. The result is called a **marketspace**—a marketplace extended beyond traditional boundaries and removed from a temporal and geographic location. From a consumer point of view, ubiquity reduces *transaction costs*—the costs of participating in a market. To transact, it is no longer necessary that you spend time and money traveling to a market. At a broader level, the ubiquity of e-commerce lowers the cognitive energy required to transact in a marketspace. *Cognitive energy* refers to the mental effort required to complete a task. Humans generally seek to reduce cognitive energy outlays. When given a choice, humans will choose the path requiring the least effort—the most convenient path (Shapiro and Varian, 1999; Tversky and Kahneman, 1981).

ubiquity
available just about everywhere, at all times

marketspace
marketplace extended beyond traditional boundaries and removed from a temporal and geographic location

Global Reach

E-commerce technology permits commercial transactions to cross cultural and national boundaries far more conveniently and cost-effectively than is true in traditional commerce. As a result, the potential market size for e-commerce merchants is roughly equal to the size of the world's online population (about 1.67 billion as of June 30, 2009, and growing) (Internet Worldstats, 2009). The total number of users or customers an e-commerce business can obtain is a measure of its **reach** (Evans and Wurster, 1997).

reach
the total number of users or customers an e-commerce business can obtain

In contrast, most traditional commerce is local or regional—it involves local merchants or national merchants with local outlets. Television and radio stations, and newspapers, for instance, are primarily local and regional institutions with limited but powerful national networks that can attract a national audience. In contrast to e-commerce technology, these older commerce technologies do not easily cross national boundaries to a global audience.

Universal Standards

One strikingly unusual feature of e-commerce technologies is that the technical standards of the Internet, and therefore the technical standards for conducting e-commerce, are **universal standards**—they are shared by all nations around the world. In contrast, most traditional commerce technologies differ from one nation to the next. For instance, television and radio standards differ around the world, as does cell phone technology. The universal technical standards of the Internet and e-commerce greatly lower *market entry costs*—the cost merchants must pay just to bring their goods to market. At the same time, for consumers, universal standards reduce *search costs*—the effort required to find suitable products. And by creating a single, one-world marketspace, where prices and product descriptions can be inexpensively displayed for all to see, *price discovery* becomes simpler, faster, and more accurate (Banerjee, et al., 2005; Bakos, 1997; Kambil, 1997). Users of the

universal standards
standards that are shared by all nations around the world

Internet, both businesses and individuals, also experience *network externalities—*benefits that arise because everyone uses the same technology. With e-commerce technologies, it is possible for the first time in history to easily find many of the suppliers, prices, and delivery terms of a specific product anywhere in the world, and to view them in a coherent, comparative environment. Although this is not necessarily realistic today for all or even many products, it is a potential that will be exploited in the future.

Richness

Information **richness** refers to the complexity and content of a message (Evans and Wurster, 1999). Traditional markets, national sales forces, and small retail stores have great richness: they are able to provide personal, face-to-face service using aural and visual cues when making a sale. The richness of traditional markets makes them a powerful selling or commercial environment. Prior to the development of the Web, there was a trade-off between richness and reach: the larger the audience reached, the less rich the message (see **Figure 1.2**). The Internet has the potential for offering considerably more information richness than traditional media such as printing presses, radio, and television because it is interactive and can adjust the message to individual users. Chatting with an online sales person, for instance, comes very close to the customer experience in a small retail shop. The richness of the Web allows retail and

richness
the complexity and content of a message

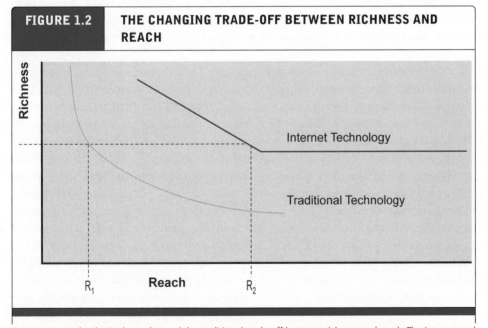

| FIGURE 1.2 | THE CHANGING TRADE-OFF BETWEEN RICHNESS AND REACH |

E-commerce technologies have changed the traditional trade-off between richness and reach. The Internet and Web can deliver, to an audience of millions, "rich" marketing messages with text, video, and audio, in a way not possible with traditional commerce technologies such as radio, television, or magazines.

SOURCE: Evans and Wurster, 2000.

service merchants to market and sell "complex" goods and services that heretofore really did require a face-to-face presentation by a sales force. Complex goods have multiple attributes, are typically expensive, and cannot be compared easily, such as used cars, non-standard financial instruments, and even diamond rings (Fink, et al., 2004).

Interactivity

Unlike any of the commercial technologies of the twentieth century, with the possible exception of the telephone, e-commerce technologies allow for interactivity, meaning they enable two-way communication between merchant and consumer. Traditional television, for instance, cannot ask viewers questions or enter into conversations with them, or request that customer information be entered into a form. In contrast, all of these activities are possible on an e-commerce Web site. **Interactivity** allows an online merchant to engage a consumer in ways similar to a face-to-face experience, but on a much more massive, global scale.

interactivity
technology that allows for two-way communication between merchant and consumer

Information Density

The Internet and the Web vastly increase **information density**—the total amount and quality of information available to all market participants, consumers, and merchants alike. E-commerce technologies reduce information collection, storage, processing, and communication costs. At the same time, these technologies increase greatly the currency, accuracy, and timeliness of information—making information more useful and important than ever. As a result, information becomes more plentiful, less expensive and of higher quality.

information density
the total amount and quality of information available to all market participants

A number of business consequences result from the growth in information density. In e-commerce markets, prices and costs become more transparent. *Price transparency* refers to the ease with which consumers can find out the variety of prices in a market; *cost transparency* refers to the ability of consumers to discover the actual costs merchants pay for products (Sinha, 2000). But there are advantages for merchants as well. Online merchants can discover much more about consumers; this allows merchants to segment the market into groups willing to pay different prices and permits them to engage in *price discrimination*—selling the same goods, or nearly the same goods, to different targeted groups at different prices. For instance, an online merchant can discover a consumer's avid interest in expensive exotic vacations, and then pitch expensive exotic vacation plans to that consumer at a premium price, knowing this person is willing to pay extra for such a vacation. At the same time, the online merchant can pitch the same vacation plan at a lower price to more price-sensitive consumers. Merchants also have enhanced abilities to differentiate their products in terms of cost, brand, and quality.

Personalization/Customization

E-commerce technologies permit **personalization**: merchants can target their marketing messages to specific individuals by adjusting the message to a person's name, interests, and past purchases. The technology also permits **customization**—changing the delivered product or service based on a user's preferences or prior behavior. Given the interactive nature of e-commerce technology, much information about the consumer can be gathered in the marketplace at the moment of purchase. With the increase in information density, a great deal of information about the consumer's past purchases and behavior can be stored and used by online merchants. The result is a level of personalization and customization unthinkable with existing commerce technologies. For instance, you may be able to shape what you see on television by selecting a channel, but you cannot change the contents of the channel you have chosen. In contrast, the online version of *The Wall Street Journal* allows you to select the type of news stories you want to see first, and gives you the opportunity to be alerted when certain events happen. Personalization and customization allow firms to precisely identify market segments and adjust their messages accordingly.

personalization
the targeting of marketing messages to specific individuals by adjusting the message to a person's name, interests, and past purchases

customization
changing the delivered product or service based on a user's preferences or prior behavior

Social Technology: User Content Generation and Social Networking

In a way quite different from all previous technologies, the Internet and e-commerce technologies have evolved to be much more social by allowing users to create and share content in the form of text, videos, music, and photos with a worldwide community. Using these forms of communication, users are able to create new social networks and strengthen existing ones. All previous mass media in modern history, including the printing press, use a broadcast model (one-to-many) where content is created in a central location by experts (professional writers, editors, directors, actors, and producers) and audiences are concentrated in huge aggregates to consume a standardized product. The telephone would appear to be an exception but it is not a "mass communication" technology. Instead the telephone is a one-to-one technology. The new Internet and e-commerce technologies have the potential to invert this standard media model by giving users the power to create and distribute content on a large scale, and permit users to program their own content consumption. The Internet provides a many-to-many model of mass communications that is unique.

WEB 2.0: PLAY MY VERSION

Many of the unique features of e-commerce and the Internet come together in a set of applications and social media technologies referred to as Web 2.0. The Internet started out as a simple network to support e-mail and file transfers among remote computers. Communication among experts was the purpose. The Web started out as a way to use the Internet to display simple pages and allow the user to navigate among the pages by linking them together electronically. You can think of this as Web 1.0—the first Web. By 2007 something else was happening. The Internet and the Web have evolved to the point where users can now create, edit, and distribute content to millions of others; share with one another their preferences, bookmarks, and online personas; participate in virtual lives; and build online communities. This "new" Web is called by many "**Web 2.0**," and while it draws heavily on the "old" Web 1.0, it is nevertheless a clear evolution from the past.

Let's look at some examples of Web 2.0 applications and sites:

Web 2.0

a set of applications and technologies that allows users to create, edit, and distribute content; share preferences, bookmarks, and online personas; participate in virtual lives; and build online communities

- YouTube, owned by Google after a $1.65 billion purchase, has become the largest online consumer-generated video posting site, although it is still searching for a profitable business model. Over 10 billion videos were viewed in August 2009 by 120 million visitors and over 20 hours of video are uploaded to the site every minute. This one site accounts for over 40% of all videos watched online (comScore, 2009a; Nielsen, 2009).

- MySpace ("a place for friends") and Facebook, discussed in the opening case, rocket to the lead of online social networking sites, while LinkedIn attracts additional millions of adults looking for online business connections. Twitter is another fast-growing social network that allows members to send short text-based messages ("tweets") of 140 characters or less via the Web or cell phone to "followers" (other users who have subscribed to them).

- Photobucket offers users an easy way to post and share photos and videos via e-mail, instant messages, and mobile phone. It also provides convenient "one-click share" links to MySpace, Facebook, Blogger and Live Journal. Photobucket has over 80 million users worldwide and stores over 7 billion consumer-generated images and videos (Photobucket.com, 2009).

- The Apple iPhone supports mobile versions of Web 2.0 applications such as Word-Press for the iPhone (which enables users to write posts, post photos, and manage comments to their blog via an iPhone or iPod touch), Mint (a personal financial manager), Borange (an iPhone app for sharing social availability), TagItLikeItsHot (a social bookmarking application), and thousands more.

- Google attracts the largest Internet audience with around 161 million unique monthly U.S. visitors in August 2009, and over 775 million international users. Google provides a continual stream of innovations such as Google Apps (a group of Web-based services offering free office productivity tools such as Google Docs, calendar, and other collaborative tools), Google Desktop, Google Maps, Google StreetView (a photo database of U.S. neighborhoods from the street level), Google Chrome (Web browser), Gmail, Google Scholar, and Google Health. Over 25% of Google search results on the world's top 20 brands provide links to consumer-generated content such as reviews, blogs, and photos (comScore, 2009b, c; Google, 2009).

- Second Life is a 3-D virtual world populated by around 600,000 active users ("residents") who have established lives by creating avatars in "The World," spending Linden dollars, owning real estate, and building, sharing, and purchasing "creations," which include custom "skins" for avatars, clothing, buildings, furniture, vehicles, and a host of other items. Residents spend over $50 million real dollars each month (and more than $500 million in total in 2009) to buy things on the site for their virtual lives, converting the real dollars to Lindens (LindenLab, 2009).

• Wikipedia allows contributors around the world to share their knowledge and in the process has become the most successful online encyclopedia, far surpassing early "professional" encyclopedias such as Encarta or even Britannica. Wikipedia is one of the largest collaboratively edited reference projects in the world. As of September 2009, there were over 3 million articles in English, and over 75,000 active contributors working on more than 13 million articles in 260 languages. Wikipedia relies on volunteers, makes no money, and accepts no advertising. The Wikimedia Foundation, Inc., a not-for-profit organization that relies on fund-raising and donations to survive, owns Wikipedia. Wikipedia is one of the top 10 most visited sites on the Web with about 65 million monthly visitors (Wikipedia.org, 2009; comScore, 2009b).

• Digg allows users to "tag" Web pages and share those tags with other users. Users "vote" on what they like best, and those that are most popular are promoted to the front page of the site, where millions can view and comment. In August 2009, Digg had around 44 million monthly unique visitors (Compete.com, 2009). StumbleUpon, Reddit, Delicious, Kaboodle, Mixx, Newsvine, Diigo, and offer similar social bookmarking or tagging systems.

• WordPress is a blogging platform that allows you to create easily create and publish a blog on the Web. WordPress is an open source project and available for use free of charge. As of September 2009, WordPress is reportedly used by over 62.8 million in the United States, and over 200 million worldwide (Peterson, 2009).

What do all these Web 2.0 applications and sites have in common? First, they rely on user- and consumer-generated content. These are all "applications" created by people, especially people in the 18–34 year-old demographic, and in the 7–17 age group as well. "Regular" people (not just experts or professionals) are creating, sharing, modifying, and broadcasting content to huge audiences. Second, easy search capability is a key to their success. Third, they are inherently highly interactive, creating new opportunities for people to socially connect to others. They are "social" sites because they support interactions among users. Fourth, they rely on broadband connectivity to the Web. Fifth, with the exception of Google, they are currently marginally profitable, and their business models unproven despite considerable investment. Sixth, they attract extremely large audiences when compared to traditional Web 1.0 applications, exceeding in many cases the audience size of national broadcast and cable television programs. These audience relationships are intensive and long-lasting interactions with millions of people. In short, they attract eyeballs in very large numbers. Hence, they present marketers with extraordinary opportunities for targeted marketing and advertising. They also present consumers with the opportunity to rate and review products, and entrepreneurs with ideas for future business ventures. Last, these sites act as application development platforms where users can contribute and use software applications for free. Briefly, it's a whole new world from what has gone before. You'll learn more about Web 2.0 in later chapters.

TABLE 1.3	MAJOR TYPES OF E-COMMERCE
TYPE OF E-COMMERCE	EXAMPLE
B2C—Business-to-Consumer	Amazon is a general merchandiser that sells consumer products to retail consumers.
B2B—Business-to-Business	Go2Paper.com is an independent third-party marketplace that serves the paper industry.
C2C—Consumer-to-Consumer	On a large number of Web auction sites such as eBay, and listing sites such as Craigslist, consumers can auction or sell goods directly to other consumers.
P2P—Peer-to-Peer	BitTorrent is a software application that permits consumers to share videos and other high-bandwidth content with one another directly, without the intervention of a market maker as in C2C e-commerce.
M-commerce—Mobile commerce	Wireless mobile devices such as personal digital assistants and cell phones can be used to conduct commercial transactions.

TYPES OF E-COMMERCE

There are a variety of different types of e-commerce and many different ways to characterize them. **Table 1.3** lists the five major types of e-commerce discussed in this book.[1] For the most part, we distinguish different types of e-commerce by the nature of the market relationship—who is selling to whom. The exceptions are P2P and m-commerce, which are technology-based distinctions

Business-to-Consumer (B2C) E-commerce

Business-to-Consumer (B2C) e-commerce
online businesses selling to individual consumers

The most commonly discussed type of e-commerce is **Business-to-Consumer (B2C) e-commerce**, in which online businesses attempt to reach individual consumers. Even though B2C is comparatively small (about $228 billion in 2009), it has grown exponentially since 1995, and is the type of e-commerce that most consumers are likely to encounter. Within the B2C category, there are many different types of business models. Chapter 2 has a detailed discussion of seven different B2C business models: portals, online retailers, content providers, transaction brokers, service providers, and community providers.

Business-to-Business (B2B) E-commerce

Business-to-Business (B2B) e-commerce
online businesses selling to other businesses

Business-to-Business (B2B) e-commerce, in which businesses focus on selling to other businesses, is the largest form of e-commerce, with about $3.36 trillion in transactions in the United States in 2009. There was an estimated $11.5 trillion in business-to-business exchanges of all kinds, online and offline, suggesting that B2B e-commerce has significant growth potential. The ultimate size of B2B e-commerce

[1]For the purposes of this text, we subsume Business-to-Government (B2G) e-commerce within B2B e-commerce, viewing the government as simply a form of business when it acts as a procurer of goods and/or services.

is potentially huge. There are two primary business models used within the B2B arena: Net marketplaces, which include e-distributors, e-procurement companies, exchanges and industry consortia, and private industrial networks, which include single firm networks and industry-wide networks.

Consumer-to-Consumer (C2C) E-commerce

Consumer-to-Consumer (C2C) e-commerce provides a way for consumers to sell to each other, with the help of an online market maker such as the auction site eBay or the classifieds site Craigslist. Given that in 2009, eBay is expected to generate between $50 billion and $60 billion in gross merchandise volume around the world, it is probably safe to estimate that the size of the global C2C market in 2009 is over $70 billion (eBay, 2009). In C2C e-commerce, the consumer prepares the product for market, places the product for auction or sale, and relies on the market maker to provide catalog, search engine, and transaction-clearing capabilities so that products can be easily displayed, discovered, and paid for.

Consumer-to-Consumer (C2C) e-commerce
consumers selling to other consumers

Peer-to-Peer (P2P) E-commerce

Peer-to-peer technology enables Internet users to share files and computer resources directly without having to go through a central Web server. In peer-to-peer's purest form, no intermediary is required, although in fact, most P2P networks make use of intermediary "super servers" to speed operations. Since 1999, entrepreneurs and venture capitalists have attempted to adapt various aspects of peer-to-peer technology into **Peer-to-Peer (P2P) e-commerce**. To date, the most widely used P2P networks are BitTorrent (which is used for downloading large video files) and eDonkey (used mostly for music files). P2P network programs account for between 43%–70% of all Internet traffic worldwide, depending on the region—a startling figure (Ipoque, 2009). Some of this downloading and sharing is legal, but most is not. Legal commercial applications of P2P networking are beginning to emerge as Hollywood film studios move towards a digital distribution platform. The business models that support P2P e-commerce are often unusual, in many cases illegal, and under constant attack by authorities.

Peer-to-Peer (P2P) e-commerce
use of peer-to-peer technology, which enables Internet users to share files and computer resources directly without having to go through a central Web server, in e-commerce

Napster, which helped Internet users find and share online music files, was the most well-known example of P2P e-commerce until it was forced out of business in 2001 by a series of negative court decisions. Other file-sharing networks, such as Kazaa and Grokster, that emerged to take Napster's place, were also ultimately shut down by the courts, but once again have been replaced by a new crop of sites. Read the case study at the end of the chapter on The Pirate Bay for a further look at how the music industry has been transformed both by file-sharing networks and legal sites such as Apple's iTunes.

Mobile Commerce (M-commerce)

Mobile commerce, or **m-commerce**, refers to the use of wireless digital devices to enable transactions on the Web. Described more fully in Chapter 3, m-commerce involves the use of wireless networks to connect personal computers, netbooks,

mobile commerce (m-commerce)
use of wireless digital devices to enable transactions on the Web

and smartphones such the iPhone, Palm Pre, Android G1, and BlackBerry to the Web. Once connected, mobile consumers can conduct transactions, including stock trades, in-store price comparisons, banking, travel reservations, and more. M-commerce is expected to grow rapidly in the United States over the next five years.

GROWTH OF THE INTERNET AND THE WEB

Internet

worldwide network of computer networks built on common standards

The technology juggernauts behind e-commerce are the Internet and the Web. Without both of these technologies, e-commerce as we know it would be impossible. We describe the Internet and the Web in some detail in Chapter 3. The **Internet** is a worldwide network of computer networks built on common standards. Created in the late 1960s to connect a small number of mainframe computers and their users, the Internet has since grown into the world's largest network. It is impossible to say with certainty exactly how many computers and other wireless access devices such as smartphones are connected to the Internet worldwide at any one time, but the number is clearly over 1 billion. The Internet links businesses, educational institutions, government agencies, and individuals together, and provides users with services such as e-mail, document transfer, shopping, research, instant messaging, music, videos, and news.

Figure 1.3 illustrates one way to measure the growth of the Internet, by looking at the number of Internet hosts with domain names. (An *Internet host* is defined by the Internet Systems Consortium, which conducts this survey, as any IP address that returns a domain name in the in-addr.arpa domain, which is a special part of the DNS namespace that resolves IP addresses into domain names.) In January 2009, there were over 625 million Internet hosts in over 245 countries, up from just 70 million in 2000. (Internet Systems Consortium, 2009).

The Internet has shown extraordinary growth patterns when compared to other electronic technologies of the past. It took radio 38 years to achieve a 30% share of U.S. households. It took television 17 years to achieve a 30% share. It took only 10 years for the Internet/Web to achieve a 53% share of U.S. households once a graphical user interface was invented for the Web in 1993.

World Wide Web (the Web)

the most popular service that runs on the Internet; provides easy access to Web pages

The **World Wide Web (the Web)** is the most popular service that runs on the Internet infrastructure. The Web is the "killer application" that made the Internet commercially interesting and extraordinarily popular. The Web was developed in the early 1990s and hence is of much more recent vintage than the Internet. We describe the Web in some detail in Chapter 3. The Web provides access to billions of Web pages indexed by Google and other search engines. These pages are created in a language called *HTML (HyperText Markup Language)*. HTML pages can contain text, graphics, animations, and other objects. You can find an exceptionally wide range of information on Web pages, ranging from the entire catalog of Sears Roebuck, to the entire collection of public records from the Securities and Exchange Commission, to the card catalog of your local library, to millions of music tracks (some of them legal) and videos. The Internet prior to the Web was primarily used for text communications, file transfers, and remote computing. The Web introduced far more powerful and commercially interesting, colorful multimedia capabilities of direct relevance to commerce. In essence, the Web added color, voice, and video to

| FIGURE 1.3 | THE GROWTH OF THE INTERNET, MEASURED BY THE NUMBER OF INTERNET HOSTS WITH DOMAIN NAMES |

Growth in the size of the Internet 1993–2009 as measured by the number of Internet hosts with domain names.
SOURCE: Based on data from Internet Systems Consortium, Inc., 2009.

the Internet, creating a communications infrastructure and information storage system that rivals television, radio, magazines, and even libraries.

There is no precise measurement of the number of Web pages in existence, in part because today's search engines index only a portion of the known universe of Web pages, and also because the size of the Web universe is unknown. It is estimated that Google currently indexes between 40 and 50 billion pages. Google has also reported that its system had, as of July 2008, identified 1 trillion unique URLs, although many of those pages did not necessarily contain unique content. Cuil.com, a rival search engine, claimed in July 2008 to have indexed 120 billion Web pages, "more than 3 times than any other search engine." There are also an estimated 900 billion Web pages in the so-called "deep Web" that are not indexed by ordinary search engines such as Google. What is indisputable, however, is that Web content has grown exponentially since 1993.

Read *Insight on Technology: Spider Webs, Bow Ties, Scale-Free Networks, and the Deep Web* on pages 26–27 for the latest view of researchers on the structure of the Web.

ORIGINS AND GROWTH OF E-COMMERCE

It is difficult to pinpoint just when e-commerce began. There were several precursors to e-commerce. In the late 1970s, a pharmaceutical firm named Baxter Healthcare initiated a primitive form of B2B e-commerce by using a telephone-based modem that permitted hospitals to reorder supplies from Baxter. This system was later expanded during the 1980s into a PC-based remote order entry system and was widely copied throughout the United States long before the Internet became a commercial environment. The 1980s saw the development of Electronic Data Interchange (EDI) standards that permitted firms to exchange commercial documents and conduct digital commercial transactions across private networks.

In the B2C arena, the first truly large-scale digitally enabled transaction system was deployed in France in 1981. The French Minitel was a videotext system that combined a telephone with an 8-inch screen. By the mid-1980s, more than 3 million Minitels were deployed, and over 13,000 different services were available, including ticket agencies, travel services, retail products, and online banking. The Minitel service continued in existence until December 31, 2006, when it was finally discontinued by its owner, France Telecom.

However, none of these precursor systems had the functionality of the Internet. Generally, when we think of e-commerce today, it is inextricably linked to the Internet. For our purposes, we will say e-commerce begins in 1995, following the appearance of the first banner advertisements placed by AT&T, Volvo, Sprint, and others on Hotwired.com in late October 1994, and the first sales of banner ad space by Netscape and Infoseek in early 1995. Since then, e-commerce has been the fastest growing form of commerce in the United States. **Figure 1.4** and **Figure 1.5** (on page 28) chart the development of B2C e-commerce and B2B e-commerce, respectively, with projections for the next several years. Both graphs show a strong projected growth rate, but the dollar amounts of B2B e-commerce dwarf those of B2C.

TECHNOLOGY AND E-COMMERCE IN PERSPECTIVE

Although in many respects, e-commerce is new and different, it is also important to keep e-commerce in perspective. First, the Internet and the Web are just two of a long list of technologies that have greatly changed commerce in the United States and around the world. Each of these other technologies spawned business models and strategies designed to leverage the technology into commercial advantage and profit. They were also accompanied by explosive early growth, which was characterized by the emergence of thousands of entrepreneurial start-up companies, followed by painful

| FIGURE 1.4 | THE GROWTH OF B2C E-COMMERCE |

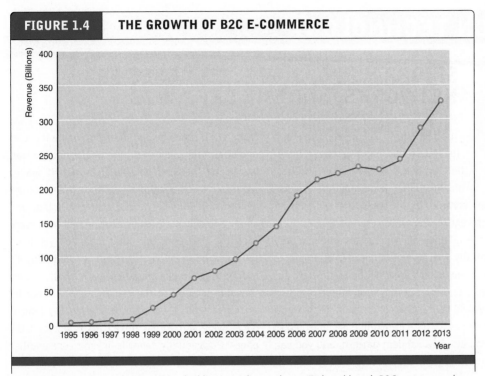

In the early years, B2C e-commerce was doubling or tripling each year. Today, although B2C e-commerce has been flat for the past year due to the economic recession, it is expected to resume growing at around 10% a year beginning in 2010.

SOURCES: Based on data from eMarketer, Inc., 2009a; U.S. Census Bureau, 2009b; authors' estimates.

retrenchment, and then a long-term successful exploitation of the technology by larger established firms. In the case of automobiles, for instance, in 1915, there were over 250 automobile manufacturers in the United States. By 1940, there were five. In the case of radio, in 1925, there were over 2,000 radio stations across the United States, with most broadcasting to local neighborhoods and run by amateurs. By 1990, there were fewer than 500 independent stations. There is every reason to believe e-commerce will follow the same pattern—with notable differences discussed throughout the text.

Second, although e-commerce has grown explosively, there is no guarantee it will continue to grow forever at these rates and much reason to believe e-commerce growth will cap as it confronts its own fundamental limitations. For instance, B2C e-commerce is still a small part (about 6%) of the overall $3.9 trillion retail market. Under current projections, in 2013, all of B2C commerce will still be less than Wal-mart's 2008 revenue. Wal-Mart is the world's largest and most successful retailer. On the other hand, with only 6% of all retail sales revenue now being generated online, there is tremendous upside potential.

INSIGHT ON TECHNOLOGY

SPIDER WEBS, BOW TIES, SCALE-FREE NETWORKS, AND THE DEEP WEB

In July 2008, Google reported that its system had identified over 1 trillion unique URLs, or Web pages. Although this is a mind-boggling number, consider that it constitutes only a fraction of the entire Web universe. To make matters worse, the number of Web pages is expanding exponentially every year, hindering attempts to catch up, keep up, and truly understand what's out there. Despite this, researchers continue to try.

The World Wide Web conjures up images of a giant spider web where everything is connected to everything else in a random pattern, and you can go from one edge of the Web to another by just following the right links. Theoretically, that's what makes the Web different from a typical index system: you can follow hyperlinks from one page to another. In 1968, sociologist Stanley Milgram put forth the "small-world" theory for social networks by positing that every human was separated from any other human by only six degrees of separation. In the "small world" theory of the Web, every Web page was thought to be separated from any other Web page by an average of about 19 clicks. The theory was supported by early research on a small sampling of Web sites. But subsequent research conducted jointly by scientists at IBM, Compaq, and AltaVista found something entirely different. These scientists used a Web crawler to identify 200 million Web pages and follow 1.5 billion links on those pages.

The researchers discovered that the Web was not like a spider web at all, but rather like a bow tie. The bow-tie Web had a "strongly connected component" (SCC) composed of about 56 million Web pages. On the right side of the bow tie was a set of 44 million OUT pages that you could get to from the center, but could not return to the center from. OUT pages tended to be corporate intranet and other Web site pages that are designed to trap you at the site when you land. On the left side of the bow tie was a set of 44 million IN pages from which you could get to the center, but that you could not travel to from the center. These were recently created pages that had not yet been linked to by many center pages. In addition, 43 million pages were classified as "tendrils," pages that did not link to the center and could not be linked to from the center. However, the tendril pages were sometimes linked to IN and/or OUT pages. Occasionally, tendrils linked to one another without passing through the center (these they called "tubes"). Finally, there were 16 million pages totally disconnected from everything.

Further evidence for the non-random and structured nature of the Web is provided in research performed by Albert-Lazlo Barabasi at the University of Notre Dame. Barabasi's team found that far from being a random, exponentially exploding network of billions of Web pages, activity on the Web was actually highly concentrated in "very-connected super nodes" that provided the connectivity to less well-connected nodes. Barabasi dubbed this type of network a "scale-free" network and found parallels in the growth of cancers, disease transmission, and computer viruses. As its turns out, scale-free networks are highly vulnerable to destruction: destroy their super nodes, and transmission of messages breaks down rapidly. On the upside, if you are a marketer trying to "spread the message" about your products, place your products on one of the super nodes and watch the news spread. Or build super nodes and attract a huge audience.

Thus, the picture of the Web that emerges from this research is quite different from earlier reports. The notion that most pairs of Web pages are separated by a handful of links, almost always under 20, and that the number of connections would grow exponentially with the size of the Web, is not supported. In fact, there is a 75% chance that there is no path from one randomly chosen page to another.

With this knowledge, it now becomes clear why the most advanced Web search engines only index a very small percentage of all Web pages, and only about 2% of the overall population of Internet hosts (about 625 million). Search engines cannot find most Web sites because their pages are not well-connected or linked to the central core of the Web.

The problem becomes more severe as the Internet goes global. Google's English language crawler does not crawl Chinese Web sites, and you will rarely see a Chinese language answer to a Google English query. The crawl-able Web of about one trillion pages is only some unknown part a much larger "deep Web," which arguably could include another 1 trillion pages or more that are not indexed at all. These pages are not easily accessible to Web crawlers that most search engine companies use. Instead, these pages are either proprietary (not available to crawlers and non-subscribers), such as the pages of *The Wall Street Journal*, airline schedule and price information, and medical research findings, or are stuck in databases that themselves are not linked to other pages. The existence of the deep Web means that search engines are often unable to answer common questions like "What's the cheapest fare to Europe from New York this week?"

A number of projects are under way to explore deep Web contents. Kosmix.com is a start-up company that attempts to categorize the databases on the Web, and then searches within those categories, which it presents in magazine format to users. Kosmix says its system allows users to effectively navigate the Web even when they don't know exactly what they are looking for. "Deep Peep" is an ambitious project at the University of Utah led by Professor Juliana Freire that aims to crawl and index every database on the public Internet even if they are not well-connected to other pages.

Given this new understanding of the structure of the Web, the implications for entrepreneurs and marketers are clear. Because e-commerce revenues inherently depend on customers being able to find a Web site using search engines, Web site managers need to take steps to ensure their Web pages are part of the connected central core, or "super nodes" of the Web. One way to do this is to make sure the site has as many links as possible to and from other relevant sites, especially to other sites within the SCC. If your site is part of the deep Web, get out, and make it more accessible to crawlers. If you want to be global, develop foreign language versions of your main site. If you want to optimize your search engine rankings, put a lot of links on your pages to pages on other sites (become a hub). Last, get as many other sites to link to your pages as you possibly can (become an authority). It's called search engine optimization, and the more you know about the structure of the real Internet, the more effective your Web sites will be.

SOURCES: Deeppeep.org, "About Us," August 2009; Kosmix.com, "About Kosmix," August 2009; "III-COR Discovering and Organizing Hidden-Web Sources," by Juliana Freire, University of Utah. Grant application. National Science Foundation, IIS Division of Information & Intelligent Systems. IIS -0713637. April 2009; "Exploring a 'Deep Web' That Google Can't Grasp," by Alex Wright, *New York Times*, February 23, 2009; "Writing the Web's Future in Numerous Languages," by Daniel Sorid, *New York Times*, December 31, 2008; "Invisible or Deep Web: What it is, Why it exists, How to find it, and Its inherent ambiguity," http://www.lib.berkeley.edu, accessed August, 2008; "Accessing the Deep Web," by Bin He, Mitesh Patel, Zhen Zhang, and Kevin Chen-Chuan Chang; *Communications of the ACM (CACM)* 50 (2): 94-101, May 2007; "The Bowtie Theory Explains Link Popularity," by John Heard, Searchengineposition.com, June 1, 2000; "Graph Structure in the Web," by A. Broder, R. Kumar, F. Maghoul, P. Raghaven, S. Rajagopalan, R. Stata, A. Tomkins, and J. Wiener, *Proceedings of the 9th International World Wide Web Conference*, Amsterdam, The Netherlands, pages 309-320. Elsevier Science, May 2000; "Authoritative Sources in a Hyperlinked Environment," by Jon M. Kleinberg, Journal of the ACM 46 (5): 604-632, 1999.

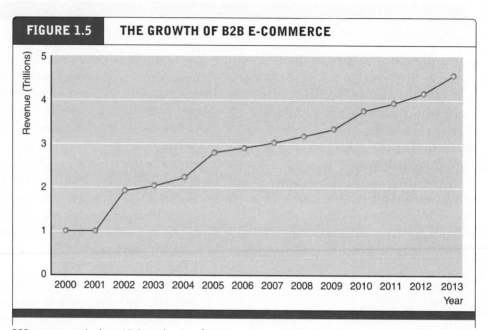

FIGURE 1.5 | **THE GROWTH OF B2B E-COMMERCE**

B2B e-commerce is about 10 times the size of B2C e-commerce. In 2013, B2B e-commerce is projected to be about $4.75 trillion. (Note: Does not include EDI transactions.)

SOURCES: Based on data from U.S. Census Bureau, 2009a; authors' estimates.

POTENTIAL LIMITATIONS ON THE GROWTH OF B2C E-COMMERCE

The data suggests that, over the next five years, B2C e-commerce will continue to grow by about 10% annually, slower than in earlier years, but much faster than traditional retail sales (about 4%). Nevertheless, there are several reasons to believe that e-commerce revenues from goods and services together will not expand forever at these rates. As online sales become a larger percentage of all sales, which typically grow in the 5%–6% range annually, online sales growth will likely decline to that growth level. This point still appears to be a long way off. Online service sales, everything from music, to video, medical information, games, and entertainment, have an even longer period to grow before they hit any ceiling effects.

There are other limitations on B2C e-commerce that have the potential to cap its growth rate and ultimate size. **Table 1.4** describes some of these limiting factors.

Some of these limitations may be minimized in the next decade. For instance, the price of an entry-level computer such as a netbook has fallen to $200 to $300, although this still represents a substantial amount of money to many. Other Internet-client gadgets such as smartphones are within this price range now. This, coupled with enhancements in capabilities such as integration with television, access to entertainment film libraries on a pay-per-view basis, and other software enhancements, will likely raise U.S. Internet household penetration rates to the

TABLE 1.4	LIMITATIONS ON THE GROWTH OF B2C E-COMMERCE
LIMITING FACTOR	**COMMENT**
Expensive technology	Using the Internet requires an investment of at least $200 to $300 for a computer and a connect charge ranging from about $10 to $50 depending on the speed of service.
Sophisticated skill set	The skills required to make effective use of the Internet and e-commerce capabilities are far more sophisticated than, say, for television or newspapers.
Persistent cultural attraction of physical markets and traditional shopping experiences	For many, shopping is a cultural and social event where people meet directly with merchants and other consumers. This social experience has not yet been fully duplicated in digital form (although social shopping is a major new development).
Persistent global inequality limiting access to telephones and personal computers	Much of the world's population does not have telephone service, PCs, or cell phones.
Saturation and ceiling effects	Growth in the Internet population slows as its approaches the size of the total population.

level of cable television penetration (about 80%) by 2013. The PC operating system will also likely evolve from the current Windows platform to far simpler interfaces similar to that found on iPhones and Palm OS handheld devices.

The most significant technology that can reduce barriers to Internet access is wireless Web technology (described in more detail in Chapter 3). Today, consumers can access the Internet via a variety of different mobile devices, such as mobile computers, smartphones, and personal digital assistants (PDAs). In 2009, almost 74 million people (around 37% of Internet users in the United States) use a mobile device to access the Internet, and this number is expected to grow to almost double (to 134 million) by 2013 (eMarketer, 2009f). **Figure 1.6** (on page 30) illustrates the rapid growth projected for mobile Internet access during the period 2008–2013.

On balance, the current technological limits on e-commerce growth, while real, are likely to recede in importance over the next decade. The social and cultural limitations of e-commerce are less likely to change as quickly, but the Web is fast developing virtual social shopping experiences and virtual realities that millions find as entertaining as shopping or seeing their friends face-to-face.

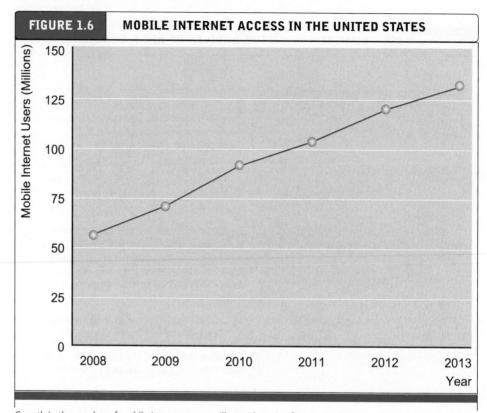

FIGURE 1.6   MOBILE INTERNET ACCESS IN THE UNITED STATES

Growth in the number of mobile Internet users will provide a significant stimulus to mobile e-commerce.
SOURCES: Based on data from eMarketer, Inc., 2009e.

1.2 E-COMMERCE: A BRIEF HISTORY

Although e-commerce is not very old, it already has a tumultuous history. The history of e-commerce can be usefully divided into three periods. The early years of e-commerce were a period of explosive growth and extraordinary innovation, beginning in 1995 with the first widespread use of the Web to advertise products. This period of explosive growth was capped in March 2000 when stock market valuations for dot-com companies reached their peak and thereafter began to collapse. A sobering period of reassessment occurred, followed by strong double-digit growth. In 2006, e-commerce entered a period of redefinition with the appearance of social networking and user-generated content sharing Web sites that have attracted huge audiences.

E-COMMERCE 1995–2000: INNOVATION

The early years of e-commerce were one of the most euphoric of times in American commercial history. It was also a time when key e-commerce concepts were developed and explored. Thousands of dot-com companies were formed, backed by over $125 billion in financial capital—one of the largest outpourings of venture capital in United States history (PricewaterhouseCoopers, National Venture Capital

Association MoneyTree Report, Data: Thomson Financial, 2009). **Figure 1.7** depicts the amounts invested by venture capital firms in Internet-related businesses in the period 1995–2008. While venture investment has trended markedly lower since 2000, it is still significantly larger than pre-1996 levels, and investing in dot-com and Internet businesses has begun to increase once again in the second half of 2009 after dramatically decreasing in the latter half of 2008 and early 2009 due to the recession.

For computer scientists and information technologists, the early success of e-commerce was a powerful vindication of a set of information technologies that had developed over a period of 40 years—extending from the development of the early Internet to the PC, to local area networks. The vision was of a universal communications and computing environment that everyone on Earth could access

FIGURE 1.7	AMOUNTS RAISED BY INTERNET-RELATED VENTURE-BACKED FIRMS

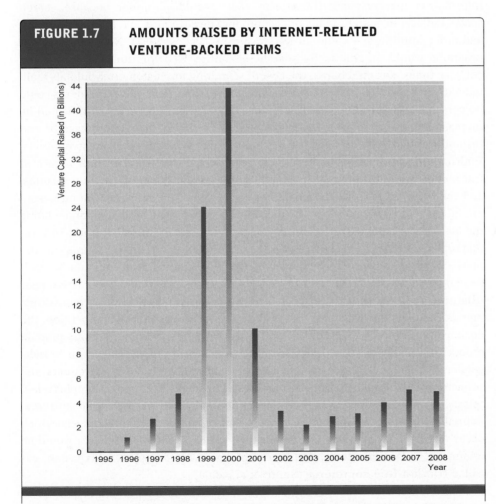

The amounts raised by Internet-related venture-backed firms peaked during the 1999–2001 period, but the amount raised in the 2002–2008 period is still much higher than that raised in the periods prior to 1999.

SOURCES: Based on data from PricewaterhouseCoopers/National Venture Capital Association MoneyTree Report, Data: Thomson Financial, 2009.

with cheap, inexpensive computers—a worldwide universe of knowledge stored on HTML pages created by hundreds of millions of individuals and thousands of libraries, governments, and scientific institutes. Technologists celebrated the fact that the Internet was not controlled by anyone or any nation, but was free to all. They believed the Internet—and the e-commerce that rose on this infrastructure—should remain a self-governed, self-regulated environment.

For economists, the early years of e-commerce raised the realistic prospect of a nearly perfect competitive market: where price, cost, and quality information is equally distributed, a nearly infinite set of suppliers compete against one another, and customers have access to all relevant market information worldwide. The Internet would spawn digital markets where information would be nearly perfect—something that is rarely true in other real-world markets. Merchants in turn would have equal direct access to hundreds of millions of customers. In this near-perfect information marketspace, transaction costs would plummet because search costs—the cost of searching for prices, product descriptions, payment settlement, and order fulfillment—would all fall drastically (Bakos, 1997). New shopping bot programs would automatically search the entire Web for the best prices and delivery times. For merchants, the cost of searching for customers would also fall, reducing the need for wasteful advertising. At the same time, advertisements could be personalized to the needs of every customer. Prices and even costs would be increasingly transparent to the consumer, who could now know exactly and instantly the worldwide best price, quality, and availability of most products. Information asymmetry would be greatly reduced. Given the instant nature of Internet communications, the availability of powerful sales information systems, and the low cost involved in changing prices on a Web site (low menu costs), producers could dynamically price their products to reflect actual demand, ending the idea of one national price, or one suggested manufacturer's list price. In turn, market middlemen—the distributors, wholesalers, and other factors in the marketplace who are intermediates between producers and consumers, each demanding a payment and raising costs while adding little value—would disappear (**disintermediation**). Manufacturers and content originators would develop direct market relationships with their customers. The resulting intense competition, the decline of intermediaries, and the lower transaction costs would eliminate product brands, and along with it, the possibility of *monopoly profits* based on brands, geography, or special access to factors of production. Prices for products and services would fall to the point where prices covered costs of production plus a fair, "market rate" of return on capital, plus additional small payments for entrepreneurial effort (that would not last long). Unfair competitive advantages (which occur when one competitor has an advantage others cannot purchase) would be eliminated, as would extraordinary returns on invested capital. This vision was called **friction-free commerce** (Smith et al., 2000).

For real-world entrepreneurs, their financial backers, and marketing professionals, the idea of friction-free commerce was far from their own visions. For these players, e-commerce represented an extraordinary opportunity to earn far above normal returns on investment. The e-commerce marketspace represented access to mil-

disintermediation
displacement of market middlemen who traditionally are intermediaries between producers and consumers by a new direct relationship between manufacturers and content originators with their customers

friction-free commerce
a vision of commerce in which information is equally distributed, transaction costs are low, prices can be dynamically adjusted to reflect actual demand, intermediaries decline, and unfair competitive advantages are eliminated

lions of consumers worldwide who used the Internet and a set of marketing communications technologies (e-mail and Web pages) that was universal, inexpensive, and powerful. These new technologies would permit marketers to practice what they always had done—segmenting the market into groups with different needs and price sensitivity, targeting the segments with branding and promotional messages, and positioning the product and pricing for each group—but with even more precision. In this new marketspace, extraordinary profits would go to **first movers**—those firms who were first to market in a particular area and who moved quickly to gather market share. In a "winner take all" market, first movers could establish a large customer base quickly, build brand name recognition early, create an entirely new distribution channel, and then inhibit competitors (new entrants) by building in *switching costs* for their customers through proprietary interface designs and features available only at one site. The idea for entrepreneurs was to create near monopolies online based on size, convenience, selection, and brand. Online businesses using the new technology could create informative, community-like features unavailable to traditional merchants. These "communities of consumption" also would add value and be difficult for traditional merchants to imitate. The thinking was that once customers became accustomed to using a company's unique Web interface and feature set, they could not easily be switched to competitors. In the best case, the entrepreneurial firm would invent proprietary technologies and techniques that almost everyone adopted, creating a network effect. A **network effect** occurs where all participants receive value from the fact that everyone else uses the same tool or product (for example, a common operating system, telephone system, or software application such as a proprietary instant messaging standard or an operating system such as Windows), all of which increase in value as more people adopt them.[2] Successful first movers would become the new intermediaries of e-commerce, displacing traditional retail merchants and suppliers of content, and becoming profitable by charging fees of one sort or another for the value customers perceived in their services and products.

To initiate this process, entrepreneurs argued that prices would have to be very low to attract customers and fend off potential competitors. E-commerce was, after all, a totally new way of shopping that would have to offer some immediate cost benefits to consumers. However, because doing business on the Web was supposedly so much more efficient when compared to traditional "bricks-and-mortar" businesses (even when compared to the direct mail catalog business) and because the costs of customer acquisition and retention would supposedly be so much lower, profits would inevitably materialize out of these efficiencies. Given these dynamics, market share, the number of visitors to a site ("eyeballs"), and gross revenue became far more important in the earlier stages of an online firm than earnings or profits. Entrepreneurs and their financial backers in the early years of e-commerce expected that extraordinary profitability would come, but only after several years of losses.

Thus, the early years of e-commerce were driven largely by visions of profiting from new technology, with the emphasis on quickly achieving very high market

first mover
a firm that is first to market in a particular area and that moves quickly to gather market share

network effect
occurs where users receive value from the fact that everyone else uses the same tool or product

[2]The network effect is quantified by Metcalfe's Law, which argues that the value of a network grows by the square of the number of participants.

visibility. The source of financing was venture capital funds. The ideology of the period emphasized the ungoverned "Wild West" character of the Web and the feeling that governments and courts could not possibly limit or regulate the Internet; there was a general belief that traditional corporations were too slow and bureaucratic, too stuck in the old ways of doing business, to "get it"—to be competitive in e-commerce. Young entrepreneurs were therefore the driving force behind e-commerce, backed by huge amounts of money invested by venture capitalists. The emphasis was on *deconstructing* (destroying) traditional distribution channels and disintermediating existing channels, using new pure online companies who aimed to achieve impregnable first-mover advantages. Overall, this period of e-commerce was characterized by experimentation, capitalization, and hypercompetition (Varian, 2000a). Read *Insight on Business: The Internet Investment Rollercoaster* for a further look at the financing of e-commerce ventures.

The crash in stock market values for Internet-related companies throughout 2000 is a convenient marker for ending the early period in the development of e-commerce. Looking back at the first years of e-commerce, it is apparent that e-commerce has been, for the most part, a stunning technological success as the Internet and the Web ramped up from a few thousand to billions of e-commerce transactions per year, generating $228 billion in B2C revenues and around $3.36 trillion in B2B revenues in 2009, with around 123 million online buyers in the United States. With enhancements and strengthening, described in later chapters, it is clear that e-commerce's digital infrastructure is solid enough to sustain significant growth in e-commerce during the next decade. The Internet scales well. The "e" in e-commerce has been an overwhelming success.

From a business perspective, though, the early years of e-commerce were a mixed success, and offered many surprises. Only about 10% of dot-coms formed since 1995 have survived as independent companies in 2009. Only a very tiny percentage of these survivors are profitable. Yet online B2C sales of goods and services are still growing. Consumers have learned to use the Web as a powerful source of information about products they actually purchase through other channels, such as at a traditional "bricks-and-mortar" store. This is especially true of expensive consumer durables such as appliances, automobiles, and electronics. This "Internet-influenced" commerce is very difficult to estimate, but is believed to be somewhere around $750 billion in 2009 (eMarketer, Inc., 2008b). Altogether then, B2C e-commerce (both actual purchases and purchases influenced by Web shopping but actually buying in a store) amounts to almost $1 trillion in 2009, or about 25% of total retail sales. The "commerce" in e-commerce is basically very sound, at least in the sense of attracting a growing number of customers and generating revenues.

E-COMMERCE 2001–2006: CONSOLIDATION

E-commerce entered a period of consolidation beginning in 2001 and lasting until 2006. Emphasis shifted to a more "business-driven" approach rather than technology driven; large traditional firms learned how to use the Web to strengthen their market positions; brand extension and strengthening became more important than creating new brands; financing shrunk as capital markets shunned start-up firms; and traditional bank financing based on profitability returned.

INSIGHT ON BUSINESS

THE INTERNET INVESTMENT ROLLERCOASTER

It's reasonable to think that in the midst of the worst global recession since the 1930s, speculative investments in Internet start-ups would come to a complete halt. But this has not happened, and in 2009, high tech was the place to be from an investor point of view.

E-commerce was built on Internet technology, but what makes it run is money—big money. Between 1998 and 2000, venture capitalists (VCs) poured an estimated $120 billion into approximately 12,450 dot-com start-up ventures. Investment bankers then took 1,262 of these companies public in what is called an initial public offering (IPO) of stock. To prepare for an IPO, investment bankers analyze a company's finances and business plans and attempt to arrive at an estimate of the company's "worth"—how much the investing public might be willing to pay for the shares and how many shares might be purchased by the public and other institutions. The bankers then underwrite the stock offering and sell the stock on a public stock exchange, making enormous fees for underwriting in the process. The basic process has not changed over time, but the style and fashions have changed since the good old "bad days" of e-commerce.

In the early years of e-commerce, from 1998 to 2000, dot-com IPO shares often skyrocketed within minutes of hitting the trading floor. Some shares tripled and quadrupled in the first day, and a 50% "pump" (or increase in value) was considered just a reasonable showing. IPO shares for dot-com companies were often targeted to open at around $15 per share, and it was not uncommon for them to be trading at $45 a share or even much more later the same day. Therefore, getting in on the ground floor of an IPO—which meant arranging to purchase a fixed number of shares prior to actual trading on the first day—was a privilege reserved for other large institutions, friends of the investment bankers, or other investment bankers. In what was called "stock spinning," the underwriter would sell IPO shares to entrepreneurs it hoped to obtain business from in the future. The Securities and Exchange Commission made this practice illegal in 1999.

What has happened to the dot-com IPOs of this period? According to a financial services research firm, Thomson Financial, 12% of the companies that went public between 1998 and 2000 were trading at $1 or less a share in April 2001, a fairly shocking development when one considers that just a relatively short time previously, those companies' shares were trading at upwards of 10 to 100 times that price. By 2007, seven years after the peak of the dot-com frenzy, at least 5,000 Internet companies had either been acquired or shut down. On a more positive note, research shows that the attrition rate of these early firms was about 20% a year, on par with what occurred in other industries during their early boom years. More than half the early dot.coms were still in business in 2007.

After the big bust of March 2000, the Thermidor period began. Venture capitalists turned away from the "Get Big Fast" and "First-Mover Advantage" religion, and instead focused on companies that demonstrated a profitable prior history. In this second period, investors spent over $200 billion on the purchase of over 4,000 Web companies. Hot properties included Internet retail shopping sites (such as Shopping.com, purchased for $620 million by eBay, and Shopzilla, purchased for $525 million by The E.W. Scripps Company), Internet advertising firms (such as DoubleClick, purchased for $1.1 billion by buyout firm Hellman & Friedman), search engine properties (such as Ask Jeeves [now Ask.com], purchased by IAC/InterActive Corp for $1.85 billion), and community sites (such as About.com, purchased by The New York Times for $410 million). The iconic event of this period, however, was Google's IPO in late 2004. Google had been prof-

(continued)

itable for three years before going public and its search-based advertising model was churning out profits. Social networking was just beginning and few thought there was any money in it. Yet in July 2005, Rupert Murdoch's News Corp.'s Fox Interactive Media division purchased MySpace for the unheard of price of $580 million.

By 2006, the period of fiscal discipline began to end, and VCs started once again to make big plays for "get big fast" companies. Tech was "in" again, and once again, audience size became the most important investment criteria. Google's shares soared from its $85 offering price in 2004 to almost $750 in November 2007. About 62% of tech firms going public in 2006–2008 were not profitable companies (still short of the all-time 85% unprofitable in 2000). So far, the King of the Get Big Fast mentality remains YouTube, an unprofitable company with an estimated $200 million in revenue in 2008, for which Google paid $1.65 billion in the belief that YouTube's then 32 million users would be worth something in the future. With a $30 billion cash hoard at the time, this was a small price to pay for a potential gold mine, at least from Google's perspective. Wall Street got the message.

Google's purchase of YouTube put the stamp of approval on what some investors have called the "social networking bubble." Sites such as Facebook, which began in 2004 with a series of small investments from venture capital firms, started receiving huge investments not from VCs but from private equity firms and established giants such as Microsoft. The reasoning behind these investments was the same as Google's: social networking sites are "winner take all" markets where, once a firm establishes a lead position, others sites simply cannot compete, and soon a single winner emerges while the rest consolidate or close their doors.

In 2007, Microsoft, having failed to perceive the explosive growth and potential value of social networking sites, and realizing that to start its own social network would be difficult given the lead of MySpace and Facebook, invested $240 million in Facebook for a 1.5% share of the company. In return, Microsoft became the exclusive third-party advertiser on Facebook. This deal valued Facebook as worth $15 billion despite the absence of profits! In 2009, a Russian investment firm paid $200 million for 1.96% of Facebook, valuing the company at $10 billion.

In late 2008 and early 2009, with the decline in the economy, venture capital investments dropped off the table, to levels not seen since 1997. The IPO market virtually shut down for e-commerce and Internet firms. In a hopeful sign, however, angel investors who make investments in early stage start-ups continued to make hundreds of investments in the $500,000 to $1 million range. Helped by the fact that the cost of building new Web sites has fallen drastically from the early days, small investments using today's technology are sufficient to test the viability of an idea on the Internet. By the second quarter of 2009, things were beginning to look up, with several high-tech IPOs scheduled, including, most notably, OpenTable (a popular but not yet profitable restaurant reservation site with $41 million in revenues and a small net loss of $149,000). OpenTable successfully went public in May 2009.

While the number of IPOs scheduled for 2009 is down, Internet e-commerce for both retail goods and services continues to weather the storm far better than their offline counterparts, and offers high growth potential. Investors seem to agree: in the first five months of 2009, the S&P index advanced 2% while the IPO Index (an index that tracks the post-issuance returns of IPOs) has risen 22% with little volatility.

SOURCES: "It's Safe to Play IPOs Again," by Jon Markman, MSNmoney.com, June 20, 2009; "A Comeback in the IPO Market," by Steve Hamm and Spencer Ante, BusinessWeek.com, May 27, 2009; "OpenTable IPO Lifts Hopes on the Stock Exchange," by Deborah Gage, SFGate.com, May 22, 2009;, "Super Angels Shake Up Venture Capital," by Spencer Ante, BusinessWeek.com, May 21, 2009; "Venture Capital Investment Sinks," by Claire Cain Miller, *New York Times*, April 28, 2009; "OpenTable Files For IPO, And Reveals Its Finances," by Erick Schonfeld, TechCrunch.com, January 30, 2009; "Microsoft Signs Two-Part Facebook Deal," by David Kirkpatrick, CNNMoney.com, October 25, 2007; "Silicon Valley Start-Ups Awash in Dollars, Again," by Brad Stone and Matt Richtel, *New York Times*, October 17, 2007; "Tech Companies Bleeding Red Ink Pursue IPO Gold," by Pui-Wing Tam, *Wall Street Journal*, March 13, 2007; "Was There Too Little Entry During the Dot Com Era?" by Brent Goldfarb, David Kirsch, and David Miller, Robert H. Smith School Research Paper No. RHS 06-029, April 24, 2006.

E-COMMERCE 2006—PRESENT: REINVENTION

E-commerce entered a third period in 2006 that extends through the present day and into the uncertain future. Google has been one of the driving forces, but so have other large media firms who have quickly bought out very fast-moving entrepreneurial firms, such as MySpace. It is a period of reinvention involving the extension of Internet technologies, and the discovery of new business models based on consumer-generated content and social networking. This period is as much a sociological phenomenon as it is a technological or business phenomenon. Few of the new models have been able to monetize their huge audiences into profitable operations yet, but many eventually will.

Table 1.5 summarizes e-commerce in each of these three periods.

TABLE 1.5	EVOLUTION OF E-COMMERCE	
1995–2000 INNOVATION	2001–2006 CONSOLIDATION	2006–PRESENT RE-INVENTION
Technology driven	Business driven	Audience, customer, and community driven
Revenue growth emphasis	Earnings and profits emphasis	Audience and social network growth emphasis
Venture capital financing	Traditional financing	Smaller VC investments; early small-firm buyouts by large online players
Ungoverned	Stronger regulation and governance	Extensive government surveillance
Entrepreneurial	Large traditional firms	Large pure Web-based firms
Disintermediation	Strengthening intermediaries	Proliferation of small online intermediaries renting business processes of larger firms
Perfect markets	Imperfect markets, brands, and network effects	Continuation of online market imperfections; commodity competition in select markets
Pure online strategies	Mixed "bricks-and-clicks" strategies	Return of pure online strategies in new markets; extension of bricks and clicks in traditional retail markets
First-mover advantages	Strategic-follower strength; complimentary assets	First-mover advantages return in new markets as traditional Web players catch up
Low-complexity retail products	High-complexity retail products	Services

ASSESSING E-COMMERCE: SUCCESSES, SURPRISES, AND FAILURES

Although e-commerce has grown at an extremely rapid pace in customers and revenues, it is clear that many of the visions, predictions, and assertions about e-commerce developed in the early years have not have been fulfilled. For instance, economists' visions of "friction-free" commerce have not been entirely realized. Prices are sometimes lower on the Web, but the low prices are sometimes a function of entrepreneurs selling products below their costs. Consumers are less price sensitive than expected; surprisingly, the Web sites with the highest revenue often have the highest prices. There remains considerable persistent and even increasing price dispersion on the Web: the difference between the lowest price and the average price for a basket of goods increased from 8% of the average price in 2000 to 10% in 2009 (Nash-equilibrium.com, 2009). In other words, the standard deviation in Web prices is about 10% of the average price for the same product on the Web. Shop around! The concept of one world, one market, one price has not occurred in reality as entrepreneurs discover new ways to differentiate their products and services. While for the most part Internet prices save consumers about 20% on average when compared to in-store prices, sometimes prices on the Web are higher than for similar products purchased offline, especially if shipping costs are considered. For instance, prices on books and CDs vary by as much as 50%, and prices for airline tickets as much as 20% (Baye, 2004; Baye, et al., 2004; Bailey, 1998a, b; Brynjolfsson and Smith, 2000; Aguiar and Hurst, 2008; Alessandria, 2009). Merchants have adjusted to the competitive Internet environment by engaging in "hit-and-run pricing" or changing prices every day or hour so competitors never know what they are charging (neither do customers); by making their prices hard to discover and sowing confusion among consumers by "baiting and switching" customers from low-margin products to high-margin products with supposedly "higher quality." Finally, brands remain very important in e-commerce—consumers trust some firms more than others to deliver a high-quality product on time (Slatalla, 2005).

The "perfect competition" model of extreme market efficiency has not come to pass. Merchants and marketers are continually introducing information asymmetries. Search costs have fallen overall, but the overall transaction cost of actually completing a transaction in e-commerce remains high because users have a bewildering number of new questions to consider: Will the merchant actually deliver? What is the time frame of delivery? Does the merchant really stock this item? How do I fill out this form? Many potential e-commerce purchases are terminated in the shopping cart stage because of these consumer uncertainties. For some product areas, it is easier to call a trusted catalog merchant on the telephone than order on a Web site. Finally, intermediaries have not disappeared as predicted. Most manufacturers, for instance, have not adopted the Dell model of online sales (direct sales by the manufacturer to the consumer), and Dell itself has moved towards a mixed model heavily reliant on in-store sales where customers can "kick the tires" by trying the keyboard and viewing the screen. Apple Stores are very successful physical retail locations, and marketing devices. People still like to shop in a physical store.

If anything, e-commerce has created many new opportunities for middlemen to aggregate content, products, and services into portals and search engines and thereby introduce themselves as the "new" intermediaries. Yahoo, MSN, and Amazon, along with third-party travel sites such as Travelocity, Orbitz and Expedia, are all examples of this kind of new intermediary. As illustrated in **Figure 1.8**, e-commerce did not drive existing retail chains and catalog merchants out of business, although it has created opportunities for new entrepreneurial Web-only firms to succeed. In fact, existing retail chains with physical stores as well as Web sites earned the largest portion of online sales in 2008.

The visions of many entrepreneurs and venture capitalists for e-commerce have not materialized exactly as predicted either. First-mover advantage appears to have succeeded only for a very small group of sites. Historically, first movers have been long-term losers, with the early-to-market innovators usually being displaced by established "fast-follower" firms with the right complement of financial, marketing, legal, and production assets needed to develop mature markets, and this has proved true for e-commerce as well. Many e-commerce first movers, such as eToys, FogDog (sporting goods), WebVan (groceries), and Eve.com (beauty products) are out of business. Customer acquisition and retention costs during the early years of e-commerce were extraordinarily high, with some firms, such as E*Trade and other financial service firms, paying up to $400 to acquire a new customer. The overall costs of doing business on the Web—including the costs of technology, site design and maintenance, and warehouses for fulfillment—are no lower than the costs faced by the most efficient bricks-and-mortar stores. A large warehouse costs tens of millions of dollars regardless of a firm's Web presence. The knowledge of how to run the warehouse is priceless, and not easily moved. The start-up costs can be staggering. Attempting to achieve profitability by raising prices has often led to large customer defections. From the e-commerce merchant's perspective, the "e" in e-commerce does not stand for "easy."

FIGURE 1.8	SHARE OF RETAIL ONLINE SALES BY TYPE OF COMPANY

Web-only firms account for less than one-third of online retail firm revenues.
SOURCE: eMarketer, Inc., 2009g.

PREDICTIONS FOR THE FUTURE: MORE SURPRISES

Given that e-commerce has changed greatly in the last several years, its future cannot be predicted except to say "Watch for more surprises." There are five main factors that will help define the future of e-commerce. First, there is little doubt that the technology of e-commerce—the Internet, the Web, and the growing number of wireless Internet devices that make up the emerging "mobile digital platform," including smartphones such as the iPhone, Palm Pre, Android G1, and BlackBerry, will continue to propagate through all commercial activity. After a flat year in 2009, the overall revenues from e-commerce (goods and services) are expected to continue to rise, most likely in the range of 10%–12% per year through 2013. The number of products and services sold on the Web and the size of the average purchase order will both continue to grow at double-digit rates. The number of online shoppers in the United States will also continue to grow, although at a more modest rate of less than 5% per year. There has also been a significant broadening of the online product mix compared to the early years when books, computer software, and hardware dominated e-commerce (see **Table 1.6**). This trend will continue as trust in e-commerce transactions grows. (See Chapter 9 for changes in retail products and services.)

TABLE 1.6	ONLINE RETAIL SALES BY CATEGORY, 2008
CATEGORY	**ANNUAL SALES (IN BILLIONS)**
	2008
Mass merchant/department store	$35.5
Computers/electronics	$23.7
Office supplies	$17.7
Apparel/accessories	$14.0
Books/CDs/DVDs	$4.3
Housewares/Home furnishings	$3.8
Specialty/non-apparel	$3.8
Health/beauty	$2.9
Food/drug	$3.3
Sporting goods	$1.7
Flower/gifts	$1.4
Hardware/home improvement	$1.4
Toys/hobbies	$1.2
Jewelry	$1.1

SOURCES: Based on data from Internet Retailer, 2009; authors' estimates.

Second, e-commerce prices will rise to cover the real costs of doing business on the Web, and to pay investors a reasonable rate of return on their capital. Third, e-commerce *margins* (the difference between the revenues from sales and the cost of goods) and profits will rise to levels more typical of all retailers. Fourth, the cast of players will change radically. Traditional well-endowed, experienced Fortune 500 companies will play a growing and dominant role in e-commerce while at the same time new start-up ventures will quickly gain large online audiences for new products and services not dominated by the large players. There will also be a continuation of audience consolidation on the Internet in general, with the top 25 sites garnering over 90% of the audience share, and nearly one-third of all online sales. **Table 1.7** lists the top 25 online retailers, as ranked by 2008 online sales. The table shows an unmistakable trend toward the appearance of some very well-known, traditional brands from strong traditional businesses, with Staples, Office Depot, OfficeMax, Sears, Best Buy, Sony, Costco, Wal-Mart and Hewlett Packard all in the top 15.

Fifth, the number of successful pure online companies will remain smaller than integrated online/offline stores that combine traditional sales channels such as physical stores and printed catalogs with online efforts. For instance, traditional catalog sales firms such as L.L.Bean have transformed themselves into integrated online and direct mail firms with more than half of their sales coming from the online channel. Procter & Gamble will continue to develop informative Web sites such as Tide.com; and the major automotive companies will continue to improve the content and value of their Web sites even if they do not enter into direct sales relationships with consumers, but instead use the Web to assist sales through dealers (thereby strengthening traditional intermediaries and channels).

The future of e-commerce will include the growth of regulatory activity both in the United States and worldwide. Governments around the world are challenging the early vision of computer scientists and information technologists that the Internet should be a self-regulating and self-governing phenomenon. The Internet and e-commerce have been so successful and powerful, so all-pervasive, that they directly involve the social, cultural, and political life of entire nations and cultures. Throughout history, whenever technologies have risen to this level of social importance, power, and visibility, they become the target of efforts to regulate and control the technology to ensure that positive social benefits result from their use and to guarantee the public's health and welfare. Radio, television, automobiles, electricity, and railroads are all the subject of regulation and legislation. Likewise, with e-commerce. In the U.S. Congress, there have already been a number of bills passed (as well as hundreds proposed) to control various facets of the Internet and e-commerce, from consumer privacy to pornography, gambling, and encryption. We can expect these efforts at regulation in the United States and around the world to increase as e-commerce extends its reach and importance.

A relatively new factor that will influence the growth of e-commerce is the cost of energy, in particular gasoline and diesel. As fuel costs rise, traveling to shop at physical locations can be a very expensive. Buying online can save customers time and energy costs. There is growing evidence that shoppers are changing their shop-

TABLE 1.7	TOP 25 ONLINE RETAILERS RANKED BY ONLINE SALES
ONLINE RETAILER	ONLINE SALES (2008) (IN BILLIONS)
Amazon	$19.1
Staples	$ 7.7
Office Depot	$ 4.8
Dell.com	$ 4.8
Apple Computer	$ 3.6
OfficeMax	$ 3.1
Sears Holdings Corporation	$ 2.7
CDW Corp	$ 2.6
Newegg.com	$ 2.1
QVC Corp	$ 2.0
Best Buy Co.	$ 2.0
SonyStyle.com	$ 1.8
Costco Wholesale Corp.	$ 1.7
Wal-Mart Stores	$ 1.7
HP Home and Home Office	$ 1.5
JC Penney	$ 1.5
Circuit City Stores	$ 1.4
Netflix.com	$ 1.3
Victoria's Secret Direct	$ 1.3
Target Corp.	$ 1.2
Systemax Inc.	$ 1.1
Williams Sonoma Inc.	$ 1.0
L.L. Bean	$ 1.0
GAP	$ 1.0
HSN	$ 1.0

SOURCES: Based on data from Internet Retailer, 2009; company reports on Form 10-K filed with the Securities and Exchange Commission; eMarketer, Inc., 2009h.

ping habits and locales because of fuel costs, and pushing the sales of online retailers to higher levels.

In summary, the future of e-commerce will be a fascinating mixture of traditional retail, service, and media firms extending their brands to online markets; early-period e-commerce firms such as Amazon and eBay strengthening their financial results and dominant positions; and a bevy of entirely new entrepreneurial firms with the potential to rocket into prominence by developing huge new audiences in months. Firms that fit this pattern include Facebook, Twitter, MySpace, and PhotoBucket.

1.3 UNDERSTANDING E-COMMERCE: ORGANIZING THEMES

Understanding e-commerce in its totality is a difficult task for students and instructors because there are so many facets to the phenomenon. No single academic discipline is prepared to encompass all of e-commerce. After teaching the e-commerce course for several years and writing this book, we have come to realize just how difficult it is to "understand" e-commerce. We have found it useful to think about e-commerce as involving three broad interrelated themes: technology, business, and society. We do not mean to imply any ordering of importance here because this book and our thinking freely range over these themes as appropriate to the problem we are trying to understand and describe. Nevertheless, as in previous technologically driven commercial revolutions, there is an historic progression. Technologies develop first, and then those developments are exploited commercially. Once commercial exploitation of the technology becomes widespread, a host of social, cultural, and political issues arise.

TECHNOLOGY: INFRASTRUCTURE

The development and mastery of digital computing and communications technology is at the heart of the newly emerging global digital economy we call e-commerce. To understand the likely future of e-commerce, you need a basic understanding of the information technologies upon which it is built. E-commerce is above all else a technologically driven phenomenon that relies on a host of information technologies as well as fundamental concepts from computer science developed over a 50-year period. At the core of e-commerce are the Internet and the World Wide Web, which we describe in detail in Chapter 3. Underlying these technologies are a host of complementary technologies: personal computers, handheld cell phone/computers such as the iPhone, local area networks, relational databases, client/server computing, cloud computing, and fiber-optic switches, to name just a few. These technologies lie at the heart of sophisticated business computing applications such as enterprise-wide computing systems, supply chain management systems, manufacturing resource planning systems, and customer relationship management systems. E-commerce relies on all these basic technologies—not just the Internet. The Internet—while representing a sharp break from prior corporate computing and communications technologies—is nevertheless just the latest development in the evolution of corporate computing and part of the continuing chain of computer-based innovations in business. **Figure 1.9** illustrates the major stages in the development of corporate computing and indicates how the Internet and the Web fit into this development trajectory.

To truly understand e-commerce, then, you will need to know something about packet-switched communications, protocols such as TCP/IP, client/server and cloud computing, mobile digital platforms, Web servers, HTML, and software programming tools such as JavaScript and AJAX. All of these topics are described fully in Part 2 of the book (Chapters 3–5).

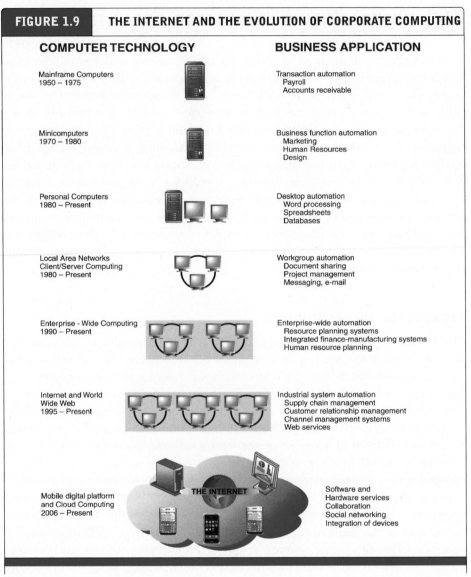

FIGURE 1.9 THE INTERNET AND THE EVOLUTION OF CORPORATE COMPUTING

The Internet and World Wide Web , and the emergence of a mobile digital platform held together by the Internet cloud, are the latest in a chain of evolving technologies and related business applications, each of which builds on its predecessors.

BUSINESS: BASIC CONCEPTS

While the technology provides the infrastructure, it is the business applications—the potential for extraordinary returns on investment—that create the interest and excitement in e-commerce. New technologies present businesses and entrepreneurs with new ways of organizing production and transacting business. New technologies change the strategies and plans of existing firms: old strategies are made obsolete and new ones need to be invented. New technologies are the birthing grounds where thousands of new companies spring up with new products and services. New technologies are the graveyard of many traditional businesses, such as record stores. To truly understand e-commerce, you will need to be familiar with some key business concepts, such as the nature of digital electronic markets, digital goods, business models, firm and industry value chains, value webs, industry structure, and consumer behavior in digital markets, as well as basic concepts of financial analysis. We'll examine these concepts further in Chapter 2 , Chapters 6 and 7, and also Chapters 9 through 12.

SOCIETY: TAMING THE JUGGERNAUT

With around 200 million adult Americans now using the Internet, many for e-commerce purposes, and over 1.67 billion users worldwide, the impact of the Internet and e-commerce on society is significant and global. Increasingly, e-commerce is subject to the laws of nations and global entities. You will need to understand the pressures that global e-commerce places on contemporary society in order to conduct a successful e-commerce business or understand the e-commerce phenomenon. The primary societal issues we discuss in this book are individual privacy, intellectual property, and public welfare policy.

Since the Internet and the Web are exceptionally adept at tracking the identity and behavior of individuals online, e-commerce raises difficulties for preserving privacy—the ability of individuals to place limits on the type and amount of information collected about them, and to control the uses of their personal information. Read *Insight on Society: Privacy Online: Does Anybody Care?* to get a view of some of the ways e-commerce sites use personal information.

Because the cost of distributing digital copies of copyrighted intellectual property—tangible works of the mind such as music, books, and videos—is nearly zero on the Internet, e-commerce poses special challenges to the various methods societies have used in the past to protect intellectual property rights.

The global nature of e-commerce also poses public policy issues of equity, equal access, content regulation, and taxation. For instance, in the United States, public telephone utilities are required under public utility and public accommodation laws to make basic service available at affordable rates so everyone can have telephone service. Should these laws be extended to the Internet and the Web? If goods are purchased by a New York State resident from a Web site in California, shipped from a center in Illinois, and delivered to New York, what state has the right to collect a sales tax? Should some heavy Internet users who consume extraordinary amounts of bandwidth be charged extra for service, or should the Internet be neutral with respect to usage? If some societies choose to ban selected images, selected commercial activity (such as gambling), or political messages from their public media, then how can that society exercise content and activity control over a global e-commerce site? What rights do nation-states and their citizens have with respect to the Internet, the Web, and e-commerce? We address issues such as these in Chapter 8, and also throughout the text

INSIGHT ON SOCIETY

PRIVACY ONLINE: DOES ANYBODY CARE?

Ever have the feeling you've lost control over your personal information on the Internet? Feel people are following you around online? Do you ever have the feeling that you no longer control what appears on your computer screen, or in your e-mail inbox? Have you ever read a privacy statement at a Web site and felt totally confused? Join the crowd: most Internet users often feel this way too. Today, upwards of 80% of all e-mail is unsolicited junk mail called spam. In a year, thousands of "display" ads (banners) will appear on your screen that you never asked for and are often irrelevant to you. Yet one of the virtues (or vices, depending on your perspective) of e-commerce technology is that it permits online merchants to send you advertising that supposedly reflects personal information the merchant has gathered about you. This is called "one-to-one" marketing or "personalization." This personal information may include such things as the Web sites you have visited, the pages you have viewed, the products you have previously purchased, how you arrived at the various sites (what Web sites you visited previously), and even your specific clicking behavior. This "clickstream" then becomes the basis for constructing a digital profile of you. Your clickstream and resulting profile is a marketer's and merchant's gold mine: if you know what people like and what they have recently purchased, you stand a good chance of being able to sell them something else. How does a Web-based company find out about your clickstream?

Let's start with Google, a site that millions of people use every day. Most people think that Google is a search engine. This is only partly true. In fact, Google is also the largest marketing firm by revenue in the world, and the largest collector of online clickstream behavioral data. A 2009 survey of online tracking identified Google Analytics and DoubleClick (an online advertising network now owned by Google) as the leading trackers, found on 70%–80% of Web sites (followed by Microsoft on 60% of Web sites). So what does Google know about your clicks? Here's a sampler:

- Google Search: Search terms you have used
- Google Desktop: Index of your computer files, e-mail, music, photos, and chat and Web browser history
- Google Talk: Your instant message chats
- Google Maps: Addresses, including your home address
- Gmail: Your e-mail history
- Google Calendar: Your schedules
- YouTube: Your video viewing history
- Google Checkout: Your credit card, payment information
- Google Analytics/DoubleClick: Your online behavior at hundreds of other Web sites connected to Google Analytics or DoubleClick's networks.

Google keeps this information for 18–24 months, and uses it to pitch ads to you. Google claims it does not really know who you are, only your computer's IP address and browser information. But critics point out that nearly 90% of Americans can be identified by name with just three pieces of information: birth date, gender, and ZIP code. Actually, just about any four pieces of information stored by Google from the list above would identify the vast majority of users by name. There are no legal or technical restrictions on how Google uses this personally identifiable information.

Social networking sites are also ideal places to collect personal information. In fact, the primary commercial purpose of social networking sites is to collect personal information and sell that information (and access to you) to merchants. For

(continued)

instance, Facebook's Beacon program would have broadcast user activities on other sites to their friends. Consumer backlash forced Facebook to allow this sharing only with user consent.

Another way your clickstream gets privatized by Web marketers is through advertising networks such as DoubleClick, ValueClick Media, and 24/7 Real Media. These advertising networks insert themselves between you and the merchant, and track your movements through their networks. They do this so well that Google bought DoubleClick in April 2007 for $3.1 billion; Yahoo bought RightMedia in the same month for $580 million; and Microsoft, fast on their heels, bought aQuantive for $6 billion in May 2007. There's money to be made invading people's privacy. When you visit any of thousands of Web sites in these ad networks, the network firms log your access to the site, and then follow your movements through the site (as does the merchant). Your clickstream behavior is merged with that of thousands of other consumers, and then these firms pop banner ads on your browser when visiting the other network sites.

Merchant sites also keep a complete contact log of every click you make and every object you choose to see on their Web sites. This data is stored and can be mined to create a profile of your behavior on the site. Most Web sites uses cookies and many use Web bugs. A cookie is a small text file downloaded onto your hard drive by a Web site. The cookie file contains whatever identifying information the merchant chooses to put in it. It can be read by other Web sites you visit and used to track your movement among sites. A Web bug is a tiny graphic, typically one pixel wide and one pixel deep, embedded within a Web page or e-mail. It usually is transparent or blends into the background color. A Web bug is placed in a Web page by a third party, and it acts as a hidden identifier of the third party. When a user views a Web page, it sends the visitor's IP address, cookie information, and referring URL back to the sending server or to the server of a third party thtat "owns" the Web bug, such as a Web advertising company. In a recent survey of 393,829 unique Web domains (URLs), 117 unique Web bug servers were identified.

All of this tracking behavior by large advertising, media, and retail firms makes many Web users nervous and distrustful. In an insightful study of public privacy attitudes and policies of companies and governments conducted by a group of graduate students at the University of California-Berkeley in 2009, researchers found users were most concerned about the loss of control over the use of their personal information, followed by the public display of their information (or sharing with others). Users want more control over their personal information, but lack awareness of data collection practices, and don't know who to complain to. Unfortunately, current online government and private privacy policies make control difficult or impossible, are opaque to users, and offer few opportunities for redress. In other words, there's a huge gap between public fears about privacy, and what privacy policies of any kind offer.

Many people feel that efforts to market products and services based on their online behavior is an invasion of their privacy. More than 50% of Internet users refuse to click on Web site ads in part out of fear their privacy will be lost. In its annual Digital Future Report, the USC Annenberg School found 93% of Internet users reported some level of concern about the lack of online privacy, and 46% were "very or extremely concerned" about privacy while shopping online. More intensive users of the Internet were less concerned than other users.

On the other hand, we live in a new era of online disclosure where millions of social network participants voluntarily post personal information for their friends and others to see. Pundits say the popularity of these sites (300 million worldwide) has dissolved the line between individual privacy and public information. Other millions willingly give up their e-mail addresses and preferences in

(continued)

order to receive a premium product or service. Does this mean, as some in the computer industry say, that Internet users don't really care about their privacy? As one reporter noted, if everyone's a friend on Facebook, is anything private?

The answer appears to be a qualified "Yes, people do care about their online privacy." Consider the experience of Facebook, the world's largest social networking site, which seems to upset its users with privacy-invading policies once every year. Apparently not learning much from the Beacon debacle, on February 4, 2009, Facebook issued a new Terms of Use policy in which it asserted broad, permanent rights to users' personal information, even after users deleted their profiles. The new policy was picked up by The Consumerist, a popular consumer information site, on February 15. Within a few days, over 500,000 Facebook users had formed groups on Facebook to oppose the policy. A flood of angry posts and petitions filled blogs and Facebook Walls. Three days later, on February 18, Facebook withdrew the new policy, reinstated the old policy, and created a site governance forum for all members to discuss and vote on a new Terms of Use policy. On April 14, a new Facebook Principles and Statement of Rights and Responsibilities was approved by 75% of the voters. The new policy explicitly stated that users "own and control their information." Facebook also improved account deletion features, limited sublicenses of information about users, and reduced data exchanges with outside developers. These moves quieted the uproar.

Still, as one commentator noted, "you'd have to be pretty dumb to think they [users] are getting any privacy from Facebook or MySpace. All they are doing is voluntarily supplying valuable personal information to these sites, who sell it to third parties." A visit to the "new" Facebook site shows that Facebook offers over 40 settings that can be tweaked to affect your privacy. But there are few restrictions on what "third party" software can see in a network of friends, or how user information is used by third parties who purchase that information from Facebook. Unless settings are changed, an application installed by a friend can vacuum up and store many categories of information. For 15 of 19 categories of information, Facebook sets the default setting to "share" information with third party servers beyond its control. Few users go to the trouble of changing any of the default privacy settings on Facebook. Facebook claims 20% of users have made some change to the settings. The new policy does not identify the mysterious "third parties," or how to figure out how they use your information.

Can you protect your privacy in the Internet age (and still use the Web for convenient shopping)? There are several kinds of solutions: merchant privacy policy, industry standards, advertising network privacy policy, technology, enforcement of existing laws, passage of new laws, and consumer market resistance. Companies such as Anonymizer.com have developed software packages and their own Web servers that you can use to hide your identity online. Software programs such as SpySweeper and Ad-aware can help remove spyware programs. Open source programs such as Ghoster can identify all the Web bugs on pages you visit. Yet these are highly limited solutions. Laws and aggressive prosecutors can also help, but as we describe in later chapters (especially Chapter 8), efforts to regulate online privacy and create new laws to protect online commercial privacy have not been widely successful, although self-regulation by advertising networks has produced some progress. Current privacy policies are so difficult to understand that one lawmaker proposed companies should not put their privacy policies into their privacy policy statements, but instead write a new document that clearly spells out what they do with consumers' personal information.

Most Web merchants are learning that it pays to be sensitive to customers' concerns about privacy. Trust is critical to successful e-commerce. Almost all sites have "opt-out" check boxes that allow visitors the option to not receive e-mail and other marketing information from the site. Many sites have "opt-in" policies that require customers to check a box if they want to receive additional marketing messages. All of the Web's top 25 e-merchants, as well as many others, have privacy policies posted on their sites. The question remains: Do these Web site privacy policies achieve what consumers want or do they simply legitimate whatever the sites believe are in their commercial interests?

SOURCES: "Social Networking Privacy," Electronic Privacy Information Center, June 10, 2009; "Google Is Top Tracker of Surfers in Study," by Miguel Helft, *New York Times*, June 2, 2009; "Know Privacy," by Joshua Gomez, Travis Pinnick, Ashkan Soltani. UC Berkeley School of Information, June 1, 2009; "Results of the Inaugural Facebook Site Governance Vote," by Ted Ullyot, blog.facebook.com, April 23, 2009; "Annual Internet Survey by the Center for the Digital Future Finds Large Increases in Use of Online Newspapers," USC Annenberg School Center for the Digital Future, April 23, 2009; "When Everyone's Your Friend, Is Anything Private?" by Randall Stross, *New York Times*, March 8, 2009; "The Blog That Ignited a Privacy Debate on Facebook," by Jenna Wortham, *New York Times*, February 19, 2009; "Agency Skeptical of Internet Privacy Policies," by Saul Hansell, *New York Times*, February 13, 2009; "The End of Internet Privacy," by Dan Slater, *Wall Street Journal*, July 7, 2008; "Facebook Dims the Beacon Spotlight," by Catherine Holahan, *BusinessWeek*, November 30, 2007; "Is it OK that Google Owns Us?" by Lisa Vaas, *eWeek*, June 17, 2007; "Internet Giants Vie to Snap Up Web Ad Firms," by Miguel Helft, *New York Times*, May 19, 2007; "Online Ads vs. Privacy," by Dan Mitchell, *New York Times*, May 12, 2007.

ACADEMIC DISCIPLINES CONCERNED WITH E-COMMERCE

The phenomenon of e-commerce is so broad that a multidisciplinary perspective is required (see **Figure 1.10**). There are two primary approaches to e-commerce: technical and behavioral.

Technical Approaches

Computer scientists are interested in e-commerce as an exemplary application of Internet technology. They are concerned with the development of computer

FIGURE 1.10	DISCIPLINES CONCERNED WITH E-COMMERCE

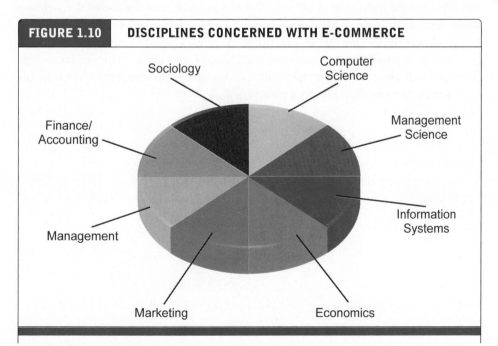

Many disciplines are directly involved in the study and understanding of e-commerce.

hardware, software, and telecommunications systems, as well as standards, encryption, and database design and operation. Management scientists are primarily interested in building mathematical models of business processes and optimizing these processes. They are interested in e-commerce as an opportunity to study how business firms can exploit the Internet to achieve more efficient business operations.

Behavioral Approaches

In the behavioral area, information systems researchers are primarily interested in e-commerce because of its implications for firm and industry value chains, industry structure, and corporate strategy. The information systems discipline spans the technical and behavioral approaches. For instance, technical groups within the information systems specialty also focus on data mining, search engine design, and artificial intelligence. Economists have focused on consumer behavior at Web sites, pricing of digital goods, and on the unique features of digital electronic markets. The marketing profession is interested in marketing, brand development and extension, consumer behavior on Web sites, and the ability of Internet technologies to segment and target consumer groups, and differentiate products. Economists share an interest with marketing scholars who have focused on e-commerce consumer response to marketing and advertising campaigns, and the ability of firms to brand, segment markets, target audiences, and position products to achieve above-normal returns on investment.

Management scholars have focused on entrepreneurial behavior and the challenges faced by young firms who are required to develop organizational structures in short time spans. Finance and accounting scholars have focused on e-commerce firm valuation and accounting practices. Sociologists—and to a lesser extent, psychologists—have focused on general population studies of Internet usage, the role of social inequality in skewing Internet benefits, and the use of the Web as a social networking and group communications tool. Legal scholars are interested in issues such as preserving intellectual property, privacy, and content regulation.

No one perspective dominates research about e-commerce. The challenge is to learn enough about a variety of academic disciplines so that you can grasp the significance of e-commerce in its entirety.

Internet Piracy:
The Pirate Bay

The Pirate Bay (www.thepiratebay.org), a Web site located in Sweden, has become one of the world's most popular pirated music and content sites, offering free access to millions of copyrighted songs and thousands of copyrighted Hollywood movies. In February 2009, the site reported that it had 22 million simultaneous users. To put that number in perspective, consider that that is more than twice the population of Sweden itself (9 million). The Pirate Bay has spearheaded a European social and political movement that opposes copyrighted content and demands that music, videos, TV shows, and other digital content be free and unrestricted. In the words of the Pirate Party, which organized parties and protests outside the Stockholm Court throughout spring 2009, "The Pirate Bay is a unique platform for distributing culture between regular people and independent artists, and that's something we want to preserve." According to John Kennedy, head of the International Federation of the Phonographic Industry (IFPI), The Pirate Bay has become "The world's No. 1 source of illegal music," following successful court actions four years ago against the P2P file-sharing sites Grokster in the United States and Kazaa in Australia.

In a unique twist on prior organized efforts to provide "free" music, The Pirate Bay does not operate a database of copyrighted content. Neither does it operate a network of computers owned by "members" who store the content, nor create, own, or distribute software (like BitTorrent and most other so-called P2P networks) that permit such networks to exist in the first place. These were the old techniques for ripping off music. Instead, The Pirate Bay simply provides a search engine that responds to user queries for free music, or specific movie titles, and generates a list of search results that include P2P networks around the world where the titles can be found. By clicking on a selected link, users gain access to the copyrighted content.

Voila! "No body, no crime." What could be illegal? The Pirate Bay claims it is merely a search engine providing pointers to existing P2P networks that it does not itself control. It claims that it cannot control what content users ultimately find on those P2P networks, and that it is no different from any other search engine, such as Google or Bing, which are not held responsible for the content found on sites listed is search results. From a broader standpoint, The Pirate Bay's founders also claim that copyright laws in general unjustly interfere with the free flow of information on the Internet, and that in any event, they were not violating Swedish copyright law, which they felt should be the only law that applied. And they further claimed they did not encourage, incite, or enable, illegal downloading.

However, in a ruling that puts to rest the notion that the law is always behind the development of technology, on April 2009, the First Swedish Court in Stockholm declared the four founders guilty of violating Swedish copyright law, and sentenced each to one year in prison and payment of $3.5 million in restitution to the plaintiffs, all Swedish divisions of the major record label firms (Warner Music, Sony, and EMI Group among them).

The court said "By providing a website with ... well-developed search functions, easy uploading and storage possibilities, and with a tracker linked to the website, the accused have incited the crimes that the file sharers have committed." The court also said that the four defendants had been aware of the fact that copyrighted material was shared with the help of their site. The prison sentence was justified by "extensive accessibility of others' (copy)rights and the fact that the operation was conducted commercially and in an organized fashion." In other words, the court believed the defendants were engaged in a commercial enterprise the basis of which was encouraging visitors to violate the copyrights of owners. In fact, the primary purpose of The Pirate Bay was to violate copyrights in order to make money for the owners (commercial intent).

"Enable," "induce," and "encourage" copyright infringement and "intent to sell" are key words in this ruling and the Pirate Bay case. These concepts grounded in Western law are not "disabled" by new technology, but instead can be, and are, extensible to new technologies, and used to shape technology to society's needs and wishes. Indeed, there's a consensus developing among prosecutors and courts worldwide that infringement is not justified simply because it's technically possible to do it on the Internet.

The defendants' initial appeal to Sweden's Supreme Court based on potential bias of the judge who decided the case was dismissed, but a further appeal remains pending and as of this writing, thepiratebay.org continues to operate as before. The defendants did not deny theirs was a commercial enterprise. Despite all the talk by the Pirate Party calling for the free, unfettered spread of culture, The Pirate Bay was a money-making operation from the beginning, designed to produce profits for its founders, with advertising as the primary source of revenue. On June 30, 2009, the founders announced that they had entered into an agreement with a Swedish company, Global Gaming Factory X (GGFX), that specializes in Internet café management software, to sell The Pirate Bay for an amount equivalent to about $7.7 million. GGFX claims that it intends to turn the Web site into a legitimate venture, much to the dismay of many of The Pirate Bay's users.

Meanwhile, the U.S. government pressured the Swedish government to strengthen its copyright laws to discourage rampant downloading. In Sweden, downloading music and videos from illegal sites is very popular, engaged in by 43% of the Swedish Internet population. To strengthen its laws, Sweden adopted the European Union convention on copyrights, which allows content owners to receive from Internet providers the names and addresses of people suspected of sharing pirated files. As a result, Internet traffic in Sweden declined by 40%, and has stayed there.

The Pirate Bay case is just the latest in a saga of court cases involving the record industry, which wants to preserve its monopolies on copyrighted music, and Internet users who want free music. In 2005, after several years of heated court battles, the case of *Metro-Goldwyn-Mayer Studios v. Grokster, et al.* finally reached the U.S. Supreme Court. In June 2005, the Court handed down its unanimous decision: Internet file-sharing services such as Grokster, StreamCast, BitTorrent, and Kazaa could be held liable for copyright infringement because they intentionally sought to induce, enable, and encourage users to share music that was owned by record companies. Indeed, it was their business model: steal the music, gather a huge audience, and monetize the audience by advertising or through subscription fees. Since the court ruling, Kazaa, Morpheus, Grokster, BearShare, iMesh, and many others have either gone out of business or settled with the record firms and converted themselves into legal file-sharing sites by entering into relationships with music industry firms.

But these legal victories have not proven to be the magic bullet that miraculously solves all the problems facing the music industry. In addition to the issue of illegal downloads, legitimate digital music sales have so far failed to make up for falling CD sales revenues. These two problems are interrelated: if customers can get the music for free, why should they buy a digital copy or a CD?

Downloading music—legally or illegally—is a major American pastime. About 65 million people downloaded music files in 2009, making the Internet the music box of choice for Americans. Approximately 33 million of these people used illegal P2P networks, while the rest downloaded from legal sites that charge for music. Those who use illegal free sites are predominantly young, tech-savvy males in the 14–21 year age group. People older than 21 tend to use legitimate downloading sites such as iTunes. The presence of so many young people on illegal P2P sites makes selling advertising on these sites very lucrative. Every month, about 1 billion songs are shared on illegal file-sharing P2P networks. In contrast, it took Apple iTunes about two years to achieve that many downloads! Illegal downloads are about 90% of the total music tracks download traffic. In other words, illegal downloaders tend to download a great many songs. How can this be if the Supreme Court declared these networks illegal?

For the record labels, the consequences of downloading music has been significant, although not yet catastrophic. The record industry has historically been based on a few physical products: acetate and vinyl records, and CDs (collections of 12 or more songs in a physical bundle). CD sales have continued to slide, leading to a poor financial performance not just at the record firms but also among their music distributors—the large retail outlets that sell CDs such as Tower Records, Sam Goody, Wal-Mart, and Best Buy. The big three record labels (EMI, Warner Music, and Sony Music) used to make nearly all their money selling CDs. Sales of CDs started falling in 2004 as the Internet ramped up its broadband connectivity. In 2007, sales of CDs plunged 20% in one year, and continued to plunge at that rate through 2009. Album sales of 12 or more songs both digital and on CD are also down 15% annually over the same period. Since 2003, 3,100 retail music stores have closed, and Wal-Mart has cut back shelf space devoted to CDs and now carries only the top titles.

The hopeful sign is that online music sales are growing rapidly. Sales of digital music at iTunes, Rhapsody, and eMusic have been growing at about 50% per year since 2006. Apple dominates the musical download scene and has become the largest retailer of music in the United States, replacing Wal-Mart. To date, Apple's iTunes Store has served up more than 5 billion songs, and its revenues are up 34% in the last year. Firing this performance of course are the sales of its i-devices. Apple has sold over 100 million iPods (all models) and over 17 million iPhones by mid-2009.

While a hopeful sign, these revenues are typically generated by sales of individual songs at 99 cents each, not entire albums at $12–$18 retail. Even though the record firms receive 90% of every iTunes sale, digital music sales have just not been strong enough to compensate for the plunging CD sales. Instead, users are "unbundling" the album and purchasing just the songs they like.

The record industry strategy to date has been to attempt to discourage illegal downloading, expand digital sales, and tightly control legal online distribution. Most illegal downloading occurs through P2P networks. So far, despite all the victories in court, the music industry has been unable to shut down the illegal downloading. Why is this proving so difficult?

P2P computer networks rely on the computing power of participants in the network rather than on a single central server or group of servers. A software program coordinates the communications among the participant computers who "donate" their storage, communication, and processing power. As more people join the network, the more power it has, and the faster you can find and exchange files. Contemporary P2P networks do not require a central control point (although in fact such networks have several busy points where most of the dispatching of requests are handled).

P2P networks followed in the footsteps of Napster—the first world champion of free music downloads. Founded in 1999, Napster had over 80 million users worldwide by 2001, but it was put out of business by a U.S. federal court decision in 2001 that required Napster to shut down its central servers that indexed music titles stored on users' computers. By maintaining a central index of available music located on network members' computers, Napster was directly enabling the sharing of music and the violation of copyright protections, i.e., users were not paying the owners of the music for listening.

A much more powerful P2P network, BitTorrent, was created by Bram Cohen in 2001, and is distributed by BitTorrent Inc. Ideally suited for sharing movies online, BitTorrent is a protocol (and a client program) in which very large files are distributed in chunks over a large number of Internet client computers. When you request a file (such as a movie), the BitTorrent program finds machines in your vicinity that are storing parts of the movie, and requests their download to your client computer. The downloading process is much faster than downloading from a single server.

In the past, P2P networks could be very profitable for their operators. They made money by downloading spyware and adware programs that in turn go out on the Internet and request pop-up advertisements and unsolicited e-mail from vendors who pay for this service. In that sense, P2P networks were advertising-supported networks even if they masqueraded as something more elevating like "freeing information from the copyright prison," as one site put it, or "helping independent music bands to reach a huge audience." With few variations, P2P networks used popular copyrighted music to create an audience that downloads software, which in turn displays ads on users' computers.

Successful lawsuits against the major P2P networks in the United States. removed the profit potential. Settling their lawsuits with the record labels in 2006, sites such as Kazaa have cleaned up their acts and no longer force users to accept spyware or adware. Instead, they make money from legitimate music sales, advertising placed directly on their sites (they are popular among millions of people) and through their distributed software. BitTorrent itself has changed its business model under the threat of law suits from both the record and movie industries. Today BitTorrent works with the major content owners to distribute their content through legal, digital channels.

However, despite the fact that the major U.S. P2P networks have been shut down or changed their business models to become legitimate music vendors, the software itself has propagated throughout the Web, and many new open source P2P programs have also propagated (such as eDonkey, the most popular). Anyone can download the programs and protocols for P2P file sharing.

The result is that hundreds of user-supported P2P networks have sprung up around the world, many in foreign countries such as Russia where they cannot be held liable for illegal sharing of music. Sites in these countries claim to be operating within the copyright laws of their countries. An estimated 95% of online music in Russia is pirated. The Russian authorities shut down the leading Russian site, AllofMP3.com, during President Putin's visit to the United States in July 2007 and it has operated only intermittently since then. However, a similar Russian site, MP3Sparks.com, has since opened and is available online today. It offers heavily discounted downloads based on file size. For instance, the American band Green Day published its new album "21st Century Breakdown" on May 15, 2009, and it was immediately available as a download from MP3Sparks for $2.96. The retail price of the album is $10–$12. According to the Recording Industry Association of America, neither AllofMP3 or MP3Sparks has ever remitted payments to the music companies.

SOURCES: "After Sale, Can Pirate Bay Survive?", by David Kravits, Wired.com, June 30, 2009; "After Sale, Can Pirate Bay Survive?", by David Kravits, Wired.com, June 30, 2009; "Pirate Bay Judge Ruled Unbiased," by Mats Lewan, CNET News, June 26, 2009; "Music Sales Down…and Out," eMarketer. April 29, 2009; "File-Sharing Site Violated Copyright, Court Says," Eric Pfanner, *New York Times*, April 18, 2009; "Four Convicted in Sweden in Internet Piracy Case," by Eric Pfanner, *New York Times,* April 18, 2009; "The Pirate Bay Operators: Heroes or Criminals," Law Blog, *Wall Street Journal*, April 13, 2009, "Court Nears Decision on File-Sharing Web Site," by Aaron Patrick, *Wall Street Journal*, April 13, 2009; "Universal Music Takes Another Stab Online," by Ethan Smith, *Wall Street Journal,* May 15, 2009; "Why are iPhone Users Willing to Pay for Content", by Saul Hansell, *New York Times*, February 26, 2009; "Amazon to Sell Music Without Copy Protection," by Brad Stone and Jeff Leeds, *New York Times*, May 17, 2007; "The Album, a Commodity in Disfavor," by Jeff Leeds, *New York Times*, March 26, 2007; "Record Labels Turn Piracy Into a Marketing Opportunity," *Wall Street Journal*, October 18, 2006.

The music industry has been justly criticized for allowing the digital theft of its music by burying its head in the sand, denial of reality, failing to develop legitimate online channels, forcing digital rights management software on users, and hence failing to answer its customers' needs for digital music, whether online or via smartphones. It's not for lack of trying: the major record companies have spent more than $1 billion attempting to develop digital outlets and business models with little to show for the effort.

There are signs of change in 2009. The major record firms have struck deals with Amazon making their songs available in an MP3 format without any limitations on sharing or playing (no digital rights management [DRM]). You can listen to the latest songs (and in some cases the entire backlist of albums) from Green Day, Lionel Ritchie, Neil Young, and hundreds of other popular groups on MySpace music and video streams, which generate sales of downloaded and physical versions. Apple has also decided to make all of its iTunes song catalog available on a DRM-free basis with its iTunes Plus service. Both YouTube and Facebook are cutting deals with record companies for access to music videos and songs. Universal Music has assigned its top digital business executive to a new project called Vevo. Being developed in concert with Google, Vevo will provide a controlled online environment operated by Universal for music videos (the main profit driver for YouTube, and social networking sites). Universal hopes to generate significantly higher advertising revenue than it obtains from YouTube and other sites using its content.

The experience of Apple also provides a sign of hope: the first generation of Internet users grew up expecting digital entertainment to be free. As they grow older, they are much more likely to pay for entertainment at iTunes or Amazon, and other online services. iTunes has trained a whole new generation to pay for music, videos, TV shows, ring tones (often based on music available for free on P2P networks), and games. The record industry hopes if it works for cell phones it might just work for the Internet.

Case Study Questions

1. How did The Pirate Bay business make money? What was its business model?

2. What is the business model of P2P networks that operate today without any corporate sponsorship?

3. What social and legal issues are raised by P2P file-sharing protocols and programs such as Pirate Bay and other P2P networks? Is the record industry justified in attempting to shut them down? Why or why not?

4. Will the Swedish Courts decision in The Pirate Bay case, and the U.S. Supreme Court's decision that Internet file-sharing services infringed copyrights, reduce the illegal sharing of music files in the United States?

5. Why do people older than 21 feel more comfortable paying for downloadable content whereas younger people often use illegal sites?

6. Do the major record companies perform a legitimate role in the creation and distribution of music which justifies their revenues?

1.5 REVIEW

KEY CONCEPTS

■ **Define e-commerce and describe how it differs from e-business.**

- E-commerce involves digitally enabled commercial transactions between and among organizations and individuals. Digitally enabled transactions include all those mediated by digital technology, meaning, for the most part, transactions that occur over the Internet and the Web. Commercial transactions involve the exchange of value (e.g., money) across organizational or individual boundaries in return for products or services.
- E-business refers primarily to the digital enabling of transactions and processes within a firm, involving information systems under the control of the firm. For the most part, e-business does not involve commercial transactions across organizational boundaries where value is exchanged.

■ **Identify and describe the unique features of e-commerce technology and discuss their business significance.**

There are eight features of e-commerce technology that are unique to this medium:
- *Ubiquity*—available just about everywhere, at all times, making it possible to shop from your desktop, at home, at work, or even from your car.
- *Global reach*—permits commercial transactions to cross cultural and national boundaries far more conveniently and cost-effectively than is true in traditional commerce.
- *Universal standards*—shared by all nations around the world. In contrast, most traditional commerce technologies differ from one nation to the next.
- *Richness*—refers to the complexity and content of a message. It enables an online merchant to deliver marketing messages with text, video, and audio to an audience of millions, in a way not possible with traditional commerce technologies such as radio, television, or magazines.
- *Interactivity*—allows for two-way communication between merchant and consumer and enabling the merchant to engage a consumer in ways similar to a face-to-face experience, but on a much more massive, global scale.
- *Information density*—is the total amount and quality of information available to all market participants. The Internet reduces information collection, storage, processing, and communication costs while increasing the currency, accuracy, and timeliness of information.
- *Personalization* and *customization*—merchants can target their marketing messages to specific individuals by adjusting the message to a person's name,

interests, and past purchases. Because of the increase in information density, a great deal of information about the consumer's past purchases and behavior can be stored and used by online merchants. The result is a level of personalization and customization unthinkable with existing commerce technologies.

- *Social technology*—provides a many-to-many model of mass communications. Millions of users are able to generate content consumed by millions of other users. The result is the formation of social networks on a wide scale and the aggregation of large audiences on social network platforms.

■ **Describe and identify Web 2.0 applications**

- A new set of applications has emerged on the Internet, loosely referred to as Web 2.0. These applications attract huge audiences and represent significant new opportunities for e-commerce revenues. Web 2.0 applications such as social networks, photo-and video-sharing sites, Wikipedia, and virtual life sites support very high levels of interactivity compared to other traditional media.

■ **Describe the major types of e-commerce.**

There are five major types of e-commerce:
- B2C involves businesses selling to consumers and is the type of e-commerce that most consumers are likely to encounter. In 2009, consumers spent about $228 billion in B2C transactions.
- B2B e-commerce involves businesses selling to other businesses and is the largest form of e-commerce, with an estimated $3.36 trillion in transactions in 2009.
- C2C is a means for consumers to sell to each other. In C2C e-commerce, the consumer prepares the product for market, places the product for auction or sale, and relies on the market maker to provide catalog, search engine, and transaction clearing capabilities so that products can be easily displayed, discovered, and paid for.
- P2P technology enables Internet users to share files and computer resources directly without having to go through a central Web server. Music and file-sharing services, such as BitTorrent, Kazaa, and eDonkey, are prime examples of this type of e-commerce, because consumers can transfer files directly to other consumers without a central server involved.
- M-commerce involves the use of wireless digital devices to enable transactions on the Web.

■ **Understand the evolution of e-commerce from its early years to today.**

E-commerce has gone through three stages: innovation, consolidation, and reinvention. The early years of e-commerce were a period of explosive growth, beginning in 1995 with the first widespread use of the Web to advertise products and ending in 2000 with the collapse in stock market valuations for dot-com ventures.
- The early years of e-commerce were a technological success, with the digital infrastructure created during the period solid enough to sustain significant growth in e-commerce during the next decade, and a mixed business success, with significant revenue growth and customer usage, but low profit margins.
- E-commerce during its early years did not fulfill economists' visions of the perfect Bertrand market and friction-free commerce, or fulfill the visions of

entrepreneurs and venture capitalists for first-mover advantages, low customer acquisition and retention costs, and low costs of doing business.

- E-commerce entered a period of consolidation beginning in March 2000 and extending through 2005.
- E-commerce entered a period of reinvention in 2006 with the emergence of social networking and Web 2.0 applications that attracted huge audiences in a very short time span.

■ **Identify the factors that will define the future of e-commerce.**

Factors that will define the future of e-commerce include the following:

- E-commerce technology will continue to propagate through all commercial activity, with overall revenues from e-commerce, the number of products and services sold over the Web, and the amount of Web traffic all rising.
- E-commerce prices will rise to cover the real costs of doing business on the Web.
- E-commerce margins and profits will rise to levels more typical of all retailers.
- Traditional well-endowed and experienced Fortune 500 companies will play a growing and more dominant role.
- Entrepreneurs will continue to play an important role in pioneering new social applications.
- The number of successful pure online companies will continue to decline and most successful e-commerce firms will adopt an integrated, multi-channel bricks-and-clicks strategy.
- Regulation of e-commerce and the Web by government will grow both in the United States and worldwide.

■ **Describe the major themes underlying the study of e-commerce.**

E-commerce involves three broad interrelated themes:

- *Technology*—To understand e-commerce, you need a basic understanding of the information technologies upon which it is built, including the Internet and the World Wide Web, and a host of complimentary technologies—personal computers, local area networks, client/server computing, packet-switched communications, protocols such as TCP/IP, Web servers, HTML, and relational databases, among others.
- *Business*—While technology provides the infrastructure, it is the business applications—the potential for extraordinary returns on investment—that create the interest and excitement in e-commerce. New technologies present businesses and entrepreneurs with new ways of organizing production and transacting business. Therefore, you also need to understand some key business concepts such as electronic markets, information goods, business models, firm and industry value chains, industry structure, and consumer behavior in electronic markets.
- *Society*—Understanding the pressures that global e-commerce places on contemporary society is critical to being successful in the e-commerce marketplace. The primary societal issues are intellectual property, individual privacy, and public policy.

■ **Identify the major academic disciplines contributing to e-commerce.**

There are two primary approaches to e-commerce: technical and behavioral. Each of these approaches is represented by several academic disciplines. On the technical side:

- Computer scientists are interested in e-commerce as an application of Internet technology.
- Management scientists are primarily interested in building mathematical models of business processes and optimizing them to learn how businesses can exploit the Internet to improve their business operations.
- Information systems professionals are interested in e-commerce because of its implications for firm and industry value chains, industry structure, and corporate strategy.
- Economists have focused on consumer behavior at Web sites, and on the features of digital electronic markets.

On the behavioral side:

- Sociologists have focused on studies of Internet usage, the role of social inequality in skewing Internet benefits, and the use of the Web as a personal and group communications tool.
- Finance and accounting scholars have focused on e-commerce firm valuation and accounting practices.
- Management scholars have focused on entrepreneurial behavior and the challenges faced by young firms who are required to develop organizational structures in short time spans.
- Marketing scholars have focused on consumer response to online marketing and advertising campaigns, and the ability of firms to brand, segment markets, target audiences, and position products to achieve higher returns on investment.

QUESTIONS

1. What is e-commerce? How does it differ from e-business? Where does it intersect with e-business?
2. What is information asymmetry?
3. What are some of the unique features of e-commerce technology?
4. What is a marketspace?
5. What are three benefits of universal standards?
6. Compare online and traditional transactions in terms of richness.
7. Name three of the business consequences that can result from growth in information density.
8. What is Web 2.0? Give examples of Web 2.0 sites and explain why you included them in your list.
9. Give examples of B2C, B2B, C2C, and P2P Web sites besides those listed in the chapter materials.
10. How are the Internet and the Web similar to or different from other technologies that have changed commerce in the past?
11. Describe the three different stages in the evolution of e-commerce.
12. What are the major limitations on the growth of e-commerce? Which is potentially the toughest to overcome?

13. What are three of the factors that will contribute to greater Internet penetration in U.S. households?
14. Define disintermediation and explain the benefits to Internet users of such a phenomenon. How does disintermediation impact friction-free commerce?
15. What are some of the major advantages and disadvantages of being a first mover?
16. Discuss the ways in which the early years of e-commerce can be considered both a success and a failure.
17. What are five of the major differences between the early years of e-commerce and today's e-commerce?
18. What factors will help define the future of e-commerce over the next five years?
19. Why is a multidisciplinary approach necessary if one hopes to understand e-commerce?

PROJECTS

1. Search the Web for an example of each of the five major types of e-commerce described in Section 1.1. Create a PowerPoint slide presentation or written report describing each Web site (take a screenshot of each, if possible), and explain why it fits into one of the five types of e-commerce.

2. Choose an e-commerce Web site and assess it in terms of the eight unique features of e-commerce technology described in Table 1.2. Which of the features does the site implement well, and which features poorly, in your opinion? Prepare a short memo to the president of the company you have chosen detailing your findings and any suggestions for improvement you may have.

3. Given the development and history of e-commerce in the years from 1995–2009, what do you predict we will see during the next five years of e-commerce? Describe some of the technological, business, and societal shifts that may occur as the Internet continues to grow and expand. Prepare a brief PowerPoint slide presentation or written report to explain your vision of what e-commerce looks like today.

4. Follow up on events at Facebook and MySpace subsequent to September 2009 (when the opening case was prepared). Has Facebook continued to challenge the dominance of MySpace (the world's largest social networking site)? What are its current prospects for success or failure? Prepare a short report on your findings.

WEB SITE RESOURCES azimuth-interactive.com/ecommerce6e

- Additional projects, exercises, and tutorials
- Careers: Explore career opportunities in e-commerce
- Raising capital and business plans

CHAPTER 2

E-commerce Business Models and Concepts

LEARNING OBJECTIVES

After reading this chapter, you will be able to:

- Identify the key components of e-commerce business models.
- Describe the major B2C business models.
- Describe the major B2B business models.
- Recognize business models in other emerging areas of e-commerce.
- Understand key business concepts and strategies applicable to e-commerce.

Tweet Tweet:
What's Your Business Model?

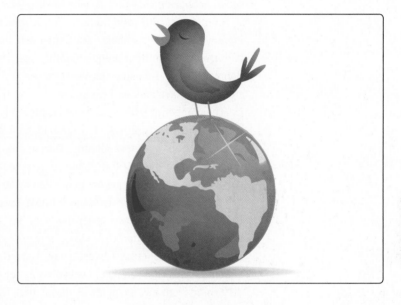

Twitter, the social networking site based on 140-character text messages, is the latest in a series of unpredicted developments on the Internet. You can think of these as "Black Swan" events that have for the most part had very positive consequences. In fact most of the wildly successful Internet applications and e-commerce businesses were not predicted by the world's leading experts and technology gurus whom we expect to tell us about the future. Who could have predicted, for instance, that in 2009, in the United States, 167 million people would use search engines to conduct 10 to 14 billion online searches, 160 million would watch videos online, and 96 million would read blogs? Who knew that America's population was so starved for communication? No one, least of all the Internet technorati.

In 2009, social networking sites continue this long tradition of surprising everyone. Twitter is the buzz social networking phenomenon of the year. Like all social networking sites, such as Facebook, MySpace, YouTube, Flickr, and others, Twitter provides a platform for users to express themselves, by creating content and sharing it with their "friends", in this case "followers" who sign up to receive someone's "tweets." And like most social networking sites, Twitter faces the problem of how to make money. As of October 2009, Twitter has yet to take in a single cent in revenue as its management ponders how best to exploit the buzz and user base it has created.

Twitter began in 2006 as a Web-based version of popular text messaging services provided by cell phone carriers. There are around 3 to 4 billion cell phones worldwide, and SMS text messaging is the most popular service after voice. The idea originated in March 2006 within a podcasting company called Odeo as executives searched for a new product or service to grow revenues. Jack Dorsey, originator of the idea, along with other executives, bought out other venture investors in Odeo, and eventually split Twitter off from Odeo to become a stand-alone, private company called Twitter.com.

The basic idea was to marry short text messaging on cell phones with the Web and its ability to create social groups. You start by establishing a Twitter account online, and identifying the friends that you would like to receive your messages. By sending a text message called a "tweet" to a short code on your cell phone (40404), you can tell your friends what you are doing, your location, and whatever else you might want to say. You are limited to 140 characters, but there is no installation and no charge. Kaboom: a social network messaging service to keep your buddies informed. Smash success.

Coming up with solid numbers for Twitter is not easy because the firm is not releasing any "official" numbers. By September 2009 Twitter, according to some estimates, had around 20 million unique monthly users in the United States, and perhaps 50 million worldwide. Industry observers believe Twitter is the third largest social networking site behind Facebook and MySpace.

The number of individual tweets is also only known by the company. According to the company, by early 2007, Twitter had transmitted 20,000 tweets, which jumped to 60,000 tweets in a few months. During the Iran rebellion in June 2009, there were reported to be over 200,000 tweets per hour worldwide. On the other hand, experts believe that 80% of tweets are generated by only 10% of users, and that the median number of tweet readers per tweet is 1 (most Tweeters tweet to one follower). In contrast, Britney Spears routinely generates over 100,000 followers to her tweets. Assuming there's about 20 million U.S. users, only 10% or 2 million will generate a tweet. Assuming these users generate 1 tweet a day, that would be 2 million a day, or 60 million tweets a month. This is probably a low estimate, but not by an order of magnitude. Even more disturbing from a value point of view is that Twittter has a 60% churn rate: only 40% of users remain more than one month. Obviously, many users lose interest in learning about their friends' breakfast menu, and many feel "too connected" to their "friends," who in fact may only be distant acquaintances, if that.

The answer to these questions about unique users, numbers of tweets, and churn rate are critical to understanding the business value of Twitter as a firm. To date, Twitter has generated losses and has unknown revenues, but in February 2009, it raised a $35 million in a deal that valued the company at $255 million. Investors included Jeff Bezos (Amazon founder), Benchmark Capital, and Spark Capital. Then in September 2009, Twitter announced it had raise $100 million in additional funding, from private equity firms, previous invetors, and mutal fund giant T.Rowe Price, based on a company valuation of a staggering $1 billion! Quite a jump in seven short months

So how can Twitter make money from its users, and their tweets? What's their business model and how might it evolve over time? To start, consider the company's assets and customer value proposition. The main asset is user attention and audience size (eyeballs per day). An equally important asset is the database of tweets that contains the comments, observations, and opinions of the audience, and the search engine that mines those tweets for patterns. These are "real-time" and spontaneous observations.

Yet another asset has emerged in the last year: Twitter is a powerful alternative media platform for the distribution of news, videos, and pictures. Once again, no one predicted that Twitter would be the first to report on terrorist attacks in Mumbai, the landing of a passenger jet in the Hudson River, or the Iranian rebellion in June 2009.

How can these assets be monetized? Twitter could ask users to pay a subscription fee, especially for premium services such as videos and music downloads. However, it may be too late for this idea because users have come to expect the service to be free. Twitter could sell display ads or text ads on its screens, something it is testing in Japan. But social media sites are known to be poor advertising venues with very low response rates, although this could change with better targeting. Twitter could charge advertisers to pay a fee for inserting messages into individual tweets. Message your friend to meet you in Times Square, and the message contains an ad for a nearby restaurant. Possible. Twitter could charge service providers such as doctors, dentists, lawyers, and hair salons for providing their customers with unexpected appointment availabilities. But Twitter's most likely steady revenue source might be its database of hundreds of millions of real-time tweets. Major firms such as Starbucks, Amazon, Intuit (makers of QuickBooks and the Mint.com site), and Dell have used Twitter to understand how their customers are reacting to products, services and Web sites, and then making corrections or changes in those services and products.

The possibilities are endless, and just about any of the above scenarios offers some solution to the company's problem, which is a lack of revenue (forget about profits). The company is coy about announcing its business model, what one pundit described as hiding behind a "Silicon Valley Mona Lisa smile." These Wall Street pundits are thought to be party poopers in the Valley. In a nod to Apple's iTunes and Amazon's merchant services, Twitter has turned over its messaging capabilities and software platform to others, one of which is CoTweet.com, a company that organizes multiple Twitter exchanges for customers so they can be tracked more easily. Google is selling ad units based around a company's last five tweets (ads are displayed to users who have created or viewed tweets about a company). Twitter is not charging for this service. In the meantime, observers wonder if Twitter is twittering away its assets.

SOURCES: :Twitter Snags $100 Million Investment, New Backers," by Alexei Oreskovic, Reuters, September 25, 2009; "Putting Twitter's World to Use," by Claire Cain Miller, New York Times, April 14, 2009; "Twitter Makes a Racket. But Revenues?" by Jon Fine, BusinessWeek magazine, April 9, 2009; "Firms Seek Profit in Twitter's Chatter," by Jessica Vascellaro, Wall Street Journal, March 26, 2009; "Twitter's Analytical Business Plan," by Taylor Buley, Forbes, February 15, 2009; "The Trouble With Twitter," by Ben Kunz, BusinessWeek.com, August 18, 2008.

Т
he story of Twitter illustrates the difficulties of turning a good business idea with a huge audience into a successful business model that produces revenues and even profits.

In the early days of e-commerce, thousands of firms discovered they could spend other people's invested capital much faster than they could get customers to pay for their products or services. In most instances of failure, the business model of the firm was faulty from the very beginning. In contrast, successful e-commerce firms have business models that are able to leverage the unique qualities of the Web, provide customers real value, develop highly effective and efficient operations, avoid legal and social entanglements that can harm the firm, and produce profitable business results. In addition, successful business models must scale. The business must be able to achieve efficiencies as it grows in volume. But what is a business model, and how can you tell if a firm's business model is going to produce a profit?

In this chapter, we focus on business models and basic business concepts that you must be familiar with in order to understand e-commerce.

| 2.1 | E-COMMERCE BUSINESS MODELS |

INTRODUCTION

business model
a set of planned activities designed to result in a profit in a marketplace

business plan
a document that describes a firm's business model

e-commerce business model
a business model that aims to use and leverage the unique qualities of the Internet and the World Wide Web

A **business model** is a set of planned activities (sometimes referred to as *business processes*) designed to result in a profit in a marketplace. A business model is not always the same as a business strategy although in some cases they are very close insofar as the business model explicitly takes into account the competitive environment (Magretta, 2002). The business model is at the center of the business plan. A **business plan** is a document that describes a firm's business model. A business plan always takes into account the competitive environment. An **e-commerce business model** aims to use and leverage the unique qualities of the Internet and the World Wide Web (Timmers, 1998).

EIGHT KEY ELEMENTS OF A BUSINESS MODEL

If you hope to develop a successful business model in any arena, not just e-commerce, you must make sure that the model effectively addresses the eight elements listed in **Table 2.1**. These elements are: value proposition, revenue model, market opportunity, competitive environment, competitive advantage, market strategy, organizational development, and management team (Ghosh, 1998). Many writers focus on a firm's value proposition and revenue model. While these may be the most important and most easily identifiable aspects of a company's business model, the other elements are equally important when evaluating business models and plans, or when attempting to understand why a particular company has succeeded or failed (Kim and Mauborgne, 2000). In the following sections, we describe each of the key business model elements more fully.

TABLE 2.1	KEY ELEMENTS OF A BUSINESS MODEL
COMPONENTS	KEY QUESTIONS
Value proposition	Why should the customer buy from you?
Revenue model	How will you earn money?
Market opportunity	What marketspace do you intend to serve, and what is its size?
Competitive environment	Who else occupies your intended marketspace?
Competitive advantage	What special advantages does your firm bring to the marketspace?
Market strategy	How do you plan to promote your products or services to attract your target audience?
Organizational development	What types of organizational structures within the firm are necessary to carry out the business plan?
Management team	What kinds of experiences and background are important for the company's leaders to have?

Value Proposition

A company's value proposition is at the very heart of its business model. A **value proposition** defines how a company's product or service fulfills the needs of customers (Kambil, Ginsberg, and Bloch, 1998). To develop and/or analyze a firm's value proposition, you need to understand why customers will choose to do business with the firm instead of another company and what the firm provides that other firms do not and cannot. From the consumer point of view, successful e-commerce value propositions include: personalization and customization of product offerings, reduction of product search costs, reduction of price discovery costs, and facilitation of transactions by managing product delivery (Kambil, 1997; Bakos, 1998).

For instance, before Amazon existed, most customers personally traveled to book retailers to place an order. In some cases, the desired book might not be available and the customer would have to wait several days or weeks, and then return to the bookstore to pick it up. Amazon makes it possible for book lovers to shop for virtually any book in print from the comfort of their home or office, 24 hours a day, and to know immediately whether a book is in stock. Amazon's primary value propositions are unparalleled selection and convenience.

value proposition
defines how a company's product or service fulfills the needs of customers

Revenue Model

A firm's **revenue model** describes how the firm will earn revenue, generate profits, and produce a superior return on invested capital. We use the terms *revenue model* and *financial model* interchangeably. The function of business organizations is both to generate profits and to produce returns on invested capital that exceed

revenue model
describes how the firm will earn revenue, produce profits, and produce a superior return on invested capital

alternative investments. Profits alone are not sufficient to make a company "successful" (Porter, 1985). In order to be considered successful, a firm must produce returns greater than alternative investments. Firms that fail this test go out of existence.

Retailers, for example, sell a product, such as a personal computer, to a customer who pays for the computer using cash or a credit card. This produces revenue. The merchant typically charges more for the computer than it pays out in operating expenses, producing a profit. But in order to go into business, the computer merchant had to invest capital—either by borrowing or by dipping into personal savings. The profits from the business constitute the return on invested capital, and these returns must be greater than the merchant could obtain elsewhere, say, by investing in real estate or just putting the money into a savings account.

Although there are many different e-commerce revenue models that have been developed, most companies rely on one, or some combination, of the following major revenue models: the advertising model, the subscription model, the transaction fee model, the sales model, and the affiliate model.

advertising revenue model
a company provides a forum for advertisements and receives fees from advertisers

In the **advertising revenue model**, a Web site that offers its users content, services, and/or products also provides a forum for advertisements and receives fees from advertisers. Those Web sites that are able to attract the greatest viewership or that have a highly specialized, differentiated viewership and are able to retain user attention ("stickiness") are able to charge higher advertising rates. Yahoo, for instance, derives a significant amount of revenue from search engine and other forms of online advertising.

subscription revenue model
a company offers its users content or services and charges a subscription fee for access to some or all of its offerings

In the **subscription revenue model**, a Web site that offers its users content or services charges a subscription fee for access to some or all of its offerings. For instance, the online version of *Consumer Reports* provides access to premium content, such as detailed ratings, reviews, and recommendations, only to subscribers, who have a choice of paying a $5.95 monthly subscription fee or a $26.00 annual fee. Experience with the subscription revenue model indicates that to successfully overcome the disinclination of users to pay for content on the Web, the content offered must be perceived as a high-value-added, premium offering that is not readily available elsewhere nor easily replicated. Companies successfully offering content or services online on a subscription basis include Match.com and eHarmony (dating services), Ancestry.com (see **Figure 2.1**) and Genealogy.com (genealogy research), Microsoft's Xboxlive.com (video games), and Rhapsody.com (music), among others.

transaction fee revenue model
a company receives a fee for enabling or executing a transaction

In the **transaction fee revenue model**, a company receives a fee for enabling or executing a transaction. For example, eBay provides an online auction marketplace and receives a small transaction fee from a seller if the seller is successful in selling the item. E*Trade, an online stockbroker, receives transaction fees each time it executes a stock transaction on behalf of a customer.

sales revenue model
a company derives revenue by selling goods, information, or services

In the **sales revenue model**, companies derive revenue by selling goods, information, or services to customers. Companies such as Amazon (which sells

FIGURE 2.1   **ANCESTRY.COM SUBSCRIPTION SERVICES**

Ancestry.com offers a variety of different membership options for different subscription fees.
SOURCE: Ancestry.com, 2009.

books, music, and other products), LLBean.com, and Gap.com, all have sales revenue models.

In the **affiliate revenue model**, sites that steer business to an "affiliate" receive a referral fee or percentage of the revenue from any resulting sales. For example, MyPoints makes money by connecting companies with potential customers by offering special deals to its members. When they take advantage of an offer and make a purchase, members earn "points" they can redeem for freebies, and MyPoints receives a fee. Community feedback sites such as Epinions receive much of their revenue from steering potential customers to Web sites where they make a purchase.

Table 2.2 summarizes these major revenue models.

Market Opportunity

The term **market opportunity** refers to the company's intended **marketspace** (i.e., an area of actual or potential commercial value) and the overall potential financial opportunities available to the firm in that marketspace. The market opportunity is usually divided into smaller market niches. The realistic market opportunity is defined by the revenue potential in each of the market niches where you hope to compete.

affiliate revenue model
a company steers business to an affiliate and receives a referral fee or percentage of the revenue from any resulting sales

market opportunity
refers to the company's intended marketspace and the overall potential financial opportunities available to the firm in that marketspace

marketspace
the area of actual or potential commercial value in which a company intends to operate

TABLE 2.2	FIVE PRIMARY REVENUE MODELS	
REVENUE MODEL	EXAMPLES	REVENUE SOURCE
Advertising	Yahoo	Fees from advertisers in exchange for advertisements
Subscription	WSJ.com Consumerreports.org	Fees from subscribers in exchange for access to content or services
Transaction Fee	eBay E*Trade	Fees (commissions) for enabling or executing a transaction
Sales	Amazon L.L.Bean Gap JCPenny.com	Sales of goods, information, or services
Affiliate	MyPoints	Fees for business referrals

For instance, let's assume you are analyzing a software training company that creates software-learning systems for sale to corporations over the Internet. The overall size of the software training market for all market segments is approximately $70 billion. The overall market can be broken down, however, into two major market segments: instructor-led training products, which comprise about 70% of the market ($49 billion in revenue), and computer-based training, which accounts for 30% ($21 billion). There are further market niches within each of those major market segments, such as the Fortune 500 computer-based training market and the small business computer-based training market. Because the firm is a start-up firm, it cannot compete effectively in the large business, computer-based training market (about $15 billion). Large brand-name training firms dominate this niche. The start-up firm's real market opportunity is to sell to the thousands of small business firms who spend about $6 billion on computer-based software training and who desperately need a cost-effective training solution. This is the size of the firm's realistic market opportunity (see **Figure 2.2**).

Competitive Environment

competitive environment

refers to the other companies operating in the same marketspace selling similar products

A firm's **competitive environment** refers to the other companies selling similar products and operating in the same marketspace. It also refers to the presence of substitute products and potential new entrants to the market, as well as the power of customers and suppliers over your business. We discuss the firm's environment later in the chapter. The competitive environment for a company is influenced by several factors: how many competitors are active, how large their operations are, what the market share of each competitor is, how profitable these firms are, and how they price their products.

FIGURE 2.2   **MARKETSPACE AND MARKET OPPORTUNITY IN THE SOFTWARE TRAINING MARKET**

Instructor-Led Training $49 Billion

Small Business $19 Billion

Small Business $6 Billion

Computer-Based Training $21 Billion

Fortune 500 $15 Billion

Fortune 500 $30 Billion

Marketspaces are composed of many market segments. Your realistic market opportunity will typically focus on one or a few market segments.

Firms typically have both direct and indirect competitors. Direct competitors are those companies that sell products and services that are very similar and into the same market segment. For example, Priceline and Travelocity, both of whom sell discount airline tickets online, are direct competitors because both companies sell identical products—cheap tickets. Indirect competitors are companies that may be in different industries but still compete indirectly because their products can substitute for one another. For instance, automobile manufacturers and airline companies operate in different industries, but they still compete indirectly because they offer consumers alternative means of transportation. CNN.com, a news outlet, is an indirect competitor of ESPN.com, not because they sell identical products, but because they both compete for consumers' time online.

The existence of a large number of competitors in any one segment may be a sign that the market is saturated and that it may be difficult to become profitable. On the other hand, a lack of competitors could either signal an untapped market niche ripe for the picking or a market that has already been tried without success because there is no money to be made. Analysis of the competitive environment can help you decide which it is.

Competitive Advantage

Firms achieve a **competitive advantage** when they can produce a superior product and/or bring the product to market at a lower price than most, or all, of their competitors (Porter, 1985). Firms also compete on scope. Some firms can develop global markets, while other firms can only develop a national or regional market. Firms that can provide superior products at lowest cost on a global basis are truly advantaged.

competitive advantage
achieved by a firm when it can produce a superior product and/or bring the product to market at a lower price than most, or all, of its competitors

Firms achieve competitive advantages because they have somehow been able to obtain differential access to the factors of production that are denied to their competitors—at least in the short term (Barney, 1991). Perhaps the firm has been able to obtain very favorable terms from suppliers, shippers, or sources of labor. Or perhaps the firm has more experienced, knowledgeable, and loyal employees than any competitors. Maybe the firm has a patent on a product that others cannot imitate, or access to investment capital through a network of former business colleagues or a brand name and popular image that other firms cannot duplicate. An **asymmetry** exists whenever one participant in a market has more resources—financial backing, knowledge, information, and/or power—than other participants. Asymmetries lead to some firms having an edge over others, permitting them to come to market with better products, faster than competitors, and sometimes at lower cost.

For instance, when Steven Jobs, CEO and founder of Apple Computer, announced iTunes, a new service offering legal, downloadable individual song tracks for 99 cents a tune that would be playable on Apple iPods or Apple desktops, the company was given better-than-average odds of success simply because of Apple's prior success with innovative hardware designs, and the large stable of music labels which Apple had meticulously lined up to support its online music catalog. Few competitors could match the combination of cheap, legal songs and powerful hardware to play them on.

One rather unique competitive advantage derives from being first mover. A **first-mover advantage** is a competitive market advantage for a firm that results from being the first into a marketplace with a serviceable product or service. If first movers develop a loyal following or a unique interface that is difficult to imitate, they can sustain their first-mover advantage for long periods (Arthur, 1996). Amazon provides a good example. However, in the history of technology-driven business innovation, most first movers lack the **complementary resources** needed to sustain their advantages, and often follower firms reap the largest rewards (Rigdon, 2000; Teece, 1986). Indeed, many of the success stories we discuss in this book are those of companies that were slow followers—businesses that gained knowledge from failure of pioneering firms and entered into the market late.

Some competitive advantages are called "unfair." An **unfair competitive advantage** occurs when one firm develops an advantage based on a factor that other firms cannot purchase (Barney, 1991). For instance, a brand name cannot be purchased and is in that sense an "unfair" advantage. As we will discuss in Chapter 6, brands are built upon loyalty, trust, reliability, and quality. Once obtained, they are difficult to copy or imitate, and they permit firms to charge premium prices for their products.

In **perfect markets**, there are no competitive advantages or asymmetries because all firms have access to all the factors of production (including information and knowledge) equally. However, real markets are imperfect, and asymmetries leading to competitive advantages do exist, at least in the short term. Most competitive advantages are short term, although some—such as the competitive advantage enjoyed by Coca-Cola because of the Coke brand name—can be sustained for very

asymmetry
exists whenever one participant in a market has more resources than other participants

first-mover advantage
a competitive market advantage for a firm that results from being the first into a marketplace with a serviceable product or service

complementary resources
resources and assets not directly involved in the production of the product but required for success, such as marketing, management, financial assets, and reputation

unfair competitive advantage
occurs when one firm develops an advantage based on a factor that other firms cannot purchase

perfect market
a market in which there are no competitive advantages or asymmetries because all firms have equal access to all the factors of production

long periods. But not forever: Coke is increasingly being challenged by fruit, health, and unique flavor drinks.

Companies are said to **leverage** their competitive assets when they use their competitive advantages to achieve more advantage in surrounding markets. For instance, Amazon's move into the online grocery business leverages the company's huge customer database and years of e-commerce experience.

leverage
when a company uses its competitive advantages to achieve more advantage in surrounding markets

Market Strategy

No matter how tremendous a firm's qualities, its marketing strategy and execution are often just as important. The best business concept, or idea, will fail if it is not properly marketed to potential customers.

Everything you do to promote your company's products and services to potential customers is known as marketing. **Market strategy** is the plan you put together that details exactly how you intend to enter a new market and attract new customers.

For instance, Twitter, YouTube, and PhotoBucket have a social network marketing strategy which encourages users to post their content on the sites for free, build personal profile pages, contact their friends, and build a community. In these cases, the customer is the marketing staff!

market strategy
the plan you put together that details exactly how you intend to enter a new market and attract new customers

Organizational Development

Although many entrepreneurial ventures are started by one visionary individual, it is rare that one person alone can grow an idea into a multi-million dollar company. In most cases, fast-growth companies—especially e-commerce businesses—need employees and a set of business procedures. In short, all firms—new ones in particular—need an organization to efficiently implement their business plans and strategies. Many e-commerce firms and many traditional firms who attempt an e-commerce strategy have failed because they lacked the organizational structures and supportive cultural values required to support new forms of commerce (Kanter, 2001).

Companies that hope to grow and thrive need to have a plan for **organizational development** that describes how the company will organize the work that needs to be accomplished. Typically, work is divided into functional departments, such as production, shipping, marketing, customer support, and finance. Jobs within these functional areas are defined, and then recruitment begins for specific job titles and responsibilities. Typically, in the beginning, generalists who can perform multiple tasks are hired. As the company grows, recruiting becomes more specialized. For instance, at the outset, a business may have one marketing manager. But after two or three years of steady growth, that one marketing position may be broken down into seven separate jobs done by seven individuals.

organizational development
plan describes how the company will organize the work that needs to be accomplished

For instance, eBay founder Pierre Omidyar started an online auction site, according to some sources, to help his girlfriend trade PEZ dispensers with other collectors, but within a few months the volume of business had far exceeded what he alone could handle. So he began hiring people with more business experience to help out. Soon the company had many employees, departments, and managers who were responsible for overseeing the various aspects of the organization.

Management Team

management team

employees of the company responsible for making the business model work

Arguably, the single most important element of a business model is the **management team** responsible for making the model work. A strong management team gives a model instant credibility to outside investors, immediate market-specific knowledge, and experience in implementing business plans. A strong management team may not be able to salvage a weak business model, but the team should be able to change the model and redefine the business as it becomes necessary.

Eventually, most companies get to the point of having several senior executives or managers. How skilled managers are, however, can be a source of competitive advantage or disadvantage. The challenge is to find people who have both the experience and the ability to apply that experience to new situations.

To be able to identify good managers for a business start-up, first consider the kinds of experiences that would be helpful to a manager joining your company. What kind of technical background is desirable? What kind of supervisory experience is necessary? How many years in a particular function should be required? What job functions should be fulfilled first: marketing, production, finance, or operations? Especially in situations where financing will be needed to get a company off the ground, do prospective senior managers have experience and contacts for raising financing from outside investors?

Read *Insight on Business: Online Grocers: Finding and Executing the Right Model* for a detailed look at how FreshDirect developed a successful business model in an arena—online groceries—in which previous efforts had failed.

CATEGORIZING E-COMMERCE BUSINESS MODELS: SOME DIFFICULTIES

There are many e-commerce business models, and more are being invented every day. The number of such models is limited only by the human imagination, and our list of different business models is certainly not exhaustive. However, despite the abundance of potential models, it is possible to identify the major generic types (and subtle variations) of business models that have been developed for the e-commerce arena and describe their key features. It is important to realize, however, that there is no one correct way to categorize these business models.

Our approach is to categorize business models according to the different e-commerce sectors—B2C, B2B, C2C, etc.—in which they are utilized. You will note, however, that fundamentally similar business models may appear in more than one sector. For example, the business models of online retailers (often called e-tailers) and e-distributors are quite similar. However, they are distinguished by the market focus of the sector in which they are used. In the case of e-tailers in the B2C sector, the business model focuses on sales to the individual consumer, while in the case of the e-distributor, the business model focuses on sales to another business.

The type of e-commerce technology involved can also affect the classification of a business model. M-commerce, for instance, refers to e-commerce conducted over wireless networks. The e-tail business model, for instance, can also be used in m-commerce, and while the basic business model may remain fundamentally the same as that used in the B2C sector, it will nonetheless have to be adapted to the special challenges posed by the m-commerce environment.

INSIGHT ON BUSINESS

ONLINE GROCERS: FINDING AND EXECUTING THE RIGHT MODEL

What could be easier than ordering all your groceries online and having them delivered to your doorstep at a time you choose? No more driving to the store, wasting gas and time, pushing carts down aisles, jostling with over-anxious shoppers, waiting in the check out lines. For those who don't mind giving up the "social experience" of shopping, as well as aspects like thumping melons to test for freshness, tearing off a shock of sweet corn to smell for mold, or sampling a cut of salami before ordering, online grocery shopping provides a compelling value proposition. In 2009, an estimated 4 million online shoppers, who are expected to generate $8.7 billion in online grocery sales at over 250 online grocers, made that trade-off.

Online grocery sales have grown 340% since 2003, and are expected to grow 17% annually to $13.7 billion by 2013. In fact, online grocery sales are growing at nearly three times the rate of traditional grocery sales offline. In a recession, driven by the high cost of restaurant food, as well as gas for cars, consumers are cooking at home more often, and looking for food deals and convenience online. Online recipe sites are seeing a doubling of traffic. Still, there's a lot of room for future growth: online groceries still account for only 1% of all grocery sales in the U.S.

There are three online grocery business models: start fresh, leverage out, and local build. The history of large-scale online grocery begins with the "start fresh" approach of Webvan, launched in 1999 with $400 million of venture funding, and another $600 million of stock sales to the public. Webvan's business plan was audacious: start a totally new nationwide, online, grocery distribution system serving 10 cities at first, and expanding to additional major cities in a few years.

When Webvan flamed out in July 2001 after having spent almost $1 billion trying to build the Web's largest online grocery store based on huge distribution warehouses in seven U.S. cities, most pundits and investors thought the entire online grocery business model was either a failure or a fraud. Facing the costs of building an entirely new distribution system of warehouses and truck fleets to compete with existing grocery businesses, not to mention the expense of marketing, and a huge IT infrastructure, Webvan compounded its problems by offering below-market prices and free delivery of even small orders at just about any time of the day or night in urban areas often clogged with traffic. Webvan is generally considered to be the largest and most spectacular e-commerce failure in history. That said, it was also ahead of its time: very few customers felt comfortable ordering "high-touch" goods online in 2001. Today, the culture of online purchasing has changed.

Despite Webvan's failure, the pundits have proven to be wrong again. Online grocery is alive, well, growing rapidly, but with different aspirations and business models. Pundits did not count on Manhattan's FreshDirect (and hundreds of other local niche online grocers) or the ability of traditional grocery chains to move into the ashes of the online grocery business to create solid, profitable businesses. These firms are learning how to exploit this potential market with profitable business models.

The largest online players today are traditional firms such as California's huge Safeway Stores, APSupermarket.com, and Shoprite.com in the North East, and Royal Ahold (Dutch owner of the U.S. Stop & Shop and Giant food stores, among others, and the Internet firm Peapod.com). Big-box discount stores such as

(continued)

Costco, BJ's, and Sam's Club also offer online grocery services. These firms are leveraging their existing nationwide distribution and supply chain systems, as well as their thousands of local stores, to provide shoppers with the opportunity of selecting what they want online, and then picking it up at the local stores or having it delivered by the local stores. These U.S. firms followed the lead of the successful British grocer Tesco. Tesco is the largest chain of supermarkets in Britain and opened an online division in 1990. It is considered to be the largest and most successful online grocery store in the world.

In the United States, Safeway's wholly-owned subsidiary GroceryWorks.com provides online shopping and delivery services for Safeway stores in California, Oregon, Washington, Arizona, Maryland, Virginia, and the District of Columbia; and for Vons stores in Southern California and Las Vegas, Nevada. Customers register online, entering their personal information, including their frequent shopper cards. They are shown lists of recently purchased items to speed selection. The prices of goods are the same as those in the stores. Safeway has so-called "pickers" roam the aisles of nearby stores using a computerized picklist that directs them through the store in an efficient pattern, and even specifies the order of packing goods into bags. The orders are put into a van and delivered to the customer within a two-hour window for a fee of $10.

At Royal AHold's Peapod.com, which serves its Stop & Shop and Giant Food store customers in 18 regional markets, shoppers can view both their online ordering history and their offline purchases at nearby stores during the previous four months. The Web site also features a shopping list that displays items in the order they can be found at the customer's local store. Customers have the option of ordering online and picking it up at the store, or

printing the shopping list and taking it to the store. For these traditional supermarket chains, the value being offered to customers is convenience and time savings at prices only marginally higher than self-shopping.

FreshDirect exemplifies the third and most common online grocery business model: local build. Other well-known local niche players include Inland Marine (Houston), Gopher Grocery (St. Paul), and Greenling (Austin), all with revenues greater than $1 million. These local online grocers focus on knowing their local customers, high-quality fresh produce, low costs, and convenient delivery.

In July 2002, Joe Fedele and Jason Ackerman founded FreshDirect as a new kind of high-quality and high-tech food preparation and delivery service in Manhattan, and raised $120 million in venture funding. Operating out of a 300,000-square-foot plant in Queens just across the river from Manhattan, FreshDirect trucks deliver groceries to densely populated Manhattan, Brooklyn, and Queens at prices 25% below what most New York grocers charge. It charges a $5.49–$6.79 delivery fee, depending on location and size of order, and requires a minimum order of $30. The value proposition to consumers is convenience and time savings, but also higher quality at lower prices.

How can FreshDirect succeed at these prices? One answer is that FreshDirect concentrates on very fresh perishable foods and stays away from low-margin dry goods. For instance, the FreshDirect Web site features around 3,000 perishables and 3,000 packaged goods compared to the typical 25,000 packaged goods and 2,200 perishable items that a typical grocery store offers. To do so, FreshDirect created the most modern automated perishable food processing plant in the United States. While most of the factory is kept at 36 degrees to ensure freshness and quality control, dedi-

(continued)

cated areas vary from a low of minus 25 degrees for frozen foods to a high of 62 degrees in one of its specially designed fruit and vegetable rooms. At the factory, FreshDirect butchers meat from whole carcasses, makes its own sausage, cuts up its own fish, grinds coffee, bakes bread and pastries, and cooks entire prepared meals. FreshDirect employs the same "make-to-order," manufacturer-direct philosophy as does Dell. Cleanliness is an obsession—the factory was built to exceed U.S. Department of Agriculture standards.

Critical to the success of FreshDirect is a power IT infrastructure that seamlessly connects online customers to inventory, billing, and then to truck delivery. The firm uses SAP software (an enterprise resource planning system) to track inventory, compile financial reports, tag products to fulfill customers' orders, and precisely control production down to the level of telling bakers how many bagels to cook each day and what temperature to use. It uses automated carousels and conveyors to bring orders to food-prep workers and packers. The FreshDirect Web site is powered by BEA Systems' Weblogic platform, which can track customer preferences, such as the level of fruit ripeness desired, or the preferred weight of a cut of meat. FreshDirect also uses NetTracker, Web site traffic and online behavior analysis software, to help it better understand and market to its online customers. At peak times, the Web site has handled up to 18,000 simultaneous shopping sessions. The final piece in the formula for profit is a supply chain that includes dealing directly with manufacturers and growers, thus cutting out the costs of middle-level distributors and the huge chains themselves.

FreshDirect does not accept slotting fees—payments made by manufacturers for shelf space. Instead, it asks suppliers to help it direct market to consumers and to lower prices. To further encourage lower prices from suppliers, FreshDirect pays them in four business days after delivery, down from the industry pattern of 35 days.

FreshDirect was profitable for the first time in 2008. The key to profitability has been improving their execution of the initial concept. In recent years, they have introduced the following "customer centric" ideas:

• Produce: Employed experts to rate the freshness of all produce and set prices accordingly. This reduces customer concerns about not being able to feel the product.

• Packaging: Eliminated the use of foam, and reduced the number of cardboard boxes by 1.5 million in response to customer complaints.

• Favorites: Developed a customer relationship management system that tracks each customers' past purchases, and presents them on-screen for re-ordering. Increased order size by 10%.

• Recommender system: Added a YMAL (You-Might-Also-Like) cross-selling tool, which recommends products that other customers purchased. Added 5% to total revenue.

With these features and direct mail campaigns, FreshDirect increased customer loyalty and reduced its churn rate (the number of customers who leave the service). Currently, 65% of its total customer base are repeat, loyal customers, whose average order size is over $100, and who contribute 80% of FreshDirect revenues.

SOURCES: "FreshDirect-Help- FAQs," FreshDirect.com, August 1, 2009; "A Look Inside Peapod - Online Grocery Delivery Service," by Wendy Thomas, simplethrift.wordpress.com, June 26, 2009; "These Online Grocers Got It Right," by Jeff Wurio, BusinessWeek, June 5, 2009; "Defying Odds, FreshDirect Delivers Gains," byt Lisa Fickensher, Crainsnewyork.com, May 31, 2009; "Lessons of Internet Marketing From Fresh Direct," by Rick Braddock, *Wall Street Journal*, May 11, 2009; "Web Recipes Are Cooking With Gas," by Elizabeth Holmes, *Wall Street Journal*, May 5, 2009; "Fresh Direct Takes a New Approach to Customer Service," Internet Retailer, January 7, 2009; Internet Retailer, *Top 500 Guide 2009 Edition*, 2009; "Food and Beverage Industry Online," eMarketer, December 2008.

Finally, you will also note that some companies use multiple business models. For instance, eBay can be considered as a B2C market maker. At the same time, eBay can also be considered as having a C2C business model. If eBay adopts wireless mobile computing, allowing customers to bid on auctions from their cell phone or wireless Web devices, then eBay may also be described as having a B2C m-commerce business model. We can expect many companies will have closely related B2C, B2B, and m-commerce variations on their basic business model. The purpose will be to leverage investments and assets developed with one business model into a new business model.

2.2 MAJOR BUSINESS-TO-CONSUMER (B2C) BUSINESS MODELS

Business-to-consumer (B2C) e-commerce, in which online businesses seek to reach individual consumers, is the most well-known and familiar type of e-commerce. **Table 2.3** illustrates the major business models utilized in the B2C arena.

PORTAL

portal

offers users powerful Web search tools as well as an integrated package of content and services all in one place

Portals such as Yahoo, MSN, and AOL offer users powerful Web search tools as well as an integrated package of content and services, such as news, e-mail, instant messaging, calendars, shopping, music downloads, video streaming, and more, all in one place. Initially, portals sought to be viewed as "gateways" to the Internet. Today, however, the portal business model is to be a destination site. They are marketed as places where consumers will want to start their Web searching and hopefully stay a long time to read news, find entertainment, and meet other people (think of destination resorts). Portals do not sell anything directly—or so it seems—and in that sense they can present themselves as unbiased. The market opportunity is very large: in 2009, about 200 million people in the United States had access to the Internet at work or home. Portals generate revenue primarily by charging advertisers for ad placement, collecting referral fees for steering customers to other sites, and charging for premium services. AOL, MSN (in conjunction with Verizon), and Yahoo (in conjunction with AT&T)—which in addition to being portals are also Internet Service Providers (ISPs) that provide access to the Internet and the Web—add an additional revenue stream: monthly subscription fees for access.

Although there are numerous portal/search engine sites, the top five sites (Google, Yahoo, MSN/Bing, AOL, and Ask.com) gather more than 95% of the search engine traffic because of their superior brand recognition (Nielsen Online, 2009). Many of the top sites were among the first to appear on the Web and therefore had first-mover advantages. Being first confers advantage because customers come to trust a reliable provider and experience switching costs if they change to late arrivals in the market. By garnering a large chunk of the marketplace, first movers—just like a single telephone network—can offer customers access to commonly shared ideas, standards, and experiences (something called *network externalities* that we describe in later chapters).

TABLE 2.3	B2C BUSINESS MODELS			
BUSINESS MODEL	VARIATIONS	EXAMPLES	DESCRIPTION	REVENUE MODEL
Portal	Horizontal/General	Yahoo AOL MSN	Offers an integrated package of content and content-search services: news, e-mail, chat, music downloads, video streaming, calendars, etc. Seeks to be a user's home base	Advertising, subscription fees, transaction fees
	Vertical/Specialized (Vortal)	Sailnet	Offers services and products to specialized marketplace	Same
	Search	Google Ask.com	Focuses primarily on offering search services	Advertising, affiliate referral
E-tailer	Virtual Merchant	Amazon	Online version of retail store, where customers can shop at any hour of the day or night without leaving their home or office	Sales of goods
	Bricks-and-Clicks	Walmart.com Sears.com	Online distribution channel for a company that also has physical stores	Same
	Catalog Merchant	LLBean.com LillianVernon.com	Online version of direct mail catalog	Same
	Manufacturer-Direct	Dell.com Mattel.com SonyStyle.com	Manufacturer uses online channel to sell direct to customer	Same
Content Provider		WSJ.com Sportline.com CNN.com ESPN.com Rhapsody.com	Information and entertainment providers such as newspapers, sports sites, and other online sources that offer customers up-to-date news and special interest how-to guidance and tips and/or information sales	Advertising, subscription fees, affiliate referral fees
Transaction Broker		E*Trade Expedia Monster Travelocity Hotels.com Orbitz	Processors of online sales transactions, such as stockbrokers and travel agents, that increase customers' productivity by helping them get things done faster and more cheaply	Transaction fees
Market Creator		eBay Priceline	Web-based businesses that use Internet technology to create markets that bring buyers and sellers together	Transaction fees
Service Provider		VisaNow.com xDrive.com Linklaters BlueFlag	Companies that make money by selling users a service, rather than a product	Sales of services
Community Provider		Facebook MySpace Twitter iVillage	Sites where individuals with particular interests, hobbies, common experiences, or social networks can come together and "meet" online	Advertising, subscription, affiliate referral fees

Comcast

Yahoo, AOL, MSN, and others like them are considered to be horizontal portals because they define their marketspace to include all users of the Internet. Vertical portals (sometimes called vortals) attempt to provide similar services as horizontal portals, but are focused around a particular subject matter or market segment. For instance, Sailnet specializes in the consumer sailboat market that contains about 8 million Americans who own or rent sailboats. Although the total number of vortal users may be much lower than the number of portal users, if the market segment is attractive enough, advertisers are willing to pay a premium in order to reach a targeted audience. Also, visitors to specialized niche vortals spend more money than the average Yahoo visitor. Google and Ask.com can also be considered portals of a sort, but focus primarily on offering search and advertising services. They generate revenues primarily from search engine advertising sales and also from affiliate referral fees. For more information, *see Insight on Technology: Can Bing Bong Google?*

E-TAILER

e-tailer
online retail store

Online retail stores, often called **e-tailers**, come in all sizes, from giant Amazon to tiny local stores that have Web sites. E-tailers are similar to the typical bricks-and-mortar storefront, except that customers only have to connect to the Internet to check their inventory and place an order. Some e-tailers, which are referred to as "bricks-and-clicks," are subsidiaries or divisions of existing physical stores and carry the same products. JCPenney, Barnes & Noble, Wal-Mart, and Staples are four examples of companies with complementary online stores. Others, however, operate only in the virtual world, without any ties to physical locations. Amazon, BlueNile.com, and Drugstore.com are examples of this type of e-tailer. Several other variations of e-tailers—such as online versions of direct mail catalogs, online malls, and manufacturer-direct online sales—also exist.

Given that the overall retail market in the United States in 2009 is estimated to be around $3.9 trillion, the market opportunity for e-tailers is very large (U.S. Census Bureau, 2009). Every Internet user is a potential customer. Customers who feel time-starved are even better prospects, since they want shopping solutions that will eliminate the need to drive to the mall or store (Bellman, Lohse, and Johnson, 1999). The e-tail revenue model is product-based, with customers paying for the purchase of a particular item.

barriers to entry
the total cost of entering a new marketplace

This sector is extremely competitive, however. Since **barriers to entry** (the total cost of entering a new marketplace) into the Web e-tail market are low, tens of thousands of small e-tail shops have sprung up on the Web. Becoming profitable and surviving is very difficult, however, for e-tailers with no prior brand name or experience. The e-tailer's challenge is differentiating its business from existing stores and Web sites.

Companies that try to reach every online consumer are likely to deplete their resources quickly. Those that develop a niche strategy, clearly identifying their target market and its needs, are best prepared to make a profit. Keeping expenses low, selection broad, and inventory controlled are keys to success in e-tailing, with inventory being the most difficult to gauge. Online retail is covered in more depth in Chapter 9.

INSIGHT ON TECHNOLOGY

CAN BING BONG GOOGLE?

After years of trying to develop a search engine and related search-based advertising platform that would be competitive with Google, on May 28, 2009, Microsoft unveiled its newest effort, called Bing. Why Bing? Allegedly, the name connotes the feeling you get when you discover something (as in "bada bing!"), it's one syllable, and potentially can become a verb (as in "Bing it!") with as much cultural weight as "Google it!" The interface is simple, but much richer and more interesting than Google's in part because each day a new full-page nature photo is shown. In fact, Bing is downright elegant according to many observers and users. Google, in contrast, under the influence of computer scientist Marissa Meyer, who controls Google's homepage, has not changed its minimalist, stark, white interface since its inception. In March 2009, Google's top designer, Doug Bowman, quit because he couldn't deal with Google's data-driven approach to page design, which in one instance caused Google to test 41 different shades of blue to use on its screens. In contrast, Bing presents a much richer customer experience.

Microsoft calls Bing a "decision engine" because of its focus on helping users make decisions in four areas: shopping, health, travel, and local business. For instance, a Bing search on "flights from Seattle to San Francisco" will produce a link that shows the lowest extant round-trip fare, and an icon for calculating the likely future cost of the ticket based on historic trends over the next seven days. There are also links to a Bing travel site from which users can link to airline sites and hotels. In contrast, a similar search on Google and Yahoo returns links to airline and other booking sites, but no information on fares or their future price.

Bing may be just the solution Microsoft needs to break into the big leagues of ad-based search. In April 2009, the industry leader Google commanded the pole position with 65% of U.S. searches, Yahoo 20.1%, and Microsoft 8%. By the middle of June, Microsoft had jumped to 12% of online searches (a 50% pop for Bing in just a few weeks), with both Yahoo and Google giving up some share. This marked the first time in history that Google's and Yahoo's share of the search market declined. Score one for Microsoft.

When the Web was first invented, no one envisaged that by 2009 online search would grow to a $12 billion dollar business. In fact, early pundits thought that online search would be a commodity business, at best a small niche player in e-commerce. Of course, no one envisaged that search could be married to advertising, and that search was in essence a huge new advertising platform. Today, search ad spending is nearly 50% of all online advertising. The search engine market is booming, along with the larger Internet advertising marketplace, now estimated at about $25 billion for all types of online advertising. It is apparent that search has become a major Web-based industry driven in large part by advances in technology, both hardware and software. What is less apparent is who exactly will dominate this marketspace and what role technology (as opposed to marketing muscle or economics) will play in the ultimate outcome. Where's the money in search and who's going to get it? A related question is how many search engines will remain when the competition is over. Is this a "winner-take-all market" or can search continue to support an oligopolistic market with two or three major players?

Today, five Web sites account for over 95% of all Web searches: Google, Yahoo, Microsoft/Bing, AOL (3.5%), and Ask.com

(continued)

ers (authorities). HITS (Hyperlinked Induced Topic Search) is an algorithm for automatically identifying the leading hubs and authorities in a network of hyperlinked pages. In other words, when you search on a topic, the HITS algorithm takes you to those pages that are ranked both high in authority on the topic, and high in the links they have to other sites related to that topic. For instance, if you search for a term such as "measles," the HITS algorithm will often show the Mayo Clinic page on this topic in the top results (first page). This is because the Mayo site receives a large number of links for this topic (it is an authority), and also links to a lot of other sites related to measles (it's a hub for information on the topic). Almost all search engines today use some form of the HITS algorithm, which as a set of ideas is not restricted by patent or copyright.

(2.1%), with the rest accounted for by over 100 less popular and specialized search engines such as Kosmix. Of these firms, Google stands out as the only "pure" search engine for which search is the major line of business, whereas the other firms are either also content portals (Yahoo and AOL) or, in the case of Microsoft, the provider of 95% of the world's desktop computer operating systems.

Google achieved its early and powerful lead in the search business through superior software technology, a highly efficient computer hardware architecture, and excellent Web site design. Google was started in 1998 by two enterprising Stanford grad students, Sergey Brin and Larry Page, who were studying data mining and the process of analyzing data for patterns. Early search engines such as Alta Vista (which once had 90% of the search market) merely counted how many times a search term appeared in a given Web site to determine where to rank a particular page. Brin and Page's research reflected the work of Jon Kleinberg, professor of Computer Science at Cornell, who originated an algorithm that rates pages based on the number of links to other pages (hubs) as well as the links they receive from oth-

Google's version of the HITS algorithm also uses the popularity of Web pages as the most important criteria for ranking pages, as well as the page content. The more other Web pages link to a particular page, the higher it jumps in Google's ranking structure, called PageRank. This is called "link analysis" and is run independently of the query being made. Once all the Web's indexed pages are ranked, Google also factors in other information, such as the number of links that a site contains to other sites, the text content of a page, its link structure, proximity of search words to one another on the page, fonts, heading, and text of nearby pages. Since the PageRank algorithm was invented by Brin and Page while they were students at Stanford, it is patented and

(continued)

owned by Stanford University, which licenses its use to Google.

However, Google is much more than a page rank algorithm. It's also a hardware superpower. It possesses the largest civilian computing system in the world with an undisclosed number of servers (rumored to be anywhere from 500,000 to 1 million, many of which today have dual- or quad- core processors or "computers") in 16 server "farms" throughout the world. The overall number of computer processors is estimated to be about 3 million.

Google also leads in two related areas: network management software, which permits parallel processing of search queries, and information management software. Google pioneered the concept of using hundreds of thousands of cheap PCs to process huge amounts of data (queries and responses) in microseconds using free Linux software. Searching an index of over 1 billion Web pages requires exceptional software that can coordinate the work of all these PCs. Want to know how many people search on "BMW" on Sundays from 8 a.m. to 8 p.m. in the New York metro area? Where did they come from (prior search), and what was their next search term? Or, maybe you would like to calculate queries and click-throughs for each hour in a 24-hour period in the United States for a single text ad paid for by a customer. To answer these and related marketing driven questions, Google uses an open source program called HADOOP (named after a toy elephant). HADOOP enables search engines to break large sets of data into smaller chunks stored across thousands of PCs, and then ask questions of this data, and receive responses in seconds.

However, it is unclear if Google can maintain its technological edge in search given the investments being made by Microsoft, as well as the proliferation of several other smaller but popular search engines. Google only has an exclusive license to the original PageRank patent until 2011. In the competition among search engines, it is clear that search software alone is not the key ingredient, just the foundation for the winning hand. It's a necessary but insufficient condition for success.

In 2004, Google became a public company, greatly expanding its capital foundation to support further growth. Google's strategy has been to extend its advantages in search into two areas and try to "out-invent" the competition. These areas are advertising and applications: in the words of CEO Eric Schmidt, Google is all about "search, ads, and apps." It has extended search to include images, books, scholars, content, finance, and news. It has extended its advertising services through its AdWords and AdSense programs. AdWords is an auction program that allows advertisers to bid for placement on Google pages. AdSense allows Google to place ads on publisher Web sites (basically any Web site is a "publisher" Web site) based on the content of that site's Web pages. Other services include Google Geo (Maps, Earth, and local content), and Google Checkout (an online wallet). No other online competitor has approached the success of Google's advertising platform Where to put Google's $1.65 billion purchase of YouTube? Wall Street analysts have had a tough time with this question too. YouTube is all three: it's an online application for storing and sharing videos; it's a search system for videos; and it's an advertiser's dream come true: over 120 million viewers watched more than 10 billion user-posted videos in August 2009. At this point, YouTube is not yet profitable because advertisers have not signed up for its display and text ad services for fear of losing control of ad placement.

Bing is arguably the only real competition for Google in the future. Microsoft is deadly serious about search as the centerpiece of its online revenues. How serious? In May 2008, Microsoft offered to pay $47.5 billion for a 16% share of Yahoo, and outright ownership of Yahoo's search engine, and the banner and search engine ad business built on Yahoo's huge Internet audience of over 150 million in the United States. The deal would have netted Yahoo over $1 billion a year in revenue. Rejected by Yahoo's then president (later fired by its Board for refusing the offer), Microsoft launched Bing with a $120 million marketing effort backed up by another $100 million in "partnership deals" with HP, Dell, and Verizon. Whether you want it or not, Bing will likely appear as the featured search engine on many hardware devices you purchase. Then, in July 2009, Microsoft finally convinced Yahoo to partner with it on search, using Bing as the carrot, and setting the stage for a renewed assault on Google. Bing will become Yahoo's search engine in a 10-year deal that gives Microsoft access to the Internet's search engine audience. Yahoo will retain 88% of its search engine ad revenue without having to continue investing in search engine technology. But some analysts are not so sure giving up control over a core technology is such a smart move for Yahoo. One noted, "With something as important as search, you don't want to give away the technology you need to compete with everybody else." How this will all play out for Google, Microsoft, and Yahoo remains anybody's guess, so stay tuned for the next installment of Search Engine Wars.

SOURCES: "With Microsoft Deal, Yahoo Tosses in the Search Engine Towel," by Sharon Gaudin, *Computerworld*, July 30, 2009; "Bing's Share Rises Again," *Wall Street Journal*, by John Letzing, Wall Street Journal, June 18, 2009; "Bing Is Off to a Good Start, ComScore Says," by Miguel Helft, *New York Times*, June 9, 2009; "Google: One Million Servers and Counting," Pandia.com, June 2009; "Microsoft Bing No Sure Thing," by Nick Wingfield and Jessioca Vascellaro, *Wall Street Journal*, May 30, 2009; "Microsoft Effort to Best Google Yields Results," by Katherine Boehret, *Wall Street Journal*, June 3, 2009; "Bloodied by Google, Microsoft Tries Again in Search," *New York Times*, by Miguel Helt, May 29, 2009; "US Online Advertising Spending," by David Hallerman, eMarketer, April 2009; "HADOOP, a Free Software Program, Finds Use Beyond Search," *New York Times*, March 17, 2009; "Just Don't Compare Kosmix to Google," by Miguel Helft, *New York Times*, March 15, 2009; Google Inc. Form 10-K for the year ended December 31, 2008 filed with the Securities and Exchange Commission, February 15, 2009; "Search Ad Spending," by David Hallerman, eMarketer, January 2009.

CONTENT PROVIDER

intellectual property
refers to all forms of human expression that can be put into a tangible medium such as text, CDs or on the Web

content provider
distributes information content, such as digital news, music, photos, video, and artwork, over the Web

Although there are many different ways the Internet can be useful, "information content," which can be defined broadly to include all forms of intellectual property, is one of the largest types of Internet usage. **Intellectual property** refers to all forms of human expression that can be put into a tangible medium such as text, CDs, or the Web (Fisher, 1999). **Content providers** distribute information content, such as digital video, music, photos, text, and artwork, over the Web. According to the Online Publishers Association, in 2005, U.S. consumers spent $2 billion for online content (Online Publishers Association, 2006). Since then, digital music, movies, and television have become an increasingly important part of the market, and are expected to generate over $3.9 billion in revenues alone during 2009 (eMarketer, Inc. 2009, 2007c; author estimates).

Content providers make money by charging a subscription fee. For instance, in the case of Rhapsody.com, a monthly subscription fee provides users with access to thousands of song tracks. Other content providers, such as WSJ.com (*The Wall Street Journal's* online newspaper), *Harvard Business Review*, and many others, charge customers for content downloads in addition to or in place of a subscription fee. Micropayment systems technology provides content providers with a cost-effective method for processing high volumes of very small monetary transactions (anywhere from $.25 to $5.00 per transaction). Micropayment systems have greatly enhanced the revenue model prospects of content providers who wish to charge by the download.

Of course, not all online content providers charge for their information: just look at CBSSports.com, CIO.com, CNN.com, and the online versions of many newspapers and magazines. Users can access news and information at these sites without paying a cent. These popular sites make money in other ways, such as through advertising and partner promotions on the site. Increasingly, however, "free content" is limited to headlines and text, whereas premium content—in-depth articles or video delivery—is sold for a fee.

Generally, the key to becoming a successful content provider is owning the content. Traditional owners of copyrighted content—publishers of books and newspapers, broadcasters of radio and television content, music publishers, and movie studios—have powerful advantages over newcomers to the Web who simply offer distribution channels and must pay for content, often at oligopolistic prices.

Some content providers, however, do not own content, but syndicate (aggregate) and then distribute content produced by others. *Syndication* is a major variation of the standard content provider model. Another variation here is Web aggregators, who collect information from a wide variety of sources and then add value to that information through post-aggregation services. For instance, Shopping.com collects information on the prices of thousands of goods online, analyzes the information, and presents users with tables showing the range of prices and Web locations. Shopping.com adds value to content it aggregates, and resells this value to advertisers who advertise on its site (Madnick and Siegel, 2001).

Any e-commerce start-up that intends to make money by providing content is likely to face difficulties unless it has a unique information source that others cannot access. For the most part, this business category is dominated by traditional content providers.

Online content is discussed in further depth in Chapter 10.

TRANSACTION BROKER

Sites that process transactions for consumers normally handled in person, by phone, or by mail are **transaction brokers**. The largest industries using this model are financial services, travel services, and job placement services. The online transaction broker's primary value propositions are savings of money and time. In addition, most transaction brokers provide timely information and opinions. Sites such as Monster.com offer job searchers a national marketplace for their talents and employers a national resource for that talent. Both employers and job seekers are attracted by the convenience and currency of information. Online stock brokers charge commissions that are considerably less than traditional brokers, with many offering substantial deals, such as cash and a certain number of free trades, to lure new customers (Bakos, Lucas, et al., 2000).

transaction broker
site that processes transactions for consumers that are normally handled in person, by phone, or by mail

Given rising consumer interest in financial planning and the stock market, the market opportunity for online transaction brokers appears to be large. However, while millions of customers have shifted to online brokers, many have been wary about switching from their traditional broker who provides personal advice and a brand name. Fears of privacy invasion and the loss of control over personal financial information also contribute to market resistance. Consequently, the challenge for online brokers is to overcome consumer fears by emphasizing the security and privacy measures in place, and, like physical banks and brokerage firms, providing a broad range of financial services and not just stock trading. This industry is covered in greater depth in Chapter 9.

Transaction brokers make money each time a transaction occurs. Each stock trade, for example, nets the company a fee, based either on a flat rate or a sliding scale related to the size of the transaction. Attracting new customers and encouraging them to trade frequently are the keys to generating more revenue for these companies. Job sites generate listing fees from employers up front, rather than charging a fee when a position is filled.

Competition among brokers has become more fierce in the past few years, due to new entrants offering ever more appealing offers to consumers to sign on. Those who prospered initially were the first movers such as E*Trade, Ameritrade, Datek, and Schwab. During the early days of e-commerce, many of these firms engaged in expensive marketing campaigns and were willing to pay up to $400 to acquire a single customer. However, online brokerages are now in direct competition with traditional brokerage firms who have joined the online marketspace. Significant consolidation is occurring in this industry. The number of job sites has also multiplied, but the largest sites (those with the largest number of job listings) are pulling ahead of smaller niche companies. In both industries, only a few, very large firms are likely to survive in the long term.

MARKET CREATOR

market creator
builds a digital environment where buyers and sellers can meet, display products, search for products, and establish a price for products

Market creators build a digital environment in which buyers and sellers can meet, display products, search for products, and establish prices. Prior to the Internet and the Web, market creators relied on physical places to establish a market. Beginning with the medieval marketplace and extending to today's New York Stock Exchange, a market has meant a physical space for transacting. There were few private digital network marketplaces prior to the Web. The Web changed this by making it possible to separate markets from physical space. A prime example is Priceline, which allows consumers to set the price they are willing to pay for various travel accommodations and other products (sometimes referred to as a reverse auction) and eBay, the online auction site utilized by both businesses and consumers.

For example, eBay's auction business model is to create a digital electronic environment for buyers and sellers to meet, agree on a price, and transact. This is different from transaction brokers who actually carry out the transaction for their customers, acting as agents in larger markets. At eBay, the buyers and sellers are their own agents. Each sale on eBay nets the company a commission based on the percentage of the item's sales price, in addition to a listing fee. eBay is one of the few

Web sites that has been profitable virtually from the beginning. Why? One answer is that eBay has no inventory or production costs. It is simply a middleman.

The market opportunity for market creators is potentially vast, but only if the firm has the financial resources and marketing plan to attract sufficient sellers and buyers to the marketplace. At the end of June 2009, eBay had about 88.4 million active users, and this makes for an efficient market (eBay, 2009). There are many sellers and buyers for each type of product, sometimes for the same product, for example, laptop computer models. New firms wishing to create a market require an aggressive branding and awareness program to attract a sufficient critical mass of customers. Some very large Web-based firms such as Amazon have leveraged their large customer base and started auctions. Many other digital auctions have sprung up in smaller, more specialized vertical market segments such as jewelry and automobiles.

In addition to marketing and branding, a company's management team and organization can make a difference in creating new markets, especially if some managers have had experience in similar businesses. Speed is often the key in such situations. The ability to become operational quickly can make the difference between success and failure.

SERVICE PROVIDER

While e-tailers sell products online, **service providers** offer services online. There's been an explosion in online services that is often unrecognized. Web 2.0 applications such as photo sharing, video sharing, and user-generated content (in blogs and social networking sites) are all services provided to customers. Google has led the way in developing online applications such as Google Maps, Google Docs and Spreadsheets, and Gmail. ThinkFree and Buzzword are online alternatives to Microsoft Word provided as services rather than boxed software (a product). More personal services such as online medical bill management, financial and pension planning, and travel recommender sites are showing strong growth.

service provider
offers services online

Service providers use a variety of revenue models. Some charge a fee, or monthly subscriptions, while others generate revenue from other sources, such as through advertising and by collecting personal information that is useful in direct marketing. Some services are free but are not complete. For instance, Google Apps' basic edition is free, but a "Premier" model with virtual conference rooms and advanced tools costs $50 per employee a year. Much like retailers who trade products for cash, service providers trade knowledge, expertise, and capabilities, for revenue.

Obviously, some services cannot be provided online. For example, dentistry, medical services, plumbing, and car repair cannot be completed via the Internet. However, online arrangements can be made for these services. Online service providers may offer computer services, such as information storage, provide legal services, such as at Linklaters BlueFlag, or offer advice and services to high-net-worth individuals, such as at HarrisMyCFO.com. Grocery shopping sites such as FreshDirect and Peapod are also providing services.[1] To complicate matters a bit, most financial transaction brokers (described previously) provide services such as college tuition and pension planning. Travel brokers also provide vacation-planning services, not

[1]FreshDirect and other e-commerce businesses can also be classified as online retailers insofar as they warehouse commonly purchased items and make a profit based on the spread between their buy and sell prices.

just transactions with airlines and hotels. Indeed, mixing services with your products is a powerful business strategy pursued by many hard-goods companies (for example, warranties are services).

The basic value proposition of service providers is that they offer consumers valuable, convenient, time-saving, and low-cost alternatives to traditional service providers or—in the case of search engines and most Web 2.0 applications—they provide services that are truly unique to the Web. Where else can you search 50 billion Web pages, or share photos with as many people instantly? Research has found, for instance, that a major factor in predicting online buying behavior is *time starvation*. Time-starved people tend to be busy professionals who work long hours and simply do not have the time to pick up packages, buy groceries, send photos, or visit with financial planners (Bellman, Lohse, and Johnson, 1999). The market opportunity for service providers is as large as the variety of services that can be provided and potentially is much larger than the market opportunity for physical goods. We live in a service-based economy and society; witness the growth of fast-food restaurants, package delivery services, and wireless cellular phone services. Consumers' increasing demand for convenience products and services bodes well for current and future online service providers.

Marketing of service providers must allay consumer fears about hiring a vendor online, as well as build confidence and familiarity among current and potential customers. Building confidence and trust is critical for service providers just as it is for retail product merchants. Kodak, for instance, has a powerful brand name over a century old, and has translated that brand into a trusted online provider of photo services. In the process, Kodak is transforming itself from a products-only company (cameras and paper) into a more contemporary digital services company.

COMMUNITY PROVIDER

Although community providers are not a new entity, the Internet has made such sites for like-minded individuals to meet and converse much easier, without the limitations of geography and time to hinder participation. **Community providers** are sites that create a digital online environment where people with similar interests can transact (buy and sell goods); share interests, photos, videos; communicate with like-minded people; receive interest-related information; and even play out fantasies by adopting online personalities called avatars. The social networking sites Facebook, MySpace, and Twitter, and hundreds of other smaller, niche sites such as Doostang and Sportsvite, all offer users community building tools and services.

The basic value proposition of community providers is to create a fast, convenient, one-stop site where users can focus on their most important concerns and interests, share the experience with friends, and learn more about their own interests. Community providers typically rely on a hybrid revenue model that includes subscription fees, sales revenues, transaction fees, affiliate fees, and advertising fees from other firms that are attracted by a tightly focused audience.

community provider
sites that create a digital online environment where people with similar interests can transact (buy and sell goods); share interests, photos, and videos; communicate with like-minded people; and receive interest-related information

Community sites such as iVillage make money through affiliate relationships with retailers and from advertising. For instance, a parent might visit Babystyle for tips on diapering a baby and be presented with a link to Huggies.com; if the parent clicks the link and then makes a purchase from Huggies.com, Babystyle gets a commission. Likewise, banner ads also generate revenue. At About.com, visitors can share tips and buy recommended books from Amazon, giving About.com a commission on every purchase. Some of the oldest communities on the Web are Well.com, which provides a forum for technology and Internet-related discussions, and The Motley Fool (Fool.com), which provides financial advice, news, and opinions. The Well offers various membership plans ranging from $10 to $15 a month. Motley Fool supports itself through ads and selling products that start out "free" but turn into annual subscriptions.

Consumers' interest in communities is mushrooming. Community is, arguably, the fastest growing online activity. While many community sites have had a difficult time becoming profitable, over time many have succeeded. Newer community sites such as Facebook and MySpace may not be profitable at this time, but they are quickly developing advertising revenues as their main source of revenue. Both the very large social networking sites such as Facebook, MySpace, and LinkedIn as well as niche sites with smaller dedicated audiences are ideal marketing and advertising territories. Traditional online communities such as the Well, iVillage, and WebMD (which provides medical information to members) find that breadth and depth of knowledge at a site is an important factor. Community members frequently request knowledge, guidance, and advice. Lack of experienced personnel can severely hamper the growth of a community, which needs facilitators and managers to keep discussions on course and relevant. For the newer community social networking sites, the most important ingredients of success appear to be ease and flexibility of use, and a strong customer value proposition. For instance, Facebook has leapfrogged over its rival MySpace by encouraging users to build their own revenue-producing applications that run on their profiles, and even take in advertising and affiliate revenues.

Online communities benefit significantly from offline word-of-mouth, viral marketing. Online communities tend to reflect offline relationships. When your friends say they have a profile on Facebook, and ask you to visit, you are encouraged to build your own online profile.

2.3 MAJOR BUSINESS-TO-BUSINESS (B2B) BUSINESS MODELS

In Chapter 1, we noted that business-to-business (B2B) e-commerce, in which businesses sell to other businesses, is more than 10 times the size of B2C e-commerce, even though most of the public attention has focused on B2C. For instance, it is estimated that revenues for all types of B2C e-commerce (including spending on online leisure travel and digital content) in 2009 will total around $228 billion, compared to over $3.36 trillion for all types of B2B e-commerce in 2009. Clearly, most of the dollar revenues in e-commerce involve B2B e-commerce. Much of this activity is unseen and unknown to the average consumer.

Table 2.4 lists the major business models utilized in the B2B arena.

E-DISTRIBUTOR

e-distributor

a company that supplies products and services directly to individual businesses

Companies that supply products and services directly to individual businesses are **e-distributors**. W.W. Grainger, for example, is the largest distributor of maintenance, repair, and operations (MRO) supplies. MRO supplies are thought of as indirect inputs to the production process—as opposed to direct inputs. In the past, Grainger relied on catalog sales and physical distribution centers in metropolitan areas. Its catalog of equipment went online in 1995 at Grainger.com, giving businesses access to more than 475,000 items. Company purchasing agents can search by type of product, such as motors, HVAC, or fluids, or by specific brand name.

TABLE 2.4	B2B BUSINESS MODELS		
BUSINESS MODEL	EXAMPLES	DESCRIPTION	REVENUE MODEL
(1) NET MARKETPLACE			
E-distributor	Grainger.com Partstore.com	Single-firm online version of retail and wholesale store; supply maintenance, repair, operation goods; indirect inputs	Sales of goods
E-procurement	Ariba Perfect Commerce	Single firm creating digital markets where sellers and buyers transact for indirect inputs	Fees for market-making services; supply chain management, and fulfillment services
Exchange	OceanConnect ChemConnect	Independently owned vertical digital marketplace for direct inputs	Fees and commissions on transactions
Industry Consortium	Exostar Quadrem Elemica	Industry-owned vertical digital market open to select suppliers	Fees and commissions on transactions
(2) PRIVATE INDUSTRIAL NETWORK			
Single Firm	Wal-Mart Procter & Gamble	Company-owned network that coordinates supply chains with a limited set of partners	Cost absorbed by network owner and recovered through production and distribution efficiencies
Industry-wide	1 SYNC Agentrics	Industry-owned network that sets standards, coordinates supply and logistics for the industry	Contributions from industry member firms and recovered through production and distribution efficiencies; fees for transactions and services.

E-distributors are owned by one company seeking to serve many customers. However, as with exchanges (described on the next page), critical mass is a factor. With e-distributors, the more products and services a company makes available on its site, the more attractive that site is to potential customers. One-stop shopping is always preferable to having to visit numerous sites to locate a particular part or product.

E-PROCUREMENT

Just as e-distributors provide products to other companies, **e-procurement firms** create and sell access to digital electronic markets. Firms such as Ariba, for instance, have created software that helps large firms organize their procurement process by creating mini-digital markets for a single firm. Ariba creates custom-integrated online catalogs (where supplier firms can list their offerings) for purchasing firms. On the sell side, Ariba helps vendors sell to large purchasers by providing software to handle catalog creation, shipping, insurance, and finance. Both the buy and sell side software is referred to generically as "value chain management" software.

e-procurement firm
creates and sells access to digital electronic markets

B2B service providers make money through transaction fees, fees based on the number of workstations using the service, or annual licensing fees. They offer purchasing firms a sophisticated set of sourcing and supply chain management tools that permit firms to reduce supply chain costs. In the software world, firms such as Ariba are sometimes also called **application service providers (ASPs)**; they are able to offer firms much lower costs of software by achieving scale economies. **Scale economies** are efficiencies that result from increasing the size of a business, for instance, when large, fixed-cost production systems (such as factories or software systems) can be operated at full capacity with no idle time. In the case of software, the marginal cost of a digital copy of a software program is nearly zero, and finding additional buyers for an expensive software program is exceptionally profitable. This is much more efficient than having every firm build its own supply chain management system, and it permits firms such as Ariba to specialize and offer their software to firms at a cost far less than the cost of developing it.

B2B service provider
sells business services to other firms

application service provider (ASP)
a company that sells access to Internet-based software applications to other companies

scale economies
efficiencies that arise from increasing the size of a business

EXCHANGES

Exchanges have garnered most of the B2B attention and early funding because of their potential market size even though today they are a small part of the overall B2B picture. An **exchange** is an independent digital electronic marketplace where hundreds of suppliers meet a smaller number of very large commercial purchasers (Kaplan and Sawhney, 2000). Exchanges are owned by independent, usually entrepreneurial start-up firms whose business is making a market, and they generate revenue by charging a commission or fee based on the size of the transactions conducted among trading parties. They usually serve a single vertical industry such as steel, polymers, or aluminum, and focus on the exchange of direct inputs to production and short-term contracts or spot purchasing. For buyers, B2B exchanges make it possible to gather information, check out suppliers, collect prices, and keep up to date on the latest happenings all in one place. Sellers, on the other hand, benefit from expanded access to buyers. The greater the number of sellers and buyers, the lower the sales cost and the higher the chances of making a sale. The ease, speed, and volume of transactions are summarily referred to as *market liquidity*.

exchange
an independent digital electronic marketplace where suppliers and commercial purchasers can conduct transactions

In theory, exchanges make it significantly less expensive and time-consuming to identify potential suppliers, customers, and partners, and to do business with each other. As a result, they can lower transaction costs—the cost of making a sale or purchase. Exchanges can also lower product costs and inventory-carrying costs—the cost of keeping a product on hand in a warehouse. In reality, as discussed in Chapter 12, B2B exchanges have had a difficult time convincing thousands of suppliers to move into singular digital markets where they face powerful price competition, and an equally difficult time convincing businesses to change their purchasing behavior away from trusted long-term trading partners. As a result, the number of exchanges has fallen to less than 200, down from over 1,500 in 2002, although the surviving firms have experienced some success (Ulfelder, 2004; Day, Fein, Ruppersberger, 2003).

INDUSTRY CONSORTIA

industry consortia
industry-owned vertical marketplaces that serve specific industries

Industry consortia are industry-owned *vertical marketplaces* that serve specific industries, such as the automobile, aerospace, chemical, floral, or logging industries. In contrast, *horizontal marketplaces* sell specific products and services to a wide range of companies. Vertical marketplaces supply a smaller number of companies with products and services of specific interest to their industry, while horizontal marketplaces supply companies in different industries with a particular type of product and service, such as marketing-related, financial, or computing services. For example, Exostar is an online trading exchange for the aerospace and defense industry, founded by BAE Systems, Boeing, Lockheed Martin, Raytheon, and Rolls-Royce in 2000. Exostar connects with over 300 procurement systems in 20 different countries and has registered more than 40,000 trading partners worldwide.

Industry consortia have tended to be more successful than independent exchanges in part because they are sponsored by powerful, deep-pocketed industry players, and also because they strengthen traditional purchasing behavior rather than seek to transform it.

PRIVATE INDUSTRIAL NETWORKS

private industrial networks
digital network designed to coordinate the flow of communications among firms engaged in business together

Private industrial networks (sometimes referred to as *private trading exchanges* or *PTXs*) constitute about 75% of all B2B expenditures by large firms and far exceed the expenditures for all forms of Net marketplaces. Private industrial networks are digital networks (often but not always Internet-based networks) designed to coordinate the flow of communications among firms engaged in business together. For instance, Wal-Mart operates one of the largest private industrial networks in the world for its suppliers, who on a daily basis use Wal-Mart's network to monitor the sales of their goods, the status of shipments, and the actual inventory level of their goods. B2B e-commerce relies overwhelmingly on a technology called electronic data interchange (EDI) (U.S. Census Bureau, 2009b). EDI is useful for one-to-one relationships between a single supplier and a single purchaser, and originally was designed for proprietary networks, although it is migrating rapidly to the Internet. Many firms have begun to supplement their EDI systems, however, with more powerful Web technologies that can enable many-to-one, and many-to-many market relationships where there are many suppliers selling to a single or small group of very large purchasers, or, in the case of independent exchanges, there may be many sellers and many buyers simultaneously in the marketplace. EDI is not designed for these types of relationships. There are two types of private industrial networks: single-firm networks and industry-wide networks.

Single-firm private industrial networks are the most common form of private industrial network. These single-firm networks are owned by a single large purchasing firm, such as Wal-Mart or Procter & Gamble. Participation is by invitation only to trusted long-term suppliers of direct inputs. Single-firm networks typically evolve out of a firm's own enterprise resource planning (ERP) system, and they are an effort to include key suppliers in the firm's own business decision making (eMarketer, Inc., 2004).

Industry-wide private industrial networks often evolve out of industry associations. These networks are usually owned by a consortium of the large firms in an industry and have the following goals: providing a neutral set of standards for commercial communication over the Internet; having shared and open technology platforms for solving industry problems; and in some cases, providing operating networks that allow members of an entire industry to closely collaborate. To some extent, these industry-wide networks are a response to the success of single-firm private industrial networks. For instance, Wal-Mart has refused to open its very successful network to other members of the retail industry, in effect to become an industry standard, for fear it will be sharing technology secrets with other retailers like Sears.

In response, Sears and other retailers around the world have created their own set of organizations and networks that are open to all in the industry. For instance, Agentrics is an industry-wide private industrial network for retailers and suppliers designed to facilitate and simplify trading among retailers, suppliers, partners, and distributors. Agentrics' members currently include more than half of the world's top 25 retailers and over 250 suppliers from Africa, Asia, Europe, North America, and South America. Agentrics provides collaborative design tools; planning and management; negotiations and auctions; order execution; demand aggregation; worldwide item management; worldwide logistics; and a global catalog in English, French, German, and Spanish containing trading relationship data for member-sponsored suppliers totaling more than 30,000 items (Agentrics LLC, 2009). From this list of services and capabilities, it is clear that industry-wide private industrial networks offer much more functionality than industry consortia, although the two models appear to be moving closer together (Gebauer and Zagler, 2000). We discuss these developments and other nuances of B2B commerce in Chapter 12.

2.4 BUSINESS MODELS IN EMERGING E-COMMERCE AREAS

When we think about a business, we typically think of a business firm that produces a product or good, and then sells it to a customer. But the Web has forced us to recognize new forms of business, such as consumer-to-consumer e-commerce, peer-to-peer e-commerce, and m-commerce. **Table 2.5** lists some of the business models that can be found in these emerging markets.

TABLE 2.5	BUSINESS MODELS IN EMERGING E-COMMERCE AREAS		
BUSINESS	EXAMPLES	DESCRIPTION	REVENUE MODEL
Consumer-to-consumer	eBay Half.com	Helps consumers connect with other consumers to conduct business	Transaction fees
Peer-to-peer	The Pirate Bay Cloudmark	Technology enabling consumers to share files and services via the Web, without a common server	Subscription fees, advertising, transaction fees
M-commerce	eBay Mobile PayPal Mobile Checkout AOL Mobile-Moviefone	Extending business applications using wireless technology	Sales of goods and services

CONSUMER-TO-CONSUMER (C2C) BUSINESS MODELS

Consumer-to-consumer (C2C) ventures provide a way for consumers to sell to each other, with the help of an online business. The first and best example of this type of business is eBay, utilizing a market creator business model.

Before eBay, individual consumers used garage sales, flea markets, and thrift shops to both dispose of and acquire used merchandise. With the introduction of online auctions, consumers no longer had to venture out of their homes or offices in order to bid on items of interest, and sellers could relinquish expensive retail space that was no longer needed in order to reach buyers. In return for linking like-minded buyers and sellers, eBay takes a small commission. The more auctions, the more money eBay makes. In fact, it is one of the few Web companies that has been profitable from day one—and has stayed so for several years.

Consumers who don't like auctions but still want to find used merchandise can visit Half.com (also owned by eBay), which enables consumers to sell unwanted books, movies, music, and games to other consumers at a fixed price. In return for facilitating the transaction, Half.com takes a commission on the sale, ranging from 5%–15%, depending on the sale price, plus a fraction of the shipping fee it charges.

PEER-TO-PEER (P2P) BUSINESS MODELS

Like the C2C models, P2P business models link users, enabling them to share files and computer resources without a common server. The focus in P2P companies is on helping individuals make information available for anyone's use by connecting users on the Web. Historically, peer-to-peer software technology has been used to allow the sharing of copyrighted music files in violation of digital copyright law. The challenge for P2P ventures is to develop viable, legal business models that will enable them to make money. In Chapter 1, we discussed the difficulties faced by The Pirate Bay, one of the most prominent examples of a P2P business model in action. To date, there are few if any examples of successful P2P e-commerce business models outside of the music and content file- swapping sites. However, one company that has successfully used this model outside those two arenas is Cloudmark, which offers a P2P anti-spam solution called Cloudmark Desktop. Cloudmark currently protects over 850 million e-mailboxes around the world.

M-COMMERCE BUSINESS MODELS

M-commerce, short for *mobile-commerce*, takes traditional e-commerce models and leverages emerging new wireless technologies—described more fully in Chapter 3—to permit mobile access to the Web. Wireless Web technology is being used to enable the extension of existing Web business models to service the mobile work force and consumer of the future. Wireless networks utilize newly available bandwidth and communication protocols to connect mobile users to the Internet. These technologies have already taken off in Asia and Europe, and will expand greatly in the United States in a few years. The major advantage of m-commerce is that it provides Internet access to anyone, anytime, and anywhere, using wireless devices. The key technologies here are cell phone-based 3G (third-generation wireless), Wi-Fi (wireless local area networks), and Bluetooth (short-range radio frequency Web devices).

There are many more cell phone subscribers (an estimated 3–4 billion worldwide in 2009) than there are Internet users (eMarketer, 2009b). Cell phone usage is still considerably higher in Asia and Europe than it is in the United States. However, in the United States, the introduction of the iPhone in June 2007, the 3G version in July 2008, and the 3GS version in June 2009 has brought about a resurgence of interest in 3G technologies and their potential role in e-commerce. The standards implementing Wi-Fi were first introduced in 1997, and since then it has exploded in the United States and elsewhere. Analysts estimate that there are 280,000 wireless hot spots (locations that enable a Wi-Fi–enabled device to connect to a nearby wireless LAN and access the Internet) worldwide in 2009 (JiWire.com, 2009). Likewise, the number of Bluetooth-enabled cell phones is also expanding exponentially. Two other wireless technologies that may have an impact are Ultrawideband (wireless USB technology), which will be able to transfer large files such as movies over short distances, and Zigbee, which, like Bluetooth, will connect devices to each other but at a longer range and with lower power requirements.

Prior to 2009, mobile commerce in the United States had been a disappointment. However, with the introduction of the iPhone and other phones with similar capabilities, this has begun to change (**Figure 2.3** on page 98). For instance, many of the top 100 largest online retailers, such as Amazon, Newegg, 1-800-Flowers.com, and others now have Web sites optimized for mobile commerce or offer shopping applications that can be downloaded onto smart phones, and more are joining them every day (Internet Retailer, 2009). The server-side hardware and software platform is in place, and the basic bandwidth is ready. As with all areas of e-commerce, the challenge for businesses will be finding ways to use m-commerce to make money while serving customer needs. Currently, demand is highest for digital content such as customized ring tones, games, and wallpaper. With the introduction of the iPhone, mobile search applications have become more popular. Consumer applications are also beginning to appear in high-volume personal transaction areas, such as AOL's Moviefone reservation system, eBay's Mobile system, and mobile payment platforms such as PayPal's Mobile Checkout.

M-commerce business models that rely on location-based advertising, as described in *Insight on Society: Where R U?* are becoming increasingly popular, but raise a number of thorny social issues.

INSIGHT ON SOCIETY

WHERE R U?

First, the Internet made the world flat. Location no longer mattered. You could find and purchase products around the world just as easily as ones in your hometown. Now with the advent of GPS chip and software technology that enables your smart phone to track your exact position, where you are located has once again become important to Internet entrepreneurs and marketers. Manufacturers of netbooks and laptops are adding similar location functionality to their products as well. With these new capabilities come new business opportunities, accompanied by some familiar concerns about privacy and security.

For instance, Loopt is a free social networking application that allows you to share your status and track the location of friends via smart phones such as the iPhone, BlackBerry, Google Android, and over 100 other mobile devices. Loopt has more than 1 million users. Loopt doesn't sell information to advertisers, but does post ads based on user location: its privacy policy allows it to disclose "some personally identifiable, registration, profile, or location information to subsidiaries, affiliated companies, or other businesses or persons ... in order to serve relevant advertisements." Loopt's target is to deal with advertisers at the walking level (within 200 to 250 meters).

Although the mobile advertising market is currently small ($760 million), it is fast-growing (up 17% from last year and expected to grow to over $3.3 billion by 2013), as more and more companies seek ways to exploit new databases of location-specific information. For example, in May 2009, Alcatel-Lucent announced a new service to be managed by 1020 Placecast that will identify cell phone users within a specified distance of an advertiser's nearest outlet and notify them of the outlet's address and phone number, perhaps including a link to a coupon or other promotion. 1020 Placecast's clients include Hyatt, FedEx and Avis Rent A Car. Burger King and Suburu have recently run trial campaigns using Useful Networks' Store Finder application that allowed users to click a mobile banner ad to find the nearest store location. The trial showed that the location-enabled campaign significantly increased Store Finder conversion rates compared to users who had to manually enter zip codes to find locations.

While there's no denying the potential usefulness of such a service, the specter of "Big Brother"-like location tracking has privacy advocates raising the alarm. Privacy experts such as Lauren Gelman, executive director of Stanford Law School's Center for Internet and Society wonder, "How are we going to get all the benefits that come from doing geolocation without sacrificing people's privacy?"

To date, wireless location-based services remain largely unregulated. The Wireless Communications and Public Safety Act (often called the "911 Act") added the term "location" to the definition of customer proprietary network information (CPNI) held by telecommunication carriers, to make it eligible for certain privacy protections offered by the Communications Act of 1934. The 911 Act also required that the Federal Communications Commission (FCC) establish rules regarding how telecommunications carriers treat CPNI. The FCC did so in July 2002, adopting an approach that requires an individual's affirmative consent (opt-in) for some circumstances and assuming consent is granted unless an individual indicates otherwise (opt-out) in others.

The 2003 CAN-SPAM Act required the FCC to issue rules to protect wireless subscribers from unwanted mobile service commercial messages, and provides that consumers can list their cell phone numbers in the National Do Not Call Registry. In August 2004, the FCC proposed regulations, most of which went into effect in October 2004. The FCC prohibits sending wireless commercial e-mail messages unless the individual addressee has given the sender express prior authorization. The FCC also created a publicly available list of wireless domain

(continued)

names list used for mobile service messaging so that senders of commercial mail could more easily determine which addresses are directed at mobile services. In 2009, the law was used to force three firms responsible for the infamous "car warranty" scam cell phone calls to cease and pay restitution to consumers.

Congress continues to debate how to protect wireless subscribers further, but thus far no laws have passed since CAN-SPAM in 2003. Europe and Japan, in contrast, have strong government privacy protection policies forbidding the use of location-based data without user consent, and there are strict limitations on selling the information to third parties. The wireless industry, mindful of the privacy issues raised in the online e-commerce context, has issued calls for stringent self-regulation in an attempt to avoid government-imposed regulation. In July 2008, the Mobile Marketing Association (MMA) adopted a global code of conduct for wireless marketing campaigns, broadening the scope of privacy guidelines it had previously issued for the United States. The code focuses on five basic tenets:

• Notice: Users should be informed of the marketer's identity and the purpose for which location information is being captured and used.

• Choice and consent: Opt-in consent should be obtained and a simple opt-out process provided.

• Customization and constraint: Customer data should be handled responsibly and only used for the purpose of providing relevant and valuable services.

• Security: Sufficient security to protect consumer data from unauthorized third-party access and use, should be provided.

• Enforcement and accountability: MMA members are expected must comply with the code of conduct, and should self-certify that they are doing so.

In addition, some companies are offering technological solutions. For instance, WaveMarket provides a location aggregation platform called Veriplace that serves as middleware between mobile application developers and wireless carriers. The platform allows developers to access real-time user location data in their application. WaveMarket identifies the platform's "Privacy Engine" as one of its core features. The Privacy Engine allows end users full control over disclosure of their location. For instance, an end user can decide to share or not share location information based on days of the week or hours of the day, or to generalize location information from street-corner level to zip code or city level. End users can also view a history of all location requests, so they can always see who is trying to locate them. Whether consumers will actually use these capabilities to protect their location and other personal information is a question whose answer remains to be seen, however.

SOURCES: "MetaPlaces 09: Location-based Ads and Privacy," TheWhereBusiness.com, July 16, 2009; "Alcatel Gets Into Mobile Ads," by Sara Silver and Emily Steel, *Wall Street Journal*, May 21, 2009; "LBS Apps Drive Higher Accuracy; Advertisers Follow," by Thomas Hallauer," TheWhereBusiness.com, May 21, 2009; "Burger King, Suburu Trial Location-based Mobile Advertising," by Dan Butcher, Mobile Marketer.com, May 16, 2009; "WaveMarket's Joel Grossman Addresses Privacy and Location-based Advertising," by Joe Francica, Directions Magazine, May 13, 2009; "Cellphone Tracking Services: Friend Finder or Big Brother," by Michael B. Farrell, *Christian Science Monitor*, May 1, 2009; "Mobile Advertising and Usage," eMarketer, April 2009; "A Call to Legislate Internet Privacy," by Saul Hansell, *New York Times*, March 13, 2009; "Agency Skeptical of Internet Privacy Policies," by Saul Hansell, *New York Times*, February 13, 2009; "Wireless Communications: Voice and Data Privacy" and "When a Cell Phone Is More Than a Phone: Protecting Your Privacy in the Age of the Smartphone," Privacy Rights Clearinghouse, http://www.privacyrights.org (undated, accessed July 31, 2009).

FIGURE 2.3	APPLE iPHONE: INTERNET IN YOUR POCKET

The Apple iPhone combines both cellular voice and Internet, as well as Wi-Fi local area network access to the Web. Over 17 million iPhones in various versions have been sold in the United States since it was first introduced in June 2007. SOURCE: Apple, Inc., 2009.

E-COMMERCE ENABLERS: THE GOLD RUSH MODEL

Of the nearly 500,000 miners who descended on California in the Gold Rush of 1849, less than 1% ever achieved significant wealth. However, the banking firms, shipping companies, hardware companies, real estate speculators, and clothing companies such as Levi Strauss built long-lasting fortunes. Likewise in e-commerce. No discussion of e-commerce business models would be complete without mention of a group of companies whose business model is focused on providing the infrastructure necessary for e-commerce companies to exist, grow, and prosper. These are the e-commerce enablers: the Internet infrastructure companies. They provide the hardware, operating system software, networks and communications technology, applications software, Web designs, consulting services, and other tools that make e-commerce over the Web possible (see **Table 2.6**). While these firms may not be conducting e-commerce per se (although in many instances, e-commerce in its traditional sense is in fact one of their sales channels), they as a group have perhaps profited the most from the development of e-commerce. We will discuss many of these players in the following chapters.

TABLE 2.6	E-COMMERCE ENABLERS
INFRASTRUCTURE	PLAYERS
Hardware: Web Servers	IBM, HP, Dell, Sun
Software: Operating Systems and Server Software	Microsoft, RedHat Linux, Sun, Apache Software Foundation
Networking: Routers	Cisco, JDS Uniphase, Lucent
Security: Encryption Software	VeriSign, Check Point, Entrust, RSA, Thawte
E-commerce Software Systems (B2C, B2B)	IBM, Microsoft, Ariba, Broadvision, Oracle (BEA Systems)
Streaming and Rich Media Solutions	Real Networks, Microsoft, Apple, Adobe
Customer Relationship Management Software	Oracle, SAP, GSI Commerce, Escalate Retail
Payment Systems	VeriSign, PayPal, Cybersource, Chase Paymentech
Performance Enhancement	Akamai, Limelight Networks
Databases	Oracle, Microsoft, Sybase, IBM
Hosting Services	IBM, WebIntellects, Qwest, Rackspace, Web.com

2.5 HOW THE INTERNET AND THE WEB CHANGE BUSINESS: STRATEGY, STRUCTURE, AND PROCESS

Now that you have a clear grasp of the variety of business models used by e-commerce firms, you also need to understand how the Internet and the Web have changed the business environment in the last decade, including industry structures, business strategies, and industry and firm operations (business processes and value chains). We will return to these concepts throughout the book as we explore the e-commerce phenomenon. In general, the Internet is an open standards system available to all players, and this fact inherently makes it easy for new competitors to enter the marketplace and offer substitute products or channels of delivery. The Internet tends to intensify competition. Because information becomes available to everyone, the Internet inherently shifts power to buyers who can quickly discover the lowest-cost provider on the Web. On the other hand, the Internet presents many new opportunities for creating value, for branding products and charging premium prices, and for enlarging an already powerful offline physical business such as Wal-Mart or Sears.

Recall Table 1.2 in Chapter 1 that describes the truly unique features of e-commerce technology. **Table 2.7** suggests some of the implications of each unique feature for the overall business environment—industry structure, business strategies, and operations.

TABLE 2.7	EIGHT UNIQUE FEATURES OF E-COMMERCE TECHNOLOGY
FEATURE	SELECTED IMPACTS ON BUSINESS ENVIRONMENT
Ubiquity	Alters industry structure by creating new marketing channels and expanding size of overall market. Creates new efficiencies in industry operations and lowers costs of firms' sales operations. Enables new differentiation strategies.
Global reach	Changes industry structure by lowering barriers to entry, but greatly expands market at same time. Lowers cost of industry and firm operations through production and sales efficiencies. Enables competition on global scope.
Universal standards	Changes industry structure by lowering barriers to entry and intensifying competition within an industry. Lowers costs of industry and firm operations by lowering computing and communications costs. Enables broad scope strategies.
Richness	Alters industry structure by reducing strength of powerful distribution channels. Changes industry and firm operations cost by reducing reliance on sales forces. Enhances post-sales support strategies.
Interactivity	Alters industry structure by reducing threat of substitutes through enhanced customization. Reduces industry and firm costs by reducing reliance on sales forces. Enables Web-based differentiation strategies.
Personalization/ Customization	Alters industry structure by reducing threats of substitutes, raising barriers to entry. Reduces value chain costs in industry and firms by lessening reliance on sales forces. Enables personalized marketing strategies.
Information density	Changes industry structure by weakening powerful sales channels, shifting bargaining power to consumers. Reduces industry and firm operations costs by lowering costs of obtaining, processing, and distributing information about suppliers and consumers.
Social networking technologies	Changes industry structure by shifting programming and editorial decisions to consumers; creates substitute entertainment products; energizes a large group of new suppliers.

industry structure
refers to the nature of the players in an industry and their relative bargaining power

industry structural analysis
an effort to understand and describe the nature of competition in an industry, the nature of substitute products, the barriers to entry, and the relative strength of consumers and suppliers

INDUSTRY STRUCTURE

E-commerce changes industry structure, in some industries more than others. **Industry structure** refers to the nature of the players in an industry and their relative bargaining power. An industry's structure is characterized by five forces: *rivalry among existing competitors*, the *threat of substitute products, barriers to entry into the industry*, the *bargaining power of suppliers*, and the *bargaining power of buyers* (Porter, 1985). When you describe an industry's structure, you are describing the general business environment in an industry and the overall profitability of doing business in that environment. E-commerce has the potential to change the relative strength of these competitive forces (see **Figure 2.4** on page 101).

When you consider a business model and its potential long-term profitability, you should always perform an industry structural analysis. An **industry structural analysis** is an effort to understand and describe the nature of competition in an

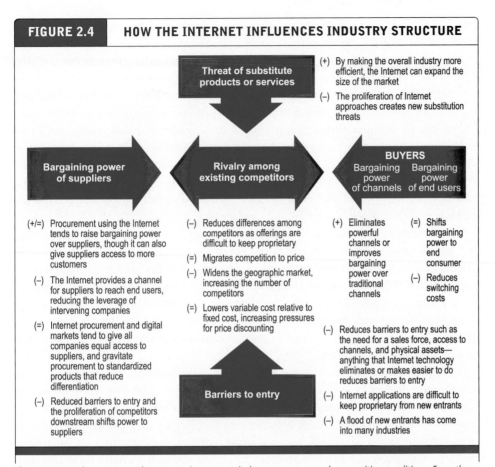

FIGURE 2.4   HOW THE INTERNET INFLUENCES INDUSTRY STRUCTURE

The Internet and e-commerce have many impacts on industry structure and competitive conditions. From the perspective of a single firm, these changes can have negative or positive implications. In this figure, "+" indicates a positive development for the firm, "−" a negative development, and "=" that neither positive nor negative impacts can be predicted. Each industry will be affected differently and must be analyzed separately. SOURCE: Porter, 2001.

industry, the nature of substitute products, the barriers to entry, and the relative strength of consumers and suppliers.

E-commerce can affect the structure and dynamics of industries in very different ways. Consider the recorded music industry, an industry that has experienced significant change because of the Internet and e-commerce. Historically, the major record label firms owned the exclusive rights to the recorded music of various artists. With the entrance into the marketplace of substitute providers such as Napster and Kazaa, millions of consumers began to use the Internet to bypass traditional music labels and their distributors entirely. In the travel industry, entirely new middlemen such as Travelocity have entered the market to compete with traditional travel agents. After Travelocity, Expedia, CheapTickets, and other travel services demonstrated the power of e-commerce marketing for airline tickets, the actual owners of the airline seats—the major airlines—banded together to form their own Internet outlet for tickets, Orbitz, for direct sales to consumers (although ultimately selling the company to a private investor group). Clearly, e-commerce and the Internet create *new industry dynamics* that can best be described as the give and take of the marketplace, the changing fortunes of competitors.

Yet in other industries, the Internet and e-commerce have strengthened existing players. In the chemical and automobile industries, e-commerce is being used effectively by manufacturers to strengthen their traditional distributors. In these industries, e-commerce technology has not fundamentally altered the competitive forces—bargaining power of suppliers, barriers to entry, bargaining power of buyers, threat of substitutes, or rivalry among competitors—within the industry. Hence, each industry is different and you need to examine each one carefully to understand the impacts of e-commerce on competition and strategy.

New forms of distribution created by new market entrants can completely change the competitive forces in an industry. For instance, if a software firm such as Microsoft discovers that consumers will gladly substitute a $50 or even free encyclopedia on a CD-ROM (a digital information product) for a $2,500 set of Britannica encyclopedias (a physical information product), then the competitive forces in the encyclopedia industry are radically changed. Even if the substitute is an inferior product, consumers are able to satisfy their anxieties about their children's education at a much lower cost (Gerace, 1999).

Inter-firm rivalry (competition) is one area of the business environment where e-commerce technologies have had an impact on most industries. In general, the Internet has increased price competition in nearly all markets. It has been relatively easy for existing firms to adopt e-commerce technology and attempt to use it to achieve competitive advantage vis-à-vis rivals. For instance, the Internet inherently changes the scope of competition from local and regional to national and global. Because consumers have access to global price information, the Internet produces pressures on firms to compete by lowering prices (and lowering profits). On the other hand, the Internet has made it possible for some firms to differentiate their product or services from others. Amazon has patented one-click purchasing for instance, while eBay has created a unique, easy-to-use interface and a differentiating brand name. REI, Inc.—a specialty mountain climbing-oriented sporting goods company— has been able to use its Web site to maintain its strong niche focus on outdoor gear. Therefore, although the Internet has increased emphasis on price competition, it has also enabled businesses to create new strategies for differentiation and branding so that they can retain higher prices.

It is impossible to determine if e-commerce technologies have had an overall positive or negative impact on firm profitability in general. Each industry is unique, so it is necessary to perform a separate analysis for each one. Clearly, e-commerce has shaken the foundations of some industries, in particular, information product industries (such as the music, newspaper, book, and software industries) as well as other information-intense industries such as financial services. In these industries, the power of consumers has grown relative to providers, prices have fallen, and overall profitability has been challenged. In other industries, especially manufacturing, the Internet has not greatly changed relationships with buyers, but has changed relationships with suppliers. Increasingly, manufacturing firms in entire industries have banded together to aggregate purchases, create industry digital exchanges or marketplaces, and outsource industrial processes in order to obtain better prices from suppliers. Throughout this book, we will document these changes in industry structure and market dynamics introduced by e-commerce and the Internet.

INDUSTRY VALUE CHAINS

While an industry structural analysis helps us understand the impact of e-commerce technology on the overall business environment in an industry, a more detailed industry value chain analysis can help identify more precisely just how e-commerce may change business operations at the industry level (Benjamin and Wigand, 1995). One of the basic tools for understanding the impact of information technology on industry and firm operations is the value chain. The concept is quite simple. A **value chain** is the set of activities performed in an industry or in a firm that transforms raw inputs into final products and services. Each of these activities adds economic value to the final product; hence, the term *value chain* as an interconnected set of value-adding activities. **Figure 2.5** illustrates the six generic players in an industry value chain: suppliers, manufacturers, transporters, distributors, retailers, and customers.

By reducing the cost of information, the Internet offers each of the key players in an industry value chain new opportunities to maximize their positions by lowering costs and/or raising prices. For instance, manufacturers can reduce the costs they pay for goods by developing Web-based B2B exchanges with their suppliers. Manufacturers can develop direct relationships with their customers through their own Web sites, bypassing the costs of distributors and retailers. Distributors can develop highly efficient inventory management systems to reduce

value chain
the set of activities performed in an industry or in a firm that transforms raw inputs into final products and services

| FIGURE 2.5 | E-COMMERCE AND INDUSTRY VALUE CHAINS |

Every industry can be characterized by a set of value-adding activities performed by a variety of actors. E-commerce potentially affects the capabilities of each player as well as the overall operational efficiency of the industry.

their costs, and retailers can develop highly efficient customer relationship management systems to strengthen their service to customers. Customers in turn can use the Web to search for the best quality, fastest delivery, and lowest prices, thereby lowering their transaction costs and reducing prices they pay for final goods. Finally, the operational efficiency of the entire industry can increase, lowering prices and adding value to consumers, and helping the industry to compete with alternative industries. Dell, for instance, employs a number of these stratagems, most notably a sales model for personal computers that bypasses traditional retail distribution channels by selling directly to consumers over the Web. Dell also has developed a highly efficient supply chain management system to reduce its costs, and an equally efficient customer relationship management system to support customers and add to the value of its products.

FIRM VALUE CHAINS

The concept of value chain can be used to analyze a single firm's operational efficiency as well. The question here is: How does e-commerce technology potentially affect the value chains of firms within an industry? A **firm value chain** is the set of activities a firm engages in to create final products from raw inputs. Each step in the process of production adds value to the final product. In addition, firms develop support activities that coordinate the production process and contribute to overall operational efficiency. **Figure 2.6** illustrates the key steps and support activities in a firm's value chain.

The Internet offers firms many opportunities to increase their operational efficiency and differentiate their products. For instance, firms can use the Internet's communications efficiency to outsource some primary and secondary activities to

firm value chain
the set of activities a firm engages in to create final products from raw inputs

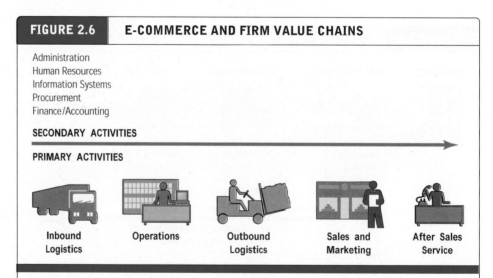

Every firm can be characterized by a set of value-adding primary and secondary activities performed by a variety of actors in the firm. A simple firm value chain performs five primary value-adding steps: inbound logistics, operations, outbound logistics, sales and marketing, and after sales service.

specialized, more efficient providers without such outsourcing being visible to the consumer. In addition, firms can use the Internet to more precisely coordinate the steps in the value chains and reduce their costs. Finally, firms can use the Internet to provide users with more differentiated and high-value products. For instance, Amazon uses the Internet to provide consumers with a much larger inventory of books to choose from, at a lower cost, than traditional book stores. It also provides many services—such as instantly available professional and consumer reviews, and information on buying patterns of other consumers—that traditional bookstores cannot.

FIRM VALUE WEBS

While firms produce value through their value chains, they also rely on the value chains of their partners—their suppliers, distributors, and delivery firms. The Internet creates new opportunities for firms to cooperate and create a value web. A **value web** is a networked business ecosystem that uses Internet technology to coordinate the value chains of business partners within an industry, or at the first level, to coordinate the value chains of a group of firms. **Figure 2.7** illustrates a value web.

value web
networked trans-business system that coordinates the value chains of several firms

FIGURE 2.7   INTERNET-ENABLED VALUE WEB

STRATEGIC ALLIANCE AND PARTNER FIRMS

DIRECT SUPPLIERS

CUSTOMERS

FIRM/INDUSTRY

ERP Systems
Legacy Systems

Supply Chain
Management Systems:
Private Industrial Networks
Net Marketplaces

Customer Relationship
Management (CRM) Systems

INDIRECT SUPPLIERS (MRO)

Internet technology enables firms to create an enhanced value web in cooperation with their strategic alliance and partner firms, customers, and direct and indirect suppliers.

A value web coordinates a firm's suppliers with its own production needs using an Internet-based supply chain management system. We discuss these B2B systems in Chapter 12. Firms also use the Internet to develop close relationships with their logistics partners. For instance, Amazon relies on UPS tracking systems to provide its customers with online package tracking, and it relies on the U.S. Postal Service systems to insert packages directly into the mail stream. Amazon has partnership relations with hundreds of firms to generate customers and to manage relationships with customers. (Online customer relationship management systems are discussed in Chapter 6.) In fact, when you examine Amazon closely, you realize that the value it delivers to customers is in large part the result of coordination with other firms and not simply the result of activities internal to Amazon. The value of Amazon is, in large part, the value delivered by its value web partners. This is difficult for other firms to imitate in the short run.

BUSINESS STRATEGY

business strategy
a set of plans for achieving superior long-term returns on the capital invested in a business firm

A **business strategy** is a set of plans for achieving superior long-term returns on the capital invested in a business firm. A business strategy is therefore a plan for making profits in a competitive environment over the long term. **Profit** is simply the difference between the price a firm is able to charge for its products and the cost of producing and distributing goods. Profit represents economic value. Economic value is created anytime customers are willing to pay more for a product than it costs to produce. Why would anyone pay more for a product than it costs to produce? There are multiple answers. The product may be unique (there are no other suppliers), it may be the least costly product of its type available, consumers may be able to purchase the product anywhere in the world, or it may satisfy some unique needs that other products do not. Each of these sources of economic value defines a firm's strategy for positioning its products in the marketplace. There are four generic strategies for achieving a profitable business: differentiation, cost, scope, and focus. We describe each of these below. The specific strategies that a firm follows will depend on the product, the industry, and the marketplace where competition is encountered.

profit
the difference between the price a firm is able to charge for its products and the cost of producing and distributing goods

Although the Internet is a unique marketplace, the same principles of strategy and business apply. As we will see throughout the book, successful e-commerce strategies involve using the Internet to leverage and strengthen existing business (rather than destroy your business), and to use the Internet to provide products and services your competitors cannot copy (in the short term anyway). That means developing unique products, proprietary content, distinguishing processes (such as Amazon's one-click shopping), and personalized or customized services and products (Porter, 2001). Let's examine these ideas more closely.

differentiation
refers to all the ways producers can make their products unique and different to distinguish them from those of competitors

Differentiation refers to all the ways producers can make their products unique and distinguish them from those of competitors. The opposite of differentiation is **commoditization**—a situation where there are no differences among products or services, and the only basis of choosing a product is price. As economists tell us, when price alone becomes the basis of competition and there are many suppliers and many customers, eventually the price of the good falls to the cost to produce it (marginal revenues from the nth unit equal marginal costs). And then profits are zero! This is an unacceptable situation for any business person.

commoditization
a situation where there are no differences among products or services, and the only basis of choosing products is price

The solution is to differentiate your product and to create a monopoly-like situation where you are the only supplier.

There are many ways businesses differentiate their products. A business may start with a core generic product, but then create expectations among users about the "experience" of consuming the product—"Nothing refreshes like a Coke!" or "Nothing equals the experience of driving a BMW." Businesses may also augment products by adding features to make them different from those of competitors. And businesses can differentiate their products further by enhancing the products' abilities to solve related consumer problems. For instance, tax programs such as TurboTax can import data from spreadsheet programs, as well as be used to electronically file tax returns. These capabilities are enhancements to the product that solve a customer's problems. The purpose of marketing is to create these differentiation features and to make the consumer aware of the unique qualities of products, creating in the process a "brand" that stands for these features. We discuss marketing and branding in Chapter 6.

In their totality, the differentiation features of a product constitute the customer value proposition we described in earlier sections of this chapter. The Internet and the Web offer some unique ways to differentiate products. The ability of the Web to personalize the shopping experience and to customize the product or service to the particular demands of each consumer are perhaps the most significant ways in which the Web can be used to differentiate products. E-commerce businesses can also differentiate products by leveraging the ubiquitous nature of the Web (by making it possible to purchase the product from home, work, or on the road); the global reach of the Web (by making it possible to purchase the product anywhere in the world); richness and interactivity (by creating Web-based experiences for people who use the product, such as unique interactive content, videos, stories about users, and reviews by users); and information density (by storing and processing information for consumers of the product, such as warranty information on all products purchased through a site or income tax information online).

Adopting a *strategy of cost competition* means a business has discovered some unique set of business processes or resources that other firms cannot obtain in the marketplace. Business processes are the atomic units of the value chain. For instance, the set of value-creating activities called Inbound Logistics in Figure 2.6 is in reality composed of many different collections of activities performed by people on the loading docks and in the warehouses. These different collections of activities are called business processes—the set of steps or procedures required to perform the various elements of the value chain.

When a firm discovers a new, more efficient set of business processes, it can obtain a cost advantage over competitors. Then it can attract customers by charging a lower price, while still making a handsome profit. Eventually, its competitors go out of business as the market decisively tilts toward the lowest-cost provider. Or, when a business discovers a unique resource, or lower-cost supplier, it can also compete effectively on cost. For instance, switching production to low-wage-cost areas of the world is one way to lower costs.

Competing on cost can be a short-lived affair and very tricky. Competitors can also discover the same or different efficiencies in production. And competitors can also move production to low-cost areas of the world. Also, competitors may decide to lose money for a period as they compete on cost.

The Internet offers some new ways to compete on cost, at least in the short term. Firms can leverage the Internet's ubiquity by lowering the costs of order entry (the customer fills out all the forms, so there is no order entry department); leverage global reach and universal standards by having a single order entry system worldwide; and leverage richness, interactivity, and personalization by creating customer profiles online and treating each individual consumer differently— without the use of an expensive sales force that performed these functions in the past. Finally, firms can leverage the information intensity of the Web by providing consumers with detailed information on products, without maintaining either expensive catalogs or a sales force.

While the Internet offers powerful capabilities for intensifying cost competition, making cost competition appear to be a viable strategy, the danger is that competitors have access to the same technology. The *factor markets*—where producers buy their supplies—are open to all. Assuming they have the skills and organizational will to use the technology, competitors can buy many of the same cost-reducing techniques in the marketplace. Even a skilled labor force can be purchased, ultimately. However, self-knowledge, proprietary tacit knowledge (knowledge that is not published or codified), and a loyal, skilled workforce are in the short term difficult to purchase in factor markets. Therefore, cost competition remains a viable strategy.

Two other generic business strategies are scope and focus. A *scope strategy* is a strategy to compete in all markets around the globe, rather than merely in local, regional, or national markets. The Internet's global reach, universal standards, and ubiquity can certainly be leveraged to assist businesses in becoming global competitors. Yahoo, for instance, along with all of the other top 20 e-commerce sites, has readily attained a global presence using the Internet. A *focus strategy* is a strategy to compete within a narrow market segment or product segment. This is a specialization strategy with the goal of becoming the premier provider in a narrow market. For instance, L.L.Bean uses the Web to continue its historic focus on outdoor sports apparel; and W.W.Grainger—the Web's most frequently visited B2B site—focuses on a narrow market segment called MRO: maintenance, repair, and operations of commercial buildings. The Internet offers some obvious capabilities that enable a focus strategy. Firms can leverage the Web's rich interactive features to create highly focused messages to different market segments; the information intensity of the Web makes it possible to focus e-mail and other marketing campaigns on small market segments; personalization—and related customization—means the same product can be customized and personalized to fulfill the very focused needs of specific market segments and consumers.

Industry structure, industry and firm value chains, value webs, and business strategy are central business concepts used throughout this book to analyze the viability of and prospects for e-commerce sites. In particular, the signature case studies found at the end of each chapter are followed with questions that may ask you to identify the competitive forces in the case, or analyze how the case illustrates changes in industry structure, industry and firm value chains, and business strategy.

CASE STUDY

Priceline.com
and the Search for a Business Model that Works

Priceline is one of the Web's most well-known companies. Its "Name Your Own Price" reverse-auction pricing system is a unique business model that uses the information sharing and communications power of the Internet to create a new way of pricing products and services. At Priceline, consumers can enter a bid for travel, hotels, rental cars, and even home financing. Priceline then queries its databases in which participating suppliers file secure discounted rates not generally available to the public. The company then determines if it can fulfill the customer's offer and decide whether it wants to accept the offer at the price designated by the consumer. Unlike other trends in online information which emphasize transparency, Priceline's business model is based on opaqueness, where consumers and suppliers have incomplete information about price, brand, and timing. In return, customers receive a much lower price than other sites can provide.

Priceline offers a compelling value proposition to customers, allowing them to save money by trading off flexibility about brands, product features, and/or sellers in return for lower prices. Vendors also can gain additional revenue by selling products they might not otherwise be able to sell by accepting below-retail price offers, without disrupting their existing distribution channels or retail pricing structure. Priceline is an example of using the Web to achieve efficient price discrimination: suppliers can charge some consumers much more than others for the same product. Priceline acts as the middleman to make that happen. In 2008, Priceline sold about 4.9 million airline tickets (up 40%), 41 million hotel room nights (up 46%), and 10 million rental car days (up 14%).

Business models are never as simple as seem. If they were, they could be easily copied. Priceline's business model has several elements. Priceline hides the names of suppliers so they won't damage their brand image and this in turn has increased support among the suppliers of the inventory (hotels, airlines, car reservation companies, and others) by buying the inevitable excess capacity of the travel industry, acting in a sense as electronic liquidators. Hiding the name of providers prior to purchase is acceptable to a wide swath of the travel market who does not care about brand names as much as price. Playing at Priceline is sort of like gambling in Las Vegas—you never know ahead of time exactly where you will end up. A third element of Priceline's business model is a powerful technology infrastructure that can match offered bids with available sellers in a customer friendly way. A superb customer experience results. These other elements can be difficult for competitors to imitate, as experience has shown in the case of Expedia, which has its own "name your price" site named Hotwire, but that has not met with much success. Perhaps most important, Priceline's business model provides customers with the lowest cost travel services on the Internet.

Priceline offers a classic example of a company that started with a unique business model, struggled to make a profit, tried to scale it up to a wider variety of consumer products, failed, and then returned to the original model while refining its key elements. By 2009, it had developed a strategic edge over several very formidable competitors and was showing strong growth in a down market. Despite the economic downturn of 2008–2009, which caused other travel sites' revenues and profits to plunge, Priceline's revenues expanded to $1.9 billion in 2008, up 34% from 2007. And its net profit jumped 24% to $193 million. For the first quarter of 2009, revenues continued expanding by 14%, and profits by 15%.

The original vision of Priceline's founder Jay Walker was called "demand collection." Walker poured millions into the concept of a one-stop shopping center for goods and services from trucks, to toothpaste, to vacation travel. But for much of its early history, Priceline was not profitable. In 1999, it lost over $1 billion. It pared losses to $15 million by 2001, but then, as travel declined after the September 11, 2001, World Trade Center tragedy, regressed in 2002, posting a $23 million dollar loss. Key executives resigned. Headlines such as "Priceline on the Ropes" and "Curtain Call for Priceline.com" predominated. However, in 2003, Priceline recorded its first ever annual profit, recording $10.4 million in net income. The good news has continued since. From 2004 to 2008, Priceline's revenues shot from $900 million to $1.9 billion, and its net profits from $31 million to $193 million.

Priceline commenced operations on April 6, 1998, with the sale of airline tickets. To purchase a Name Your Own Price ticket, a customer logs onto Priceline's Web site, specifies the origin and destination of the trip, the dates he or she wishes to depart, the price the customer is willing to pay, and a valid credit card to guarantee the offer. The customer must agree to fly on any major airline, leave at any time of day between 6 a.m. and 10 p.m., accept at least one stop or connection, receive no frequent flier miles or upgrades, and accept tickets that cannot be refunded or changed. Upon receiving the offer, Priceline checks the available fares, rules, and inventory provided by its participating airlines and determines whether it will fulfill the order at the requested price. If so, it notifies the customer within an hour that his or her offer has been accepted. On the consumer side, a central premise of Priceline's Name Your Own Price business model is that in many product and service categories, there are a significant number of consumers for whom brands, product features, and sellers are interchangeable, particularly if agreeing to a substitution among brands or sellers will result in saving money. On the vendor side, the Priceline Name Your Own Price business model is predicated on the assumption that sellers almost invariably have excess inventory or capacity that they would sell at lower prices, if they could do so without either lowering their prices to retail customers or advertising that lower prices are available. Priceline believed that its business model was ideally suited to industries characterized by expiring or rapidly aging inventory (for example, airline seats not sold by the time a flight takes off or hotel rooms not rented), although it did not think that it would be limited to such industries.

Priceline extended its initial airline-only system to hotel reservations in October 1998, and introduced home financing services (name your own mortgage terms). It went public in March 1999, and later that year, it added rental cars and even new cars to the mix. To promote its products and the Priceline brand, Priceline embarked on an extensive (and expensive) advertising campaign, hiring William Shatner to become the voice of Priceline, and it quickly became one of the most recognizable brands on the Web. Problems for the company started when its founder attempted to aggressively expand the company into entirely new consumer product areas, and extend the franchise to the global market place. Priceline licensed the Name Your Own Price business model to several affiliates, including Priceline Webhouse Club, which attempted to extend the model to groceries and gasoline, and Perfect Yardsale, which used the model to sell used goods online, and added long distance calling and travel insurance. Priceline also had ambitious plans to expand internationally, and licensed its business model to companies planning to set up similar operations in Asia and Australia.

However, by fall 2000, the picture no longer looked so rosy. In October 2000, after only 10 months of operation, Priceline's affiliate Priceline Webhouse Club was unable to raise additional financing and had to shut down its business, after spending $363 million. The financial climate at the time, with its renewed emphasis on profitability, made it impossible for Jay Walker, Priceline's founder, to raise the additional hundreds of millions that would be required before Webhouse might become profitable. Walker did not see the closure as a failure of the Priceline business model, however. Instead, he characterized it as the result of the "fickle sentiments" of investors. Many analysts did not accept Walker's characterization. Instead, they pointed to other factors. First, many of the major manufacturers of food and dried goods chose not to participate in

Priceline Webhouse. So, to generate consumer interest, Priceline Webhouse subsidized discounts on most products itself. Although some major manufacturers, such as Kellogg's and Hershey's, did eventually sign up, many, such as Kraft, Procter & Gamble, and Lever Brothers, did not. The second miscalculation was that bidding on groceries and gasoline did not exactly provide a "hassle-free" way to shop. Customers were required to bid on and pay for groceries online, then use a special identification card to pick them up at a participating supermarket. If the particular items purchased were not available at the store, the customer would either have to go to another store or return at another time. To many, the demise of Priceline Webhouse highlighted potential cracks in the Priceline business model and raised strong concerns about its ultimate extensibility. Priceline's founder Jay Walker resigned in December 2000.

New management sharply curtailed Priceline's expansion and laid off over 1,000 employees. Priceline Chairman Richard Braddock said, "Priceline will entertain selective expansion... with stringent financial controls. We're going to make money on this and move forward." In 2002, Priceline focused on its core business of travel reservations, shedding its auto sales and long distance telephone units. Its only non-travel business today is its 49% interest in Priceline Mortgage. And in 2003–2004, it tweaked its business model once again, adding new discount "retail" airline ticket and rental car services to complement its hallmark Name Your Own Price offerings, in order to compete more effectively with firms such as Expedia, Travelocity, Hotwire, and Orbitz for the business of the consumer who prefers to book a specific airline or rental car. Although these services are not as lucrative as the Name Your Own Price model (it takes 1.5 to 2.5 retail plane tickets to bring in the same gross profit as a single Name Your Own Price ticket), and to a certain extent "cannibalize" its Name Your Own Price tickets, Priceline has made up at least some of the difference in increased volume. To further support this strategy, Priceline acquired a majority interest in TravelWeb, a consortium of five large hotel chains that provides Priceline with access to discount hotel rooms; purchased Active Hotels and Bookings B.V., a European hotel reservation service; and in 2005 extended its retail strategy to the hotel market. In 2006 and 2007, Priceline focused on adding to its full-service travel offerings in the United States, and recognizing that the growth of the domestic online market for travel services had slowed, on building its brand in Europe and Asia. Its international business represented approximately 62% of its gross bookings in 2008.

In 2008, Priceline eliminated the $5 to $11 booking fee that nearly all travel sites charge for airline bookings. In 2009, other sites such as Expedia started dropping their fees in response, but this will have a significant impact on their profit margins far greater than Priceline's because in many instances, such fees were the main source of their revenue. Priceline has become the undisputed low cost air reservation site. Priceline has also introduced "social features" to its Web site through an online blog called Ekspert, which provides customers with suggestions for travel, hot deals, and general travel news. In February 2009, Priceline's European subsidiary Booking.com announced a distribution deal with Hilton Hotels Corporation allowing Booking to access Hilton's worldwide portfolio of hotels, and give Hilton access to Booking.com's 30 million monthly visitors (the largest travel booking operation in Europe). Priceline also continues to enhance the customer experience of booking hotels by providing hotel tours, guest scorecards, Zagat reviews, more hotels (75,000 worldwide), and an expanded Winning Bids feature that reduces some of the opaqueness and uncertainty in their business model by displaying winning bids for hotels, helping customers to better understand the "market price" for Priceline offerings.

Like many other survivors of the dot-com era, Priceline has followed a twisting path to long-term sustainability and profits. However, although Priceline is currently "in the black," a rosy future is by no means assured. Priceline faces industry-wide shrinkage in all forms of travel caused by the fear of terrorism, war, high fuel prices and economic recession. In addition, Priceline faces extraordinary competition, not just from other online middlemen such as Expedia, Travelocity, Hotels.com, Hotwire, and CheapTickets, but also from the direct discount sales by airlines. Priceline is largely restricted to the travel market, having failed to extend the model to other sectors. But, just like discount retailers performing well in a recession, Priceline is in a good position to weather the storm as the industry-leading low cost provider of a unique, differentiated service.

Case Study Questions

1. What are the core components of Priceline's business model?

2. Do you think Priceline will ultimately succeed or fail? Why?

3. How has Priceline (and similar online services) impacted the travel services industry?

4. Follow up on developments at Priceline since August 2009 when this case study was prepared. Has its business model and/or strategy changed at all, and if so, how? Who are its strongest competitors? What will be the impact on the industry of eliminating booking fees?

SOURCES: "Priceline.com Launches New, Enhanced Hotel Reservation Service," Priceline.com June 10, 2009; "Expedia Ends Air Booking and Cancellation Fees," by Kristen Lee, BusinessWeek, May 27, 2009; "Priceline's Profit Rises 82%, Boosted by Strong Bookings," *Wall Street Journal*, by Kerry Grace, May 11, 2009; "Priceline's Differences Appeal," by Gregory Zuckerman, *Wall Street Journal*, April 20, 2009; "Booking.com and Hilton Sign Global Distribution Deal," Priceline.com, February 23, 2009; Priceline.com Incorporated Form 10-Q Quarterly Report for quarterly period ended December 31, 2008, filed with the Securities and Exchange Commission on February 28, 2009; "Introducing Travel Ekspert, A New Travel Blog From Priceline," Priceline.com, January 22, 2009; "Place Your Bets in Priceline's Online Casino," by Joe Starkey, *New York Times*, January 13, 2009; "Hot Growth Companies: Priceline Is Really Going Places," by Aaron Pressman, BusinessWeek Online, May 29, 2008; "Priceline Outshines Its Rivals," by Rick Munarriz, The Motley Fool, May 12, 2008.

2.7 REVIEW

KEY CONCEPTS

■ Identify the key components of e-commerce business models.

A successful business model effectively addresses eight key elements:

- *Value proposition*—how a company's product or service fulfills the needs of customers. Typical e-commerce value propositions include personalization, customization, convenience, and reduction of product search and price delivery costs.

- *Revenue model*—how the company plans to make money from its operations. Major e-commerce revenue models include the advertising model, subscription model, transaction fee model, sales model, and affiliate model.
- *Market opportunity*—the revenue potential within a company's intended marketspace.
- *Competitive environment*—the direct and indirect competitors doing business in the same marketspace, including how many there are and how profitable they are.
- *Competitive advantage*—the factors that differentiate the business from its competition, enabling it to provide a superior product at a lower cost.
- *Market strategy*—the plan a company develops that outlines how it will enter a market and attract customers.
- *Organizational development*—the process of defining all the functions within a business and the skills necessary to perform each job, as well as the process of recruiting and hiring strong employees.
- *Management team*—the group of individuals retained to guide the company's growth and expansion.

■ **Describe the major B2C business models.**

There are a number of different business models being used in the B2C e-commerce arena. The major models include the following:

- *Portal*—offers powerful search tools plus an integrated package of content and services; typically utilizes a combined subscription/advertising revenue/ transaction fee model; may be general or specialized (vortal).
- *E-tailer*—online version of traditional retailer; includes virtual merchants (online retail store only), bricks-and-clicks e-tailers (online distribution channel for a company that also has physical stores), catalog merchants (online version of direct mail catalog), and manufacturers selling directly over the Web.
- *Content provider*—information and entertainment companies that provide digital content over the Web; typically utilizes an advertising, subscription, or affiliate referral fee revenue model.
- *Transaction broker*—processes online sales transactions; typically utilizes a transaction fee revenue model.
- *Market creator*—uses Internet technology to create markets that bring buyers and sellers together; typically utilizes a transaction fee revenue model.
- *Service provider*—offers services online.
- *Community provider*—provides an online community of like-minded individuals for networking and information sharing; revenue is generated by advertising, referral fees, and subscriptions.

■ **Describe the major B2B business models.**

The major business models used to date in the B2B arena include:

- *E-distributor*—supplies products directly to individual businesses.
- *E-procurement*—single firms create digital markets for thousands of sellers and buyers.
- *Exchange*—independently owned digital marketplace for direct inputs, usually for a vertical industry group.
- *Industry consortium*—industry-owned vertical digital market.

- *Private industrial network*—industry-owned private industrial network that coordinates supply chains with a limited set of partners.

■ Recognize business models in other emerging areas of e-commerce.

A variety of business models can be found in the consumer-to-consumer e-commerce, peer-to-peer e-commerce, and m-commerce areas:
- *C2C business models*—connect consumers with other consumers. The most successful has been the market creator business model used by eBay.
- *P2P business models*—enable consumers to share files and services via the Web without common servers. A challenge has been finding a revenue model that works.
- *M-commerce business models*—take traditional e-commerce models and leverage emerging wireless technologies to permit mobile access to the Web.
- *E-commerce enablers*—focus on providing the infrastructure necessary for e-commerce companies to exist, grow, and prosper.

■ Understand key business concepts and strategies applicable to e-commerce.

The Internet and the Web have had a major impact on the business environment in the last decade, and have affected:
- *Industry structure*—the nature of players in an industry and their relative bargaining power by changing the basis of competition among rivals, the barriers to entry, the threat of new substitute products, the strength of suppliers, and the bargaining power of buyers.
- *Industry value chains*—the set of activities performed in an industry by suppliers, manufacturers, transporters, distributors, and retailers that transforms raw inputs into final products and services by reducing the cost of information and other transaction costs.
- *Firm value chains*—the set of activities performed within an individual firm to create final products from raw inputs by increasing operational efficiency.
- *Business strategy*—a set of plans for achieving superior long-term returns on the capital invested in a firm by offering unique ways to differentiate products, obtain cost advantages, compete globally, or compete in a narrow market or product segment.

QUESTIONS

1. What is a business model? How does it differ from a business plan?
2. What are the eight key components of an effective business model?
3. What are Amazon's primary customer value propositions?
4. Describe the five primary revenue models used by e-commerce firms.
5. Why is targeting a market niche generally smarter for a community provider than targeting a large market segment?
6. Besides music, what other forms of information could be shared through peer-to-peer sites? Are there legitimate commercial uses for P2P commerce?
7. Would you say that Amazon and eBay are direct or indirect competitors? (You may have to visit the Web sites to answer.)

8. What are some of the specific ways that a company can obtain a competitive advantage?
9. Besides advertising and product sampling, what are some other market strategies a company might pursue?
10. What elements of FreshDirect's business model may be faulty? Does this business scale up to a regional or national size?
11. Why is it difficult to categorize e-commerce business models?
12. Besides the examples given in the chapter, what are some other examples of vertical and horizontal portals in existence today?
13. What are the major differences between virtual storefronts, such as Drugstore.com, and bricks-and-clicks operations, such as Walmart.com? What are the advantages and disadvantages of each?
14. Besides news and articles, what other forms of information or content do content providers offer?
15. What is a reverse auction? What company is an example of this type of business?
16. What are the key success factors for exchanges? How are they different from portals?
17. What is an application service provider?
18. What are some business models seen in the C2C and P2P e-commerce areas?
19. How have the unique features of e-commerce technology changed industry structure in the travel business?
20. Who are the major players in an industry value chain and how are they impacted by e-commerce technology?
21. What are four generic business strategies for achieving a profitable business?

PROJECTS

1. Select an e-commerce company. Visit its Web site and describe its business model based on the information you find there. Identify its customer value proposition, its revenue model, the marketspace it operates in, who its main competitors are, any comparative advantages you believe the company possesses, and what its market strategy appears to be. Also try to locate information about the company's management team and organizational structure. (Check for a page labeled "the Company," "About Us," or something similar.)

2. Examine the experience of shopping on the Web versus shopping in a traditional environment. Imagine that you have decided to purchase a digital camera (or any other item of your choosing). First, shop for the camera in a traditional manner. Describe how you would do so (for example, how you would gather the necessary information you would need to choose a particular item, what stores you would visit, how long it would take, prices, etc.). Next, shop for the item on the Web. Compare and contrast your experiences. What were the advantages and disadvantages of each? Which did you prefer and why?

3. Visit eBay and look at the many types of auctions available. If you were considering establishing a rival specialized online auction business,

what are the top three market opportunities you would pursue, based on the goods and auction community in evidence at eBay? Prepare a report or slide presentation to support your analysis and approach.

4. During the early days of e-commerce, first-mover advantage was touted as one way to success. On the other hand, some suggest that being a market follower can yield rewards as well. Which approach has proven to be more successful— first mover or follower? Choose two e-commerce companies that prove your point, and prepare a brief presentation to explain your analysis and position.

5. Prepare a research report (3 to 5 pages) on the current and potential future impacts of e-commerce technology on the book publishing industry.

WEB SITE RESOURCES www.azimuth-interactive.com/ecommerce6e

- Additional projects, exercises and tutorials
- Careers: Explore career opportunities in e-commerce
- Raising capital and business plans

PART **2**

Technology Infrastructure for E-commerce

CHAPTER 3

The Internet and World Wide Web: E-commerce Infrastructure

After reading this chapter, you will be able to:

- Discuss the origins of the Internet.
- Identify the key technology concepts behind the Internet.
- Describe the role of Internet protocols and utility programs.
- Explain the current structure of the Internet.
- Understand the limitations of today's Internet.
- Describe the potential capabilities of Internet II.
- Understand how the World Wide Web works.
- Describe how Internet and Web features and services support e-commerce.

W i k i t u d e . m e

Walk down the street in any major metropolitan area and count the number of people pecking away at their iPhones or BlackBerries. Roam your campus—how many of your friends are texting as they speak, using Twitter, or watching a YouTube video on their smartphone? Ride the train, and observe how many fellow travelers are reading an online newspaper on their phone. In a few years, the primary means of accessing the Internet, both in the United States and worldwide, will be through highly portable netbooks and smart phones such as the Apple iPhone, BlackBerry Curve, and others. Traditional desktop and laptop PCs will of course remain important e-commerce and Internet tools, but the action has shifted to the mobile platform. This means that the primary platform for e-commerce products and services will also change to a mobile platform. The number of mobile Internet users is expected grow to 63% of all Internet users by 2013.

Wikitude.me is an example of a online mobile platform "points of interest" service that uses the same kind of wiki tools that power Wikipedia, the online encyclopedia. Wikitude.me focuses on information about where you are currently located. Wikitude provides a special kind of browser for smart phones equipped with a built-in GPS and compass that can identify your precise location and where the phone is pointed. Using information from over 800,000 points of interest available on Wikipedia.com, the browser overlays information about the points of interest you are looking at, and displays that information on your smart phone screen, overlayed on a map or photograph that you just snapped. Mobilizy GmbH, the Austrian firm that invented the browser, refers to these techniques as "augmented reality applications." Wikitude.me also allows users to geo-tag the world around them, and then submit the tags to Wikitude in order to share content with other users around the world. This user-generated database adds thousands of local sites that are not identified on Wikipedia. Users can point their smart phone cameras towards mountains from a tour bus and see the names and heights of the mountains displayed on the screen. Lost in a European medieval city, or downtown Los Angeles? Open up the Wikitude browser, point your camera at a building, and then find the address and other interesting details. At Wimbledon in 2009, Mobilizy worked with IBM to develop an application for TMobile's G1 phone that displayed real-time information about matches in progress, and players, along with dining and transportation information.

Mobilizy and Wikitude are currently in the development stage and have not yet begun to exploit the commercial application of augmented reality. But it's not hard to figure out where the e-commerce might reside in these tools. How would you like your restaurant, or fruit stand, or service company, or movie theater, to show up on the cell phones of users visiting or searching for points of interest in your neighborhood? How much would you pay to have an online travel guide with you all the time for that next trip abroad?

SPRXmobile, a Dutch company, has developed a similar augmented reality, location-based application called Layar. Users can download Layar for free in Amsterdam. Starting up the Layar application automatically activates the smartphone camera. The embedded GPS automatically knows the location of the phone, and the compass determines in which direction the phone is facing. Commercial partners provide location coordinates with relevant information that forms a digital layer. By tapping the side of the screen, the user easily switches between layers—from a simple picture, to a picture augmented with information, to a map. Local firms, which include restaurants, theaters, financial service firms, and businesses looking for employees, pay a fee to SPRXmobile and can then look through their Android smart phone cameras and see information about ATMs on the street, restaurants, bars, healthcare providers, and job openings displayed in the front of the buildings that house these services and opportunities. The first country in which Layar has been launched is The Netherlands. Partners include local market leaders ING (bank), Funda (real estate firm), Hyves (social network), Tempo-team (temporary employment agency) and Zekur.nl (healthcare provider).

Mobile digital platform services are also extending to more traditional online activities such as shopping for retail goods and finding the best prices. Slifter is a location-based shopping service that you can use on the Web or download to your BlackBerry or iPhone. Forgot your tie at the hotel on the way to an important business meeting? Or forget the wedding shoes? Not a problem. Slifter will tell you where you can find ties and shoes based on the GPS location of your smart phone. Slifter also tells you the price, whether the product is in stock, provides product information, images, special promotions, and maps. You can save products and promotions into a mobile Shopping List and share finds with friends using Twitter or several social networks. Slifter is based on the premise that most shopping in America takes place in local stores. True: less than 5% of the $3.9 trillion retail goods marketplace in the United States is online, the rest is offline at local stores. Helping consumers find the right store is possibly a much larger market and more solid business model than helping consumers find the right product and lowest price online.

Other players in this space are Nearbynow and Krillion. Related competitors include ShopSavvy, which allows consumers to hold their mobile phone cameras up to a product's UPC code sitting on a retailer's shelf, scan the code, ping the ShopSavvy servers, and receive back information on the best prices both locally and on the Web. Quattro Wireless provides another example of the potential for mobile online location-based services. Quattro Wireless, a mobile advertising network, has combined its service with one of the iPhone's most popular applications called WHERE. WHERE is a mobile app that provides users with information about the people, places, and things around them. Local content available through WHERE includes everything from the weather, news, and restaurant reviews, to the cheapest gas, movie show times, and the ability to connect with other users through Buddy Beacon and the WHERE Wall. The combined service sells location-based keyword searches, sponsored widgets, and local search terms. For instance, a consumer pharmacy chain such as Walgreens can purchase mobile keywords such as "headache," "stomach ache," or "back pain" to drive consumers to the nearest Walgreen's pharmacy.

Location-based services are in their infancy, producing about $134 million in revenue in 2009, but this is expected to grow to over $700 million by 2013. Other revenue streams generated by the new mobile digital platform in 2009 include software apps sales at stores such as iTunes ($3 billion); entertainment downloads of ringtones, music, video, and TV shows (about $1 billion); mobile display advertising ($760 million); direct shopping services such as Slifter ($200 million); and e-book sales ($100 million). While these numbers are still relatively small, mobile e-commerce is the fastest growing form of e-commerce, expanding at the rate of 50% or more a year. By 2013, the mobile platform is expected to generate about 7% of all online B2C e-commerce.

SOURCES: "Kicking Reality Up a Notch," by Leslie Berlin, *New York Times*, July 12, 2009; "IBM Unveils Smart New Mobile Applications to Keep Up to Date With Wimbledon 2009," IBM, June 17, 2009; 'Mobile Applications," by Noah Elkin, eMarketer, June 2009; "The Future of Touch," by Kathy Sandler, *Wall Street Journal*, June 2, 2009; "Mobile Advertising and Usage," eMarketer, April 2009; "The Expanding and Complex World of Mobile Computing," by John Dickinson, Verizon Business, April 2009; "Can the Cellphone Industry Keep Growing," by Matt Richtel, *New York Times*, February 4, 2009; "Play Flute, Name a Tune (or Make a Call)," by Matt Richtel and Laura M. Holson, New York Times, January 2, 2009; "Away From the Desk...Always," by David Pauleen, *Wall Street Journal*, December 15, 2008; "iPhone Software Sales Take Off: Apple's Jobs," by Nick Wingfield, *Wall Street Journal*, August 11, 2008 "Augmented Reality: Another (Virtual) Brick in the Wall," by Michelle Delio, *MIT Technology Review*, February 15, 2005.

This chapter examines the Internet and World Wide Web of today and tomorrow, how it evolved, how it works, and how the present and future infrastructure of the Internet and the Web enables new business opportunities.

The opening case about the new mobile digital platform illustrates how important it is for business people to understand how the Internet and related technologies work, and to be aware of what's new on the Internet. It could change your business drastically, and open up new opportunities as well. Operating a successful small business on the Web and implementing key Web business strategies such as personalization, customization, market segmentation, and price discrimination, all require that business people understand Web technology and keep track of Web developments.

The Internet and its underlying computer technology is not a static phenomenon in history, but instead is changing very rapidly. The Internet happened, but it is also happening. Computers have merged with cell phone services; broadband access in the home and broadband wireless access to the Internet via wireless devices are expanding rapidly; self-publishing on the Web via blogging, social networking, and podcasting now engages millions of Internet users; and new software technologies such as Web services, cloud computing, and peer-to-peer applications are being deployed. Looking forward a few years to the emerging Internet II of 2013, the business strategies of the future will require a firm understanding of these new technologies to deliver products and services to consumers.

3.1   THE INTERNET: TECHNOLOGY BACKGROUND

What is the Internet? Where did it come from, and how did it support the growth of the World Wide Web? What are the Internet's most important operating principles? How much do you really need to know about the technology of the Internet?

Let's take the last question first. The answer is: it depends on your career interests. If you are on a marketing career path, or general managerial business path, then you need to know the basics about Internet technology, which you'll learn in this and the following chapter. If you are on a technical career path and hope to become a Web designer, or pursue a technical career in Web infrastructure for businesses, you'll need to start with those basics and then build from there. You'll also need to know about the business side of e-commerce, which you will learn about throughout this book.

Internet

an interconnected network of thousands of networks and millions of computers linking businesses, educational institutions, government agencies, and individuals

As noted in Chapter 1, the **Internet** is an interconnected network of thousands of networks and millions of computers (sometimes called *host computers* or just *hosts*) linking businesses, educational institutions, government agencies, and individuals. The Internet provides approximately 1.67 billion people around the world (including about 200 million people in the United States) with services such as e-mail, newsgroups, shopping, research, instant messaging, music, videos, and news (Internetworldstats.com, 2009). No single organization controls the Internet or how it functions, nor is it owned by anybody, yet it has provided the infrastructure for a transformation in commerce, scientific research, and culture. The word Internet is derived from the word *internetwork*, or the connecting together of two or more computer networks. The **World Wide Web**, or **Web** for short, is one of the Internet's most popular services, providing access to billions, perhaps trillions of Web pages, which are documents created in a programming language called HTML that can contain text, graphics, audio, video, and other objects, as well as "hyperlinks" that permit users to jump easily from one page to another.

THE EVOLUTION OF THE INTERNET: 1961—THE PRESENT

Today's Internet has evolved over the last 40 or so years. In this sense, the Internet is not "new;" it did not happen yesterday. Although journalists talk glibly about "Internet" time—suggesting a fast-paced, nearly instant, worldwide global change mechanism, in fact, it has taken over 40 years of hard work to arrive at today's Internet.

The history of the Internet can be segmented into three phases (see **Figure 3.1**). In the first phase, the *Innovation Phase,* from 1961 to 1974, the fundamental building blocks of the Internet were conceptualized and then realized in actual hardware and software. The basic building blocks are: packet-switching hardware, client/server computing, and a communications protocol called TCP/IP (all described more fully later in this section). The original purpose of the Internet, when it was conceived in the 1960s, was to link large mainframe computers on different college campuses. This kind of one-to-one communication between campuses was previously only possible through the telephone system or postal mail.

In the second phase, the *Institutionalization Phase,* from 1975 to 1994, large institutions such as the Department of Defense and the National Science Foundation

World Wide Web (Web)

one of the Internet's most popular services, providing access to over 50 billion Web pages

FIGURE 3.1	STAGES IN THE DEVELOPMENT OF THE INTERNET

Innovation
1961 – 1974

Institutionalization
1975 – 1995

Commercialization
1995 →

The Internet developed in three stages over a 40-year period from 1961 to the present. In the Innovation stage, basic ideas and technologies were developed; in the Institutionalization stage, these ideas were brought to life; in the Commercialization stage, once the ideas and technologies had been proven, private companies brought the Internet to millions of people worldwide.

(NSF) provided funding and legitimization for the fledging invention called the Internet. Once the concepts behind the Internet had been proven in several government-supported demonstration projects, the Department of Defense contributed $1 million to further develop them into a robust military communications system that could withstand nuclear war. This effort created what was then called ARPANET (Advanced Research Projects Agency Network). In 1986, the NSF assumed responsibility for the development of a civilian Internet (then called NSFNET) and began a 10-year-long $200 million expansion program.

In the third phase, the *Commercialization Phase*, from 1995 to the present, government agencies encouraged private corporations to take over and expand both the Internet backbone and local service to ordinary citizens—families and individuals across America and the world who were not students on campuses. By 2000, the Internet's use had expanded well beyond military installations and research universities. See **Table 3.1** for a closer look at the development of the Internet from 1961 on.

THE INTERNET: KEY TECHNOLOGY CONCEPTS

In 1995, the Federal Networking Council (FNC) took the step of passing a resolution formally defining the term *Internet* (see **Figure 3.2**).

Based on that definition, the Internet means a network that uses the IP addressing scheme, supports the Transmission Control Protocol (TCP), and makes services available to users much like a telephone system makes voice and data services available to the public.

FIGURE 3.2	RESOLUTION OF THE FEDERAL NETWORKING COUNCIL

"The Federal Networking Council (FNC) agrees that the following language reflects our definition of the term 'Internet.'

'Internet' refers to the global information system that—

(i) is logically linked together by a globally unique address space based on the Internet Protocol (IP) or its subsequent extensions/follow-ons;

(ii) is able to support communications using the Transmission Control Protocol/Internet Protocol (TCP/IP) suite or its subsequent extensions/ follow-ons, and/or other IP-compatible protocols; and

(iii) provides, uses or makes accessible, either publicly or privately, high level services layered on the communications and related infrastructure described herein."

Last modified on October 30, 1995.

SOURCE: Federal Networking Council, 1995.

TABLE 3.1	DEVELOPMENT OF THE INTERNET TIMELINE

YEAR EVENT	SIGNIFICANCE
INNOVATION PHASE 1961–1974	
1961 Leonard Kleinrock (MIT) publishes a paper on "packet switching" networks.	The concept of packet switching is born.
1972 E-mail is invented by Ray Tomlinson of BBN. Larry Roberts writes the first e-mail utility program permitting listing, forwarding, and responding to e-mails.	The first "killer app" of the Internet is born.
1973 Bob Metcalfe (XeroxPark Labs) invents Ethernet and local area networks.	**Client/server computing is invented.** Ethernet permitted the development of local area networks and client/server computing in which thousands of fully functional desktop computers could be connected into a short-distance (<1,000 meters) network to share files, run applications, and send messages. Although the Apple and IBM personal computers had not yet been invented, at XeroxPark Labs, the first powerful desktop computers connected into a local network were created in the late 1960s.
1974 "Open architecture" networking and TCP/IP concepts are presented in a paper by Vint Cerf (Stanford) and Bob Kahn (BBN).	**TCP/IP invented.** The conceptual foundation for a single common communications protocol that could potentially connect any of thousands of disparate local area networks and computers, and a common addressing scheme for all computers connected to the network, are born.
	These developments made possible "peer-to-peer" "open" networking. Prior to this, computers could only communicate if they shared a common proprietary network architecture, e.g., IBM's System Network Architecture. With TCP/IP, computers and networks could work together regardless of their local operating systems or network protocols.
INSTITUTIONAL PHASE 1975–1995	
1980 TCP/IP is officially adopted as the DoD standard communications protocol.	The single largest computing organization in the world adopts TCP/IP and packet-switched network technology.
1980 Personal computers are invented.	Altair, Apple, and IBM personal desktop computers are invented. These computers become the foundation for today's Internet, affording millions of people access to the Internet and the Web.
1984 Apple Computer releases the HyperCard program as part of its graphical user interface operating system called Macintosh.	The concept of "hyperlinked" documents and records that permit the user to jump from one page or record to another is commercially introduced.
1984 Domain Name System (DNS) introduced.	DNS provides a user-friendly system for translating IP addresses into words that people can easily understand.

(continued)

TABLE 3.1	DEVELOPMENT OF THE INTERNET TIMELINE (CONTINUED)

YEAR EVENT	SIGNIFICANCE
1989 Tim Berners-Lee of the physics lab CERN in Switzerland proposes a worldwide network of hyperlinked documents based on a common markup language called HTML—HyperText Markup Language.	**The concept of an Internet-supported service called the World Wide Web based on HTML pages is born.** The Web would be constructed from "pages" created in a common markup language, with "hyperlinks" that permitted easy access among the pages. The idea does not catch on rapidly and most Internet users rely on cumbersome FTP and Gopher protocols to find documents.
1990 NSF plans and assumes responsibility for a civilian Internet backbone and creates NSFNET.[1] ARPANET is decommissioned.	The concept of a "civilian" Internet open to all is realized through non-military funding by NSF.
1993 The first graphical Web browser called Mosaic is invented by Mark Andreesen and others at the National Center for Supercomputing at the University of Illinois.	Mosaic makes it very easy for ordinary users to connect to HTML documents anywhere on the Web. The browser-enabled Web takes off.
1994 Andreesen and Jim Clark form Netscape Corporation.	The first commercial Web browser—Netscape—becomes available.
1994 The first banner advertisements appear on Hotwired.com in October 1994.	**The beginning of e-commerce.**

COMMERCIALIZATION PHASE 1995–PRESENT

YEAR EVENT	SIGNIFICANCE
1995 NSF privatizes the backbone, and commercial carriers take over backbone operation.	**The fully commercial civilian Internet is born.** Major long-haul networks such as AT&T, Sprint, GTE, UUNet, and MCI take over operation of the backbone. Network Solutions (a private firm) is given a monopoly to assign Internet addresses.
1995 Jeff Bezos founds Amazon; Pierre Omidyar forms AuctionWeb (eBay).	E-commerce begins in earnest with pure online retail stores and auctions.
1998 The U.S. federal government encourages the founding of Internet Corporation for Assigning Numbers and Names (ICANN).	Governance over domain names and addresses passes to a private nonprofit international organization.
1999 The first full-service Internet-only bank, First Internet Bank of Indiana, opens for business.	Business on the Web extends into traditional services.
2003 The Internet2 Abilene high-speed network is upgraded to 10 Gbps. Internet2 now has over 200 university, 60 corporate, and 40 affiliate members.	A major milestone toward the development of ultra-high-speed transcontinental networks several times faster than the existing backbone is achieved.
2005 NSF proposes the Global Environment for Networking Investigations (GENI) Initiative to develop new core functionality for the Internet, including new naming, addressing, and identity architectures; enhanced capabilities, including additional security architecture and a design that supports high availability; and new Internet services and applications.	Recognition that future Internet security and functionality needs may require the thorough rethinking of existing Internet technology.

[1] "Backbone" refers to the U.S. domestic trunk lines that carry the heavy traffic across the nation, from one metropolitan area to another. Universities are given responsibility for developing their own campus networks that must be connected to the national backbone.

(continued)

TABLE 3.1	DEVELOPMENT OF THE INTERNET TIMELINE (CONTINUED)

YEAR EVENT	SIGNIFICANCE
2006 The U.S. Senate Committee on Commerce, Science, and Transportation holds hearings on "Network Neutrality."	The debate grows over differential pricing based on utilization that pits the backbone utility owners against the online content and service providers, and device makers.
2007 BBN Technologies selected by the NSF to plan and design the next generation Internet (GENI).	Work begins on the new Internet, which can provide differential service levels, guaranteed service levels, and differential pricing.
2008 The Internet Society (ISOC) identifies Trust and Identity as a primary design element for every layer of the Internet, and launches an initiative in 2008–2010 to address these issues.	The leading Internet policy group recognizes the current Internet is threatened by breaches of security and trust that are built into the existing network.
2008 National LambdaRail develops the first 40 gigabit per second network, and the first transcontinental Ethernet network.	Using Cisco optical routers, this leading consortium of universities and businesses provides a nationwide platform for experimentation in very high-speed Internet platforms.
2008 Internet "cloud computing" becomes a billion dollar industry.	Internet capacity is sufficient to support on-demand computing resources (processing and storage), as well as software applications, for large corporations and individuals.
2009 Internet-enabled smartphones become a major new Web access platform	Smartphones extend the reach and range of the Internet to more closely realize the promise of the Internet anywhere, anytime, anyplace
2009 Broadband stimulus package and Broadband Data Improvement Act enacted	President signs stimulus package containing $7.2 billion for the expansion of broadband access in the United States.

SOURCES: Based on Leiner, et al., 2000; Zakon, 2005; Gross, 2005; Geni.net, 2007; nlr.org, 2008; ISOC.org, 2008.

Behind this formal definition are three extremely important concepts that are the basis for understanding the Internet: packet switching, the TCP/IP communications protocol, and client/server computing. Although the Internet has evolved and changed dramatically in the last 30 years, these three concepts are at the core of the way the Internet functions today and are the foundation for Internet II.

Packet Switching

Packet switching is a method of slicing digital messages into discrete units called **packets**, sending the packets along different communication paths as they become available, and then reassembling the packets once they arrive at their destination (see **Figure 3.3**). Prior to the development of packet switching, early computer networks used leased, dedicated telephone circuits to communicate with terminals and other computers. In circuit-switched networks such as the telephone system, a complete point-to-point circuit is put together, and then communication can proceed. However, these "dedicated" circuit-switching techniques were expensive and wasted available communications capacity—the circuit would be maintained regardless of whether any data was being sent. For nearly 70% of the time, a dedicated voice circuit is not being fully used because of pauses between words and delays in assembling the

packet switching
a method of slicing digital messages into packets, sending the packets along different communication paths as they become available, and then reassembling the packets once they arrive at their destination

packet
the discrete units into which digital messages are sliced for transmission over the Internet

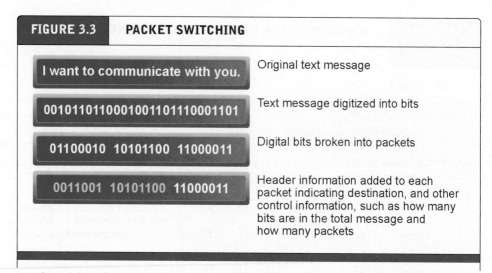

| FIGURE 3.3 | PACKET SWITCHING |

I want to communicate with you. — Original text message

0010110110001001101110001101 — Text message digitized into bits

01100010 10101100 11000011 — Digital bits broken into packets

0011001 10101100 11000011 — Header information added to each packet indicating destination, and other control information, such as how many bits are in the total message and how many packets

In packet switching, digital messages are divided into fixed-length packets of bits (generally about 1,500 bytes). Header information indicates both the origin and the ultimate destination address of the packet, the size of the message, and the number of packets the receiving node should expect. Because the receipt of each packet is acknowledged by the receiving computer, for a considerable amount of time, the network is not passing information, only acknowledgments, producing a delay called latency.

circuit segments, both of which increase the length of time required to find and connect circuits. A better technology was needed.

The first book on packet switching was written by Leonard Kleinrock in 1964 (Kleinrock, 1964), and the technique was further developed by others in the defense research labs of both the United States and England. With packet switching, the communications capacity of a network can be increased by a factor of 100 or more. (The communications capacity of a digital network is measured in terms of bits per second.[1]) Imagine if the gas mileage of your car went from 15 miles per gallon to 1,500 miles per gallon—all without changing too much of the car!

In packet-switched networks, messages are first broken down into packets. Appended to each packet are digital codes that indicate a source address (the origination point) and a destination address, as well as sequencing information and error-control information for the packet. Rather than being sent directly to the destination address, in a packet network, the packets travel from computer to computer until they reach their destination. These computers are called routers. A **router** is a special-purpose computer that interconnects the different computer networks that make up the Internet and routes packets along to their ultimate destination as they travel. To ensure that packets take the best available path toward their destination, routers use a computer program called a **routing algorithm**.

Packet switching does not require a dedicated circuit, but can make use of any spare capacity that is available on any of several hundred circuits. Packet switching makes nearly full use of almost all available communication lines and capacity.

router

special-purpose computer that interconnects the computer networks that make up the Internet and routes packets to their ultimate destination as they travel the Internet

routing algorithm

computer program that ensures that packets take the best available path toward their destination

[1] A bit is a binary digit, 0 or 1. A string of eight bits constitutes a byte. A home telephone dial-up modem connects to the Internet usually at 56 Kbps (56,000 bits per second). Mbps refers to millions of bits per second, whereas Gbps refers to billions of bits per second.

Moreover, if some lines are disabled or too busy, the packets can be sent on any available line that eventually leads to the destination point.

Transmission Control Protocol/Internet Protocol (TCP/IP)

While packet switching was an enormous advance in communications capacity, there was no universally agreed upon method for breaking up digital messages into packets, routing them to the proper address, and then reassembling them into a coherent message. This was like having a system for producing stamps but no postal system (a series of post offices and a set of addresses). The answer was to develop a **protocol** (a set of rules and standards for data transfer) to govern the formatting, ordering, compressing, and error-checking of messages, as well as specify the speed of transmission and means by which devices on the network will indicate they have stopped sending and/or receiving messages.

In 1974, Vint Cerf and Bob Kahn laid the conceptual foundation for **Transmission Control Protocol/Internet Protocol (TCP/IP)**, which has become the core communications protocol for the Internet (Cerf and Kahn, 1974). **TCP** establishes the connections among sending and receiving Web computers, and makes sure that packets sent by one computer are received in the same sequence by the other, without any packets missing. **IP** provides the Internet's addressing scheme and is responsible for the actual delivery of the packets.

TCP/IP is divided into four separate layers, with each layer handling a different aspect of the communication problem (see **Figure 3.4**). The **Network Interface Layer** is responsible for placing packets on and receiving them from the network medium, which could be a LAN (Ethernet) or Token Ring network, or other network technology. TCP/IP is independent from any local network technology and can adapt to changes at the local level. The **Internet Layer** is responsible for addressing, packaging, and routing messages on the Internet. The **Transport Layer** is responsible for providing communication with the application by acknowledging and sequencing the packets to and from the application. The **Application Layer** provides a wide variety of applications with the ability to access the services of the lower layers. Some of the best known applications are HyperText Transfer Protocol (HTTP), File Transfer Protocol (FTP), and Simple Mail Transfer Protocol (SMTP), all of which we will discuss later in this chapter.

IP Addresses

The IP addressing scheme answers the question "How can 500 million computers attached to the Internet communicate with one another?" The answer is that every computer connected to the Internet must be assigned an address—otherwise it cannot send or receive TCP packets. For instance, when you sign onto the Internet using a dial-up, DSL, or cable modem, your computer is assigned a temporary address by your Internet Service Provider. Most corporate and university computers attached to a local area network have a permanent IP address.

There are two versions of IP currently in use. IPv4 (Version 4) is still the most frequently used version. An IPv4 **Internet address** is a 32-bit number that appears as a series of four separate numbers marked off by periods, such as 64.49.254.91.

protocol
a set of rules and standards for data transfer

Transmission Control Protocol/Internet Protocol (TCP/IP)
the core communications protocol for the Internet

TCP
protocol that establishes the connections among sending and receiving Web computers and handles the assembly of packets at the point of transmission, and their reassembly at the receiving end

IP
protocol that provides the Internet's addressing scheme and is responsible for the actual delivery of the packets

Network Interface Layer
responsible for placing packets on and receiving them from the network medium

Internet Layer
responsible for addressing, packaging, and routing messages on the Internet

Transport Layer
responsible for providing communication with the application by acknowledging and sequencing the packets to and from the application

Application Layer
provides a wide variety of applications with the ability to access the services of the lower layers

Internet address
Internet address expressed as a 32-bit number that appears as a series of four separate numbers marked off by periods, such as 64.49.254.91

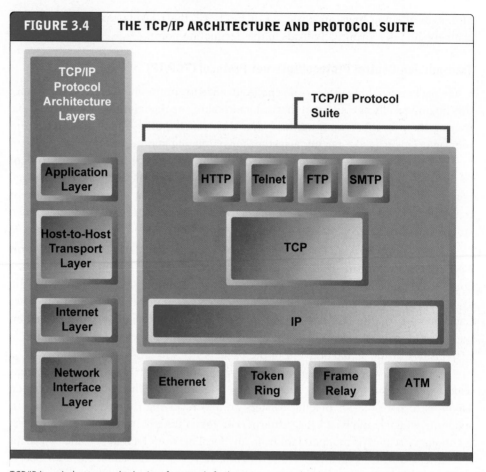

TCP/IP is an industry-standard suite of protocols for large internetworks. The purpose of TCP/IP is to provide high-speed communication network links.

Each of the four numbers can range from 0–255. This "dotted quad" addressing scheme contains up to 4 billion addresses (2 to the 32nd power). In a typical Class C network, the first three sets of numbers identify the network (in the preceding example, 64.49.254 is the local area network identification) and the last number (91) identifies a specific computer.

Because many large corporate and government domains have been given millions of IP addresses each (to accommodate their current and future work forces), and with all the new networks and new Internet-enabled devices requiring unique IP addresses being attached to the Internet, a newer version of the IP protocol, called IPv6, has been developed. IPv6 provides for 128-bit addresses, or about 1 quadrillion (10 to the 15th power) (National Research Council, 2000).

Figure 3.5 illustrates how TCP/IP and packet switching work together to send data over the Internet.

FIGURE 3.5 — ROUTING INTERNET MESSAGES: TCP/IP AND PACKET SWITCHING

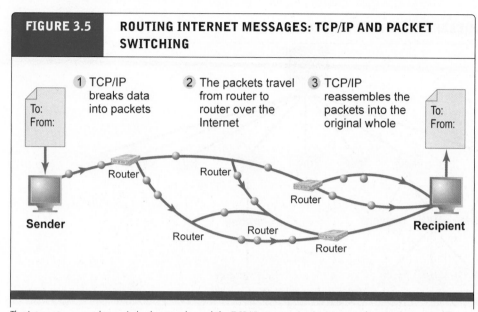

The Internet uses packet-switched networks and the TCP/IP communications protocol to send, route, and assemble messages. Messages are broken into packets, and packets from the same message can travel along different routes.

Domain Names, DNS, and URLs

Most people cannot remember 32-bit numbers. An IP address can be represented by a natural language convention called a **domain name**. The **Domain Name System (DNS)** allows expressions such as Cnet.com to stand for a numeric IP address (cnet.com's numeric IP is 216.239.113.101).[2] A **Uniform Resource Locator (URL)**, which is the address used by a Web browser to identify the location of content on the Web, also uses a domain name as part of the URL. A typical URL contains the protocol to be used when accessing the address, followed by its location. For instance, the URL http://www.azimuth-interactive.com/flash_test refers to the IP address 208.148.84.1 with the domain name "azimuth-interactive.com" and the protocol being used to access the address, HTTP. A resource called "flash_test" is located on the server directory path /flash_test. A URL can have from two to four parts; for example, name1.name2.name3.org. We discuss domain names and URLs further in Section 3.4. **Figure 3.6** illustrates the Domain Name System and **Table 3.2** summarizes the important components of the Internet addressing scheme

Client/Server Computing

While packet switching exploded the available communications capacity and TCP/IP provided the communications rules and regulations, it took a revolution in computing to bring about today's Internet and the Web. That revolution is called client/server computing and without it, the Web—in all its richness—would not exist. **Client/server computing** is a model of computing in which powerful personal computers called

domain name
IP address expressed in natural language

Domain Name System (DNS)
system for expressing numeric IP addresses in natural language

Uniform Resource Locator (URL)
the address used by a Web browser to identify the location of content on the Web

client/server computing
a model of computing in which powerful personal computers are connected in a network together with one or more servers

[2]You can check the IP address of any domain name on the Internet. In Windows, or use Start/Run/cmd to open the DOS prompt. Type "ping <Domain Name>". You will receive the IP address in return.

FIGURE 3.6	THE HIERARCHICAL DOMAIN NAME SYSTEM

The Domain Name System is a hierarchical namespace with a root server at the top. Top-level domains appear next and identify the organization type (such as .com, .gov, .org, etc.) or geographic location (such as .uk [Great Britain] or .ca [Canada]). Second-level servers for each top-level domain assign and register second-level domain names for organizations and individuals such as IBM.com, Microsoft.com, and Stanford.edu. Finally, third-level domains identify a particular computer or group of computers within an organization, e.g., www.finance.nyu.edu.

client

a powerful personal computer that is part of a network

server

networked computer dedicated to common functions that the client computers on the network need

clients are connected in a network to one or more server computers. These clients are sufficiently powerful to accomplish complex tasks such as displaying rich graphics, storing large files, and processing graphics and sound files, all on a local desktop or handheld device. **Servers** are networked computers dedicated to common functions that the client computers on the network need, such as file storage, software applications, utility programs such as Web connections, and printers (see **Figure 3.7**). The Internet is a giant example of client/server computing in which millions of Web

TABLE 3.2	PIECES OF THE INTERNET PUZZLE: NAMES AND ADDRESSES
IP addresses	Every device connected to the Internet must have a unique address number called an Internet Protocol (IP) address.
Domain names	The Domain Name System allows expressions such as Pearsoned.com (Pearson Education's Web site) to stand for numeric IP locations.
DNS servers	DNS servers are databases that keep track of IP addresses and domain names on the Internet.
Root servers	Root servers are central directories that list all domain names currently in use for specific domains; for example, the .com root server. DNS servers consult root servers to look up unfamiliar domain names when routing traffic.

FIGURE 3.7 — **THE CLIENT/SERVER COMPUTING MODEL**

In the client/server model of computing, client computers are connected in a network together with one or more servers.

servers located around the world can be easily accessed by millions of client computers, also located throughout the world.

To appreciate what client/server computing makes possible, you must understand what preceded it. In the mainframe computing environment of the 1960s and 1970s, computing power was very expensive and limited. For instance, the largest commercial mainframes of the late 1960s had 128k of RAM and 10 megabyte disk drives, and occupied hundreds of square feet. There was insufficient computing capacity to support graphics or color in text documents, let alone sound files or hyperlinked documents and databases.

With the development of personal computers and local area networks during the late 1970s and early 1980s, client/server computing became possible. Client/server computing has many advantages over centralized mainframe computing. For instance, it is easy to expand capacity by adding servers and clients. Also, client/server networks are less vulnerable than centralized computing architectures. If one server goes down, backup or mirror servers can pick up the slack; if a client computer is inoperable, the rest of the network continues operating. Moreover, processing load is balanced over many powerful smaller computers rather than being concentrated in a single huge computer that performs processing for everyone. Both software and hardware in client/server environments can be built more simply and economically.

Today there are over 1.25 billion personal computers in existence worldwide (Gartner, 2009). Personal computing capabilities are also moving to handheld devices such as netbooks and smart phones such as Apple's iPhones, RIMs BlackBerries, and T-Mobile's Android G1(much "thinner clients"). In the process, more computer processing will be performed by central servers (reminiscent of mainframe computers of the past). Read *Insight on Business: P2P Dukes It Out with Streaming Video* for a discussion of a form of computing that does not directly involve central servers.

INSIGHT ON BUSINESS

P2P DUKES IT OUT WITH STREAMING VIDEO

Let's face it: the future of the Internet is video entertainment. Just about any kind of video will do, including cats and dogs riding skateboards. With Hollywood movies, popular TV shows, independent video artists, music videos, and online advertisements all moving towards Web distribution, the Internet public is fascinated when their computer screen performs like a television.   In August 2009, 160 million people watched over 25 billion videos on the Internet. About 40% of this viewing took place at YouTube, but the rest came at Web sites operated by ESPN (sports videos), national news broadcasters (e.g. CNN, Time Magazine), Viacom and Hulu (Hollywood feature movies), Fox (MySpace), and other smaller players. Today, the Internet audience rivals the television audience in total size (although Americans spend many more hours watching TV than they do on Internet).

But fulfilling this demand for Internet video raises both business and technology issues. For instance, nearly 40 million people in the United States watched President Obama's inauguration on television on January 20, 2009. No problem. On the Internet, about 10 million individuals tried to watch the inauguration online, but experienced server breakdowns at the major distributors, missing frames and no audio. The truth is that the Internet is not quite ready for prime time.

On the technology side there are two ways to get video to millions of people: peer-to-peer (P2P) and streaming technology. Both of these methods have issues. For instance, if everyone tried to watch TV or movies online it would brown out the Internet. Nobody would get service. Scale is a problem. The ideal of course is "point, click, watch" as in cable television interactive TV and pay-per-view. Point, click, watch means instant gratification: You can watch a movie online at the spur of the moment. No waiting for the Netflix mailer, no standing at the register at Blockbuster.

Let's look at P2P networks as a type of video distribution. The most commonly used P2P network software today is BitTorrent. Bram Cohen, a programmer, designed the protocol in April 2001, under the aegis of his company BitTorrent, Inc. BitTorrent accounts for 30–50% of all Internet traffic in the United States, and the majority of users are located on college campuses. Its primary use is distributing copyrighted material such as movies, music, games, and TV shows without the permission of copyright owners. The software was released to the public as an open source program available to anyone. The BitTorrent P2P network uses the computing power and bandwidth of hundreds, even thousands, of participants rather than the power of central file and application servers in a typical client/server network. In P2P computing, two things happen. First, client computers can establish file sharing and sharing workspaces with one another without the intervention of a central server. Second, idle computers on the network can be used to share hard drives, processing power, and bandwidth for collective complex tasks. When a client computer seeks a movie file, a P2P network will fetch parts of the file distributed across hundreds of other nearby client computers logged into the network, and then reassemble them on your computer. The larger the network, the more people logged on, the more computing power connected, the faster the network becomes. Scale problem solved. Arguably, P2P networks are the most efficient and scalable technology for downloading very large video files, especially really large files required for High Definition (HD) video.

While this sounds simple, achieving this objective is anything but. P2P requires that hundreds of people keep their computers on around the clock to serve up files to their peers, or that a single company owns thousands of these distributed computers. The size of the network, and therefore its efficiency, is variable. The speed of the network may depend on who is sleeping, or on vacation. A greatly compressed movie can be downloaded on a P2P network in a little over an hour (compared to seconds for a single song) and the result is jerky small video. A television-quality movie that can fill your 17" laptop screen (or digital TV) takes at least three hours to download with a cable high-speed connection, and overnight for slower connections. Hardly point, click, and watch. High definition DVD-quality can take 24 hours to download. The same is true for television shows. Hold the popcorn till morning, folks, or just rent a DVD. In terms of what the user gets, there are plenty of quality issues such as sketchy audio, poor video if the video was produced using a camcorder in a theater, and missing frames. Yet, if you're a high school or college student with little money, waiting around for a free movie to download, or getting a copy from a friend who has paid the "price" (time), then P2P networks are an attractive alternative.

From the business perspective of copyright owners of videos and TV shows, not to mention the writers and actors who receive royalties from legitimate sales, P2P networks are a nightmare. In June 2005, the Supreme Court ruled that P2P file-sharing networks could be held liable for copyright infringement. However, the Court did not rule P2P networks themselves illegal, and the ruling does not impair the future development of this technology for legitimate purposes. By and large, the Court's ruling has has little impact on illegal music video and music file sharing although the movie and television industries have begun to succeed in getting adult Internet users to pay for high-quality video experiences at Web sites such as Hulu and iTunes. It is simply too difficult to prosecute the users of the Bit-Torrent protocol (at least to date) even though it is technically possible to identify the key players who make their computers available to the network. BitTorrent advocates, usually critics of copyright in general, argue that P2P networks can easily scale up to handle any workload. While technically true, in fact P2P file sharing jams up college campus and corporate networks very easily. When P2P traffic consumes more than 50% of a campus network, or local area network, administrators generally act to put a stop to the activity.

There are legitimate P2P companies that use the BitTorrent protocol, including BitTorrent Inc. The company has developed a BitTorrent streaming service called BitTorrent DNA that provides video distributors with a highly distributed, controlled P2P environment offering the ideal point, click, watch capability. But from a business perspective, it is still considered extremely risky to allow your $100 million blockbuster movie to be distributed by a network of thousands of clients that the distributor does not control. If you had $100 million in cash, would you trust its management to a P2P network of client computers strung out around the country?

The other method of online video distribution is to stream video content. In streaming video, instead of downloading the entire movie file and saving it to your hard drive, the file is sent by a centrally controlled server in chunks over the Internet and stored in cache memory on your computer, and then played almost instantly. The movie can only be played once, and is not stored on your hard drive. You don't own it, and you can't replay it.

When video files are streamed from a single server, or downloaded from a single server, that server and the routers along the way can load up very quickly. The result is a slowdown in transmission, overwhelming other traffic on the Web.

The solution to streaming large video and other media files is to distribute copies of the content to servers in metropolitan areas. Many companies use Akamai, a company that maintains a large distributed network of 48,000 servers in 70 countries and in 1,000 networks. Companies such as Akamai are referred to as content delivery networks (CDNs). Akamai distributes copies of large, popular files to its servers closest to the ultimate consumer, spreading the load on the Internet across thousands of servers and networks rather than overtaxing a single server. About 20% of all Internet traffic is handled by Akamai, and 20% of Fortune 500 companies use its distributed network. If you're Netflix or ESPN or the National Basketball League and you want to distribute video, Akamai can provide a one-hop route to your customers. You will learn more about Akamai in the closing case study for this chapter.

There are technology limits even with streaming. Some metropolitan areas (New York, Los Angeles, Chicago) can get overloaded and slow to a trickle if a few videos become very popular. Home and business network traffic can also slow the stream as bandwidth is shared with other users. Yet from a business point of view, a distributed computer network where a single company controls all the distributed servers and can provide good security, is a much safer bet.

SOURCES: "Google Sites Surpasses 10 Billion Video Views in August," by comScore, September 28, 2009; "Obama Inauguration Audience Trumped Jackson Memorial," by Paola Messana, AFP, July 8, 2009; "Pirate's Bay Weird New Business Plan," by Mark Scott, BusinessWeek.com, July 1, 2009; "Buyer of Pirate Bay, a File-Sharing Site, Plans to Go Legal," by Eric Pfanner, *New York Times,* June 30, 2009; "Study: P2P Customers Are Hollywood's Best Friends-Really!" by Nate Anderson, arstechnica.com, June 2, 2009; "Netflix Trying for Consistent Excellence on Streaming ," by Neil Hunt, Netflix Corporation, http://blog.netflix.com, March 20, 2009; "VUZE Applauds FCC in Setting Traffic-Throttling Hearing," Vuze Corporation, February 12, 2009; "Increasing Legitimacy Through Partnerships & Getting More Social," by Chris Crum, Webpronews.com, February 9, 2009; "Obama crashes Internet on Inauguration Day," Businessreviewonline.com; January 21, 2009; "Open Source P2P Streaming Getting Ready to Disrupt CDN Business Models," by Janko Roettgers, New-teevee.com, July 24, 2008; "Special Delivery: High Def Video," by Jan Ozer, Streamingmedia.com, February 15, 2008; "Promoting New TV Through P2P," *Los Angeles Times*, June 10, 2008; "Off New York Streets, Film Piracy is Online," by Eric Taub, *New York Times*, April 14, 2008.

THE NEW CLIENT: THE EMERGING MOBILE PLATFORM

There's a new client in town. In a few years, the primary means of accessing the Internet both in the United States and world-wide will be through highly portable netbooks and smartphones, and not traditional desktop or laptop PCs. This means that the primary platform for e-commerce products and services will also change to a mobile platform.

The change in hardware has reached a tipping point. In 2009, worldwide PC sales shipments slumped to 257 million units from over 300 million in 2008. Desktop shipments declined 31%, while portable laptops rose 3%, and the even smaller netbooks rose 79% to more than 21 million units (Sha, 2009). U.S. PC markets reflected these changes as well, with overall PC shipments sagging to 67 million units in 2009. While there are an estimated 1.25 billion PCs in the world, the number of cell phones long ago exceeded the population of PCs. In 2009, there are an estimated 3–4 billion cell phone subscribers, with nearly 300 million in the United States, 700 million in China, and 400 million in India. The population of cell phone subscribers is at least three times that of PC owners. About 25%, or 1 billion, of the world's cell phones are "smartphones," capable of accessing the Internet using broadband cell networks. In the United States, about 74 million people access the Internet using mobile devices, mostly cell phones. In 2009, there will be more than 1 billion cell phones sold world-wide, and about 146 million of those will be smartphones.

Netbooks are a part of the mobile digital platform because they are designed to connect to the Internet using wireless networks. Netbooks are small computers weighing less than 2 pounds, with 8" displays, no hard drives, solid state memory, often using new energy saving non-Intel chips, and a variety of operating systems from Linux to Windows XP. Netbooks are designed to connect to the wireless Internet (Wi-Fi or cellular) for software applications and data storage, although most can also run scaled-down office applications locally. Netbooks are priced from $200 to $400.

Smartphones are a disruptive technology that radically alters the personal computing and e-commerce landscape. Smartphones involve a major shift in computer processors, and software that is disrupting the 40-year dual monopolies established by Intel and Microsoft, whose chips, operating systems and software applications have dominated the PC market since 1982. Virtually no cell phones use Intel chips, which power 90% of the world's PCs; only 12% of smartphones use Microsoft's operating systems and that's mostly in Asia (Windows Mobile). Instead smartphone manufacturers either purchase operating systems such as Symbian, the world leader, or build their own such as Apple's iPhone OS and Blackberry's OS, typically based on Linux and Java platforms. Ninety percent of the billion cell phones shipped each year use some version of Advanced RISC Machine (ARM) chips, licensed by ARM Inc. and manufactured by many firms (Hansell, 2009). For instance, Apple's latest 3G iPhone uses an ARM 11 chip with a 600 megahertz (MHz) processor speed, and that uses only .45 milliwatts of power (compared to a typical laptop dual core mobile Intel processor that uses 25 watts—about 500 times more power consumption). Apple has not officially released information on the chip or its manufacturer. Smartphones do not need fans. Cell phones do not use power-hungry hard drives but instead use flash memory chips with storage up to 32 megabytes. While the latest Energy Star 4 laptop disk drives consume 500 milliwatts at idle, and 1 watt writing and reading, flash memory chips consume about 50 milliwatts writing and reading data (20 times less power).

The emerging mobile platform has profound implications for e-commerce because it influences how, where, and when consumers shop and buy.

THE INTERNET "CLOUD COMPUTING" MODEL: SOFTWARE AND HARDWARE AS A SERVICE

The growing bandwidth power of the Internet has pushed the client/server model one step further, towards what is called the "cloud computing model."

Cloud computing refers to a model of computing in which firms and individuals obtain computing power and software applications over the Internet, rather than purchasing the hardware and software, and installing it on their own computers. Currently, cloud computing is the fastest growing form of computing, with an estimated market size in 2009 of $56 billion, and a projected size of $150 billion in 2013, according to Gartner research analysts (Robinson, 2009).

cloud computing
model of computing in which firms and individuals obtain computing power and software over the Internet

FIGURE 3.8 | **THE CLOUD COMPUTING MODEL**

THE INTERNET

Software and
Hardware services
Collaboration
Social networking
Integration of devices

In the cloud computing model, hardware and software services are provided on the Internet by vendors operating very large server farms and data centers.

Hardware firms such as IBM, HP, and Dell are building very large, scalable cloud computing centers that provide computing power, data storage, and high-speed Internet connections to firms that rely on the Internet for business software applications.

Software firms such as Google, Microsoft, SAP, Oracle, and Salesforce.com sell software applications that are Internet-based. Instead of software as a product, in the cloud computing model, software is a service provided over the Internet. For instance, over 1.75 million firms in 2009 use Google Apps, a suite of office software applications such as word processing, spreadsheets, and calendars, that firms access over the Internet (Google, 2009). In 2009, more than 55,000 firms worldwide will be using Salesforce.com's customer relationship management software, some on their iPhones or Android G1s.

Microsoft, which in the past has depended on selling boxed software to firms and individuals, is adapting to this new marketplace with its own "software plus service" (buy the boxed version and get "free" online services), Windows Live, and Online Technology initiatives.

Cloud computing has many significant implications for e-commerce. For e-commerce firms, cloud computing radically reduces the cost of building and operating Web sites because the necessary hardware infrastructure and software can be licensed as a service from Internet providers at a fraction of the cost of purchasing these services as products. This means firms can adopt "pay-as-you-go" and "pay-as-you-grow" strategies when building out their Web sites. For instance, according to Amazon, hundreds of thousands of customers use Amazon's Web Services arm, which provides storage services, computing services, database services, messaging services, and payment services (Sperling, 2009). For individuals, cloud computing means you no longer need a powerful laptop or desktop computer to engage in e-commerce or other activities. Instead you can use much less expensive netbooks or smart phones that cost a few hundred dollars. For corporations, cloud computing means that a significant part of hardware and software costs (infrastructure costs) can be reduced because firms can obtain these services online for a fraction of the cost of owning, and they do not have to hire an IT staff to support the infrastructure. These benefits come with some risks: firms become totally dependent on their cloud service providers.

OTHER INTERNET PROTOCOLS AND UTILITY PROGRAMS

There are many other Internet protocols and utility programs that provide services to users in the form of Internet applications that run on Internet clients and servers. These Internet services are based on universally accepted protocols—or standards—that are available to everyone who uses the Internet. They are not owned by any organization, but they are services that have been developed over many years and made available to all Internet users.

Internet Protocols: HTTP, E-mail Protocols, FTP, Telnet, and SSL

HyperText Transfer Protocol (HTTP) is the Internet protocol used to transfer Web pages (described in the following section). HTTP was developed by the World Wide Web Consortium (W3C) and the Internet Engineering Task Force (IETF). HTTP runs in the Application Layer of the TCP/IP model shown in Figure 3.4 on page 132. An HTTP session begins when a client's browser requests a resource, such as a Web page, from a remote Internet server. When the server responds by sending the page requested, the HTTP session for that object ends. Because Web pages may have many objects on them—graphics, sound or video files, frames, and so forth—each object must be requested by a separate HTTP message. The most common HTTP request message is Get, which is used to request a resource (typically a Web page) by specifying its URL. For more information about HTTP, you can consult RFC 2616, which details the standards for HTTP/1.1, the version of HTTP most commonly used today (ISOC, 1999). (An RFC is a document published by the Internet Society [ISOC] or one of the other organizations involved in Internet governance that sets forth the standards for various Internet-related technologies. You will learn more about the organizations involved in setting standards for the Internet later in the chapter).

E-mail is one of the oldest, most important, and frequently used Internet services. Like HTTP, the various Internet protocols used to handle e-mail all run in the Application Layer of TCP/IP. **Simple Mail Transfer Protocol (SMTP)** is the Internet protocol used to send e-mail to a server. SMTP is a relatively simple, text-based protocol that was developed in the early 1980s. SMTP handles only the sending of e-mail. To retrieve e-mail from a server, the client computer uses either **Post Office Protocol 3 (POP3)** or **Internet Message Access Protocol (IMAP)**. You can set POP3 to retrieve e-mail messages from the server and then delete the messages on the server, or retain them on the server. IMAP is a more current e-mail protocol supported by all browsers and most servers and ISPs. IMAP allows users to search, organize, and filter their mail prior to downloading it from the server. For more information about SMTP, POP3 and IMAP, you can consult RFCs 2821

HyperText Transfer Protocol (HTTP)
the Internet protocol used for transferring Web pages

Simple Mail Transfer Protocol (SMTP)
the Internet protocol used to send mail to a server

Post Office Protocol 3 (POP3)
a protocol used by the client to retrieve mail from an Internet server

Internet Message Access Protocol (IMAP)
a more current e-mail protocol that allows users to search, organize, and filter their mail prior to downloading it from the server

File Transfer Protocol (FTP)

one of the original Internet services. Part of the TCP/IP protocol that permits users to transfer files from the server to their client computer, and vice versa

Telnet

a terminal emulation program that runs in TCP/IP

Secure Sockets Layer (SSL)

a protocol that secures communications between the client and the server

Ping

a program that allows you to check the connection between your client and the server

(SMTP), 1939 (POP3), and 3501 (IMAP) (Internet Society, 2001, 1996, 2003). You also can see how your browser handles SMTP, and POP or IMAP, by looking in your browser's Preferences or Tools section, where the e-mail settings are defined.

File Transfer Protocol (FTP) is one of the original Internet services. FTP runs in TCP/IP's Application Layer and permits users to transfer files from a server to their client computer, and vice versa. The files can be documents, programs, or large database files. FTP is the fastest and most convenient way to transfer files larger than 1 megabyte, which some e-mail servers will not accept. More information about FTP is available in RFC 0959 (Internet Society, 1985).

Telnet is a network protocol that also runs in TCP/IP's Application Layer and is used to allow remote login on another computer. The term Telnet also refers to the Telnet program, which provides the client part of the protocol and enables the client to emulate a mainframe computer terminal. (The industry-standard terminals defined in the days of mainframe computing are VT-52, VT-100, and IBM 3250.) You can then attach yourself to a computer on the Internet that supports Telnet and runs programs or download files from that computer. Telnet was the first "remote work" program that permitted users to work on a computer from a remote location. The specifications for Telnet are set forth in RFC 854 (Internet Society, 1983).

Secure Sockets Layer (SSL) is a protocol that operates between the Transport and Application Layers of TCP/IP and secures communications between the client and the server. SSL helps secure e-commerce communications and payments through a variety of techniques such as message encryption and digital signatures that we will discuss further in Chapter 5.

Utility Programs: Ping, Tracert, and Pathping

Packet InterNet Groper (Ping) allows you to check the connection between a client computer and a TCP/IP network (see **Figure 3.9**). Ping will also tell you the time it takes for the server to respond, giving you some idea about the speed of the server and the Internet at that moment. You can run Ping from the DOS prompt on a

FIGURE 3.9	THE RESULT OF A PING

```
Command Prompt                                              _ □ ×
C:\>
C:\>
C:\>ping www.yahoo.com

Pinging www.yahoo.com [204.71.200.72] with 32 bytes of data:

Reply from 204.71.200.72: bytes=32 time=100ms ITL=240
Reply from 204.71.200.72: bytes=32 time=100ms ITL=240
Reply from 204.71.200.72: bytes=32 time=130ms ITL=240
Reply from 204.71.200.72: bytes=32 time=100ms ITL=240

C:\>_
```

A ping is used to verify an address and test the speed of the round trip from a client computer to a host and back.

personal computer with a Windows operating system by typing: ping <domain name>. We will discuss Ping further in Chapter 5, because one way to slow down or even crash a domain computer is to send it millions of ping requests.

Tracert is one of a several route-tracing utilities that allow you to follow the path of a message you send from your client to a remote computer on the Internet. **Figure 3.10** shows the result of route tracking a message sent to a remote host using a visual route-tracing program called VisualRoute (available from Visualware).

The **Pathping** utility combines the functionality offered by Ping and Tracert. Pathping provides the details of the path between two hosts and statistics for each node in the path based on samples taken over a period of time, depending on the number of nodes between the start and end host.

Tracert
one of several route-tracing utilities that allow you to follow the path of a message you send from your client to a remote computer on the Internet

Pathping
combines the functionality offered by Ping and Tracert

3.2 THE INTERNET TODAY

In 2009, there were an estimated 1.67 billion Internet users worldwide, up from 100 million users at year-end 1997. While this is a huge number, it represents only about 23% of the world's population (Internetworldstats.com, 2009). Although Internet user growth has slowed in the United States to about 1% annually, in Asia, Internet growth is about 10% annually, and by 2012, it is expected that there will be over 2 billion Internet users worldwide. One would think that with such incredible growth, the Internet would be overloaded. However, this has not been true for several reasons. First, client/server computing is highly extensible. By simply adding servers and clients, the population of Internet users can grow indefinitely. Second, the Internet architecture is built in layers so that each layer can change without disturbing devel-

FIGURE 3.10   TRACING THE ROUTE A MESSAGE TAKES ON THE INTERNET

(a) (b)

VisualRoute and other tracing programs provide some insight into how the Internet uses packet switching. This particular message traveled from a computer in Ashburn, Virginia, to San Antonio, Texas.
SOURCE: Visualware, Inc., 2007.

Network Technology Substrate layer
layer of Internet technology that is composed of telecommunications networks and protocols

Transport Services and Representation Standards layer
layer of Internet architecture that houses the TCP/IP protocol

Applications layer
layer of Internet architecture that contains client applications

opments in other layers. For instance, the technology used to move messages through the Internet can go through radical changes to make service faster without being disruptive to your desktop applications running on the Internet.

Figure 3.11 illustrates the "hourglass" and layered architecture of the Internet. The Internet can be viewed conceptually as having four layers: the Network Technology Substrate, Transport Services and Representation Standards, Middleware Services, and Applications.[3] The **Network Technology Substrate layer** is composed of telecommunications networks and protocols. The **Transport Services and Representation Standards layer** houses the TCP/IP protocol. The **Applications layer** contains client applications such as the World Wide Web, e-mail, and audio or

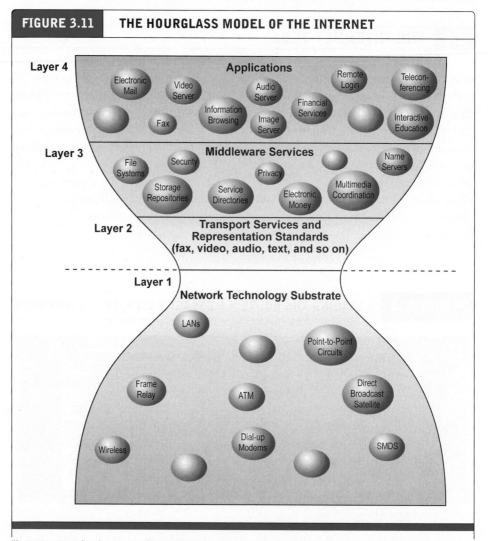

FIGURE 3.11   **THE HOURGLASS MODEL OF THE INTERNET**

The Internet can be characterized as an hour-glass modular structure with a lower layer containing the bit-carrying infrastructure (including cables and switches) and an upper layer containing user applications such as e-mail and the Web. In the narrow waist are transportation protocols such as TCP/IP.
SOURCE: Adapted from Computer Science and Telecommunications Board (CSTB), 2000.

[3]Recall that the TCP/IP communications protocol also has layers, not to be confused with the Internet architecture layers.

video playback. The **Middleware Services layer** is the glue that ties the applications to the communications networks, and includes such services as security, authentication, addresses, and storage repositories. Users work with applications (such as e-mail) and rarely become aware of middleware that operates in the background. Because all layers use TCP/IP and other common standards linking all four layers, it is possible for there to be significant changes in the network layer without forcing changes in the applications layer. The Network Technology Substrate layer is further described.

THE INTERNET BACKBONE

Figure 3.12 illustrates some of the main physical elements of today's Internet. Originally, the Internet had a single backbone, but today's Internet has several backbones that are physically connected with each other and which transfer information from one private network to another. These private networks are referred to as **Network Service Providers (NSPs)**, which own and control the major backbone networks (see **Table 3.3**). For the sake of clarity we will refer to these networks of backbones as a single "backbone." The **backbone** has been likened to a giant pipeline that transports data around the world in milliseconds. In the United States, the backbone is composed entirely of fiber-optic cable with bandwidths ranging

Middleware Services layer
the "glue" that ties the applications to the communications networks, and includes such services as security, authentication, addresses, and storage repositories

Network Service Provider (NSP)
owns and controls one of the major networks comprising the Internet's backbone

backbone
high-bandwidth fiber-optic cable that transports data across the Internet

FIGURE 3.12	INTERNET I NETWORK ARCHITECTURE

Today's Internet has a multi-tiered open network architecture featuring multiple national backbones, regional hubs, campus area networks, and local client computers.

TABLE 3.3	MAJOR U.S INTERNET BACKBONE OWNERS
AT&T	NTT/Verio
AOL Transit Data Network (ATDN)	Qwest
Cable & Wireless	Sprint
Global Crossing	Verizon
Level 3	

bandwidth

measures how much data can be transferred over a communications medium within a fixed period of time; is usually expressed in bits per second (bps), kilobits per second (Kbps), megabits per second (Mbps),or gigabits per second (Gbps)

redundancy

multiple duplicate devices and paths in a network

from 155 Mbps to 2.5 Gbps. **Bandwidth** measures how much data can be transferred over a communications medium within a fixed period of time, and is usually expressed in bits per second (bps), kilobits (thousands of bits) per second (Kbps), megabits (millions of bits) per second (Mbps), or gigabits (billions of bits) per second (Gbps).

Connections to other continents are made via a combination of undersea fiber-optic cable and satellite links. The backbones in foreign countries typically are operated by a mixture of private and public owners. The U.S. backbone is one of the most developed because the Internet's infrastructure was developed here. The backbone has built-in redundancy so that if one part breaks down, data can be rerouted to another part of the backbone. **Redundancy** refers to multiple duplicate devices and paths in a network.

INTERNET EXCHANGE POINTS

Internet Exchange Point (IXP)

hub where the backbone intersects with local and regional networks and where backbone owners connect with one another

In the United States, there are a number of hubs where the backbone intersects with regional and local networks, and where the backbone owners connect with one another (see **Figure 3.13**). These hubs were originally called Network Access Points (NAPs) or Metropolitan Area Exchanges (MAEs), but now are more commonly referred to as **Internet Exchange Points (IXPs)**. IXPs use high-speed switching computers to connect the backbone to regional and local networks, and exchange messages with one another. The regional and local networks are owned by local Bell operating companies (RBOCs—pronounced "ree-bocks"), and private telecommunications firms; they generally are fiber-optic networks operating at over 100 Mbps. The regional networks lease access to ISPs, private companies, and government institutions.

CAMPUS AREA NETWORKS

campus area network (CAN)

generally, a local area network operating within a single organization that leases access to the Web directly from regional and national carriers

Campus area networks (CANs) are generally local area networks operating within a single organization—such as New York University or Microsoft Corporation. In fact, most large organizations have hundreds of such local area networks. These organizations are sufficiently large that they lease access to the Web directly from regional and national carriers. These local area networks generally are running Ethernet (a local area network protocol) and have network operating systems such as Windows Server, Novell NetWare, or Linux that permit desktop clients to connect to the Internet through a local Internet server attached to their campus networks. Connection speeds in campus area networks are in the range of 10–100 Mbps to the desktop.

FIGURE 3.13	SOME MAJOR U.S. INTERNET EXCHANGE POINTS (IXPs)		
Region	**Name**	**Location**	**Operator**
EAST	MAE East	Virginia and Miami	MCI
	New York International Internet Exchange (NYIIX)	New York	Telehouse
	Peering and Internet Exchange (PAIX)	New York, Philadelphia and Northern Virginia	Switch and Data
	NAP of the Americas	Miami	Terramark
CENTRAL	MAE Chicago	Chicago	MCI
	Chicago NAP	Chicago	SBC
	MAE Central	Dallas and Atlanta	MCI
	Peering and Internet Exchange (PAIX)	Atlanta	Switch and Data
WEST	MAE West	San Jose and Los Angeles	MCI
	Peering and Internet Exchange (PAIX)	Palo Alto, San Jose, and Seattle	Switch and Data
	Los Angeles International Internet Exchange (LAIIX)	Los Angeles	Telehouse

INTERNET SERVICE PROVIDERS

Internet Service Provider (ISP)

firm that provides the lowest level of service in the multi-tiered Internet architecture by leasing Internet access to home owners, small businesses, and some large institutions

The firms that provide the lowest level of service in the multi-tiered Internet architecture by leasing Internet access to home owners, small businesses, and some large institutions are called **Internet Service Providers (ISPs)**. ISPs are retail providers—they deal with "the last mile of service" to the curb—homes and business offices. ISPs typically connect to IXPs with high-speed telephone or cable lines (45 Mbps and higher).

There are a number of major ISPs, such as AOL, Earthlink, AT&T, Comcast (Optimum Online), Verizon, Sprint, Qwest, as well as thousands of local ISPs in the United States, ranging from local telephone companies offering dial-up and DSL telephone access to cable companies offering cable modem service, to small "mom-and-pop" Internet shops that service a small town, city, or even county with mostly dial-up phone access. If you have home or small business Internet access, an ISP likely provides the service to you. Satellite firms also offer Internet access, especially in remote areas where broadband service is not available.

narrowband

the traditional telephone modem connection, now operating at 56.6 Kbps

broadband

refers to any communication technology that permits clients to play streaming audio and video files at acceptable speeds—generally anything above 100 Kbps

Table 3.4 summarizes the variety of services, speeds, and costs of ISP Internet connections. There are two types of ISP service: narrowband and broadband. **Narrowband** service is the traditional telephone modem connection now operating at 56.6 Kbps (although the actual throughput hovers around 30 Kbps due to line noise that causes extensive resending of packets). This used to be the most common form of connection worldwide but is quickly being replaced by broadband connections in the United States, Europe, and Asia. Broadband service is based on DSL, cable modem, telephone (T1 and T3 lines), and satellite technologies. **Broadband**—in the context of Internet service—refers to any communication technology that permits clients to play streaming audio and video files at acceptable speeds—generally anything above 100 Kbps. In the United States, broadband users surpassed dial-up users in 2004, and in 2009 there were 80.5 million broadband households and only 6.7 million dial-up households (eMarketer, Inc., 2009a).

TABLE 3.4	ISP SERVICE LEVELS AND BANDWIDTH CHOICES	
SERVICE	COST/MONTH	SPEED TO DESKTOP (KBPS)
Telephone modem	$10–$25	30–56 Kbps
DSL	$15–$50	768 Kbps–5 Mbps
Cable modem	$20–$50	1 Mbps–20 Mbps
Satellite	$20–$50	768 Kbps–5 Mbps
T1	$300–$`1,200	1.54 Mbps
T3	$2,500–$10,000	45 Mbps

The actual throughput of data will depend on a variety of factors including noise in the line and the number of subscribers requesting service. Service level speeds quoted are typically only for downloads of Internet content; upload speeds tend to be much slower. T1 lines are publicly regulated utility lines that offer a guaranteed level of service, but the actual throughput of the other forms of Internet service is not guaranteed.

Digital Subscriber Line (DSL) service is a telephone technology that provides high-speed access to the Internet through ordinary telephone lines found in a home or business. Service levels range from about 768 Kbps up to 7 Mbps. DSL service requires that customers live within two miles (about 4,000 meters) of a neighborhood telephone switching center.

Cable modem refers to a cable television technology that piggybacks digital access to the Internet using the same analog or digital video cable providing television signals to a home. Cable Internet is a major broadband alternative to DSL service, generally providing faster speeds and a "triple play" subscription: telephone, television, and Internet for a single monthly payment. Cable modem services range from 1 Mbps up to 15 Mbps. Comcast, Time Warner Road Runner, and Cox are the largest cable Internet providers.

T1 and T3 are international telephone standards for digital communication. **T1** lines offer guaranteed delivery at 1.54 Mbps, while T3 lines offer delivery at a whopping 45 Mbps. T1 lines cost about $300–$1,200 per month, and **T3** lines between $2,500 and $10,000 per month. These are leased, dedicated, guaranteed lines suitable for corporations, government agencies, and businesses such as ISPs requiring high-speed guaranteed service levels.

Satellite companies provide high-speed broadband Internet access, primarily to homes and offices located in rural areas where DSL or cable access is not available. Access speeds and monthly costs are comparable to DSL and cable, but typically require a higher initial payment for installation of a small (18-inch) satellite dish. Satellite providers typically have policies that limit the total megabytes of data that a single account can download within a set period, usually 24 hours. Accounts that exceed the threshold are penalized by reduced download speeds for a period of time. The purpose of these policies is to deter heavy users from using excessive amounts of the provider's bandwidth, which has the effect of slowing down data transfer rates overall. The four major satellite providers are HughesNet, Bluewild, Skyway, and StarBand.

Prices are falling drastically to as low as $14.95 per month for DSL service. Cable broadband accounts for around 55% of all broadband users and nearly all large business firms and government agencies have broadband connections to the Internet. Demand for broadband service has grown so rapidly simply because it greatly speeds up the process of downloading Web pages and increasingly large video and audio files located on Web pages (see **Table 3.5**). As the quality of Internet service offerings expands to include Hollywood movies, music, games, and other rich media-streaming content, the demand for broadband access will continue to swell. In order to compete with cable companies, telephone companies have introduced an advanced form of DSL called FiOS (fiber-optic service) that provides up to 50 Mbps speeds for households, which is much faster than cable systems.

Digital Subscriber Line (DSL)
delivers high-speed access through ordinary telephone lines found in homes or businesses

cable modem
piggybacks digital access to the Internet on top of the analog video cable providing television signals to a home

T1
an international telephone standard for digital communication that offers guaranteed delivery at 1.54 Mbps

T3
an international telephone standard for digital communication that offers guaranteed delivery at 45 Mbps

TABLE 3.5	TIME TO DOWNLOAD A 10-MEGABYTE FILE BY TYPE OF INTERNET SERVICE
TYPE OF INTERNET SERVICE	TIME TO DOWNLOAD
NARROWBAND SERVICES	
Telephone modem	25 minutes
BROADBAND SERVICES	
DSL @ 1 Mbps	1.33 minutes
Cable modem @ 10 Mbps	8 seconds
T1	52 seconds
T3	2 seconds

INTRANETS AND EXTRANETS

The very same Internet technologies that make it possible to operate a worldwide public network can also be used by private and government organizations as internal networks. An **intranet** is a TCP/IP network located within a single organization for purposes of communications and information processing. Internet technologies are generally far less expensive than proprietary networks, and there is a global source of new applications that can run on intranets. In fact, all the applications available on the public Internet can be used in private intranets. The largest provider of local area network software is Microsoft, followed by open source Linux, both of which use TCP/IP networking protocols.

intranet
a TCP/IP network located within a single organization for purposes of communications and information processing

Extranets are formed when firms permit outsiders to access their internal TCP/IP networks. For instance, General Motors permits parts suppliers to gain access to GM's intranet that contains GM's production schedules. In this way, parts suppliers know exactly when GM needs parts, and where and when to deliver them.

extranet
formed when firms permit outsiders to access their internal TCP/IP networks

Intranets and extranets generally do not involve commercial transactions in a marketplace, and they are mostly beyond the scope of this text. Extranets will receive some attention as a technology that supports certain types of B2B exchanges (described in Chapter 12).

WHO GOVERNS THE INTERNET?

Aficionados and promoters of the Internet often claim that the Internet is governed by no one, and indeed cannot be governed, and that it is inherently above and beyond the law. What these people forget is that the Internet runs over private and public telecommunications facilities that are themselves governed by laws, and subject to the same pressures as all telecommunications carriers. In fact, the Internet is tied into a complex web of governing bodies, national legislatures, and international professional societies. There is no one single governing organization that controls activity on the Internet. Instead, there are several organizations that influence the system and monitor its operations. Among the governing bodies of the Internet are:

- The *Internet Architecture Board (IAB)*, which helps define the overall structure of the Internet.
- The *Internet Corporation for Assigned Names and Numbers (ICANN)*, which assigns IP addresses and manages the top-level domain name system. ICANN was created in 1998 by the U.S. Department of Commerce.
- The *Internet Engineering Steering Group (IESG)*, which oversees standard setting with respect to the Internet.
- The *Internet Engineering Task Force (IETF)*, a private-sector group that forecasts the next step in the growth of the Internet, keeping watch over its evolution and operation.
- The *Internet Society (ISOC)*, which is a consortium of corporations, government agencies, and nonprofit organizations that monitors Internet policies and practices.
- The *World Wide Web Consortium (W3C)*, a largely academic group that sets HTML and other programming standards for the Web.
- The *International Telecommunication Union (ITU)*, which helps set technical standards.

While none of these organizations has actual control over the Internet and how it functions, they can and do influence government agencies, major network owners, ISPs, corporations, and software developers with the goal of keeping the Internet operating as efficiently as possible.

In addition to these professional bodies, the Internet must also conform to the laws of the sovereign nation-states in which it operates, as well as the technical infrastructures that exist within the nation-state. Although in the early years of the Internet there was very little legislative or executive interference, this situation is changing as the Internet plays a growing role in the distribution of information and knowledge, including content that some find objectionable.

The U.S. Department of Commerce originally created ICANN with the intent that it take over control of the Domain Name System and the 13 root servers that are at the heart of the Internet addressing scheme. However, this is no longer the case. The United States changed its policy in June 2005, when the Department of Commerce announced it would retain oversight over the root servers. There were several reasons for this move, including the use of the Internet for basic communications services by terrorist groups, and the uncertainty that might be caused should an international body take over. In 2008, the Department of Commerce reaffirmed this stance, stating that it "has no plans to transition management of the authoritative root zone file to ICANN" (U.S. Department of Commerce, 2008).

Read *Insight on Society: Government Regulation and Surveillance of the Internet* for a further look at the issue of censorship of Internet content and substance.

INSIGHT ON SOCIETY

GOVERNMENT REGULATION AND SURVEILLANCE OF THE INTERNET

In June 2009, the video of Neda Adha Soltan, who had been shot by a squad of Iranian riot police and was bleeding to death on the streets of Tehran, quickly raced around the world via the Internet and cell phone networks despite the efforts of the Iranian government, which had completely shut down text messaging in the country; blocked access to selected sites such as YouTube, MySpace, and Facebook; and slowed all Internet traffic in Iran by 90% so it could sift through e-mail messages. In the protests that followed the disputed Iranian election of June 12, 2009, Twitter became the primary organizing tool of the protestors, and an important source of information for the rest of the world, along with YouTube and other social sites to which protestors were able to connect, despite the best efforts of Iranian government censors.

Iran's Internet surveillance of its citizens is considered by security experts to be "one of the world's most sophisticated mechanisms for controlling and censoring the Internet, allowing it to examine the content of individual online communications on a massive scale," far more sophisticated than even China's Internet surveillance activities. The Iranian system goes far beyond preventing access to specific sites such as BBC World News, Google, and Facebook. Because the techniques for getting around government site access censorship are widely known (generally find a proxy server in another country that will allow you access to a forbidden site), governments need to do much more to control access and to figure out what their citizens are really thinking. One technique is deep packet inspection of every e-mail, text, or Twitter tweet. Deep packet inspection allows governments to read messages, alter their contents for disinformation purposes,

and identify senders and recipients. It is accomplished by installing computers in the line between users and ISPs, opening up every digitized packet, inspecting for keywords and images, reconstructing the message, and sending it on. This is done for all Internet traffic including Skype, Facebook, e-mail, tweets, and messages sent to proxy servers. These operations can slow down Internet service, but this delay can be avoided by installing additional servers.

Iran's Internet Monitoring Center is located in the government telecommunications monopoly, a central choke point for all Internet traffic in the country. Iran has some of the world's finest deep packet monitoring equipment supplied by a joint venture called Nokia Siemens Networks. There are of course reasons why Iran's government did not simply shut down the Internet entirely. Some traffic is required for business purposes, and keeping the Internet functioning allows the state to identify its enemies and critics.

The Internet is often hailed as a unique media that empowers average citizens to make their voices heard. The Internet is a giant public playground. True. At the same time the Internet is a playground for all governments that want to listen in on what people are saying and thinking. Some people believe they are anonymous on the Internet. After all, who could possibly be reading the billions of e-mail messages that are sent daily in the United States alone? Many people assume that because the Internet is so widely dispersed, it must be difficult to control or monitor. Legions of youthful music pirates believe they are anonymous on the Internet and cannot possibly be held accountable for whatever they want to do. "Information," they say, "wants to be free!" Unfortunately, with contemporary surveillance technologies, these statements are either false or misleading.

In reality, state-sponsored surveillance of the Internet and its content turns out to be pretty easy and very widespread. According to the Berkman Center for Internet and Society, about three dozen governments, from Iran, China, and Cuba, to Uzbekistan and Russia, control citizen access to the Internet. The United States, various state governments, as well as many European countries, also exercise Web site access control over Internet users. The number of countries that monitor e-mail and text messages is much larger, and once again, includes the United States, all European nations and Japan. In fact, just about all governments assert some kind of control and surveillance over Internet content and messages. There's a tug of war going on between young sophisticated users of the Internet and cell networks, and state-sponsored censors and security police around the world.

In another example, on July 4, 2009, a Tunis court convicted Khedija Arfaoui and sentenced her to eight years in prison on a charge of "disturbing public order" for posting a message about the rumored abduction of children for their organs in Tunisia on Facebook. In April 2009, the government of Bahrain sentenced three reporters to prison for posting articles to Web sites that were considered harmful to the state. They then issued a decree that "telecommunication companies and Internet Service Providers are required to prohibit any means that allow access to sites blocked by the ministry, whether by Internet address, use of a proxy server or any other means." Around 600 Web sites are currently blocked in Bahrain including access to the Washington-based news Web site Aafaq.org, Ghada Jamsheer's women's rights blog Bahraineve and the blog aggregator Bahrainblogs.org. In China, citizens who use the Internet to make their voices heard run the risk of losing their freedom, and sometimes their lives. For instance, on July 8, 2009, two cyber-dissidents and human rights activists, Zhang Qi and Zhang Peng, were sentenced to custodial custody and "re-education" for criticizing the government online.

Internet traffic in all countries runs through huge fiber-optic trunk lines. In China, there are three such lines, and China requires the companies that own these lines to configure their routers for both internal and external service requests. When a request originates in China for a Web page in Chicago, the Chinese routers examine the request to see if the site is on a blacklist, and then examine words in the requested Web page to see if they contain blacklisted terms. The most famous blacklisted terms are "falun" (a suppressed religious group in China) and "Tiananmen Square massacre" (or any symbols that might lead to such results such as "198964" which signifies June 4, 1989, the date of the massacre). The system is often referred to as "The Great Firewall of China," and is implemented with the assistance of Cisco Systems—the U.S. firm that is the largest manufacturer of routers in the world. Other U.S. Internet firms are also involved in China's censorship and surveillance efforts.

In addition to the Great Firewall of China, the Chinese government relies on a much more effective tactic called "self censorship" (or intimidation). For instance, in 2002, the Chinese government summarily shut off access to Google's servers from inside China. Even before this action, Google's results were often slowed by the Great Firewall. After this incident, Google decided to locate its servers on Chinese soil (Google.cn), where they became directly subject to China's censorship regime, which bans from the Internet anything that "damages the honor or interests of the state," "disturbs the public order," or "infringes upon national customs and habits." Why does Google, an American company whose mottos are "Don't be evil," and "Organize the world's information," and other Internet companies who do business in China, such as Cisco, Yahoo and Microsoft, collaborate with a repressive regime? In response, these firms say they are simply abiding by the laws of the countries where they do business. Google claims it is not identifying specific individuals to Chinese authorities because it operates no e-mail or bulletin board services in China, just search services, which it censors to avoid trouble with the Chinese government. Cisco says it does not cooperate with governments for such uses, though it notes the hardware "can be used for many different purposes." Yahoo and Microsoft said they were exploring a voluntary approach and have suggested to the U.S. government raising the issue of Internet service directly with Beijing. "Our leverage and ability to influence government policies in various countries is severely limited," the companies said. They are looking for U.S. government help to avoid having to comply with foreign government requests for surveillance and censorship.

In June 2009, the Chinese government issued a directive that all personal computers sold in China after July 1 would have to include pre-installed software that can filter out pornography and other "unhealthy" information. Called "Green Dam," the software can be automatically updated by Chinese authorities whenever a new "unhealthy" site appears on the Chinese Internet. Manufacturers such as Lenovo, Dell, and HP were able to persuade the Chinese government to allow them more time to install the software. China has extended its Internet restrictions to "vulgar" sites, popular blogs, Twitter, YouTube, Flickr, and Live.com, and extended its surveillance to Skype phone calls.

Not to be outdone, both Europe and the United States have at various times taken steps to control access to Internet sites, censor Web content, and engage in extensive communications, although not to the extent of Iran, China, and many other nations. For instance, Britain has a list of blocked sites, as does Germany and France.

The Australian Communications and Media Authority has developed a list of several hundred Web sites that have been refused registration in Australia, mostly violent video game and online pornography sites. The United States and European countries generally ban the sale, distribution, and/or possession of online child pornography. Both France and Germany bar online Nazi memorabilia. The United States has passed laws attempting to restrict ordinary pornographic content, but most of these have been struck down by courts. The United States does ban Internet gambling, and has arrested several European entrepreneurs on U.S. soil for promoting or engaging in Internet gambling sites.

In response to terrorism threats, both European governments and the U.S. government have also initiated deep packet inspection of e-mail and text communications. This surveillance is not limited to cross-border international data flows, and includes large-scale domestic surveillance of "ordinary" e-mail. Although it may seem preposterous that any government agency of government could read an estimated 150 billion daily e-mails in the United States, this task is, in reality, only slightly more complicated than Google's handling of 10 to 12 billion search queries per month. With the cooperation of the major Internet trunk carriers (AT&T, Verizon, and Sprint), and a dedicated signals intelligence computing capacity equal to Google's, near total e-mail, text, and Twitter surveillance is possible. In 2008, Congress modified FISA (the Foreign Intelligence Surveillance Act) and exempted telecommunications companies from any liability for cooperating with the National Security Agency to pursue extensive Internet surveillance, and removed this activity from the oversight of the FISA court. In 2009, both President Obama and Congress have continued to permit warrantless mass surveillance techniques.

While the Internet has unleashed an explosion of expression, and even enabled several rebellions and revolutions around the globe, at the same time it has become a testing center and proving ground for new surveillance capabilities and repressive governments.

There is the distinct possibility that the single World Wide Web will become a collection of loosely connected country Webs, each with its own form of censorship. The irony here is that the Internet was developed as a means of fostering global communication.

■ **SOURCES**: "Foreign Intelligence Surveillance Act (FISA)," *New York Times*, July 23, 2009; "US and European Countries Jointly Responsible for Internet Censorship," Reporters Without Borders, www.rsf.org, July 23, 2009; "Senate Approves Bill to Broaden Wiretap Powers," by Eric Lichtblau, *New York Times*, July 10, 2009; "In a Death Seen Around the World, a Symbol of Iranian Protests," by Nazila Fathi, *New York Times*, June 23, 2009; "Iran's Web Spying Aided By Western Technology. European Gear Used in Vast Effort to Monitor Communications," by Christopher Rhoads, *Wall Street Journal*, June 22, 2009; "Iranians Continue to Tweet Amid Internet Clampdown," *Wall Street Journal*, June 17, 2009; "Social Networks Spread Defiance Online," by Brad Stone and Noam Cohen, *New York Times*, June 16, 2009; "Ahmadinejad Confirmed Victor; Violent Protests Erupt in Tehran," by Farnaz Fassihi, *Wall Street Journal*, June 13, 2009; "Officials Say U.S. Wiretaps Exceeded Law," by Eric Lichtblau and James Risen, *New York Times*, April 16, 2009; "Circumvention Landscape Report: Methods, Uses, and Tools," Berkman Center for Internet and Society, Harvard University, March 05, 2009; "Court Affirms Wiretapping Without Warrants," by James Risen and Eric Lichtblau, *New York Times*, January 16, 2009..

3.3   INTERNET II: THE FUTURE INFRASTRUCTURE

The Internet is changing as new technologies appear and new applications are developed. We refer to the future infrastructure as Internet II. The second era of the Internet is being built today by private corporations, universities, and government agencies. To appreciate the benefits of Internet II, you must first understand the limitations of the Internet's current infrastructure.

LIMITATIONS OF THE CURRENT INTERNET

Much of the Internet's current infrastructure is several decades old (equivalent to a century in Internet time). It suffers from a number of limitations, including:

- *Bandwidth limitations.* There is insufficient capacity throughout the backbone, the metropolitan switching centers, and most importantly, the "last mile" to the house and small businesses. The result is slow peak-hour service (congestion) and a limited ability to handle high volumes of video and voice traffic.

- *Quality of service limitations.* Today's information packets take a circuitous route to get to their final destinations. This creates the phenomenon of **latency**—delays in messages caused by the uneven flow of information packets through the network. In the case of e-mail, latency is not noticeable. However, with streaming video and synchronous communication, such as a telephone call, latency is noticeable to the user and perceived as "jerkiness" in movies or delays in voice communication. Today's Internet uses "best-effort" quality of service (QOS), which makes no guarantees about when or whether data will be delivered, and provides each packet with the same level of service, no matter who the user is or what type of data is contained in the packet. A higher level of service quality is required if the Internet is to keep expanding into new services, such as video on demand and telephony.

latency
delays in messages caused by the uneven flow of information packets through the network

- *Network architecture limitations.* Today, a thousand requests for a single music track from a central server will result in a thousand efforts by the server to download the music to each requesting client. This slows down network performance as the same music track is sent out a thousand times to clients that might be located in the same metropolitan area. This is very different from television, where the program is broadcast once to millions of homes.

- *Language development limitations.* HTML, the language of Web pages, is fine for text and simple graphics, but poor at defining and communicating "rich documents," such as databases, business documents, or graphics. The tags used to define an HTML page are fixed and generic.

- *Wired Internet.* The Internet is based on cables—fiber-optic and coaxial copper cables. Copper cables use a centuries-old technology, and fiber-optic cable is expensive to place underground. The wired nature of the Internet restricts mobility of users although it is changing rapidly as Wi-Fi hotspots proliferate, and cellular phone technology advances. However, cellular systems are often overloaded due to the growth in the number of smartphones.

Now imagine an Internet at least 100 times as powerful as today's Internet, one that is not subjected to the limitations of bandwidth, protocols, architecture, physical connections, and language detailed previously. Welcome to the world of Internet II, and the next generation of e-commerce services and products!

THE INTERNET2® PROJECT

Internet2®
a consortium of more than 200 universities, government agencies, and private businesses that are collaborating to find ways to make the Internet more efficient

Internet2® is a consortium of more than 200 universities working in partnership with government agencies and private businesses in an effort to make the Internet more efficient.[4] Their work is a continuation of the kind of cooperation among government, private, and educational organizations that created the original Internet.

The idea behind Internet2 is to create a "giant test bed" where new technologies can be tested without impacting the existing Internet. The three primary goals of Internet2 are to:

- Create a leading-edge very high-speed network capability for the national research community

- Enable revolutionary Internet applications

- Ensure the rapid transfer of new network services and applications to the broader Internet community

GigaPoP
a regional Gigabit Point of Presence, or point of access to the Internet2 network, that supports at least one gigabit (1 billion bits) per second information transfer

Some of the areas Internet2 participants are focusing on in this pursuit are advanced network infrastructure, new networking capabilities, middleware, and advanced applications. The advanced networks created and in use by Internet2 members provide the environment in which new technologies can be tested and enhanced. Several new networks have been established, including Abilene and vBNS. Abilene and vBNS (short for *very high performance Backbone Network Service*) are high-performance backbone networks with bandwidths ranging from 2.5 Gbps to 10 Gbps that interconnect the GigaPoPs used by Internet2 members to access the network. A **GigaPoP** is a regional Gigabit Point of Presence, or point of access to the Internet2 network that supports data transfers at the rate of 1 Gbps or higher

[5]The Internet2® project is just one aspect of the larger second generation Internet we call Internet II.

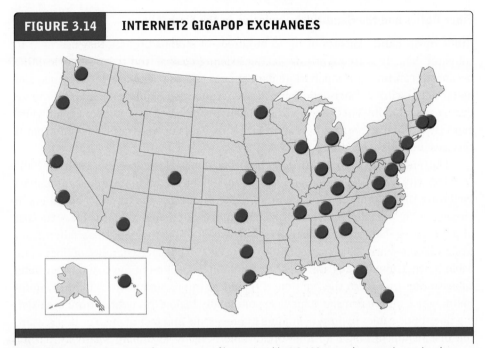

FIGURE 3.14   **INTERNET2 GIGAPOP EXCHANGES**

The backbone of the Internet2 infrastructure is a fiber-optic cable OC-192 network connecting regional GigaPoP servers (represented by the blue circles) that operate at billions of bits per second.
SOURCE: Internet2.edu, 2008.

(see **Figure 3.14**). In February 2004, Internet2 upgraded all segments of the Abilene network to 10 Gbps. In 2007, Internet2 deployed a 100 Gbps East-West link. At these speeds, the ability of the network to process data begins to exceed the speed at which client computers can pull data off their hard drives. With a 100 Gbps Internet, a high-quality version of the movie "The Matrix" could be sent in a few seconds rather than half a minute over the current Internet2 and two days over a typical home broadband line.

THE LARGER INTERNET II TECHNOLOGY ENVIRONMENT: THE FIRST MILE AND THE LAST MILE

The Internet2 project is just the tip of the iceberg when it comes to near-term future enhancements to the Internet. In 2007, the NSF began work on the Global Environment for Networking Innovations (GENI) Initiative to develop new core functionality for the Internet, including new naming, addressing and identity architectures; enhanced capabilities, including additional security architecture and a design that supports high availability; and new Internet services and applications (Geni.net, 2008). The most significant privately initiated (but often government-influenced) changes are coming in two areas: fiber-optic trunk line bandwidth and wireless Internet services. Fiber optics is concerned with the first mile or backbone Internet services that carry bulk traffic long distances. Wireless Internet is concerned with the last mile—from the larger Internet to the user's cell phone or laptop.

Fiber Optics and the Bandwidth Explosion in the First Mile

fiber-optic cable

consists of up to hundreds of strands of glass or plastic that use light to transmit data

Fiber-optic cable consists of up to hundreds of strands of glass that use light to transmit data. It is frequently replacing existing coaxial and twisted pair cabling because it can transmit much more data at faster speeds, with less interference and better data security. Fiber-optic cable is also thinner and lighter, taking up less space during installation. The hope is to use fiber optics to expand network bandwidth capacity in order to prepare for the expected increases in Web traffic once Internet II services are widely adopted.

The enormous increase in long-haul backbone capacity from 1998 to 2001, coupled with a decline in demand, caused over 60 telecommunications companies including WorldCom and Global Crossing Ltd. to declare bankruptcy and others to struggle with large deficits, leading to painful losses in shareholder value. The cost of a 1.5 Mbps dedicated line between Los Angeles and New York has fallen from $1.8 million in early 2000 down to $100,000 in 2009. Thousands of miles of fiber-optic cable in the United States are "dark" or "unlit." The decline in the cost of fiber-optic cable is due in part to the continued technical improvement in switching equipment, which allows firms to achieve exponentially higher throughput from the existing fiber-optic cables by improvements in processors and technique. For this reason, the installation of long-haul fiber-optic cable is likely to remain relatively flat for years to come, and the prices companies can charge for long-haul digital transmission will also likely remain flat through 2013.

However, there is a silver lining in this cloudy picture. The fiber-optic cable will not disappear or degrade over time, and it represents a vast digital highway that is currently being exploited by YouTube (Google), Facebook, MySpace, and other high-bandwidth applications; telecommunications companies are re-capitalizing and building new business models based on market prices for digital traffic. The net result is that society will ultimately benefit from extraordinarily low-cost, long-haul, very high-bandwidth communication facilities that are already paid for.

Demand for fiber-optic cable is likely to strengthen as consumers demand integrated telephone, broadband access, and video from a single source. Interactive online television, online Hollywood movies, inexpensive Voice over Internet Protocol (VoIP) telephone, and Internet access all from the same company that provides a single cable into the home is the vision driving Verizon, other local Bells, and cable firms. In 2004, Verizon began building its FiOS, network infrastructure, and since then has spent $23 billion expanding the service. As of July 2009, there are about 3.3 million Verizon FiOS broadband customers. FiOS costs consumers from $40 to $200 a month, and provides download speeds of up to 50 Mbps and upload speeds of up to 10 Mbps. This so-called Fiber to the Premises (FTTP) will be the fastest growing form of broadband connection in the next decade.

photonics

the study of communicating with light waves

Table 3.6 describes some of the **photonic** technologies that are being used to expand the capacity of the installed long-haul fiber lines. Together, these improvements will allow the Internet to move from narrowband to broadband digital services, and from stationary Web access to mobile Web access.

Figure 3.15 gives a comparative look at bandwidth demand for various applications.

TABLE 3.6	MAJOR PHOTONICS OPPORTUNITIES AND PLAYERS	
TECHNOLOGY	OPPORTUNITY	PLAYERS
Dense Wavelength Division Multiplexing	Transform single strand of fiber-optic cable into multiple virtual fibers	Cisco, Cogent Communications
Optical switches and transmission equipment	Expand capacity, drop costs, speed service	Glimmerglass; Aurora Networks
Gigabit Ethernet over fiber switches	Increased access to metro regional equipment networks	Ciena, Zuma Networks
Optical service accounting platforms	Packet size metering and billing; bytes to bucks	Ellacoya Networks
Optical switching	Building blocks for all optical systems conponents	ADC Telecommunications, JDS Uniphase, Oclaro
Optical integrated circuits	Powerful optical chips with mirrors and lasers	Oclaro
Passive Optical Networks (PON)	Low-cost, high-performance networks	Zhone, Broadlight
Fiber-optic cable	The highway material	Corning, AT&T

The Last Mile: Mobile Wireless Internet Access

Fiber-optic networks carry the long-haul bulk traffic of the Internet—and in the future will play an important role in bringing BigBand to the household and small business. But along with fiber optics and photonics, arguably the most significant development

FIGURE 3.15 BANDWIDTH DEMAND OF VARIOUS WEB APPLICATIONS

Narrowband	**Broadband**	**BigBand**
Peripheral sharing	Video conferencing	TV, HDTV
	Multimedia distance learning	Interactive TV
Telemetry	File transfer	Hollywood on the Web
Radio e-mail	WWW voice	Internet II:
		Extensive ASP/LSP possible
		Medical images
Wireless alarms, pagers, text, e-mail	CD transfer rates	Remote labs
	Simulations	Multi-person video conferencing
	High-definition graphics	Ubiquitous netpliance computing
	ASPs/LSPs possible	

1 Kbps   1 Mbps   1 Gbps   1 Tbps

Protocol: Modem vbis90 56.6Kbps Ethernet 10Mbps FDDI/SONET 100Mbps ATM

Media: Cellular/WAP   Twisted Pair   DSL   Coax Cable   Fiber Cable   OC-68

The really exciting e-commerce applications such as high definition television (HDTV) and interactive TV and movies require higher levels of bandwidth to the home than are typically currently available. in the United States. Verizon's FiOS fiber optic network operating at 15 Mbps is a suitable option.

for the Internet and Web in the last five years has been the emergence of mobile wireless Internet access.

Wireless Internet is concerned with the last mile of Internet access to the user's home, office, car, or cell phone anywhere. Up until 2000, the last-mile access to the Internet—with the exception of a small satellite Internet connect population—was bound up in land lines of some sort: copper coaxial TV cables or telephone lines or, in some cases, fiber-optic lines to the office. Internet II will increasingly rely on wireless technology to connect users' smartphones and computers to the Web and LANs.

In 2008, for the first time, more portable notebook computers (most with wireless networking functionality built in) were sold in the United States than desktop computers, and in 2009, this is expected to be true of worldwide sales of notebook computers as well (Stross, 2009). As more and more smartphones continue to add Wi-Fi capabilities, such as Apple's iPhone or T-Mobile's Android G1, millions of smartphone users will also gain Internet access. Clearly, a large part of the future Internet will be mobile, access—anywhere, broadband service for the delivery of video, music, and Web search. According to eMarketer, there are already 74 million mobile Internet users in the United States in 2009, and 600 million worldwide. Those numbers are expected to grow significantly in the next four years, almost doubling in the United States to 134 million in 2013 and increasing even more worldwide to 1.22 billion (eMarketer, 2009b, c).

Telephone-based versus Computer Network-based Wireless Internet Access There are two different basic types of wireless Internet connectivity: telephone-based and computer network-based systems.

Telephone-based wireless Internet access connects the user to a global telephone system (land, satellite, and microwave) that has a long history of dealing with thousands of users simultaneously and already has in place a large-scale transaction billing system and related infrastructure. Cellular telephones and the telephone industry are currently the largest providers of wireless access to the Internet today. In 2008, there were over 1 billion cell phones sold worldwide, with a similar amount expected to be sold in 2009. The percentage of smartphones sold is continuing to climb (eMarketer, Inc., 2009d).

The first generation of cellular networks were analog-based. Second generation (2G) cellular networks are relatively slow circuit-switched digital networks that can transmit data at about 10 Kbps—one fifth of the speed of a home modem. A 2.5G network provides speeds of 60 to 144 Kbps using General Packet Radio Services (GPRS), a packet-switching technology that is much more efficient (and hence faster) than dedicated circuit-switched networks. An enhanced version of GPRS called EDGE can carry data at up from 384 Kbps to around 2 Mbps.

In the United States, there are two basic types of 3G networks - those based on Global System for Mobile Communications (GSM) standards (used worldwide, and in the United States by AT&T and T-Mobile) and those based on Code Division Multiple Access (CDMA, used primarily in the United States, by Verizon and Sprint). Cell phone providers have also begun to offer what they call 3G+ or 3.5G service, which can provide speeds of up to 14.4 Mbps. Just around the corner are 4G networks using

Wi-Max technology and a technology known as Long-Term Evolution (LTE) (adopted by both AT&T and Verizon). A 4G network using Wi-Max can deliver downloads at up to 72 Mbps, while LTE has the potential to provide up to 300 Mbps. **Table 3.7** summarizes the various telephone technologies used for wireless Internet access.

Regardless of which standard is involved, the advent of higher speed cellular networks has created an entire new class of Web appliances that utilize a new kind of telecommunications service called "hybrid PCS," or just PCS for personal

TABLE 3.7	WIRELESS INTERNET ACCESS TELEPHONE TECHNOLOGIES		
TECHNOLOGY	SPEED	DESCRIPTION	PLAYERS
2G			
Global System for Mobile Communications (GSM)	10 Kbps	European and some American companies' basic cell phone service; text messaging; uses TDMA.	Vodafone (Europe), Cingular, T-Mobile
Time Division Multiple Access (TDMA)	10 Kbps	An early standard for cell phone service. Used by GSM networks worldwide.	GSM networks in Europe and Japan
CDMA	10 Kbps	American standard for basic cell phone service; text messaging. Developed by Qualcomm.	Verizon, Sprint
2.5G			
General Packet Radio Services (GPRS) EDGE CDMA2000 1xRTT	30–170 Kbps	Interim step toward 3G in the United States. Fast enough for Web access.	AT&T, T-Mobile, Vodafone, Verizon, Sprint
3G (THIRD GENERATION)			
CDMA2000 EV-DO HSPA (W-CDMA)	144 Kbps–2 Mbps	High-speed, mobile, always on for e-mail, browsing, instant messaging. Implementing technologies include versions of CDMA2000 EV-DO (used by CDMA providers) and HSPDA (used by GSM providers). Truly a broadband cellular service as fast as Wi-Fi.	Verizon, Sprint AT&T, T-Mobile, Vodafone
3.5G (3G+)			
CDMA2000 EV-DO, Rev.B	Up to 14.4 Mbps	Enhanced version of CDMA 2000 EV-DO.	Verizon, Sprint
HSPA+	Up to 11 Mbps	Enhanced version of HSPA	AT&T, T-Mobile
4G (FOURTH GENERATION)			
Long-Term Evolution (LTE)	Up to 100–300 Mbps	True broadband on cell phone.	AT&T, Verizon
Wi-Max	72 Mbps	Alternative to LTE.	Clearwire/Sprint

communication devices. Also known as smart phones, these devices combine the functionality of a PDA with that of a cell phone, such as an Apple iPhone, T-Mobile Android G1/G2, or RIM BlackBerry, and that of a mobile laptop computer with Wi-fi capability. This makes it possible to combine in one device music, video, Web access, and telephone service. When these same cellular devices also can provide Wi-Fi connections to the Web, and switch seamlessly from one network to the other, they are referred to as *fully converged devices*. **Table 3.8** describes some of the most popular smartphones available as of August 2009.

Once a connection is established with a user's smartphone, there are a number of different ways to deliver Web pages. The Apple iPhone has a such a high resolution and large screen that Web pages are delivered as ordinary HTML pages and the user can scroll around the page to navigate. Likewise with BlackBerry Storm. Older devices with less-capable screens either use Wireless Application Protocol (WAP) or iMode, a proprietary standard owned by the Japanese company NTT DoCoMo.

Wireless local area network (WLAN)-based Internet access derives from a completely different background from telephone-based wireless Internet access. Popularly known as Wi-Fi, WLANs are based on computer local area networks where the task is to connect client computers (generally stationary) to server computers within local areas of, say, a few hundred meters. WLANs function by sending radio signals that are broadcast over the airwaves using certain radio frequency ranges (2.4 gigahertz [GHz] to 5.875 GHz, depending on the type of stan-

TABLE 3.8	POPULAR SMARTPHONES			
DEVICE	APPLE IPHONE 3GS	PALM PRE	ANDROID G2	BLACKBERRY STORM
Functionality	Phone, Internet access, e-mail, GPS, camera, video recording, voice commands	Phone, Internet access, e-mail, GPS, camera	Phone, Internet access, e-mail, GPS, camera, video recording	Phone, Internet access, e-mail, GPS camera, video recording
Applications	ITunes App Store; 65,000 apps	Palm App Catalog, 30 apps	Android Marketplace, 5,000 apps	BlackBerry App World, 2,000 apps
Hardware	Touch screen, 16/32 GB storage, Bluetooth	Touch screen, 8 GB storage, Bluetooth, keyboard	Touch screen, 16 GB storage, Bluetooth	Touch screen, Bluetooth
Operating System	iPhone OS	Web OS	Google Android	Blackberry OS 4.7
Storage	16/32 GB	8 GB	1 GB, expandable	1 GB + 8GB removable
Provider/Network	AT&T 3G/Wi-Fi	Sprint 3G/Wi-Fi	T-Mobile 3G/Wi-Fi	Verizon 3G/Wi-Fi

dard involved). The major technologies here are the various versions of the Wi-Fi standard and Bluetooth. Emerging WLAN technologies include WiMax, Ultra-Wideband (UWB), and ZigBee (see **Table 3.9**).

IEEE 802.11b (also referred to as **Wi-Fi**) was the first commercially viable standard for wireless local networks in the 2.4 GHz frequency range set aside by the U.S. government for unregulated use. Subsequent versions offered greater speed. Version 802.11n became the standard in 2008.

In a Wi-Fi network, a *wireless access point* (also known as a "hot spot") connects to the Internet directly via a broadband connection (cable, DSL telephone, or T1 line) and then transmits a radio signal to a transmitter/receiver installed in a laptop computer or PDA, either as a PCMCIA card or built-in at manufacture (such as Intel's Centrino processor, which provides built-in support for Wi-Fi in portable devices). **Figure 3.16** illustrates how a Wi-Fi network works.

Wi-Fi offers high bandwidth capacity of from 11 Mbps to 70 Mbps—far greater than any 3G service even planned—but has a limited range of 300 meters, with the exception of WiMax discussed below. Wi-Fi is also exceptionally inexpensive. The cost of creating a corporate Wi-Fi network in a single 14-story building with an access

Wi-Fi

also referred to as 802.11b, 802.11a (Wi-Fi5), and 802.16 (WiMAX). Wireless standard for Ethernet networks with greater speed and range than Bluetooth

TABLE 3.9	WIRELESS INTERNET ACCESS NETWORK TECHNOLOGIES		
TECHNOLOGY	RANGE/SPEED	DESCRIPTION	PLAYERS
Wi-Fi (IEEE 802.11a –802.11n)	300 feet/11–70 Mbps	Evolving high-speed, fixed broadband wireless local area network for commercial and residential use	Linksys, Cisco, and other Wi-Fi router manufacturers; entrepreneurial network developers
WiMax (IEEE 802.16)	30 miles/50–70 Mbps	High-speed, medium-range, broadband wireless metropolitan area network	Clearwire, Sprint, Fujitsu, Intel, Alcatel, Proxim/Terabeam
Bluetooth (wireless personal area network)	1–30 meters/ 1–3 Mbps	Modest-speed, low-power, short-range connection of digital devices	Ericsson, Nokia, Apple, HP, and other device makers
Ultra-Wideband (UWB) (wireless personal area network)	30 feet/5–10 Mbps	Low-power, short-range, high-bandwidth network technology useful as cabling replacement in home and office networks	Ultrawideband Forum, Intel, Freescale
ZigBee (wireless personal area network)	30 feet/250 Kbps	Short-range, very low-power, wireless network technology useful for remotely controlling industrial, medical, and home automation devices	ZigBee Alliance, Chipcon, Freescale, Mitsubishi, Motorola, MaxStream, San Juan Software

| FIGURE 3.16 | WI-FI NETWORKS |

In a Wi-Fi network, wireless access points connect to the Internet using a land-based broadband connection. Clients, which could be laptops, desktops, cell phones, or suitably equipped PDAs, connect to the access point using radio signals.

point for each floor is less than $100 an access point. It would cost well over $500,000 to wire the same building with Ethernet cable. Admittedly, the Ethernet cable would be operating at a theoretical 100 Mbps—ten times as fast as Wi-Fi. However, in some cases, this capacity is not needed and Wi-Fi is an acceptable alternative.

While initially a grass roots, "hippies and hackers" public access technology, billions of dollars have subsequently been poured into private ventures seeking to create for-profit Wi-Fi networks. The most prominent network has been created by Boingo Wireless with over 100,000 hot spots around the globe (Boingo Wireless, Inc., 2009). Wayport (now owned by AT &T) s created another large network that provides Wi-Fi service at hotels, airports, McDonalds, IHOPs, and Hertz airport rental offices, with almost 20,000 hot spots in the United States (Wayport, Inc., 2008). T-Mobile and Sprint have also established nationwide Wi-Fi services at 2,000 Starbuck's coffee shops, and thousands of other public locations. Apple, in turn, has made Wi-Fi automatically available to iPhone handsets as an alternative to the more expensive and much slower 2.5G cellular systems such as EDGE.

Will WLAN compete directly against far more expensive telephone 3G services? The answer is "eventually, but not right now." Wi-Fi was originally a local area network technology of limited range, for stationary client computers, but with high capacity suitable for most Web surfing and some corporate uses with modest bandwidth demands. Cellular phone systems are wide area networks of nearly unlimited range, for mobile client computers and handhelds, and with modest but rapidly increasing capacity suitable for e-mail, photos, and Web browsing (on very small screens). However, the rock bottom price of Wi-Fi coupled with ambitious plans for a 30-mile- range WiMax (802.16) service suggests that Wi-Fi could drain significant business from far more capital-intensive cellular systems.

A second WLAN technology for connecting to the Internet, and for connecting Internet devices to one another, is called Bluetooth. Bluetooth is an industry standard that emanated from Scandinavian telecommunications firms such as Ericsson, Nokia, and Siemens in the 1990s. **Bluetooth** is a personal connectivity technology that enables links between mobile computers, mobile phones, PDAs, and connectivity to the Internet (Bluetooth SIG, 2005). Bluetooth is the universal cable cutter, promising to get rid of the tangled mess of wires, cradles, and special attachments that plague the current world of personal computing. With Bluetooth, users wear a cell phone wireless earbud, share files in a hallway or conference room, synchronize their PDA with their laptop without a cradle, send a document to a printer, and even pay a restaurant bill from the table to a Bluetooth-equipped cash register. Bluetooth also is an unregulated media operating in the 2.4 GHz spectrum but with very limited range of 30 feet or less. It uses a frequency hopping signal with up to 1,600 hops per second over 79 frequencies, giving it good protection from interference. Bluetooth-equipped devices—which could be cell phones, PDAs, or laptops—constantly scan their environments looking for connections to compatible devices. Today, almost all cell phones and PDAs are Bluetooth-enabled.

A more recent arrival on the wireless connectivity front is ZigBee. **ZigBee** is a less-expensive, low-power, and simpler form of radio network operating in the 2.4 GHz frequency range that allows small appliances and sensors to communicate with one another. The current focus of ZigBee is developing simple networks for industrial controls, medical devices, smoke and intruder alarms, building automation, and home automation. These networks use very small amounts of power, so individual devices might run for a year or two with a single alkaline battery (ZigBee Alliance, 2009).

Table 3.10 summarizes some of the e-commerce services that can be supported by wireless Internet access. Some of these services are *push services*—the transmission of data at a predetermined time, or under determined conditions. This could include unsolicited information such as news delivery or stock market values. Other services are *pull services*—transmission of data resulting from user requests. Geographical information services—advertising for local pizza shops, restaurants, and museums—are a major growth area for cell phone services in part due to the Wireless Communications and Public Safety Act of 1999, which required all cell phone carriers in the United States to feature E911 technology by 2006. E911 (Enhanced 911) service allows a person's cell phone to be located at a physical address when that person calls the 911 emergency number used throughout the United States. This requires all cell phones to be equipped with GPS receivers, which provide a fairly precise latitude and longitude location. In fact, all cell phone carriers can identify the GPS location of a cell phone regardless of what number is called. This enhanced geographic locating capability can easily be used to send locally based advertising to cell phone users either over the Web or using the cellular network itself.

Bluetooth
new technology standard for short-range wireless communication under 10 meters

ZigBee
a less-expensive, low-power, and simpler form of radio network operating in the 2.4 GHz band and other bands that allows small appliances and sensors to talk with one another

TABLE 3.10	POTENTIAL WIRELESS INTERNET E-COMMERCE SERVICES
SERVICE	DESCRIPTION
Horizontal Market Services	**Services that apply across industries and firms**
Personalized information	Stock values, news, quotes based on user profiles and needs
Geographical-based local content	Local maps, hotel finders, movie locations and times, and restaurant locations and reviews
Media services	Video, photos, news, and music
Banking services	Balance checking, money transfer, bill payment, and overdraft alerts
Financial services	Trading, stock alerts, and interest rates based on user account information
Vertical Market Services	**Services that apply within a firm or industry**
Sales support	Stock and production information, remote orders, calendars, and planning information
Reservation systems	Airline, train, hotel, and event reservations coordinated with inventory
Dispatching	Communication of job details, parts information, and repair routines
Fleet management	Control of fleet delivery or service staff; monitoring locations and work schedules
Parcel delivery	Tracking of packages, queries, and performance monitoring
Home automation	Coordinating alarm and other digital services and devices in a home
Industrial automation	Coordinating machine controllers in a factory

BENEFITS OF INTERNET II TECHNOLOGIES

The increased bandwidth and expanded wireless network connectivity of the Internet II era will result in benefits beyond faster access and richer communications. First-mile enhancements created by fiber-optic networks will enhance reliability and quality of Internet transmissions and create new business models and opportunities. Some of the major benefits of these technological advancements include IP multicasting, latency solutions, guaranteed service levels, lower error rates, and declining costs. Widespread wireless access to the Internet will also essentially double or even triple the size of the online shopping marketspace because consumers will be able to shop and make purchases just about anywhere. This is equivalent to doubling the physical floor space of all shopping malls in America. We describe some of these benefits in more detail in the following sections.

IP Multicasting

The future of the Internet is clearly to become the entertainment center of American life, replacing radio, television, and movie theaters. This means Hollywood movies, television shows, and all the music ever digitized will have to routinely move across the Internet from coast to coast on demand from 200 million users. Today, this would cause a near collapse of the Internet. Internet II will potentially solve this problem. One capability of Internet II is IP multicasting.

IP multicasting is a set of technologies that enables efficient delivery of very large files to many locations on a network. Rather than making multiple copies of a message intended to be distributed to multiple recipients at the point of origin of a message, multicasting initially sends just one message and does not copy it to the individual recipients until it reaches the closest common point on the network, thereby minimizing the bandwidth consumed (see **Figure 3.17**). At that point, routers make copies as needed to serve requesting clients, and the sender sends only a single copy over the Internet. Network performance is significantly improved because it isn't bogged down with the processing and transmission of

IP multicasting
a set of technologies that enables efficient delivery of data to many locations on a network

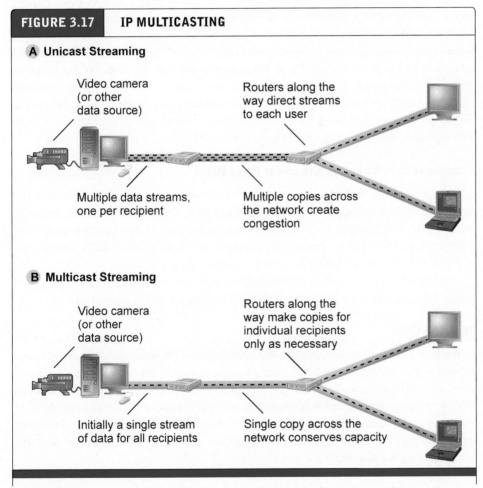

FIGURE 3.17	IP MULTICASTING

A Unicast Streaming

Video camera (or other data source)

Routers along the way direct streams to each user

Multiple data streams, one per recipient

Multiple copies across the network create congestion

B Multicast Streaming

Video camera (or other data source)

Routers along the way make copies for individual recipients only as necessary

Initially a single stream of data for all recipients

Single copy across the network conserves capacity

IP multicasting is a method for efficiently sending high-bandwidth video files to clients without causing Internet congestion and delay for other traffic.

SOURCES: Adapted from Cisco Systems, 2007; Internet2.edu, 2000.

several large data files; each receiving computer doesn't have to query the transmitting server for the file. Multicasting technologies are already making their way into today's Internet through the use of Mbone (a special-purpose backbone for delivering video data). Used in combination with protocols like BitTorrent, IP multicasting has the potential to scale up to serve an entire nation of Internet users.

Latency Solutions

One of the challenges of packet switching, where data is divided into chunks and then sent separately to meet again at the destination, is that the Internet does not differentiate between high-priority packets, such as video clips, and those of lower priority, such as self-contained e-mail messages. Because the packets cannot yet be simultaneously reassembled, the result can be distorted audio and video streams.

differentiated quality of service (diffserv)
a new technology that assigns levels of priority to packets based on the type of data being transmitted

Internet II holds the promise of **diffserv**, or differentiated quality of service—a new technology that assigns levels of priority to packets based on the type of data being transmitted. Video conference packets, for example, which need to reach their destination almost instantaneously, would receive much higher priority than e-mail messages. In the end, the quality of video and audio will skyrocket without undue stress on the network. Live and on-demand television and movies will be possible once Internet II is completed. But differential service is very controversial because it means some users will get more bandwidth than others, and potentially they may have to pay a higher price for more bandwidth.

Guaranteed Service Levels and Lower Error Rates

In today's Internet, there is no service-level guarantee and no way to purchase the right to move data through the Internet at a fixed pace. Today's Internet promises only "best effort." The Internet is democratic—it speeds or slows everyone's traffic alike. With Internet II, it will be possible to purchase the right to move data through the network at a guaranteed speed in return for higher fees.

Improved capacity and packet switching will also inevitably impact quality of data transmissions, reducing error rates and boosting customer satisfaction.

Declining Costs

As the Internet pipeline is upgraded, the availability of broadband service will expand beyond major metropolitan areas, significantly reducing the costs of access. More users means lower cost, as products and technology catch on in the mass market. Higher volume usage enables providers to lower the cost of both access devices, or clients, and the service required to use such products. Both broadband and wireless service fees are expected to decline as geographic service areas increase, in part due to competition for that business.

3.4 THE WORLD WIDE WEB

Without the Web, there would be no e-commerce. The invention of the Web brought an extraordinary expansion of digital services to millions of amateur computer users, including color text and pages, formatted text, pictures, animations, video, and sound. In short, the Web makes nearly all the rich elements of human expression needed to establish a commercial marketplace available to nontechnical computer users worldwide.

While the Internet was born in the 1960s, the Web was not invented until 1989–1991 by Dr. Tim Berners-Lee of the European Particle Physics Laboratory, better known as CERN (Berners-Lee et al., 1994). Several earlier authors—such as Vannevar Bush (in 1945) and Ted Nelson (in the 1960s)—had suggested the possibility of organizing knowledge as a set of interconnected pages that users could freely browse (Bush, 1945; Ziff Davis Publishing, 1998). Berners-Lee and his associates at CERN built on these ideas and developed the initial versions of HTML, HTTP, a Web server, and a browser, the four essential components of the Web.

First, Berners-Lee wrote a computer program that allowed formatted pages within his own computer to be linked using keywords (hyperlinks). Clicking on a keyword in a document would immediately move him to another document. Berners-Lee created the pages using a modified version of a powerful text markup language called SGML (Standard Generalized Markup Language).

Berners-Lee called this language HyperText Markup Language, or HTML. He then came up with the idea of storing his HTML pages on the Internet. Remote client computers could access these pages by using HTTP (introduced earlier in Section 3.2 and described more fully in the next section). But these early Web pages still appeared as black and white text pages with hyperlinks expressed inside brackets. The early Web was based on text only; the original Web browser only provided a line interface.

Information being shared on the Web remained text-based until 1993, when Marc Andreesen and others at the National Center for Supercomputing Applications (NCSA) at the University of Illinois created a Web browser with a graphical user interface (GUI) called **Mosaic** that made it possible to view documents on the Web graphically—using colored backgrounds, images, and even primitive animations. Mosaic was a software program that could run on any graphically based interface such as Macintosh, Windows, or Unix. The Mosaic browser software read the HTML text on a Web page and displayed it as a graphical interface document within a graphical user interface (GUI) operating system such as Windows or Macintosh. Liberated from simple black and white text pages, HTML pages could now be viewed by anyone in the world who could operate a mouse and use a Macintosh or PC.

Aside from making the content of Web pages colorful and available to the world's population, the graphical Web browser created the possibility of **universal computing**, the sharing of files, information, graphics, sound, video, and other objects across all computer platforms in the world, regardless of operating system. A browser could be made for each of the major operating systems, and the Web pages created for one system, say, Windows, would also be displayed exactly the

Mosaic
Web browser with a graphical user interface (GUI) that made it possible to view documents on the Web graphically

universal computing
the sharing of files, information, graphics, sound, video, and other objects across all computer platforms in the world, regardless of operating system

same, or nearly the same, on computers running the Macintosh or Unix operating systems. As long as each operating system had a Mosaic browser, the same Web pages could be used on all the different types of computers and operating systems. This meant that no matter what kind of computer you used, anywhere in the world, you would see the same Web pages. The browser and the Web have introduced us to a whole new world of computing and information management that was unthinkable prior to 1993.

Netscape Navigator
the first commercial Web browser

In 1994, Andreesen and Jim Clark founded Netscape, which created the first commercial browser, **Netscape Navigator**. Although Mosaic had been distributed free of charge, Netscape initially charged for its software. In August 1995, Microsoft Corporation released its own version of a browser, called **Internet Explorer**. In the ensuing years, Netscape has faltered, falling from a 100% market share to less than .5% in 2009. The fate of Netscape illustrates an important e-commerce business lesson. Innovators usually are not long-term winners, whereas smart followers often have the assets needed for long-term survival.

Internet Explorer
Microsoft's Web browser

HYPERTEXT

Web pages can be accessed through the Internet because the Web browser software on your PC can request Web pages stored on an Internet host server using the HTTP protocol. **Hypertext** is a way of formatting pages with embedded links that connect documents to one another, and that also link pages to other objects such as sound, video, or animation files. When you click on a graphic and a video clip plays, you have clicked on a hyperlink. For example, when you type a Web address in your browser such as http://www.sec.gov, your browser sends an HTTP request to the sec.gov server requesting the home page of sec.gov.

Hypertext
a way of formatting pages with embedded links that connect documents to one another, and that also link pages to other objects such as sound, video, or animation files

HTTP is the first set of letters at the start of every Web address, followed by the domain name. The domain name specifies the organization's server computer that is housing the document. Most companies have a domain name that is the same as or closely related to their official corporate name. The directory path and document name are two more pieces of information within the Web address that help the browser track down the requested page. Together, the address is called a Uniform Resource Locator, or URL. When typed into a browser, a URL tells it exactly where to look for the information. For example, in the following URL:

http://www.megacorp.com/content/features/082602.html

http = the protocol used to display Web pages

www.megacorp.com = domain name

content/features = the directory path that identifies where on the domain Web server the page is stored

082602.html = the document name and its format (an html page)

The most common domain extensions (known as general top-level domains, or gTLDs) currently available and officially sanctioned by ICANN are shown in **Table 3.11**. Countries also have domain names, such as .uk, .au, and .fr (United Kingdom, Australia, and France, respectively). These are sometimes referred to as

TABLE 3.11		TOP-LEVEL DOMAINS	
GENERAL TOP-LEVEL DOMAIN (gTLD)	YEAR(S) INTRODUCED	PURPOSE	SPONSOR/ OPERATOR
.com	1980s	Unrestricted (but intended for commercial registrants)	VeriSign
.edu	1980s	U.S. educational institutions	Educause
.gov	1980s	U.S. government	U.S. General Services Administration
.mil	1980s	U.S. military	U.S. Department of Defense Network Information Center
.net	1980s	Unrestricted (but originally intended for network providers, etc.)	VeriSign
.org	1980s	Unrestricted (but intended for organizations that do not fit elsewhere)	Public Interest Registry (was operated by VeriSign until December 31, 2002)
.int	1998	Organizations established by international treaties between governments	Internet Assigned Numbers Authority (IANA)
.aero	2001	Air-transport industry	Societe Internationale de Telecommunications Aeronautiques SC (SITA)
.biz	2001	Businesses	NeuLevel
.coop	2001	Cooperatives	DotCooperation LLC
.info	2001	Unrestricted use	Afilias LLC
.museum	2001	Museums	Museum Domain Name Association (MuseDoma)
.name	2001	For registration by individuals	Global Name Registry Ltd.
.pro	2002	Accountants, lawyers, physicians, and other professionals	RegistryPro Ltd
.jobs	2005	Job search	Employ Media LLC
.travel	2005	Travel search	Triallance Corporation
.mobi	2005	Web sites specifically designed for mobile phones	mTLD Top Level Domain, Ltd.
.cat	2005	Individuals, organizations, and companies that promote the Catalan language and culture	Fundació puntCAT
.asia	2006	Regional domain for companies, organizations, and individuals based in Asia	DotAsia Organization
.tel	2006	Telephone numbers and other contact information	Telnic, Ltd.

SOURCES: Based on data from ICANN, 2009.

country-code top-level domains, or ccTLDs. In 2008, ICANN approved a significant expansion of gTLDs, with potential new domains representing cities (such as .berlin), regions (.africa), ethnicity (.eus), industry/activities (such as .health), and even brands (such as .deloitte). In 2009, ICANN began the process of implementing these guidelines.

MARKUP LANGUAGES

Although the most common Web page formatting language is HTML, the concept behind document formatting actually had its roots in the 1960s with the development of Generalized Markup Language (GML).

Standard Generalized Markup Language (SGML)

In 1986, the International Standards Organization adopted a variation of GML called Standard Generalized Markup Language, or SGML. The purpose of SGML was to help very large organizations format and categorize large collections of documents. The advantage of SGML is that it can run independent of any software program but, unfortunately, it is extremely complicated and difficult to learn. Probably for this reason, it has not been widely adopted.

HyperText Markup Language (HTML)

HyperText Markup Language (HTML)
one of the next generation of GMLs that is relatively easy to use in Web page design. HTML provides Web page designers with a fixed set of markup "tags" that are used to format a Web page

HyperText Markup Language (HTML) is a GML that is relatively easy to use. HTML provides Web page designers with a fixed set of markup "tags" that are used to format a Web page (see **Figure 3.18**). When these tags are inserted into a Web page, they are read by the browser and interpreted into a page display. You can see the source HTML code for any Web page by simply clicking on the "Page Source" command found in all browsers. In Figure 3.18, the HTML code in the first screen produces the display in the second screen.

HTML defines the structure and style of a document, including the headings, graphic positioning, tables, and text formatting. Since its introduction, the major browsers have continuously added features to HTML to enable programmers to further refine their page layouts. Unfortunately, some browser enhancements may work only in one company's browser. Whenever you build an e-commerce site, you should take care that the pages can be viewed by the major browsers, even outdated versions of browsers. HTML Web pages can be created with any text editor, such as Notepad or WordPad, using Microsoft Word (simply save the Word document as a Web page) or any one of several Web page development tools such as Expression Web or Dreamweaver.[5]

eXtensible Markup Language (XML)

eXtensible Markup Language (XML)
a markup language specification developed by the World Wide Web Consortium (W3C) that is designed to describe data and information

eXtensible Markup Language (XML) takes Web document formatting a giant leap forward. XML is a markup language specification developed by the World Wide Web Consortium (W3C) that is similar to HTML, but has a very different purpose. Whereas the purpose of HTML is to control the "look and feel" and display of data on the Web page, XML is designed to describe data and information. For example, consider the sample XML document in **Figure 3.19**. The first line in the sample document is the

[5]A detailed discussion of how to use HTML is beyond the scope of this text.

FIGURE 3.18 **EXAMPLE HTML CODE (A) AND WEB PAGE (B)**

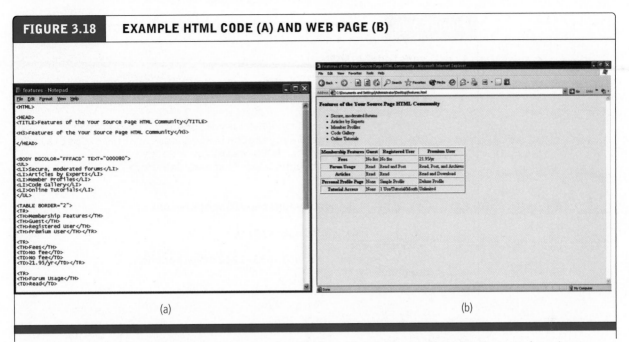

(a)   (b)

HTML is a text markup language used to create Web pages. It has a fixed set of "tags" that are used to tell the browser software how to present the content on screen. The HTML shown in Figure 3.18 (a) creates the Web page seen in Figure 3.18 (b).

XML declaration, which is always included; it defines the XML version of the document. In this case, the document conforms to the 1.0 specification of XML. The next line defines the first element of the document (the root element): < note >. The next four lines define four child elements of the root (to, from, heading, and body). The last line defines the end of the root element. Notice that XML says nothing about how to display the data, or how the text should look on the screen. HTML is used for information display in combination with XML, which is used for data description.

FIGURE 3.19 **A SIMPLE XML DOCUMENT**

```
<?xml version="1.0"?>
<note>
<to>George</to>
<from>Carol</from>
<heading>Just a Reminder</heading>
<body>Don't forget to order the groceries from FreshDirect!</body>
</note>
```

The tags in this simple XML document, such as <note>, <to>, and <from> are used to describe data and information, rather than the look and feel of the document.

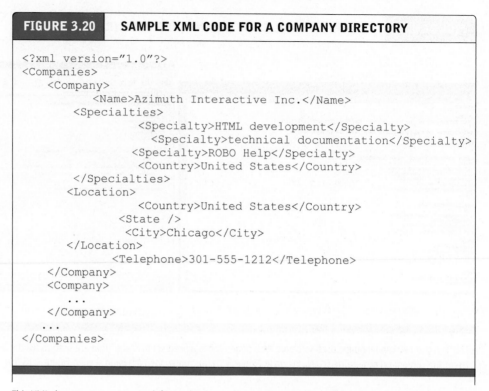

FIGURE 3.20	SAMPLE XML CODE FOR A COMPANY DIRECTORY

```
<?xml version="1.0"?>
<Companies>
    <Company>
            <Name>Azimuth Interactive Inc.</Name>
        <Specialties>
                <Specialty>HTML development</Specialty>
                    <Specialty>technical documentation</Specialty>
                <Specialty>ROBO Help</Specialty>
                <Country>United States</Country>
        </Specialties>
        <Location>
                <Country>United States</Country>
            <State />
             <City>Chicago</City>
        </Location>
                <Telephone>301-555-1212</Telephone>
    </Company>
    <Company>
        . . .
    </Company>
    . . .
</Companies>
```

This XML document uses tags to define a database of company names.

Figure 3.20 shows how XML can be used to define a database of company names in a company directory. Tags such as < Company >, < Name >, and < Specialty > can be defined for a single firm, or an entire industry. On an elementary level, XML is extraordinarily easy to learn and is very similar to HTML except that you can make up your own tags. At a deeper level, XML has a rich syntax and an enormous set of software tools, which make XML ideal for storing and communicating many types of data on the Web.

XML is "extensible," which means the tags used to describe and display data are defined by the user, whereas in HTML the tags are limited and predefined. XML can also transform information into new formats, such as by importing information from a database and displaying it as a table. With XML, information can be analyzed and displayed selectively, making it a more powerful alternative to HTML. This means that business firms, or entire industries, can describe all of their invoices, accounts payable, payroll records, and financial information using a Web-compatible markup language. Once described, these business documents can be stored on intranet Web servers and shared throughout the corporation.

XML is not yet a replacement for HTML; however, most contemporary browsers support XML. Currently, XML and HTML work side by side on the same Web pages.

WEB SERVERS AND CLIENTS

We have already described client/server computing and the revolution in computing architecture brought about by client/server computing. You already know that a server is a computer attached to a network that stores files, controls peripheral devices, interfaces with the outside world—including the Internet—and does some processing for other computers on the network.

But what is a Web server? **Web server software** refers to the software that enables a computer to deliver Web pages written in HTML to client computers on a network that request this service by sending an HTTP request. The two leading brands of Web server software are Apache, which is free Web server shareware that accounts for about 46% of the market, and Microsoft's Internet Information Services (IIS), which accounts for about 22% of the market (Netcraft.com, 2009).

Aside from responding to requests for Web pages, all Web servers provide some additional basic capabilities such as the following:

Web server software
software that enables a computer to deliver Web pages written in HTML to client computers on a network that request this service by sending an HTTP request

- *Security services*—These consist mainly of authentication services that verify that the person trying to access the site is authorized to do so. For Web sites that process payment transactions, the Web server also supports SSL, the Internet protocol for transmitting and receiving information securely over the Internet. When private information such as names, phone numbers, addresses, and credit card data needs to be provided to a Web site, the Web server uses SSL to ensure that the data passing back and forth from the browser to the server is not compromised.

- *FTP*—This protocol allows users to transfer files to and from the server. Some sites limit file uploads to the Web server, while others restrict downloads, depending on the user's identity.

- *Search engine*—Just as search engine sites enable users to search the entire Web for particular documents, search engine modules within the basic Web server software package enable indexing of the site's Web pages and content, and permit easy keyword searching of the site's content. When conducting a search, a search engine makes use of an index, which is a list of all the documents on the server. The search term is compared to the index to identify likely matches.

- *Data capture*—Web servers are also helpful at monitoring site traffic, capturing information on who has visited a site, how long the user stayed there, the date and time of each visit, and which specific pages on the server were accessed. This information is compiled and saved in a log file, which can then be analyzed. By analyzing a log file, a site manager can find out the total number of visitors, average length of each visit, and the most popular destinations, or Web pages.

The term *Web server* is also used to refer to the physical computer that runs Web server software. Leading manufacturers of Web server computers include IBM, Dell, and Hewlett-Packard. Although any personal computer can run Web server software, it is best to use a computer that has been optimized for this purpose. To be a Web server, a computer must have the Web server software installed and be connected to the Internet. Every public Web server computer has an IP address. For example, if you type http://www.pearsonhighered.com/laudon in your browser, the browser software sends a request for HTTP service to the Web server whose domain name is pearson-

database server
server designed to access specific information with a database

ad server
server designed to deliver targeted banner ads

mail server
server that provides e-mail messages

video server
server that serves video clips

Web client
any computing device attached to the Internet that is capable of making HTTP requests and displaying HTML pages, most commonly a Windows PC or Macintosh

highered.com. The server then locates the page named "laudon" on its hard drive, sends the page back to your browser, and displays it on your screen. Of course, firms also can use Web servers for strictly internal local area networking in intranets.

Aside from the generic Web server software packages, there are actually many types of specialized servers on the Web, from **database servers** that access specific information within a database, to **ad servers** that deliver targeted banner ads, to **mail servers** that provide e-mail messages, and **video servers** that provide video clips. At a small e-commerce site, all of these software packages might be running on a single computer, with a single processor. At a large corporate site, there may be hundreds or thousands of discrete server computers, many with multiple processors, running specialized Web server functions. We discuss the architecture of e-commerce sites in greater detail in Chapter 4.

A **Web client**, on the other hand, is any computing device attached to the Internet that is capable of making HTTP requests and displaying HTML pages. The most common client is a Windows or Macintosh computer, with various flavors of Unix/Linux computers a distant third. However, the fastest growing category of Web clients are not computers at all, but cell phones and handheld PDAs outfitted with wireless Web access software. In general, Web clients can be any device—including a refrigerator, stove, home lighting system, or automobile instrument panel—capable of sending and receiving information from Web servers.

WEB BROWSERS

Web browsers are software programs whose primary purpose is to display Web pages. Browsers also have added features, such as e-mail and newsgroups (an online discussion group or forum). The leading Web browsers are Internet Explorer, with about 67% of the market as of August 2009. Firefox (Mozilla) is currently the second most popular Web browser, with about 23% of the U.S. Web browser market (Net Applications, 2009). First released in 2004, Firefox is a free, open source Web browser for the Windows, Linux and Macintosh operating systems, based on Mozilla open source code (which originally provided the code for Netscape). It is small and fast and offers many new features such as pop-up blocking and tabbed browsing. Google provides over 85% of the funding for the Mozilla Foundation, creators of Firefox.

In September 2008, Google released a beta version of its entry into the Web browser competition, a small, yet technologically advanced open-source browser called Chrome. With the development of Chrome, Google hopes to create a browser that improves upon other browsers' speed, security, and stability, while also serving as a streamlined platform for even the most complex Web pages as well as a wide variety of applications. In the process, the company hopes to make inroads against the market share of Firefox and, more importantly, Internet Explorer. As of July 2009, Chrome had a market share of about 3%.

Other browsers include Apple's Safari, Opera, and Netscape Navigator, which collectively make up about 5% of the market.

3.5 THE INTERNET AND THE WEB: FEATURES

The Internet and the Web have spawned a number of powerful new software applications upon which the foundations of e-commerce are built. You can think of these all as Web services, and it is interesting as you read along to compare these services to other traditional media such as television or print media. If you do, you will quickly realize how rich is the Internet environment.

E-MAIL

Since its earliest days, **electronic mail**, or **e-mail**, has been the most-used application of the Internet. Worldwide, an estimated 1.4 billion people use e-mail, sending an estimated 247 billion messages a day! (Radicati Group, 2009). Estimates vary on the amount of spam, ranging from 40% to 90%. E-mail marketing and spam are examined in more depth in Chapter 7.

E-mail uses a series of protocols to enable messages containing text, images, sound, and video clips to be transferred from one Internet user to another. Because of its flexibility and speed, it is now the most popular form of business communication—more popular than the phone, fax, or snail mail (the U.S. Postal Service). In addition to text typed within the message, e-mail also allows **attachments**, which are files inserted within the e-mail message. The files can be documents, images, sounds, or video clips.

INSTANT MESSAGING

One of the fastest growing forms of online human communication is **instant messaging (IM)**. An instant messenger is a client software program that signs onto an instant messaging server. IM sends text messages in real time, one line at a time, unlike e-mail. E-mail messages have a time lag of several seconds to minutes between when messages are sent and received. IM displays lines of text entered on a computer almost instantaneously. Recipients can then respond immediately to the sender the same way, making the communication more like a live conversation than is possible through e-mail. To use IM, users create a buddy list they want to communicate with, and then enter short text messages that their buddies will receive instantly (if they are online at the time). And although text remains the primary communication mechanism in IM, users can insert audio clips or photos into their instant messages, and even participate in video conferencing.

The major IM systems are AOL (which first introduced IM as a proprietary consumer service in 1997), Microsoft's Windows Live Messenger, Yahoo Messenger, and Google Talk. Facebook and MySpace also offer instant messaging services. IM systems were initially developed as proprietary systems, with competing firms offering versions that did not work with one another. However, in 2006, Yahoo and Microsoft joined together to provide a level of interoperability between their respective systems, and in June 2008, Google has announced talks with Yahoo to do the same.

Meebo is a service that allows users to communicate across IM platforms, and has over 50 million members. Digsby offers a similar service. Users of instant mes-

electronic mail (e-mail)
the most-used application of the Internet. Uses a series of protocols to enable messages containing text, images, sound, and video clips to be transferred from one Internet user to another

attachment
a file inserted within an e-mail message

instant messaging (IM)
displays words typed on a computer almost instantaneously. Recipients can then respond immediately to the sender the same way, making the communication more like a live conversation than is possible through e-mail

saging are increasingly moving to mobile platforms as well. According to Nielsen Mobile estimates, the mobile version of Yahoo Messenger has about 11.7 million individuals who use the service at least once a month, AOL, 10.5 million, MSN Messenger, 7.1 million, and Google Talk, 4.5 million (eMarketer, 2009). Worldwide, the leading IM platform is Microsoft Windows Live, with 330 million active users, while in the United States, Yahoo's Messenger platform leads with 33 million unique monthly visitors (Microsoft, 2009; Yahoo, 2009).

SEARCH ENGINES

No one knows for sure how many Web pages there really are. The surface Web is that part of the Web that search engines visit and record information about. For instance, Google currently searches about 40 to 50 billion Web pages and stores information about those pages in its massive computer network located throughout the United States. But there is also a "deep Web" that could contain over a trillion additional Web pages, many of them proprietary (such as the pages of the online version of *The Wall Street Journal*, which cannot be visited without an access code) or behind corporate firewalls (Zillman, 2005).

But obviously with so many Web pages, finding Web-specific pages that can help you or your business, nearly instantly, is an important problem. The question is: how can you find the one or two Web pages you really want and need out of the 50 billion indexed Web pages?

search engine
identifies Web pages that appear to match keywords, also called queries, typed by the user and provides a list of the best matches

Search engines solve the problem of finding useful information on the Web nearly instantly, and, arguably, they are the "killer app" of the Internet era. About 168 million Americans use a search engine at least once a month, generating about 10 to 14 billion queries a month (eMarketer, 2009f, comScore 2009; Nielsen Company, 2009). There are hundreds of different search engines in the world, but the vast majority of the search results are supplied by the top five providers (see **Figure 3.21**).

Web search engines started out in the early 1990s shortly after Netscape released the first commercial Web browser. Early browsers were relatively simple software programs that roamed the nascent Web, visiting pages, and gathering information about the content of each Web page. These early programs were called variously crawlers, spiders, and wanderers; the first full-text crawler that indexed the contents of an entire Web page was called WebCrawler, released in 1994. AltaVista (1995), one of the first widely used search engines, was the first to allow "natural language" queries such as "history of Web search engines" rather than "history + Web search + search engine".

The Google search engine is continuously crawling the Web, indexing the content of each page, calculating its popularity, and caching the pages so that it can respond quickly to your request to see a page. The entire process takes about one-half of a second.

The first search engines employed simple keyword indexes of all the Web pages visited. They would count the number of times a word appeared on the Web page, and store this information in an index. These search engines could be easily fooled by Web designers who simply repeated words on their home pages. The real innovations in search engine development occurred through a program funded by the Department of Defense called the Digital Library Initiative, designed to help the Pentagon find

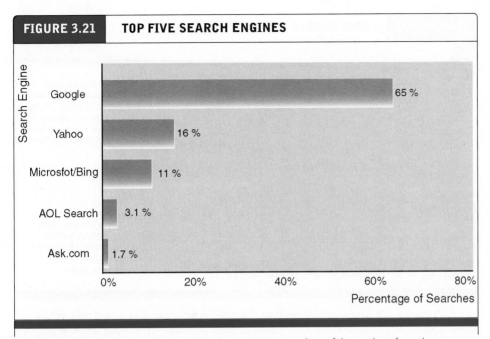

FIGURE 3.21   TOP FIVE SEARCH ENGINES

Google is, by far, the leading search engine based on its percentage share of the number of searches.
SOURCE: Based on data from Nielsen Online, 2009; comScore 2009.

research papers in large databases. Stanford, Berkeley, and three other universities became hotbeds of Web search innovations in the mid-1990s. At Stanford in 1994, two computer science students, David Filo and Jerry Yang, created a hand-selected list of their favorite Web pages and called it "Yet Another Hierarchical Officious Oracle," or Yahoo!. Yahoo initially was not a real search engine, but rather an edited selection of Web sites organized by categories the editors found useful. Yahoo has since developed "true" search engine capabilities.

In 1998, Larry Page and Sergey Brin, two Stanford computer science students, released their first version of Google. This search engine was different: not only did it index each Web page's words, but Page had discovered that the AltaVista search engine not only collected keywords from sites but also calculated what other sites linked to each page. By looking at the URLs on each Web page, they could calculate an index of popularity. AltaVista did nothing with this information. Page took this idea and made it a central factor in ranking a Web page's appropriateness to a search query. He patented the idea of a Web page ranking system (PageRank System), which essentially measures the popularity of the Web page. Brin contributed a unique Web crawler program that indexed not just keywords on a Web page, but combinations of words (such as authors and their article titles). These two ideas became the foundation for the Google search engine (Brandt, 2004). **Figure 3.22** illustrates how Google works.

Search engine Web sites have became so popular and easy to use that they also serve as major portals for the Internet (see Chapter 11). The search marketplace has become very competitive despite the dominance of Google. Both Microsoft and Yahoo have invested over a billion dollars each to match Google's search engine. In 2009, Yahoo finally threw in the towel and agreed to adopt

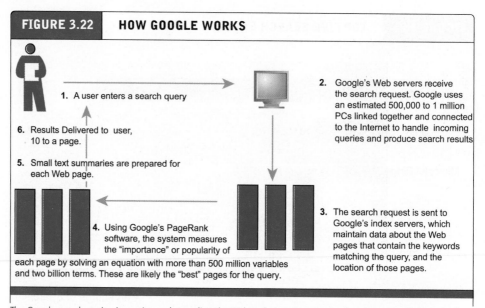

FIGURE 3.22   HOW GOOGLE WORKS

1. A user enters a search query

2. Google's Web servers receive the search request. Google uses an estimated 500,000 to 1 million PCs linked together and connected to the Internet to handle incoming queries and produce search results

6. Results Delivered to user, 10 to a page.

5. Small text summaries are prepared for each Web page.

3. The search request is sent to Google's index servers, which maintain data about the Web pages that contain the keywords matching the query, and the location of those pages.

4. Using Google's PageRank software, the system measures the "importance" or popularity of each page by solving an equation with more than 500 million variables and two billion terms. These are likely the "best" pages for the query.

The Google search engine is continuously crawling the Web, indexing the content of each page, calculating its popularity, and caching the pages so that it can respond quickly to your request to see a page. The entire process takes about one-half of a second.

Microsoft's Bing search engine instead, in return for 88% of the advertising revenues generated by search on Yahoo's sites.

Initially, few understood how to make money from search engines. That changed in 2000 when Goto.com (later Overture) allowed advertisers to bid for placement on their search engine results, and Google followed suit in 2003 with its AdWords program, which allowed advertisers to bid for placement of short text ads on Google search results. The spectacular increase in Internet advertising revenues (which have been growing over the last few years at around 20%–25% annually), has helped search engines transform themselves into major shopping tools and created an entire new industry called "search engine marketing." Search engine marketing has been the fastest growing form of advertising in the United States, reaching about $12 billion in 2009. When users enter a search term at Google, Bing, Yahoo, or any of the other Web sites serviced by these search engines, they receive two types of listings: sponsored links, for which advertisers have paid to be listed (usually at the top of the search results page), and unsponsored "organic" search results. In addition, advertisers can purchase small text ads on the right side of the search results page. Although the major search engines are used for locating general information of interest to users, search engines have also become a crucial tool within e-commerce sites. Customers can more easily search for the product information they want with the help of an internal search program; the difference is that within Web sites, the search engine is limited to finding matches from that one site. In addition, search engines are extending their services to include maps, satellite images, computer images, e-mail, group calendars, group meeting tools, and indexes of scholarly papers. Outside of e-mail, search engines are the most common online daily activity and produce the largest online audiences.

INTELLIGENT AGENTS (BOTS)

An **intelligent agent** (also known as a software robot, or bot, for short) is a software program that gathers and/or filters information on a specific topic, and then provides a list of results for the user ranked in a number of ways, such as from lowest price to availability or to delivery terms. Intelligent agents were originally invented by computer scientists interested in the development of artificial intelligence (a family of related technologies that attempt to imbue computers with human-like intelligence). However, with the advent of e-commerce on the Web, interest quickly turned to exploiting intelligent agent technology for commercial purposes. Today, there are a number of different types of bots used in e-commerce on the Web (see **Table 3.12**).

For instance, as previously noted, many search engines employ Web crawlers or spiders that crawl from server to server, compiling lists of URLs that form the database for the search engine. These Web crawlers and spiders are actually bots, automated programs that search the Web for a variety of reasons.

The shopping bot is another common type of bot. Shopping bots search online retail sites all over the Web and then report back on the availability and pricing of a range of products. For instance, you can use MySimon's shopping bot to search for a Sony digital camera. The bot provides a list of online retailers that carry a particular camera model, as well as report about whether it is in inventory and the price and shipping charges. Orbitz provides bots that find the lowest prices for airfares, hotels, and rental cars. Yahoo Shopping is a leading comparison shopping Web site with an estimated 22 million unique monthly visitors in 2009, followed by Shopzilla.com with an estimated 10–12 million, and Shopping.com with an estimated 6–7 million. Over 50% of respondents to an August 2008 survey said they would use a comparison shopping site more frequently this year due to economic circumstances.

intelligent agent
software program that gathers and/or filters information on a specific topic and then provides a list of results for the user

TABLE 3.12	TYPES OF WEB BOTS
TYPE	**EXAMPLES**
Search bot	Webcrawler.com Altavista.com
Shopping Bot	Shopzilla.com Shopping.com MySimon.com Orbitz.com
Web Monitoring Bot	WebSite-Watcher TimelyWeb.com
News Bot	WebClipping.com
Chatter Bot	Anna (Ikea) Ask Vic (Qantas) Virtual Advisor (Ultralase)

Another type of bot, called a Web monitoring bot, allows you to monitor for updated materials on the Web, and will e-mail you when a selected site has new or changed information. News bots will create custom newspapers or clip articles for you in newspapers around the world. Really Simple Syndication (RSS), discussed later in this chapter, is also a kind of automated program that sends updates and news to subscribers, and is quickly becoming the most common type of Web content monitoring tool. Chatter bots are intelligent agent online customer support tools.

ONLINE FORUMS AND CHAT

online forum
a Web application that allows Internet users to communicate with each other, although not in real time

An **online forum** (also referred to as a message board, bulletin board, discussion board, discussion group, or simply a board or forum) is a Web application that enables Internet users to communicate with each other, although not in real time. A forum provides a container for various discussions (or "threads") started (or "posted") by members of the forum, and depending on the permissions granted to forum members by the forum's administrator, enables a person to start a thread and reply to other people's threads. Most forum software allows more than one forum to be created. The forum administrator typically can edit, delete, move, or otherwise modify any thread on the forum. Unlike an electronic mailing list (such as a listserv), which automatically sends new messages to a subscriber, an online forum typically requires that the member visit the forum to check for new posts. Some forums offer an "e-mail notification" feature that notifies users that a new post of interest to them has been made.

online chat
enables users to communicate via computer in real time, that is, simultaneously. Unlike IM, chat can occur among several users

Online chat differs from an online forum in that, like IM, chat enables users to communicate via computer in real time, that is, simultaneously. However, unlike IM, which works only between two people, chat can occur among several users. Typically, users log in to a "chat room" where they can text message others. Some chat rooms offer virtual chat, which enable users to incorporate 2-D and 3-D graphics along with avatars (an icon or representation of the user) into their chat, or offer the ability to communicate via audio and/or video. Chat systems include Internet Relay Chat (IRC), Jabber, and a number of proprietary systems based on the Microsoft Windows or Java platform. E-commerce firms typically use online forums and online chat to help develop community and as customer service tools. We will discuss the use of online forums as a community-building tool further in Chapter 11.

STREAMING MEDIA

streaming media
enables music, video, and other large files to be sent to users in chunks so that when received and played, the file comes through uninterrupted

Streaming media enables live Web video, music, video, and other large-bandwidth files to be sent to users in a variety of ways that enable the user to play back the files. In some situations, such as live Web video, the files are broken into chunks and served by specialized video servers to users in chunks. Client software puts the chunks together and plays the video. In other situations, such as YouTube, a single large file is downloaded from a standard Web server to users who can begin playing the video before the entire file is downloaded. Streamed files must be viewed "live"; they cannot be stored on client hard drives without special software. Streamed files are "played" by a software program such as Microsoft's Media Player, Apple QuickTime, Flash, and RealMedia Player. There are a number of tools used to create streaming files, but one of the most common is Adobe's Flash program. The Flash player has the advantage of being built into most client browsers; no plug-in is required to play Flash files.

Sites such as YouTube, Metacafe, and Google Video have popularized user-generated video streaming. Web advertisers increasingly use video to attract viewers. Streaming audio and video segments used in Web ads and news stories are perhaps the most frequently used streaming services. As the capacity of the Internet grows, streaming media will play an even larger role in e-commerce.

COOKIES

A **cookie** is a tool used by a Web site to store information about a user. When a visitor enters a Web site, the site sends a small text file (the cookie) to the user's computer so that information from the site can be loaded more quickly on future visits. The cookie can contain any information desired by the Web site designers, including customer number, pages visited, products examined, and other detailed information about the behavior of the consumer at the site. Cookies are useful to consumers because the Web site will recognize returning patrons and not ask them to register again. Cookies are also used by advertisers to ensure visitors do not receive the same advertisements repeatedly. Cookies can also help personalize a Web site by allowing the site to recognize returning customers and make special offers to them based on their past behavior at the site. Cookies allow Web marketers to customize products and segment markets—the ability to change the product or the price based on prior consumer information (described more fully in later chapters). As we will discuss throughout the book, cookies also can pose a threat to consumer privacy, and at times they are bothersome. Many people clear their cookies at the end of every day. Some disable them entirely using tools built into most browsers.

cookie
a tool used by Web sites to store information about a user. When a visitor enters a Web site, the site sends a small text file (the cookie) to the user's computer so that information from the site can be loaded more quickly on future visits. The cookie can contain any information desired by the site designers

WEB 2.0 FEATURES AND SERVICES

Today's broadband Internet infrastructure has greatly expanded the services available to users. These new capabilities have formed the basis for new business models. Digital content and digital communications are the two areas where innovation is most rapid.

Blogs

There are so many "killer apps" on the Web that it's hard to pick one super app. But blogs arguably are a super app. A **blog**, (originally called a weblog), is a personal Web page that typically contains a series of chronological entries (newest to oldest) by its author, and links to related Web pages. The blog may include a blogroll (a collection of links to other blogs) and trackbacks (a list of entries in other blogs that refer to a post on the first blog). Most blogs allow readers to post comments on the blog entries as well. The act of creating a blog is often referred to as "blogging." Blogs are either hosted by a third-party site such as Blogger.com (owned by Google), LiveJournal, TypePad, Xanga, WordPress, or Microsoft's Windows Live Spaces, or prospective bloggers can download software such as Movable Type and bBlog to create a blog that is hosted by the user's ISP. Blog pages are usually variations on templates provided by the blogging service or software and hence require no knowledge of HTML. Therefore, millions of people without HTML skills of any kind can post their own Web pages, and share content with friends and relatives. The totality of blog-related Web sites is often referred to as the "blogoshpere."

blog
personal Web page that is created by an individual or corporation to communicate with readers

The content of blogs range from individual musings to corporate communications. Blogs have had a significant impact on political affairs, and have gained increasing notice for their role in breaking and shaping the news. Blogs have become hugely popular. While estimates on the number of blogs vary, Technorati, a blog research firm, claims there were over 133 million blogs as of 2009 (Technorati, 2009). According to eMarketer, there are 28 million active U.S. bloggers, and 97 million U.S. blog readers (eMarketer, 2009h). No one knows how many of these blogs are kept up to date or just yesterday's news. And no one knows how many of these blogs have a readership greater than one (the blog author). In fact, there are so many blogs you need a blog search engine just to find them (such as Google's or Technorati's search engine), or you can just go to a list of the most popular 100 blogs and dig in. We discuss blogs further in Chapters 6 and 7 as a marketing and advertising mechanism, and in Chapter 10 as a part of the significant growth in user-generated content.

Really Simple Syndication (RSS)

Really Simple Syndication (RSS)
program that allows users to have digital content, including text, articles, blogs and podcast audio files, automatically sent to their computers over the Internet

The rise of blogs is correlated with a new distribution mechanism for news and information from Web sites that regularly update their content. **Really Simple Syndication (RSS)** is an XML format that allows users to have digital content, including text, articles, blogs, and podcast audio files, automatically sent to their computers over the Internet. An RSS aggregator software application that you install on your computer gathers material from the Web sites and blogs that you tell it to scan and it brings new information from those sites to you. Sometimes this is referred to as "syndicated" content because it is distributed by news organizations and other syndicators (or distributors). Users download RSS aggregators and then "subscribe" to the RSS "feeds." When you go to your RSS aggregator's page, it will display the most recent updates for each channel to which you have subscribed.

RSS has rocketed from a "techie" pastime to a broad-based movement. No one knows how many people have downloaded RSS client programs, but at the New York Times, the subscriber base for RSS feeds (which include headlines, summaries, and links to full articles) went from 500,000 when first introduced in 2003 to more than 8 million today. In fact, so many users are requesting RSS feeds that online publishers are developing ways to present advertising along with the content. Microsoft has included an integrated RSS reader in Windows 7, the current version of its Windows operating system, and Google and Yahoo are selling advertising options for RSS.

Podcasting

podcast
an audio presentation—such as a radio show, audio from a movie, or simply personal audio presentations—stored as an audio file and posted to the Web

A **podcast** is an audio presentation—such as a radio show, audio from a movie, or simply personal audio presentations—stored as an audio file and posted to the Web. Listeners download the files from the Web and play them on their players or computers. While commonly associated with Apple's iPod portable music player, you can listen to MP3 podcast files with any MP3 player. Podcasting has transitioned from an amateur independent producer media in the "pirate radio" tradition, to a professional news and talk content distribution channel. According to eMarketer, about 22 million Americans listen to a podcast at least once a month, and this number is expected to grow to about 38 million by 2013 (eMarketer, 2009i).

Celebrities such as Ashton Kutcher and Fortune 500 firms now vie with thousands of independent producers by posting podcasts to get their messages out. Major advertisers are using podcasts as a new advertising channel. Microsoft has included podcast creation tools in Windows 7. No one knows for sure how many podcasts exist, but Apple's iTunes Web site provides a directory to over 100,000 podcasts. Podcasting is discussed further in Chapter 10 as one aspect of the growth in user-generated digital content.

Wikis

A **wiki** is a Web application that allows a user to easily add and edit content on a Web page. (The term wiki derives from the "wiki wiki" (quick or fast) shuttle buses at Honolulu Airport.) Wiki software enables documents to be written collectively and collaboratively. Most wiki systems are open source, server-side systems that store content in a relational database. The software typically provides a template that defines layout and elements common to all pages, displays user-editable source code (usually plain text), and then renders the content into an HTML-based page for display in a Web browser. Some wiki software allows only basic text formatting, whereas others allow the use of tables, images, or even interactive elements, such as polls and games. Since wikis by their very nature are very open in allowing anyone to make changes to a page, most wikis provide a means to verify the validity of changes via a "Recent Changes" page, which enables members of the wiki community to monitor and review the work of other users, correct mistakes, and hopefully deter "vandalism."

wiki
Web application that allows a user to easily add and edit content on a Web page

Wikis are another Web 2.0 killer app. The most well-known wiki is Wikipedia, an online encyclopedia that contains over 3 million English-language articles on a variety of topics. The Wikimedia Foundation, which operates Wikipedia, also operates a variety of related projects, including Wikibooks, a collection of collaboratively written free textbooks and manuals; Wikinews, a free content news source; and Wikitionary, a collaborative project to produce a free multilingual dictionary in every language, with definitions, etymologies, pronunciations, quotations, and synonyms. Wikimedia's sites had 60 to 65 million unique visitors in July 2009 and are routinely among the top 10 visited sites on the Web (comScore, 2009b). Wikis are also discussed further in Chapter 10.

New Music and Video Services

With the low-bandwidth connections of the early Internet, audio and video files were difficult to download and share, but with the huge growth in broadband connections, these files are not only commonplace but at major universities and other places where those under 25 years of age log on, they are the majority of Web traffic. Spurred on by the worldwide sales of more than 200 million iPods and iPhones through July 2009, as well as millions of other smartphones and MP3 players, the Internet has become a virtual digital river of music files. In 2005, Apple introduced video files to its iTunes service, offering music videos licensed from the major record labels, Pixar short films, and hit TV shows. Today, the iTunes Store has a catalog with over 10 million tracks, 40,000 television episodes, and over 5,000 movies (Apple, 2009) Onlive video viewing has also exploded in popularity, In August 2009, around 160 million Americans watched an average of 157 online videos per viewer (comScore., 2009c)!.

Video clips, Flash animations, and photo images are now routinely displayed either as part of Web sites or sent as attached files. Companies that want to demonstrate use of their products have found video clips to be extremely effective. And audio reports and discussions have also become commonplace, either as marketing materials or customer reports.

Digital video on demand is considered by many to be the "killer app" for the future Internet. Future digital video networks will be able to deliver better-than-broadcast-quality video over the Internet to computers and other devices in homes and on the road. High-quality interactive video and audio makes sales presentations and demonstrations more effective and lifelike and enable companies to develop new forms of customer support. New video, audio, and presentation approaches are also dramatically changing the nature of the media and news business. One can easily foresee the Internet as a major new distribution channel for Hollywood movies (see Chapter 10).

Internet Telephony

If the telephone system were to be built from scratch today, it would be an Internet-based packet-switched network using TCP/IP because it would be less expensive and more efficient than the alternative existing system, which involves a mix of circuit-switched legs with a digital backbone. Likewise, if cable television systems were built from scratch today, they most likely would use Internet technologies for the same reasons.

IP telephony

a general term for the technologies that use VoIP and the Internet's packet-switched network to transmit voice and other forms of audio communication over the Internet

Voice over Internet Protocol (VoIP)

protocol that allows for transmission of voice and other forms of audio communication over the Internet

Already, nearly all pre-paid long distance phone cards use the Internet for the long distance portion of calls. About 30% of the international calls from or to the United States use the Internet. Internet telephony is not entirely new. **IP telephony** is a general term for the technologies that use **Voice over Internet Protocol (VoIP)** and the Internet's packet-switched network to transmit voice, fax, and other forms of audio communication over the Internet. VoIP avoids the long distance charges imposed by traditional phone companies.

There are about 26 million residential VoIP subscribers in the United States in 2009, and this number is expanding rapidly as cable systems provide telephone service as part of their "triple play": voice, Internet, and TV as a single package. VoIP's share of international traffic has grown even faster, rising from 0.2% in 1998 to over 20% of the 417 billion minutes of international voice traffic worldwide in 2008. Skype, the most popular VoIP service in the United States, accounts for 8% of all international calling (eMarketer, 2008a; Voip.biz-news.com, 2009).

VoIP is a disruptive technology. In the past, voice and fax were the exclusive provenance of the regulated telephone networks. With the convergence of the Internet and telephony, however, this dominance is already starting to change, with local and long distance telephone providers and cable companies becoming ISPs, and ISPs getting into the phone market (see **Table 3.13**). Independent service providers such as VoIP pioneers Vonage and Skype accounted for over 60% of VoIP service in the United States in 2004, but this percentage dropped significantly by 2008 as traditional players such as Comcast, Time Warner, Verizon, AT&T, Cox, and other telephone and cable companies moved aggressively into the market. ISPs are also joining the fray: AOL developed its own Internet phone service; Yahoo bought Dialpad Communications, a VoIP service provider; and Microsoft moved to build its presence in the market with the purchase of Internet phone company Teleo Inc. In September 2005, eBay purchased Skype for $2.6 billion, but was forced to write down the value of its investment by $900 million in 2007, and is trying to sell Skype in 2009.

Internet Television

There are three ways in which people watch television over the Internet: as a streaming Flash-based video (such as YouTube videos), as download videocasts from a variety of sites such as Apple's iTunes store, or as very high definition streaming files that use the IPTV protocol. By far the most common type of Internet video is provided by YouTube, with more than 10 billion video streams a month, some of them short clips taken from television networks. Television and movie producers use videocasts as a marketing tool, and sites such as Apple's iTunes and independent sites such as videopodcasts.tv distribute millions of television downloads a month. There is very little data on the amount of television content per se (syndicated television shows vs. movies or home-made videos) that is being download. Clearly, the largest source of legal, paid television content is the iTunes store where you can purchase entire seasons of TV shows.

IPTV, the third method of watching television on the Internet, uses high-bandwidth Internet connections to deliver television programming to the home. Standard quality television requires about 3 Mbps Internet connectivity using MPEG2 compression, but high definition TV requires about 19 Mbps. MPEG4 compression requires about half as much bandwidth, but still a substantial connection.

The definition of IPTV is still fluid and many different protocols are used, such as IP multicasting to move compressed digital television streams over the Internet. Quality is an issue, and typical broadband connection speeds can support standard quality television streams, but HDTV requires much more bandwidth. Commercial IPTV is

IPTV
uses high-bandwidth Internet connections to deliver television programming to the home

TABLE 3.13	KEY IP TELEPHONY PLAYERS
SPECIALTY	COMPANY
Independent Facilities-based Service Providers	Vonage Time Warner Digital Comcast Digital Voice Cablevision/Optimum Voice Cox Digital Phone Verizon AT&T SBC
Client-based Service Providers	Skype (eBay) Net2Phone MSN Yahoo Messenger Google Talk AOL Phoneline

growing in Europe, where it has approximately 11 million subscribers. In North America, there are currently around 4.5 million subscribers (Point Topic, 2009).

Telepresence and Video Conferencing

Although video conferencing has been available for years, few have used it due to the cost of video equipment and telephone line rental fees. However, in recent years, Internet-based video conferencing has begun to overtake traditional telephone-based systems. Internet video conferencing is accessible to anyone with a broadband Internet connection and a Web camera (webcam). The most widely used Web conferencing suite of tools is WebEx (now owned by Cisco). VoIP companies such as Skype also provide more limited Web conferencing capabilities.

Telepresence takes video conferencing up several notches. Rather than single persons "meeting" by using Web cams, telepresence creates an environment in a room using multiple cameras, and screens, which surround the users. The experience is uncanny and strange at first because as you look at the people in the screens, they are looking at you directly. Broadcast quality and higher screen resolutions help create the effect. Users have the sensation of "being in the presence of their colleagues" in a way that is not true for traditional Webcam meetings. Providers of telepresence software and hardware include Cisco, HP, and Teliris.

Online Software and Web Services: Web Apps, Widgets, and Gadgets

We are all used to installing software on our PCs. But as the Web and e-commerce moves towards a service model, applications increasingly will be running off Web servers. Instead of buying a "product" in a box, you will be paying for a Web service instead. There are many kinds of Web services now available, many free, all the way from full-function applications, to much smaller chunks of code called "widgets" and "gadgets."

Widgets pull content and functionality from one place on the Web to a place where you want it, such as on your Web page, blog, or Facebook page. You can see Web widget services most clearly in photo sites such as Picnik.com, which offers a free photo editing application that is powerful and simple to use. Or drag a copy of iLike to your Facebook page and share your favorite musicians, songs, movies, and concert plans with your friends. Over 50 million people use iLike's Music applications on Facebook and other platforms. Wal-Mart, eBay, and Amazon, along with many other retailers, are creating shopping widgets that users can drag to their blogs or profile pages on various social networks so visitors can shop at a full-function online store without having to leave the page. Yahoo, Google, MSN, and Apple all have collections of hundreds of widgets available on their Web sites, and companies are expected to spend over $70 million on widgets in 2009 as marketing tools (eMarketer, 2009j).

Gadgets are closely related to widgets. They are small chunks of code that usually supply a single limited function such as a clock, calendar, or diary. You can see a collection of gadgets at http://desktop.google.com/plugins.

As bandwidth capabilities of the Internet have increased, major software firms have begun to move away from the boxed model and towards Web distribution of software as a service. The clear leader here is Google, which has online versions of word processing, spreadsheet, and presentation programs, all of which are becoming competitive with Microsoft's Office suite. Microsoft is planning for a future where Microsoft Office is a Web application, but the revenue implications are uncertain.

In the business world, digital libraries of software applications have begun that permit companies and individuals to rent software (or purchase software services) rather than buy it. For instance, SalesForce.com sells customer and sales force management software services to companies over the Internet for a subscription fee instead of a purchase price. Accessing a Web server enables a user to download the desired software. Most enterprise software firms such as SAP and Oracle are moving towards a Web services model for small businesses. This service is especially useful for expensive software packages, such as graphic design or software development tools, that few individuals or small businesses can afford.

Application Service Providers (ASPs) can assist both in processing data and in storing it, dispersing it to multiple servers rather than having it reside on just one. Backing up online has many advantages. You do not need to buy extra hard drives, and your information is backed up entirely offline in a secure environment run by professional staff. Both iBackup.com and Box.net offer backup and data distribution services such as FTP servers for sharing large media and other files.

The case study *Insight on Technology: All Mashed Up* gives you some further background on some new Web applications and services.

M-commerce Applications: The Next Big Thing

In many places around the world, mobile commerce is a viable part of e-commerce. Combining voice, data, images, audio, and video on a handheld wireless device in a high-bandwidth network is common in Japan and parts of southeast Asia. In Japan, NTT DoCoMo, Japan's largest wireless and landline phone company, offers cell phones with embedded credit cards. These permit mobile consumers to make payments easily from their cell phones, unleashing a torrent of potential "mobile commerce" applications. Already in Korea and Europe, mobile payments systems of various types are becoming firmly established. In the United States, though, up until 2007 there was very little mobile e-commerce simply because there was no truly mobile (handheld) device capable of accessing the Internet, very few Internet-based mobile services or applications, and only slow 2G cellular networks. Once the iPhone was launched in 2007 , a flood of similar devices from many manufacturers began arriving, along with thousands of applications (many of them free). 3G networks have finally become commonlplace, and 4G networks are on the horizon.

So, from nearly zero mobile commerce prior to 2007, today, mobile e-commerce revenues in the United States from mobile advertising, entertainment, location-based services, e-book sales, and app sales are finally starting to take off, and are expected to reach an estimated $5 billion (about 2% of all e-commerce) in 2009. By 2013, mobile e-commerce revenues are expected to grow to $27 billion (about 7% of all e-commerce). There is more complete coverage of these topics in later chapters

The implications for e-commerce of the "always on" mobile platform are very positive: for the first time consumers will truly be able to shop from anywhere, anytime, and from any location. The transaction costs and infrastructure costs of shopping will decline significantly, making e-commerce even more comfortable and affordable than fixed-place, physical shopping venues. Mobile e-commerce, talked about for years, is finally poised to take off.

INSIGHT ON TECHNOLOGY

ALL MASHED UP

Mashups were initially developed by the music industry. Disk jockeys developed a new remix style, known as a mashup, in which two or more songs are melded together. Often, the resulting track features the melody of one song and the vocals of another. The idea is to take different sources and produce a new work that is "greater" than the sum of its parts. Similarly, Web mashups combine the capabilities of two or more online applications to create a hybrid that provides more customer value than the original sources alone.

So far, the area of greatest innovation involves the mashup of mapping and satellite image software with local content. For instance, the City of Portland, Oregon, created a site called PortlandMaps.com that integrates Google Earth's satellite imagery with city data on land use, zoning, street construction, household income, crime rates, and other data locked in city computers. GasBuddy.com provides searchable maps showing current gasoline prices. And thousands of real estate agents have integrated Google Earth or Microsoft Maps into their Web sites so customers can see online what a house and neighborhood really looks like.

In May 2007, Google introduced Google Gears, an open source toolkit that allows users to easily integrate Google applications such as Web search, chat, maps, calendars, scheduling, and advertising into Web sites. For instance, Google's My Maps service makes it easy for users to create customized maps. Google also has collected thousands of gadgets (small stand-alone applications), many created by users, that can be added to any user Web page and provide services and newsfeeds, everything from To Do lists and calendars, to tweets and Facebook entries from your friends. Yahoo and Microsoft provide similar tools. You can think of mashups as a kind of software Legos.

While building communication links among software applications using Web-based tools is not new (these are called Web services), online mashup applications are driving a whole new set of recombinant applications. The Web services movement is being driven by the increased use of the programming language eXtensible Markup Language (XML) and a new set of computer communication standards that make it possible for computer programs to "talk" with one another without special programming. For Calin Uioreanu, creator of a site called Simplest-shop.com, Web services means that he can offer his customers the same functionality as Amazon—because it is Amazon's system he is using. Uioreanu rents a server that communicates with Amazon servers throughout the day and night to obtain continual updates on prices, availability, products, and shipping information. On some items, customers have a choice of buying from Amazon or from Simplest-Shop.com. Uioreanu makes a 15% referral fee on Amazon sales, and a full markup on products he sells. Uioreanu won't discuss profits or revenue, but claims he has about 2 million monthly hits.

What's different about the mashup programs of today is that the major vendors have greatly simplified the process of building mashups, which can involve as little work as inserting four lines of JavaScript into a program. With publicly available application programming interfaces (APIs), programmers are able to get the tools needed to pull data from many different Web sites and to combine it with other information to make an entirely new Web service. The result is that instead of the Web being merely a collection of pages, it is becoming a collection of capabilities, a platform that enables programmers to create new services quickly and inexpensively.

Probably the fastest growing type of mashups are geomashups, which combine maps with spe-

(continued)

cialized niche information and knowledge. Since Google released My Maps in April 2007, users have created over 15 million customized maps. Examples include HealthMap.org, a site that provides a global mapping of current infectious diseases, and Chicagocrime.org, which uses Google Maps to display where crimes occur in Chicago. Non-map-based mashups include Plaxo.com, a site that provides the integration of your contact information including built-in calendar and schedules; Bookburro.com, which allows users to compare book prices based on Amazon's API and other screen-scrapping tools that scour the Web for other book sites' prices; and Indeed.com, which pulls job listings from many different Web job sites and organizes them by city. The YouTube Plugin allows you to search YouTube, select a video from the results, and add it to your site. Even the browser developers are getting into the action. An add-on to the Firefox browser called Greasemonkey allows users to install scripts on their computer that customize the way a Web site works on a specific computer.

Mashups are also being taken seriously by business. IBM developed the IBM Mashup Center in February 2008. It allows employees and customers (even those that are non-technical) to create mashups by remixing information from a myriad of sources, such as Web sites and feeds, spreadsheets, databases, applications, and unstructured text from an e-mail, video, and audio to gain business insight and do their jobs more efficiently. Mashups also make it easy for businesses to create "digital dashboards," Web pages that pull together data feeds and information needed by managers to monitor their company's performance.

Mashups are also infiltrating the news business. Who was the first to report on US Airlines Flight 1549 landing in the Hudson River and the protests on the streets of Tehran? It wasn't any of the traditional services—but Twitter, quickly becoming the fastest way to find out what's going on in the world. Yahoo BOSS (Yahoo's open Build your Own Search Service) engineer Vik Singh created TweetNews. TweetNews uses Twitter as an index for determining the importance of breaking stories, which are indexed by the BOSS search engine. The result is a search engine mashup that tracks breaking news stories ranked by Twitter search results. According to Singh, using Twitter's API and the open BOSS search engine, less than 100 lines of code were required to build this mashup in about a week.

How do mashups affect e-commerce? Mashups represent one of the key technologies that is driving down the costs of building Web sites and applications. This, in turn, drives down the cost of Web entrepreneurship, the cost of initial financing, and increases the number of new Web applications that can be built. Mashups make it possible for thousands of Web entrepreneurs to create Web sites using free or very low-cost applications built by much larger firms. For large Web players, such as Google, Microsoft, Yahoo, and others who create plug-in program modules, mashups enable them to distribute their brand names across the Web at no cost. Frequently, advertising opportunities will result: you can place Google's AdSense advertising on your Web site to display Web ads with just a few lines of code. Mashups are also likely to cause an eruption of e-commerce tied to local destinations-an area today where the Web is somewhat weak. The advertising industry is looking for ways to contact consumers when they are seeking local addresses: contextual advertising tied to specific locations. With a Google or Microsoft map mashup, you can easily direct customers to local restaurants, museums, and sites. Potentially, there are billions of dollars of e-commerce revenues waiting to be developed by local advertising that occurs just at the right moment for consumers.

SOURCES: IBM Mashup Center, www-01.ibm.com/software/info/mashup-center, accessed August 11, 2009; "Mashups for Learning," By Ryann K. Ellis, American Society for Training and Development, astd.org, accessed July 16, 2009; "Flickr2Twitter: Flickr Enters the Twitter Stream," by Adam Ostrow, Mashable.com, June 30, 2009; "Gnip Adds Facebook Data To Its API Mashup," by Leena Rao, TechCrunch.com, May 18, 2009; "5 Impressive Mashups of Twitter and Flickr," by Ben Parr, Mashable.com, May 11, 2009; "Google Maps: 100+ Best Tools and Mashups," by Cameron Chapman, Mashable.com, January 8, 2009; "Social Media Will Change Your Business," by Stephen Baker and Heather Green, BusinessWeek, February 20, 2008; 'With Tools on Web, Amateurs Reshape Mapmaking," *New York Times*, July 27, 2007; "Businesses Embrace 'Mashups,'" by Lee Gomes, *Wall Street Journal*, July 3, 2007

CASE STUDY

Akamai Technologies:

The Web's Invisible Accelerator

O n January 20, 2009, the Internet experienced an unheralded meltdown that generally escaped public notice or concern. It was the inauguration day of Barack Obama in Washington D.C. More than 10 million people tried to watch the event on the Internet, but many were not able to view the live video feed because the Internet did not have the capacity to handle the traffic. Not only did 3 million users not receive any video, but many of the 7 million who were able to establish a connection were treated to burpy audio, freeze-frame video, and lost backgrounds. Cable and broadcast television viewers had no problem. Hardly the stuff of a bright future for mass audience video over the Web.

Most people love the Web, but hate the wait and the stumble that can occur. Studies have shown that most people won't stay on a Web site if the Web page and its contents take more than a few seconds to load. Other studies show that if a video ad or sports video takes too long to buffer, shows jerky frames, or poor visual quality, over half the customers will seek out a competitor's Web site. For online publishers and retailers, online video is rapidly becoming a serious component of their business strategies. In order for these initiatives to pay off, the viewing experience needs to be nearly flawless. For marketers who increasingly are using video to establish a more intimate relationship with the consumer and the brand, the quality of the Internet video experience is critical. For Web sites such as NBA.com, ESPN, CNN, MySpace, and YouTube, whose entire business model depends on delivery of high-quality video and audio, the need for high speed and quality media is vital to their success.

In today's broadband cable and DSL environment, the threshold of patience is probably much lower than a few seconds. Increased video and audio customer expectations are bad news for anyone seeking to use the Web for delivery of high-quality multimedia content such as CD-quality music and high definition video. YouTube and MySpace have unleashed a torrent of video downloads, causing total Internet traffic to expand yearly at somewhere between 50% and 100%. BitTorrent files used to share videos now account for half of U.S. Internet traffic, and on college campuses more than 80% of campus Internet use. If you are SIRIUS/XM Radio and you want to stream online music to a several million users a day, you will definitely need some help. If you are MTV and want to stream music video to your 6 million customers online, or Apple iTunes and want to download music or video files to your 50 million online customers, you will also need some help. Akamai is one of the Web's major helpers, and each of the preceding companies, along with the Web's top 2,000 domains, use Akamai's services to speed the delivery of content. Akamai serves over 1 million simultaneous media streams on a typical day.

Slow-loading Web pages and Web content—from music to video—sometimes results from poor design, but more often than not, the problem stems from the underlying infrastructure of the Internet. As you have learned in this chapter, the Internet was originally developed to carry text-based e-mail messages among a relatively small group of researchers, not bandwidth-hogging graphics, sound, and video files to tens of millions of people all at once. The Internet is a collection of networks that has to pass information from one network to another. Sometimes the handoff is not smooth. Every 1,500-byte packet of information sent over the Internet must be verified by the receiving server and an acknowledgment sent to the sender. This slows down not only the distribution of content such as music, but also slows down interactive requests, such as purchases, that require the client computer to interact with an online shopping cart. Moreover, each packet may go through many different servers on its way to its final destination, multiplying by several orders of magnitude the number of acknowledgments required to move a packet from New York to San Francisco. The Internet today spends much of its time and capacity verifying packets, contributing to a problem called "latency" or delay.

Today's Internet traffic has also changed drastically. Instead of handling only text messages, the Internet must devote 50% of its total capacity to moving BitTorrent videos and P2P network music! Music lovers dominate the Web's traffic, although video will soon surpass music traffic. On average, there are over 500,000 visitors per minute to U.S. music sites. Another 20% of capacity is devoted to video sites that spew out everything from full-length movies and trailers, to television shows and short marketing videos. At current growth rates, video traffic of all kinds will increase to more than 50% of Internet capacity by 2013 according to Cisco, the Internet networking giant. The explosion in user-generated content sites, streaming news sites, music, movies, games, and Big-Band applications such as high definition television and video, all point to a potential crisis for the Internet, leading to delays and break-downs. In 2013, according to Cisco, Internet video will be nearly 700 times the capacity of the U.S. Internet backbone in 2000. It would take well over half a million years to watch all the online video that will cross the network each month in 2013. Internet video will generate over 18 exabytes per month in 2013. Akamai, and other firms in the CDN (content distribution network) industry are one of the reasons why the Web has not already disintegrated under the load. It is not clear at this time if the entire CDN industry will be able to meet the expected demand in 2013.

There are many other causes of Internet delay or failure, including bandwidth constraints at the end-user site, Internet traffic exceeding the capacity of routers at local ISPs, malfunctioning peering points at the hand-off of data between ISPs, and traffic bottlenecks at corporate data centers. The result is that, realistically, and without special efforts, the average throughput on a busy day from San Francisco to New York is about 30 Kbps-enough for text e-mail but not enough for CNN news videos or music downloads. The solution Akamai came up with is Edge Network: it places copies of content close to the user so the content only has to move across country once and can be delivered to users from local servers.

Akamai (which means intelligent, clever, or "cool" in Hawaiian) Technologies was founded by Tom Leighton, an MIT professor of applied mathematics, and Daniel Lewin, an MIT grad student, with the idea of expediting Internet traffic to overcome these limitations. When Timothy Berners-Lee, founder of the World Wide Web, realized that congestion on the Internet was becoming an enormous problem, he issued a challenge to Leighton's research group to invent a better way to deliver Internet content. The result was a set of breakthrough algorithms that became the basis for Akamai. Lewin received his masters degree in electrical engineering and computer science in 1998. His master's thesis was the theoretical starting point for the company. It described storing copies of Web content such as pictures or video clips at many different locations around the Internet so that one could always retrieve a nearby copy, making Web pages load faster.

Officially launched in August 1998, Akamai's main product is EdgeSuite, a suite of services that allows corporations to maximize their Web performance and minimize costs while distributing their content on the Internet. EdgeSuite allows customers to move their Web content closer to end users so a user in New York City, for instance, will be served L.L.Bean pages from the New York Metro area Akamai servers, while users of the L.L.Bean site in San Francisco will be served pages from Akamai servers in San Francisco. Presto! Faster Internet. Akamai has a wide range of large corporate and government clients, from SIRIUS/XM Radio, Apple iTunes, and Yahoo to NAS-DAQ, General Motors, the National Basketball Association, and FedEx. Today, Akamai has over 20,000 corporate and government customers and operates over 48,000 servers worldwide, which makes it possible for customers' Web pages and other content to load and run quickly. In 2009, Akamai delivers between 15% and 20% of all Web traffic in the United States. Other competitors in the CDN industry include Blue-Coat, LimeLight, SAVVIS, and Mirror Image Internet.

Accomplishing this seemingly simple task—what Akamai calls "edge computing"—requires that Akamai monitor the entire Internet, locating potential sluggish areas and devising faster routes for information to travel. Frequently used portions of a client's Web site, or large video or audio files that would be difficult to send to users quickly, are stored on Akamai's 48,000 servers on 1,100 networks located in 70 countries around the world. When a user requests a song or a video file, his or her request is redirected to an Akamai server nearby and the content served from this local server. Akamai's servers are placed in Tier 1 backbone supplier networks, large ISPs, universities, and other networks. Akamai's software determines which server is optimum for the user and then transmits the "Akamaized" content locally. Web sites that are "Akamaized" can be delivered anywhere from four to ten times as fast as non-Akamaized content. Akamai has developed a number of other business services based on its Internet savvy, including content targeting of advertising based on user location and zip code, content security, business intelligence, disaster recovery, on-demand bandwidth, and computing capacity during spikes in Internet traffic in partnership with IBM, storage, global traffic management, and streaming services.

For marketing and advertising firms, Akamai offers a product called EdgeScape. EdgeScape provides enterprises with intelligence generated by the Internet's most accurate and comprehensive knowledge base of Internet network activity. Akamai's massive server deployment and relationships with networks throughout the world enable optimal collection of geography and bandwidth-sensing information. As a result of these unparalleled data-gathering techniques, Akamai provides a highly accurate knowledge base with worldwide coverage. Customers integrate a simple program into their Web server or application server. This program communicates with the Akamai database to retrieve the very latest information. The Akamai global network of servers is constantly mapping the Internet, and at the same time, each enterprise's EdgeScape software is in continual communication with the Akamai network. The result: data is always current. Advertisers can deliver ads based on country, region, city, market area, area code, county, zip code, connection type, and speed. You can see several interesting visualizations of the Internet that log basic real-time Web activity by visiting the Akamai Web site and clicking on "Data Visualizations."

While Akamai is one of the leaders in its field, its stock was severely impacted by the crash of 2008, losing 75% of value and selling at $10 per share. By July 2009, however, it had started to regroup, and it now trades in the $20 range, with Akamai showing steady, if slow, revenue growth in this recession period of about 12% a year. Akamai had $791 million in revenue in 2008, and is clearly advantaged by the strong growth in Internet video and television. Some analysts believe that Akamai's technology is challenged by new upstart companies using less expensive technology such as P2P video delivery networks. In fact, many of the formerly illegal P2P sites have entered into the legitimate CDN business of distributing video and other files through their highly distributed networks. However, Akamai can always counter P2P networks by adopting the same distribution technology. Moreover, while P2P networks are excellent for distributing titles that are not in high demand by a mass simultaneous audience, Akamai's technology has more capability to deliver videos and TV shows that are in very high demand. There are no P2P commercial networks with 100,000

SOURCES: "F.C.C. Chief Would Bar Comcast From Imposing Web Restrictions," By Saul Hansell, *New York Times*, July 12, 2008; "State of the Internet," by Akamai, Inc., June, 2008; Akamai Technologies Inc. Form 10-K for the fiscal year ended December 31, 2007, filed with the Securities and Exchange Commission on March 30, 2008; "Video Surge Divides Web Watchers," by Kevin Delaney and Bobby White, *Wall Street Journal*, August 14, 2007; "Akamai, Exxon Slide, While Apple Shines," by Thomas Gryta, *Wall Street Journal*, July 27, 2007.

servers under their direct control, and located so close to today's users. Because of the growing demand for video by very large audiences, many still remain positive about Akamai's prospects, and feel that that the company's infrastructure, "best of breed" status, and Fortune 500 client base will help it stave off competition.

Case Study Questions

1. Why does Akamai need to geographically disperse its servers to deliver its customers' Web content?

2. If you wanted to deliver software content over the Internet, would you sign up for Akamai's service? Why or why not?

3. What advantages does an advertiser derive from using Akamai's EdgeScape service? What kinds of products might benefit from this kind of service?

4. Why should Akamai be wary of P2P networks? How could it counter competition from P2P networks?

5. With the demand for high-bandwidth music and video exploding, why isn't Akamai's stock performing better? If you were an investor, what factors would encourage you to invest in Akamai? What factors would discourage you?

3.7 REVIEW

KEY CONCEPTS

■ Discuss the origins of the Internet.

The Internet has evolved from a collection of mainframe computers located on a few U.S. college campuses to an interconnected network of thousands of networks and millions of computers worldwide. The history of the Internet can be divided into three phases:

- During the *Innovation Phase* (1961–1974), the Internet's purpose was to link researchers nationwide via computer.
- During the *Institutionalization Phase* (1975–1994), the Department of Defense and National Science Foundation provided funding to expand the fundamental building blocks of the Internet into a complex military communications system and then into a civilian system.
- During the *Commercialization Phase* (1995 to the present), government agencies encouraged corporations to assume responsibility for further expansion of the network, and private business began to exploit the Internet for commercial purposes.

■ Identify the key technology concepts behind the Internet.

The Internet's three key technology components are:
- *Packet switching*, which slices digital messages into packets, routes the packets along different communication paths as they become available, and then reassembles the packets once they arrive at their destination.
- *TCP/IP*, which is the core communications protocol for the Internet. TCP establishes the connections among sending and receiving Web computers and makes sure that packets sent by one computer are received in the sequence by the other, without any packets missing. IP provides the addressing scheme and is responsible for the actual delivery of the packets.
- *Client/server technology*, which makes it possible for large amounts of information to be stored on Web servers and shared with individual users on their client computers (which may be desktop PCs, laptops, netbooks, or smartphones).

■ Describe the role of Internet protocols and utility programs.

Internet protocols and utility programs make the following Internet services possible:
- *HTTP* delivers requested Web pages, allowing users to view them.
- *SMTP* and *POP* enable e-mail to be routed to a mail server and then picked up by the recipient's server, while *IMAP* enables e-mail to be sorted before being downloaded by the recipient.
- *SSL* ensures that information transmissions are encrypted.
- *FTP* is used to transfer files from servers to clients and vice versa.
- *Telnet* is a utility program that enables work to be done remotely.
- *Ping* is a utility program that allows users to verify a connection between client and server.
- *Tracert* lets you track the route a message takes from a client to a remote computer.
- *Pathping* combines the functionality offered by Ping and Tracert.

■ Explain the structure of the Internet today.

The main structural elements of the Internet are:
- The *backbone*, which is composed primarily of high-bandwidth fiber-optic cable operated by a variety of providers.
- *IXPs*, which are hubs that use high-speed switching computers to connect the backbone with regional and local networks.
- *CANs*, which are local area networks operating within a single organization that connect directly to regional networks.
- *ISPs*, which deal with the "last mile" of service to homes and offices. ISPs offer a variety of types of service, ranging from dial-up service to broadband DSL, cable modem, T1 and T3 lines, and satellite link service.
- *Governing bodies*, such as IAB, ICANN, IESG, IETF, ISOC, W3C, and ITU. Although they do not control the Internet, have influence over it and monitor its operations.

■ Understand the limitations of today's Internet.

To envision what the Internet of tomorrow—Internet II—will look like, we must first look at the limitations of today's Internet:

- *Bandwidth limitations.* Today's Internet is slow and incapable of effectively sharing and displaying large files, such as video and voice files.
- *Quality of service limitations.* Data packets don't all arrive in the correct order, at the same moment, causing latency; latency creates jerkiness in video files and voice messages.
- *Network architecture limitations.* Servers can't keep up with demand. Future improvements to Internet infrastructure will improve the way servers process requests for information, thus improving overall speed.
- *Language development limitations.* The nature of HTML restricts the quality of "rich" information that can be shared online. Future languages will enable improved display and viewing of video and graphics.
- *Limitations arising from the "wired" nature of the Internet.* The Internet is based primarily on physical cables, which restricts the mobility of users.

■ Describe the potential capabilities of Internet II.

Internet2 is a consortium working together to develop and test new technologies for potential use on the Internet. Internet2 participants are working in a number of areas, including advanced network infrastructure, new networking capabilities, middleware, and advanced applications that incorporate audio and video to create new services.

In addition to the Internet2 project, other groups are working to expand Internet bandwidth via improvements to fiber optics and photonics. Wireless LAN and 3G telephone technologies will provide users of cellular phones and PDAs with increased access to the Internet and its various services.

The increased bandwidth and expanded connections of the Internet II era will result in a number of benefits, including IP multicasting, which will enable more efficient delivery of data; latency solutions; guaranteed service levels; lower error rates; and declining costs.

■ Understand how the World Wide Web works.

The Web was developed during 1989–1991 by Dr. Tim Berners-Lee, who created a computer program that allowed formatted pages stored on the Internet to be linked using keywords (hyperlinks). In 1993, Marc Andreesen created the first graphical Web browser, which made it possible to view documents on the Web graphically and created the possibility of universal computing. The key concepts you need to be familiar with in order to understand how the Web works are the following:

- *Hypertext,* which is a way of formatting pages with embedded links that connect documents to one another and that also link pages to other objects.
- *HTTP,* which is the protocol used to transmit Web pages over the Internet.
- *URLs,* which are the addresses at which Web pages can be found.
- *HTML,* which is the programming language used to create most Web pages and which provides designers with a fixed set of tags that are used to format a Web page.

- *XML*, which is a newer markup language that allows designers to describe data and information.
- *Web server software*, which is software that enables a computer to deliver Web pages written in HTML to client computers that request this service by sending an HTTP request. Web server software also provides security services, FTP, search engine, and data capture services. The term Web server also is used to refer to the physical computer that runs the Web server software.
- *Web clients*, which are computing devices attached to the Internet that are capable of making HTTP requests and displaying HTML pages.
- *Web browsers*, which display Web pages and also have added features such as e-mail and newsgroups.

■ Describe how Internet and Web features and services support e-commerce.

Together, the Internet and the Web make e-commerce possible by allowing computer users to access product and service information and to complete purchases online. Some of the specific features that support e-commerce include:

- *E-mail*, which uses a series of protocols to enable messages containing text, images, sound, and video clips to be transferred from one Internet user to another. E-mail is used in e-commerce as a marketing and customer support tool.
- *Instant messaging*, which allows messages to be sent between two users almost instantly, allowing parties to engage in a two-way conversation. In e-commerce, companies are using instant messaging as a customer support tool.
- *Search engines*, which identify Web pages that match a query submitted by a user. Search engines assist users in locating Web pages related to items they may want to buy.
- *Intelligent agents (bots)*, which are software programs that gather and/or filter information on a specific topic and then provide a list of results for the users.
- *Online forums* (message boards), which enable users to communicate with each other, although not in real time, and online chat, which allows users to communicate in real time (simultaneously), are being used in e-commerce as community-building tools.
- *Streaming media*, which enables music, video, and other large files to be sent to users in chunks so that when received and played, the file comes through uninterrupted. Like standard digital files, streaming media may be sold as digital content and used as a marketing tool.
- *Cookies*, which are small text files that allow a Web site to store information about a user, are used by e-commerce as a marketing tool. Cookies allow Web sites to personalize the site to the user and also permit customization and market segmentation.

The Internet II infrastructure will permit the rapid deployment of new services and greatly expand e-commerce opportunities. Emerging services include:

- *Blogs*, which are personal Web pages that typically contain a series of chronologyical entries (newest to oldest) by the author and links to related Web pages.
- *RSS*, which is an XML format that allows users to have digital content, including text, articles, blogs and podcast audio files, automatically sent to their computers over the Internet.

- *Podcasts*, which are audio presentations—such as a radio show, audio from a movie, or simply personal audio presentations—stored as an audio file and posted to the Web.
- *Wikis*, which are Web applications that allow a user to easily add and edit content on a Web page.
- *New music and video services*, such as iTunes and digital video on demand.
- *Internet telephony*, which uses VoIP to transmit audio communication over the Internet, and *Internet television (IPTV)*.
- *Online software and services*, such as Web apps, widgets, gadgets, and distribution of software applications and distributed storage offered by ASPs.
- *M-commerce applications*, which permit mobile consumers to make payments easily from their cell phones.

QUESTIONS

1. What are the three basic building blocks of the Internet?
2. What is latency, and how does it interfere with Internet functioning?
3. Explain how packet switching works.
4. How is the TCP/IP protocol related to information transfer on the Internet?
5. What technological innovation made client/server computing possible? What impact has client/server computing had on the Internet?
6. Despite the number of PCs connected to the Internet, rich information sharing is still limited. Why?
7. Why isn't the Internet overloaded? Will it ever be at capacity?
8. What types of companies form the Internet backbone today?
9. What function do the IXPs serve?
10. What is a campus area network, and who uses them?
11. Compare and contrast intranets, extranets, and the Internet as a whole.
12. What are the four major limitations of today's Internet?
13. What are some of the challenges of policing the Internet? Who has the final say when it comes to content?
14. Compare and contrast the capabilities of Wi-Fi and 3G wireless networks.
15. What are some of the new wireless standards, and how are they relevant to Internet II?
16. What are the major technological advancements that are anticipated will accompany Internet II? Define and discuss the importance of each.
17. Why was the development of the browser so significant for the growth of the Web?
18. Name the different Web markup languages and explain the differences among them.
19. Name and describe five services currently available through the Web.
20. What are at least three new services that will be available through the next generation of the Internet?

PROJECTS

1. Visit the MySimon.com Web site and investigate the following types of purchases: an iPod, a copy of the book *The Lost Symbol* (by Dan Brown), and a

dozen red roses. What did you find as you searched for these items? Describe the process, the search results, and any limitations you encountered. What are the major advantages and disadvantages of such intelligent agents?

2. Locate where cookies are stored on your computer. (They are probably in a folder entitled "cookies" within your browser program.) List the top 10 cookies you find and write a brief report describing the kinds of sites that placed the cookies. What purpose do you think the cookies serve? Also, what do you believe are the major advantages and disadvantages of cookies? In your opinion, do the advantages outweigh the disadvantages, or vice versa?

3. Call a local ISP, cable provider, and DSL provider to request information on their Internet services. Prepare a brief report summarizing the features, benefits, and costs of each. Which is the fastest? What, if any, are the downsides of selecting any of the three for Internet service (such as additional equipment purchases)?

4. Select two countries (excluding the United States) and prepare a short report describing their basic Internet infrastructure. Are they public or commercial? How and where do they connect to backbones within the United States?

5. We have mentioned several high-speed gigabit networks throughout this chapter. Investigate the topic of high-speed networks on the Web and try to find the fastest recorded network (usually used for research purposes). Then try to find the fastest commercial network handling routine Internet traffic.

WEB SITE RESOURCES www.azimuth-interactive.com/ecommerce6e

- Additional projects, exercises, and tutorials
- Careers: Explore career opportunities in e-commerce
- Raising capital and business plans

CHAPTER 4

Building an E-commerce Web Site

After reading this chapter, you will be able to:

- Explain the process that should be followed in building an e-commerce Web site.
- Describe the major issues surrounding the decision to outsource site development and/or hosting.
- Identify and understand the major considerations involved in choosing Web server and e-commerce merchant server software.
- Understand the issues involved in choosing the most appropriate hardware for an e-commerce site.
- Identify additional tools that can improve Web site performance.

Right-Sizing a Web Site

L et's say you've decided to create a Web site for your successful garden equipment company. You've been in business for five years, have established a regional brand for high-quality gardening tools, and have about 12,000 retail customers and 21 wholesale dealers who purchase from you. Based on a marketing report you commissioned, you expect that in the first year your Web site will have about 1,400 visitors a day. The average visitor will look at eight pages, producing about 4 million page views a year. About 10% will purchase something, and the rest will browse to explore prices and products. However, in peak times (during the months of April, May, June, and December), you expect peak loads of 3,000 customers a day, concentrated during the hours of 9 a.m. to 5 p.m. local time, producing about 375 visitors per hour or 6 per second. During this time, your Web site will have to serve up about 40 screens per second, with most of the content being read from a database of product and price information. Pages must be served up within 2 seconds of a customer click during peak times or customers may lose patience and go elsewhere. You've decided to operate your own on-site Web infrastructure, including hardware and software. You have contracted out the Web site design to a design firm and have made arrangements with the local phone company to provide an Internet connection.

Before you can proceed, there are some questions you will need answered. How many Web servers will your site require? How many CPUs should each server have? How powerful does the site's database server need to be? What kind of connection speed do you need to the Internet? How about power? Is the local utility reliable, and do you need backup diesel-powered generators? Until recently, finding the answers to questions such as these was often done on a trial-and-error basis. However, hardware and software vendors such as IBM, Microsoft, and Hewlett-Packard have developed a number of simulation tools that can help you find the right answers.

IBM's simulator is called the On Demand Performance Advisor (OPERA) (formerly known as the High Volume Web Sites Simulator). OPERA enables users to estimate the performance and capacity of a Web server based on workload patterns, performance objectives, and specific hardware and software. OPERA has a very easy-to-use interface that includes pre-built workload patterns for various e-commerce applications, such as shopping, banking, brokerage, auction, portal, B2B, and reservation systems, that can be modified as necessary based on the user's own data or assumptions. It can provide what-if analyses for various performance parameters such as throughput, response time, resource utilization, number of concurrent users, and page view rate. It also provides special algorithms to address increases in Web traffic during peak usage periods. The simulator includes built-in performance characteristics for various types of hardware (such IBM, Sun, and HP servers), software, and infrastructure models. OPERA uses an analytic model to generate reports that allow users to assess the adequacy of proposed hardware and software configurations, forecast performance, and graphically identify bottlenecks that might develop. IBM also offers Sonoma, a Web service based on OPERA, that can be used to estimate the performance and capacity of service-oriented architecture (SOA) workloads.

Users of the simulator have included Charles Schwab, Aetna, Fidelity, Visa, Bank of America, Walmart.com, and eBay, among others. eBay first turned to the simulator when it was attempting to cope with dramatic increases in customer demand. In its early years, eBay needed to serve up only about 1 million pages per hour, but as its customer base grew, and the number of page views per hour significantly increased, its original Web site hardware and software became insufficient, creating customer resistance. After running a simulation of its current and likely future workload, eBay decided to rebuild its auction system around IBM's WebSphere application that integrates a variety of software tools into an integrated Web site design. Later, eBay returned to OPERA to examine the performance of its Sell Your Item application on its new three-tier Web server architecture. The simulation enabled eBay to determine both the number of servers (36) and the optimal CPU (the IBM x335, which provided a 30% performance increase due to a higher-speed CPU, increased amount of RAM, and faster bus speed) required to meet current workloads and future growth targets.

But let's say you're not eBay or Fidelity, and are just creating the proverbial "one-person-in-a-garage-just-getting-started" kind of Web site. For instance, Dave Novak created Steamshowers4Less.com using a MacBook Pro computer in a spare bedroom. SteamShowers4Less.com is an eBay success story. Its Web site offers products for luxury bathrooms on a budget, and focuses on the do-it-yourself (DIY) market. The company specializes in walk-in and whirlpool computerized steam showers and claims to be the first company to manufacture its own iPod-compatible unit. Luxe bath? Its models have FM stereo, speakers, computer control, LED lighting, foot massagers and much more. Novak now sells over $1 million a year in bath fixtures.

For really small sites, micro-businesses with just a few people, there are many less costly alternatives to using a sophisticated tool like IBM's OPERA. Nevertheless, you still face the same problems as the big Web sites: how many computers, what size, how large a pipe to the Internet, and what kind of database? For a really small company, it generally does not make sense to spend the time and money to DIY. Instead it makes more sense to let the professionals worry about these problems. For instance, one solution is to build a Web site using pre-built templates offered by Yahoo Merchant Solutions, Amazon, eBay, Design.NetworkSolutions.com, or hundreds of other online sites. Fees range from a few hundred dollars to several thousand. These firms host your Web site and they worry about capacity and scale issues as your firm grows. For instance, Yahoo Merchant Solutions offers three different packages—Starter, Standard, and Professional. As the business grows, you can move up to a more comprehensive package. Amazon will even handle the fulfillment of orders for you and probably do a much better job than you or your limited staff can do.

Another solution is to hire a local professional designer (for about $1,000 to $5,000) and have them build you an e-commerce installation that runs off a single computer and broadband connection to your office. You can grow by trial and error. If your site becomes popular, and you need more computing power, buy a newer PC with multicore processors, greater speed, and a much larger hard drive or hard drive array. You can always upgrade your Web connection to a faster speed if users experience a slow down in your Web site. Still another solution is to do everything yourself (design the Web site, procure and build the Web servers, and connect to the Internet) at first until you start attracting customers.

The cost of building Web sites has fallen drastically, not just because of the fall in hardware costs, but also because the cost of software needed to build and operate Web sites has fallen also, sometimes to zero. There are thousands of open source software tools available to develop Web sites and associated databases that will cost you nothing. Many of these tools can be used by amateurs, some are as simple to use as blog software tools, while others require a technical background and training. Analysts believe that a Web site costing over $1 million in 2000 could be built for less than $50,000 in 2009. For instance, you can obtain the Linux operating system to run your Web site for next to nothing, along with osCommerce, an open source shopping cart order system. In the past, building your own custom shopping cart could easily cost $250,000 and up. Google provides more than 20 Web site management and operations tools for free. However, in both of these DIY solutions, you will have to worry about how to keep up with growth, about the stability of local power supplies, the ability of your computers to meet peak demands, and the ability of your local Internet connection provider to supply your needs for continuous Internet connectivity. Even if you decide to let an outside vendor host your new Web site, you will still need to address these questions. Remember, the "e" in e-commerce does not stand for easy.

SOURCES: "The Open Source Web Design Toolbox: 100 Web Design Template Sources, Tools and Resources," by Emil Mustafa, Designvitality.com, July 28, 2009"; Home-based Hits That Do Big Business," StartupNation, July 28, 2009; "23 Google Tools for Your Website," by Tom Now, StartupNation, July 18th, 2009; "End-to-End Banking Transformation in the Product Domain" by Chin Huang, Nimesh Bhatia, and Steve Chu. IBM High Performance On Demand Solutions (HiPODS), May 2009; "Why Your Web Startup Will Fail," by Eric Shelkie, Ideasonideas.com. January 2nd, 2009; "Sonoma:Web Service for Estimating Capacity and Performance of Service-Oriented Architecture (SOA) Workloads," by Eugene Hung, Qi He, Jinzy Zhu, IBM Working Paper, October 9, 2006; "HiPODs Model: An eBay Case Study," by Noshir C.Wadia, Jayashree Subrahmonia, and Umesh Talwalkar, IBM Conference on Performance Engineering and Best Practices, June 21, 2004; "More About High Volume Web Sites," by High-Volume Web Sites Team, IBM Redbook, March 8, 2004; "HVWS Simulator: An eBay Case Study," High Performance On Demand Solutions Team and eBay, February 27, 2004.

I n Chapter 3, you learned about the infrastructure of the Internet and the Web, e-commerce's technological foundation. Now it's time to focus on the next step: building an e-commerce site. In this chapter, you will examine the important factors that a manager needs to consider when building an e-commerce site. The focus will be on the managerial and business decisions you must make before you begin to build Web pages and Web sites, and which you will continually need to make during the life of your Web site. Although building a sophisticated e-commerce site isn't easy, today's tools for building Web sites are much less expensive and far more powerful than they were during the early days of e-commerce. You do not have to be Amazon or eBay to create a successful Web site. In this chapter, we focus on both small and medium-sized businesses that want to build a Web site, and much larger corporate entities that serve thousands of customers a day, or even an hour. As you will see, although the scale may be very different, the principles and considerations are basically the same.

4.1 BUILDING AN E-COMMERCE WEB SITE: A SYSTEMATIC APPROACH

Building a successful e-commerce site requires a keen understanding of business, technology, and social issues, as well as a systematic approach. E-commerce is just too important to be left totally to technologists and programmers.

The two most important management challenges in building a successful e-commerce site are (1) developing a clear understanding of your business objectives and (2) knowing how to choose the right technology to achieve those objectives. The first challenge requires you to build a plan for developing your firm's site. The second challenge requires you to understand some of the basic elements of e-commerce infrastructure. Let the business drive the technology.

Even if you decide to outsource the entire e-commerce site development and operation to a service provider, you will still need to have a site development plan and some understanding of the basic e-commerce infrastructure issues such as cost, capability, and constraints. Without a plan and a knowledge base, you will not be able to make sound management decisions about e-commerce within your firm (Laudon and Laudon, 2009).

PIECES OF THE SITE-BUILDING PUZZLE

Let's assume you are a manager for a medium-sized, industrial parts firm of around 10,000 employees worldwide, operating in 10 countries in Europe, Asia, and North America. Senior management has given you a budget of $1 million to build an e-commerce site within one year. The purpose of this site will be to sell and service the firm's 20,000 customers, who are mostly small machine and metal fabricating shops around the world. Where do you start?

FIGURE 4.1	PIECES OF THE E-COMMERCE SITE-BUILDING PUZZLE

Building an e-commerce Web site requires that you systematically consider the many factors that go into the process.

First, you must be aware of the main areas where you will need to make decisions (see **Figure 4.1**). On the organizational and human resources fronts, you will have to bring together a team of individuals who possess the skill sets needed to build and manage a successful e-commerce site. This team will make the key decisions about technology, site design, and the social and information policies that will be applied at your site. The entire site development effort must be closely managed if you hope to avoid the disasters that have occurred at some firms.

You will also need to make decisions about your site's hardware, software, and telecommunications infrastructure. Although you will have technical advisors help you make these decisions, ultimately the operation of the site is your responsibility. The demands of your customers should drive your choices of technology. Your customers will want technology that enables them to find what they want easily, view the product, purchase the product, and then receive the product from your warehouses quickly. You will also have to carefully consider your site's design. Once you have identified the key decision areas, you will need to think about a plan for the project.

PLANNING: THE SYSTEMS DEVELOPMENT LIFE CYCLE

Your second step in building an e-commerce site will be creating a plan document. In order to tackle a complex problem such as building an e-commerce site, you will have to proceed systematically through a series of steps. One methodology for developing an e-commerce site plan is the systems development life cycle (see **Figure 4.2**).

FIGURE 4.2 WEB SITE SYSTEMS DEVELOPMENT LIFE CYCLE

**systems development
life cycle (SDLC)**

a methodology for
understanding the business
objectives of any system
and designing an
appropriate solution

The **systems development life cycle (SDLC)** is a methodology for understanding the business objectives of any system and designing an appropriate solution. Adopting a life cycle methodology does not guarantee success, but it is far better than having no plan at all. The SDLC method also helps in creating documents that communicate to senior management the objectives of the site, important milestones, and the uses of resources. The five major steps involved in the systems development life cycle for an e-commerce site are:

- Systems analysis/planning
- Systems design
- Building the system
- Testing
- Implementation

SYSTEMS ANALYSIS/PLANNING: IDENTIFY BUSINESS OBJECTIVES, SYSTEM FUNCTIONALITY, AND INFORMATION REQUIREMENTS

The systems analysis/planning step of the SDLC tries to answer the question, "What do we want the e-commerce site to do for our business?" The key lesson to be learned here is to let the business decisions drive the technology, not the reverse. This will ensure that your technology platform is aligned with your business. We will assume here that you have identified a business strategy and chosen a business model to achieve your strategic objectives (see Chapter 2). But how do you translate your strategies, business models, and ideas into a working e-commerce site?

One way to start is to identify the specific business objectives for your site, and then develop a list of system functionalities and information requirements. **Business objectives** are simply capabilities you want your site to have.

System functionalities are types of information systems capabilities you will need to achieve your business objectives. The **information requirements** for a system are the information elements that the system must produce in order to achieve the business objectives. You will need to provide these lists to system developers and programmers so they know what you as the manager expect them to do.

Table 4.1 describes some basic business objectives, system functionalities, and information requirements for a typical e-commerce site. As shown in the table, there are nine basic business objectives that an e-commerce site must deliver. These objectives must be translated into a description of system functionalities and ultimately into a set of precise information requirements. The specific information requirements for a system typically are defined in much greater detail than Table 4.1 indicates. To a large extent, the business objectives of an e-commerce site are not that different from those of an ordinary retail store. The real difference lies in the system functionalities and information requirements. In an e-commerce site,

business objectives
capabilities you want your site to have

system functionalities
types of information systems capabilities you will need to achieve your business objectives

information requirements
the information elements that the system must produce in order to achieve the business objectives

TABLE 4.1	SYSTEM ANALYSIS: BUSINESS OBJECTIVES, SYSTEM FUNCTIONALITY, AND INFORMATION REQUIREMENTS FOR A TYPICAL E-COMMERCE SITE	
BUSINESS OBJECTIVE	**SYSTEM FUNCTIONALITY**	**INFORMATION REQUIREMENTS**
Display goods	Digital catalog	Dynamic text and graphics catalog
Provide product information (content)	Product database	Product description, stocking numbers, inventory levels
Personalize/customize product	Customer on-site tracking	Site log for every customer visit; data mining capability to identify common customer paths and appropriate responses
Execute a transaction payment	Shopping cart/payment system	Secure credit card clearing; multiple options
Accumulate customer information	Customer database	Name, address, phone, and e-mail for all customers; online customer registration
Provide after-sale customer support	Sales database	Customer ID, product, date, payment, shipment date
Coordinate marketing/advertising	Ad server, e-mail server, e-mail, campaign manager, ad banner manager	Site behavior log of prospects and customers linked to e-mail and banner ad campaigns
Understand marketing effectiveness	Site tracking and reporting system	Number of unique visitors, pages visited, products purchased, identified by marketing campaign
Provide production and supplier links	Inventory management system	Product and inventory levels, supplier ID and contact, order quantity data by product

the business objectives must be provided entirely in digital form without buildings or salespeople, twenty-four hours a day, seven days a week.

SYSTEM DESIGN: HARDWARE AND SOFTWARE PLATFORMS

Once you have identified the business objectives and system functionalities, and have developed a list of precise information requirements, you can begin to consider just how all this functionality will be delivered. You must come up with a **system design specification**—a description of the main components in the system and their relationship to one another. The system design itself can be broken down into two components: a logical design and a physical design. A **logical design** includes a data flow diagram that describes the flow of information at your e-commerce site, the processing functions that must be performed, and the databases that will be used. The logical design also includes a description of the security and emergency backup procedures that will be instituted, and the controls that will be used in the system.

A **physical design** translates the logical design into physical components. For instance, the physical design details the specific model of server to be purchased, the software to be used, the size of the telecommunications link that will be required, the way the system will be backed up and protected from outsiders, and so on.

Figure 4.3(a) presents a data flow diagram for a simple high-level logical design for a very basic Web site that delivers catalog pages in HTML in response to HTTP requests from the client's browser, while **Figure 4.3(b)** shows the corresponding physical design. Each of the main processes can be broken down into lower-level designs that are much more precise in identifying exactly how the information flows and what equipment is involved.

BUILDING THE SYSTEM: IN-HOUSE VERSUS OUTSOURCING

Now that you have a clear idea of both the logical and physical design for your site, you can begin considering how to actually build the site. There are many choices here and much depends on how much money you are willing to spend. Choices range from outsourcing everything (including the actual systems analysis and design) to building everything yourself (in-house). **Outsourcing** means that you will hire an outside vendor to provide the services involved in building the site that you cannot perform with in-house personnel. You also have a second decision to make: will you host (operate) the site on your firm's own servers or will you outsource the hosting to a Web host provider? These decisions are independent of each other, but they are usually considered at the same time. There are some vendors who will design, build, and host your site, while others will either build or host (but not both). **Figure 4.4** on page 212 illustrates the alternatives.

Build Your Own versus Outsourcing

Let's take the building decision first. If you elect to build your own site, there are a range of options. Unless you are fairly skilled, you should use a pre-built template to create the Web site. For example, Yahoo Merchant Solutions, Amazon Stores, and eBay

system design specification
description of the main components in a system and their relationship to one another

logical design
describes the flow of information at your e-commerce site, the processing functions that must be performed, the databases that will be used, the security and emergency backup procedures that will be instituted, and the controls that will be used in the system

physical design
translates the logical design into physical components

outsourcing
hiring an outside vendor to provide the services you cannot perform with in-house personnel

FIGURE 4.3 A LOGICAL AND PHYSICAL DESIGN FOR A SIMPLE WEB SITE

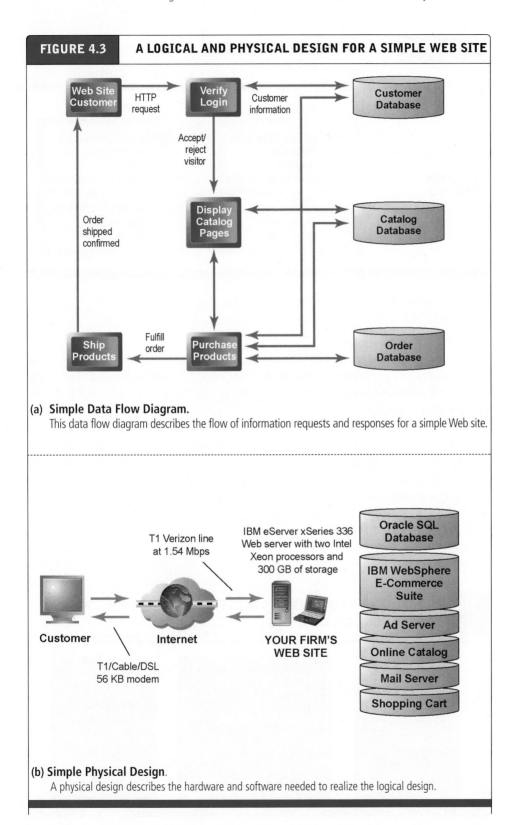

(a) **Simple Data Flow Diagram.**
This data flow diagram describes the flow of information requests and responses for a simple Web site.

(b) **Simple Physical Design**.
A physical design describes the hardware and software needed to realize the logical design.

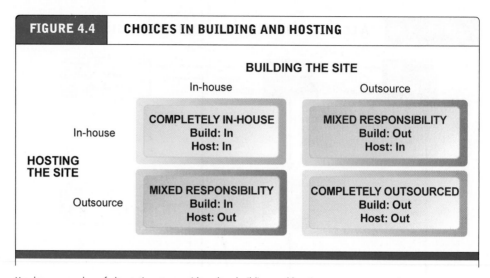

FIGURE 4.4   CHOICES IN BUILDING AND HOSTING

You have a number of alternatives to consider when building and hosting an e-commerce site.

all provide templates that merely require you to input text, graphics, and other data, as well as the infrastructure to run the Web site once it has been created. This is the least costly and simplest solution but you will be limited to the "look and feel" and functionality provided by the template and infrastructure.

If you have some experience with computers, you might decide to build the site yourself "from scratch." There is a broad variety of tools, ranging from those that help you build everything truly "from scratch," such as Adobe Dreamweaver and Microsoft Expression, to top-of-the-line prepackaged site-building tools that can create sophisticated sites customized to your needs. **Figure 4.5** illustrates the spectrum of tools available. We will look more closely at the variety of e-commerce software available in Section 4.2.

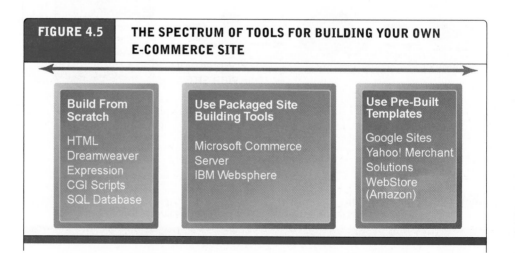

FIGURE 4.5   THE SPECTRUM OF TOOLS FOR BUILDING YOUR OWN E-COMMERCE SITE

The decision to build a Web site on your own has a number of risks. Given the complexity of features such as shopping carts, credit card authentication and processing, inventory management, and order processing, the costs involved are high, as are the risks of doing a poor job. You will be reinventing what other specialized firms have already built, and your staff may face a long, difficult learning curve, delaying your entry to market. Your efforts could fail. On the positive side, you may be better able to build a site that does exactly what you want, and more important, develop the in-house knowledge to allow you to change the site rapidly if necessary due to a changing business environment.

If you choose more expensive site-building packages, you will be purchasing state-of-the art software that is well tested. You could get to market sooner. However, to make a sound decision, you will have to evaluate many different packages and this can take a long time. You may have to modify the packages to fit your business needs and perhaps hire additional outside vendors to do the modifications. Costs rise rapidly as modifications mount. A $4,000 package can easily become a $40,000 to $60,000 development project (see **Figure 4.6**). If you choose the template route, you will be limited to the functionality already built into the templates, and you will not be able to add to the functionality or change it.

In the past, bricks-and-mortar retailers in need of an e-commerce site typically designed the site themselves (because they already had the skilled staff in place and had extensive investments in information technology capital such as databases and telecommunications). However, as Web applications have become more sophisticated, larger retailers today rely heavily on vendors to provide sophisticated Web site capabilities, while also maintaining a substantial internal staff. Small start-ups may build their own sites from scratch using in-house technical personnel in an effort to

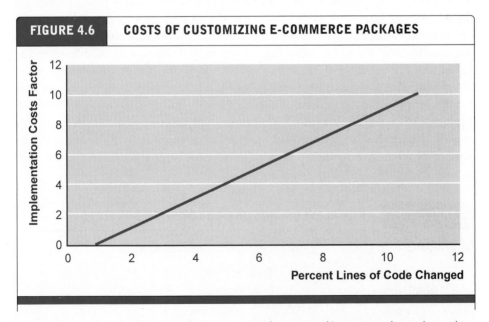

FIGURE 4.6 — **COSTS OF CUSTOMIZING E-COMMERCE PACKAGES**

While sophisticated site development packages appear to reduce costs and increase speed to market, as the modifications required to fit the package to your business needs rise, costs also rise exponentially.

keep costs low. Medium-size start-ups will often purchase a sophisticated package and then modify it to suit their needs. Very small mom-and-pop firms seeking simple storefronts will use templates. For e-commerce sites, the costs of building has dropped dramatically in the last five years, resulting in lower capital requirements for all players (see *Insight on Business: Curly Hair and MotorMouths: Getting Started on the Cheap*).

Host Your Own versus Outsourcing

Now let's look at the hosting decision. Most businesses choose to outsource hosting and pay a company to host their Web site, which means that the hosting company is responsible for ensuring the site is "live," or accessible, twenty-four hours a day. By agreeing to a monthly fee, the business need not concern itself with many of the technical aspects of setting up a Web server and maintaining it, telecommunications links, nor with staffing needs.

co-location

when a firm purchases or leases a Web server (and has total control over its operation) but locates the server in a vendor's physical facility. The vendor maintains the facility, communications lines, and the machinery

You can also choose to *co-locate*. With a **co-location** agreement, your firm purchases or leases a Web server (and has total control over its operation) but locates the server in a vendor's physical facility. The vendor maintains the facility, communications lines, and the machinery. Co-location has expanded with the spread of virtualization where one server has multiple processors (4–16) and can operate multiple Web sites at once with multiple operating systems. In this case, you do not buy the server but rent its capabilities on a monthly basis, usually at one-quarter of the cost of owning the server itself. See **Table 4.2** for a list of some of the major hosting/co-location providers. There is an extraordinary range of prices for co-hosting, ranging from $4.95 a month, to several hundred thousands of dollars per month depending on the size of the Web site, bandwidth, storage, and support requirements.

Hosting and co-location have become a commodity and a utility: costs are driven by very large providers (such as IBM and Qwest) who can achieve large economies of scale by establishing huge "server farms" located strategically around the country and the globe. What this means is that the cost of pure hosting has fallen as fast as the fall in server prices, dropping about 50% every year! Telecommunications costs have also fallen. As a result, most hosting services seek to differentiate themselves from the commodity hosting business by offering extensive site design, marketing, optimization and other services. Small, local ISPs also can be used as hosts, but service reliability is an issue. Will the small ISP be able to provide uninterrupted service, 24x7x365? Will they have service staff available when you need it?

TABLE 4.2	KEY PLAYERS: HOSTING/CO-LOCATION SERVICES
GoDaddy.com	Qwest Communications
BlueHost	NTT/Verio
IBM Global Services	Rackspace
GSI Commerce	ServerBeach

INSIGHT ON BUSINESS

CURLY HAIR AND MOTORMOUTHS: GETTING STARTED ON THE CHEAP

With so many big companies with national brand names dominating the e-commerce scene, and with the top 100 retail firms collecting over 90% of the revenues, you may wonder if there's a chance for the little guy anymore, the complete amateurs. The answer is yes: there's still at least about $23 billion left in potential online retail sales to go for, with additional money to be made from advertising revenues. As it turns out, being big does not necessarily make you nimble.

NaturallyCurly.com is a good example of a low entry cost, niche-oriented portal site. Two reporters, Gretchen Heber and Michelle Breyer, started the site with $500 in 1998.

Both had naturally curly hair. "We had long diatribes complaining about our curly hair on very muggy days," says Heber. Or they'd talk about how good it looked on other days. Based on a hunch that other people also needed help coping with curly hair issues, they launched NaturallyCurly.com. They spent $200 on the domain name, and bought some curly hair products to review on the site. The site was built with a simple Web server and the help of a 14-year-old Web page designer. The idea was to act as a content site with community feedback. They added a bulletin board for users to send in their comments.

There were no competitors at first, and even without advertising on Google, they

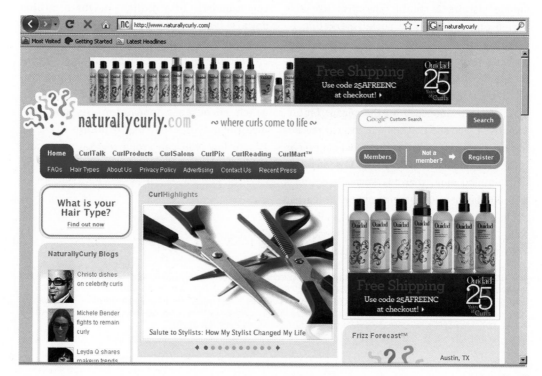

(continued)

started showing up in Google searches for "curly hair" near or at the top of the search results list. In 2000, after a year of operation, they got an e-mail from Procter & Gamble, the world's largest personal care products company, asking if they would accept advertising for $2,000 a month for two years. From there, the site grew by adding additional advertising from leading hair care products companies such as Aveda, Paul Mitchell, and Redken, among others, and now generates revenue in excess of $1 million from advertising and sales of products on curlmart.com, its online boutique for curly hair products. In May 2007, the firm received an investment of $600,000 from a venture capital firm that was used to hire a marketing person and support staff, improve its Web technology, and expand its shipping and handling operations.

By 2009, NaturallyCurly.com had 200,000 registered members and attracts about 30,000 unique visitors a month. The firm has also moved aggressively into social marketing by establishing a Facebook site, and a Twitter account, hoping to tap into the "curly hair community."

MotorMouths.com is another good example of a Web site launched on the cheap. Motor-Mouths, a Web site that summarizes car reviews and provides rankings of every model of new car, is the brain child of John Tayman. Tayman began with nothing more than his PowerBook and a $10,000 budget. Researching online, he learned about free open source software such as Ruby on Rails, and RentACoder.com and Elance.com, sites that helped him find freelance software programmers that could help him build the site. Within a few months, he had a virtual staff of 20, from five different countries, working on various pieces of his site. MotorMouths.com officially launched in January 2009, for a total cost of $9,800, and about 10 hours a week of "sweat equity" on Tayman's part. Upkeep costs him about $75 a month in server fees.

Growth within the first few months was slow and steady, with about 10,000 visitors a week who find the site primarily through word-of-mouth. Tayman is optimistic about the future: "If our current growth trends hold and the ad trends hold, MotorMouths could be a $250,000-revenue company in 18 months." Not bad for a $10,000 investment.

The moral of the story: its never been cheaper to start a Web-based company. According to Chris Gill, president of the Silicon Valley Association of Startup Entrepreneurs (SVASE), "What would have cost you a quarter of a million, maybe a million dollars two or three years ago, now costs $25,000." And in fact, the recession may be an entrepreneur's best friend. In a poor economy, failures are not so noticeable, which creates a better environment for risk-taking, which encourages innovation. As one tech investor put it: "The cost of failure is cheap. It's so low, you can swing the bat way more times."

▬ **SOURCES**: "Software and Technology Services NaturallyCurly.com, Inc., "BusinessWeek.com, July 28, 2009; "Assignment 7: Recession May Be Good Time for Startups," ABC7News.com, June 22, 2009; "NaturallyCurly.com Web Traffic," Quantcast.com, June, 2009; "The New Internet Startup Boom: Get Rich Slow," by Josh Quittner, Time.com, April 9, 2009; "About Us", NaturallyCurly.com, 2009; " Curl Tamers," *Jewish Woman*, Summer 2008; "Turning Curls into Dollar Signs," Business Opportunities Weblog, March 2008; "Bad Hair Days Lead Pair to Web Incubator and Venture Capital," by Bob Tedeschi, *New York Times*, May 21, 2007; "Naturally Curly Raises $600,000 in Funding," by Kristen Nicole, Mashable.com, May 20, 2007.

There are several disadvantages to outsourcing hosting. If you choose a vendor, make sure the vendor has the capability to grow with you. You need to know what kinds of security provisions are in place for backup copies of your site, internal monitoring of activity, and security track record. Is there a public record of a security breach at the vendor? Most Fortune 500 firms do their own hosting so they can control the Web environment. On the other hand, there are risks to hosting your own site if you are a small business. Your costs will be higher than if you had used a large outsourcing firm because you don't have the market power to obtain low-cost hardware and telecommunications. You will have to purchase hardware and software, have a physical facility, lease communications lines, hire a staff, and build security and backup capabilities yourself.

TESTING THE SYSTEM

Once the system has been built and programmed, you will have to engage in a testing process. Depending on the size of the system, this could be fairly difficult and lengthy. Testing is required whether the system is outsourced or built in-house. A complex e-commerce site can have thousands of pathways through the site, each of which must be documented and then tested. **Unit testing** involves testing the site's program modules one at a time. **System testing** involves testing the site as a whole, in the same way a typical user would when using the site. Because there is no truly "typical" user, system testing requires that every conceivable path be tested. Final **acceptance testing** requires that the firm's key personnel and managers in marketing, production, sales, and general management actually use the system as installed on a test Internet or intranet server. This acceptance test verifies that the business objectives of the system as originally conceived are in fact working. It is important to note that testing is generally under-budgeted. As much as 50% of the software effort can be consumed by testing and rebuilding (usually depending on the quality of initial design).

unit testing
involves testing the site's program modules one at a time

system testing
involves testing the site as a whole, in a way the typical user will use the site

acceptance testing
verifies that the business objectives of the system as originally conceived are in fact working

IMPLEMENTATION AND MAINTENANCE

Most people unfamiliar with systems erroneously think that once an information system is installed, the process is over. In fact, while the beginning of the process is over, the operational life of a system is just beginning. Systems break down for a variety of reasons—most of them unpredictable. Therefore, they need continual checking, testing, and repair. Systems maintenance is vital, but sometimes not budgeted for. In general, the annual system maintenance cost will roughly parallel the development cost. A $40,000 e-commerce site will likely require a $40,000 annual expenditure to maintain. Very large e-commerce sites experience some economies of scale, so that, for example, a $1 million site will likely require a maintenance budget of $500,000 to $700,000.

Why does it cost so much to maintain an e-commerce site? Unlike payroll systems, for example, e-commerce sites are always in a process of change, improvement, and correction. Studies of traditional systems maintenance have found 20% of the time is devoted to debugging code and responding to emergency situations (a new server was installed by your ISP, and all your hypertext links were lost and CGI scripts disabled—the site is down!) (Lientz and Swanson, 1980; Banker and Kemerer, 1989). Another 20% of the time is concerned with changes in reports, data files, and links to backend databases. The remaining 60% of maintenance time is devoted to general administration (making product and price changes in the catalog) and making changes and enhancements to the system. E-commerce sites are never finished: they are always in the process of being built and rebuilt. They are dynamic—much more so than payroll systems.

The long-term success of an e-commerce site will depend on a dedicated team of employees (the Web team) whose sole job is to monitor and adapt the site to changing market conditions. The Web team must be multi-skilled; it will typically include programmers, designers, and business managers drawn from marketing, production, and sales support. One of the first tasks of the Web team is to listen to customers' feedback on the site and respond to that feedback as necessary. A second task is to develop a systematic monitoring and testing plan to be followed weekly to ensure all the links are operating, prices are correct, and pages are updated. A large business may have thousands of Web pages, many of them linked, that require systematic monitoring. Other important tasks of the Web team include **benchmarking** (a process in which the site is compared with those of competitors in terms of response speed, quality of layout, and design) and keeping the site current on pricing and promotions. The Web is a competitive environment where you can very rapidly frustrate and lose customers with a dysfunctional site.

benchmarking

a process in which the site is compared with those of competitors in terms of response speed, quality of layout, and design

FACTORS IN OPTIMIZING WEB SITE PERFORMANCE

The purpose of a Web site is to deliver content to customers and to complete transactions. The faster and more reliably these two objectives are met, the more effective the Web site is from a commerce perspective. If you are a manager or marketing executive, you will want the Web site operating in a way that fulfills customers' expectations. You'll have to make sure the Web site is optimized to achieve this business objective. The optimization of Web site performance is more complicated than it seems and involves at least three factors: page content, page generation, and page delivery (see **Figure 4.7**). In this chapter, we describe the software and hardware choices you will need to make in building an e-commerce site; these are also important factors in Web site optimization.

Using efficient styles and techniques for *page design* and *content* can reduce response times by two to five seconds. Simple steps include reducing unnecessary HTML comments and white space, using more efficient graphics, and avoiding unnecessary links to other pages in the site. *Page generation* speed can be enhanced by segregating computer servers to perform dedicated functions (such as static page generation, application logic, media servers, and database servers), and using various devices from vendors to speed up these servers. Using a single server or multiple servers to perform multiple tasks reduces throughput by over 50%. *Page delivery* can be speeded up by using edge-caching services such as Akamai, or specialized content delivery networks such as RealNetworks, or by increasing local bandwidth. We will

FIGURE 4.7	FACTORS IN WEB SITE OPTIMIZATION

Page Delivery

Content delivery networks
Edge caching
Bandwidth

Page Generation

Server response time
Device-based accelerators
Efficient resource allocation
Resource utilization thresholds
Monitoring site performance

Page Content

Optimize HTML
Optimize images
Site architecture
Efficient page style

Web site optimization requires that you consider three factors: page content, page generation, and page delivery.

discuss some of these factors throughout the chapter, but a full discussion of Web site optimization is beyond the scope of this text.

WEB SITE BUDGETS

How much you spend on a Web site depends on what you want it to do. Simple Web sites can be built and hosted with a first-year cost of $5,000 or less. The Web sites of large firms that offer high levels of interactivity and linkage to corporate systems can cost several hundred thousand to millions of dollars a year to create and operate. For instance, in September 2006, Bluefly, which sells women's and men's designer clothes online, embarked on the process of developing an improved version of its Web site based on software from Art Technology Group (ATG). It launched the new site in August 2008. To date, it has capitalized over $5.3 million in connection with the redevelopment of the Web site (Bluefly, Inc., 2009).

While how much you spend to build a Web site depends on how much you can afford, and, of course, the size of the opportunity, **Figure 4.8** provides some idea of the relative size of various Web site costs. In general, the cost of hardware, software, and telecommunications for building and operating a Web site has fallen dramatically (by over 50%) since 2000, making it possible for very small entrepreneurs to build fairly sophisticated sites. At the same time, while technology has lowered the costs of system development, the costs of system maintenance and content creation have risen to make up more than half of typical Web site budgets. Providing content and smooth 24x7 operations are both labor intensive.

FIGURE 4.8 | **COMPONENTS OF A WEB SITE BUDGET**

Content design and development 15%

System maintenance 35%

Hardware 10%

Software 8%

Telecommunications 10%

System development 22%

4.2 CHOOSING SOFTWARE

Much of what you are able to do at an e-commerce site is a function of the software. As a business manager in charge of building the site, you will need to know some basic information about e-commerce software. The more sophisticated the software and the more ways you can sell goods and services, the more effective your business will be. This section describes the software needed to operate a contemporary e-commerce site. Section 4.3 discusses the hardware you will need to handle the demands of the software.

SIMPLE VERSUS MULTI-TIERED WEB SITE ARCHITECTURE

system architecture
the arrangement of software, machinery, and tasks in an information system needed to achieve a specific functionality

Prior to the development of e-commerce, Web sites simply delivered Web pages to users who were making requests through their browsers for HTML pages with content of various sorts. Web site software was appropriately quite simple—it consisted of a server computer running basic Web server software. We might call this arrangement a single-tier system architecture. **System architecture** refers to the arrangement of software, machinery, and tasks in an information system needed to achieve a specific functionality (much like a home's architecture refers to the arrangement of building materials to achieve a particular functionality). The SteamShowers4Less and NaturallyCurly sites both started this way—there were no monetary transactions. Tens of thousands of dot-com sites still perform this way. Orders can always be called in by telephone and not taken online.

However, the development of e-commerce required a great deal more interactive functionality, such as the ability to respond to user input (name and address forms), take customer orders for goods and services, clear credit card transactions on the fly, consult price and product databases, and even adjust advertising on the screen based on user characteristics. This kind of extended functionality required the development of Web application servers and a multi-tiered system architecture to handle the processing loads.

Web application servers, described more fully later in this section, are specialized software programs that perform a wide variety of transaction processing required by e-commerce.

In addition to having specialized application servers, e-commerce sites must be able to pull information from and add information to pre-existing corporate databases. These older databases that predate the e-commerce era are called *backend* or *legacy* databases. Corporations have made massive investments in these systems to store their information on customers, products, employees, and vendors. These backend systems constitute an additional layer in a multi-tiered site.

Figure 4.9 illustrates a simple two-tier and more complex multi-tier e-commerce system architecture. In **two-tier architecture**, a Web server responds to requests

two-tier architecture
e-commerce system architecture in which a Web server responds to requests for Web pages and a database server provides backend data storage

FIGURE 4.9   TWO-TIER AND MULTI-TIER E-COMMERCE ARCHITECTURES

User requests for pages   Web Server   Dynamic Content Database

(a) Two-tier Architecture
In a two-tier architecture, a Web server responds to requests for Web pages and a database server provides backend data storage.

Web Server Layer   Web Servers
Incoming Internet requests T1 Line 1.544 Mbps

Middle-tier Layer   E-commerce Servers
Application Servers
Database Servers
Ad Servers
Mail Servers

Backend Layer   Corporate applications
Finance
Production MRP
Enterprise systems
HR systems

(b) Multi-tier Architecture
In a multi-tier architecture, a Web server is linked to a middle-tier layer that typically includes a series of application servers that perform specific tasks, as well as to a backend layer of existing corporate systems.

multi-tier architecture

e-commerce system architecture in which the Web server is linked to a middle-tier layer that typically includes a series of application servers that perform specific tasks as well as to a backend layer of existing corporate systems

for Web pages and a database server provides backend data storage. In a **multi-tier architecture**, in contrast, the Web server is linked to a middle-tier layer that typically includes a series of application servers that perform specific tasks, as well as to a backend layer of existing corporate systems containing product, customer, and pricing information. A multi-tiered site typically employs several physical computers, each running some of the software applications and sharing the workload across many physical computers.

The remainder of this section describes basic Web server software functionality and the various types of Web application servers.

WEB SERVER SOFTWARE

All e-commerce sites require basic Web server software to answer requests from customers for HTML and XML pages.

When you choose Web server software, you will also be choosing an operating system for your site's computers. Looking at all servers on the Web, the leading Web server software, with about 47% of the market, is Apache, which works with Linux and Unix operating systems. Unix is the original programming language of the Internet and Web, and Linux is a derivative of Unix designed for the personal computer. Apache was developed by a worldwide community of Internet innovators. Apache is free and can be downloaded from many sites on the Web; it also comes installed on most IBM Web servers. Literally thousands of programmers have worked on Apache over the years; thus, it is extremely stable. There are thousands of utility software programs written for Apache that can provide all the functionality required for a contemporary e-commerce site. In order to use Apache, you will need staff that is knowledgeable in Unix or Linux.

Microsoft Internet Information Services (IIS) is the second major Web server software available, with about 25% of the market. IIS is based on the Windows operating system and is compatible with a wide selection of Microsoft utility and support programs. These numbers are different among the Fortune 1000 firms (25% of which use Microsoft IIS), and different again if you include blogs which are served up by Microsoft and Google at their own proprietary sites.

There are also at least 100 other smaller providers of Web server software, most of them based on the Unix or Sun Solaris operating systems. Note that the choice of Web server has little effect on users of your system. The pages they see will look the same regardless of the development environment. There are many advantages to the Microsoft suite of development tools—they are integrated, powerful, and easy to use. The Unix operating system, on the other hand, is exceptionally reliable and stable, and there is a worldwide open software community that develops and tests Unix-based Web server software.

Table 4.3 shows the basic functionality provided by all Web servers.

Site Management Tools

site management tools

verify that links on pages are still valid and also identify orphan files

In Chapter 3, we described most of the basic functionality of the Web servers listed in Table 4.3. Another functionality not described previously is site management tools. **Site management tools** are essential if you want to keep your site working, and if

TABLE 4.3	BASIC FUNCTIONALITY PROVIDED BY WEB SERVERS
FUNCTIONALITY	DESCRIPTION
Processing of HTTP requests	Receive and respond to client requests for HTML pages
Security services (Secure Sockets Layer)	Verify username and password; process certificates and private/public key information required for credit card processing and other secure information
File Transfer Protocol	Permits transfer of very large files from server to server
Search engine	Indexing of site content; keyword search capability
Data capture	Log file of all visits, time, duration, and referral source
E-mail	Ability to send, receive, and store e-mail messages
Site management tools	Calculate and display key site statistics, such as unique visitors, page requests, and origin of requests; check links on pages

you want to understand how well it is working. Site management tools verify that links on pages are still valid and also identify orphan files, or files on the site that are not linked to any pages. By surveying the links on a Web site, a site management tool can quickly report on potential problems and errors that users may encounter. Your customers will not be impressed if they encounter a "404 Error: Page Does Not Exist" on your Web site. Links to URLs that have moved or been deleted are called dead links; these can cause error messages for users trying to access that link. Regularly checking that all links on a site are operational helps prevent irritation and frustration in users who may decide to take their business elsewhere to a better functioning site.

Even more importantly, site management tools can help you understand consumer behavior on your Web site. Site management software and services, such as those provided by Webtrends, can be purchased in order to more effectively monitor customer purchases and marketing campaign effectiveness, as well as keep track of standard hit counts and page visit information. **Figure 4.10** contains two screenshots that illustrate two Web site analytics tools: WebTrends Analytics 9 and Google Analytics.

Dynamic Page Generation Tools

One of the most important innovations in Web site operation has been the development of dynamic page generation tools. Prior to the development of e-commerce, Web sites primarily delivered unchanging static content in the form of HTML pages. While this capability might be sufficient to display pictures of products, consider all the elements of a typical e-commerce site today by reviewing Table 4.1 on page 209, or visit what you believe is an excellent e-commerce site. The content of successful e-commerce sites is always changing, often day by day. There are new products and promotions, changing prices, news events, and stories of successful users. E-commerce sites must intensively

FIGURE 4.10	WEBTRENDS ANALYTICS; GOOGLE ANALYTICS

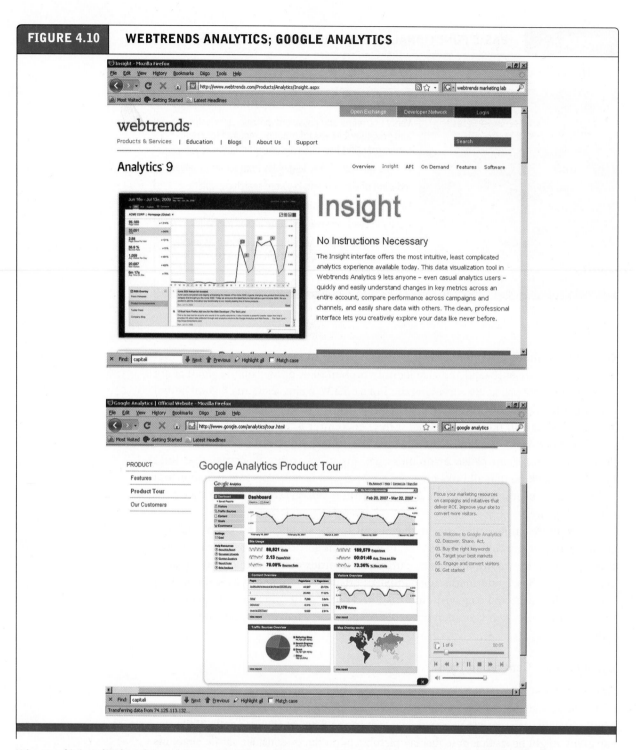

Using a sophisticated Web analytics solution such as Webtrends Analytics or Google Analytics, managers can quickly understand the return on investment of their online marketing efforts and determine how to improve conversion by drilling down into abandonment paths, product preferences, and successful campaign elements for different types of customers.

SOURCE: Webtrends, Inc., 2009; Google, 2009.

interact with users who not only request pages but also request product, price, availability, and inventory information. One of the most dynamic sites is eBay—the auction site. There, the content is changing minute by minute. E-commerce sites are just like real markets—they are dynamic. News sites, where stories change constantly, are also dynamic.

The dynamic and complex nature of e-commerce sites requires a number of specialized software applications in addition to static HTML pages. Perhaps one of the most important is dynamic page generation software. With **dynamic page generation**, the contents of a Web page are stored as objects in a database, rather than being hard-coded in HTML. When the user requests a Web page, the contents for that page are then fetched from the database. The objects are retrieved from the database using Common Gateway Interface (CGI), Active Server Pages (ASP), Java Server Pages (JSP), or other server-side programs. CGI, ASP, and JSP are described in the last section of this chapter. This technique is much more efficient than working directly in HTML code. It is much easier to change the contents of a database than it is to change the coding of an HTML page. A standard data access method called *Open Database Connectivity (ODBC)* makes it possible to access any data from any application regardless of what database is used. ODBC is supported by most of the large database suppliers such as Oracle, Sybase, and IBM. ODBC makes it possible for HTML pages to be linked to backend corporate databases regardless of who manufactured the database. Web sites must be able to pull information from, and add information to, these databases. For example, when a customer clicks on a picture of a pair of boots, the site can access the product catalog database stored in a DB2 database, and access the inventory database stored in an Oracle database to confirm that the boots are still in stock and to report the current price.

Dynamic page generation gives e-commerce several significant capabilities that generate cost and profitability advantages over traditional commerce. Dynamic page generation lowers *menu costs* (the costs incurred by merchants for changing product descriptions and prices). Dynamic page generation also permits easy online *market segmentation*—the ability to sell the same product to different markets. For instance, you might want variations on the same banner ad depending on how many times the customer has seen the ad. In the first exposure to a car ad, you might want to emphasize brand identification and unique features. On the second viewing you might want to emphasize superlatives like "most family friendly" to encourage comparison to other brands. The same capability makes possible nearly cost-free *price discrimination*—the ability to sell the same product to different customers at different prices. For instance, you might want to sell the same product to corporations and government agencies but use different marketing themes. Based on a cookie you place on client files, or in response to a question on your site that asks visitors if they are from a government agency or a corporation, you would be able to use different marketing and promotional materials for corporate clients and government clients. You might want to reward loyal customers with lower prices, say on DVDs or musical tracks, and charge full price to first-time buyers. Dynamic page generation allows you to approach different customers with different messages and prices.

dynamic page generation
the contents of a Web page are stored as objects in a database, rather than being hard-coded in HTML. When the user requests a Web page, the contents for that page are then fetched from the database

Web content management system (WCMS, WebCMS)
used to create and manage Web content

Dynamic page generation also enables the use of Web content management systems. As its name implies, a **Web content management system (WCMS or WebCMS)** is used to create and manage Web content. A WCMS separates the design and presentation of content (such as HTML documents, images, video, audio) from the content creation process. The content is maintained in a database and dynamically linked to the Web site. A WCMS usually includes templates that can be automatically applied to new and existing content, WYSIWIG editing tools that make it easy to edit and describe (tag) content, and collaboration, workflow, and document management tools. Typically, an experienced programmer is needed to install the system, but thereafter, content can be easily created and managed by non-technical staff. There are a wide range of commercial WCMSs available, from top-end enterprise systems offered by Autonomy, Interwoven, EMC, Documentum, Open Text, IBM, and Oracle, to mid-market systems by Ixiasoft, PaperThin, Ektron, and Hot Banana, as well as hosted software as a service (SaaS) versions by Clickability, CrownPeak Technology, and OmniUpdate. There are also several open source content management systems available, such as Joomla, Drupal, OpenCms, and others (CMSWatch.com, 2009).

APPLICATION SERVERS

web application server
software programs that provide specific business functionality required of a Web site

Web application servers are software programs that provide the specific business functionality required of a Web site. The basic idea of application servers is to isolate the business applications from the details of displaying Web pages to users on the front end and the details of connecting to databases on the back end. Application servers are a kind of middleware software that provides the glue connecting traditional corporate systems to the customer as well as all the functionality needed to conduct e-commerce. In the early years, a number of software firms developed specific separate programs for each function, but increasingly, these specific programs are being replaced by integrated software tools that combine all the needed functionality for an e-commerce site into a single development environment, a packaged software approach.

Table 4.4 illustrates the wide variety of application servers available in the marketplace. The table focuses on "sell side" servers that are designed to enable selling products on the Web. So-called "buy side" and "link" servers focus on the needs of businesses to connect with partners in their supply chains or find suppliers for specific parts and assemblies. These buy side and link servers are described more fully in Chapter 12, *B2B E-commerce, Supply Chain Management, and Collaborative Commerce*. There are several thousand software vendors that provide application server software. For Linux and Unix environments, many of these capabilities are available free on the Internet from various sites. Most businesses—faced with this bewildering array of choices—choose to use integrated software tools called merchant server software.

e-commerce merchant server software
software that provides the basic functionality needed for online sales, including an online catalog, order taking via an online shopping cart, and online credit card processing

E-COMMERCE MERCHANT SERVER SOFTWARE FUNCTIONALITY

E-commerce merchant server software provides the basic functionality needed for online sales, including an online catalog, order taking via an online shopping cart, and online credit card processing.

TABLE 4.4	APPLICATION SERVERS AND THEIR FUNCTION
APPLICATION SERVER	**FUNCTIONALITY**
Catalog display	Provides a database for product descriptions and prices
Transaction processing (shopping cart)	Accepts orders and clears payments
List server	Creates and serves mailing lists and manages e-mail marketing campaigns
Proxy server	Monitors and controls access to main Web server; implements firewall protection
Mail server	Manages Internet e-mail
Audio/video server	Stores and delivers streaming media content
Chat server	Creates an environment for online real-time text and audio interactions with customers
News server	Provides connectivity and displays Internet news feeds
Fax server	Provides fax reception and sending using a Web server
Groupware server	Creates workgroup environments for online collaboration
Database server	Stores customer, product, and price information
Ad server	Maintains Web-enabled database of advertising banners that permits customized and personalized display of advertisements based on consumer behavior and characteristics
Auction server	Provides a transaction environment for conducting online auctions
B2B server	Implements buy, sell, and link marketplaces for commercial transactions

Online Catalog

A company that wants to sell products on the Web must have a list, or **online catalog**, of its products, available on its Web site. Merchant server software typically includes a database capability that will allow for construction of a customized online catalog. The complexity and sophistication of the catalog will vary depending on the size of the company and its product lines. Small companies, or companies with small product lines, may post a simple list with text descriptions and perhaps color photos. A larger site might decide to add sound, animations, or videos (useful for product demonstrations) to the catalog, or interactivity, such as customer service representatives available via instant messaging to answer questions. Today, larger firms make extensive use of streaming video.

online catalog
list of products available on a Web site

Shopping Cart

Online **shopping carts** are much like their real-world equivalent; both allow shoppers to set aside desired purchases in preparation for checkout. The difference is that the online variety is part of a merchant server software program residing on the Web server, and allows consumers to select merchandise, review what they have

shopping cart
allows shoppers to set aside desired purchases in preparation for checkout, review what they have selected, edit their selections as necessary, and then actually make the purchase by clicking a button

selected, edit their selections as necessary, and then actually make the purchase by clicking a button. The merchant server software automatically stores shopping cart data.

Credit Card Processing

A site's shopping cart typically works in conjunction with credit card processing software, which verifies the shopper's credit card and then puts through the debit to the card and the credit to the company's account at checkout. Integrated e-commerce software suites typically supply the software for this function. Otherwise, you will have to make arrangements with a variety of credit card processing banks and intermediaries.

MERCHANT SERVER SOFTWARE PACKAGES (E-COMMERCE SUITES)

merchant server software package (e-commerce server suite)

offers an integrated environment that provides most or all of the functionality and capabilities needed to develop a sophisticated, customer-centric site

Rather than build your site from a collection of disparate software applications, it is easier, faster, and generally more cost-effective to purchase a **merchant server software package** (also called an **e-commerce server suite**). Merchant server software/e-commerce suites offer an integrated environment that promises to provide most or all of the functionality and capabilities you will need to develop a sophisticated, customer-centric site. E-commerce suites come in three general ranges of price and functionality.

Basic packages for elementary e-commerce business applications are provided by Bizland, HyperMart, and Yahoo! Merchant Solutions. FreeWebs.com also offers free Web building tools and hosting services. OSCommerce is a free, open source e-commerce suite used by many small start-up sites. PayPal can be used as a payment system on simple Web sites, and widgets can add interesting capabilities.

Midrange suites include IBM's WebSphere Commerce Express Edition and Microsoft's Commerce Server 2009. High-end enterprise solutions for large global firms are provided by IBM WebSphere's Commerce Professional and Enterprise Editions, BroadVision Commerce, and others. There are several hundred software firms that provide e-commerce suites, which raises the costs of making sensible decisions on this matter. Many firms simply choose vendors with the best overall reputation. Quite often this turns out to be expensive but ultimately a workable solution. **Table 4.5** lists some of the most widely adopted midrange and high-end e-commerce suites.

Choosing an E-commerce Suite

With all of these vendors, how do you choose the right one? Evaluating these tools and making a choice is one of the most important and uncertain decisions you will make in building an e-commerce site. The real costs are hidden—they involve training your staff to use the tools and integrating the tools into your business processes and organizational culture. The following are some of the key factors to consider:

- Functionality
- Support for different business models
- Business process modeling tools

TABLE 4.5	WIDELY USED MIDRANGE AND HIGH-END E-COMMERCE SUITES
PRODUCT	APPROXIMATE PRICE
Microsoft Commerce Server	Standard Edition, $6,999 per processor Enterprise Edition, $19,999 per processor
IBM WebSphere Commerce	Express Edition, single-user license, $3,610; Processor Value Unit (PVU) license, $20,000
	Professional Edition, PVU license, $100,000
	Enterprise Edition, PVU license, $159,000
BroadVision Commerce	$60,000 per processor
Intershop Enfinity Suite 6 Consumer Channel	$125,000–$250,000
ATG (Art Technology Group)	$380,000 for a four-CPU license

- Visual site management tools and reporting
- Performance and scalability
- Connectivity to existing business systems
- Compliance with standards
- Global and multicultural capability
- Local sales tax and shipping rules

For instance, although e-commerce suites promise to do everything, your business may require special functionality—such as streaming audio and video. You will need a list of business functionality requirements. Your business may involve several different business models—such as a retail side and a business-to-business side; you may run auctions for stock excess as well as fixed-price selling. Be sure the package can support all of your business models. You may wish to change your business processes, such as order taking and order fulfillment. Does the suite contain tools for modeling business process and work flows? Understanding how your site works will require visual reporting tools that make its operation transparent to many different people in your business. A poorly designed software package will drop off significantly in performance as visitors and transactions expand into the thousands per hour, or minute. Check for performance and scalability by stress testing a pilot edition or obtaining data from the vendor about performance under load. You will have to connect the e-commerce suite to your traditional business systems. How will this connection to existing systems be made, and is your staff skilled in making the connection? Because of the changing technical environment—in particular, changes in mobile commerce platforms—it is important to document exactly what standards the suite supports now, and what the migration path will be toward the future. Finally, your e-commerce site may have to work both globally and locally. You may need a foreign language edition using foreign currency denominations. And you will have to collect sales taxes across many local, regional, and national tax systems. Does the e-commerce suite support this level of globalization and localization?

BUILDING YOUR OWN E-COMMERCE SITE: WEB SERVICES AND OPEN SOURCE OPTIONS

While existing firms often have the financial capital to invest in commercial merchant server software suites, many small firms and start-up firms do not. They have to build their own Web sites, at least initially. There are really two options here, the key factor being how much programming experience and time you have. One option is to utilize the e-commerce merchant services provided by hosting sites such as Yahoo's Merchant Solutions. For a $50 setup fee, and a starter plan of $39.95, the service will walk you through setting up your Web site and provide Web hosting, a shopping cart, technical help by phone, and payment processing. Bigstep.com takes users step by step through the process of building an online store. Entrabase.com and Tripod provide easy-to-use site-building tools and e-commerce templates for e-commerce sites. An e-commerce template is a pre-designed Web site that allows users to customize the look and feel of the site to fit their business needs and provides a standard set of functionality. Most templates today contain ready-to-go site designs with built-in e-commerce suite functionality like shopping carts, payment clearance, and site management tools.

One of the most popular low-cost tools for creating a Web site without having to have any programming skills is Homestead.com. Building a Web site at Homestead involves three steps: choosing a design from over 2,000 templates; customizing the design with logos and content; and publishing it on the Web on Homestead servers with your own unique IP address, and e-mail. Once you build the Web site, Homestead provides a comprehensive set of services such as PayPal and credit card payment clearing, online catalog, shopping cart, real-time transaction processing, and custom shipping tables. Marketing support is available in the form of search engine optimization for your site, and advertising on Google, Amazon, and MSN. There is a 30-day free trial, and basic service for $4.99 a month, with charges for additional services.

If you have considerable, or at least some, programming background, then you can consider open source merchant server software. Open source software, as described in Chapter 3, is software developed by a community of programmers and designers, and is free to use and modify. **Table 4.6** provides a description of some open source options.

The advantage of using open source Web building tools is that you get exactly what you want, a truly customized unique Web site. The disadvantage is that it will take several months for a single programmer to develop the site and get all the tools to work together seamlessly. How many months do you want to wait before you get to market with your ideas?

One alternative to building a Web site first is to create a blog first, and develop your business ideas and a following of potential customers on your blog. Once you have tested your ideas with a blog, and attract a Web audience, you can then move on to developing a simple Web site.

TABLE 4.6	**OPEN SOURCE SOFTWARE OPTIONS**
MERCHANT SERVER FUNCTIONALITY	OPEN SOURCE SOFTWARE
Web server	Apache (the leading Web server for small and medium businesses)
Shopping cart, online catalog	Many providers: Zen-Cart.com, AgoraCart.com, X-Cart.com, OSCommerce.com
Credit card processing	Many providers: Echo Internet Gateway; ASPDotNetStorefront. Credit card acceptance is typically provided in shopping cart software but you may need a merchant account from a bank as well.
Database	MySQL (the leading open source SQL database for businesses)
Programming/scripting language	PHP (a scripting language embedded in HTML documents but executed by the server providing server-side execution with the simplicity of HTML editing). PERL is an alternative language. JavaScript programs are client-side programs that provide user interface components. Ruby on Rails (RoR, Rails) is another popular open source Web application framework.
Analytics	Analytics keep track of your site's customer activities and the success of your Web advertising campaign. You can also use Google Analytics if you advertise on Google, which provides good tracking tools; most hosting services will provide these services as well. Other open source analytic tools include Piwik, CrawlTrack, and Open Web Analytics.

4.3 CHOOSING THE HARDWARE FOR AN E-COMMERCE SITE

As the manager in charge of building an e-commerce site, you will be held accountable for its performance. Whether you host your own site or outsource the hosting and operation of your site, you will need to understand certain aspects of the computing hardware platform. The **hardware platform** refers to all the underlying computing equipment that the system uses to achieve its e-commerce functionality. Your objective is to have enough platform capacity to meet peak demand (avoiding an overload condition), but not so much platform that you are wasting money. Failing to meet peak demand can mean your site is slow, or actually crashes. Remember, the Web site may be your only or principal source of cash flow. How much computing and telecommunications capacity is enough to meet peak demand? How many hits per day can your site sustain?

To answer these questions, you will need to understand the various factors that affect the speed, capacity, and scalability of an e-commerce site.

hardware platform
refers to all the underlying computing equipment that the system uses to achieve its e-commerce functionality

RIGHT-SIZING YOUR HARDWARE PLATFORM: THE DEMAND SIDE

The most important factor affecting the speed of your site is the demand that customers put on the site. **Table 4.7** lists the most important factors to consider when estimating the demand on a site.

Demand on a Web site is fairly complex and depends primarily on the type of site you are operating. The number of simultaneous users in peak periods, the nature of customer requests, the type of content, the required security, the number of items in inventory, the number of page requests, and the speed of legacy applications that may be needed to supply data to the Web pages are all important factors in overall demand on a Web site system.

Certainly, one important factor to consider is the number of simultaneous users who will likely visit your site. In general, the load created by an individual customer on a server is typically quite limited and short-lived. A Web session initiated by the

TABLE 4.7	FACTORS IN RIGHT-SIZING AN E-COMMERCE PLATFORM				
SITE TYPE	PUBLISH/ SUBSCRIBE	SHOPPING	CUSTOMER SELF-SERVICE	TRADING	WEB SERVICES/B2B
Examples	WSJ.com	Amazon	Travelocity	E*Trade	Ariba e-procurement exchanges
Content	Dynamic Multiple authors High volume Not user specific	Catalog Dynamic items User profiles with data mining	Data in legacy applications Multiple data sources	Time sensitive High volatility Multiple suppliers and consumers Complex transactions	Data in legacy applications Multiple data sources Complex transactions
Security	Low	Privacy Non-repudiation Integrity Authentication Regulations	Privacy Non-repudiation Integrity Authentication Regulations	Privacy Non-repudiation Integrity Authentication Regulations	Privacy Non-repudiation Integrity Authentication Regulations
Percent secure pages	Low	Medium	Medium	High	Medium
Cross session information	No	High	High	High	High
Searches	Dynamic Low volume	Dynamic High volume	Non dynamic Low volume	Non dynamic Low volume	Non dynamic Moderate volume
Unique items (SKUs)	High	Medium to high	Medium	High	Medium to high
Transaction volume	Moderate	Moderate to high	Moderate	High to extremely high	Moderate
Legacy integration complexity	Low	Medium	High	High	High
Page views (hits)	High to very high	Moderate to high	Moderate to low	Moderate to high	Moderate

typical user is **stateless**, meaning that the server does not have to maintain an ongoing, dedicated interaction with the client. A Web session typically begins with a page request, then a server replies, and the session is ended. The sessions may last from tenths of a second to a minute per user. Nevertheless, system performance does degrade as more and more simultaneous users request service. Fortunately, degradation (measured as "transactions per second" and "latency" or delay in response) is fairly graceful over a wide range, up until a peak load is reached and service quality becomes unacceptable (see **Figure 4.11**).

Serving up static Web pages is **I/O intensive**, which means it requires input/output (I/O) operations rather than heavy-duty processing power. As a result, Web site performance is constrained primarily by the server's I/O limitations and the telecommunications connection, rather than speed of the processor.

There are some steps you can take to make sure that you stay within an acceptable service quality. One step is to simply purchase a server with faster CPU processors, multiple CPU processors, or larger hard disk drives. However, the improvement that results is not linear and at some point becomes cost-ineffective. **Figure 4.12** on page 235 shows the theoretical performance of a Web server as processors are added from a single processor up to eight processors. By increasing processors by a factor of eight, you get only three times more load capacity.

A second factor to consider on the demand side is the **user profile**, which refers to the nature of customer requests and customer behavior on your site (how many pages customers request and the kind of service they want). Web servers can be very efficient at serving static Web pages. However, as customers request more advanced services, such as site searches, registration, order taking via shopping carts, or downloads of large audio and video files, all of which require more processing power, performance can deteriorate rapidly.

The nature of the content your site offers is a third factor to consider. If your site uses dynamic page generation, then the load on the processor rises rapidly and performance will degrade. Dynamic page generation and business logic (such as a shopping cart) are **CPU-intensive** operations—they require a great deal of processing power. For instance, a site with only dynamic page content can expect performance of a single processor server to fall to one-tenth the levels described in Figure 4.12. Instead of effectively serving 8,000 users, you can only service 1,000 concurrent users. Any interaction with the user requiring access to a database—filling out forms, adding to carts, purchasing, and completing questionnaires—puts a heavy processing load on the server.

A final factor to consider is the telecommunications link that your site has to the Web, and also the changing nature of the client connection to the Web. **Figure 4.13** on page 236 shows that the number of hits per second your site can handle depends on the bandwidth connection between your server and the Web. The larger the bandwidth available, the more customers can simultaneously hit your site. For example, if your connection to the Web is a 1.5 Mbps DSL line, the maximum number of visitors per second for 1 kilobyte files is probably about 100. Most businesses host their sites at an ISP or other provider that contractually is (or should be) obligated to provide enough bandwidth for your site to meet peak demands. However, there are no guar-

stateless
refers to the fact that the server does not have to maintain an ongoing, dedicated interaction with the client

I/O intensive
requires input/output operations rather than heavy-duty processing power

user profile
refers to the nature of customer requests and customer behavior at a site

CPU-intensive
operations that require a great deal of processing power

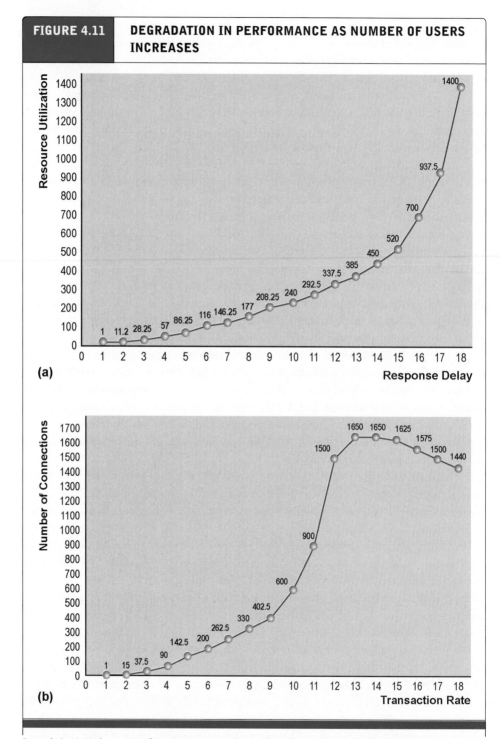

FIGURE 4.11 **DEGRADATION IN PERFORMANCE AS NUMBER OF USERS INCREASES**

(a) *Response Delay*

(b) *Transaction Rate*

Degradation in Web server performance occurs as the number of users (connections) increases, and as the systems resources (processors, disk drives) become more utilized. In (a), user-experienced delay rises gracefully until an inflection point is reached, and then delay rises exponentially to an unacceptable level. In (b), the transaction rate rises gracefully until the number of users rapidly escalates the transaction rate, and at a certain inflection point, the transaction rate starts declining as the system slows down or crashes.

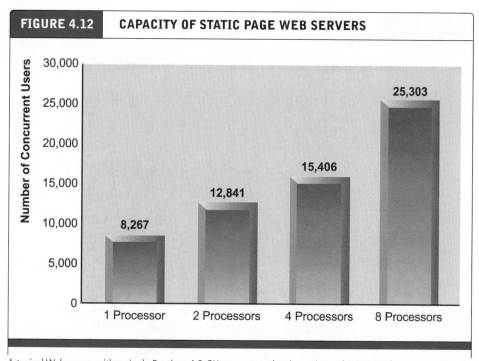

FIGURE 4.12 | **CAPACITY OF STATIC PAGE WEB SERVERS**

A typical Web server with a single Pentium 4.2 GHz processor that is serving only static Web pages can handle about 8,000 concurrent users. With eight processors, the same computer could handle about 25,000 concurrent users.

antees and ISPs can blame Web congestion for their own bandwidth limitations. Check your ISP's bandwidth and your site performance daily.

While server bandwidth connections are less a constraint today with the widespread deployment of fiber-optic cable, the connection to the client is improving and this will have implications for your customers' expectations. In 2009, there are approximately 80 million broadband households in the United States, and this number is expected to increase to around 92 million by 2013 (eMarketer, Inc., 2009). This means your customers will be able to make far more frequent requests and demand far richer content like videos, games, podcasts, and simulations. This demand will translate quickly into dynamic content and the need for additional capacity.

RIGHT-SIZING YOUR HARDWARE PLATFORM: THE SUPPLY SIDE

Once you estimate the likely demand on your site, you will need to consider how to scale up your site to meet demand. **Scalability** refers to the ability of a site to increase in size as demand warrants. There are three steps you can take to meet the demands for service at your site: scale hardware vertically, scale hardware horizontally, and/or improve the processing architecture of the site (see **Table 4.8**). **Vertical scaling** refers to increasing the processing power of individual components. **Horizontal scaling** refers to employing multiple computers to share the workload and increase the "footprint" of the installation (IBM, 2002).

scalability
refers to the ability of a site to increase in size as demand warrants

horizontal scaling
employing multiple computers to share the workload

vertical scaling
increasing the processing power of individual components

FIGURE 4.13	THE RELATIONSHIP OF BANDWIDTH TO HITS

The greater the bandwidth available, the more customers can simultaneously access a Web site without any perceived degradation in performance.
SOURCE: IBM, 2003.

TABLE 4.8	VERTICAL AND HORIZONTAL SCALING TECHNIQUES

TECHNIQUE	APPLICATION
Use a faster computer	Applies to edge servers, presentation servers, data servers, etc.
Create a cluster of computers	Use computers in parallel to balance loads
Use appliance servers	Special-purpose computers optimized for their task
Segment workload	Segment incoming work to specialized computers
Batch requests	Combine related requests for data into groups, process as a group
Manage connections	Reduce connections between processes and computers to a minimum
Aggregate user data	Aggregate user data from legacy applications in single data pools
Cache	Store frequently used data in cache rather than on the disk

You can scale your site vertically by upgrading the servers from a single processor to multiple processors (see **Figure 4.14**). You can keep adding processors to a computer depending on the operating system and upgrade to faster chip speeds as well.

FIGURE 4.14 **VERTICALLY SCALING A SYSTEM**

HP ProLiant Server
DL140 G3
Intel Xeon
Dual Core 1.6 GHz
1 GB RAM

HP ProLiant Server
DL140 G3
Intel Xeon
Dual Core 3 GHz
2 GB RAM

HP ProLiant Server
DL585 G3
AMD Opteron
Dual Core 2.8GHz
8 GB RAM

HP ProLiant Server
DL585 G3
AMD Opteron
Quad Core 2.8 GHz
16 GB RAM

You can scale a site vertically by both improving the processors and adding additional CPUs into a single physical server.

There are two drawbacks to vertical scaling. First, it can become expensive to purchase new computers with every growth cycle, and second, your entire site becomes dependent on a small number of very powerful computers. If you have two such computers and one goes down, half of your site, or perhaps your entire site, may become unavailable.

Horizontal scaling involves adding multiple single-processor servers to your site and balancing the load among the servers. You can also then partition the load so that some servers handle only requests for HTML or ASP pages, while others are dedicated to handling database applications. You will need special load-balancing software (provided by a variety of vendors such as Cisco, Microsoft, and IBM) to direct incoming requests to various servers (see **Figure 4.15**).

There are many advantages to horizontal scaling. It is inexpensive and often can be accomplished using older PCs that otherwise would be disposed of. Horizontal scaling also introduces redundancy—if one computer fails, chances are that another computer can pick up the load dynamically. However, when your site grows from a single computer to perhaps 10 to 20 computers, the size of the physical facility required (the "footprint") increases and there is added management complexity.

A third alternative—improving the processing architecture—is a combination of vertical and horizontal scaling, combined with artful design decisions. **Table 4.9** on page 239 lists some of the more common steps you can take to greatly improve performance of your site. Most of these steps involve splitting the workload into I/O-intensive activities (such as serving Web pages) and CPU-intensive activities (such as taking orders). Once you have this work separated, you can fine-tune the servers for each type of load. One of the least expensive fine-tuning steps is to simply add RAM to a few servers and store all your HTML pages in RAM. This reduces load on your hard drives and increases speed dramatically. RAM is thousands of times faster than hard disks, and RAM is inexpensive. The next most important step is to move your CPU-intensive activities, such as order taking, onto a high-end, multiple processor

FIGURE 4.15 | **HORIZONTALLY SCALING A SYSTEM**

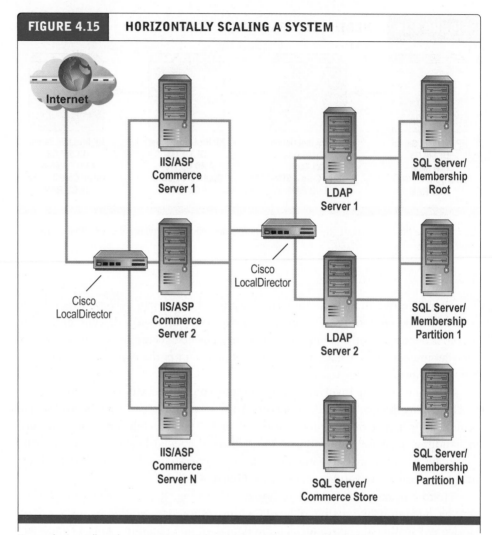

You can horizontally scale a system to meet demands by adding inexpensive single-processor servers to the site and using load-balancing software to allocate incoming customer requests to the correct server, shown in the diagram as a Cisco LocalDirector.

server that is totally dedicated to handling orders and accessing the necessary databases. Taking these steps can permit you to reduce the number of servers required to service 10,000 concurrent users from 100 down to 20, according to one estimate.

4.4 OTHER E-COMMERCE SITE TOOLS

Now that you understand the key factors that affect the speed, capacity, and scalability of your site, we can consider some other important requirements for your Web site. You will need a coherent Web site design effort that makes business sense—not necessarily a site to wow visitors or excite them, but to sell them something. You will also

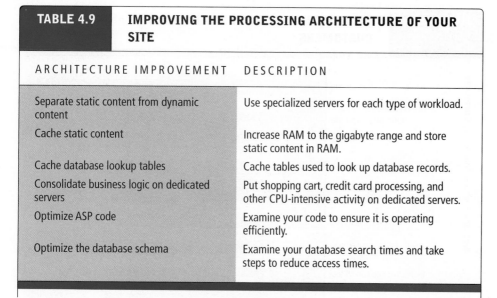

TABLE 4.9	IMPROVING THE PROCESSING ARCHITECTURE OF YOUR SITE
ARCHITECTURE IMPROVEMENT	**DESCRIPTION**
Separate static content from dynamic content	Use specialized servers for each type of workload.
Cache static content	Increase RAM to the gigabyte range and store static content in RAM.
Cache database lookup tables	Cache tables used to look up database records.
Consolidate business logic on dedicated servers	Put shopping cart, credit card processing, and other CPU-intensive activity on dedicated servers.
Optimize ASP code	Examine your code to ensure it is operating efficiently.
Optimize the database schema	Examine your database search times and take steps to reduce access times.

need to know how to build active content and interactivity into your site—not just display static HTML pages. You will definitely want to be able to track customers who come, leave, and return to your site in order to be able to greet return visitors ("Hi Sarah, welcome back!"). You will also want to track customers throughout your site so you can personalize and customize their experience. Finally, you will need to establish a set of information policies for your site—privacy, accessibility, and access to information policies.

In order to achieve these business capabilities, you will need to be aware of some design guidelines and additional software tools that can cost-effectively achieve the required business functionality.

WEB SITE DESIGN: BASIC BUSINESS CONSIDERATIONS

This is not a text about how to design Web sites. (In Chapter 7, we discuss Web site design issues from a marketing perspective.) Nevertheless, from a business manager's perspective, there are certain design objectives you must communicate to your Web site designers to let them know how you will evaluate their work. At a minimum, your customers will need to find what they need at your site, make a purchase, and leave. A Web site that annoys customers runs the risk of losing the customer forever. For instance, a survey by Hostway found that about 75% of respondents said they were extremely or somewhat likely to not visit an offending site again and to unsubscribe from the offending company's promotional messages when they encounter one of their "pet peeves," and around 71% said they might refuse to purchase from the Web site and would view the company in a negative way. About 55% said they would complain about the Web site to friends and associates, and 45% said they might even refuse to make purchases in the company's offline stores (Hostway, 2007). See **Figure 4.16** for a list of the most common consumer complaints about Web sites.

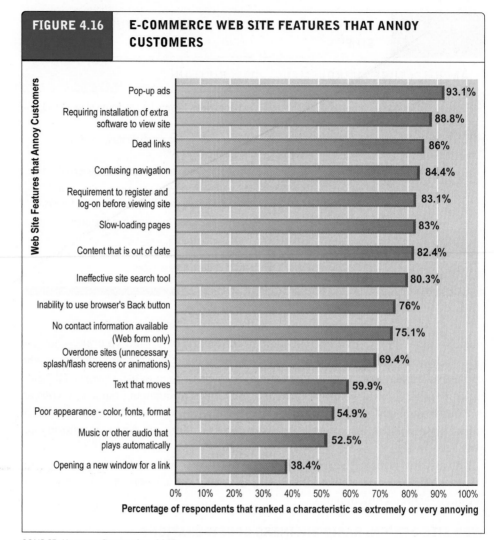

FIGURE 4.16 — E-COMMERCE WEB SITE FEATURES THAT ANNOY CUSTOMERS

SOURCE: Hostway Corporation, 2007.

Some critics believe poor design is more common than good design. It appears easier to describe what irritates people about Web sites than to describe how to design a good Web site. The worst e-commerce sites make it difficult to find information about their products and make it complicated to purchase goods; they have missing pages and broken links, a confusing navigation structure, and annoying graphics or sounds that you cannot turn off. **Table 4.10** restates these negative experiences as positive goals for Web site design.

TOOLS FOR WEB SITE OPTIMIZATION

A Web site is only as valuable from a business perspective as the number of people who visit. Web site optimization (as we use it here) means how to attract lots of people to your site. One answer, of course, is through search engines such as Google, Yahoo, MSN, Ask, and several hundred others. The first stop for most customers

TABLE 4.10	THE EIGHT MOST IMPORTANT FACTORS IN SUCCESSFUL E-COMMERCE SITE DESIGN	
FACTOR	**DESCRIPTION**	
Functionality	Pages that work, load quickly, and point the customer toward your product offerings	
Informational	Links that customers can easily find to discover more about you and your products	
Ease of use	Simple fool-proof navigation	
Redundant navigation	Alternative navigation to the same content	
Ease of purchase	One or two clicks to purchase	
Multi-browser functionality	Site works with the most popular browsers	
Simple graphics	Avoids distracting, obnoxious graphics and sounds that the user cannot control	
Legible text	Avoids backgrounds that distort text or make it illegible	

looking for a product or service is to start with a search engine, and follow the listings on the page, usually starting with the top three to five listings, then glancing to the sponsored ads to the right. The higher you are on the search engine pages, the more traffic you will receive. Page 1 is much better than Page 2. So how do you get to Page 1 in the natural (unpaid) search listings? While every search engine is different, and none of them publish their algorithms for ranking pages, there are some basic ideas that work well:

- Keywords and page titles: Search engines "crawl" your site and identify keywords as well as title pages and then index them for use in search arguments. Pepper your pages with keywords that accurately describe what you sell or do. Experiment: use different keywords to see which work. "Vintage cars" may attract more visitors than "antique cars," or "restored cars."

- Identify market niches: Instead of marketing "jewelry," be more specific, such as "Victorian jewelry," or "1950s jewelry" to attract small, specific groups who are intensely interested in period jewelry.

- Offer expertise: White papers, industry analyses, FAQ pages, guides, and histories are excellent ways to build confidence on the part of users and to encourage them to see your Web site as the place to go for help and guidance.

- Get linked up: Encourage other sites to link to your site; build a blog that attracts people and who will share your URL with others and post links in the process. List your site with Yahoo Directory for $300 a year.

- Buy ads: Complement your natural search optimization efforts with paid ads on search engines. Choose your keywords and purchase direct exposure on Web pages. You can set your budget and put a ceiling on it to prevent large losses. See what works, and observe the number of visits to your site produced by each keyword string.

- Local e-commerce: Developing a national market can take a long time. If your Web site is particularly attractive to local people, or involves products sold locally, then use keywords that connote your location so people can find you nearby. Town and city names in your keywords, or regions can be helpful, such as "Vermont cheese" or "San Francisco blues music."

TOOLS FOR INTERACTIVITY AND ACTIVE CONTENT

As a manager responsible for building a Web site, you will want to ensure that users can interact with your Web site quickly and easily. As we describe in later chapters, the more interactive a Web site is, the more effective it will be in generating sales and encouraging return visitors.

Although functionality and ease of use are the supreme objectives in site design, you will also want to interact with users and present them with a lively "active" experience. You will want to personalize the experience for customers by addressing their individual needs, and customize the content of your offerings based on their behavior or expressed desires. For example, you may want to offer customers free mortgage calculations or free pension advice, based on their interaction with programs available at your site. In order to achieve these business objectives, you will need to consider carefully the tools necessary to build these capabilities. Simple interactions such as a customer submitting a name, along with more complex interactions involving credit cards, user preferences, and user responses to prompts, all require special programs. Here is a brief description of some commonly used software tools for achieving high levels of site interactivity.

Bling for Your Blog: Web 2.0 Design Elements

widget
a small, pre-built chunk of code that executes automatically in your HTML Web page; capable of performing a wide variety of tasks

One easy way to pump up the energy on your Web site is to include some appropriate widgets (sometimes called gadgets, plug-ins, or snippets). **Widgets** are small chunks of code that execute automatically in your HTML Web page. They are pre-built and many are free. Social networks and blogs use widgets to present users with content drawn from around the Web (news headlines from specific news sources, announcements, press releases, and other routine content), calendars, clocks, weather, live TV, games, and other functionality. You can copy the code to an HTML Web page. A good place to start is Google Gadgets and Yahoo Widgets.

Mashups are a little more complicated, and as explained in Chapter 3, involve pulling functionality and data from one program and including it another. The most common mashup involves using Google Maps data and software and combining it with other data. For instance, if you have a local real estate Web site, you can download Google Maps and satellite images applications to your site so visitors can get a sense of the neighborhood. There are thousands of Google Map mashups, from maps of Myanmar political protests, to maps of the Fortune 500 companies, all with associated news stories and other content. Other mashups involve sports, photos, video, shopping, and news.

The point of these Web 2.0 applications is to enhance user interest and involvement in your site, and to easily include sophisticated functionality and unique data in your Web site.

Common Gateway Interface (CGI)

Common Gateway Interface (CGI) is a set of standards for communication between a browser and a program running on a server that allows for interaction between the user and the server. CGI permits an executable program to access all the information within incoming requests from clients. The program can then generate all the output required to make up the return page (the HTML, script code, text, etc.), and send it back to the client via the Web server. For instance, if a user clicks the Display the Contents of My Shopping Cart button, the server receives this request and executes a CGI program. The CGI program retrieves the contents of the shopping cart from the database and returns it to the server. The server sends an HTML page that displays the contents of the shopping cart on the user's screen. Notice all the computing takes place on the server side (this is why CGI programs and others like it are referred to as "server-side" programs).

CGI programs can be written in nearly any programming language as long as they conform to CGI standards. Currently, Perl is the most popular language for CGI scripting. Generally, CGI programs are used with Unix servers. CGI's primary disadvantage is that it is not highly scalable because a new process must be created for each request, thereby limiting the number of concurrent requests that can be handled. CGI scripts are best used for small to medium-sized applications that do not involve a high volume of user traffic. There are also Web server extensions available, such as FastCGI, that improve CGI's scalability (Doyle and Lopes, 2005).

Common Gateway Interface (CGI)
a set of standards for communication between a browser and a program running on a server that allows for interaction between the user and the server

Active Server Pages (ASP)

Active Server Pages (ASP) is Microsoft's version of server-side programming for Windows. Invented by Microsoft in late 1996, ASP has grown rapidly to become the major technique for server-side Web programming in the Windows environment. ASP enables developers to easily create and open records from a database and execute programs within an HTML page, as well as handle all the various forms of interactivity found on e-commerce sites. Like CGI, ASP permits an interaction to take place between the browser and the server. ASP uses the same standards as CGI for communication with the browser. ASP programs are restricted to use on Windows 2003/2000/NT Web servers running Microsoft's IIS Web server software.

Active Server Pages (ASP)
a proprietary software development tool that enables programmers using Microsoft's IIS package to build dynamic pages

Java, Java Server Pages (JSP), and JavaScript

Java is a programming language that allows programmers to create interactivity and active content on the client computer, thereby saving considerable load on the server. Java was invented by Sun Microsystems in 1990 as a platform-independent programming language for consumer electronics. The idea was to create a language whose programs (so-called Write Once Run Anywhere [WORA] programs) could operate on any computer regardless of operating system. This would be possible if

Java
a programming language that allows programmers to create interactivity and active content on the client computer, thereby saving considerable load on the server

every operating system at the time (Macintosh, Windows, Unix, DOS, and mainframe MVS systems) had a Java Virtual Machine (VM) installed that would interpret the Java programs for that environment.

By 1995, it had become clear, however, that Java was more applicable to the Web than to consumer electronics. Java programs (known as Java applets) could be downloaded to the client over the Web and executed entirely on the client's computer. Applet tags could be included in an HTML page. To enable this, each browser would have to include a Java VM. Today, the leading browsers do include a VM to play Java programs. When the browser accesses a page with an applet, a request is sent to the server to download and execute the program and allocate page space to display the results of the program. Java can be used to display interesting graphics, create interactive environments (such as a mortgage calculator), and directly access the Web server.

Different vendors, including Microsoft, IBM, HP, and others, have produced several versions of the Java language, and even different VMs. Java applets built using Microsoft Java can play well only on Microsoft's Internet Explorer browser. Therefore, the objective of having Java applets play the same on all Web clients has not succeeded. Many corporations will not allow Java applets through their firewalls for security reasons. Despite the fact that Java applets do not have access to local client system resources (they operate in a "sandbox" for security reasons), information system security managers are extremely reluctant to allow applets served from remote servers to come through the firewall. Many Java applets crash or do not perform well, wasting system resources, and when they do perform, the functions are often trivial (such as flashing logos).

Java Server Pages (JSP), like CGI and ASP, is a Web page coding standard that allows developers to use a combination of HTML, JSP scripts, and Java to dynamically generate Web pages in response to user requests. JSP uses Java "servlets," small Java programs that are specified in the Web page and run on the Web server to modify the Web page before it is sent to the user who requested it. JSP is supported by most of the popular application servers on the market today.

JavaScript is a programming language invented by Netscape that is used to control the objects on an HTML page and handle interactions with the browser. It is most commonly used to handle verification and validation of user input, as well as to implement business logic. For instance, JavaScript can be used on customer registration forms to confirm that a valid phone number, zip code, or even e-mail address has been given. Before a user finishes completing a form, the e-mail address given can be tested for validity. JavaScript appears to be much more acceptable to corporations and other environments in large part because it is more stable and also it is restricted to the operation of requested HTML pages. *Insight on Technology: Pumping Up the Customer Experience Using AJAX and Flash* further describes the use of JavaScript and other tools to create highly interactive Web sites.

ActiveX and VBScript

Microsoft—not to be outdone by Sun Microsystems and Netscape—invented the **ActiveX** programming language to compete with Java and **VBScript** to compete

---

Java Server Pages (JSP)

like CGI and ASP, a Web page coding standard that allows developers to dynamically generate Web pages in response to user requests

JavaScript

a programming language invented by Netscape that is used to control the objects on an HTML page and handle interactions with the browser

ActiveX

a programming language created by Microsoft to compete with Java

VBScript

a programming language invented by Microsoft to compete with JavaScript

INSIGHT ON TECHNOLOGY

PUMPING UP THE CUSTOMER EXPERIENCE USING AJAX AND FLASH

The truth is, despite the success of e-commerce retail and services, many people still prefer to shop in real stores so they can feel, touch, and see the goods. The online shopping experience has until recently been limited to online catalogs with pretty pictures and a cumbersome check-out procedure euphemistically called a "shopping cart." There's very little meaningful interactivity in most online retail shopping. Less than 20% of the people who visit even the best Web sites buy something, while most Web sites find less than 5% buy anything. Around 60% of shopping carts are abandoned before purchase. Over 50% of those who visit but do not buy say the main reason is that they cannot see or touch the product.

If ordinary physical retail stores performed this badly they would not call the United States a "consumer economy," and Macy's and Wal-Mart would go broke. Looked at another way: If shopping cart abandonment went to zero and everyone who visited a Web site bought something, it is likely that retail e-commerce would double to over $300 billion a year. That's the upside.

The days of static HTML pages are hopefully coming to an end, and the shopping experience made more virtual, highly interactive, and enjoyable through the use of a set of techniques called AJAX. You can see these new techniques most clearly in mapping services such as Google Maps, MapQuest, and Yahoo Maps. Once the map is drawn on the screen, you can grab the map to move it in any direction without causing the entire HTML page to reload.

But AJAX is at work in many places. In 2009, a start-up called Polyvore took on the giants of fashion Vogue, InStyle, and Lucky.

Polyvore is a user-generated fashion magazine. Using an AJAX application they call the Polyvore Editor, visitors can put together collages (called "sets") using pictures of clothing, accessories, and models drawn from across the Web. Some of the items are already on the site, and users just drag and drop the images to a work area. Polyvore also has a downloadable clipper application that allows users to bring their own images on to the site and paste them into their sets. When users click on a set, and roll their mouse over an item, the manufacturer and price appear. Click on these hot links and you're taken to a site where you can purchase the item. Along with showing display ads, that's how Polyvore makes money. Polyvore had 1.1 million unique visitors in August 2009, more than any of the top fashion magazines. Many other retail sites such as Timberland.com and Nike.com use these same interactive techniques that allow users to build custom boots and shoes with colors, initials, embroidery, and designs all in real-time, without interruption.

Despite these exciting possibilities for rich interactive consumer Web sites, most Web sites today still work on the standard Web model: a customer's client computer asks for a Web page, and a Web server delivers the page. This occurs every time you press a Continue or Search button, or click on another product. Today's highly graphical Web pages often contain several hundred kilobytes of data. But even if you have entered only a few lines of information containing a few hundred bytes of data in the traditional Web client/server model, all the processing is done on a remote server computer, and the client is not much more than a keyboard, screen, and interface. With this traditional model, entire Web

(continued)

pages of information are transferred across the Web, creating delays for the user and hogging bandwidth on the Web.

But there is a different way to create Web pages. Using "AJAX" (for Asynchronous JavaScript and XML, also sometimes just called "Rich Internet applications" or RIA), the client and server work in the background to transfer information immediately as the user enters it, and the server responds immediately, all without the user being aware of the transfer. The result is a smooth, seamless, seemingly continuous user experience. How does RIA work? There are several ways of building rich Internet applications, but they all involve downloading a small program to the client. AJAX and RIA use existing tools to improve the user experience. One method is to download a small JavaScript program to a client computer that has a Java-enabled browser. JavaScript was one of the first client-side languages and technologies with the ability to run a computer program delivered over the Web. This small program carries on a background conversation with the server, retrieving only the information the user needs at whatever interval the application program requires. This method requires that the JavaScript program be capable of running on all target client computers, which may be using any one of several different browsers, and which may or may not be Java-enabled.

A different method is supported by Adobe's Flash plug-in, which nearly 98% of U.S. client computers are currently using. In this method, a Flash program is downloaded to the client. This program runs within the Flash Player installed in most browsers. Flash provides a nearly universal client-side solution. In 2009, Nike rebuilt its online customization tools by using Adobe's Scene7 software, which stores computer models of shoes and clothing items. When users click on a product, they do not see a bitmap image but rather a computer model with the color and texture selected. Scene7 allows the user to rapidly change the color and texture for a customized product. Other innovative software can choose a colored sweater that is appropriate for a specific color of dress you just selected. Select a navy skirt, and you're likely to be shown a beige sweater. That pin-striped blue suit you selected for work probably should have a white shirt behind it, and blue tie. Black shoes.

Whatever method is chosen, the results at consumer Web sites are encouraging. How much more fun can shopping get when you can interact with other shoppers, the tastes of designers, and the ability to build your own. Tests at TJMaxx.com and HomeGoods.com showed that about 50% more customers completed a one-page, AJAX-enabled shopping cart (which combined checkout, billing, and shipping pages) compared to a multiple-page shopping cart used earlier. TravelClicks, an iHotelier unit that sells hotel reservation systems to other hotels, licenses a reservation program built using Adobe's Flex program (a program specifically designed by Adobe to create RIAs). On the roughly 2,000 hotel sites using iHotelier, customers now can see instantly the impact of changing rooms, or changing dates, without loading new pages.

As innovative software tools that allow intense user involvement spread, the original vision of the Web as a highly interactive medium—as opposed to a slow page-turner—will become a reality. And hopefully, shopping carts will not become places where transactions go to die, but instead the last stop for a pleasing customer shopping experience.

■ **SOURCES:** "Polyvore Raises Money for Do-It-Yourself Fashion Site," by Claire Cain Miller, *New York Times*, August 18, 2009; "Site Wins Fashion Fans by Letting Them Design" by Claire Cain Miller, *New York Times*, July 27, 2009; "E-tailers Add Some Glam," by Geoffrey A. Fowler, *Wall Street Journal*, April 20, 2009 "Shopping Cart Abandonment Rises," eMarketer, Inc., May 29, 2008; "The Business Benefits of Developing Applications in AJAX," by Andre Charland, Ulresourcecenter.com, 2008; "Making Web 2.0 Usable: Ajax Case Study," Molecular Inc. 2007; "Ajax Builds a Better Way to Find Ocean Carrier Timetables," by Heather Havenstein, *Computerworld*, March 9, 2007; "E-commerce: AJAX, Flash Make Websites More Engaging," by Meredith Levinson, *CIO Magazine*, March 1, 2006.

with JavaScript. When a browser receives an HTML page with an ActiveX control (comparable to a Java applet), the browser simply executes the program. Unlike Java, however, ActiveX has full access to all the client's resources—printers, networks, and hard drives. VBScript performs in the same way as JavaScript. Of course, ActiveX and VBScript work only if you are using Internet Explorer. Otherwise, that part of the screen is blank.

In general, given the conflicting standards for Java, ActiveX, and VBScript and the diversity of user client computers, many e-commerce sites choose to steer clear of these tools. CGI scripts, JSP, and JavaScript are the leading tools for providing active, dynamic content.

ColdFusion

ColdFusion is an integrated server-side environment for developing interactive Web applications. Originally developed by Macromedia and now offered by Adobe, Cold-Fusion combines an intuitive tag-based scripting language and a tag-based server scripting language (CFML) that lowers the cost of creating interactive features. ColdFusion offers a powerful set of visual design, programming, debugging, and deployment tools.

PERSONALIZATION TOOLS

You will definitely want to know how to treat each customer on an individual basis and emulate a traditional face-to-face marketplace. *Personalization* (the ability to treat people based on their personal qualities and prior history with your site) and *customization* (the ability to change the product to better fit the needs of the customer) are two key elements of e-commerce that potentially can make it nearly as powerful as a traditional marketplace, and perhaps even more powerful than direct mail or shopping at an anonymous suburban shopping mall. Speaking directly to the customer on a one-to-one basis, and even adjusting the product to the customer is quite difficult in the usual type of mass marketing, one-size-fits-all commercial transaction that characterizes much of contemporary commerce.

There are a number of methods for achieving personalization and customization. For instance, you could personalize Web content if you knew the personal background of the visitor. You could also analyze the pattern of clicks and sites visited for every customer who enters your site. We discuss these methods in later chapters on marketing. The primary method for achieving personalization and customization is through the placement of cookie files on the user's client computer. As we discussed in Chapter 3, a cookie is a small text file placed on the user's client computer that can contain any kind of information about the customer, such as customer ID, campaign ID, or purchases at the site. And then, when the user returns to the site, or indeed goes further into your site, the customer's prior history can be accessed from a database. Information gathered on prior visits can then be used to personalize the visit and customize the product.

For instance, when a user returns to a site, you can read the cookie to find a customer ID, look the ID up in a database of names, and greet the customer ("Hello Mary! Glad to have you return!"). You could also have stored a record of prior

ColdFusion
an integrated server-side environment for developing interactive Web applications

purchases, and then recommend a related product ("How about the wrench tool box now that you have purchased the wrenches?"). And you could think about customizing the product ("You've shown an interest in the elementary training programs for Word. We have a special 'How to Study' program for beginners in Office software. Would you like to see a sample copy online?").

We further describe the use of cookies and their effectiveness in achieving a one-to-one relationship with the customer in Chapter 8.

THE INFORMATION POLICY SET

privacy policy

a set of public statements declaring to your customers how you treat their personal information that you gather on the site

accessibility rules

a set of design objectives that ensure disabled users can effectively access your site

In developing an e-commerce site, you will also need to focus on the set of information policies that will govern the site. You will need to develop a **privacy policy**—a set of public statements declaring to your customers how you treat their personal information that you gather on the site. You also will need to establish **accessibility rules**—a set of design objectives that ensure disabled users can effectively access your site. There are more than 50 million Americans who are disabled and require special access routes to buildings as well as computer systems (see *Insight on Society: Designing for Accessibility in Web 2.0*). E-commerce information policies are described in greater depth in Chapter 8.

INSIGHT ON SOCIETY

DESIGNING FOR ACCESSIBLITY IN WEB 2.0

In July 2009, the National Federation of the Blind and the American Council of the Blind sued Arizona State University to stop ASU's planned use of Kindle e-book reading devices in a pilot program that would be inaccessible to blind students. ASU plans to roll out the Kindle reader campus-wide sometime in the near term. For students, Kindle textbooks are available at roughly half the price of a standard book. However, the Kindle has no audio option, which means blind students cannot select a book or have the book read aloud to them. This is just the most recent of a number of lawsuits dealing with the issue of Web site and online accessibility.

In 1998, Congress amended the Rehabilitation Act to require U.S. agencies, government contractors, and others receiving federal money to make electronic and information technology services accessible to people with disabilities. Known as Section 508, this legislation requires Web sites of federally funded organizations to be accessible to users who are blind, deaf, blind and deaf, or unable to use a mouse. However, the legislation applies only to U.S. agencies, government contractors, and others receiving federal money, and not to the broader e-commerce environment of private business firms.

In one of the first law suits seeking to enforce Section 508 for Internet services, Access Now Inc., an advocacy group for the disabled, sued Southwest Airlines in 2001 on behalf of more than 50 million disabled Americans for operating a Web site that was inaccessible to the disabled, on the grounds that this violated the 1990 Americans with Disabilities Act (ADA). In November 2002, a Federal District Court in Florida, in one of the first court decisions on the applicability of

the ADA to Web sites, ruled that ADA applies only to physical spaces, not virtual spaces. However, the judge noted in a footnote that she was surprised that a customer-oriented firm like Southwest Airlines did not "employ all available technologies to expand accessibility to its Web site for visually impaired customers who would be an added source of revenue."

Since this early decision however, both the interpretation of the law and public sentiment have resulted in many well-known Web sites attempting to conform to the spirit of Section 508, sometimes voluntarily and sometimes under threat from advocacy groups. For instance, RadioShack, Amazon, Ramada, and Priceline have entered into agreements with the American Council for the Blind, and the American Foundation for the Blind. Meanwhile, the National Federation of the Blind (NFB) brought a class-action suit against Target for failing to make its site accessible for the blind. They claimed that blind people could not use Target's shopping cart because it required use of a mouse, used inaccessible image maps and graphics, and lacked compliant alt-text, an invisible code embedded beneath graphics that allows screen reading software to vocalize a description of the image. Target claimed the ADA did not apply to Web sites.

In September 2006, a federal district court ruled that ADA did indeed apply to Web sites. The court held "the 'ordinary meaning' of the ADA's prohibition against discrimination in the enjoyment of goods, services, facilities, or privileges is that whatever goods or services the place provides, it cannot discriminate on the basis of disability in providing enjoyment of those goods and services." The court thus rejected Target's

(continued)

argument that only its physical store locations were covered by the civil rights laws, ruling instead that all services provided by Target, including its Web site, must be accessible to persons with disabilities. In October 2007, the court granted class-action status to the lawsuit.

In August 2008, Target and the NFB settled the suit. Target made no admission or concession that its Web site violated the ADA, but agreed to bring it into compliance with certain online assistive technology guidelines by February 28, 2009, and to have the NFB certify that it is compliant with those guidelines. In addition, Target agreed to pay damages of $6 million. Many accessibility advocates expressed disappointment that the resolution of the case via a settlement failed to provide any clear legal precedent. Nevertheless, a prudent e-commerce firm with a customer orientation will use available technologies to expand accessibility to its Web site for impaired customers both to expand its customer base and avoid costly and embarrassing litigation.

And it isn't just American law that a business needs to consider when designing a Web site. In 2007, a blind systems manager was unable to complete an online course provided by the Project Management Institute (PMI). The test taker was a U.K. resident and brought proceedings against PMI, a U.S.-based non-profit group, citing the U.K. Disability Discrimination Act of 1995. PMI was ultimately required to compensate the test taker.

So how does a blind person access the Web, and how should designers build in accessibility for blind persons? Most blind persons use the same PCs as everyone else. But a blind person's PC uses screen-reader software that translates text information on the screen into synthesized speech or Braille. The program used to surf the Web will most likely be Internet Explorer, although other browsers are also available, such as Lynx (a text-only browser written originally to run under Unix) and IBM's Home Page Reader, which generate their own speech.

A blind person enters a Web page by checking out the hypertext links that are on the page. This is usually accomplished by jumping from link to link with the Tab key; the screen-reader access software automatically reads the highlighted text as the focus moves from link to link. If the highlighted text is something like "How to Contact Us" or "Visit Your Shopping Cart," the blind user will be able to make some sense out of the link. If, however, the highlighted text is "Click Here," or "Here," it will be difficult if not impossible for the blind user to interpret the meaning of the link without using a different navigation strategy. With the more recent screen access software/browser combinations, it is possible for a blind Web surfer to explore the page one line at a time, thus alleviating this problem. However, being forced to examine every detail of a Web page just to learn the meaning of a hypertext link is a time-consuming process that, ideally, should be avoided. The important point to keep in mind is that the screen access software is looking for ASCII text, which it can convert to speech or Braille.

Once the desired hypertext link has been located, the blind person presses the Enter key (clicks on the link) to go where the link points. If there is a form to fill out on the page, the blind person will usually tab to the appropriate input field and type the information in the usual way. Other controls such as checkboxes, combo boxes, radio buttons, and the like can all be used if the screen-reader software can detect them. There are several simple strategies Web designers can use to improve accessibility. Embedding text descriptions behind images is one example that allows screen readers to announce those descriptions. So instead of saying "Image," when a screen reader passes over an image, the visually impaired user can hear "Photo of a cruise ship sitting in a harbor." Allowing users to set the color and font schemes can also make a difference for the visually impaired. Adding screen magnification tools and sound labels where hyperlinks appear are two additional ways to increase accessibility.

These are examples of "equivalent alternatives" to visual content that disability advocates suggest should be required, both for visual and auditory content, to ensure individuals with disabilities have equal access information that appears on screen. Guidelines for creating accessible Web pages include ensuring that text and graphics are understandable when viewed without color, using features that enable activation of page elements via a variety of input devices (such as keyboard, head wand, or Braille reader), and providing clear navigation mechanisms (such as navigation bars or a site map) to aid users.

The World Wide Web Consortium (W3C) issued Web Content Accessibility Guidelines (WCAG) 2.0 in December 2008 that provide all organizations with assistive and adaptive strategies in Web design for accommodating people with many different kinds of disabilities. Some of the problems encountered by disabled users in today's Web 2.0 are so-called "captchas" or distorted text which people are supposed to read and then reenter into a text box to gain access to a site; check out buttons that are images rather than text and cannot be read by text-reading soft-

ware; and of course YouTube videos without captions.

In general, the software industry has come up short: sophisticated screen-reader software costs about $1,000. The Apple iPhone 3GS provides an example of what is possible in hardware and software design for blind people. The iPhone has no physical keys, but it does have a VoiceOver function (in Settings->General->Accessibility). You can do everything on the iPhone by tapping the icon while the software speaks what you are touching. You can select the language, for example, and the speaking rate.

Business firms pay a cost for making their sites accessible to the blind. Today, only about 10% of all Web sites in the United States are minimally accessible and only loosely conform to the international Web Accessibility Initiative (version 1.0) of the W3C. The only large-scale survey of Web site accessibility was carried out by T. V. Rahman, a blind engineer at Google in 2006. Of several million Web pages searched, not a single Web page was totally in conformance with W3C guidelines, and only a handful of sites were reasonably in compliance. But, as graphical elements such as video come to play an ever more important role in Web content and navigation, it becomes even more important for these elements to be accessible to the blind. There are about 10 million visually impaired persons in the United States alone who represent a formidable economic force, not to mention 42 million other persons who have other disabilities, many of which impair access to today's Web 2.0.

SOURCES: W3C "Web Accessibility Initiative," WC3.org, accessed August 14, 2009; "Web Accessibility: Making Your Site Accessible to the Blind," by Curtiss Chong, National Federation of the Blind, accessed August 14, 2009; "Advocates for Blind Students Sue ASU Over Kindle Use," by Anne Ryman, *Arizona Republic*, July 27, 2009; "Making the iPhone Icons Speak," by David Pogue, *New York Times*, July 14, 2009;. "Web Accessibility and the Law," by Joseph Dolson, *Practical eCommerce*, June 30, 2009; "Accessible Design is Good Business," podcast, BusinessWeek.com, April 21, 2009; "For the Blind, Technology Does What A Guide Dog Can't," by Miguel Helt, *New York Times*, January 4, 2009; "Target Settles Lawsuit with Advocates for Blind," by Andrea K.Walker, *Baltimore Sun*, August 28, 2008; "Develop a Web Site Accessible by Visually Impaired Users and Comply with the Law," by Joe Gross, TechRepublic.com, February 21, 2008.

REI Climbs the Web Mountain

Washington-based Recreational Equipment, Inc. (REI) is one of the world's largest online retailers of outdoor gear. REI is also one of the e-commerce pioneers in the United States, having launched their first Web site in 1996. In 2009, they are on their fourth Web site design. REI's story is the story of e-commerce for large national retailers as they adapt both to changing Internet technology and changing consumer taste and culture.

Lloyd and Mary Anderson, mountain climbers from Seattle, Washington, founded REI in 1938. The Andersons imported a special ice axe from Austria for themselves and decided to set up a cooperative to help their friends and other fellow outdoor enthusiasts acquire high-quality climbing and camping gear at reasonable prices. Today, REI is the largest consumer cooperative in the United States, with 3.7 million members who have paid a one-time membership fee of $20 that entitles them to an annual dividend equal to about 10% of their annual purchases. And the business has grown. Today, REI operates 112 retail stores in 28 states, two online stores, an international mail order operation, and REI Adventures, a travel agency. Kiosks in every store allow customers to access products at either of REI's Web sites: REI.com and REI-Outlet.com. REI employs over 9,500 people, and in 2008, generated over $1.43 billion in gross revenues, about $238 million of which comes from its online stores.

REI first started exploring the Internet in the summer of 1995. Netscape, the first popular Internet browser, had just gone public, and e-commerce was just getting started. As with many business success stories, REI's online venture began with senior executives who recognized the potentially transformative power of the Web, and the mixture of opportunity and possible threat that it represented to their existing business.

Many traditional bricks-and-mortar retailers at that time feared cannibalization of their retail and/or catalog sales if they introduced an online sales outlet. Their nightmare was that starting an online store would merely "steal" their own customers from their regular sales channels. But REI wasn't deterred. As Dennis Madsen, REI's former president and chief executive officer, said, "We knew that if we could not serve our customers who were looking to shop with us online, they would turn to someone else online. It was never a question for us. Being online meant better serving the customer. Our experience has proven that cannibalization is largely a myth and that our multi-channel customers are our best customers. For instance, dual-channel customers who shopped both online and at stores spent 114% more than single-channel customers. And customers who shop three channels—retail stores, Web, and kiosks—spent 48% more than dual-channel customers."

REI launched its first Web site with a budget of approximately $500,000. At the time, Netscape was the only company offering a complete e-commerce suite, so REI chose Netscape's Merchant 4.5 Server software installed on an IBM RS/6000 server. And although Matt Hyde, the executive in charge of the launch, recognized that REI was a retailer by trade, not a programming shop, he chose to keep design of the site in-house, using off-the-shelf Web authoring tools rather than outsource creation of the Web site. The rationale: "When [we] took the leap of faith that we could launch this compelling value proposition, and that it could be big, [we] realized we needed to make this a core competency. It couldn't be outsourced."

The decision to "build their own" was not without its costs, however: managing REI.com's growth internally, with no outsourcing, strained REI's human resources. REI soon discovered that finding people with the requisite skills could be difficult, and even if they could be found, they were a lot more expensive than salespeople. In September 1996, at a time when few traditional retailers were even looking at online sales, REI.com launched, promoted primarily through direct mail and in-store notices. The first order arrived 20 minutes later. By February 1997, Hyde and his team knew they were on the right track. Traffic was up by 50% in the two months following Christmas. But that in itself posed a problem. As Hyde remembers, "We chose Netscape early on, and they were clearly the leader [at that time]. But not long after getting the system up, we realized that it was too limited. When you go from a few thousand people checking out your site to a million every month, you need a lot of infrastructure."

He also noted, "On the surface, e-commerce sounds relatively easy. It's not until you have experience trying to integrate a high-volume, high-functionality Web site into existing business processes and applications that you realize that it's a lot harder than it seems. It's like an iceberg—the view from the browser is only 10% of what it takes to build a successful and profitable Web site."

In 1998, REI initiated its second Web site design. This time they had more of a choice in the marketplace for Web software and services. They looked at offerings from all the major vendors, including Microsoft, IBM, BroadVision, and Open Market. "When you change commerce packages, there's a huge learning curve. I was going to make this change once, but I wasn't going to do it again, so I wanted to pick the right package ... for the next several years." In early 1998, REI decided on IBM's Net.Commerce server software. An important factor in the decision was IBM's ability to preserve all the custom coding REI had done over the past two years to connect its online store to its legacy system. "I had hundreds of thousands, if not millions of dollars tied up in this [system], and we didn't want to throw it away. And since Net.Commerce [would also lessen] the need to do custom coding in the future, it's a two-fold benefit." The new REI.com Web site launched in October 1998.

In 2002, REI began a third re-building of its Web site by standardizing on a single platform, IBM's WebSphere, an integrated set of e-commerce site development and operational tools. Prior to that point, REI's e-commerce infrastructure was a mixture of software applications written both in-house and by a variety of different technology vendors. In the period since REI's second re-build in 1998, IBM had developed a suite of tools and functionalities built on standards such as Java and Unix that included WebSphere Application Server and WebSphere Commerce, all running on IBM pSeries

Unix-based servers that could be configured with multiple processors as necessary in order to scale the business (see figure above). With its focus on an integrated platform from a single vendor, REI has implemented extensive customer features utilizing the platform's capabilities in personalized service and information, as well as more convenience for both online and in-store shoppers. For instance, REI gained the ability to refer new Web customers to nearby stores that are having sales. It can e-mail coupons for bike helmets redeemable at local stores or online to customers who purchased a bicycle. WebSphere can drop an image of hiking boots featured at REI on to the screen of a customer reading an REI "Learn and Share" article on backpacking.

REI's clicks-and-bricks strategy has paid off handsomely. In addition to improving relationships with existing customers, the online stores have helped create new customers. Over a third of the online customers are not members of the REI cooperative, meaning they are likely new customers, compared to 15% of REI's retail customers. And despite management's early fears, the online stores haven't cannibalized traditional store sales. In fact, the opposite has occurred: The Web site has attracted new customers and strengthened the relationship with existing customers. Two services enabled by the WebSphere Commerce platform, REI Store Pickup service, and REI's gift registry, are a case in point. REI Store Pickup service provides in-store pickup as a free shipping option for online orders. To implement the service, REI combined its Web and store fulfillment systems, shipping customer merchandise to the stores on the same trucks that deliver the store's bi-weekly stock orders. The service has proved to be a tremendous success. In its first 12 months, in-store pickups from online sales accounted for $40 million in revenue, and they now account for about a third of online sales. Today, more than 40% of all orders generated on REI.com's Web site are delivered to stores for pickup, and one-third of the customers who pick up orders purchase an additional $90 in merchandise during the visit. REI's multi-channel gift registry is another example.

With the ascendancy of Google and search engine marketing, REI realized the importance of appearing on the first page of search engine queries. REI worked with a Web firm called Netconcepts to redesign its Web pages, end the practice of using dynamic URLs for pages, and in general make the catalog Web pages more friendly to search engine Web crawlers so its pages could be properly read. The result was a 200% gain in "natural search" sales produced without making payments to search engines. In 2006, REI began using a software service, Mercent Retail, to help it better manage referrals from comparison shopping portals such as Shopping.com and manufacturer Web sites. The service, which is integrated with REI's backend retail management software systems, helps REI maintain brand and merchandising consistency between its own Web sites and the various third-party sites, and optimizes the product links sent to each of its channel partners. In 2007, REI switched from its proprietary search engine to one from Mercado Software, enabling customers to quickly search for items by brand, price, or best sellers.

In 2008, REI initiated its fourth Web site redesign. Today's Internet is more interactive, more personal, more social, and more video-oriented than in the past. REI's 2009 Web site would have been unimaginable in 1996, or even 2006. The emphasis of the new Web site is standardization, personalization, search, and social features (user-written product reviews, and lots of onsite opportunities to send messages to friends via various social channels). The focus is on enhancing the shopping experience, resulting in longer average online sessions, and more sales. The average visitor session has increased by 14% to 11 minutes and 23 seconds from 10 minutes in 2007, says Web measurement firm Hitwise.

When you run a Web site with a handful of pages, it's possible to hand-code each page. When you have 4,000 product pages, you need a standardized template in a database that allows you to make one change to the single template, and then automatically roll out those changes to the 4,000 product pages. The new site, which REI quietly launched in June, also was built with standard templates on the back end that make it easier for Web developers and programmers to make changes to home and product pages. "It was time to move REI.com into the twenty-first century," says REI vice president of e-commerce and Web strategy Brad Brown. "We can now change the product page template, republish it and each page that uses that template is updated with the change. One template for 4,000 product pages means one change results in all product pages being changed versus having to change each product page in the pre-template world."

To achieve more personalization, REI is using customer review technology from PowerReviews Inc. and survey tools from OpinionLab Inc.. REI now has 35,000 reviews posted on the site. To keep up with changing technologies and consumer culture, REI has created two free smart phone apps in 2009: Bike Your Drive, a free program that allows bikers to view their progress, save the mileage they've traveled, upload photos tagged by location, and report how much less carbon dioxide there is in the air as a result of their bike trip; and REI Snow Reports, which lets iPhone, BlackBerry, and Windows Mobile users get instant information about conditions at ski resorts and mountains in the United States, Canada, Europe, and elsewhere. Both free apps provide one-touch access to REI's e-commerce site. REI has numerous

SOURCES: "About Us," REI.com, August 2009; "REI Peddles Pedaling With a Free Tracking Program for Mobile Phones," Internet Retailer, July 8, 2009; "2008 E-commerce Sales For REI Jog Ahead by 5.3%," Internet Retailer, February 25, 2009; "Cabela's Bags In-store Traffic With Online Coupons," May 25, 2009; "Top 500 Guide, 2009 Edition," Internet Retailer, 2009; "REI Gives Skiers and Snowboarders Their Own Mobile Application," Internet Retailer, December 18, 2008; "REI's Approach to Online Music: Free and Exclusive," Internet Retailer, October 24, 2008. "REI Makes Standardization the Bedrock of Its New Web Site Design," Internet Retailer, October 1, 2008; REI Announces Bill Bauman, Vice President of Information Technology, September 2, 2008; "REI Combines 20 Sources of Customer Information into One Data Warehouse," Internet Retailer, March 18, 2008; "Driving Sales," Internet Retailer, March 2008; REI's Online Performance Climbs with Mercent Retail," March 20, 2007; "Case Study: REI," Netconcepts.com, July 28, 2006; "REI.com Expands Its Store Pickup Program," Internet Retailer, March 15, 2006; "REI Optimizes Sales with Cross-Channel Commerce Solution," IBM Case Study, August 2004; "How REI Scaled the Ecommerce Mountain, " by Megan Santosus, CIO, May 19, 2004; "REI Personalizes Online Shopping with WebSphere Commerce Suite," IBM Global Industries: Retail Case Studies, IBM Case Study, April 2003.

videos on its site, and plans more videos to augment the expert advice videos customers already can access on topics such as bike maintenance.

REI in 2009 is also implementing more rich media, videocasts, and other Web 2.0 tools. For example, shoppers can watch a video on how to change a flat bicycle tire. Links for related products appear on the same page. Rich media applications from Heck Yes Productions enable shoppers to see products in 3-D and from different angles. RSS is another new tool that REI is using. As you learned in Chapter 3, RSS is a data feed that delivers updated information from selected Web sites directly to a subscriber's desktop. REI uses RSS to drive traffic to REI-Outlet.com's "deal of the day."

Continuing to evolve with its customer base, REI has experimented with music and music videos as a marketing tool to attract its young audience and keep them on site for longer periods of time. For instance, the company launched an REI Go Playlist of 10 songs exclusive to REI that customers could download from REIGoPlaylist.com. REI developed the songs in partnership with the bands and its snow sports brands. "All tracks are exclusive to REI Go Playlist and are not on any CDs or other sites," says a spokeswoman. Brand name manufacturers sponsoring the list included Burton, K2, Marmot, Ride, Rossignol, Smith, Salomon, The North Face, and Völkl. "Through a wide range of music, we hope REI Go Playlist gets new and current customers and members excited about the upcoming skiing and snowboarding season," says Tom Vogl, REI's vice president of marketing. The program ran from October 2008 to March 2009, and was very successful.

REI is also putting the finishing touches on a three-year-long, multi-million dollar project to create a new data warehouse that will combine information collected in stores, on the Web, from call centers, and all other customer contacts into a single database. The data warehouse will allow REI to deliver highly targeted marketing messages and customer service: "People [like you] who like music by Robbers on High Street also like Rossignol skis." Staying atop the Web mountain requires both continuing innovation and investment.

Case Study Questions

1. Create a simple logical design and physical design for REI.com using information provided in the case study, supplemented as necessary by your own research.

2. After reading the case study, identify the key reasons for REI.com's success thus far.

3. Visit REI.com and rate its performance on the eight factors listed in Table 4.10 on a scale of 1 to 10 (with 1 being the lowest and 10 the highest). Provide reasons for your ratings.

4. Prepare a short industry analysis of the online outdoor sporting goods and apparel industry. Who are REI's primary competitors? How well have they developed multi-channel retailing?

4.6 REVIEW

KEY CONCEPTS

■ Explain the process that should be followed in building an e-commerce Web site.

Factors you must consider when building an e-commerce site include:
- Hardware architecture
- Software
- Telecommunications capacity
- Site design
- Human resources
- Organizational capabilities

The systems development life cycle (a methodology for understanding the business objectives of a system and designing an appropriate solution) for building an e-commerce Web site involves five major steps:

- Identify the specific business objectives for the site, and then develop a list of system functionalities and information requirements.
- Develop a system design specification (both logical design and physical design).
- Build the site, either by in-house personnel or by outsourcing all or part of the responsibility to outside contractors.
- Test the system (unit testing, system testing, and acceptance testing).
- Implement and maintain the site.

The nine basic business and system functionalities an e-commerce site should contain include:

- *Digital catalog*—allows a site to display goods using text and graphics.
- *Product database*—provides product information, such as a description, stocking number, and inventory level.
- *Customer on-site tracking*—enables a site to create a site log for each customer visit, aiding in personalizing the shopping experience and identifying common customer paths and destinations.
- *Shopping cart/payment system*—provides an ordering system, secure credit-card clearing, and other payment options.
- *Customer database*—includes customer information such as the name, address, phone number, and e-mail address.
- *Sales database*—contains information regarding the customer ID, product purchased, date, payment, and shipment to be able to provide after-sale customer support.
- *Ad server*—tracks the site behavior of prospects and customers that come through e-mail or banner ad campaigns.
- *Site tracking and reporting system*—monitors the number of unique visitors, pages visited, and products purchased.

- *Inventory management system*—provides a link to production and suppliers in order to facilitate order replenishment.

■ **Describe the major issues surrounding the decision to outsource site development and/or hosting.**

Advantages of building a site in-house include:
- The ability to change and adapt the site quickly as the market demands
- The ability to build a site that does exactly what the company needs

Disadvantages of building a site in-house include:
- The costs may be higher
- The risks of failure may be greater, given the complexity of issues such as security, privacy, and inventory management
- The process may be more time-consuming than if you had hired an outside specialist firm to manage the effort
- Staff may experience a longer learning curve that delays your entry into the market

Using design templates cuts development time, but pre-set templates can also limit functionality.

A similar decision is also necessary regarding outsourcing the hosting of the site versus keeping it in-house. Relying on an outside vendor to ensure that the site is live twenty-four hours a day places the burden of reliability on someone else, in return for a monthly hosting fee. The downside is that if the site requires fast upgrades due to heavy traffic, the chosen hosting company may or may not be capable of keeping up. Reliability versus scalability is the issue in this instance.

■ **Identify and understand the major considerations involved in choosing Web server and e-commerce merchant server software.**

Early Web sites used single-tier system architecture and consisted of a single-server computer that delivered static Web pages to users making requests through their browsers. The extended functionality of today's Web sites required the development of a multi-tiered systems architecture, which utilizes a variety of specialized Web servers, as well as links to pre-existing "backend" or "legacy" corporate databases.

All e-commerce sites require basic Web server software to answer requests from customers for HTML and XML pages. When choosing Web server software, companies are also choosing what operating system the site will run on. Apache, which runs on the Unix system, is the market leader.

Web servers provide a host of services, including:
- Processing user HTML requests
- Security services
- File transfer
- Search engine
- Data capture
- E-mail
- Site management tools

Dynamic server software allows sites to deliver dynamic content, rather than static, unchanging information. Web application server programs enable a wide range of e-commerce functionality, including creating a customer database, creating an e-mail promotional program, and accepting and processing orders, as well as many other services.

E-commerce merchant server software is another important software package that provides catalog displays, information storage and customer tracking, order taking (shopping cart), and credit card purchase processing. E-commerce suites can save time and money, but customization can significantly drive up costs. Factors to consider when choosing an e-commerce suite include its functionality, support for different business models, visual site management tools and reporting systems, performance and scalability, connectivity to existing business systems, compliance with standards, and global and multicultural capability.

- **Understand the issues involved in choosing the most appropriate hardware for an e-commerce site.**

Speed, capacity, and scalability are three of the most important considerations when selecting an operating system, and therefore the hardware that it runs on.

To evaluate how fast the site needs to be, companies need to assess the number of simultaneous users the site expects to see, the nature of their requests, the type of information requested, and the bandwidth available to the site. The answers to these questions will provide guidance regarding the processors necessary to meet customer demand. In some cases, adding additional processing power can add capacity, thereby improving system speed.

Scalability is also an important issue. Increasing processing supply by scaling up to meet demand can be done through:

- *Vertical scaling*—improving the processing power of the hardware, but maintaining the same number of servers
- *Horizontal scaling*—adding more of the same processing hardware
- *Improving processing architecture*—identifying operations with similar workloads and using dedicated tuned servers for each type of load

- **Identify additional tools that can improve Web site performance.**

In addition to providing a speedy Web site, companies must also strive to have a well-designed site that encourages visitors to buy. Building in interactivity improves site effectiveness, as does personalization techniques that provide the ability to track customers while they are visiting the site. Commonly used software tools for achieving high levels of Web site interactivity and customer personalization include:

- *Common Gateway Interface (CGI) scripts*—a set of standards for communication between a browser and a program on a server that allows for interaction between the user and the server
- *Active Server Pages (ASP)*—a Microsoft tool that also permits interaction between the browser and the server
- *Java applets*—programs written in the Java programming language that also provide interactivity
- *JavaScript*—used to validate user input, such as an e-mail address

- *ActiveX and VBScript*—Microsoft's version of Java and JavaScript, respectively
- *Cookies*—text files stored on the user's hard drive that provide information regarding the user and his or her past experience at a Web site

QUESTIONS

1. Name the six main pieces of the e-commerce site building puzzle.
2. Define the systems development life cycle and discuss the various steps involved in creating an e-commerce site.
3. Discuss the differences between a simple logical and simple physical Web site design.
4. Why is system testing important? Name the three types of testing and their relation to each other.
5. Compare the costs for system development and system maintenance. Which is more expensive, and why?
6. Why is a Web site so costly to maintain? Discuss the main factors that impact cost.
7. What are the main differences between single-tier and multi-tier site architecture?
8. Name five basic functionalities a Web server should provide.
9. What are the three main factors to consider when choosing the best hardware platform for your Web site?
10. Why is Web server bandwidth an important issue for e-commerce sites?
11. Compare and contrast the various scaling methods. Explain why scalability is a key business issue for Web sites.
12. What are the eight most important factors impacting Web site design, and how do they affect a site's operation?
13. What are Java and JavaScript? What role do they play in Web site design?
14. Name and describe three methods used to treat customers individually. Why are they significant to e-commerce?
15. What are some of the policies e-commerce businesses must develop before launching a site, and why must they be developed?

PROJECTS

1. Go to FreeWebs.com or NetworkSolutions.com. Both sites allow you to create a simple e-tailer Web site for a free trial period. Create a Web site. The site should feature at least four pages, including a home page, product page, shopping cart, and contact page. Extra credit will be given for additional complexity and creativity. Come to class prepared to present your e-tailer concept and Web site.

2. Visit several e-commerce sites, not including those mentioned in this chapter, and evaluate the effectiveness of the sites according to the eight basic criteria/functionalities listed in Table 4.10. Choose one site you feel does an excellent job on all the aspects of an effective site and create a presentation, including screen shots, to support your choice.

3. Imagine that you are the head of information technology for a fast-growth e-commerce start-up. You are in charge of development of the company's Web site. Consider your options for building the site in-house with existing staff, or outsourcing the entire operation. Decide which strategy you believe is in your company's best interest and create a brief presentation outlining your position. Why choose that approach? And what are the estimated associated costs, compared with the alternative? (You'll need to make some educated guesses here—don't worry about being exact.)

4. Choose two of the e-commerce suite software packages listed in Table 4.5 and prepare an evaluation chart that rates the packages on the key factors discussed in the section "Choosing an E-commerce Suite." Which package would you choose if you were developing a Web site of the type described in this chapter, and why?

5. Choose one of the open source Web content management systems such as Joomla or Drupal or another of your own choosing and prepare an evaluation chart similar to that required by Project 4. Which system would you choose and why?

WEB SITE RESOURCES www.azimuth-interactive.com/ecommerce6e

- Additional projects, exercises, and tutorials
- Careers: Explore career opportunities in e-commerce
- Raising capital and business plans

CHAPTER 5

Online Security and Payment Systems

After reading this chapter, you will be able to:

- Understand the scope of e-commerce crime and security problems.
- Describe the key dimensions of e-commerce security.
- Understand the tension between security and other values.
- Identify the key security threats in the e-commerce environment.
- Describe how technology helps protect the security of messages sent over the Internet.
- Identify the tools used to establish secure Internet communications channels, and protect networks, servers, and clients.
- Appreciate the importance of policies, procedures, and laws in creating security.
- Describe the features of traditional payment systems.
- Understand the major e-commerce payment mechanisms.
- Describe the features and functionality of electronic billing presentment and payment systems.

Cyberwar Becomes a Reality

On August 6, 2009, Twitter, the micro-blogging site, with more than 45 million daily users worldwide at the time, was hit with a distributed denial of service (DDoS) attack launched via a worldwide botnet. The botnet is believed to have been controlled by a group of hackers in Russia seeking to shut down the Web activities of a single blogger in Georgia (a former Russian republic) who voiced support for the Republic of Georgia in that country's continuing conflict with Russia. The attack caused a nearly day-long outage at Twitter as network administrators tried to cope with tens of millions of requests for service (pages) launched by the botnet. The Georgian blogger's other activities

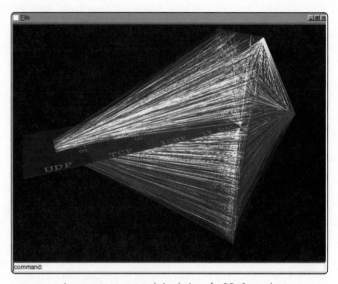

A computer-generated simulation of a DDoS attack.

on Facebook, YouTube, and LiveJournal were also targeted. However, Facebook, YouTube, and LiveJournal have better defenses and were not so severely affected. Investigators are uncertain exactly who launched the attack or where it originated. Around 45% of the computers in the botnet were located in Brazil, 9% in Turkey, 8% in India, and the remainder spread across the world. Owners of these thousands of computers were not aware their computers were involved.

The attack on Twitter is just the most recent (as of this writing) instance of cyberwarfare. Cyberwarfare is a form of war among organizations, states, and societies carried out over the Internet. During the prior month, on the July 4th holiday weekend, a number of South Korean and U.S. Web sites were similarly attacked. Eleven major government Web sites in South Korea (including the Defense Ministry, National Assembly, and Information Security Agency), the daily newspaper *Chosun Ilbo*, the Internet portal Naver.com, and Korea's Shinhan Bank were hit. Fourteen major U.S. sites were also targeted, including the White House, State Department, Treasury Department, the Secret Service, the Federal Trade Commission, and the New York Stock Exchange. Many of the government sites were knocked out for various periods of time. According to the *Washington Post*, in addition to the government sites, several commercial Web sites were also attacked, including its own, and those operated by the Nasdaq securities exchange. The attack used several botnets around the world, and it is unclear who was behind these attacks although observers speculated North Korea may have been involved.

These 2009 attacks mirror an extensive cyberattack against Estonia in April 2007, which shut down key government and financial institutions there for several days. Prior to the current attacks, the cyberattack on Estonia was the largest and most significant Internet security event among nations in the history of the Internet. In 10 large assaults, over 1 million computers worldwide slammed Estonian servers with junk messages and requests, producing streams of 90 megabits of data a second for 10 hours, far beyond the capacity of Estonia's routers, switches, and Web servers.

While cyberwar has been written about in novels, the Twitter, Korean-American, and Estonian situations, and an earlier major attack against VeriSign, illustrate that cyberwar is now a reality on a much scarier scale. VeriSign operates and maintains the root servers that keep track of nearly all Internet addresses in the United States. In the VeriSign case, several botnets involving several hundred thousand computers around the globe attempted to overwhelm all of the 13 root server systems—the top-level domains such as .com, .org, .net, and others. The attack failed but severely stressed the United States' Internet infrastructure, slowing down the Internet and demonstrating how fragile the entire system is to such attacks. In the United States, the public Web, air-traffic control systems, and telecommunications services have all been attacked. Congressional offices have been told that China has broken into their computers. Both China and Russia have been caught trying to infiltrate the U.S. electric-power grid, leaving behind software code to be used to disrupt the system. The risk of attacks to create massive power outages is so serious that the best option could be unplugging the U.S. power grid from the Internet.

Imagine: about 10% of the world's billion plus computers connected to the Internet worldwide are captured by stealth malware programs that users unintentionally install by opening e-mail attachments or clicking malicious links that download files, or as a result of using pirated "free" software. RustockB is one common stealth program that adds unwitting users to botnets. These programs then take over the computer without the user knowing and are controlled remotely by a Command and Control server. Once under control, the botnet is used to send spam. Botnets are responsible for over 80% of the spam sent throughout the world. This is the most profitable use of botnets. They are also used to collect credit card information, personal IDs, and bank information, feeding the underground economy with identity theft candidates. The botnets can be "rented" to run DDoS attacks against any site on the Internet. It could be your company, or your bank. Shadowserver, an organization of volunteer computer security experts, tracks 400,000 known infected computers (a small fraction of the total) and about 1,500 active controllers.

National defense against botnets requires a significant investment in additional computing power, as well as management attention. The Pentagon has created a Cyberwar Command to lead national security efforts in cyber defense. The Obama administration, recognizing the growing importance of cybersecurity, has proposed creating a cabinet-level post. "It's now clear this cyber threat is one of the most serious economic and national security challenges we face as a nation," Obama has said, and "We're not as prepared as we should be, as a government or as a country."

SOURCES: "Security Researchers Zero In On Twitter Hackers," by Gregg Keizer, Computerworld, August 7, 2009; "Attack on Twitter Came in Two Waves," Jenna Wortham, *New York Times*, August 7, 2009; "Webs Anonymity Makes Cyberattack Hard to Trace," by John Markoff, *New York Times*, July 17, 2009; "Cyberattacks Hit U.S. and South Korean Web Sites," by Choe Sang-Hun, *New York Times*, July 9, 2009; "Obama and Cyber Defense," by L. Gordon Crovitz, *Wall Street Journal*, June 29, 2009; "Obama Announces U.S. Cyber Security Plan," by Lolita Baldor, *New York Times*, May 29, 2009; "Vast Spy System Loots Computers in 103 Countries," by John Markoff, *New York Times*, March 29, 2009; "U.S. at Risk of Cyberattacks, Experts Say," by Brandon Griggs, cnn.com, August 18, 2008; "Georgia Takes a Beating in the Cyberwar with Russia," by John Markoff, *New York Times*, August 11, 2008; Net Attack," by Aaron Mannes and James Hendler, *Wall Street Journal*, June 5, 2007; "War Fears Turn Digital After Data Siege in Estonia," by Mark Lander and John Markoff, *New York Times*, May 29, 2007; "VeriSign Moves to Address an Internet Security Problem," by John Markoff, *New York Times*, February 8, 2007.

As *Cyberwar Becomes a Reality* illustrates, the Internet and Web are increasingly vulnerable to large-scale attacks and potentially large-scale failure. Increasingly, these attacks are led by organized gangs of criminals operating globally—an unintended consequence of globalization. However, there are steps you can take to protect your Web sites and your personal information when using online e-commerce sites.

In this chapter, we will examine e-commerce security and payment issues. First, we will identify the major security risks and their costs, and describe the variety of solutions currently available. Then, we will look at the major payment methods and consider how to achieve a secure payment environment.

5.1 THE E-COMMERCE SECURITY ENVIRONMENT

For most law-abiding citizens, the Internet holds the promise of a huge, convenient, global marketplace, providing access to people, goods, services, and businesses worldwide, all at a bargain price. For criminals, the Internet has created entirely new—and lucrative—ways to steal from the more than 1 billion consumers in the world on the Internet. From products and services to cash to information, it's all there for the taking on the Internet.

It's also less risky to steal online. Rather than rob a bank in person, the Internet makes it possible to rob people remotely and almost anonymously. Rather than steal a CD at a local record store, you can download the same music for free and almost without risk from the Internet. The potential for anonymity on the Internet cloaks many criminals in legitimate-looking identities, allowing them to place fraudulent orders with online merchants, steal information by intercepting e-mail, or simply shut down e-commerce sites by using software viruses and swarm attacks. The Internet was never designed to be a global marketplace with a billion users, and lacks many basic security features found in older networks such as the telephone system or broadcast television networks. Who ever heard of the telephone system being hacked and "brought down" by programmers in Eastern Europe? By comparison, the Internet is an open, vulnerable-design network. The actions of cybercriminals are costly for both businesses and consumers, who are then subjected to higher prices and additional security measures. However, the overall security environment is strengthening as business managers and government officials make significant investments in security equipment and business procedures.

THE SCOPE OF THE PROBLEM

Cybercrime is becoming a more significant problem for both organizations and consumers. Bot networks, DDoS attacks (described in the opening case), Trojans, phishing (fraudulently obtaining financial information from a victim, typically via e-mail), data theft, identity theft, credit card fraud, and spyware are just some of the threats that are making daily headlines. Recently, even social networks such as

Twitter have had security breaches. For example, an individual hacked into Britney Spears' Twitter account and began sending messages saying the singer had died. But despite the increasing attention being paid to cybercrime, it is difficult to accurately estimate the actual amount of such crime, in part because some companies may be hesitant to report crime due to fear of losing the trust of its customers, and because even if crime is reported, it may be difficult to quantify the actual dollar amount of the loss.

One source of information is the Internet Crime Complaint Center ("IC3"), a partnership between the National White Collar Crime Center and the Federal Bureau of Investigation. The IC3 data is useful for gauging the types of e-commerce crimes most likely to be reported by consumers and the typical amount of loss experienced. In 2008, the IC3 processed more than 275,000 Internet crime complaints and referred more than 72,000 of them to federal, state, and local law enforcement agencies. The total dollar loss from all referred cases was nearly $265 million, a 10% increase over 2007; and the average dollar loss was about $4,175, while the highest dollar loss per incident arose from check fraud (National White Collar Crime Center and the Federal Bureau of Investigation, 2009).

The Computer Security Institute's annual *Computer Crime and Security Survey* is another source of information. In 2008, the survey was based on the responses of around 525 security practitioners in U.S. corporations, government agencies, financial institutions, medical institutions, and universities. The survey reported that 49% of responding organizations experienced a computer security incident within the past year. **Figure 5.1** illustrates the various types of attacks against computer systems reported. Not all of these necessarily involve e-commerce, although many of them do. Fewer companies were willing to share numbers. Of those that did, the total loss reported was $41.5 million, with an average annual loss of $288,000. The most expensive security incidents were financial fraud, which averaged $500,000; followed by dealing with bot computers within the organization's network ($345,000) (Computer Security Institute, 2009).

Reports issued by security product providers, such as Symantec, are another source of data. Symantec, for instance, issues a semi-annual *Internet Security Threat Report*, based on 40,000 sensors monitoring Internet activity in over 180 countries, and malicious code reports from over 120 million systems that utilize Symantec's anti-virus products. In 2008, over 1,650,000 new malicious code threats were reported to Symantec, a 165% increase over 2007. It observed an average of about 75,000 active bot-infected computers per day, and there were over 55,000 phishing hosts, up 66% from the prior year (Symantec, 2009). However, Symantec does not attempt to quantify any actual crimes and/or losses related to these threats.

Online credit card fraud and phishing attacks are perhaps the most high-profile form of e-commerce crimes. Although the average amount of credit card fraud loss experienced by any one individual is typically relatively small (for instance, about $223 for those credit card/debit card fraud complaints reported in 2008 to the Internet Crime Complaint Center), the overall amount is substantial. The research firm CyberSource estimates online credit card fraud in the United States amounted to about $4 billion in 2008 (CyberSource, 2009). The overall rate of online credit card

FIGURE 5.1 TYPES OF ATTACKS AGAINST COMPUTER SYSTEMS (CYBERCRIME)

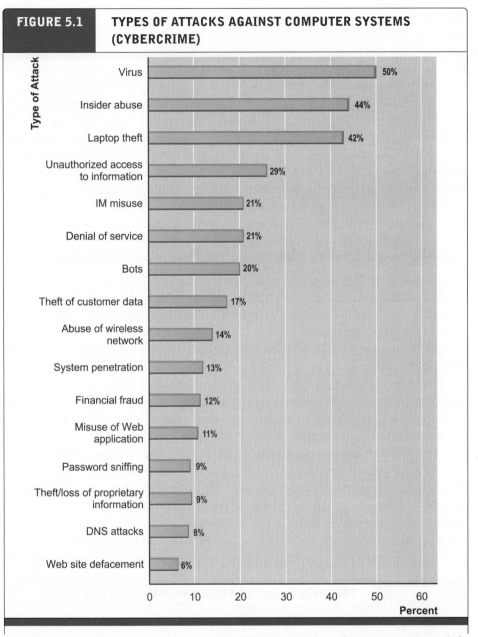

The most common attacks against computer systems are viruses, insider abuse of Internet access, laptop theft, unauthorized access to information, IM misuse, and denial of service. Some of these are specifically related to e-commerce, while others are not.

SOURCE: Based on data from Computer Security Institute, 2009.

fraud is estimated to be about 1.4% of all online card transactions, roughly twice the rate of offline credit card fraud. As a percentage of all e-commerce revenues, credit card fraud is declining as merchants and credit companies expand security systems to prevent the most common types of low-level fraud. But the nature of credit card fraud has changed greatly from the theft of a single credit card number and efforts to purchase goods at a few sites, to the simultaneous theft of millions of credit card numbers and their distributions to thousands of criminals operating as gangs of thieves. The emergence of "identify theft," described in detail later in this chapter, as a major online/offline type of fraud, may well increase markedly the incidence and amount of credit card fraud, since identity theft often includes the use of stolen credit card information and the creation of phony credit card accounts.. For instance, the 2009 Identity Fraud Survey by Javelin Strategy & Research found that in 2008, identity theft incidents were on the rise, with 4.3% of adults in the United States (9.9 million people) victims, compared to 3.6% in 2007. According to Javelin, the total loss was $48 billion (compared to $45 billion in 2007), while the average cost per consumer was $496, down from $718 in 2007, due in part to enhanced detection and resolution efforts by businesses and consumers (Javelin Research & Strategy, 2009).

The Underground Economy Marketplace: The Value of Stolen Information

Criminals who steal information on the Internet do not always use this information themselves, but instead derive value by selling the information to others on so-called "underground economy servers." There are several thousand known underground economy servers around the world that sell stolen information (about half of these are in the United States). **Table 5.1** lists some recently observed prices, which typically vary depending on the quantity being purchased.

Finding these servers is difficult for the average user (and for law enforcement agencies), and you need to be vetted by other criminals before gaining access. This vetting process takes place through e-mail exchanges of information, money, and reputation. Criminals have fairly good, personalized security!

Note that not every cybercriminal is necessarily after money. In some cases, such criminals aim to just deface, vandalize, and/or disrupt a Web site, rather than actually steal goods or services. The cost of such an attack includes not only the time and effort to make repairs to the site but also damage done to the site's reputation and image as well as revenues lost as a result of the attack.

So, what can we can conclude about the overall size of cybercrime? Cybercrime against e-commerce sites is dynamic and changing all the time, with new risks

TABLE 5.1	THE UNDERGROUND ECONOMY MARKETPLACE
Credit card	$0.06–$30
A full identity (U.S. bank account, credit card, date of birth, social security, etc.)	$0.70–$60
Bank account	$10–$1000
E-mail passwords	$1-$100
A single compromised computer	$6–$20
Social security number	$5–$7
Phishing Web site hosting	$3–$5

SOURCE: Based on data from Symantec, 2009, 2008.

appearing often. The amount of losses to businesses appears to be significant but stable, and may represent a declining percentage of overall sales, because firms have invested in security measures to protect against the simplest crimes. Individuals face new risks of fraud, many of which (unlike credit cards where federal law limits the loss to $50 for individuals) involve substantial uninsured losses involving debit cards and bank accounts. The managers of e-commerce sites must prepare for an ever-changing variety of criminal assaults, and keep current in the latest security techniques.

WHAT IS GOOD E-COMMERCE SECURITY?

What is a secure commercial transaction? Any time you go into a marketplace, you take risks, including the loss of privacy (information about what you purchased). Your prime risk as a consumer is that you do not get what you paid for. In fact, you might pay and get nothing! Worse, someone steals your money while you are at the market! As a merchant in the market, your risk is that you don't get paid for what you sell. Thieves take merchandise and then either walk off without paying anything, or pay you with a fraudulent instrument, stolen credit card, or forged currency.

E-commerce merchants and consumers face many of the same risks as participants in traditional commerce, albeit in a new digital environment. Theft is theft, regardless of whether it is digital theft or traditional theft. Burglary, breaking and entering, embezzlement, trespass, malicious destruction, vandalism—all crimes in a traditional commercial environment—are also present in e-commerce. However, reducing risks in e-commerce is a complex process that involves new technologies, organizational policies and procedures, and new laws and industry standards that empower law enforcement officials to investigate and prosecute offenders. **Figure 5.2** illustrates the multi-layered nature of e-commerce security.

To achieve the highest degree of security possible, new technologies are available and should be used. But these technologies by themselves do not solve the problem. Organizational policies and procedures are required to ensure the technologies are not subverted. Finally, industry standards and government laws are required to enforce payment mechanisms, as well as investigate and prosecute violators of laws designed to protect the transfer of property in commercial transactions.

The history of security in commercial transactions teaches that any security system can be broken if enough resources are put against it. Security is not absolute. In addition, perfect security forever is not needed, especially in the information age. There is a time value to information—just as there is to money. Sometimes it is sufficient to protect a message for a few hours, days, or years. Also, because security is costly, we always have to weigh the cost against the potential loss. Finally, we have also learned that security is a chain that breaks most often at the weakest link. Our locks are often much stronger than our management of the keys.

We can conclude then that good e-commerce security requires a set of laws, procedures, policies, and technologies that, to the extent feasible, protect individuals and organizations from unexpected behavior in the e-commerce marketplace.

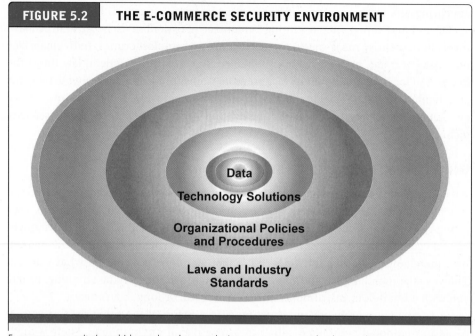

FIGURE 5.2   THE E-COMMERCE SECURITY ENVIRONMENT

Data

Technology Solutions

Organizational Policies and Procedures

Laws and Industry Standards

E-commerce security is multi-layered, and must take into account new technology, policies and procedures, and laws and industry standards.

DIMENSIONS OF E-COMMERCE SECURITY

There are six key dimensions to e-commerce security: integrity, nonrepudiation, authenticity, confidentiality, privacy, and availability (see **Table 5.2**).

Integrity refers to the ability to ensure that information being displayed on a Web site, or transmitted or received over the Internet, has not been altered in any way by an unauthorized party. For example, if an unauthorized person intercepts and changes the contents of an online communication, such as by redirecting a bank wire transfer into a different account, the integrity of the message has been compromised because the communication no longer represents what the original sender intended.

Nonrepudiation refers to the ability to ensure that e-commerce participants do not deny (i.e., repudiate) their online actions. For instance, the availability of free e-mail accounts with alias names makes it easy for a person to post comments or send a message and perhaps later deny doing so. Even when a customer uses a real name and e-mail address, it is easy for that customer to order merchandise online and then later deny doing so. In most cases, because merchants typically do not obtain a physical copy of a signature, the credit card issuer will side with the customer because the merchant has no legally valid proof that the customer ordered the merchandise.

Authenticity refers to the ability to identify the identity of a person or entity with whom you are dealing on the Internet. How does the customer know that the Web site operator is who it claims to be? How can the merchant be assured that the customer is really who she says she is? Someone who claims to be someone he is not is "spoofing" or misrepresenting himself.

integrity
the ability to ensure that information being displayed on a Web site or transmitted or received over the Internet has not been altered in any way by an unauthorized party

nonrepudiation
the ability to ensure that e-commerce participants do not deny (i.e., repudiate) their online actions

authenticity
the ability to identify the identity of a person or entity with whom you are dealing on the Internet

TABLE 5.2	CUSTOMER AND MERCHANT PERSPECTIVES ON THE DIFFERENT DIMENSIONS OF E-COMMERCE SECURITY	
DIMENSIONS	**CUSTOMER'S PERSPECTIVE**	**MERCHANT'S PERSPECTIVE**
Integrity	Has information I transmit or receive been altered?	Has data on the site been altered without authorization? Is data being received from customers valid?
Nonrepudiation	Can a party to an action with me later deny taking the action?	Can a customer deny ordering products?
Authenticity	Who am I dealing with? How can I be assured that the person or entity is who they claim to be?	What is the real identity of the customer?
Confidentiality	Can someone other than the intended recipient read my messages?	Are messages or confidential data accessible to anyone other than those authorized to view them?
Privacy	Can I control the use of information about myself transmitted to an e-commerce merchant?	What use, if any, can be made of personal data collected as part of an e-commerce transaction? Is the personal information of customers being used in an unauthorized manner?
Availability	Can I get access to the site?	Is the site operational?

Confidentiality refers to the ability to ensure that messages and data are available only to those who are authorized to view them. Confidentiality is sometimes confused with **privacy**, which refers to the ability to control the use of information a customer provides about himself or herself to an e-commerce merchant.

E-commerce merchants have two concerns related to privacy. They must establish internal policies that govern their own use of customer information, and they must protect that information from illegitimate or unauthorized use. For example, if hackers break into an e-commerce site and gain access to credit card or other information, this not only violates the confidentiality of the data, but also the privacy of the individuals who supplied the information.

Availability refers to the ability to ensure that an e-commerce site continues to function as intended.

E-commerce security is designed to protect these six dimensions. When any one of them is compromised, it is a security issue.

THE TENSION BETWEEN SECURITY AND OTHER VALUES

Can there be too much security? The answer is yes. Contrary to what some may believe, security is not an unmitigated good. Computer security adds overhead and expense to business operations, and also gives criminals new opportunities to hide their intentions and their crimes.

confidentiality
the ability to ensure that messages and data are available only to those who are authorized to view them

privacy
the ability to control the use of information about oneself

availability
the ability to ensure that an e-commerce site continues to function as intended

Ease of Use

There are inevitable tensions between security and ease of use. When traditional merchants are so fearful of robbers that they do business in shops locked behind security gates, ordinary customers are discouraged from walking in. The same can be true on the Web. In general, the more security measures added to an e-commerce site, the more difficult it is to use and the slower the site becomes. As you will discover reading this chapter, digital security is purchased at the price of slowing down processors and adding significantly to data storage demands on storage devices. Security is a technological and business overhead that can detract from doing business. Too much security can harm profitability, while not enough security can potentially put you out of business.

Public Safety and the Criminal Uses of the Internet

There is also an inevitable tension between the desires of individuals to act anonymously (to hide their identity) and the needs of public officials to maintain public safety that can be threatened by criminals or terrorists. This is not a new problem, or even new to the electronic era. The U.S. government began informal tapping of telegraph wires during the Civil War in the mid-1860s in order to trap conspirators and terrorists, and the first police wiretaps of local telephone systems were in place by the 1890s—twenty years after the invention of the phone (Schwartz, 2001). No nation-state has ever permitted a technological haven to exist where criminals can plan crimes or threaten the nation-state without fear of official surveillance or investigation. In this sense, the Internet is no different from any other communication system. Drug cartels make extensive use of voice, fax, and data encryption devices; a number of large international organized criminal groups steal information from commercial Web sites and resell it to other criminals who use it for financial fraud. Over the years, the U.S. government has successfully pursued various "carding forums" (Web sites that facilitate the sale of stolen credit card and debit card numbers), such as Shadowcrew.com and Carderplanet.com, resulting in the arrest and prosecution of a number of their members and the shutting down of the sites. However, other criminal organizations have emerged to take their place, including Cardersmarket.com, which reportedly has thousands of members worldwide, and CCpowerForums.com.

Terrorists are also fond users of the Internet and have been for many years. Encrypted files sent via e-mail were used by Ramsey Yousef—a member of the terrorist group responsible for bombing the World Trade Center in 1993—to hide plans for bombing 11 U.S. airliners. The Internet was also used to plan and coordinate the subsequent attacks on the World Trade Center on September 11, 2001. In addition, the Aum Shinrikyo religious cult in Japan that spread poison gas in the Tokyo subway in March 1995 (killing 12 and hospitalizing 6,000 people) stored their records detailing plans for attacks on other countries on computers using a powerful form of encryption called RSA, described later. Fortunately, authorities were lucky to find the encryption key stored on a floppy disk (Denning and Baugh, 1999).

More recently, Al Qaeda and its offshoots "have understood that both time and space have in many ways been conquered by the Internet," said John Arquilla, a professor at the Naval Postgraduate School who coined the term "netwar" more than a decade ago. Al Qaeda, according to security experts in the United States and Britain, use the Web as a dynamic library of training materials on poison mixing and explosive construction, tactical coordination of imminent attacks, and building a larger terrorist community of like-minded people. The Internet is both anonymous and pervasive, an ideal communication tool for criminal and terrorist groups (Peretti, 2008).

5.2 SECURITY THREATS IN THE E-COMMERCE ENVIRONMENT

From a technology perspective, there are three key points of vulnerability when dealing with e-commerce: the client, the server, and the communications pipeline. **Figure 5.3** illustrates a typical e-commerce transaction with a consumer using a credit card to purchase a product. **Figure 5.4** illustrates some of the things that can

FIGURE 5.3	A TYPICAL E-COMMERCE TRANSACTION

In a typical e-commerce transaction, the customer uses a credit card and the existing credit payment system. The transaction has many vulnerable points.

SOURCE: Boncella, 2000.

FIGURE 5.4	VULNERABLE POINTS IN AN E-COMMERCE TRANSACTION

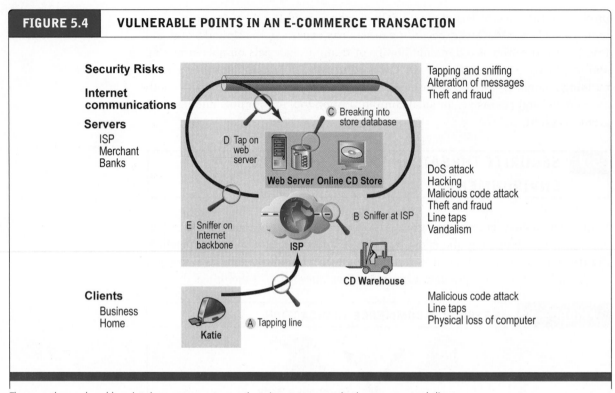

There are three vulnerable points in e-commerce transactions: Internet communications, servers, and clients.
SOURCE: Boncella, 2000.

go wrong at each major vulnerability point in the transaction—over Internet communications channels, at the server level, and at the client level.

In this section, we describe a number of the most common and most damaging forms of security threats to e-commerce consumers and site operators: malicious code, unwanted programs, phishing and identity theft, hacking and cybervandalism, credit card fraud/theft, spoofing (pharming) and spam (junk) Web sites, Denial of Service (DoS) and Distributed Denial of service (DDoS) attacks, sniffing, insider attacks, and finally, poorly designed server and client software.

MALICIOUS CODE

malicious code (malware)
includes a variety of threats such as viruses, worms, Trojan horses, and bots

virus
a computer program that has the ability to replicate or make copies of itself, and spread to other files

Malicious code (sometimes referred to as "malware") includes a variety of threats such as viruses, worms, Trojan horses, and bots. In 2009, Microsoft reported that its security products had detected a total of nearly 95 million unique malicious files in the second half of 2008 (Microsoft, 2009). Malicious code in the past often was intended simply to impair computers, and was often authored by a lone hacker, but increasingly the intent is to steal e-mail addresses, logon credentials, personal data, and financial information. Increasingly, malicious code is used to develop integrated malware networks that organize the theft of information and money.

One of the latest innovations in malicious code distribution is to embed it in the online advertising chain, including at Google and other ad networks. As the ad network chain becomes more complicated, it becomes more and more difficult for Web sites to vet ads placed on their sites to ensure they are malware-free. For instance, in 2009, Web sites as disparate as eWeek.com (a technology site) to MLB.com (Major League Baseball) to AmericanIdol.com experienced instances where ads placed on their sites either had malicious code embedded or directed clickers to malicious sites (Steel, 2009). In 2008, Flash-based ads infected with malicious script were discovered to be inserting URLS for sites offering phony security software onto the clipboards of both PCs and Macs running Windows (Keizer, 2008). Malicious code embedded in PDF files have also been discovered. Malware authors are also increasingly using links embedded within e-mail instead of the more traditional file attachments to infect computers. The links lead directly to a malicious code download or Web sites that include malicious JavaScript code. Equally important, there has been a major shift in the writers of malware from amateur hackers and adventurers to organized criminal efforts to defraud companies and individuals. In other words, it's now more about the money than ever before.

A **virus** is a computer program that has the ability to replicate or make copies of itself, and spread to other files. In addition to the ability to replicate, most computer viruses deliver a "payload." The payload may be relatively benign, such as the display of a message or image, or it may be highly destructive—destroying files, reformatting the computer's hard drive, or causing programs to run improperly. Computer viruses fall into several major categories:

- *Macro viruses* are application-specific, meaning that the virus affects only the application for which it was written, such as Microsoft Word, Excel, or PowerPoint. When a user opens an infected document in the appropriate application, the virus copies itself to the templates in the application, so that when new documents are created, they are infected with the macro virus as well. Macro viruses can easily be spread when sent in an e-mail attachment.

- *File-infecting viruses* usually infect executable files, such as *.com, *.exe, *.drv, and *.dll files. They may activate every time the infected file is executed by copying themselves into other executable files. File-infecting viruses are also easily spread through e-mails and any file transfer system.

- *Script viruses* are written in script programming languages such as VBScript (Visual Basic Script) and JavaScript. The viruses are activated simply by double-clicking an infected *.vbs or *.js file. The ILOVEYOU virus (also known as the Love Bug), which overwrites *.jpg and *.mp3 files, is one of the most famous examples of a script virus.

Viruses are often combined with a worm. Indeed, most researchers agree that classic viruses—the original malicious programs—have become much less common, while the far more dangerous worm has grown exponentially. Some of the reason is simple: viruses infect a single computer, and may destroy but produce very little cash. As the nature of the criminal changes from amateur hacker to professional criminal interested in cash, it is much more lucrative to create a worm that can propagate from one computer to another, perhaps to millions.

Instead of just spreading from file to file, a **worm** is designed to spread from computer to computer. A worm does not necessarily need to be activated by a user or program in order for it to replicate itself. For example, the Slammer worm, which

worm
malware that is designed to spread from computer to computer

targeted a known vulnerability in Microsoft's SQL Server database software, infected more than 90% of vulnerable computers worldwide within 10 minutes of its release on the Internet; crashed Bank of America cash machines, especially in the southwestern part of the United States; affected cash registers at supermarkets such as the Publix chain in Atlanta, where staff could not dispense cash to frustrated buyers; and took down most Internet connections in South Korea, causing a dip in the stock market there. The Conficker worm, which first appeared in November 2008, is the most significant worm since Slammer, and reportedly infected over 9 to 15 million computers worldwide. Other well-known worms include the MyDoom worm, the Sasser worm, the Zotob worm, and the Nymex worm (Symantec, 2007; United States Government Accountability Office, 2005).

Trojan horse

appears to be benign, but then does something other than expected. Often a way for viruses or other malicious code to be introduced into a computer system

A **Trojan horse** appears to be benign, but then does something other than expected. The Trojan horse is not itself a virus because it does not replicate, but is often a way for viruses or other malicious code such as bots or *rootkits* (a program whose aim is to subvert control of the computer's operating system) to be introduced into a computer system. The term *Trojan horse* refers to the huge wooden horse in Homer's *Iliad* that the Greeks gave their opponents, the Trojans—a gift that actually contained hundreds of Greek soldiers. Once the people of Troy let the massive horse within their gates, the soldiers revealed themselves and captured the city. In today's world, a Trojan horse may masquerade as a game, but actually hide a program to steal your passwords and e-mail them to another person. According to Symantec, of the top 10 new malicious code families detected in 2008, three were Trojans. Trojans made up 68% of the volume of the top 50 malicious code reports, a minor decrease from 2008 (Symantec, 2009). In 2007, Monster.com suffered a highly publicized attack from a Trojan horse called Infostealer.Monstres that stole more than 1.6 million records, such as names, e-mail addresses, home addresses, and phone numbers of job seekers who had filed resumes with Monster (Kreizer, 2007b).

bot

type of malicious code that can be covertly installed on a computer when attached to the Internet. Once installed, the bot responds to external commands sent by the attacker

botnet

collection of captured bot computers

Bots (short for robots) are a type of malicious code that can be covertly installed on your computer when attached to the Internet. Once installed, the bot responds to external commands sent by the attacker, and your computer becomes a "zombie," and is able to be controlled by an external third party (the "bot-herder"). **Botnets** are collections of captured computers used for malicious activities such as sending spam, participating in a Distributed Denial of Service attack (described later), stealing information from computers, and storing network traffic for later analysis. In 2008, Symantec identified an average of 75,000 active bot-infected computers per day, an increase of 31% from 2007. Arguably, bots and bot networks are the single most important threat to the Internet and e-commerce in 2009–2010 because they can be used to launch very large-scale attacks using many different techniques. In 2009, the authors of the Conficker worm used it to assemble a massive botnet that is still growing. Thus far, the botnet has not been used for other than installing fake anti-virus software, but security experts caution that it still remains a threat (Kerner, 2009).

Malicious code is a threat at both the client and the server level, although servers generally engage in much more thorough anti-virus activities than do consumers. At the server level, malicious code can bring down an entire Web site, preventing millions of people from using the site. Such incidents are infrequent. Much more frequent malicious code attacks occur at the client level, and the damage can quickly spread to millions of other computers connected to the Internet. **Table 5.3** lists some well-known examples of malicious code.

While the number of viruses and worms is increasing, so too has prosecution of those who create viruses. Increasingly, European and Asian authorities are coordinating arrests with American authorities. In the United States, the FBI's Operation BotRoast has resulted in a number of arrests (FBI, 2007). In 2006, a Moroccan teenager was sent to jail for two years for releasing the Zotob worm virus that ravaged U.S. computer networks. In July 2005, the 18-year-old creator of the Sasser worm was convicted in Germany on charges including computer sabotage.

UNWANTED PROGRAMS

In addition to malicious code, the e-commerce security environment is further challenged by unwanted programs such as adware, browser parasites, spyware, and other applications that install themselves on a computer, typically without the user's informed consent. Such programs are increasingly being found on social networking and user-generated content sites where users are fooled into downloading them. Once installed, these applications are usually exceedingly difficult to remove from the computer.

Adware (described further in Chapter 7) is typically used to call for pop-up ads to display when the user visits certain sites. While annoying, adware is not typically used for criminal activities. ZangoSearch and PurityScan are examples of adware programs that open the Web pages or display pop-up ads of partner sites when certain keywords are used in Internet searches. A **browser parasite** is a program that can monitor and change the settings of a user's browser, for instance, changing the browser's home page, or sending information about the sites visited to a remote computer. Browser parasites are often a component of adware. For example, Websearch is an adware component that modifies Internet Explorer's default home page and search settings.

browser parasite
a program that can monitor and change the settings of a user's browser

Spyware, on the other hand, can be used to obtain information such as a user's keystrokes, copies of e-mail and instant messages, and even take screenshots (and thereby capture passwords or other confidential data). One example of spyware is SpySheriff, which claims to be a spyware removal program but is actually a malicious spyware application. Spyware (along with phishing, described in the next section) is often used for identity theft.

spyware
a program used to obtain information such as a user's keystrokes, e-mail, instant messages, and so on

PHISHING AND IDENTITY THEFT

Phishing is any deceptive, online attempt by a third party to obtain confidential information for financial gain. Phishing attacks do not involve malicious code but instead rely on straightforward misrepresentation and fraud, so-called "social engineering" techniques. The most popular phishing attack is the e-mail scam letter. The scam begins with an e-mail: a rich former oil minister of Nigeria is seeking a bank account to stash millions of dollars for a short period of time, and requests your bank account number where the money can be deposited. In return, you will receive a million dollars. This type of e-mail scam is popularly known as a "Nigerian letter" scam (see **Figure 5.5**).

phishing
any deceptive, online attempt by a third party to obtain confidential information for financial gain

TABLE 5.3	NOTABLE EXAMPLES OF MALICIOUS CODE	
NAME	TYPE	DESCRIPTION
Conficker	Worm	First appeared November 2008. Targets Microsoft operating system. Uses advanced malware techniques. Largest worm infection since Slammer in 2003.
Netsky.P	Worm/Trojan horse	First appeared in early 2003; still one of the most common computer worms. It spreads by gathering target e-mail addresses from the computers it infects, and sending e-mail to all recipients from the infected computer. It is commonly used by bot networks to launch spam and Denial of Service attacks.
Storm (Peacomm, NuWar)	Worm/Trojan horse	First appeared in January 2007. It spreads in a manner similar to the Netsky.P worm. May also download and run other Trojan programs and worms.
Nymex	Worm	First discovered in January 2006. Spreads by mass mailing; activates on the 3rd of every month, and attempts to destroy files of certain types.
Zotob	Worm	First appeared in August 2005. Well-known worm that infected a number of U.S. media companies.
Sasser	Worm	First appeared in 2004. Exploited a vulnerability in LSASS, causing network problems.
Mydoom	Worm	First appeared in January 2004. One of the fastest-spreading mass-mailer worms.
Slammer	Worm	Launched in January 2003. Caused widespread problems.
Klez	Worm	Most prolific virus of 2002. Was distributed via an e-mail with a random subject line and message body. Once launched, the worm sent itself to all addresses in the Windows Address Book, the database of instant-messaging program ICQ, and local files.
CodeRed	Worm	Appeared in 2001. It achieved an infection rate of over 20,000 systems within 10 minutes of release and ultimately spread to hundreds of thousands of systems.
Melissa	Macro virus/worm	First spotted in March 1999. At the time, Melissa was the fastest-spreading infectious program ever discovered. It attacked Microsoft Word's Normal.dot global template, ensuring infection of all newly created documents. It also mailed an infected Word file to the first 50 entries in each user's Microsoft Outlook Address Book.
Chernobyl	File-infecting virus	First appeared in 1998. It wipes out the first megabyte of data on a hard disk (making the rest useless) every April 26, the anniversary of the nuclear disaster at Chernobyl.

FIGURE 5.5 **AN EXAMPLE OF A NIGERIAN LETTER E-MAIL SCAM**

This is an example of a typical Nigerian letter e-mail scam.

Thousands of other phishing attacks use other scams, some pretending to be eBay, PayPal, or Citibank writing to you for "account verification" (known as "spear phishing", or targeting a known customer of a specific bank, or other type of business). Click on a link in the e-mail and you will be taken to a Web site controlled by the scammer, and prompted to enter confidential information about your accounts, such as your account number and PIN codes (see **Figure 5.6**). On any given day, millions of these phishing attack e-mails are sent, and, unfortunately, some people are fooled and disclose their personal account information.

Phishers rely on traditional "con man" tactics, but use e-mail to trick recipients into voluntarily giving up financial access codes, bank account numbers, credit card numbers, and other personal information. Often, phishers create ("spoof") a Web site that purports to be a legitimate financial institution and con users into entering financial information, or downloads malware such as a keylogger to the victim's computer. . Phishers use the information they gather to commit fraudulent acts such as charging items to your credit cards or withdrawing funds from your bank account, or in other ways "steal your identity" (identity theft). Phishing attacks are one of the fastest-growing forms of e-commerce crime. In 2008, Symantec detected over 55,000 phishing website hosts, up 66% over 2007. Financial services are the primary brands used in phishing attacks (almost 80%) Other top brands exploited by phishing attacks were Amazon and eBay (Symantec, 2009).

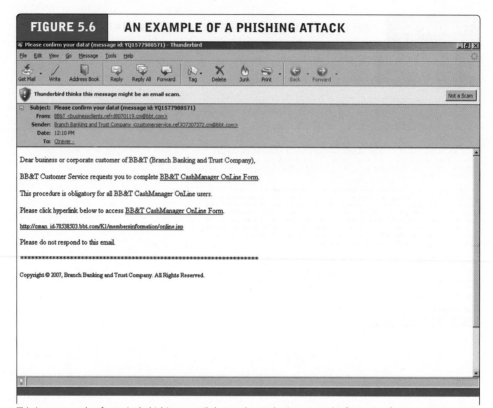

FIGURE 5.6   AN EXAMPLE OF A PHISHING ATTACK

This is an example of a typical phishing e-mail that seeks to obtain personal information from an unwary respondent.

Many of the security vulnerabilities described throughout this section use what are called "social engineering" techniques to propagate. These techniques involve fraud or misrepresentation, or in other words, pretending to be something that it is not. For instance, the Netsky.P worm uses an e-mail message that takes the form of an e-mail delivery notification to trick recipients into thinking that the e-mail is from a valid source, encouraging them to open an attached file that, in reality, is an executable program that contains a virus or worm. Once the attachment is opened, the worm begins to execute on the computer. Social engineering not only aids the worm in getting the target recipient to open the infected e-mail, it also allows the worm to evade content filters or scanners, often by masquerading as a compressed zip file.

HACKING AND CYBERVANDALISM

A **hacker** is an individual who intends to gain unauthorized access to a computer system. Within the hacking community, the term **cracker** is typically used to denote a hacker with criminal intent, although in the public press, the terms hacker and cracker tend to be used interchangeably. Hackers and crackers gain unauthorized access by finding weaknesses in the security procedures of Web sites and computer systems, often taking advantage of various features of the Internet that make it an open system that is easy to use. Hackers and crackers typically are computer aficionados excited by the challenge of breaking into corporate and government Web

hacker
an individual who intends to gain unauthorized access to a computer system

cracker
within the hacking community, a term typically used to denote a hacker with criminal intent

sites. Sometimes they are satisfied merely by breaking into the files of an e-commerce site. Others have more malicious intentions and commit **cybervandalism**, intentionally disrupting, defacing, or even destroying the site.

For instance, Robert Lyttle of San Francisco and Benjamin Stark of St. Petersburg, Florida, were convicted of breaking into and "hacking" a computer at NASA's Ames Research Center in Moffett Field, California. They stole information about members of the agency's Astrobiology Institute and used that information to deface the home page of the NASA Astrobiology Institute. Calling themselves "The Deceptive Duo," Lyttle and Stark stated that their attacks were intended to demonstrate vulnerabilities in the government's computer security systems. The pair also hacked into the Defense Department's Defense Logistics Information Service Web site and the agency's Office of Health Affairs. Lyttle pleaded guilty to the attacks, and the U.S. District Court in Oakland, California, sentenced him to four months in prison, restitution payment of $71,181, and three years probation. Stark, who also pleaded guilty, was sentenced to two years probation and to pay $29,006 in restitution (Butterfield, 2005).

The hacker phenomenon has diversified over time. In general, benign hacking and defacement hacking has receded as law enforcement and private agencies learn how to detect perpetrators. Hacker activities have broadened beyond mere system intrusion to include theft of goods and information, as well as vandalism and system damage.

Groups of hackers called *tiger teams* are sometimes used by corporate security departments to test their own security measures. By hiring hackers to break into the system from the outside, the company can identify weaknesses in the computer system's armor. These "good hackers" became known as **white hats** because of their role in helping organizations locate and fix security flaws. White hats do their work under contract, with agreement from clients that they will not be prosecuted for their efforts to break in.

In contrast, **black hats** are hackers who engage in the same kinds of activities but without pay or any buy-in from the targeted organization, and with the intention of causing harm. They break into Web sites and reveal the confidential or proprietary information they find. These hackers believe strongly that information should be free, so sharing previously secret information is part of their mission.

Somewhere in the middle are the **grey hats**, hackers who believe they are pursuing some greater good by breaking in and revealing system flaws. Grey hats discover weaknesses in a system's security, and then publish the weakness without disrupting the site or attempting to profit from their finds. Their only reward is the prestige of discovering the weakness. Grey hat actions are suspect, however, especially when the hackers reveal security flaws that make it easier for other criminals to gain access to a system.

CREDIT CARD FRAUD/THEFT

Theft of credit card data is one of the most feared occurrences on the Internet. Fear that credit card information will be stolen frequently prevents users from making online purchases. Interestingly, this fear appears to be largely unfounded. Incidences of stolen credit card information are much lower than users think, around 1.4% of all online card transactions (CyberSource, 2009).

In traditional commerce, there is substantial credit card fraud, but the consumer is largely insured against losses by federal law. In the past, the most common cause of credit card fraud was a lost or stolen card that is used by someone else, followed by employee theft of customer numbers and stolen identities (criminals applying for credit cards using false identities). Federal law limits the liability of individuals to $50 for a stolen credit card. For amounts over $50, the credit card company generally pays the amount, although in some cases, the merchant may be held liable if it failed to verify the account or consult published lists of invalid cards. Banks recoup the cost of credit card fraud by charging higher interest rates on unpaid balances, and by merchants who raise prices to cover the losses.

But today the most frequent cause of stolen cards and card information is the systematic hacking and looting of a corporate server where the information on millions of credit card purchases are stored. On of the largest and most damaging mass credit card thefts to date occurred at TJX Companies, owner of 2,500 retail stores. Information from 47.5 million credit and debit cards was stolen by hackers who gained access to TJX's customer information database via a poorly protected wireless local area network in 2003. The theft was not discovered until 2006, and was not reported until 2007. The information was sold on underground economy sites to criminals who subsequently made hundreds of thousands of purchases, both offline and online (Dash, 2007; Vijayan, 2007). More recently, Heartland, a payment processing company, announced that the personal data of over 100 million cardholders was potentially vulnerable due to a data breach that began in May 2008 and wasn't discovered until the fall. In August 2009, the U.S. Attorney General announced the indictment of Albert Gonzales and two unidentified Russians with running an international scheme to steal over 130 million credit and debit cards from Heartland, 7-Eleven, Hannaford, and two unnamed companies. Gonzales was already in custody at the time in connection with his alleged involvement with data breaches at TJMaxx, Dave & Busters, BJ's Wholesale Club, and a number of other organizations (Gaudin, 2009).

International orders have been particularly prone to repudiation. If an international customer places an order and then later disputes it, online merchants often have no way to verify that the package was actually delivered and that the credit card holder is the person who placed the order.

The solution for many Web sites is to institute new identity verification mechanisms that are currently in development; these will be discussed in the next section. Until a customer's identity can be guaranteed, online companies are at a much higher risk of loss than traditional offline companies. The federal government has attempted to address this issue through the Electronic Signatures in Global and National Commerce Act (the "E-Sign" law), which gives digital signatures the same authority as hand written signatures in commerce. This law also intended to make digital signatures more commonplace, and easier to use. Except for large businesses conducting transactions over the Internet, the law has had little impact on B2C commerce, but that may be changing.

SPOOFING (PHARMING), SPAM (JUNK) WEB SITES AND SPLOGS

Hackers attempting to hide their true identity often **spoof**, or misrepresent themselves by using fake e-mail addresses or masquerading as someone else. Spoofing a Web site is also called "pharming," which involves redirecting a Web link to an address different from the intended one, with the site masquerading as the intended destination. Links that are designed to lead to one site can be reset to send users to a totally unrelated site—one that benefits the hacker.

Although spoofing does not directly damage files or network servers, it threatens the integrity of a site. For example, if hackers redirect customers to a fake Web site that looks almost exactly like the true site, they can then collect and process orders, effectively stealing business from the true site. Or, if the intent is to disrupt rather than steal, hackers can alter orders—inflating them or changing products ordered—and then send them on to the true site for processing and delivery. Customers become dissatisfied with the improper order shipment and the company may have huge inventory fluctuations that impact its operations.

In addition to threatening integrity, spoofing also threatens authenticity by making it difficult to discern the true sender of a message. Clever hackers can make it almost impossible to distinguish between a true and a fake identity or Web address. Spam (junk) Web sites are a little different. These are sites that promise to offer some product or service, but in fact are a collection of advertisements for other sites, some of which contain malicious code. For instance, you may search for "[name of town] weather," and then click on a link that promises your local weather, but then discover that all the site does is display ads for weather-related products or other Web sites.

Junk or spam Web sites typically appear on search results, and do not involve e-mail. These sites cloak their identities by using domain names similar to legitimate firm names, and redirect traffic to known spammer-redirection domains such as topsearch10.com.

Splogs (spam blogs) are fake blogs created solely to raise the search engine rank of affiliated Web sites. Estimates of the number of splogs range from 33% to almost 80% of all blogs (Mullenweg, 2008). Even blogs that are legitate are plagued by spam, with spammers taking advantage of the Comment feature of most blogs to comments with links to spam sites.

DENIAL OF SERVICE (DOS) AND DISTRIBUTED DENIAL OF SERVICE (DDOS) ATTACKS

In a **Denial of Service (DoS)** attack, hackers flood a Web site with useless page requests that inundate and overwhelm the site's Web servers. Increasingly, DoS attacks involve the use of bot networks and so-called "distributed attacks" built from thousands of compromised client computers. DoS attacks typically cause a Web site to shut down, making it impossible for users to access the site. For busy e-commerce sites, these attacks are costly; while the site is shut down, customers cannot make purchases. And the longer a site is shut down, the more damage is

spoof
to misrepresent oneself by using fake e-mail addresses or masquerading as someone else

splog
fake blog created solely to raise the search engine rank of affiliated Web sites

Denial of Service (DoS) attack
flooding a Web site with useless traffic to inundate and overwhelm the network

done to a site's reputation. Although such attacks do not destroy information or access restricted areas of the server, they can destroy a firm's online business. Often, DoS attacks are accompanied by attempts at blackmailing site owners to pay tens or hundreds of thousands of dollars to the hackers in return for removing the DoS attack.

Distributed Denial of Service (DDoS) attack

using numerous computers to attack the target network from numerous launch points

A **Distributed Denial of Service (DDoS)** attack uses numerous computers to attack the target network from numerous launch points. DoS and DDoS attacks are threats to a system's operation because they can shut it down indefinitely. Major Web sites such as Yahoo and Microsoft have experienced such attacks, making the companies aware of their vulnerability and the need to continually introduce new measures to prevent future attacks. The largest DDoS attack to date occurred in 2007, when a botnet composed of several thousand computers attempted to bring down the part of the Internet domain name system operated by VeriSign. The attack affected 13 domain name servers operated by VeriSign, including the .com and .org domains (Markoff, 2007). The attack impeded but did not bring down any of the servers. Had it succeeded, the Internet itself would have failed for a period of time.

Hackers continue to use DDoS to attack Web sites, and in 2009, as you learned in the opening case, politically motivated DDoS attacks were launched against a number of South Korean, and U.S. government and commercial Web sites, and also shut down Twitter for almost a day.

SNIFFING

sniffer

a type of eavesdropping program that monitors information traveling over a network

A **sniffer** is a type of eavesdropping program that monitors information traveling over a network. When used legitimately, sniffers can help identify potential network trouble-spots, but when used for criminal purposes, they can be damaging and very difficult to detect. Sniffers enable hackers to steal proprietary information from anywhere on a network, including e-mail messages, company files, and confidential reports. For instance, in March 2009, hackers inserted code on the servers of Network Solutions (which provides domain registration and hosting services) that sniffed and intercepted credit and debit card and personal identifying information of more than 573,000 customers (Channelinsider.com, 2009). The threat of sniffing is that confidential or personal information will be stolen or made public.

E-mail wiretaps are a variation on the sniffing threat. An e-mail wiretap is hidden code in an e-mail message that allows someone to monitor all succeeding messages forwarded with the original message. E-mail wiretaps can be installed on servers and client computers. For instance, the USA PATRIOT Act permits the FBI to compel ISPs to install a black box on their mail servers that can impound the e-mail of a single person or group of persons for later analysis. In the case of American citizens communicating with other citizens, an FBI agent or government lawyer need only certify to a judge on the secret 11-member U.S. Foreign Intelligence Surveillance Court (FISC) that the information sought is "relevant to an ongoing criminal investigation" to get permission to install the program. Judges have no discretion. They must approve wiretaps based on government agents' unsubstantiated assertions (Associated Press, 2005). Congress adopted a new amendment to the 1978 Foreign Intelligence Surveillance Act, known as FISA, that provides new powers to the National Security Agency to monitor international e-mail and telephone communications where one person is in the United States, and where the purpose of such interception is to collect foreign intelligence (Foreign Intelligence Surveillance Act of 1978; Protect America Act of 2007).

INSIDER ATTACKS

We tend to think of security threats to a business as originating outside the organization. In fact, the largest financial threats to business institutions come not from robberies but from embezzlement by insiders. Bank employees steal far more money than bank robbers. The same is true for e-commerce sites. Some of the largest disruptions to service, destruction to sites, and diversion of customer credit data and personal information have come from insiders— once trusted employees. Employees have access to privileged information, and in the presence of sloppy internal security procedures, they are often able to roam throughout an organization's systems without leaving a trace. The 2009 CSI survey reports that insider abuse of systems was the second most frequent type of attack during the preceding 12 months, and that around 44% of survey respondents believed that insiders contributed to some portion of the firm's financial losses during the previous year (Computer Security Institute, 2009). A Michigan State University study found that as much as 70% of all identity theft, including credit card theft, is the work of "insiders" (Borden, 2007). In some instances, the insider might not have criminal intent, but inadvertently expose data that can then be exploited by others. For instance, a Ponemon Institute study found that 75% of organizations surveyed in the United States, United Kingdom, France, and Germany had suffered data breaches caused by negligent insiders. (Ponemon Institute, 2008).

POORLY DESIGNED SERVER AND CLIENT SOFTWARE

Many security threats prey on poorly designed server and client software, sometimes in the operating system and sometimes in the application software, including browsers. The increase in complexity and size of software programs, coupled with demands for timely delivery to markets, has contributed to an increase in software flaws or vulnerabilities that hackers can exploit. Each year, security firms identify about thousands of software vulnerabilities in Internet and PC software. For instance, in 2008, Symantec identified 47 vulnerabilities in Internet Explorer, 99 in Mozilla browsers, 40 in Apple Safari, 35 in Opera, and 11 in Google Chrome. Some of these vulnerabilities were critical (Symantec, 2009). The top 5 Internet attacks launched in 2008 were attacks against Microsoft Windows server and client software, exploiting various weaknesses. The very design of the personal computer includes many open communication ports that can be used, and indeed are designed to be used, by external computers to send and receive messages. The port typically attacked is TCP port 445. However, given their complexity and design objectives, all operating systems and application software, including Linux and Macintosh, have vulnerabilities. There are also a growing number of "zero-day" vulnerabilities, where the vulnerability is unknown to security experts and is actively exploited before there is a patch available, requiring firms to scurry to develop patches. In the single week of August 17, 2009, the U.S. Computer Emergency Readiness Team (US-CERT; Department of Homeland Security) reported on 153 newly discovered vulnerabilities in server and application software, 69 of them rated "high severity" (US-CERT, 2009).

5.3 TECHNOLOGY SOLUTIONS

At first glance it might seem like there is not much that can be done about the onslaught of security breaches on the Internet. Reviewing the security threats in the previous section, it is clear that the threats to e-commerce are very real, potentially devastating, and likely to be increasing in intensity along with the growth in e-commerce. But in fact a great deal of progress has been made by private security firms, corporate and home users, network administrators, technology firms, and government agencies. There are two lines of defense: technology solutions and policy solutions. In this section, we consider some technology solutions, and in the following section, we look at some policy solutions that work.

The first line of defense against the wide variety of security threats to an e-commerce site is a set of tools that can make it difficult for outsiders to invade or destroy a site. **Figure 5.7** illustrates the major tools available to achieve site security. In the next section, we describe these tools in greater detail.

PROTECTING INTERNET COMMUNICATIONS

Because e-commerce transactions must flow over the public Internet, and therefore involve thousands of routers and servers through which the transaction packets flow, security experts believe the greatest security threats occur at the level of Internet communications. This is very different from a private network where a dedicated communication line is established between two parties. A number of tools are available to protect the security of Internet communications, the most basic of which is message encryption.

ENCRYPTION

encryption

the process of transforming plain text or data into cipher text that cannot be read by anyone other than the sender and the receiver. The purpose of encryption is (a) to secure stored information and (b) to secure information transmission

Encryption is the process of transforming plain text or data into **cipher text** that cannot be read by anyone other than the sender and the receiver. The purpose of encryption is (a) to secure stored information and (b) to secure information transmission. Encryption can provide four of the six key dimensions of e-commerce security referred to in Table 5.2 on page 271:

- *Message integrity*—provides assurance that the message has not been altered.
- *Nonrepudiation*—prevents the user from denying he or she sent the message.
- *Authentication*—provides verification of the identity of the person (or computer) sending the message.
- *Confidentiality*—gives assurance that the message was not read by others.

cipher text

text that has been encrypted and thus cannot be read by anyone other than the sender and the receiver

---

FIGURE 5.7 **TOOLS AVAILABLE TO ACHIEVE SITE SECURITY**

There are a number of tools available to achieve site security.

This transformation of plain text to cipher text is accomplished by using a key or cipher. A **key** (or **cipher**) is any method for transforming plain text to cipher text.

Encryption has been practiced since the earliest forms of writing and commercial transactions. Ancient Egyptian and Phoenician commercial records were encrypted using substitution and transposition ciphers. In a **substitution cipher**, every occurrence of a given letter is replaced systematically by another letter. For instance, if we used the cipher "letter plus two"—meaning replace every letter in a word with a new letter two places forward—then the word "Hello" in plain text would be transformed into the following cipher text: "JGNNQ." In a **transposition cipher**, the ordering of the letters in each word is changed in some systematic way. Leonardo Da Vinci recorded his shop notes in reverse order, making them readable only with a mirror. The word "Hello" can be written backwards as "OLLEH." A more complicated cipher would (a) break all words into two words and (b) spell the first word with every other letter beginning with the first letter, and then spell the second word with all the remaining letters. In this cipher, "HELLO" would be written as "HLO EL."

Symmetric Key Encryption

In order to decipher these messages, the receiver would have to know the secret cipher that was used to encrypt the plain text. This is called **symmetric key encryption** or **secret key encryption**. In symmetric key encryption, both the sender and the receiver use the same key to encrypt and decrypt the message. How

key (cipher)
any method for transforming plain text to cipher text

substitution cipher
every occurrence of a given letter is replaced systematically by another letter

transposition cipher
the ordering of the letters in each word is changed in some systematic way

symmetric key encryption (secret key encryption)
both the sender and the receiver use the same key to encrypt and decrypt the message

do the sender and the receiver have the same key? They have to send it over some communication media or exchange the key in person. Symmetric key encryption was used extensively throughout World War II and is still a part of Internet encryption.

The possibilities for simple substitution and transposition ciphers are endless, but they all suffer from common flaws. First, in the digital age, computers are so powerful and fast that these ancient means of encryption can be broken quickly. Second, symmetric key encryption requires that both parties share the same key. In order to share the same key, they must send the key over a presumably *insecure* medium where it could be stolen and used to decipher messages. If the secret key is lost or stolen, the entire encryption system fails. Third, in commercial use, where we are not all part of the same team, you would need a secret key for each of the parties with whom you transacted, that is, one key for the bank, another for the department store, and another for the government. In a large population of users, this could result in as many as n(n–1) keys. In a population of millions of Internet users, thousands of millions of keys would be needed to accommodate all e-commerce customers (estimated at about 120 million in the United States). Potentially, 120 million^2 different keys would be needed. Clearly this situation would be too unwieldy to work in practice.

Modern encryption systems are digital. The ciphers or keys used to transform plain text into cipher text are digital strings. Computers store text or other data as binary strings composed of 0s and 1s. For instance, the binary representation of the capital letter "A" in ASCII computer code is accomplished with eight binary digits (bits): 01000001. One way in which digital strings can be transformed into cipher text is by multiplying each letter by another binary number, say, an eight-bit key number 0101 0101. If we multiplied every digital character in our text messages by this eight-bit key, sent the encrypted message to a friend along with the secret eight-bit key, the friend could decode the message easily.

The strength of modern security protection is measured in terms of the length of the binary key used to encrypt the data. In the preceding example, the eight-bit key is easily deciphered because there are only 2^8 or 256 possibilities. If the intruder knows you are using an eight-bit key, then he or she could decode the message in a few seconds using a modern desktop PC just by using the brute force method of checking each of the 256 possible keys. For this reason, modern digital encryption systems use keys with 56, 128, 256, or 512 binary digits. With encryption keys of 512 digits, there are 2^{512} possibilities to check out. It is estimated that all the computers in the world would need to work for 10 years before stumbling upon the answer.

The **Data Encryption Standard (DES)** was developed by the National Security Agency (NSA) and IBM in the 1950s. DES uses a 56-bit encryption key. To cope with much faster computers, it has been improved by *Triple DES*—essentially encrypting the message three times each with a separate key. Today, the most widely used symmetric key encryption algorithm is **Advanced Encryption Standard (AES)**, which offers key sizes of 128, 192, and 256 bits. There are also many other symmetric key systems with keys up to 2,048 bits.[1]

Data Encryption Standard (DES)

developed by the National Security Agency (NSA) and IBM. Uses a 56-bit encryption key

Advanced Encryption Standard (AES)

the most widely used symmetric key encryption algorithm. Offers 128-, 192-, and 256-bit keys.

[1]For instance: DESX and RDES with 168-bit keys; the RC Series: RC2, RC4, and RC5 with keys up to 2,048 bits; and the IDEA algorithm, the basis of PGP, e-mail public key encryption software described later in this chapter, which uses 128-bit keys.

Public Key Encryption

In 1976, a new way of encrypting messages called **public key cryptography** was invented by Whitfield Diffie and Martin Hellman. Public key cryptography solves the problem of exchanging keys. In this method, two mathematically related digital keys are used: a public key and a private key. The private key is kept secret by the owner, and the public key is widely disseminated. Both keys can be used to encrypt and decrypt a message. However, once the keys are used to encrypt a message, that same key cannot be used to unencrypt the message. The mathematical algorithms used to produce the keys are *one-way functions*. A one-way irreversible mathematical function is one in which, once the algorithm is applied, the input cannot be subsequently derived from the output. Most food recipes are like this. For instance, it is easy to make scrambled eggs, but impossible to retrieve whole eggs from the scrambled eggs. Public key cryptography is based on the idea of irreversible mathematical functions. The keys are sufficiently long (128-, 256-, and 512-bit keys) that it would take enormous computing power to derive one key from the other using the largest and fastest computers available. **Figure 5.8** illustrates a simple use of public key cryptography and takes you through the important steps in using public and private keys.

Public Key Encryption Using Digital Signatures and Hash Digests

In public key encryption, some elements of security are missing. Although we can be quite sure the message was not understood or read by a third party (message confidentiality), there is no guarantee the sender really is the sender; that is, there is no authentication of the sender. This means the sender could deny ever sending the message (repudiation). And there is no assurance the message was not altered somehow in transit. For example, the message "Buy Cisco @ $25" could have been accidentally or intentionally altered to read "Sell Cisco @ $25." This suggests a potential lack of integrity in the system.

A more sophisticated use of public key cryptography can achieve authentication, nonrepudiation, and integrity. **Figure 5.9** on page 291 illustrates this more powerful approach.

To check the integrity of a message and ensure it has not been altered in transit, a hash function is used first to create a digest of the message. A **hash function** is an algorithm that produces a fixed-length number called a *hash* or *message digest*. A hash function can be simple, and count the number of digital 1s in a message, or it can be more complex, and produce a 128-bit number that reflects the number of 0s and 1s, the number of 00s, 11s, and so on. Standard hash functions are available (MD4 and MD5 produce 128- and 160-bit hashes) (Stein, 1998). These more complex hash functions produce hashes or hash results that are unique to every message. The results of applying the hash function are sent by the sender to the recipient. Upon receipt, the recipient applies the hash function to the received message and checks to verify the same result is produced. If so, the message has not been altered. The sender then encrypts both the hash result and the original message using the recipient's public key (as in Figure 5.8), producing a single block of cipher text.

One more step is required. To ensure the authenticity of the message and to ensure nonrepudiation, the sender encrypts the entire block of cipher text one more

public key cryptography

two mathematically related digital keys are used: a public key and a private key. The private key is kept secret by the owner, and the public key is widely disseminated. Both keys can be used to encrypt and decrypt a message. However, once the keys are used to encrypt a message, that same key cannot be used to unencrypt the message

hash function

an algorithm that produces a fixed-length number called a hash or message digest

FIGURE 5.8	PUBLIC KEY CRYPTOGRAPHY—A SIMPLE CASE

STEP	DESCRIPTION
1. The sender creates a digital message.	The message could be a document, spreadsheet, or any digital object.
2. The sender obtains the recipient's public key from a public directory and applies it to the message.	Public keys are distributed widely and can be obtained from recipients directly.
3. Application of the recipient's key produces an encrypted ciphertext message.	Once encrypted using the public key, the message cannot be reverse-engineered or unencrypted using the same public key. The process is irreversible.
4. The encrypted message is sent over the Internet.	The encrypted message is broken into packets and sent through several different pathways, making interception of the entire message difficult (but not impossible).
5. The recipient uses his/her private key to decrypt the message.	The only person who can decrypt the message is the person who has possession of the recipient's private key. Hopefully, this is the legitimate recipient.

In the simplest use of public key cryptography, the sender encrypts a message using the recipient's public key, and then sends it over the Internet. The only person who can decrypt this message is the recipient, using his or her private key. However, this simple case does not ensure integrity or an authentic message.

FIGURE 5.9   PUBLIC KEY CRYPTOGRAPHY WITH DIGITAL SIGNATURES

STEP	DESCRIPTION
1. The sender creates an original message.	The message could be any digital file.
2. The sender applies a hash function, producing a 128-bit hash result.	Hash functions create a unique digest of the message based on the message contents.
3. The sender encrypts the message and hash result using recipient's public key.	This irreversible process creates a cipher text that can be read only by the recipient using his or her private key.
4. The sender encrypts the result, again using his or her private key.	The sender's private key is a digital signature. There is only one person who could create this digital mark.
5. The result of this double encryption is sent over the Internet.	The message traverses the Internet as a series of independent packets.
6. The receiver uses the sender's public key to authenticate the message.	Only one person could send this message, namely, the sender.
7. The receiver uses his or her private key to decrypt the hash function and the original message. The receiver checks to ensure the original message and the hash function results conform to one another.	The hash function is used here to check the original message. This ensures the message was not changed in transit.

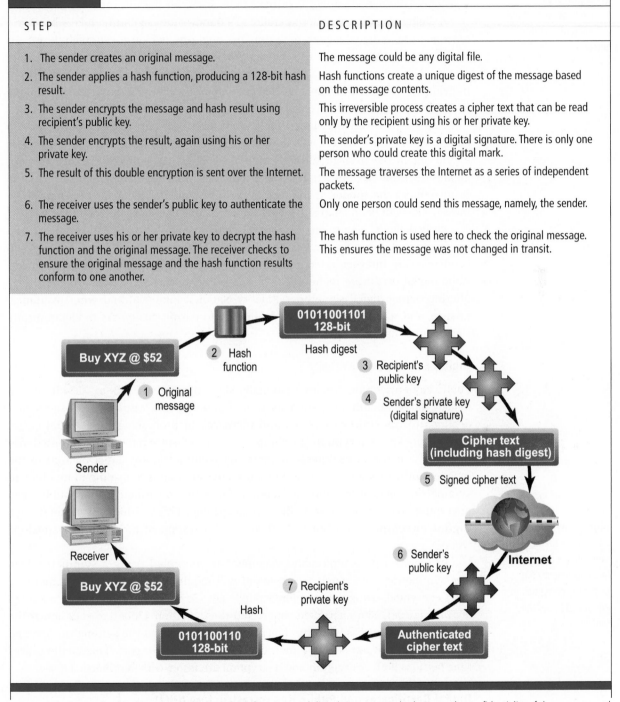

A more realistic use of public key cryptography uses hash functions and digital signatures to both ensure the confidentiality of the message and authenticate the sender. The only person who could have sent the above message is the owner or the sender using his/her private key. This authenticates the message. The hash function ensures the message was not altered in transit. As before, the only person who can decipher the message is the recipient, using his/her private key.

digital signature (e-signature)

"signed" cipher text that can be sent over the Internet

time using the sender's private key. This produces a **digital signature** (also called an *e-signature*) or "signed" cipher text that can be sent over the Internet.

A digital signature is a close parallel to a handwritten signature. Like a handwritten signature, a digital signature is unique—only one person presumably possesses the private key. When used with a hash function, the digital signature is even more unique than a handwritten signature. In addition to being exclusive to a particular individual, when used to sign a hashed document, the digital signature is also unique to the document, and changes for every document.

The recipient of this signed cipher text first uses the sender's public key to authenticate the message. Once authenticated, the recipient uses his or her private key to obtain the hash result and original message. As a final step, the recipient applies the same hash function to the original text, and compares the result with the result sent by the sender. If the results are the same, the recipient now knows the message has not been changed during transmission. The message has integrity.

Early digital signature programs required the user to have a digital certificate, and were far too difficult for an individual to use. Newer programs from several small companies are Internet-based and do not require users to install software, or understand digital certificate technology. DocuSign, EchoSign, and Sertifi are companies offering online digital signatures. Fidelity National Financial and other insurance, finance, and surety companies are beginning to permit customers to electronically sign documents.

Digital Envelopes

digital envelope

a technique that uses symmetric encryption for large documents, but public key encryption to encrypt and send the symmetric key

Public key encryption is computationally slow. If one used 128- or 256-bit keys to encode large documents—such as this chapter or the entire book—significant declines in transmission speeds and increases in processing time would occur. Symmetric key encryption is computationally faster, but as we pointed out previously, it has a weakness—namely, the symmetric key must be sent to the recipient over insecure transmission lines. One solution is to use the more efficient symmetric encryption and decryption for large documents, but public key encryption to encrypt and send the symmetric key. This technique is called using a **digital envelope**. See **Figure 5.10** for an illustration of how a digital envelope works.

In Figure 5.10, a diplomatic document is encrypted using a symmetric key. The symmetric key—which the recipient will require to decrypt the document—is itself encrypted, using the recipient's public key. So we have a "key within a key" (a *digital envelope*). The encrypted report and the digital envelope are sent across the Web. The recipient first uses his/her private key to decrypt the symmetric key, and then the recipient uses the symmetric key to decrypt the report. This method saves time because both encryption and decryption are faster with symmetric keys.

Digital Certificates and Public Key Infrastructure (PKI)

There are still some deficiencies in the message security regime described previously. How do we know that people and institutions are who they claim to be? Anyone can make up a private and public key combination and claim to be someone

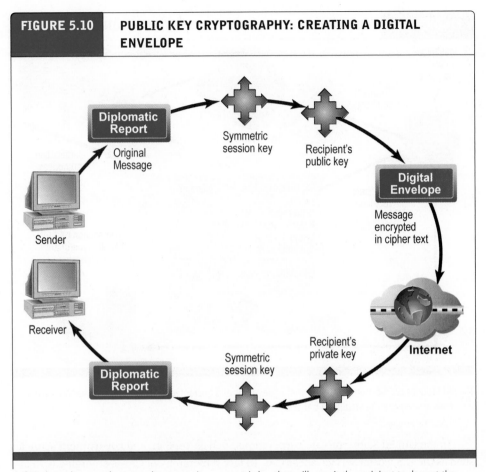

| FIGURE 5.10 | PUBLIC KEY CRYPTOGRAPHY: CREATING A DIGITAL ENVELOPE |

A digital envelope can be created to transmit a symmetric key that will permit the recipient to decrypt the message and be assured the message was not intercepted in transit.

they are not. Before you place an order with an online merchant such as Amazon, you want to be sure it really is Amazon.com you have on the screen and not a spoofer masquerading as Amazon. In the physical world, if someone asks who you are and you show a social security number, they may well ask to see a picture ID or a second form of certifiable or acceptable identification. If they really doubt who you are, they may ask for references to other authorities and actually interview these other authorities. Similarly, in the digital world, we need a way to know who people and institutions really are.

Digital certificates, and the supporting public key infrastructure, are an attempt to solve this problem of digital identity. A **digital certificate** is a digital document issued by a trusted third-party institution known as a **certification authority (CA)** that contains the name of the subject or company, the subject's public key, a digital certificate serial number, an expiration date, an issuance date, the digital signature of the certification authority (the name of the CA encrypted using the CA's private key), and other identifying information (see **Figure 5.11**).

digital certificate
a digital document issued by a certification authority that contains the name of the subject or company, the subject's public key, a digital certificate serial number, an expiration date, an issuance date, the digital signature of the certification authority, and other identifying information

certification authority (CA)
a trusted third party that issues digital certificates

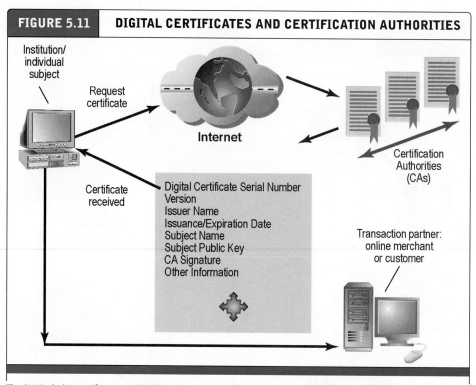

FIGURE 5.11 | DIGITAL CERTIFICATES AND CERTIFICATION AUTHORITIES

The PKI includes certification authorities that issue, verify, and guarantee digital certificates that are used in e-commerce to assure the identity of transaction partners.

In the United States, private corporations such as VeriSign and government agencies such as the U.S. Postal Service act as CAs. In fact, a hierarchy of CAs is emerging with less well-known CAs being certified by larger and better-known CAs, creating a community of mutually verifying institutions. **Public key infrastructure (PKI)** refers to the CAs and digital certificate procedures that are accepted by all parties.

To create a digital certificate, the user generates a public/private key pair and sends a request for certification to a CA along with the user's public key. The CA verifies the information (how this is accomplished differs from CA to CA). The CA issues a certificate containing the user's public key and other related information. Finally, the CA creates a message digest from the certificate itself (just like a hash digest) and signs it with the CA's private key. This signed digest is called the *signed certificate*. We end up with a totally unique cipher text document—there can be only one signed certificate like this in the world.

There are several ways the certificates are used in commerce. Before initiating a transaction, the customer can request the signed digital certificate of the merchant and decrypt it using the merchant's public key to obtain both the message digest and the certificate as issued. If the message digest matches the certificate, then the merchant and the public key are authenticated. The merchant may in return request certification of the user, in which case the user would send the merchant his or her individual certificate. There are many types of certificates: personal, institutional, Web server, software publisher, and CAs themselves.

public key infrastructure (PKI)

CAs and digital certificate procedures that are accepted by all parties

You can easily obtain a public and private key for personal, noncommercial use at the International PGP Home Page Web site, Pgpi.org. **Pretty Good Privacy (PGP)** was invented in 1991 by Phil Zimmerman, and has become one of the most widely used e-mail public key encryption software tools in the world. Using PGP software installed on your computer, you can compress and encrypt your messages as well as authenticate both yourself and the recipient. The *Insight on Society* story, *In Pursuit of E-mail Security*, describes additional efforts to ensure e-mail security.

Pretty Good Privacy (PGP)

a widely used e-mail public key encryption software program

Limitations to Encryption Solutions

PKI is a powerful technological solution to security issues, but it has many limitations. PKI applies mainly to protecting messages in transit on the Internet and is not effective against insiders—employees—who have legitimate access to corporate systems including customer information. Most e-commerce sites do not store customer information in encrypted form. Other limitations are apparent. For one, how is your private key to be protected? Most private keys will be stored on insecure desktop or laptop computers.

There is no guarantee the person using your computer—and your private key—is really you. Under many digital signature laws (such as those in Utah and Washington), you are responsible for whatever your private key does even if you were not the person using the key. This is very different from mail-order or telephone order credit card rules, where you have a right to dispute the credit card charge. Second, there is no guarantee the verifying computer of the merchant is secure. Third, CAs are self-selected organizations seeking to gain access to the business of authorization. They may not be authorities on the corporations or individuals they certify. For instance, how can a CA know about all the corporations within an industry to determine who is or is not legitimate? A related question concerns the method used by the CA to identify the certificate holder. Was this an e-mail transaction verified only by claims of applicants who filled out an online form? For instance, VeriSign acknowledged in one case that it had mistakenly issued two digital certificates to someone fraudulently claiming to represent Microsoft. Digital certificates have been hijacked by hackers, tricking consumers into giving up personal information. Last, what are the policies for revoking or renewing certificates? The expected life of a digital certificate or private key is a function of the frequency of use and the vulnerability of systems that use the certificate. Yet most CAs have no policy or just an annual policy for re-issuing certificates (Ellison and Schneier, 2000).

SECURING CHANNELS OF COMMUNICATION

The concepts of public key encryption are used routinely for securing channels of communication.

Secure Sockets Layer (SSL)

The most common form of securing channels is through the *Secure Sockets Layer (SSL)* of TCP/IP (described briefly in Chapter 3). When you receive a message from a server on the Web with which you will be communicating through a secure channel, this means you will be using SSL to establish a secure negotiated session. (Notice that the

INSIGHT ON SOCIETY

IN PURSUIT OF E-MAIL SECURITY

You just sent a poisonous e-mail to a friend about a colleague at work with whom you compete for position and recognition. Now you wish you could expunge that e-mail because you now remember that the two share several common friends and you are afraid the e-mail will make the rounds of friends of friends. You just wish you could say "kablooey" and away it would go.

You are in New York and you would like to use e-mail to negotiate a deal with another company in London but are afraid they will forward your offer to competitors seeking the same deal and seek a higher price than you are willing to start with. You are looking for a private deal, not a public conversation.

You sent an e-mail to a distributor telling them to stop shipment of a train-car load of parts to a retail dealer that just went bankrupt. If the goods are shipped and received by the retailer, they will be tied up in bankruptcy proceedings as that company's assets. You need undeniable evidence your distributor received the message. If the distributor shipped, then it is liable, not you. What you need is a registered, certified, and return receipt capability like regular postal mail. Good luck!

About 250 billion e-mail messages are generated every day worldwide, according to the Radicati Group. Most e-mail programs offer little if any help in terms of controlling who sees your e-mail, how long it remains live, and who if anyone received it. E-mail is easily denied or altered. In fact, your e-mail theoretically can be seen by anybody, forever, or by no one if they so choose. Therefore, you need to think carefully about what you say, how you say it, and in the end you might want to avoid e-mail altogether. But help is on the way.

There are now a number of free services that allow users to send self-destructing emails, which expire/disappear automatically after a specified time interval. One example is BigString, which recalls or retracts a message after it has been sent, based on the number of times the message is read, and/or the age of the e-mail message. It also blocks the recipient from copying, forwarding, or printing the message. There is also a plug-in being developed to allow those using the services to do so through any e-mail client. Self-destructing-email.com, which works with Web-based e-mail clients to enable the user to create a one-time secure page for the recipient, is another example. The message is accessed through a specific URL, and then it is deleted. Kicknotes.com's messages self-destruct based on times read and age; Stealthmessage.com stores encrypted messages anonymously (the user can set the self-destruct options and messages cannot be forwarded); Sdmessage.com (Self Destruct Message) is web-based, and messages self-destruct 60 seconds after they are viewed.

If you've ever wondered why e-mail can't be "registered" like postal mail, a solution is now provided by RPost.com as an add-on to Microsoft Outlook. For a monthly fee of $14.75, RPost alerts the sender that an e-mail was received and opened. It can also verify that the content of the e-mail was not altered.

According to Microsoft's William Kennedy, general manager of Office communications services, Microsoft will be adding many of these features to its Outlook 2007 application over time, such as electronic postmarks (the mail was processed and delivered), non-forwarding mail, and non-printing mail.

But the ability to eliminate, delete, destroy, or alter e-mail runs flat up against the drift of

(continued)

modern corporate law. E-mail is increasingly playing a role similar to postal mail and contracts in courts. It is used as evidence of action, intention, and consequence. Corporate e-mail messages have achieved the same status as other commonly used business documents. The Sarbanes-Oxley Act of 2002 (also known as SOX, or the Public Company Accounting Reform and Investor Protection Act of 2002) requires all public firms to develop a reasonable policy of business record retention, including e-mail and instant messages. The retention period must be "reasonable" and clearly set in the policy. A good retention policy cannot be selective—all documents need to be saved. As a result, most public firms are storing all e-mail and IMs in perpetuity. Under SOX, if you are convicted of changing, altering, or deleting business e-mail that is needed for a judicial process, you can be sentenced for up to 20 years in jail. In the current environment, therefore, you will need to be careful to balance user control over e-mail with corporate responsibilities for record retention.

SOURCES: Bigstring.com, "Email Rewards Program Unveiled by BigString," July 29, 2009; "Companies Finding Ways to Cope with Large Volumes of Electronic Messages," by Chris Starrs, OnlineAthens.com, August 22, 2008; "Unintentional Employee Misuse Top Driver for Enterprise Email Risk," Messagegate.com, July 9, 2008; "Office Space: Career Couch. The Risk Is All Yours in Office E-Mail," by Matt Villano, *New York Times*, August 31, 2007; "Key Issues for Electronic Discovery," by Whit Andrews, EMC White Paper, August 20, 2007; "Don't Let Your E-Evidence Get Trashed," by Jerold S. Solovy and Robert L. Byman, *National Law Journal*, June 11, 2007; "10 Free Services to Send Self-destructing Emails which Expire/Disappear Automatically after a Specified Time Interval," Tech.blog.com, July 25, 2007; "Sarbanes-Oxley Has Major Impact on Electronic Evidence," by Michele Lange, *National Law Journal*, January 2, 2007.

URL changes from HTTP to HTTPS.) A **secure negotiated session** is a client-server session in which the URL of the requested document, along with the contents, contents of forms, and the cookies exchanged, are encrypted (see **Figure 5.12**). For instance, your credit card number that you entered into a form would be encrypted. Through a series of handshakes and communications, the browser and the server establish one another's identity by exchanging digital certificates, decide on the strongest shared form of encryption, and then proceed to communicate using an agreed-upon session key. A **session key** is a unique symmetric encryption key chosen just for this single secure session. Once used, it is gone forever. Figure 5.12 shows how this works.

secure negotiated session
a client-server session in which the URL of the requested document, along with the contents, contents of forms, and the cookies exchanged, are encrypted

session key
a unique symmetric encryption key chosen for a single secure session

In practice, most private individuals do not have a digital certificate. In this case, the merchant server will not request a certificate, but the client browser will request the merchant certificate once a secure session is called for by the server.

The SSL protocol provides data encryption, server authentication, optional client authentication, and message integrity for TCP/IP connections. SSL is available in 40-bit and 128-bit levels, depending on what version of browser you are using. The strongest shared encryption is always chosen.

SSL was designed to address the threat of authenticity by allowing users to verify another user's identity or the identity of a server. It also protects the integrity of the messages exchanged. However, once the merchant receives the encrypted credit and order information, that information is typically stored in unencrypted format on the merchant's servers.

While the SSL protocol provides secure transactions between merchant and consumer, it only guarantees server-side authentication. Client authentication is optional.

FIGURE 5.12   SECURE NEGOTIATED SESSIONS USING SSL

Certificates play a key role in using SSL to establish a secure communications channel.

In addition, SSL cannot provide irrefutability—consumers can order goods or download information products, and then claim the transaction never occurred. Other protocols for protecting financial transactions such as Secure Electronic Transaction Protocol (SET), which requires all parties to a transaction to use digital certificates, have been developed. However, SET has not been widely adopted.

Secure Hypertext Transfer Protocol (S-HTTP)

Secure Hypertext Transfer Protocol (S-HTTP)

a secure message-oriented communications protocol designed for use in conjunction with HTTP. Cannot be used to secure non-HTTP messages

A competing method is called **Secure Hypertext Transfer Protocol (S-HTTP)**. S-HTTP is a secure message-oriented communications protocol designed for use in conjunction with HTTP. It is designed to coexist with HTTP and to be easily integrated with HTTP applications. Whereas SSL is designed to establish a secure connection between two computers, S-HTTP is designed to send individual messages securely. Not all browsers and not all Web sites support S-HTTP. You know you are dealing with a supporting site when the URL starts with "SHTTP." The use of this as part of an anchor tag indicates that the target server is S-HTTP capable. Using S-HTTP, any message may be signed, authenticated, encrypted, or any combination of these. Basically, S-HTTP attempts to make HTTP more secure.

Virtual Private Networks (VPNs)

A **virtual private network (VPN)** allows remote users to securely access internal networks via the Internet, using the **Point-to-Point Tunneling Protocol (PPTP)**. PPTP is an encoding mechanism that allows one local network to connect to another using the Internet as the conduit. A remote user can dial into a local ISP, and PPTP makes the connection from the ISP to the corporate network as if the user had dialed into the corporate network directly. The process of connecting one protocol (PPTP) through another (IP) is called *tunneling,* because PPTP creates a private connection by adding an invisible wrapper around a message to hide its content. As the message travels through the Internet between the ISP and the corporate network, it is shielded from prying eyes by PPTP's encrypted wrapper.

A VPN is "virtual" in the sense that it appears to users as a dedicated secure line when in fact it is a temporary secure line. The primary use of VPNs is to establish secure communications among business partners—larger suppliers or customers. A dedicated connection to a business partner can be very expensive. Using the Internet and PPTP as the connection method significantly reduces the cost of secure communications.

PROTECTING NETWORKS

Once you have protected communications as well as possible, the next set of tools to consider are those that can protect your networks, as well as the servers and clients on those networks.

Firewalls

Firewalls and proxy servers are intended to build a wall around your network and the attached servers and clients, just like physical-world firewalls protect you from fires for a limited period of time. Firewalls and proxy servers share some similar functions, but they are quite different.

A **firewall** refers to either hardware or software that filters communication packets and prevents some packets from entering the network based on a security policy. The firewall controls traffic to and from servers and clients, forbidding communications from untrustworthy sources, and allowing other communications from trusted sources to proceed. Every message that is to be sent or received from the network is processed by the firewall, which determines if the message meets security guidelines established by the business. If it does, it is permitted to be distributed, and if it doesn't, the message is blocked. Firewalls can filter traffic based on packet attributes such as source IP address, destination port or IP address, type of service (such as WWW or HTTP), the domain name of the source, and many other dimensions. Most hardware firewalls that protect local area networks connected to the Internet have default settings that require little if any administrator intervention and accomplish simple but effective rules that deny incoming packets from a connection that does not originate from an internal request—the firewall only allows connections from servers that you requested service from. A common default setting on hardware firewalls (DSL and cable modem routers) simply ignores efforts to communicate with TCP port 445, the most commonly attacked port. The increasing use of firewalls by home and business Internet users has

virtual private network (VPN)
allows remote users to securely access internal networks via the Internet, using the Point-to-Point Tunneling Protocol (PPTP)

Point-to-Point Tunneling Protocol (PPTP)
an encoding mechanism that allows one local network to connect to another using the Internet as the conduit

firewall
refers to either hardware or software that filters communication packets and prevents some packets from entering the network based on a security policy

greatly reduced the effectiveness of attacks, and forced hackers to focus more on e-mail attachments to distribute worms and viruses.

There are two major methods firewalls use to validate traffic: packet filters and application gateways. *Packet filters* examine data packets to determine whether they are destined for a prohibited port or originate from a prohibited IP address (as specified by the security administrator). The filter specifically looks at the source and destination information, as well as the port and packet type, when determining whether the information may be transmitted. One downside of the packet filtering method is that it is susceptible to spoofing, since authentication is not one of its roles.

Application gateways are a type of firewall that filters communications based on the application being requested, rather than the source or destination of the message. Such firewalls also process requests at the application level, farther away from the client computer than packet filters. By providing a central filtering point, application gateways provide greater security than packet filters, but can compromise system performance.

proxy server (proxy)
software server that handles all communications originating from or being sent to the Internet, acting as a spokesperson or bodyguard for the organization

Proxy servers (proxies) are software servers (usually located on a dedicated computer) that handle all communications originating from or being sent to the Internet, acting as a spokesperson or bodyguard for the organization. Proxies act primarily to limit access of internal clients to external Internet servers, although some proxy servers act as firewalls as well. Proxy servers are sometimes called *dual home systems* because they have two network interfaces. To internal computers, a proxy server is known as the *gateway*, while to external computers it is known as a *mail server* or *numeric address*.

When a user on an internal network requests a Web page, the request is routed first to the proxy server. The proxy server validates the user and the nature of the request, and then sends the request onto the Internet. A Web page sent by an external Internet server first passes to the proxy server. If acceptable, the Web page passes onto the internal network Web server and then to the client desktop. By prohibiting users from communicating directly with the Internet, companies can restrict access to certain types of sites, such as pornographic, auction, or stock-trading sites. Proxy servers also improve Web performance by storing frequently requested Web pages locally, reducing upload times, and hiding the internal network's address, thus making it more difficult for hackers to monitor. **Figure 5.13** illustrates how firewalls and proxy servers protect a local area network from Internet intruders and prevent internal clients from reaching prohibited Web servers.

PROTECTING SERVERS AND CLIENTS

Operating system features and anti-virus software can help further protect servers and clients from certain types of attacks.

Operating System Security Enhancements

The most obvious way to protect servers and clients is to take advantage of Microsoft's and Apple's automatic computer security upgrades. Windows Server 2008/2003 and the Windows XP and Windows Vista client operating systems are continuously being upgraded by Microsoft to patch vulnerabilities discovered by hackers. These patches are autonomic; that is, when using Windows XP or Vista on the Internet, you are

FIGURE 5.13 | FIREWALLS AND PROXY SERVERS

The primary function of a firewall is to deny access by remote client computers to local computers. The primary purpose of a proxy server is to provide controlled access from local computers to remote computers.

prompted and informed that operating system enhancements are available. Users can easily download these security patches for free. The most common known worms and viruses can be prevented by simply keeping your server and client operating systems and applications up to date. Application vulnerabilities are also fixed in the same manner. For instance, both the Mozilla and Internet Explorer browsers are updated automatically with little user intervention.

Anti-Virus Software

The easiest and least expensive way to prevent threats to system integrity is to install anti-virus software. Programs by McAfee, Symantec (Norton AntiVirus), and many others provide inexpensive tools to identify and eradicate the most common types of malicious code as they enter a computer, as well as destroy those already lurking on a hard drive. Anti-virus programs can be set up so that e-mail attachments are inspected prior to you clicking on them, and the attachments are eliminated if they contain a known virus or worm. It is not enough, however, to simply install the software once. Since new viruses are developed and released every day, daily routine updates are needed in order to prevent new threats from being loaded. Some premium-level anti-virus software is updated hourly.

Anti-virus suite packages and stand-alone programs are available to eliminate intruders such as bot programs, adware, and other security risks. Such programs work much like anti-virus software in that they look for recognized hacker tools or signature actions of known intruders. Designed to trigger an alarm when such an action is noted, these systems must be monitored by staff members or intrusion detection services in order to work properly.

5.4   MANAGEMENT POLICIES, BUSINESS PROCEDURES, AND PUBLIC LAWS

U.S. business firms and government agencies spend about 12% of their information technology budgets on security hardware, software, and services. That will add up to about $120 billion in 2009 (Forrester Research, 2009).

However, most CEOs and CIOs of existing e-commerce operations believe that technology is not the sole answer to managing the risk of e-commerce. The technology provides a foundation, but in the absence of intelligent management policies, even the best technology can be easily defeated. Public laws and active enforcement of cybercrime statutes are also required to both raise the costs of illegal behavior on the Internet and guard against corporate abuse of information. Let's consider briefly the development of management policy.

A SECURITY PLAN: MANAGEMENT POLICIES

In order to minimize security threats, e-commerce firms must develop a coherent corporate policy that takes into account the nature of the risks, the information assets that need protecting, and the procedures and technologies required to address the risk, as well as implementation and auditing mechanisms. **Figure 5.14** illustrates the key steps in developing a solid security plan.

risk assessment

an assessment of the risks and points of vulnerability

A security plan begins with **risk assessment**—an assessment of the risks and points of vulnerability. The first step is to inventory the information and knowledge assets of the e-commerce site and company. What information is at risk? Is it customer information, proprietary designs, business activities, secret processes, or other internal information, such as price schedules, executive compensation, or payroll? For each type of information asset, try to estimate the dollar value to the firm if this information were compromised, and then multiply that amount by the probability of the loss occurring. Once you have done so, rank order the results. You now have a list of information assets prioritized by their value to the firm.

security policy

a set of statements prioritizing the information risks, identifying acceptable risk targets, and identifying the mechanisms for achieving these targets

Based on your quantified list of risks, you can start to develop a **security policy**—a set of statements prioritizing the information risks, identifying acceptable risk targets, and identifying the mechanisms for achieving these targets. You will obviously want to start with the information assets that you determined to be the highest priority in your risk assessment. Who generates and controls this information in the firm? What existing security policies are in place to protect the information? What enhancements can you recommend to improve security of these most valuable assets? What level of risk are you willing to accept for each of these assets? Are you willing, for instance, to lose customer credit data once every

FIGURE 5.14	DEVELOPING AN E-COMMERCE SECURITY PLAN

There are five steps involved in building an e-commerce security plan.

10 years? Or will you pursue a 100-year hurricane strategy by building a security edifice for credit card data that can withstand the once-in-100-year disaster? You will need to estimate how much it will cost to achieve this level of acceptable risk. Remember, total and complete security may require extraordinary financial resources. By answering these questions, you will have the beginnings of a security policy.

Next consider an **implementation plan**—the steps you will take to achieve the security plan goals. Specifically, you must determine how you will translate the levels of acceptable risk into a set of tools, technologies, policies, and procedures. What new technologies will you deploy to achieve the goals, and what new employee procedures will be needed?

To implement your plan, you will need an organizational unit in charge of security, and a security officer—someone who is in charge of security on a daily basis. For a small e-commerce site, the security officer will likely be the person in charge of Internet services or the site manager, whereas for larger firms, there typically is a dedicated team with a supporting budget. The **security organization** educates and trains users, keeps management aware of security threats and breakdowns, and maintains the tools chosen to implement security.

The security organization typically administers access controls, authentication procedures, and authorization policies. **Access controls** determine which outsiders and insiders can gain legitimate access to your networks. Outsider access controls

implementation plan
the action steps you will take to achieve the security plan goals

security organization
educates and trains users, keeps management aware of security threats and breakdowns, and maintains the tools chosen to implement security

access controls
determine who can gain legitimate access to a network

authentication procedures

include the use of digital signatures, certificates of authority, and public key infrastructure

biometrics

the study of measurable biological or physical characteristics

authorization policies

determine differing levels of access to information assets for differing levels of users

authorization management system

establishes where and when a user is permitted to access certain parts of a Web site

security audit

involves the routine review of access logs (identifying how outsiders are using the site as well as how insiders are accessing the site's assets)

include firewalls and proxy servers, while insider access controls typically consist of login procedures (usernames, passwords, and access codes).

Authentication procedures include the use of digital signatures, certificates of authority, and PKI. Now that e-signatures have been given the same legal weight as an original pen-and-ink version, companies are in the process of devising ways to test and confirm a signer's identity. Companies frequently have signers type their full name and click on a button indicating their understanding that they have just signed a contract or document.

Biometric devices are used along with digital signatures to verify physical attributes associated with an individual, such as a fingerprint or retina (eye) scan or speech recognition system. (**Biometrics** is the study of measurable biological, or physical, characteristics.) A company could require, for example, that an individual undergo a fingerprint scan before being allowed access to a Web site, or before being allowed to pay for merchandise with a credit card. Biometric devices make it even more difficult for hackers to break into sites or facilities, significantly reducing the opportunity for spoofing.

Authorization policies determine differing levels of access to information assets for differing levels of users. **Authorization management systems** establish where and when a user is permitted to access certain parts of a Web site. Their primary function is to restrict access to private information within a company's Internet infrastructure. Although there are several authorization management products currently available, most operate in the same way: the system encrypts a user session to function like a passkey that follows the user from page to page, allowing access only to those areas that the user is permitted to enter, based on information set at the system database. By establishing entry rules up front for each user, the authorization management system knows who is permitted to go where at all times.

The last step in developing an e-commerce security plan is performing a security audit. A **security audit** involves the routine review of access logs (identifying how outsiders are using the site as well as how insiders are accessing the site's assets). A monthly report should be produced that establishes the routine and non-routine accesses to the systems and identifies unusual patterns of activities. As previously noted, tiger teams are often used by large corporate sites to evaluate the strength of existing security procedures. Many small firms have sprung up in the last five years to provide these services to large corporate sites.

The *Insight on Technology* story, *Securing Your Information: Cleversafe Hippie Storage*, discusses a new method for securing information using the Internet.

THE ROLE OF LAWS AND PUBLIC POLICY

The public policy environment today is very different from the early days of e-commerce. The net result is that the Internet is no longer an ungoverned, unsupervised, self-controlled technology juggernaut. Just as with financial markets in the last 70 years, there is a growing awareness that e-commerce markets work only when a powerful institutional set of laws and enforcement mechanisms are in place. These laws help ensure orderly, rational, and fair markets. This growing public policy environment is becoming just as global as e-commerce itself. Despite some spectacu-

INSIGHT ON TECHNOLOGY

SECURING YOUR INFORMATION: CLEVERSAFE HIPPIE STORAGE

Normally when you think of keeping your computer data secure, you think about making multiple copies of the information and putting them on separate storage devices, such as backing up your desktop files to a central server, and/or or copying them to a USB jump drive and taking it home at night. Three copies are generally considered the corporate norm for securing data in a distributed file system method known as LOCKSS: lots of copies keeps stuff safe. This is the method offered by Microsoft and most data security companies to e-commerce firms. But there are just a few problems with this brute force method.

LOCKSS increases the number of servers and storage devices by at least 200% just to store files. This makes hard disk and server manufacturers happy but ends up being very costly to firms. In a world that's swimming in digital information, this does not seem like an intelligent choice. For instance, Google stores so much information that it was forced to create one of the world's largest data storage facilities (68,000 square feet of disk drives and PCs) in Dalles, Oregon, on the banks of the Columbia River—one of America's largest—so it could take advantage of cheap Columbia River hydroelectric power and the cooling waters of the river to keep its PCs humming. With the amount of digital information now exceeding 5 exabytes (roughly 37,000 Libraries of Congress) and doubling every three years, it is conceivable that at some point there won't be enough electricity on earth to make three copies of our really important files.

Also, traditional methods are not very secure: if one storage system is hacked, or if one laptop containing a copy is misplaced, you lose all security. Ask TJMaxx, which lost control of over 47 million customer credit card records because one storage system was hacked. Their files were all backed up with multiple copies, some buried inside mountains, but one server was compromised. Moreover, communicating the data to remote storage locations increases the risk of interception.

Cleversafe, an open source company located at the Illinois Institute of Technology, is developing a different system. Whereas Google aims to organize all the world's information, Cleversafe wants to store all the world's information. In this method—variously called hippie storage or grid storage—an algorithm known as an information dispersal algorithm is used to slice the information into pieces, encrypt the pieces, and distribute them to different servers across the Internet. The algorithm adds redundancy, error checking, and encryption as it moves through the data file. The idea is similar to the SETI@Home project, a shared computing system that allows individual PC users to contribute their idle computer time to create a distributed computer project that looks for meaning in signals from space.

Based on a paper by computer scientist Adi Shamir ("How to Share a Secret"), the original data can be reconstructed from a majority of the slices. In most examples of this method, the data is distributed to 11 interconnected servers on the Internet, and can be reconstructed from any four of these servers. Depending on your needs and risks, you can determine how many dispersed servers to use and how many are needed to reconstruct your data. This is referred to as a computing grid: an interconnected set of computers that share the processing load across all computers on the grid. Losing anywhere from one to six of the servers to fire, flood, hacking or

(continued)

another problem, and your data is still available from the four remaining servers. If hackers break into one or two servers, or three or four, not a problem: they would need to crack into more to reconstruct your data. The overhead cost is a fraction of the LOCKSS brute force strategy. The largest cost reduction comes from eliminating separate copies for backups, archives, or disaster recovery. Compared with ratios of 5-to-1 or 6-to-1 of "extra" versus original data in copy-based storage environments, Cleversafe requires ratios of 1.3-to-1 or less.

In March 2008, Cleversafe launched its first commercial dispersed storage product. The product divides digital content into slices using information dispersal algorithms and disperses the slices to multiple storage nodes on a dispersed storage network. A typical configuration of equipment that includes 24 terabytes of raw storage capacity costs $127,000. In August 2008, Cleversafe announced a partnership with five key partners, a U.S-based consortium of ISPs, hosting companies, and telecommunications providers, to deploy the product. In April 2009, Cleversafe released software upgrades for its dispersed storage product. The new release unveils Smart Client, the foundation for next-generation content delivery networks (CDNs). Smart Client technology allows organizations to distribute rich content to both wire, and wireless devices in a secure and cost-effective way. In addition, Cleversafe announced reductions in the amount of power needed and increases in storage capcity to its Smart Client product.

With more than 1 billion PCs connected to the Web, and grid computing becoming more common, it is likely in the near future that confidential data generated in e-commerce will be stored and shared across thousands of Internet computers, in plain site. It's an economical and "green" way of sharing secrets to protect them.

■ **SOURCES:** "Cleversafe's New Smart Client Integrates Scalable Storage with Effective Content Delivery," April 14, 2009, "Cleversafe Launches First 'Dispersed' Storage Network," by Chris Preimesberger, Eweek.com, August 21, 2008; "First Steps into the Cloud," by George Crump, *Information Week*, July 11, 2008; "Cleversafe Announces Availability of First Commercial Products to Create Dispersed Storage Networks," Reuters, February 19, 2008; "Cleversafe's Dispersed Storage," by Robert Scheier, *Computerworld*, August 20, 2007; "Cleversafe Presents Alternative to Google's Triple Storage Philosophy at Linux World," by Alexander Ljungberg, *Linux/Unix/Open Source*, August 10, 2007; "How to Share a Secret," by Adi Shamir, *Communications of the ACM*, November, 1979.

lar internationally based attacks on U.S. e-commerce sites, the sources and persons involved in major harmful attacks have almost always been uncovered and, where possible, prosecuted.

Voluntary and private efforts have played a very large role in identifying criminal hackers and assisting law enforcement. Since 1995, as e-commerce has grown in significance, national and local law enforcement activities have expanded greatly. New laws have been passed that grant local and national authorities new tools and mechanisms for identifying, tracing, and prosecuting cybercriminals. **Table 5.4** lists the most significant federal e-commerce security legislation.

Following passage of the National Information Infrastructure Protection Act of 1996, which makes DoS attacks and virus distribution federal crimes, the FBI and the Department of Justice established the National Infrastructure Protection Center (NIPC). Now subsumed within the National Cyber Security Division of the Department of Homeland Security, this organization's sole mission is to identify and combat threats against the United States' technology and telecommunications infrastructure.

By increasing the punishment for cybercrimes, the U.S. government is attempting to create a deterrent to further hacker actions. And by making such actions federal

TABLE 5.4	E-COMMERCE SECURITY LEGISLATION
LEGISLATION	**SIGNIFICANCE**
Computer Fraud and Abuse Act (1986)	Primary federal statute used to combat computer crime
Electronic Communications Privacy Act (1986)	Imposes fines and imprisonment for individuals who access, intercept, or disclose the private e-mail communications of others
National Information Infrastructure Protection Act (1996)	Makes DoS attacks illegal; creates NIPC in the FBI
Cyberspace Electronic Security Act (2000)	Reduces export restrictions
Computer Security Enhancement Act (2000)	Protects federal government systems from hacking
Electronic Signatures in Global and National Commerce Act (the "E-Sign Law") (2000)	Authorizes the use of electronic signatures in legal documents
USA PATRIOT Act (2001)	Authorizes use of computer-based surveillance of suspected terrorists
Homeland Security Act (2002)	Authorized establishment of the Department of Homeland Security, which is assigned responsibility for developing a comprehensive national plan for security of the key resources and critical infrastructures of the United States; DHS becomes the central coordinator for all cyberspace security efforts
CAN-SPAM Act (2003)	Although primarily a mechanism for civil and regulatory lawsuits against spammers, the CAN-SPAM Act also creates several new criminal offenses intended to address situations in which the perpetrator has taken steps to hide his or her identity or the source of the spam from recipients, ISPs, or law enforcement agencies. Also contains criminal sanctions for sending sexually explicit e-mail without designating it as such.
U.S. SAFE WEB Act (2006)	Enhances FTC's ability to obtain monetary redress for consumers in cases involving spyware, spam, Internet fraud, and deception; also improves FTC's ability to gather information and coordinate investigations with foreign counterparts

crimes, the government is able to extradite international hackers and prosecute them within the United States.

After September 11, 2001, Congress passed the USA PATRIOT Act, which broadly expanded law enforcement's investigative and surveillance powers. The act has provisions for monitoring e-mail and Internet use. Currently, this is a temporary act, but there are efforts to make it permanent and to further expand law enforcement's monitoring powers. The Homeland Security Act of 2002 also attempts to fight cyberterrorism and increases the government's ability to compel information disclosure by computer and ISP sources.

Private and Private-Public Cooperation Efforts

The good news is that e-commerce sites are not alone in their battle to achieve security on the Internet. Several organizations—some public and some private—are devoted to tracking down criminal organizations and individuals engaged in attacks against Internet and e-commerce sites. One of the better-known private organizations is the **CERT Coordination Center** (formerly known as the Computer Emergency Response Team) at Carnegie Mellon University. CERT monitors and tracks online criminal activity reported to it by private corporations and government agencies that seek out its help. CERT is composed of full-time and part-time computer experts who can trace the origins of attacks against sites despite the complexity of the Internet. Its staff members also assist organizations in identifying security problems, developing solutions, and communicating with the public about widespread hacker threats. The CERT Coordination Center also provides product assessments, reports, and training in order to improve the public's knowledge and understanding of security threats and solutions. The U.S. Department of Homeland Security (DHS) operates the **United States Computer Emergency Readiness Team (US-CERT)**, which coordinates cyber incident warnings and responses across both the government and private sectors.

Government Policies and Controls on Encryption Software

As noted in the beginning of this chapter, governments have sought to restrict availability and export of encryption systems as a means of detecting and preventing crime and terrorism. In the United States, both Congress and the executive branch have sought to regulate the uses of encryption. At the international level, four organizations have influenced the international traffic in encryption software: the Organization for Economic Cooperation and Development (OECD), G-7/G-8 (the heads of state of the top eight industrialized countries in the world), the Council of Europe, and the Wassnaar Arrangement (law enforcement personnel from the top 33 industrialized counties in the world) (EPIC, 2000). Various governments have proposed schemes for controlling encryption software or at least preventing criminals from obtaining strong encryption tools (see **Table 5.5)**.

OECD Guidelines

In July 2002, the OECD formally released its *Guidelines for the Security of Information Systems and Networks: Towards a Culture of Security*. The guidelines consist of nine principles that aim to increase public awareness, promote education, share information, and provide training that can lead to a better understanding of online security and the adoption of best practices. "A culture of security" represents a new way of thinking—one in which everyone using computers and networks like the Internet has a role to play. The Guidelines represent the consensus views of all 30 OECD member countries and support the OECD's larger goal of promoting economic growth, trade, and development.

CERT Coordination Center
monitors and tracks online criminal activity reported to it by private corporations and government agencies that seek out its help

US-CERT
division of the U.S. Department of Homeland Security that coordinates cyber incident warnings and responses across government and private sectors

TABLE 5.5	GOVERNMENT EFFORTS TO REGULATE AND CONTROL ENCRYPTION
REGULATORY EFFORT	**IMPACT**
Restrict export of strong security systems	Supported primarily by the United States. Widespread distribution of encryption schemes weakens this policy. The policy is changing to permit exports except to pariah countries.
Key escrow/key recovery schemes	France, the United Kingdom, and the United States supported this effort in the late 1990s, but now have largely abandoned it. There are few trusted third parties.
Lawful access and forced disclosure	Growing support in recent U.S. legislation and in OECD countries.
Official hacking	All countries are rapidly expanding budgets and training for law enforcement "technical centers" aimed at monitoring and cracking computer-based, encryption activities of suspected criminals.

5.5 PAYMENT SYSTEMS

TYPES OF PAYMENT SYSTEMS

In order to understand e-commerce payment systems, you first need to be familiar with the various types of generic payment systems. Then you will be able to clarify the different requirements that e-commerce payments systems must meet and identify the opportunities provided by e-commerce technology for developing new types of payment systems. There are five main types of payment systems: cash, checking transfer, credit cards, stored value, and accumulating balance.

Cash

Cash, which is legal tender defined by a national authority to represent value, is the most common form of payment in terms of number of transactions. The key feature of cash is that it is instantly convertible into other forms of value without the intermediation of any other institution. For instance, free airline miles are not cash because they are not instantly convertible into other forms of value—they require intermediation by a third party (the airline) in order to be exchanged for value (an airline ticket). Private organizations sometimes create a form of private cash called *scrip* that can be instantly redeemed by participating organizations for goods or cash. Examples include trading stamps, "point" programs, and other forms of consumer loyalty currency.

Why is cash still so popular today? Cash is portable, requires no authentication, and provides instant purchasing power for those who possess it. Cash allows for micropayments (payments of small amounts). The use of cash is "free" in that neither merchants nor consumers pay a transaction fee for using it. Using cash does not

cash
legal tender defined by a national authority to represent value

require any complementary assets, such as special hardware or the existence of an account, and it puts very low cognitive demands on the user. Cash is anonymous and difficult to trace, and in that sense it is "private." Other forms of payment require significant use of third parties and leave an extensive digital or paper trail.

On the other hand, cash is limited to smaller transactions (you can't easily buy a car or house with cash), it is easily stolen, and it does not provide any "**float**" (the period of time between a purchase and actual payment for the purchase); when it is spent, it is gone. With cash, purchases tend to be final and irreversible (i.e., they are irrefutable) unless otherwise agreed by the seller.

float

the period of time between a purchase and actual payment for the purchase

Checking Transfer

A **checking transfer**, which represents funds transferred directly via a signed draft or check from a consumer's checking account to a merchant or other individual, is the second most common form of payment in the United States in terms of number of transactions, and the most common in terms of total amount spent.

Checks can be used for both small and large transactions, although typically they are not used for micropayments (less than $1). Checks have some float (it can take up to 10 days for out-of-state checks to clear), and the unspent balances can earn interest. Checks are not anonymous and require third-party institutions to work. Checks also introduce security risks for merchants: They can be forged more easily than cash, so authentication is required. For merchants, checks also present some additional risk compared to cash because they can be canceled before they clear the account or they may bounce if there is not enough money in the account.

checking transfer

funds transferred directly via a signed draft or check from a consumer's checking account to a merchant or other individual

Credit Card

A **credit card** represents an account that extends credit to consumers, permits consumers to purchase items while deferring payment, and allows consumers to make payments to multiple vendors at one time. **Credit card associations** such as Visa and MasterCard are nonprofit associations that set standards for the **issuing banks**—such as Citibank—that actually issue the credit cards and process transactions. Other third parties (called **processing centers** or **clearinghouses**) usually handle verification of accounts and balances. Credit card issuing banks act as financial intermediaries, minimizing the risk to transacting parties.

Credit cards offer consumers a line of credit and the ability to make small and large purchases instantly. They are widely accepted as a form of payment, reduce the risk of theft associated with carrying cash, and increase consumer convenience. Credit cards also offer consumers considerable float. With a credit card, for instance, a consumer typically need not actually pay for goods purchased until receiving a credit card bill 30 days later. Merchants benefit from increased consumer spending resulting from credit card use, but they pay a hefty transaction fee of 3% to 5% of the purchase price to the issuing banks. In addition, federal Regulation Z places the risks of the transaction (such as credit card fraud, repudiation of the transaction, or nonpayment) largely on the merchant and credit card issuing bank. Regulation Z limits cardholder liability to $50 for unauthorized transactions that occur before the card issuer is notified. Once a card is reported stolen, consumers are not liable for any subsequent charges.

credit card

represents an account that extends credit to consumers, permits consumers to purchase items while deferring payment, and allows consumers to make payments to multiple vendors at one time

credit card association

nonprofit association that sets standards for issuing banks

issuing bank

bank that actually issues credit cards and processes transactions

processing center (clearinghouse)

institution that handles verification of accounts and balances

Credit cards have less finality than other payment systems because consumers can refute or repudiate purchases under certain circumstances, and they limit risk for consumers while raising risk for merchants and bankers.

Stored Value

Accounts created by depositing funds into an account and from which funds are paid out or withdrawn as needed are **stored-value payment systems**. Stored-value payment systems are similar in some respects to checking transfers—which also store funds—but do not involve writing a check. Examples include debit cards, gift certificates, prepaid cards, and smart cards (described in greater detail later in the chapter). **Debit cards** immediately debit a checking or other demand-deposit account. For many consumers, the use of a debit card eliminates the need to write a paper check. Today, there are nearly 300 million debit cards in use nationwide. However, because debit cards are dependent on funds being available in a consumer's bank account, larger purchases are still typically paid for by credit card, and their use in the United States still lags behind that of other developed nations, in part because they do not have the protections provided by Regulation Z and they do not provide any float.

Peer-to-peer (P2P) payment systems such as PayPal (discussed further in Section 5.6) are variations on the stored value concept. P2P payment systems do not insist on prepayment, but do require an account with a stored value, either a checking account with funds available or a credit card with an available credit balance. PayPal is often referred to as a P2P payment system because it allows small merchants and individuals to accept payments without using a merchant bank or processor to clear the transaction.

Accumulating Balance

Accounts that accumulate expenditures and to which consumers make periodic payments are **accumulating balance payment systems**. Traditional examples include utility, phone, and American Express accounts, all of which accumulate balances, usually over a specified period (typically a month), and then are paid in full at the end of the period.

Table 5.6 summarizes how payment systems differ on a variety of dimensions and highlights a number of points about payment systems. First, evaluating payment systems is a complex process; there are many dimensions that must be considered. Table 5.6 suggests how difficult it is for entrepreneurs to devise new payment mechanisms to displace current payment systems (cash, checks, and credit cards). As we will discuss below, consumers in the United States have not, as a general matter, accepted alternative online payment systems and rely primarily on credit cards for online payments.

Table 5.6 also suggests that the various parties that have an interest in payment systems (stakeholders) may have different preferences with respect to the different dimensions. The main stakeholders in payment systems are consumers, merchants, financial intermediaries, and government regulators.

Consumers are interested primarily in low-risk, low-cost, refutable (able to be repudiated or denied), convenient, and reliable payment mechanisms. Consumers

stored-value payment system
account created by depositing funds into an account and from which funds are paid out or withdrawn as needed

debit card
immediately debits a checking or other demand-deposit account

accumulating balance payment system
account that accumulates expenditures and to which consumers makes periodic payments

TABLE 5.6	DIMENSIONS OF PAYMENT SYSTEMS				
DIMENSION	CASH	PERSONAL CHECK	CREDIT CARD	STORED VALUE (DEBIT CARD)	ACCUMULATING BALANCE
Instantly convertible without intermediation	yes	no	no	no	no
Low transaction cost for small transactions	yes	no	no	no	yes
Low transaction cost for large transactions	no	yes	yes	yes	yes
Low fixed costs for merchant	yes	yes	no	no	no
Refutable (able to be repudiated)	no	yes	yes	no (usually)	yes
Financial risk for consumer	yes	no	up to $50	limited	no
Financial risk for merchant	no	yes	yes	no	yes
Anonymous for consumer	yes	no	no	no	no
Anonymous for merchant	yes	no	no	no	no
Immediately respendable	yes	no	no	no	no
Security against unauthorized use	no	some	some	some	some
Tamper-resistant	yes	no	yes	yes	yes
Requires authentication	no	yes	yes	yes	yes
Special hardware required	no	no	yes—by merchant	yes—by merchant	yes—by merchant
Buyer keeps float	no	yes	yes	no	yes
Account required	no	yes	yes	yes	yes
Has immediate monetary value	yes	no	no	yes	no

SOURCE: Adapted from MacKie-Mason and White, 1996.

have demonstrated they will not use new payment mechanisms unless they are equally or more beneficial to them than existing systems. In general, most consumers use cash, checks, and/or credit cards. The specific payment system chosen will change depending on the transaction situation. For instance, cash may be preferred to keep certain transactions private and anonymous, but the same consumer may want a record of transaction for the purchase of a car.

Merchants are interested primarily in low-risk, low-cost, irrefutable (i.e., final), secure, and reliable payment mechanisms. Merchants currently carry much of the risk of checking and credit card fraud, refutability of charges, and much of the hardware cost of verifying payments. Merchants typically prefer payments made by cash, check, and to a lesser extent credit cards, which usually carry high fees and allow transactions to be repudiated after the fact by consumers.

Financial intermediaries, such as banks and credit card networks, are primarily interested in secure payment systems that transfer risks and costs to consumers and merchants, while maximizing transaction fees payable to themselves. The preferred payment mechanisms for financial intermediaries are checking transfers, debit cards, and credit cards.

Government regulators are interested in maintaining trust in the financial system. Regulators seek to protect against fraud and abuse in the use of payment systems; ensure that the interests of consumers and merchants are balanced against the interests of the financial intermediaries whom they regulate; and enforce information reporting laws. The most important regulations of payment systems in the United States are Regulation Z, Regulation E, and the Electronic Funds Transfer Act (EFTA) of 1978, regulating ATM machines. Regulation Z limits the risk to consumers when using credit cards. In contrast, EFTA and Regulation E place more risk on consumers when using debit or ATM cards. For instance, if you lose an ATM card or debit card, you are potentially liable for any losses to the account. However, in reality, Visa and MasterCard have issued policies that limit consumer risk for loss of debit cards to the same $50 that applies to credit cards.

5.6 E-COMMERCE PAYMENT SYSTEMS

The emergence of e-commerce has created new financial needs that in some cases cannot be effectively fulfilled by traditional payment systems. For instance, new types of purchasing relationships—such as auctions between individuals online—have resulted in the need for peer-to-peer payment methods that allow individuals to e-mail payments to other individuals. New types of online information products such as iTunes, video purchases and rentals, newspaper and magazine articles, and other information services require micropayments of less than $5. Yet, for the most part, existing payment mechanisms used in most societies have been able to adapt to the new online environment. E-commerce technology offers a number of possibilities for creating new payment systems that substitute for existing systems, as well as for creating enhancements to existing systems. In this section, we provide an overview of e-commerce payment systems in use today.

In the United States, the primary form of online payment is still the existing credit card system, although the use of alternative payment methods is increasing. In 2009, credit cards are estimated to account for around 55% of online transactions in the United States, with debit cards accounting for about 28%. **Figure 5.15** illustrates the approximate usage of various payment types. PayPal is the most popular alternative to usage of credit and debit cards online. (see the "Online Stored Value Payment Systems" section for more information on PayPal).

In other parts of the world, e-commerce payments can be very different depending on traditions and infrastructure. Credit cards are not nearly as dominant a form of online payment as in the United States. If you plan on operating a Web site in Europe, Asia, or Latin America, you will need to develop different payment systems for each region. Consumers in Europe rely for the most part on bank debit cards (especially in Germany) and some credit cards. Online purchases in China are typically paid for by check or cash when the consumer picks up the goods at a local store. In Japan, consumers use postal and bank transfers and CODs, using local convenience stores (konbini) as the pickup and payment point. Japanese consumers also use

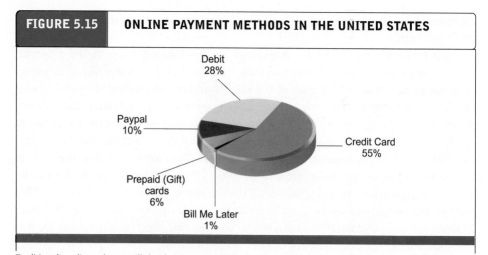

| FIGURE 5.15 | ONLINE PAYMENT METHODS IN THE UNITED STATES |

Debit
28%

Paypal
10%

Credit Card
55%

Prepaid (Gift)
cards
6%

Bill Me Later
1%

Traditional credit cards are still the dominant method of payment for online purchases, although alternative methods such as PayPal are gaining ground.

SOURCE: Based on data from Javelin Strategy & Research, 2008; Cardline, 2008; authors' estimates.

accumulated balance accounts with the telephone company for Internet purchases made from their home computers.

ONLINE CREDIT CARD TRANSACTIONS

Because credit cards are the dominant form of online payment, it is important to understand how they work and to recognize the strengths and weaknesses of this payment system. Online credit card transactions are processed in much the same way that in-store purchases are, with the major differences being that online merchants never see the actual card being used, no card impression is taken, and no signature is available. Online credit card transactions most closely resemble *Mail Order-Telephone Order (MOTO)* transactions. These types of purchases are also called *Cardholder Not Present (CNP)* transactions and are the major reason that charges can be disputed later by consumers. Since the merchant never sees the credit card, nor receives a hand-signed agreement to pay from the customer, when disputes arise, the merchant faces the risk that the transaction may be disallowed and reversed, even though he has already shipped the goods or the user has downloaded a digital product.

Figure 5.16 illustrates the online credit card purchasing cycle. There are five parties involved in an online credit card purchase: consumer, merchant, clearinghouse, merchant bank (sometimes called the "acquiring bank"), and the consumer's card issuing bank. In order to accept payments by credit card, online merchants must have a merchant account established with a bank or financial institution. A **merchant account** is simply a bank account that allows companies to process credit card payments and receive funds from those transactions.

As shown in Figure 5.16, an online credit card transaction begins with a purchase (1). When a consumer wants to make a purchase, he or she adds the item to the merchant's shopping cart. When the consumer wants to pay for the items in the

merchant account
a bank account that allows companies to process credit card payments and receive funds from those transactions

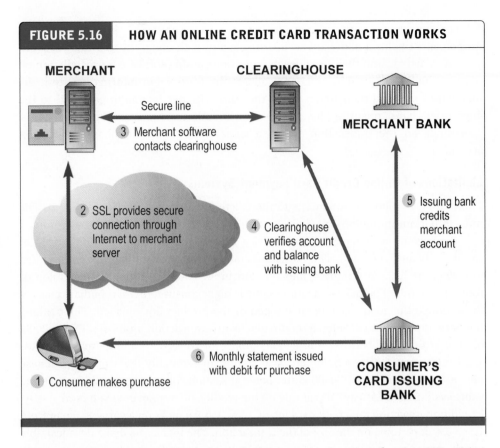

FIGURE 5.16   HOW AN ONLINE CREDIT CARD TRANSACTION WORKS

MERCHANT

CLEARINGHOUSE

Secure line

3 Merchant software contacts clearinghouse

MERCHANT BANK

2 SSL provides secure connection through Internet to merchant server

4 Clearinghouse verifies account and balance with issuing bank

5 Issuing bank credits merchant account

6 Monthly statement issued with debit for purchase

1 Consumer makes purchase

CONSUMER'S CARD ISSUING BANK

shopping cart, a secure tunnel through the Internet is created using SSL. Using encryption, SSL secures the session during which credit card information will be sent to the merchant and protects the information from interlopers on the Internet (2). SSL does not authenticate either the merchant or the consumer. The transacting parties have to trust one another.

Once the consumer credit card information is received by the merchant, the merchant software contacts a clearinghouse (3). As previously noted, a clearinghouse is a financial intermediary that authenticates credit cards and verifies account balances. The clearinghouse contacts the issuing bank to verify the account information (4). Once verified, the issuing bank credits the account of the merchant at the merchant's bank (usually this occurs at night in a batch process) (5). The debit to the consumer account is transmitted to the consumer in a monthly statement (6).

Credit Card E-commerce Enablers

Companies that have a merchant account still need to buy or build a means of handling the online transaction; securing the merchant account is only step one in a two-part process. Today, Internet payment service providers can provide both a merchant account and the software tools needed to process credit card purchases online.

For instance, Authorize.net is an Internet payment service provider. Authorize.net helps a merchant secure an account with one of its merchant account provider partners and then provides payment processing software for installation on the merchant's server. The software collects the transaction information from the merchant's site and then routes it via the Authorize.net "payment gateway" to the appropriate bank, ensuring that customers are authorized to make their purchases. The funds for the transaction are then transferred to the merchant's merchant account.

Limitations of Online Credit Card Payment Systems

There are a number of limitations to the existing credit card payment system. The most important limitations involve security, merchant risk, cost, and social equity.

The existing system offers poor security. Neither the merchant nor the consumer can be fully authenticated. The merchant could be a criminal organization designed to collect credit card numbers, and the consumer could be a thief using stolen or fraudulent cards. The risk facing merchants is high: consumers can repudiate charges even though the goods have been shipped or the product downloaded. The banking industry attempted to develop a secure electronic transaction protocol (SET) in 2000, but this effort failed because it was too complex for consumers and merchants alike.

Credit costs for merchants are also significant—roughly 3.5% of the purchase plus a transaction fee of 20–30 cents per transaction, plus other setup fees. Stored value systems such as PayPal that rely on the credit card system are even more costly: in addition to paying the credit card fee of 3.5%, PayPal tacks on a variable fee of from 1.5%–3% depending on the size of the transaction. The high costs make it undesirable to sell goods that cost less than $10 on the Web. The sale of individual articles, music tracks, or other small items is not particularly feasible with credit cards. One way around this problem is to aggregate a consumer's purchases over a period of time before actually charging the credit card. This is the tack taken by Apple's iTunes Music Store, which now uses a variable pricing system of 69 cents for older songs, 99 cents for most other songs, and $1.29 for hits and "hot" songs. Instead of charging your credit card for each individual song, Apple aggregates any purchases you make within a 24-hour period so that they're posted to your credit card account as a total for the period, not as individual song purchases. iTunes barely breaks even on a single sale, but can start making money if you purchase several songs. In general, credit companies are opposed to "aggregating" because it reduces their profits.

Credit cards are not very democratic, even though they seem ubiquitous. Millions of young adults do not have credit cards, along with almost 100 million other adult Americans who cannot afford cards or who are considered poor risks because of low incomes.

DIGITAL WALLETS

Aside from credit cards, there are also a number of new forms of payment that have been attempted, with mixed success. These include digital wallets, digital cash, online stored value payment systems, digital accumulating balance systems, and digital checking systems

A **digital wallet** seeks to emulate the functionality of a regular wallet that you carry on your person. The most important functions of a digital wallet are to (a) authenticate the consumer through the use of digital certificates or other encryption methods, (b) store and transfer value, and (c) secure the payment process from the consumer to the merchant. Early efforts by many companies failed to popularize the idea of a digital wallet. Even Microsoft, which offered a proprietary server-side digital wallet with first Passport and then MSN Wallet, ultimately abandoned the effort in February 2005. The latest effort to develop something like a digital wallet is Google's Checkout, which is a payment processing system designed to make online shopping more convenient and easier. It does not store value like PayPal, but communicates a shopper's credit card and personal information necessary for a transaction to the merchant. The merchant receives some additional transaction guarantees that the user has been authenticated by Google. It is not clear at this time how successful this system will be. As of September 2009, despite aggressively promoting Checkout to its search advertisers, Google has yet to match PayPal's strength or popularity, in part due to eBay's refusal to allow merchants to use Checkout.

digital wallet
emulates the functionality of a regular wallet by authenticating the consumer, storing and transferring value, and securing the payment process from consumer to merchant

DIGITAL CASH

Digital cash (sometimes called *e-cash*) was one of the first forms of alternative payment systems developed for e-commerce. The basic idea behind all digital cash systems is payment over the Internet by transmitting unique, authenticated tokens representing cash value from consumers to merchants. In these schemes, users would deposit money in a bank or provide a credit card. Banks would issue digital tokens (unique encrypted numbers) for various denominations of cash, and consumers could "spend" these at merchants' sites. Merchants would in turn deposit these electronic tokens in their banks. DigiCash, First Virtual, and Millicent, all early pioneers in digital cash, no longer offer services in the form originally envisioned. In general, the protocols and practices required to make digital cash a reality were far too complex. However, there are still several firms that are continuing to pursue the idea of digital cash. Some firms, such as E-gold and GoldMoney, have focused on electronic currency backed by gold bullion.

digital cash
an alternative payment system developed for e-commerce in which unique, authenticated tokens representing cash value are tramsmitted from consumers to merchants

ONLINE STORED VALUE PAYMENT SYSTEMS

Online stored value payment systems permit consumers to make instant, online payments to merchants and other individuals based on value stored in an online account.

PayPal (purchased by eBay in 2002) enables individuals and businesses with e-mail accounts to make and receive payments up to a specified limit. PayPal transferred about $32 billion in payments among individuals and businesses during the first six months of 2009, a 11% increase over the same period in 2008. PayPal is now available in 190 countries and, as of June 30, 2009, had about 75 million active accounts. PayPal builds on the existing financial infrastructure of the countries in which it operates. You establish a PayPal account by specifying a credit, debit, or checking account you wish to have charged or paid when conducting online transactions. When you make a payment using PayPal, you e-mail the payment to

online stored value payment system
permits consumers to make instant, online payments to merchants and other individuals based on value stored in an online account

the merchant's PayPal account. PayPal transfers the amount from your credit or checking account to the merchant's bank account. The beauty of PayPal is that no personal credit information has to be shared among the users, and the service can be used by individuals to pay one another even in small amounts. Issues with PayPal include its high cost, and lack of consumer protections when a fraud occurs or a charge is repudiated. PayPal is discussed in further depth in the case study at the end of the chapter.

There are also several different categories of online stored value systems in addition to PayPal. Some, such as Valista, are merchant platforms. Others, such as QPass, are primarily aimed at the micropayments market for wireless carriers and publishers selling individual articles.

smart card

a credit-card sized plastic cards with an embedded chip that stores personal information; can be used to support mobie wireless e-commerce payments

Smart cards are another kind of stored value system based on credit-card-sized plastic cards with embedded chips that store personal information that can be used to support mobile wireless e-commerce payments. They are not used from home PCs to purchase goods, but can be used to pay for generally small ticket items by waving the card at a reader, or passing it through a reader. Whereas credit cards store a single charge account number in the magnetic strip on the back, smart cards can hold 100 times more data, including multiple credit card numbers and information regarding health insurance, transportation, personal identification, bank accounts, and loyalty programs, such as frequent flyer accounts. This capacity makes them an attractive alternative to carrying a dozen or so credit and ID cards in a physical wallet. Smart cards can also require a password, unlike credit cards, adding another layer of security.

There are actually two types of smart cards—*contact and contactless*—depending on the technology embedded. In order for contact cards to be read, they must be physically placed into a card reader, while contactless cards have an antenna built in that enables transmission of data without direct contact using RFID technology. **Radio frequency identification (RFID)** is a method of automatic identification that uses short range radio signals to identify objects and users. A stored-value smart card, such as a retail gift card purchased in a certain dollar value, is an example of a contact card because it must be swiped through a smart card reader in order for payment to be processed. A highway toll payment system such as EZPass is an example of a contactless smart card because the EZPass device in the card is read by a remote sensor, with the appropriate toll automatically deducted from the card at the end of the trip.

radio frequency identification (RFID)

a method of automatic identification that uses short range radio signals to identify objects and users

Smart cards as payment vehicles are more common in Europe and Asia. The Mondex card is one of the original smart cards, invented in 1990 by NatWest Bank in England. The card allows users to download cash from a bank account to the card via a Mondex-compatible telephone or a card reader attached to a PC, and spend large or small amounts. It can carry five different currencies simultaneously and can be accepted by merchants who have readers installed. Mondex is part of MasterCard's worldwide suite of smart card products.

The Octopus card is a rechargeable contactless stored value smart card used in Hong Kong. The card debuted in 1997 as a fare collection system for Hong Kong's mass transit system. Today, it has become the world's most successful stored value smart card. It can be used to pay not only for public transportation, but also to make payments at convenience stores and fast-food restaurants and for parking, and point-of-sale applications such as gas and vending machines. There are over 17 million Octopus cards in circulation, used to conduct over 10 million transactions a day. The card can be recharged online, over the counter, or via special-purpose "add-value" machines. So far, smart cards have played a limited role in supporting electronic transactions on the fly, where the user is mobile (as in a subway train passenger) and wants to make small payments. However, in the future, smart card technology will be integrated with cell phones, and wireless payment, to support mobile e-commerce will become more widespread.

DIGITAL ACCUMULATING BALANCE PAYMENT SYSTEMS

Digital accumulating balance payment systems allow users to make micropayments and purchases on the Web, accumulating a balance for which they are billed at the end of the month. Like a utility or phone bill, consumers are expected to pay the entire balance at the end of the month using a checking or credit card account. Digital accumulating balance systems are ideal for purchasing intellectual property on the Web such as single music tracks, chapters of books, or articles from a newspaper. such as ringtones and games. A good example is Valista's PaymentsPlus, a system for accumulating balances for small transactions. PaymentsPlus is used by companies such as AOL, Vodafone, NTT DoCoMo, Tiscali, and T-Online, among others.

Clickshare takes a different approach. Consumers have one account at a Web site of their choice, and then can use that account to purchase digital content from other Web sites without having to reenter credit card or other personal information. Clickshare has found its greatest acceptance with the online newspaper and publishing industry.

BillMeLater offers a variation on the digital accumulating balance system. BillMeLater, owned by eBay, identifies itself as an open-ended credit account. Users select the BillMeLater option at checkout and are asked to provide their birthdate and the last four digits of their social security number. They are then billed for the purchase by BillMeLater within 10-14 days. BillMeLater appeals to consumers who do not wish to enter their credit card information online. It is currently accepted by over 1000 online merchants.

DIGITAL CHECKING PAYMENT SYSTEMS

In December 2004, the Federal Reserve announced that for the first time in history, the number of electronic payment transactions (credit, debit, and other forms of electronic payment) exceeded the number of paper checks. However, the venerable check is not yet moving into retirement. According to the 2007 Federal Reserve Payments Study, over 30 billion checks were written in the United States in 2007. **Digital checking payment systems** seek to extend the functionality of existing checking accounts for use as online shopping payment tools.

PayByCheck's system is based on the consumer's existing checking account. When a consumer wishes to pay by check at a merchant site that offers this service,

digital accumulating balance payment system
allows users to make micropayments and purchases on the Web, accumulating a balance for which they are billed at the end of the month

digital checking payment system
seeks to extend the functionality of existing checking accounts for use as online shopping payment tools

an online authorization form appears that mimics the appearance of a paper check. The user is prompted to fill in checking account information, including a valid check number, bank routing number, and bank account number. To authorize payment, a user must type his or her full name, and in some instances, if required by the merchant, the last four digits of his or her social security number. The payment information is matched against PayByCheck's various databases containing information on known bad check writers, real-time information from the customer's bank about current bank account status, fraud databases, and an address verification system to verify the customer's name and address. Bio identification in the form of a fingerprint scanner attached to a PC can also be used. PayByCheck then produces a check or electronic debit for the amount of the purchase as indicated on the check, and delivers it to the merchant. The check is deposited by the merchant and routed to the consumer's bank for payment, just like a check written from a checkbook. eBillme is another option. eBillme links to a customer's online banking account. Digital checking has not been successful so far because of the difficulties of verifying the consumer online.

WIRELESS PAYMENT SYSTEMS

There are around 3 to 4 billion cell phones in use around the world, and in China, the number of cell phones in 2009 exceeded 700 million, more than twice the entire population of the United States. The United States' cell phone population is around 300 million. These numbers dwarf the global personal computer population of about 1.25 billion. In Japan, more than 95% of households have cell phones.

Use of mobile handsets as payment devices is already well established in Europe, Japan, and South Korea. Japan is arguably the most advanced in terms of providing non-voice services to consumers, that is, real mobile commerce. Japanese cell phones can act as bar code readers, GPS locators, FM radios, voice recorders and analog TV tuners, and purchase things such as train tickets, newspapers, restaurant meals, groceries, books, and a host of common retail goods and services. Three kinds of mobile payments systems are used in Japan, and these provide a glimpse of the future of mobile payments in the United States. Japanese cell phones support e-money (stored value systems charged by credit cards or bank accounts), mobile debit cards (tied to personal bank accounts), and mobile credit cards. Japanese cell phones act like mobile wallets, containing a variety of payment mechanisms. Consumers can pay merchants by simply waving the cell phone at a merchant payment device that can accept payments. How do the cell phones communicate with merchants when, say, buying a newspaper at a train station or restaurant meal? Japan's largest phone company, NTT DoCoMo, introduced wireless RFID cell phones and a related payment system (FeliCa) in 2004. Currently more than 50 million phones equipped with the "Osaifu-Keitai" (literally "wallet phone") system have been sold in Japan (Davies, 2009).

In the United States, the cell phone has not yet evolved into a fully capable mobile commerce and payment system. A 2008 Nielsen Mobile poll found that only 9.2 million U.S. mobile subscribers had purchased goods or service with their cell phones. The vast majority (almost 80%) of cell phone revenues in the United States

($148 billion in 2008) come from voice services (CTIA, 2009). In the United States, the most popular mobile purchases are digital content to be used on the cell phone itself such as ringtones, music, e-books, and software applications that are billed for by the cell phone provider. The cell phone in the United States is not connected to the wide network of financial institutions, but instead resides behind the walled garden of the telephone providers. In comparison, in Europe and Asia, cell phone users can pay for a very wide variety of real goods and services, and there, phones are integrated into a wide array of financial institutions (eMarketer, Inc., 2009). However, surveys indicate that consumers are starting to grow more comfortable with the idea of wireless payment systems. A 2009 Harris Interactive Study found that about half of U.S. adults surveyed felt that it was safe to make a purchase via their cell phone (Shields, 2009). The *Insight on Business* story, *Mobile Payment's Future: WavePayMe, TextPayMe* provides a look at the future of mobile commerce in the United States.

5.7 ELECTRONIC BILLING PRESENTMENT AND PAYMENT

In 2007, for the first time, the number of bill payments made online exceeded the number of physical checks written (Fiserv, 2007). In the $13.8 trillion U.S. economy with an $9.7 trillion consumer sector for goods and services, there are a lot of bills to pay. No one knows for sure, but some experts believe the life-cycle cost of a paper bill for a business, from point of issuance to point of payment, ranges from $3 to $7. This calculation does not include the value of time to consumers, who must open bills, read them, write checks, address envelopes, stamp, and then mail remittances. The billing market represents an extraordinary opportunity for using the Internet as an electronic billing and payment system that potentially could greatly reduce both the cost of paying bills and the time consumers spend paying them. Estimates vary, but online payments are believed to cost between only 20 to 30 cents to process.

Electronic billing presentment and payment (EBPP) systems are systems that enable the online delivery and payment of monthly bills. EBPP services allow consumers to view bills electronically and pay them through electronic funds transfers from bank or credit card accounts. More and more companies are choosing to issue statements and bills electronically, rather than mailing out paper versions. But even those businesses that do mail paper bills are increasingly offering online bill payment as an option to customers, allowing them to immediately transfer funds from a bank or credit card account to pay a bill somewhere else.

electronic billing presentment and payment (EBPP) system
new form of online payment systems for monthly bills

MARKET SIZE AND GROWTH

There were just 12 million U.S households (11% of all households) using online bill payment in 2001. Today, according to Forrester Research, that figure has grown to around 48 million households (about 40% of all households), with Forrester forecasting a 5.4% compounded annual growth rate to 63 million households in 2014. An alternative survey, performed by Harris Interactive and The Marketing Workshop on behalf of Fiserv (formerly CheckFree), estimated that 64.4 million households in 2009

INSIGHT ON BUSINESS

MOBILE PAYMENT'S FUTURE: WAVEPAYME, TEXTPAYME

Mobile commerce—in the United States, at least—has so far been a disappointment. But that may finally be about to change. With the advent of smartphones such as the iPhone and Black-Berry Storm, the cell phone can now be used as a mobile payment platform. Before the cell phone, smart cards were the primary means of mobile payments in Asian and European countries but not in the United States. Smart cards store value based on a customer's bank balances, and act like electronic debit cards. They can be charged at a variety of locations, and used to pay for services or products without an elaborate online verification system like credit cards use. But cell phones are far more prevalent these days than smart cards, and who needs another card anyway?

Several large-scale experiments around the globe are developing the technology that will make the cell phone the centerpiece of contactless payment. Contactless payment systems do not require the user to swipe a credit card. All that's needed is for the customer to come within several meters of a reader and wave his or her cell phone at the reader to make a payment. In Japan, millions of consumers already use their cell phones to wave-pay for train tickets, coffee, meals, newspapers, and other small-ticket items purchased on the street. Specially equipped Nokia mobile phones come with built-in RFID chips. RFID is a collection of devices, both readers and tags, which communicate with one another using radio frequencies and help identify people and objects. In payment applications, when you wave the phone at a reader, the RFID chip returns the customers' account information to a reader device. The reader asks for a user verification code (like a PIN). Once the user enters the code, the amount of the purchase is transferred from the customer's account to the merchant's account. It takes just seconds. If someone steals your phone, they cannot use it for payments without the personal verification code.

In the United States, in 2008, the number of contactless payment cards issued by banks and credit card companies totaled around 35 million. Industry experts estimate that there are now more than 400,000 contactless readers in place at over 80,000 merchant locations, and that usage is on the rise, especially with consumers in the 25–34 year-old age group, almost 10% of whom report using a contactless payment system at least once a week or more.

The real future is the mobile digital wallet in the form of a cell phone. So-called smart phones are equipped with Near Field Communication (NFC) chips. NFC is a kind of short-range RFID technology that allows the chips to communicate with readers up to about 10 inches away. Nokia is building the chips into some of its cell phones. Motorola is also building handsets. Visa, Cingular, JPMorgan Chase, and Nokia have built a cellular test platform in Atlanta at the Philips Stadium (home to the Atlanta Hawks and the Thrashers hockey team). MasterCard and the 7-Eleven convenience store chain have also launched trial systems based on Nokia's cell phone. You can also use these phones to do mobile banking and check balances, make payments, and transfer funds. Wave your cell phone at a blouse and it's yours!

Not be outdone, PayPal, along with several start-up firms, are using cell phone text messaging to make P2P payments possible on the fly. PayPal Mobile is built on the PayPal infrastructure that customers use to make purchases on

(continued)

eBay. Users register their phone with PayPal, and open an account if they don't already have one. They enter a PIN code as well, which is used in the authorization process. When they want to buy something, they text message PayPal requesting the payment. PayPal calls them back to confirm, and after confirmation, sends the money to the recipient. Other similar services have been developed by Obopay. Citigroup uses Obopay to run its mobile payment service. And in March 2009, Nokia invested $35 million in Obopay. Previous investors included Citigroup and Qualcomm. In May, MasterCard launched MoneySend, a person-to-person mobile payments platform for its issuers in the United States powered by Obopay. In August 2009, Nokia and Obopay announced a similar mobile payment service called Nokia Money. And let's not forget about Google. In 2007, it applied for a patent for gPay, a platform-independent text-message-based payment system. Google has not yet announced its plans for gPay.

The advantage of these texting methods is that you don't need a special NFC-equipped cell phone. New companies are entering this market as well. Boku raised $13 million in venture financing and launched in June 2009. Boku allows users to buy digital goods using text messaging, with billing being handled by the cell phone provider. Zong, another company, offers a similar service.

It is likely that both the RFID cell phone and texting methods of mobile payment will grow exceptionally fast once the cell phone networks in the United States get behind the technology. To date, American carriers have been exceptionally slow in pushing advanced cell phone features in the United States. But this will change once the potential revenue of mobile payments becomes clear to the carriers, and once customers demand a level of service at least equal to that in Europe and Asia.

SOURCES: "Mobile Payments Are Taking Off. But Which One to Use?," by Chris Dannen, Fast Company, September 1, 2009; "Nokia, Obopay Launch Mobile Payment Service, by Chris Harnick, MobileMarketer.com, August 27, 2009; "MasterCard Launches MoneySend Mobile Payments Platform," by Dan Butcher, MobileMarketer.com, May 15, 2009; "Investors Bet on Payments via Cellphone," by Claire Cain Miller and Matt Richtel, _New York Times,_ June 21, 2009; "Nokia Sends $35 Million to Obopay to Develop Mobile Payments," by Claire Cain Miller, New York Times, March 25, 2009; "Visa Launches New Mobile Payment Services; Continues Mobile Technology Momentum Globally," Business Wire, September 3, 2008; "Payment via Mobiles to Hit $300B by 2013," by Natasha Lomas, BusinessWeek Online, July 1, 2008; "Google, Gpay, Patent Reveals Plans for Mobile Payments," by Joel Hruska, Arstechnica.com, September 5, 2007; "Swiping Your Credit Card Is So Yesterday," by Robert Mitchell, TechNewsWorld, June 22, 2007; "Verizon Announces Deal With Mobile-Payment Firm Obopay," by Jessica Vascellaro, Wall Street Journal, June 20, 2007; "Cell Phone Banking Is Coming of Age," by John Quain, New York Times, May 24, 2007; "New Form of Impulse: Shopping via Text Message," by Louise Story, New York Times, April 16, 2007.

paid at least one bill online. It is clear that online bill payment is becoming widely accepted (Forrester Research, 2009; Fiserv, 2009).

One major reason for the surge in EBPP usage is that companies are starting to realize how much money they can save through online billing. Not only is there the savings in postage and processing, but payments can be received more quickly (3 to 12 days faster, compared to paper bills sent via regular mail), thereby improving cash flow. In order to realize these savings, many companies are becoming more aggressive in encouraging their customers to move to EBPP by instituting a charge for the privilege of continuing to receive a paper bill.

Financials don't tell the whole story, however. Companies are discovering that a bill is a both sales opportunity and a customer retention opportunity, and that the electronic medium provides many more options when it comes to marketing and promotion. Rebates, savings offers, cross-selling, and upselling are all possible in the digital realm.

Consumers are also becoming more receptive to online bill payment. The Fiserv survey found that around 80% of those surveyed said they preferred to pay bills online because it was faster than other payment methods. Ease of use, cost savings on stamps, and greater control over timing of payments were also cited by 70% as leading benefits. Environmental concerns were also relevant to about 60% of the respondents.

EBPP BUSINESS MODELS

There are two main competing business models in the EBPP marketspace: biller-direct and consolidator. The biller-direct system was originally created by utility companies that send millions of bills each month. Their purpose is to make it easier for their customers to pay their utility bills routinely online. Today, telephone and credit card companies also frequently offer this service, as well as a number of individual stores. Companies implementing a biller-direct system can either develop their own system in-house (usually only an option for the very largest companies), install a system acquired from a third-party EBPP software vendor, use a third-party EBPP service bureau (the service bureau hosts a biller-branded Web site that enables consumers to view and pay bills and handles all customer enrollment, bill presentment, and payment processing), or use an application service provider (similar to a service bureau, but runs on the biller's Web site rather than being hosted on the service provider's Web site).

Currently, the biller-direct model is the dominant EBPP model, although Forrester predicts that by 2012, the consolidator model will surpass it. In the consolidator model, a third party, such as a financial institution or portal (either a general portal such as Yahoo! Bill Pay, or a focused portal such as Bills.com or Intuit's Paytrust.com), aggregates all bills for consumers and ideally permits one-stop bill payment (pay anyone). Within this model are two submodels—"thick" consolidation and "thin" consolidation. In thick consolidation, both the bill summary and bill detail are stored at the consolidator's site, while in thin consolidation, only the summary bill information is available, and the consumer must click on a link to access a detailed bill that is stored at another location, such as the biller's site or elsewhere. Currently, financial institutions have been more successful than portals in attracting online bill payers. The consolidator model faces several challenges. For billers, using the consolidator model means an increased time lag between billing and payment, and also inserts an intermediary between the company and its customer. For consumers, security continues to be major issue. Most consumers are unwilling to pay any kind of fee to pay bills online, and many are concerned about sharing personal financial information with non-financial institutions. Today, more and more banks are offering online bill payment free to some or all of their customers as an enticement.

Supporting these two primary business models are infrastructure providers such as Harbor Payments, Online Resources (which acquired Princeton eCom in 2006), Yodlee, Fiserv (which also offers its own bill payment portal, Mycheckfree.com), Metavante, MasterCard RPPS (Remote Payment and Presentment Service), Corillian, and others that provide the software to create the EBPP system or handle billing and payment collection for the biller. **Figure 5.17** categorizes the major players in the EBPP marketspace.

FIGURE 5.17   MAJOR PLAYERS IN THE EBPP MARKETSPACE

The main business models in the EBPP marketspace are biller-direct and consolidator. Infrastructure providers support both of these competing models.

5.8   CASE STUDY

PayPal Has Company

PayPal—the online payment processor now owned by eBay—was the first truly successful Internet-based e-commerce payment system. Its origins were quite simple. On November 16, 1999, Peter Theil sat with friends at a restaurant. When the bill arrived, Theil used his Palm Pilot to "beam" his share to a friend sitting across the table. Theil and fellow co-founder Max Levchin had built a system that would allow them to send money to one another via a Palm Pilot's infrared links. From this idea sprang one of the first "peer-to-peer" payment systems: a system that allows individuals to send money to one another via e-mail.

PayPal emphasizes ease of use for both senders and receivers of cash. Here's a brief synopsis of how it works. First, you create a PayPal account at the PayPal Web site by filling out a one-page application form and providing credit or debit card or bank account information. Only PayPal is privy to this information, not the receiving party. Then, when you use PayPal to pay for a purchase, money is drawn from the credit card or bank account and transmitted to the Automated Clearing House (ACH) Network, a privately operated financial intermediary that tracks and transfers funds between financial institutions. The party who is to receive the payment is notified via e-mail that money is waiting. If the receiving party has a PayPal account, the funds are automatically deposited into the account; if the person does not have a PayPal account, he or she must set one up, and then the money is credited to his or her account. Once the funds are in the PayPal account, the recipient can then transfer them electronically to a checking account, request a paper check, or use PayPal to send the funds to someone else.

Levchin and Theil originally conceived of PayPal as a method for "beaming" money to users of handheld PDAs. When this idea did not pan out, they changed their target to arranging payments between individuals who knew one another. However, they quickly realized that it would also work for a company such as eBay, providing purchasers and sellers with a way to short-cut the time-consuming and cumbersome process of mailing checks and money orders and waiting for checks to clear before shipping items. Moreover, for small merchants selling items on the Web, it is difficult and expensive to obtain the capability to accept credit cards. Credit companies extend these merchant services only to bona fide businesses, usually requiring a physical place of business as a requirement.

Today, PayPal is the largest and most popular online payment service, growing from a handful of users when it launched in late 1999 to around 185 million accounts in 2009, of which about 75 million can be characterized as active. In 2008, PayPal processed $60 billion in payments, and according to the company, has a 15% share of the U.S. consumer e-commerce payments market and a 9% share of the global market. One reason PayPal has grown so fast is because it experiences the benefits of network economics or the "viral effect": the more people who accept and use PayPal, the greater the benefit to the consumer. If I send you a PayPal payment via e-mail, then you are incentivised to open a PayPal account to receive the funds. If PayPal is to continue growing, it will have to break out of the eBay marketspace and find new payment opportunities.

PayPal earns money in many different ways. First, online sellers (who may be individuals or small businesses that do not want the difficulties associated with obtaining a merchant credit card account) pay a transaction fee for the service (30 cents plus 1.9%–2.9% of the proceeds of the transaction). This generally works out to 3.3% of the transaction on a $100 transaction. Credit card firms generally charge about the same or 0.3% more due to their higher customer acquisition costs. PayPal, in other words, can be slightly less costly than credit cards for merchants.

One advantage for merchants on eBay is that they are not required to have a merchant bank account, which is required by credit card issuers. Merchant banks clear credit card transactions and charge fees. Consumers are not charged directly for the use of their PayPal account although they do pay ultimately because retailers need to recover the costs of the transaction by raising the prices on goods sold using PayPal. Second, PayPal earns revenue by collecting the interest earned on consumer funds not yet transferred out of the PayPal system. PayPal has charges for transferring funds to foreign banks, converting currencies, and new financial products such as a PayPal credit card.

Part of the strength of PayPal lies in its simplicity: it piggybacks on existing credit card and checking payment systems. This is also one of its weaknesses, however.

PayPal reportedly suffers relatively high levels of fraud related to the credit card system on which it relies. To protect against fraud, PayPal requires special authorization for payments over $200.

In 2002, PayPal went public and issued shares in an initial public offering. One of the main reasons PayPal grew so rapidly was because of its popularity on eBay. In an effort not to lose this lucrative transaction business to PayPal, eBay spent over $100 million promoting its own similar system called Billpoint—but to no avail. In October 2002, eBay purchased PayPal for $1.5 billion—about $20 a share. At the time, analysts felt the price was too high, but eBay has had the last laugh. Today, PayPal accounts for an increasing share of of eBay's revenue (around 30% in 2008), a trend that is expected to continue. In 2008, PayPal generated around $30 billion of its net total payment volume from eBay.com transactions, which represented approximately 51% of PayPal's total volume for the year. For the first time, in the second half of 2008, the payment volume generated by PayPal's merchant services business exceeded its volume from eBay. This trend has continued in 2009 as well. PayPal's revenue in 2008 increased by about 25%, from $1.9 billion in 2007 to $2.4 billion. This is a lower growth rate than the prior year, mostly due to a decrease in overall consumer purchases, particularly in the second half of the year. But even this lower growth rate is impressive when one considers that, in contrast, eBay's auction revenue for the year grew only 4%.

For a brief period, PayPal enjoyed its position as the only widely adopted online platform (aside from the credit card companies). But this is changing rapidly. Looming on the horizon are no less than Facebook, Apple, Google, and Amazon. During the summer of 2009, Facebook began to gradually expand the scope of a virtual currency called "Pay with Facebook" credits (purchased with a credit card) that allow users to buy items in Facebook's Gift Shop. In May 2009, the service was extended to include a few third-party game developers and virtual gift makers. In June, Facebook began accepting 14 new currencies, in addition to the U.S. dollar. In August 2009, Facebook revealed that it was testing a system that would allow users to buy physical merchandise via its payment system. It also launched a test to let some users buy Facebook Credits by billing their mobile phones. Analysts believe that Facebook will try to establish its payment system as an on-site "wallet" and then leverage Facebook Connect to deliver one-click purchasing across the Web.

Apple, which already has developed an extremely successful micropayment processing system with its iTunes Stores, may entering the fray. Some analysts believe Apple is considering the idea of extending that system to third-party vendors selling digital goods on the Internet. iPhone users can already use their iTunes account to buy some third-party virtual and subscription goods. Currently, however, Apple charges developers 30% per transaction, much higher than PayPal's take.

Google has already made its foray into the market with Google Checkout. Google Checkout stores a user's financial information, including credit card information, and then presents this information to merchants when the user checks out. The customer does not have to fill out forms or reveal credit information to online merchants. Checkout does not support P2P payments, at least not yet. Google has been careful not to directly challenge PayPal in the P2P market, if only because eBay (the owner of PayPal) is the largest single advertiser on Google, and Google directs a significant traffic volume to eBay. They need one another. Google also uses Checkout to support its advertising network. Ads for online stores that accept Checkout are highlighted with an icon, increasing the chances that users will click on those sites. Once users click on an ad, they are more likely to purchase. Merchants who accept Checkout on their sites receive more traffic simply for offering the convenience of the service, and Google has frequent promotions where it eliminates all processing fees for periods of time, saving merchants the 2% plus 20 cents it charges for transactions.

Amazon has also entered the payments market with Amazon Payments. Amazon Payments allows participating vendors to give customers the option of checking out using their Amazon account information. Amazon Payments also offers mobile purchase (Amazon TextBuyIt) and payment services (Amazon TextPayMe). Amazon's Flexible Payment Services (FPS) allows developers to integrate Amazon Payments into third-party applications.

An even more direct challenge is coming from another source: cell phone carriers such as AT&T and Verizon, especially in P2P payments. PayPal is built upon the existing credit card system. What if you could eliminate the credit card intermediaries? Mobile payment company Obopay allows subscribers to transfer money and make purchases through their cell phones. Users can send money to anyone with a cell phone on any wireless network. Obopay has deals with Verizon, Nokia, BlackBerry, Citigroup, and Mastercard. Currently, Obopay customers have to load their Obopay accounts at the Obopay Web site with a credit or debit card, or a bank account. But in the future, Obopay hopes to integrate its service with the cell phone providers' monthly billing service, thereby eliminating credit card companies altogether from the payment loop, reducing transaction costs for merchants and customers, and making it easier to use the service. That's what start-ups Boku and Zong hope to do.

To compete with these new services, in June 2009, PayPal announced that it will open up its API to software developers in order to allow them to integrate PayPal functionality into programs created for mobile phones and social networks like Facebook PayPal is also pursuing a number of other growth initiatives. PayPal signed up both Napster and Apple's iTunes Music Store as merchants in its first foray into the micropayments market. The experience proved so successful that PayPal introduced a micropayments pricing plan designed to increase and encourage the purchase of low-priced digital goods. PayPal is also pursuing an overseas expansion strategy. It has added localized Web sites in 18 different markets.. In 2009, businesses or consumers with e-mail could use PayPal to send online payments in 190 countries, and receive payments in 65 of those countries. Payments can be made or accepted in any one of 19 different currencies. PayPal is expanding beyond eBay sales by setting up preferred merchant relationships with other large Internet retailers such as Yahoo and Amazon, with mixed success. Amazon has its own credit card and preferred methods of payment, but Yahoo uses PayPal as a recommended payment method. PayPal also expanded its presence to e-commerce sites such as American Airlines, Omaha Steaks, Walmart.com, Zappos, and Ferrari. PayPal continues to enhance its mobile text message payment system, which allows cell phone users to pay for goods and services by texting PayPal payments to merchants.

PayPal also faces other challenges. PayPal's brand is closely associated with smaller merchants, P2P money transfers, and low-cost auctions. As a result, some larger firms might not want the PayPal brand image associated with their brands, although as PayPal has become popular, this has become less of an issue. PayPal's business also makes it a natural target for fraud, both by merchants that do not deliver goods or services paid for by its customers, and from outside forces who send fraudulent e-mails to its customers, attempting to steal the customers' password, credit card numbers, or other personal information. As a result, PayPal has been forced to institute a number of costly measures to combat fraud in the attempt to enhance its customers' confidence in its services. But these measures are working: in 2008, PayPal's transaction loss was $171.5 million, .29% of its total payment volume. PayPal's protections for consumers are also still somewhat weaker than what credit card companies are required to offer. For instance, you can deny a credit card charge and have a $50 maximum liability if your credit card information is stolen and used in commerce. With PayPal, you may or may not receive your money back, depending on whether PayPal can receive its money back, and a host of other conditions. PayPal has developed a consumer protection program, but it also settled in 2006 with 28 state attorneys general involving concerns about certain business practices. Chief among these practices was encouraging users to allow PayPal to directly debit consumer bank accounts, because PayPal can avoid paying credit companies a 2% funds transfer fee, making the direct deduction option more profitable for PayPal. If you have given PayPal both your credit card information and bank account information, the default payment method used by PayPal is your bank account. Once funds are withdrawn from your bank account, they cannot be recovered, unlike credit card transactions. Hence, the risk to consumers is substantially greater. Credit card companies can retrieve funds from misbehaving merchants more quickly by simply reverse-crediting their merchant bank accounts. In its latest attempt to address these issues, eBay paid $169 million to buy a company called Fraud Services, to accelerate the next generation of fraud detection and enhance PayPal's risk management.

Despite the challenges, however, the future for PayPal appears bright. In fact, some analysts believe that PayPal may someday become an even bigger phenomenon than its acquirer, eBay.

SOURCES: "Mobile Payments are Taking Off. But Which One to Use?" by Chris Dannen, September 1, 2009; "Facebook Sets Sights on Online Payments Business, cnnmoney.com, August 31, 2009; "eBay's PayPal Faces Increasing Competition in Payments Space," by Ina Steiner, Auctionbytes.com, August 27, 2009; "Apple Wants to Build a PayPal Killer, Say Wall Street Gossips," by Nicholas Carlson, Silicon Alley Insider, August 4, 2009, "Why Pay Pal Wants to Know Where Everybody Lives," by Saul Hensell, *New York Times*, June 29, 2009; "PayPal Q1 2009 Fast Facts," Paypal.com, April 30, 2009; "Chief Promises a New eBay and Talks Up PayPal," by Laura Silva Laughlin and Jeff Segal, *New York Times*, March 11, 2009; eBay, Inc. Report on 10-K for the fiscal year ended December 31, 2008; filed with the Securities and Exchange Commission, February 19, 2009.

Case Study Questions

1. What is the value proposition that PayPal offers consumers? How about merchants?

2. What are some of the risks of using PayPal when compared to credit cards and debit cards?

3. What strategies would you recommend that PayPal pursue in order to maintain its growth over the next five years?

4. Why are cell phone networks a threat to PayPal's future growth?

5.9 REVIEW

KEY CONCEPTS

■ **Understand the scope of e-commerce crime and security problems.**

While the overall size of cybercrime is unclear at this time, cybercrime against e-commerce sites is growing rapidly, the amount of losses is growing, and the management of e-commerce sites must prepare for a variety of criminal assaults.

■ **Describe the key dimensions of e-commerce security.**

There are six key dimensions to e-commerce security:
- *Integrity*—ensures that information displayed on a Web site or sent or received via the Internet has not been altered in any way by an unauthorized party.
- *Nonrepudiation*—ensures that e-commerce participants do not deny (repudiate) their online actions.
- *Authenticity*—verifies an individual's or business's identity.
- *Confidentiality*—determines whether information shared online, such as through e-mail communication or an order process, can be viewed by anyone other than the intended recipient.
- *Privacy*—deals with the use of information shared during an online transaction. Consumers want to limit the extent to which their personal information can be divulged to other organizations, while merchants want to protect such information from falling into the wrong hands.
- *Availability*—determines whether a Web site is accessible and operational at any given moment.

■ **Understand the tension between security and other values.**

Although computer security is considered necessary to protect e-commerce activities, it is not without a downside. Two major areas where there are tensions between security and Web site operations include:
- *Ease of use*—The more security measures that are added to an e-commerce site, the more difficult it is to use and the slower the site becomes, hampering ease of use. Security is purchased at the price of slowing down processors and adding significantly to data storage demands. Too much security can harm profitability, while not enough can potentially put a company out of business.
- *Public safety*—There is a tension between the claims of individuals to act anonymously and the needs of public officials to maintain public safety that can be threatened by criminals or terrorists.

■ **Identify the key security threats in the e-commerce environment.**

The nine most common and most damaging forms of security threats to e-commerce sites include:

- *Malicious code*—viruses, worms, Trojan horses, and bot networks are a threat to a system's integrity and continued operation, often changing how a system functions or altering documents created on the system.
- *Unwanted programs (adware, spyware, etc.)*—a kind of security threat that arises when programs are surreptitiously installed on your computer or computer network with
- *Phishing*—any deceptive, online attempt by a third party to obtain confidential information for financial gain.
- *Hacking and cybervandalism*—intentionally disrupting, defacing, or even destroying a site.
- *Credit card fraud/theft*—one of the most-feared occurrences and one of the main reasons more consumers do not participate in e-commerce. The most common cause of credit card fraud is a lost or stolen card that is used by someone else, followed by employee theft of customer numbers and stolen identities (criminals applying for credit cards using false identities).
- *Spoofing*—occurs when hackers attempt to hide their true identities or misrepresent themselves by using fake e-mail addresses or masquerading as someone else. Spoofing also can involve redirecting a Web link to an address different from the intended one, with the site masquerading as the intended destination.
- *Denial of Service (DoS) attacks*—hackers flood a Web site with useless traffic to inundate and overwhelm the network, frequently causing it to shut down and damaging a site's reputation and customer relationships.
- *Sniffing*—a type of eavesdropping program that monitors information traveling over a network, enabling hackers to steal proprietary information from anywhere on a network, including e-mail messages, company files, and confidential reports. The threat of sniffing is that confidential or personal information will be made public.
- *Insider jobs*—although the bulk of Internet security efforts are focused on keeping outsiders out, the biggest threat is from employees who have access to sensitive information and procedures.
- *Poorly designed server and client software*—the increase in complexity and size of software programs has contributed to an increase in software flaws or vulnerabilities that hackers can exploit weaknesses.

■ **Describe how technology helps protect the security of messages sent over the Internet.**

Encryption is the process of transforming plain text or data into cipher text that cannot be read by anyone other than the sender and the receiver. Encryption can provide four of the six key dimensions of e-commerce security:

- *Message integrity*—provides assurance that the sent message has not been altered.
- *Nonrepudiation*—prevents the user from denying that he or she sent a message.
- *Authentication*—provides verification of the identity of the person (or computer) sending the message.
- *Confidentiality*—gives assurance that the message was not read by others.

There are a variety of different forms of encryption technology currently in use. They include:

- *Symmetric key encryption*—Both the sender and the receiver use the same key to encrypt and decrypt a message. Advanced Encryption Standard (AES) is the most widely used symmetric key encryption system on the Internet today.
- *Public key cryptography*—Two mathematically related digital keys are used: a public key and a private key. The private key is kept secret by the owner, and the public key is widely disseminated. Both keys can be used to encrypt and decrypt a message. Once the keys are used to encrypt a message, the same keys cannot be used to unencrypt the message.
- *Public key encryption using digital signatures and hash digests*—This method uses a mathematical algorithm called a hash function to produce a fixed-length number called a hash digest. The results of applying the hash function are sent by the sender to the recipient. Upon receipt, the recipient applies the hash function to the received message and checks to verify that the same result is produced. The sender then encrypts both the hash result and the original message using the recipient's public key, producing a single block of cipher text. To ensure both the authenticity of the message and nonrepudiation, the sender encrypts the entire block of cipher text one more time using the sender's private key. This produces a digital signature or "signed" cipher text that can be sent over the Internet to ensure the confidentiality of the message and authenticate the sender.
- *Digital envelope*—This method uses symmetric encryption to encrypt and decrypt the document, but public key encryption to encrypt and send the symmetric key.
- *Digital certificates and public key infrastructure*—This method relies on certification authorities who issue, verify, and guarantee digital certificates (a digital document that contains the name of the subject or company, the subject's public key, a digital certificate serial number, an expiration date, an issuance date, the digital signature of the certification authority, and other identifying information).

■ Identify the tools used to establish secure Internet communications channels and protect networks, servers, and clients.

In addition to encryption, there are several other tools that are used to secure Internet channels of communication, including:
- *Secure Sockets Layer (SSL)*—This is the most common form of securing channels. The SSL protocol provides data encryption, server authentication, client authentication, and message integrity for TCP/IP connections.
- *Secure Hypertext Transfer Protocol (S-HTTP)*—S-HTTP secures only Web protocols and cannot be used to secure non-HTTP messages.
- *Virtual private networks (VPNs)*—These allow remote users to securely access internal networks via the Internet, using the Point-to-Point Tunneling Protocol (PPTP), an encoding mechanism that allows one local network to connect to another using the Internet as the conduit.

After communications channels are secured, tools to protect networks, the servers, and clients should be implemented. These include:
- *Firewalls*—software applications that act as filters between a company's private network and the Internet itself, denying unauthorized remote client computers from attaching to your internal network.
- *Proxies*—software servers that act primarily to limit access of internal clients to external Internet servers and are frequently referred to as the gateway.

- *Operating system controls*—built-in username and password requirements that provide a level of authentication. Some operating systems also have an access control function that controls user access to various areas of a network.
- *Anti-virus software*—a cheap and easy way to identify and eradicate the most common types of viruses as they enter a computer, as well as to destroy those already lurking on a hard drive.

■ **Appreciate the importance of policies, procedures, and laws in creating security.**

In order to minimize security threats:
- E-commerce firms must develop a coherent corporate policy that takes into account the nature of the risks, the information assets that need protecting, and the procedures and technologies required to address the risk, as well as implementation and auditing mechanisms.
- Public laws and active enforcement of cybercrime statutes are also required to both raise the costs of illegal behavior on the Internet and guard against corporate abuse of information.

The key steps in developing a security plan are:
- *Perform a risk assessment*—an assessment of the risks and points of vulnerability.
- *Develop a security policy*—a set of statements prioritizing the information risks, identifying acceptable risk targets, and identifying the mechanisms for achieving these targets.
- *Create an implementation plan*—a plan that determines how you will translate the levels of acceptable risk into a set of tools, technologies, policies, and procedures.
- *Create a security team*—the individuals who will be responsible for ongoing maintenance, audits, and improvements.
- *Perform periodic security audits*—routine reviews of access logs and any unusual patterns of activity

■ **Describe the features of traditional payment systems.**

Traditional payment systems include:
- *Cash*, whose key feature is that it is instantly convertible into other forms of value without the intermediation of any other institution.
- *Checking transfers*, which are funds transferred directly through a signed draft or check from a consumer's checking account to a merchant or other individual; these are the second most common form of payment.
- *Credit card accounts*, which are accounts that extend credit to a consumer and allow consumers to make payments to multiple vendors at one time.
- *Stored value systems*, which are created by depositing funds into an account and from which funds are paid out or are withdrawn as needed. Stored value payments systems include debit cards, phone cards, and smart cards.
- *Accumulating balance systems*, which accumulate expenditures and to which consumers make periodic payments.

■ **Understand the major e-commerce payment mechanisms.**

The major types of digital payment systems include:

- *Online credit card transactions,* which are the primary form of online payment system. There are five parties involved in an online credit card purchase: consumer, merchant, clearinghouse, merchant bank (sometimes called the "acquiring bank"), and the consumer's card issuing bank. However, the online credit card system has a number of limitations involving security, merchant risk, cost, and social equity.
- *Digital wallets,* which emulate the functionality of a traditional wallet containing personal identifying information and store value in some form.
- *Digital cash,* which are online numeric tokens based on bank deposits or credit card accounts.
- *Online stored value systems,* which permit consumers to make instant, online payments to merchants and other individuals based on value stored in an online account. Some stored value systems require the user to download a digital wallet, while others require users to simply sign up and transfer money from an existing account into an online stored value account.
- *Digital accumulating balance systems,* which allow users to make purchases on the Web, accumulating a debit balance for which they are billed at the end of the cycle (such as at the end of a day or month); consumers are then expected to pay the entire balance using a checking or credit card account. Accumulating balance systems are ideal for purchasing digital content such as music tracks, chapters of books, or articles from a newspaper.
- *Digital checking payment systems,* which are extensions to the existing checking and banking infrastructure.
- *Wireless payment systems,* which are cell phone-based payment systems that enable mobile payments.

■ Describe the features and functionality of electronic billing presentment and payment systems.

EBPP systems are a form of online payment systems for monthly bills. EBPP services allow consumers to view bills electronically and pay them through electronic funds transfers from bank or credit card accounts. Major players in the EBPP marketspace include:
- *Biller-direct systems,* which were originally created by large utilities to facilitate routine payment of utility bills, but which are increasingly being used by other billers.
- *Consolidators,* which attempt to aggregate all bills for consumers in one place and ideally permit one-stop bill payment.
- *Infrastructure providers* which support the biller-direct and consolidator business models.

QUESTIONS

1. Why is it less risky to steal online? Explain some of the ways criminals deceive consumers and merchants.
2. Explain why an e-commerce site might not want to report being the target of cybercriminals.
3. Give an example of security breaches as they relate to each of the six dimensions of e-commerce security. For instance, what would be a privacy incident?

4. How would you protect your firm against a Denial of Service attack?
5. Explain why the U.S. government wants to restrict the export of strong encryption systems. And why would other countries be against it?
6. Name the major points of vulnerability in a typical online transaction.
7. How does spoofing threaten a Web site's operations?
8. Why is adware or spyware considered to be a security threat?
9. What are some of the steps a company can take to curtail cybercriminal activity from within a business?
10. Explain some of the modern-day flaws associated with encryption. Why is encryption not as secure today as it was earlier in the century?
11. Briefly explain how public key cryptography works.
12. Compare and contrast firewalls and proxy servers and their security functions.
13. Is a computer with anti-virus software protected from viruses? Why or why not?
14. Identify and discuss the five steps in developing an e-commerce security plan.
15. How do biometric devices help improve security? What particular type of security breach do they particularly reduce?
16. What are tiger teams, who uses them, and what are some of the tactics they use in their work?
17. How do the interests of the four major payment systems stakeholders impact each other?
18. Compare and contrast stored value payment systems and checking transfers.
19. Why is a credit card not considered an accumulating balance payment system?
20. Name six advantages and six disadvantages of using cash as a form of payment.
21. Describe the relationship between credit card associations and issuing banks.
22. What is Regulation Z, and how does it protect the consumer?
23. Briefly discuss the disadvantages of credit cards as the standard for online payments. How does requiring a credit card for payment discriminate against some consumers?
24. Describe the major steps involved in an online credit card transaction.
25. Compare and contrast smart cards and traditional credit cards.
26. How is money transferred in transactions using wireless devices?
27. Discuss why EBPP systems are becoming increasingly popular.
28. How are the two main types of EBPP systems both alike and different from each other?

PROJECTS

1. Imagine you are the owner of an e-commerce Web site. What are some of the signs that your site has been hacked? Discuss the major types of attacks you could expect to experience and the resulting damage to your site. Prepare a brief summary presentation.

2. Given the shift toward mobile commerce, do a search on mobile commerce crime .Identify and discuss the new security threats this type of technology creates. Prepare a presentation outlining your vision of the new opportunities for cybercrime.

3. Find three certification authorities and compare the features of each company's digital certificates. Provide a brief description of each company as well, including number of clients. Prepare a brief presentation of your findings.

4. Research the challenges associated with payments across international borders and prepare a brief presentation of your findings. Do most e-commerce companies conduct business internationally? How do they protect themselves from repudiation? How do exchange rates impact online purchases? What about shipping charges? Summarize by describing the differences between a U.S. customer and an international customer who each make a purchase from a U.S. e-commerce merchant.

WEB SITE RESOURCES www.azimuth-interactive.com/ecommerce6e

- Additional projects, exercises, and tutorials
- Careers: Explore career opportunities in e-commerce
- Raising capital and business plans

PART **3**

- **CHAPTER 6**
- E-commerce Marketing Concepts
- **CHAPTER 7**
  E-commerce Marketing
  Communications
- **CHAPTER 8**
  Ethical, Social, and Political Issues in
  E-commerce

Business Concepts
and Social Issues

C H A P T E R 6

E-commerce Marketing Concepts

After reading this chapter, you will be able to:

- Identify the key features of the Internet audience.
- Discuss the basic concepts of consumer behavior and purchasing decisions.
- Understand how consumers behave online.
- Describe the basic marketing concepts needed to understand Internet marketing.
- Identify and describe the main technologies that support online marketing.
- Identify and describe basic e-commerce marketing and branding strategies.

Netflix Develops and Defends Its Brand

Netflix is the largest online entertainment subscription service in the United States, providing more than 10 million customers in 2009 with access to over 100,000 DVD titles (and more than 55 million DVDs in stock). Netflix's basic business is renting DVD titles on a subscription basis, with different plans ranging from $4.99 a month to $16.99 a month. The more you pay, the larger the number of DVDs you can possess simultaneously, and the more movies you can stream to your PC or TV. Since 1999, Netflix subscribers have grown at an annual rate of 79%, and its revenues have grown at 113%. If you're looking for a success story in 2009, Netflix is a good candidate. Its 2008 annual revenues hit $1.3 billion, 13% higher than 2007. In 2009, second quarter results were even better: revenue and profits up 22% over the previous year. Netflix is adding about 300,000 subscribers a month in 2009. In April, it delivered its 2 billionth movie. If you ever wondered how many of its 100,000 DVD titles are rented at least once on a typical day, the answer is an astounding 51,000. Most people guess about 1,000, and they seriously underestimate the breadth of American tastes in movies, and the overall demand for Hollywood fare.

But how did Netflix build up a nationally recognized successful brand in a marketplace filled with established brand names such as behemoth Blockbuster, which has over 50 million customers and 90,000 rental DVD titles distributed by over 7,000 local neighborhood stores and 500 kiosks (with plans to expand to 10,000 by 2010)?

Netflix started out in Los Gatos, California (in the heart of Silicon Valley and the San Francisco Bay Area) as a regionally based online movie store. It offered Bay Area customers a simple list of videos arranged by title and lead actor. Rentals were mailed out, and renters were charged the usual late fees for failure to return within a week. Despite the simplicity of its business model and regional character, Netflix had gross revenues of over $1 million in 1998, but lost over $11 million. It was hardly an auspicious beginning, even though these first years demonstrated a market for online video rentals. Many doubted the U.S. Postal Service was up to the task of delivering DVDs in the region, let alone hundreds of thousands daily on a national scale.

In 2000, Netflix changed its business model to that of a nationally based subscription model, entered into a number of relationships with Hollywood producers to speed up access to recent titles, expanded the functionality of its Web site, and changed its strategic marketing objectives toward becoming a nationally recognized online brand name. Unlike most neighborhood video rental stores at the time, Netflix changed from charging a fee for each video rental to assessing a monthly service charge for unlimited video rentals. Customers can rent as many videos as they want (with its most popular plan allowing a limit of three videos signed out at any given time) every month. For hard-core video fans, Netflix has developed a $16.99 a month plan that allows eight movies to be checked out at once. Moreover, Netflix eliminated late fees—the single largest complaint of video store customers around the country. To fulfill orders on a national basis, Netflix established video warehouse operations in various metropolitan areas around the United States (now totaling 58) and entered into a long-term relationship with the U.S. Postal Service to ensure delivery within one or two days for 95% of its subscribers in most parts of the country at very low cost for high-volume deliveries. Netflix provides a pre-stamped mailer for postal returns, absorbing the cost by using revenues from sales of DVDs to some renters.

To build national brand awareness, Netflix used every method in the e-commerce playbook. Netflix marketed its service by purchasing pay-for-performance banner advertising from Yahoo, MSN, and AOL. The familiar Netflix red banner ad is one of the most frequently seen leave-behind ads on the Web. It used search engine marketing and pay-for-placement ads on major search engines and permission-based e-mail. It also developed an active affiliate marketing program where third parties can automatically download Netflix ads and logos, place them on their sites, and collect revenues for steering customers to Netflix. Netflix also entered into a relationship with Best Buy—an online and offline electronics store—to place Netflix flyers offering a free 14-day trial of Netflix service inside every DVD player Best Buy shipped, and place Netflix on its site as the sole provider of DVDs.

On its own Web site, Netflix offered free trial periods and experienced high conversion rates. Hollywood studios typically distribute their filmed entertainment to the home video market six months after the theater release, to the pay-per-view (PPV) market seven months after theater release, to premium satellite and cable systems one year after release, and to general broadcast television and basic cable about two to three years after release. Rather than invest heavily in the purchase of DVDs from Hollywood, Netflix entered into a revenue-sharing arrangement with several studios, which allowed Netflix to purchase the DVDs below cost but to share the revenues from rentals with the studios. In this way, Netflix was able to build a bigger inventory faster and with less investment.

But building a brand also involves building a trusted high-value relationship with the customer, a unique value proposition that the customer cannot obtain elsewhere and might even pay a premium to receive. To build this relationship, Netflix enlarged its titles library from a few thousand to over 100,000 titles, providing customers 10 times more titles than can be found in the typical large Blockbuster store (and adding customer value through the "library effect" described later in the chapter).

A major focus of Netflix is "the customer experience" on-site. In an effort to provide personalized video rental advice, Netflix also added a recommender system to its Web site. Using its own customers as a knowledge base, it asked customers to submit online reviews, comments, and recommendations on videos they rented. So far, Netflix has gathered over 1 billion customer recommendations, which it then makes available to the entire online customer base—a valuable and inimitable resource. In 2006, the company started a contest offering $1 million to any person or group who could improve Netflix's recommendations by 10%. In 2009, a team from AT&T Research called BelKor Pragmatic Chaos was one of two teams to pass the 10% improvement mark. Using data mining techniques and a collaborative filtering tool similar to Amazon's, Netflix is able to recommend to its customers new videos based on each customer's personal profile of previous rentals and the rentals of other similar customers. Netflix sends e-mail to its customer base offering recently released videos that, given the customer's previous rental history, might be of special interest to that customer.

Providing a superior customer experience based on convenience, selection, personalization, and service, Netflix has been able to best its major competitors such as Blockbuster, at least for now. Wall Street analysts have been predicting a slide at Netflix for many years despite its growth because of the possibility of serious competition and bruising price wars for subscribers with Blockbuster, not to mention the growth of alternative online video streaming sites. Sales of DVDs are down 20% over the last few years and millions watch YouTube. So far Netflix has defied predictions of a fall off in DVD rentals and also has surprised analysts by building a very successful DVD streaming business with more than 12,000 movies available for instant viewing, free with most rental plans. In August 2009, Netflix inked a deal with Disney-ABC to stream prior-season hit ABC TV series to its subscribers.

In 2008, Netflix stock was hammered down to $20 in October, and then popped back up to $40 based on its solid performance in 2009. Blockbuster developed its own subscription service in 2006 and has grown the initial 1 million subscribers to over 4 million in 2009. However, Blockbuster has had a difficult time moving from a physical rental store model to an online DVD rental model. In 2005, it began the transition with a Total Service Plan that allows customers to drop off rental DVDs at any of the 20,000 local stores, and even exchange them for other DVDs. It also offers digital downloads of selected videos to customer PCs, and in August 2007, acquired Movielink, a movie download service provider. Blockbuster forced Netflix to drop subscription prices as well. In 2009, Blockbuster experienced steep declines in rentals and streaming, as revenues plummeted 22% in the second quarter, its stock sank from $4 to .75 cents, with bankruptcy a likely outcome. DVD kiosk operator Redbox, which allows customers to burn DVDs at supermarkets, also took business from Blockbuster.

In the meantime, Amazon has entered the fray by offering a movie download service to Tivo subscribers for direct play on television. Hollywood's own efforts at digital distribution (at sites such as Hulu, CinemaNow, HBO, and Showtime) have increased their selections and are more competitive with Netflix. To counter this competition, Netflix is building on its customer service strength by offering real human telephone customer service (as opposed to online digital help), and its newer service of streaming selected videos to subscriber PCs for free. As the competition heats up, Netflix's founder and CEO Reed Hastings says, "We have a lot of room to grow. Our relative execution will determine what the share split is between Netflix and Blockbuster."

SOURCES: "Netflix Announces Agreement with Disney-ABC Television Group to Stream Several Hit ABC Series," Netflix, August 3, 2009; "Netflix Announces Q2 2009 Financial Results," Netflix, July 23, 2009; Netflix Inc Form 10-K for the fiscal year ended December 31, 2008, filed with the Securities and Exchange Commission on March 15, 2009; "Netflix Passes 10 Million Subscribers, With 600,00 Net Additions Since January," Netflix, February 12, 2009; "Netflix Competitors Learn the Power of Teamwork," by Steve Lohr, *New York Times*, July 28, 2009; "Blockbuster's Loss Exceeds Forecast," Associated Press, April 14, 2009; "Blockbuster's Loss Widens As Same-Store Sales Climb," by Shara Tibken, *Wall Street Journal*, August 7, 2008; "Netflix to Sell a Device for Instantly Watching Movies on TV Sets," by Saul Hansell, *New York Times*, May 20, 2008.

Netflix provides an example of how the Internet has changed the nature of entire industries and how it enables new types of businesses to thrive even in highly competitive environments. But perhaps no area has been more affected than marketing and marketing communications. As a communications tool, the Internet affords marketers new ways of contacting millions of potential customers at costs far lower than traditional media. The Internet also provides new ways—often instantaneous and spontaneous—to gather information from customers, adjust product offerings, and increase customer value. In the case of Netflix, and in the other cases in this and the following chapter, the Internet has spawned entirely new ways to identify and communicate with customers, including search engine marketing, data mining, recommender systems, and targeted e-mail.

In the Web 2.0 environment of 2009 and 2010, advertisers are following huge shifts in audience away from traditional media and towards social networking, user-generated content, and online content destinations. For instance, according to Internet Retailer, almost 75% of its Top 500 e-retailers have a presence on at least one of the major social networking or social shopping sites. (Internet Retailer, 2009a). Another survey of marketing executives found that 43% expected to increase the amount of their online advertising budget allocated to social media in 2009 (Datran Media, 2009). In this chapter and Chapter 7, we discuss avenues for marketing and advertising on the Internet. This chapter focuses on the basic marketing concepts you need to understand to evaluate e-commerce marketing programs. Here, we examine consumer behavior on the Web, brands, the unique features of electronic markets, and special technologies that support new kinds of branding activities. For some of you, this will be a useful review of material you first learned in marketing classes, while for others this will be a first-time exposure to basic marketing concepts. Chapter 7 discusses e-commerce marketing communications, including advertising and other tools.

6.1 CONSUMERS ONLINE: THE INTERNET AUDIENCE AND CONSUMER BEHAVIOR

Before firms can begin to sell their products online, they must first understand what kinds of people they will find online and how those people behave in the online marketplace. In this section, we focus primarily on individual consumers in the B2C arena. However, many of the factors discussed apply to the B2B arena as well, insofar as purchasing decisions by firms are made by individuals.

THE INTERNET AUDIENCE

We will start with an analysis of some basic background demographics of Web consumers in the United States. The first principle of marketing and sales is "know thy customer." Who uses the Web, who shops on the Web and why, and what do they buy?

INTERNET TRAFFIC PATTERNS: THE ONLINE CONSUMER PROFILE

In 2009, around 200 million people and over 87 million U.S. households (about 72% of all U.S. households) will have access to the Internet (eMarketer, Inc., 2009a). By comparison, 98% of all U.S. households currently have televisions and 94% have telephones.

Although the number of new online users increased at a rate of 30% a year or higher in the late 1990s, over the last several years, this growth rate has slowed to about 2%–3% a year. Because of the cost and complexity of computer use required for Internet access, it is unlikely that Internet use will equal that of television or radio use in the near future, although this may change as computers become less expensive and complex. E-commerce businesses can no longer count on an annual 30% growth rate in the online population to fuel their revenues. The days of extremely rapid growth in the U.S. Internet population are over.

Intensity and Scope of Usage

The slowing rate of growth in the U.S. Internet population is compensated for in part by an increasing intensity and scope of use. Several studies show that a greater amount of time is being spent online by Internet users. Overall, users are going online more frequently, with 73% of adult users in the United States (115 million people) logging on in a typical day (Pew Internet & American Life Project, 2009a). The more time users spend online, becoming more comfortable and familiar with Internet features and services, the more services they are likely to explore, according to the Pew Internet & American Life Project.

People who go online are engaging in a wider range of activities than in the past. While e-mail remains the most-used Internet service, other popular activities include using search engines, researching products and services, catching up on news, gathering hobby-related information, seeking health information, conducting work-related research, and reviewing financial information. **Table 6.1** identifies the range of online activities for the typical adult U.S. Internet user. Each percent translates into about 1.57 million people.

Demographics and Access

The demographic profile of the Internet—and e-commerce—has changed greatly since 1995. Up until 2000, single, white, young, college-educated males with high incomes dominated the Internet. This inequality in access and usage led to concerns about a possible "digital divide." However, in recent years, there has been a marked increase in Internet usage by females, minorities, and families with modest incomes, resulting in a notable decrease—but not elimination—in the earlier inequality of access and usage. The following discussion is based on data collected in surveyed conducted by the Pew Internet & American Life Project.

Gender A fairly equal percentage of both men (81%) and women (77%) use the Internet. Women are also almost as likely to use the Internet on a daily basis as men, although somewhat less likely to purchase online.

TABLE 6.1	A GROWING RANGE OF ONLINE ACTIVITIES: AN AVERAGE DAY IN THE LIFE OF AN INTERNET USER
ACTIVITY	**PERCENT OF INTERNET USERS WHO REPORTED ENGAGING IN ACTIVITY "YESTERDAY"**
	2009
Use the Internet	73%
Send or read e-mail	57%
Use a search engine to find information	50%
Get news	38%
Go online just for fun or to pass time	38%
Check the weather	33%
Look online for political news/information	25%
Do banking online	20%
Use an online social networking site	19%
Watch a video on a video-sharing site	16%
Look for information on Wikipedia	12%
Get financial information online	12%
Send instant messages	11%
Visit a government Web site	10%
Read an online journal or blog	10%
Look for health/medical information	10%
Use online classified ads or sites	9%
Look online for job information	9%
Buy a product	8%
Search for information about someone you know or might meet	8%
Look for "how-to," "do-it-yourself" information	7%
Use Twitter or other status update service	5%
Look for religious/spiritual information	4%
Rate a product, service, or person using an online rating system	3%
Create or work on own online journal or blog	3%
Buy or make a reservation for travel	3%
Download a podcast	3%
Download or share files using P2P file sharing networks	3%
Participate in an online auction	3%
Use an online dating Web site	2%
Participate in an online discussion group	1%
Buy or sell stocks, bonds, or mutual funds	1%

SOURCE: Pew Internet & American Life Project, 2009a.

Age Young adults (18–29) form the age group with the highest percentage of Internet access at 92%. Adults in the 30–49 group (87%) are also strongly represented and growing their Internet presence. The percentage of the very young (under 12) and teens (12–17) going online is also growing dramatically, in part due to increased access to computers and the Internet both at school and at home. Another fast growing group online is the 65 and over segment, 42% of whom now use the Internet, more than double the level of 2002.

Ethnicity Variation across ethnic groups is not as wide as across age groups. In 2002, there were significant differences among ethnic groups, but this has receded. The percentage of Hispanics with Internet access now exceeds that of whites. African-Americans continue to lag somewhat behind, with 67%, but this number is increasing over time. The growth rates for both Hispanics and African-Americans over the period from 2002 to 2009 is higher than those for whites, which has helped close the gap.

Community Type Historically, Internet access rates have been lower in rural areas than other kinds of communities. Internet penetration in rural areas has grown significantly since 2002, but continues to lag 10 percentage points below that of urban areas.

Income Level About 95% of households with income levels above $75,000 have Internet access, compared to only 69% of households earning less than $30,000. However, those households with lower earnings are gaining Internet access at faster rates than households with incomes of $75,000 and above. Over time, income differences have declined, but they remain significant.

Education Amount of education also makes a significant difference when it comes to online access. Of those individuals with a high school education, just 50% were online in 2009, compared to 94% of individuals with a college degree or more. Even a high school education boosted Internet usage, with that segment reaching 67% accessing the Web. In general, educational disparities far exceed other disparities in Internet access and usage.

Overall, there remains a strong relationship between age, income, ethnicity, and education on one hand and Internet usage on the other. The so-called "digital divide" has indeed moderated, but it still persists along the income, education, age, and ethnic dimensions. **Table 6.2** summarizes some of the major intergroup differences discussed above and their pace of change.

Type of Internet Connection: Broadband Impacts

In 2009, around 81 million households had broadband service in their homes—66.5% of all households (eMarketer, 2009a). Research suggests the broadband audience is different from the dial-up audience (see **Table 6.3**) and marketers need to take this into account when devising marketing plans. The broadband audience is more educated, wealthier, and more middle-aged. The broadband audience is much more intensely involved with the Internet and much more capable of using the Internet. For marketers, this audience offers unique opportunities for the use of multimedia advertis-

TABLE 6.2	CHANGING DEMOGRAPHIC DIFFERENCES IN INTERNET ACCESS	
GROUP	THE PERCENT OF EACH GROUP ONLINE	
	2009	2002
Total Adults	79%	50%
Women	81%	56%
Men	77%	60%
AGE		
18–29	92%	74%
30–49	87%	67%
50–64	79%	52%
65+	42%	18%
RACE/ETHNICITY		
White, Non-Hispanic	79%	60%
Black, Non-Hispanic	67%	45%
Hispanic (English-speaking)	84%	54%
COMMUNITY TYPE		
Urban	75%	67%
Suburban	77%	66%
Rural	65%	52%
HOUSEHOLD INCOME		
Less than $30,000/yr	60%	38%
$30,000–$50,000	80%	65%
$50,000–$75,000	88%	74%
More than $75,000	94%	86%
EDUCATIONAL ATTAINMENT		
Less than High School	50%	N/A
High School	69%	45%
Some College	88%	72%
College +	94%	82%

SOURCE: Based on data from Pew Internet & American Life Project, 2009b, 2005a, 2005b.

ing and marketing campaigns, and for the positioning of products especially suited for this audience.

Community Effects: Social Contagion

For a physical retail store, the most important factor in shaping sales is location, location, and location. If you are located where thousands of people pass by every day, you will tend to do well. But for Internet retailers, physical location has almost no consequence as long as customers can be served by shipping services such as UPS or the post office. What does make a difference for consumer purchases on the Internet is whether or not the consumer is located in "neighborhoods" where others purchase on the Internet. These so-called neighborhood effects, and the role of social emulation in consumption decisions, are well-known for other goods such as personal computers. Research on an Internet grocery found that being located nearby other users of the online grocery increased the likelihood of purchasing at the site by 50% (Bell and Song, 2004). Online marketers are beginning to realize the importance of online and offline social ties, and communities, for branding and sales. Social networking sites, blogs, and social tagging sites are increasingly influential in consumer behavior as you will see throughout this chapter.

TABLE 6.3	THE IMPACT OF BROADBAND ON INTERNET ACTIVITIES	
ACTIVITY	HOME DIAL-UP	HOME BROADBAND
Use an online search engine	80%	94%
Check weather reports	75%	84%
Get news	61%	80%
Visit a state or local government Web site	55%	72%
Look for information on the 2008 election	37%	62%
Watch a video on a video-sharing site like YouTube or Google Video	29%	60%
Look online for information about a job	36%	50%
Send instant messages	38%	44%
Read someone else's blog	15%	40%
Use a social networking site	21%	33%
Make a donation to a charity online	9%	23%
Download a podcast	8%	22%
Download or share files	17%	17%
Create or work on your blog	8%	15%

SOURCE: Pew Internet & American Life Project, 2008.

Lifestyle and Sociological Impacts

There are some worrisome potential impacts to intensive Internet use. Ask many parents of young teenagers, and they will often complain their children are spending too much time instant messaging and playing games online. Early research suggested that the Internet might be causing a decline in traditional social activities, such as talking face-to-face with neighbors and family members, encouraging users to spend less time with family and friends, and more time working, whether at home or at the office. According to an early study performed at Stanford University by a group of political scientists, Internet users lose touch with those around them; individuals spending just two to five hours a week online spend far less time talking with friends and family face-to-face and on the phone. Users who spend up to five hours a week online frequently experience an increase in time spent working while at home, while those who spend more than five hours a week online find themselves working more at work as well; the Internet is taking up a larger portion of what used to be free time for some workers. On the other hand, e-mail, instant messaging, and chat groups, all decidedly social activities, albeit not face-to-face ones, are among the most popular uses of the Internet.

More recent research has found that the use of the Internet strengthens and compliments traditional face-to-face relationships. While Internet use involves a single user sitting in front of a screen—much like television—it is very different from television because of the high levels of social interaction possible on the Internet. Insofar as Internet use deters children from face-to-face interaction or from undirected "play" out of doors, undesirable effects on child social development may result (Nie and Erbring, 2000). On the other hand, a recent study demonstrated that the Internet has strengthened ties among cousins (the "clicking cousins effect"), children, and parents through the use of e-mail to stay in touch on a daily basis. A meta-analysis of multiple studies on the impact of the Internet on social interaction from 1995–2003 found mixed results, with offline and online interaction stimulating one another, but online communication did not translate into more visiting face-to-face (Saunders and Chester, 2008; Shklovski, et al., 2004).

Media Choices and Multitasking: The Internet versus Other Media Channels

What may be of even more interest to marketers, however, is that the more time individuals spend using the Internet, "the more they turn their back on traditional media," according to the Stanford study. For every additional hour users spend online, they reduce their corresponding time spent with traditional media, such as television, newspapers, and radio. Traditional media are competing with the Internet for consumer attention, and so far, the Internet appears to be gaining on print media (newspapers and magazines) but not television. Media multitasking is rising: over 100 million U.S. adult Internet users watch television while going online. Others listen to the radio, read magazines, or newspapers (eMarketer, Inc., 2008a). We discuss media consumption in greater depth in Chapter 10.

CONSUMER BEHAVIOR MODELS

consumer behavior
a social science discipline that attempts to model and understand the behavior of humans in a marketplace

Once firms have an understanding of who is online, they need to focus on how consumers behave online. The study of **consumer behavior** is a social science discipline that attempts to model and understand the behavior of humans in a marketplace. Several social science disciplines play roles in this study, including sociology, psychology, and economics. Models of consumer behavior attempt to predict or "explain" what consumers purchase and where, when, how much, and why they buy. The expectation is that if the consumer decision-making process can be understood, firms will have a much better idea how to market and sell their products. **Figure 6.1** illustrates a general consumer behavior model that takes into account a wide range of factors that influence a consumer's marketplace decisions.

Consumer behavior models seek to predict the wide range of decisions that consumers make on the basis of background demographic factors, and on a set of intervening, more immediate variables that shape the consumer's ultimate decisions.

Background factors are cultural, social, and psychological in nature. Firms must recognize and understand the behavioral significance of these background factors and adjust their marketing efforts accordingly. **Culture** is the broadest factor in consumer behavior because it shapes basic human values, wants, perceptions, and behaviors. Culture creates basic expectations that consumers bring to the marketplace, such as what should be bought in different markets, how things should be bought, and how things should be paid for. Generally, culture affects an entire nation, and takes on major significance in international marketing. For instance, an American-style e-commerce site that sells cooking spices might have difficulty in an Asian culture such as China or Japan, where food and spice shopping takes place at local neighborhood markets, large food stores do not exist, and shoppers tend to pick out and smell each spice before purchasing it.

culture
shapes basic human values, wants, perceptions, and behaviors

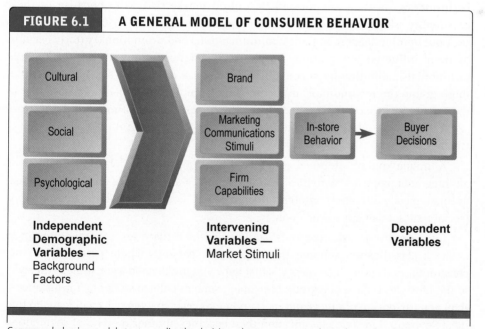

FIGURE 6.1 **A GENERAL MODEL OF CONSUMER BEHAVIOR**

Consumer behavior models try to predict the decisions that consumers make in the marketplace.
SOURCE: Adapted from Kotler and Armstrong, 2009.

subculture
subset of cultures that form around major social differences

Within nations, subcultures are extremely important in consumer behavior. **Subcultures** are subsets of cultures that form around major social differences such as ethnicity, age, lifestyle, and geography. In the United States, ethnicity plays a very large role in consumer behavior. There are an estimated 41 million African-Americans with an annual purchasing power of over $913 billion, about 47 million Hispanics with a total annual purchasing power of $951 billion, and almost 15.5 million Asian-Americans with a total purchasing power of over $509 billion. (U.S. Census Bureau, 2009, Humphreys, 2009). Each of these ethnic groups represents a significant market segment that firms can target. For instance, Toyota was one of the first automotive manufacturers to use the Internet to target Hispanic customers. Toyota places Web advertisements on Spanish-language portals such as MSN Latino, Yahoo en Espanol, AOL Latino, Univision, and Terra to direct Hispanic customers to its Toyota.com Spanish-language Web site. As a result, Toyota now ranks 1st in the new vehicle sales registered by Latinos. Best Buy also has a Spanish language Web site. Among the important social factors that shape consumer behavior are the many reference groups to which all consumers "belong," either as direct participating members, or as indirect members by affiliation, association, or aspiration. **Direct reference groups** include one's family, profession or occupation, religion, neighborhood, and schools. **Indirect reference groups** include one's life-cycle stage, social class, and lifestyle group (discussed later). For instance, the concept of community-based Web sites is based on the notion that people choose to be members of groups and subgroups that express and reflect their interests, such as the home-schooling community, personal health-related-issues communities, and recreational activity communities.

direct reference groups
one's family, profession or occupation, religion, neighborhood, and schools

indirect reference groups
one's life-cycle stage, social class, and lifestyle group

opinion leaders (viral influencers)
influence the behavior of others through their personality, skills, or other factors

Within each of these reference groups, there are **opinion leaders** (or **viral influencers**, as they are termed by online marketers), who because of their personality, skills, or other factors, influence the behavior of others. Marketers seek out opinion leaders in their communications and promotional efforts because of their influence over other people. For instance, many Web sites include testimonials submitted by successful adopters of a product or service. Generally, those giving the testimonials are portrayed as opinion leaders— "smart people in the know." At Procter & Gamble's Web site, for example, testimonials come from "P&G Advisors," who are consumers who take an active interest in Procter & Gamble products.

lifestyle group
an integrated pattern of activities, interests, and opinions

A unique kind of reference group is a **lifestyle group**, which can be defined as an integrated pattern of activities (hobbies, sports, shopping likes and dislikes, social events typically attended), interests (food, fashion, family, recreation), and opinions (social issues, business, government).

Lifestyle group classification systems—of which there are several—attempt to create a classification scheme that captures a person's whole pattern of living, consuming, and acting. The theory is that once you understand a consumer's lifestyle, or the lifestyles typical of a group of people—such as college students, for instance—then you can design products and marketing messages that appeal specifically to that lifestyle group. Lifestyle classification then becomes another method of segmenting the market.

In addition to lifestyle classification, marketers are interested in a consumer's psychological profile. A **psychological profile** is a set of needs, drives, motivations, perceptions, and learned behaviors—including attitudes and beliefs. Marketers attempt to appeal to psychological profiles through product design, product positioning, and marketing communications. For instance, many health e-commerce sites emphasize that they help consumers achieve a sense of control over their health destiny by providing them with information about diseases and treatments. This message is a powerful appeal to the needs of a wealthy, educated, professional, and technically advanced set of Web users for self-control and mastery over what might be a complex, health-threatening situation.

Marketers cannot influence demographic background factors, but they can adjust their branding, communications, and firm capabilities to appeal to demographic realities. For instance, the National Basketball Association's Web site, NBA.com, appeals to a variety of basketball fan subgroups from avid fans interested in specific team statistics, to fashion-conscious fans who can purchase clothing for specific NBA teams, to fans who want to auction memorabilia.

psychological profile
set of needs, drives, motivations, perceptions, and learned behaviors

PROFILES OF ONLINE CONSUMERS

Online consumer behavior parallels that of offline consumer behavior with some obvious differences. It is important to first understand why people choose the Internet channel to conduct transactions. **Table 6.4** illustrates the main reasons consumers choose the online channel.

While price appears on this list, overwhelmingly, consumers shop on the Web because of convenience, which in turn is produced largely by saving them time. Overall transaction cost reduction appears to be the major motivator for choosing the online channel, followed by other cost reductions in the product or service.

TABLE 6.4	WHY CONSUMERS CHOOSE THE ONLINE CHANNEL
REASON	PERCENTAGE OF RESPONDENTS
Can shop at any time of day	88%
Can research many products at the same time	66%
Can find products that are not available in stores	54%
Do not need to deal with salespeople	53%
Can get better information on products online	45%
Easier to find information on Web sites than it is to find in-store employees to help	44%
Prices are better online	40%
Products are usually in stock	40%

SOURCES: Based on data from eMarketer, Inc., 2007a; Sterling Commerce and Deloitte Consulting, 2007.

THE ONLINE PURCHASING DECISION

Once online, why do consumers actually purchase a product or service at a specific site? There are many models and several research studies that attempt to provide answers to this question. **Psychographic research** (research that combines both demographic and psychological data and divides a market into different groups based on social class, lifestyle, and/or personality characteristics) on the profile of active e-commerce shoppers attempts to understand the characteristics of users—in particular their various lifestyles—that lead to online buying behavior. For instance, in a study by the Wharton Forum on Electronic Commerce, a panel of 2,500 people was surveyed to understand the factors that predict e-commerce purchases. As shown in **Figure 6.2**, the survey found that the most important factors in predicting buying behavior were (1) looking for product information online, (2) leading a "wired lifestyle" (one where consumers spend a considerable amount of their working and home lives online), and (3) recently ordering from a catalog.

But aside from individual characteristics, you need to consider how buyers make the actual decision to purchase and how the Internet environment affects consumers' decisions. There are five stages in the consumer decision process: awareness of need, search for more information, evaluation of alternatives, the actual purchase decision,

psychographic research

divides a market into different groups based on social class, lifestyle, and/or personality characteristics

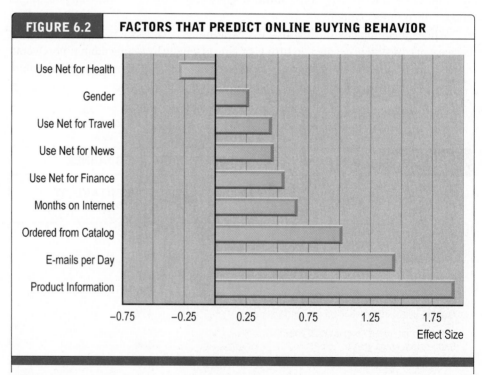

FIGURE 6.2   **FACTORS THAT PREDICT ONLINE BUYING BEHAVIOR**

Actively looking for product information, the number of e-mails sent per day, and whether someone has recently ordered from a catalog are the most significant variables in predicting whether someone will purchase online (variables are listed from lowest to highest effect).
SOURCE: Lohse, Bellman, and Johnson, 2000.

and post-purchase contact with the firm (Kotler and Armstrong, 2009). **Figure 6.3** shows the consumer decision process and the types of offline and online marketing communications that support this process and seek to influence the consumer before, during, and after the purchase decision.

As shown in Figure 6.3, traditional mass media, along with catalogs and direct mail campaigns, are used to drive potential buyers to Web sites. What's new about online purchasing is the new media marketing communications capabilities afforded by the Web: search engines, social media such as blogs, social networks and social shopping sites, online product reviews, video ads, targeted banner ads and permission e-mail, bulletin boards, chat rooms and the like. Simply put, the Web offers marketers an extraordinary increase in marketing communications tools and power, and the ability to envelop the consumer in a very rich information and purchasing environment (Awad, et al, 2007). In Chapter 7, we describe these new communications techniques and gauge their effectiveness in greater detail.

Both offline and online communications tools can be used to support the online consumer decision process at each of the five stages of the process.

A MODEL OF ONLINE CONSUMER BEHAVIOR

Is offline consumer behavior fundamentally different from online consumer behavior? Arguably not. Consumer behavior offline and online has both similarities and differences. The e-commerce world is not quite so revolutionary as some would have us believe. For instance, the stages of the consumer decision process are basically the same whether the consumer is offline or online. On the other hand, the general model of consumer behavior requires modification to take into account new factors. In **Figure 6.4**, we have modified the general model of consumer

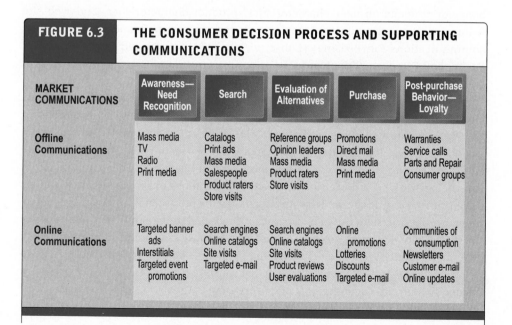

FIGURE 6.3	THE CONSUMER DECISION PROCESS AND SUPPORTING COMMUNICATIONS				
MARKET COMMUNICATIONS	Awareness— Need Recognition	Search	Evaluation of Alternatives	Purchase	Post-purchase Behavior— Loyalty
Offline Communications	Mass media TV Radio Print media	Catalogs Print ads Mass media Salespeople Product raters Store visits	Reference groups Opinion leaders Mass media Product raters Store visits	Promotions Direct mail Mass media Print media	Warranties Service calls Parts and Repair Consumer groups
Online Communications	Targeted banner ads Interstitials Targeted event promotions	Search engines Online catalogs Site visits Targeted e-mail	Search engines Online catalogs Site visits Product reviews User evaluations	Online promotions Lotteries Discounts Targeted e-mail	Communities of consumption Newsletters Customer e-mail Online updates

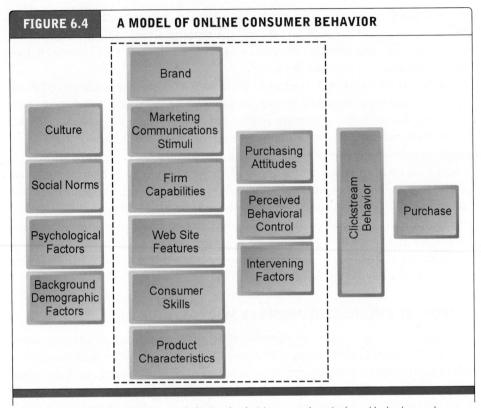

| FIGURE 6.4 | A MODEL OF ONLINE CONSUMER BEHAVIOR |

In this general model of online consumer behavior, the decision to purchase is shaped by background demographic factors, several intervening factors, and finally influenced greatly by clickstream behavior very near to the precise moment of purchase.

behavior to focus on user characteristics, product characteristics, and Web site features, along with traditional factors such as brand strength and specific market communications (advertising) (Lohse, et. al. 2000; Pavlou and Fygenson, 2005, Pavlou and Dimoka, 2006). Figure 6.4 attempts to summarize and simplify current research.

In the online model, Web site features, along with consumer skills, product characteristics, attitudes towards online purchasing, and perceptions about control over the Web environment come to the fore. Web site features include latency (delay in downloads), navigability, and confidence in a Web site's security. (We examine Web site design issues as they relate to marketing more fully in Chapter 7.) There are parallels in the analog world. For instance, it is well known that consumer behavior can be influenced by store design, and that understanding the precise movements of consumers through a physical store can enhance sales if goods and promotions are arranged along the most likely consumer tracks. For instance, because consumers almost invariably enter a store and move to the right, high-margin items—jewelry and cosmetics—tend to be located there. And because it is known that consumers purchase fresh dairy products frequently, they are put at the back of grocery stores. Wal-Mart uses consumer-tracking databases within its stores to optimize the convenience to consumers—putting clothing nearest the entry, and electronics and cameras toward the back. Proper store design and precision tracking of consumers is not new—but its technical implementation on the Web, its lowered cost, its ubiquity, and its comprehensiveness on the Web are new.

Consumer skills refers to the knowledge that consumers have about how to conduct online transactions (which increases with experience). *Product characteristics* refers to the fact that some products can be easily described, packaged, and shipped over the Internet (such as books, software, and DVDs), whereas others cannot. Combined with traditional factors, such as brand, advertising, and firm capabilities, these factors lead to specific attitudes about purchasing at a Web site (trust in the Web site and favorable customer experience) and a sense that the consumer can control his or her environment on the Web site.

Clickstream behavior refers to the transaction log that consumers establish as they move about the Web, from search engine, to a variety of sites, then to a single site, then to a single page, and then, finally, to a decision to purchase. These precious moments are similar to "point-of-purchase" moments in traditional retail.

clickstream behavior
the transaction log that consumers establish as they move about the Web

A number of researchers have argued that understanding the background demographics of Internet users is no longer necessary, and not that predictive in any event. In most studies of consumer behavior, background demographics usually account for less than 5% of the observed behavior. Many believe instead that the most important predictors of online consumer behavior are the session characteristics and the clickstream behavior of people online very close to the moment of purchase. The theory is that this information will enable marketers to understand what the consumer was looking for at each moment, and how much they were willing to pay, thus allowing the marketers to precisely target their communications in an effort to sway the purchase decision in their favor.

For instance, a study by Booz Allen & Hamilton and NetRatings found that background demographics alone, and even background demographics with attitudinal and lifestyle factors, fail to take into account the different types of user sessions and different clickstream patterns. Analyzing the clickstream behavior of 2,466 individuals engaged in 186,797 user sessions, the study identified seven categories of user sessions: "Quickies," "Just the Facts," "Single Mission," "Do It Again," "Loitering," "Information Please," and "Surfing." Researchers called these segments "occasions," and suggested "occasion-based" marketing is more effective than static market segmentation based on demographics and/or consumer attitudes. Segmenting the market in this way, they found that in some types of sessions, users are more likely to buy, whereas in other sessions, they appear to be immune to online advertising. A study of over 10,000 visits to an online wine store found that detailed and general clickstream behavior were as important as customer demographics and prior purchase behavior in predicting a current purchase (Van den Poel and Buckinx, 2005). The most important clickstream factors were:

- Number of days since last visit
- Speed of clickstream behavior
- Number of products viewed during last visit
- Number of pages viewed
- Number of products viewed

- Supplying personal information (trust)
- Number of days since last purchase
- Number of past purchases

Clickstream marketing takes maximum advantage of the Internet environment. It presupposes no prior knowledge of the customer (and in that sense is "privacy-regarding"), and can be developed dynamically as customers use the Internet. For instance, the success of search engine marketing (the display of paid advertisements on Web search pages) is based in large part on what the consumer is looking for at the moment and how they go about looking (detailed clickstream data). After examining the detailed data, general clickstream data is used (days since last visit, past purchases). If available, demographic data is used (region, city, and gender).

SHOPPERS: BROWSERS AND BUYERS

The picture of Internet use sketched in the previous section emphasizes the complexity of behavior online. Although the Internet audience still tends to be concentrated among the well educated, affluent, and youthful, increasingly the audience is becoming more diverse. Clickstream analysis shows us that people go online for many different reasons. Online shopping is similarly complex. Beneath the surface of the $228 billion B2C e-commerce market in 2009 are substantial differences in how users shop online.

For instance, as shown in **Figure 6.5**, about 70% of online users are "buyers" who actually purchase something entirely online. Another 16% of online users research products on the Web ("browsers"), but purchase them offline. This combined group, referred to as "shoppers," constitutes approximately 86% of the online Internet audience. With the adult U.S. Internet audience (14 years or older) estimated at about 175 million in 2009, online shoppers (the combination of buyers and browsers) add up to a market size of around 150 million consumers. Most marketers find this number exciting.

| FIGURE 6.5 | ONLINE SHOPPERS AND BUYERS |

Did not shop or buy online
14%

Buy online
70%

Research, shop online
but did not buy
16%

About 86% of the online audience shops online, either by researching products or by purchasing products online. The percentage of the online audience actually purchasing has increased by 7% since 2005 to 70%.
SOURCE: Based on data from eMarketer, Inc., 2009b.

The significance of online browsing for offline purchasing should not be underestimated. Although it is difficult to precisely measure the amount of offline sales that occur because of online product research, several different studies have found that about one-third of all offline retail purchasing is influenced by online product research, blogs, banner ads, and other Internet exposure. The offline influence varies by product. This amounts to about $1 trillion in annual retail sales, a truly extraordinary number (eMarketer, Inc., 2008b).

E-commerce is a major conduit and generator of offline commerce. The reverse is also true: online traffic is driven by offline brands and shopping. While online research influences offline purchase, it is also the case that offline marketing media heavily influence online behavior including sales. Traditional print media (magazines and newspapers) and television are by far the most powerful media for reaching and engaging consumers with information about new products and directing them to the Web (see **Table 6.5**). Online communities and blogging are also very influential but not yet as powerful as traditional media.

TABLE 6.5	MEDIA THAT INFLUENCE CONSUMERS TO START SEARCH FOR MERCHANDISE ONLINE
MEDIA	PERCENTAGE OF RESPONDENTS
Magazines	47%
Reading an article	43%
Broadcast TV	43%
Newspapers	41%
Cable TV	36%
Coupons	36%
Face-to-face communication	34%
Radio	30%
Direct mail	30%
E-mail advertising	29%
In-store promotions	27%
Online advertising	26%
Outdoor billboards	12%
Online communities	10%
Instant messaging	9%
Mobile phone	8%
Blogs	8%
Yellow pages	7%
Mobile pictures/video	5%
Text messaging	5%
Other	6%

SOURCES: Based on data from eMarketer, Inc., 2008c; BigResearch and the Retail Advertising and Marketing Association, 2008.

These considerations strongly suggest that e-commerce and traditional commerce are coupled and should be viewed by merchants (and researchers) as part of a continuum of consuming behavior and not as radical alternatives to one another. Commerce is commerce; the customers are often the same people. Customers use a wide variety of media, sometimes multiple media at once. The significance of these findings for marketers is very clear. Online merchants should build the information content of their sites to attract browsers looking for information, build content to rank high in search engines, put less attention on selling per se, and promote services and products (especially new products) in offline media settings in order to support their online stores.

WHAT CONSUMERS SHOP FOR AND BUY ONLINE

You can look at online sales as divided roughly into two groups: small-ticket and big-ticket items. Big-ticket items include computer equipment and consumer electronics, where orders can easily be over $500. Small-ticket items include apparel, books, health and beauty supplies, office supplies, music, software, videos, and toys, where the average purchase is typically less than $100. In the early days of e-commerce, sales of small-ticket items vastly outnumbered those of large-ticket items for a variety of reasons. First movers on the Web sold these products early on; the purchase price was low (reduced consumer risk); the items were physically small (shipping costs were low); margins were high (at least on CDs and software); and there was a broad selection of products (e-commerce vendors could compete on scope when compared to traditional offline stores). But the recent growth of big-ticket items such as computer hardware, consumer electronics, furniture, and jewelry has changed the overall sales mix. Consumers are now much more confident spending online for big-ticket items. Although furniture and large appliances were initially perceived as too bulky to sell online, these categories have rapidly expanded in the last few years. The types of purchases made also depend on levels of experience with the Web (U.S.C. Annenberg School Center for the Digital Future, 2004). New Web users tend primarily to buy small-ticket items, while experienced Web users are more willing to buy large-ticket items in addition to small-ticket items. **Figure 6.6** illustrates how much consumers spent online for various categories of goods at the top 500 Internet retailers in 2008.

INTENTIONAL ACTS: HOW SHOPPERS FIND VENDORS ONLINE

Given the prevalence of "click here" banner ads, one might think customers are "driven" to online vendors by spur-of-the-moment decisions. In fact, only a tiny percentage of shoppers click on banners to find vendors. Once they are online, 37% of consumers use search engines as their preferred method of research or purchasing a product; 33% go directly to the company Web site. Comparison shopping sites (17%) and product rating sites (15%) also play a role (eMarketer, 2007b). E-commerce shoppers are highly intentional. Typically, they are focused browsers looking for specific products, companies, and services. Merchants can convert these "goal-oriented," intentional shoppers into buyers if the merchants can target their communications to the shoppers and design their sites in such a way as

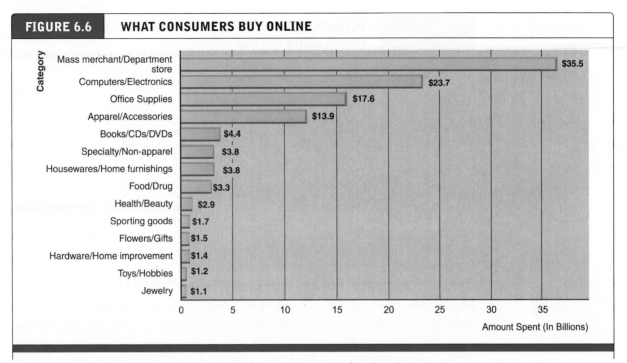

FIGURE 6.6   WHAT CONSUMERS BUY ONLINE

This figure illustrates how much consumers spent online for various categories of goods at the top 500 Internet retailers in 2008.
SOURCES: Based on data from Internet Retailer, 2009a; eMarketer, 2009b; authors' estimates.

to provide easy-to-access and useful product information, full selection, and customer service and do this at the very moment the customer is searching for the product (Wolfinbarger and Gilly, 2001). No small task. There are, of course, exceptions. Some people go on the Web and are not quite clear what they are looking for. StumbleUpon.com is a site for these unintentional searchers who, for the most part, are subject and community searchers rather than product searchers. StumbleUpon identifies the general topic of interest for the user, and then relies on collaborative filtering tools to direct visitors to other sites on the Web that similarly interested people have visited and found interesting.

WHY MORE PEOPLE DON'T SHOP ONLINE

A final consumer behavior question to address is: Why don't more online Web users shop online? **Table 6.6** lists the major online buying concerns among Internet users in the United States.

Arguably, the largest factor preventing more people from shopping online is the "trust factor," the fear that online merchants will cheat you, lose your credit card information, or use personal information you give them to invade your personal privacy, bombarding you with unwanted e-mail, and pop-up ads. Secondary factors can be summarized as "hassle factors," like shipping costs, returns, and inability to touch and feel the product (Doolin, et al, 2007).

TABLE 6.6	INTERNET USERS' MAJOR CONCERNS ABOUT PURCHASING ONLINE
Uneasy about online credit card use	44%
Concerns about privacy of data	42%
Shipping charges	37%
No need to purchase online	33%
Prefer to touch and feel product before purchase	32%
Returning a product too difficult	27%
Not seen anything online interested in buying	21%

SOURCES: Based on data from eMarketer, Inc., 2007b; Internet Retailer, 2006.

TRUST, UTILITY, AND OPPORTUNISM IN ONLINE MARKETS

Recent research shows that the two most important factors shaping the decision to purchase online are utility and trust (Ba and Pavlou, 2002). The decision to purchase anything on the Web is strongly affected by these two factors. Consumers want good deals, bargains, convenience, and speed of delivery. In short, consumers are looking for utility. On the other hand, in any seller-buyer relationship, there is an asymmetry of information. The seller usually knows a lot more than the consumer about the quality of goods and terms of sale. This can lead to opportunistic behavior by sellers (Akerlof, 1970; Williamson, 1985; Mishra, 1998). Consumers need to trust a merchant before they make a purchase. Sellers can develop trust among online consumers by building strong reputations of honesty, fairness, and delivery of quality products—the basic elements of a brand. Feedback forums such as Epinions.com (now merged with DealTime to form Shopping.com), Amazon's book reviews from reviewers, and eBay's feedback forum are examples of trust-building online mechanisms (Opinion Research Corporation, 2009). Online sellers who develop trust among consumers are able to charge a premium price for their online products and services (Kim and Benbaset, 2006; Kim and Benbasat, 2007; Pavlou, 2002). A review of the literature suggests that the most important factors leading to a trusting online relationship are perception of Web site credibility, ease of use, and risk (Corritore, et al., 2006).

marketing
the strategies and actions firms take to establish a relationship with a consumer and encourage purchases of its products or services

Internet marketing
using the Web—as well as traditional channels—to develop a positive, long-term relationship with customers, thereby creating a competitive advantage for the firm by allowing it to charge a higher price for products or services than its competitors can charge

6.2   BASIC MARKETING CONCEPTS

In Section 6.1, we discussed who's on the Web and online behavior as it relates to purchase decisions. In this section, we expand our focus to look at the broader topic of **marketing**—the strategies and actions firms take to establish a relationship with a consumer and encourage purchases of its products or services. The key objective of **Internet marketing** is to use the Web—as well as traditional channels—to develop a positive, long-term relationship with customers (who may be online or offline) and thereby create a competitive advantage for the firm by allowing it to charge a higher price for products or services than its competitors can charge.

To begin, you must first be familiar with some basic marketing concepts. Recall from Chapter 2 (Section 2.5) that the profitability of an industry depends on (1) the ease with which substitute products or services can enter the market, (2) the ease with which new entrants can enter the industry, (3) the power of customers and suppliers to influence pricing, and (4) the nature of competition within the industry. Competitive markets are ones that have lots of substitutes, easy entry, and customers and suppliers who possess strong bargaining power.

Marketing directly addresses the competitive situation of industries and firms. Marketing seeks to create unique, highly differentiated products or services that are produced or supplied by one trusted firm ("little monopolies"). There are few, if any, substitutes for an effectively marketed product or service, and new entrants have a difficult time matching the product or service's **feature set** (the bundle of capabilities and services offered by the product or service). When successful, these little monopolies reduce the bargaining power of consumers because they are the sole sources of supply; they also enable firms to exercise significant power over their suppliers.

Marketing is designed to avoid pure price competition and to create markets where returns on investment are above average, competition is limited, and consumers are willing to pay premium prices for products that have no substitute because they are perceived as unique. Marketing encourages customers to buy on the basis of nonmarket (i.e., nonprice) qualities of a product. Firms use marketing to prevent their products and services from becoming commodities. A **commodity** is a good or service for which there are many dealers supplying the same product and all products in the segment are essentially identical. Price and delivery terms are the only basis for consumer choice. Examples of commodities include wheat, corn, and steel.

FEATURE SETS

A central task of marketing is to identify and then communicate to the customer the unique, differentiated capabilities and services of a product or service's feature set. **Figure 6.7** illustrates the three levels of a product or service: core, actual, and augmented. Although the example given is for a physical product, the concept applies equally to a digital product or service.

The core product is at the center of the feature set. The **core product** is the core benefit the customer receives from the product. Let's say, for example, that the core product is a cell phone. The **actual product** is the set of characteristics designed to deliver the product's core benefits. Marketers must identify the features of the cell phone that differentiate it from those of other manufacturers. In the case of a "cell phone" like Apple's iPhone, the actual product is a cell phone and music player with a wide screen that connects through wireless networks to the Internet. It comes with the Apple name and with certain features and capabilities, such as high-speed network connectivity, a large screen for Web browsing, design elegance, extraordinary packaging, and selected utility programs. The **augmented product** is a product with additional benefits to customers beyond the core benefits embodied in the actual product. In the case of the iPhone, the augmented product

feature set
the bundle of capabilities and services offered by the product or service

commodity
a good or service for which there are many dealers supplying the same product, and all products in the segment are essentially identical

core product
the core benefit the customer receives from the product

actual product
the set of characteristics designed to deliver the product's core benefits

augmented product
a product with additional benefits to customers beyond the core benefits embodied in the actual product

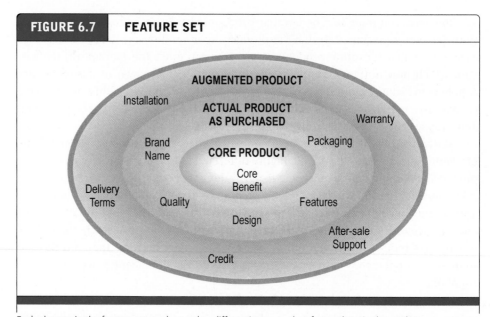

FIGURE 6.7 | **FEATURE SET**

Each element in the feature set can be used to differentiate a product from others in the market.

includes a standard one-year warranty, an available AppleCare Protection Plan that extends the warranty and support for an additional year, iPhone support Web pages, and other after-sale support. The augmented product forms the basis for building the iPhone brand (a process known as *branding*) described next. The augmented product is the foundation for the product brand.

PRODUCTS, BRANDS, AND THE BRANDING PROCESS

brand
a set of expectations that consumers have when consuming, or thinking about consuming, a product or service from a specific company

What makes products truly unique and differentiable in the minds of consumers is the product's brand. A **brand** is a set of expectations that a consumer has when consuming, or thinking about consuming, a product or service from a specific company. These expectations are based in part on past experiences the consumer has had actually using the product, on the experiences of trusted others who have consumed the product, and on the promises of marketers who extol the unique features of the product in a variety of different channels and media.

The most important expectations created by brands are quality, reliability, consistency, trust, affection, loyalty, and ultimately, reputation. Marketers create promises, and these promises engender consumer expectations. As Charles Revson, the founder of Revlon noted, "In the factory we make cosmetics; in the store we sell hope" (Kotler and Armstrong, 2008). The promise made by cosmetic manufacturers to consumers is: "If you use this product, you will perceive yourself to be more beautiful." In the case of Apple's iPhone, marketers (including Steve Jobs himself) have artfully created expectations among users for superb industrial design, quality construction, and unique products. The Apple iPhone brand connotes to iPhone owners a cool, hip, technologically advanced style of life. Consumers are willing to pay a premium price for Apple iPhones not only because of the augmented product features, but also because of these brand expectations. **Figure 6.8** illustrates the process of brand creation or **branding**.

Marketers identify the differentiating features of the actual and augmented product. They engage in a variety of marketing communications activities to transmit the feature set to the consumer. Based on the consumers' experiences and the promises made by marketers in their communications, consumers develop expectations about a product. For instance, when a consumer purchases an Apple iPhone, he or she expects to receive a unique, high-quality, very easy-to-use cell phone. Consumers are willing to pay a premium price in order to obtain these qualities. If iPhones do not in fact perform according to these expectations, the brand will be weakened and consumers will be less willing to pay a premium price. In other words, a strong brand requires a strong product. But if iPhones do perform according to expectations, then customers will feel loyal to the product; they will purchase again or recommend it to others; and they will trust, feel affection for, and ascribe a good reputation to both the product and the company that makes it.

Ideally, marketers directly influence the design of products to ensure the products have desirable features, high quality, correct pricing, product support, and reliability. When marketers are able to directly influence the design of a core product based on market research and feedback, this is called **closed loop marketing**. While ideal, it is more often the case that marketers are hired to "sell" a product that has already been designed. E-commerce—as we see next—offers some unique opportunities to achieve closed loop marketing.

branding
process of brand creation

closed loop marketing
when marketers are able to directly influence the design of the core product based on market research and feedback from the market

FIGURE 6.8   **MARKETING ACTIVITIES: FROM PRODUCTS TO BRANDS**

Marketers aim to create a "brand identity" for a product, based on consumer perceptions of trust, affection, loyalty, and reputation.

brand strategy

a set of plans for differentiating a product from its competitors, and communicating these differences effectively to the marketplace

Marketers devise and implement brand strategies. A **brand strategy** is a set of plans for differentiating a product from its competitor, and communicating these differences effectively to the marketplace. In developing new e-commerce brands, the ability to devise and develop a brand strategy has been crucial in the success and failure of many companies, as described throughout this book.

What kinds of products can be branded? According to many marketing specialists, there is no limit. Every product can potentially be branded. Sneakers that make you soar from Nike, cars from Volvo that make you feel safe on dark rainy nights, shirts from Polo that make you appear as if you were on the way to a country club—these are all examples of products with extraordinary brand names for which consumers pay premium prices.

brand equity

the estimated value of the premium customers are willing to pay for using a branded product when compared to unbranded competitors

How much is a brand worth? Brands differ in their power and value in the marketplace. A brand can represent corporate value as an asset, it can also represent customer loyalty or attachment, and it can be seen as a set of associations that consumers have about products. **Brand equity** is the estimated value of the premium customers are willing to pay for using a branded product when compared to unbranded competitors (Feldwick, 1996). According to Interbrand's 2009 World's Most Valuable Brands survey, the top five brands and their estimated equity value are Coca-Cola ($68.7 billion), IBM ($60.2 billion), Microsoft ($56.6 billion), General Electric ($47.7 billion), and Nokia ($34.8 billion) (Interbrand, 2009). Brand equity also affects stock prices insofar as brands strengthen future revenue streams, and insofar as brands are intangible assets that have a market value. There are several methodologies used to calculate brand value, but this discussion is beyond the scope of this book (Berg, et al., 2007; Ailawadi, 2003).

SEGMENTING, TARGETING, AND POSITIONING

Markets are not unitary, but in fact are composed of many different kinds of customers with different needs. Firms seek to segment markets into distinct groups of customers who differ from one another in terms of product needs. Once the segments are established, each segment can be *targeted* with differentiated products. Within each segment, the product is *positioned* and branded as a unique, high-value product, especially suited to the needs of segment customers.

There are six major ways in which marketers segment and target markets (**Table 6.7**). By segmenting markets, firms can differentiate their products to more closely fit the needs of customers in each segment. Rather than charge one price for the same product, firms can maximize revenues by creating several different variations on the same product and charging different prices in each market segment. While segmenting and targeting are not new, the Internet offers an unusual opportunity for very fine-grained segmenting down to the level of the individual. Potentially, with enough personal information, marketers on the Internet can personalize market messages to precisely fit an individual's needs and wants. In the physical world of marketing using other technologies like newspapers, radio, and television, it is more difficult to personalize messages.

TABLE 6.7	MAJOR TYPES OF ONLINE MARKET SEGMENTATION AND TARGETING
Behavioral	Segmenting on the basis of behavior in the marketplace. In traditional stores, this involves observing how customers walk through stores. On the Internet, Web site owners and members of advertising networks can dynamically assign users to groups, and merge their behavioral information with other data.
Demographic	Using age, ethnicity, religion, and other demographic factors to segment. On the Internet, using registration data or other self-revelations. Sites visited also serves as proxy measures of age, e.g., music sites are visited by young persons.
Psychographic	Using common interests, values, and opinions along with personality, attitude, and lifestyle preferences to segment consumers into groups. On the Internet, Web sites visited can substitute for direct measurement, e.g., the fashion Web sites visited by consumers reflect a self-chosen lifestyle and values.
Technical	Using information gathered by a shopping technology as a basis for segmentation. Nearly everyone who shops at malls owns a car. On the Internet, each consumer visit generates a record of the user's domain, IP address, browser, computer platform, and connection type, as well as what URL the user linked to the site from and the date and time. People who connect using broadband media, for instance, are much more likely to download music from the Internet.
Contextual	Using the context of an event, or the content of an event, as a basis for segmentation. People who attend rock concerts tend to purchase music CDs as well. On the Internet, people who read the online *Wall Street Journal* are very good targets for financial service advertising.
Search	Using consumers' explicitly expressed interest at this moment to segment and target. Perhaps the simplest of all segmenting, search direct response follows the ageless maxim "sell them what they want."

Once markets are segmented, the branding process proceeds within each segment by appealing to the segment members. For instance, automobile manufacturers segment their markets on many dimensions: demographics (age, sex, income, and occupation), geographic (region), benefits (special performance features), and psychographics (self-image and emotional needs). For each market segment, they offer a uniquely branded product.

ARE BRANDS RATIONAL?

Coca-Cola is one of the most enduring, powerful brands in U.S. commercial history. The core product is colored, flavored, carbonated sugar water. The augmented branded product is a delightful, refreshing, reputable, unique-tasting drink available worldwide, based on a secret formula that consumers are willing to pay up to twice as much for when compared to unbranded grocery store cola. Coca-Cola is a marketing-created micro-monopoly. There is only one Coke and only one supplier. Why would consumers pay twice as much for Coke compared to unbranded cola drinks? Is this rational?

The answer is a qualified yes. Brands introduce market efficiency by reducing the search costs and decision-making costs of consumers. Strong brands signal strong products that work. Brands carry information. Confronted with many different drinks, the choice of Coke can be made quickly, without much thought, and with the assurance that you will have the drinking experience you expect based on prior use of the product. Brands reduce consumer risk and uncertainty in a crowded marketplace. Brands are like an insurance policy against nasty surprises in the marketplace for which consumers willingly pay a premium—better safe than sorry.

The ability of brands to become a corporate asset (to attain brand equity) based on future anticipated premiums paid by consumers also provides an incentive for firms to build products that serve customer needs better than other products. Therefore, although brands create micro-monopolies, increase market costs, and lead to above-average returns on investment (monopoly rents), they also introduce market efficiencies for the consumer.

For business firms, brands are a major source of revenue and are obviously rational. Brands lower customer acquisition costs and increase customer retention. The stronger the brand reputation, the easier it is to attract new customers. **Customer acquisition costs** refer to the overall costs of converting a prospect into a consumer, and include all marketing and advertising costs. **Customer retention costs** are those costs incurred in convincing an existing customer to purchase again. In general, it is much more expensive to acquire a new customer than to retain an existing customer. For instance, Reichheld and Schefter calculated that e-commerce sites lose from $20 to $80 on each customer in the first year because of the high cost of acquiring a customer, but potentially can make up for this loss in later years by retaining loyal customers (Reichheld and Schefter, 2000). In some instances, however, e-commerce companies have gone out of business before they ever reached that point.

A successful brand can constitute a long-lasting, impregnable unfair competitive advantage. As we discussed in Chapter 2, a competitive advantage is considered "fair" when it is based on innovation, efficient production processes, or other factors that theoretically can be imitated and/or purchased in the marketplace by competitors. An "unfair competitive advantage" cannot be purchased in the factor markets and includes such things as patents, copyrights, secret processes, unusually skilled or dedicated employees and managers, and, of course, brand names. Brands cannot be purchased (unless one buys the entire company).

customer acquisition costs

the overall costs of converting a prospect into a consumer

customer retention costs

costs incurred in convincing an existing customer to purchase again

DO BRANDS LAST FOREVER?

Brands, however, do not necessarily last forever, and the micro-monopolies they create may not be stable over the long term. In a study of brand endurance, Golder found that between 1923 and 1997, only 23% of the firms that ranked first in market share in 1923 were still in the market-leading position in 1997, while 28% of the leaders failed altogether (Golder, 2000). Less than 10% of the Fortune 500 companies of 1917 still exists (Starbuck and Nystrom, 1997). Life at the top is sweet, but often short, and market efficiency is restored long-term as entrepreneurs exploit new technologies and new public tastes at a faster rate than the incumbent market leaders.

CAN BRANDS SURVIVE THE INTERNET? BRANDS AND PRICE DISPERSION ON THE INTERNET

As we noted in Chapter 1, during the early days of e-commerce, many academics and business consultants postulated that the Web would lead to a new world of information symmetry and "frictionless" commerce. In this world, newly empowered customers, using intelligent shopping agents and the nearly infinite product and price information available on the Internet, would shop around the world (and around the clock) with minimal effort, driving prices down to their marginal cost and driving intermediaries out of the market as customers began to deal directly with producers (Wigand and Benjamin, 1995; Rayport and Sviolka, 1995; Evans and Wurster, 1999; Sinha 2000).[1] The result was supposed to be an instance of the "**Law of One Price**": with complete price transparency in a perfect information marketplace, one world price for every product would emerge. "Frictionless commerce" would, of course, mean the end of marketing based on brands.

But it didn't work out this way. Price has not proven to be the only determinant of online consumer behavior. E-commerce firms continue to rely heavily on brands to attract customers and charge premium prices. For instance, online retailers use "flash pricing," where some popular products are marked down significantly for a day or even a few hours to create market buzz, and then are increased significantly the next day. Internet technologies can be used to infinitely differentiate products by using personalization, customization, and community marketing techniques (described in the next section), thereby overcoming the price-lowering effects of lower search costs and a large number of worldwide suppliers for goods. By introducing information asymmetries into the marketplace, merchants can avoid direct price competition.

Whether or not prices are lower online than offline is still a point of debate. For instance, Bailey and Brynjolfsson (1997) found that prices for books, music CDs, and software were not substantially lower at e-commerce sites than in traditional stores or catalogs (see also Clay, et al., 1999 for similar results). Later studies found that prices at e-commerce sites were 9%–16% lower than at conventional retail outlets for musical CDs (depending on whether taxes and shipping costs were included in the price), but also found substantial price dispersion—nearly as much as in traditional markets for the same goods (Brynjolfsson and Smith, 2000). Other research finds that online prices vary with season, and that during the holiday season of October-December online prices rise, and then fall in the Spring. This phenomenon is not dissimilar from traditional retail stores.

Price dispersion refers to the difference between the highest and lowest prices in a market. In a perfect market, with perfect information, there is not supposed to be any price dispersion. Other evidence suggests that many suppliers and price comparisons can overwhelm consumers, and that consumers achieve efficiencies by quickly purchasing from a trusted, high-price provider. In general, the most frequently visited and used e-commerce sites are not the lowest-price sites (Smith, et al., 1999).

Law of One Price
with complete price transparency in a perfect information marketplace, there will be one world price for every product

price dispersion
the difference between the highest and lowest prices in a market

---

[1]The theory of frictionless commerce is not unique to the Internet. Computerized stock and options markets over the last 20 years have also attempted to achieve low-friction transactions.

Research on brands and price dispersion illustrates the complexities of Internet marketing as well as the continuing power of brands, customer loyalty, and information symmetries. Some found that online prices were higher relative to offline prices (Baye, et al., 2002a; Scholten and Smith, 2002). Others found that, in general, online prices were less than offline prices depending on the product category and other variables. Price dispersion, a measure of competitiveness, typically is less for commodities (memory chips) than for books or other differentiated products. Moreover, Internet-savvy users systematically seek out the lowest prices by visiting shopping comparison sites, while other Internet users choose not to inform themselves and just purchase from a well-known online brand like Amazon. Sellers invest heavily in ways to differentiate their product or service—they create online brands that permit charging a premium for many products. The result is large differences in price sensitivity for the same products. For instance, researchers estimate that a 1% increase in prices at Amazon decreases sales by about 0.5%, while at Barnes & Noble, a 1% increase in prices results in a decrease in sales of about 4% (Baye, et al., 2002b). Price dispersion is also heavily influenced by "market thickness," the number of competitors selling the same undifferentiated goods. The more sellers in an online market (like photography), the less the price dispersion (Leiter and Warin, 2007). Nash-equilibrium.com, a site run by economists Michael Bay, John Morgan, and Patrick Sholten, charts market thickness, relative price dispersion, and other economic indicators on the Web (see **Figure 6.9**).

library effect

an attempt to appeal to consumers on the basis of the total number of products offered

Another tactic used by online sellers is the "**library effect**" (or "catalog effect"). How much is it worth to you to shop at a store that has everything? Just one stop, and chances are that you can get what you want. Would you rather visit a library with 10 million volumes, or one with a few hundred thousand? The number of books on sale at Amazon is 23 times larger than the number of books found at a typical Barnes & Noble superstore, and 57 times larger than the number of books typically found at a large independent bookstore. One analysis put the gain in economic value (or "consumer welfare") produced by online bookstores at about $1 billion annually, five times larger than the gain in economic value produced by lower prices on the Internet (Brynjolfsson, Smith, and Hu, 2003). Stores such as Amazon make the size of their product offerings a part of their brand image and marketing communications in order to charge premium prices. Obviously, library effects apply only where there is a large number of SKUs or products available to sell—like music, DVDs, CDs, books, travel arrangements, airline tickets, and many of the products available on the Web—but not for unique collector items.

We can conclude from the research evidence that brands are alive and well on the Web, that consumers are willing to pay premium prices for products and services they perceive as differentiated, that consumers are willing to shop online as opposed to offline at stores where product variety is high, and that in many instances Web prices may be higher than those available in retail stores because of the premium consumers will pay for convenience. The evidence also suggests some solid reasons for the adage popular during the early days of e-commerce: "Get Big Fast." Selection, not price, may be your e-commerce site's biggest advantage and largest contributor to consumer welfare. Another strategic way to look at these data is to expect growing ownership concentration among Internet merchants as they pursue scale economies and library effects that derive from size.

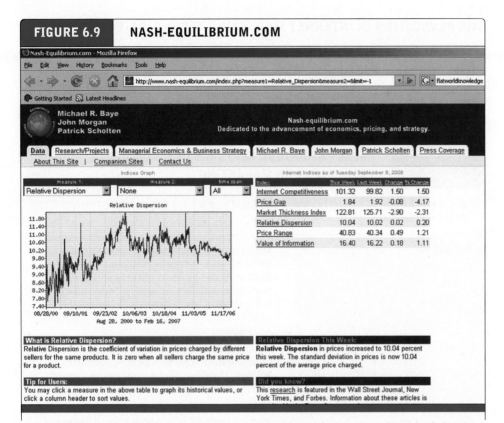

FIGURE 6.9   NASH-EQUILIBRIUM.COM

Nash-equilibrium.com is a Web site run by economists Michael Baye, John Morgan, and Patrick Scholten that provides a variety of economic indices related to the Internet, including Internet competitiveness, price gaps, price ranges, and relative dispersion statistics.

SOURCE: Nash-equilibrium.com, 2008.

Now that you have covered these basic concepts, the next section describes what makes Internet marketing different from ordinary marketing.

6.3   INTERNET MARKETING TECHNOLOGIES

Internet marketing has many similarities to and differences from ordinary marketing. The objective of Internet marketing—as in all marketing—is to build customer relationships so that the firm can achieve above-average returns (both by offering superior products or services and by communicating the feature set to the consumer). But Internet marketing is also very different from ordinary marketing because the nature of the medium and its capabilities are so different from anything that has come before. In order to understand just how different Internet marketing can be and in what ways, you first need to become familiar with some basic Internet marketing technologies.

In Chapter 7, we will describe marketing communications channels, and advertising, including search engine marketing, which tends to be used more for sales rather than marketing and branding.

THE REVOLUTION IN INTERNET MARKETING TECHNOLOGIES

In Chapter 1, we listed eight unique features of e-commerce technology. **Table 6.8** describes how marketing has changed as a result of these new technical capabilities.

On balance, the Internet has had three very broad impacts on marketing. First, the Internet, as a communications medium, has broadened the scope of

TABLE 6.8	IMPACT OF UNIQUE FEATURES OF E-COMMERCE TECHNOLOGY ON MARKETING
E-COMMERCE TECHNOLOGY DIMENSION	**SIGNIFICANCE FOR MARKETING**
Ubiquity	Marketing communications have been extended to the home, work, and mobile platforms; geographic limits on marketing have been reduced. The marketplace has been replaced by "marketspace" and is removed from a temporal and geographic location. Customer convenience has been enhanced, and shopping costs have been reduced.
Global reach	Worldwide customer service and marketing communications have been enabled. Potentially hundreds of millions of consumers can be reached with marketing messages.
Universal standards	The cost of delivering marketing messages and receiving feedback from users is reduced because of shared, global standards of the Internet.
Richness	Video, audio, and text marketing messages can be integrated into a single marketing message and consuming experience.
Interactivity	Consumers can be engaged in a dialog, dynamically adjusting the experience to the consumer, and making the consumer a co-producer of the goods and services being sold.
Information density	Fine-grained, highly detailed information on consumers' real-time behavior can be gathered and analyzed for the first time. "Data mining" Internet technology permits the analysis of terabytes of consumer data everyday for marketing purposes
Personalization/Customization	This feature potentially enables product and service differentiation down to the level of the individual, thus strengthening the ability of marketers to create brands.
Social technology	User-generated content and social networking sites, along with blogs, have created new, large, online audiences where the content is provided by users. These audiences have greatly expanded the opportunity for marketers to reach new potential customers in a nontraditional media format. Entirely new kinds of marketing techniques are evolving. These same technologies expose marketers to the risk of falling afoul of popular opinion by providing more market power to users who now can "talk back."

marketing communications—in the sense of the number of people who can be easily reached. Second, the Internet has increased the richness of marketing communications by combining text, video, and audio content into rich messages. Arguably, the Web is richer as a medium than even television or video because of the complexity of messages available, the enormous content accessible on a wide range of subjects, and the ability of users to interactively control the experience. Third, the Internet has greatly expanded the information intensity of the marketplace by providing marketers (and customers) with unparalleled fine-grained, detailed, real-time information about consumers as they transact in the marketplace.

WEB TRANSACTION LOGS

How can e-commerce sites know more than a department store does about consumer behavior? A primary source of consumer information on the Web is the transaction log maintained by all Web servers. A **transaction log** records user activity at a Web site. The transaction log is built into Web server software. **Figure 6.10** shows one second from the Web transaction log for Azimuth-interactive.com, a Web-based software training site. The log has been edited to eliminate the names of real persons and show only a few entries for each visitor. In fact, visitors usually create tens or hundreds of entries in the log, one entry for each page or object they request.

Table 6.9 lists the data elements contained in a Web transaction log and shows how these elements can be used in marketing, using the first entry in the transaction log in Figure 6.10 as an example.

Webtrends, discussed in Chapter 4, is a leading log file analysis tool. Transaction log data becomes even more useful when combined with two other visitor-generated data trails: registration forms and the shopping cart database. Users are enticed through various means (such as free gifts or special services) to fill out registration forms. **Registration forms** gather personal data on name, address, phone, zip code, e-mail address (usually required), and other optional self-confessed information on interests and tastes. When users make a purchase, they also enter additional information into the shopping cart database. The **shopping cart database** captures all the item selection, purchase, and payment data. Other potential additional sources of data are information users submit on product forms, contribute to chat groups, or send via e-mail messages using the "Contact Us" option on most sites.

For a Web site that has a million visitors per month, and where, on average, a visitor makes 15 page requests per visit, there will be 15 million entries in the log each month. These transaction logs, coupled with data from the registration forms and shopping cart database, represent a treasure trove of marketing information for both individual sites and the online industry as a whole. Nearly all the new Internet marketing capabilities are based on these data-gathering tools. For instance, here are just a few of the interesting marketing questions that can be answered by examining a site's Web transaction logs, registration forms, and shopping cart database:

- What are the major patterns of interest and purchase for groups and individuals?
- After the home page, where do most users go first, and then second and third?

transaction log
records user activity at a Web site

registration forms
gather personal data on name, address, phone, ZIP code, e-mail address, and other optional self-confessed information on interests and tastes

shopping cart database
captures all the item selection, purchase, and payment data

FIGURE 6.10	ONE SECOND FROM THE WEB TRANSACTION LOG OF AZIMUTH-INTERACTIVE.COM

dsl254-068-173.nyc1.dsl.speakeasy.net - - [22/Oct/2009:11:29:32 -0400] "GET /masthead.cgi?page=hompage&ad=1 HTTP/1.1" 200 3646 "http://www.azimuth-interactive.com/" "Mozilla/5.0 (Windows; U; Windows NT 5.0; en-US; rv:1.6) Gecko/20040113"

dsl254-068-173.nyc1.dsl.speakeasy.net - - [22/Oct/2009:11:29:32 -0400] "GET /images/newredspacer.gif HTTP/1.1" 200 35 "http://www.azimuth-interactive.com/homepage2.php" "Mozilla/5.0 (Windows; U; Windows NT 5.0; en-US; rv:1.6) Gecko/20040113"

dsl254-068-173.nyc1.dsl.speakeasy.net - - [22/Oct/2009:11:29:32 -0400] "GET /images/azimuthweblogo2.gif HTTP/1.1" 200 1494 "http://www.azimuth-interactive.com/masthead.cgi?page=hompage&ad=1" "Mozilla/5.0 (Windows; U; Windows NT 5.0; en-US; rv:1.6) Gecko/20040113"

dsl254-068-173.nyc1.dsl.speakeasy.net - - [22/Oct/2009:11:29:32 -0400] "GET /images/newmastheadart.gif HTTP/1.1" 200 26349 "http://www.azimuth-interactive.com/masthead.cgi?page=hompage&ad=1" "Mozilla/5.0 (Windows; U; Windows NT 5.0; en-US; rv:1.6) Gecko/20040113"

dsl254-068-173.nyc1.dsl.speakeasy.net - - [22/Oct/2009:11:29:32 -0400] "GET /images/whitespacer.gif HTTP/1.1" 200 45 "http://www.azimuth-interactive.com/masthead.cgi?page=hompage&ad=1" "Mozilla/5.0 (Windows; U; Windows NT 5.0; en-US; rv:1.6) Gecko/20040113"

dsl254-068-173.nyc1.dsl.speakeasy.net - - [22/Oct/2009:11:29:32 -0400] "GET /images/corpsolutionsnav.gif HTTP/1.1" 200 206 "http://www.azimuth-interactive.com/masthead.cgi?page=hompage&ad=1" "Mozilla/5.0 (Windows; U; Windows NT 5.0; en-US; rv:1.6) Gecko/20040113"

dsl254-068-173.nyc1.dsl.speakeasy.net - - [22/Oct/2009:11:29:32 -0400] "GET /images/softcoursesnav.gif HTTP/1.1" 200 239 "http://www.azimuth-interactive.com/masthead.cgi?page=hompage&ad=1" "Mozilla/5.0 (Windows; U; Windows NT 5.0; en-US; rv:1.6) Gecko/20040113"

dsl254-068-173.nyc1.dsl.speakeasy.net - - [22/Oct/2009:11:29:32 -0400] "GET /images/coursebooksnav.gif HTTP/1.1" 200 165 "http://www.azimuth-interactive.com/masthead.cgi?page=hompage&ad=1" "Mozilla/5.0 (Windows; U; Windows NT 5.0; en-US; rv:1.6) Gecko/20040113"

dsl254-068-173.nyc1.dsl.speakeasy.net - - [22/Oct/2009:11:29:32 -0400] "GET /images/onlinecoursesnav.gif HTTP/1.1" 200 174 "http://www.azimuth-interactive.com/masthead.cgi?page=hompage&ad=1" "Mozilla/5.0 (Windows; U; Windows NT 5.0; en-US; rv:1.6) Gecko/20040113"

dsl254-068-173.nyc1.dsl.speakeasy.net - - [22/Oct/2009:11:29:32 -0400] "GET /images/onlinetestingnav.gif HTTP/1.1" 200 175 "http://www.azimuth-interactive.com/masthead.cgi?page=hompage&ad=1" "Mozilla/5.0 (Windows; U; Windows NT 5.0; en-US; rv:1.6) Gecko/20040113"

TABLE 6.9	MARKETING USES OF DATA FROM WEB TRANSACTION LOGS
DATA ELEMENT	**MARKETING USE**
IP address of the visitor: dsl254-068-173.nyc1.dsl.speakeasy.net	Can be used to send return e-mails for marketing when the visitor is using a dedicated URL as opposed to a dial-in modem. Dial-in modems use temporary IPs and cannot be used for return mail.
Date and time stamp: [22/Oct/2009:11:29:32 -0400]	Used to understand patterns in the time of day and year of consumer activity.
Pages and objects requested and visited ("Get" statements): "GET /masthead.cgi?page=hompage& ad=1 HTTP/1.1"	Used to understand what this specific consumer was interested in finding (the clickstream). Can be used later to send "personalized" messages, "customized products," or simply return mail regarding related products.
Response of site server: 200	Used to monitor for broken links, pages not returned.
Size of pages sent (bytes of information): 3646	Used to understand capacity demands on servers and communications links.
Name of page or site from which the consumer came to this site: "http://www.azimuth-interactive.com/"	Used to understand how consumers come to a site, and once there, their patterns of behavior.
Name and version of the browser used: "Mozilla/5.0 (Windows; U; Windows NT 5.0; en-US; rv:1.6) Gecko/20040113"	Useful for understanding target browsers, ensuring your site is compatible with browsers being used.
Name and version of the operating system of the consumer's client computer: (Windows; U; Windows NT 5.0; en-US; rv:1.6)	Useful for understanding the capabilities of target client computers; more recent operating systems indicates new computer, or technically savvy user.
History of all the pages and objects visited during a session at the site.	Used to establish personal profiles of individuals, analyze site activity, and understand the most popular pages and resources.

- What are the interests of specific individuals (those we can identify)?
- How can we make it easier for people to use our site so they can find what they want?
- How can we change the design of the site to encourage visitors to purchase our high-margin products?
- Where are visitors coming from (and how can we optimize our presence on these referral sites)?
- How can we personalize our messages, offerings, and products to individual users?

Answering these questions requires some additional technologies. As noted by Jupiter Research, businesses can choke on the massive quantity of information found in a typical site's log file. We describe some technologies that help firms more effectively utilize this information below.

SUPPLEMENTING THE LOGS: COOKIES AND WEB BUGS

While transaction logs create the foundation of online data collection, they are supplemented by two other data collection techniques: cookies and Web bugs. As described in Chapter 3, a cookie is small text file that Web sites place on the hard disk of visitors' client computers every time they visit, and during the visit, as specific pages are visited. Cookies allow a Web site to store data on a user's computer and then later retrieve it. The Firefox Cookies dialog box in **Figure 6.11** shows the components in a typical cookie file on a client computer (in this case, a cookie from the *New York Times* Web site). The cookie typically includes a name, a unique ID number for each visitor that is stored on the user's computer, the domain (which specifies the Web server/domain that can access the cookie), a path (if a cookie comes from a particular part of a Web site instead of the main page, a path will be given), a security setting that provides whether the cookie can only be transmitted by a secure server, and an expiration date (not required). First-party cookies come from the same domain name as the page the user is visiting, while third-party cookies come from another domain, such as ad serving or adware companies, affiliate marketers, or spyware servers.

A cookie provides Web marketers with a very quick means of identifying the customer and understanding his or her prior behavior at the site. Web sites use cookies to determine how many people are visiting the site, whether they are new or repeat visitors, and how often they have visited, although this data may be somewhat

FIGURE 6.11 **FIREFOX COOKIES DIALOG BOX**

Firefox's Cookies dialog box identifies the various components of a typical cookie file on your computer.

inaccurate because people share computers, they often use more than one computer, and cookies may have been inadvertently or intentionally erased. Cookies make shopping carts and "quick checkout" options possible by allowing a site to keep track of a user as he or she adds to the shopping cart. Each item added to the shopping cart is stored in the site's database along with the visitor's unique ID value.

The location of cookie files on a computer depends on the browser version being used. Cookie files can be accessed on a computer using Mozilla Firefox by opening the Tools menu, clicking Options, selecting the Privacy tab, and clicking the Show Cookies button. Firefox neatly organizes all your cookies in an alphabetically arranged file based on the name of the vendor placing the cookie. You can delete individual cookies or all cookies in Firefox. In Internet Explorer 7.0, and even more so with IE 8.0 released in 2008, users have a bit more control over the level of privacy. You can set the level of privacy you desire all the way from rejecting all cookies (Block All Cookies option) or accepting some cookies from third and first parties if they have a privacy policy in place (Medium) or accepting all cookies (Accept All Cookies option). In Internet Explorer 7.0, select Tools, Internet Options, and then the Privacy tab. You adjust the level of privacy you want by using the slider. In the latest browsers, users can opt for a privacy mode that extinguishes all records of browsing activity on the client computer.

Reports from a variety of Internet research firms indicate that most Americans do not delete cookies from their computers in large part because around 70% of U.S. computer users do not know how to do this (eMarketer, 2008c). Nevertheless, a large study of Yahoo (first-party) and DoubleClick (third-party) cookies in over 400,000 U.S. households found that about 58% of the cookies placed by these firms had been reset (deleted) (eMarketer Inc., 2007c). Over time, as users become more familiar with cookies, acceptance levels have gone up, and the number of users who report "never blocking cookies" has risen (Insight Express, 2008). The more cookies are deleted, the less accurate are Web page and ad server metrics, and the less likely marketers will be able to understand who is visiting their sites or where they came from.

Although cookies are site-specific (a Web site can only receive the data it has stored on a client computer and cannot look at any other cookie), when combined with Web bugs, they can be used to create cross-site profiles. We discuss this practice further in the "Advertising Networks" section later in this chapter.

Web bugs are tiny (1-pixel) graphic files embedded in e-mail messages and on Web sites. Web bugs are used to automatically transmit information about the user and the page being viewed to a monitoring server. For instance, when a recipient opens an e-mail in HTML format or opens a Web page, a message is sent to a server calling for graphic information. This tells the marketer that the e-mail was opened, indicating that the recipient was at least interested in the subject header. Web bugs are often clear or colored white so they are not visible to the recipient. You may be able to determine if a Web page is using Web bugs by using the View Source option of your browser and examining the IMG (image) tags on the page. As noted above, Web bugs are typically 1 pixel in size and contain the URL of a server that differs from the one that served the page itself (see http://w2.eff.org/Privacy/Marketing/web_bug.html). *Insight on Society: Marketing with Web Bugs* examines the use of Web bugs.

INSIGHT ON SOCIETY

MARKETING WITH WEB BUGS

Images called "clear GIFs," "Web beacons," and "invisible GIFs" don't sound too threatening. But when they're referred to as "Web bugs," Internet users begin to get a better sense of their true purpose. Web bugs come in several different varieties, but the basic idea is that they are objects (in the form of an image or a tiny pixel) that are embedded invisibly on Web pages and in an e-mail that cause a part of the Web page (usually that image or pixel) to be retrieved by a completely different third-party Web site by sending a signal to that third-party site. As a result, the third-party Web site knows that you visited the original Web site, and they can know much more if they want to, such as where you've been and what you've bought.

Marketers using Web bugs claim they have two purposes. One is to improve the efficiency of display ads by aiding in collecting detailed information about Web usage, including how many visitors a particular site has had, which pages on a site are most popular, and which banner ads are providing the best results. A second purpose involves improving the efficiency of marketing and advertising by targeting ads to individuals based on their prior behavior on the Web. This is variously called "behavioral targeting," "targeting advertising," "performance driven advertising," or what Yahoo calls and sells as SmartAds. The idea is to display banner ads to individuals no matter where they browse on the Web based on their personal preferences revealed in prior Web visits, searches, and purchases. In general, banner ads have very poor response rates, less than 1%, much less than search engine ads. A Microsoft-sponsored study found that targeted ads increased click-through rates six fold.

Search engine marketing and portal companies such as Google, Microsoft, and AOL use them, as do advertising networks such as DoubleClick. Canadian Web security firm Security Space periodically samples over 15 million Web pages from 1.5 million Web domains to identify the top 100 bug-using sites. The leading Web bugger is Google Analytics followed by Google Syndication, Google, Yahoo, Amazon, and your favorite Web 2.0 sites, YouTube, Photobucket, Flickr, and GeoCities. Anytime you use these sites, your every move is bugged. SecuritySpace also collects data on Web traffic that is bugged to identify who is bugging the most Web traffic. The leading traffic bugger is the advertising network DoubleClick, followed by Akamai, other ad networks, ISPs such as Lycos, and of course, Google and Amazon. Collectively, these sites capture a significant portion of the Web behavior of 124 million daily Internet users in the United States.

In 2009, Google announced the launch of "interest-based advertising," which will target banner ads on its DoubleClick ad network based not just on context but on the Web pages you previously viewed. The system is driven by Web bugs and cookies placed on your browser, and you may end up receiving ads based on another user's behavior (e.g., your children) using that browser. Privacy advocates fear that interest-based advertising is just the first step toward more highly targeted advertising that draws upon everything Google knows about your behavior on Google sites, including YouTube, Picassa, and other applications. Mike Zaneis, vice president of public policy at the Internet Advertising Bureau, acknowledges that highly targeted advertising can be creepy. But, he says, "creepiness is not in and of itself a consumer harm."

(continued)

Google does allow users to opt-out of the DoubleClick targeted advertising program at the Google Privacy Center. But to find the Center, you would need to read this book or other sources. Google's Chief Privacy Officer claims its personal information policy is based on three bedrock principles: "We don't sell it. We don't collect it without permission. We don't use it to serve ads without permission." He failed to note that you have to opt-out at the Privacy Center to exercise your permission, otherwise you're in.

Web bugs are used to track billions of monthly advertising promotions. Without such data, advertisers argue, they would be unable to determine which marketing techniques to use. All information collected is anonymous—so they say—and, on its own, cannot be linked back to any particular individual. For that reason, advertisers claim Web bugs are innocuous. Yet offline marketing information obtained from supermarkets and credit companies and collected by firms such as Acxiom is routinely sold to firms for targeted marketing. Therefore, there is no reason to believe firms abstain from mixing online behavioral data with offline personal information.

If Web bugs are so harmless, why go to the trouble of hiding them? Why not just let people know the site is bugged, perhaps using a yellow caution sign on each bug? That's what privacy advocates are asking. And what they've learned is that although Web bugs may have been designed to simply provide traffic counts, when combined with information from third-party sources, bugs can give marketers an all too complete picture of an individual consumer—right down to home address, online account balances, account numbers, and whatever else the user has entered into his or her computer.

Bugs enable marketers to know who's online, which Web sites they've visited, where they've spent money, what their address is, and more. When the technology is used by a network of sites linked to a third-party, such as DoubleClick, consumer profiling becomes even more detailed, leading to a potentially significant loss of privacy. Use of Web bug technology is rising sharply as marketers seek to gain a foothold in Web 2.0 communities such as Facebook, MySpace, YouTube, and Photobucket. Personal pages and user-generated content are favorite locations for buggers to place their works. Collecting information on consumers is nothing new, but the extent to which data can now be accumulated and combined to form very specific profiles of Internet users has led to calls for regulation.

The Privacy Foundation has issued guidelines for Web bug usage. The guidelines suggest that Web bugs should be visible as an icon on the screen, the icon should be labeled to indicate its function, and it should identify the name of the company that placed the Web bug on the page. In addition, if a user clicks on the Web bug, it should display a disclosure statement indicating what data is being collected, how the data is used after it is collected, what companies receive the data, what other data the Web bug is combined with, and whether or not a cookie is associated with the Web bug. Users should be able to opt-out of any data collection done by the Web bug, and the Web bug should not be used to collect information from Web pages of a sensitive nature, such as medical, financial, job-related, or sexual matters.

In an effort to address growing congressional concerns about privacy, and build consumer trust online, an industry advertising group, the Network Advertising Initiative (NAI), released self-regulatory guidelines for the industry. Major advertising industry groups have adopted Self Regulatory Principles for Online Behavioral Advertising that emphasize transparency (tell consumers how you use their information), and choice (opt-in, and opt-out). The NAI renamed Web bugs as "Web beacons" and requires online firms to notify customers of Web bug usage

(continued)

whether in e-mail or on Web sites, state the purpose of their use, and disclose any data that could be released to third parties. The NAI also called for users to be given a choice (whether opt-in or opt-out) of any release of personally identifiable information (PII) to third parties, and to provide an opt-in choice for any release of information related to PII. These restrictions do not apply to the Web site itself (agents). In addition, the NAI provides a capability open to all Web users to opt out of online advertising networks collecting non-personal information on them. However, for this to work, users need to have a cookie downloaded to their browser that will inform the networks not to collect information on this user.

Currently, Internet users are not protected by government regulation against Web bugs or other forms of behavioral targeting.

SOURCES: "NAI Principles Roadmap for OBA," Networkadvertising.org, September, 2009; "The Google Opt-Out Village Launches [Parody Video]," by Adam Ostrow, August 11th, 2009. Mashable.com; "The Paradox of Privacy," by Eric Pfanner, *New York Times*, July 13, 2009; "Network Advertising Initiative Applauds New Self-Regulation Principles by Industry Associations," Network Advertising Initiative, July 2, 2009; "What Google Knows About You," by Richard Mitchell, *Computerworld*, May 11, 2009; "Google to Offer Ads Based on Interests," by Miguel Helft, *New York Times*, March 21, 2009; "More Web Ads Improve Their Aim," by Jessica Vascellaro and Emily Steel, *Wall Street Journal*, February 2, 2009; "A Push to Limit the Tracking of Web Surfers' Clicks," by Louise Story, *New York Times*, March 20, 2008; "Web Bug Report," SecuritySpace, October 1, 2007.

DATABASES, DATA WAREHOUSES, AND DATA MINING: DEVELOPING PROFILES

database
a software application that stores records and attributes

Databases, data warehouses, data mining, and the variety of marketing decision-making techniques loosely called *profiling* are at the heart of the revolution in Internet marketing. Together, these techniques attempt to identify precisely who the online customer is and what they want, and then, to fulfill the customer's criteria exactly. These techniques are more powerful and far more precise and fine-grained than the gross levels of demographic and market segmentation techniques used in mass marketing media or by telemarketing.

database management system (DBMS)
a software application used by organizations to create, maintain, and access databases

In order to understand the data in transaction logs, registration forms, shopping carts, cookies, Web bugs, and other sources, Internet marketers need massively powerful and capacious databases, database management systems, and data modeling tools. Just examine the transaction log in Figure 6.10 again, and then imagine trying to find the patterns in millions of entries each day!

structured query language (SQL)
an industry-standard database query and manipulation language used in relational databases

Databases

relational databases
represent data as two-dimensional tables with records organized in rows and attributes in columns; data within different tables can be flexibly related as long as the tables share a common data element

The first step in interpreting huge transaction streams is to store the information systematically. A **database** is a software application that stores records and attributes. A telephone book is a physical database that stores records of individuals and their attributes such as names, addresses, and phone numbers. A **database management system (DBMS)** is a software application used by organizations to create, maintain, and access databases. The most common DBMS are DB2 from IBM and a variety of SQL databases from Oracle, Sybase, and other providers. **structured query language (SQL)** is an industry-standard database query and manipulation language used in relational databases. **Relational databases** such as DB2 and SQL represent data as two-dimensional tables with records organized in rows, and attributes in columns, much like a spreadsheet. The tables—and all the data in them—can be flexibly related to one another as long as the tables share a common data element.

Relational databases are extraordinarily flexible and allow marketers and other managers to view and analyze data from different perspectives very quickly. **Figure 6.12** illustrates a relational database view of customers. The data are organized into four tables: customer, order, product, and supplier. The tables all share at least one data element. Using this model, it would be possible to query the database for a list of all customers who bought a certain product, or to message a supplier when the inventory falls below a certain level (and message a customer automatically via e-mail that the product is temporarily out of stock).

Data Warehouses and Data Mining

A **data warehouse** is a database that collects a firm's transactional and customer data in a single location for offline analysis by marketers and site managers. The data originate in many core operational areas of the firm, such as Web site transaction logs, shopping carts, point-of-sale terminals (product scanners) in stores, warehouse

data warehouse
a database that collects a firm's transactional and customer data in a single location for offline analysis

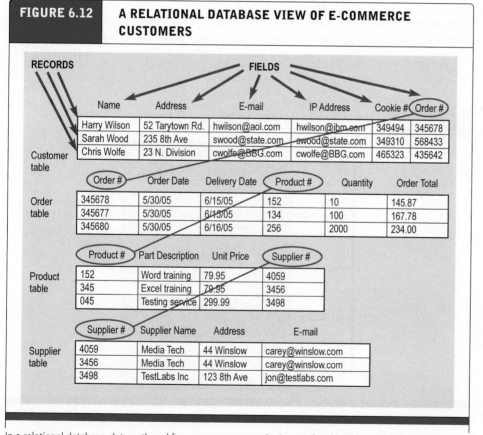

FIGURE 6.12   A RELATIONAL DATABASE VIEW OF E-COMMERCE CUSTOMERS

In a relational database, data gathered from an e-commerce site is stored on hard drives and presented to managers of sites in the form of interrelated tables.

inventory levels, field sales reports, external scanner data supplied by third parties, and financial payment data. The purpose of a data warehouse is to gather all the firm's transaction and customer data into one logical repository where it can be analyzed and modeled by managers without disrupting or taxing the firm's primary transactional systems and databases. Data warehouses grow quickly into storage repositories containing terabytes of data (trillions of bytes) on consumer behavior at a firm's stores and Web sites. With a data warehouse, firms can answer such questions as: What products are the most profitable by region and city? What regional marketing campaigns are working? How effective is store promotion of the firm's Web site? Data warehouses can provide business managers with a more complete awareness of customers through data that can be accessed quickly.

data mining

a set of analytical techniques that look for patterns in the data of a database or data warehouse, or seek to model the behavior of customers

customer profile

a description of the typical behavior of a customer or a group of customers at a Web site

Data mining is a set of different analytical techniques that look for patterns in the data of a database or data warehouse, or seek to model the behavior of customers. Web site data can be "mined" to develop profiles of visitors and customers (see **Figure 6.13**). A **customer profile** is simply a set of rules that describe the typical behavior of a customer or a group of customers at a Web site. Customer profiles help to identify the patterns in group and individual behavior that occur online as millions of visitors use a firm's Web site. For example, almost every financial transaction you engage in is processed by a data mining application to detect fraud. Phone companies closely monitor your cell phone use as well to detect stolen phones and unusual calling patterns. Financial institutions and cell phone firms use data mining to develop fraud profiles. When a user's behavior conforms to a fraud profile, the transaction is not allowed or terminated (Mobasher, 2007).

FIGURE 6.13   **DATA MINING AND PERSONALIZATION**

Personalization of content and marketing is based on data mining techniques that can produce reliable profiles of individual consumer behavior.

SOURCE: Adomavicius and Tuzhilin, 2001b. ©2001 IEEE.

There are many different types of data mining. The simplest type is **query-driven data mining**, which is based on specific queries. For instance, based on hunches of marketers who suspect a relationship in the database or who need to answer a specific question, such as "What is the relationship between time of day and purchases of various products at the Web site?", marketers can easily query the data warehouse and produce a database table that rank-orders the top 10 products sold at a Web site by each hour of the day. Marketers can then change the content of the Web site to stimulate more sales by highlighting different products over time or placing particular products on the home page at certain times of day or night.

Another form of data mining is model-driven. **Model-driven data mining** involves the use of a model that analyzes the key variables of interest to decision makers. For example, marketers may want to reduce the inventory carried on the Web site by removing unprofitable items that do not sell well. A financial model can be built showing the profitability of each product on the site so that an informed decision can be made.

A more interesting kind of data mining is rule-based. **Rule-based data mining** examines demographic and transactional data of groups and individuals at a Web site and attempts to derive general rules of behavior for visitors. There are factual and behavioral approaches as well as different levels of granularity, from market segments down to individuals. In the *factual approach*, factual demographic and transactional data (purchase price, products purchased) and material viewed at the site are analyzed and stored in a customer profile table in order to segment the marketplace into well-defined groups. For instance, female customers who purchased items worth more than $50 in an average visit and who viewed travel articles might be shown a vacation travel advertisement. The rules are specified by marketing managers as a set of *filters* based on their expert opinions, as well as trial and error, and are applied to aggregate groups of visitors or market segments. There can be thousands of different types of visitors, and hence thousands of marketing decisions or filters that marketers have to make.

A different *behavioral approach* to data mining is **collaborative filtering** (see *Insight on Technology: The Long Tail: Big Hits and Big Misses*). Behavioral approaches try to "let the data speak for itself" rather than impose rules set by expert marketers. Collaborative filtering was first developed at the MIT Media Lab and commercialized by an MIT Media Lab–backed start-up company, Firefly. Rather than having expert marketers make decisions based on their own "rules of thumb," experience, and corporate needs (a need to move old inventory, for instance), site visitors collaboratively classify themselves based on common selections. The idea is that people classify themselves into "affinity groups" characterized by common interests. A query to the database can isolate the individuals who all purchased the same products. Later, based on purchases by other members of the affinity group, the system can recommend purchases based on what other people in the group have bought recently. For example, visitors who all purchased books on amateur flying could be pitched a video that illustrates small-plane flying techniques. And then later, if several members of this "amateur flying interest group" purchased books on parachuting, then all members of the group would be pitched a recommendation to buy parachuting books, based on what other people collaboratively "like themselves" were purchasing. This pitch would be made regardless of the demographic background of the individuals.

query-driven data mining
data mining based on specific queries

model-driven data mining
involves the use of a model that analyzes the key variables of interest to decision makers

rule-based data mining
examines demographic and transactional data of groups and individuals at a Web site and attempts to derive general rules of behavior for visitors

collaborative filtering
site visitors classify themselves into affinity groups characterized by common interests; products are then recommended based on what other people in the group have recently purchased

INSIGHT ON TECHNOLOGY

THE LONG TAIL: BIG HITS AND BIG MISSES

The "Long Tail" is a colloquial name given to various statistical distributions characterized by a small group of events of high amplitude and a very large group of events with low amplitude. Coined by *Wired Magazine* writer Chris Anderson in 2004, the Web's Long Tail has since gone on to perplex academics and challenge online marketers. The concept is straightforward. Think Hollywood movies: there are big hits that really hit big, and thousands of films that no one ever hears about. In economics, it's the Pareto principle: 20% of anything produces 80% of the effects. That means 20% of the hits produce 80% of the revenue, and by extension, 80% of the product line only returns 20% of the revenue. It's these non-hit misses that make up the Long Tail. Anderson claims to have discovered a new 98% rule: no matter how much content you put online, someone, somewhere will show up to buy it. eBay would seem to be a perfect example. The online tag sale contains millions of items drawn from every Aunt Tilly's closet in the world and still seems to find a buyer somewhere for just about anything.

On the Internet, where search costs are tiny, and storage and distribution costs are near zero, Amazon is able to offer millions of books for sale compared to a typical large bookstore with 40,000–100,000 titles. The same is true of CDs, DVDs, digital cameras, and portable MP3 players. Wherever you look on the Web, you find huge inventories, and a great many items that few people are interested in buying. But someone is almost always searching for something. With a billion people online, even a one-in-a-million product will find 1,000 buyers. According to Anderson, online music sites sell access to 98% of their titles once a quarter. According to Netflix, over 50% of its 100,000 titles are rented at least once a day by someone.

Unlike physical stores such as Wal-Mart and Sears, online merchants have much lower overhead costs because they do not have physical stores and have lower labor costs. Therefore they can load up on inventory, including items that rarely sell. Researchers argue that one impact of the Internet is to alter the 80:20 rule to something more like 70:30, where the niche products make up a larger share of the revenues than in traditional catalogs or stores.

There are several implications of the Long Tail phenomenon for Web marketing. Some writers such as Anderson claim that the Internet revolutionizes digital content by making even niche products highly profitable, and that the revenues produced by small niche products will ultimately outweigh the revenues of hit movies, songs, and books. For Hollywood, and all content producers, this means less focus on the blockbusters that bust the budget, and more emphasis on the steady base-hit titles that have smaller audiences but make up for it in numbers of titles. The Long Tail is a democratizing phenomenon: even less-well-known movies, songs, and books can now find a market on the Web. There's hope for your blog and garage band! For economists, the Long Tail represents a net gain for social welfare because now customers can find exactly the niche content they really want rather than accept the "big hits" on the shelf. The Web's Long Tail makes more customers happy, and the possibility of making money on niche products should encourage more production of "indy" music and film.

The problem with all these misses in the Long Tail is that few people can find them because they are—by definition—largely unknown. Search engines help but return so much information that choice is difficult. Faced with hundreds of titles the user never heard of is perplexing, delays decision,

(continued)

raises consumer anxiety levels, and potentially wastes consumer time. Hence, in their native state, the revenue value of low-demand products is locked up in collective ignorance. Here's where recommender systems come into play: they can guide consumers to obscure but wonderful works based on the recommendations of others.

Recommender systems use historical data on user preferences or behavior to predict how new users will behave. Memory-based systems use the entire database to make predictions, and model-based systems use past data to build a model of consumer behavior and then apply the model to new consumers. Using a similarity metric, which is a means of segmenting the user base, a sub-segment of users are selected whose behavior or preferences are similar to the user seeking recommendations. An average purchase propensity for a specific product by members of that sub-segment is calculated, with a recommendation made based on that average.

In many cases, recommendations are made based on past purchasing behavior of the user, which may or may not reflect the needs or preferences of the user today. The ability to narrow down the list of potential options, however, makes the information-gathering process more efficient and, for many users, very helpful. It's also possible that social networks make the long-tail phenomenon even stronger. One online person discovers an unheard-of niche product and shares his or her feelings with others.

But recent research casts some doubt on the revenue potential in the Long Tail. In an odd twist, the number of DVD titles online that never get played is increasing rapidly, while at the same time the big blockbuster "winner-take-all" titles are increasing. Solid "best sellers" have expanded and

produce the vast part of online DVD revenues. Over time, the number of titles in the Long Tail has exploded, and the "no play" rate has expanded at music sites from 2% to 12%. A massive study of millions of digital downloads in England found that 75% of the digital titles were not downloaded even once. The Long Tail is a very lonely, quiet place. Even in illegal P2P music markets, the hits account for the vast majority of sales, while millions of tracks from niche bands and singers sit idle. Pirates are just like everybody else: they like popular songs. In reality there seems to be more selling of less (the hits) than less selling of more (the misses). A U.S. study similarly found that 10% of music titles at Rhapsody, a music site, produced 78% of the revenues. Hits, so-called "blockbuster" music and videos, appear to be growing in importance as the Internet reduces communication costs, widely sharing popular views. Think the "wisdom of crowds." As much as we celebrate the Internet for making indie music and movies available to a new mass audience, there is some reason to believe the indie producers are a smaller share of market revenue than before the Internet.

Both the Long Tail and the winner-take-all approaches have implications for marketers and product designers. In the Long Tail approach, online merchants, especially those selling digital goods such as content, should build up huge libraries of content because they can make significant revenues from niche products that have small audiences. In the winner-take-all approach, the niche products produce little revenue, and firms should concentrate on hugely popular titles and services. Surprisingly, contrary to what Anderson originally theorized, the evidence for online digital content increasingly supports a winner-take-all perspective.

SOURCES: "The Long Tail of P2P," by Will Page and Eric Garland, *Economic Insight*, August 14, 2009; "Chopping the Long Tail Down to Size," by Andrew Orlowski, *The Register*, November 7, 2008. "Should You Invest in the Long Tail,? by Anita Elberse, *Harvard Business Review*, July–August 2008; "How Big Is the Free Economy?" by Kevin Kelly, Longtail.com, July 30, 2008; "The Dynamics of Viral Marketing," by Jure Leskovec, Lada A. Adamic, and Bernardo A. Huberman, ACM Transactions on the Web, Vol. 1, No. 1, Article 5, May 2007. "Superstars and Underdogs: An Examination of the Long Tail Phenomenon in Video Sales," by Anita Elberse and Felix Oberholzer-Gee, Harvard Business School Working Paper Series, No. 07-015, December, 2006; "It May Be a Long Time Before the Long Tail Is Wagging the Web," by Lee Gomes, *Wall Street Journal*, July 26, 2006; "From Niches to Riches: Anatomy of the Long Tail," by Eric Brynjolfsson, Yu Hu, and Michael Smith, *MIT Sloan Management Review*, Summer 2006; "The Long Tail," by Chris Anderson, *Wired Magazine*, October 2004.

A more fine-grained behavioral approach that seeks to deal with individuals as opposed to market segments or affinity groups derives rules from individual consumer behavior (along with some demographic information) and seeks to deal specifically with individuals (Adomavicius and Tuzhilin, 2001a; Chan, 1999; Fawcett and Provost, 1996, 1997). Here, the pages actually visited by specific users are stored as a set of conjunctive rules. For example, if an individual visits a site and typically ("as a rule") moves from the home page to the financial news section to the Asian report section, and then often purchases articles from the "Recent Developments in Banking" section, then this person—based on purely past behavioral patterns—might be shown an advertisement for a book on Asian money markets. These rules can be constructed to follow an individual across many different Web sites.

There are many drawbacks to all these techniques, not least of which is that there may be millions of rules, many of them nonsensical, and many others of short-term duration. Hence, the rules need extensive validation and culling (Adomavicius and Tuzhilin, 2001a). Also, there can be millions of affinity groups and other patterns in the data that are temporal or meaningless. The difficulty is isolating the valid, powerful (profitable) patterns in the data and then acting on the observed pattern fast enough to make a sale you would otherwise not have made. As we see later, there are practical difficulties and trade-offs involved in achieving these levels of granularity, precision, and speed.

CUSTOMER RELATIONSHIP MANAGEMENT (CRM) SYSTEMS

customer relationship management (CRM) system

a repository of customer information that records all of the contacts that a customer has with a firm and generates a customer profile available to everyone in the firm with a need to "know the customer"

Customer relationship management systems are another important Internet marketing technology. A **customer relationship management (CRM) system** is a repository of customer information that records all of the contacts that a customer has with a firm (including Web sites) and generates a customer profile available to everyone in the firm with a need to "know the customer." CRM systems also supply the analytical software required to analyze and use customer information. Customers come to firms not just over the Web but also through telephone call centers, customer service representatives, sales representatives, automated voice response systems, ATMs and kiosks, in-store point-of-sale terminals, and mobile devices (m-commerce). In the past, firms generally did not maintain a single repository of customer information, but instead were organized along product lines, with each product line maintaining a customer list (and often not sharing it with others in the same firm).

In general, firms did not know who their customers were, how profitable they were, or how they responded to marketing campaigns. For instance, a bank customer might see a television advertisement for a low-cost auto loan that included an 800-number to call. However, if the customer came to the bank's Web site instead, rather than calling the 800-number, marketers would have no idea how effective the television campaign was because this Web customer contact data was not related to the 800-number call center data. **Figure 6.14** illustrates how a CRM system integrates customer contact data into a single system.

CRMs are part of the evolution of firms toward a customer-centric and marketing-segment-based business, and away from a product-line-centered business. CRMs are essentially a database technology with extraordinary capabilities for addressing the

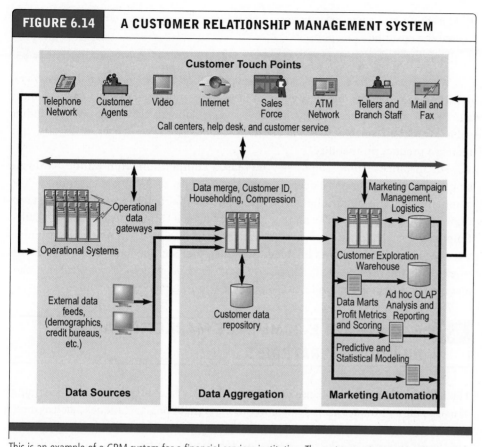

FIGURE 6.14 | A CUSTOMER RELATIONSHIP MANAGEMENT SYSTEM

This is an example of a CRM system for a financial services institution. The system captures customer information from all customer "touch" points as well as other data sources, merges the data, and aggregates it into a single customer data repository or data warehouse where it can be used to provide better service, as well as to construct customer profiles for marketing purposes. Online Analytical Processing (OLAP) allows managers to dynamically analyze customer activities to spot trends or problems involving customers. Other analytical software programs analyze aggregate customer behavior to identify profitable and unprofitable customers as well as customer activities.

SOURCE: Compaq, 1998.

needs of each customer and differentiating the product or service on the basis of treating each customer as a unique person. Customer profiles can contain the following information:

- A map of the customer's relationship with the institution
- Product and usage summary data
- Demographic and psychographic data
- Profitability measures
- Contact history summarizing the customer's contacts with the institution across most delivery channels

- Marketing and sales information containing programs received by the customer and the customer's responses
- E-mail campaign responses

With these profiles, CRMs can be used to sell additional products and services, develop new products, increase product utilization, reduce marketing costs, identify and retain profitable customers, optimize service delivery costs, retain high lifetime value customers, enable personal communications, improve customer loyalty, and increase product profitability.

For instance, Home Depot saw increased competition from online hardware stores and decided to emphasize e-commerce as part of its business strategy. The company sought a comprehensive CRM solution that could organize and analyze information from both clicks and mortar. They used a CRM software package called Epiphany Insight to gain a better understanding of which Home Depot products were selling on the Web and enabled their customer service focus from their stores to exist on the Web as well. Epiphany has since been acquired by Infor. Other leading CRM vendors include SAP, SalesForce.com, Oracle, Kana, and eGain.

6.4 B2C AND B2B E-COMMERCE MARKETING AND BRANDING STRATEGIES

The new marketing technologies described previously have spawned a new generation of marketing techniques and added power to some traditional techniques (such as direct mail campaigns with Web site addresses displayed). In this section, we describe a variety of Internet marketing strategies for market entry, customer acquisition, customer retention, pricing, and dealing with channel conflict. It is important to note that although B2C and B2B e-commerce do have differentiating features (for instance, in B2C e-commerce, marketing is aimed at individual consumers, whereas in B2B e-commerce, typically more than just one individual is involved with the purchase decision), the strategies discussed in this section in most instances can be, and are, applied in both the B2C and B2B arenas.

MARKET ENTRY STRATEGIES

Both new firms and traditional existing firms have choices about how to enter the market, and ways to establish the objectives of their online presence. **Figure 6.15** illustrates four basic market entry strategies.

Let's examine the situation facing new firms—quadrants 1 and 2 in Figure 6.15. In the early days of e-commerce, the typical entry strategy was pure clicks/first-mover advantage, utilized by such companies as Amazon, eBay, and E*Trade (quadrant 1). Indeed, this strategy was at the heart of the so-called new economy movement, and provided the capital catch basin into which billions of investment dollars flowed. The ideas are beguiling and simplistic: enter the market first and experience "first-mover" advantages—heightened user awareness, followed rapidly by successful consumer transactions and experiences—and grow brand strength. According to leading consultants of this era, first movers would experience a short-lived

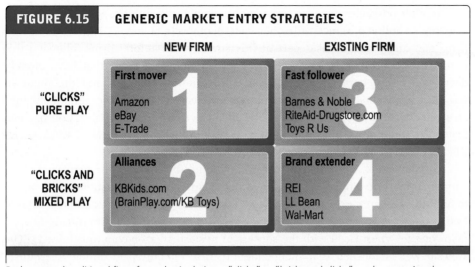

| FIGURE 6.15 | GENERIC MARKET ENTRY STRATEGIES |

Both new and traditional firms face a basic choice—"clicks" or "bricks and clicks"—when entering the e-commerce marketplace.

mini-monopoly. They would be the only providers for a few months, and then other copycats would enter the market because entry costs were so low. To prevent new competitors from entering the market, growing audience size very rapidly became the most important corporate goal rather than profits and revenue.

Firms following this strategy typically spent the majority of their marketing budget (which, in and of itself, may have constituted a large part of their available capital) on building brand (site) awareness by purchasing high-visibility advertising in traditional mass media such as television (Super Bowl game ads), radio, newspapers, and magazines. If the first mover gathered most of the customers in a particular category (pets, wine, gardening supplies, and so forth), the belief was that new entrants would not be able to enter because customers would not be willing to pay the switching costs. Customers would be "locked in" to the first-mover's interface. Moreover, the strength of the brand would inhibit switching, even though competitors were just a click away.

In retrospect, it is now clear that pursuing first-mover advantage as a marketing strategy was not particularly successful for most firms. Although first movers may have interesting advantages, they also have significant liabilities. The history of first movers in most areas of business is that statistically, they are losers for the most part because they lack the complementary assets and resources required to compete over the long term. While innovative, first movers usually lack financial depth, marketing and sales resources, loyal customers, strong brands, and production or fulfillment facilities needed to meet customer demands once the product succeeds (Teece, 1986). Research on Internet advertising indicates that while expensive ad campaigns may have increased brand awareness, the other components of a brand such as trust, loyalty, and reputation did not automatically follow, and more important, site visits did not necessarily translate into purchases (Ellison, 2000).

Another possibility for new firms is to pursue a mixed bricks-and-clicks strategy, coupling an online presence with other sales channels (quadrant 2). However, few new firms can afford the "bricks" part of this strategy. Therefore, firms following this entrance strategy often ally themselves with established firms that have already developed brand names, production and distribution facilities, and the financial resources needed to launch a successful Internet business. For instance, BrainPlay, Inc., an e-tailer of children's goods, entered into an alliance with the established Consolidated Stores Corporation KB Toys unit to form a new online presence called KBkids.com. KBkids was later closed, but KBToys.com survives today.

Now let's look at traditional firms. Traditional firms face some similar choices, with of course one difference: they have significant amounts of cash flow and capital to fund their e-commerce ventures over a long period of time. For example, Barnes & Noble, the world's largest book retailer, formed Barnesandnoble.com (quadrant 3), a follower site, when faced with the success of upstart Amazon.com (quadrant 1). The Web site was established as an independent firm, a Web pure-play, although obviously making use of the Barnes & Noble brand name. Likewise, Rite Aid followed the success of online pharmacies by establishing its own Web site (Riteaid.com) and then forming an alliance with Drugstore.com to fulfill and service prescriptions ordered online at Drugstore.com (and perform backend processing of insurance payments).

The most common strategy for existing firms is to extend their businesses and brands by using a mixed bricks-and-clicks strategy in which online marketing is closely integrated with offline physical stores (quadrant 4). These "brand-extension" strategies characterize REI, L.L.Bean, Wal-Mart, and many other established retail firms. Like fast followers, they have the advantage of existing brands and relationships. However, even more than fast followers, the brand extenders do not set up separate pure-play online stores, but instead typically integrate the online firm with the traditional firm from the very beginning. L.L.Bean and Wal-Mart both saw the Web as an extension of their existing order processing and fulfillment, marketing, and branding efforts.

Each of the market entry strategies discussed above has seen its share of successes and failures. While the ultimate choice of strategy depends on a firm's existing brands, management strengths, operational strengths, and capital resources (Gulati and Garino, 2000), today most firms are opting for a mixed bricks-and-clicks strategy in the hope that it will enable them to reach profitability more quickly.

ESTABLISHING THE CUSTOMER RELATIONSHIP

Once a firm chooses a market entry strategy, the next task is establishing a relationship with the customer. Traditional public relations and advertising media (newsprint, direct mail, magazines, television, and even radio) remain vital for establishing awareness of the firm. However, a number of unique Internet marketing techniques have emerged that have proven to be very powerful drivers of Web site traffic and purchases. Here we discuss several of these new techniques, including advertising networks, permission marketing, affiliate marketing, viral marketing, blog marketing, and social network marketing. The use of keyword purchases and pay-for-placement and rank on search engines (so-called "search engine marketing") is discussed in some detail in Chapter 8 as a special type of advertising or marketing communications.

Advertising Networks

In the early years of e-commerce, firms placed ads on the few popular Web sites in existence, but by early 2000, there were hundreds of thousands of sites where ads could be displayed. Most firms by themselves, even very large firms, did not have the capabilities to place banner ads and marketing messages on thousands of Web sites, and monitor the results. Specialized marketing firms called **advertising networks** appeared to help firms take advantage of the powerful tracking and marketing potential of the Internet.

Advertising networks represent the most sophisticated application of Internet database capabilities to date, and illustrate just how different Internet marketing is from traditional marketing. These networks sell advertising and marketing opportunities (slots) to companies who wish to buy exposure to an online audience. Advertising networks obtain their inventory of ad opportunities from a network of participating sites that want to display ads on their sites in return for receiving a payment from advertisers. These sites are usually referred to as Web publishers. The advertising network shares the revenue with the publisher. Advertising networks have developed software that tracks customer movements among the network members, say, from Amazon, to Travelocity, to Google, Yahoo, and eBay. At each visit the ad network software decides which banner ads, videos, and other ads to show the customer based in part on the customer's behavior at various sites on the network. For instance, at Travelocity, the customer may research a vacation to England. On Google, the customer may search for English cities. When the customer goes to Yahoo, he or she may be shown ads for raincoats. The advertiser works with the network to determine the rules for showing ads. If you wonder, for instance, why you see so many ads for home mortgages despite the fact you have never looked at an apartment or house for sale, it is because the advertising mortgage company and the ad network have determined your age demographic and geographic location, and on that basis, show mortgage ads to everyone meeting those criteria regardless of previous network behavior. Ad networks are not always very discriminating in their behavior.

Perhaps the best-known advertising network is DoubleClick, which released its first-generation tracking system, DART, in 1996. Google purchased DoubleClick for $3.1 billion in April 2007. Other advertising networks include 24/7 Real Media's Open AdStream (purchased by WPP, the world's largest advertising firm, for $649 million in June 2007), and aQuantive (purchased by Microsoft for $6.1 billion in May 2007).

Why are billions of dollars being invested in these companies? For technology firms such as Google and Microsoft, purchasing these companies allows them to buy large chunks of the online display advertising business, which amounts to about $3 billion a year in revenue. For marketing firms such as WPP, the purchase of 24/7 Real Media allows it to extend its traditional business of creating and placing ads, and develop a third line of business in the Internet display ad market.

DoubleClick serves about 60 billion ads per month (in round numbers, about 24,000 ads per second) and maintains over 100 million user profiles on individual Web

advertising networks
present users with banner advertisements based on a database of user behavioral data

consumers. Specialized ad servers are used to store and send to users the appropriate banner ads. All these systems rely on cookies, Web bugs, and massive backend user profile databases to pitch banner ads to users and record the results, including sales. This process allows feedback from the market to be entered into the database. For instance, DoubleClick's Intelligent Targeting service allows advertisers to send ads to consumers who have indicated a specific interest area, either through recent or frequent visits to particular types of Web sites, while its Boomerang service allows a Web site to target visitors to that site by advertising to those anonymous visitors when they visit other DoubleClick client sites.

Figure 6.16 illustrates how these systems work. Advertising networks begin with a consumer requesting a page from a member of the advertising network (1). A connection is established with the third-party ad server (2). The ad server identifies the user by reading the cookie file on the user's hard drive and checks its user profile database for the user's profile (3). The ad server selects an appropriate banner ad based on the user's previous purchases, interests, demographics, or other data in the profile (4). Whenever the user later goes online and visits any of the network member sites, the ad server recognizes the user and serves up the same or different ads regardless of the site content. The advertising network follows users from site to site through the use of Web bugs (5).

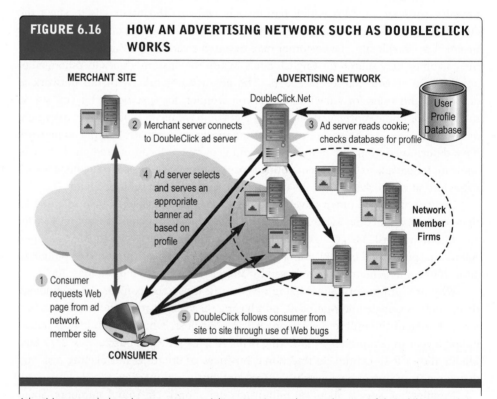

| FIGURE 6.16 | HOW AN ADVERTISING NETWORK SUCH AS DOUBLECLICK WORKS |

Advertising networks have become controversial among privacy advocates because of their ability to track individual consumers across the Internet. We discuss privacy issues further in Chapter 8.

Permission Marketing

The phrase "**permission marketing**" was coined by author and consultant Seth Godin to describe the strategy of obtaining permission from consumers before sending them information or promotional messages (Godin, 1999). Godin's premise was that by obtaining permission to send information to consumers up front, companies are much more likely to be able to develop a customer relationship. When consumers agree to receive promotional messages, they are *opting-in*; when they decide they do not want to receive such messages, they *opt-out*.

Most consumers need an incentive to spend time reading promotional material, or to provide personal information companies can use to improve their own marketing. Godin's former company, Yoyodyne, pioneered the creation of online sweepstakes and games that gathered information from participants in return for the chance to win money and prizes. Another company, portal Iwon.com, gives users the chance to win money each week for visiting the site; each month, the company offers special bonus prizes to users who are willing to complete a more in-depth survey about their personal life. The site gains useful personal information, and the user earns the chance to win a free prize.

A key component of e-mail involves permission marketing. Typically, when placing an order online, consumers are given the option of receiving newsletters or announcements of products and sales via e-mail. In the United States, the default is usually "opt-in," and the consumer is required to check off an option to not receive e-mail. Federal law now requires merchants sending e-mail to consumers to provide an Unsubscribe link for all e-mail. We discuss e-mail as a marketing communication tool in greater detail in Chapter 7

permission marketing
marketing strategy in which companies obtain permission from consumers before sending them information or promotional messages

Affiliate Marketing

In the offline world, referrals are one of the best sources of qualified leads. **Affiliate marketing** is the online application of this marketing method, where one Web site agrees to pay another Web site or an individual writing a blog a commission for new business opportunities it refers to the site. The affiliate adds a link to the company's Web site on its own site and encourages its visitors to patronize its marketing partner. Some affiliates are paid a commission based on any sales that are generated, while others may be paid a fee based on number of click-throughs or new registrations, or a flat fee, or some combination of these.

For instance, Amazon has a strong affiliate program consisting of more than 1 million participant sites, called Associates, which receive up to 15% on sales their referrals generate. Members of eBay's Affiliates Program can earn between $20 and $35 for each active registered user sent to eBay. Amazon, eBay, and other large e-commerce companies with affiliate programs typically administer such programs themselves. Smaller e-commerce firms who wish to use affiliate marketing often decide to join an *affiliate network* (sometimes called an *affiliate broker*), which acts as an intermediary. The affiliate network brings would-be affiliates and merchants seeking affiliates together, helps affiliates set up the necessary links on their Web site, tracks all activity, and arranges all payments. Leading affiliate networks include Commission Junction and LinkShare. In return for their services, affiliate networks typically take

affiliate marketing
one Web site agrees to pay another Web site a commission for new business opportunities it refers to the site

about 20% of any fee that would be payable to the affiliate. The total size of the affiliate market is not known, but industry experts estimate that around 10% of all retail online sales are generated through affiliate programs (as compared, say, to search engine ads which account for over 30% of online sales).

A key benefit of affiliate marketing is the fact that it typically operates on a "pay-for-performance" basis. Affiliates provide qualified sales leads in return for pre-agreed upon compensation. Another advantage, however, is the existence of an established user base that a marketer can immediately tap into through an affiliate. For affiliates, the appeal is a steady income—potentially large—that can result from such relationships. In addition, the presence of another company's logo or brand name can provide a measure of prestige and credibility.

Affiliate marketing can have some drawbacks, however, if not managed carefully. Too many links that are not relevant to a firm's primary focus can lead to brand confusion, for instance. Affiliate marketing works best when affiliates choose products and services that match and supplement the content of their own Web site. Web sites with affiliate links also risk "losing" those customers who click on a link and then never return, unless the Web site takes action to prevent this, such as by having the link open a new window that when closed returns the customer to the original site.

Viral Marketing in the Web 2.0 Milieu

viral marketing

the process of getting customers to pass along a company's marketing message to friends, family, and colleagues

Just as affiliate marketing involves using a trusted Web site to encourage users to visit other sites, **viral marketing** is the process of getting customers to pass along a company's marketing message to friends, family, and colleagues. It's the online version of word-of-mouth advertising, which spreads even faster than in the real world. In the offline world, next to television, word of mouth is the second most important means by which consumers find out about new products. Millions of online adults in the United States are "influencers" who share their opinions about products in a variety of online settings. In addition to increasing the size of a company's customer base, customer referrals also have other advantages: they are less expensive to acquire since existing customers do all the acquisition work, and they tend to use online support services less, preferring to turn back to the person who referred them for advice. Also, because they cost so little to acquire and keep, referred customers begin to generate profits for a company much earlier than customers acquired through other marketing methods. There are a number of online venues where viral marketing appears in the Web 2.0 era. E-mail used to be the primary online venue for e-mail marketing ("please forward this e-mail to your friends"), but Web 2.0 venues such as blogs and social networking sites are beginning to play a major role as described below (eMarketer, 2008e).

Half.com's Take Five! program is an example of viral marketing, where registered users at the site selling used books, music, movies, and games are given an incentive (coupons) to tell their friends about the site. When a user submits a friend's name and e-mail address on Half.com's Take Five page, Half.com sends the friend a coupon valid for $5 off the friend's first order of $10 or more. Then, when the friend uses the Take Five coupon, Half.com gives the referring user a $5 coupon that also can be used on a $10 order. The process of viral marketing can also involve users who do not know each other. When a consumer decides to make a major purchase, such as a new mountain bike, getting advice and opinions from people who own such bikes is usually the first step. And with the Internet, it is fairly easy to find and read reviews of various bike models written by knowledge-able consumers. Sites such as Epinions.com and ConsumerReports.org provide objective product reviews by people who have bought and used a long list of products and services. Armed with feedback and input from online aficionados, consumers can then click through to an e-commerce site and make a purchase. Epinions has links to a number of affiliate online retailers who pay a fee back to the site for each purchase that originates there.

Blog Marketing

Blogs have become a part of mainstream online culture (see Chapter 3 for a description of blogs and RSS). Around 97 million Americans read a blog at least once a month in 2009, and around 28 million have created blogs. The number of blog readers is expected to grow to about 128 million, and blog creators to 38 million by 2013. (eMarketer, 2009c). Thousands of high-ranking corporate officials, politicians, journalists, academics, and government officials have created blogs, along, of course, with the rest of us. Blog creators tend to be young, broadband users, Internet veter-ans, wealthy, and educated. It did not take long for marketers to discover this large number of "eyeballs" and seek out ways to market and advertise to them. Because blogs are based on the personal opinions of the writers, they are ideal locations to start a viral marketing campaign.

Blogs, like ordinary Web sites, can be used to display both branding ads not geared towards sales, as well as advertising aimed at making sales. But because blogs are usually created by private individuals wishing to make a public statement, bloggers do not have the Web marketing and advertising resources of large corporations, and the number of eyeballs viewing any one site is miniscule compared to portal Web sites such as Yahoo. The problem is how to efficiently aggregate these tiny audiences into a significant block of eyeballs worthy of an advertiser's attention.

One solution is to build an advertising network of bloggers and allow bloggers to sub-scribe to this network, agreeing to display ads on their blogs, and then paying them a fee for each visitor who clicks on the ad. Within the last two years, two major players in the blogging industry, Technorati and Six Apart, have launched blog advertising networks designed to connect blog sites with advertisers. Blogads.com provides a similar service.

Google's AdSense is also a major blog marketer. The AdSense service "reads" a blog and identifies the subject of the blog's postings. Then AdSense will place appropriate ads on the blog, adjusted to the blog's content. For instance, BoingBoing.net, a very popular technology blog known for its love of gadgets, displays ads from major advertisers like HP, Verizon, and RackSpace.

Given the growth of this phenomenon—well over 50% a year in the past few years—and the novelty, blog marketing will likely show substantial gains over the next several years. In 2009, blog advertising revenue is estimated to be about $530 million, growing to about $746 million by 2012, although this estimate does not take into account the impact of the recession (eMarketer, 2008f). There may also be limits on this phenomenon just as with e-mail marketing. The *blogosphere* (the Internet's aggregate blogging community) is already buzzing about blogs set up merely for personal financial gain. The founder of one site on asbestos litigation, for instance, freely admits he set up the site in order to tap into the revenues flowing to individuals and law firms in connection with asbestos litigation (Rodgers, 2005). Firms are tempted to hire bloggers to report favorably on their products, leading to what one wag called "blogola." This behavior reduces the credibility and effectiveness of blog marketing, and makes larger advertisers fearful of advertising on blogs when they cannot control the content of the blog.

We cannot leave a discussion of blog marketing without mentioning Twitter. As you learned in Chapter 2, Twitter is an example of microblogging—mini-blog postings (tweets) of 140 characters or less. Twitter has attracted enormous attention in the popular press in 2009, and marketers (and Twitter) are still figuring out how best to exploit the service. Twitter currently does not accept paid advertising. Marketers are currently using Twitter to gather and share information from and with consumers, and deliver special offers. Some marketers are also experimenting with applications that aggregate or segment Twitter feeds, such as Federated Media's ExecTweets (eMarketer, Inc, 2009d).

Social Network Marketing and Social Shopping

Social networks in the offline world are collections of people who voluntarily communicate with one another over an extended period of time. Online social networks, such as Facebook, MySpace, LinkedIn, Xanga, Orkut, Friendster, Buzznet, and Bebo, are Web sites that enable users to communicate with one another, form close group and individual relationships, and share interests, values, and ideas. Individuals establish online profiles, which may include pictures, and then invite their friends to create their own profiles and link to their profile. The network grows by word of mouth and through e-mail links. In May 2009, according to comScore Media Metrix, the top 20 social networking sites had an aggregate of 147 million unique visitors, up 12 % from 2008. Marketers will spend about $1.1 million on social network marketing in 2009, about 5% of all online marketing. It is estimated that Facebook, the most popular social network, will generate about $230 million in online ad revenues in 2009, and MySpace, about $495 million. These two sites together account for over 60% of all online social networking ad revenues. (eMarketer Inc., 2009d).

social shopping
sharing product choices with friends online

Firms are beginning to harness the spectacular popularity and growth of social networking sites by marketing to participants. The idea is that consumers will tend to buy what their friends buy and recommend. At Yub.com, which has several patents on **social shopping**, users can view their friends' purchases and interests, click an image of the products, and link to a Web site where they can buy the products. Yub.com keeps the referral fees of 10%–15%. Friendster uses similar techniques to send customers to Amazon, keeping a referral fee. Other online retail sites are attempting to create their own user communities. At Overstock.com, users of that site's auction service are invited to create free online profiles, and share news of their recent purchases with friends at the site. The *Insight on Business* story, *Social Network Marketing: New Influencers Among the Chattering Masses*, further examines the emergence of social network marketing.

INSIGHT ON BUSINESS

SOCIAL NETWORK MARKETING: NEW INFLUENCERS AMONG THE CHATTERING MASSES

Social network marketing is arguably the single most exciting and fastest growing online marketing development in the last 10 years. Social networking sites of all kinds are ideal locations for a conversation to occur between brands and customers. With over 150 million unique visitors a month in 2009, social networking sites such as MySpace, Facebook, Twitter, Flickr, YouTube, and scores of niche sites are natural targets for marketers who want to be where their customers are. Alongside these sites are social news/social bookmarking sites such as Digg, Reddit, Delicious (formerly Newsvine), and StumbleUpon, which attract additional millions of viewers. At social news/bookmarking sites, visitors send links to stories or their favorite bookmarked sites to their friends and colleagues. The fate of news stories and blogs depends on how well these recommendations are received. Blogs are yet another online forum for writers to express themselves and readers to respond, creating a community of responses. The top 25 most popular blogs tracked by comScore Media Metrix draw over 70 million unique visitors a day! There are an estimated 27 million "influential" people on social networking sites who express opinions on products and brands. Social networking sites are the equivalent of offline word-of-mouth networks, which are the most powerful influence on consumer behavior. It's word of mouth on digital steroids.

A whole new lexicon has emerged to describe the new social network marketing opportunities:

- Online word-of-mouth-marketing: Giving people a reason to talk about your products online
- Buzz marketing: Using high-profile entertainment, games, or news to get people talking about your products online
- Online viral marketing: Creating messages designed to be passed along by e-mail, blogging, or networking with others

- Online community marketing: Forming online niche communities to share interests about your brand
- Online grassroots marketing: Organizing volunteers or paying people to reach out to their friends online
- Influencer marketing: Finding people in online communities who are opinion leaders or key influencers
- Conversation marketing: Interesting or fun online advertising to start word-of-mouth campaigns via e-mail, blogs, and networking profiles
- Brand blogging: Creating blogs, or participating on blogs, or hiring bloggers to share and promote the value of your brands

Marketers are starting to follow the opportunity, though: it is estimated that social network marketing will hit $1.3 billion in 2010, still less than one-tenth of all online marketing, but growing at 13% a year. This makes social marketing the fastest growing form of online marketing just at a time when search engine marketing growth is slowing.

There are risks, however. For instance, you cannot control what bloggers, tweeters, chatters, and networkers say about your brand or products, and while they may provide valuable feedback that is useful for product design and improvement, unfair characterizations of your products, intentions, or policies can kill sales. You will not want your brand name associated with some raunchy content found at YouTube and Facebook. How do you know what the chattering masses are saying about your brand, and what can you do about it? Ford is taking a gamble on social network marketing: giving away 100 Ford Fiestas to young people and asking them to submit videos about their experience on YouTube without any editorial control.

Social network marketing is very different from traditional media marketing where the firm can control the message and the medium. Social network

(continued)

marketing is a no-holds barred dialogue between the customer and the company. A number of firms have sprung up to help solve this problem. For instance, Nielsen BuzzMetrics is a company formed by the media ratings firm A.C. Nielsen that uses search engines to sweep the Internet for phrases, opinions, keywords, sentences, and images that impact one of its customers' brands. It then analyzes the vocabulary, language patterns, and phrasing to determine if the comments are positive or negative, and the demographics of the people making the comments wherever possible. In a sense, it is using the Internet as an online focus group. BuzzMetrics warns "Every day, millions of consumers converse in online communities, discussion boards, blogs and social networks. They turn to the Internet to share opinions, advice, grievances and recommendations. Are you listening, connecting and responding in a way that protects and promotes your brand?" Other firms performing similar services are Umbria, Cymfony,

and Biz360. Coke has used BuzzMetrics to gauge responses to a video it posted on YouTube; ConAgra has used these techniques to anticipate lifestyle and food trends; Sony has used these firms to track interest in its computer games.

The online brand intelligence field is also moving towards real-time monitoring of the social network ecosystem. VML, based in Kansas City, a unit of WPP Group, tracks the blogosphere in real time with its SEER ™ brand management tool and produces visual maps of the blogosphere that pinpoint the originators of comments about a firm, the subscribers, and the links among them (see screenshot below). They can tell a customer such as Adidas that the blogosphere is complaining about fading colors on the Predator, a new soccer cleat. As a result, Adidas began telling customers at the point of purchase to treat the leather before wearing the cleats, and then changed the formulation of dyes used in the color process.

SOURCES: "Social Network Ad Spending: A Brighter Outlook for Next Year," by Debra Aho Williamson, eMarketer, July 2009; "How Facebook Will Upend Advertising," by Jonathon Yarmis, BusinessWeek, May 27, 2009; "Ford Takes Online Gamble With New Fiesta," by Matthew Dolan, *Wall Street Journal*, April 8, 2009; "U.S. Advertising Spending: the New Reality," by David Hallerman, eMarketer, April 2009; "The Blogosphere: A-Twitter With Activity," by Paul Verna, eMarketer, April 2009; "Social Networks: Five Consumer Trends," by Debra Aho Williamson, eMarketer, February 2009; "Use Social Media to Bond With Consumers," by Kelly Spors, *Wall Street Journal*, September 3, 2008; "Make Social Networking Work for Your Business," by Kelly Spors, *Wall Street Journal*, July 8, 2008.

Marketing Based on the Wisdom of Crowds

So far we have described Web 2.0 social marketing techniques in which firms push the message to the customer by purchasing advertising, sending e-mails, and promoting events, and contests. This certainly is one way of establishing a relationship with the customer. But in the Web 2.0 era, there are a number of techniques where the customer speaks to the firm, and the firm adjusts its products and services accordingly. In this new relationship, the customers are in charge of the message, and this is not always a very comfortable position for a firm if the message is negative.

The Wisdom of the Crowds Is it possible that decisions, predictions, or estimates made by a large group of people are better and more accurate than decisions made by any individual, or small group of experts, in the group? In 2004, James Surowiecki wrote a book titled *The Wisdom of Crowds* exploring this thesis. There are plenty of precedents for the notion that large aggregates produce better estimates and judgments than individuals or small groups of experts. For instance, one premise of democracy is that a very large number of diverse and independent voters will over the long run produce superior political decisions than a single dictator, king, bureaucrat, or committee. Economists have studied the problem of how to find the best restaurant in a strange town. Answer: the restaurant with the largest crowds (surely the locals know where there's good food). In financial theory, the best estimate of the current value of a firm can be found in free, open markets where millions of participants vote with their pocketbooks. In statistics, the best estimate of the value of a parameter is the mean or average arrived at by taking thousands of independent samples of the population.

In general, crowds are wise when there are many decision makers who make decisions independent of one another, come from diverse backgrounds, and where there is a mechanism (like a market) that can aggregate opinions to produce a single outcome or choice. However, there are many crowds which do not fit these conditions, and the result can be a failure of collective judgment. Mobs, herds, and runaway stock market bubbles are examples of where crowds can produce very bad estimates and decisions. In these cases, the lack of diversity and independence among participants can lead to an "information cascade," which prevents independent judgments.

Nevertheless, when the four conditions of wise crowds are met, Surowiecki argues, crowds produce superior judgments, forecasts, and estimates. In the eyes of many, the conditions for crowds to be "wise" are quite rare, especially so in a "connected" Internet world where millions of people are blogging, networking, and e-mailing. Being connected to others—millions of others—reduces the independence of participants and makes them more susceptible to manipulation and hysteria (Surowiecki, 2004).

The idea of the social basis of wisdom and knowledge is reflected in many Web 2.0 applications. For instance, Wikipedia is based on the idea that millions of diverse contributors can produce an encyclopedia of knowledge that is superior to those produced by small groups of experts. In marketing, the "wisdom of crowds" concept suggests that firms should consult with thousands of customers first as a way of establishing a relationship with them, and second, to better understand how their products and services are used and appreciated by their customers (or why they are rejected by customers). Actively soliciting the comments of your customers builds trust and sends the message to your customers that you care what they are thinking, and that you need their advice. There are new forums where firms can apply these techniques.

Prediction Markets While all markets make predictions or estimates of value based on buy-sell transactions among a group of participants, or bets among a group of bettors with a "gambling house" clearing the bets, prediction markets are established as peer-to-peer betting markets where participants make bets on specific outcomes of, say, quarterly sales of a new product, designs for new products, or outcomes of political elections. Participants make bets with their own funds that a certain outcome will occur. Others bet against that outcome. The result is that an asset is created (a contract, for example), which reflects the market's aggregate value for that outcome.

The world's largest commercial prediction market is Betfair.com, founded in 2000, where you bet for or against specific outcomes on football games, horse races, and whether or not the Dow Jones will go up or down in a single day. The Iowa Electronic Markets (IEM) is an academic market focused on elections. You can place bets on the outcome of local and national elections. The IEM allows traders to buy and sell contracts based on political election results and economic indicators. The contract is the asset with a value determined by long buyers and short sellers. Positions are limited to $500

Let's say you trying to decide which of two Web site designs works best for your firm. Rather than have a small internal committee make the decision, or a few senior executives, why not let thousands of your customers bet which Web site is most effective by placing bets on a contest Web site. You will of course have to hand out $100 worth of script money (not legal tender) to each customer, and offer them a chance to buy and sell shares in a market based on their opinion of which would be the most successful with your customers. After a week of buying and selling, the market closes and the winning Web site will have the highest share price. The reward for participating and having chosen the winning site can be anything from $100 in cash to a year's supply of your services.

Folksonomies and Social Tagging Another application of the "wisdom of crowds" to marketing is the use of a large number of people to classify objects, which could be movies, photos, books, PowerPoint slides, or consumer products. Folksonomy is a play on the term "taxonomy," which refers to any classification schema for organizing a collection of objects. Generally, taxonomies are created by individuals or a group of experts. Folksonomies are created by groups of people looking at a set of objects, and then tagging them (or bookmarking them) using their own criteria. Folksonomies are a bottom-up, self-organizing activity in which thousands of people classify objects.

A related phenomenon that relies on large numbers of online users to identify and classify products, services, events, and content is social tagging. Social tagging sites allow millions of people to post their bookmarks or "favorite" content to a single site where others can review the links. If your Diggs become popular as other people Digg them, they will bounce to the top of the list of Diggs where millions more people can see and review them.

As an online marketer, how can you use social tagging and folksonomies to your advantage? One way to influence social tagging sites is to organize the placement of social tags by customers who love your products. Alternatively, ask your customers on your Web site to tag your site, and send it to their friends. Setting aside the ethics of such moves, to a large extent these phenomena are inherently difficult to manipulate, and the act of attempted manipulation can bring aspersion down on a firm.

Leveraging Brands

Brand leveraging is one of the most successful online customer acquisition strategies (Carpenter, 2000). **Brand leveraging** refers to the process of using the power of an existing brand to acquire new customers for a new product or service. For instance, while Tab was the first to discover a huge market for diet cola drinks, Coca-Cola ultimately succeeded in dominating the market by leveraging the Coke brand to a new product called Diet Coke.

In the online world, some researchers predicted that offline brands would not be able to make the transition to the Web because customers would soon learn who was offering products at the cheapest prices and brand premiums would disappear (price transparency). But this has not occurred. In retail, firms such as Wal-Mart and JCPenney have leaped into the top 10 online retail firms in a very short period in large part because of the strength of their offline brand, which gave them the ability to attract millions of their offline customers to their Web sites. In the financial service industry sector, firms such as Wells Fargo, Citibank, Fidelity, and Merrill Lynch have all succeeded in acquiring millions of online customers based on their large offline customer bases and brands. In the content provider industry, the *Wall Street Journal* and *Consumer Reports* have become among the most successful subscription-based content providers. In manufacturing and retail, Dell has been very successful in leveraging its brand of custom-built computers ordered by telephone into a made-to-order computer ordered over the Internet (Kraemer, et al., 2000). A major advantage of brand leveraging—when compared to a start-up venture with no brand recognition—is that it significantly reduces the costs of acquiring new customers (Kotler and Armstrong, 2008).

brand leveraging
using the power of an existing brand to acquire new customers for a new product or service

CUSTOMER RETENTION: STRENGTHENING THE CUSTOMER RELATIONSHIP

The Internet offers several extraordinary marketing techniques for building a strong relationship with customers and for differentiating products and services.

Personalization and One-to-One Marketing

No Internet-based marketing technique has received more popular and academic comment than "one-to-one" or "personalized marketing." **One-to-one marketing** segments the market on the basis of individuals (not groups), based on a precise and timely understanding of their needs, targeting specific marketing messages to these individuals, and then positioning the product vis-à-vis competitors to be truly unique (Peppers and Rogers, 1997). One-to-one marketing is the ultimate form of market segmentation, targeting, and positioning—where the segments are individuals.

The movement toward market segmentation has been ongoing since the development of systematic market research and mass media in the 1930s. However, e-commerce and the Internet are different in that they enable personalized one-to-one marketing to occur on a mass scale. **Figure 6.17** depicts the continuum of marketing: from mass marketing of undifferentiated products, where one size and one price fits all, to personalized one-to-one marketing.

one-to-one marketing
segmenting the market based on a precise and timely understanding of an individual's needs, targeting specific marketing messages to these individuals, and then positioning the product vis-à-vis competitors to be truly unique

FIGURE 6.17	THE MASS MARKET-PERSONALIZATION CONTINUUM

MARKETING STRATEGIES	MARKETING ATTRIBUTES			
	Product	**Target**	**Pricing**	**Techniques**
Mass Marketing	Simple	All consumers	One nation, one price	Mass media
Direct Marketing	Stratified	Segments	One price	Targeted communications, e.g., mail and phone
Micromarketing	Complex	Micro-segments	Variable pricing	Segment profiles
Personalized, One-to-One Marketing	Highly complex	Individual	Unique pricing	Individual profiles

Personalized one-to-one marketing is part of a continuum of marketing strategies. The choice of strategy depends on the nature of the product as well as the technologies that are available to enable various strategies.

Mass marketing, based on national media messages aimed at a single national audience and with a single national price, is appropriate for products that are relatively simple and attractive to all consumers in a single form. Think of Coke, Tide, and McDonalds. *Direct marketing*, which is based on direct mail or phone messages and aimed at segments of the market likely to purchase and which has little variation in price (but special offers to loyal customers), is most often used for products that can be stratified into different categories. *Micromarketing*, which is aimed at geographical units (neighborhoods, cities) or specialized market segments (technology buffs), is the first form of true database marketing. Frito-Lay, for instance, maintains a national sales database for each of 10,000 route sales personnel and over 50,000 store outlets. Frito-Lay marketers know precisely at the end of every day how many small bags of Salsa Chips sell in Los Angeles, and how many bags of Ranch Chips sell in Cambridge, Massachusetts, store by store. Although seemingly simple, the corn chip can take on fairly complex and nuanced taste experiences that attract different customers in different neighborhoods. Using its database, Frito-Lay dynamically adjusts prices to market conditions and competitor product and pricing, every day.

Personalized one-to-one marketing is suitable for products (1) that can be produced in very complex forms, depending on individual tastes, (2) whose price can be adjusted to the level of personalization, and (3) where the individual's tastes and preferences can be effectively gauged.

A good example of personalization at work is Amazon or Barnesandnoble.com. Both sites greet registered visitors (based on cookie files), recommend recent books based on user preferences (based on a user profile in their database), and expedite checkout procedures based on prior purchases.

Several U.S. firms such as the New York Times and Orbitz have adopted a form of permission-based, personalized "direct-messaging" banner advertising in which customers are shown ads addressed to them by name, mentioning some of their past purchases. Dotomi Direct Messages differ from banner ads and e-mail messages because consumers agree to receive messages from various companies, and the ads are personal in the sense of being based on the consumer's prior purchases and behavior. Invented by Yair Goldfinger, who created instant messaging while working for AOL, the system uses cookies to identify returning visitors to a network of sites. In a sense, the ads are specially built for each unique user. The response rate to traditional banner ads is currently about 0.5%, whereas the response rate to personalized banner ads is about 34% (Giuliani, 2009). Unfortunately, consumers who sign up for this service do not receive fewer of the old-style, mass market, banner ads.

Is Web-based personalization as good as the personal attention you would receive from a local, independent bookstore owner? Probably not. Nevertheless, these Web-based techniques use more individual knowledge and personalization than traditional mass media, and more than a direct mail post card.

Personalization is not necessarily an unmitigated good, however. Research indicates that most consumers appreciate personalization when it increases their sense of control and freedom, such as through personalized order tracking, purchase histories, databases of personalized information to ensure quicker transactions during future sessions, and opt-in e-mail notification of new products and special deals. The online buyers participating in Wolfinbarger and Gilly's focus groups saw personalization as negative, however, when it resulted in unsolicited offers or reduced anonymity; such features are perceived to take away user control and freedom (Wolfinbarger and Gilly, 2001). Furthermore, although personalization technologies have made significant advances over the past several years, it is still difficult for a computer to accurately understand and anticipate the interests and needs of a customer. "Personalized" offers that miss the mark can lead to more customer disdain than satisfaction (Waltner, 2001). How often do you open up a Web site such as Yahoo and find ads that are totally irrelevant to your interests?

customization
changing the product, not just the marketing message, according to user preferences

Customization and Customer Co-Production

Customization is an extension of personalization. **Customization** means changing the product—not just the marketing message—according to user preferences. **Customer co-production** means the users actually think up the innovation and help create the new product. For instance, studies of new and improved products find that many come directly from intensive users. The operating system Linux is entirely built by users, and

customer co-production
in the Web environment, takes customization one step further by allowing the customer to interactively create the product

innovations in mountain bikes, sail boards, sailboats and gear, ski equipment, and thousands of other industrial products often came from "lead users" (von Hippel, 2005, 1994). Customer co-production in the Web environment takes customization one step further by allowing the customer to interactively create the product.

Many leading companies now offer "build-to-order" customized products on the Internet on a large scale, creating product differentiation and, hopefully, customer loyalty. Customers appear to be willing to pay a little more for a unique product. The key to making the process affordable is to build a standardized architecture that lets consumers combine a variety of options. For example, Nike has been offering customized sneakers through its Nike iD program on its Web site since 1999. Consumers can choose the type of shoe, colors, material, and even a logo of up to eight characters. Nike transmits the orders via computers to specially equipped plants in China and Korea. The sneakers cost only $10 extra and take about three weeks to reach the customer. At the Shop M&M's Web site, customers can get their own message printed on custom-made M&Ms; Timberland.com also offers online customization of its boots.

Information goods—goods whose value is based on information content—are also ideal for this level of differentiation. For instance, the New York Times—and many other content distributors—allows customers to select the news they want to see on a daily basis. Many Web sites, particularly portal sites such as Yahoo, MSN, Netscape, and AOL, allow customers to create their own customized version of the Web site. Such pages frequently require security measures such as usernames and passwords to ensure privacy and confidentiality.

Transactive Content

According to several studies, the most common reasons people go online are to communicate (e-mail) and to find information. As we noted in Section 6.1, shopping is not the primary Internet consumer activity.

Marketers have adjusted their Web marketing strategies accordingly. The result is "transactive content," a term originally coined by Forrester Research (Forrester Research, 1997, 1998). **Transactive content** results from the combination of traditional content, such as articles and product descriptions, with dynamic information—such as new product announcements—culled from product databases, tailored to each user's profile. Such applications dynamically respond to user needs and preferences, for instance, by featuring a product within a price range typically preferred by the customer on the order page. You might be reading an article on travel to Africa at Iexplore.com, a travel company with an extensive Web site for adventure-travel advice, products, and services. Based on data drawn from your user profile as well as real-time clickstream behavior (for instance, you had previously expressed an interest in water sports), you might be served a link to information on kayaking safaris in Africa. Transactions, content, and interactivity are combined into a seamless experience.

transactive content
results from the combination of traditional content, such as articles and product descriptions, with dynamic information culled from product databases, tailored to each user's profile

Customer Service

A Web site's approach to customer service can significantly help or hurt its marketing efforts. Online customer service is more than simply following through on order fulfillment; it has to do with users' ability to communicate with a company and obtain desired information in a timely manner. Customer service can help reduce consumer frustration, cut the number of abandoned shopping carts, and increase sales.

According to Wolfinbarger and Gilly, most consumers want to, and will, serve themselves as long as the information they need to do so is relatively easy to find. Online buyers largely do not expect or desire "high-touch" service unless they have questions or problems, in which case they want relatively speedy answers that are responsive to their individual issue. Wolfinbarger and Gilly noted that participants in their study said that the first opportunity to cement them to an online brand came when they had a problem with the order; customer loyalty increased substantially when online buyers learned that customer service representatives were available online or at an 800-number and were willing and able to resolve the situation quickly. Conversely, online buyers who did not receive satisfaction at these critical incidents terminated their relationship and became willing to do business with a site that might charge more, but offered better customer service (Wolfinbarger and Gilly, 2001).

There are a number of tools that companies can use to encourage interaction with prospects and customers and provide customer service—FAQs, customer service chat systems, intelligent agents, and automated response systems—in addition to the customer relationship management systems described in the preceding section.

Frequently asked questions (FAQs), a text-based listing of common questions and answers, provide an inexpensive way to anticipate and address customer concerns. Adding an FAQ page on a Web site linked to a search engine helps users track down needed information more quickly, enabling them to help themselves resolve questions and concerns. By directing customers to the FAQs page first, Web sites can give customers answers to common questions. If a question and answer do not appear, it is important for sites to make contact with a live person simple and easy. Offering an e-mail link to customer service at the bottom of the FAQs page is one solution.

frequently asked questions (FAQs)
a text-based listing of common questions and answers

Real-time customer service chat systems (in which a company's customer service representatives interactively exchange text-based messages with one or more customers on a real-time basis) are an increasingly popular way for companies to assist online shoppers during a purchase. Chats with online customer service representatives can provide direction, answer questions, and troubleshoot technical glitches that can kill a sale. Leading vendors of customer service chat systems include LivePerson and InstantService. Vendors claim that chat is significantly less expensive than telephone-based customer service. However, critics point out this conclusion may be based on optimistic assumptions that chat representatives can assist three or four customers at once, and that chat sessions are shorter than phone sessions. Also, chat sessions are text sessions, and not as rich as talking with a human being over the phone. On the plus side, chat has been reported to raise per-order sales figures, providing sales assistance by allowing companies to "touch" customers during the decision-making process. According to comScore, anecdotal evidence suggests that chat can lower shopping cart abandonment rates, increase the number of items purchased per transaction, and increase the dollar value of transactions. In 2009, about 54% of U.S. online retailers offer live chat and another 27% indicated that they planned to add the feature

real-time customer service chat systems
a company's customer service representatives interactively exchange text-based messages with one or more customers on a real-time basis

to their Web sites in 2009 (Briggs, 2009; Internet Retailer, 2009b). "Click to call" or "live call" is another version of a real-time online customer service system, in which the customer clicks a link or accepts an invitation to have a customer service representative call them on the telephone.

Intelligent agent technology, described in Chapter 3, is another way customers are providing assistance to online shoppers. Intelligent agents are part of an effort to reduce costly contact with customer service representatives. **Automated response systems** send e-mail order confirmations and acknowledgments of e-mailed inquiries, in some cases letting the customer know that it may take a day or two to actually research an answer to their question. Automating shipping confirmations and order status reports are also common. Although the upfront expenditure to install and implement automated systems may be costly, the potential reduction in calls to live telephone operators and online help centers is an incentive for companies to increasingly automate as many aspects of the online shopping experience as possible. Firms must use and monitor automated response systems carefully, however, or they may backfire. Many customers still resent automated communications, even if they appear personalized. If automated replies are not useful, they may drive consumers to use live support even more.

NET PRICING STRATEGIES

In a competitive market, firms compete for customers through price as well as product features, scope of operations, and focus. **Pricing** (putting a value on goods and services) is an integral part of marketing strategy. Together, price and quality determine customer value. Pricing of e-commerce goods has proved very difficult for both entrepreneurs and investors to understand.

In traditional firms, the prices of traditional goods—such as books, drugs, and automobiles—are usually based on their fixed and variable costs as well as the market's **demand curve** (the quantity of goods that can be sold at various prices). Fixed costs are the costs of building the production facility. *Variable costs* are costs involved in running the production facility—mostly labor. In a competitive market, with undifferentiated goods, prices tend toward their *marginal costs* (the incremental cost of producing the next unit) once manufacturers have paid the fixed costs to enter the business.

Firms usually "discover" their demand curves by testing out various price and volume bundles, closely watching their cost structure. Normally, prices are set to maximize profits. A profit-maximizing company sets its prices so that the *marginal revenue* (the revenue a company receives from the next unit sold) from a product just equals its marginal costs. If a firm's marginal revenue is higher than its marginal costs, it would want to lower prices a bit and sell more product (why leave money on the table when you can sell a few more units?). If its marginal revenue for selling a product is lower than its marginal costs, then the company would want to reduce volume a bit and charge a higher price (why lose money on each additional sale?).

During the early days of e-commerce, something unusual happened. Sellers were pricing their products far below their marginal costs. Some sites were losing money on every sale. How could this be? New economics? New technology? The Internet

automated response system
sends e-mail order confirmations and acknowledgments of e-mailed inquiries

pricing
putting a value on goods and services

demand curve
the quantity of goods that can be sold at various prices

Age? No. Internet merchants could sell below their marginal costs (even giving away products for free) simply because a large number of entrepreneurs and their venture capitalist backers thought this was a worthwhile activity, at least in the short term. The idea was to attract "eyeballs" with free goods and services, and then later, once the consumer was part of a large, committed audience, charge advertisers enough money to make a profit, and (maybe) charge customers subscription fees for value-added services (the so-called *"piggy-back" strategy* in which a small number of users can be convinced to pay for premium services that are piggy-backed upon a larger audience that receives standard or reduced value services). To a large extent, social networking sites and user-generated content sites have resurrected this revenue model with a focus on the growth in audience size and not short-term profits. To understand the behavior of entrepreneurial firms, it is helpful to examine a traditional demand curve (see **Figure 6.18**).

A small number of customers are willing to pay a great deal for the product—far above P_1. A larger number of customers would happily pay P_1, and an even larger number of customers would pay less than P_1. If the price were zero, the demand might approach infinity! Ideally, in order to maximize sales and profits, a firm would like to pick up all the money in the market by selling the product at the price each customer is willing to pay. This is called **price discrimination**—selling products to different people and groups based on their willingness to pay. If some people really want the product, sell it to them at a high price. But sell it to indifferent people at a much lower price; otherwise, they will not buy. This only works if the firm can (a)

price discrimination
selling products to different people and groups based on their willingness to pay

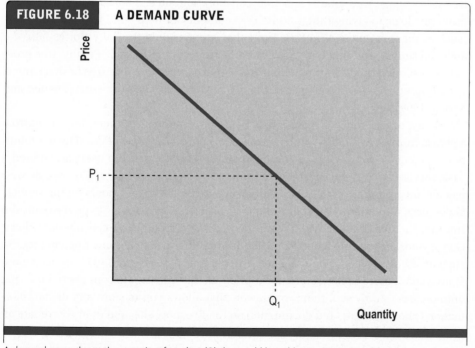

FIGURE 6.18	A DEMAND CURVE

A demand curve shows the quantity of product (Q) that could be sold at various prices (P).

identify the price each individual would be willing to pay, and (b) segregate the customers from one another so they cannot find out what the others are paying. Therefore, most firms adopt a fixed price for their goods (P_1), or a small number of prices for different versions of their products.

During the early days of e-commerce, and even today in the case of Web 2.0 firms, e-commerce firms were willing to charge far below their costs, sometimes giving away valuable services, in order to attract huge audiences. Millions of visitors accepted free or nearly free services and products being sold below their cost.

What if the marginal cost of producing a good is zero? What should the price be for these goods? It would be impossible then to set prices based on equalizing marginal revenue and marginal cost—because marginal cost is zero. The Internet is primarily filled with information goods—from music to research reports, to stock quotes, stories, weather reports, articles, pictures, and opinions—whose marginal cost of production is zero when distributed over the Internet. Thus, another reason certain goods, such as information goods, may be free on the Internet is that they are "selling" for what it costs to produce them—nothing. Content that is stolen from television, CDs, and Hollywood movies has zero production costs. Content that is contributed by users also has zero production costs for the Web sites themselves.

Free and Freemium

Let's examine free pricing of Internet services. Everyone likes a bargain, and the best bargain is something for free. Businesses give away free PCs, free data storage, free music, free Web sites, free photo storage, and free Internet connections. Free is not new: banks used to give away "free" toasters to depositors in the 1950s. Google offers free office apps, free email, and free collaboration sites. There can be a sensible economic logic to giving things away. Free content can help build market awareness (such as the free online *New York Times* that contains only the daily stories—not the archived stories) and can lead to sales of other follow-on products. Finally, free products and services knock out potential and actual competitors (the free browser Internet Explorer from Microsoft spoiled the market for Netscape's browser) (Shapiro and Varian, 1999).

Today, online "free" is increasingly being implemented as "freemium" to borrow a phrase from Chris Anderson's book *Free: The Future of a Radical Price.* The freemium pricing model is a cross-subsidy online marketing strategy where users are offered a basic service for free, but must pay for premium or add-on services. The people who pay for the premium services hopefully will pay for all the free riders on the service. Skype uses a freemium model: millions of users can call other Skype users on the Internet for free, but there's a charge for calling a landline or cell phone. Flickr, Google Sites, Yahoo, and a host of others offer premium services at a price in order to support "free" services. Even YouTube is launching a premium movie service where Hollywood movies are streamed for a price. In 2009, Evernote.com started offering online users a "universal memory drawer" that allows you to store any digital information (photos, videos, and documents) on the Evernote site, and then coordinate all of your digital devices from laptops, desktops, and smartphones. The basic service is free, but additional storage and special services cost $5 a month (Darlin, 2009).

"Free" and "freemium" as pricing strategies do have limits. In the past, many e-commerce businesses found it difficult to convert the eyeballs into paying customers. YouTube is still not profitable. Free sites attract hundreds of millions of price-sensitive "free loaders" who have no intention of ever paying for anything, and who switch from one free service to another at the very mention of charges. The piggyback strategy has not been a universal success. "Free" eliminates a rich price discrimination strategy. Clearly some of the free loaders would indeed pay a small amount each month, and this revenue is lost to the firms who offer significant services for free. Some argue that everything digital will one day be free in part because Internet users expect it to be so. But the history of "free" includes broadcast television, which used to be "free" (it was advertising-supported) but the public eventually had no problem moving to cable television and DVDs as paid services. The exceptions to "free" are really valuable streams of information that are exclusive, not widely distributed, unique, and have immediate consumption or investment value. Even in the age of the Internet, these digital streams will sell for a price greater than zero. There probably is no free lunch after all, at least not one that's worth eating.

Versioning

One solution to the problem of free information goods is **versioning**—creating multiple versions of the goods and selling essentially the same product to different market segments at different prices. In this situation, the price depends on the value to the consumer. Consumers will segment themselves into groups that are willing to pay different amounts for various versions (Shapiro and Varian, 1998). Versioning fits well with a modified "free" strategy. A reduced value version can be offered for free, while premium versions can be offered at higher prices. What makes a "reduced-value version?" Low-priced—or in the case of information goods, even "free"—versions might be less convenient to use, less comprehensive, slower, less powerful, and offer less support than the high-priced versions. Just as there are different General Motors car brands appealing to different market segments (Cadillac, Buick, Chevrolet, and Pontiac), and within these divisions, hundreds of models from the most basic to the more powerful and functional, so can information goods be "versioned" in order to segment and target the market and position the products. In the realm of information goods, online magazines, music companies, and book publishers offer sample content for free, but charge for more powerful content. The *New York Times*, for instance, offers free daily content for several days after publication, but then charges per article for access to the more powerful archive of past issues. Writers, editors, and analysts are more than willing to pay for access to archived, organized content. Some Web sites offer "free services" with annoying advertising, but turn off the ads for a monthly fee.

versioning
creating multiple versions of information goods and selling essentially the same product to different market segments at different prices

Bundling

"Ziggy" Ziegfeld, a vaudeville entrepreneur at the turn of the twentieth century in New York, noticed that nearly one-third of his theater seats were empty on some Friday nights, and during the week, matinee shows were often half empty. He came up with an idea for bundling tickets into "twofers": pay for one full-price ticket and get the next ticket free. Twofers are still a Broadway theater tradition in New York. They are based on the idea that (a) the marginal cost of seating another patron is zero, and (b) a great many people who would not otherwise buy a single ticket would buy a "bundle" of tickets for the same or even a slightly higher price.

Bundling of information goods online extends the concept of a twofer. **Bundling** offers consumers two or more goods for one price. The key idea behind the concept of bundling is that although consumers typically have very diverse ideas about the value of a single product, they tend to agree much more on the value of a bundle of products offered at a fixed price. In fact, the per-product price people are willing to pay for the bundle is often higher than when the products are sold separately. Bundling reduces the variance (dispersion) in market demand for goods. **Figure 6.19** illustrates how the demand curve changes when information goods are offered in a bundle.

Examples of bundling abound in the information goods marketplace. Microsoft bundles its separate Office tools (Word, Excel, PowerPoint, and Access) into a single Microsoft Office package. Even though many people want to use Word and Excel, far fewer want Access or PowerPoint. However, when all products are put into a single bundle, a very large number of people will agree that about $399 (or around $100 per tool) is a "fair" price for so many products. Likewise, the more software applications that Microsoft bundles with its basic operating system, the more the marketplace agrees that as a package of functionality, it is reasonably priced. On the Web, many content sites bundle as opposed to charge individual prices. Electronic libraries such as NetLibrary.com offer access to thousands of publications for a fixed annual fee. Theoretically, bundlers have distinct competitive advantages over those who do not or cannot bundle. Specifically, on the supply side, bundler firms can pay higher prices

bundling

offers consumers two or more goods for one price

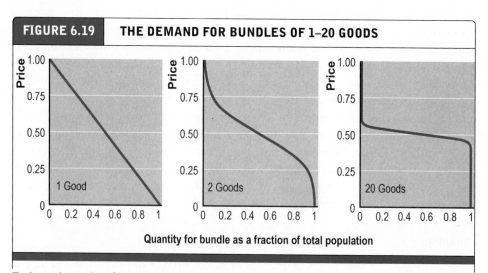

FIGURE 6.19   **THE DEMAND FOR BUNDLES OF 1–20 GOODS**

Quantity for bundle as a fraction of total population

The larger the number of goods bundled in a package, the higher the per-product price consumers are willing to pay.

SOURCE: Bakos and Brynjolfsson, 1999.

for content, and on the demand side, bundlers can charge higher prices for their bundles than can single-good firms (Bakos and Brynjolfsson, 2000).

However, bundling of digital goods does not always work. It depends on the bundle and the price. For instance, Reed Elsevier, the world's largest publisher of scientific journals, created a bundle of 1,500 digital scientific journals for American universities, and priced the bundle at a substantial markup to what universities were paying for a much smaller number of journals. It then raised the price to universities that did not want the bundle. The result was a marketplace rebellion shaped in part by the fact that much of the research in these journals was paid for by taxpayers through government grants.

Dynamic Pricing

The pricing strategies we have discussed so far are all fixed-price strategies. Versions and bundles are sold for fixed prices based on the firm's best effort at maximizing its profits. But what if there is product still left on the shelf along with the knowledge that someone, somewhere, would be willing to pay something for it? It might be better to obtain at least some revenue from the product, rather than let it sit on the shelf, or even perish. Imagine also that there are some people in every market who would pay a hefty premium for a product if they could have it right away. In other situations, such as for an antique, the value of the product has to be discovered in the marketplace (usually because there is a belief that the marketplace would value the product at a much higher price than its owner paid as a cost). In other cases, the value of a good is equal to what the market is willing to pay (and has nothing to do with its cost). Here is where dynamic pricing mechanisms come to the fore, and where the strengths of the Internet can be seen.

Two prevalent kinds of *dynamic pricing mechanisms* are auctions and yield management. Auctions have been used for centuries to establish the instant market price for goods. Auctions are flexible and efficient market mechanisms for pricing unique or unusual goods, as well as commonplace goods such as computers, flower bundles, and cameras.

Yield management is quite different from auctions. In *auctions*, thousands of consumers establish a price by bidding against one another. In *yield management*, managers set prices in different markets, appealing to different segments, in order to sell excess capacity. Airlines exemplify yield management techniques. Every few minutes during the day, they adjust prices of empty airline seats to ensure at least some of the 50,000 empty airline seats are sold at some reasonable price—even below marginal cost of production. Frito-Lay, as mentioned earlier, also uses yield management techniques to ensure products move off the shelf in a timely fashion.

Yield management works under a limited set of conditions. Generally, the product is perishable (an empty airline seat perishes when the plane takes off without a full load); there are seasonal variations in demand; market segments are clearly defined; markets are competitive; and market conditions change rapidly (Cross, 1997). In general, only very large firms with extensive monitoring and database systems in place have been able to afford yield management techniques.

The Internet has truly revolutionized the possibilities to engage in dynamic, and even misleading pricing strategies. With millions of consumers using a site every hour, and access to powerful databases, merchants can raise prices one minute, and drop them another minute when a competitor threatens. Bait-and-switch tactics become more common: a really low-price on one product is used to attract people to a site where in fact the product is not available.

We discuss dynamic pricing, auctions, and yield management techniques in greater detail in Chapter 11.

CHANNEL STRATEGIES: MANAGING CHANNEL CONFLICT

channel

refers to different methods by which goods can be distributed and sold

channel conflict

occurs when a new venue for selling products or services threatens to destroy existing venues for selling goods

In the context of commerce, the term **channel** refers to different methods by which goods can be distributed and sold. Traditional channels include sales by manufacturers, both directly and through intermediaries such as manufacturer representatives, distributors, and retailers. The emergence of e-commerce on the Web has created a new channel and has led to channel conflict. **Channel conflict** occurs when a new venue for selling products or services threatens to destroy existing venues for selling goods. Channel conflict is not new, but the Web creates incentives for producers of goods and services to establish direct relationships with consumers and thereby eliminate "middle persons" such as distributors and retailers.

For instance, Levi Strauss & Co. decided to begin selling Levi's jeans and Dockers on its Levi.com and Dockers.com sites. Initially, it forbade retailers (such as Macy's—one of Levi's largest retailers) from selling Levi products on the Web. However, the storm of protest from retailers, falling sales, and drooping profits forced Levi to allow retailers to sell through their Web channels.

Rather than engage in direct confrontation with alternative channels, some manufacturers have turned toward a partnership model. For instance, Ethan Allen developed its own Web site for direct sales of its entire line of furniture. At the same time, Ethan Allen recognizes the importance of its independent retail stores for delivery, service, and support, and pays dealers in a local area 25% of the Internet sale for delivery and service, and 10% of the Internet sale even if the dealer does not participate in any way.

At the other end of the spectrum, some manufacturers use the Web solely as a marketing and branding mechanism in order to prevent channel conflict. For instance, Ford, General Motors, and most automobile manufacturers continue to rely on sales made by their dealerships rather than attempt to sell their cars directly online.

CASE STUDY

Liquidation.com:
B2B Marketing Success Story

What would you do if you wanted to sell 1,300 pounds of scrap titanium? A truckload of new kitchen cabinets or four pallets of used Dell computers? How about 200 designer Hannah Montana Disney girls wallets? Or six German-made circular knitting machines worth about $42,000 each when new but no longer needed because of changes in the U.S. textile marketplace? You might want to unload that strip mall in San Francisco now that real estate prices have tanked. If you wanted to sell these industrial goods, large lot sizes, and real estate, you would look for an online B2B liquidator site such as Liquidation.com or Bid4assets.com. These and other smaller firms provide eBay-style auctions that create a market for production overruns, store returns, and goods of bankrupt firms. These firms live off the misfortunes of some, while creating fortunes for other entrepreneurs who can buy large lots of goods at pennies on the dollar and resell them for large profits. In the case of the used Dell computers, the seller at Liquidation.com squeezed out nearly $200 for each of the computers, which in the past might have been sold to a traditional liquidator for $50 a piece. On average, sellers who use online liquidation services receive 20%–200% more than if they had used traditional liquidators. But how do these liquidation firms compete against their much larger rival eBay, which also provides liquidation services? The answer is precision online marketing and branding.

Liquidity Services, Inc. operates four online auction marketplaces: Liquidation.com, Govliquidation.com, Liquibiz.com, and a wholesale industry portal, GoWholesale.com, that connects advertisers with buyers seeking products for resale and related business services. Liquidity Services is in what is called the "reverse supply chain business." We normally think of the supply chain business as one where firms work through a variety of mechanisms to pull together the resources needed to produce goods. In the reverse supply chain, firms start with finished products and try to dispose of them. While a well-established forward supply chain exists for the procurement of assets, most manufacturers, retailers, corporations, and government agencies have not made significant investments in the reverse supply chain process. The reverse supply chain addresses the redeployment and remarketing of wholesale, surplus, and salvage assets. These assets generally consist of retail customer returns, overstock products, and end-of-life goods from both the corporate and government sectors. According to D.F. Blumberg Associates, Inc., a research and consulting firm, the estimated reverse logistics market in North America will be $69.5 billion in 2009, up from $38 billion in 2004.

Liquidity Services is utilizing online marketplaces, B2B product sales, and marketing expertise, and value-added services to complete more than 500,000 bulk sale transactions in 2009. Liquidity Services, which went public in February 2006, had $263 million in revenue in 2008 (32% growth over 2007) and has been profitable since 2002. The company has been affected by the recession, with 2009 quarterly revenues down 5% in the first quarter, to 19% in the third quarter, although earnings advanced about 9% in 2009 through cost-cutting efforts. Transaction volume is up about 12% as sellers try to raise cash and pay down debt. It has over 550 employees worldwide and is head-quartered in Washington, D.C. While the offline world of liquidation is populated with discount hunters, local wholesalers, scrap yards, and musty warehouses, and where returns for sellers are a few pennies on the dollar, at Liquidation.com, sellers are offered a global marketplace, complete support for presentation on the Web site (including graphics and text), and support for transactions (an auction and bidding engine). Liquidation.com offers sellers at least twice as much value as they would recover in the offline world. The firm is used by over 900,000 qualified professional buyers who purchase bulk products from Fortune 500 retailers, leading e-tailers, manufacturers, and distributors. About 80% of the items listed are actually sold. These buyers may be retailers, wholesalers, or eBay PowerSellers located in the United States and around the world in about 116 countries. The sellers tend to be manufacturers, distributors, and large retailers. At large retail stores such as Wal-Mart and JCPenney, over 6% of in-store sales are returned. For e-commerce online transactions, the return rate is an astounding 12% of sales. Most of these items cannot be re-sold because the original packaging or the item itself is damaged in some way. Hence they must be sold off at the best available price.

Liquidation.com has a federal contract as the exclusive liquidator for the U.S. Department of Defense, and is one of eight firms liquidating materials from other federal agencies. The U.S. government alone disposes of 10,000 computers a month. How much money is involved in "surplus"? In a recent deal, Liquidator Services signed an agreement with U.S. Defense Department to pay 3.26% of the original value on usable surplus gear and gets to keep all the profits. At its Govliquidation.com site you probably will not find Indiana Jones' Ark of the Covenant, but you can find surplus Army five-ton trucks, camping gear, generators, boots, and boats. The Defense Department is the largest single consumer in the world, and they have a lot of surplus equipment to unload. Over 10,000 new items are added every week.

Auctions at Liquidation.com close every two to three days, and there is no sniping allowed. (*Sniping* is the practice of standing on the sidelines and not bidding, and then coming into the bidding in the last few seconds and winning the auction.) Bidding is extended every three minutes until there is just one bidder left. Extending the auction when there are multiple bidders allows time for bidders to raise their bids, and also creates a sense of fairness among bidders.

When it first began, Liquidation.com faced some difficult issues of marketing and branding. First, it had to discover how to attract buyers to its Web site when the inventory itself changes daily, and the potential buyer never knows what will be for sale on any day. Second, it had to appeal to a very broad audience of potential purchasers who might be interested in anything at the right price. This was not targeted marketing so much as shotgun marketing to a world audience of businesses. Last, it had to build trust by ensuring that customers received exactly what they bid for even though Liquidation.com does not own the goods. Like eBay, Liquidation.com provides the transaction platform for buyers and sellers. However, it also provides a wide range of value-added services for both buyers and sellers, taking, on average, a 20% profit-share cut or commission from sellers. Communicating the wide range of value-added services to potential users has proved to be difficult. Sellers tended to think of Liquidation.com simply as a place to get rid of large lots of surplus goods, and were unaware of all the other services available. One marketing challenge was informing sellers and buyers about these other services. The figure below illustrates the broad range of services provided by Liquidity Services to buyers and sellers.

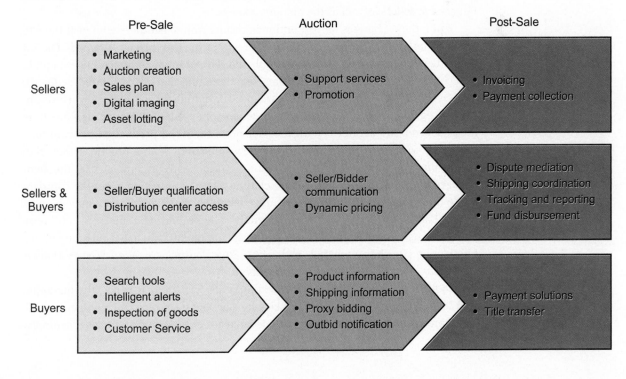

Some of the tactics Liquidation.com used to build a site that looks trustworthy are a home page with links on top, bottom, and side to customer service; logos of Dun & Bradstreet, VeriSign, PayPal, and TrustE on the bottom of many pages; and a news section for press releases and press mentions so that the site looks as if it is well known by trusted third parties (such as the Wall Street Journal, which occasionally mentions Liquidation. com).

The marketing team at Liquidation.com knew it needed to understand what was working at the Web site and how it worked, and then focus on driving customers to the Web site. Liquidation.com first invested in building a tracking program that focused on conversion metrics such as the average number of auctions viewed per name, average number of bids placed, average number of transactions, percentage of opt-in e-mail, and percentage of visitors who registered. The marketing team discovered that first-time visitors did not like to fill out the existing five-page registration form, so it was simplified to a half page. That increased registrations and opt-in to e-mail messages. They also discovered that first-time visitors rarely purchased anything, and the average length of time from first visit to first bid was 60 days. Therefore, the team reasoned it was important to keep in touch with first-time visitors and registrants through e-mail or other means. Looking at the sales metrics, the marketing and sales teams can use the information collected over the past eight years to lot and merchandise incoming inventory into batches that are attractive to its buyer base. In some instances, there is more demand and higher bids from smaller buyers who might be able to handle 100 briefcases as opposed to a lot of 1,000 briefcases. In other cases, larger buyers are increasingly attracted to truckload lots to help stock discount stores, flea market kiosks, and other small businesses. As Liquidation.com increases the volume of goods on its site from large retailers and manufacturers, it has the flexibility to provide a broad range of product offerings to better suit customer demand and increase the total amount returned to sellers as well as the amount it keeps.

While these changes helped optimize results from customers who visit the site, the question of how to bring people to the site in the first place remained. The initial budget for marketing was very small, and the potential audience huge. Liquidation.com's first tactic was to start using search engine marketing offered by Google and Overture (now Yahoo). They purchased hundreds of words on Overture and Google that would point directly to Liquidation.com product pages. At the same time, they checked the "organic" listings on Google to see if the product pages were turning up on their own as a result of Google's Web-based search engine. If not, they would purchase keywords. To drive more traffic without much cost, the team engaged in guerilla marketing public relations campaigns, trying to get the company name into major media business coverage wherever possible. When a huge blizzard hit the East Coast, the PR team immediately called reporters at metropolitan newspapers to suggest stories about retailers using Liquidation.com to get rid of inventory. Liquidation.com has appeared in the *Wall Street Journal*, *Christian Science Monitor*, *USA Today*, and *Business Week*, among others.

Looking at how his competitors used print ads in trade magazines, the marketing staff laid copies of all the magazines side by side and discovered the competitors' ads were "pretty cheesy looking." They decided to place a small number of ads that emphasized a professional level of service, efficient business processes, and the trustworthiness of their company.

While Liquidation.com is primarily intended as a site that makes it easy for bulk sellers to find retail buyers, Liquidity Services realized there was also a market for a Web site that would cater to retailers seeking out suppliers. In June 2004, Liquidity Services launched GoWholesale.com for retailers seeking long-term wholesale suppliers. Taking a page from Google, GoWholesale lets wholesalers bid on keywords for sponsored listings on the site. Retailers will see sponsored listings first, and then unsponsored links.

Perhaps the most effective tactic for driving traffic is e-mail marketing. Liquidation.com rents a small number of opt-in e-mail lists that have proved effective. Two precautions they have taken are to assume people on these lists may already be customers, and not to rent too frequently and annoy customers. But the most effective use of e-mail turns out to be mailing to the over 900,000 registered buyers on a regular basis, offering new products each time. About one-quarter of the mailing list receives a targeted mailing for a specific item at auction. On the registration page, users are asked to describe their interests in broad terms, and these self-selections (like a collaborative filter) are used to target e-mail campaigns. The open, click, and conversion rates on these targeted mailings is 20% higher than the general campaigns.

As a result of its successful marketing and branding campaigns, Liquidation.com has turned a murky world of inefficient, local liquidation markets into a global, trusted, online niche in the expanding Web liquidation industry. In 2007, Liquidity Services won three international Web awards for outstanding Web site development. Among the features cited in the awards were a robust search engine, customized e-mail alerts to keep buyers informed, superior product information, shipping quotes to assure final prices for buyers, and real-time tracking of transactions.

SOURCES: "Liquidity Services Inc. Marks 10 Years," JD Kathuria, ExecutiveBiz.com, August 11, 2009; "Liquidity Services Helps Companies Clear Shelves," by T.A. Ritter, nj.com/business, March, 2009; "One Man's Surplus Is...." by Tim Feran, *The Columbus Dispatch*, May 12, 2009; "Government Liquidation Opens Oklahoma Warehouse," by Jennifer Palmer, newsok.com, May 8, 2009; Liquidity Services Inc. Form 10-k, for the fiscal year ending September 30, 2008, filed with the Securities and Exchange Commission, December 22, 2008; "Liquidity Services, Inc. Awarded New Surplus Contract with the U.S. Department of Defense," Liquidity Services, Inc., August 4, 2008; "Casting a Web From Business to Business," by Peter Morton, Canada.com, May 26, 2007; "Liquidity Services, Inc. Honored With Three International WebAwards for Outstanding Web Site Development," Liquiditiy Services, Inc., October 15, 2007.

Case Study Questions

1. Why is Liquidation.com able to compete against eBay?

2. How did Liquidation.com build trust in its site and services?

3. Why would retailers rather have a site dedicated to finding wholesalers rather than use the existing Liquidation.com site?

4. What are the key elements in Liquidation.com's core product and how does it create an augmented product?

5. Find a product on the Liquidation.com site that is also for sale on eBay. Compare the prices per unit. What accounts for the price differential?

6.6   REVIEW

KEY CONCEPTS

■   Identify the key features of the Internet audience.

Key features of the Internet audience include:

*   *The number of users online in the United States.* In 2009, around 200 million. However, the rate of growth in the U.S. Internet population has begun to slow.
*   *Intensity and scope of use.* Both are increasing, with around 73% of adult users in the United States logging on in a typical day and engaging in a wider set of activities, including sending and reading e-mail, gathering hobby-related information, catching up on news, browsing for fun, buying products, seeking health information, conducting work-related research, and reviewing financial information.
*   *Demographics and access.* Although the Internet population is growing increasingly diverse, some demographic groups have much higher percentages of online usage than other groups, and different patterns of usage exist across various groups.
*   *Lifestyle impacts.* Intensive Internet use may cause a decline in traditional social activities. The social development of children who use the Internet intensively instead of engaging in face-to-face interactions or undirected play out of doors may also be negatively impacted.
*   *Media choices.* The more time individuals spend using the Internet, the less time they spend using traditional media.

■   Discuss the basic concepts of consumer behavior and purchasing decisions.

Models of consumer behavior attempt to predict or explain what consumers purchase, and where, when, how much, and why they buy. Factors that impact buying behavior include:

*   Cultural factors
*   Social factors
*   Psychological factors

There are five stages in the consumer decision process:

*   Awareness of need
*   Search for more information
*   Evaluation of alternatives
*   The actual purchase decision
*   Post-purchase contact with the firm

The online consumer decision process is basically the same, with the addition of two new factors:

*   *Web site capabilities*—the content, design, and functionality of a site.
*   *Consumer clickstream behavior*—the transaction log that consumers establish as they move about the Web and through specific sites. Analysts believe the most important predictors of online consumer behavior are the session characteristics and the clickstream behavior of people online, rather than demographic data.

■ **Understand how consumers behave online.**

Clickstream analysis shows us that people go online for many different reasons, at different times, and for numerous purposes.

- About 70% of online users are "buyers" who actually purchase something entirely online. Another 16% of online users research products on the Web, but purchase them offline. This combined group, referred to as "shoppers," constitutes approximately 86% of the online Internet audience.

- Online sales are divided roughly into two groups: small-ticket and big-ticket items. In the early days of e-commerce, sales of small-ticket items vastly out-numbered those of large-ticket items. However, the recent growth of big-ticket items such as computer hardware and consumer electronics has changed the overall sales mix.

- There are a number of actions that e-commerce vendors could take to increase the likelihood that shoppers and non-shoppers would purchase online more frequently. These include better security of credit card information and privacy of personal information, lower shipping costs, and easier returns.

■ **Describe the basic marketing concepts needed to understand Internet marketing.**

The key objective of Internet marketing is to use the Web—as well as traditional channels—to develop a positive, long-term relationship with customers (who may be online or offline) and thereby create a competitive advantage for the firm by allowing it to charge a higher price for products or services than its competitors can charge.

- Firms within an industry compete with one another on four dimensions: differentiation, cost, focus, and scope. "Competitive markets" are ones with lots of substitute products, easy entry, low differentiation among suppliers, and strong bargaining power of customers and suppliers.

- Marketing is an activity designed to avoid pure price competition, and to create imperfect markets where returns on investment are above average, competition is limited, and consumers are convinced to pay premium prices for products that have no substitute because they are unique. Marketing encourages customers to buy on the basis of perceived and actual nonmarket, that is, non-price, qualities of products.

- A product's brand is what makes products truly unique and differentiable in the minds of consumers. A brand is a set of expectations, such as quality, reliability, consistency, trust, affection, and loyalty, that consumers have when consuming, or thinking about consuming, a product or service from a specific company.

- Marketers devise and implement brand strategies—a set of plans for differentiating a product from its competitors and communicating these differences effectively to the marketplace. Segmenting the market, targeting different market segments with differentiated products, and positioning products to appeal to the needs of segment customers are key parts of brand strategy.

- Brand equity is the estimated value of the premium customers are willing to pay for using a branded product when compared to unbranded competitors.

Consumers are willing to pay more for branded products in part because they reduce consumers' search and decision-making costs. The ability of brands to attain brand equity also provides incentive for firms to build products that serve customer needs better than other products. Brands also lower customer acquisition cost and increase customer retention.

- Although some predicted that the Web would lead to "frictionless commerce" and the end of marketing based on brands, recent research has shown that brands are alive and well on the Web and that consumers are still willing to pay price premiums for products and services they perceive and differentiate.

■ Identify and describe the main technologies that support online marketing.

- *Web transaction logs*—records that document user activity at a Web site. Coupled with data from the registration forms and shopping cart database, these represent a treasure trove of marketing information for both individual sites and the online industry as a whole.
- *Cookies*—small text files that Web sites place on visitors' client computers every time they visit, and during the visit, as specific pages are visited. Cookies provide Web marketers with a very quick means of identifying the customer and understanding his or her prior behavior at the site.
- *Web bugs*—tiny (1 pixel) graphic files hidden in marketing e-mail messages and on Web sites. Web bugs are used to automatically transmit information about the user and the page being viewed to a monitoring server.
- *Databases, data warehouses, data mining, and "profiling"*—technologies that allow marketers to identify exactly who the online customer is and what they want, and then to present the customer with exactly what they want, when they want it, for the right price.
- *CRM systems*—a repository of customer information that records all of the contacts that a customer has with a firm and generates a customer profile available to everyone in the firm who has a need to "know the customer."

■ Identify and describe basic e-commerce marketing and branding strategies.

The marketing technologies described above have spawned a new generation of marketing techniques and added power to some traditional techniques.

- Internet marketing strategies for market entry for new firms include pure clicks/first-mover and mixed bricks-and-clicks/alliances; and for existing firms include pure clicks/fast-follower and mixed bricks-and-clicks/brand extender.
- Online marketing techniques to online customers include the use of advertising networks, permission marketing, affiliate marketing, viral marketing, blog marketing, social network marketing, and brand leveraging.
- Online techniques for strengthening customer relationships include one-to-one marketing, customization and customer co-production, transactive content, and customer service (such as CRMs, FAQs, live chat, intelligent agents, and automated response systems).
- Online pricing strategies include offering products and services for free, versioning, bundling, and dynamic pricing.

- Companies operating in the e-commerce environment must also have marketing strategies in place to handle the possibility of channel conflict.

QUESTIONS

1. Is growth of the Internet, in terms of users, expected to continue indefinitely? What will cause it to slow, if anything?
2. Other than search engines, what are some of the most popular uses of the Internet?
3. Would you say that the Internet fosters or impedes social activity? Explain your position.
4. Why would the amount of experience someone has using the Internet likely increase future Internet usage?
5. Research has shown that many consumers use the Internet to investigate purchases before actually buying, which is often done in a physical storefront. What implication does this have for online merchants? What can they do to entice more online buying, rather than pure research?
6. Name four improvements Web merchants could make to encourage more browsers to become buyers.
7. Name the five stages in the buyer decision process and briefly describe the online and offline marketing activities used to influence each.
8. Why are "little monopolies" desirable from a marketer's point of view?
9. Describe a perfect market from the supplier's and customer's perspective.
10. Explain why an imperfect market is more advantageous for businesses.
11. What are the components of the core product, actual product, and augmented product in a feature set?
12. List some of the major advantages of having a strong brand. How does a strong brand positively influence consumer purchasing?
13. How are product positioning and branding related? How are they different?
14. List the differences among databases, data warehouses, and data mining.
15. Name some of the drawbacks to the four data mining techniques used in Internet marketing.
16. Why have advertising networks become controversial? What, if anything, can be done to overcome any resistance to this technique?
17. Which of the four market entry strategies is most lucrative?
18. Compare and contrast four marketing strategies used in mass marketing, direct marketing, micromarketing, and one-to-one marketing.
19. What pricing strategy turned out to be deadly for many e-commerce ventures during the early days of e-commerce? Why?
20. Is price discrimination different from versioning? If so, how?
21. What are some of the reasons that freebies, such as free Internet service and giveaways, don't work to generate sales at a Web site?
22. Explain how versioning works. How is this different from dynamic pricing?
23. Why do companies that bundle products and services have an advantage over those that don't or can't offer this option?

PROJECTS

1. Go to the SRI site (www.sric-bi.com/VALS/presurvey.shtml). Take the survey to determine which lifestyle category you fit into. Then write a brief two-page paper describing how your lifestyle and values impact your use of the Web for e-commerce. How is your online consumer behavior affected by your lifestyle?

2. Find an example of a Web site that you feel does a good job appealing to both goal-directed and experiential consumers. Explain your choice.

3. Choose a digital content product available on the Web and describe its feature set.

4. Visit Eluxury.com and create an Internet marketing plan for it that includes each of the following:

   - One-to-one marketing
   - Affiliate marketing
   - Viral marketing
   - Blog marketing
   - Social network marketing

   Describe how each plays a role in growing the business, and create a Power-Point slide presentation of your marketing plan.

WEB SITE RESOURCES www.azimuth-interactive.com/ecommerce6e

- Additional projects, exercises, and tutorials
- Careers: Explore career opportunities in e-commerce
- Raising capital and business plans

CHAPTER 7

E-commerce Marketing Communications

LEARNING OBJECTIVES

After reading this chapter, you will be able to:

- Identify the major forms of online marketing communications.
- Understand the costs and benefits of online marketing communications.
- Discuss the ways in which a Web site can be used as a marketing communications tool.

Video Ads Cure Banner Blindness:

String Master

The age of online video ads is upon us, just in case you haven't noticed. Improvements in video production tools, and better streaming quality, have fueled an online video surge. Video production is no longer the exclusive province of just a few major players in New York and Hollywood, but instead has expanded to a much larger group of potential creators. In addition, the ways online video can be viewed has also expanded, from desktop PCs and laptops to smartphones, netbooks, and Web-enabled television sets.

The online audience for videos is huge. In 2009, over 160 million people (80% of all U.S. Internet users) watched online videos. In August 2009, YouTube streamed a staggering 10 billion videos! This makes video an obvious advertising medium. And just in time: Internet users have learned how to avoid traditional banner ads by instinctively moving their eyes to a different part of the screen. Click-throughs on banner ads are miniscule. Videos are another story: next to search engine marketing, and focused e-mail campaigns, videos have the highest click-through rate. Firms are using online video for marketing in two primary ways. Many companies produce their own videos to promote their brands and sell products. Other companies attach a text or ad to videos created by others to support their brand or make sales.

Evan Sofron's company, Actiontuners, is an example of the first type of online video promotion. String Master is a robotic guitar tuner that uses a computer-based listening device and a geared motor to tune a guitar to a perfect pitch. Evan initially used Google AdWords and text ads in both keyword and site-targeted campaigns. He saw a 15% increase in sales, but felt it was difficult to convey the features of his product, or what it looked like, with just text ads. Evan was also disappointed that the click-through rates for the ads were only 0.5%. Several years ago, Google began developing the capability to distribute video ads on its AdSense network. Evan created a 30-second video that demonstrated how String Master actually worked. Then, working with the Google Content Network, he chose various guitar, music, and musician sites on which the video ad would be displayed. Evan focused on optimizing the number of plays for his video and the time viewers spent watching his ads on the various sites. In a few weeks he could tell which sites were most productive, and focused his ads on these sites while removing them from the other sites. In a few months, Evan increased sales of String Master by 40%. Click-through rates averaged 8.5% across all sites, and went as high as 30% on some sites.

Major Fortune 500 companies have learned a similar lesson: people are far more likely to watch a video, and pay attention to the content, than look at a banner ad or remember a text ad on Google. Many large firms are moving into the online video advertising marketplace with sophisticated campaigns and big budgets. For instance, Dove Soap (owned by Unilever) has created a number of very successful online viral videos to promote the Dove Self-Esteem Fund. One of the videos in the series, Evolution, has been viewed on YouTube over 12 million times. Dove's experience also illustrates the perils of video advertising on YouTube: there are thousands of user-generated videos that disparage the Dove video and brand name.

Other big-name firms using online video include the The Gap, HP, and Allstate. The Gap, struggling to get back into the high fashion jeans market, is promoting its new 1969 Premium Jeans line at borntofit.com with a video interview featuring Patrick Robinson, the jeans' designer. Allstate has an entire YouTube channel devoted to explaining storm risks to its potential customers and building its brand name. Many Fortune 500 firms have YouTube channels where they control the video content and ad environment.

Sony Music's use of the famous Jill Peterson and Kevin Heinz "JK" wedding dance entrance video shot in a Minnesota church is an example of the second type of online video marketing. The video became a global hit with more than 12 million views in the first week alone. Sony Music used YouTube's content management tools to request YouTube to overlay a click-to-buy ad for its copyrighted song "Forever" by Chris Brown, which the wedding couple used as its wedding entrance song on the video. The ad directed viewers to either iTunes or Amazon. Sales of the song leaped to #4 on the iTunes chart, and #3 on Amazon's MP3 store. Although in this instance, the maker of the wedding video (the wedding couple) did not personally profit from it, YouTube has also enabled the monetizing of popular amateur videos through its YouTube Partnership program. When a video becomes really popular, YouTube e-mails the maker an "Enable revenue sharing" message that allows the maker to earn revenue from ads placed with the video.

People care and get excited about videos far more than banner ads and e-mail. This makes them an ideal advertising medium. The challenge is figuring out how to package advertising messages more directly with the videos, and how to piggyback advertising onto millions of user-generated video, and measure the impact on sales. Google, Yahoo, AOL, and literally hundreds of smaller firms, are hard at work trying to attach the right ads to the right videos, a tricky process since computers cannot "understand" the content of videos (although they can "understand" the audio script—sort of). No one wants their product ads attached to stolen, pornographic, or inappropriate videos. Another challenge is to figure out how to show the ad while the video plays without destroying the viewing experience. The final challenge is to avoid turning the viewer off, and causing a kind of video blindness on a mass scale.

SOURCES: "Video Content. A Premium Opportunity," by Paul Verna, eMarketer, August 2009; "YouTube Wedding Spurs Music Sales," by Brad Stone, *New York Times*, July 30, 2009; "Covering Many Bases for a Brand of Blue Jeans," by Stuart Elliot, *New York Times*, August 13, 2009; "YouTube to Share Ad Money With More Video Makers," by Reuters, *New York Times*, August 25, 2009; "What Works in Online Video Advertising," by Douglas MacMillion, *BusinessWeek*, January 2009; "Camera Ready: New Tools and Services for Small Companies to Create Video Ads," by Shelly Banjo, *Wall Street Journal*, August 28, 2008; "Lights! Camera! Sales!," by Raymund Flandez, *Wall Street Journal*, November 26, 2007; "Marketers See a Banner-Blindness Cure," by Emily Steel, *Wall Street Journal*, June 20, 2007; "Case Study: Using Video Advertising to Engage Your Customers," by Feng and Vivian, *Inside AdWords*, May 18, 2007.

The opening case provides an interesting glimpse into how the new broadband video capacity of homes and businesses, coupled with new Internet technologies, and widespread distribution of digital video cameras, is being used to influence consumer choice and build brand awareness. It also illustrates some of the challenges that marketers should be aware of when using these new forms of advertising.

In the last few years, Internet advertising has been on a tear. While the recession in late 2008 and 2009 slowed the growth of Internet advertising expenditures in 2009 to about 4.5%, analysts expect that this is a temporary state of affairs, and that advertising budgets will once again be increasing in 2010. In the meantime, the advertising industry as a whole—both offline and online—is going through a period of tumultuous change. The Internet and online advertising are disrupting the traditional advertising business, which was dominated by television and print media. Advertising budgets are following customer eyeballs and moving onto the Web, while expenditures for print and television are static or declining. **Table 7.1** summarizes the significant changes in the advertising industry for 2009–2010.

After taking a steep plunge in 2001 following the dot-com bust, aggressive forms of "push" advertising such as animated banners, and pop-ups that greet you on entering and leaving Web sites have exploded, along with unsolicited e-mail or "spam," which now consumes about 80%–90% of all e-mail traffic on the Internet. Paid search advertising (also called "pull" advertising)—where consumers search for and find information and advertisers pay for text ads, such as that offered by Google, Yahoo, MSN, and many others, has skyrocketed in popularity to become the single largest online ad form. Video advertising is still a small part of the overall Internet ad pie, but it is the fastest growing form of advertising. Internet advertising has become more costly as demand has exploded but still costs far less than traditional media advertising.

In Chapter 6, we described brands as a set of expectations that consumers have about products offered for sale. We discussed some of the marketing activities that companies engage in to create those expectations. In this chapter, we focus on understanding **online marketing communications**—all the major methods that online firms use to communicate to the consumer, create strong brand expectations, and drive sales. What are the best methods for attracting people to a Web site and converting them into customers? We also examine the Web site as a marketing communications tool. How does the design of a Web site affect sales? How can you optimize a Web site for search engines?

online marketing communications
methods used by online firms to communicate to the consumer and create strong brand expectations

TABLE 7.1	WHAT'S NEW IN INTERNET ADVERTISING 2009–2010
TREND	IMPACT
Internet advertising grows as a share of the total advertising budget at the expense of traditional media.	Online advertising in the United States will grow in 2009—2010 to around 10%–11% of the total spending for all forms of advertising.
Online ad spending increases, even as the total ad budget declines.	Despite the recession, online advertising grows in 2009 by 4.5% to $24.5 billion and will keep growing, by 9% in 2010, while total ad spending slips.
Search engine advertising spending continues to be the dominant form of spending on online advertising, accounting for about 50% of all online spending.	Search engine advertising grows in 2009 by 13.3% to almost $12 billion, and will keep growing, to $13.5 billion in 2010, over 2.5 times the size of the display banner ad format ($4.8 billion). However, the rate of growth is slowing.
Industry giants embrace Internet advertising.	Major packaged goods companies from Procter & Gamble to Budweiser move additional ad spending to the Web with an emphasis on interactive branding formats like video, brand sites (BudTV), Twitter, and social network sites.
Video, games, widgets, and virtual lives: New ad formats	The banner display ad, in all its forms, gives way to an explosion in video ads, games and in-game ads, ads in widgets, and ads on virtual sites.
Behavioral advertising, and personalized Web experiences	Behavioral marketing technologies come closer to the ideal of showing ads at the right time, to the right person, as well as personalizing the Web experience. Privacy protests grow.
Social networking sites seek to monetize their audience through display and interactive ad formats.	Social networking site ad revenues grow to $12.8 billion as ads follow the eyeballs.
Google, AOL, Microsoft, and Yahoo enter the display ad industry.	Declining growth rate in search advertising causes search and portal companies to leverage their online positions in search advertising into the display ad industry by purchasing online ad networks.
Metrics: challenges and solutions	Lack of industry standards, and new technologies like AJAX, complicate the problem of measuring the impact of online ads, and understanding how much these ads are worth.

7.1 MARKETING COMMUNICATIONS

Marketing communications have a dual purpose: branding and sales. One purpose of marketing communications is to develop and strengthen a firm's brands by informing consumers about the differentiating features of the firm's products and services. In addition, marketing communications are used to promote sales directly by encouraging the consumer to buy products (the sooner, the better). The distinction between the branding and sales purposes of marketing communications is subtle but important because branding communications differ from promotional communications. **Promotional sales communications** almost always suggest that the consumer "buy now," and they make offers to encourage immediate purchase. **Branding communications** rarely encourage consumers to buy now, but instead emphasize the differentiable benefits of consuming the product or service.

There are many different forms of online marketing communications, including online advertising, e-mail marketing, and public relations. Even the Web site itself can be viewed as a marketing communications tool.

ONLINE ADVERTISING

Advertising is the most common and familiar marketing communications tool. Companies will spend an estimated $250 billion on advertising in 2009, and an estimated $24.5 billion of that amount on **online advertising** (defined as a paid message on a Web site, paid search listing, video, widget, game, or other online medium, such as instant messaging) (see **Figure 7.1**) (eMarketer, Inc., 2009a).

In the last five years, advertisers have aggressively increased online spending and cut outlays on traditional channels such as radio, television, and newspapers. However, although online advertising is the fastest growing form of advertising, it will still remain a small part of total advertising for some time to come, reaching only 15% of all advertising by 2013.

Spending on online advertising among different industries is highly skewed. The top five industries—consumer (retail, automotive, travel, and packaged goods), financial services, computers, telecommunications, and media (television and radio broadcasting and print publishing)—account for 80% of all online advertising (Interactive Advertising Bureau/PricewaterhouseCoopers, 2009). Online advertising has both advantages and disadvantages when compared to advertising in traditional media, such as television, radio, and print (magazines and newspapers). One big advantage for online advertising is that the Internet is where the audience is moving, especially the very desirable 18–34 year olds, as well as the ballooning baby boomers who are over-65 years of age. A second large advantage for online advertising is the ability to target ads to narrow segments and track performance of advertisements in almost real time. **Ad targeting**, the sending of market messages to specific subgroups in the population in an effort to increase the likelihood of a purchase, is as old as advertising itself. Ad targeting is also the foundation of price discrimination: the ability to charge different types of consumers different prices for the same product or service. The six major online

promotional sales communications
suggest the consumer "buy now" and make offers to encourage immediate purchase

branding communications
focus on extolling the differentiable benefits of consuming the product or service

online advertising
a paid message on a Web site, online service, or other interactive medium

ad targeting
the sending of market messages to specific subgroups in the population

FIGURE 7.1	ONLINE ADVERTISING FROM 2002–2013

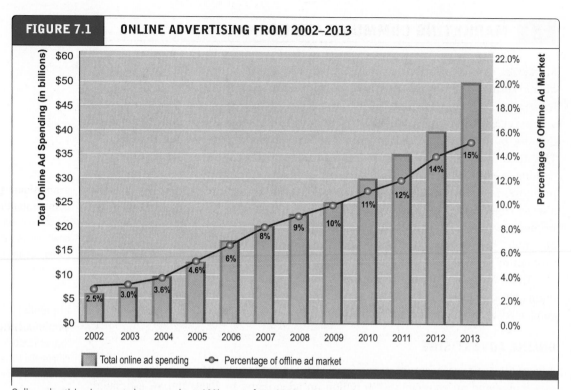

Online advertising is expected to grow about 10% a year from 2009 to 2013, and to comprise an increasing percentage of total advertising expenditures.

SOURCES: Based on data from eMarketer, Inc., 2009a.

segmentation and targeting methods (behaviorial, demographic, pyschographic, technical, contextual, and search) were described in Table 6.7 in Chapter 6. We further discuss ad targeting later in this section.

Theoretically, online advertising can personalize every ad message to precisely fit the needs, interests, and values of each consumer. In practice, as we all know from spam and constant exposure to pop-up ads that are of little interest, the reality is very different. Online advertisements also provide greater opportunities for interactivity—two-way communication between advertisers and potential customers. The primary disadvantages of online advertising are concerns about its cost versus its benefits, how to adequately measure its results, and the supply of good venues to display ads. For instance, the owners of Web sites who sell advertising space ("publishers") do not have agreed-upon standards or routine audits to verify their claimed numbers as do traditional media outlets. We examine the costs and benefits of online advertising as well as research on its effectiveness in Section 7.2.

There are a number of different forms of online advertisement:

- Display ads (banners and pop-ups)
- Rich media ads
- Video ads

- Search engine advertising
- Social network, blog, and game advertising
- Sponsorships
- Referrals (affiliate relationship marketing)
- E-mail marketing
- Online catalogs

Table 7.2 provides some comparative data on the amount of spending for certain advertising formats. The online advertising format that currently produces the highest revenue is paid search, followed by display ads, but the fastest growing online ad format is rich media/video ads. We discuss the various online ad formats in more depth next.

Display Ads: Banners and Pop-Ups

Display ads were the first Internet advertisements. A **banner ad** displays a promotional message in a rectangular box at the top or bottom of a computer screen. A banner ad is similar to a traditional ad in a printed publication but has some added advantages. If clicked on, it can bring a potential customer directly to the advertiser's Web site. It also is much more dynamic than a printed ad: it can present multiple images or otherwise change its appearance.

Banner ads sometimes feature Flash video and animations or animated GIFs, which display different images in relatively quick succession, creating an animated effect. The Interactive Advertising Bureau (IAB), an industry organization, has established voluntary industry guidelines for banner ads. A full banner, the most common, is 468 pixels wide by 60 pixels high with a resolution of 72 dpi (dots per inch) and a maximum file size of 13 KB.

banner ad
displays a promotional message in a rectangular box at the top or bottom of a computer screen

TABLE 7.2	ONLINE ADVERTISING SPENDING FOR SELECTED FORMATS (IN BILLIONS)		
FORMAT	2009	2013	%CHANGE
Search	$11.95	$18.34	53%
Display ads	$4.65	$5.54	19%
Video ads	$1.05	$4.09	290%
Classified	$2.67	$2.97	11%
Rich media	$1.69	$2.64	56%
Lead generation (affiliate marketing/referrals)	$1.76	$2.60	48%
E-mail	$0.39	$0.52	33%
Sponsorships	$0.32	$0.48	50%
Total	$24.5	$37.2	52%

SOURCES: Based on data from eMarketer, Inc., 2009a; authors' estimates.

The IAB guidelines include specifications for virtually all types of ads and buttons, including skyscrapers (a tall, narrow banner ad almost three times the height of the traditional vertical banner ad), rectangles of various sizes, and a square pop-up (which opens in a separate window), to allow marketers to develop ads featuring enhanced interactivity as well as expanded creativity. The various types of ads (including the rich media/video ads discussed in the next section) are designed to help advertisers break through the "noise" and clutter created by the high number of display ad impressions that a typical user is exposed to within a given day. Advertising networks such as DoubleClick serve over 500 billion impressions of various types in a single year, and research firms estimate that Internet users are exposed to over 1,000 display ads per day. **Figure 7.2** shows examples of some of the different types of display ads, as specified by the IAB.

pop-up ad

banners and buttons that appear on the screen without the user calling for them

Pop-up ads are those banners and buttons that appear on the screen without the user calling for them. Generally, these ads conform to the size specifications of the IAB banner and button specifications. One type of pop-up ad is the **pop-under ad**, which opens underneath a user's active browser window and does not appear until the user closes the active window. The ad remains visible until the user takes action to close it. Pop-ups can appear prior to display of the consumer's target page, during, or after the display on leaving.

pop-under ad

opens underneath a user's active browser window and does not appear until the user closes the active window

Multiple surveys have found that pop-up ads that appear over a user's Web page cause negative consumer sentiment. Online consumers rate pop-ups right next to telemarketing as the most annoying form of marketing communication. A number of ISPs and search engine/portal sites, such as Yahoo, Google, AOL, and Earthlink, now offer consumers pop-up blocking toolbars, as do Web browsers such as Mozilla Firefox and Internet Explorer 7 and 8. Unfortunately, studies have found that pop-up ads are twice as effective in terms of click-through rates than normal banner ads (although this may occur because people get confused about how to close the ads and end up unintentionally clicking to the advertised site). As a result, despite the backlash, although the number of pop-ups and pop-unders are likely to decline, they will not disappear entirely.

Rich Media Ads

rich media ads

ad employing Flash, DHTML, and Java, and streaming audio and/or video

Rich media ads are ads that employ animation, sound, and interactivity, using Flash, dynamic HTML (DHTML), Java, and JavaScript. Rich media ads will account for about $1.7 billion in online advertising expenditures (about 7% of total online advertising) in 2009 and are expected to grow to about $2.64 billion by 2013. Rich media ads tend to be more about branding than driving sales per se and have been found to be more effective than display ads. For instance, one research report found that exposure to rich media ads boosted brand awareness by 10% over a control group. The same methodology applied to normal banner ads found that it took three exposures to a large rectangle ad to produce a similar increase, six exposures to a skyscraper unit to get an 8% increase, and ten exposures to a regular banner ad to get a 6% increase (Dynamic Logic, 2004).

interstitial ad

a way of placing a full-page message between the current and destination pages of a user

Interstitial ads are typically considered a kind of "rich media" ad. An **interstitial ad** (interstitial means "in between") is a way of placing a full-page message between the current and destination pages of a user. Interstitials are usually inserted within a

FIGURE 7.2	TYPES OF DISPLAY ADS

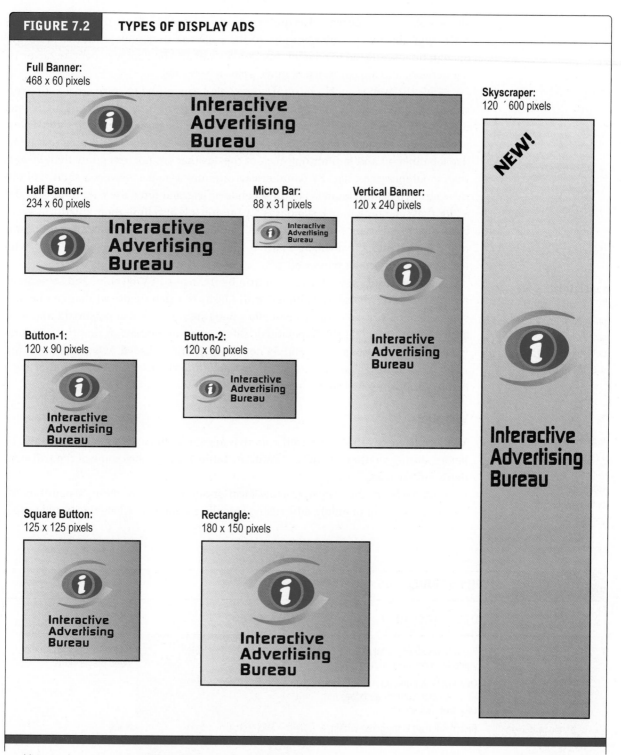

In addition to the various display ads shown above, IAB also provides standards for a medium, large, and vertical rectangle, a square pop-up, a wide skyscraper, a half-page ad, and an ad it calls a "leaderboard" (728 x 90 pixels).

SOURCE: Interactive Advertising Bureau, 2008.

single Web site, and displayed as the user moves from one page to the next. The interstitial typically moves automatically to the page the user requested after allowing enough time for the ad to be read. Interstitials can also be deployed over an advertising network and appear as users move among Web sites.

Since the Web is such a busy place, people have to find ways to cope with over-stimulation. One means of coping is known as sensory input filtering. This means that people learn to filter out the vast majority of the messages coming at them. Internet users quickly learn at some level to recognize banner ads or anything that looks like a banner ad and to filter out most of the ads that are not exceptionally relevant. Interstitial messages, like TV commercials, attempt to make viewers a captive of the message. Typical interstitials last 10 seconds or less and force the user to look at the ad for that time period. IAB standards for pre-roll ads also limit their length. To avoid boring users, ads typically use animated graphics and music to entertain and inform them. A good interstitial will also have a "skip through" or "stop" option for users who have no interest in the message.

superstitial
a rich media ad that is pre-loaded into a browser's cache and does not play until fully loaded and the user clicks to another page

A **superstitial** (now offered by a firm by the name of Viewpoint and sometimes referred to as a Unicast Transitional with Flash) is a rich media ad that can be any screen display size up to full screen 900 x 500 (the full-screen superstitial), and with a file size of up to 600 KB. Superstitials differ from interstitials in that they are pre-loaded into a browser's cache and do not play until fully loaded. When the file is finished downloading, like an interstitial, it waits until the user clicks to another page before popping up in a separate window.

Video Ads

video ad
TV-like advertisement that appears as an in-page video commercial or before, during, or after, content

Video ads are TV-like advertisements that appear as in-page video commercials or before, during, or after a variety of content. **Table 7.3** describes some of the IAB standards for video ads.

Video ads are the fastest growing form of online advertisement, accounting for about $1.05 billion in online advertising spending, which is expected to almost triple

TABLE 7.3	TYPES OF VIDEO ADS		
FORMAT	DESCRIPTION	WHEN USED	USED WITH
Linear video ad	Pre-roll; takeover; ad takes over video for a certain period of time	Before, between, after video	Text, banners, rich media video player skins
Non-linear video ad	Overlay; Web bugs; ad runs at same time as video content and does not take over full screen	During, over, or within video	
In-banner video ad	Rich media; ad is triggered within banner, may expand outside banner	Within Web page, generally surrounded by content	None
In-text video ad	Rich media; ad is delivered when user mouses over relevant text	Within Web page, identified as a highlighted word within relevant content	None

to $4.0 billion by 2013. However, from a total revenue standpoint, online video ads are still very small when compared to the amount spent on search engine advertising, and of course, are dwarfed by the amount spent on television advertising (eMarketer, 2009b).

The explosion of online video content across major news and entertainment sites, Web portals, and humor and user-generated sites has created huge opportunities for brand marketers to better reach their target audiences. About 80% of the entire U.S. Internet audience (around 160 million viewers) now watch online videos(comScore, 2009). Online video has become the audience aggregator of the twenty-first century, displacing television broadcast networks and Hollywood film producers .

Exactly how to take advantage of this opportunity is still a puzzle. Internet users are willing to listen to advertising in order to see short video clips as long as the ads don't interfere, and the ads are not too long. There are many formats for displaying ads with videos. Currently, the most widely used format is the "pre-roll" (followed by the mid-roll and the post-roll) where users are forced to watch an ad, often another video, either before, in the middle, or at the end of the video they originally clicked on. While advertising firms have been successful in selling the video ad format to firms, the major video sites such as YouTube and MySpace have had a difficult time selling their ad space and monetizing their huge audiences.

There are many specialized video advertising networks such as VideoEgg, Advertsing.com, Broadband, Roo, and others who run video advertising campaigns for national advertisers and place these videos on their respective network of Web sites. Firms can also establish their own video and television sites to promote their products. For instance Anheuser Busch has created Bud.tv, where "beer drinkers to kick back and take a break with original comedy, sports, and web video entertainment.".

Regardless of the type of advertising, most large advertisers work through intermediaries such as advertising networks (e.g., DoubleClick), or advertising agencies that have an ad placement and creative staff. Other options include swapping ad space with other sites, and dealing directly with the publisher (the Web site that will post the advertisement). **Banner swapping** arrangements among firms allow each firm to have its banners displayed on other affiliate sites for no cost. **Advertising exchanges** arrange for banner swapping among firms, usually small firms that cannot afford expensive ad networks such as DoubleClick. By displaying the banners of other firms, the firm can earn credits toward the display of its banner on other Web sites. Smaller firms have many more opportunities than in the past to place banner ads inexpensively using Yahoo Advertising, Google Ads, and Microsoft's Digital Advertising Solutions. Each of these firms provides targeting, segmentation, cross-selling techniques, and ad customization.

banner swapping
an arrangement among firms that allows each firm to have its banners displayed on other affiliate sites for no cost

advertising exchanges
arrange for banner swapping among firm

Search Engine Advertising: Paid Search Engine Inclusion and Placement

Arguably, the most significant change in online marketing in the past five years has been the explosive growth in search engine marketing. More than any other form of online advertising, search engine marketing has altered the entire marketing communications industry. This form of marketing communications has been one of the fastest growing: revenues generated by search engine marketing have grown from 1% of total online advertising spending in 2000 to almost 50% in 2009 (see **Figure 7.3**), although the rate of growth is slowing to around 10%–13% a year (eMarketer, Inc. 2009a). The search engine audience is huge—almost as big as the e-mail user population. On an average day in the United States, around 78.5 million American adults (around 50% of the adult online population) will use a search engine (Pew Internet & American Life Project, 2009). Collectively, they generate around 10–15 billion searches a month. Briefly, this is where the eyeballs are (at least for a few moments) and this is where advertising can be very effective by responding with ads that match the interests and intentions of the user. The click-through rate for search marketing generally is 10%–15% and has been fairly steady over the years.

Today there are hundreds of search engines on the Internet, with about 25 "major" search sites that generate most of the search traffic. Search engine marketing is highly concentrated. The top three search engine providers (Google, Yahoo, and MSN) supply over 95% of all the searches to these top 20 sites (see Figure 3.21).

Types of Search Engine Marketing There are at least three different types of search engine marketing: keyword paid inclusion or rank, advertising keywords, and search engine-based advertising networks. Search engine sites originally performed unbiased searches of the Web's huge collection of Web pages and derived most of their revenue from banner advertisements. This form of search engine results is often

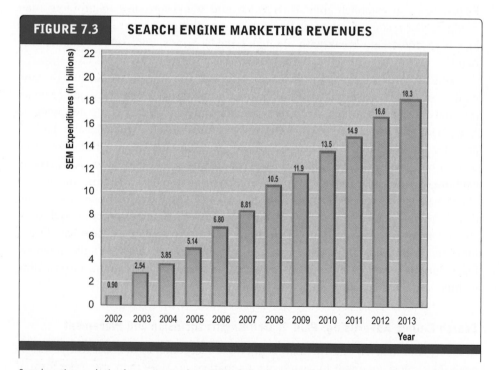

FIGURE 7.3 **SEARCH ENGINE MARKETING REVENUES**

Search engine marketing has grown to about 50% of all online advertising. However, its growth rate has slowed considerably to the low double digits.

SOURCES: Based on data from eMarketer, Inc., 2009, 2007a, 2005.

called **organic search** because the inclusion and ranking of Web sites depends on a more or less "unbiased" application of a set of rules (an algorithm) imposed by the search engine. Since 1998, search engine sites have slowly been transforming themselves into digital yellow pages, where firms pay for inclusion in the search engine index and/or pay for specific locational placement or rank in the results of searches—so-called paid placement or paid rank.

Most search engines offer **paid inclusion** programs which, for a fee, guarantee a Web site's inclusion in its list of search results, more frequent visits by its Web crawler, and suggestions for improving the results of organic searching. Search engines claim that these payments—costing some merchants hundreds of thousands a year do not influence the organic ranking of a Web site in search results, just inclusion in the results. However, it is the case that page inclusion ads get more hits, and the rank of the page appreciates, causing the organic search algorithm to rank it higher in the organic results.

Some search engines do not have a paid inclusion program, but do charge for placing small text ads in either sponsored link areas of the results pages or sometimes mixed with organic results (unbeknownst to the user). Google claims it does not permit firms to pay for their rank in the organic results, although it does allocate two to three sponsored links at the very top of their pages, albeit labeling them as "Sponsored Links." Some search engines make it very difficult for the user to know if the top-listed results of a search are paid inclusions or the result of objective search criteria. Merchants who refuse to pay for inclusion typically fall far down on the list and off the first page of results, which is akin to commercial death.

Research demonstrates the significance of rank in both organic and paid placements, and equally important, the greater power that users attach to organic search results (see **Figure 7.4**). Researchers used an eye-tracking tool to gauge Web users' behavior at search engines. They discovered an "F" shaped pattern in which viewers scan search result pages from top to bottom, with greater attention to the left side of the page looking for clues. They spend less time on the right side of the page looking at paid text advertisements, and usually only at the top three advertisements. Users always viewed the first three organic listings, but were much less likely to view the sponsored listings. These results have been replicated several times using eye heat maps (Shrestha and Lenz, 2007; Nielsen, 2006).

The two other types of search engine marketing rely on selling keywords in online auctions.

In **keyword advertising**, merchants purchase keywords through a bidding process at search sites, and whenever a consumer searches for that word, their advertisement shows up somewhere on the page, usually as a small text-based advertisement on the right, but also as a listing on the very top of the page. The more merchants pay, the higher the rank and greater the visibility of their ads on the page. Generally, the search engines do not exercise editorial judgment about quality or content of the ads although they do monitor the use of language. In addition, some search engines rank the ads in terms of their popularity rather than merely the money paid by the advertiser so that the rank of the ad depends both on the amount paid and the number of clicks per unit time. Google's keyword advertising program is called AdWords, Yahoo's is called Sponsored Search, and Microsoft's is called adCenter.

organic search
inclusion and ranking of sites depends on a more or less unbiased application of a set of rules imposed by the search engine

paid inclusion
for a fee, guarantees a Web site's inclusion in its list of sites, more frequent visits by its Web crawler, and suggestions for improving the results of organic searching

keyword advertising
merchants purchase keywords through a bidding process at search sites, and whenever a consumer searches for that word, their advertisement shows up somewhere on the page

FIGURE 7.4	THE IMPORTANCE OF RANK FOR CUSTOMER VIEWING BY TYPE OF SEARCH

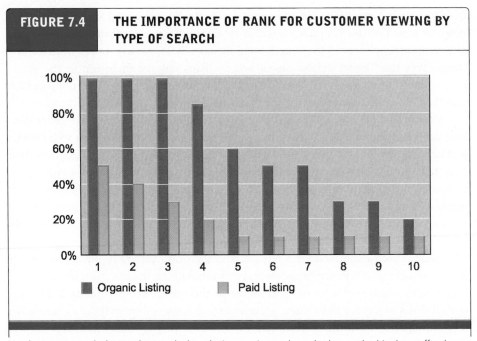

Nearly everyone reads the top three-ranked results in organic search results, but readership drops off rather dramatically for the 4th through 10th-ranked results. Sponsored links are heavily discounted by readers—only 50% read the top-ranked sponsored results listed, and readership drops off sharply after that.

SOURCE: Based on data from Hotchkiss, et al., 2007.

network keyword advertising (context advertising)

network of publishers accepts ads placed by Google on their Web sites, and receive a fee for any click-throughs from those ads

Network keyword advertising (**context advertising**), introduced by Google in 2002, differs from ordinary keyword advertising described previously. Here's how these search engine networks operate. Publishers (Web site owners) join the network, and allow the search engine to place "relevant" ads on their sites. The ads are paid for by advertisers who want their messages to appear across the Web. Google-like text messages are the most common. The revenue from the resulting clicks is split between the search engine and the site publisher although in some cases the publisher gets much more than half. The publisher has no direct control over what ads are shown on his/her site. The advertiser has no control over where their ads appear either. But the search engines use a variety of tools (keyword analysis and propinquity of keywords) to ensure only "relevant" and "appropriate" ads appear. For this reason, network keyword advertising is often called "context marketing" because an effort is made to understand the context where the ad will be shown. Google calls this "AdSense," knowing where to place ads based on the surrounding context. Yahoo's program is called Content Match. Together, keyword and network keyword advertising account for most of the revenue growth in search engine marketing. About half of Google's revenue comes from AdWords and the rest comes from AdSense.

In this manner, the search engines have greatly extended their keyword advertising beyond their own sites (where users do not linger) to tens of thousands of other sites on the Web. Unfortunately, these programs have also led to the creation of "junk AdSense" sites composed of re-hashed links from the Web, and an entire industry of illegitimate poachers who nevertheless are paid when their Web site visitors click on an adSense link.

Keywords for both types of keyword advertising range in price from a few pennies per click, to $25 or above for high-priced popular items (see **Figure 7.5**). The highest keyword prices are paid for potential litigation customers by law firms. The family of "mesothelioma" keywords sell for up to $800 a click. How much would you pay (or should you pay) to place your company's listing in front of the consumer just at the precise moment the consumer is looking for products provided by your company? This depends, of course, on how much customers are likely to spend at your site. And it depends on how much your competitors are willing to pay for the same keyword. In an auction environment, it is easy to overpay or under pay.

Search engine marketing is nearly an ideal targeted marketing technique: at precisely the moment that a consumer is looking for a product, an advertisement for that product is presented. While originally this was the idea behind advertising networks such as DoubleClick and Real Media 24/7, their database techniques cannot deliver the advertisement with as much accuracy or speed at the moment of interest.

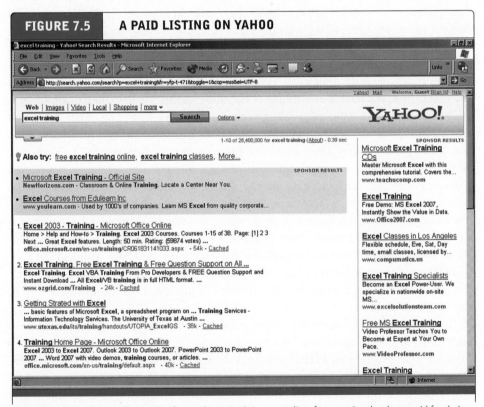

FIGURE 7.5   **A PAID LISTING ON YAHOO**

A search on "Excel training" on Yahoo's search engine brings up a list of companies that have paid for their inclusion and placement on the search results list.

SOURCE: Yahoo.com . Reproduced with permission of Yahoo! Inc. © 2008 Yahoo! Inc. YAHOO! and the YAHOO! logo are trademarks of Yahoo! Inc.

Unlike traditional online and offline targeted marketing approaches, which are based on searching large databases for customer profiles and information, search engine marketing is based on the much more efficient idea of responding to keyword searches at that moment (although prior searches from the IP address, or keywords gleaned from other sources such as Google's Gmail can also influence the results). No databases on clickstream behavior or background demographics are generally used. The most important fact for search engine marketers is that the customer is looking for a product like the one sold by the merchant.

In some cases, search engines do not inform the user that the results of a query have been paid for by participating firms, or they make it difficult to tell what is paid and what is the result of unbiased search. Some analysts argue that users don't care if merchants pay for listings—just as they don't care when they use the yellow pages—as long as the searches produce relevant results. Some have even argued that informing the user about the commercial nature of placement and listings would harm e-commerce because users have been trained by the industry to "avoid anything that looks commercial." Users might actually not pursue appropriate and relevant links if they thought the listing was commercially influenced. A number of complaints had been filed with the Federal Trade Commission (FTC) that search engines that fail to clearly indicate they accept payments for higher search ranking are engaging in deceptive practices. In July 2002, the FTC recommended to the search engine industry that it should improve the disclosure of paid content within search results (Sullivan, 2003). A follow-up study by Consumer Reports WebWatch found that paid inclusion was not satisfactorily disclosed or explained by any of the search engines tested; meta-engines, which present results from several search engines simultaneously, repeatedly failed to adequately disclose the presence of paid placement and paid inclusion within search results; and disclosures when made are generally hard to find, making them easy for consumers to overlook. The report also found that information disclosed by Web sites about business practices with advertisers—and how these practices may affect search results—was often confusing and jargon-laden. Some search engines, such as Google (one of the few major search engines not named in the original FTC complaint) took pains to visually segregate paid results from non-paid results (Consumer Reports WebWatch, 2004, 2005). The search engine industry has the online population pretty confused about where the results come from. A Pew Internet & American Life Project study found that 62% of search engine users were not aware of the difference between paid and unpaid results, and 70% accepted the concept of sponsored results. Half said they would stop using a search engine if they felt it was not being honest about how the results are produced (Pew Internet & American Life Project, 2005).

Why does search engine marketing work so well and why is it so popular with both merchants and consumers? For merchants, search engine marketing is close to ideal for sales promotion. Paid search engine inclusion and placement is one of the most effective marketing communications tools on the Web, given that on any given day about 89 million American adults use a search engine to find products and information.

The major search engines have been very helpful to small businesses that cannot afford large marketing campaigns. Because shoppers are looking for a specific product or service when they use search engines, they are what marketers call "hot prospects"—people who are looking for information and often intending to buy. Moreover, search engines charge only for click-throughs to a site. Merchants do not have to pay for ads that don't work. Last, merchants do not have to be at the mercy of search engine ranking and listing rules that they—and most others—cannot understand. No one really knows, for instance, exactly how or why Google decides to organically rank one company over another, or to refuse a company a listing in the front pages. No one really knows how to improve their rankings (although there are hundreds of firms who claim otherwise). In fact, according to Google's own self-description of its search engine, listings are biased toward already popular Web sites to whom many consumers connect, and ignore new startup companies or put them on back pages. Google editors intervene in unknown ways to punish certain Web sites and reward others. Search engines such as Google maintain a stranglehold over small companies trying to get national market exposure. Paid listings change much of this. A company simply pays Google or another search engine and has the certain knowledge that its ad will appear on the page and with a rank that reflects its bid. For many merchants who can afford this, the reduction in uncertainty is worth the price.

What about consumers? Consumers benefit from search engine marketing because ads for merchants appear only when consumers are looking for a specific product. There are no pop-ups, Flash animations, videos, interstitials, e-mails, or other irrelevant communications to deal with. Thus, search engine marketing saves consumers cognitive energy. Search engine marketing works because it is primarily pull-oriented: consumers pull the information they are looking for.

Search Engine Click Fraud and Ad Nonsense The Achilles' heel of search engine marketing is "click fraud." Just as spam has greatly reduced the utility of e-mail marketing, so has click fraud raised the costs and reduced the attractiveness of search engine marketing to merchants. So much of the Internet depends on openness, trust, and ethical behavior by participants. Click fraud strikes at the heart of these assumptions.

Anyone, including competitors, can click on search engine ads, driving up a merchant's costs, without ever purchasing anything. If you are a Web site publisher, you can increase your revenue by having friends and relatives click on the ads Google or Microsoft place on your site. **Click fraud** occurs when (a) a competitor fraudulently clicks on another competitor's ads in order to drive up their marketing costs, or (b) a Web site publisher fraudulently clicks on ads posted on their sites in order to increase ad revenue. Some fraudsters have developed "click bots" that automatically click on ads from hundreds of different IP addresses, and utilize zombie computers (unprotected clients on the Web that have been captured by adware programs) to generate the clicks, which are untraceable. A related type of click fraud involves fraudsters who call up a search results page where their competitors' ads appear, and then fail to click on competitor ads. This results in a low ad popularity rank for these Google AdWords and AdSense ads, which in turn can result in their being pushed down the rank order of ads onto the lower part of the page.

click fraud
occurs when a competitor hires third parties (typically from low-wage countries) to fraudulently click on another competitor's ads

Search engines attempt to monitor and prevent this behavior by observing traffic patterns, but find it difficult to trace fraudulent clicks because defrauders can hide their offshore IP addresses. Current research suggests the click fraud rate in the United States is around 13% of all clicks (Click Forensics, 2009). The amount of publisher-originated click fraud is not known. SEMPO, the Search Engine Marketing Professional Organization (a trade association of marketers in part sponsored by search engine firms), reports that 40% of large advertisers felt click fraud was a problem, 19% of advertisers attempt to track click fraud, and about 50% of advertisers have reduced their keyword search budgets because of click fraud (Fair Isaac Corporation, 2007). Click fraud can be difficult but not impossible to detect. The typical click fraud pattern is one where clicks increase and sales remain the same or decline. Large departures from historical click rates (such as one standard deviation or more) are suspect. Search engine firms such as Google and Yahoo do refund charges in suspicious situations. A somewhat less severe issue is the appearance of "ad nonsense," which occurs because Google's AdSense program places ads on thousands of Web sites using a computer program that attempts to understand the content of the Web page. Sometimes, the computer program makes mistakes, such as when a search on the term "lost dogs" produces ads on Google offering "great deals" on lost dogs, and ads for "disease," "sewage," and "rot." Even more disturbing to advertisers, sometimes ads for products show up on Web sites totally unrelated to that product. For instance, Kraft Foods ads for cheese appeared on a Web site of a "White Nationalist" hate group that used the words "Thanksgiving" on its Web site. Advertisers lose control over where their ads appear when they use the Google AdSense program.

Sponsorships

sponsorship
a paid effort to tie an advertiser's name to information, an event, or a venue in a way that reinforces its brand in a positive yet not overtly commercial manner

A **sponsorship** is a paid effort to tie an advertiser's name to particular information, an event, or a venue in a way that reinforces its brand in a positive yet not overtly commercial manner. Sponsorships typically are more about branding than immediate sales. A common form of sponsorship is targeted content (or advertorials), in which editorial content is combined with an ad message to make the message more valuable and attractive to its intended audience. For instance, WebMD.com, the leading medical information Web site in the United States, offers "sponsorship sites" on the WebMD Web site to companies such as Phillips to describe their home defibrillators, and Lilly to describe their pharmaceutical solutions for attention deficit disorders among children. According to eMarketer, sponsorships accounted for around $320 million in online advertising revenues in 2008 (eMarketer, Inc., 2009a).

Referrals (Affiliate Relationship Marketing)

affiliate relationships
permit a firm to put its logo or banner ad on another firm's Web site from which users of that site can click through to the affiliate's site

An **affiliate relationship** permits a firm (the originating Web site) to place its logo, banner ad, or text link on another firm's Web site (called the affiliate) from which users of that site can click through to the originating site. Millions of personal Web sites have Amazon and other logos that when clicked will take the visitor to Amazon, and generate revenue for the Web site. Among large firms, affiliate relationships are sometimes called "tenancy deals" because they allow a firm to become a long-term "tenant" on another site. Amazon has tenancy relationships with a number of retailers. In some cases, the firms share a single corporate parent or investor group that is seeking to optimize the performance of all its Web sites by creating links among its "children" sites. In other cases, two Web sites may sell complementary products and the firms may strike an affiliate relationship to make it easier for their customers to find the products they are looking for.

E-MAIL MARKETING AND THE SPAM EXPLOSION

In the early days of e-commerce, **direct e-mail marketing** (e-mail marketing messages sent directly to interested users) was one of the most effective forms of marketing communications. Direct e-mail marketing messages were sent to an "opt-in" audience of Internet users who, at one time or another, had expressed an interest in receiving messages from the advertiser. Unsolicited e-mail was not common. By sending e-mail to an opt-in audience, advertisers were targeting interested consumers. Response rates to legitimate, opt-in e-mail campaigns average just over 6%, depending on the targeting and freshness of the list. By far, in-house e-mail lists are more effective than purchased e-mail lists. Because of the comparatively high response rates and low cost, direct e-mail marketing remains a common form of online marketing communications. In 2009, the total amount U.S. companies spent on e-mail marketing was about $520 million (eMarketer, 2009a). Click rates for legitimate e-mails depend on the promotion (the offer), the product, and the amount of targeting, but they average in the 5%–6% range, higher than postal mail response rates (less than 2%–4%) (Epsilon, 2009). Despite the deluge of spam mail, e-mail remains a highly cost-effective way of communicating with existing customers, and to a lesser extent finding new customers.

direct e-mail marketing
e-mail marketing messages sent directly to interested users

E-mail marketing and advertising is inexpensive and somewhat invariant to the number of mails sent. The cost of sending 1,000 mails is about the same as the cost to send 1 million. The primary cost of e-mail marketing is for the purchase of the list of names to which the e-mail will be sent. This generally costs anywhere from 5 to 20 cents a name, depending on how targeted the list is. Sending the e-mail is virtually cost-free. In contrast, a direct mail 5 x 7-inch post card mailing costs about 15 cents per name, but printing and mailing costs raise the overall cost to around 75 to 80 cents a name. While the cost of legitimate e-mail messages based on high-quality commercial opt-in e-mail lists is $5 to $10 per thousand, the direct mail cost is $500 to $700 per thousand when all costs are added up.

In 2009, however, e-mail no longer commands quite as much respect as it once did because of three factors: spam, software tools used to control spam that eliminate much e-mail from user in-boxes, and poorly targeted purchased e-mail lists. **Spam** is "junk e-mail" and spammers are people who send unsolicited e-mail to a mass audience of Internet users who have expressed no interest in the product. Worse, spammers tend to market pornography, fraudulent deals and services, outright scams, and other products not widely approved in most civilized societies. Legitimate direct opt-in e-mail marketing is not growing as fast as behaviorally targeted banners, pop-ups, and search engine marketing because of the explosion in spam. Consumer response to even legitimate e-mail campaigns has

spam
unsolicited commercial e-mail

become more sophisticated. Almost three-quarters of Internet users say they see value in e-mail from companies they do business with, while only 17% saw value when the e-mail came from companies they do not do business with. As Internet users become more experienced with spam filters, more and more (currently around 70%) delete spam before opening based on the "From" line or the "Subject" line. Over 60% of users find e-mail commercial spam unpleasant and 20% report reduced overall use of e-mail because of spam (eMarketer, Inc., 2007b). In general, e-mail works well for maintaining the customer relationship, but poorly in acquiring new customers.

While click fraud may be the Achilles' heel of search engine marketing, spam is the nemesis of effective e-mail marketing and advertising. The percentage of all e-mail that is spam is estimated at around 80%–90% in 2009 (Symantec MessageLabs, 2009) (see **Figure 7.6**).

Figure 7.7 illustrates the average breakdown for the most common categories of spam, as recorded by Symantec and its subsidiary Brightmail, a San Francisco-based anti-spam software company, during 2008.

The cost of entry to the spam business or "mass bulk e-mailing business" is small. Hundreds of programs that can be purchased on the Web allow spammers to harvest e-mail addresses across the Web from message boards and chat rooms; downloads of millions of names are available. Spammers do not generally pay anything for the cost of distributing their spam because they send the messages using captured client and

FIGURE 7.6 | **PERCENTAGE OF E-MAIL THAT IS SPAM**

Spam Rate

88.5%

Last Month:	89.4%
Six Month Avg.:	89.6%

Top 5 Geographies	
93.4%	Hong Kong
92.6%	Denmark
92.5%	China
91.6%	United Kingdom
91.1%	Luxembourg

Top 5 Verticals	
93.4%	Engineering
93.2%	Education
92.5%	Automotive
91.9%	Marketing/Media
91.8%	Telecoms

By Horizontal	
90.5%	1–250
90.3%	251–500
90.8%	501–1000
90.5%	1001–1500
91.7%	1501–2500
89.8%	2501 +

2005   2006   2007   2008   2009

88.5%

August 2009

After a period of decline, spam volume has resumed growth largely because of the greater number and sophistication of "spam zombies" and "bot networks," which consist of thousands of captured PCs that can initiate and relay spam messages. Spam is seasonally cyclical, and varies monthly due to the impact of new technologies (both supportive and discouraging of spammers), new prosecutions, and seasonal demand for products and services. Spam seems to peak in June.

SOURCE: Symantec MessageLabs, 2009.

FIGURE 7.7	SPAM CATEGORIES

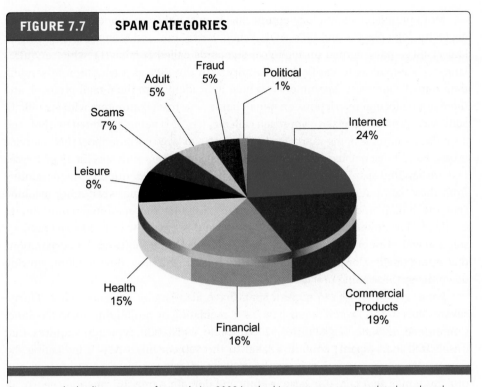

On average, the leading category of spam during 2008 involved Internet or computer-related goods and services, followed by commercial products, financial services and health products (drugs).
SOURCE: Symantec, 2009.

server computers. The explosion in spam has led to many unsuccessful efforts to control the deluge. There are four solutions to spam: technology, government legislation, voluntary self-regulation, and volunteer efforts to identify spammers and either shut them down or inform authorities. Obviously, none of these approaches has been successful to date, each approach has many advocates and entrepreneurs, and all approaches combined just might make a difference.

Filtering software on client computer browsers has helped companies and individual users cope with spam, but spammers purchase the same software to understand how to defeat them. Moreover, company mail servers still fill up with spam messages. Filters on corporate servers are more effective and reduce server loads by deleting spam or compressing it in smaller files. Large ISPs such as AOL and MSN are able to filter a lot of, but not all, spam, as spammers are able to capture thousands of unprotected client computers in homes and offices and to use them to originate spam mail without the owner's knowledge. ISPs set up "honey pots"— dummy e-mail accounts—that quickly receive spam mail to study the subject lines of spam and to develop filters on specific words and phrases. Spammers reply by creating new variations on words, often with dummy characters such as "V1agra" and "F*A*S*T M*O*N*E*Y".

More promising technology approaches may result from cooperation among the big technology players and ISPs. AOL, Yahoo, EarthLink, and Microsoft—the nation's largest ISPs—have agreed on technical standards called Sender ID, which requires large-scale e-mailers to verify their identity with the ISPs as a condition of sending their e-mail. Currently, spammers can hide their identity in the e-mail protocol, and there are no formal restrictions on e-mail being sent from computers with specific IP addresses. A more aggressive approach called FairUCE is being marketed by IBM, and a similar program is being marketed by Symantec to large corporations. IBM's service is based on a huge database that identifies actual computers with specific IP addresses that are sending spam, and adds them to a spam list. Once identified, e-mails coming from these computers are immediately returned to the actual spamming machine (not the e-mail address in the From: field), causing the spammer computer to overload, slow down, and choke. It is not clear at this time how well IBM's technology solution will work on a large scale. Symantec has developed software for corporations that intentionally slows down their bit rate to that of a very slow modem, slowing down the spam sending process.

Legislative attempts to control spam have also largely not succeeded. Thirty-seven states in the United States have laws regulating or prohibiting spam (National Conference of State Legislatures, 2008). State legislation typically requires that unsolicited mail (spam) contain a label in the subject line ("ADV") indicating the message is an advertisement, require a clear opt-out choice for consumers, and prohibit e-mail that contains false routing and domain name information (nearly all spammers hide their own domain, ISP, and IP address). Some states, such as California and Delaware, are much stricter and prohibit all unsolicited e-mail to or from state citizens and require a specific "opt-in" choice before consumers can be sent e-mail. In Virginia, sending spam is a criminal felony offense.

Congress passed the first national anti-spam law ("Controlling the Assault of Non-Solicited Pornography and Marketing" or CAN-SPAM Act) in 2003, and it went into effect in January 2004. The act does not prohibit unsolicited e-mail (spam) but instead requires unsolicited commercial e-mail messages to be labeled (though not by a standard method) and to include opt-out instructions and the sender's physical address. It prohibits the use of deceptive subject lines and false headers in such messages. The FTC is authorized (but not required) to establish a "do-not-e-mail" registry. State laws that require labels on unsolicited commercial e-mail or prohibit such messages entirely are pre-empted, although provisions merely addressing falsity and deception may remain in place. The act imposes fines of $10 for each unsolicited pornographic e-mail and authorizes state attorneys general to bring lawsuits against spammers. The act obviously makes lawful legitimate bulk mailing of unsolicited e-mail messages (what most people call spam), yet seeks to prohibit certain deceptive practices and provide a small measure of consumer control by requiring opt-out notices. In this sense, critics point out, CAN-SPAM ironically legalizes spam as long as spammers follow the rules. For this reason, large spammers have been among the bill's biggest supporters, and consumer groups have been the Act's most vociferous critics. Major business interest groups also lobbied against the CAN-SPAM bill. Citicorp, Schwab, Procter & Gamble, the National Retail Foundation, the Securities Industry Association, and the American Insurance Association all argued that the act would harm legitimate e-mail marketing and put e-commerce at a disadvantage.

There have been a number of state and federal prosecutions of spammers, and private civil suits by large ISPs such as Microsoft. For instance, in May 2007, Robert Soloway, a 27-year-old Seattle man also known as the "Spam King," was arrested after being indicted by a federal grand jury on 16 counts of mail fraud, e-mail fraud, wire fraud, and aggravated identity theft. According to the indictment, Soloway, operating under the name "Newport Internet Marketing," claimed to have a list of 158 million e-mail addresses, and charged $495 for a typical blast of 20 million e-mails sent over 15 days. Soloway obtained the e-mail addresses from "harvesting" programs and spyware programs that read lists from infected computers. He sold the lists to businesses claiming they contained only the addresses of "opt-in" prospects. Then, using remote botnets, he sent out blast e-mails of 20 to 100 million spam messages at a time. In 2007, prosecutors won a $7.8 million judgment against the King, and in March 2008 he pleaded guilty to federal criminal charges that he failed to pay income taxes on his spam income. Soloway faces 26 years in prison. Currently the FBI and Justice Department have over 100 spam and phishing investigations under way.

Volunteer efforts by industry are another potential control point. Notably, the Direct Marketing Association (DMA), an industry trade group that represents companies that use the postal mail system as well as e-mail for solicitations, is now strongly supporting legislative controls over spam, in addition to its voluntary guidelines. The DMA would like to preserve the legitimate use of e-mail as a marketing technique. The DMA has formed a 15-person anti-spam group and spends $500,000 a year trying to identify spammers; the DMA also is a supporter of the National Cyber-Forensics & Training Alliance, a purportedly non-profit organization with "close ties" to the FBI, which operates a program called Operation Slam Spam that seeks to identify the IP addresses of the largest spammers and has a database of over 400 known spam addresses.

ONLINE CATALOGS

Online catalogs are the equivalent of a paper-based catalog. Online catalogs were popular in the early years of e-commerce but quickly went out of favor among advertisers because the pages took so long to load. But with about 92% of the online households using broadband high-speed connections in 2009, graphic-intense pages load quickly, and the possibilities for advertisers to re-use their paper catalog photos increase. Web publishers such as Google Catalogs and Catalog.com have made it far easier for even small merchants to find an audience and re-purpose their expensive four-color offline catalogs. The result is a resurgence in online catalogs. The number of online catalogs in 2009 has more than doubled since 2005. E-catalog sales have risen to about 36% of U.S. multi-channel retailers (Direct Marketing Association, 2008; eMarketer, Inc., 2008a).

The basic function of a catalog is to display the merchant's wares (see **Figure 7.8**). The electronic version typically contains a color image of each available product and a description of the item, as well as size, color, material composition, and

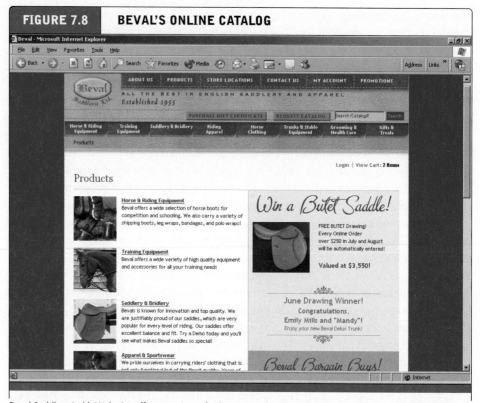

FIGURE 7.8 **BEVAL'S ONLINE CATALOG**

Beval Saddlery Ltd.'s Web site offers a variety of riding apparel and equipment. Customers can click on one of the product categories listed on the left side of the screen and are taken to a page listing products within that category. Clicking on a particular product takes the customer to a page with a description and photo of the product and an order button.

SOURCE: Beval Saddlery, Ltd., 2008.

pricing information. There are two different types of online catalogs: full-page spreads and grid displays. Most online retailers use a grid display in which multiple products are shown in very small postage-stamp photos. This is typical of Amazon, LLBean.com, and Gap.com. The other alternative is to use larger page spreads using large photos to display one or two products; HammacherSchlemmer.com, Landsend.com, and Restorationhardware.com use this approach, among others. The cost of building an online catalog ranges from $30,000—$50,000 for smaller Web sites, to several million for an online catalog with thousands of products and images.

How do companies integrate online catalogs with physical catalogs? Most direct mail catalog companies continue to use physical direct mail catalogs, and pure online companies have begun to supplement their online advertising with physical catalogs. Direct mail companies can increase their operational efficiency by sending electronic catalogs to customers before sending out the physical catalogs. This evens out the flow of orders. In general, merchants find that online and offline catalogs are complementary and do not cannibalize or substitute for one another. The flow of orders increases as the overall awareness of the company brand increases when both channels are used simultaneously. On the other hand, research suggests that the effects are subtle, and that much depends on the type of customer ("good" versus "best" customers) and their prior Internet experience (Anderson, et al., 2005).

SOCIAL MARKETING: BLOGS, SOCIAL NETWORKS, AND GAMES

The two key elements of Web 2.0 are the rapid growth of user-generated content and the use of the Internet for socializing and sharing. Around 45% of Internet users visit a social networking site at least once a month (eMarketer, 2009c). With 92 million Facebook users, 64 million MySpace users, 97 million blog readers, and over 120 million YouTube visitors, it's little wonder that marketers and advertisers are joyous at the prospect of connecting with this new audience. Microsoft's purchase of an interest in Facebook, and Google's purchase of YouTube, suggest the excitement in the marketing community for the advertising potential of social networking. Although in the past, major brands have been reluctant to risk advertising on sites whose content they cannot control, they are beginning to experiment with a number of new formats. In 2009, all forms of social marketing are expected to generate around $2 billion in revenues.

It is difficult to define "social marketing" precisely, but a working definition might be that it is advertising that adopts a many-to-many model as opposed to a one-to-many model of traditional advertising, where a central broadcaster sends the same message to millions of people. For instance, over 400,000 viewers saw Microsoft's Halo 3 trailer on YouTube in a single month after being posted by a handful of posters. About 2,500 added the video to their favorites lists, which are broadcast to all their friends. So an existing social network composed of many people distributes the Microsoft message to a great many other people.

This kind of marketing is "social" because, like traditional word-of-mouth and viral marketing, it relies on pre-existing social networks to spread the message. However, in this case, the social networks exist on the Internet, and they are digitally enabled networks whose members have extraordinary tools to spread the message far, wide, and very quickly. The vast majority of online social network members are also friends offline, or friends of friends offline (Ellison, et. al., 2006). Hence the offline world and the online world are intimately connected.

The three main areas of social marketing are blog, social network, and game advertising.

Blog Advertising

Blogs are very high on the list of advertising tactics that marketing executives consider. In 2009, blog advertising revenue will be about $530 million (out of a total online ad spend of $24.5 billion) during that year. However, it is expected to grow to $746 million by 2012 (eMarketer, Inc., 2008b). Blogs have proved difficult to monetize because few blogs attract large audiences, and the subject matter of most blogs is highly personal and idiosyncratic. Search engines have a difficult time "reading" blogs, understanding their content, and making a judgment about the appropriateness of their ad inventory. Advertising dollars are therefore concentrated in the top 100 blogs, which have a coherent theme that consistently attracts larger audiences. Because blog readers and creators tend to be more educated, have higher incomes, and be opinion leaders, they are ideal recipients of ads for many products and services that cater to this kind of an audience. Advertising networks that specialize in blogs provide some efficiency in placing ads, as do blog networks, which are collections of a small number of popular blogs, coordinated by a central management team, and which can deliver a larger audience to advertisers.

Social Network Advertising

Although still in its infancy, social network advertising is the largest and fastest growing form of social marketing, generating about $1.1 billion in revenue for 2009. There are a number of different types of social networks from general purpose (Facebook), to niche networks of professionals and hobbyists, to sponsored networks created by firms. However, most of the advertising action centers on the leading sites—MySpace ($495 million), Facebook ($230 million), and YouTube (unknown, but estimated to be between $240–500 million in 2009) (eMarketer, 2009d).

Social networks offer advertisers all the formats found on portal and search sites including banner ads (the most common), short pre-roll and post-roll ads before a video, and sponsorship of content. For instance, Adidas, Burger King, General Electric, Toyota Yaris, and Verizon have profile pages on MySpace, and other national brand names have posted videos on YouTube. Chevrolet, Geico, and Mars have encouraged users to create their own ads, and sponsored contests to choose the best ads.

There are several dangers to social network advertising. User-generated ads can obviously generate negative messages that are widely distributed. The content of many YouTube videos and MySpace profiles is repugnant to many American consumers and could taint brands associated with sites that permit this kind of content although entertainment firms may benefit from this milieu. While Google and YouTube have developed ways to display text and background ads alongside playing videos, many advertisers do not yet trust the software used to select the appropriate videos for an ad.

It is easy to overstate the growth in social marketing, and it is risky to ignore it. Currently, the three major search engines/portals have a much higher Internet audience share of the U.S. online population visiting their sites on a daily and weekly basis than even the largest social networking sites, or even all of the social sites combined. Google and Yahoo each have more than 155 million unique visitors a month, Microsoft about 130 million, and AOL 100 million. Still the social media sites have substantial audiences. Therefore, marketers should continue investing in search engine and portal display advertising, while experimenting in social marketing. In the longer term of the next five years, with current trends, it is likely that social networking sites will equal the audience share of major portals and search engines, challenging these "older" venues for dominance in advertising platforms.

Game Advertising

According to a report published by the Cable & Telecommunications Association for Marketing, there is a video game console in around 40% of American households (50 million) (Cable & Telecommunications Association for Marketing, 2009). From January to June 2009, over 15 million Microsoft Xbox 360s, Nintendo Wiis, and Sony Playstation 3s were sold (eMarketer, 2009e). Today most games are played in social environments with multiple players in the same room, or over the Internet. We include them in a discussion of social marketing because of the mutually influential social environment in which most digital video games are played today. There are, of course, many kinds of games that are broadcast by a game sponsor—over 800 million sponsored games were downloaded in 2008 to millions of users. So-called "advergames" are sponsored games to promote brands. Coca-Cola, Burger King, and Taco Bell, along with many other national brands, have used advergames. These kinds of games could be considered a unique kind of display ad that is highly interactive, but not necessarily social.

U.S. video in-game advertising will generate about $443 million in 2009, and it is estimated that it will increase to over $680 million million by 2013. While we tend to think of online gamers as mostly male, in fact over 40% of gamers are female, a percentage that increased significantly with the introduction of the Nintendo Wii. One quarter of gamers are over 50, and half of gamers are 18–49 (eMarketer, 2008c).

The limitations of game advertising are due in part to game content, which tends to be attractive to young males and females, but not to a much larger audience. Many advertisers do not want their brands to be associated with violence, mayhem, and war-like scenarios, or sexual content that is often present in video games. *Insight on Society: Marketing to Children of the Web in the Age of Social Networks* considers some of the social issues that marketing to children on the Web present.

BEHAVIORAL TARGETING: GETTING PERSONAL

In Chapter 6, you learned about the six major ways that marketers target markets (refer to Table 6.7)—through behavioral, demographic, psychographic, technical, contextual, and search data collected online. Behavioral targeting of ads involves using the online and offline behavior of consumers to adjust the advertising message, even the screens they are shown. One of the original promises of the Web has been that it can deliver a marketing message tailored to each consumer based on this data, and then measure the results in terms of click-throughs and purchases. There are three methods that online advertisers use to behaviorally target ads: search engine queries, and the collection of data on individual browsing history online (in the past, generally not personally identifiable data), and increasingly, the integration of this online data with offline data like income, education, address, purchase patterns, credit records, driving records, and hundreds of other personal descriptors tied to specific, identifiable persons. The use of offline and online data to follow consumers across the Internet is referred to as tracking. On average, offline information bureaus maintain 1,500 data elements on each adult person.

In Chapter 7 we described search engine marketing in some detail. Search engine advertising has turned out to be the most effective online advertising format by several orders of magnitude, and provides 98% of the revenue of Google, the world's largest online advertising agency. Why is search engine advertising so effective? Most agree that when users enter a query into a search engine, it reveals a very specific intention to shop, compare, and possibly purchase. When ads are shown at these very

INSIGHT ON SOCIETY

MARKETING TO CHILDREN OF THE WEB IN THE AGE OF SOCIAL NETWORKS

Children grow up today in an Internet world where 75% of all American households are online. There are around 38 million kids under the age of 18 online, with tens of millions of them visiting Web sites such as Wrigley's Candystand.com ("the sweetest games online"), Postopia.com ("a fun site for kids"), and Millsberry.com ("a town full of kids just like you and me"). Millsberry is a General Mills-sponsored site with games encouraging kids to watch Lucky Charms webisodes and play games to hunt for Reese's Puffs online. Kids spend more time on these sites than they do watching TV commercials. Industry self-regulation requires firms not to advertise to children younger than 12, but sites such as Kraft's NabiscoWorld.com includes games that appeal to younger audiences, such as Oreos Race for the Stuf, whereby a player-controlled character can twist, lick, and dunk oversize Oreo cookies. An FTC report in 2008 concluded that U.S. food firms were spending $1.6 billion on advertising to children, about half of that to children under 12. Critics argue, and the FTC expresses concern, that most of this advertising is for foods that make children obese and pose a health threat.

Children as young as three or four years old can often recognize brands and status items before they can even read, and almost 75% of four-year-olds generally ask their parents for specific brands. These findings are cause for celebration for some marketers. In the United States, 56 million school-age children spend approximately $100 billion annually of their own and their family's money on food, drinks, video and electronic products, toys, and clothing, and they influence family spending decisions valued at another $165 billion.

In order to capture a portion of this spending and position themselves for future purchases as the child ages, marketers are becoming increasingly interested in advertising aimed at children. In addition to investing in television advertising, which accounts for around 70% of the total amount spent on advertising to children in the United States, marketers focused on children are now migrating to the Web, where over 20% of all Internet users are children, totaling more than 38 million users under the age of 18, split fairly evenly between the 2–11 year age group (18 million) and the 12–17 year old age group (19.8 million).

The Web provides marketers an entirely new arsenal to influence really young children. What's in the arsenal? Here are some of the most common child-advertiser tools: mobile phone marketing; behavioral profiling; digital "360 buzz" campaigns; commercialized online "communities," viral videos; game advertising; and avatar advertising. Using online custom banner ads, product characters, games, virtual worlds, and surveys, marketers are both influencing behaviors and gathering valuable data about purchasing preferences and family members. Coupled with in-bedroom televisions, video games, cell phones, and other digital paraphernalia, a children's "digital culture" has been created with built-in avenues to the psyche of very young minds—minds that are so young they are unlikely to know when they are being marketed to and when they are given misleading or even harmful information.

And as if this wasn't enough—then came social networking sites, virtual worlds aimed at kids, and social bookmarking sites. By January 2009, 112 virtual worlds aimed at children under

(continued)

18 were already up and running worldwide, and another 81 were in development. Over 16 million children in the United States visit virtual worlds on a regular basis, and 17 million visit social networking sites. A study funded by Microsoft, News Corp. (MySpace), and Verizon found that 70% of children visit social networking sites weekly and over 50% had participated in some kind of advertiser-branded activity such as visiting a company profile page in the past month. Marketers are moving aggressively to use online social networks and viral marketing to get kids hooked on brands early in life. For instance, Red Bull does little traditional TV advertising in the 100 countries where it sells energy drinks. Instead it has been using Web-based contests and games such as the Red Bull Art of the Can, where youngsters create sculptures out of Red Bull cans and submit photos of their handiwork. The prize: a trip for two to Switzerland.

You may not have heard of Axe (a product of Unilever), a deodorant for young men that apparently drives girls crazy for them. Axe Vice President Russell Taylor's goal is for the brand to become truly global. The sales pitch is simple: "Hey, dude, spray Axe deodorant all over your body, and you will become irresistible to beautiful young women." The branding message: a female wolf whistle and the phrase "Bom Chicka Wah Wah," expressed in a woman's sexy voice. Armed with this powerful message to the world's teenagers, Axe launched the product in the United States by posting online videos that supposedly show the "Axe effect" of women chasing men who used the spray (viewable at TheAxeEffect.com). The response was sensational: millions of people forwarded the videos to friends by e-mail in a massive viral outpouring. Marketers also created an online game wherein guys indicated the kind of young woman they were interested in and got recommendations on which Axe fragrance to buy. You can bet that many of these postings and shared experiences were by children under the age

of 13. Using social networks, blogs, and YouTube, in a way much more powerful than earlier Web marketing to children, marketers are able to circumvent what few restrictions on marketing to children exist.

While such moves may be savvy marketing, are they ethical? Some people say no. Research conducted in 1996 by the Center for Media Education (CME), showed that young children cannot understand the potential effects of revealing their personal information; neither can they distinguish between substantive material on Web sites and the advertisements surrounding it. While some parents tried to monitor their children's use of the Internet services, many of them failed due to lack of time, computer skills, or awareness of risk. Targeting of children by marketing techniques resulted in the release of a large amount of private information into the market and triggered the need for regulation.

Experts argue that since children don't understand persuasive intent until they are eight or nine years old, it is unethical to advertise to them before they can distinguish between advertising and the real world. Others believe that fair advertising is an important, and necessary, part of the maturation process for future adults in today's society. But does that argument hold when children are gaining increased access to information about unhealthy activities, such as beer drinking through Web sites geared to a younger audience? Although brewers admit they are targeting a younger market segment—twenty-somethings—they have set up warning screens and registration pages that require users to enter a birth date proving they are of legal drinking age. Of course, there is no process to verify such data, making it easy for underage consumers to gain access to, and be influenced by, entertaining content at drinking oriented Web sites.

In 1998, Congress passed the Children's Online Privacy Protection Act (COPPA) after the FTC discovered that 80% of Web sites were

(continued)

collecting personal information from children, but only 1% required their parents' permission. Under COPPA, companies must post a privacy policy on their Web sites, detailing exactly how they collect information from consumers, how they'll use it, and the degrees to which they'll protect consumer privacy. Companies are not permitted to use personal information collected from children under 13 years of age without the prior, verifiable consent of parents. But the problem is that the FTC and others have been unable to specify exactly what "verifiable consent" means. Until technologies such as digital signatures are widely available, there appears to be no reliable way to provide verifiable consent online. The FTC recognized this fact by issuing a temporary ruling (now permanent) requiring a "sliding scale of verifiable parental consent." If firms want to use the personal information of children for internal uses only, the FTC requires an e-mail from the parent plus one other form of verification (such as a credit card or phone number). A stricter standard is required of firms who want to sell personal information about children: these Web sites are required to use one of the following means of verification in addition to an e-mail: a print-and-send consent form, credit card transaction, a toll free number staffed by trained personnel, or an e-mail with a password or PIN.

Since the law took effect, the FTC has obtained a number of settlements and issued fines as high as $1 million. For instance, in December 2008, Sony BMG Music Entertainment (Sony Music) got clipped for $1 million as part of a settlement to resolve FTC charges that it violated COPPA. The Commission's complaint alleged that, through its music fan Web sites, Sony Music improperly collected, maintained, and disclosed personal information from thousands of children under the age of 13, without their parents' consent. The civil penalty paid by Sony Music matches the largest penalty ever in a COPPA case. Previously, the operators of

imbee.com, a social networking site specifically targeting kids and "tweens," agreed to settle FTC charges that their data-collection practices violated federal law. Their fine: $130,000, a mere pittance in comparison. Industrious Kid, Inc., and owner Jeanette Symons, promoted the imbee.com Web site as a "free, secure, social networking and blogging destination specifically designed for kids ages 8 to 14." In addition, the Web site was promoted as "purposely designed to ensure the greatest level of safety and satisfaction for young members," and as "safer than other social networking sites." According to the FTC, imbee.com collected and maintained personal information from children under the age of 13 without first notifying parents and obtaining their consent. In an earlier enforcement action, Xanga paid up $1 million in part because it collected, used, and disclosed personal information from children under the age of 13 without first notifying parents and obtaining their consent. The complaint charged that the defendants had actual knowledge they were collecting and disclosing personal information from children. The Xanga site stated that children under 13 could not join, but then allowed visitors to create Xanga accounts even if they provided a birth date indicating they were under 13. Further, they failed to notify the children's parents of their information practices or provide the parents with access to and control over their children's information. The defendants created 1.7 million Xanga accounts for users who submitted age information indicating they were under 13. Previous FTC COPPA cases included Mrs. Fields' Original Cookies, Hershey Foods, UMG recordings, and Bonzi Software. These cases involved no actual intent or knowledge, just lack of attention.

While in general, voluntary compliance with COPPA has been good, and most Web sites are careful to avoid gathering personal information on children as a part of their marketing effort,

(continued)

some Web sites are directly aimed at very young children. Sites such as ClubPenguin, Webkinz (the most popular children's site), and NeoPets provide online tools and play environments that enable young users to interact, adopt pets, play sponsored advergames, and reveal personal information. In the process of playing the games, children produce marketing information for product designers. While each of these Web sites' privacy policies claim strict adherence to the restrictions of COPPA, it is unclear how they ascertain who is over 13 and who is under 13, or if those under 13 have parental consent. Even less clear is how social networking sites where marketers are posting brand videos can protect the identities and privacy of children who expose their friends' e-mails every time they favorite a video. In March 2009, the FTC started its own online ad campaign aimed at kids called the Children's Online Advertising Initiative which is intended to inform children between 8 and 12 years of age to become better informed about marketing and advertising. Some state governments have also stepped in. Maine enacted the Act to Prevent Predatory Marketing Practices Against Minors law, which became effective September 12, 2009, and imposed even stricter standards than those set by COPPA.

SOURCES: "The Maine Act: Preventing Predatory Marketing Practices Against Minors," by Eric Sinrod, Blog.findlaw.com/technologist, August 11, 2009; "Kids and Teens: Growing Up Virtual," by Debra Aho Williamson, eMarketer, May 2009; "FTC Launching Its Own Marketing Campaign for Kids," Consumer Advertising Law Blog, March 19, 2009; "Ad It Up: Kids in a Commercial World," Federal Trade Commission, March 12, 2009; "US Internet Users," by Lisa Phillips, eMarketer, February 2009; "Sony Music Settles Charges Its Music Fan Websites Violated the Children's Online Privacy Protection Act," Federal Trade Commission, December 11, 2008; "Online Age Verification for Children Brings Privacy Worries," by Brad Stone, *New York Times*, November 16, 2008; "Crying Foul Over Online Junk Food Marketing," by Catherine Holahan, *BusinessWeek*, August 12, 2008; "No Escape: Marketing to Kids in the Digital Age," by Jeff Chester and Kathryn Montgomery, *Multinational Monitor*, July/August 2008; "Marketing Food to Children and Adolescents. A Review of Industry Expenditures, Activities, and Self-Regulation," Federal Trade Commission, July 2008.

moments on customer behavior, they are four to ten times as effective as other formats. In 2003, the author John Battelle coined the phrase and the notion that the Web is a database of intentions:

"The Database of Intentions is simply this: The aggregate results of every search ever entered, every result list ever tendered, and every path taken as a result. It lives in many places, but three or four places in particular hold a massive amount of this data (i.e., MSN, Google, and Yahoo). This information represents, in aggregate form, a place holder for the intentions of humankind—a massive database of desires, needs, wants, and likes that can be discovered, subpoenaed, archived, tracked, and exploited to all sorts of ends. Such a beast has never before existed in the history of culture, but is almost guaranteed to grow exponentially from this day forward. This artifact can tell us extraordinary things about who we are and what we want as a culture. And it has the potential to be abused in equally extraordinary fashion." (Battelle, 2003.)

The decline in the growth rate of search engine advertising from the early days of double-digit growth, to today's growth of high single digits, has caused the major search engine firms to seek out alternative forms of future growth. Likewise with banner display portals like Yahoo and AOL: the effectiveness of banner ads has fallen, and so have their prices. Portal firms are turning to behavioral targeting in the effort to secure their future growth in Internet advertising. Advertising agencies are willing to pay a great deal more for targeted ads than non-targeted ads.

Behavioral targeting seeks to optimize consumer response by using information that Web visitors reveal about themselves online, and if possible, combine this with offline identity and consumption information gathered by companies such as Acxiom. Behavioral targeting is based on real-time information about visitors use' of Web sites, including pages visited, content viewed, search queries, ads clicked, videos watched, content shared, and products they purchase. Once this information is collected and analyzed on the fly, behavioral targeting programs attempt to develop profiles of individual users, and then show advertisements most likely to be of interest to the user. In 2010, U.S. firms will spend more than an estimated $2 billion on behavioral targeting, and this is expected to double by 2014, growing at the rate of 50% a year, the fastest growing form of online marketing techniques (eMarketer, Inc. 2008a). Twenty-three percent of online display advertising will be behaviorally targeted in 2014. Interest in this area has spurred four recent acquisitions: Google-DoubleClick, Yahoo-Right Media, WPP Group-24/7 Media, and Microsoft-aQuantive. You cannot target consumers on the Internet without a very large-scale advertising network than can follow people's movements closely and display ads. Many of these techniques are not new, just extensions of offline techniques. The difference is obtaining this information online, unobtrusively, without the user knowing, dynamically analyzing the information on the fly, and taking the appropriate action within a tolerable 1 to 2 seconds of response time.

For a variety of technical and other reasons, this vision has, thus far, not been widely achieved. The quality of the data, largely owned by the online advertising networks, is quite good, but the ability to understand and respond—the business intelligence and analytics—are weak, preventing companies from being able to respond quickly in meaningful ways when the consumer is online. Although in general targeted ads are four to ten times more effective than non-targeted ads, this is not always the case and depends on the product, and nearness of a consumer decision. And marketing companies are not yet prepared to accept the idea that there needs to be several hundred or a thousand variations on the same display ad depending on the customer's profile. Such a move would raise costs. Last, consumer resistance to targeting is allowing more consumers to escape the tracking net.

As a result, just about everyone using the major Web portals is exposed to advertising that has nothing to do with their personal interests, or intentions. Second, search-engine marketing is still the only technique that reliably comes close to revealing consumers' intentions.

Nevertheless, firms are experimenting with more precise targeting methods. Snapple used behavioral targeting methods (with the help of an online ad firm Tacoda) to identify the types of people attracted to Snapple Green Tea. Answer: people who like the arts and literature, travel internationally, and visit health sites. Microsoft offers MSN advertisers access to personal data derived from 270 million worldwide Windows Live users. Some advertisers have reported over 50% increases in click-through rates. General Motors uses Digitas (a Boston-based online ad firm) to create several hundred versions of a single ad for its new Acadia crossover vehicle. Viewers are initially shown ads that emphasize brand, features, and communities. On subsequent viewing, they are shown different ads based on demographics, lifestyle, and behavioral considerations. Men are shown versions of the ads emphasizing engines, specifications, performance, while women are shown versions that emphasize comfort, accessibility, and families (Story, 2007).

The growth in the power, reach, and scope of behavioral targeting has drawn the attention of privacy groups and the Federal Trade Commission (FTC). In November 2007, the FTC opened hearings to consider proposals from privacy advocates to develop a "do not track list," develop visual online cues for people to alert them to tracking, and allow people to opt out. In June 2008, the Senate held hearings on behavioral marketing and privacy. While Google, Microsoft, and Yahoo pleaded for legislation to protect them from consumer lawsuits, the FTC refused to consider new legislation to protect the privacy of Internet users. Instead, the FTC proposed industry self-regulation. In 2009, a consortium of advertising firms (Network Advertising Initiative) responded positively to FTC proposed principles to regulate online behavioral advertising. In the Senate, hearings on behavioral targeting are on-going throughout 2009. All of these regulatory efforts emphasize transparency, user control over their information, security, and the temporal stability of privacy promises (unannounced and sudden changes in information privacy may not be allowed). Currently there are few, if any, industry or government regulations on behavioral targeting.

Perhaps the central question is understanding what rights individuals have in their own personally identifiable Internet profiles. Are these "ownership" rights, or merely an "interest" in an underlying asset? Do consumers have viewing and editing rights for their profiles? Why not? Can consumers opt-out using a federal "Do Not Track" list? Who can possibly "own" the intentions of an entire culture? We consider these issues further in Chapter 8.

MIXING OFFLINE AND ONLINE MARKETING COMMUNICATIONS

Many early proponents of e-commerce believed that the traditional world of marketing based on mass media was no longer relevant to the exploding online commercial world and that in the "new Internet economy," nearly all marketing communications would be online. As it turned out, this did not happen. What did happen is that offline marketing powerhouses in consumer-oriented industries learned how to use the Web to extend their brand images and sales campaigns to an educated, wealthy, and computer-literate, online audience. The large advertising agencies that specialized in mass media opened up Internet practices, and learned quickly how to integrate online and offline campaigns. Pure online companies learned how to use traditional print and television advertising as a means for driving sales to their Web sites.

The marketing communications campaigns most successful at driving traffic to a Web site have incorporated both online and offline tactics, rather than relying solely on one or the other. The objective is to draw the attention of people who are already online and persuade them to visit a new Web site, as well as attract the attention of people who will be going online in the near future in order to suggest that they, too, visit the Web site. Several research studies have shown that the most effective online advertisements are those that use consistent imagery with campaigns running in other media at the same time (Briggs, 1999). Offline mass media such as television and radio have nearly a 100% market penetration into the 121 million households in the United States. U.S. daily newspapers have a total circulation of around 48 million. It would be foolish for pure online companies not to use these popular media to drive traffic to the online world of commerce. In the early days of e-commerce, the Internet audience was quite different from the general population, and perhaps was best reached by using online marketing alone. This is no longer true as the Internet population becomes much more like the general population.

Many online ventures have used offline marketing techniques to drive traffic to their Web sites, increase awareness, and build brand equity. For instance, LendingTree.com has used television advertising to direct people to its Web site to look for mortgages. Barnes & Noble, as well as JCPenney and REI Inc., use print media to inform customers of their in-store Web kiosks. Such "tie-ins" between a print product and a firm's Web site have proven to be very successful in driving Web traffic.

Another example of the online/offline marketing connection is the use of print catalogs by heretofore entirely online ventures. Some online ventures have created paper catalogs and mailed them to their customers to improve their relationship with that group.

The development of multi-channel marketing and communications reflects the fact that the behavior of consumers is increasingly multi-channel (see Chapter 9). Around 60% of all consumers research products online before buying in a store, and 56% of the online retail sales generated by Internet Retailer's Top 500 Web sites were made by multi-channel retailers—retailers who had physical stores and catalogs in addition to Web sites (eMarketer, Inc., 2009f).

Insight on Business: Are The Very Rich Are Different from You and Me? examines how luxury goods providers use online marketing in conjunction with their offline marketing efforts.

7.2   UNDERSTANDING THE COST AND BENEFITS OF ONLINE MARKETING COMMUNICATIONS

As we saw in Section 7.1, online marketing communications still comprise only a very small part of the total marketing communications universe. While there are several reasons why this is the case, two of the main ones are concerns about whether online advertising really works and about how to adequately measure the costs and benefits of online advertising. We will address both of these topics in this section. But first, we will define some important terms used when examining the effectiveness of online marketing.

INSIGHT ON BUSINESS

ARE THE VERY RICH DIFFERENT FROM YOU AND ME?

"The very rich are different from you and me," Nick Carroway observed, in a memorable line from *The Great Gatsby*, a novel by F. Scott Fitzgerald about life among the very wealthy in the 1920s. Palm Beach has its Worth Avenue, New York has its Fifth Avenue, Los Angeles has its Rodeo Drive, and Chicago has the Magnificent Mile. So where do the rich go on the Web to get that $5,000 cocktail dress, or that $3,000 Italian suit? How about a Jimmy Choo handbag? Well, today, it turns out they may not be so different from the rest of us: they look for online deals, say, the $5,000 cocktail dress for only $3,500. Or they might try eBay for the white-studded leather tote bag for only $510. Who could resist?

Yes, the recession has hit even the really rich. Let's say you have a "mere" $5 million in net worth (placing you in the "minor rich"), including the house, the second house, three cars (all still with money owed on them), and stocks and bonds, and then all this booty sinks in value by 30% to 40%? What to do? You have a job, so you cut back on spending, sell one of the cars, engage in a little "cheap chic" by shopping at Wal-Mart, and look for incredible sales at luxe spending stores such as Tiffany, Neiman Marcus, and Marni. Online, you learn to pay attention to your e-mail.

The problem is the real luxe online stores typically don't have sales. Luxe retailers are loathe to offer sales because they believe sales detract from their reputations for timeless quality. As a vice president at Tiffany's noted, "We certainly don't engage in price promotion. We say, 'Here's the product, and here's the price, and the price is justified.'"

But luxe retailers are in fact offering more discounts—but they're secret. How can a sale be secret? Whispered discounts at the physical stores ("Shhhh! There's a special sale in the dress department!") have their online counterpart in flash e-mail campaigns and "private online sales" in which selected online customers are e-mailed alerts such as "A $3,000 handbag on sale for the next two hours for $800." Neiman Marcus calls them "midday dash" sales. Two-hour online-only sales promise 50% off on luxe goods that can be purchased only by clicking on a link in the e-mail. One week's "dash sale" featured a $697 Burberry handbag, marked down from $1,395. A Carmen Marc Valvo chiffon gown, just right for that special charity party, was offered at $575, down from $1,150. Cole Haan flats only $82, down from $165.

With in-store sales suffering as a result of the recession, the action has moved to the Internet where luxe retailers can offer discrete sales to a select group of customers without tarnishing the brand, preserving exclusivity, and create a sense of urgency by limiting the time to purchase. At the same time, they can deny they discount their items. If prices were public, customers would know that the $800 Marni skirt they bought today was sold the next day on sale for $400. They might conclude that none of these goods are worth the price charged, certainly not the retail price, no matter what it is. Online dash sales are sort of like impulse buying at Wal-Mart, but instead of 20 batteries for $5, it's more like one Burberry bag for a $1,000. Rich people can indulge bigger impulses. But like the rest of us, the rich just can't seem to get enough of a good thing, especially if its half price.

(continued)

Overall, times are not great for online luxe retailers, but they are not so bad either. While the physical store retail world struggles with 20%-30% declines in revenues, online retail has been flat or slightly down. The bright spot is luxe online sales have only declined only 8%. Through rapid cost cutting, and inventory control, luxe retailers have managed to remain profitable throughout the period. Tiffany, the quintessential luxe firm, experienced lower profits in the 2009 second quarter, but they were still positive. Sales of $50,000+ items are off, while increased sales of silver and gold fashion jewelry is making up most of the difference. Tiffany's strategy, echoed by Hermes, is not to lower prices, but to add more lowered-price items to the marketing mix. For instance, pendants are going for $150 to only $15,000 (those are the ones with the big shiny things). Neiman Marcus, Saks Inc. and Hermes International reported similar results despite the recession.

There are 16 million affluent households in the United States with a net worth of more than $500,000. Those with incomes of greater than $100,000 account for 40% of all online spending. Around 80% of U.S. consumers with a net worth greater than $5 million use the Web everyday, and shop on the Web for clothes, jewelry, as well as more common items such as music and videos. Around 60% of rich Internet users hobnob on social sites. Households with more than $100,000 in income increased their online spending by 17% in 2009. So much for the recession.

U.S. luxury e-commerce sales in 2009 are expected to be around $3.5 billion, essentially flat from 2008 numbers. The second fastest growing Web site category is jewelry/luxury goods/accessories. U.S. online jewelry sites experienced growth in 2009 of 1%, and overall revenues of just over $1 billion. Yoox, Saks.com, Zagliani, and Marni all report their online sales are now approaching the sales of their flagship stores.

Many who lost 30% of their net worth apparently still have a lot left over.

Yet luxury retailers such as Neiman Marcus, Tiffany, Armani, and Christian Dior have had a difficult time developing an online presence for their wealthy customers. Critics argue they have had a difficult time understanding their wealthy online customers. A recent report from the Luxury Institute found that online luxe goods retailers fall short in community building. Most sites do not track online customer comments on rating, review sites, and blogs (let alone Twitter), although most use search engine optimization. When you're really good and charging accordingly, why ask customers what they think?

Luxury brands and retailers do face a difficult market where they must try to please not only their wealthy older customers, but also their children and grandchildren who are used to shopping online. And they have had a hard time coming up with a credible online image that supports their brand, but is still an online site that appeals to the online customer.

For instance, when Neiman Marcus introduced its first Web site with two virtual boutiques, featuring tours of Kate Spade handbags and John Hardy silver cuff links, Web designers were awed by the display of graphics and motion. But most customers were turned off because they could not find enough goods for sale, and could not easily navigate the site. Pretty snazzy stuff, but today it's all gone. Neimanmarcus.com no longer features any animations or Flash graphics, but instead has much more merchandise neatly arranged by category and designer: in short, an online catalog much like JCPenney's. The current Neiman Marcus Web site gets generally high marks for the simplicity of design and efficiency of navigation, although critics point out that it's still somewhat difficult to find the online version of Neiman Marcus' most popular off-line market-

(continued)

ing tool: its Christmas catalog that features "beyond the pale" luxury items such as a "his and hers" double portrait in chocolate for $100,000 and an underwater personal submarine for $1.4 million.

Developing an online marketing approach that increases a company's access to consumers while retaining an image of exclusivity was the challenge faced by the world-renowned jeweler Tiffany & Co. when it redesigned its Web site in 1999. The company was in the enviable position of being perhaps the most famous jewelry company in the United States. Tiffany's offline marketing communications sought to engender feelings of beauty, quality, and timeless style—all hallmarks of the Tiffany brand. How could Tiffany maintain its approach on the Web, a medium that often emphasizes speed and flashy graphics over grace and elegance, and low-cost bargains over high-priced exclusive fashion? The Web, at least in its early days, was all about low prices and great deals—concepts that are anathema to the high fashion merchant.

Tiffany's first effort on the Web was designed by Oven Digital Inc., who built a Web site that used soft, neutral colors throughout, sparse wording, and pictures that faded slowly onto the screen. The shopping portion of the Web site showed just one large item, with some smaller photos that could be enlarged by clicking at the bottom of the screen. The Web site also included information on buying and caring for jewelry. Caroline Naggiar, Tiffany's senior vice president of marketing at the time, characterized the site "as an enormous exercise in reserve." But that same "reserved" quality made it difficult for consumers to find out what was for sale. Critics complained that the Tiffany Web site had too few products online, the Flash graphics were slow, there were too many animations, and the product line available was poorly organized. While Tiffany claimed there were 2,000 products online, finding them and buying them was an arduous process. Critics complained the Web site was dull with all the white space, surfing was tedious, and only those not in a hurry could navigate it. The site was redesigned by an in-house team with a view toward making it more focused. Today, Tiffany has shifted more of its direct marketing effort from the offline catalog to the online catalog. The results improved dramatically. It has opened new sites in Canada, the United Kingdom, and Japan. Tiffany sites carry over 2,800 products in five categories of goods: diamonds, jewelry, watches, table settings, gifts, and accessories. By 2008, Tiffany's online sales were over $140 million, 5% of their $2.8 billion worldwide sales.

Other cutting-edge fashion houses such as Christian Dior, Armani, and Bottega Veneta insisted in their first efforts on managing their own Web sites. The results were not impressive. The Web sites were typically a collection of photos with directions to the nearest store. Embracing the Internet ran counter to their strategies to keep tight control over their images and customers. As a result of the difficulties they encountered, some luxury sites began reluctantly to outsource their Web sites. For instance, Louis Vuitton, DKNY, and Armani have all outsourced their online boutiques to Web operations outfits such as Yoox, a fashion retailer with a long experience on the Web. In the case of Armani, Emporio Armani personally directed the online effort. To avoid the cheaper catalog look, he had his store design team hand over architectural plans to the flagship store in Milan so that Yoox could use it as a metaphor and model for the Web site. Now visitors can turn left or right as they would at the Milan store, and take a virtual tour of the goods on display. Armani wanted a three-dimensional look, and the ability to shine bright lights on the products being examined, a

(continued)

trick used in his stores to impart the sense of elegance. Robert Trefus, Armani's vice president in charge of the Web site, expects the Internet Boutique to become the line's biggest store in a few years. The cost of opening the site has been a fraction of the cost of launching a new store, and less risky. "At least we don't have to worry about the location, or opening a store on the wrong corner." A trip to the Armani Web site is a trip all unto itself: stunning video images of the latest seasonal collections, Armani Jeans, and the Armani Exchange, where you can actually buy something from the Emporio Armani retail collection.

SOURCES: "CEO Helps Jimmy Choo Diversify," Jimmychoo.com, September 2, 2009; "High End Retailers Offering More Discounts," by Stephanie Rosenblum, *New York Times*, August 1, 2009; "In Luxury Sector, Discounting Can Be Dangerous," by Brian Burnsaid, *BusinessWeek*, July 23, 2009; "Luxury Goods Retailers Fall Short in Online Community Building," *Internet Retailer*, July 3, 2009; "Affluents Online: Living the Life in Private," by Lisa Phillips, eMarketer, May 2009; "How the Luxury Consumer Will Spend in 2009," by Lauren Sherman, *Forbes*, January 13, 2009; ""Getting Luxury Goods Online," by Thomas Grose, *Time Magazine*, June 23, 2008; "Luxury Brands Lag in Adopting e-Commerce," Internet Retailer, May 30, 2008; "Affluent Hobnob on Social Networks," eMarketer, March 19, 2008.

ONLINE MARKETING METRICS: LEXICON

impressions
number of times an ad is served

click-through rate (CTR)
the percentage of people exposed to an online advertisement who actually click on the banner

view-through rate (VTR)
measures the 30-day response rate to an ad

hits
number of http requests received by a firm's server

page views
number of pages requested by visitors

stickiness (duration)
average length of time visitors remain at a site

In order to understand the process of attracting prospects to your firm's Web site via marketing communications and converting them into customers, you will need to be familiar with Web marketing terminology. **Table 7.4** lists some terms commonly used to describe the impacts and results of online marketing.

The first nine metrics focus primarily on the success of a Web site in achieving audience or market share by "driving" shoppers to the site. In the early years of e-commerce, these measures often substituted for solid information on sales revenue as e-commerce entrepreneurs sought to have investors and the public focus on the success of the Web site in "attracting eyeballs" (viewers).

Impressions are the number of times an ad is served. **Click-through rate (CTR)** measures the percentage of people exposed to an online advertisement who actually click on the advertisement. Because not all ads lead to an immediate click, the industry has invented a new term for a long-term hit called **view-through rate** (VTR), which measures the 30-day response rate to an ad. **Hits** are the number of HTTP requests received by a firm's server. Hits can be misleading as a measure of Web site activity because a "hit" does not equal a page. A single page may account for several hits if the page contains multiple images or graphics. A single Web site visitor can generate hundreds of hits. For this reason, hits are not an accurate representation of Web traffic or visits, even though they are generally easy to measure; the sheer volume of hits can be huge—and sound impressive—but not be a true measure of activity. **Page views** are the number of pages requested by visitors. However, with increased usage of Web frames that divide pages into separate sections, a single page that has three frames will generate three page views. Hence, page views per se are also not a very useful metric.

Stickiness (sometimes called *duration*) is the average length of time visitors remain at a Web site. Stickiness is important to marketers because the longer the

TABLE 7.4	**MARKETING METRICS LEXICON**
COMMON MARKETING E-METRICS	**DESCRIPTION**
Impressions	Number of times an ad is served
Click-through rate (CTR)	The percentage of times an ad is clicked
View-through rate (VTR)	The percentage of times an ad is not clicked immediately but the Web site is visited within 30 days.
Hits	Number of HTTP requests
Page views	Number of pages viewed
Stickiness (duration)	Average length of stay at a Web site
Unique visitors	Number of unique visitors in a period
Loyalty	Measured variously as the number of page views, frequency of single-user visits to the Web site, or percentage of customers who return to the site in a year to make additional purchases
Reach	Percentage of Web site visitors who are potential buyers; or the percentage of total market buyers who buy at a site
Recency	Time elapsed since the last action taken by a buyer, such as a Web site visit or purchase
Acquisition rate	Percentage of visitors who indicate an interest in the Web site's product by registering or visiting product's pages
Conversion rate	Percentage of visitors who become customers
Browse to buy ratio	Ratio of items purchased to product views
View to cart ratio	Ratio of "Add to cart" clicks to product views
Cart conversion rate	Ratio of actual orders to "Add to cart" clicks
Checkout conversion rate	Ratio of actual orders to checkouts started
Abandonment rate	Percentage of shoppers who begin a shopping cart purchase but then leave the Web site without completing a purchase (similar to above)
Retention rate	Percentage of existing customers who continue to buy on a regular basis (similar to loyalty)
Attrition rate	Percentage of customers who do not return during the next year after an initial purchase
E-MAIL METRICS	
Open rate	Percentage of e-mail recipients who open the e-mail and are exposed to the message
Delivery rate	Percentage of e-mail recipients who received the e-mail
Click-through rate (e-mail)	Percentage of recipients who clicked through to offers
Bounce-back rate	Percentage of e-mails that could not be delivered
Unsubscribe rate	Percentage of recipients who click unsubscribe
Conversion rate (e-mail)	Percentage of recipients who actually buy

unique visitors
the number of distinct, unique visitors to a site

loyalty
percentage of purchasers who return in a year

reach
percentage of the total number of consumers in a market who will visit a site

recency
average number of days elapsed between visits

acquisition rate
measures the percentage of visitors who register or visit product pages

conversion rate
percentage of visitors who purchase something

browse-to-buy ratio
ratio of items purchased to product views

view-to-cart ratio
ratio of "Add to cart" clicks to product view

cart conversion rate
average number of days elapsed between visits

checkout conversion ratio
ratio of actual orders to checkouts started

abandonment rate
percentage of shoppers who begin a shopping cart form, but then fail to complete the form

retention rate
percentage of existing customers who continue to buy on a regular basis

amount of time a visitor spends at a Web site, the greater the probability of a purchase. For instance, eBay, which is one of the stickiest and most profitable sites on the Web, is often held up as evidence that stickiness correlates with success. However, experience at other Web sites counters this argument, calling into question the relevance of stickiness as a measure. Search engine Google, for example, is a very popular destination and yet reports very low stickiness ratings (Weber, 2001). Its founders take this as a sign that they have achieved their objective—sending users to their desired destination quickly.

The number of unique visitors is perhaps the most widely used measure of a Web site's popularity. The measurement of **unique visitors** counts the number of distinct, unique visitors to a Web site, regardless of how many pages they view. **Loyalty** measures the percentage of visitors who return in a year. This can be a good indicator of a site's Web following, and perhaps the trust shoppers place in a site. **Reach** is typically a percentage of the total number of consumers in a market who visit a Web site; for example, 10% of all book purchasers in a year will visit Amazon at least once to shop for a book. This provides an idea of the power of a Web site to attract market share. **Recency**—like loyalty—measures the power of a Web site to produce repeat visits and is generally measured as the average number of days elapsed between shopper or customer visits. For example, a recency value of 25 days means the average customer will return once every 25 days.

The metrics described so far do not say much about commercial activity or help understand the conversion from visitor to customer. Several other measures are more helpful in this regard. **Acquisition rate** measures of the percentage of visitors who register or visit product pages (indicating interest in the product). **Conversion rate** measures the percentage of visitors who actually purchase something. Conversion rates can vary widely, depending on the success of the site. E-tailing Group's 8th Annual Merchant Survey found that 44% of the respondents reported conversion rates in the 1%–3% range, 21% in the 3%–5% range, and 17% in the 5%–8% range (e-Tailing Group, 2009). The **browse-to-buy ratio** measures the ratio of items purchased to product views. The **view-to-cart ratio** calculates the ratio of "Add to cart" clicks to product views. **Cart conversion rate** measures the ratio of actual orders to "Add to cart" clicks. **Checkout conversion rate** calculates the ratio of actual orders to checkouts started. **Abandonment rate** measures the percentage of shoppers who begin a shopping cart form but then fail to complete the form and leave the Web site. Abandonment rates can signal a number of potential problems—poor form design, lack of consumer trust, or consumer purchase uncertainty caused by other factors. A study by PayPal and comScore found that 45% of U.S. online shoppers had abandoned shopping carts multiple times in the three weeks prior to being surveyed. The average cost of the abandoned goods was over $100. Among the reasons for abandonment were security concerns (21%), couldn't find customer support (22%), couldn't find preferred payment option (24%) and the item being unavailable at checkout (23%) (eMarketer, 2009g). Given that more than 80% of online shoppers generally have a purchase in mind when they visit a Web site, a high abandonment rate signals many lost sales.

Retention rate indicates the percentage of existing customers who continue to buy on a regular basis. **Attrition rate** measures the percentage of customers who purchase once but never return within a year (the opposite of loyalty and retention rates).

E-mail campaigns have their own set of metrics. **Open rate** measures the percentage of customers who open the e-mail and are exposed to the message. Generally, open rates are quite high, in the area of 50% or greater. However, some browsers open mail as soon as the mouse cursor moves over the subject line, and therefore this measure can be difficult to interpret. **Delivery rate** measures the percentage of e-mail recipients who received the e-mail. **Click-through rate (e-mail)** measures the percentage of e-mail recipients who clicked through to the offer. Finally, **bounce-back rate** measures the percentage of e-mails that could not be delivered.

There is a lengthy path from simple online ad impressions, Web site visits, and page views to the purchase of a product and the company making a profit (see **Figure 7.9**). You first need to make customers aware of their needs for your product and somehow drive them to your Web site. Once there, you need to convince them you

attrition rate
percentage of customers who purchase once, but do not return within a year

open rate
percentage of customers who open the e-mail and are exposed to the message

delivery rate
percentage of e-mail recipients who received the e-mail

click-through rate (e-mail)
percentage of e-mail recipients who clicked through to the offer

bounce-back rate
percentage of e-mails that could not be delivered

FIGURE 7.9	AN ONLINE CONSUMER PURCHASING MODEL

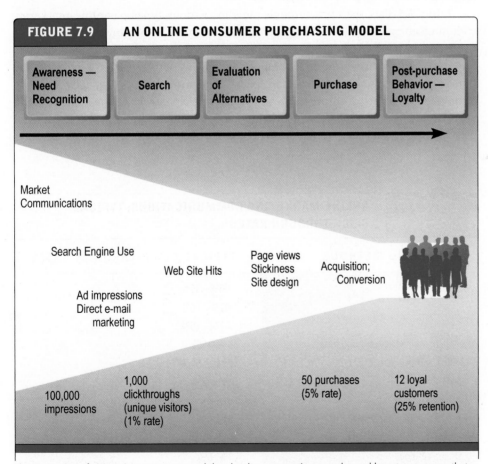

The conversion of visitors into customers, and then loyal customers, is a complex and long-term process that may take several months.

have the best value—quality and price—when compared to alternative providers. You then must persuade them to trust your firm to handle the transaction (by providing a secure environment and fast fulfillment). Based on your success, a percentage of customers will remain loyal and purchase again or recommend your Web site to others.

HOW WELL DOES ONLINE ADVERTISING WORK?

What is the most effective kind of online advertising? How does online advertising compare to offline advertising? The answers depend on the goals of the campaign, the nature of the product, and the quality of the Web site you direct customers toward. The answers also depend on what you measure. Click-through rates are interesting, but ultimately it's the return on the investment in the ad campaign that counts. A broader understanding of the matter requires that you consider the cost of purchasing the promotional materials and mailing lists, and the studio production costs for radio and TV ads. Also, each media has a different revenue per contact potential because the products advertised differ. For instance, online purchases tend to be for smaller items when compared to newspaper, magazine, and television ads (although this too seems to be changing).

Table 7.5 lists the click-through rates for various types of online marketing communications tools. There is a great deal of variability within any of these types so the figures in Table 7.4 should be viewed as just very general estimates." Click-through rates on all these formats are a function of personalization, and other targeting techniques. Search engine ads have the highest click-through rates, typically 5%-15%. Permission e-mail click-through rates have been fairly consistent over the last five years, in the 5%–6% range. Putting the recipient's name in the subject line can double the click-through rate. (For unsolicited e-mail and outright spam, response rates

TABLE 7.5	ONLINE MARKETING COMMUNICATIONS: TYPICAL CLICK-THROUGH RATES
MARKETING METHODS	TYPICAL CLICK-THROUGH RATES
Display ads	.06%–.35%
Interstitials	.02%–.16%
Superstitials	.02%–.16%
Search engine keyword purchase	5%–15%
Video and rich media	.5%–2.65%
Sponsorships	1.5%–3%
Affiliate relationships	.2%–.4%
E-mail marketing in-house list	5%–6%
E-mail marketing purchased list	.01%–1.5%
Online catalogs	3%–6%

SOURCES: Based on data from Doubleclick, 2009a, 2009b; eMarketer, 2009a, Jansen and Spink, 2009.

are much lower even though about 20% of U.S. e-mail users report clicking occasionally on an unsolicited e-mail.)

The click-through rates for video ads may seem low, but it is twice as high as the rate for display ads. The "interaction rate" (sometimes referred to as "dwell rate") with rich media ads and video ads videos is quite high, about 7%–8%. "Interaction" means the user clicks on the video, plays it, stops it, or takes some other action (possibly skips the ad altogether) (eMarketer, 2009h, Eyeblaster, 2009).

As consumers become more accustomed to new online advertising formats, click-through rates tend to fall. Response rates to banner ads have fallen about 50% over the last four years, and e-mail response has also fallen from its initial high rates. This is not true of video and rich media where response rates have remained steady, perhaps due to the growing quality and novelty of online video.

How effective is online advertising when compared to offline advertising? **Figure 7.10** provides some insight into this question. In general, the online channels (e-mail, banner ads, and video) compare favorably with traditional channels. Search engine marketing over the last two years has grown to be the most cost-effective form of marketing communications and accounts for large part in the growth of Google, as

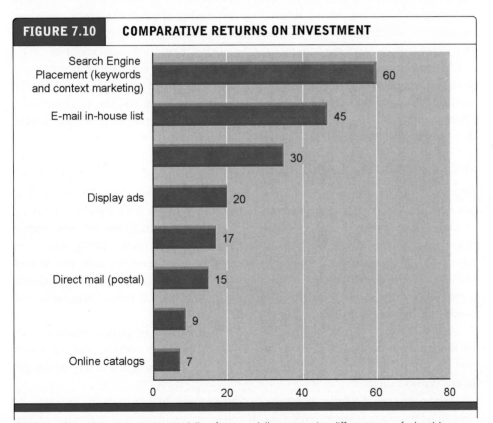

| FIGURE 7.10 | COMPARATIVE RETURNS ON INVESTMENT |

This figure shows the average returns in dollars for every dollar spent using different types of advertising techniques. Search engine placement has replaced e-mail as the most cost-effective form of online advertising. These amounts are estimates and will vary by product, ad effectives, page placement, and degree of targeting.

SOURCES: Industry sources; author's estimates.

well as other search engines. The cost-effectiveness of targeted, opt-in e-mail remains very strong.

There is growing evidence that the cost-effectiveness of search engine marketing has peaked, and may actually be declining because the cost of keywords has grown significantly, and the number of keywords being purchased has also expanded as retailers branch out from their core keywords into more peripheral words. The result is a rising cost per click and a declining efficacy of keywords that are peripheral to the brand. Growth in search engine advertising revenues are likely to slow in the near future, and search engine firms such as Google and Microsoft are seeking other opportunities for growth by purchasing advertising networks, and moving into the ad brokerage business for traditional media like radio, newspapers, and television.

A study of the comparative impacts of offline and online marketing concluded that the most powerful marketing campaigns used multiple forms of marketing, including online, catalog, television, radio, newspapers, and retail store. Traditional media like television and print media remain the primary means for consumers to find out about new products even though advertisers have reduced their budgets for print media ads. The consensus conclusion is that consumers who shop multiple channels are spending more than consumers who shop only with a single channel, in part because they have more discretionary income but also because of the combined number of "touch points" which marketers are making with the consumers. The fastest growing channel in consumer marketing is the multi-channel shopper.

Banner ads can be made far more effective if they are targeted to specific occasions (occasion-based marketing), particular keyword search arguments, or users who have an identified user profile and can be pitched the ad at just the right moment. Usually, this kind of precision ad pitching requires the services of an advertising network firm such as DoubleClick or 24/7 Real Media.

THE COSTS OF ONLINE ADVERTISING

cost per thousand (CPM)
advertiser pays for impressions in 1,000-unit lots

Effectiveness cannot be considered without an analysis of costs. Initially, most online ads were sold on a barter or **cost per thousand (CPM)** (M is the symbol for thousand in Latin) basis, with advertisers purchasing impressions in 1,000-unit lots. Today, other pricing models have developed, including **cost per click (CPC)**, where the advertiser pays a prenegotiated fee for each click an ad receives, **cost per action (CPA)**, where the advertiser pays a prenegotiated amount only when a user performs a specific action, such as a registration or a purchase, and hybrid arrangements, combining two or more of these models (see **Table 7.6**).

cost per click (CPC)
advertiser pays prenegotiated fee for each click an ad receives

While in the early days of e-commerce, a few online sites spent as much as $400 on marketing and advertising to acquire one customer, the average cost was never that high. **Table 7.7** shows the estimated average cost per acquisition for various different types of media.

cost per action (CPA)
advertiser pays only for those users who perform a specific action

While the costs for offline customer acquisition are higher than online, typically the offline items are far more expensive. If you advertise in the *Wall Street Journal*, you are tapping into a wealthy demographic interested in buying islands, jets, other corporations, and expensive homes in France. A full-page black and white ad in the *Wall Street Journal* National Edition costs about $200,000, whereas other papers are in

TABLE 7.6	DIFFERENT PRICING MODELS FOR ONLINE ADVERTISEMENTS
PRICING MODEL	DESCRIPTION
Barter	Exchange of ad space for something of equal value
Cost per thousand (CPM)	Advertiser pays for impressions in 1,000 unit lots
Cost per click (CPC)	Advertiser pays pre-negotiated fee for each click ad receives
Cost per action (CPA)	Advertiser pays only for those users who perform a specific action, such as registering, purchasing, etc.
Hybrid	Two or more of the above models used together
Sponsorship	Term-based; advertiser pays fixed fee for a slot on a Web site

the $100,000 range. For these kinds of prices you will need to either sell quite a few apples, or a small number of corporate jet lease agreements.

One of the advantages of online marketing is that online sales can generally be directly correlated with online marketing efforts. The online merchant can measure precisely just how much revenue is generated by specific banners or e-mail messages sent to prospective customers. One way to measure the effectiveness of online marketing is by looking at the ratio of additional revenue received divided by the cost of the campaign (Revenue/Cost). Any positive whole number means the campaign was worthwhile.

A more complex situation arises when both online and offline sales revenues are affected by an online marketing effort. A large percentage of the online audience uses the Web to "shop," but not buy. These shoppers buy at physical

TABLE 7.7	AVERAGE COST PER CUSTOMER ACQUISITION FOR SELECT MEDIA IN THE UNITED STATES, 2009
Internet search engine	$8.50
Yellow pages	$15.00
Online display ads	$25.00
E-mail	$10.00
Direct mail	$50.00
Newspaper	$25.00
Magazine	$19.00
Television	$11.00

SOURCES: Industry sources; authors' estimates.

stores. Merchants such as Sears and Wal-Mart will use e-mail to inform their registered customers of special offers available for purchase either online or at stores. Unfortunately, purchases at physical stores cannot be tied precisely with the online e-mail campaign. In these cases, merchants have to rely on less precise measures such as customer surveys at store locations to determine the effectiveness of online campaigns.

In either case, measuring the effectiveness of online marketing communications—and specifying precisely the objective (branding versus sales)—is critical to profitability. To measure marketing effectiveness, you need to understand the costs of various marketing media and the process of converting online prospects into online customers.

In general, online marketing communications are more costly on a CPM basis than traditional mass media marketing, but are more efficient in producing sales. **Table 7.8** shows costs for typical online and offline marketing communications. For instance, a local television spot (30 seconds) can cost $4,000–$40,000 to run the ad and an additional $40,000 to produce the ad, for a total cost of $44,000–$80,000. The ad may be seen by a population of, say, 2 million persons (impressions) in a local area for a CPM ranging from 2 to 4 cents, which makes television very inexpensive for reaching large audiences quickly. A Web site banner ad costs virtually nothing to produce and can be purchased at Web sites for a cost of from $2 to $15 per thousand impressions. Direct postal mail can cost 80 cents to $1 per household drop for a post card, but e-mail can be sent for virtually nothing and costs only $5–$15 per thousand targeted names. Hence e-mail is far less expensive than postal mail on a CPM basis.

SOFTWARE FOR MEASURING ONLINE MARKETING RESULTS

A number of software programs are available to automatically calculate activities at a Web site. **Figure 7.11** illustrates the information that a Web site activity analysis might provide.

Other software programs and services assist marketing managers in identifying exactly which marketing initiatives are paying off and which are not. See *Insight on Technology: It's 10 P.M. Do You Know Who Is On Your Web Site?* on pages 473–475 for a description of one such program, offered by Visual Sciences.

7.3 THE WEB SITE AS A MARKETING COMMUNICATIONS TOOL

One of the strongest online marketing communications tools is a functional Web site that customers can find easily, and once there, locate what they are looking for quickly. In some ways, a Web site can be viewed as an extended online advertisement. An appropriate domain name, search engine optimization, and proper Web site design are integral parts of a coordinated marketing communications strategy and ultimately, necessary conditions for e-commerce success.

TABLE 7.8	TRADITIONAL AND ONLINE ADVERTISING COSTS COMPARED
TRADITIONAL ADVERTISING	
Local television	$4,000 for a 30-second commercial during a movie; $45,000 for a highly rated show
Network television	$80,000–$600,000 for a 30-second spot during prime time; the average is $120,000 to $140,000
Cable television	$5,000–$8,000 for a 30-second ad during prime time
Radio	$200–$1,000 for a 60-second spot, depending on the time of day and program ratings
Newspaper	$120 per 1,000 circulation for a full-page ad
Magazine	$50 per 1,000 circulation for an ad in a regional edition of a national magazine, versus $120 per 1,000 for a local magazine
Direct mail	$15–$20 per 1,000 delivered for coupon mailings; $25–$40 per 1,000 for simple newspaper inserts
Billboard	$5,000–$25,000 for a 1–3 month rental of a freeway sign
ONLINE ADVERTISING	
Banner ads	$2–$15 per 1,000 impressions on a Web site, depending on how targeted the ad is (the more targeted, the higher the price)
Video and rich media	$20–$25 per 1,000 ads, depending on the Web site's demographics
E-mail	$5–$15 per 1,000 targeted e-mail addresses
Sponsorships	$30–$75 per 1,000 viewers, depending on the exclusivity of the sponsorship (the more exclusive, the higher the price)

DOMAIN NAMES

One of the first communications an e-commerce Web site has with a prospective customer is via its URL. Domain names play an important role in reinforcing an existing brand and/or developing a new brand. There are a number of considerations to take into account in choosing a domain name. Ideally, a domain name should be short, memorable, not easily confused with others, and difficult to misspell. The name of a Web site may or may not reflect the nature of the company's business. The name of most major brands do not. Companies that choose a name unrelated to the nature of their business must be willing to spend extra time, effort, and money to establish the name as a brand. Dot-com domain names (as opposed to .net or .org) are still considered the most preferable, especially in the United States.

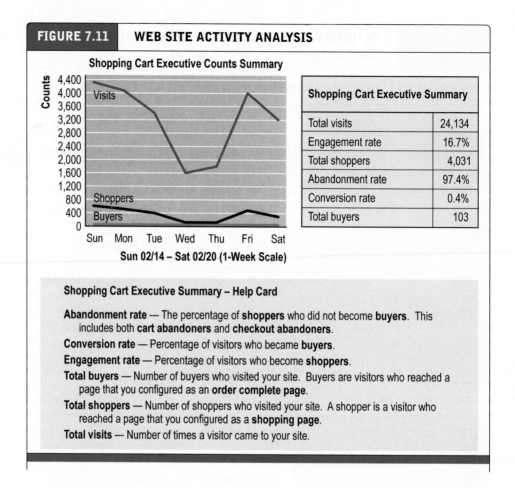

FIGURE 7.11   **WEB SITE ACTIVITY ANALYSIS**

Shopping Cart Executive Counts Summary

Shopping Cart Executive Summary	
Total visits	24,134
Engagement rate	16.7%
Total shoppers	4,031
Abandonment rate	97.4%
Conversion rate	0.4%
Total buyers	103

Sun 02/14 – Sat 02/20 (1-Week Scale)

Shopping Cart Executive Summary – Help Card

Abandonment rate — The percentage of **shoppers** who did not become **buyers**. This includes both **cart abandoners** and **checkout abandoners**.

Conversion rate — Percentage of visitors who became **buyers**.

Engagement rate — Percentage of visitors who become **shoppers**.

Total buyers — Number of buyers who visited your site. Buyers are visitors who reached a page that you configured as an **order complete page**.

Total shoppers — Number of shoppers who visited your site. A shopper is a visitor who reached a page that you configured as a **shopping page**.

Total visits — Number of times a visitor came to your site.

Today, however, it may be difficult to find a domain name that satisfies all of the above criteria. Many of the "good" .com domain names have already been taken. A number of companies exist that list domain names for sale (such as GreatDomains.com and BuyDomains.com). Most of the online domain registration sites such as Networksolutions.com, Godaddy.com, and Register.com have tools that can help you find appropriate names.

SEARCH ENGINE OPTIMIZATION

Given that around 78 million Americans use search engines daily, it makes sense for a company to optimize its Web site for search engine recognition. Despite the fact that, with the exception of Google, most major search engines allow Web sites to pay for inclusion in their search results listing (but not the organic ranking), and most major search engines have also adopted a paid search engine advertising model, it is still advisable to take the steps needed to objectively improve a Web site's visibility to search engines. Even if you use paid search engine marketing, by optimizing your Web site to improve its rank in the organic listings, you increase the chances of being noticed by consumers on the all important first page of search results, and reduce

INSIGHT ON TECHNOLOGY

IT'S 10 P.M. DO YOU KNOW WHO IS ON YOUR WEB SITE?

Chances are you don't, but if you used a Web site analytics company such as Omniture you would. And if you did pay attention to these matters, you most surely would be making more money from your Web site. Why? Because if you knew in real time what types of people were on your Web site hour by hour, minute by minute, you would be able to adjust your marketing and advertising messages, adjust your product mix, change product placement, and greatly improve the conversion process from mere visitors to actual purchasers.

In an industry where the players cannot seem to agree on standards for measuring Web site performance, and where webmasters are overwhelmed with literally millions of bits of information about the behavior of consumers on their Web sites, Omniture is working to help Web managers make sense out of their clickstream traffic. Omniture is an software as a service (SaaS) provider that sells Web site analytics and optimization services to other firms. In 2008, Omniture generated $297 million in revenue, double its revenue of 2007! The company has approximately 5,100 customers in the United States and Europe, including Newsweek, Delta, Macy's, TV Guide, Kohl's, and Scotts. Most customers subscribe to its flagship product SiteCatalyst, a collection of tools that allow managers to see in real time who is on their site, how customers flow through their site, and which are the most popular and profitable pages. The company was founded in 1996, and began selling on-demand Web site optimization and management tools in 2002. Since then, the company has made several acquisitions to grow its business rapidly. It has been so successful that in September 2009, Adobe announced that it was purchasing Omniture for $1.8 billion.

Other competitors in the same business include Coremetrics and Nedstat; network management software and business intelligence vendors such as NetIQ and SPSS, which offer Web analytics as part of their larger product offerings; and digital marketing and e-commerce services providers such as Microsoft Advertising (formerly aQuantive) and Digital River, which incorporate Web analytics in their services.

Omniture SiteCatalyst allows webmasters to monitor and analyze their Web traffic in real time, collect visitor intelligence, and enable faster adjustments to underperforming pages. It also provides most, if not all, of the answers to questions about performance and return on investment (ROI) that Web site marketing managers want.

SiteCatalyst collects, processes, stores, and reports on Internet user behavior based on browser activity. Reports allow customers to measure which marketing initiatives visitors responded to, what search engines they used, what keywords they entered, how much time they spent on pages, what they bought online, when they abandoned shopping carts, and where they live. The available reports and features include Web site navigation analysis, conversion rate analysis including calculating the long-term value of customers, marketing campaign measurement, and executive dashboards.

SiteCatalyst can evaluate a page-by-page navigation path a visitor has taken through a Web site. The service works by embedding a small piece of code into each HTML page a client wants to track and analyze. One benefit to clients is that SiteCatalyst eliminates the need to capture, store, and process log files, which are expensive to run and maintain and consume

(continued)

a good bit of a company's time and resources. SiteCatalyst does not need to be installed on a customer's own computers and infrastructure, but instead operates as a Web service (SaaS, software as a service) model. There is no "installation" involved. Hence maintenance and operational costs are borne by Omniture.

SiteCatalyst is able to segment customers live, in real-time, as they poke around a Web site. For instance, some visitors come for replacement parts, and can be cross-sold to other products from your firm in the process. Looking for a printer cartridge? Why not consider buying a whole new printer on sale today? Most visitors come to Web sites (especially brand-name Web sites like Microsoft, HP, or Macy's) looking for specific products. But as long as they are on your site, why not entice them to consider related products or services? If an L.L.Bean customer comes to LLBean.com looking for pajamas, Omniture is able to determine which ads and prompts lead to additional sales. In general, people looking for pajamas can be sold sleep- and warmth-related products like underwear, blankets, and pillows.

Not to be left behind by Web 2.0, Omniture also provides "Social Networking Optimization" tools. If you have social networking elements on your Web site like user comments, user-generated content, video with sharing possibilities, or bookmarking, Omniture networking optimization can help you understand the consumption and creation habits of visitors, identify how much the social networking elements add to sales, engage users with content that is motivational, and help create emotional links to your products and brand.

The National Geographic Society, one of the world's largest non-profit organizations devoted to exploration and geographic knowledge, reported in 2009 that Omniture SiteCatalyst and SearchCenter services had increased its Web site visits by 150%. Ted McDonald, Web analytics manager at National Geographic, said "Prior to using Omniture, we didn't have the data needed to understand the value of different parts of our site to our visitors or how our keyword advertising was translating into subscriptions. Using SiteCatalyst and SearchCenter together has given us insight into our paid search spend and return on every part of our site, which has been invaluable to our business." National Geographic deployed Search-Center to optimize its paid search initiatives with the goal of realizing a specific return on ad spend. Its primary goal from paid search was to drive subscriptions, and using SearchCenter, it discovered that 90% of the company's keywords were losing money. As a result, the National Geographic team identified which keyword variations were ineffective and reallocated spend to the remaining profitable 10%, turning all of the company's paid search ads profitable, it reports. "With SearchCenter, we've optimized our ads to a point where we don't need to change them often, which increases the productivity of the team and allows us to focus on more valuable tasks," says McDonald. "When the profitability changes, I have dashboards set up that show the return on investment for each search campaign and I can make changes accordingly."

HP, one of the world's largest PC and printer manufacturers, uses Omniture SiteCatalyst to manage its Web site, HP.com. An incredibly complex business, HP is segmented into largely independent product and service groups: such as printers, PCs, commercial servers, and software. It is further segmented into market groups: home/office, small business, enterprise business, government systems, and graphic arts. A visit to the Web site shows the complexity of having a single Web site to deliver service to customers coming from all of these segments. Behind the scenes, in the past HP had no systemic way of understanding how well users navigated the site, found what they want, and purchased a product. It did not have tracking data on customers visiting the site. Therefore, it did not know if printer customers were also PC

(continued)

or corporate customers. Also the independent business groups contributed their own ideas to how the user would be treated, creating many different and inconsistent marketing messages. HP did use surveys of visitors and specialized reports performed by various HP employees on an ad hoc basis. The absence of an overall coordinated Web site management tool meant that HP could not run its business as an integrated, cohesive firm. HP began using SiteCatalyst with the goal of complete customer tracking, a unified set of reports available on demand and nearly instantly to more than 1,300 HP managers, and a full 360-degree view of their customers. HP tripled its conversion rates for its e-mail campaigns, largely due to knowing who visited the site, capturing their e-mail, and sending appropriate marketing e-mails for products and services. HP was also able to improve the navigation of its Web site by examining closely the click-path that users followed on the HP site. When people get lost on a Web site, it usually results in nearly randomized clicking in an effort by the user to find their way. Understanding these faulty navigation areas, HP revised its navigation to minimize "the lost user" phenomenon. For instance, the Customer Experience Group (a newly formed group responsible for the overall operation of HP.com) discovered that visitors seeking parts were more likely to buy online from HP if they arrived at the Parts store in one or two clicks (rather than a much more lengthy navigation path for the old site). HP estimates this change in navigation produced an annual increase of $775,000 in revenue from the Parts store.

■ **SOURCES:** "Buying Your Brand On Search—Up To 23% Revenue Lift!," Omniture Articles, September 1, 2009; "Omniture, Inc. Form 10-K for the fiscal year ended December 31, 2008 filed with the Securities and Exchange Commission on February 27, 2009;"National Geographic Increases Site Visits, Page Views and Return on Ad Spend With Omniture SearchCenter and Omniture SiteCatalyst," Case Study, Omniture, August 26, 2009; "HP Uses Omniture to Get a 360 Degree View of Its Customers," Case Study, Omniture.com, September, 2008; "SiteCatalyst Business Optimizations: Social Networking Optimization," White Paper, Omniture.com, September, 2008; "The Interactive Marketing Metrics You Need," by Rebecca Jennings, Forrester Research Group, May 30, 2008; "Omniture's SiteCatalyst Turns 14," By Enid Burns, The ClickZ Network, Mar 5, 2008.

your customer acquisition costs. For small firms, organic ranking is the primary tool for driving sales.

Search engines today operate primarily with the use of Web crawlers, software programs that search the Web for pages, index their content, identify the number of sites linking to the page, and report the content to very large databases where it can be searched.

The method of indexing and ranking Web pages varies across search engines, and is proprietary. There are many consulting firms, books, and online sources that provide guidance on how to enhance the visibility of a Web site to crawler programs. Most of this advice is quite commonsensical and none of it is guaranteed to work despite the promises.

The first step in improving a firm's search engine ranking is to register with as many search engines as possible, so that a user looking for similar Web sites has a chance of coming across the firm's site. Nearly all search engines have registration pages, and some may charge an "inclusion fee" of around $50 per year.

The second step to improve a firm's ranking is to ensure that keywords used in the Web site description match keywords likely to be used as search terms by prospective customers. Using the keyword "lamps," for example, will not help your search engine ranking if most prospective customers are searching for "lights." Search engines differ, but most search engines read home page title tags, metatags, and other text on the home page in order to understand and index the content of the page.

Third, place keywords in a Web site's metatag and page title. A metatag is an HTML tag containing a list of words describing the Web site. Metatags are heavily used by search engines to determine the relevance of Web sites to search terms used frequently by users. The title tag provides a brief description of the Web site's content. The words in both the metatags and the title tags should match words on the home page. In addition, it is wise to include many references on the home page to the subject matter of likely consumer searches. Most crawlers will index the text content of the home page and may not go deeper into the Web site's secondary pages.

Fourth, link the Web site to as many other Web sites as possible, both in-coming links and out-going links. Search engines evaluate both kinds of links, and their quality to identify how popular a page is and how linked it is to other content on the Web. Search engines such as Google are guessing that when you enter a query for a product, chances are good that the product is located at one of the highly connected Web sites. The assumption is that the more links there are to a Web site, the more useful the Web site must be. How can a firm increase links to its Web site? Placing advertising is one way: banner ads, buttons, interstitials, and superstitials are all links to a firm's Web site. You can also create Web sites, even hundreds of Web sites, whose only function is to link to your main Web site although search engines can discover this and place you on the last page of search returns. Entering into affiliate relationships with other Web sites is another method. Search engines attempt to cancel out all efforts to mislead their search engines with varying and unknown success.

While the steps listed above are a beginning, increasing a firm's ranking is still a bit of an art form and usually requires a full-time professional effort to tweak metatags, keywords, and network links before solid results are obtained. The task often requires several months and is complicated by the fact that each search engine uses slightly different indexing methods, and changes their indexing methods in order to fool search engine optimizers.

WEB SITE FUNCTIONALITY

Attracting users to a company's Web site is the objective of marketing, but once a consumer is at a Web site, the sales process begins. This means that whatever brought the individuals to the Web site becomes much less relevant, and what they find at the Web site will ultimately determine whether they will make a purchase or return. Recall that a Web page and Web site are, first and foremost, a software interface. The question is: What makes for an effective software interface? In general, people use software interfaces that they perceive to be useful and easy to use (a literature that is referred to as the "technology acceptance model"). Utility and ease of use are, therefore, the main factors to focus on when designing a site. Other factors involved in the credibility and trust that users place in a Web site—both very important for making decisions—are described in a growing literature on Web site design (Fogg, et al., 2003). In an exploratory study of Web site credibility based on 2,600 participants, the top three factors in Web site credibility were design look, information design/structure, and information focus (Fogg, et al., 2003) (see **Figure 7.12.**). Similar

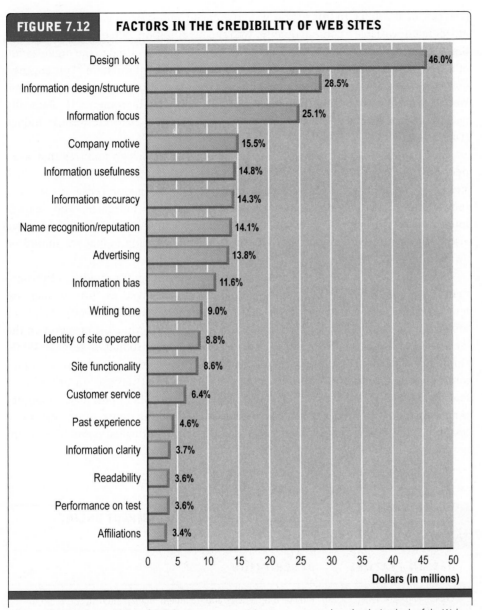

| FIGURE 7.12 | FACTORS IN THE CREDIBILITY OF WEB SITES |

When evaluating the credibility of a Web site, survey participants commented on the design look of the Web site more than any other Web site feature.

SOURCE: Based on data from Fogg, et al., 2003.

results were reported by Flanigan and Metzger in a 2007 study (Flanigan and Metzger, 2007). The message is: design counts.

The authors of this study were disappointed that users were most impressed by the design look of a Web site rather than its utility or ease of use.

Research on Web site utilization has found that the way information is organized on a Web site, while important for first-time users, declines in importance over time. Gradually, information content becomes the major factor attracting further visits

(Davern, et al., 2001). In this research, frequency of Web site use is a function of four independent variables: content quality, Web site organization, perceived usefulness of the Web site, and perceived ease of use. Over time, people get used to the organization of a Web site and learn how to use it effectively to gather information. This suggests that improving content and usefulness ought to be the first priority of a firm, and that Web site redesign should be implemented carefully and incrementally. Radically redesigning a site runs the risk of losing the "lock-in" effects that Web sites can induce (Davern, et al., 2001).

In Chapter 4 (Section 4.4), we identified eight basic design features that were necessary, from a business point of view, to attract and retain customers. The Web site must be functional, informative, employ simple navigation (ease of use), use redundant navigation, make it easy for customers to purchase, and feature multi-browser functionality, simple graphics, and legible text. Researchers have also found a number of other design factors that marketing managers should be aware of (see **Table 7.9**).

Sites that offer a "compelling experience" in the sense of providing entertainment with commerce or interactivity, or that are perceived as "fun" to use, are more successful in attracting and keeping visitors (Novak, et al., 2000). Web sites with editorial content that informs users also increases the time users spend on the Web site and increases the chance of them purchasing a product or service. While simplicity of design is hard to define, Lohse et al. (2000) found that the most important factor in predicting monthly sales was product list navigation and choice features that save consumers time. Thus, Amazon's "one-click" purchase capability is a powerful tool for increasing sales. In difficult economic times, more customers "fantasy shop": enter the purchase process and pull out at the last possible moment before purchase.

TABLE 7.9	WEB SITE DESIGN FEATURES THAT IMPACT ONLINE PURCHASING
DESIGN FEATURE	**DESCRIPTION**
Compelling experience	Provide interactivity, entertainment, human interest; site is fun to use.
Editorial content	Provide helpful content, opinions, and features on subjects of interest to visitors in order to increase stickiness.
Fast download times	Quicker is better; if longer, provide amusement.
Easy product list navigation	Consumers can easily find the products they want.
Few clicks to purchase	The shorter the click list, the greater the chance of a sale.
Customer choice agents	Recommendation agents/configurators help the consumer make quick, correct choices.
Responsiveness	Personal e-mail response; 1–800 phone capability shown on Web site.

More and more Web sites are using interactive consumer-decision aids to help the shopper make choices. Recommendation agents are programs that can suggest a product based on either consumer surveys or a review of a consumer's profile. Dell uses an online configurator to help consumers decide what computer to order.

Responsiveness of Web sites is also important to credibility. Firms are improving but have a long way to go. A study of large firms found that while 90% of firms have a privacy policy, 75% don't tell users how to have their personal information destroyed so it can't be used by others, 12% of large companies did not respond to e-mail queries, and 21% responded only to half the queries sent to their Web sites. In general, large companies with Web sites receive favorable respect ratings for "simplicity of design and use" but weak ratings on responding to customers (Walker, 2004; Customer Respect Group, 2005). Other researchers have found that consumers purchase more at sites where there are strong privacy policies and these are known to visitors (Tsai, et. al., 2007).

No matter how successful the offline and online marketing campaign, a Web site that fails to deliver information, customer convenience, and responsiveness spells disaster. Attention to these Web site design features will help ensure success.

Adware, Spyware, Ad Bombs, Ambush Marketing, and Customer Hijacking:

Invasive Marketing Techniques Grow on the Web

Imagine you turn on your television and tune in *American Idol*, looking forward to another exciting evening. At 9:00 p.m., the show comes on, but suddenly the opening credits are blocked by a pop-up ad that takes up half the screen and lasts for 30 seconds. You fiddle with the remote, but it doesn't stop. Other pop-ups continue to appear throughout the show, preventing you from really enjoying it. Finally, you turn it off. Of course, this doesn't happen on TV, or the radio, or with the telephone system. At least not yet. But on the Web, it happens all the time.

Spying, phishing, and spamming. Sometimes you have to wonder if the Web will just self-destruct and take most of e-commerce with it. The holy grail of advertising and marketing is to deliver the right message to the right person at the right time. If this were possible, no one would receive ads they did not want to see and then no advertising dollars would be wasted, reducing the costs to end users and increasing the efficiency of each ad dollar. One early vision of e-commerce was a trade-off between privacy and efficiency: let us know a little more about you and we will show you only the advertising and products you are interested in seeing, and even offer free content. E-commerce was supposed to end the mass advertising that exploded in the television era. But you quickly learn on the Web that your e-mail address can easily be discovered by marketing firms—who often share your address with one another—and thereafter you are treated to hundreds of e-mail messages a week offering "free" credit cards, cash prizes, coupons, no-money-down mortgages, lifetime income without work, and other get-rich quick schemes. Thousands of banner ads are displayed on the Web sites you visit that rarely have anything to do with your interests. Rather than achieve the holy grail of advertising, much of Web-based marketing is extraordinarily ignorant of who you are or what you are looking for.

Sometimes the technology can lead aggressive marketers in the opposite direction, increasing the chances that you will see the wrong ads at the wrong time without your consent. Adware and spyware are technologies that would seem to defeat the very purpose of the Internet, namely, a global interactive information environment under user control.

Adware is a kind of malware installed without the user's informed consent that calls outside servers to deliver ads based upon the user's browser behavior. For instance, when the user points his/her browser to LLBean.com, an adware program will call out for an ad from a competitor, and display that ad until the user closes it down. Once the adware ad window is closed, the LLBean.com home page is displayed. The entire process is one kind of "customer hijacking," where your customers are diverted to other sites without their consent.

Spyware is a bit more aggressive. Spyware is also a program installed without user consent, but the intent of spyware is to record your keystrokes as you enter information into other legitimate Web sites (such as your online banking account) and then to transmit this information to spyware servers and data centers where the information can be used to steal funds from your accounts, or is sold on the Internet to other hackers. Spyware uses key loggers to monitor your keystrokes, screen capture devices, and Trojan horses. In some cases, spyware may be a legitimate program used by parents or corporations to track use of the Internet by children or employees, or by law enforcement or intelligence agencies. However, typically, it is used for malicious purposes.

To get a better understanding of how adware works, let's follow an "ad bomb" as it moves through the system that is not protected by an adware blocker. Suppose a 10 year-old relative visits your house and wants to "play with the computer" as adults go about their business. You have DSL service. Surfing to a game site, she sees an offer for $100 in "free" prizes. She clicks and up pops the following proposition: "Click Here to Get Your Free Prizes." She clicks and up pops pictures of ten free prizes, ranging from free CDs to free clothing. But in the background a program is loaded onto your computer that automatically—without your intervention—requests that pop-up advertisements served by an advertising network be displayed every few minutes whenever you are using your computer. It is not even necessary to have launched your browser because the program automatically launches your browser whenever it wants to serve up an ad. Thankfully, however, most of the ads served up are appropriate for a 10-year-old (more offers of free prizes, CDs for children, and clothing), although there are some inappropriate advertisements, such as those for credit cards.

Following one of these ads back to its originator, you discover a direct marketing firm called Zango.com that specializes in putting together a network of millions of users offering free videos, games, screen savers, and music. There, in order to actually obtain your free content, you are required to register and give your name and e-mail address. Zango adds your name to millions of other consumers. Then, when you download your free content, Zango automatically installs a program that tracks your every online movement, and reports back to Zango servers. Zango then sells this information to marketers looking for specific market segments. For instance, as a marketer for a sportswear site, you might want to pop an ad for your monogrammed t-shirts every time a user enters a search term for t-shirts on Google, or enters the URL of L.L.Bean. In this case, both Google and L.L.Bean are denied revenue, and their customers are hijacked to another competing site. In an effort to rid your computer of the offending ad bomb, you contact the ad network. Technicians explain in an e-mail that they are just serving the ads and bear no responsibility for the downloaded program. They explain that "you may have unknowingly downloaded an application from one of these sites. An application downloaded from one of these sites may be requesting an advertisement from our ad server. Please note that we do not download any applications to your computer. We do not control these Web sites who did download the program to your computer." The ad network technicians fail to mention that they are paid by the advertisers involved to respond to the ads. The network does offer to help, however. Technical support advises you to close down ad windows as they appear, or press CTRL + N to display the URL of the advertisers and then send the URLs to the network, which will, in turn notify the advertisers to unsubscribe you from their lists. Finally, you open Windows' Programs and Features utility in the hope of identifying the program and removing it. After scanning the list of programs, you discover an unfamiliar program. Guessing this oddly named program is the offender, you remove it, and finally the ad bomb event is over. Sometimes. In other cases, the adware is hidden from Windows altogether. Zango's position, and that of other adware distributors, is that consumers voluntarily consent to receive the ads when they install the file-swapping or other programs that typically have notices on install pages in very small print that say "You agree to receive occasional advertising messages from us directly or our affiliates." Consumer groups and the federal government think otherwise. They claim the programs are installed without consumer consent or knowledge.

Claria (formerly Gator.com) was one of the first to use an adware technique that could be called ambush advertising. Claria originally started business as a provider of a client-side digital wallet that stored personal information and automatically filled out Web forms. From there, Claria added a product called the OfferCompanion that could follow a consumer's movements on the Web, and when the user surfed to a site such as Staples.com, notify Claria's servers, which would search their ad database for an ad purchased by a Staples competitor such as OfficeMax, and then serve that as a "mini-billboard" that would appear directly over the Staples Web site. The IAB—a trade group that represents Internet advertising agencies—announced its opposition to OfferCompanion, charging that it infringed on the trademark, copyright, and intellectual property rights of Web site publishers and other advertisers whose ads were being covered up by the mini-billboard. IAB demanded that Claria cease use of the program. Claria in turn sued the IAB in a California federal court for IAB's "malicious disparagement" of its products.

While many early purveyors of adware, under pressure from consumer groups, Internet security firms, and the FTC, have closed shop, others persisted and thousands of new adware firms have emerged. The most notorious and persistent was Zango.com (formerly ePIPO, and 180Solutions), mentioned previously. Identified by security firms such as McAfee and Symantec as "an adware downloader" and a "potentially unwanted program," Zango downloaded programs to user computers that display pop-up ads without user consent. It automatically ran on startup, and could not be shut down by the user or removed without requesting a separate uninstall program. In 2008, Zango was discovered on social networking sites like Facebook and MySpace hawking an application called "Crush Calculator." This application that tells Facebook members that one of their friends has a crush on them, and then leads users through several screens where they reveal their friends' e-mail addresses and other personal information. In April 2009, Zango finally closed its doors after nearly a decade of hijacking customers. The entire $40 million investment by Spectrum Equity in 2004 was lost in a bankruptcy settlement. Apparently, Silicon Valley investors thought malware was a wonderful business model in 2004. Adware often infects social networks and user-generated content sites. Security firms have discovered thousands of user pages on MySpace and Facebook that have videos that look like YouTube videos but when clicked, automatically install adware toolbars and games. Users are sent to a site called Youtube.info where prizes, games, music, and sports entertainment are offered. It's all "free," but you pay the "price" by installing more adware. In 2009, another typical malware application came in the form of a Web game that can be downloaded. For instance, the online game ABC Scrabble from 2MGames.com was identified as a 2009 Top Ten champion "badware" because it installs additional applications—including spyware and badware components—without telling the user; it attempts to install additional software well after the initial installation; it adds programs to the user's startup folder without disclosure; and it fails to uninstall bundled software when the main program is uninstalled. ABC Scrabble generates revenue from advertisers and other Web sites by sending them information on Internet users, or diverting users to these other domains. ABC Scrabble bundles the webHancer Customer Companion and webHancer Survey Companion, which are commonly considered spyware (see Symantec, DoxDesk, and Spyware Guide). WebHancer monitors Web sites visited by the user and reports this information to a remote server. This potential transmission of personal information is not disclosed to the user during the installation process.

How big a problem is adware and spyware? Well over 120 billion ad impressions a month are flashed in front of Internet users paid for by thousands of firms. No one has any idea how many of these billions of ads are served up by adware. The FTC believes that about 10% of all ad impressions are generated by spyware. An academic and industrial consortium, Stopbadware.org, a joint venture of the Harvard Berkman Center for Internet and Society and the Oxford Internet Institute, backed by Google, Lenovo, PayPal, Sun Microsystems, and VeriSign, began tracking Web sites where adware and malware is found. Malware, regardless of type, always calls out to external servers. Stopbadware.org, tracks over 400,000 malware sites on the Internet that distribute malware, and identifies the top-level domains where malware directs users. All domains on the Top 10 list are suspected to have compromised more than 10,000 Web sites on the Internet.

Why do companies use adware? They do so primarily because research shows that adware can be twice as effective as other forms of online advertising. Adware vendors point out that by using adware you can truly target consumers when they are most interested in products or services. Advertisers achieve a higher return on investment while exposing people to fewer ads than hit-or-miss pop-ups and banners. When a user searches for a product, or tries to go to a competitor's Web site (indicating interest and willingness to purchase), the user can be hit immediately either with an ad for that product, or diverted to a competitor's Web site. Obviously, many firms are hurt and threatened by adware, and consumers suffer negative externalities.

The growth of the spyware industry and resulting business and consumer complaints have generated several legislative efforts to define and control, if not eliminate, malware in all its varieties. The U.S. Senate is considering the Counter Spy Act (CSA) and conducting hearings to "examine the impact of spyware on computer performance and privacy and security risks associated with this software." The act defines and prohibits illegal activities such as zombifying a system, denial of service attacks, browser hijacking, and any software that enables identity theft are all prohibited. Similarly, the CSA states that it's illegal to steal someone's personal identification information off of their computer either via direct physical access or through a third-party program. All of these things are already illegal under federal and state law. The main concern of critics is a long list of activities it does permit: the restrictions imposed by this act do not apply to any monitoring of, or interaction with, a subscriber's Internet or other network connection or service, or a protected computer, by or at the direction of a telecommunications carrier, cable operator, computer hardware or software provider, financial institution, or provider of information services or interactive computer servicefor a variety of "legitimate" users like network or computer security, diagnostics, technical support, and authorized remote system management. The Counter Spy Act itself does not define any type of criteria under which software use shall be deemed authorized or not, gives no guidance on who has the authority to make such a ruling, and does not mandate that the software user be notified that such an investigation is taking place, as long as the investigation itself is done with the goal of "preventing unauthorized use." In other words, large software providers such as Apple and Microsoft, or ISPs like AT&T and Optimum Online, can pretty much monitor your computer anytime they want without your informed consent. In other words, the Senate is trying to make an exception for "legal spyware," certain types of malware that is used for the "right" reasons. This sort of contradiction has brought about the presence of powerful interests that indeed do want to monitor your online behavior for a variety of reasons, some commercial and some related to an ill-defined state of "security."

The group Americans For Fair Electronic Commerce Transactions (AFFECT) raised some of these points in their testimony, noting that "whether the use of a particular software is 'unauthorized,' 'fraudulent,' or 'illegal' is often subject to legitimate dispute and merits some judicial consideration before a provider is allowed to unilaterally employ a drastic remedy like remote disablement." While most groups express general support for the bill, the Direct Marketing Association (DMA) has expressed concern about the legitimate uses of cookies, which are downloaded to user computers, and which provide a record of user Internet activities that is used by advertisers to show ads. In the proposed legislation, cookies are expressly exempted from the provisions of the bill. So, according to DMA, keeping track of what Internet sites users have visited is acceptable.

While most firms are opposed to malware, defining malware is difficult. Major institutions such as hardware, software, financial services, search engines, and cell phone operators all want to be able to download programs to users that will scan computers for illicit copies of software, attempted attacks on Web sites, and other illicit activities. Start-up marketing firms looking for an edge want to install "deep packet inspection" software on ISP servers that handle your Web traffic. Deep packet inspection will allow the ISP and marketing firm to trace your every click on the

SOURCES: "Badware Websites Report 2009," Stopbadware.org, September, 2009; "Top Ten Malware Sites," by Niels Provos, Google Security Team, June 3, 2009; "Counter Spy Act Leaves Loopholes Open for "Legal" Spyware," by Joel Hruska, arstechica.com, June 17, 2009; "End of Desktop Adware Market," by John Leyden, The Register, theregister.co.uk, April 21, 2009; "Crime Ware: Understanding New Attacks and Defenses," by Markus Jakobsson and Zulfikar Ramzan, Association of Computing Machinery, 2008; "NebuAd Halts Plans for Web Tracking," by Ellen Nakashima, Washington Post.com, September 4, 2008; "Adware Vendor Zango Profits from Pirated Movies," by Gregg Keizer, *Computerworld*, August 18, 2008; "Experts: Spyware Legislation Needs More Work," by Grant Gross, *Computerworld*, June 12, 2008; "Red In the Face: Zango Adware Surfaces on Facebook," by Wendy Davis, MediaPost.com, January 4, 2008; "The Economics of Malware," by Michel J. van Eeten, J. Bauer, J. Groenwegen, and W. Lemstra, University of Delft, 35th Telecommunications Policy Research Conference, September 28, 2007.

Web. Deep packet inspection does not involve installing adware, but does accomplish the same purpose using the ISP servers, namely, tracing your online movements for the purpose of making a profit. As it turns out, distinguishing acceptable from unacceptable software applications installed without the user's informed consent proves to be far more difficult than many expected.

Case Study Questions

1. Do you believe ISPs who host adware sites should be held legally responsible for allowing adware Web sites on their networks? Do you think the ad sponsors who paid firms such as Zango should be held responsible? Why or why not?

2. Do these programs result in greater "targeting" of advertising, or are they just as mass market in nature as television ads?

3. What types of industry or government regulations might be needed to control these forms of advertising? Should some malware be allowed for certain purposes?

4. In what ways does adware contribute to a more efficient marketplace? Does it increase consumer choice, speed product search, or increase the efficiency of matching buyers and sellers?

7.5   REVIEW

KEY CONCEPTS

■ Identify the major forms of online marketing communications.

Marketing communications include promotional sales communications that encourage immediate purchases and branding communications that focus on extolling the differentiable benefits of consuming a product or service. There are a number of different forms of marketing communications:

- *Banner and rich media/video ads* are promotional messages that users can respond to by clicking on the banner and following the link to a product description or offering. Variations include different size banners, buttons, skyscrapers, pop-ups, and pop-unders. Rich media ads use Flash, DHTML, Java, and streaming audio and/or video and typically seek to involve users more deeply than static banner ads.
- *Interstitial ads* are a way of placing full-page messages between the current and destination pages of a user. They are usually inserted within a single site, and are displayed as the user moves from one page to the next; they can also be made to appear as users move among sites.
- *Superstitials* are rich media ads developed by Unicast that pre-load into a browser's cache and do not play until fully loaded and the user clicks to another page.

- *Paid search engine inclusion and placement* is a relatively recent phenomenon. Firms now pay search engines for inclusion in the search engine index (formerly free and based on "objective" criteria), receiving a guarantee that their firm will appear in the results of relevant searches.
- *Sponsorships* are paid efforts to tie an advertiser's name to particular information, an event, or a venue in a way that reinforces its brand in a positive yet not overtly commercial manner. Advertorials are a common form of online sponsorship.
- *Affiliate relationships* permit a firm to put its logo or banner ad on another firm's Web site from which users of that site can click through to the affiliate's site.
- *Direct e-mail marketing sends* e-mail directly to interested users, and has proven to be one of the most effective forms of marketing communications. The key to effective direct e-mail marketing is "interested users"—Internet users who, at one time or another, have expressed an interest in receiving messages from the advertiser (people who have "opted in").
- *Online catalogs* are the online equivalent of paper-based catalogs. Their basic function is to display an e-commerce merchant's wares.
- Offline marketing combined with online marketing communications is typically the most effective. Although many e-commerce ventures want to rely heavily on online communications, marketing communications campaigns most successful at driving traffic to a Web site have incorporated both online and offline tactics.

■ **Understand the costs and benefits of online marketing communications.**

Key terms that one must know in order to understand evaluations of online marketing communications' effectiveness and its costs and benefits include:

- *Impressions*—the number of times an ad is served.
- *Click-through rate*—the number of times an ad is clicked.
- *Hits*—the number of http requests received by a firm's server.
- *Page views*—the number of pages viewed by visitors.
- *Stickiness (duration)*—the average length of time visitors remain at a site.
- *Unique visitors*—the number of distinct, unique visitors to a site.
- *Loyalty*—the percentage of purchasers who return in a year.
- *Reach*—the percentage of total consumers in a market who will visit a site.
- *Recency*—the average number of days elapsed between visits.
- *Acquisition rate*—the percentage of visitors who indicate an interest in the site's product by registering or visiting product's pages.
- *Conversion rate*—the percentage of visitors who purchase something.
- *Browse-to-buy ratio*—the ratio of items purchased to product views
- *View-to-cart ratio*—the ratio of "Add to cart" clicks to product views.
- *Cart conversion rate*—the ratio of actual orders to "Add to cart" clicks.
- *Checkout conversion rate*—the ratio of actual orders to checkouts started.
- *Abandonment rate*—the percentage of shoppers who begin a shopping cart form, but then fail to complete the form.
- *Retention rate*—the percentage of existing customers who continue to buy on a regular basis.
- *Attrition rate*—the percentage of customers who purchase once, but do not return within a year.
- *Open rate*—the percentage of customers who open the mail and are exposed to the message.

- *Delivery rate*—the percentage of e-mail recipients who received the e-mail.
- *Click-through rate (e-mail)*—the percentage of e-mail recipients who clicked through to the offer.
- *Bounce-back rate*—the percentage of e-mails that could not be delivered

Studies have shown that low click-through rates are not indicative of a lack of commercial impact of online advertising, and that advertising communication does occur even when users do not directly respond by clicking. Online advertising in its various forms has been shown to boost brand awareness and brand recall, create positive brand perceptions, and increase intent to purchase.

Effectiveness cannot be considered without analysis of cost. Typical pricing models for online marketing communications include:
- *Barter*—the exchange of ad space for something of equal value.
- *Cost per thousand (CPM)*—the advertiser pays for impressions in 1,000-unit lots.
- *Cost per click (CPC)*—the advertiser pays a prenegotiated fee for each click an ad receives.
- *Cost per action (CPA)*—the advertiser pays only for those users who perform a specific action.
- *Hybrid models*—combines two or more other models.
- *Sponsorships*—the advertiser pays a fixed fee for a particular term.

Online marketing communications are typically less costly than traditional mass media marketing. Also, online sales can generally be directly correlated with online marketing efforts, unlike with traditional marketing communications tactics.

The online merchant can measure precisely just how much revenue is generated by specific banners or specific e-mail messages sent to prospective customers.

■ **Discuss the ways in which a Web site can be used as a marketing communications tool.**

A functional Web site that customers can find is one of the strongest online communications tools. The following are all integral parts of a coordinated marketing communications strategy:
- *Appropriate domain name*—Companies should choose a domain name that is short, memorable, hard to confuse or misspell, and indicative of a firm's business functions, and that preferably uses dot.com as its top-level domain.
- *Search engine optimization*—Companies should register with all the major search engines so that a user looking for similar sites has a better chance of finding that particular site; ensure that keywords used in the Web site description match keywords likely to be used as search terms by prospective customers; and link the site to as many other sites as possible.
- *Web site functionality*—Once at a Web site, visitors need to be enticed to stay and to buy. Web site design features that impact online purchasing include how compelling the experience of using the Web site is, download time, product list navigation, the number of clicks required to purchase, the existence of customer choice agents, and the Web site's responsiveness to customer needs.

QUESTIONS

1. Explain the difference between marketing and marketing communications.

2. Explain the difference between branding communications and sales/promotional communications.

3. What are some reasons why online advertising constitutes only about 9% of the total advertising market?

4. What kinds of products are most suited to being advertised online?

5. What is the difference between an interstitial ad and a superstitial ad?

6. What are some of the reasons for the decline in click-through rates on banner ads today? How can banner ads be made more effective?

7. Why are some affiliate relationships called "tenancy" deals? How do they differ from pure affiliate arrangements?

8. There is some controversy surrounding paid placements on search engines. What are the issues surrounding paid-placement search engines? Why might consumers object to this practice?

9. What are some of the advantages of direct e-mail marketing?

10. Why is offline advertising still important?

11. What is the difference between hits and page views? Why are these not the best measurements of Web traffic? Which is the preferred metric for traffic counts?

12. Define CTR, CPM, CPC, and CPA.

13. What are the key attributes of a good domain name?

14. What are some of the steps a firm can take to optimize its search engine rankings?

15. List and describe some Web site design features that impact online purchasing.

PROJECTS

1. Use the Online Consumer Purchasing Model (Figure 7.9) to assess the effectiveness of an e-mail campaign at a small Web site devoted to the sales of apparel to the ages 18–26 young adult market in the United States. Assume a marketing campaign of 100,000 e-mails (at 25 cents per e-mail address). The expected click-through rate is 5%, the conversion to customer rate is 10%, and the loyal customer retention rate is 25%. The average sale is $60, and the profit margin is 50% (the cost of the goods is $30). Does the campaign produce a profit? What would you advise doing to increase the number of purchases and loyal customers? What Web design factors? What communications messages?

2. Surf the Web for at least 15 minutes. Visit at least two different e-commerce sites. Make a list describing in detail all the different marketing communication tools you see being used. Which do you believe is the most effective and why?

3. Do a search for a product of your choice on at least three search engines. Examine the results page carefully. Can you discern which results, if any, are a result of a paid placement? If so, how did you determine this? What other marketing communications related to your search appear on the page?

4. Examine the use of rich media and video in advertising. Find and describe at least two examples of advertising using streaming video, sound, or other rich media technologies. (Hint: Check the sites of Internet advertising agencies for case studies or examples of their work.) What are the advantages and/or disadvantages of this kind of advertising? Prepare a short 3- to 5-page report on your findings.

5. Visit Webroot.com's Computer Security Center Spyware Information Center and Badwarebusters.org. Develop a presentation describing your findings and recommendations regarding spyware.

WEB SITE RESOURCES www.azimuth-interactive.com/ecommerce 6e

- Additional projects, exercises, and tutorials
- Careers: Explore career opportunities in e-commerce
- Raising capital and business plans

CHAPTER 8

Ethical, Social, and Political Issues in E-commerce

After reading this chapter, you will be able to:

- Understand why e-commerce raises ethical, social, and political issues.
- Recognize the main ethical, social, and political issues raised by e-commerce.
- Identify a process for analyzing ethical dilemmas.
- Understand basic concepts related to privacy.
- Identify the practices of e-commerce companies that threaten privacy.
- Describe the different methods used to protect online privacy.
- Understand the various forms of intellectual property and the challenges involved in protecting it.
- Understand how governance of the Internet has evolved over time.
- Explain why taxation of e-commerce raises governance and jurisdiction issues.
- Identify major public safety and welfare issues raised by e-commerce.

Discovering Law and Ethics in a Virtual World

Second Life is a massively multiplayer online role playing game (MMORPG) experience where over half a million active monthly users engage in online "virtual life." For the most part, players come not to compete with one another, but to entertain themselves, escape their real worlds, and have some fun. Some come to make money. With liquidity provided by Linden dollars that can be purchased with real dollars (currently $1=250–270 Linden dollars), avatars that users create can buy and sell virtual assets—goods and services—from handbags and cars, to furniture, buildings, real estate, avatar design, clothing, and accessories service businesses. The global market for virtual goods is estimated to be approximately $1.5 billion a year,

and Second Life plays a significant role in this market. In 2009, residents of Second Life will purchase and sell around USD $500 million of virtual goods and services. Shopping for virtual goods has become one of the most compelling and popular aspects of the Second Life experience, with over 680,000 items typically listed for sale.

Others come to create mischief. Mischief, so much a part of the real world where law and custom aim to hold it in check, poses an interesting challenge for virtual worlds where there are no laws, and yet where actions taken online can injure people and corporations offline. It's like the Old West, where law and order were not quite established and people sought solutions, looking at times for a strong High Noon sheriff to bring order. Every now and then, the Sheriff sets down the law in Second Life, when its owners declare certain activities illegal and attempt to set up a system of self-regulation (if not quite law).

For instance, many of the assets, goods, and services sold on Second Life do not "belong" to the people who are selling them. You can buy virtual Gucci bags, Ferrari cars (L$1,995—what a deal!), Rolex watches, Rayban sunglasses, Prada and Oakley clothes for your avatars, Nike shoes, and Apple iPods. In a small study conducted by several lawyers, of 10 randomly selected virtual stores on Second Life, seven sold knockoff goods that exhibited obvious trademark infringements. Some stores sold nothing but brand-name goods. But because this is all virtual, none of the mentioned trademark owners have thus far brought a lawsuit against residents. As lawyers point out, if and when companies seek to develop their trademarks on virtual sites, they will not want to compete with hundreds or thousands of residents selling knockoffs. And unless companies actively enforce their trademarks in the face of infringement, they can lose the trademark altogether. In 2009, one company finally did. Taser, the maker of real world stun guns, filed a lawsuit in the U.S. District Court, District of Arizona, charging that Linden Lab had damaged its reputation and hurt sales by allowing virtual Tasers to be sold within the Second Life world. The case was later dropped after Linden Lab's management removed the offending products from the Web site. Linden Lab does indeed have an intellectual property rights policy as a part of its terms of service, which tells users "You should not use copyrighted, trademarked, or celebrity material in Second Life, unless of course you are the intellectual property owner or have permission from the intellectual property owner." However, its enforcement of these terms is haphazard and is triggered largely from complaints by trademark owners.

In a further sign of emerging legal and ethical issues, six major content creators on Second Life filed a real-world copyright and trademark infringement lawsuit against Thomas Simon, a Queens, New York, resident. Simon allegedly found a flaw in the Second Life program, and used a third-party copy program to make thousands of copies of the creators' products. Included in the alleged theft were avatar clothing, skins and shapes, scripted objects, furniture, and other objects. To complicate matters, the plaintiffs "broke into" his skybox to find the evidence of infringement. In the real world, the evidence obtained by unlawful means would be disallowed. The plaintiffs settled the lawsuit, with Simon agreeing to pay $525 in damages for profits made as a result of unauthorized copying of the plaintiff's intellectual property. Linden Lab takes the position that it is an ISP under the Digital Millennium Copyright Act and thus is not itself responsible for any copyright infringement by its users.

Linden Lab has been forced to confront other issues of governance and ethics on Second Life. It has banned six behaviors: intolerance (including slurs against groups), harassment, assault (including use of software tools to attack people's avatars), disclosure of information about other people's real-world lives, indecency (sexual behavior outside areas rated as mature), and disturbing the peace. Violations prompt warnings, suspension or banishment, enforced by Linden managers. There is no appeal process or due process.

The large-scale trademark and copyright infringements on Second Life raise concerns about virtual life and real-life law and statutes. Stealing in virtual life would seem to parallel stealing in real life. Gambling is another matter. Linden Lab's terms of service ban any illegal activity, but the company itself was not sure whether in-world gambling crossed the line. The FBI and federal prosecutors were invited to visit Second Life gambling operations in 2007, but issued no opinion on the legality of the operation. According to Ginsu Yoon, Vice President of Business Affairs, "It's not always clear to us whether a 3-D simulation of a casino is the same thing as a casino, legally speaking— and it's not clear to the law enforcement authorities we have asked." Even if the law were clear, he said the company would have no way to monitor or prevent in-world gambling, much as law enforcement cannot police every neighborhood poker game or office basketball pool. "There are millions of registered accounts and tens of millions of different objects in Second Life; there is simply no way for us to monitor content prospectively even if we wanted to," Yoon said. "That would be a harder task than pre-monitoring all e-mail sent through Yahoo Mail or Gmail, and no one expects those services to prevent all possible use of e-mail for illegal activity." This sounds like no one is in control, and real-world laws just don't apply, an argument that used to be made by P2P music sites. Ultimately, the Supreme Court in the real world shut down those music sites because they intentionally established a mechanism to violate copyright laws. Later in 2007, Linden Lab decided to outlaw all forms of gambling.

Linden Lab and Second Life have a strong libertarian history. Its founders envisaged Second Life as a self-regulating community where good people could amuse themselves in a fantasy world. But in 2009, Linden Lab has launched several efforts to integrate Second Life into the real world. At the beginning of the year, it purchased OnRez and xStreet SL, two Web-based marketplaces for virtual goods to aid in its effort to build an internal Amazon-like market where citizens can buy and sell virtual goods (and Linden can earn transaction fees). It also launched AvaLine, a service that allows its residents to receive cell, landline, or VoIP calls in-world from people outside Second Life. Linden Lab has also focused on enticing real-world companies such as IBM, Northrop, Nike, and Coca-Cola to increase their use of Second Life for business meetings, product introductions, product training, marketing events, and conferences. The future of Second Life is that it becomes a support system for real-world corporations, and an economically viable platform for e-commerce. Given this likely future, Second Life managers probably need to more closely integrate their ethics and legal practices with those of the real world. If not, real-world businesses may abandon the site. Second Life needs a second life in which it develops as a legitimate platform for conducting business.

SOURCES: "Trademarked, Copyrighted, and Celebrity Material in Second Life," http://wiki.secondlife.com/wiki/Intellectual_Property, accessed September 7, 2009; "Linden Lab Hires VP of Web Development to Help Users More Closely Integrate Second Life with their Online Lives," Press Release, Linden Lab, August 31, 2009; "Taser Sues 'Second Life' for Trademark Infringement," by Ian Rowan, switched.com, April 24, 2009; "A Second Chance for Second Life," by Scott Morrison, *Wall Street Journal*, April 10, 2009; "Linden Goes Shopping, Buys Virtual Goods Marketplace to Integrate Web Shopping With Second Life," Press Release, Linden Lab, January 20, 2009; "Ethics of Practice in Virtual Worlds," by Benjamin Duranske, Virtuallyblind.com, November 2, 2008; "Virtual Knockoffs," by Steven Seidenberg, Inside Counsel, March 2008; "Second Life Content Creators' Lawsuit Against Thomas Simon (aka Avatar 'Rase Kenzo') Settles; Signed Consent Judgment Filed," Virtuallyblind.com, January 2008; "Rapid Trademark Infringement in Second Life Costs Millions, Undermines Future Enforcement," by Benjamin Duranske, Virtuallyblind.com, October 30, 2007; "Second Life Players Bring Virtual Reality to Court," by Emil Steiner, Washingtonpost.com, October 29, 2007; "Second Life Virtual Gamblers Told to Fold," by Mike Musgrove, *Washington Post*, August 1, 2007.

D etermining how to regulate virtual behavior that may have a real-world impact is just one of many ethical, social, and political issues raised by the rapid evolution of the Internet and e-commerce. These questions are not just ethical questions that we as individuals have to answer; they also involve social institutions such as family, schools, and business firms. And these questions have obvious political dimensions because they involve collective choices about how we should live and what laws we would like to live under.

In this chapter, we discuss the ethical, social, and political issues raised in e-commerce, provide a framework for organizing the issues, and make recommendations for managers who are given the responsibility of operating e-commerce companies within commonly accepted standards of appropriateness.

8.1 UNDERSTANDING ETHICAL, SOCIAL, AND POLITICAL ISSUES IN E-COMMERCE

The Internet and its use in e-commerce have raised pervasive ethical, social, and political issues on a scale unprecedented for computer technology. Entire sections of daily newspapers and weekly magazines are devoted to the social impact of the Internet. But why is this so? Why is the Internet at the root of so many contemporary controversies? Part of the answer lies in the underlying features of Internet technology itself, and the ways in which it has been exploited by business firms. Internet technology and its use in e-commerce disrupt existing social and business relationships and understandings.

Consider for instance Table 1.2 (in Chapter 1), which lists the unique features of Internet technology. Instead of considering the business consequences of each unique feature, **Table 8.1** examines the actual or potential ethical, social, and/or political consequences of the technology.

We live in an "information society," where power and wealth increasingly depend on information and knowledge as central assets. Controversies over information are often disagreements over power, wealth, influence, and other things thought to be valuable. Like other technologies, such as steam, electricity, telephones, and television, the Internet and e-commerce can be used to achieve social progress, and for the most part, this has occurred. However, the same technologies can be used to commit crimes, despoil the environment, and threaten cherished social values. Before automobiles, there was very little interstate crime and very little federal jurisdiction over crime. Likewise with the Internet: before the Internet, there was very little "cybercrime."

Many business firms and individuals are benefiting from the commercial development of the Internet, but this development also exacts a price from individuals, organizations, and societies. These costs and benefits must be carefully considered by those seeking to make ethical and socially responsible decisions in this new environment. The question is: How can you as a manager make reasoned

TABLE 8.1	UNIQUE FEATURES OF E-COMMERCE TECHNOLOGY AND THEIR POTENTIAL ETHICAL, SOCIAL, AND/OR POLITICAL IMPLICATIONS
E-COMMERCE TECHNOLOGY DIMENSION	**POTENTIAL ETHICAL, SOCIAL, AND POLITICAL SIGNIFICANCE**
Ubiquity—Internet/Web technology is available everywhere: at work, at home, and elsewhere via mobile devices, anytime.	Work and shopping can invade family life; shopping can distract workers at work, lowering productivity; use of mobile devices can lead to automobile and industrial accidents. Presents confusing issues of "nexus" to taxation authorities.
Global reach—The technology reaches across national boundaries, around the Earth.	Reduces cultural diversity in products; weakens local small firms while strengthening large global firms; moves manufacturing production to low-wage areas of the world; weakens the ability of all nations—large and small—to control their information destiny.
Universal standards—There is one set of technology standards, namely Internet standards.	Increases vulnerability to viruses and hacking attacks worldwide affecting millions of people at once. Increases the likelihood of "information" crime, crimes against systems, and deception.
Richness—Video, audio, and text messages are possible.	A "screen technology" that reduces use of text and potentially the ability to read by focusing instead on video and audio messages. Potentially very persuasive messages that may reduce reliance on multiple independent sources of information.
Interactivity—The technology works through interaction with the user.	The nature of interactivity at commercial sites can be shallow and meaningless. Customer e-mails are frequently not read by human beings. Customers do not really "co-produce" the product as much as they "co-produce" the sale. The amount of "customization" of products that occurs is minimal, occurring within predefined platforms and plug-in options.
Information density—The technology reduces information costs, raises quality.	While the total amount of information available to all parties increases, so does the possibility of false and misleading information, unwanted information, and invasion of solitude. Trust, authenticity, accuracy, completeness, and other quality features of information can be degraded. The ability of individuals and organizations to make sense of out of this plethora of information is limited.
Personalization/Customization—The technology allows personalized messages to be delivered to individuals as well as groups.	Opens up the possibility of intensive invasion of privacy for commercial and governmental purposes that is unprecedented.
Social technology—The technology enables user content generation and social networking.	Creates opportunities for cyberbullying, abusive language, and predation; challenges concepts of privacy, fair use, and consent to use posted information; creates new opportunities for surveillance by authorities and corporations into private lives.

judgments about what your firm should do in a number of e-commerce areas—from securing the privacy of your customer's clickstream to ensuring the integrity of your company's domain name?

A MODEL FOR ORGANIZING THE ISSUES

E-commerce—and the Internet—have raised so many ethical, social, and political issues that it is difficult to classify them all, and hence complicated to see their relationship to one another. Clearly, ethical, social, and political issues are interrelated. One way to organize the ethical, social, and political dimensions surrounding e-commerce is shown in **Figure 8.1**. At the individual level, what appears as an ethical issue—"What should I do?"—is reflected at the social and political levels—"What should we as a society and government do?" The ethical dilemmas you face as a manager of a business using the Web reverberate and are reflected in social and political debates. The major ethical, social, and political issues that have developed around e-commerce over the past nine to 10 years can be loosely categorized into four major dimensions: information rights, property rights, governance, and public safety and welfare.

Some of the ethical, social, and political issues raised in each of these areas include the following:

- **Information rights:** What rights to their own personal information do individuals have in a public marketplace, or in their private homes, when Internet technologies make information collection so pervasive and efficient? What rights do individuals have to access information about business firms and other organizations?
- **Property rights:** How can traditional intellectual property rights be enforced in an Internet world where perfect copies of protected works can be made and easily distributed worldwide in seconds?

FIGURE 8.1	THE MORAL DIMENSIONS OF AN INTERNET SOCIETY

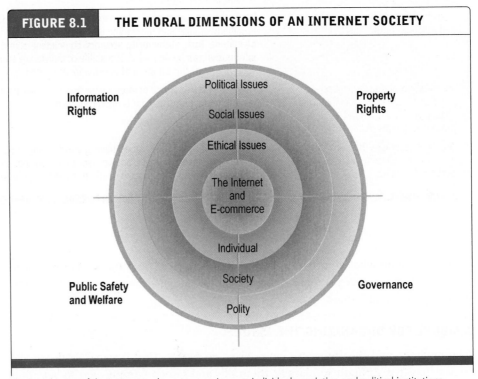

The introduction of the Internet and e-commerce impacts individuals, societies, and political institutions. These impacts can be classified into four moral dimensions: property rights, information rights, governance, and public safety and welfare.

- **Governance:** Should the Internet and e-commerce be subject to public laws? And if so, what law-making bodies have jurisdiction—state, federal, and/or international?

- **Public safety and welfare:** What efforts should be undertaken to ensure equitable access to the Internet and e-commerce channels? Should governments be responsible for ensuring that schools and colleges have access to the Internet? Are certain online content and activities—such as pornography and gambling—a threat to public safety and welfare? Should mobile commerce be allowed from moving vehicles?

To illustrate, imagine that at any given moment, society and individuals are more or less in an ethical equilibrium brought about by a delicate balancing of individuals, social organizations, and political institutions. Individuals know what is expected of them, social organizations such as business firms know their limits, capabilities, and roles, and political institutions provide a supportive framework of market regulation, banking, and commercial law that provides sanctions against violators.

Now, imagine we drop into the middle of this calm setting a powerful new technology such as the Internet and e-commerce. Suddenly, individuals, business firms, and political institutions are confronted by new possibilities of behavior. For instance, individuals discover that they can download perfect digital copies of music tracks from Web sites without paying anyone, something that, under the old technology of CDs, would have been impossible. This can be done, despite the fact that these music tracks still "belong" as a legal matter to the owners of the copyright—musicians and record label companies. Then, business firms discover that they can make a business out of aggregating these digital musical tracks—or creating a mechanism for sharing musical tracks—even though they do not "own" them in the traditional sense. The record companies, courts, and Congress were not prepared at first to cope with the onslaught of online digital copying. Courts and legislative bodies will have to make new laws and reach new judgments about who owns digital copies of copyrighted works and under what conditions such works can be "shared." It may take years to develop new understandings, laws, and acceptable behavior in just this one area of social impact. In the meantime, as an individual and a manager, you will have to decide what you and your firm should do in legal "gray" areas, where there is conflict between ethical principles but no clear-cut legal or cultural guidelines. How can you make good decisions in this type of situation?

Before examining the four moral dimensions of e-commerce in greater depth, we will briefly review some basic concepts of ethical reasoning that you can use as a guide to ethical decision making, and provide general reasoning principles about the social and political issues of the Internet that you will face in the future.

BASIC ETHICAL CONCEPTS: RESPONSIBILITY, ACCOUNTABILITY, AND LIABILITY

Ethics is at the heart of social and political debates about the Internet. **Ethics** is the study of principles that individuals and organizations can use to determine right and wrong courses of action. It is assumed in ethics that individuals are free moral agents who are in a position to make choices. When faced with alternative courses of action,

ethics
the study of principles that individuals and organizations can use to determine right and wrong courses of action

what is the correct moral choice? Extending ethics from individuals to business firms and even entire societies can be difficult, but it is not impossible. As long as there is a decision-making body or individual (such as a Board of Directors or CEO in a business firm, or a governmental body in a society), their decisions can be judged against a variety of ethical principles.

If you understand some basic ethical principles, your ability to reason about larger social and political debates will be improved. In western culture, there are three basic principles that all ethical schools of thought share: responsibility, accountability, and liability. **Responsibility** means that as free moral agents, individuals, organizations, and societies are responsible for the actions they take. **Accountability** means that individuals, organizations, and societies should be held accountable to others for the consequences of their actions. The third principle—**liability**—extends the concepts of responsibility and accountability to the area of law. Liability is a feature of political systems in which a body of law is in place that permits individuals to recover the damages done to them by other actors, systems, or organizations. **Due process** is a feature of law-governed societies and refers to a process in which laws are known and understood and there is an ability to appeal to higher authorities to ensure that the laws have been applied correctly.

You can use these concepts immediately to understand some contemporary Internet debates. For instance, consider the *Metro-Goldwyn-Mayer v. Grokster* lawsuit noted in the case study at the end of Chapter 1. MGM and other studios that joined it in the case argued that because the primary and intended use of Internet P2P file-sharing services such as Grokster, StreamCast, and Kazaa was the swapping of copyright-protected music and video files, the file-sharing services should be held accountable, and shut down. Although Grokster and the other networks acknowledged that the most common use of the software was for illegal digital music file-swapping, they argued that there were substantial, nontrivial uses of the same networks for legally sharing files. They also argued they should not be held accountable for what individuals do with their software, any more than Sony could be held accountable for how people use VCRs, or Xerox for how people use copying machines. Ultimately, the Supreme Court ruled that Grokster and other P2P networks could be held accountable for the illegal actions of their users if it could be shown that they intended their software to be used for illegal downloading and sharing, and had marketed the software for that purpose. The court relied on copyright laws to arrive at its decisions, but these laws reflect some basic underlying ethical principles of responsibility, accountability, and liability.

Underlying the *Grokster* Supreme Court decision is a fundamental rejection of the notion that the Internet is an ungoverned "Wild West" environment that cannot be controlled. Under certain defined circumstances, the courts will intervene into the uses of the Internet. No organized civilized society has ever accepted the proposition that technology can flaunt basic underlying social and cultural values. Through all of the industrial and technological developments that have taken place, societies have intervened by means of legal and political decisions to ensure that the technology serves socially acceptable ends without stifling the positive consequences of innovation and wealth creation. The Internet in this sense is no different, and we can

---

responsibility

as free moral agents, individuals, organizations, and societies are responsible for the actions they take

accountability

individuals, organizations, and societies should be held accountable to others for the consequences of their actions

liability

a feature of political systems in which a body of law is in place that permits individuals to recover the damages done to them by other actors, systems, or organizations

due process

a process in which laws are known and understood and there is an ability to appeal to higher authorities to ensure that the laws have been applied correctly expect societies around the world to exercise more regulatory control over the Internet and e-commerce in an effort to arrive at a new balance between innovation and wealth creation, on the one hand, and other socially desirable objectives on the other. This is a difficult balancing act, and reasonable people will arrive at different conclusions.

ANALYZING ETHICAL DILEMMAS

Ethical, social, and political controversies usually present themselves as dilemmas. A **dilemma** is a situation in which there are at least two diametrically opposed actions, each of which supports a desirable outcome. When confronted with a situation that seems to present an ethical dilemma, how can you analyze and reason about the situation? The following is a five-step process that should help:

1. **Identify and clearly describe the facts.** Find out who did what to whom, and where, when, and how. In many instances, you will be surprised at the errors in the initially reported facts, and often you will find that simply getting the facts straight helps define the solution. It also helps to get the opposing parties involved in an ethical dilemma to agree on the facts.

2. **Define the conflict or dilemma and identify the higher-order values involved.** Ethical, social, and political issues always reference higher values. Otherwise, there would be no debate. The parties to a dispute all claim to be pursuing higher values (e.g., freedom, privacy, protection of property, and the free enterprise system). For example, supporters of the use of advertising networks such as DoubleClick argue that the tracking of consumer movements on the Web increases market efficiency and the wealth of the entire society. Opponents argue this claimed efficiency comes at the expense of individual privacy, and advertising networks should cease their activities or offer Web users the option of not participating in such tracking.

3. **Identify the stakeholders.** Every ethical, social, and political issue has stakeholders: players in the game who have an interest in the outcome, who have invested in the situation, and usually who have vocal opinions. Find out the identity of these groups and what they want. This will be useful later when designing a solution.

4. **Identify the options that you can reasonably take.** You may find that none of the options satisfies all the interests involved, but that some options do a better job than others. Sometimes, arriving at a "good" or ethical solution may not always be a balancing of consequences to stakeholders.

5. **Identify the potential consequences of your options.** Some options may be ethically correct, but disastrous from other points of view. Other options may work in this one instance, but not in other similar instances. Always ask yourself, "What if I choose this option consistently over time?"

Once your analysis is complete, you can refer to the following well-established ethical principles to help decide the matter.

dilemma
a situation in which there are at least two diametrically opposed actions, each of which supports a desirable outcome

CANDIDATE ETHICAL PRINCIPLES

Although you are the only one who can decide which ethical principles you will follow and how you will prioritize them, it is helpful to consider some ethical principles with deep roots in many cultures that have survived throughout recorded history:

- **The Golden Rule:** Do unto others as you would have them do unto you. Putting yourself into the place of others and thinking of yourself as the object of the decision can help you think about fairness in decision making.

- **Universalism:** If an action is not right for all situations, then it is not right for any specific situation (Immanuel Kant's categorical imperative). Ask yourself, "If we adopted this rule in every case, could the organization, or society, survive?"

- **Slippery Slope:** If an action cannot be taken repeatedly, then it is not right to take at all (Descartes' rule of change). An action may appear to work in one instance to solve a problem, but if repeated, would result in a negative outcome. In plain English, this rule might be stated as "once started down a slippery path, you may not be able to stop."

- **Collective Utilitarian Principle:** Take the action that achieves the greater value for all of society. This rule assumes you can prioritize values in a rank order and understand the consequences of various courses of action.

- **Risk Aversion:** Take the action that produces the least harm, or the least potential cost. Some actions have extremely high failure costs of very low probability (e.g., building a nuclear generating facility in an urban area) or extremely high failure costs of moderate probability (speeding and automobile accidents). Avoid the high-failure cost actions and choose those actions whose consequences would not be catastrophic, even if there were a failure.

- **No Free Lunch:** Assume that virtually all tangible and intangible objects are owned by someone else unless there is a specific declaration otherwise. (This is the ethical "no free lunch" rule.) If something someone else has created is useful to you, it has value and you should assume the creator wants compensation for this work.

- **The *New York Times* Test (Perfect Information Rule):** Assume that the results of your decision on a matter will be the subject of the lead article in the *New York Times* the next day. Will the reaction of readers be positive or negative? Would your parents, friends, and children be proud of your decision? Most criminals and unethical actors assume imperfect information, and therefore they assume their decisions and actions will never be revealed. When making decisions involving ethical dilemmas, it is wise to assume perfect information markets.

- **The Social Contract Rule:** Would you like to live in a society where the principle you are supporting would become an organizing principle of the entire society?

For instance, you might think it is wonderful to download illegal copies of music tracks, but you might not want to live in a society that did not respect property rights, such as your property rights to the car in your driveway, or your rights to a term paper or original art.

None of these rules is an absolute guide, and there are exceptions and logical difficulties with all of them. Nevertheless, actions that do not easily pass these guidelines deserve some very close attention and a great deal of caution because the appearance of unethical behavior may do as much harm to you and your company as the actual behavior.

Now that you have an understanding of some basic ethical reasoning concepts, let's take a closer look at each of the major types of ethical, social, and political debates that have arisen in e-commerce.

8.2 PRIVACY AND INFORMATION RIGHTS

Privacy is the moral right of individuals to be left alone, free from surveillance or interference from other individuals or organizations, including the state. Privacy is a girder supporting freedom: Without the privacy required to think, write, plan, and associate independently and without fear, social and political freedom is weakened, and perhaps destroyed. **Information privacy** is a subset of privacy. The right to information privacy includes both the claim that certain information should not be collected at all by governments or business firms, and the claim of individuals to control the use of whatever information that is collected about them. Individual control over personal information is at the core of the privacy concept.

Due process also plays an important role in defining privacy. The best statement of due process in record keeping is given by the Fair Information Practices doctrine developed in the early 1970s and extended to the online privacy debate in the late 1990s (described later in this section).

There are two kinds of threats to individual privacy posed by the Internet. One threat originates in the private sector and concerns how much personal information is collected by commercial Web sites and how it will be used. A second threat originates in the public sector and concerns how much personal information federal, state, and local government authorities collect, and how they use it. While these threats are conceptually distinct, in practice they are related as the federal government increasingly relies on Internet companies to provide intelligence on specific individuals and groups, and as Internet records held by search engine companies and others (like Amazon) are sought by legal authorities and attorney's.

Privacy claims—and thinking about privacy—mushroomed in the United States at the end of the nineteenth century as the technology of photography and tabloid journalism enabled the invasion of the heretofore private lives of wealthy industrialists. For most of the twentieth century, however, privacy thinking and legislation focused on restraining the government from collecting and using personal information. With the explosion in the collection of private personal information by Web-based marketing firms since 1995, privacy concerns are increasingly directed toward restraining the activities of private firms in the collection and use of information on the Web. Claims to privacy are also involved at the workplace. Millions of employees are subject to various forms of electronic surveillance that in many

privacy
the moral right of individuals to be left alone, free from surveillance or interference from other individuals or organizations, including the state

information privacy
includes both the claim that certain information should not be collected at all by governments or business firms, and the claim of individuals to control the use of whatever information that is collected about them

cases is enhanced by firm intranets and Web technologies. For instance, the majority of U.S. companies monitor which Web sites their workers visit, as well as employee e-mail and instant messages. Employee posts on message boards and blogs are also coming under scrutiny.

In general, the Internet and the Web provide an ideal environment for both business and government to invade the personal privacy of millions of users on a scale unprecedented in history. Perhaps no other recent issue has raised as much widespread social and political concern as protecting the privacy of 200 million Web users in the United States alone. The major ethical issues related to e-commerce and privacy include the following: Under what conditions should we invade the privacy of others? What legitimates intruding into others' lives through unobtrusive surveillance, market research, or other means? The major social issues related to e-commerce and privacy concern the development of "expectations of privacy" or privacy norms, as well as public attitudes. In what areas of life should we as a society encourage people to think they are in "private territory" as opposed to public view? The major political issues related to e-commerce and privacy concern the development of statutes that govern the relations between record keepers and individuals. How should both public and private organizations—which may be reluctant to remit the advantages that come from the unfettered flow of information on individuals—be restrained, if at all? In the following section, we look first at the various practices of e-commerce companies that pose a threat to privacy.

INFORMATION COLLECTED AT E-COMMERCE SITES

As you have learned in previous chapters, e-commerce sites routinely collect a variety of information from or about consumers who visit their site and/or make purchases. Some of this data constitutes **personally identifiable information (PII)**, which is defined as any data that can be used to identify, locate, or contact an individual (Federal Trade Commission, 2000a). Other data is **anonymous information**, composed of demographic and behavioral information, such as age, occupation, income, zip code, ethnicity, and other data that characterizes your life without identifying who you are. **Table 8.2** lists some of the personal identifiers routinely collected by online e-commerce sites. This is not an exhaustive list.

personally identifiable information (PII)
any data that can be used to identify, locate, or contact an individual

anonymous information
demographic and behavioral information that does not include any personal identifiers

TABLE 8.2	PERSONAL INFORMATION COLLECTED BY E-COMMERCE SITES	
Name	Bank accounts	Education
Address	Credit card accounts	Preference data
Phone number	Gender	Transaction data
E-mail address	Age	Clickstream data
Social security number	Occupation	Browser type

Advertising networks and search engines also track the behavior of consumers across thousands of popular sites, not just at one site, via cookies, spyware, and other techniques

Table 8.3 illustrates some of the major ways online firms gather information about consumers.

TABLE 8.3	THE INTERNET'S MAJOR INFORMATION GATHERING TOOLS AND THEIR IMPACT ON PRIVACY
INTERNET CAPABILITY	**IMPACT ON PRIVACY**
Advertising networks	Used to track individuals as they move among thousands of Web sites.
Social networks	Used to gather information on user provided content such as books, music, and other interests, preferences, and life styles.
Cookies	Used to track individuals at a single site.
Third-party cookies	Cookies placed by outside third-party advertising networks. Used to monitor and track online behavior, searches, and sites visited across thousands of sites that belong to the advertising network for the purpose of displaying "relevant" advertising.
Spyware	Can be used to record all the keyboard activity of a user, including Web sites visited and security codes used; also used to display advertisements to users based on their searches or other behavior.
Search engine behavioral targeting (Google, and other search engines)	Uses prior search history, demographic, expressed interests, geographic, or other user-entered data to target advertising.
Deep packet inspection	Uses software installed at the ISP level to track all user clickstream behavior, sells this information to advertisers, and then attempts to show users "relevant ads."
Shopping carts	Can be used to collect detailed payment and purchase information.
Forms	Online forms that users voluntarily fill out in return for a promised benefit or reward that are linked with clickstream or other behavioral data to create a personal profile.
Site transaction logs	Can be used to collect and analyze detailed information on page content viewed by users.
Search engines	Can be used to trace user statements and views on newsgroups, chat groups, and other public forums on the Web, and profile users' social and political views. Google returns name, address, and links to a map with directions to the address when a phone number is entered.
Digital wallets (single sign-on services)	Client-side wallets and software that reveal personal information to Web sites verifying the identity of the consumer.
Digital Rights Management (DRM)	Software (Windows Media Player) that requires users of online media to identify themselves before viewing copyrighted content.
Trusted Computing Environments	Hardware and software that controls the viewing of copyrighted content and requires users identification.

SOCIAL NETWORKS AND PRIVACY

Social networks pose a unique challenge for the maintenance of personal privacy because they encourage people to reveal details about their personal lives (passions, loves, favorites, photos, videos and personal interests), and to share them with their friends. Some social networkers share these personal details with everyone on the social network! On the face of it, this would seem to indicate that people who participate in social networks voluntarily give up their rights to personal privacy. How could they claim an expectation of privacy? When everything is shared, what's private?

But the reality is that many adult (over 17 years) participants in social networks have a very keen sense of their personal privacy. Every time a leading social network has sought to use the personal information provided by participants as a method of monetizing social networks by displaying ads and targeting individuals, it has been vociferously rejected by members of the networks. Facebook is a prime example of a senior management that just didn't get it when it comes to members' sense of their privacy. In December 2007, Facebook CEO Mark Zuckerberg announced the Beacon Program, sponsored by over 40 large firms, that would track what Facebook members purchased at their corporate sites, send the information to Facebook, who would then share that information with their friends without asking permission. In a few days, hundreds of thousands of members had organized a fierce resistance to the program. Management then declared that members could opt-out of the program and turn it off completely. Coca-Cola withdrew from sponsorship because it thought the program was an opt-in program only. Other corporate sponsors started pulling out from the program, as member resistance mounted. In 2009, Beacon still exists, but keeps a lower profile. Many open source programs exist on the Internet to block Beacon, and the Firefox browser has a Beacon Blocker add-on to prevent corporate sites from sending any information to Facebook.

In a similar gaffe, in February 2009, Facebook sought to change its information retention and collection policy (Terms of Service) which had the effect of granting Facebook nearly unlimited data collection and control over user-generated information forever, without redress. Management acted without warning, provided no opportunity for public comment, and applied the new policy to personal information that had been collected under the old policy. Over a hundred thousand people joined various blog sites and privacy groups to protest, based on the belief that their information belonged to them, not Facebook. Within days the firm retreated to the old policy, and set up user forums to discuss the Terms of Service and user attitudes about personal information. In the meantime, though, millions of people on Facebook continue to use third-party quiz applications (such as "Which Cocktail Best Suits Your Personality?") without realizing the extent to which developers of the quizzes and other applications have access to personal information. Facebook's default privacy settings allow nearly unfettered access to a user's profile information. Only "sensitive information" such as contact information is not available.

The result of these conflicts suggests that social network participants do indeed have a strong expectation of privacy in the sense that they want to control how "their" information is used. People who contribute user-generated content have a strong sense of ownership over that content that is not diminished by posting the information on a social network for one's friends. What's involved are some basic tenets of privacy thinking: personal control over the uses of personal information, choice, informed consent, participation in formulation of information policies, and due process. Some of these ideas are foreign to managers and owners seeking to monetize huge social network audiences. As for members who post information to everyone, not just friends, these should be seen as "public performances" where the contributors voluntarily publish their performances, just as writers or other artists do. This does not mean they want the entirety of their personal lives thrown open to every Web tracking automaton on the Internet.

PROFILING AND BEHAVIORAL TARGETING

On an average day, around 115 million adult Americans go online (Pew Internet & American Life Project, 2009). Marketers would like to know who these people are, what they are interested in, and what they buy. The more precise the information, the more complete the information, the more valuable it is as a predictive and marketing tool. Armed with this information, marketers can make their ad campaigns more efficient by targeting specific ads at specific groups or individuals, and they can even adjust the ads for specific groups.

Many Web sites allow third parties—including online advertising networks such as Microsoft Advertising (formerly aQuantive), DoubleClick, and others—to place "third-party" cookies on a visitor's hard drive in order to engage in profiling the user's behavior across thousands of Web sites. A third-party cookie is used to track users across hundreds or thousands of other Web sites who are members of the advertising network. **Profiling** is the creation of digital images that characterize online individual and group behavior. **Anonymous profiles** identify people as belonging to highly specific and targeted groups, for example, 20-to 30-year-old males, with college degrees and incomes greater than $30,000 a year, and interested in high-fashion clothing (based on recent search engine use). **Personal profiles** add a personal e-mail address, postal address, and/or phone number to behavioral data. Increasingly, online firms are linking their online profiles to personal offline consumer data collected by database firms tracking credit card purchases, as well as established retail and catalog firms. In the past, individual stores collected data on customer movement through a single store in order to understand consumer behavior and alter the design of stores accordingly. Also, purchase and expenditure data was gathered on consumers purchasing from multiple stores—usually long after the purchases were made—and the data was used to target direct mail and in-store campaigns, in addition to mass-media advertising.

The online advertising networks such as DoubleClick and 24/7 Real Media have added several new dimensions to established offline marketing techniques. First, they have the ability to precisely track not just consumer purchases, but all browsing behavior on the Web at thousands of the most popular member sites, including browsing book lists, filling out preference forms, and viewing content pages. Second, they can dynamically adjust what the shopper sees on screen—including prices. Third, they can build and continually refresh high-resolution data images or behavioral pro-

profiling
the creation of digital images that characterize online individual and group behavior

anonymous profiles
identify people as belonging to highly specific and targeted groups

personal profiles
add a personal e-mail address, postal address, and/or phone number to behavioral data

files of consumers (Laudon, 1996). Other advertising firms have created spyware software that, when placed on a consumer's computer, can report back to the advertiser's server on all consumer Internet use, and is also used to display advertising on the consumer's computer.

A different kind of profiling and a more recent form of behavioral targeting is Google's results-based personalization of advertising. Google has a patent on a program that allows advertisers using Google's AdWord program to target ads to users based on their prior search histories and profiles, which Google constructs based on user searches, along with any other information the user submits to Google or that Google can obtain, such as age, demographics, region, and other Web activities (such as blogging). Google also applied for a second patent on a program that allows Google to help advertisers select keywords and design ads for various market segments based on search histories, such as helping a clothing Web site create and test ads targeted at teenage females. In August 2007, Google began to put some of those ideas into practice, using behavioral targeting to help it display more relevant ads based on keywords. According to Google, the feature is aimed at capturing a more robust understanding of user intent, and thereby delivering a better ad. Google's Gmail, a free e-mail service, offers a powerful interface, and as of September 2009, 7.3 gigabytes of free storage. In return, Google computers read all incoming and outgoing e-mail and place "relevant" advertising in the margins of the mail. Profiles are developed on individual users based on the content in their e-mail. Google's Chrome browser has a Suggest feature that automatically suggests related queries and Web sites when the user enters a search. Critics pointed out this was a "key logger" device that would record every keystroke of users forever. Google has since announced it will anonymize the data within 24 hours.

deep packet inspection

a technology for recording every key stroke at the ISP level

Deep packet inspection is another technology for recording every key stroke at the ISP level of everyone (no matter where they ultimately go on the Web), and then use that information to make suggestions, and target ads. While advertising networks are limited, and even Google does not constitute the universe of search, deep packet inspection at the ISP level really does capture the universe of all Internet users. The leading firm in this technology is NebuAd. After testing the hardware and software with several ISPs in 2008, the outcry from privacy advocates and Congress caused these ISPs to withdraw from the experiment, and NebuAd withdrew the product from the market (Nakashima, 2008).

What is different about these efforts at online profiling and behavioral targeting (when compared to offline methods used in the past) is the scope and intensity of the data dragnet, and the ability to manipulate the shopping environment to the advantage of the merchant. Most of this activity occurs in the background without the knowledge of the shopper, and it takes place dynamically online in less than a second. Arguably, no other Web-based technique comes so close to being a real-world implementation of George Orwell's novel *1984* and its lead character, Big Brother. Here's an illustration of online profiling from "Online Profiling: A Report to Congress," an FTC report:

Online consumer Joe Smith goes to a Web site that sells sporting goods. He clicks on the pages for golf bags. While there, he sees a banner ad, which he ignores as it does not interest him. The ad was placed by USAad Network. He then goes to a travel site and enters a search on "Hawaii." The USAad Network also serves ads on this site, and Joe sees an ad for rental cars there. Joe then visits an online bookstore and browses through books about the world's best golf courses. USAad Network serves ads there as well. A week later, Joe visits his favorite online news site, and notices an ad for golf vacation packages in Hawaii. Delighted, he clicks on the ad, which was served by USAad Network. Later, Joe begins to wonder whether it was a coincidence that this particular ad appeared and, if not, how it happened (Federal Trade Commission, 2000b).

The sample online profile illustrates several features of such profiles. First, the profile created for Joe Smith was completely anonymous and did not require any personal information, such as a name, e-mail address, or social security number. Obviously, this profile would be more valuable if the system did have personal information because then Joe could be sent e-mail marketing. Second, ad networks do not know who is operating the browser. If other members of Joe's family used the same computer to shop the Web, they would be exposed to golf vacation ads, and Joe could be exposed to ads more appropriate to his wife or children. Third, profiles are usually very imprecise, the result of "best guesses" and just plain guesses. Profiles are built using a product/service scoring system that is not very detailed, and as a result, the profiles tend to be very crude.

In the preceding example, Joe is obviously interested in golf and travel because he intentionally expressed these interests. However, he may have wanted to scuba dive in Hawaii, or visit old friends, not play golf. The profiling system in the example took a leap of faith that a golf vacation in Hawaii is what Joe really wants. Sometimes these guesses work, but there is considerable evidence to suggest that simply knowing Joe made an inquiry about Hawaii would be sufficient to sell him a trip to Hawaii for any of several activities and the USAad Network provided little additional value.

Network advertising firms argue that Web profiling benefits both consumers and businesses. Profiling permits targeting of ads, ensuring that consumers see advertisements mostly for products and services in which they are actually interested. Businesses benefit by not paying for wasted advertising sent to consumers who have no interest in their product or service. The industry argues that by increasing the effectiveness of advertising, more advertising revenues go to the Internet, which in turn subsidizes free content on the Internet. Last, product designers and entrepreneurs benefit by sensing demand for new products and services by examining user searches and profiles.

Critics argue that profiling undermines the expectation of anonymity and privacy that most people have when using the Internet, and change what should be a private experience into one where an individual's every move is recorded. As people become aware that their every move is being watched, they will be far less likely to explore sensitive topics, browse pages, or read about controversial issues. In most cases, the profiling is invisible to users, and even hidden. Consumers are not notified that profiling is occurring. Profiling permits data aggregation on hundreds or even thousands of unrelated sites on the Web. The cookies placed by ad networks are persistent, and they can be set to last days, months, years, or even forever. Their tracking occurs over an extended period of time and resumes each time the individual logs on to the Internet. This clickstream data is used to create profiles that can include hundreds of distinct data fields for each consumer. Associating so-called

weblining

charging some customers more money for products and services based on their profiles

anonymous profiles with personal information is fairly easy, and companies can change policies quickly without informing the consumer. Some critics believe profiling permits **weblining**—charging some customers more money for products and services based on their profiles. Although the information gathered by network advertisers is often anonymous (non-PII data), in many cases, the profiles derived from tracking consumers' activities on the Web are linked or merged with personally identifiable information. DoubleClick and other advertising network firms have attempted to purchase offline marketing firms that collect offline consumer data for the purpose of matching offline and online behavioral data at the individual level. However, public reaction was so negative that no network advertising firm publicly admits to matching offline PII with online profile data. Nevertheless, client Web sites encourage visitors to register for prizes, benefits, or content access in order to capture personal information such as e-mail addresses and physical addresses. Anonymous behavioral data is far more valuable if it can be linked with offline consumer behavior, e-mail addresses, and postal addresses.

This consumer data can also be combined with data on the consumers' offline purchases, or information collected directly from consumers through surveys and registration forms. As the technology of connection to the Internet for consumers moves away from telephone modems where IP addresses are assigned dynamically, and toward static assigned IP addresses used by DSL and cable modems, then connecting anonymous profiles to personal names and e-mail addresses will become easier and more prevalent.

From a privacy protection perspective, the advertising network raises issues about who will see and use the information held by private companies, whether the user profiles will be linked to actual personally identifying information (such as name, Social Security number, and bank and credit accounts), the absence of consumer control over the use of the information, the lack of consumer choice, the absence of consumer notice, and the lack of review and amendment procedures.

The pervasive and largely unregulated collection of personal information online has raised significant fears and opposition among consumers. According to a 2008 survey of 1,105 respondents, 57% said they were uncomfortable with advertisers using browsing history to serve relevant ads,and 54% delete cookies every two to three months. Forty-four percent would click a button that said "Reduce unwanted ads," and 42% would sign up for a online registry to ensure advertisers are not able to track browsing behavior. Even worse for advertisers, 87% said that less than 25% of the ads they do see online are relevant. Another study found that over six in 10 U.S. Web searchers do not trust search engines with their information. One result of the lack of trust toward online firms and specific fears of privacy invasion is a reduction in online purchases. For instance, one survey found that over 70% of respondents had decided against registering or making a purchase online because those actions required them to provide information that they did not want to divulge. A Gartner survey found that nearly half of online U.S. adults said that concerns about theft of information, data breaches, or Internet-based attacks affected their purchasing, payment, online transaction, or e-mail behavior. The actual amount of lost sales is unknown, but if 25% of consumers stopped purchasing online, that would add up to a hefty $57 billion in lost sales. If even just 10% of this number turned out to be accurate, that would still be a $22.8 billion loss in sales. A Harris survey in 2008 found that 45% of Internet users were not very comfortable with Web sites that target ads based on browser history or clickstreams (eMarketer, Inc., 2009, 2007a, 2007b).

The Internet and e-commerce—as we have seen in previous chapters—strengthen the ability of private firms to collect, store, and analyze personal information at a level never envisioned by privacy thinkers and legislators. With Web technologies, the invasion of individual privacy is low-cost, profitable, and effective.

The Internet and Government Invasions of Privacy: E-commerce Surveillance

Today, the e-commerce behavior, profiles, and transactions of consumers are routinely available to a wide range of government agencies and law enforcement authorities, contributing to rising fears among online consumers, and in many cases, their withdrawal from the online marketplace. While the Internet used to be thought of as impossible for governments to control or monitor, nothing could be actually further from the truth. Law enforcement authorities have long claimed the right under numerous statutes to monitor any form of electronic communication pursuant to a court order and judicial review and based on the reasonable belief that a crime is being committed. This includes the surveillance of consumers engaged in e-commerce. In the case of the Internet, this is accomplished by placing sniffer software and servers at the ISP being used by the target suspect, in a manner similar to pen registers and trap-and-trace devices used for telephone surveillance. The Communications Assistance for Law Enforcement Act (CALEA), the USA PATRIOT Act, the Cyber Security Enhancement Act, and the Homeland Security Act all strengthen the ability of law enforcement agencies to monitor Internet users without their knowledge and, under certain circumstances when life is purportedly at stake, without judicial oversight. In addition, government agencies are among the largest users of private sector commercial data brokers, such as ChoicePoint, Acxiom, Experian, and TransUnion Corporation, that collect a vast amount of information about consumers from various offline and online public sources, such as public records and the telephone directory, and non-public sources, such as "credit header" information from credit bureaus (which typically contains name, aliases, birth date, social security number, current and prior addresses, and phone numbers). Information contained in individual reference services' databases ranges from purely identifying information (e.g., name and phone number) to much more extensive data (e.g., driving records, criminal and civil court records, property records, and licensing records). This information can be linked to online behavior information collected from other commercial sources to compile an extensive profile of individual's online and offline behavior (Frackman, Ray, and Martin, 2002; Federal Trade Commission, 1997).

In June 2006, the Justice Department appointed a task force to investigate a proposal that Internet companies retain records that would allow the government to identify which individuals visited certain Web sites and conducted searches using certain terms, and also records about whom users exchange e-mail with, for as long two years. The European Parliament had passed similar legislation in December 2005. In 2007, the four major search engines (Google, Yahoo, MSN, and Ask.com) all announced new policies on how long they would retain search information, ranging from 18 months (Google and MSN) to 13 months (Yahoo), while Ask.com announced a new tool, Ask Eraser, that would allow users to block any retention of specific search terms and the user's IP address (Hansell and Lichtblau, 2006; Zeller, 2006; Leidtke, 2007). In April 2008, the European Parliament's Data Protection Working Party called for search engines to set their data retention at six months. Currently, the EU requires search engines to set their data retention limit at 18 months. In September 2008, under pressure from European regulators, Google announced that it would reduce the amount of time it stores IP addresses on its server logs to nine months in both the United States and Europe. In December 2008, Yahoo went a step better, and announced that going forward, it would delete a users' personally identifiable information (the last 8 bits in the users' IP address) from its records within three months. Yahoo also said it would hide cookie data related to each log, and strip out any personally identifiable information, such as a name, phone, address, or social security number, from queries. The policy also extends to other types of data it collects, such as page view, page clicks, ad views, and ad clicks.

Congress, aware of the dangers of unregulated government intrusion into Internet communications, and its threat to e-commerce privacy, created a Privacy and Civil Liberties Oversight Board in the Office of the President in 2004 to ensure anti-terrorism laws do not decimate other privacy protection laws. The Board began meeting in 2006, and issued its first annual report to Congress in April 2007. However, since that time the Board has been inactive.

LEGAL PROTECTIONS

In the United States, Canada, and Germany, rights to privacy are explicitly granted in, or can be derived from, founding documents such as constitutions, as well as in specific statutes. In England and the United States, there is also protection of privacy in the common law, a body of court decisions involving torts or personal injuries. For instance, in the United States, four privacy-related torts have been defined in court decisions involving claims of injury to individuals caused by other private parties: intrusion on solitude, public disclosure of private facts, publicity placing a person in a false light, and appropriation of a person's name or likeness (mostly concerning celebrities) for a commercial purpose (Laudon, 1996). In the United States, the claim to privacy against government intrusion is protected primarily by the First Amendment guarantees of freedom of speech and association, the Fourth Amendment protections against unreasonable search and seizure of one's personal documents or home, and the Fourteenth Amendment's guarantee of due process.

In addition to common law and the Constitution, there are both federal laws and state laws that protect individuals against government intrusion and in some cases define privacy rights vis-à-vis private organizations such as financial, educational, and media institutions (cable television and video rentals) (see **Table 8.4**).

TABLE 8.4	FEDERAL AND STATE PRIVACY LAWS
NAME	**DESCRIPTION**
GENERAL FEDERAL PRIVACY LAWS	
Freedom of Information Act of 1966	Gives people the right to inspect information about themselves held in government files; also allows other individuals and organizations the right to request disclosure of government records based on the public's right to know.
Privacy Act of 1974, as amended	Regulates the federal government's collection, use, and disclosure of data collected by federal agencies. Gives individuals a right to inspect and correct records.
Electronic Communications Privacy Act of 1986	Makes conduct that would infringe on the security of electronic communications illegal.
Computer Matching and Privacy Protection Act of 1988	Regulates computerized matching of files held by different government agencies.
Computer Security Act of 1987	Makes conduct that would infringe on the security of computer-based files illegal.
Driver's Privacy Protection Act of 1994	Limits access to personal information maintained by state motor vehicle departments to those with legitimate business purposes. Also gives drivers the option to prevent disclosure of driver's license information to marketers and the general public.
E-Government Act of 2002	Regulates the collection and use of personal information by federal agencies.
FEDERAL PRIVACY LAWS AFFECTING PRIVATE INSTITUTIONS	
Fair Credit Reporting Act of 1970	Regulates the credit investigating and reporting industry. Gives people the right to inspect credit records if they have been denied credit and provides procedures for correcting information.
Family Educational Rights and Privacy Act of 1974	Requires schools and colleges to give students and their parents access to student records and to allow them to challenge and correct information; limits disclosure of such records to third parties.
Right to Financial Privacy Act of 1978	Regulates the financial industry's use of personal financial records; establishes procedures that federal agencies must follow to gain access to such records.
Privacy Protection Act of 1980	Prohibits government agents from conducting unannounced searches of press offices and files if no one in the office is suspected of committing a crime.
Cable Communications Policy Act of 1984	Regulates the cable industry's collection and disclosure of information concerning subscribers.
Video Privacy Protection Act of 1988	Prevents disclosure of a person's video rental records without court order or consent.
Child Online Privacy Protection Act (1998)	Prohibits deceptive practices in connection with the collection, use, and/or disclosure of personal information from and about children on the Internet.
Financial Modernization Act (Gramm-Leach-Bliley Act) (1999)	Requires financial institutions to inform consumers of their privacy policies and permits consumers some control over their records.
Health Insurance Portability and Accountability Act of 1996 (HIPAA)	Requires health care providers and insurers and other third parties to promulgate privacy policies to consumers and establishes due process procedures.

TABLE 8.4	FEDERAL AND STATE PRIVACY LAWS (CONT'D)
NAME	**DESCRIPTION**
SELECTED STATE PRIVACY LAWS	
Online privacy policies	The California Online Privacy Protection Act of 2003 was the first state law in the United States requiring owners of commercial Web sites or online services to post a privacy policy. The policy must, among other things, identify the categories of PII collected about site visitors and categories of third parties with whom the information may be shared. Failure to comply can result in a civil suit for unfair business practices. Nebraska and Pennsylvania prohibit false and misleading statements in online privacy policies. At least 16 states require government Web sites to establish privacy policies or procedures or incorporate machine-readable privacy policies into their Web sites.
Spyware legislation	A number of states, including California, Utah, Arizona, Arkansas, and Virginia, among others, have passed laws that make the installation of spyware on a user's computer without consent, illegal.
Disclosure of security breaches	In 2002, California enacted legislation that requires state agencies or businesses that own or license computer data with personal information to notify state residents if they experience a security breach involving that information; today, nearly every state has enacted similar legislation
Privacy of personal information	Two states, Nevada and Minnesota, require ISPs to keep their customers' PII private unless the customer consents to disclose the information. Minnesota also requires ISPs to get permission from subscribers before disclosing information about subscribers' online surfing habits.
Data encryption	In October 2007, Nevada passed the first law that requires encryption for the transmission of customer personal information. The law took October 1, 2008.

Informed Consent

informed consent

consent given with knowledge of all material facts needed to make a rational decision

The concept of **informed consent** (defined as consent given with knowledge of all material facts needed to make a rational decision) also plays an important role in protecting privacy. In the United States, business firms (and government agencies) can gather transaction information generated in the marketplace and then use that information for other marketing purposes, without obtaining the informed consent of the individual. For instance, in the United States, if a Web shopper purchases books about baseball at a site that belongs to an advertising network such as DoubleClick, a cookie can be placed on the consumer's hard drive and used by other member sites to sell the shopper sports clothing without the explicit permission or even knowledge of the user. This online preference information may also be linked with personally identifying information. In Europe, this would be illegal. A business in Europe cannot use marketplace transaction information for any purpose other than supporting the current transaction, unless of course it obtains the individual's consent in writing or by filling out an on-screen form.

There are traditionally two models for informed consent: opt-in and opt-out. The **opt-in** model requires an affirmative action by the consumer to allow collection and use of information. For instance, using opt-in, consumers would first be asked if they approved of the collection and use of information, and then directed to check a selection box if they agreed. Otherwise, the default is not to approve the collection of data. In the **opt-out** model, the default is to collect information unless the consumer takes an affirmative action to prevent the collection of data by checking a box, or by filling out a form.

Until recently, many U.S e-commerce companies rejected the concept of informed consent and instead simply published their information use policy on their site. U.S. businesses argue that informing consumers about how the information will be used is sufficient to obtain the users' informed consent. Most U.S. sites that offer informed consent make opting in the default option, and require users to go to special pages to request to opt-out of promotional campaigns. Some sites have an opt-out selection box at the very bottom of their information policy statements where the consumer is unlikely to see it. Privacy advocates argue that many information/privacy policy statements on U.S. Web sites are obscure, difficult to read, and legitimate just about any use of personal information. For instance, Yahoo's privacy policy begins with the statement that "Yahoo! takes your privacy seriously." It then states that it "does not rent, sell, or share personal information about you with other people or non-affiliated companies." However, there are a number of exceptions that significantly weaken this statement. For instance, Yahoo may share the information with "trusted partners," which could be anyone that Yahoo does business with, although perhaps not a company that the user might choose to do business with.

opt-in

requires an affirmative action by the consumer to allow collection and use of consumer information

opt-out

the default is to collect information unless the consumer takes an affirmative action to prevent the collection of data

The FTC's Fair Information Practices Principles

In the United States, the FTC has taken the lead in conducting research on online privacy and recommending legislation to Congress. The FTC is a cabinet-level agency charged with promoting the efficient functioning of the marketplace by protecting consumers from unfair or deceptive practices and increasing consumer choice by promoting competition. In addition to reports and recommendations, the FTC enforces existing legislation by suing corporations it believes are in violation of federal fair trade laws.

In 1995, the FTC began a series of investigations of online privacy based on its belief that online invasion of privacy potentially involved deceit and unfair behavior. In 1998, the FTC issued its Fair Information Practice (FIP) principles, on which it has based its assessments and recommendations for online privacy. **Table 8.5** describes these principles. Two of the five are designated as basic, "core" principles that must be present to protect privacy, whereas the other practices are less central. The FTC's FIP principles restate and strengthen in a form suitable to deal with online privacy the Fair Information Practices doctrine developed in 1973 by a government study group (U.S. Department of Health, Education and Welfare, 1973).

The FTC's FIP principles set the ground rules for what constitutes due process privacy protection procedures at e-commerce and all other Web sites—including government and nonprofit Web sites—in the United States.

TABLE 8.5	FEDERAL TRADE COMMISSION'S FAIR INFORMATION PRACTICE PRINCIPLES
Notice/Awareness (core principle)	Sites must disclose their information practices before collecting data. Includes identification of collector, uses of data, other recipients of data, nature of collection (active/inactive), voluntary or required, consequences of refusal, and steps taken to protect confidentiality, integrity, and quality of the data
Choice/Consent (core principle)	There must be a choice regime in place allowing consumers to choose how their information will be used for secondary purposes other than supporting the transaction, including internal use and transfer to third parties. Opt-in/opt-out must be available.
Access/Participation	Consumers should be able to review and contest the accuracy and completeness of data collected about them in a timely, inexpensive process.
Security	Data collectors must take reasonable steps to assure that consumer information is accurate and secure from unauthorized use.
Enforcement	There must be in place a mechanism to enforce FIP principles. This can involve self-regulation, legislation giving consumers legal remedies for violations, or federal statutes and regulation.

SOURCE: Based on data from Federal Trade Commission, 1998, 2000a.

At this point, the FTC's FIP principles are guidelines, not laws. They have stimulated private firms and industry associations to develop their own private guidelines (discussed next). However, the FTC's FIP guidelines are being used as the basis of new legislation. The most important online privacy legislation to date that was directly influenced by the FTC's FIP principles is the Children's Online Privacy Protection Act (COPPA) (1998), which requires Web sites to obtain parental permission before collecting information on children under 13 years of age.

In July 2000, the FTC recommended legislation to Congress to protect online consumer privacy from the threat posed by advertising networks. **Table 8.6** summarizes the Commission's recommendations. The FTC profiling recommendations significantly strengthen the FIP principles of notification and choice, while also including restrictions on information that may be collected.[1] Although the FTC supports industry efforts at self-regulation, it nevertheless recommended legislation to ensure that all Web sites using network advertising and all network advertisers comply. To date, however, Congress has not passed such legislation.

---

[1]Much general privacy legislation affecting government, e.g., the Privacy Act of 1974, precludes the government from collecting information on political and social behavior of citizens. The FTC restrictions are significant because they are the FTC's first effort at limiting the collection of certain information.

TABLE 8.6	FTC RECOMMENDATIONS REGARDING ONLINE PROFILING
PRINCIPLE	DESCRIPTION OF RECOMMENDATION
Notice	Complete transparency to user by providing disclosure and choice options on the host Web site. "Robust" notice for PII (time/place of collection; before collection begins). Clear and conspicuous notice for non-PII.
Choice	Opt-in for PII, opt-out for non-PII. No conversion of non-PII to PII without consent. Opt-out from any or all network advertisers from a single page provided by the host Web site.
Access	Reasonable provisions to allow inspection and correction.
Security	Reasonable efforts to secure information from loss, misuse, or improper access.
Enforcement	Done by independent third parties, such as seal programs and accounting firms.
Restricted collection	Advertising networks will not collect information about sensitive financial or medical topics, sexual behavior or sexual orientation, or use social security numbers for profiling.

In November 2007, the FTC held a two-day workshop on online advertising, behavioral targeting, and online privacy. Consumer privacy groups have asked for the institution of a "Do Not Track" list similar to the FTC's "Do Not Call" telemarketing list, which would permit people to more easily opt out of behavioral tracking programs, as well as disclosure notices that tracking is occurring, and the ability for consumers to view and edit any profiles about themselves that ad networks build. The online advertising industry, not surprisingly, believes that FTC regulation would stifle innovation in the industry. At least one FTC member suggested at the conference that rules about privacy policies might need to be established, and that the FTC needed to increase its scrutiny of the online targeting (Story, 2007).

In 2008, the growing fear of widespread behavioral targeting, strengthened by the buyouts of the largest advertising networks by search engines (e.g. Google's purchase of DoubleClick), led to a Congressional hearings in June. Industry leaders such as Google and Microsoft called for new privacy legislation that would legitimate their behavioral targeting programs. In August 2008, four legislators sent a letter to 33 Internet companies, including the top search engines, requesting detailed explanations of their privacy policies (Clifford, 2008).

In February 2009, the FTC held hearings to discuss its program for voluntary industry principles for regulating behavioral targeting. The online advertising trade group Network Advertising Initiative (discussed later in this section), published its own self-regulatory principles that largely agreed with the FTC. Nevertheless, the government, privacy groups, and the online ad industry are still at loggerheads over two issues. Privacy advocates want both an opt-in policy at all sites and a national Do Not Track list. The industry opposes these moves and continues to insist on an opt-out capability being the only way to avoid tracking (Federal Trade Commission, 2009).

The European Directive on Data Protection

In Europe, privacy protection is much stronger than it is in the United States. In the United States, private organizations and businesses are permitted to use PII gathered in commercial transactions for other business purposes without the prior consent of the consumer (so-called secondary uses of PII). In the United States, there is no federal agency charged with enforcing privacy laws. Instead, privacy laws are enforced largely through self-regulation by businesses, and by individuals who must sue agencies or companies in court to recover damages. This is expensive and rarely done. The European approach to privacy protection is more comprehensive and regulatory in nature. European countries do not allow business firms to use PII without the prior consent of consumers. They enforce their privacy laws by creating data protection agencies to pursue complaints brought by citizens and to actively enforce privacy laws.

On October 25, 1998, the European Commission's Directive on Data Protection went into effect, standardizing and broadening privacy protection in the European Union (EU) nations. The Directive is based on the Fair Information Practices doctrine, but extends the control individuals can exercise over their personal information. The Directive requires companies to inform people when they collect information about them and to disclose how it will be stored and used. Customers must provide their informed consent before any company can legally use data about them, and they have the right to access that information, correct it, and request that no further data be collected. Further, the directive prohibits the transfer of PII to organizations or countries that do not have similarly strong privacy protection policies. This means that data collected in Europe by American business firms cannot be transferred or processed in the United States (which has weaker privacy protection laws). This would potentially interfere with a $350 billion annual trade flow between the United States and Europe.

safe harbor
a private self-regulating policy and enforcement mechanism that meets the objectives of government regulators and legislation but does not involve government regulation or enforcement

The Department of Commerce, working with the European Commission, developed a safe harbor framework for U.S. firms. A **safe harbor** is a private self-regulating policy and enforcement mechanism that meets the objectives of government regulators and legislation, but does not involve government regulation or enforcement. The government plays a role in certifying safe harbors, however. Organizations that decide to participate in the safe harbor program must develop policies that meet European standards, and they must publicly sign on to a Web-based register maintained by the Department of Commerce. Enforcement occurs in the United States and relies to a large extent on self-policing and regulation, backed up by government enforcement of fair trade statutes. For more information on the safe harbor procedures and the EU Data Directive, see www.export.gov/safeharbor.

PRIVATE INDUSTRY SELF-REGULATION

The online industry in the United States has historically opposed privacy legislation, arguing that industry can do a better job of protecting privacy than government. However, individual firms such as AOL, Yahoo, and Google have adopted policies on their own in an effort to address the concerns of the public about personal privacy on the Internet. The online industry formed the Online Privacy Alliance (OPA) in 1998 to encourage self-regulation in part as a reaction to growing public concerns and the threat of legislation being proposed by FTC and privacy advocacy groups.

Private industry in the United States has created the idea of safe harbors from government regulation. For instance, COPPA includes a provision enabling industry groups or others to submit for the FTC's approval self-regulatory guidelines that implement the protections of the FIP principles and FTC rules. In May 2001, the FTC approved the TRUSTe Internet privacy protection program under the terms of COPPA as a safe harbor.[2]

OPA has developed a set of privacy guidelines that members are required to implement. The primary focus of industry efforts has been the development of online "seals" that attest to the privacy policies on a site. The Better Business Bureau (BBB), TRUSTe, WebTrust, and major accounting firms—among them PricewaterhouseCoopers' BetterWeb—have established seals for Web sites. To display a seal, Web site operators must conform to certain privacy principles, a complaint resolution process, and monitoring by the seal originator. Around 2,500 sites now display the TRUSTe seal, and over 57,000 display the BBB's Reliability seal. Nevertheless, online privacy seal programs have had a limited impact on Web privacy practices. Critics argue that the seal programs are not particularly effective in safeguarding privacy. For these reasons, the FTC has not deemed the seal programs as "safe harbors" yet (with the exception of TRUSTe's children's privacy seal under COPPA), and the agency continues to push for legislation to enforce privacy protection principles.

The advertising network industry has also formed an industry association, the Network Advertising Initiative (NAI), to develop privacy policies. NAI member companies include Advertising.com, Atlas, DoubleClick, Revenue Science, Tacoda, and 24/7 Real Media. The NAI has developed a set of privacy principles in conjunction with the FTC. The NAI policies have two objectives: to offer consumers a chance to opt-out of advertising network programs (including e-mail campaigns), and to provide consumers redress from abuses. In order to opt-out, the NAI has created a Web site—Networkadvertising.org—where consumers can use a global opt-out feature to prevent network advertising agencies from placing their cookies on a user's computer. If a consumer has a complaint, the NAI has a link to the Truste.org Web site where the complaints can be filed. Consumers still receive Internet advertising just as before, but the ads will not be targeted to their browsing behavior (Network Advertising Initiative, 2009a).

Responding to public concerns about tracking people online, AOL established an opt-out policy that allows users of its site to not be tracked. Yahoo follows the NAI guidelines and also allows opt out for tracking and Web beacons (Web bugs). Google has reduced retention time for tracking data.

---

[2]Another longstanding industry group with a safe harbor program for children online is the Children's Advertising Review Unit (CARU), founded in 1974 as the advertising industry's self-regulation program for the protection of children.

In 2009, the NAI published its version of behavioral tracking self-regulation guidelines, which emphasize their agreement with the FTC's set of principles. The self regulatory principles are: transparency, choice, security and data retention, and changes to privacy policies (Network Advertising Initiative, 2009b).

In general, industry efforts at self-regulation in online privacy have not succeeded in reducing American fears of privacy invasion during online transactions, or in reducing the level of privacy invasion. At best, self-regulation has offered consumers notice about whether a privacy policy exists, but usually says little about the actual use of the information, does not offer consumers a chance to see and correct the information or control its use in any significant way, offers no promises for the security of that information, and offers no enforcement mechanism (Hoofnagle, 2005). At the same time, the FTC and Congress point to efforts at self-regulation as a reason for not legislating in this area. Read *Insight on Business: Chief Privacy Officers* to see a different approach to industry self-regulation.

PRIVACY ADVOCACY GROUPS

There are a number of privacy advocacy groups on the Web that monitor developments in privacy. Some of these sites are industry-supported, while others rely on private foundations and contributions. Some of the better-known sites are listed in **Table 8.7**.

TECHNOLOGICAL SOLUTIONS

There are a number of privacy-enhancing technologies for protecting user privacy during interactions with Web sites that have been developed (see **Table 8.8**) on page 521. Most of these tools emphasize security—the ability of individuals to protect their communications and files from illegitimate snoopers. This is just one element of privacy. The other is the development of private and public policies that enable consumers to control the collection and use of information that is gathered in the course of market transactions.

The growth in consumer use of spyware blockers, cookie blockers, and pop-up controls on browsers threatens the online advertising industry that relies on cookies,

TABLE 8.7	PRIVACY ADVOCACY GROUPS
ADVOCACY GROUP	FOCUS
Epic.org (Electronic Privacy Information Center)	Washington-based watch-dog group
Privacyinternational.org	Tracks international privacy developments
Cdt.org (Center for Democracy and Technology)	Foundation- and business-supported group with a legislative focus
Privacy.org	Clearinghouse sponsored by EPIC and Privacy International
Privacyrights.org	Educational clearinghouse
Privacyalliance.org	Industry-supported clearinghouse

INSIGHT ON BUSINESS

CHIEF PRIVACY OFFICERS

How can you tell if your own corporate practices actually conform to the privacy policy stated on your Web site? How can your business keep track of all the new privacy legislation and changes in European policies? How can you avoid taking some embarrassing action that insults your customers' sense of what's an acceptable use of their personal information?

The answer for many corporations is to create an executive position—chief privacy officer (CPO). The position is a relatively new one that firms first started to create about 10 years ago, but today is one of fastest growing in corporate management. The use of personal information on commercial Web sites in the United States is largely unregulated, and a potential minefield for companies whose business relies on using the personal information of their customers for financial gain. Industries that have added CPOs include health care, financial services, technology, and consumer goods, in part due to growing regulatory requirements with respect to data privacy. Examples include Facebook, Google, IBM, AT&T, Verizon, DoubleClick (owned by Google), New York Life, Intel, Loopt, ChoicePoint, and Microsoft. The International Association of Privacy Professionals (IAPP), a professional group composed of chief privacy officers, now has 6,000 members across the globe, 85% of whom are located in the United States, up 30% over the last two years. In a recent survey, privacy leaders rank high in their organizations, with 61% one or two reporting levels away from the CEO; around 60% of privacy leaders reported two or more full-time employees; 36% indicated their privacy program was at the mature stage.

What does a CPO do? The job has several aspects. Often, a CPO's first job is to plan and then implement a privacy plan for the firm to follow. Once a plan is in place, it needs to be enforced, and monitored, and the company's business units and employees may need to be educated about the plan and the importance of privacy. For instance, at Marriott International, Chris Zoladz, vice president of information protection and privacy, notes that "Good privacy is good business." When Marriott marketing executives proposed personalizing the information that appears on the hotel chain's Web site so that it was customized based on personal information collected from guests as part of the reservation process, Zoladz got involved to make sure the information was used properly.

Another job is helping the company avoid privacy "land mines," which are mistakes in policy or technology that, had any one thought about it, would obviously be embarrassing to the company because of the potential for a storm of protest from privacy protection groups. It seems that at least once a year, a major firm makes a mistake and issues a policy or takes an action which communicates to customers that they have lost control over their personal private information. In 2009, it was Facebook's turn: the social networking site released a new Terms of Service agreement in February 2009 that gave the impression that, as one commentator put it, "we [Facebook] can do anything we want with your content. Forever." Facebook CEO Mark Zuckerberg initially defended the new policy, claiming it did not change anything of importance, but a firestorm of protests involving hundreds of thousands of Facebook users led the company to revert back to its old policy. It also established a users group to define privacy settings, and ultimately, adopted a policy that gives users considerable control over the uses of their private personal

(continued)

information. Social networking sites make money ("monetize their audience" in Wall Street lingo) by selling information about their members to advertisers who can use this information to target their ads. The more information Facebook can sell to advertisers, the more money it makes. Privacy invasion is very profitable. Facebook's Chief Privacy Officer Chris Kelly has been a voice within the firm advocating for user controls and opt-in functionality for personal information. According to Kelly, the new privacy policy at Facebook is that "Facebook users own all their data." This is music to the ears of most privacy advocates even though the concept of "ownership of private personal information" itself is controversial.

In other cases, in the absence of a CPO, disaster is possible. U.S. Bancorp decided to sell personal financial data to a direct-marketing company in violation of its own stated policies. This cost Bancorp $3 million in a legal settlement in Minnesota. Real Networks had to apologize to users and change its data collection policies after a disclosure that the company's RealJukebox Internet music software captured data about users' preferences. A string of data losses, criminal intrusions, and accidents at data brokerage firms such as ChoicePoint and Reed Elsevier's LexisNexis unit resulted in the diversion and theft of hundreds of thousands of complete personal profiles. This in turn has led to Congressional investigations, fines, and the threat of restrictive legislation for the entire data brokerage industry.

The new corporate emphasis on privacy has also created a new business for the big accounting firm PricewaterhouseCoopers. PWC has conducted hundreds of privacy audits. Companies are taking this issue very seriously because data theft or loss and invasions of privacy directly threaten the brand names of firms. Privacy audits identify the risks that firms face and prescribe corrective actions with a view to avoiding

class-action suits, Internet-based protests, and shareholder enmity. And what do the auditors find? About 80% of the companies audited by PWC do not follow their own stated privacy policies. Most of the time this is the result of poor training and human error. After Expedia completed a privacy audit led by PWC, it changed its information collection policy from opt-out to opt-in. Now Expedia's customers have to actively click a button and ask to be informed of new offers from the travel site. The result is that far fewer customers ask to unsubscribe from mailing solicitations. Expedia executives believe trust and privacy are major concerns of their customers, and anything they can do to enhance trust is good for their business.

What do CPOs worry about? They often have a hard time with their own employees taking privacy seriously and changing policies to cope with the risks. After ChoicePoint lost 145,000 personal dossiers to criminals posing as real companies, ChoicePoint decided to hire a CPO to report directly to the Board of Directors and the CEO. The CPO discovered that ChoicePoint did not verify the authenticity or legitimacy of people claiming a business need to access their databases.

Another challenge facing CPOs is federal legislation that requires companies to inform consumers of their privacy policies, and the trend towards a narrow legalistic emphasis on compliance. The Gramm-Leach-Bliley Act of 1999 requires all financial service firms to inform consumers of their privacy policies. This results in tens of millions of pamphlets being sent to consumers, often written in confusing legal jargon that few can understand. HIPAA, designed to make the transfer of records among health care agencies more efficient as well as to safeguard the privacy of those records, has also unleashed a flood of privacy pamphlets that few can understand. HIPAA requires that all health care providers and insurers have a privacy officer, even

(continued)

in small medical practices with seven doctors. Professional associations such as the International Association of Privacy Professionals openly worry that legalistic compliance with federal laws fails to take into account the real interests of consumers and the strategic implications for the firm.

Currently the Obama administration is faced with demands that the executive branch and Congress develop a legal framework for the uses of personal information on the Internet. It is likely that CPOs will continue to be much in demand and have much work to do in the near future.

SOURCES: "IAPP Membership Climbs to 6,000,"International Association of Privacy Professionals, July 14, 2009; Facebook's Chief Privacy Officer: Balancing Needs of Users with the Business of Social Networks," by C.G. Lynch, *CIO Magazine*, April 1, 2009; "Facebook's Chief Privacy Officer: Users Own All Their Data," Insidefacebook.com, February 22nd, 2009; "Facebook's About-Face on Data," by Jessica Vascellaro, *Wall Street Journal*, February 10, 2009; "Online Privacy Decisions Confront Obama," by Kim Hart, *Washington Post*, January 13, 2009; "Q&A: Jules Polonetsky, Chief Privacy Officer, AOL" by Kenneth Corbin, Internetnews.com, May 12, 2008; "Gartner for IT Leaders Overview: The Chief Privacy Officer," by Arabella Hallawell and Paul E. Proctor, October 1, 2007; "Why Your Company Needs a Chief Privacy Officer," by Cara Garretson, *Network World*, May 22, 2007.

TABLE 8.8	TECHNOLOGICAL PROTECTIONS FOR ONLINE PRIVACY	
TECHNOLOGY	**PRODUCTS**	**PROTECTION**
Spyware blockers	Spyware Doctor, ZoneAlarm, Ad-Aware and Spybot—Search & Destroy (Spybot-S&D) (freeware)	Detects and removes spyware and adware, keyloggers, and other malware
Pop-up blockers	Browsers: Firefox, Internet Explorer 6.0 SP2 and 7, Safari, Opera Toolbars: Google, Yahoo, MSN Add-on programs: STOPzilla, Adblock, NoAds	Prevents calls to ad servers that push pop-up, pop-under, and leave-behind ads; restricts downloading of images at user request
Secure e-mail	ZL Technologies; SafeMessage.com, Hushmail.com, Pretty Good Privacy (PGP)	E-mail and document encryption
Anonymous remailers	W3-Anonymous Remailer, Jack B Nymble, Java Anonymous Proxy	Send e-mail without trace
Anonymous surfing	Freedom Websecure, Anonymizer.com, Tor, GhostSurf	Surf without a trace
Cookie managers	CookieCrusher, and most browsers	Prevents client computer from accepting cookies
Disk/file erasing programs	Mutilate File Wiper, Eraser, DiskVac 2.0	Completely erases hard drive and floppy files
Policy generators	OECD Privacy Policy Generator	Automates the development of an OECD privacy compliance policy
Privacy Policy Reader	P3P	Software for automating the communication of privacy policies to users
Public Key Encryption	PGP Desktop	Program that encrypts your mail and documents

placed mostly by advertising networks, although thus far, it has not appreciably reduced reliance on these techniques by advertisers.

Perhaps the most comprehensive technological privacy protection effort is **P3P**, the **Platform for Privacy Preferences** sponsored by W3C (the World Wide Web Consortium—an international, nonprofit, industry-supported Web standards group). P3P is a standard designed to communicate a Web site's privacy policy to Internet users, and to compare that policy to the user's own preferences, or to other standards such as the FTC's FIP principles or the EU Data Protection Directive. P3P does not establish privacy standards and relies on government and industry to develop them. The basic idea behind P3P and subsequent efforts like TAMI (MIT) and PRIME (Europe) is to allow individuals to express their privacy preferences in a machine readable form that all Web sites can universally understand.

P3P works through a user's Web browser. On the server side, P3P enables sites to translate their privacy policies into a standardized machine-readable XML format that can be read either by the browser or by installed software plug-ins. On the user client side, the browser automatically fetches a Web site's privacy policy and informs the user. **Figure 8.2(A)** illustrates how this could work.

Platform for Privacy Preferences (P3P)
a standard designed to communicate to Internet users a Web site's privacy policy, and to compare that policy to the user's own preferences, or to other standards such as the FTC's FIP guidelines or the EU Data Protection Directive

FIGURE 8.2(A)   HOW P3P WORKS

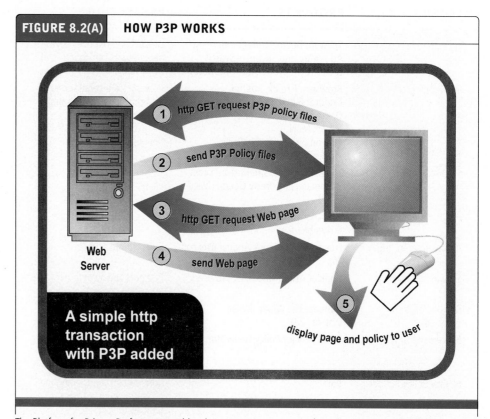

The Platform for Privacy Preferences enables the automatic communication of privacy policies between e-commerce sites and consumers.
SOURCE: W3C Platform for Privacy Preferences Initiative, 2003.

P3P is now built into browsers such as Firefox and Internet Explorer 6.0/8.0. By using a slider, users can set the privacy policy they desire; their browser will automatically read the privacy policy of sites they visit and warn them when a site does not match their preferences (see **Figure 8.2 (B)**). According to a Carnegie Mellon study, about 10% of Web sites overall, and more than 20% of e-commerce sites, now feature P3P, as well as about one-third of the top 100 Web sites (eMarketer, Inc., 2007c).

While P3P is one step in the direction of increasing consumer awareness and understanding of Web site privacy, it fails to achieve other goals of fair information policies such as limits on what information is collected, the use of personal information, user control of personal information, security, and enforcement of privacy rights. In this sense, it has failed to increase the consumer's sense of trust when shopping online. Most users simply leave the default settings for P3P at "medium," not knowing exactly what this means (Van Kirk, 2005).

Insight on Technology: The Privacy Tug of War: Advertisers vs. Consumers describes some other new technologies being used to both invade and protect privacy.

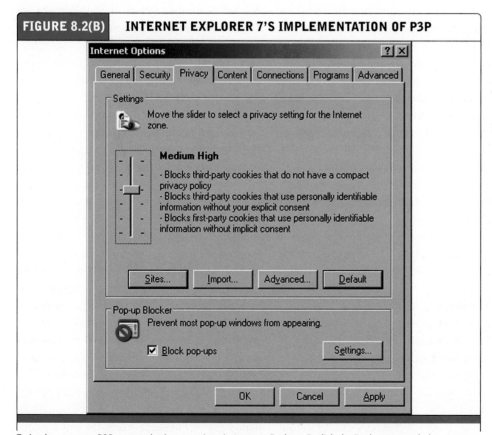

FIGURE 8.2(B)	**INTERNET EXPLORER 7'S IMPLEMENTATION OF P3P**

To implement your P3P personal privacy settings in Internet Explorer 7, click the Tools command, then Internet Options. Then click the Privacy tab in the Internet Options dialog box.

INSIGHT ON TECHNOLOGY

THE PRIVACY TUG OF WAR: ADVERTISERS VS. CONSUMERS

In the "old days," as the famous *New Yorker* cartoon put it, "On the Internet, nobody knows you are a dog." But that was then. On today's Internet, online marketers and data companies not only know you're not a dog, but they also can find out much more about you, such as your income, credit score, home ownership, the car you drive, what car you're interested in buying, and whether or not you have any traffic offenses, as well as your online behavior, such as the music you listen to, the books you've ordered from Amazon, the frequency of your purchases, and your use of Twitter and iPhone apps. In the past, offline marketers and data companies knew much more personal information about you than online companies did. For instance, one of the biggest offline tracking firms is Acxiom. Acxiom estimates it stores more than 1,500 data items on each American adult. But the separation of offline and online, the separation of data bases, and the isolation of information in unconnected "pools" is changing as offline market information firms merge their data with online marketers. It's the total coordination of the technological means of tracking individuals that is new. The result is that all of us leave a huge digital footprint (total Web activities) on the Internet. You can check the size of your digital footprint at emc.com. Ken Laudon's footprint , for instance, is over 427 gigabytes.

We are all engaged in a technological tug of war between technologies that make invading customer privacy very easy versus technologies and policies that make protecting privacy easier for us, the consumer. On the privacy invasion side, Google has become the largest tracker on the Internet, and as one commentator put it, "Google knows more about you than your mother." With its treasure trove of data developed from users of its search service, Gmail, Google Sites, Google Health, and a host of other applications, Google has entered a new phase of behavioral targeting. In the past, Google engaged in "context advertising": enter a search argument, and Google would display "relevant" ads. Today Google is moving into what it calls "interest-based" advertising, what people on the sell side of ads call "performance-based advertising" and what everyone else calls behavioral targeting. For instance, mention in a Gmail to your doctor that you're having acid stomach problems, and you'll be shown ads for stomach acid products. Now that Google owns the largest online advertising network, DoubleClick, it's quite likely you will be shown stomach acid banner ads wherever you go on the Internet for an indeterminate period of time.

Experian links Web sites to its database and provides the names and addresses of visitors to the sites in real time. Other companies such as Acxiom combine offline and online purchasing and behavioral data into one central database. Acxiom's service, Relevance-X, draws on that database to determine which online ads to show. MySpace has developed its HyperTargeting ad program, which scours user profiles for interests and then delivers related ads. In 2007, Facebook introduced Beacon, an advertising system that broadcast members' activities on other Web sites (such as what you had purchased) to their friends on Facebook. Beacon was launched with the support of 40 other firms from Coca-Cola to Verizon. Beacon created a fire storm of resistance from Facebook members, and privacy groups. By the end of 2007, Facebook CEO, Mark Zuckerberg, apologized to Facebook members and changed the Beacon program so that users needed to

(continued)

explicitly approve of their activities being shared with others. In August 2008, Facebook was sued in a class action suit for violating several federal and state laws that prohibit the unauthorized release of personal information. Currently, Beacon requires users to opt in to the program. Opt-in is a strong form of consumer protection.

Advertisers justify their intrusions into our private lives and our private use of the Internet with two arguments. They point out that the Internet is not really free. According to senior executives at advertising networks such as DoubleClick: the implicit bargain underlying the "free" Internet is that consumers get content because they are looking at ads. Never mind that you paid around $1,000 for your computer system, and $20–$50 monthly for Internet service. Take away the ads, and some other way will have to be found to pay for what you get on the Internet. Take away the targeted ads, Web sites make less money, and they will provide less service. No more "free" Picassa. Expect charges for even minimal service. The second rationale behind all these intrusive behaviors is marketing efficiency and effectiveness: the more advertisers know about you, the more they can customize and personalize the advertising to exactly what you are looking for at the right time, and, of course, the more they can charge their customers, the firms that pay for the advertising. Online advertisers believe that consumers are saying, "Take my privacy, but please send the content and the services for free." But is this really what consumers are saying? Arguably not.

In one of the more insightful studies of consumer attitudes towards Internet privacy, a group of Berkeley students conducted surveys of online users, and of complaints filed with the Federal Trade Commission involving privacy issues. Here's some of their results. User concerns: people feel they have no control over the information collected about them, and they don't know who to

complain to. Web site practices: Web sites collect all this information, but do not let users have access; the policies are unclear; they share data with "affiliates" but never identify who the affiliates are and how many there are. (MySpace, owned by NewsCorp, has over 1,500 affiliates with whom it shares online information.) Web bug trackers: they are ubiquitous and we are not informed they are on the pages we visit. The results of this study and others suggest that consumers are not saying "take my privacy, I don't care, send me the service for free." They are saying "We want access to the information, we want some controls on what can be collected, what is done with the information, the ability to opt out of the entire tracking enterprise, and some clarity on what the policies really are, and we don't want those policies changed without our participation and permission." (The full report is available at knowprivacy.org).

Confirming these views, an industry-backed survey of over 1,000 Web users found that only 14% said they liked giving information to Web sites in order to receive customized content, and 71% said they disliked it but did so only if necessary to obtain content or information. Another survey found that 41% said that, in the past six months, they had provided inaccurate information to Web sites that required personal information, which respondents did not want to share. They seem to be saying, "Send the content, but let me keep my privacy!" While some studies suggest that many teenagers and young adults do not care as much about privacy as older adults, privacy experts believe that this is because they do not understand how much information is being gathered about them.

On the privacy protection side, there are some tools available to consumers. Admittedly, P3P, an industry-sponsored effort to provide users some choice in privacy by making them aware of

(continued)

Web site privacy policies, has not been too successful. But ISPs and independent software companies now provide a host of tools that work wonders and are easy to use. AOL offers a "Do Not Track" service that links consumers directly to opt-out lists offered by the large advertising networks. Google has followed: anyone may opt out of the DoubleClick cookie (for AdSense partner sites, DoubleClick ad serving, and certain Google services using the DoubleClick cookie) at any time by clicking a button on the Google Privacy Center page (assuming you know enough to go to that page). Using a tool created by the Network Advertising Initiative, you can opt out of several third-party ad servers' and networks' cookies simultaneously. Web browsers have effective pop-up and image blockers. Adoption rates of cookie blockers and anti-spyware software are increasing as software makers such as Symantec make them available as a part of their software suites that install automatically. For instance, a recent survey found that anti-virus, anti-spyware, and firewall software are used by over 80% of U.S. adult Internet users, and that over two-thirds had configured their browser or operating system to block pop-ups, reject cookies or block specific Web sites. Even if these estimates are off by 50%, a significant number of targeted ads are not actually being shown to consumers. Consumers who opt out are still shown ads, but they are not based on tracking or user interests or prior Web behavior.

The most important spur to industry initiatives protecting privacy is the growing public pressure to do something that gets reflected in congressional hearings, and ultimately legislation. As public concern over behavioral targeting has grown, with calls for greater transparency and accountability, the pressure from Washington on the industry also grows, and attitudes have changed. Gone are the days when Silicon Valley leaders who profit from the invasion of Internet users' privacy could announce to the American public: "Privacy is dead. Get over it!" Instead a broad consensus between industry, privacy advocates, and Congress has emerged that users want transparency, control, choice, security, and data retention rules, and no changes in privacy promises. Facebook users don't want to wake up some morning and discover that Mark Zuckerberg has decided to sell all their personal information to "affiliates." The leading advertising industry associations have adopted "Self Regulatory Principles for Online Behavioral Advertising," which address many but not all concerns described above. Disagreement persists on questions of user access to the data collected, opt-out vs. opt-in, how "transparency" will be implemented, and the sharing of information with so-called affiliates. The Center for Democracy and Technology supports the idea of a Web-based Do Not Track List where users could sign up at one government site, and all Web advertisers would have to consult that database before targeting ads at users. The industry believes this would be too easy for consumers, and thereby too successful, preventing them from effectively exploiting consumers' personal information.

SOURCES: "Know Privacy. The Current State of Web Privacy, Data Collection, and Information Sharing," Knowprivacy.org, accessed September 8, 2009; "Ads Follow Web Users, and Get More Personal," by Stephanie Clifford, *New York Times*, July 31, 2009; "The Paradox of Privacy," by Eric Pfanner, *New York Times*, July 13, 2009; "Web Privacy Efforts Targeted. Facing Rules, Ad Firms Give Consumers More Control," by Emily Steel, *Wall Street Journal*, June 25, 2009; "Social Networking Sites Could Be Embroiled in Privacy Crackdown," *Telegraph*, June 18, 2009; "Google to Offcer Ads Based on Interests," by Miguel Helft, *New York Times*, March 11, 2009; "When Everyone's a Friend, Is Anything Private," by Randall Stross, *New York Times*, March 8, 2009; "Link by Link. As Data Collecting Grows, Privacy Erodes," by Noam Cohen, *New York Times*, February 16, 2009; "Self-Regulatory Principles For Online Behavioral Advertising. Behavioral Advertising, Tracking, Targeting, and Technology," Federal Trade Commission Staff Report, Washington D.C., February 2009; "Many See Privacy on Web as Big Issue, Survey Says," by Stephanie Clifford, *New York Times*, March 16, 2009; "A Call to Legislate Internet Privacy," by Saul Hansell, *New York Times*, March 13, 2009; "Facebook Rules," *New York Times*, February 18, 2009; "Agency Skeptical of Internet Privacy Policies," by Saul Hansell, New York Times, February 13, 2009.

8.3   INTELLECTUAL PROPERTY RIGHTS

Congress shall have the power to "promote the progress of science and useful arts, by securing for limited times to authors and inventors the exclusive right to their respective writings and discoveries."

—Article I, Section 8, Constitution of the United States, 1788.

Next to privacy, the most controversial ethical, social, and political issue related to e-commerce is the fate of intellectual property rights. Intellectual property encompasses all the tangible and intangible products of the human mind. As a general rule, in the United States, the creator of intellectual property owns it. For instance, if you personally create an e-commerce site, it belongs entirely to you, and you have exclusive rights to use this "property" in any lawful way you see fit. But the Internet potentially changes things. Once intellectual works become digital, it becomes difficult to control access, use, distribution, and copying. These are precisely the areas that intellectual property seeks to control.

Digital media differ from books, periodicals, and other media in terms of ease of replication, transmission, and alteration; difficulty in classifying a software work as a program, book, or even music; compactness—making theft easy; and difficulty in establishing uniqueness. Before widespread use of the Internet, copies of software, books, magazine articles, or films had to be stored on physical media, such as paper, computer disks, or videotape, creating some hurdles to distribution.

The Internet technically permits millions of people to make perfect digital copies of various works—from music to plays, poems, and journal articles—and then to distribute them nearly cost-free to hundreds of millions of Web users. The proliferation of innovation has occurred so rapidly that few entrepreneurs have stopped to consider who owns the patent on a business technique or method their site is using. The spirit of the Web has been so free-wheeling that many entrepreneurs ignored trademark law and registered domain names that can easily be confused with another company's registered trademarks. In short, the Internet has demonstrated the potential for destroying traditional conceptions and implementations of intellectual property law developed over the last two centuries.

The major ethical issue related to e-commerce and intellectual property concerns how we (both as individuals and as business professionals) should treat property that belongs to others. From a social point of view, the main questions are: Is there continued value in protecting intellectual property in the Internet age? In what ways is society better off, or worse off, for having the concept of property apply to intangible ideas? Should society make certain technology illegal just because it has an adverse impact on some intellectual property owners? From a political perspective, we need to ask how the Internet and e-commerce can be regulated or governed to protect the institution of intellectual property while at the same time encouraging the growth of e-commerce and the Internet.

TYPES OF INTELLECTUAL PROPERTY PROTECTION

There are three main types of intellectual property protection: copyright, patent, and trademark law. In the United States, the development of intellectual property law begins in the U.S. Constitution in 1788, which mandated Congress to devise a system of laws to promote "the progress of science and the useful arts." Congress passed the first copyright law in 1790 to protect original written works for a period of 14 years, with a 14-year renewal if the author was still alive. Since then, the idea of copyright has been extended to include music, films, translations, photographs, and most recently (1998), the designs of vessels under 200 feet (Fisher, 1999). The copyright law has been amended (mostly extended) 11 times in the last 40 years.

The goal of intellectual property law is to balance two competing interests—the public and the private. The public interest is served by the creation and distribution of inventions, works of art, music, literature, and other forms of intellectual expression. The private interest is served by rewarding people for creating these works through the creation of a time-limited monopoly granting exclusive use to the creator.

Maintaining this balance of interests is always challenged by the invention of new technologies. In general, the information technologies of the last century—from radio and television to CD-ROMs, DVDs, and the Internet—have at first tended to weaken the protections afforded by intellectual property law. Owners of intellectual property have often but not always been successful in pressuring Congress and the courts to strengthen the intellectual property laws to compensate for any technological threat, and even to extend protection for longer periods of time and to entirely new areas of expression. In the case of the Internet and e-commerce technologies, once again, intellectual property rights are severely challenged. In the next few sections, we discuss the significant developments in each area: copyright, patent, and trademark.

COPYRIGHT: THE PROBLEM OF PERFECT COPIES AND ENCRYPTION

copyright law

protects original forms of expression such as writings, art, drawings, photographs, music, motion pictures, performances, and computer programs from being copied by others for a minimum of 70 years

In the United States, **copyright law** protects original forms of expression such as writings (books, periodicals, lecture notes), art, drawings, photographs, music, motion pictures, performances, and computer programs from being copied by others for a period of time. Up until 1998, the copyright law protected works of individuals for their lifetime plus 50 years beyond their life, and for works created for hire and owned by corporations such as Mickey Mouse of the Disney Corporation, 75 years after initial creation. Copyright does not protect ideas—just their expression in a tangible medium such as paper, cassette tape, or handwritten notes.

In 1998, Congress extended the period of copyright protection for an additional 20 years, for a total of 95 years for corporate-owned works, and life plus 70 years of protection for works created by individuals (the Copyright Term Extension Act, also known as CETA). In *Eldred v. Ashcroft*, the Supreme Court ruled on January 16, 2003, that CETA was constitutional, over the objections of groups arguing that Congress had given copyright holders a permanent monopoly over the expression of ideas, which ultimately would work to inhibit the flow of ideas and creation of new works by making existing works too expensive (Greenhouse, 2003a). Librarians, academics, and others who depend on inexpensive access to copyrighted material opposed the legislation.

Since the first federal Copyright Act of 1790, the congressional intent behind copyright laws has been to encourage creativity and authorship by ensuring that creative people receive the financial and other benefits of their work. Most industrial nations have their own copyright laws, and there are several international conventions and bilateral agreements through which nations coordinate and enforce their laws.

In the mid-1960s, the Copyright Office began registering software programs, and in 1980, Congress passed the Computer Software Copyright Act, which clearly provides protection for source and object code and for copies of the original sold in commerce, and sets forth the rights of the purchaser to use the software while the creator retains legal title. For instance, the HTML code for a Web page—even though easily available to every browser—cannot be lawfully copied and used for a commercial purpose, say, to create a new Web site that looks identical.

Copyright protection is clear-cut: it protects against copying of entire programs or their parts. Damages and relief are readily obtained for infringement. The drawback to copyright protection is that the underlying ideas behind a work are not protected, only their expression in a work. A competitor can view the source code on your Web site to see how various effects were created and then reuse those techniques to create a different Web site without infringing on your copyright.

Look and Feel

"Look and feel" copyright infringement lawsuits are precisely about the distinction between an idea and its expression. For instance, in 1988, Apple Computer sued Microsoft Corporation and Hewlett-Packard Inc. for infringing Apple's copyright on the Macintosh interface. Among other claims, Apple claimed that the defendants copied the expression of overlapping windows. Apple failed to patent the idea of overlapping windows when it invented this method of presenting information on a computer screen in the late 1960s. The defendants counterclaimed that the idea of overlapping windows could only be expressed in a single way and, therefore, was not protectable under the "merger" doctrine of copyright law. When ideas and their expression merge (i.e., if there is only one way to express an idea), the expression cannot be copyrighted, although the method of producing the expression might be patentable (*Apple v. Microsoft*, 1989). In general, courts appear to be following the reasoning of a 1992 case—*Brown Bag Software vs. Symantec Corp.*—in which the court dissected the elements of software alleged to be infringing. There, the Federal Circuit Court of Appeals found that neither similar concept, function, general functional features (e.g., drop-down menus), nor colors were protectable by copyright law (*Brown Bag vs. Symantec Corp.*, 1992).

Fair Use Doctrine

Copyrights, like all rights, are not absolute. There are situations where strict copyright observance could be harmful to society, potentially inhibiting other rights such as the right to freedom of expression and thought. As a result, the doctrine of fair use has been created. The **doctrine of fair use** permits teachers and writers to use copyrighted materials without permission under certain circumstances. **Table 8.9** describes the five factors that courts consider when assessing what constitutes fair use.

The fair use doctrine draws upon the First Amendment's protection of freedom of speech (and writing). Journalists, writers, and academics must be able to refer to, and cite from, copyrighted works in order to criticize or even discuss copyrighted works. Professors are allowed to clip a contemporary article just before class, copy it, and hand it out to students as an example of a topic under discussion. However, they are not permitted to add this article to the class syllabus for the next semester without compensating the copyright holder.

What constitutes fair use has been at issue in a number of recent cases, including the Google Book Search Project described in the case study at the end of the chapter, and in several recent lawsuits. In *Kelly v. ArribaSoft* (2003) and *Perfect 10, Inc. v. Amazon.com, Inc.* (2007), the Federal Circuit Court of Appeals for the 10th Circuit held that the display of thumbnail images in response to search requests constituted fair use. A similar result was reached by the district court for the District of Nevada with respect to Google's storage and display of Web sites from cache memory, in *Field v. Google, Inc.* (2006). In all of these cases, the courts accepted the argument that caching the material and displaying it in response to a search request was not only a public benefit, but also a form of marketing of the material on behalf of its copyright owner, thereby enhancing the material's commercial value. Fair use is also at issue in the lawsuit filed by Viacom against Google and YouTube in March 2007, described further in the next section.

doctrine of fair use

under certain circumstances, permits use of copyrighted material without permission

TABLE 8.9	FAIR USE CONSIDERATIONS TO COPYRIGHT PROTECTIONS
FAIR USE FACTOR	**INTERPRETATION**
Character of use	Nonprofit or educational use versus for-profit use.
Nature of the work	Creative works such as plays or novels receive greater protection than factual accounts, e.g., newspaper accounts.
Amount of work used	A stanza from a poem or a single page from a book would be allowed, but not the entire poem or a book chapter.
Market effect of use	Will the use harm the marketability of the original product? Has it already harmed the product in the marketplace?
Context of use	A last-minute, unplanned use in a classroom versus a planned infringement.

The Digital Millennium Copyright Act of 1998

The Digital Millennium Copyright Act (DMCA) of 1998 is the first major effort to adjust the copyright laws to the Internet age. This legislation was the result of a confrontation between the major copyright holders in the United States (publishing, sheet music, record label, and commercial film industries), ISPs, and users of copyrighted materials such as libraries, universities, and consumers. While social and political institutions are sometimes thought of as "slow" and the Internet as "fast," in this instance, powerful groups of copyright owners anticipated Web music services such as Napster by several years. Napster was formed in 1999, but work by the World Intellectual Property Organization (WIPO)—a worldwide body formed by the major copyright-holding nations of North America, Europe, and Japan—began in 1995. **Table 8.10** summarizes the major provisions of the DMCA.

> **Digital Millennium Copyright Act (DMCA)**
> the first major effort to adjust the copyright laws to the Internet age

The penalties for willfully violating the DMCA include restitution to the injured parties of any losses due to infringement. Criminal remedies are available to federal prosecutors that include fines up to $500,000 or five years imprisonment for a first offense, and up to $1 million in fines and 10 years in prison for repeat offenders. These are serious remedies.

The DMCA attempts to answer two vexing questions in the Internet age. First, how can society protect copyrights online when any practical encryption scheme imaginable can be broken by hackers and the results distributed worldwide? Second, how can society control the behavior of thousands of ISPs, who often host infringing Web sites, or who provide Internet service to individuals who are routine infringers? ISPs claim to be like telephone utilities—just carrying messages—and they do not

TABLE 8.10	THE DIGITAL MILLENNIUM COPYRIGHT ACT
SECTION	**IMPORTANCE**
Title I, WIPO Copyright and Performances and Phonograms Treaties Implementation	Makes it illegal to circumvent technological measures to protect works for either access or copying or to circumvent any electronic rights management information.
Title II, Online Copyright Infringement Liability Limitation	Requires ISPs to "take down" sites they host if they are infringing copyrights, and requires search engines to block access to infringing sites. Limits liability of ISPs and search engines.
Title III, Computer Maintenance Competition Assurance	Permits users to make a copy of a computer program for maintenance or repair of the computer.
Title IV, Miscellaneous Provisions	Requires the copyright office to report to Congress on the use of copyright materials for distance education; allows libraries to make digital copies of works for internal use only; extends musical copyrights to include "webcasting."

SOURCE: Based on data from United States Copyright Office, 1998.

want to put their users under surveillance or invade the privacy of users. The DMCA recognizes that ISPs have some control over how their customers use their facilities.

The DMCA implements the WIPO Copyright treaty of 1996, which declares it illegal to make, distribute, or use devices that circumvent technology-based protections of copyrighted materials, and attaches stiff fines and prison sentences for violations. WIPO is an organization within the United Nations. Recognizing that these provisions alone cannot stop hackers from devising circumventions, the DMCA makes it difficult for such inventors to reap the fruits of their labors by making the ISPs (including universities) responsible and accountable for hosting Web sites or providing services to infringers once the ISP has been notified. ISPs are not required to intrude on their users. However, when copyright holders inform the ISP that a hosted site or individual users are infringing, they must "take down" the site immediately to avoid liability and potential fines. ISPs must also inform their subscribers of the ISP's copyright management policies. Copyright owners can subpoena the personal identities of any infringers using an ISP. There are important limitations on these ISP prohibitions that are mostly concerned with the transitory caching of materials for short periods without the knowledge of the ISP. However, should the ISP be deriving revenues from the infringement, it is as liable as the infringer, and is subject to the same penalties.

Title I of the DMCA provides a partial answer to the dilemma of hacking. It is probably true that skilled hackers can easily break any usable encryption scheme, and the means to do so on a large scale through distribution of decryption programs already exists. The WIPO provisions accept this possibility and simply make it illegal to do so, or to disseminate or to enable such dissemination, or even store and transmit decrypted products or tools. These provisions put large ISPs on legal notice.

There are a number of exceptions to the strong prohibitions against defeating a copyright protection scheme outlined above. There are exceptions for libraries to examine works for adoption, for reverse engineering to achieve interoperability with other software, for encryption research, for privacy protection purposes, and for security testing. Many companies, such as YouTube, Google, and MySpace have latched on to the provision of the DMCA that relates to removing infringing material upon request of the copyright owner as a "safe harbor" that precludes them from being held responsible for copyright infringement. This position is currently being tested in a $1 billion lawsuit brought by Viacom against Google and YouTube for willful copyright infringement.

In the Viacom case, Viacom alleges that YouTube and Google engaged in massive copyright infringement by deliberately building up a library of infringing works to draw traffic to the YouTube site and enhance its commercial value. In response, Google and YouTube claim that they are protected by the DMCA's safe harbor and fair use, and that it is often impossible to know whether a video is infringing or not. YouTube also does not display ads on pages where consumers can view videos unless it has an agreement with the content owner. In October 2007, Google announced a filtering system aimed at addressing the problem. It requires content owners to give Google a copy of their content so Google can load it into an auto-identification system. The copyright owner can specify whether it will allow others to post the material. Then after a video is uploaded to YouTube, the system attempts to match it with its database of copyrighted material, and removes any unauthorized material. Whether content owners will be satisfied with this system is unknown, particularly since guidelines issued by a coalition of major media and Internet companies with respect to the handling of copyrighted videos on user-generated Web sites calls for the use of filtering technology that can block infringing material before it is posted online. As of September 2009, the case remained mired in the discovery process.

The disturbing truth facing YouTube and its owner Google, is that amateur videos attract few viewers, and cannot be easily monetized because advertisers are loath to have their products displayed against cats-on-skateboard amateur videos. And the only videos that routinely draw huge audiences on YouTube are copyrighted music videos, Hollywood trailers, and parts of feature movies. These videos can indeed be monetized. As a result, YouTube has dramatically changed its attitude towards copyright owners and the concept of copyright. Whereas in the initial years YouTube encouraged users to post whatever videos they wanted, since 2008, YouTube has begun to work closely with content owners to either take down copyrighted material, or to place ads next to the material and share the revenues with the owners. Hollywood and New York production studios have changed their attitudes towards YouTube as well from that of an adversary, to that of a new, lucrative distribution network.

PATENTS: BUSINESS METHODS AND PROCESSES

"Whoever invents or discovers any new and useful process, machine, manufacture, or composition of matter, or any new and useful improvement thereof, may obtain a patent therefore, subject to the conditions and requirements of this title."

—Section 101, U.S. Patent Act

A **patent** grants the owner a 20-year exclusive monopoly on the ideas behind an invention. The congressional intent behind patent law was to ensure that inventors of new machines, devices, or industrial methods would receive the full financial and other rewards of their labor and still make widespread use of the invention possible by providing detailed diagrams for those wishing to use the idea under license from the patent's owner. Patents are obtained from the United States Patent and Trademark Office (USPTO), created in 1812. Obtaining a patent is much more difficult and time-consuming than obtaining copyright protection (which is automatic with the creation of the work). Patents must be formally applied for, and the granting of a patent is determined by Patent Office examiners who follow a set of rigorous rules. Ultimately, federal courts decide when patents are valid and when infringement occurs.

patent
grants the owner an exclusive monopoly on the ideas behind an invention for 20 years

Patents are very different from copyrights because patents protect the ideas themselves and not merely the expression of ideas. There are four types of inventions for which patents are granted under patent law: machines, man-made products, compositions of matter, and processing methods. The Supreme Court has determined that patents extend to "anything under the sun that is made by man" (*Diamond v. Chakrabarty*, 1980) as long as the other requirements of the Patent Act are met. There are three things that cannot be patented: laws of nature, natural phenomena, and abstract ideas. For instance, a mathematical algorithm cannot be patented unless it is realized in a tangible machine or process that has a "useful" result (the mathematical algorithm exception).

In order to be granted a patent, the applicant must show that the invention is new, original, novel, nonobvious, and not evident in prior arts and practice. As with copyrights, the granting of patents has moved far beyond the original intent of Congress's first patent statute that sought to protect industrial designs and machines. Patent protection has been extended to articles of manufacture (1842), plants (1930), surgical and medical procedures (1950), and software (1981). The Patent Office did not accept applications for software patents until a 1981 Supreme Court decision that held that computer programs could be a part of a patentable process. Since that time, thousands of software patents have been granted. Virtually any software program can be patented as long as it is novel and not obvious.

Essentially, as technology and industrial arts progress, patents have been extended to both encourage entrepreneurs to invent useful devices and promote widespread dissemination of the new techniques through licensing and artful imitation of the published patents (the creation of devices that provide the same functionality as the invention but use different methods) (Winston, 1998). Patents encourage inventors to come up with unique ways of achieving the same functionality as existing patents. For instance, Amazon's patent on one-click purchasing caused Barnesandnoble.com to invent a simplified two-click method of purchasing.

The danger of patents is that they stifle competition by raising barriers to entry into an industry. Patents force new entrants to pay licensing fees to incumbents, and thus slow down the development of technical applications of new ideas by creating lengthy licensing applications and delays.

E-commerce Patents

Much of the Internet's infrastructure and software was developed under the auspices of publicly funded scientific and military programs in the United States and Europe. Unlike Samuel F. B. Morse, who patented the idea of Morse code and made the telegraph useful, most of the inventions that make the Internet and e-commerce possible were not patented by their inventors. The early Internet was characterized by a spirit of worldwide community development and sharing of ideas without consideration of personal wealth (Winston, 1998). This early Internet spirit changed in the mid-1990s with the commercial development of the World Wide Web.

In 1998, a landmark legal decision, *State Street Bank & Trust v. Signature Financial Group, Inc.*, paved the way for business firms to begin applying for "business methods" patents. In this case, a Federal Circuit Court of Appeals upheld the claims of Signature Financial to a valid patent for a business method that allows managers to monitor and record financial information flows generated by a partner fund. Previously, it was thought business methods could not be patented. However, the court ruled there was no reason to disallow business methods from patent protection, or any "step by step process, be it electronic or chemical or mechanical, [that] involves an algorithm in the broad sense of the term" (*State Street Bank & Trust Co. v. Signature Financial Group*, 1998). The State Street decision led to an explosion in applications for e-commerce "business methods" patents, with over 13,000 in 2008 (see **Figure 8.3**). Note that the

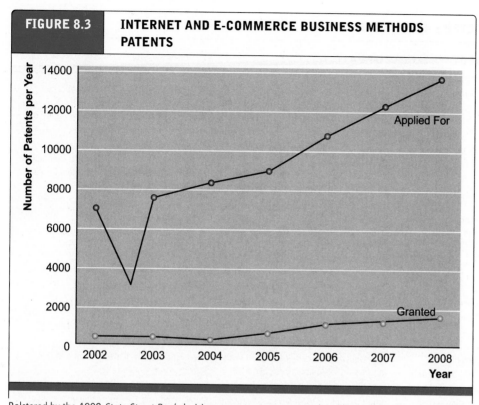

FIGURE 8.3 | **INTERNET AND E-COMMERCE BUSINESS METHODS PATENTS**

Bolstered by the 1998 *State Street Bank* decision, patents on computer-related business methods increased exponentially from 1998 when 1,337 applications were filed, to 2001, when 9,288 applications were submitted. During the period 2002–2005, applications dropped off somewhat and remained relatively steady at around 7,500–8,500 per year, but in 2006, they increased significantly again, to over 10,000 applications. SOURCE: Based on data from U.S. Patent and Trademark Office, 2009.

overall number of patent applications filed has also increased dramatically, from about 237,000 in 1995 to over 485,000 in 2008.

Table 8.11 lists some of the better-known, controversial e-commerce patents. Reviewing these, you can understand the concerns of commentators and corporations. Some of the patent claims are very broad (for example, "name your price" sales methods), have historical precedents in the pre-Internet era (shopping carts), and seem "obvious" (one-click purchasing). Critics of online business methods patents argue that the Patent Office has been too lenient in granting such patents and that in most instances, the supposed inventions merely copy pre-Internet business methods and thus do not constitute "inventions" (Harmon, 2003; Thurm, 2000; Chiappetta, 2001). The Patent Office argues, on the contrary, that its Internet inventions staff is composed of engineers, lawyers, and specialists with many years of experience with Internet and network technologies, and that it consults with outside technology experts before granting patents. To complicate matters, the European Patent Convention and the patent laws of most European countries do not recognize

TABLE 8.11	SELECTED E-COMMERCE PATENTS	
COMPANY	**SUBJECT**	**UPDATE**
Leon Stambler	Secure communications	Private inventor with seven patents (1992–1998) covering creation of an authentication code to be used in electronic communications. In 2003, a Delaware jury found that RSA Security and VeriSign did not infringe on the patents. Stambler's appeal to the U.S. Court of Appeals for the Federal Circuit was rejected in February 2005.
Amazon	One-click purchasing	Amazon attempted to use patent originally granted to it in 1999 to force changes to Barnes & Noble's Web site, but a federal court overturned a previously issued injunction. Eventually settled out of court. In September 2007, a USPTO panel rejected most of the patent because of evidence another patent predated it, sending it back to the patent examiner for reconsideration.
Eolas Technologies	Embedding interactive content in a Web site	Eolas Technologies, a spin-off of the University of California, obtained patent in 1998. Eolas filed suit against Microsoft in 1999 for infringing the patent in Internet Explorer and was awarded a $520 million judgment in 2003. Decision was partially reversed in 2005, and sent back to district court for a new trial. The patent was reaffirmed in September 2005 by the USPTO. In August 2007, Eolas and Microsoft finally settled the suit on undisclosed terms.
Priceline	Buyer-driven "name your price" sales	Originally invented by Walker Digital, an intellectual property laboratory, and then assigned to Priceline. Granted by the USPTO in 1999. Shortly thereafter, Priceline sued Microsoft and Expedia for copying its patented business method. Expedia settled and agreed to pay a royalty in 2001.
Sightsound	Music downloads	Sightsound won a settlement in 2004 against Bertelsmann subsidiaries CDNow and N2K music sites for infringing its patent.
Akamai	Internet content delivery global hosting system	A broad patent granted in 2000 covering techniques for expediting the flow of information over the Internet. Akamai sued Digital Island (subsequently acquired by Cable & Wireless) for violating the patent and, in 2001, a jury found in its favor. In 2004, Akamai accepted a damages payment to finally settle the suit.
DoubleClick	Dynamic delivery of online advertising	The patent underlying DoubleClick's business of online banner ad delivery, originally granted in 2000. DoubleClick sued competitors 24/7 Real Media and L90 for violating the patent and ultimately reached a settlement with them.
Overture	Pay for performance search	System and method for influencing position on search result list generated by computer search engine, granted in 2001. Competitor FindWhat.com sued Overture, charging that patent was obtained illegally; Overture countered by suing both FindWhat and Google for violating patent. Google agreed to pay a license fee to Overture in 2004 to settle the suit, and the lawsuit with FindWhat resulted in a hung jury in 2005, with both sides claiming victory.
Acacia Technologies	Streaming video media transmission	Patents for the receipt and transmission of streaming digital audio and or video content originally granted to founders of Greenwich Information Technologies in 1990s. Patents were purchased by Acacia, a firm founded solely to enforce the patents, in 2001. Acacia has subsequently secured dozens of licenses.
Soverain Software	Purchase technology	The so-called "shopping cart" patent for network-based systems, which involves any transaction over a network involving a seller, buyer, and payment system. In other words, e-commerce! Originally owned by Open Markets, then Divine Inc., and now Soverain. Soverain filed suit against Amazon for patent infringement in 2004; Amazon settled for $40 million in August 2005.
MercExchange (Thomas Woolston)	Auction technology	Patents on person-to-person auctions and database search, originally granted in 1995. eBay ordered to pay $25 million in 2003 for infringing on patent. In July 2007, the U.S. district court denied a motion for permanent patent injunction against eBay using the "Buy It Now" feature, and moved to the final stages of allowing the damages award to be paid. Issues related to a second patent were deferred pending a USPTO office reexamination.
Google	Search technology	Google PageRank patent was filed in 1998 and granted in 2001.

business methods per se unless the method is implemented through some technology (Takenaka, 2001).

Patent Reform

Issues related to business method patents, patent "trolls" (companies such as Acacia Technologies that buy up broadly-worded patents on a speculative basis and then use them to threaten companies that are purportedly violating the patent), and confusing legal decisions have led to increasing calls for patent reform over the last few years, particularly by companies in the technology sector. One target of such legislation are firms that produce nothing but simply collect patents and then seek to enforce them. In 2000, Nathan Myhrvold formed a new kind of patent investment firm called Intellectual Ventures. A former Microsoft Chief Technology Officer, Myhrvold has amassed a collection of over 20,000 patents in the digital technology field, including e-commerce by purchasing them from small companies and entrepreneurs. He discovers large firms that are violating those patents and threatens to sue. Sony, Verizon, Google, Verizon, and many other large firms pay up, and in addition, invest in the company so they can participate in future revenues (Sharma and Clark, 2008).

In September 2007, the House of Representatives passed its version of a patent reform bill that includes provisions that change the patent system from a "first to invent" system to a "first to file" system, change the way damages for patent infringement are calculated, provide a new way to challenge patents out of court, limit where patent suits can be filed (to prevent suits from being filed in districts that have a reputation for being more favorable), and impose heightened standards for a finding of willful infringement. The Senate Judiciary Committee voted in April 2009 to send the bill to the full Senate, and as of September 2009 it remained under consideration.

TRADEMARKS: ONLINE INFRINGEMENT AND DILUTION

> Trademark is "any word, name, symbol, or device, or any combination thereof ... used in commerce ... to identify and distinguish ... goods . . . from those manufactured or sold by others and to indicate the source of the goods."
>
> —The Trademark Act, 1946

Trademark law is a form of intellectual property protection for **trademarks**—a mark used to identify and distinguish goods and indicate their source. Trademark protections exist at both the federal and state levels in the United States. The purpose of trademark law is twofold. First, the trademark law protects the public in the marketplace by ensuring that it gets what it pays for and wants to receive. Second, trademark law protects the owner—who has spent time, money, and energy bringing the product to the marketplace—against piracy and misappropriation. Trademarks have been extended from single words to pictures, shapes, packaging, and colors. Some things may not be trademarked: common words that are merely descriptive ("clock"), flags of states and nations, immoral or deceptive marks, or marks belonging to others. Federal trademarks are obtained, first, by use in interstate commerce, and

trademark
a mark used to identify and distinguish goods and indicate their source

second, by registration with the USPTO. Trademarks are granted for a period of 10 years, and can be renewed indefinitely.

Disputes over federal trademarks involve establishing infringement. The test for infringement is twofold: market confusion and bad faith. Use of a trademark that creates confusion with existing trademarks causes consumers to make market mistakes, or misrepresents the origins of goods is an infringement. In addition, the intentional misuse of words and symbols in the marketplace to extort revenue from legitimate trademark owners ("bad faith") is proscribed.

In 1995, Congress passed the Federal Trademark Dilution Act, which created a federal cause of action for dilution of famous marks. This legislation dispenses with the test of market confusion (although that is still required to claim infringement), and extends protection to owners of famous trademarks against **dilution**, which is defined as any behavior that would weaken the connection between the trademark and the product. Dilution occurs through blurring (weakening the connection between the trademark and the goods) and tarnishment (using the trademark in a way that makes the underlying products appear unsavory or unwholesome).

dilution

any behavior that would weaken the connection between the trademark and the product

Trademarks and the Internet

The rapid growth and commercialization of the Internet have provided unusual opportunities for existing firms with distinctive and famous trademarks to extend their brands to the Internet. These same developments have provided malicious individuals and firms the opportunity to squat on Internet domain names built upon famous marks, as well as attempt to confuse consumers and dilute famous or distinctive marks (including your personal name or a movie star's name). The conflict between legitimate trademark owners and malicious firms was allowed to fester and grow because Network Solutions Inc. (NSI), originally the Internet's sole agency for domain name registration for many years, had a policy of "first come, first served." This meant anyone could register any domain name that had not already been registered, regardless of the trademark status of the domain name. NSI was not authorized to decide trademark issues (Nash, 1997).

Anticybersquatting Consumer Protection Act (ACPA)

creates civil liabilities for anyone who attempts in bad faith to profit from an existing famous or distinctive trademark by registering an Internet domain name that is identical, or confusingly similar, or "dilutive" of that trademark

cybersquatting

involves the registration of an infringing domain name, or other Internet use of an existing trademark, for the purpose of extorting payments from the legitimate owners

In response to a growing number of complaints from owners of famous trademarks who found their trademark names being appropriated by Web entrepreneurs, Congress passed the **Anticybersquatting Consumer Protection Act (ACPA)** in November 1999. The ACPA creates civil liabilities for anyone who attempts in bad faith to profit from an existing famous or distinctive trademark by registering an Internet domain name that is identical, confusingly similar, or "dilutive" of that trademark. The act does not establish criminal sanctions. The act proscribes using "bad-faith" domain names to extort money from the owners of the existing trademark (**cybersquatting**), or using the bad-faith domain to divert Web traffic to the bad-faith domain that could harm the good will represented by the trademark, create market confusion, tarnish, or disparage the mark (**cyberpiracy**). The Act also proscribes the use of a domain name that consists of the name of a living person, or a name confusingly similar to an existing personal name, without that

cyberpiracy

involves the same behavior as cybersquatting, but with the intent of diverting traffic from the legitimate site to an infringing site

TABLE 8.12	INTERNET AND TRADEMARK LAW EXAMPLES	
ACTIVITY	**DESCRIPTION**	**EXAMPLE CASE**
Cybersquatting	Registering domain names similar or identical to trademarks of others to extort profits from legitimate holders.	*E. & J. Gallo Winery v. Spider Webs Ltd.*, 129 F. Supp. 2d 1033 (S.D. Tex., 2001) aff'd 286 F. 3d 270 (5th Cir.,2002)
Cyberpiracy	Registering domain names similar or identical to trademarks of others to divert Web traffic to their own sites.	*Ford Motor Co. v. Lapertosa*, 2001 U.S. Dist. LEXIS 253 (E.D. Mich., 2001); *PaineWebber Inc. v. Fortuny*, Civ. A. No. 99-0456-A (E.D. Va., 1999); *Playboy Enterprises, Inc. v. Global Site Designs, Inc.*, 1999 WL 311707 (S.D. Fla., 1999), *Audi AG and Volkswagen of America Inc. v. Bob D'Amato* (No. 05-2359; 6th Cir., November 27, 2006).
Metatagging	Using trademark words in a site's metatags.	*Bernina of America, Inc. v. Fashion Fabrics Int'l, Inc.*, 2001 U.S. Dist. LEXIS 1211 (N.D. Ill., 2001); *Nissan Motor Co., Ltd. v. Nissan Computer Corp.*, 289 F. Supp. 2d 1154 (C.D. Cal., 2000), aff'd, 246 F. 3rd 675 (9th Cir., 2000).
Keywords	Placing trademarked keywords on Web pages, either visible or invisible.	*Playboy Enterprises, Inc. v. Netscape Communications, Inc.*, 354 F. 3rd 1020 (9th Cir., 2004); *Nettis Environment Ltd. v. IWI, Inc.*, 46 F. Supp. 2d 722 (N.D. Ohio, 1999); *Government Employees Insurance Company v. Google, Inc.*, Civ. Action No. 1:04cv507 (E.D. VA, 2004); *Google, Inc. v. American Blind & Wallpaper Factory, Inc.*, Case No. 03-5340 JF (RS) (N.D. Cal., April 18, 2007)
Linking	Linking to content pages on other sites, bypassing the home page.	*Ticketmaster Corp. v. Tickets.com*, 2000 U.S. Dist. Lexis 4553 (C.D. Cal., 2000)
Framing	Placing the content of other sites in a frame on the infringer's site.	*The Washington Post, et al. v. TotalNews, Inc., et al.*, (S.D.N.Y., Civil Action Number 97-1190)

person's consent, if the registrant is registering the name with the intent to profit by selling the domain dame to that person. In addition, there are five arbitration panels established to hear trademark disputes: WIPO, ICANN, the National Arbitration Forum (Minneapolis), eResolutions Consortium (Amherst, Massachusetts), and C.P.R. Institute for Dispute Resolutions in New York.

Trademark abuse can take many forms on the Web. **Table 8.12** lists the major behaviors on the Internet that have run afoul of trademark law, and the some of the court cases that resulted.

Cybersquatting

In one of the first cases involving the ACPA, E. & J. Gallo Winery, owner of the registered mark "Ernest and Julio Gallo" for alcoholic beverages, sued Spider Webs Ltd. for using the domain name Ernestandjuliogallo.com. Spider Webs Ltd. was a domain name speculator that owned numerous domain names consisting of famous company names. The Ernestandjuliogallo.com Web site contained information on the risks of alcohol use, anti-corporate articles about E. & J. Gallo Winery, and was poorly constructed. The court concluded that Spider Webs Ltd. was in violation of the ACPA and that its actions constituted dilution by blurring because the Ernestandjuliogallo.com domain name appeared on every page printed off the Web site accessed by that name, and that Spider Webs Ltd. was not free to use this particular mark as a domain name (*E. & J. Gallo Winery v. Spider Webs Ltd.*, 2001). In 2008, incidents of cybersquatting increased by 18%, according to MarkMonitor's Brandjacking Index, with a total of over 440,000 instances identified in the 4th quarter of 2008 alone! (MarkMonitor, 2009). In August 2009, a court upheld the largest cybersquatting judgment to date: a $33 million verdict in favor of Verizon against OnlineNIC, an Internet domain registration company that had used over 660 names that could easily be confused with legitimate Verizon domain names.

Cyberpiracy

Cyberpiracy involves the same behavior as cybersquatting, but with the intent of diverting traffic from the legitimate site to an infringing site. In *Ford Motor Co. v. Lapertosa*, Lapertosa had registered and used a Web site called Fordrecalls.com as an adult entertainment Web site. The court ruled that Fordrecalls.com was in violation of the ACPA in that it was a bad-faith attempt to divert traffic to the Lapertosa site and diluted Ford's wholesome trademark (*Ford Motor Co. v. Lapertosa*, 2001).

The Ford decision reflects two other famous cases of cyberpiracy. In the *Paine Webber Inc. v. Fortuny* case, the court enjoined Fortuny from using the domain name Wwwpainewebber.com—a site that specialized in pornographic materials—because it diluted and tarnished Paine Webber's trademark and diverted Web traffic from Paine Webber's legitimate site—Painewebber.com (*Paine Webber Inc. v. Fortuny*, 1999). In the *Playboy Enterprises, Inc. v. Global Site Designs, Inc.* case, the court enjoined the defendants from using the Playboy and Playmate marks in their domain names Playboyonline.net and Playmatesearch.net and from including the Playboy trademark in their metatags. In these cases, the defendants' intention was diversion for financial gain (*Playboy Enterprises, Inc. v. Global Site Designs, Inc.*, 1999).

In a more recent case, *Audi AG and Volkswagen of America Inc. v. Bob D'Amato*, the Federal Circuit Court of Appeals for the Sixth Circuit affirmed the district court's ruling that the defendant Bob D'Amato infringed and diluted the plaintiffs' Audi, Quattro, and Audi Four Rings logo marks, and violated the ACPA by operating the Audisport.com Web site (*Audi AG and Volkswagen of America Inc. v. Bob D'Amato*, 2006).

Typosquatting is a form of cyberpiracy in which a domain name contains a common misspelling of another site's name. Often the user ends up at a site very different from one they intended to visit. For instance, John Zuccarini is an infamous typosquatter who was jailed in 2002 for setting up pornographic Web sites with URLs based on misspellings of popular children's brands, such as Bob the Builder and Teletubbies. The FTC fined him again in October 2007 for engaging in similar practices (McMillan, 2007).

Metatagging

The legal status of using famous or distinctive marks as metatags is more complex and subtle. The use of trademarks in metatags is permitted if the use does not mislead or confuse consumers. Usually this depends on the content of the site. A car dealer would be permitted to use a famous automobile trademark in its metatags if the dealer sold this brand of automobiles, but a pornography site could not use the same trademark, nor a dealer for a rival manufacturer. A Ford dealer would most likely be infringing if it used "Honda" in its metatags, but would not be infringing if it used "Ford" in its metatags. (Ford Motor Company would be unlikely to seek an injunction against one of its dealers.)

In the *Bernina of America, Inc. v. Fashion Fabrics Int'l, Inc.* case, the court enjoined Fashion Fabrics, an independent dealer of sewing machines, from using the trademarks "Bernina" and "Bernette," which belonged to the manufacturer Bernina, as metatags. The court found the defendant's site contained misleading claims about Fashion Fabrics' knowledge of Bernina products that were likely to confuse customers. The use of the Bernina trademarks as metatags per se was not a violation of ACPA, according to the court, but in combination with the misleading claims on the site would cause confusion and hence infringement (*Bernina of America, Inc. v. Fashion Fabrics Int'l, Inc.*, 2001).

In the *Nissan Motor Co. Ltd. v. Nissan Computer Corp.* case, Uzi Nissan had used his surname "Nissan" as a trade name for various businesses since 1980, including Nissan Computer Corp. He registered Nissan.com in 1994 and Nissan.net in 1996. Nissan.com had no relationship with Nissan Motor, but over the years began selling auto parts that competed with Nissan Motor. Nissan Motor Company objected to the use of the domain name Nissan.com and the use of "Nissan" in the metatags for both sites on grounds it would confuse customers and infringe on Nissan Motor's trademarks. Uzi Nissan offered to sell his sites to Nissan Motor for several million dollars. Nissan Motor refused. The court ruled that Nissan Computer's behavior did indeed infringe on Nissan Motor's trademarks, but it refused to shut the site down. Instead, the court ruled Nissan Computer could continue to use the Nissan name, and metatags, but must post notices on its site that it was not affiliated with Nissan Motor (*Nissan Motor Co. Ltd. v. Nissan Computer Corp.*, 2000). In November 2002, a U.S. district court issued a permanent injunction, allowing Mr. Nissan to keep the domains, but restricting the commercial, advertising, and anti-Nissan Motor content that could be placed on the Web sites. Mr. Nissan appealed, and in August 2004, the Ninth Circuit Court of Appeals found that while Nissan Computer in fact capitalized on Nissan Motors' goodwill in the Nissan trademark to the extent that use of the mark for automobiles captured the attention of customers interested in Nissan cars, Nissan Motor could not gain protection against any resultant dilution of the trademark because Nissan Computer had made its first commercial use of the mark over five years before Nissan Motor's mark became famous in the United States. In addition, requiring that the Web site not contain links to anti-Nissan Web sites was inconsistent with free speech rights. The court of appeals therefore reversed the previous ruling, ordering Mr. Nissan to refrain only from showing car-related ads, and remanded the case back to the district court for consideration as to whether the injunction should be broadened to include the transfer of the domains. In April 2005, the U.S. Supreme Court turned down an appeal made by Nissan Motor.

Keywording

The permissibility of using trademarks as keywords on search engines is also subtle and depends on the extent to which such use is considered to be a "use in commerce," causes "initial customer confusion" and on the content of the search results.

In *Playboy Enterprises, Inc. v. Netscape Communications, Inc.*, Playboy objected to the practice of Netscape's and Excite's search engines displaying banner ads unrelated to Playboy Magazine when users entered search arguments such as "playboy," "playmate," and "playgirl." The Ninth Circuit Court of Appeals denied the defendant's motion for a summary judgment and held that when an advertiser's banner ad is not labeled so as to identify its source, the practice could result in trademark infringement due to consumer confusion (*Playboy Enterprises, Inc. v. Netscape Communications, Inc.*, 2004).

In the *Nettis Environment Ltd. v. IWI, Inc.* case, Nettis and IWI Inc. were competitors in the ventilation business. IWI had registered the trademarks "nettis" and "nettis environmental" on over 400 search engines, and in addition, used these marks as metatags on its site. The court required IWI to remove the metatags and de-register the keywords with all search engines because consumers would be con fused—searching for Nettis products would lead them to an IWI Web site (*Nettis Environment Ltd. v. IWI, Inc.*, 1999).

Google has also faced lawsuits alleging that its advertising network illegally exploits others' trademarks. For instance, insurance company GEICO challenged Google's practice of allowing competitors' ads to appear when a searcher types "Geico" as the search query. In December 2004, a U.S. district court ruled that this practice did not violate federal trademark laws as long as the word "Geico" was not used in the ads' text (*Government Employees Insurance Company v. Google, Inc.*, 2004). Google quickly discontinued allowing the latter, and settled the case (Associated Press, 2005). Google settled another similar lawsuit, *Google Inc. v American Blind & Wallpaper Factory, Inc.*, in August 2007, following a court ruling in April that Google's display of competitor's ads as part of Google's AdWords program was a use of those marks in commerce, and allowing American Blind to proceed with trademark infringement claims arising from the use of those marks, finding that American Blind had presented sufficient evidence of consumer confusion to survive Google's motion for summary judgment on the matter. However, these settlements have not prevented other companies from also suing Google. For instance, in July 2009, Rosetta Stone, the language-learning software firm, filed a lawsuit against Google for trademark infringement, alleging its AdWords program allowed other companies to use Rosetta Stone's trademarks for online advertisements without permission. The suit is one of nine similar lawsuits against Google instituted since May 2009, when Google expanded to more than 190 new countries its policy of allowing anyone to buy someone else's trademark as a trigger for ads. Google also announced in May 2009 that it would allow the limited use of other companies' trademarks in the text of some search ads, even if the trademark owner objects. Thus far, although Google has lost some trademark cases in Europe, no definitive ruling against it has been issued in the United States.

The state of Utah attempted to pre-empt the issue and passed a controversial Trademark Protection Act in March 2007 that banned advertisers from using the trademarked terms of their competitors to target ads to Utah users. The statute also established an "electronic registration mark" protecting trademark owners that file marks with a registry the state intends to create. Not surprisingly, the statute was severely criticized by search providers such as Google, AOL, Yahoo, and Microsoft, aand in 2008, Utah quietly amended the act to repeal many of the provisions that search providers found objectionable.

Linking

Linking refers to building hypertext links from one site to another site. This is obviously a major design feature and benefit of the Web. **Deep linking** involves bypassing the target site's home page and going directly to a content page. In *Ticketmaster Corp. v. Tickets.com*, Tickets.com—owned by Microsoft—competed directly against Ticketmaster in the events ticket market. When Tickets.com did not have tickets for an event, it would direct users to Ticketmaster's internal pages, bypassing the Ticketmaster home page. Even though its logo was displayed on the internal pages, Ticketmaster objected on the grounds that such "deep linking" violated the terms and conditions of use for its site (stated on a separate page altogether and construed by Ticketmaster as equivalent to a shrink-wrap license), and constituted false advertising, as well as the violation of copyright. The court found, however, that deep linking per se is not illegal, no violation of copyright occurred because no copies were made, the terms and conditions of use were not obvious to users, and users were not required to read the page on which the terms and conditions of use appeared in any event. The court refused to rule in favor of Ticketmaster, but left open further argument on the licensing issue. In an out-of-court settlement, Tickets.com nevertheless agreed to stop the practice of deep linking (*Ticketmaster v. Tickets.com*, 2000).

Framing

Framing involves displaying the content of another Web site inside your own Web site within a frame or window. The user never leaves the framer's site and can be exposed to advertising while the target site's advertising is distorted or eliminated. Framers may or may not acknowledge the source of the content. In *The Washington Post, et al. v. TotalNews, Inc. case*, *The Washington Post*, CNN, Reuters, and several other news organizations filed suit against TotalNews Inc., claiming that TotalNews's use of frames on its Web site, TotalNews.com, infringed upon the respective plaintiffs' copyrights and trademarks, and diluted the content of their individual Web sites. The plaintiffs claimed additionally that TotalNews's framing practice effectively deprived the plaintiffs' Web sites of advertising revenue.

TotalNews's Web site employed four frames. The TotalNews logo appeared in the lower left frame, various links were located on a vertical frame on the left side of the screen, TotalNews's advertising was framed across the screen bottom, and the "news frame," the largest frame, appeared in the center and right. Clicking on a specific

linking
building hypertext links from one site to another site

deep linking
involves bypassing the target site's home page, and going directly to a content page

framing
involves displaying the content of another Web site inside your own Web site within a frame or window

news organization's link allowed the reader to view the content of that particular organization's Web site, including any related advertising, within the context of the "news frame." In some instances, the framing distorted or modified the appearance of the linked Web site, including the advertisements, while the appearance of Total-News's advertisements, in a separate frame, remained unchanged. In addition, the URL remained fixed on the TotalNews address, even though the content in the largest frame on the Web site was from the linked Web site. The "news frame" did not, however, eliminate the linked Web site's identifying features.

The case was settled out of court. The news organizations allowed TotalNews to link to their Web sites, but prohibited framing and any attempt to imply affiliation with the news organizations (*The Washington Post, et al. v. TotalNews, Inc.*, 1997).

CHALLENGE: BALANCING THE PROTECTION OF PROPERTY WITH OTHER VALUES

In the areas of copyright, patent law, and trademark law, societies have moved quickly to protect intellectual property from challenges posed by the Internet. In each of these areas, traditional concepts of intellectual property have not only been upheld, but often strengthened. The DMCA seems to restrict journalists and academics from even accessing copyrighted materials if they are encrypted, a protection not true of traditional documents (which are rarely encrypted anyway). Patents have been extended to Internet business methods, and trademarks are more strongly protected than ever because of fears of cybersquatting. In the early years of e-commerce, many commentators believed that Internet technology would sweep away the powers of corporations to protect their property (Dueker, 1996). The experience of the music industry in the past decade is a powerful example of how a new technology can disrupt an entrenched business model and an entire industry. The music industry has not hesitated to use the legal system and in many instances has been victorious. However, despite these legal victories, the software for file sharing itself is now widely distributed (BitTorrent, for instance, is in the public domain and can be used by anyone with a computer). Because shared music files can be split up across thousands of user computers on these networks, there is no one in charge, no corporate entity to sue. On the other hand, industry associations can identify and sue not only the operators of computing systems on the networks who act as primary repositories and distributors of stolen music, but also individuals.

For instance, in 2008 and 2009, the Recording Industry Association of America (RIAA) successfully pursued a number of civil suits against individuals storing even modest numbers of music tracks on their computers and making them available to others for downloading, as well as against universities who permit their servers to download stolen files. (By 2009, the RIAA had filed over 30,000 separate lawsuits.) In September 2008, the Federal Bureau of Investigation arrested a Los Angeles man on copyright-infringement charges for posting on his Web site nine songs from a yet-to-be-released album by the rock band Guns N' Roses. This is only the second criminal prosecution for piracy in U.S. history, but it may signal a growing belief among copyright owners that the reality of going to jail can stop illegal file sharing.

It is apparent that corporations have some very powerful legal tools for protecting their digital properties. The difficulty now may be in going too far to protect the property interests of the powerful and the rich, preventing parody sites or parody content from receiving wide distribution and recognition, and in this sense interfering with the exercise of First Amendment guarantees of freedom of expression.

8.4 GOVERNANCE

Governance has to do with social control: Who will control the Internet? Who will control the processes of e-commerce, the content, and the activities? What elements will be controlled, and how will the controls be implemented? A natural question arises and needs to be answered: Why do we as a society need to "control" e-commerce? Because e-commerce and the Internet are so closely intertwined (though not identical), controlling e-commerce also involves regulating the Internet.

governance
has to do with social control: who will control e-commerce, what elements will be controlled, and how the controls will be implemented

TABLE 8.13	THE EVOLUTION OF GOVERNANCE OF E-COMMERCE
INTERNET GOVERNANCE PERIOD	**DESCRIPTION**
Government Control 1970–1994	DARPA and the National Science Foundation control the Internet as a fully government-funded program.
Privatization 1995–1998	Network Solutions Inc. is given a monopoly to assign and track high-level Internet domains. Backbone is sold to private telecommunications companies. Policy issues are not decided.
Self-Regulation 1995–present	President Clinton and the Department of Commerce encourage the creation of a semiprivate body, the Internet Corporation for Assigning Numbers and Names (ICANN), to deal with emerging conflicts and establish policies. ICANN currently holds a contract with the Department of Congress to govern some aspects of the Internet.
Governmental Regulation 1998–present	Executive, legislative, and judicial bodies worldwide begin to implement direct controls over the Internet and e-commerce.

WHO GOVERNS E-COMMERCE AND THE INTERNET?

Governance of both the Internet and e-commerce has gone through four stages. **Table 8.13** summarizes these stages in the evolution of e-commerce governance.

Prior to 1995, the Internet was a government program. Beginning in 1995, private corporations were given control of the technical infrastructure as well as the process of granting IP addresses and domain names. However, the NSI monopoly created in this period did not represent international users of the Internet, and was unable to cope with emerging public policy issues such as trademark and intellectual property protection, fair policies for allocating domains, and growing concerns that a small group of firms were benefiting from growth in the Internet.

In 1995, President Clinton, using funds from the Department of Commerce, encouraged the establishment of an international body called the Internet Corporation for Assigned Names and Numbers (ICANN) that hopefully could better represent a wider range of countries and a broad range of interests, and begin to address emerging public policy issues. ICANN was intended to be an Internet/ e-commerce industry self-governing body, not another government agency.

The explosive growth of the Web and e-commerce created a number of issues over which ICANN had no authority. Content issues such as pornography, gambling, and offensive written expressions and graphics, along with commercial issue of intellectual property protection, ushered in the current era of growing governmental regulation of the Internet and e-commerce throughout the world. Currently, we are in a mixed-mode policy environment where self-regulation through a variety of Internet policy and technical bodies co-exists with limited government regulation.

Today, ICANN remains in charge of the domain name system that translates domain names (such as www.company.com) into IP addresses. It has subcontracted the work of maintaining the databases of the domain registries to several private corporations. The U.S. government controls the "A-root" server. However, these arrangements are increasingly challenged by other countries, including China, Russia, Saudi Arabia, and most of the European Union, all of whom want the United States to give up control over the Internet to an international body such as the International Telecommunication Union (ITU) (a UN agency). In November 2005, an Internet Summit sponsored by the ITU agreed to leave control over the Internet domain servers with the United States and instead called for an international forum to meet in future years to discuss Internet policy issues (Miller and Rhoads, 2005). For its part, the United States is currently loath to give up control over the Internet as originally envisaged by earlier presidents.

Can the Internet Be Controlled?

Early Internet advocates argued that the Internet was different from all previous technologies. They contended that the Internet could not be controlled, given its inherent decentralized design, its ability to cross borders, and its underlying packet switching technology that made monitoring and controlling message content impossible. Many still believe this to be true today. The slogans are "Information wants to be free," and "The Net is everywhere" (but not in any central location). The implication of these slogans is that the content and behavior of e-commerce sites—indeed Internet sites of any kind—cannot be "controlled" in the same way as traditional media such as radio and television. However, attitudes have changed as many governments and corporations extend their control over the Internet and the World Wide Web (Markoff, 2005).

In fact, the Internet is technically very easily controlled, monitored, and regulated from central locations (such as network access points, as well as servers and routers throughout the network). For instance, in China, Saudi Arabia, Iran, North Korea, Thailand, Singapore, and many other countries, access to the Web is controlled from government-owned centralized routers that direct traffic across their borders and within the country, such as China's "Great Firewall of China," which permits the government to block access to certain U.S. or European Web sites, or via tightly regulated ISPs operating within the countries. In China, for instance, all ISPs need a license from the Ministry of Information Industry (MII), and are prohibited from disseminating any information that may harm the state or permit pornography, gambling, or the advocacy of cults. In addition, ISPs and search engines such as Google, Yahoo, and MSN typically self-censor their Asian content by using only government-approved news sources. MySpace also self-censors content it believes might upset the Chinese government. Despite this, in October 2007, it was reported that China was redirecting traffic from search engines operated by Google, Microsoft, and Yahoo to Chinese-operated Baidu.com (Ho, 2007; Elgin and Einhorn, 2006). In the 2008 Olympics, China routinely censored access by Western media to common Internet sites, including BBC.com.

In some instances, the firms have also cooperated with the Chinese government's pursuit of bloggers and journalists as a condition of its continuing business in China. For instance, Yahoo has been roundly denounced for helping the Chinese government convict and sentence a man to 10 years in jail for posting information to a U.S. Web site.

Following the outbreak of street demonstrations in June 2009 protesting a rigged election, the Iranian government unleashed one of the world's most sophisticated mechanisms for controlling and censoring the Web. Built with the assistance of Western companies like Siemens, and Nokia, the system uses deep packet inspection to open every packet, look for keywords, re-seal it, and send it on the network.

In the United States, as we have seen in our discussion of intellectual property, e-commerce sites can be put out of business for violating existing laws, and ISPs can be forced to "take down" offending content, or stolen content. Government security agencies such as the FBI can obtain court orders to monitor ISP traffic and engage in widespread monitoring of millions of e-mail messages. Under the USA PATRIOT Act, passed after the World Trade Center attack on September 11, 2001, American intelligence authorities are permitted to tap into whatever Internet traffic they believe is relevant to the campaign against terrorism, in some circumstances without judicial review. Working with the large ISP firms such as AT&T, Verizon, and others, U.S. security agencies have access to nearly all Internet communications through the country. And many American corporations are developing restrictions on their employees' at-work use of the Web to prevent gambling, shopping, and other activities not related to a business purpose.

In the United States, efforts to control media content on the Web have run up against equally powerful social and political values that protect freedom of expression, including several rulings by the Supreme Court which have struck down laws attempting to limit Web content in the United States. The U.S. Constitution's First Amendment says "Congress shall make no law ... abridging the freedom of speech, or of the press." As it turns out, the 200-year-old Bill of Rights has been a powerful brake on efforts to control twenty-first-century e-commerce content.

PUBLIC GOVERNMENT AND LAW

The reason we have governments is ostensibly to regulate and control activities within the borders of the nation. What happens in other nations, for the most part, we generally ignore, although clearly environmental and international trade issues require multinational cooperation. E-commerce and the Internet pose some unique problems to public government that center on the ability of the nation-state to govern activities within its borders. Nations have considerable powers to shape the Internet.

TAXATION

Few questions illustrate the complexity of governance and jurisdiction more potently than taxation of e-commerce sales. In both Europe and the United States, governments rely on sales taxes based on the type and value of goods sold. In Europe, these taxes are collected along the entire value chain, including the final sale to the consumer, and are called "value-added taxes" (VAT), whereas in the United States, taxes are collected on final sales to consumers and are called consumption taxes. In the United States, there are 50 states, 3,000 counties, and 12,000 municipalities, each with unique tax rates and policies. Cheese may be taxable in one state as a "snack food" but not taxable in another state (such as Wisconsin), where it is considered a basic food. Consumption taxes are generally recognized to be regressive because they disproportionately tax poorer people, for whom consumption is a larger part of total income.

Sales taxes were first implemented in the United States in the late 1930s as a Depression era method of raising money for localities. Ostensibly, the money was to be used to build infrastructure such as roads, schools, and utilities to support business development, but over the years the funds have been used for general government purposes of the states and localities. In most states, there is a state-based sales tax, and a smaller local sales tax. The total sales tax ranges from zero in some states (North Dakota) to as much as 13% in New York City.

The development of "remote sales" such as mail order/telephone order (MOTO) retail in the United States in the 1970s broke the relationship between physical presence and commerce, complicating the plans of state and local tax authorities to tax all retail commerce. States sought to force MOTO retailers to collect sales taxes for them based on the address of the recipient, but Supreme Court decisions in 1967 and 1992 established that states had no authority to force MOTO retailers to collect state taxes unless the businesses had a "nexus" of operations (physical presence) in the state. Congress could, however, create legislation giving states this authority. But every congressional effort to tax catalog merchants has been beaten back by a torrent of opposition from catalog merchants and consumers, leaving intact an effective tax subsidy for MOTO merchants.

The explosive growth of e-commerce, the latest type of "remote sales," has once again raised the issue of how—and if—to tax remote sales. Since its inception, e-commerce has benefited from a tax subsidy of up to 13% for goods shipped to high sales tax areas. Local retail merchants have complained bitterly about the e-commerce tax subsidy. E-commerce merchants have argued that this new form of commerce needs to be nurtured and encouraged in its early years, and that in any event, the crazy quilt of sales and use tax regimes would be difficult to administer for Internet merchants. State and local governments meanwhile see a potential source of new revenue slipping from their reach.

In 1998, Congress passed the Internet Tax Freedom Act, which placed a moratorium on "multiple or discriminatory taxes on electronic commerce" as well as on taxes on Internet access, for three years until October 2001, and in November 2001, extended the moratorium to November 2003. In November 2002, delegates from 32 states approved model legislation designed to create a system to tax Web sales. Spearheaded by the National Governor's Association (NGA), the Streamlined Sales Tax Project (SSTP) requires participating states to have only one tax rate for personal property or services effective by the end of 2005. By 2007, 15 states had agreed to support the SSTP. The governors are trying to get Congress to override judicial opinions and force online merchants to start collecting taxes. Nevertheless, in December 2004, Congress enacted the Internet Tax Nondiscrimination Act (Public Law 108–435), which extended the moratorium on states and local governments imposing taxes on Internet access and taxes on electronic commerce through November 1, 2007. In October 2007, Congress extended the moratorium once again, this time for an additional seven years (Gross, 2007).

The merger of online e-commerce with offline commerce further complicates the taxation question. Currently, almost all of the top 100 online retailers collect taxes when orders ship to states where these firms have a physical presence. But others, like eBay, still refuse to collect and pay local taxes, arguing that the so-called tax simplification project ended up with taxes for each of 49,000 zip codes, hardly a simplification. The taxation situation is also very complex in services. For instance, none of the major online travel sites collect the full amount of state and local hotel occupancy taxes, or state and local airline taxes. Instead of remitting sales tax on the full amount of the consumer's purchase, these sites instead collect taxes on the basis of the wholesale price they pay for the hotel rooms or tickets.

The states have not given up on collecting hundreds of millions of dollars from Internet merchants. In 2009, they are using two strategies. One is to define "nexus" to include having affiliates in a state which they argue is the equivalent of a store. Amazon, Blue Nile, and Overstock have eliminated their affiliate programs in states adopting this tactic. A second tactic is to agree to a tax simplification plan. Congress and the courts have at least considered taxing e-commerce if the states had a simplified and uniform state tax system. To date, 20 states have adopted the simplified system although none of them are large states.

The taxation situation in Europe, and trade between Europe and the United States, is similarly complex. The Organization for Economic Cooperation and Development (OECD), the economic policy coordinating body of European, American, and Japanese governments, is currently investigating different schemes for applying consumption and business profit taxes for e-commerce digitally downloaded goods. The EU began collecting a VAT on digital goods such as music and software delivered to consumers by foreign companies in 2003. Previously, European Union companies were required to collect the VAT on sales to EU customers, but U.S. companies were not. This gave American companies a huge tax edge.

Thus, there is no integrated rational approach to taxation of domestic or international e-commerce (Varian, 2001). In the United States, the national and international character of Internet sales is wreaking havoc on taxation schemes that were built in the 1930s and based on local commerce and local jurisdictions. Although there appears to be acquiescence among large Internet retailers such as Amazon to the idea of some kind of sales tax on e-commerce sales, their insistence on uniformity will probably delay taxation for many years, and any proposal to tax e-commerce will likely incur the wrath of around 150 million U.S. e-commerce consumers. Congress is not likely to ignore their voices.

NET NEUTRALITY

"Net neutrality" is more a political slogan than a concept. It means different things to different people. Currently, all Internet traffic is treated equally (or "neutrally") by Internet backbone owners in the sense that all activities—word processing, e-mailing, video downloading, etc.—are charged the same flat rate regardless of how much bandwidth is used. However, the telephone and cable companies that provide the Internet backbone would like to be able to charge differentiated prices based on the amount of bandwidth consumed by content being delivered over the Internet. They would also like to ration bandwidth so that in times of excessive demand they would slow down some traffic ("bandwidth hogs") so that other traffic such as e-mail can proceed more quickly. There are two ways to achieve this rationing: pricing or speed (bandwidth controls). Heavy bandwidth users can be charged higher usage fees if they overstep a limit. This is referred to as "congestion pricing" or "Web metering."

Heavy bandwidth users can also have their applications slowed down based on metering of their usage. In addition, high bandwidth vendors such as YouTube could be charged additional fees. The content of companies that pay an additional fee would be given preferential treatment in terms of delivery speed. The content of companies that refused to pay would be delivered at a slower rate.

Likewise, individual home users who downloaded enormous movie files would be charged a higher monthly fee for Internet service compared to neighbors who use the Internet only for email and surfing. For instance, in 2008, Comcast, the largest ISP in the U.S., began to slow down traffic using the BitTorrent protocol not because the content was pirated but because these video users were consuming huge chunks of the Comcast network capacity during peak load times. Comcast claims its policy was a legitimate effort to manage capacity. The FCC disagreed, and ruled in August 2008 that Comcast illegally inhibited users of its high-speed network from using file-sharing software. Comcast has appealed and filed suit against the FCC in the U.S. Court of Appeals for the District of Columbia. Currently, Time Warner Cable is experimenting with Web metering in Beaumont, Texas, charging $1 for every gigabyte over a 5 gigabyte base service.

Those who oppose the idea of "net metering" and charging more for heavy users of bandwidth have been lobbying Congress to create a new layer of Internet regulation that would require network providers to manage their networks in a nondiscriminatory manner. In 2009, the FCC began developing a national broadband strategy in connection with the enactment of the government stimulus package. As part of the plan, the FCC is expected to issue regulations as to what sort of rules, if any, should be applied to guarantee delivery of Internet traffic. The plan is subject to public and industry comment and due to be issued by February 2010. In the meantime, in September 2009 the FCC has indicated that it will propose a rule in favor of net neutrality that will provide that broadband companies, including wireless cell phone carriers not be allowed to discriminate against any particular Internet content or applications.

8.5 PUBLIC SAFETY AND WELFARE

Governments everywhere claim to pursue public safety, health, and welfare. This effort produces laws governing everything from weights and measures to national highways, to the content of radio and television programs. Electronic media of all kinds (telegraph, telephone, radio, and television) have historically been regulated by governments seeking to develop a rational commercial telecommunications environment and to control the content of the media—which may be critical of government or offensive to powerful groups in a society. Historically, in the United States, newspapers and print media have been beyond government controls because of constitutional guarantees of freedom of speech. Electronic media such as radio and television have, on the other hand, always been subject to content regulation because they use the publicly owned frequency spectrum. Telephones have also been regulated as public utilities and "common carriers," with special social burdens to provide service and access, but with no limitations on content.

In the United States, critical issues in e-commerce center around the protection of children, strong sentiments against pornography in any public media, efforts to control gambling, and the protection of public health through restricting sales of drugs and cigarettes.

PROTECTING CHILDREN

Pornography is an immensely successful Internet business. The most recent statistics with respect to revenues generated by online pornography are now several years old. However, it is probably safe to estimate that the online pornography industry in 2009 generates over $3 billion in revenue. Adult Web sites reportedly attract over 75 million unique visitors a month and make up 12% of the Internet. (New York Times, 2009; Worthen, 2009).

To control the Web as a distribution medium for pornography, in 1996, Congress passed the Communications Decency Act (CDA). This act made it a felony criminal offense to use any telecommunications device to transmit "any comment, request, suggestion, proposal, image or other communications which is obscene, lewd, lascivious, filthy, or indecent" to anyone, and in particular, to persons under the age of 18 years of age (Section 502, Communications Decency Act of 1996). In 1997, the Supreme Court struck down the CDA as an unconstitutional abridgement of freedom of speech protected by the First Amendment. While the government argued the CDA was like a zoning ordinance designed to allow "adult" Web sites for people over 18 years of age, the Court found the CDA was a blanket proscription on content and rejected the "cyberzoning" argument as impossible to administer. Another 1996 law, the Child Pornography Prevention Act, which made it a crime to create, distribute, or posses "virtual" child pornography that uses computer-generated images or young adults rather than real children, was also struck down as overly broad by the Supreme Court in 2002, in the *Ashcroft v. Free Speech Coalition* case.

In 1998, Congress passed the Children's Online Protection Act (COPA). This act made it a felony criminal offense to communicate for "commercial purposes" "any material harmful to minors." Harmful material was defined as prurient, depicting sexual acts, and lacking value for minors. The act differed from the CDA by focusing on "commercial speech" and minors exclusively. In February 1999, a federal district court in Pennsylvania struck down COPA as an unconstitutional restriction on Web content that was protected under the First Amendment. The court nevertheless recognized the interest of Congress and society to protect children on the Internet and in e-commerce. In May 2002, the U.S. Supreme Court returned the case to the court of appeals for a decision, leaving in place an injunction barring enforcement of the law. In March 2003, the Third Circuit Court of Appeals ruled for the second time that COPA was unconstitutional, finding that the law violated the First Amendment because it improperly restricted access to a substantial amount of online speech that is lawful for adults. In 2004, the Supreme Court blocked enforcement of the law again, saying that it likely violated the First Amendment, but remanded it to the district court for a further trial examining Internet filtering technologies that might be used to achieve the law's goals. In January 2006, it was revealed that in preparation for this trial, the Department of Justice had issued subpoenas to Google, AOL, Yahoo, and MSN seeking a week's worth of search queries and a random sampling of 1 million Web addresses in the effort to understand the prevalence of material that could be deemed harmful to minors and the effectiveness of filtering technology, raising a storm of additional controversy. AOL, MSN, and Yahoo all agreed to supply the requested data, but Google refused on a variety of grounds, including protection of its trade secrets, privacy, and public relations (Hafner and Richtel, 2006). In response, the court limited the subpoena to just a sample of URLs in Google's database. In March 2007, the district court struck down COPA, ruling once again that the law violated the First and Fifth Amendments, and issued an order permanently enjoining the government from enforcing COPA. The government once again appealed, and in July 2008, the Third Circuit Court of Appeals upheld the district court opinion that COPA violated the First amendment. On January 21, 2009, the Supreme Court refused an appeal of the circuit court decision, putting an end to the saga- of litigation over the act.

The 2003 Protect Act is an omnibus bill intended to prevent child abuse that includes prohibitions against computer-generated child pornography." Part of that statute was previously held to be unconstitutional by the Eleventh Circuit Court of Appeals, but in May 2008, the Supreme Court reversed the circuit court, and upheld the provision (Greenhouse, 2008).

Although Congress has had a difficult time framing constitutionally acceptable legislation to protect children and other consumers from pornography, in the Children's Online Privacy Protection Act (COPPA) (1998) (described in Section 8.2), it appears to have been successful in preventing e-commerce sites from collecting information on minors without parental consent. Pornographers who collect information on children without parental consent are potential felons. Because COPPA does not regulate e-commerce content per se, to date it has not been challenged in the courts.

In 2001, Congress passed the Children's Internet Protection Act (CIPA), which required schools and libraries in the United States to install "technology protection measures" (filtering software), in an effort to shield children from pornography. In June 2003, the Supreme Court upheld CIPA, overturning a federal district court that found the law interfered with the First Amendment guarantee of freedom of expression. The Supreme Court, in a 6–3 opinion, held that the law's limitations on access to the Internet posed no more a threat to freedom of expression than limitations on access to books that librarians choose for whatever reason not to acquire. The dissenting justices found this analogy inappropriate and instead argued the proper analogy was if librarians were to purchase encyclopedias and then rip out pages they thought were or might be offensive to patrons. All the justices agreed that existing blocking software was overly blunt, unable to distinguish child pornography from sexually explicit material (which is protected by the First Amendment), and generally unreliable (Greenhouse, 2003b). Other legislation such as the 2002 Domain Names Act seeks to prevent unscrupulous Web site operators from luring children to pornography using misleading domain names or characters known to children, while the 2002 Dot Kids Act authorizes the creation of a second-level domain on the Internet where all Web sites would have to declare they contain no material harmful to children. An alternative plan, to create an .xxx domain for adult Web site content, was rejected by ICANN for the third time in March 2007 (Moore, 2007).

In addition to government regulation, private pressure from organized groups has also been successful in forcing some Web sites to eliminate the display of pornographic materials. In June 2008, in response to pressure from Andrew Cuomo, New York's attorney general, Verizon, Time Warner Cable, and Sprint, agreed to limit access to some or all Usenet groups in an effort to block access to child pornography. AT&T, AOL, and Comcast followed suit in July 2008.

CIGARETTES, GAMBLING, AND DRUGS: IS THE WEB REALLY BORDERLESS?

In the United States, both the states and the federal government have adopted legislation to control certain activities and products in order to protect public health and welfare. Cigarettes, gambling, medical drugs, and of course addictive recreational drugs, are either banned or tightly regulated by federal and state laws (see *Insight on Society: The Internet Drug Bazaar*). Yet these products and services are ideal for

INSIGHT ON SOCIETY

THE INTERNET DRUG BAZAAR

In July 2009, a U.S. District Judge in Orlando sentenced Jude Lacour to eight years in federal prison for drug trafficking and money laundering. Along with six doctors, a pharmacist, and clerical workers, Lacour was convicted of operating an Internet drug operation referred to as Jive Network that distributed controlled substances and prescription drugs to customers who did not have prescriptions, who were never examined by a doctor, and without performing a proper health history. Jive Network filled over 500,000 customer orders for controlled substances, and generated in excess of $85 million in revenue during the three years of its operation. Lacour was required to make a cash payment to the government in the amount of $9.8 million.

In another case, Jared Wheat, the president of Hi- Tech Pharmaceuticals and three other company officers pleaded guilty to conspiracy charges in connection with the importation and distribution of adulterated and unapproved drugs without valid prescriptions. The company used spam e-mail to market inexpensive, generic versions of Valium, Xanax, Ambien, Vioxx, Viagra and Cialis, among others, that were supposedly made in Canada, but were instead produced in an unsanitary four-room house in Belize. Wheat was sentenced to over four years in federal prison, and assessed a $3 million forfeiture. The company sold millions of dollars worth of pharmaceuticals before being shut down.

According to a study done by the Treatment Research Institute at the University of Pennsylvania, addictive and potentially lethal medications are available without prescription from more than 2 million Web sites around the world, with many sites based in countries that impose little if any regulation on pharmaceuticals. MarkMonitor, a company specializing in online brand protection, studied 2,968 online pharmacies and found questionable business practices were more the norm than the exception. A Google search on "drugs" "no prescription" returns over 2 million results, and a Bing search on "Internet drugstore" returns 16 million hits. According to a study conducted by an online compliance and Web-based pharmacy verification service, 89.7% of the reviewed drugstore ads on Microsoft's Bing came from illegal pharmacies. A similar situation exists on Google. The study scoured the paid search ads delivered when queries for prescription-based pain medications and erectile dysfunction drugs were submitted. Most of the top advertisers proved to be bogus, offshore pharmacies that don't ask for prescriptions or perform age verification checks. A study of Yahoo found that 80% of online pharmacy ads were from online pharmacies that did not conform to legal requirements of the United States. As it turns out, search engine operators make money from ads placed predominantly by illegal online drugstores.

The International Narcotics Control Board, a U.N. narcotics watchdog agency, issued guidelines in March 2009 that provide guidelines and a framework fpr governments struggling to contain growing abuse of prescription drugs on the Internet. According to the report, a U.S. study found that only 2 of 365 so-called Internet pharmacies it surveyed were legitimate. In many countries, the report said, trafficking in illegal prescription drugs now equals or exceeds the sale of heroin, cocaine, and amphetamines. In November 2008, police in nine countries raided businesses suspected of supplying medicines illegally over the Internet in the first such global swoop coordinated by Interpol. The U.N. report noted that

(continued)

properly regulated, Internet pharmacies offer a valuable service by increasing competition and access to treatments in underserved regions

The sale of drugs without a prescription is not the only danger posed by the Internet drug bazaar. Rogue online pharmacy sites may be selling counterfeit drugs, or unapproved drugs. For instance, in the past, the FDA has issued warnings that a number of consumers who had purchased Ambien, Xanax, and Lexapro online from several different Web sites had instead received a product containing haloperial, a powerful anti-psychotic drug.

Drug pushers on the Internet also include legitimate U.S. pharmaceutical firms who have discovered search engine advertising. Enter a search for "high cholesterol" on Bing or Google and you will be faced with multiple ads extolling the benefits of Lipitor (Pfizer's leading statin drug). In 2009, the FDA issued a warning to these firms that their search engine ads violated laws that required them to clearly state the risks of drugs they are marketing.

But despite these dangers, online pharmacies remain alluring and are one of the fastest growing business models, with, oddly, senior citizens—usually some of the most law-abiding citizens—leading the charge for cheaper drugs. The top 1,000 Internet pharmacies are estimated to generate about $4 billion in revenue. The main attraction of online drug sites is price. Typically, online pharmacies are located in countries where prescription drugs are price-controlled, or where the price structure is much lower, such as Canada, the U.K., and European countries, as well as India and Mexico. U.S. citizens can often save 50%–75% by purchasing from online pharmacies located in other countries. For instance, choose any common prescription drug, and compare prices of that drug with U.S.- based pharmacies (such as Drugstore.com), and Canadian and European pharmacies. Generally, the European pharmacies offer the same drugs at half the American price, while Canada offers a 50% discount from U.S. prices. Using offshore, online pharmacies can save people up to half of their pharmaceutical budget.

Currently a patchwork regulatory structure governs the sale of drugs online. At the federal level, the 1938 Food, Drug, and Cosmetic Act (FDCA) requires that certain drugs may only be purchased with a valid doctor's prescription and must be dispensed by a state-licensed pharmacy. To get around this requirement, some online pharmacies use questionnaires to diagnose disease and have these questionnaires reviewed by doctors who write the prescription. This practice has not been allowed by U.S. courts. Congress has considered legislation to establish a federal definition of what constitutes a valid prescription, but to date such legislation has not passed. Complicating matters is the fact that many online pharmacies operate offshore, making it difficult for federal and state authorities to exercise jurisdiction over them. In September 2008, Congress strengthened its regulation of online pharmacies considerably by passing the Ryan Haight Online Pharmacy Consumer Protection Act, which bans the sale of prescription drugs over the Internet without a legitimate prescription issued by a medical practitioner that has examined the patient in person at least once. The bill is named after teenager Ryan Haight, who died from a drug overdose using drugs purchased on the Internet. The act requires online pharmacies to comply with pharmacy licensing laws in every state where they do business, and to register with the FDA before beginning to sell drugs online. The last requirement is virtually unenforceable because foreign online pharmacies can easily develop their Web sites offshore. The act does not prohibit online pharmacies anywhere in the world from providing drugs based on a legitimate doctor's prescription.

(continued)

In the meantime, the Food and Drug Administration recommends that consumers look for the National Association of Boards of Pharmacy (NABP) Verified Internet Pharmacy Practices Sites (VIPPS) Seal, which verifies that the site is legitimate with respect to conformance with state laws, and requiring a prescription for controlled drugs. So far, 17 major Internet pharmacies have signed on, including Drugstore.com, Caremark.com, CVS.com, Walgreens.com, and many other U.S. online pharmacies. Unfortunately, as an American trade association, the NABP never considers Canadian or European pharmacies, and locks the American consumer into high-priced drugs. That leaves thousands of sites that consumers should approach with a "buyer beware" attitude.

SOURCES: "Rogue Pharmacies Still a Problem For Search Engines," by Lance Whitney, CNET News, August 19, 2009; "Eleven Members of Internet Drug Organization Sentenced," United States Attorney's Office, Middle District of Florida, July 29, 2009; "Microsoft's Bing Hit With Illegal Pharmacy Ads," By Rick Aristotle Munarriz, Fool.com August 19, 2009; "Report on Yahoo! Rogue Internet Pharmacy Ads," LegitScript.com, August 18, 2009; "FDA Warns Drug Firms Over Internet Ads," by Jerod Favole, *Wall Street Journal*, April 4, 2009; "U.N. Issues Guidelines on Illegal Web Pharmacies," by Reuters, *PC Magazine*, March 17, 2009; "Don't Put Your Health in the Hands of Crooks," Federal Bureau of Investigation, Headline Archives, March 3, 2009; "Owner of Hi-Tech Pharmaceuticals and Co-conspirators Sentenced in Prescription Drug Importation Ring," U.S. Department of Justice, Press Release, February 3, 2009; "MarkMonitor Reports Continuing Rise in Online Abuse of Top Drug Brands," Markmonitor.com, August 26, 2008; "Ryan Haight Online Pharmacy Consumer Protection Act," H.R. 6353, 110th Congress, 2008.

distribution over the Internet through e-commerce sites. Because the sites can be located offshore, they can operate beyond the jurisdiction of state and federal prosecutors. Or so it seemed until recently. In the case of cigarettes, state and federal authorities have been quite successful in shutting down tax-free cigarette Web sites within the United States by pressuring PayPal and credit card firms to drop cigarette merchants from their systems. The major shipping companies—UPS, FedEx and DHL—have been pressured into refusing shipment of untaxed cigarettes. Phillip Morris has also agreed not to ship cigarettes to any resellers that have been found to be engaging in illegal Internet and mail order sales. However, East European sites and Web sites located on American Indian reservations continue to operate using checks and money orders as payments and the postal system as logistics partner, but their level of business has plummeted as consumers fear state tax authorities will present them with huge tax bills if they are discovered using these sites. As a result of these pressures and the threat of ultimately collecting taxes from consumers who purchase at these sites, online tax-free cigarette sales have dropped precipitously. Legislation has also been introduced in Congress making it a felony to sell tobacco in violation of any state tax law and requiring the U.S. Postal Service to stop shipping cigarettes, although it had not passed as of September 2009.

Gambling also provides an interesting example of the clash between traditional jurisdictional boundaries and claims to a borderless, uncontrollable Web. The online gambling market, based almost entirely offshore—primarily in United Kingdom and various Caribbean Islands—grew by leaps and bounds between 2000 and 2006, generating as much as $50 billion to $60 billion a year, and with much of the action (some estimate up to 50%) coming from customers based in the United States. Although the federal government contended online gambling was illegal under U.S. federal law, they were initially unable to stop it, with various federal courts offering mixed opinions. However, in the summer of 2006, federal officials turned up the heat and arrested two executive officers of offshore gambling operations as they passed through the United States, leading their companies to cease U.S. operations. Then in October 2006, Congress passed the Unlawful Internet Gambling Enforcement Act, which makes it a crime to use credit cards or online payment systems for Internet betting. This effectively bars online gambling companies from operating legally in the United States, and shortly thereafter a number of the leading, publicly traded companies suspended their business in the United States. However, the bill has not eliminated all online gambling in the United States, with some smaller companies still offering offshore gambling. An association of online gambling groups challenged the law as unconstitutional, claiming that Internet gambling is protected by First Amendment privacy rights and that filtering technology exists to make sure that children and compulsive gamblers cannot access offshore betting sites. These arguments were rejected by the Third Circuit Court of Appeals in September 2009. Several countries are also seeking compensation from the United States on the basis of a World Trade Organization ruling that American Internet gambling restrictions are illegal (Reuters, 2009).

In September 2008, Representative Barney Frank, chairman of the House Financial Services Committee, introduced a bill that would require federal agencies to define the term "unlawful Internet gambling," on the grounds that existing legislation and regulation failed to define to do so, leaving financial institutions to figure out for themselves whether or not it was legal to process a given transaction. That bill did not pass, but in fall 2009, new legislation that would establish a framework to permit licensed gambling operators to accept wagers from individuals located in the United Staes was re-introduced in both the House and the Senate, with proponents expressing higher hopes for success.

The Google Book Settlement:

Is It Fair?

I n the Internet age, books are supposed to die off and go away. Who wants to read books when YouTube streams over 10 billion videos a month in 2009, covering most topics known to man, and Google can provide online access to the world's information? Steve Jobs noted in an interview about the Kindle e-book reader, "It doesn't matter how good or bad the product [e-book reader] is, the fact is that people don't read anymore. Forty percent of the people in the U.S. read one book or less last year. The whole conception is flawed at the top because people don't read anymore."

Actually, in 2009, over 3 billion books will be sold in the United States, generating over $40 billion in revenue, down only 1.5% from the previous year's revenues. Americans in fact read 10 books per year per person on average, and people over 17 tend to read many more than that. In a recession when "not down much" is actually "up," the book industry is holding very steady, much better than industrials, consumer products, and of course financial services, which tanked, and a little better than the high tech Silicon Valley firms. Books are surprisingly a very hot topic in 2009 as Google battles the

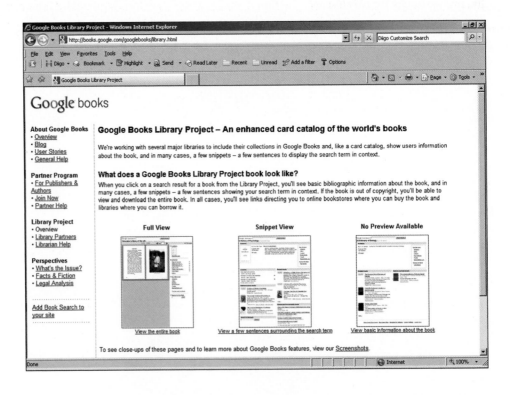

major heavy-hitter tech companies, authors, publishing firms, the United States Congress, the Department of Justice, and the European Commission over the future of online digital books.

Google is on a tear to put everything digital on its servers and then, as the founders promise in ceaseless self-congratulatory announcements, provide access to "all the world's information" through its efforts. And make a buck, as it turns out, by selling ads aimed at you that are "relevant" to your searches. A problem arises, however, when what Google wants to put on its servers does not belong to them. We're all familiar with the copyrighted music and video situation, where firms often operating offshore, beyond the law (or so they think) and enable, induce, and encourage Internet users to illegally download copyrighted material without paying a dime for it, while in the meantime raking in millions of advertising dollars from companies willing to advertise on their networks.

But Google is no criminal organization. For a firm who's motto is "Don't be evil," it seems out of character for it to initiate a program of scanning millions of copyrighted books it does not own and then, without permission, providing its search engine users with access to those books without charge, while selling ad space and pocketing millions for its own account without sharing that revenue with publishers or authors. One major difference between Google and most file-sharing firms is that Google has very deep pockets filled with cash, and they are based in the United States, making it an excellent legal target.

It all started with Google's secret 2002 project to scan all the books in libraries and make parts ("snippets") available online, and of course, display ads next to the results of book searches, even on the pages of snippets. In 2004, Google announced a program it first called Google Print and now just calls Google Books. There are two parts to the project. Under the Partner Program (previously called the Publisher Program), publishers give permission to Google to scan their books, or make scans available, and then make parts of the work, or simply bibliographic information (title, author, and publisher), available on Google's search engine. No problem there: publishers and authors get a chance to find a wider market, and Google sells more ads. Publishers may even choose to sell online editions of their books. And publishers were promised a hefty 70% of the display ad revenues and book sales (far better than Amazon's cut of book sales which is about 50%).

It's the second part of the project that became controversial. Under the Library Project, Google proposed to scan millions of books in university and public libraries and then allow users to search for key phrases, and display "relevant" portions of the text (what it calls "snippets"), all without contacting the publisher or seeking permission or paying a royalty fee. Google said it would "never show a full page without the right from the copyright holder," just the "relevant" portion. Google gave the publishing industry until November 2005 to opt-out by providing Google with a list of books they did not want to be included. In addition, Google proposed to scan millions of books for which the copyright has lapsed and make those available on its servers for free. In these early days, Google's public stance towards authors and publishers was "Stop us if you can."

Google has the backing of a number of prestigious libraries, such as the University of Michigan, Harvard University, Stanford University, the New York Public

Library, and Oxford University. But not all librarians agree. Some believe this is a marvelous extension of public access to library collections, while other librarians fear it is harmful to book authors and publishers. A number of well-known libraries, such as the Smithsonian Institution, and the Boston Public Library, as well as a consortium of 19 research and academic libraries in the Northeast, have refused to participate, in part because of restrictions that Google wants to place on the collection. Libraries that work with Google must agree to make the material unavailable to other commercial search services. Google claims it is performing a public service by making an index of books, and relevant portions, available to millions on the Internet, and perhaps even helping publishers sell new copies of books that currently sit on dusty library shelves.

In 2005, the publishing industry struck back at Google's book scanning program and two lawsuits were filed in federal court in New York, one a class-action suit by the Authors Guild, and the second by five major publishing companies (McGraw Hill, Pearson Education, Penguin Group, Simon & Schuster, and John Wiley & Sons), claiming copyright infringement. The publishers' consortium, the American Association of Publishers (AAP), alleged that Google was claiming the right to "unilaterally change copyright law and copy anything unless somebody tells [them] "No" [making it] impossible for people in the intellectual property community to operate. They [Google] keep talking about doing this because it is good for the world. That has never been a principle in law. They 'do no evil' except they are stealing people's property." Or, as one commentator put it, it's like having a thief break into your house and clean the kitchen—it's still breaking and entering.

Google, on the other hand, claimed its use was "fair" under the "fair use" doctrine that has emerged from a number of court decisions issued over the years, and which is codified in the Copyright Act in 1976. The copying and lending of books by libraries has been considered a fair use since the late 1930s under a "gentleman's agreement" between libraries and publishers, and a library exemption was codified as Section 108 of the Copyright Act of 1976. Libraries loan books to patrons for a limited period, and they must purchase at least one copy. Many people read books borrowed from libraries and recommend them to friends, who often buy the books rather than take the time and effort to go to a library. Libraries are also considered by many in the publishing industry as helping to market a book to a larger public, and libraries are believed to be performing a public service by increasing literacy and education.

In 2008, Google agreed to a settlement of the lawsuit with the authors and publishers. Google decided to cut a deal for cash and other considerations. In return for the nonexclusive right to sell books scanned into its database, place advertisements on those pages, display snippets, and make other commercial uses of its database of scanned books, Google agreed to pay $125 million to the parties. Of this amount, $15 million will be used to reimburse legal expenses and establish a fund to aid authors and publishers in pursuing their rights; $45 million will be put into the settlement fund for books digitized prior to an opt-out deadline (September 1, 2009); $34.5 million will be used to fund the launch of a central registry of books involved in the program; and the remaining $31 million will be used to pay for administrative and operating expenses of the registry. In addition, Google agreed to pay the registry 70% of Google's revenues from the project, less 10% for operating expenses. No provision is made in the agreement for (a) public domain books (government and out-of-copyright books) and (b) "orphaned books" where the copyright holders cannot be identified. All books that Google digitizes will be listed in the central registry available to the public on the Internet.

In 2009, a flurry of companies such as Microsoft, Yahoo, and Amazon; university groups; private organizations such as the American Association of Publishers; members of the Author's guild; and publishers in the European Union all filed briefs with the court disputing the settlement. The technology companies formed the Open Book Alliance to oppose the settlement. They were joined by privacy protection groups who claimed (not without merit) that Google would be able to track whatever e-books people accessed and read. Sony is the only technology company supporting Google. European publishers, authors, and copyright holders have also objected to the proposed settlement in the American courts. In September 2009, representatives of those groups spoke out at a hearing sponsored by the European Commission against the proposed deal. They said it would give Google too much power, including exclusive rights to sell out-of-print works that remain under copyright, a category that includes millions of books.

The Justice Department is investigating the antitrust implications of the settlement. Critics argue the settlement will create a de facto monopoly position for Google, make it difficult for competitors to enter the field, and give Google broad copyright immunity. The settlement provides that Google's access to publishers' books is "non exclusive," but competitors would have to scan all the same books over again in order to establish a competitive position, something that experts believe is financially prohibitive. Google, and settlement parties, including the AAP and Author's Guild, argue the settlement will expand digital access to millions of books that are gathering dust on library shelves. Critics retort that Google's database of books will be exclusive, not available to other firms or non-profit groups, and the costs of developing an open source, competing database of scanned books would be prohibitive. Google, they argue, would end up owning the digital book, which is like owning the libraries of the future.

SOURCES: "11th Hour Filings Oppose Google's Book Settlement," by Miguel Helft, *New York Times*, September 9, 2009; "Congress to Weigh Google Books Settlement," *New York Times*, September 9, 2009; "Tech Heavyweightgs Put Google's Books Deal in Crosshairs," by Jessica Vascellaro and Geoffrey Fowler, *Wall Street Journal*, August 21, 2009; "Probe of Google Book Dweal Heats Up," by Elizabeth Williamson, J. Tarchtenberg, and J. Vascellaro, *Wall Street Journal*, June 10, 2009; "Preparing to Sell E-books, Google Takes on Amazon," by Motoko Rich, *New York Times*, June 1, 2009; "Justice Department Opens Antitrust Inquiry Into Google Books Deal," by Miguel Helft, *New York Times*, April 29, 2009; The Authors Guild, Inc., Association of American Publishers, Inc., et al., v. Google Inc., Preliminary Settlement, Case 1:05-cv-08136-JES Document 56, Filed 10/28/2008; The McGraw Hill Companies, et. al., v. Google Inc., United States Southern District Court, Southern District of New York, October 19, 2005.

Case Study Questions

1. Who is harmed by Google's Library Project? Make a list of harmed groups, and for each group, try to devise a solution that would eliminate or lessen the harm.

2. Why is Google pursuing the Library Project program? What is in it for Google? Make a list of benefits to Google.

3. If you were a librarian, would you support Google's Library Project? Why or why not?

4. Why do firms like Amazon, Yahoo, and Microsoft opposed the Google book project? Why would Sony support Google?

5. Do you think Google's book project will result in a de facto monopoly in e-books, or will there be other competitors?

8.7 REVIEW

KEY CONCEPTS

■ **Understand why e-commerce raises ethical, social, and political issues.**

Internet technology and its use in e-commerce disrupts existing social and business relationships and understandings. Suddenly, individuals, business firms, and political institutions are confronted by new possibilities of behavior for which understandings, laws, and rules of acceptable behavior have not yet been developed. Many business firms and individuals are benefiting from the commercial development of the Internet, but this development also has costs for individuals, organizations, and societies. These costs and benefits must be carefully considered by those seeking to make ethical and socially responsible decisions in this new environment, particularly where there are as yet no clear-cut legal or cultural guidelines.

■ **Recognize the main ethical, social, and political issues raised by e-commerce.**

The major issues raised by e-commerce can be loosely categorized into four major dimensions:

- *Information rights*—What rights do individuals have to control their own personal information when Internet technologies make information collection so pervasive and efficient?
- *Property rights*—How can traditional intellectual property rights be enforced when perfect copies of protected works can be made and easily distributed worldwide via the Internet?
- *Governance*—Should the Internet and e-commerce be subject to public laws? If so, what law-making bodies have jurisdiction—state, federal, and/or international?
- *Public safety and welfare*—What efforts should be undertaken to ensure equitable access to the Internet and e-commerce channels? Do certain online content and activities pose a threat to public safety and welfare?

■ **Identify a process for analyzing ethical dilemmas.**

Ethical, social, and political controversies usually present themselves as dilemmas. Ethical dilemmas can be analyzed via the following process:
- Identify and clearly describe the facts.
- Define the conflict or dilemma and identify the higher-order values involved.
- Identify the stakeholders.
- Identify the options that you can reasonably take.
- Identify the potential consequences of your options.
- Refer to well-established ethical principles, such as the Golden Rule, Universalism, Descartes' Rule of Change, the Collective Utilitarian Principle, Risk Aversion, the No Free Lunch Rule, the *New York Times* Test, and the Social Contract Rule to help you decide the matter.

■ **Understand basic concepts related to privacy.**

To understand the issues concerning online privacy, you must first understand some basic concepts:

- *Privacy* is the moral right of individuals to be left alone, free from surveillance or interference from others.
- *Information privacy* includes both the claim that certain information should not be collected at all by governments or business firms, and the claim of individuals to control the use of information about themselves.
- *Due process* as embodied by the Fair Information Practices doctrine, informed consent, and opt-in/opt-out policies also play an important role in privacy.

■ **Identify the practices of e-commerce companies that threaten privacy.**

Almost all e-commerce companies collect some personally identifiable information in addition to anonymous information and use cookies to track clickstream behavior of visitors. Advertising networks and search engines also track the behavior of consumers across thousands of popular sites, not just at one site, via cookies, spyware, search engine behavioral targeting, and other techniques

■ **Describe the different methods used to protect online privacy.**

There are a number of different methods used to protect online privacy. They include:

- Legal protections deriving from constitutions, common law, federal law, state laws, and government regulations. In the United States, rights to online privacy may be derived from the U.S. Constitution, tort law, federal laws such as the Children's Online Privacy Protection Act (COPPA), the Federal Trade Commission's Fair Information Practice principles, and a variety of state laws. In Europe, the European Commission's Directive on Data Protection has standardized and broadened privacy protection in the European Union nations.
- Industry self-regulation via industry alliances, such as the Online Privacy Alliance and the Network Advertising Initiative, that seek to gain voluntary adherence to industry privacy guidelines and safe harbors. Some firms also hire chief privacy officers.
- Privacy-enhancing technological solutions include secure e-mail, anonymous remailers, anonymous surfing, cookie managers, disk file-erasing programs, policy generators, and privacy policy readers.

■ **Understand the various forms of intellectual property and the challenge of protecting it.**

There are three main types of intellectual property protection: copyright, patent, and trademark law.

- *Copyright law* protects original forms of expression such as writings, drawings, and computer programs from being copied by others for a minimum of 70 years. It does not protect ideas—just their expression in a tangible medium. "Look and feel" copyright infringement lawsuits are precisely about the distinction between an idea and its expression. If there is only one way to express an idea, then the expression cannot be copyrighted. Copyrights, like all rights, are not absolute. The doctrine of fair use permits certain parties under certain circumstances to use copyrighted material without permission. The Digital Millennium Copyright Act (DMCA) is the first major effort to adjust the copyright laws to the Internet Age. The DMCA implements a World Intellectual Property Organization treaty, which declares it illegal to make, distribute, or use devices that circumvent technology-based protections of copyrighted materials, and attaches stiff fines and prison sentences for violations.

- *Patent law* grants the owner of a patent an exclusive monopoly to the ideas behind an invention for 20 years. Patents are very different from copyrights in that they protect the ideas themselves and not merely the expression of ideas. There are four types of inventions for which patents are granted under patent law: machines, man-made products, compositions of matter, and processing methods. In order to be granted a patent, the applicant must show that the invention is new, original, novel, non-obvious, and not evident in prior arts and practice. Most of the inventions that make the Internet and e-commerce possible were not patented by their inventors. This changed in the mid-1990s with the commercial development of the World Wide Web. Business firms began applying for "business methods" and software patents.

- *Trademark protections* exist at both the federal and state levels in the United States. The purpose of trademark law is twofold. First, trademark law protects the public in the marketplace by ensuring that it gets what it pays for and wants to receive. Second, trademark law protects the owner who has spent time, money, and energy bringing the product to market against piracy and misappropriation. Federal trademarks are obtained, first, by use in interstate commerce, and second, by registration with the U.S. Patent and Trademark Office (USPTO). Trademarks are granted for a period of 10 years and can be renewed indefinitely. Use of a trademark that creates confusion with existing trademarks, causes consumers to make market mistakes, or misrepresents the origins of goods is an infringement. In addition, the intentional misuse of words and symbols in the marketplace to extort revenue from legitimate trademark owners ("bad faith") is proscribed. The Anticybersquatting Consumer Protection Act (ACPA) creates civil liabilities for anyone who attempts in bad faith to profit from an existing famous or distinctive trademark by registering an Internet domain name that is identical, confusingly similar, or "dilutive" of that trademark. Trademark abuse can take many forms on the Web. The major behaviors on the Internet that have run afoul of trademark law include cybersquatting, cyberpiracy, metatagging, keywording, linking, and framing.

■ **Understand how governance of the Internet has evolved over time.**

Governance has to do with social control: who will control e-commerce, what elements will be controlled, and how the controls will be implemented. Governance of both the Internet and e-commerce has gone through four stages:

- *Government control (1970–1994).* During this period, DARPA and the National Science Foundation controlled the Internet as a fully government funded program.

- *Privatization (1995–1998).* Network Solutions was given a monopoly to assign and track high-level Internet domain names. The backbone was sold to private telecommunications companies and policy issues remained undecided.

- *Self-regulation (1995–present).* President Clinton and the Department of Commerce encouraged creation of ICANN, a semi-private body, to deal with emerging conflicts and to establish policies.

- *Governmental regulation (1998–present).* Executive, legislative, and judicial bodies worldwide began to implement direct controls over the Internet and e-commerce.

We are currently in a mixed-mode policy environment where self-regulation, through a variety of Internet policy and technical bodies, co-exists with limited government regulation.

■ **Explain why taxation of e-commerce raises governance and jurisdiction issues.**

E-commerce raises the issue of how—and if—to tax remote sales. The national and international character of Internet sales is wreaking havoc on taxation schemes in the United States that were built in the 1930s and based on local commerce and local jurisdictions. E-commerce has benefited from a tax subsidy since its inception. E-commerce merchants have argued that this new form of commerce needs to be nurtured and encouraged, and that in any event, the crazy quilt of sales and use tax regimes would be difficult to administer for Internet merchants. In 1998, Congress passed the Internet Tax Freedom Act, which placed a moratorium on multiple or discriminatory taxes on electronic commerce, and any taxation of Internet access, and since that time has extended the moratorium three times, most recently until November 2014. In November 2002, delegates from 32 states approved model legislation designed to create a system to tax Web sales, and by 2007, 15 states had agreed to support the program. Although there appears to be acquiescence among large Internet retailers to the idea of some kind of sales tax on e-commerce sales, insistence on uniformity will delay taxation for many years, and any proposal to tax e-commerce will likely incur the wrath of U.S. e-commerce consumers.

■ **Identify major public safety and welfare issues raised by e-commerce.**

Critical public safety and welfare issues in e-commerce include:
- The protection of children and strong sentiments against pornography. The Children's Online Protection Act (COPA) of 1998 made it a felony criminal offense to communicate for commercial purposes any material harmful to minors. This law has thus far been struck down as an unconstitutional restriction on Web content that is protected under the First Amendment. The Children's Internet Protection Act (CIPA), which requires schools and libraries in the United States to install "technology protection measures" (filtering software) in an effort to shield children from pornography, has however, been upheld by the Supreme Court. In addition to government regulation, private pressure from organized groups has also been successful in forcing some Web sites to eliminate the display of pornographic materials.
- Efforts to control gambling and restrict sales of cigarettes and drugs. In the United States, cigarettes, gambling, medical drugs, and addictive recreational drugs are either banned or tightly regulated by federal and state laws. Yet these products and services are often distributed via offshore e-commerce sites operating beyond the jurisdiction of federal and state prosecutors. At this point, it is not clear that the Web will remain borderless or that e-commerce can continue to flaunt national, state, and local laws with impunity.

QUESTIONS

1. What basic assumption does the study of ethics make about individuals?
2. What are the three basic principles of ethics? How does due process factor in?

3. Explain Google's position that YouTube does not violate the intellectual property rights of copyright owners.

4. Define universalism, slippery slope, the *New York Times* test, and the social contract rule as they apply to ethics.

5. Explain why someone with a serious medical condition might be concerned about researching his or her condition online, through medical search engines or pharmaceutical sites, for example. What is one technology that could prevent one's identity from being revealed?

6. Name some of the personal information collected by Web sites about their visitors.

7. How does information collected through online forms differ from site transaction logs? Which potentially provides a more complete consumer profile?

8. How is the opt-in model of informed consent different from opt-out? In which type of model does the consumer retain more control?

9. What are the two core principles of the FTC's Fair Information Practice principles?

10. How do safe harbors work? What is the government's role in them?

11. Name three ways online advertising networks have improved on, or added to, traditional offline marketing techniques.

12. Explain how Web profiling is supposed to benefit both consumers and businesses.

13. What are some of the challenges that chief privacy officers (CPOs) face in their jobs?

14. How could the Internet potentially change protection given to intellectual property? What capabilities make it more difficult to enforce intellectual property law?

15. What does the Digital Millennium Copyright Act attempt to do? Why was it enacted? What types of violations does it try to prevent?

16. Define cybersquatting. How is it different from cyberpiracy? What type of intellectual property violation does cybersquatting entail?

17. What is deep linking and why is it a trademark issue? Compare it to framing—how is it similar and different?

18. What are some of the tactics illegal businesses, such as betting parlors and casinos, successfully use to operate outside the law on the Internet?

PROJECTS

1. Go to Google and click on the Search Settings link (at the top right corner of the home page). Examine its SafeSearch filtering options available on the Preferences page. Surf the Web in search of content that could be considered objectionable for children using each of the options. What are the pros and cons of such restrictions? Are there terms that could be considered inappropriate to the filtering software but be approved by parents? Name five questionable terms. Prepare a brief presentation to report on your experiences and to explain the positive and negative aspects of such filtering software.

2. Develop a list a privacy protection features that should be present if a Web site is serious about protecting privacy. Then, visit at least four well-known Web sites and examine their privacy policies. Write a report that rates each of the Web sites on the criteria you have developed.

3. Review the provisions of the Digital Millennium Copyright Act of 1998. Examine each of the major sections of the legislation and make a list of the protections afforded property owners and users of copyrighted materials. Do you believe this legislation balances the interests of owners and users appropriately? Do you have suggestions for strengthening "fair use" provisions in this legislation?

4. Visit at least four Web sites that take a position on e-commerce taxation, beginning with the National Conference of State Legislatures (Ncsl.org) and the National Governor's Association (Nga.org). You might also include national associations of local businesses or citizen groups opposed to e-commerce taxation. Develop a reasoned argument for, or against, taxation of e-commerce.

5. Consider the issue of the Department of Justice's subpoena of search query records discussed on page 552. Prepare a list of reasons why the firms subpoenaed should or should not have complied with this request. What moral dilemmas are presented? What higher-order values, and what kind of value conflicts, are revealed in this list? How do you propose that we as a society resolve these dilemmas? You might conclude by applying each of the Candidate Ethical Principles described in Section 8.1.

WEB SITE RESOURCES www.azimuth-interactive.com/ecommerce6e

- ■ Additional projects, exercises, and tutorials
- ■ Careers: Explore career opportunities in e-commerce
- ■ Raising capital and business plans

E-commerce in Action

CHAPTER 9

Online Retail and Services

Blue Nile Sparkles
for Your Cleopatra

Men: looking for that special gift for your Cleopatra, but don't want to spend a lot of time shopping? Want to give the "Big Rock" certified by the independent Gemological Institute of America (GIA) or the American Gem Society Laboratories (AGSL) without spending a mountain of cash for the engagement experience? How about 35% less than retail prices? Not sure about the future value of diamonds? Then how about pearls, gold, or platinum?

Your answer has arrived: BlueNile.com offers you an online selection of over 60,000 diamonds for that special someone. You can buy them cut and polished, or put them into settings like rings, bracelets, earrings, necklaces, pendants, watches, and broaches that you can choose online. All the diamonds are graded by the 4Cs: carats (size), cut, color, and clarity, and a report for each diamond prepared by the GIA is available online. To make it easier, fellas, the carats are translated into milligrams, and one carat is exactly 200 milligrams of mass (if that helps). Just ask her what size she wants, and then look in your wallet. Although the majority of visitors to the site are women, about 85% of Blue Niles customers are men.

In June 2007, Blue Nile sold the biggest item in Internet history, a $1.5 million single diamond of around 10 carats, a size that would cover your finger with a penny-size rock. That's about 2,000 milligrams, the biggest mouse click ever. The mouse that roared?

BlueNile.com started out as RockShop.com in March 1999 in Seattle, Washington. In May 1999, the company purchased Williams and Son, a Seattle jeweler with a Web site, and changed its name to Internet Diamonds, Inc. In November 1999, the company launched the Blue Nile brand and changed its name to Blue Nile Inc., opening up its Web site, BlueNile.com, in December 1999. In May 2004, Blue Nile went public at $20, and jumped to $28 (a 38% pop) in the first day of trading. The received wisdom of Web gurus in 1999 was that the Internet would never be a place where fine jewelry could be sold. Why? CDs and books are what everyone thought the Web was good at back then.

Purchasing jewelry, especially high-cost diamonds, is what marketers call a "significant event." Typically, gifts of diamonds are associated with a significant emotional event, such as an engagement, marriage, or an anniversary. Generally, the event is shared with a significant other and often involves shopping together for the gem. Shopping on the Web (alone or together) hardly matches the emotional impact of walking into Tiffany's or another established retail store, with marvelous clear glass cases filled with brilliantly shining baubles, attended by a small army of unctuous perfumed sales clerks that make you feel so special. Diamonds represent a significant cost, and there is significant uncertainty about their value and pricing. Surveys show that most shoppers believe jewelry is highly overpriced, but they lack the knowledge and information to negotiate a better price or even judge the quality of what they are buying. Consumers generally have no rational way to compare diamonds, and face a limited selection at a single store, often in a high-pressured environment where sales employees are helping several customers at the same time. Most experts thought that, given the emotional significance and uncertainty of purchasing diamonds, few consumers would heighten the built-in anxiety by going to a strange Web site and plunking down $5,000 or more for a diamond they could not see or touch for several days.

But jewelry and high fashion retailers are leading the second act of online retailing, bursting on the scene in 2004 with high growth rates and spectacular average sales transaction levels. As it turns out, the retail jewelry industry is an ideal candidate for Web sales. Here's why.

The $60 billon traditional jewelry industry is a byzantine, fragmented collection of over 50,000 physical stores in the United States. About 95% of all retail jewelry firms operate only a single store. To supply this fragmented market, several layers of wholesalers and middlemen intervene, from rough diamond brokers, diamond cutters, diamond wholesalers, jewelry manufacturers, jewelry wholesalers, and finally, regional distributors. Oddly, the source of raw mined diamonds is monopolized by a single company, De Beers, which controls over two-thirds of the world market. The fragmented supply and distribution chains add to huge markups based on monopoly-set prices for the raw diamonds. Currently, the typical retail store markup for diamonds is between 50% and 100%. Blue Nile's markup is around 30%.

In 2008 and early 2009, the entire offline and online jewelry industry was hit hard by the recession as wealthy buyers and young lovers cut back their purchases. Even still, overall online jewelry sales are estimated at $1 billion, with Blue Nile accounting for about 30% of that number. In 2008, its revenues were $295 million, down 7.5% from $319 million in 2007, although the firm still earned a profit of $11.6 million. Another bright spot in 2008 was a 62% growth rate in international sales to $27.7 million, or 9% of total sales. In the first half of 2009, sales continued to decline, but only by 5%, and profits were still positive at $2.8 million. It might be a recession, but for at least some, love still trumps the pocketbook.

Blue Nile's main competitor with $205 million in revenue in 2008 is Bidz.com, a Web jewelry discount site. Other competitors include Tiffany.com and Ice.com, and even Amazon. Together, these companies are transforming the Byzantine jewelry business. Blue Nile, for instance, has simplified the supply-side of diamonds by only ordering and paying for a diamond after the customer has ordered it. Blue Nile has cut out several supply-side layers of middlemen and instead deals directly with wholesale diamond owners and jewelry manufacturers.

Blue Nile minimizes its inventory costs and limits its risk of inventory markdowns. On the sell side of distribution, Blue Nile has eliminated the expensive stores, sales clerks, and beautiful but expensive glass cases. Instead, Blue Nile offers a single Web site at which it can aggregate the demand of thousands of unique visitors for diamonds and present them with a more attractive shopping experience than a typical retail store. The result of rationalizing the supply and distribution chain is much lower markups. For example, Blue Nile will purchase a pair of oval emerald and diamond earrings from a supplier for $850 and charge the consumer $1,020. A traditional retailer would charge the consumer $1,258.

Blue Nile has improved the shopping experience primarily by creating a trust- and knowledge-based environment that reduces consumer anxiety about the value of diamonds. In essence, Blue Nile and the other online retailers give the consumer as much information as a professional gemologist would give them. The Web site contains educational guides to diamonds and diamond grading systems, and provides independent quality ratings for each diamond provided by non-profit industry associations, such as the GIA. There's a 30-day, money-back, no-questions-asked guarantee.

In 2009, for the first time in a decade, Blue Nile rebuilt its Web site, strengthening its appeal to its mostly male customer base while at the same time attempting to draw more women to the site. The new site removed the left menu so common to older Web designs, enlarged the pictures, added visualization software so visitors can see the jewelry with shadows and sparkles, expanded the product detail, and improved the search engine. The site's "Build Your Own Ring" feature has a new layout that's easier to use and to see more precisely what you're building.

Despite its lower gross margins due to its low prices, Blue Nile has higher net operating margins than its chief offline physical store competitor, Zales Inc., the country's largest jewelry chain. To get an idea of Blue Nile's efficiency, in order to sell $300 million in jewelry, a traditional physical store chain such as Zales would need around 300 stores. Blue Nile achieves $300 million in sales with three Web sites, two warehouses, and 170 workers.

After a strong 2007 when Blue Nile's stock hit $70, it tanked down to $20 in December, 2008, as the recession-induced weak holiday market took its toll. But the bounce back was extraordinary, and in September 2009 its stock was in the $60 range. The average ticket price for Blue Nile diamonds is $5,500, compared to $2,500 in typical retail stores.

So far the "Blue Nile" effect of lower margins and Internet efficiency has mainly impacted the small mom and pop jewelry stores. About 3,000 small retailers have disappeared in the last few years for a variety of reasons. The big retailers, such as Tiffany, Zales, and others sell more than Blue Nile, and continue to benefit from consumer interest in diamond engagement and wedding rings. Both Tiffany and Zales have online Web sites. Tiffany's site is primarily a branding site, but it has greatly improved its online graphics and online sales capabilities. The Zales site is a much more effective sales site than Tiffany's, with a marvelous build-a-ring capability, but still not quite up to the level of Blue Nile with respect to certification. Still, the success of Blue Nile, and the size of its competitors, mean that Blue Nile will have to keep a keen watch on its competitors who are not far behind. But for now, the future of Blue Nile looks, well, sparkling.

SOURCES: "Blue Nile Gets Makover to Please Ladies," by Geoffrey Fowler, *Wall Street Journal*, September 1, 2009; "New Blue Site Hits Web," *New York Times*, September 1, 2009; "Blue Niles Aims to Sparkle With Re-designed Web Site," *Internet Retailer*, September 1, 2009; Blue Nile Inc. Report on Form 10-Q for the fiscal quarter ended June 4, 2009, filed with the Securities and Exchange Commission on August 13, 2009; Blue Nile Inc. Report on Form 10-K for the fiscal year ended January 4, 2008, filed with the Securities and Exchange Commission on March 5, 2009; "Blue Nile: A Guy's Best Friend," Jay Greene, *Business Week*, May 29, 2008.

The Blue Nile case illustrates some of the advantages that a pure-play, start-up retail company has over traditional offline retailers, and some of the disadvantages. A pure-play consumer service company can radically simplify the existing industry supply chain and develop an entirely new Web-based distribution system that is far more efficient than traditional retail outlets. At the same time, an online pure-play retailer can create a better value proposition for the customer, improving customer service and satisfaction in the process. On the other hand, pure-play start-up companies often have razor-thin profit margins, lack a physical store network to bolster sales to the non-Internet audience, and are often based on unproven business assumptions that, in the long term may not prove out. In contrast, large offline retailers, such as Wal-Mart, JCPenney, Sears, and Target, have established brand names, a huge real estate investment, a loyal customer base, and extraordinarily efficient inventory control and fulfillment systems. As we shall see in this chapter, traditional offline catalog merchants are even more advantaged. We will also see that, in order to leverage their assets and core competencies, established offline retailers need to cultivate new competencies and a carefully developed business plan to succeed on the Web.

As with retail goods, the promise of pure-online service providers is that they can deliver superior-quality service and greater convenience to millions of consumers at a lower cost than established bricks-and-mortar service providers, and still make a respectable return on invested capital. The service sector is one of the most natural avenues for e-commerce because so much of the value in services is based on collecting, storing, and exchanging information—something for which the Web is ideally suited. And, in fact, online services have been extraordinarily successful in attracting banking, brokerage, travel, and job-hunting customers. The quality and amount of information online to support consumer decisions in finance, travel, and career placement is extraordinary, especially when compared to what was available to consumers before e-commerce.

The online service sector—like online retail—has shown both explosive growth and some recent impressive failures. Despite the failures, online services have established a significant beachhead and are coming to play a large role in consumer time on the Internet. In areas such as brokerage, banking, and travel, online services are an extraordinary success story, and are transforming their industries. As with the retail sector, many of the early innovators—delivery services such as Kozmo and WebVan and consulting firms such as BizConsult.com—are gone. However, some early innovators, such as E*Trade, Schwab, Expedia, and Monster, have been successful, while many established service providers, such as Citigroup, JPMorgan Chase, Wells Fargo, Bank of America, and the large airlines, have developed successful online e-commerce service delivery sites. In Sections 9.5–9.7 of this chapter, we take a close at three of these most successful online services: financial services (including insurance and real estate), travel services, and career services.

9.1 THE ONLINE RETAIL SECTOR

Table 9.1 summarizes some of these leading trends in online retailing for 2009–2010. Perhaps the most important theme in online retailing is the effort by retailers—both offline and online—to integrate their operations so they can serve customers in the various ways they want to be served.

TABLE 9.1	WHAT'S NEW IN ONLINE RETAIL, 2009–2010

- Continued rapid growth in social networks and user-generated content sites encourages "social shopping," where users pass on their opinions and recommendations to others in several online viral networks.

- During the recession, the average annual amount of online purchases for individuals remained flat, but overall retail online e-commerce grew in the low single digits, and sales at the Internet Top 500 online retailers grew 11%. Amazon's sales grew by 29%.

- Online retailers remain generally profitable, despite the recession, by focusing on revenue growth, increasing the size of average purchase amounts, and improving efficiency of operations.

- Online retail remains the fastest growing retail channel, and should surpass the mail order/telephone order (MOTO) catalog sales channel by 2010 at current growth rates.

- Buying online has become a normal, mainstream, everyday experience. Around 86% of Internet users in the United States are now online shoppers.

- The selection of goods for purchase online continues to increase to include luxury goods, such as jewelry, gourmet groceries, furniture, and wine, as customer trust and experience increase.

- Informational shopping for big-ticket items such as cars and appliances continues to expand rapidly to include nearly all retail goods (both durables and non-durables).

- Specialty retail sites show the most rapid growth in online retail as they develop customized retail goods and customer online configuration of goods.

- Online retailers place an increased emphasis on providing an improved "shopping experience," including ease of navigation and use, online inventory updates, interactive tools, and customer feedback and ratings.

- Online retailers increase the use of interactive multimedia marketing technologies and Web 2.0 techniques such as blogs, user-generated content, and video that exploit the dominance of broadband connections and offer features such as zoom, color switch, product configuration, and virtual simulations of households and businesses.

- Retail intermediaries strengthen in many areas, including groceries, automobiles, appliance, and furniture dealers.

- Retailers become increasingly efficient in integrating multiple retailing channels, beyond "bricks-and-clicks" to "click-and-drive" and in-store Web kiosk ordering.

- Personalized goods, especially in apparel, become financially successful and begin to spread to many sites beyond specialty retailers.

- Online shopping becomes more multi-seasonal and less gift-oriented as consumers come to accept the Web as a routine shopping venue that is neither a novelty nor a special-occasion marketplace.

- More than half of online shopping and nearly a third of online purchases occur at work. However, growth of at-home broadband connections increases, making evening purchases from home the fastest growing time segment for retail purchases online, relieving some pressure on workplace purchasing.

By any measure, the size of the U.S. retail market is huge. In a $13.8 trillion economy, personal consumption of retail goods and services accounts for over $9.7 trillion (about 70%) of the total gross domestic product (GDP)—or over two-thirds of all economic activity (U.S. Census Bureau, 2009).

If we examine the personal consumption sector more closely, we find that about 60% of personal consumption is for services, 11% is for durable goods, and 29% is for nondurable goods. Services include medical, educational, financial, and food services. **Durable goods** are those that are consumed over a longer period of time (generally more than a year), such as automobiles, appliances, and furniture. **Nondurable goods** are consumed quickly and have shorter life spans, and include general merchandise, clothing, music, drugs, and groceries.

The distinction between a "good" and a "service" is not always clear-cut, and is becoming more ambiguous over time. Increasingly, manufacturers and retailers of physical goods sell support services that add value to the physical product. It is difficult to think of a sophisticated physical good that does not include significant services in the purchase price. The movement toward "product-based services" can be seen in the packaged software market. Microsoft offers purchasers of its Windows and Office suite products additional value-added services from a variety of Microsoft Web sites. Charging for services, particularly on a monthly subscription basis, can be highly profitable. For instance, warranties, insurance policies, after-sale repairs, and purchase loans are increasingly a large source of revenue for manufacturers and retailers. Nevertheless, in this chapter, retail goods refer to physical products, and retailers refer to firms that sell physical goods to consumers, recognizing that retail goods include many services.

durable goods

goods that are consumed over a longer period of time (generally more than a year)

nondurable goods

goods that are consumed quickly and have shorter life spans

THE RETAIL INDUSTRY

The retail industry is composed of many different types of firms. **Figure 9.1** divides the retail industry into eight segments: clothing, durable goods, general merchandise, groceries, specialty stores, gasoline and fuel, eating and drinking, MOTO, and online retail firms.

Each of these segments offers opportunities for online retail, and yet in each segment, the uses of the Internet may differ. Some eating and drinking establishments use the Web to inform people of their physical locations and menus, while others offer delivery via Web orders (although this has not been a successful model). Retailers of durable goods typically use the Web as an informational tool rather than as a direct purchasing tool, although this is beginning to change as consumers have begun to purchase furniture and building supplies over the Internet. For instance, automobile manufacturers still do not sell cars over the Web, but they do provide information to assist customers in choosing among competing models. In fact, almost 90% of the respondents in a January 2009 survey said that they viewed products, services, and rates on company or dealership Web sites when comparison shopping for a car (Microsoft, 2009).

The largest segment of the U.S. retail market is consumer durables, followed by general merchandise. These segments, particularly general merchandise, are highly concentrated, with large firms dominating sales. These very large firms have

FIGURE 9.1	**COMPOSITION OF THE U.S. RETAIL INDUSTRY**

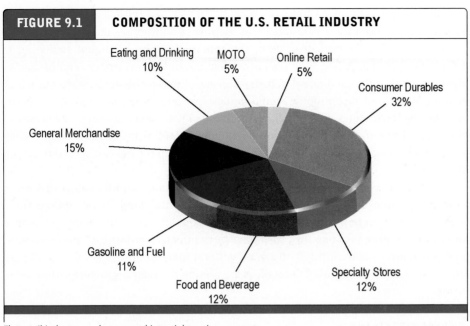

The retail industry can be grouped into eight major segments.
SOURCE: Based on data from U.S. Census Bureau, 2009.

developed highly automated real-time inventory control systems (systems that collect point-of-sale data from cash registers, update inventory records, and inform vendors of stock levels), large national customer bases, and customer databases containing detailed purchasing information.

General merchandisers have always competed against a more traditional form of retail commerce called specialty retailers. In fact, modern retail trade began as a collection of small retail shops in a concentrated location that customers visited in serial order. Shopping used to mean a visit to a shoemaker, dressmaker, pharmacy, butcher, and dry goods store. While mass-market general department stores were the fastest growing form of retail commerce for most of the twentieth century, in the 1960s, boutique and specialty stores catering to much smaller market segments with higher priced goods became the fastest growing form of physical retail stores. Stores such as The Gap, Banana Republic, Athlete's Foot, Sports Authority, Victoria's Secret, Staples, and many others developed national and international chain store strategies based on upscale youth market segments. The success of specialty retailing depends on building unique products for a market segment, offering strong customer service, and providing a persuasive shopping experience to support the brand image.

The MOTO sector is the most similar to the online retail sales sector. In the absence of physical stores, MOTO retailers distribute millions of physical catalogs (their largest expense) and operate large telephone call centers to accept orders. They have developed extraordinarily efficient order fulfillment centers that generally ship customer orders within 24 hours of receipt. MOTO was the fastest growing retail segment throughout the 1970s and 1980s. It grew as a direct result of improvements in the national toll-free call system, the implementation of digital switching in telephone systems, falling long distance telecommunications prices, and of course, the expansion of the credit card industry and associated technologies, without which neither MOTO nor e-commerce would be possible on a large national scale. MOTO was the last "technological" retailing revolution that preceded e-commerce. Because of their experience in fulfilling small orders rapidly, MOTO firms are advantaged when competing in e-commerce, and the transition to e-commerce has not been difficult for these firms.

Like general merchandisers, MOTO retailers have sophisticated inventory control systems, substantial customer databases, and large scale, giving them significant market power over vendors. In addition, MOTO retailers are advantaged in online retailing because they also have very effective order fulfillment systems and procedures—something with which general merchandisers have little experience. For these reasons, MOTO retailers are among the fastest growing online retail firms.

ONLINE RETAILING

Online retail is perhaps the most high-profile sector of e-commerce on the Web. Over the past decade, this sector has experienced both explosive growth and spectacular failures.

Many of the early pure-play online-only firms that pioneered the retail marketspace failed. Entrepreneurs and their investors seriously misjudged the factors needed to succeed in this market. But the survivors of this early period emerged much stronger, and along with traditional offline general and specialty merchants, as well as new start-ups, the e-tail space is growing very rapidly and is increasing its reach and size.

E-commerce Retail: The Vision

In the early years of e-commerce, literally thousands of entrepreneurial Web-based retailers were drawn to the marketplace for retail goods, simply because it was one of the largest market opportunities in the U.S. economy. Many entrepreneurs initially believed it was easy to enter the retail market. Early writers predicted that the retail industry would be revolutionized, literally "blown to bits"—as prophesized by two consultants in a famous Harvard Business School book (Evans and Wurster, 2000). The basis of this revolution would be fourfold. First, because the Internet greatly reduced both search costs and transaction costs, consumers would use the Web to find the lowest-cost products. Several results would follow. Consumers would increasingly drift to the Web for shopping and purchasing, and only low-cost, high-service, quality online retail merchants would survive. Economists assumed that the Web consumer was rational and cost-driven—not driven by perceived value or brand, both of which are nonrational factors.

Second, it was assumed that the entry costs to the online retail market were much less than those needed to establish physical storefronts, and that online merchants were inherently more efficient at marketing and order fulfillment than offline stores. The costs of establishing a powerful Web site were thought to be minuscule compared to the costs of warehouses, fulfillment centers, and physical stores. There would be no difficulty building sophisticated order entry, shopping cart, and fulfillment systems because this technology was well known, and the cost of technology was falling by 50% each year. Even the cost of acquiring consumers was thought to be much lower on the Web because of search engines that could almost instantly connect customers to online vendors.

Third, as prices fell, traditional offline physical store merchants would be forced out of business. New entrepreneurial companies—such as Amazon—would replace the traditional stores. It was thought that if online merchants grew very quickly, they would have first-mover advantages and lock out the older traditional firms that were too slow to enter the online market.

Fourth, in some industries—such as electronics, apparel, and digital content— the market would be disintermediated as manufacturers or their distributors entered to build a direct relationship with the consumer, destroying the retail intermediaries or middlemen. In this scenario, traditional retail channels—such as physical stores, sales clerks, and sales forces—would be replaced by a single dominant channel: the Web.

Many predicted, on the other hand, a kind of hypermediation based on the concept of a virtual firm in which online retailers would gain advantage over established offline merchants by building an online brand name that attracted millions of customers, and outsourcing the expensive warehousing and order fulfillment functions—the original concept of Amazon and Drugstore.com.

As it turned out, few of these assumptions and visions were correct, and the structure of the retail marketplace in the United States, with some notable exceptions, has not been blown to bits, disintermediated, or revolutionized in the traditional meaning of the word revolution. With several notable exceptions, online retail has often not been successful as an independent platform on which to build a successful "pure-play" Web-only business. As it turns out, the consumer is not primarily price-driven when shopping on the Internet but instead considers brand name, trust, reliability, and delivery time as at least as important as price (Brynjolfsson, Dick, and Smith, 2004).

However, the Internet has created an entirely new venue for multi-channel firms that have a strong offline brand, and in some cases, the Internet has supported the development of pure-play online-only merchants, both general merchandisers as well as specialty retailers. As predicted, online retail has indeed become the fastestgrowing and most dynamic retail channel in the sense of channel innovation. The Web has created a new marketplace for millions of consumers to conveniently shop. The Internet and Web have continued to provide new opportunities for entirely new firms using new business models and new online products—such as Blue Nile, as previously described. The new online channel can conflict with a merchant's other channels, such as direct sales forces, physical stores, and mail order, but this multi-channel conflict can be managed and turned into a strength.

The Online Retail Sector Today

Although online retailing is one of the smallest segments of the retail industry, constituting about 5% of the total retail market today, it is growing at a faster rate than its offline counterparts, with new functionality and product lines being added every day (see **Figure 9.2**). Due to the recession, online retail revenues were basically flat in 2009 compared to 2008, but they are expected to resume their upward trajectory at the rate of 10%–15% a year during the period between 2010 and 2013. When we refer to online retail, we will not be including online services revenues such as travel, job-hunting, or the purchase of digital downloads such as software applications and music. Instead, for the purposes of this chapter, online retail refers solely to sales of physical goods over the Internet. The Internet provides a number of unique advantages and challenges to online retailers. **Table 9.2** summarizes these advantages and challenges.

Despite the high failure rate of online retailers in the early years, more consumers than ever are shopping online. For most consumers, the advantages of shopping on the Web overcome the disadvantages. In 2009, it is estimated that around 70% of Internet users over the age of 14 (around 123 million people) bought at an online retail store, generating about $132 billion in online retail sales. While the number of new Internet users in the United States is not growing as rapidly at it was, with around 71% of the U.S. population over 14 years of age already on the Internet, this slowdown will not necessarily slow the growth in online retail e-commerce because the average shopper

FIGURE 9.2	ONLINE RETAIL AND B2C E-COMMERCE IS ALIVE AND WELL

Online retail revenues were flat in 2008–2009, but are expected to reach $145 billion by 2010 and $201 billion by 2013. Total B2C e-commerce revenues (including travel, other services and digital downloads) are projected to reach around $329 billion by 2013.

SOURCES: Based on data from eMarketer, Inc., 2009a; U.S. Department of Commerce, 2009; Forrester Research, 2008; authors' estimates.

TABLE 9.2	ADVANTAGES AND CHALLENGES TO ONLINE RETAIL
ADVANTAGES	**CHALLENGES**
Lower supply chain costs by aggregating demand at a single site and increasing purchasing power	Consumer concerns about the security of transactions
Lower cost of distribution using Web sites rather than physical stores	Consumer concerns about the privacy of personal information given to Web sites
Ability to reach and serve a much larger geographically distributed group of customers	Delays in delivery of goods when compared to store shopping
Ability to react quickly to customer tastes and demand	Inconvenience associated with return damaged or exchange goods
Ability to change prices nearly instantly	Overcoming lack of consumer trust in online brand names
Ability to rapidly change visual presentation of goods	
Avoidance of direct marketing costs of catalogs and physical mail	
Increased opportunities for personalization, customization	
Ability to greatly improve information and knowledge delivered to consumer	
Ability to lower consumers' overall market transaction costs	

is spending more on the Internet each year, and finding many new categories of items to buy. For instance, in 2003, the average annual amount spent online by users was $675, but by 2009, it had jumped to $1,069 (eMarketer, Inc., 2009a, 2005a). Also, as noted in Chapter 6, millions of additional consumers research products on the Web and are influenced in their purchase decisions at offline stores.

The primary beneficiaries of this growing consumer support are not only the first-mover dot-com companies, but also the established offline retailers who have the brand-name recognition, supportive infrastructure, and financial resources to enter the online marketplace successfully. Table 1.7 on page 42 lists the top online retail firms ranked by online sales. The list contains pure-play online retailers for whom the Internet is the only sales channel, such as Amazon (in first place) and Newegg (in 10th); multi-channel firms that have established brand names and for whom e-commerce plays a relatively small role when compared to their offline physical store channels, such as Staples (2nd), Office Depot (3rd), Office Max (6th), Sears (8th), Best Buy (13th), JCPenney (14th), and Wal-Mart (15th), and manufacturers of computer and electronic equipment, such as Dell (3rd), Apple (7th), Sony (12th). The top 15 retailers account for about one-third of all online retail. For pure-play firms heavily dependent on Web sales, the challenge is to turn visitors into customers, and to develop efficient operations that permit them to achieve long-term profitability. For traditional firms that are much less dependent on e-commerce sales, their challenge is to integrate the offline and online channels so customers can move seamlessly from one environment to another.

Multi-Channel Integration

Clearly one of the most important e-commerce retail themes of 2009–2010 and into the future, is the ability of offline traditional firms such as Wal-Mart, Target, JCPenney, Staples, and others to continue to integrate their Web operations with their physical store operations in order to provide an "integrated shopping customer experience," and leverage the value of their physical stores. **Table 9.3** illustrates some of the various ways in which traditional retailers have integrated the Web and store operations to develop nearly seamless multi-channel shopping. This list is not exclusive, and retailers continue to develop new links between channels.

In the past, it has generally been traditional physical store retailers moving towards the development of powerful Web operations, but in the future, online, pure-play retailers such as Amazon and eBay may develop physical retail stores in

TABLE 9.3	RETAIL E-COMMERCE: MULTI-CHANNEL INTEGRATION METHODS
INTEGRATION TYPE	**DESCRIPTION**
Online order, in-store pickup	Probably one of the first types of integration.
Online order, store directory and inventory	When items are out of stock online, customer is directed to physical store network inventory and store location.
In-store kiosk Web order, home delivery	When retail store is out of stock, customer orders in store and receives at home. Presumes customer is Web familiar.
In-store retail clerk Web order, home delivery	Similar to above, but the retail clerk searches Web inventory if local store is out of stock as a normal part of the in-store check out process.
Web order, in-store returns and adjustments	Defective or rejected products ordered on the Web can be returned to any store location.
Online Web catalog	Online Web catalog supplements offline physical catalog and often the online catalog has substantially more product on display.
Manufacturers use online Web site promotions to drive customers to their distributors' retail stores	Consumer product manufacturers such as Colgate-Palmolive and Procter & Gamble use their Web channels to design new products and promote existing product retail sales.
Gift card, loyalty program points can be used in any channel	Recipient of gift card, loyalty program points can use it to purchase in-store, online, or via catalog, if offered by merchant.

order to process returns or even sell products. For instance, some local entrepreneurs have opened up eBay "drop-off" stores. Like a traditional consignment shop, eBay drop-off stores take in merchandise from people who are too busy or not interested in running an eBay auction and then attempt to sell the merchandise on eBay, keeping as much as 50% of the proceeds for themselves.

Rather than demonstrate disintermediation, online retailing provides an example of the powerful role that intermediaries continue to play in retail trade. Established offline retailers have rapidly gained online market share. Increasingly, consumers are attracted to stable, well-known, trusted retail brands and retailers. The online audience is very sensitive to brand names (as described in Chapter 6) and is not primarily cost-driven. Other factors such as reliability, trust, fulfillment, and customer service are equally important.

9.2 ANALYZING THE VIABILITY OF ONLINE FIRMS

In this and the following chapters, we analyze the viability of a number of online companies that exemplify specific e-commerce models. We are primarily interested in understanding the near-to-medium term (1–3 years) economic viability of these firms and their business models. **Economic viability** refers to the ability of firms to survive as profitable business firms during the specified period. To answer the question of economic viability, we take two business analysis approaches: strategic analysis and financial analysis.

economic viability
refers to the ability of firms to survive as profitable business firms during a specified period

STRATEGIC ANALYSIS

Strategic approaches to economic viability focus on both the industry in which a firm operates and the firm itself (see Chapter 2, Sections 2.2 and 2.5). The key industry strategic factors are:

- *Barriers to entry*: Can new entrants be barred from entering the industry through high capital costs or intellectual property barriers (such as patents and copyrights)?
- *Power of suppliers*: Can suppliers dictate high prices to the industry or can vendors choose from among many suppliers? Have firms achieved sufficient scale to bargain effectively for lower prices from suppliers?
- *Power of customers*: Can customers choose from many competing suppliers and hence challenge high prices and high margins?
- *Existence of substitute products*: Can the functionality of the product or service be obtained from alternative channels or competing products in different industries? Are substitute products and services likely to emerge in the near future?
- *Industry value chain*: Is the chain of production and distribution in the industry changing in ways that benefit or harm the firm?
- *Nature of intra-industry competition*: Is the basis of competition within the industry based on differentiated products and services, price, scope of offerings, or focus of offerings? How is the nature of competition changing? Will these changes benefit the firm?

The strategic factors that pertain specifically to the firm and its related businesses include:

- *Firm value chain*: Has the firm adopted business processes and methods of operation that allow it to achieve the most efficient operations in its industry? Will changes in technology force the firm to realign its business processes?
- *Core competencies*: Does the firm have unique competencies and skills that cannot be easily duplicated by other firms? Will changes in technology invalidate the firm's competencies or strengthen them?
- *Synergies*: Does the firm have access to the competencies and assets of related firms either owned outright or through strategic partnerships and alliances?
- *Technology*: Has the firm developed proprietary technologies that allow it to scale with demand? Has the firm developed the operational technologies (e.g., customer relationship management, fulfillment, supply chain management, inventory control, and human resource systems) to survive?
- *Social and legal challenges*: Has the firm put in place policies to address consumer trust issues (privacy and security of personal information)? Is the firm the subject of lawsuits challenging its business model, such as intellectual property ownership issues? Will the firm be affected by changes in Internet taxation laws or other foreseeable statutory developments?

FINANCIAL ANALYSIS

Strategic analysis helps us comprehend the competitive situation of the firm. Financial analysis helps us understand how in fact the firm is performing. There are two parts to a financial analysis: the statement of operations and the balance sheet. The statement of operations tells us how much money (or loss) the firm is achieving based on current sales and costs. The balance sheet tells us how many assets the firm has to support its current and future operations.

Here are some of the key factors to look for in a firm's Statement of Operations:

- *Revenues*: Are revenues growing and at what rate? Many e-commerce companies have experienced impressive, even explosive revenue growth, as an entirely new channel is created.
- *Cost of sales*: What is the cost of sales compared to revenues? Cost of sales typically includes the cost of the products sold and related costs. The lower the cost of sales compared to revenue, the higher the gross profit.
- *Gross margin*: What is the firm's gross margin, and is it increasing or decreasing? **Gross margin** is calculated by dividing gross profit by net sales revenues. Gross margin can tell you if the firm is gaining or losing market power vis á vis its key suppliers.
- *Operating expenses*: What are the firm's operating expenses, and are they increasing or decreasing? Operating expenses typically include the cost of marketing, technology, and administrative overhead. They also include, in accordance with professional accounting standards (see below), stock-based compensation to

gross margin
gross profit divided by net sales

employees and executives, amortization of goodwill and other intangibles, and impairment of investments. In e-commerce companies, these turn out to be very important expenses. Many e-commerce firms compensated their employees with stock shares (or options), and many e-commerce firms purchased other e-commerce firms as a part of their growth strategy. Many of the companies were purchased at extremely high values using company stock rather than cash; in numerous instances, the purchased companies fell dramatically in market value. All these items are counted as normal operating expenses.

- *Operating margin*: What did the firm earn from its current operations? **Operating margin** is calculated by dividing operating income or loss by net sales revenue. Operating margin is an indication of a company's ability to turn sales into pre-tax profit after operating expenses have been deducted. Operating margin tells us if the firm's current operations are covering its operating expenses, not including interest expenses and other non-operating expenses.

- *Net margin*: **Net margin** tells us the percentage of its gross sales revenue the firm was able to retain after all expenses are deducted. Net margin is calculated by dividing net income or loss by net sales revenue. Net margin sums up in one number how successful a company has been at the business of making a profit on each dollar of sales revenues. Net margin also tells us something about the efficiency of the firm by measuring the percentage of sales revenue it is able retain after all expenses are deducted from gross revenues, and within a single industry can be used to measure the relative efficiency of competing firms. Net margin takes into account many non-operating expenses such as interest and stock compensation plans.

When examining the financial announcements of e-commerce companies, it is important to realize that online firms often choose not to announce their net income according to generally accepted accounting principles (GAAP). These principles have been promulgated by the Financial Accounting Standards Board (FASB), a board of professional accountants that establishes accounting rules for the profession, and which has played a vital role since the 1934 Securities Act, which sought to improve financial accounting during the Great Depression. Many e-commerce firms in the early years instead reported an entirely new calculation called *pro forma earnings* (also called EBITDA—earnings before income taxes, depreciation, and amortization). Pro forma earnings generally do not deduct stock-based compensation, depreciation, or amortization. The result is that pro forma earnings are always better than GAAP earnings. The firms that report in this manner typically claim these expenses are non-recurring and special and "unusual." In 2002 and 2003, the SEC issued new guidelines (Regulation G) that prohibit firms from reporting pro forma earnings in official reports to the SEC, but still allow firms to announce pro forma earnings in public statements (Weil, 2003). Throughout this book, we consider a firm's income or loss based on GAAP accounting standards only.

A **balance sheet** provides a financial snapshot of a company's assets and liabilities (debts) on a given date. **Assets** refer to stored value. **Current assets** are those assets such as cash, securities, accounts receivable, inventory, or other

operating margin
calculated by dividing operating income or loss by net sales revenue

net margin
the percentage of its gross sales revenue the firm is able to retain after all expenses are deducted; calculated by dividing net income or loss by net sales revenue

balance sheet
provides a financial snapshot of a company on a given date and shows its financial assets and liabilities

assets
refers to stored value

current assets
assets such as cash, securities, accounts receivable, inventory, or other investments that are likely to be able to be converted to cash within one year

liabilities
outstanding obligations of the firm

current liabilities
debts of the firm that will be due within one year

long-term debt
liabilities that are not due until the passage of a year or more

working capital
firm's current assets minus current liabilities

investments that are likely to be able to be converted to cash within one year. **Liabilities** are outstanding obligations of the firm. **Current liabilities** are debts of the firm that will be due within one year. Liabilities that are not due until the passage of a year or more are characterized as **long-term debt**. For a quick check of a firm's short-term financial health, examine its **working capital** (the firm's current assets minus current liabilities). If working capital is only marginally positive, or negative, the firm will likely have trouble meeting its short-term obligations. Alternatively, if a firm has a large amount of current assets, it can sustain operational losses for a period of time.

9.3 E-COMMERCE IN ACTION: E-TAILING BUSINESS MODELS

So far, we have been discussing online retail as if it were a single entity. In fact, as we briefly discussed in Chapter 2, there are four main types of online retail business models: virtual merchants, multi-channel merchandisers (sometimes referred to as bricks-and-clicks or clicks-and-bricks), catalog merchants, and manufacturer-direct firms. In addition, there are small "mom and pop" retailers that use eBay, Amazon, and Yahoo Stores sales platforms, as well as affiliate merchants whose primary revenue derives from sending traffic to their "mother" sites. Each of these different types of online retailers faces a different strategic environment, as well as different industry and firm economics.

VIRTUAL MERCHANTS

virtual merchant
single-channel Web firms that generate almost all of their revenue from online sales

Virtual merchants are single-channel Web firms that generate almost all their revenue from online sales. Virtual merchants face extraordinary strategic challenges. They must build a business and brand name from scratch, quickly, in an entirely new channel and confront many virtual merchant competitors (especially in smaller niche areas). Because these firms are totally online stores, they do not have to bear the costs associated with building and maintaining physical stores, but they face large costs in building and maintaining a Web site, building an order fulfillment infrastructure, and developing a brand name. Customer acquisition costs are high, and the learning curve is steep. Like all retail firms, their gross margins (the difference between the retail price of goods sold and the cost of goods to the retailer) are low. Therefore, virtual merchants must achieve highly efficient operations in order to preserve a profit, while building a brand name as quickly as possible in order to attract sufficient customers to cover their costs of operations. Most merchants in this category adopt low-cost and convenience strategies, coupled with extremely effective and efficient fulfillment processes to ensure customers receive what they ordered as fast as possible. In the following *E-commerce in Action* section, we take an in-depth look at the strategic and financial situation of Amazon, the leading online virtual merchant. In addition to Amazon, other successful virtual merchants include Newegg, Netflix, Zappos, Drugstore.com, Buy.com, Blue Nile (profiled in the opening case), Bluefly, Bidz.com, and eBags.com.

E-COMMERCE IN ACTION

AMAZON.COM

Amazon, the Seattle-based pure-online merchant is one of the most best-known names on the Web. Never suffering from modesty, Amazon's founder, Jeff Bezos, has proclaimed in its annual report that the objective of Amazon is to "offer the Earth's Biggest Selection and to be Earth's most customer-centric company where customers can find and discover anything they may want to buy." Just exactly what these claims mean, and how it might be possible to achieve them, is still a matter of speculation for both customers and investors. Yet this has not stopped Bezos and his team from becoming the Web's most successful and innovative pure-play, online retailer.

Few business enterprises have experienced a similar roller-coaster ride from explosive early growth, to huge losses, and then on to profitability. No Internet business has been both so hotly reviled and so hotly praised. Its stock reflects these changing fortunes, hitting a high of $106 a share in the second quarter of 1999, and a low of $6 a share in 2001, climbing back up to $60 a share in 2003, bouncing between $30 to $50 during 2004–2005, dropping down to a low of $27 a share in 2006, then climbing back up to into the $90s in 2007, before dropping down again into the $40s in the latter half of 2008, then back again into the $80s by the fall of 2009. The story for now is that Amazon is an Internet survivor, one that is likely to succeed in the long term. It had its first profitable quarter in fall 2002, and its first profitable year in 2003. While controversial, Amazon has also been one of the most innovative online retailing stories in the history of e-commerce. From the earliest days of e-commerce, Amazon has continuously adapted its business model based both on its market experience and its insight into the online consumer.

The Vision

The original vision of founder Jeff Bezos and his friends was that the Internet was a revolutionary new form of commerce and that only companies that became really big early on (ignoring profitability) would survive. The path to success, according to founder Bezos, was to offer consumers three things: the lowest prices, the best selection, and convenience (which translates into feature-rich content, user-generated reviews of books and products, fast and reliable fulfillment, and ease of use). Currently Amazon offers consumers millions of unique new, used, and collectible items in 12 major categories: books; movies, music and games; digital downloads; Kindle e-book reader products; computers and office; electronics; home and garden; grocery, health and beauty; toys, kids and baby; clothing, shoes and jewelry; sports and outdoors; and tools, auto and industrial. And if Amazon does not carry it, they have created systems for helping you find it at online merchants who rent space from Amazon, or even at other places on the Web. In short, Amazon has come close to becoming the largest, single one-stop merchant on the Web, a kind of combined "shopping portal" and "product search portal" that puts it in direct competition with other large online general merchants, eBay, and general portals such as Yahoo, MSN, and even Google. As Amazon has succeeded in becoming the world's largest online store, it expanded its original vision to become one of the Web's largest supplier of merchant and search services.

Business Model

Amazon's business is currently organized into two basic segments, North American and Retail. Within those segments, it serves not only retail customers, but also merchants and developers. The retail component of the business sells goods that Amazon has purchased and then resells to consumers just like a traditional retailer.

The second major component of Amazon's business is its third-party merchant segment. Amazon Services' enables third parties to integrate their products into Amazon's Web site, and use Amazon's customer technologies. In the early years of its business, Amazon entered into partnerships with large merchants such as Toys "R" Us, Borders, and Target, and created storefronts for these companies within the larger Amazon site. Today, Amazon has increasingly left the enterprise-level business to competitors (Target announced it was ending its partnership with Amazon in 2011), although it still runs Web sites for Bebe (a youth retailer), OshKosh B'Gosh (children's clothing), Timex, and Marks & Spencer (an English department store). Instead it has been focusing its efforts on small and medium-sized retail merchants.

Thousands of these types of merchants have signed on with Amazon, offering products that in some instances even compete with those that Amazon itself sells. For instance, a single product on the Amazon Web site may be listed for sale simultaneously by Amazon, by a large branded merchant participant such as Target, and by a business or individual selling a new, used, or collectible version of the product through Amazon Marketplace, Amazon Auctions, or an Amazon WebStore created by the merchant. For these types of merchants, Amazon is not the seller of record, does not own these products, and the shipping of products is usually handled by the third party (although in some instances, Amazon provides fulfillment services as well). Amazon collects a monthly fixed fee, sales commission (generally estimated to be between 10% and 20% of the sale), per-unit activity fee, or some combination thereof from the third party. In this segment, Amazon acts as an online shopping mall, collecting "rents" from other merchants and providing "site" services such as order entry and payment.

In many respects, Amazon's third-party seller segment is an effort to compete directly with eBay, the Web's most successful third-party merchant sales platform, which has, at any given time, a registered trading community of active buyers and sellers of over 84 million people. Amazon has even developed its own version of PayPal: Checkout by Amazon. At the same time, eBay itself has moved closer to Amazon's business model by encouraging merchants to sell rather than auction goods on its sites. ("Buy It Now", eBay stores, and other fixed-price trading features now accounts for around 40% of all products sold by eBay.)

The third major part of Amazon's business is Amazon Web Services. Through this segment, Amazon offers a variety of Web services that provide developers with direct access to Amazon's technology platform, and allow them to build their own applications based on that platform. The company launched the program in 2002, and five years later, Amazon had over 200,000 volunteers building applications and services, strengthening the business. Bezos, however, was not satisfied with only a slew of cool new applications for his company's Web site. In March 2006, Amazon introduced the first of several new services that Bezos hoped would transform the future of Amazon as a business. With Simple Storage Service (S3) and, later, Elastic Compute Cloud (EC2), Amazon entered the utility computing market. The company realized that the benefits of its $2 billion investment in technology could also be valuable to other companies. Amazon has tremendous computing capacity, but like most companies, only uses a small portion of it at any one time. Moreover, the Amazon infrastructure is considered by many to be among the most robust in the world. Amazon began to sell its computing power on a per-usage basis, just like a power company sells electricity.

S3, for example, is a data storage service that is designed to make Web-scale computing easier and more affordable for developers. United States customers pay 15 cents per gigabyte of data for up to the first 50 terabytes stored per month on Amazon's network of disk drives, and a declining amount for additional storage. There is also a charge of 10 cents per gigabyte for data transferred in and 17 cents per gigabyte for the first 10 terabytes of data transferred out, again with a declining amount for additional transfers over that amount. Customers pay for exactly what they use and no more. Working in conjunction with S3, EC2 enables businesses to utilize Amazon's servers for computing tasks, such as testing software. Using EC2 incurs charges of 10 cents per standard (small instance) hour consumed for Linux/Unix usage and 12.5 cents per hour for Windows usage.. A standard "small instance" supplies the user with the equivalent of 1.7 GB of RAM, 1.0–1.2 GHz Opteron or Xeon processor, a 160 GB hard drive, a 32-bit platform, and 250 MB/s of bandwidth on the network. Other "Infrastructure" Web services offered by Amazon include Simple Queue Service (SQS), which offers a hosted queue for storing messages as they travel between computers; SimpleDB, a database Web service; CloudFront, a content delivery Web service; and Elastic MapReduce, a Web service that enables users to perform data-intensive tasks.

In addition to these Web services, Amazon also offers Virtual Private Cloud, which can be used to create a VPN between the Amazon cloud and a company's existing IT infrastructure. Flexible Payments Service (FPS) provides a payments service for developers. DevPay is an online billing and account management service for developers who create Amazon cloud applications. Amazon Mechanical Turk provides a marketplace for work that requires human intelligence. Alexa Web Information Services provides Web traffic data and information for developers. Fulfillment Web Services (FWS) allows merchants to access Amazon's fulfillment capabilities through a simple Web services interface.

As yet, it is not possible to quantify the impact and success of the Amazon Web Services initiative since Amazon does not provide a breakout of its revenues in its financial reports. For now, Amazon continues to generate revenue primarily by selling products. While Amazon started out as an online merchant of books, CDs, and DVDs, since 2002 it has diversified into becoming a general merchandiser of millions of other products. In 2008, around 58% of its revenue came from media sales such as books, CDs, DVDs, and music, while 39% came from electronics and other general merchandise. Its dependence on media sales has been declining each year, however, and in 2009, it is expected that worldwide sales of media products will be surpassed for the first time by sales of electronics and other general merchandise.

In addition to Amazon.com in the United States, Amazon also operates localized sites in Japan, Germany, United Kingdom, France, and Canada. The success of its international business often does not attract much attention. For instance, in 2008, Amazon derived almost $9 billion, or over 45%, of its $19.16 billion of gross revenues offshore, and international sales grew by 33% for the year. In 2008, Amazon opened 12 new Web stores and continued to develop new technology and new products like the Kindle, an electronic reader. Kindle 2 was introduced on February 23, 2009, and is selling briskly. It offers the ability to store 1,500 books, there are 250,000 titles to choose from, and each book takes less than 60 seconds to download.

Financial Analysis

Amazon's revenues have increased from about $600 million in 1998 to $19.17 billion in 2008. In the last three years, Amazon's revenues have grown an incredible 56% (see **Table 9.4**). This is very impressive, explosive revenue growth. In an effort to attract sales, Amazon has offered free shipping on orders over $25, and this has increased its operating costs and lowered net margins, a move that worries investors. This policy is one of a number of factors that contribute to Amazon's pattern of increasing revenues and decreasing profits.

However, Amazon has been able to compensate for the cost of its low price strategy and free shipping policies by reducing operating expenses and by eliminating marketing in offline magazines and television. Costs have remained steady at a little over 2% of revenues despite a 30% increase in sales in 2008. General and administrative costs as a percentage of sales have also remained nearly constant. This means that Amazon's increase in sales did not come about by increases in marketing, head count, or administrative overhead. Amazon instead relies heavily on affiliates and third-party merchants to drive sales. In addition, it has demonstrated an ability to scale its operations without rapidly increasing its administrative expenditures. As a result of its cost-saving measures, Amazon was able to grow its net income by a factor of almost 20 from 2003 ($35 million) to 2008 ($645 million). Net margin has fluctuated from a low of .7% in 2003, to a high of 8.5% in 2004, and was 3.4% in 2008. For every dollar in net sales in 2008, Amazon was earning a profit of about 3 cents—positive but not wonderful and not any better than a lot of bricks-and-mortar retailers. The reason for this fall off in net margin is clearly related to its free shipping policy and low cost policies. Nevertheless, the prospect for Amazon based on this financial analysis looks much improved from earlier years when it was showing negative margins and losing money on every sale.

Amazon's balance sheet shows a company with a still heavy reliance on long-term debt , although significantly reduced from 2007. At the end of December 2008, it had about $3.7 billion in cash and marketable securities. The cash and securities were obtained from sales, sales of stock and notes to the public, venture

| TABLE 9.4 | **AMAZON'S CONSOLIDATED STATEMENTS OF OPERATIONS AND SUMMARY BALANCE SHEET DATA 2006–2008** |

CONSOLIDATED STATEMENTS OF OPERATIONS (in thousands)

For the fiscal year ended December 31,	2008	2007	2006
Revenue			
Net sales	$ 19,166,000	$ 14,835,000	$10,711,000
Cost of sales	14,896,00	$11,482,000	8,255,000
Gross profit	**4,270,000**	**3,353,000**	**2,456,000**
Gross margin	**22%**	**23%**	**23%**
Operating expenses			
Marketing	482,000	344,000	263,000
Fulfillment	1,658,000	1,292,000	937,000
Technology and content	1,033,000	818,000	662,000
General and administrative	279,000	235,000	195,000
Other operating expense, net	(24,000)	(9,000)	(10,000)
Total operating expenses	3,428,000	2,698,000	2,067,000
Income from operations	**842,000**	**655,000**	**389,000**
Operating margin	**4.4%**	**4.4%**	**3.6%**
Total non-operating income (expense)	59,000	5,000	(12,000)
Income before income taxes	901,000	660,000	377,000
Provision for income taxes	(247,000)	(184,000)	
Equity-method investment activity, net of tax	(9,000)	—	—
Income before change in accounting principle	—	476,000	190,000
Cumulative effect of change in accounting principle	—	—	—
Net income (loss)	**645,000**	**476,000**	**190,000**
Net margin	**3.4%**	**3.2%**	**1.8%**

SUMMARY BALANCE SHEET DATA (in thousands)

At December 31,	2008	2007	2006
Assets			
Cash, cash equivalents and marketable securities	3,727,000	3,112,000	$2,019,000
Total current assets	6,157,000	5,164,000	3,373,000
Total assets	8,314,000	6,485,000	4,363,000
Liabilities			
Total current liabilities	4,746,000	3,714,000	2,532,000
Long-term debt and other	896,000	1,574,000	1,400,000
Working capital	1,411,000	1,450,000	841,000
Stockholders' Equity (Deficit)	2,672,000	1,197,000	431,000

SOURCE: Amazon.com ,Inc., 2009.

capital investors, and institutional investors in return for equity (shares) in the company or debt securities. Total assets are listed at $8.3 billion. The company emphasizes the strength of its "free cash flow" as a sign of financial strength, suggesting it has more than enough cash available to cover short-term liabilities (such as financing holiday season purchasing). The balance sheet has improved over the last three years since 2006 as asset-debt ratios are improving. In 2008, Amazon decreased it long-term debt significantly. Amazon's cash assets should certainly be enough to cover future short-term deficits should they occur. However, the company continues to carry over $400 million in long-term debt and other liabilities, and $71 million a year in interest expense. It is fair to conclude that Amazon's management is still under pressure to maintain consistent profitability and reduce its long-term debt.

Strategic Analysis—Business Strategy

Amazon engages in a number of business strategies that seek to maximize growth in sales volume, while cutting prices to the bare bones. Its two main revenue growth strategies include moving towards a broader trading platform by expanding the third-party seller segment, and moving towards greater product focus by grouping its offerings into major categories called stores. In the past two years, Amazon has created 28 new online stores that group together sellers and products: such as an Outdoor recreation store, an AmazonWireless store offering cell phones and service plans, and others focused on beauty, gourmet food, sporting goods, jewelry and watches, health and personal care, office supplies, a Software en Espanol store for Spanish-language and bilingual software products, and a motorcycle and ATV store. Early results suggest these stores are growing faster than Amazon as a whole, particularly jewelry and watches. Amazon is still following Wal-Mart's and eBay's examples by attempting to be a mass-market, low-price, high-volume online supermarket where you can get just about anything. To achieve profitability in this environment, Amazon has invested heavily in supply chain management and fulfillment strategies to reduce its costs to the bare minimum while still providing excellent customer service and even free shipping.

Specific programs to increase revenues are the continuation of free shipping from Amazon Retail (a strategy that has increased order sizes by 25%), Amazon Prime (which for $79 a year provides free two-day shipping and one-day delivery upgrades for $3.99), greater product selection, and shorter order fulfillment times. Amazon's management is experimenting with "accelerated shipping" by offering customers next-day or even same-day shipping in selected areas such as Manhattan, while not charging additional fees. Internet customers have long been frustrated both by high shipping and handling charges as well as long delays in receiving goods. A ticking clock can be seen next to some Amazon sale items indicating the hours remaining for an order to make it to the customer by the next day.

Amazon also made several strategic acquisitions in 2008 and 2009, including Audible.com, a leading online provider of audio books and other digital spoken word audio content; Abebooks.com, an online marketplace primarily for used, rare and out-of-print books;, Fabric.com, an online fabric store that offers custom measured and cut fabrics, as well as patterns, sewing tools, and accessories; and Zappos.com, a popular online shoe shopping destination.

Amazon is increasingly moving into the mobile shopping space as well, launching a shopping app for the iPhone in December 2008, the BlackBerry in April 2009, and the Android in August 2009. In 2009, Amazon also introduced significant enhancements to its wireless Kindle e-book reader, with two new versions, the Kindle 2 and the Kindle DX, a large screen version more appropriate for newspapers, magazines and textbooks, and a Kindle for iPhone app. By the end of June 2009, its Kindle Store was offering more than 320,000 books.

On the cost side, Amazon has taken significant steps to lower costs in the past two years. Important initiatives included the hiring of mathematicians and operations specialists to optimize the location of storing goods in Amazon's six warehouses, optimizing the size of shipments, and consolidating orders into larger batches prior to shipping. The company increasingly uses "postal injection" for shipping, in which Amazon trucks deliver pre-posted packages to U.S. Postal System centers.

Strategic Analysis—Competition

Amazon's competitors are general merchandisers who are both offline and online, and increasingly both. This includes the largest online competitor, eBay, and multi-channel retailers such as Wal-Mart, Sears, and JCPenney. Amazon also competes with catalog merchants such as L.L.Bean and Lands' End in a number of product areas. As the Web's largest bookseller, Amazon is in competition with bookstores such as Barnesandnoble.com. Insofar as other portal sites such as MSN and Yahoo are involved in operating online stores or auctions, or selling their own products, Amazon also competes with these portals. In addition, Amazon competes with other firms who sell Web services such as hosting, shopping cart, and fulfillment services. Amazon has also engaged iTunes, Netflix, and Blockbuster in competition by offering video and audio downloads. In 2007, Amazon started selling MP3 music files without the Digital Rights Management (DRM) shackles that prevent iTunes users from playing their downloaded music on anything but an iPod, and by September 2009, was offering over 8 million DRM-free MP3 songs from all four major music labels and thousands of independent labels that can be played on virtually any hardware device and managed with any music software. In September 2008, Amazon also introduced Amazon Video On Demand Service, which offers thousands of movies and television shows that can be viewed instantly on a PC or Mac, as well as downloaded onto a computer or Tivo box. In April 2009, Amazon added high definition movies and television episodes to the service.

Strategic Analysis—Technology

The person who said that "IT doesn't make a difference" clearly does not know much about Amazon. Amazon arguably has the largest and most sophisticated collection of online retailing technologies available at any single site on the Web. Amazon has implemented numerous Web site management, search, customer interaction, recommendation, transaction processing, and fulfillment services and systems using a combination of its own proprietary technologies and commercially available, licensed technologies. Amazon's transaction-processing systems handle millions of items, a number of different status inquiries, gift-wrapping requests, and multiple shipment methods. These systems allow customers to choose whether to receive single or several shipments based on availability and to track the progress of each order. Amazon's technology extends to its employees as well. Every warehouse worker carries a shoehorn-size device that combines a bar code scanner, a display screen, and a two-way data transmitter. In 2008, Amazon spent over $1 billion on technology and new content, and is on track to spend a similar amount in 2009.

Strategic Analysis—Social and Legal Challenges

Amazon is currently facing a number of lawsuits concerning various aspects of its business. One series of lawsuits alleges that Amazon wrongfully failed to collect and remit sales and use taxes for sales of personal property and knowingly created records and statements falsely stating it was not required to collect or remit such taxes. Amazon historically has also been faced with a number of patent infringement suits, which it typically settles out of court. Currently, there are several pending suits.

Perhaps the most troubling lawsuit against Amazon, however, is the suit filed by its previous partner Toys"R"Us in 2004. Toys"R"Us sued Amazon over what it claimed was its exclusive right to sell toys on Amazon, and the fee which is reported to be $200 million for that right until 2010. This lawsuit aimed squarely at Amazon's Third Party Seller segment business. Toys"R"Us claimed the two companies agreed that Toys"R"Us would be the exclusive toy purveyor on the site. While in general this seems to be true because it is difficult to find toys on the Amazon site outside of the Toys"R"Us store, nevertheless Toys"R"Us is claiming some 4,000 items have slipped through the cracks. Amazon filed counter claims against Toys"R"Us. In March 2006, the Superior Court of New Jersey ruled in favor of Toys"R"Us, granting the toy company release from its contract with Amazon, but awarding no damages. Amazon is appealing the decision with the goal of reinstating the contract and compelling Toys"R"Us to pay the damages requested in the counterclaim. Because Amazon has come to rely heavily on the brand power of the largest third-party merchants, it would be particularly harmful to Amazon if it is deemed to have entered into "exclusivity" covenants with those retailers. For instance, eBay has no such exclusivity arrangement with any of its sellers.

In May 2008, Amazon filed a lawsuit against the State of New York, which in April 2008 amended its sales tax law to specifically cover sales by out-of-state online retailers who get customers through New York-based affiliate Web sites. Amazon has charged that the statute is unconstitutional and overly broad and vague. The NY State Supreme Court rejected Amazon's position in January 2009, but Amazon has appealed, and the case remains pending as of September 2009.

Future Prospects

Amazon clearly has improved its financial performance through consistent gains in operational efficiency and extraordinary growth in sales. In 2008, net sales grew 30% to $19.17 billion, and net income rose by 36% to $645 million, . Through the second quarter of 2009, even in the midst of a recessionary period, Amazon showed significant gains over the previous year in net sales, operating income, and net income. For the first six months of the year, the company registered over $8.2 billion in sales, as opposed to $5.9 billion for the same period in 2008, paced by increases in sales of electronics and general merchandise. . Net income for the period was $319 million compared to $301 million. Projections for the third quarter indicated a growth in net sales of between 11% and 23%. Although many worry about its ability to maintain high levels of customer service, Amazon routinely ranks among the top five online e-commerce sites for customer service, accuracy of delivery, and speed of fulfillment.

However, when compared to Wal-Mart, a very profitable retailing giant, Amazon comes up short because its net margins are paper. Although it seems to have turned the corner and achieved several years of consecutive profitability, when compared to Wal-Mart's return on invested capital and consistent growth rate in sales and profits, Amazon still has a long way to go. Analysts express a mix of optimism and caution over Amazon's future in 2010 and beyond.

MULTI-CHANNEL MERCHANTS: BRICKS-AND-CLICKS

Also called multi-channel merchants, **bricks-and-clicks** companies have a network of physical stores as their primary retail channel, but also have introduced online offerings. These are multi-channel firms such as Wal-Mart, JCPenney, Sears, and other brand-name merchants. While bricks-and-clicks merchants face high costs of physical buildings and large sales staffs, they also have many advantages such as a brand name, a national customer base, warehouses, large scale (giving them leverage with suppliers), and a trained staff. Acquiring customers is less expensive because of their brand names, but these firms face challenges in coordinating prices across channels and handling returns of Web purchases at their retail outlets. However, these retail players are used to operating on very thin margins and have invested heavily in purchasing and inventory control systems to control costs, and in coordinating returns from multiple locations. Bricks-and-clicks companies face the challenge of leveraging their strengths and assets to the Web, building a credible Web site, hiring new skilled staff, and building rapid-response order entry and fulfillment systems. According to Internet Retailer, in 2008, the chain retailers accounted for around $45 billion (almost 40%) of all online retail sales. However, there remains much room for growth. (Internet Retailer, 2009).

JCPenney.com (rebranded as JCP.com in 2007) is a prime example of a traditional merchant based on physical stores and an ailing catalog operation moving successfully to a multi-channel online store. Other examples include Sears.com, NeimanMarcus.com, Target.com and, of course, Walmart.com.

James Cash Penney founded JCPenney in 1902. Penney's original vision was to create a nationwide chain of stores based on the newly emerging business model called a "department store," which aggregated a wide variety of general merchandise at a central location, usually near local transportation hubs formed by streets, highways, and street car lines. In addition, Penney envisioned a national catalog mail-order business to rival the successful Sears model. Today, JCPenney is one of the largest national department store chains, with more than 1,000 department stores in the United States and Puerto Rico. In addition to its department stores, JCPenney operates one of the largest catalog operations in the United States, distributing over 400 million catalogs annually.

Like many traditional retailers, however, JCPenney has had to change its business model to accommodate the Internet and consumer demands for low cost

bricks-and-clicks
companies that have a network of physical stores as their primary retail channel, but also have introduced online offerings

and unparalleled product depth and selection, which could only be achieved by enhancing its Web operations. JCPenney opened its Web site for business in 1998 and placed its full catalog inventory online. Its department stores and Internet channels primarily serve the same target market: "modern spenders" and "starting-outers," or two-income families with median annual incomes of $50,000.

At JCPenney.com, customers can buy family clothing, jewelry, shoes, accessories, and home furnishings. And whether they buy merchandise in a bricks-and-mortar store, through the catalog, or on the Internet, customers can return items either at a store or through the mail. Indeed, the current essence of multi-channel retailing is the nearly complete integration of offline and online sales and operations while presenting a single branded experience to the customer. A second feature of successful multi-channel retailing is understanding customer preferences so that each channel sells products appropriate to that channel. For instance, not only can customers pick up and return at a local store what they order from JCPenney.com, but they can also order from the store's counters items not in the store but available online. The in-store point-of-sale system is integrated with Penney's Web catalog, and they both share a common inventory system. Many items are too expensive to hold in physical store inventory, but they can be offered economically on the Web site. The company is also investing in state-of-the-art interactivity and imaging tools for the Web site, such as a tool that lets shoppers mix and match 142,000 combinations of window treatments, and fitting guides that enable shoppers to zoom in on products such as jeans and create more custom-fitted orders.

The company has achieved online success through some savvy decisions: putting approximately 250,000 products online, from lingerie to home furnishings, surpassing the competition in terms of selection, targeting women as the primary consumer, and making it easy to move from one category to the next on the site. JCPenney is able to directly compete against Amazon given its large selection, especially in apparel lines. In doing so, online sales are attracting new, younger JCPenney shoppers, 25% of whom have never bought anything in a JCPenney store. According to Internet Retailer, in 2008, 90% of JCPenney Web customers also shopped in their stores. Online sales are complementing, rather than cannibalizing, store and catalog sales. Shoppers who buy through all three channels spend four times more—$1,000—than the shopper who makes purchases only at the retail store.

As a result, JCPenney appears to have successfully made the transition from department store/catalog merchant to store/Web merchant. Web sales in 2008 were $1.5 billion, about the same as in 2007, due to the recession, but a bright light when compared to an almost 7% overall decline in sales from its other operations. In the fourth quarter of 2008, Web sales declined 8.6%, but by February 2009 they were growing again. Continued improvement in this segment, coupled with a strong focus on high-margin apparel products for families, an area where Amazon and eBay are weak, offers a chance for continuing improved long-term performance. (JCPenney, 2009; Internet Retailer, 2009).

CATALOG MERCHANTS

Catalog merchants such as Lands' End, L.L.Bean, Eddie Bauer, Victoria's Secret, and Lillian Vernon are established companies that have a national offline catalog operation that is their largest retail channel, but who have also developed online capabilities. JCPenney could also be included here, given the large scale of its catalog operation. Catalog merchants face very high costs for printing and mailing millions of catalogs each year—many of which have a half-life of 30 seconds after the customer receives them. Nevertheless, catalog merchants have the highest margins in the retail sector because they have achieved very efficient operations. They generally have few, if any, physical stores. They also typically have developed centralized fulfillment and call centers, extraordinary service, and excellent fulfillment in partnership with package delivery firms such as FedEx and UPS. Catalog firms have suffered in recent years as catalog sales growth rates have fallen to levels that are still far above general retail but much slower than the early years of the 1980s, when annual revenues were growing at 30% a year. As a result, catalog merchants have had to diversify their channels either by building stores (L.L.Bean), being bought by store-based firms (Sears purchased Lands' End), or by building a strong Web presence.

Catalog merchants face many of the same challenges as bricks-and-mortar stores—they must leverage their existing assets and competencies to a new technology environment, build a credible Web presence, and hire new staff. Catalog firms are uniquely advantaged, however, because they already possess very efficient, fast response order entry and fulfillment systems. In 2008, according to Internet Retailer, catalog merchants generated combined Web sales of almost $20 billion.

Arguably one of the most successful online catalog merchants is LandsEnd.com. Lands' End started out in 1963 in a basement of Chicago's tannery district selling sailboat equipment and clothing, handling 15 orders on a good day. Since then it expanded into a direct catalog merchant, distributing over 200 million catalogs annually and selling a much expanded line of "traditionally" styled sport clothing, soft luggage, and products for the home. Lands' End launched its Web site in 1995 with 100 products and travelogue essays. Located in Racine, Wisconsin, it has since grown into one of the Web's most successful apparel sites.

Land's End has always been on the leading edge of online retailing technologies, most of which emphasize personal marketing and customized products. Among these technologies are My Virtual Model, which allows customers to create a 3-D model of themselves to "try on" clothing; Lands' End Live, which enables customers to chat online with customer service representatives; and Lands' End Custom, which allows customers to create custom-crafted clothing built for their personal measurements. While customized clothing built online was thought to be a gimmick in the early years of online retailing, today 40% of Lands' End clothing sold online is customized, and 25% of My Virtual Model customers are first-time customers. In 2003, Lands' End was purchased by Sears (which itself was purchased by Kmart in 2004) but retains an independent online presence and catalog operation. Sears has incorporated many of Lands' End's online techniques into its own Web site, Sears.com (Landsend.com, 2009).

catalog merchants
established companies that have a national offline catalog operation that is their largest retail channel, but who have recently developed online capabilities

MANUFACTURER-DIRECT

manufacturer-direct
single- or multi-channel manufacturers who sell directly online to consumers without the intervention of retailers

Manufacturer-direct firms are either single- or multi-channel manufacturers that sell directly online to consumers without the intervention of retailers. Manufacturer-direct firms were predicted to play a very large role in e-commerce, but this has generally not happened. The primary exception is computer hardware, where firms such as Dell, Hewlett-Packard, Sony, Apple, and Gateway, account for over 70% of computer retail sales online. Some of these firms had retail experience prior to the Web (Dell was built on the direct sales model), while others—such as Hewlett-Packard—had no prior direct sales experience.

As discussed in Chapter 6, manufacturer-direct firms face channel conflict challenges. Channel conflict occurs when physical retailers of products must compete on price and currency of inventory directly against the manufacturer, who does not face the cost of maintaining inventory, physical stores, or sales staffs. Firms with no prior direct marketing experience face the additional challenges of developing a fast-response online order and fulfillment system, acquiring customers, and coordinating their supply chains with market demand. Switching from a **supply-push model** (where products are made prior to orders received based on estimated demand and then stored in warehouses awaiting sale) to a **demand-pull model** (where products are not built until an order is received) has proved extremely difficult for traditional manufacturers. Yet for many products, manufacturer-direct firms have the advantage of an established national brand name, an existing large customer base, and a lower cost structure than even catalog merchants because they are the manufacturer of the goods and thus do not pay profits to anyone else. Therefore, manufacturer-direct firms should have higher margins.

supply-push model
products are made prior to orders received based on estimated demand

demand-pull model
products are not built until an order is received

The most frequently cited successful manufacturer-direct retailer is Dell Inc., the world's largest direct computer systems supplier, providing corporations, government agencies, small-to-medium businesses, and individuals with computer products and services ordered straight from the manufacturer's headquarters in Austin, Texas. Although sales representatives support corporate customers, individuals and smaller businesses buy direct from Dell by phone, fax, and via the Internet, with about $4 billion in sales generated online.

When Michael Dell started the company in 1984 in his college dorm room, his idea was to custom-build computers for customers, to eliminate the middleman, and more effectively meet the technology needs of his customers. Today, the company sells much more than individual computer systems; it also offers enterprise systems, desktop, and laptop computers, as well as installation, financing, repair, and management services. By relying on a build-to-order manufacturing process, the company achieves faster inventory turnover (five days), and reduced component and finished goods inventory levels; this strategy virtually eliminates the chance of product obsolescence.

The direct model simplifies the company's operations, eliminating the need to support a wholesale and retail sales network, as well as cutting out the costly associated markup, and gives Dell complete control over its customer database. In addition, Dell can build and ship custom computers nearly as fast as a mail-order supplier can pull a computer out of inventory and ship it to the customer.

To extend the benefits of its direct sales model, Dell has aggressively moved sales, service, and support online. Each month, the company typically has 15–16 million unique visitors at Dell.com, where it maintains an estimated 80 country-specific Web sites. The Premier.Dell.com service enables companies to investigate product offerings, complete order forms and purchase orders, track orders in real time, and review order histories all online. For its small business customers, it has created an online virtual account executive, as well as a spare-parts ordering system and virtual help desk with direct access to technical support data. Dell has also continued to broaden its offerings beyond pure product sales, adding warranty services, product integration and installation services, Internet access, software, peripherals, and technology consulting, referring to them as "beyond the box" offerings. These include nearly 30,000 software and peripheral products from leading manufacturers that can be bundled with Dell products. In 2009, Dell opened a download store in the United States, United Kingdom, France, and Germany, that enables customers to download software purchases rather than wait to receive them on a CD. Dell has also embraced Web 2.0, adding Web site features such as instruction on how to create and maintain a blog, edit and post online vidoes, and build and share online photo scrapbooks. Dell Lounge allows visitors to create video and audio mashups, while StudioDell shows how to work with digital photo and videos and allows visitors to upload videos they've created showing how they use Dell technology.

To improve customer service, Dell has established call center operations in Canada that feature advanced online customer service applications, such as DellConnect. DellConnect allows a customer service representative to remotely connect to a customer's computer via a broadband link to troubleshoot customer problems (Dell, Inc., 2009; Internet Retailer, 2009).

COMMON THEMES IN ONLINE RETAILING

We have looked at some very different companies in the preceding section, from entrepreneurial Web-only merchants to established offline giants. Online retail e-commerce is indeed alive and well for some retailers, particularly for established offline retailers with existing brands. Online retail is the fastest growing channel in retail on a revenue basis, has the fastest growing consumer base, and has growing penetration across many categories of nonessential goods. On the other hand, profits for new start-up ventures have been difficult to achieve, and it took even Amazon until 2003 to show its first profit.

The reasons for the difficulties experienced by online retailers in achieving profits are also now clear. The path to success in any form of retail involves having a central location in order to attract a larger number of shoppers, charging high enough prices to cover the costs of goods as well as marketing, and developing highly efficient inventory and fulfillment systems so that the company can offer goods at lower costs than competitors and still make a profit. In the early years, many online merchants failed to follow these fundamental ideas, and lowered prices below the total costs of goods and operations, failed to develop efficient business processes, or spent far too much on customer acquisition and marketing. In recent years, however, online retail firms have begun to raise prices, often matching the prices in some categories of offline stores. Consumers have been willing to accept higher prices in return for the convenience of shopping online, and avoiding the costs of shopping at stores and malls.

For the most part, disintermediation did not occur and the retail middleman did not disappear. Indeed, virtual merchants, along with powerful offline merchants who moved online, maintained their powerful grip on the retail customer, with some notable exceptions in electronics and software. Manufacturers—with the exception of electronic goods—have used the Web primarily as an informational resource, driving consumers to the traditional retail channels for transactions.

The most significant online growth has been that of offline general merchandiser giants such as Wal-Mart and JCPenney and catalogers such as Lands' End and L.L. Bean. Many of the first-mover, Web pure-play merchants failed to achieve profitability and closed their doors en masse in 2000 and 2001 as their venture capital funds were depleted. Traditional retailers are the fast followers (although many of them cannot be characterized as particularly "fast") most likely to succeed on the Web by extending their traditional competencies and assets. In this sense, e-commerce technological innovation is following the historical pattern of other technology-driven commercial changes, from automobiles to radio and television.

To succeed online, established merchants need to create an integrated shopping environment that combines their catalog, store, and online experiences into one. Established retailers have significant fulfillment, inventory management, supply chain management, and other competencies that apply directly to the online channel. And although established merchants have moved online, their e-commerce operations are not always profitable. To succeed online, established retailers need to extend their brands, provide incentives to consumers to use the online channel, avoid channel conflict, and build partnerships with online portals such as AOL, MSN, and Yahoo.

A second area of very rapid online growth is a new crop of specialty merchants selling high-end, fashionable and luxury goods, such as Blue Nile, the online diamond merchant, or selling discounted electronics, such as BestBuy.com (electronics), or apparel (Gap.com), or office products (OfficeDepot.com). For instance, at Gap, Inc., its Web sales provided the only bright spot in 2008—while store sales fell 12%, online sales grew by 14%. These firms are demonstrating the vitality and openness of the Internet for innovation and extending the range of products available on the Web. Many virtual merchants have developed large, online customer bases, as well as the online tools required to market to their customer base. These online brands can be strengthened further through alliances and partnerships that add the required competencies in inventory management and fulfillment services. Virtual merchants need to build operational strength and efficiency before they can become profitable.

Both Web-only and established offline retailers wishing to strengthen their e-commerce revenues will be favorably affected in the future by new retailing technologies—from extending high-speed Internet access to the majority of potential consumers, to mobile commerce using cell phones, to new services such as enhanced comparison shopping sites, as described in *Insight on Technology: Using the Web to Shop 'Till You Drop.*

INSIGHT ON TECHNOLOGY

USING THE WEB TO SHOP 'TILL YOU DROP

The original idea was simple and leveraged many of the unique features of e-commerce technology: Create a Web site listing thousands of products where consumers can compare prices, features, consumer reviews of the actual product performance, and reputations of merchants. Then, when visitors click on a product and price they like, they are taken to the merchant's Web site where they can make the purchase. The merchant pays the Web site a fee or commission for sending the customer, as well as a listing fee usually determined by bidding on key words. The idea: Shoppers would not have to shop till they dropped, but instead could conveniently price compare at one site, and then buy from the lowest-price merchant on the Web. Merchants would support this service because they would obtain additional customers and sales. Merchants join the shopping services and provide a digital feed to the comparison sites providing information on both products and prices.

The idea first appeared in the mid-1990s in academic papers on potential uses of the Web and Internet, and was referred to as "shopping robots." Shopping robots are essentially search engines that scour the Web for prices on specific products. Now referred to much more descriptively as comparison shopping sites, they have become big business, with products tracked numbering in the millions. No one knows for sure, but observers believe there are over 100 price comparison sites on the Web in 2009. The top sites are BizRate, NexTag, PriceGrabber, Shopzilla, and Pronto. The most popular site, BizRate, typically attracted over 20 million unique monthly visitors in 2009, while the number five site Pronto received around 11 million visitors.

Shopping comparison sites have become attractive acquisition candidates because they have done very well in attracting visitors, and are also profitable. For instance, Shopping. com, with an estimated 7 million unique monthly visitors in 2009, was purchased in 2005 by eBay for $634 million. (Shopping.com was formerly known as Dealtime.com, and also includes Epinions.com, an online consumer review and ratings platform.) Shopzilla was purchased in 2005 by E.W. Scripps Co. for $525 million. Competitors that have not yet been acquired include NexTag and PriceGrabber. General merchandisers such as Amazon, portals such as Yahoo and AOL, and search engines such as Google have also developed their own comparison shopping capabilities. Shopping sites make money by charging participating merchants on a per-click basis regardless of whether a sale is made. A twist on shopping search engines is comparison shopping coupon systems. Sites like Wow-Coupons, CurrentCodes, and FatWallet search the Web for deals and coupons.

About 60% of consumers have used a comparison shopping Web site, according to Jupiter Research. Up until the recession in 2009, shopping sites had been growing in double digits, but in 2009, all the top shopping sites lost from 10% to 15% of their visitors. The exception was PriceGrabber, which popped up 48%.

Comparison shopping sites focused originally on tracking online prices for electronic consumer goods and computers. Consumer electronics are fairly commoditized products by a few branded manufacturers, with standard features, making it fairly easy to compare one product to another. Type in "digital camera", select the number of megapixels you want, enter the zoom range and price, press the Enter key on your keyboard, and you will receive a long list of cameras and deal-

(continued)

ers. You can refine your search as you move along the purchase process, and explore the reputations of dealers before you decide to purchase.

However, although Shopping.com tracks over 60 million products, very few of these items are so-called "soft goods" purchased by women, who have risen to equal the purchasing power of men on the Web. In 1998, 65% of Web purchases were made by men, while today, over 60% are made by women who are much more likely to be looking for soft goods, such as apparel, jewelry, accessories, luggage, and gifts. In fact, these are among the fastest growing consumer product categories on the Web. For this reason, the shopping comparison sites are currently adding soft goods to their services.

But the process of comparison shopping for soft goods is not as simple as for hard goods such as digital TVs or digital cameras. The strength of a comparison shopping site is to present highly similar or identical items from different merchants at varying prices and reputation levels. Generally, these kinds of electronic goods have a limited number of suppliers (mostly solid brand names) and limited features. But in more complex product areas, such as apparel or jewelry, such standards do not exist. In fact, manufacturers of these products emphasize their uniqueness, not their similarity. One solution is to focus on the brands of soft goods and not the price: bags from Gucci, sweaters from Benetton, and mountain climbing gear from REI. Yahoo and search engines such as MSN and Google are moving closer to the brand model of comparison shopping as price becomes a less powerful factor in consumer purchases of soft goods.

As more attention focuses on comparison shopping sites, the sites themselves continue to innovate and add features, and they attempt to go beyond simply finding customers the lowest-price products. Shopping.com tracks its visitors to help consumers decide what to buy, and where to buy. It does this by showing visitors the most popular sites for each category of product selected. Shopzilla has developed a data categorization technology that it calls Robozilla, designed to help expedite the shopping process. In 2009, Shopzilla redesigned its Web site seeking to enhance the customer experience by adding speed, a better search engine, and more product detail. Shopzilla was able to reduce the search time for products from 6 to 9 seconds, down to 1.2 seconds on average. PriceGrabber is focused on adding product tours and more content, such as user and third-party reviews, and discussion boards. NexTag offers consumers e-mail price alerts and product price history charting, and for merchants, a new data feed auto-import option. Most of the larger sites are adding user-generated reviews and opinions of products.

Companies are also continuing to enter the market every day. HealthPricer lists over 360,000 health products. StylePath focuses on soft goods from jewelry, to clothing, and bed linens, and finds consumers products based on their tastes and interests that they reveal to the shopping engine. StylePath features 100,000 products from 1,500 online merchants. Discount-More relaunched its search engine to include a search of all the Web's shopping sites. The site enables consumers to get results from the top 26 shopping sites all on one page. Why not shop all shopping sites at once from a single site?

Despite these innovations, visitors to shopping comparison sites continue to be primarily price motivated: 85% of visitors press the "sort by price" button despite the search engines' efforts to provide more qualitative assessments of quality and reliability. The comparison sites are obviously in competition with search engines, such as Google (which has its own comparison service). As keyword prices have risen on search engines, shopping comparison sites become an excellent bargain. But in 2009, some merchants began to complain the comparison sites are getting greedy, and charging excessively high commissions for steering traffic their way. Google Product Search (formerly Froogle) is the most popular comparison shopping engine for merchants in 2009 (72% of the top 500 Internet retailers list with Google Product Search) in large part because it is free. Merchants do not have to bid for keywords or listing, are not charged a commission, and can use Google Analytics to understand their Web performance. Google makes money on this service by placing ads next to the merchant's offering using its AdSense system. Google's efforts have not yet paid off in terms of visitors, but its user base is growing at greater than 10% a year, and may put downward pressure on the keyword listing fees and commissions charged by other comparison shopping sites.

SOURCES: "8 Top Sites for Online Shopping Deals," by Jennifer Mulrean, moneycentral.msn.com, September 14, 2009; "Shopzilla Site Redo- You Get What You Measure," by Philip Dixon, en.oreilly.com, June 24, 2009; "Google Gets Top Marks in a Ranking of Comparison Shopping Engines," Internet Retailer, May 29, 2009; "Shopping Engine Traffic Review for January 2009," Retail-ecommerce.com, March 4, 2009; "Comparison Shopping Engines Primer," mivamerchant.com, October 2008.

9.4 THE SERVICE SECTOR: OFFLINE AND ONLINE

The service sector is typically the largest and most rapidly expanding part of the economies in advanced industrial nations such as the United States, and in European and some Asian countries. In the United States, services (broadly defined) employ about 108 million people (76% of the labor force) and account for about $7.7 trillion (about 58%) of the U.S.'s gross domestic product (GDP) (U.S. Census Bureau, 2009). Less than one-quarter of the U.S. workforce is involved in the production of physical goods.

On the other hand, productivity in the service sector has lagged far behind productivity in factories and on farms. Productivity in the service sector over the last decade has averaged about 1%, while farm and factory productivity has averaged about 5% (U.S. Census Bureau, 2009). While the explosion in information technology capital investment since 1995 has certainly added to overall productivity, "white collar" service sector employees did not benefit from this as much as factory employees. In part, this is because the very nature of services—performing activities for others in a highly personalized and customized manner—is somewhat immune to the beneficial aspects of computerization. The productivity of doctors, lawyers, accountants, and business consultants—all service occupations—has not been markedly affected in terms of unit output per unit time by the explosion in information technology, although the quality of their work has undoubtedly improved. Unfortunately, increases in quality of service are not measured by productivity statistics. Being able to find the lowest price in the United States for a flight from New York to Los Angeles in a matter of minutes (as opposed to many hours in the past) will never be measured in productivity statistics. What this means for e-commerce is that the service sector offers extraordinary opportunities insofar as e-commerce sites can deliver information, knowledge, and transaction efficiencies.

WHAT ARE SERVICES?

service occupations
occupations concerned with performing tasks in and around households, business firms, and institutions

Just what are services? The U.S. Department of Labor defines **service occupations** as "concerned with performing tasks" in and around households, business firms, and institutions (U.S. Department of Labor, 1991). The U.S. Census Bureau defines **service industries** as those "domestic establishments providing services to consumers, businesses, governments, and other organizations" (U.S. Census Bureau, 2001). The major service industry groups are finance, insurance, real estate, travel, professional services such as legal and accounting, business services, health services, and educational services. Business services include activities such as consulting, advertising and marketing, and information processing.

service industries
establishments providing services to consumers, businesses, governments, and other organizations

CATEGORIZING SERVICE INDUSTRIES

transaction brokering
acting as an intermediary to facilitate a transaction

Within these service industry groups, companies can be further categorized into those that involve **transaction brokering** (acting as an intermediary to facilitate a transaction) and those that involve providing a "hands-on" service. For instance, one type of financial services involves stockbrokers who act as the middle person in a transaction between buyers and sellers. Online mortgage companies such as Tree.com (formerly LendingTree) refer customers to mortgage companies that actually issue the mortgage. Employment agencies put a seller of labor in contact with a buyer of labor. The service involved in all these examples is brokering a transaction.

In contrast, legal, medical, accounting, and other such industries perform specific hands-on activities for consumers. In order to provide their service, these professionals need to interact directly and personally with the "client." For these service industries, the opportunities for e-commerce are somewhat different. Currently, doctors and dentists cannot treat patients over the Internet. However, the Internet can assist their services by providing consumers with information, knowledge, and communication.

KNOWLEDGE AND INFORMATION INTENSITY

With some exceptions (for example, providers of physical services, such as cleaning, gardening, and so on), perhaps the most important feature of service industries (and occupations) is that they are knowledge- and information-intense. In order to provide value, service industries process a great deal of information and employ a highly skilled, educated work force. For instance, to provide legal services, you need lawyers with law degrees. Law firms are required to process enormous amounts of textual information. Likewise with medical services. Financial services are not so knowledge-intensive, but require much larger investments in information processing just to keep track of transactions and investments. In fact, the financial services sector is the largest investor in information technology, with over 80% of invested capital going to information technology equipment and services (Laudon and Laudon, 2009).

For these reasons, many services are uniquely suited to e-commerce applications and the strengths of the Internet, which are to collect, store, and disseminate high-value information and to provide reliable, fast communication.

PERSONALIZATION AND CUSTOMIZATION

Services differ in the amount of personalization and customization required, although just about all services entail some personalization or customization. Some services, such as legal, medical, and accounting services, require extensive personalization—the adjustment of a service to the precise needs of a single individual or object. Others, such as financial services, benefit from customization by allowing individuals to choose from a restricted menu. The ability of Internet and e-commerce technology to personalize and customize service, or components of service, is a major factor undergirding the extremely rapid growth of e-commerce services. Future expansion of e-services will depend in part on the ability of e-commerce firms to transform their customized services—choosing from a list—into truly personalized services, such as providing unique advice and consultation based on a digital yet intimate understanding of the client (at least as intimate as professional service providers).

9.5 ONLINE FINANCIAL SERVICES

Financial services (finance, insurance, and real estate) contribute over $2.7 trillion to the U.S. GDP. The online financial services sector is a shining example of an e-commerce success story, but one with many twists and turns. While the innovative, pure-online firms such as E*Trade have been instrumental in transforming the brokerage industry, the impacts of e-commerce on the large, powerful banking, insurance, and real estate firms have been delayed by consumer resistance and the lack of industry innovation. For instance, online-only banks have not displaced or transformed the large national banks or even regional and local banks. But e-commerce has nevertheless transformed the banking and financial industries, as the major institutions have deployed their own online applications to service an increasingly connected online customer base. Four out of five online households now use online banking. Over 3 million people are now using mobile banking applications on iPhones and BlackBerries. About one-quarter of the large commercial banks in the United States now have blogs, and even use Twitter. Insurance has become more standardized and easier to purchase on the Web. In the meltdown of financial institutions in 2008, consumers turned to online financial advice and tracking services as they lost confidence in banks. Consumers are much more willing to trust online sites with their financial information than in the past. Entrepreneurial start-up firms such as Mint.com, SmartyPig, Cake Financial, Wesabe, and Credit Karma showed double-digit growth in 2008 and 2009. Multi-channel, established financial services firms—the slow followers—also continue to show strong growth in online transactions.

FINANCIAL SERVICES INDUSTRY TRENDS

The financial services industry provides four generic kinds of services: storage of and access to funds, protection of assets, means to grow assets, and movement of funds. Historically, in the United States and elsewhere, separate institutions provided these financial services (see **Table 9.5**).

TABLE 9.5	TRADITIONAL PROVIDERS OF FINANCIAL SERVICES
FINANCIAL SERVICE	INSTITUTIONAL PROVIDER
Storage of and access to funds	Banking, lending
Protection of assets	Insurance
Growth	Investment and brokerage firms
Movement of funds (payment)	Banks, credit card firms

However, two important global trends in the financial services industry that have direct consequences for online financial services firms are changing the institutional structure of financial services. The first trend is industry consolidation (see **Figure 9.3**).

In the United States, the banking, finance, brokerage, and insurance industries were legally separated by the Glass-Steagall Act of 1934, which prohibited banks, insurance firms, and brokerages from having significant financial interests in one another in order to prevent a repetition of the calamitous financial institution failures that followed the stock market crash of 1929 and the ensuing Depression. The Glass-Steagall Act also prevented large banks from owning banks in other states. This

FIGURE 9.3	INDUSTRY CONSOLIDATION AND INTEGRATED FINANCIAL SERVICES

The major trends in financial services are industry consolidation and the provision of integrated financial services to consumers.

legal separation meant that financial institutions in the United States could not provide customers with integrated financial services, and could not operate nationwide. One result was the proliferation of small, inefficient, local banks in the United States, arguably the most "over-banked" country in the world. West European and Japanese financial institutions did not face similar restrictions, putting the American industry at a disadvantage. The Financial Reform Act of 1998 amended Glass-Steagall and permitted banks, brokerages, and insurance firms to merge and to develop nationwide banks. This new law touched off an avalanche of financial service sector consolidations.

The financial meltdown of 2008 demonstrated the risks of permitting financial institution consolidation. The rapid growth of risk-transfer instruments (credit default swaps), and collateralized debt obligations, which began in the late 1990s, greatly expanded the pools of capital available for investment, allowing banks to greatly expand their leverage, and to make loans to subprime customers. The merger of commercial banks with insurance and investment banking meant that they now shared risks: if investment banks failed, so would commercial banks, and the insurance companies that guaranteed all these new instruments. When the U.S. housing and credit markets collapsed in 2007 and 2008, so did the foundation of banking and investment institutions worldwide. Suddenly, what looked like solid assets were worth very little, sometimes nothing. One result is that large money center banks are buying up failed regional and local commercial banks, as well as investment banks and brokerage firms. Consolidation in the banking and investment sphere continues on an accelerated schedule.

A second related trend is the movement toward integrated financial services. Once banks, brokerages, and insurance companies are permitted to own one another, it becomes possible to provide consumers with what countless surveys have documented they really want: trust, service, and convenience. The movement toward financial service integration began in the 1980s when Merrill Lynch developed the first "cash management account" that integrated the brokerage and cash management services provided to Merrill Lynch's customers into a single account. Spare cash in each customer account was invested at the close of business each day into a money market fund. In the 1990s, Citibank and other large money center banks developed the concept of a financial supermarket, where consumers can find any financial product or service at a single physical center or branch bank. Nearly all large national banks now provide some form of financial planning and investment service. As a result of the financial meltdown in 2008, Bank of America took over a failed Merrill Lynch (brokerage and investment banking). Citibank, largely owned by the federal government, continues its former integrated business model of banking, investment banking, insurance, and brokerage.

The Internet has created the technical foundations for an online financial supermarket to operate, but, for the most part, it has still not arrived. It is not yet possible to arrange for a car loan, obtain a mortgage, receive investment planning advice, and establish a pension fund at any single financial institution with one account. Nevertheless, this is the direction in which large banking institutions are attempting to move.

The promise of the Internet in the long term is to take the financial supermarket model one step further by providing a truly personalized, customized, and integrated offering to consumers based on a complete understanding of the consumer and his or her financial behavior, life cycle status, and unique needs. It will take many years to develop the technical infrastructure, as well as change consumer behavior toward a much deeper relationship with online financial services institutions.

ONLINE FINANCIAL CONSUMER BEHAVIOR

Surveys show that consumers are attracted to financial sites because of their desire to save time and access information rather than save money, although saving money is an important goal among the most sophisticated online financial households. About 67% of generation Xer's and 57% of generation Y users go online to obtain financial information or use online banking or other financial services (Pew Internet & American Life Report, 2009b; USC Annenberg School Center for the Digital Future, 2009). In addition, 69.7 million households use online banking and 64.4 million pay at least one bill online (Fiserv, 2009). Most online consumers use financial services sites for mundane financial management, such as checking balances of existing accounts, and paying bills most of which were established offline. Once accustomed to performing mundane financial management activities, consumers move on to more sophisticated capabilities such as using personal financial management tools, making loan payments, and considering offers from online institutions. **Table 9.6** shows the results of a survey of consumer interest in a wide variety of personal financial services, indicating that consumers are expanding their expectations of online banking.

Currently, the greatest deterrent to increased usage of online financial services is fears about security and confidentiality of sensitive financial information. In general, consumers are much more reluctant to conduct financial transactions online than they are to shop online. For instance, surveys by both The Conference Board and TNS NFO have found that online households are much more concerned

TABLE 9.6	INTEREST IN ONLINE PERSONAL FINANCIAL SERVICES
ONLINE BANKING SERVICES	PERCENTAGE OF RESPONDENTS INTERESTED
Free identity theft services	63%
Free credit score monitoring	52%
Personal financial management	37%
Chat/Instant messaging service	30%
Widget	27%
Blog	20%

SOURCES: Based on data from comScore, 2009; Reuters.com, 2009.

about the security of their financial transactions than about purchasing products online, communicating online, or using search engines. For instance, a Computer Associates July 2008 survey found that 58% of the respondents felt that major financial institutions do not spend enough on online security (Computer Associates, 2008). Consumers are particularly concerned about the possibility of identity theft, fraud, and the risk of account intrusion.

ONLINE BANKING AND BROKERAGE

NetBank and Wingspan pioneered online banking in the United States in 1996 and 1997, respectively. Traditional banks had developed earlier versions of telephone banking, but did not use online services until 1998. Although late by a year or two, the established brand-name national banks have taken a substantial lead in market share as the percentage of their customers who bank online has grown rapidly. **Table 9.7** lists the top five online banks in 2009, ranked by the percentage of all Web visits to online banks. The top banks are all large, national and international banks. Pure online banks such as ING Direct and VirtualBank continue to offer higher returns to consumers, but have not grown at the rates initially expected. NetBank, one of the original piooners, declared bankruptcy in 2007, primarily as a result of the subprime mortgage loan crisis.

According to eMarketer, 105 million U.S. consumers are expected to conduct some online banking activity in 2009, an increase of about 15% over 2008, and this number is expected to grow to around 192 million by 2013 (eMarketer, 2009a) (see **Figure 9.4**).

The history of online brokerage has been similar to that of online banking. Early innovators such as E*Trade have been displaced from their leadership positions in terms of numbers of online accounts by discount broker pioneer Charles Schwab and financial industry giant Fidelity (which has more mutual fund customers and more funds under management than any other U.S. firm).

Today, according to Nielsen Net Ratings, 20 million U.S. investors trade online, a number expected to increase to approximately 29 million by 2013. According to a survey of online financial activities over the previous 12 months among U.S. adult Internet users, 20% traded stocks (eMarketer, Inc., 2009). According to

TABLE 9.7	TOP ONLINE BANKS: SEPTEMBER 2009
BANK (RANKED BY VISITORS)	PERCENTAGE OF TOTAL WEB BANK VISITS
Bank of America Online Banking	7.4%
Chase Online	5.8%
Wells Fargo-Online Banking	4.0%
Wachovia Online Services	2.3%
Capital One Onine Banking	1.6%

SOURCES: Based on data from Hitwise,2009; .

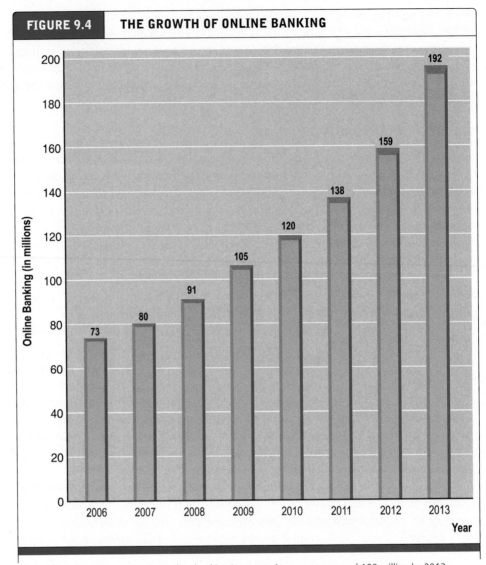

| FIGURE 9.4 | THE GROWTH OF ONLINE BANKING |

The number of Internet users using online banking is expected to grow to around 192 million by 2013. Increases in mobile banking may impact these numbers over the next three years.

SOURCES: Based on data from eMarketer, Inc., 2008a, authors' estimates.

Nielsen, in terms of unique visitors, the top trading Web site among U.S. Internet users in 2009 was Fidelity Investments, with over 4.8 million (see **Table 9.8**).

Multi-channel vs. Pure Online Financial Services Firms

Online consumers prefer to visit financial services sites that have physical outlets or branches. In general, multi-channel financial services firms that have both physical branches or offices and solid online offerings are growing faster than pure-online firms that have no physical presence, and they are assuming market leadership as well. Traditional banking firms have literally thousands of branches

TABLE 9.8	TOP ONLINE BROKERAGES JULY 2009	
FIRM	NUMBER OF UNIQUE VISITORS (JULY 2009)
Fidelity.com	5.2 million
ShareBuilder	2.0 million
Scottrade	2.0 million
E*Trade	1.8 million
Vanguard	1.8 million
Ameritrade	1.7 million
Charles Schwab	1.4 million
SaneBull	1.1 million

SOURCES: Based on data from MarketingCharts.com, 2009; Nielsen/NetRatings Netview, 2009.

where customers can open accounts, deposit money, take out loans, find home mortgages, and rent a safety deposit box. Top online brokerage firms do not have the same physical footprint as the banks do, but each has a strong physical presence or telephone presence to strengthen its online presence. Fidelity has urban walk-in service center branches, but it primarily relies on the telephone for interacting with investors. Charles Schwab has decided to open investment centers around the country as an integral part of its online strategy. Pure-online banks and brokerages cannot provide customers with many services that still require a hands-on interaction.

Internet-only banks and brokerages lack physical client acquisition channels and therefore must rely on their Web sites and advertising to acquire customers, whereas established multi-channel institutions can convert existing branch customers into online customers at a far lower cost. In terms of loyalty and intensity, a different picture emerges. Users of pure-online institutions utilize these sites more intensively for a wide variety of services that used to be performed at branches, whereas the established multi-channel site users make fewer online transactions and visit the site less often. However, customers of pure-online institutions comparison shop more, are more price-driven, and are less loyal than customers of established multi-channel players.

Financial Portals and Account Aggregators

Financial portals are sites that provide consumers with comparison shopping services, independent financial advice, and financial planning. Independent portals do not themselves offer financial services, but act as steering mechanisms to online providers. They generate revenue from advertising, referral fees, and subscription fees. For example, Yahoo's financial portal, Yahoo Finance, offers consumers credit card purchase tracking, market overviews, real-time stock

financial portals
sites that provide consumers with comparison shopping services, independent financial advice, and financial planning

quotes, news, financial advice, streaming-video interviews with financial leaders, and Yahoo Bill Pay, an EBPP system. Other independent financial portals include Intuit's Quicken.com, MSN's MSN Money, CNN Money, and America Online's Money and Finance channel. A host of new, smaller financial portal sites have sprung up to help consumers with financial management and planning such as Mint.com, SmartPiggy, Wesabe, and Credit Karma.

In general, the financial portals do not offer financial services (they make their money from advertising); instead, they add to the online price competition in the industry and run counter to the strategy of large banking institutions to ensnare consumers into a single branded, financial institutional system, with a single account and high switching costs.

account aggregation
the process of pulling together all of a customer's financial (and even nonfinancial) data at a single personalized Web site

Account aggregation is the process of pulling together all of a customer's financial (and even nonfinancial) data at a single personalized Web site, including brokerage, banking, insurance, loans, frequent flyer miles, personalized news, and much more. For example, a consumer can see his or her TD Ameritrade brokerage account, Fidelity 401(k) account, Travelers Insurance annuity account, and American Airlines frequent flyer miles all displayed on a single site. The idea is to provide consumers with a holistic view of their entire portfolio of assets, no matter what financial institution actually holds those assets.

The leading provider of account aggregation technology is Yodlee. It uses screen-scraping and other techniques to pull information from over 8,000 different data sources. A smart-mapping technology is also used so that if the underlying Web sites change, the scraping software can adapt and still find the relevant information. Today, Yodlee has more than 20 million personal financial management (PFM) users worldwide and is used by six of the top 10 U.S. banks (Yodlee, 2009).

Account aggregation raises a number of issues. In order to use account aggregation services, consumers must release all their login and password information to the aggregator. If one institution holds all account information, consumers face the risk of losing control over their information, which heretofore was spread across many largely inaccessible sites. Financial aggregators may be tempted to "cross sell" products to consumers at their sites, raising the possibility of fairly intense marketing campaigns, although aggregator sites claim they will not use their customers' information to promote products without explicit permission.

ONLINE MORTGAGE AND LENDING SERVICES

During the early days of e-commerce, hundreds of firms launched pure-play online mortgage sites to capture the U.S. home mortgage market. Early entrants hoped to radically simplify and transform the traditional mortgage value chain process, dramatically speed up the loan closing process, and share the economies with consumers by offering lower rates.

By 2003, over half of these early-entry, pure-online firms had failed. Early pure-play online mortgage institutions had difficulties developing a brand name at an affordable price and failed to simplify the mortgage generation process. They ended up suffering from high start-up and administrative costs, high customer acquisition costs, rising interest rates, and poor execution of their strategies.

Despite this rocky start, the online mortgage market is slowly growing; it is dominated by established online banks and other online financial services firms, traditional mortgage vendors, and a few successful online mortgage firms.

About $1.5 trillion worth of home mortgages were originated in 2009, down from over $2 trillion in 2008 due to the collapse of the housing market and weakness in the banking sector (Curran, 2008; U.S. Census Bureau, 2009). More than half of all mortgage shoppers research mortgages online, but few actually apply online because of the complexity of mortgages. Most mortgages today are written by intermediary mortgage brokers, with banks still playing an important origination role but generally not servicing mortgages they originate.

Although online mortgage originations currently represent a small percentage of all mortgages, their number is expected to continue to grow slowly but surely over the next several years, although in 2009 the number of mortgages being originated in all forms has been negatively impacted by the subprime mortgage crisis.

There are three kinds of online mortgage vendors:

- Established banks, brokerages, and lending organizations such as Chase, Bank of America/Countrywide Credit Industries, Wells Fargo, Ameriquest Mortgage, and Citigroup (which operates Mortgage.com).

- Pure online mortgage bankers/brokers such as E-Loan, Quicken Loans, and E*Trade Mortgage. These companies aim to expedite the mortgage shopping and initiation process, but still require extensive paperwork to complete a mortgage.

- Mortgage brokers such as Tree.com (formerly LendingTree), owned by IAC/Inter-activeCorp, and comparison shopping site NexTag. These companies offer visitors access to hundreds of mortgage vendors who bid for their business.

Consumer benefits from online mortgages include reduced application times, market interest rate intelligence, and process simplification that occurs when participants in the mortgage process (title, insurance, and lending companies) share a common information base. Mortgage lenders benefit from the cost reduction involved in online processing of applications, while charging rates marginally lower than traditional bricks-and-mortar institutions.

Nevertheless, the online mortgage industry has not transformed the process of obtaining a mortgage. A significant brake on market expansion is the complexity of the mortgage process, which requires physical signatures and documents, multiple institutions, and complex financing details—such as closing costs and points—that are difficult for shoppers to compare across vendors (Perkins, 2004). Nevertheless, as in other areas, the ability of shoppers to find low mortgage rates on the Web has helped reduce the fees and interest rates charged by traditional mortgage lenders.

ONLINE INSURANCE SERVICES

In 1995, the price of a $500,000 20-year term life policy for a healthy 40-year-old male was $995 a year. In 2009, the same policy could be had for around $400—a decline of about 60%—while other prices have risen 15% in the same period (Hough, 2009). In a study of the term life insurance business, Brown and Goolsbee discovered that Internet usage led to an 8%–15% decline in term life insurance prices industry-wide (both offline and online), and increased consumer surplus by about $115 million per year (and hence reduced industry profits by the same amount) (Brown and Goolsbee, 2000). Price dispersion for term life policies initially increased, but then fell as more and more people began using the Internet to obtain insurance quotes.

Unlike books and CDs, where online price dispersion is higher than offline, and in many cases online prices are higher than offline, term life insurance stands out as one product group supporting the conventional wisdom that the Internet will lower search costs, increase price comparison, and lower prices to consumers. Term life insurance is a commodity product, however, and in other insurance product lines, the Web offers insurance companies new opportunities for product and service differentiation and price discrimination.

The insurance industry forms a major part of the $2.7 trillion financial services sector. It has four major segments: automobile, life, health, and property and casualty. Insurance products can be very complex. For example, there are many different types of non-automotive property and casualty insurance: liability, fire, homeowners, commercial, workers' compensation, marine, accident, and other lines such as vacation insurance. Writing an insurance policy in any of these areas is very information-intense, often necessitating personal inspection of the properties, and it requires considerable actuarial experience and data. The life insurance industry has also developed life insurance policies that defy easy comparison and can only be explained and sold by an experienced sales agent. Historically, the insurance industry has relied on thousands of local insurance offices and agents to sell complex products uniquely suited to the circumstances of the insured person and the property. Complicating the insurance marketplace is the fact that the insurance industry is not federally regulated, but rather is regulated by 50 different state insurance commissions that are strongly influenced by local insurance agents. Before a Web site can offer quotations on insurance, it must obtain a license to enter the insurance business in all the states where it provides quotation services or sells insurance.

Like the online mortgage industry, the online insurance industry has been very successful in attracting visitors who are looking to obtain prices and terms of insurance policies. For instance, results of a 2009 comScore survey indicated that 63% of people looking for auto insurance went online first. In 2008, there were 32 million online inquiries for auto insurance, and a record 2.4 million policies purchased (up 7% from the previous year) (comScore, 2009b). Analysts believe the online insurance market is growing stronger despite the recession.

While many national insurance underwriting companies initially did not offer competitive products directly on the Web because it might injure the business operations of their traditional local agents, the Web sites of almost all of the major firms now provide the ability to obtain an online quote. Even if consumers do not actually purchase insurance policies online, the Internet has proven to have a powerful influence on consumer insurance decisions by dramatically reducing search costs and changing the price discovery process.

See **Table 9.9** for a list and description of some of the leading online insurance services companies.

TABLE 9.9	LEADING MULTI-PRODUCT ONLINE INSURANCE SERVICES	
COMPANY	2008 REVENUES	DESCRIPTION
InsWeb	$37.5 million	Comparison shopping for consumers; insurance companies pay for client leads; also earns commissions from policies via two wholly owned insurance agencies. Auto, life, health, and homeowner's insurance quotes. Public company.
Insure.com (Quotesmith)	$15.7 million	Free quotes from 200 insurance companies on a full range of policies with no fee. Operates insurance agency and brokerage and earns revenue from insurance companies for client leads and commissions. Public company.
Insurance.com (operated by ComparisonMarket)	ND	Reportedly the nation's largest online auto insurance company. Consumers can compare quotes from 15 different carriers, and purchase policies online or from a licensed agent. Other products include life, health, and home insurance as well as travel, dental, and pet health insurance. Formerly owned by Fidelity, now privately held.
QuickQuote	ND	Free quotes on a range of policies. Revenue from advertising and client leads. Formerly owned by ING Group, now privately held.
Answer Financial	ND	One-stop insurance shopping resource, featuring auto, home, life, health, dental, and long-term care insurance as well as annuity products, pet insurance, and more. Offers the products of more than 230 providers through intranets, the Internet, and by toll-free phone staffed by licensed agents.
NetQuote	ND	Provides quotes for auto, home, health, life, and business insurance. Has relationship with over 100 insurance companies, such as GEICO, Progressive, Allstate, and others. Claims to be the most visited insurance shopping site on the Web.

ND = Not Disclosed

ONLINE REAL ESTATE SERVICES

Real estate is a $1.7 trillion industry. Commercial real estate involves around 4.9 million commercial buildings with around 72 billion square feet of floor space.

During the second quarter of 2009, there were approximately 131 million housing units in the United States, of which approximately 18.7 million were available for sale or rent. Real estate advertising expenditures account for about $11 billion a year. Finally, about $46 billion changed hands in real estate commissions for real estate transactions of all kinds. All together, despite the economic downturn, these metrics still make real estate a very attractive market (U.S. Census Bureau, 2009; Finkelstein, 2009).

During the early days of e-commerce, real estate seemed ripe for an Internet revolution that would rationalize this historically local, complex, and local agent-driven industry that monopolized the flow of consumer information. Potentially, the Internet and e-commerce might have disintermediated this huge marketspace, allowing buyers and sellers, renters, and owners to transact directly; lower search costs to near zero; and dramatically reduce prices. However, this did not happen. What did happen is extremely beneficial to buyers and sellers, as well as to real estate agents. At one point, there was an estimated 100,000 real estate sites on the Internet worldwide. Many of these sites have disappeared. However, the remaining online sites have started to make headway toward transforming the industry. In addition, most local real estate brokers in the United States have their own agency Web sites to deal with clients, in addition to participating with thousands of other agencies in multiple listing services that list homes online. See **Table 9.10** for a list of some of the major online real estate sites.

Real estate differs from other types of online financial services because it is impossible to complete a property transaction online. Clearly, the major impact of Internet real estate sites is in influencing offline decisions. The Internet has become a compelling method for real estate professionals, homebuilders, property managers and owners, and ancillary service providers to communicate with and provide information to consumers. According to a survey conducted by the National Association of Realtors, the percentage of respondents receiving leads from the Internet grew from 30% in 2005 to 50% in 2007, and 93% of those who received Internet leads indicated that the leads ultimately resulted in a sale (Center for Realtor Technology, National Association of Realtors, 2007). Another survey, the California Association of Realtors "2008 Survey of California Home Buyers," found that over 78% of all first-time homebuyers used the Internet for a significant part of the home-buying process, compared to only 28% in 2000. In general, Internet buyers were younger, wealthier, better educated, and more likely to be married than traditional buyers. According to the survey, more than nine out of 10 indicated that the Internet helped them better understand the process of buying a home. Most indicated that they preferred the dynamic online experience offered by the Internet compared to the static experience provided by newspaper advertisements. In particular, multiple pictures/slide shows, and maps showing the location of homes, were among the highest rated online features (California Association of Realtors, 2008).

The primary service offered by real estate sites is a listing of houses available. For example, Realtor.com, the official site of the National Association of Realtors, listed over 4.1 million homes, and had over 11 million unique visitors in April 2009. The offerings have become sophisticated and integrated. Listings typically feature detailed property

TABLE 9.10	MAJOR ONLINE REAL ESTATE SITES
COMPANY	DESCRIPTION
Realtor.com	Official site of the National Association of Realtors. Operated by Move, Inc. Includes a searchable database of over 1.1 million existing homes for sale; listing content from over 800 multiple listing services.
HomeGain	Online lead-generation and real estate marketing resource not affiliated with any traditional real estate agency. Acquired by Classified Ventures, a joint venture of six leading media companies, in July 2005.
RealEstate.com	Online lead generator for real estate brokers and agents. Owned by Tree.com, a spinoff of IAC/InterActive Corp.
ZipRealty	One of the first independent full-service residential real estate brokers to leverage the Internet to provide discount services. A public company with $107 million in net revenues for 2008. Currently operates in 22 states and District of Columbia. Shares a portion of its commission with buyer clients in the form of a cash rebate, and typically represents seller clients at fee levels below those offered by most traditional brokerage firms.
Move.com	Information on rental properties, builders, newly built homes, and housing plans. Owned by Move, Inc. (formerly Homestore).
Rent.com	Rental housing database with "millions" of apartments to rent. Owned by eBay.
Apartments.com	Rental housing listings. Exclusive provider of visual apartment listings for Web sites of over 140 newspapers. Owned by Classified Ventures.
Craigslist	Local community classifieds forum that includes advertisements for housing in over 570 communities around the world. Owned in part by eBay.
Loopnet	Leading online commercial real estate service with more than $500 billion of property listed for sale and 5.7 billion square feet of space for lease as of July 2009.
Zillow	Online real estate service that provides home sale data and estimates of home value.
Trulia	Similar to Zillow. Provides home sale data and estimates of home value.

descriptions, multiple photographs, and virtual 360-degree tours. Consumers can link to mortgage lenders, credit reporting agencies, house inspectors, and surveyors. There are also online loan calculators, appraisal reports, sales price histories by neighborhood, school district data, crime reports, and social and historical information on neighborhoods. Some online real estate brokers now charge substantially less than traditional offline brokers who typically charge 6% of the sale price. They can do this because the buyers (and in some cases, the seller) do much of the work of traditional real estate agents, such as prospecting, choosing neighborhoods, and identifying houses of interest prior to contacting an online agent. For instance, Move.com also offers a "Find a Neighborhood" feature that allows users to choose the type of neighborhood they want to live in by weighing factors such as the quality (and tax costs) of schools, age of the population, number of families with children nearby, and available social and recreational services.

Despite the revolution in available information, there has not been a revolution in the industry value chain. The listings available on Web sites are provided by local multiple listing services supported by local real estate agents. Sometimes, addresses of the houses are not available, and online users are directed to the local listing agent who is hired by the seller of house. Traditional hands-on real estate brokers will show the house and handle all transactions with the owner to preserve their fees, typically ranging from 5% to 6% of the transaction. See *Insight on Society: Turf Wars—Antitrust and the Online Real Estate Market* for a further examination of the real estate industry's reaction to the threats posed by the Internet to its traditional methods of doing business.

9.6 ONLINE TRAVEL SERVICES

Travel and tourism in the United States contribute over $1.1 trillion to the U.S. GDP, with online travel services becoming an ever larger part of the picture. Arguably, online travel is one of the most successful B2C e-commerce segments, accounting for more online revenues than any other online category. The Internet is becoming the most common channel used by consumers to research travel options, seek the best possible prices, and book reservations for airline tickets, hotel rooms, rental cars, cruises, and tours. According to eMarketer, 2007 was the first year in which more travel (51%) was booked online than offline. Online travel revenues declined slightly in 2009 ($92 billion) compared to 2008 ($95 billion) due to the recession, but are expected to begin growing again in 2010, increasing to around $118 billion by 2013. (see **Figure 9.5** on page 622) (eMarketer, Inc., 2009c, 2008b).

WHY ARE ONLINE TRAVEL SERVICES SO POPULAR?

Online travel sites offer consumers a one-stop, convenient, leisure and business travel experience where travelers can find content (descriptions of vacations and facilities), community (chat groups and bulletin boards), commerce (purchase of all travel elements), and customer service (usually through call centers). Online sites claim to offer much more information and many more travel options than traditional travel agents. For suppliers—the owners of hotels, rental cars, and airlines—the online sites aggregate millions of consumers into singular, focused customer pools that can be efficiently reached through onsite advertising and promotions. Online sites claim to create a much more efficient marketplace, bringing consumers and suppliers together in a low transaction cost environment.

INSIGHT ON SOCIETY

TURF WARS—ANTITRUST AND THE ONLINE REAL ESTATE MARKET

The promise of e-commerce is that it would create a fair, level playing field where thousands of suppliers and millions of consumers could negotiate prices and terms in a very efficient marketplace. These electronic markets would be more efficient in part because intermediaries—the distributors, wholesalers, and agents—would be eliminated by direct commerce between sellers and buyers. Reality can play havoc with great ideas. Distributors, wholesalers, and agents do not want to be eliminated.

Although efficient outcomes may have occurred in some e-commerce sectors, in many other sectors we see the emergence of oligopolies—near monopolies—characterized by three or four giant firms, or an even smaller number. Instead of disintermediation, e-commerce sometimes can cause a strengthening of existing intermediaries through exclusive market relationships. In certain markets, network effects occur which predispose that only a handful of competitors, and in some cases just a single provider, will exist, such as telephone markets and operating system markets. In other cases, the oligopoly is a function of market agreements among the top competitors. At times, the level of concentrated power and collusion online can become so strong that government agencies such as the U.S. Department of Justice and the Federal Trade Commission get involved.

Consider Move, Inc. (formerly Homestore, Inc.) which operates Realtor.com, the official site of the National Association of Realtors (NAR). Realtor.com lists more than 4.1 million homes based on exclusive agreements with over 800 local trade associations called multiple listing services (MLSs) that represent over 1.2 million real estate agents. In addition, Move Inc.'s recently consolidated Web site, Move.com, also handles 40,000 rental properties, representing approximately 5.5 million apartment units in more than 5,500 cities nationwide, and its New Homes section offers information on more than 66,000 new and model homes for sale in over 6,500 new home communities and planned developments in the United States. Currently, its network of real estate industry Web sites (Realtor.com, Moving.com, and Seniorhousingnet.com) is the leading consumer destination for residential real estate, rental properties, and realtor listings. Move sites attract around 10.8 million unique monthly visitors. Move is also the exclusive provider of real estate listings to AOL, City Guide, CompuServe, Netscape, MSN, and Yahoo rentals. Move's aim is to provide consumers who are in the process of moving with all the services and information they need to make a successful move.

In April 2000, the Department of Justice opened an investigation into Homestore, Realtor.com, and the NAR. At issue were the exclusive agreements that Homestore had with the NAR and the potential it had to monopolize online MLS listings. In February 2001, Homestore eliminated its largest competitor by purchasing Move.com, which at that time was owned by Cendant. The Move.com acquisition gave Homestore access to more than 25% of the industry's brokers and transactions, and enabled Homestore to tap into more than 200,000 local real estate agents. Perhaps the biggest jewel in the Move.com purchase was a 40-year exclusive listing agreement with Century 21, Coldwell Banker, and ERA, three of Cendant's prized national franchises, as well as seven-year exclusive listing pacts with the nation's largest rental market brokers (NRT and Rent.net). This meant that Homestore acquired exclusive access to three of the largest bricks-and-mortar

(continued)

real estate firm listings in the United States. The Move.com deal also raised antitrust issues because it allegedly had the potential to give Homestore control of up to 90% of all online real estate listings. Homestore executives argued they had not violated antitrust laws or "restrained trade" in any way, but they had simply been successful in growing quite large. Industry experts argued that competitor sites could obtain local listings from sources other than local MLS agencies. For instance, competitors could obtain listings from local newspapers, although this clearly would not be as efficient as having access to local MLS listings. The Department of Justice apparently was swayed by these arguments because, in July 2001, it ended its inquiry into Homestore without comment. As noted previously, Homestore is now known as Move, Inc.

However, that did not end government interest in the issue of competition in the real estate market. In March 2005, the Department of Justice filed a complaint against the Kentucky Real Estate Commission, arguing that local rules prohibiting brokers from giving consumers rebates on real estate commissions (a key strategy for online real estate brokers such as ZipRealty and RealEstate.com) violated antitrust laws. The Department of Justice next focused on policies adopted by the NAR governing the Internet display of MLS listings. In September 2005, it filed an antitrust complaint alleging that the policies put Web-based brokerages at a competitive disadvantage vis-à-vis traditional brokers. The complaint claimed that provisions in the policy that enable brokers to unilaterally withhold their MLS listings from display on competitors' Web sites (known as a "blanket opt-out"), yet at the same time allow those listings to appear on Realtor.com, violated antitrust laws. In other words, the NAR, through its rules, was preventing the operators of online real estate Web sites (sometimes called virtual office Web sites—VOW) from getting access to local MLS listings. According to

the Department of Justice, the policy allows traditional brokers to block their competitors' customers from having full online access to all MLS listings, a critical component in the ability of a broker to effectively compete. In the government's view, the policy enables brokers to discriminate against other brokers based on their usage of new technologies and business models, denying them the benefits of MLS membership available to traditional brokers, discourages competition on price and quality, and deprives consumers of benefits that would flow from new ways of competing. The move by the Department of Justice was, not surprisingly, applauded by discount and non-traditional real estate firms. In response to the suit, the NAR announced that it strongly backed its policies and had no intention of settling. It asserted that the suit mischaracterized the purpose and effect of the "blanket opt-out," which it claimed was merely intended to protect brokers' ownership rights in their property listings. In 2006, the NAR moved to have the suit dismissed. The U.S. District Court in Chicago rejected this in November 2006.

In May 2008, the Justice Department announced that it had reached a proposed settlement with the NAR in which the NAR agreed to repeal its anticompetitive policies and require affiliated MLSs to repeal their rules based on those policies. The NAR also agreed to enact a new policy that Internet-based brokerage companies will not be treated differently from traditional brokers. Under the new policy, brokers participating in a NAR-affiliated MLS will not be permitted to withhold their listings from brokers who serve their customers through VOWs. In addition, brokers will be able to use VOWs to educate consumers, make referrals, and conduct brokerage services. The NAR agreed that such brokers would not be excluded from MLS membership based on their business model.

Every year, 1.5 million homes are sold, most of them through the MLS facilities located in the

(continued)

community. It's unclear how long the NAR and its local members can maintain their stranglehold on the local MLSs, and thereby maintain their 6% commissions. In 2009, the Department of Justice reached a settlement with Consolidated Multiple Listing Service Inc. that requires CMLS to change its rules to allow low-priced and innovative brokers to compete with traditional brokers. The existing rules discouraged brokers from competing on price, unbundling their services, and using Internet-based business models. Undoubtedly, Craigslist (partially owned by eBay) and Google have their eyes on the $60 billion in annual commissions generated by traditional real estate agents. But so far neither has made a move into the local real estate market. Alternatively, the future may be exemplified by firms such as FsboMadison.com, one of the largest for-sale-by-owner sites in the country, and which currently has a 20% share of the Dane County, Wisconsin, market for real estate listings. The site charges just $150 to list a home, and provides a yard "For Sale" sign to boot. Lawyers are now offering advertisements to conduct a house closing for a fixed fee of $600. Consumers who in the past may have been frightened about the prospect of conducting a large transaction without a professional real estate agent holding their hand are now more confident they can do it themselves or with minimal help. In the current recession, sellers, turned off by the huge 6% commissions of traditional agents, are also more confident they know how much to charge for their home. The technology for setting up a database with pictures and prices is now commonplace and inexpensive. Together, all of these factors may ultimately make it impossible for the NAR to continue to conduct business as usual.

SOURCES: "Justice Department Reaches Settlement with Consolidated Multiple Listing Service Inc.," Department of Justice, May 4, 2009; "Justice Department Announces Settlement with the National Association of Realtors," Justice Department, May 27, 2008; "Court Allows Department of Justice Antitrust Lawsuit Against National Association of Realtors to Proceed," Department of Justice, December 2, 2006; "Five Multiple Listing Services Agree to Equal Treatment for Discount Brokers," by Vikas Bajaj, *New York Times*, October 16, 2006; "Court Greenlights DOJ Case Against Realtors," by Roy Mark, Internetnews.com, September 10, 2006.

Travel services appear to be an ideal service/product for the Internet, and therefore e-commerce business models should work well for this product. Travel is an information-intensive product requiring significant consumer research. It is an electronic product in the sense that travel requirements—planning, researching, comparison shopping, reserving, and payment—can be accomplished for the most part online in a digital environment. On the fulfillment side, travel does not require any "inventory": there are no physical assets. And the suppliers of the product—owners of hotels, airlines, rental cars, vacation rooms, and tour guides—are highly fragmented and often have excess capacity. Always looking for customers to fill vacant rooms and rent idle cars, suppliers will be anxious to lower prices and willing to advertise on Web sites that can attract millions of consumers. The online agencies—such as Travelocity, Expedia, and others—do not have to deploy thousands of travel agents in physical offices across the country but can instead concentrate on a single interface with a national consumer audience. Travel services may not require the kind of expensive multi-channel "physical presence" strategy required of financial services (although they generally operate centralized call centers to provide personal customer service). Therefore, travel services might "scale" better, permitting earnings to grow faster than costs.

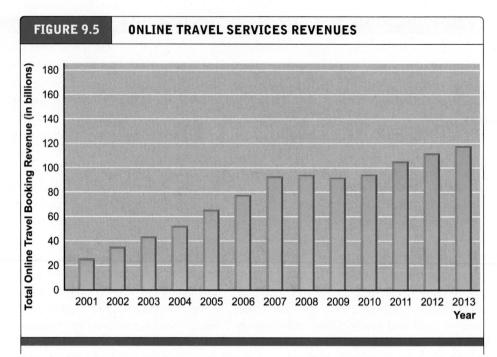

FIGURE 9.5   **ONLINE TRAVEL SERVICES REVENUES**

U.S. online leisure/unmanaged business travel service revenues were flat in the 2008–2009 time period, but are expected to resume growing in 2010.

SOURCES: Based on data from eMarketer, 2009c, 2007, 2005b.

THE ONLINE TRAVEL MARKET

There are four major sectors in the travel market: airline tickets, hotel reservations, car rentals, and cruises/tours. Airline tickets are the source of the greatest amount of revenue in online travel, accounting for an estimated $60 billion in 2009, and projected to grow at a rate of about 5%–6% a year to $75 billion in 2013. Hotels and car rentals, although not as large from a dollar standpoint as airline reservations, are also expected to grow at about the same rate (see **Figure 9.6** on page 625).

The huge size and continued robust growth in online airline reservations reflects several factors. Airline reservations are largely a commodity. They can be easily described over the Web. The same is true with car rentals; most people can reliably rent a car over the phone or the Web and expect to obtain what they ordered (see *Insight on Business: Zipcars* for a different kind of car rental business model). Although hotels are somewhat more difficult to describe, hotel branding, supplemented by Web sites that include descriptions, photographs, and virtual tours, typically provide enough information to most consumers to allow them to feel as if they know what they are purchasing, making them more comfortable making hotel reservations online.

Analysts typically also divide the travel market into two major segments: leisure/unmanaged business travel and managed business travel. The online travel industry has concentrated mostly on the leisure/unmanaged business travel market,

INSIGHT ON BUSINESS

ZIPCARS

How would you like to have all the functionality of a car but not have to deal with any of the headaches typically associated with ownership of a car, such as maintenance and insurance, garaging, or even with the rental of a car from a traditional car rental agency that requires that you go to an office, stand in line, and fill out papers in order to rent, and that mandates a minimum rental period of at least one day?

This might sound like an impossible dream, but it's not. In the late 1990s, a new business model for renting cars was imported from Europe by a group of environmentally conscious entrepreneurs that leverages the power of the Web to make the dream a reality. Today, Zipcar, along with a number of other smaller companies, are using this model on their way towards sustained growth.

Zipcar began in 1999 with a few hundred members and 25 cars in Cambridge, Massachusetts. Members ("Zipsters") could pick up cars at any one of several parking spots around the city, use them for as long as they wanted, and then return them to the same parking spot. By 2005, Zipcar had grown to 700 cars, and 50,000 members paying $35 a year; expanded to include Boston, New York, Washington D.C., and San Francisco; and achieved revenue of around $15 million. In November 2007, Zipcar merged with its largest competitor, Flexcar. Today, the combined company has 6,500 cars (up 20% over the previous year) and 350,000 members, who pay $50 a year for membership and $10 to $15 an hour for using a car depending on the city. The company operates in 28 states and the City of London.

Zipcars brings the Web 2.0 culture of sharing online videos and tweets to the car transportation market. An online application costs $25 and takes minutes to complete. Haven't been in a high-speed chase lately? There's a 90% chance that Zipcar will welcome you into its fold right away. Your Zipcard will arrive in the mail in a day or two. Zipcars are parked mostly in small clusters—between 2 and 20 —in neighborhood garages, shoulder to shoulder with the owned and leased cars of the unenlightened. There are 1,300 Zipcars in the New York area, where 4.5 million people live within a 10-minute walk of one. In Manhattan, a mix of Honda Civics, Toyotas, Volkswagens, Volvos, and BMW Mini Coopers are available. As one commentator noted: "It's such a brazen conceit that it would seem positively communist if Zipcar weren't run by a bunch of fervent free marketers. Zipcar's predicate is that sharing is to ownership what the iPod is to the eight-track, what the solar panel is to the coal mine. Sharing is clean, crisp, urbane, postmodern; owning is dull, selfish, timid, backward. In Zipcar's view, sharing is big business too—bigger, potentially, than anyone can fathom. Its claim is that the winners in the new economy will be those who crack the puzzle posed by scarce resources." Briefly, in certain circles, sharing a Zipcar is cooler than owning a BMW!

In order to make the business work, Zipcar uses a lot of technology and tries to reduce the human-customer contact as much as possible to keep expenses low. Here's how it works. Customers pay an annual subscription fee and are issued a Zipcar card. Customers go online or call an automated central number to reserve a car for around $15 an hour plus $56 a day. Once a car is rented, a central computer activates the car's key card entry system to permit a specific user to enter the car and start the engine. Customers return cars to the same locations and their credit cards are billed. Using wireless technology, the Internet, and automated voice recognition software at each city's central office, Zipcar is able to keep costs very low.

(continued)

Zipcar is supported by universities as well as city governments looking for ways to discourage car ownership, and encourage car sharing, to reduce pollution and congestion. Zipcar has exclusive arrangements with Johns Hopkins, University of Michigan, University of North Carolina, Ohio State, Wellesley College, and many others. In these deals, the universities promise the car will make a certain revenue level per year (usually about $100,000) and make up the difference if they do not hit that revenue target. In September 2009, Los Angeles Zipcar expanded its fleet to 40 cars and partnered with city officials, UCLA, and USC by moving vehicles into their neighborhoods. In San Francisco, when the Bay Bridge closed for repairs in September 2009, over 350 Zipcars were located near BART rapid transit terminals in the Bay Area so residents could take trains to stations, and hop into Zipcars to drive to their final destinations. In an emergency, Zipcars can act as a reserve mini-mass transportation system.

Zipcar's customers are not Middle America, the people who own 200 million cars. Instead, most of Zipcar's customers are young urban professionals (lots of college and advanced degrees) or college students, a market shunned by traditional car rental companies who typically will not rent to drivers under 21. Zipcar started with a fleet of VW Beetles, but now offers Honda Civics, Toyota Prius Hybrids, Ford Escapes, and Mazda 3s. The attraction to college students is that they save money compared to owning cars that sit idle while they are in classes. In urban areas, Zipcar users report they are saving over $500 a month on car operational and parking costs alone. Consider that in Manhattan, where studio apartments rent for $2,500 a month, garage parking for your personal 4-wheeler will run another $300.

Car sharing is also green: national studies show that each shared car replaces up to 20 privately owned vehicles. Some corporations in major cities are thinking about eliminating their urban fleets and using car-sharing services.

However, whether or not hourly car rental services can expand beyond large cities and universities remains to be seen. The idea might not work as well in the suburbs, because customers would have to drive a car to pick up a Zipcar rental. On the other hand, Zipcar executives see a fleet of about 1 million cars in the future just in urban areas. This fleet would replace 20 million privately owned vehicles, one-tenth of the U.S. private fleet. Who needs the burbs? Traditional car rental companies have begun to respond to Zipcar by opening small neighborhood rental shops that make it much more convenient to rent cars. But these firms are not Web-enabled like Zipcar, and lack the technology infrastructure to compete effectively. Zipcar, for instance, spent over $500,000 on a fleet reservation system that connects users, their Web site, and the cars themselves. Avis, Budget, National? Call the 800-number. But the majors are not standing still now that Zipcar has pioneered the marketplace. In 2009, Hertz started its own car-sharing service Connect by Hertz in New York, London, and Paris, with a fleet of Mini Coopers in each city. Hertz charges a flat hourly fee and its rates are lower than Zipcar's. In the New York area, Hertz has over 40,000 vehicles, many of which could ultimately be put into the program. But so far, Zipcar is not worrying, and some analysts have identified it as a potential candidate for a public offering in 2010.

■ **SOURCES:** "Zipcars Coming to Downtown Ann Arbor," by Jon Zemke, concentratemedia.com, September 15, 2009; "Zipcar Partners With City Officials, UCLA, and USC to Expand Car Sharing in Los Angeles," Reuters, September 14, 2009; "Zipcars Near BART Stations Offer Convenient Alternative During Bay Bridge Closing," Reuters, September 4, 2009; "The IPO Class of 2010," by Steve Schaefer, Forbes.com, September 2, 2009; "Share My Ride," by Mark Levine, *New York Times*, March 8, 2009; "Hertz Tosses Some Car Keys Into the Ring, Battling Zipcar," by Ken Belson, *New York Times*, December 16, 2008; "Top Car Sharing Services Join Forces," by Associated Press, *New York Times*, October 31, 2007; "The Next Disruptors: 10 Game Changing Startups," by Eric Schonfeld and Chris Morrison, CNNMoney.com, August 22, 2007.

FIGURE 9.6	PROJECTED GROWTH OF ONLINE TRAVEL MARKET SEGMENTS

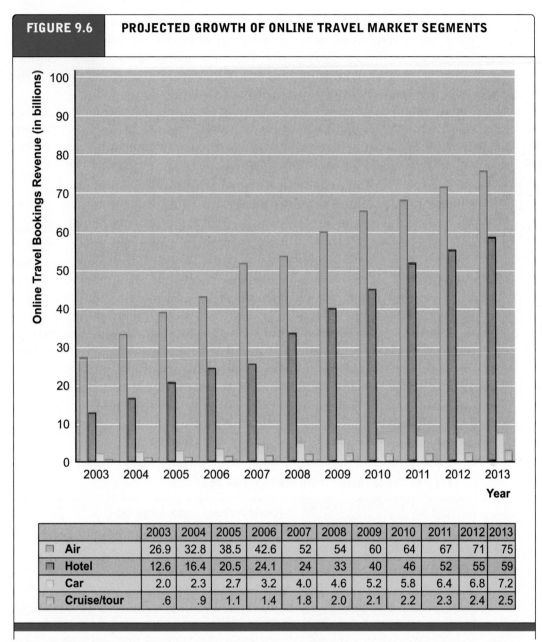

	2003	2004	2005	2006	2007	2008	2009	2010	2011	2012	2013
Air	26.9	32.8	38.5	42.6	52	54	60	64	67	71	75
Hotel	12.6	16.4	20.5	24.1	24	33	40	46	52	55	59
Car	2.0	2.3	2.7	3.2	4.0	4.6	5.2	5.8	6.4	6.8	7.2
Cruise/tour	.6	.9	1.1	1.4	1.8	2.0	2.1	2.2	2.3	2.4	2.5

Airline reservations will continue to dominate the online travel market, although hotel reservations and car reservations are growing at a faster rate.
SOURCES: Based on data from eMarketer, Inc., 2009d, 2007, 2005b; authors' estimates.

but this is expected to change in the future as the managed business travel segment offers greater growth opportunities compared to the more mature leisure/unmanaged business travel market. Managed travel business refers to mid-size and large corporations' efforts to control corporate travel costs by actively managing their employees' travel arrangements. In the past five years, corporate travel expenses have mushroomed, leading corporations to seek greater control over employee travel plans. Many corporations will not reimburse employee travel unless it is made through an approved in-house travel office or a contracted travel agency such as American Express, Rosenbluth International, or Carlson Travel, or increasingly, through Web-based solutions such as Sabre's GetThere.com.

Increasingly, corporations are outsourcing their travel offices entirely to vendors who can provide Web-based solutions, high-quality service, and lower costs. Online vendors to corporations provide **corporate online booking solutions** (**COBS**) that provide integrated airline, hotel, conference center, and auto rental services at a single site.

corporate online-booking solutions (COBS)

provide integrated airline, hotel, conference center, and auto rental services at a single site

ONLINE TRAVEL INDUSTRY DYNAMICS

Because much of what travel agency sites offer is a commodity, and thus they face the same costs, competition among online providers is intense. Price competition is difficult because shoppers, as well as online site managers, can comparison shop easily. Therefore, competition among sites tends to focus on scope of offerings, ease of use, payment options, and personalization. Some well-known travel sites are listed in **Table 9.11**.

The online travel services industry has gone through a period of consolidation with stronger offline, established firms such as Sabre Holdings (which now owns Travelocity, Lastminute, and Site59, among others) purchasing weaker and relatively inex-

TABLE 9.11	MAJOR ONLINE TRAVEL SITES
NAME	DESCRIPTION
LEISURE/UNMANAGED BUSINESS TRAVEL	
Expedia	Largest online travel service; leisure focus.
Travelocity	Second-largest online travel service; leisure focus. Owned by Sabre Holdings.
Orbitz	Began as supplier-owned reservation system; now owned by Cendant.
Priceline	"Name your price" model; leisure focus.
CheapTickets	Discount airline tickets, hotel reservations, and auto rentals. Owned by Cendant.
Hotels.com	Largest hotel reservation network; leisure and corporate focus. Owned by Expedia.
Hotwire	Seeks out discount fares based on airline excess inventory. Owned by Expedia.
MANAGED BUSINESS TRAVEL	
GetThere.com	Corporate online booking solution (COBS). Owned by Sabre Holdings.
Travelocity Business	Full-service corporate travel agency.

pensive online travel agencies in order to build stronger multi-channel travel sites. Orbitz and Expedia have also been involved in the industry consolidation. Orbitz was initially an industry consortium, then went public, then was purchased by Cendant (along with other travel firms such as CheapTickets and Trip.com), then sold by Cendant to Blackstone Group, and finally went public again in 2007. Expedia, originally begun by Microsoft, was purchased by Barry Diller's conglomerate IAC/InterActiveCorp, but has now been spun off as an independent company once again, picking up IAC's Hotels.com, Hotwire, TripAdvisor, and TravelNow in the process.

In addition to industry consolidation, the online travel industry is also being roiled by new technologies in the form of meta-search engines that scour the Web for the best prices on travel and lodging, and then collect finder or affiliate fees for sending consumers to the lowest-price sites. For instance, Kayak.com has created a one-stop Web site where consumers can find the lowest price airfares and hotels by searching over 100 other Web travel sites and presenting the fares in rank order. Similar "travel aggregator" sites are SideStep and Mobissimo. These sites, in the eyes of many industry leaders, commoditize the online travel industry even further, cause excessive price competition, and divert revenues from the leading, branded firms who have made extensive investments in inventory and systems. Kayak.com and other sites have been denied access to Expedia and Travelocity, and only search travel sites with permission, which explains why they have not been sued. Forced to work with smaller travel sites, the travel search engines have yet to show a profit but they are growing site traffic and revenues at a fast pace.

Opportunities for Disintermediation and Re-intermediation

The travel industry value chain is more complex than you may realize (see **Figure 9.7**). Suppliers such as large national airlines, international hotel chains, auto rental companies, and cruise/tour operators generally must deal through a group of intermediaries such as **global distribution systems** (**GDSs**) and travel agencies rather than directly with consumers. GDSs are merchants who buy reservations from suppliers and then resell the "inventory" to agencies, who then retail the inventory to consumers or create vacation packages that are then sold to retail agents. In the past, it was difficult if not impossible for suppliers to have a direct relationship with the consumer. Merchants and GDSs have far higher profit margins, with 50% markups not uncommon. Travel agencies, in contrast, receive fees and commissions that rarely rise above 15% of the amount of the travel booked.

global distribution systems (GDS) merchants who buy reservations from suppliers, and then resell the "inventory" to agencies, which then retail the inventory to consumers or create vacation packages that are then sold to retail

GDSs and travel agencies are under pressure from both the supply side and the corporate demand side. Suppliers—such as airlines, hotels, and auto rental firms—would like to eliminate middlemen such as GDSs and travel agencies, and develop a direct relationship with consumers. Almost all airlines and hotel chains now offer online reservations directly to the public. The major auto rental firms have all also opened direct-to-customer Web sites (Alamo.com, Budget.com, and Hertz.com) in part to reduce agency fees and to combat Priceline's sale of unused rental capacity.

At the same time, successful online travel agencies are attempting to turn themselves into merchants by purchasing large blocks of travel inventory and then

The travel services industry is composed of suppliers, distributors, retail travel agents, and business and leisure travelers. Internet travel sites are an example of how e-commerce can create new intermediaries while weakening existing intermediaries.

reselling it to the public, eliminating the global distributors and earning much higher returns (while assuming greater risk).

We examine the experience of Expedia in the online travel industry in more detail in the *E-commerce in Action* case available online at azimuth-interactive.com/ecommerce6e.

9.7   ONLINE CAREER SERVICES

Next to travel services, one of the Internet's most successful online services has been job services (recruitment sites) that provide a free posting of individual resumes, plus many other related career services; for a fee, they also list job openings posted by companies. Career services sites collect revenue from other sources as well, by providing value-added services to users and collecting fees from related service providers.

The online job market is dominated by three large players: CareerBuilder, Monster, and Yahoo HotJobs. CareerBuilder also provides job listings for AOL and MSN. Other popular sites include Job.com, Indeed.com, SimplyHired, and USAJobs. These top sites generate more than $1 billion annually in revenue from employers' fees and consumer fees. Rising unemployment during late 2008 and 2009 has led to an increasing number of Americans seeking jobs and career opportunities online, according to comScore Media Metrix, with career services and development Web sites among the top 10 fastest growing site categories, with a total of over 65 million visitors in June 2009 (comScore, 2009c).

Traditionally, companies have relied on five employee recruitment tools: classified and print advertising, career expos (or trade shows), on-campus recruiting, private employment agencies (now called "staffing firms"), and internal referral programs. In comparison to online recruiting, these tools have severe limitations. Print advertising usually includes a per-word charge that limits the amount of detail employers provide about a job opening, as well as a limited time period within which the job is posted. Career expos do not allow for pre-screening of attendees and are limited by the amount of time a recruiter can spend with each candidate. Staffing firms charge high fees and have a limited, usually local, selection of job hunters. On-campus recruiting also restricts the number of candidates a recruiter can speak with during a normal visit and requires that employers visit numerous campuses. And internal referral programs may encourage employees to propose unqualified candidates for openings in order to qualify for rewards or incentives offered.

Online recruiting overcomes these limitations, providing a more efficient and cost-effective means of linking employers and potential employees, while reducing the total time-to-hire. Online recruiting enables job hunters to more easily build, update, and distribute their resumes while gathering information about prospective employers and conducting job searches.

IT'S JUST INFORMATION: THE IDEAL WEB BUSINESS?

Online recruitment is ideally suited for the Web. The hiring process is an information-intense business process that involves discovering the skills and salary requirements of individuals and matching them with available jobs. In order to accomplish this match up, there does not initially need to be face-to-face interaction, or a great deal of personalization. Prior to the Internet, this information sharing was accomplished locally by human networks of friends, acquaintances, former employers, and relatives, in addition to employment agencies that developed paper files on job hunters. The Internet can clearly automate this flow of information, reducing search time and costs for all parties.

Table 9.12 lists some of the most popular recruitment sites.

Why are so many job hunters and employers using Internet job sites? Recruitment sites are popular largely because they save time and money for both job hunters and employers seeking recruits. For employers, the job boards expand the geographical reach of their searches, lower costs, and result in faster hiring decisions.

For job seekers, online sites are popular not only because their resumes can be made widely available to recruiters but also because of a variety of other related job-hunting services. The services delivered by online recruitment sites have greatly expanded since their emergence in 1996. Originally, online recruitment sites just provided a digital version of newspaper classified ads. Today's sites offer many other services, including skills assessment, personality assessment questionnaires, personalized account management for job hunters, organizational culture assessments, job search tools, employer blocking (prevents your employer from seeing your posting), employee blocking (prevents your employees from seeing your listings if you are their

TABLE 9.12	POPULAR ONLINE RECRUITMENT SITES
RECRUITMENT SITE	**BRIEF DESCRIPTION**
General Recruitment Sites	
CareerBuilder	Owned by Gannett, Tribune, McClatchy (all newspaper companies), and Microsoft. Provides job search centers for more than 9,000 Web sites, including AOL and MSN, and 140 newspapers; 1.6 million jobs listed.
Monster	One of the first commercial sites on the Web in 1994. Today, a public company offering general job searches in 40 countries, generating revenue of over $1.3 billion a year.
Yahoo HotJobs	General job searches. Partners with consortium of newspapers, including Hearst, Cox, MediaNews General, Scripps, and others for cross-listing of job postings.
Job.com	General job searches in 70 different disciplines. In August 2009, more than 17 million registered users, and fourth most visited site in category, according to comScore Media Metrix.
Kenexa (formerly Brassring)	Management recruitment and job searches
Craigslist	Popular classified listing service focused on local recruiting
Indeed.com	Job site aggregator
SimplyHired	Job site aggregator
Executive Search Sites	
Futurestep	Korn/Ferry site, low-end executive recruiting
Spencerstuart.com	Middle-level executive recruiting
ExecuNet	Executive search firm
Niche Job Sites	
USAJobs	Federal government jobs
HigherEdJobs	Education industry
EngineerJobs	Engineering jobs
Medzilla	Medical industry
Showbizjobs	Entertainment industry
Salesjobs	Sales and marketing
Dice	Information technology jobs
MBAGlobalNet	MBA-oriented community site

employer), and e-mail notification. Online sites also provide a number of educational services such as resume writing advice, software skills preparation, and interview tips.

For the most part, online recruitment sites work, in the sense of linking job hunters with jobs, but they are just one of many ways people actually find jobs. A survey by The Conference Board found that the majority (70%) of job seekers rely equally on both the Internet and newspapers to look for jobs, with about half relying on word-of-mouth leads, and about a quarter on employment agencies. However, most respondents felt that the Internet was the most productive in producing a job offer (eMarketer, Inc., 2006). Given that the cost of posting a resume online is zero, the marginal returns are very high.

The ease with which resumes can be posted online has also raised new issues for both job recruiters and job seekers. If you are an employer, how do you sort through and parse the thousands of resumes you may receive when posting an open job? If you are a job seeker, how do you stand out among the thousands or even millions of others? Perhaps one way is to post a video resume. In a survey by Vault, nearly nine in 10 employers said they would watch a video resume if it were submitted to them, in part because it would help them better assess a candidate's professional presentation and demeanor, and over half said they believed video would become a common addition to future job applications. CareerBuilder became the first major online job site to implement a video resume tool for job candidates, following a previous launch for an online video brand-building tool for employers.

In another sense, general online recruitment sites may be experiencing declining effectiveness. The advent of the Web and e-mail has increased the supply of resumes (the number of resumes landing on a recruiter's desktop) beyond the point where they can be rationally evaluated. On the other hand, most large companies rely heavily on their company's Web site as a source of employees. One way to avoid the clutter is to target and focus on specific companies, or, if you are a recruiter, to focus on niche sites that are likely to have people with the skills you are looking for. The use of corporate Web sites to find job candidates has also increased with the debut of the new .jobs top-level domain created to allow employers to create Web sites focused specifically at online recruiting.

Perhaps the most important function of online recruitment sites is not so much their capacity to actually match employees with job hunters but their ability to establish market prices and terms, as well as trends in the labor market. Online recruitment sites identify salary levels for both employers and job hunters, and categorize the skill sets required to achieve those salary levels. In this sense, online recruitment sites are online national marketplaces that establish the terms of trade in the labor markets. For instance, Monster.com offers its U.S. Monster Employment Index. This index monitors over 1,500 online job sites and calculates employment demand for the nation, regions, and specific occupations. The existence of these online national job sites should lead to a rationalization of wages, greater labor mobility, and higher efficiency in recruitment and operations because employers will be able to quickly find the people they need.

RECRUITMENT MARKET SEGMENTS

There are three segments in the recruitment business. General job recruitment is the largest segment and focuses on placing a wide range of individuals at all skill and salary levels. In the past, general job recruitment has been performed by government labor agencies and private placement firms, and through newspaper classified ads (a major source of revenue for newspapers). The executive search segment focuses on placing executives with annual salaries of $100,000 or more.

Specialized executive placement firms conduct executive searches for employers, generally charging one-third of the first year's salary as a fee. A third segment is specialized job placement services, which are often run by professional societies such as the Society of Plastics Engineers site (4spe.org), and the police recruiting site, Policeemployment.com.

Online recruitment has focused primarily on the largest market for general job recruitment. However, many general sites—such as Monster—have begun listing lower- and middle-level management jobs. Indeed, the largest revenue potential for the general job online sites is in executive recruiting, where fees are currently very high. The traditional executive placement agencies such as Korn/Ferry and Spencer Stuart—realizing the threat from online sites—have also developed their own Web sites for lower- and middle-level managers seeking salaries above $100,000. Pitney Bowes and Accenture are just two firms hiring mid-level and even senior executives through the Internet. They are saving $50,000 per hire by avoiding expensive executive search firms.

ONLINE RECRUITMENT INDUSTRY TRENDS

Trends for 2009–2010 in the online recruitment services industry including the following:

- **Consolidation**: The three largest job services are CareerBuilder (owned by newspapers and Microsoft), Monster, and HotJobs (owned by Yahoo). In 2009–2010, these three sites dominate the market, and are expected to do so for some time to come.

- **Diversification**: While the national online market is becoming larger and consolidating into a few general sites, there is an explosion in specialty niche employment sites that focus on specific occupations. This is creating greater online job market diversity and choice.

- **Localization**: While local classified ads in newspapers remain a significant source of jobs, the large national online sites are also developing local boards in large metropolitan areas that compete more directly against local newspapers. The local newspapers themselves have responded by building local Web sites that focus on local job markets, especially hourly and contract jobs that often do not appear on the large national job boards. Craigslist is another source of local job listings. Hence there is a growing focus on local job markets by all participants in the marketplace because this is where so many new jobs first appear.

- **Job search engines/aggregators**: As with travel services, search engines that focus specifically on jobs are posing a new threat to established online career sites. For instance, Indeed.com, SimplyHired, and JobCentral "scrape" listings from thousands of online job sites such as Monster, CareerBuilder, specialty recruiting services, and the sites of individual employers, to provide a free, searchable index of thousands of job listings in one spot. Because these firms do not charge employers a listing fee, they are currently using a pay-per-click or other advertising revenue model.

- **Social networking**: LinkedIn, probably the most well-known business-oriented social network, has grown significantly to over 47 million members representing over 150 different industries around the world as of September 2009. Consumers are using sites such as LinkedIn to establish business contacts and networks, while employers use them to conduct searches to find potential job candidates that may not be actively job hunting. For instance, LinkedIn offers companies a tool called LinkedIn Talent Advantage that includes tools that help corporate recruiters find "passive talent" (people who are not actively looking for a new job), as well as custom company profiles that are specifically designed for recruitment (LinkedIn.com, 2009). CareerBuilder offers a job and internship matching application on Facebook that allows users to receive continuously updated listings based on the information found in their profiles. Social networking sites are also being used by employers to "check up" on the background of job candidates. For instance, one survey found that 77% of recruiters surveyed used the Internet and social network sites to screen job candidates, and that over a third had eliminated a candidate based on information found there (eMarketer, 2009e). Companies are also increasingly using Twitter as a job recruitment tool, with companies as diverse as McDonald's, PepsiCo, IBM, MTV, Intel, and the U.S. Department of State and hundreds of others tweeting about available jobs (Joyce, 2009).

9.8 CASE STUDY

OpenTable:
Your Reservation Is Waiting

OpenTable is the leading supplier of reservation, table management, and guest management software for restaurants. In addition, the company operates, OpenTable.com, the world's most popular Web site for making restaurant reservations online. In 11 years, OpenTable has gone from a start-up to a successful and growing public company that counts one-third of the nation's reservation-taking restaurants as clients. And, in the first quarter of 2009, an average of 3 million diners per month made reservations using OpenTable.

Today, more than 11,000 restaurants in the United States, Canada, Mexico, United Kingdom, Germany, France, Spain, and Japan use the OpenTable hardware and software system. This system automates the reservation-taking and table management process, while allowing restaurants to build diner databases for improved guest recognition and targeted e-mail marketing. The Web site provides a fast, efficient way for diners to find available tables in real time. The Web site connects directly to the thousands of computerized reservation systems at OpenTable restaurants, and reservations are immediately recorded in a restaurant's electronic reservation book.

Restaurants subscribe to the OpenTable Electronic Reservation Book (ERB), the company's proprietary software, which is installed on a touch-screen computer system and supported by asset-protection and security tools. The ERB software provides a real-time map of the restaurant floor and enables the restaurant to retain meal patterns of all parties, serving as a customer relationship management (CRM) system for restaurants. The software is upgraded periodically, and the latest version, introduced in May 2009, was designed to provide better use of real-time data to help turn more tables, enhance guest service, personalize responses to diners, coordinate the seating process and maximize guest seating. The ERBs at OpenTable's restaurant customers connect via the Internet to form an online network of restaurant reservation books.

OpenTable's revenue comes from two sources. Restaurants pay a one-time fee for onsite installation and training, a monthly subscription fee of $199 for software and hardware, and a $1 transaction fee for each restaurant guest seated through online reservations. The online reservation service is free to diners. The business model encourages diners to assist in viral marketing. When an individual makes a reservation, the site "suggests" that they send e-vites to their dinner companions directly from OpenTable.com. The e-vites include a link back to the OpenTable site.

OpenTable is a service-based (software as service, or SaaS) e-commerce company. In other words, customers don't buy software and install it on their computers, but instead go online and get the software functionality through subscriptions. OpenTable is also an online service that does not sell goods, but instead enables diners to make reservations, like social networking sites provide services.

The restaurant industry was slow to leverage the power of the Internet. This was in part because the industry was, and continues to be, highly fragmented, and local—made up of more than 30,000 small, independent businesses or local restaurant-owning groups.

The founders of OpenTable knew the industry was fragmented, and therefore dealing with all these restaurants as a single market would be difficult. They also realized that the Internet was changing things for diners by providing them with instant access to reviews, menus, and other information about dining options. And there was no method for making reservations online—we all know reserving by phone is time-consuming, inefficient, and prone to errors. In order to make the system work, reach and scale were very important. For diners to use an online reservation system, they would need real-time access to a number of local restaurants, and the ability to instantly book confirmed reservations around the clock. If customers were planning a trip to another city, OpenTable would need participating restaurants in those cities.

The company was originally incorporated in San Francisco in 1998 as Easyeats.com. In 1999, its name was changed to OpenTable.com, Inc. When the company was founded, most restaurants did not have computers, let alone systems that would allow online reservations made through a central Web site. OpenTable's initial strategy of paying online restaurant reviewers for links to its Web site and targeting national chains for fast expansions got the company into 50 cities, but it was spending $1 million a month and bringing in only $100,000 in revenue. Not exactly a formula for success. The original investors still felt there was a viable business to be built, and they made a number of management changes, including installing investor and board member Thomas Layton, founder of CitySearch.com, as OpenTable's CEO. Mr. Layton cut staff, shut down marketing efforts, and got the company out of all but four cities: Chicago, New York, San Francisco, and Washington, DC.

The company retooled its hardware and software to create the user-friendly ERB system, and deployed a door-to-door sales force to solicit subscriptions from high-end restaurants. The combination of e-commerce, useful, user-friendly technology, and the personal touch, worked. The four markets Open Table targeted initially developed into active, local networks of restaurants and diners that continue to grow. OpenTable has implemented the same strategy across the country, and now includes approximately 10,000 OpenTable restaurant customers spanning all 50 states as well as over 1,000 plus in select markets outside of the United States. In 11 years, the company has seated approximately 100 million diners through Opentable.com.

As the company grew, investors began making plans for it to go public. Mr. Layton stepped down from his position as CEO in 2007, though he remains a board member. He was replaced by Jeffrey Jordan, former president of PayPal. Mr. Jordan had some experience with public companies from working with eBay on their acquisition of PayPal. In 2009, he chose an aggressive strategy—going ahead with an initial public offering (IPO) despite a terrible economy and worse financial markets. So far, his gamble has paid off. On its first day of trading, OpenTable's shares climbed 59%. The share price at the end of August 2009 was $27.65, well above the $17 IPO price.

Despite the challenging economy, OpenTable's numbers at the time of the IPO were strong. For the 12 months ended December 31, 2007 and 2008, revenues were $41.1 million and $55.8 million, respectively. During the three-year period from January 2006 through December 2008, OpenTable's revenue grew at an annualized rate of 43%. Despite the severe recession, results from the first quarter of 2009 showed growth as well—the number of restaurant partners increased to 10,645 from 8,404 in 2008.

The company benefitted tremendously from having e-commerce revenue streams from subscription fees and per-transaction charges, instead of from advertising at a time when advertising expenditures—by companies large and small—have dropped precipitously. Further, more than 50% of OpenTable's revenue comes from B2B subscriptions, which are typically part of long-term contracts. Restaurants that have invested in OpenTable's software package are less likely to want to incur the switching costs associated with changing to a different reservation management package.

Another reason for its success is that OpenTable has a large number of satisfied customers. Restaurant owners report that they and their staff members find the software easy to use, and it helps them manage their business better. Specifically, it streamlines operations, helps fill additional seats, and improves quality of service, providing a concrete return on investment. This has led to both high customer satisfaction and high retention rates.

OpenTable has also taken advantage of the interconnected needs of restaurants and diners. Restaurants want cost-effective ways to attract guests and manage their reservations, while diners want convenient ways to find available restaurants, choose among them, and make reservations. By creating an online network of restaurants and diners that transact with each other through real-time reservations, OpenTable has figured out how to successfully address the needs of both.

OpenTable's market is susceptible to network effects: the more people use it, the more utility the system delivers. OpenTable's growth continually provides diners with expanded choices. More diners discover the benefits of using the online reservation system, which in turn delivers value to restaurant customers, and helps attract more restaurants to the network. Diners serve as a source of viral marketing, as the OpenTable Web site encourages them to e-vite their dinner companions to the meal. When they do so, the e-mail provides links back to the OpenTable Web site. And the OpenTable link appears on the restaurant's Web site, linking directly to the reservation page. OpenTable has been able to improve its efficiency even as diners are staying home more often. The company's operating margins are now 5%, up from 1% in 2008. This occurred even while the number of staff members increased from 248 to 300.

While OpenTable is the biggest, most successful online player in the restaurant reservations market, it does have competitors. MenuPages.com offers access to restaurant menus and reviews, but no ability for visitors to the site to make reservations, and the site covers only eight U.S. cities. UrbanSpoon.com offers a reservation service, but its technology is not compatible with OpenTable, so those reservations must be entered manually into the OpenTable system. Like OpenTable, UrbanSpoon charges $1 for each diner. DinnerBroker.com offers the ability to make online reservations, and offers dining discounts for those willing to eat at off-peak hours. As of August 2009, they are working with 1,500 restaurants nationwide, far fewer than OpenTable's 10,000-plus. Foodline.com and SavvyDiner.com offer similar services; however, only OpenTable and Foodline provide the option for restaurants to track customer behavior.

While some may argue that there are better ways to make reservations that don't take visitors away from restaurant's Web sites (once someone clicks on the OpenTable link, they navigate away), restaurant owners like the OpenTable software, and diners have an enormous range of dining choices. Those two factors make this argument a relatively weak one. In the past six months, OpenTable's bookings have tripled; a good sign for the future.

The company is committed to innovation when it makes sense, for example, it recently introduced OpenTable applications for PDAs—the Palm Pre, the BlackBerry, and the iPhone. These applications help users find restaurants with the use of GPS, and make reservations.

Along with innovation, OpenTable continues to use its tried and true business model that combines technology with old-fashioned door-to-door sales. Using this model, OpenTable's new North American markets have grown predictably over time, and this growth is projected to continue. OpenTable plans a selective international expansion into countries where there are large numbers of online consumer transactions and reservation-taking restaurants. The company currently has operations in Germany, Japan, and the United Kingdom, each supported with a direct sales force, and has signed on approximately 1,000 restaurant customers in these markets.

SOURCES: OpenTable.com, September 21, 2009; "Open Table-the Hottest Spot in Town," by Maha Atal, CNNMoney.con, August 14, 2009; "OpenTable Unveils Version 2.0 of its iPhone App," AppScout.com, August 14, 2009; Open Table,. Form10-Q for quarter ended June 30, 2009, filed with the Securities and Exchange Commission, August 11, 2008; "Gadgetell: Fight for Your Dinner: Urbanspoon vs. Open Table," NewsFactor.com, August 8, 2009; "Urbanspoon is Now Taking Online Reservations: Takes on OpenTable," by Federic Lardinois, ReadWriteWeb.com, August 7, 2009; "OpenTable Launches BlackBerry App," by Jamie Lendino, PCMag.com, August 5, 2009; "OpenTable App Hits the Palm Pre," AppScout.com, July 29, 2009; "Yelp vs. OpenTable -- Where Should Restaurants Spend Their Marketing Dollars," Dinner Rush Blog, eservationdc.wordpress.com, July 19, 2009; "OpenTable IPO Rises 59%; Critics Sneer," by Lynn Cowan, *Wall Street Journal*, May 22, 2009; "OpenTable Finds Strong Demand for Shares in Offering," by Claire Cain Miller, *New York Times*, May 21, 2009; "What Media Companies Could Learn from Open Table," The Media Wonk, May 20, 2009; Open Table S-1/A Amendment #6, filed with the Securities and Exchange Commission, May 19, 2009; "OpenTable IPO Shows Advantage of Not Relying on Advertising," by Rory Maher paidContent.org, May 19, 2009; "Open Table Announces New Upgrade of its Electronic Reservation Book Software," Open Table press release, May 16, 2009; "How OpenTable Could Actually Matter," by Sarah Lacey, TechCrunch.com, May 3, 2009.

The company's international strategy is to replicate the successful U.S. model by focusing initially on building a restaurant customer base. OpenTable believes the localized versions of its software will compete favorably against competitive software offerings, enabling them to expand across a broad selection of local restaurants.

The company is well-positioned for future growth. Its size, track record of growth, and high customer satisfaction rates should continue to work in its favor.

Case Study Questions

1. Why will OpenTable competitors have a difficult time competing against OpenTable?

2. What characteristics of the restaurant market make it difficult for a reservation system to work?

3. How did OpenTable change its marketing strategy to succeed?

4. Why would restaurants find the SaaS model very attractive?

9.9   REVIEW

KEY CONCEPTS

■ **Understand the environment in which the online retail sector operates today.**

Personal consumption of retail goods and services comprise about 70% and account for over $9.7 trillion of total GDP. The retail sector can be broken down into three main categories:
- Services, which account for 60% of total retail sales
- Durable goods, which account for 11% of total retail sales
- Nondurable goods, which account for 29% of total retail sales

Although the distinction between a good and a service is not always clear-cut and "product-based services" are becoming the norm, we use the term retail goods to refer to physical products and retailers to refer to firms that sell physical goods to consumers. The retail industry can be further divided into nine major firm types:
- Clothing
- General merchandise
- Groceries
- Durable goods
- Specialty stores
- Eating and drinking
- Gasoline and fuel
- MOTO
- Online retail firms

Each type offers opportunities for online retail. The biggest opportunities for direct online sales are within those segments that sell small-ticket items (less than $100). This includes specialty stores, general merchandisers, mail-order catalogers, and grocery stores. The MOTO sector is the most similar to the online retail sales sector, and MOTO retailers are among the fastest growing online retail firms.

During the early days of e-commerce, some predicted that the retail industry would be revolutionized, based on the following beliefs:

- Greatly reduced search costs on the Internet would encourage consumers to abandon traditional marketplaces in order to find the lowest prices for goods. First movers who provided low-cost goods and high-quality service would succeed.
- Market entry costs would be much lower than those for physical storefront merchants, and online merchants would be more efficient at marketing and order fulfillment than their offline competitors because they had command of the technology (technology prices were falling sharply).
- Online companies would replace traditional stores as physical store merchants were forced out of business. Older traditional firms that were too slow to enter the online market would be locked out of the marketplace.
- In certain industries, the "middleman" would be eliminated (disintermediation) as manufacturers or their distributors entered the market and built a direct relationship with the consumer. This cost savings would ensure the emergence of the Web as the dominant marketing channel.
- In other industries, online retailers would gain the advantage over traditional merchants by outsourcing functions such as warehousing and order fulfillment, resulting in a kind of hypermediation, in which the online retailer gained the upper hand by eliminating inventory purchasing and storage costs.

Today, it has become clear that few of the initial assumptions about the future of online retail were correct. Also, the structure of the retail marketplace in the United States has not been revolutionized. The reality is that:

- Online consumers are not primarily cost-driven—instead, they are as brand-driven and influenced by perceived value as their offline counterparts.
- Online market entry costs were underestimated, as was the cost of acquiring new customers.
- Older traditional firms, such as the general merchandising giants and the established catalog-based retailers, are taking over as the top online retail sites.
- Disintermediation did not occur. On the contrary, online retailing has become an example of the powerful role that intermediaries play in retail trade.

■ Explain how to analyze the economic viability of an online firm.

The economic viability, or ability of a firm to survive during a specified time period, can be analyzed by examining the key industry strategic factors, the strategic factors that pertain specifically to the firm, and the financial statements for the firm. The key industry strategic factors include:

- *Barriers to entry*, which are expenses that will make it difficult for new entrants to join the industry.
- *Power of suppliers*, which refers to the ability of firms in the industry to bargain effectively for lower prices from suppliers.
- *Power of customers*, which refers to the ability of the customers for a particular product to shop among the firm's competitors, thus keeping prices down.

- *Existence of substitute products*, which refers to the present or future availability of products with a similar function.
- The *industry value chain*, which must be evaluated to determine if the chain of production and distribution for the industry is changing in ways that will benefit or harm the firm.
- The *nature of intra-industry competition*, which must be evaluated to determine if the competition within the industry is based on differentiated products and services, price, the scope of the offerings, or the focus of the offerings and whether any imminent changes in the nature of the competition will benefit or harm the firm.

The key firm strategic factors include:

- The *firm value chain*, which must be evaluated to determine if the firm has adopted business systems that will enable it to operate at peak efficiency and whether there are any looming technological changes that might force the firm to change its processes or methods.
- *Core competencies*, which refer to unique skills that a firm has that cannot be easily duplicated. When analyzing the economic viability of a firm, it is important to consider whether technological changes might invalidate these competencies.
- *Synergies*, which refer to the availability to the firm of the competencies and assets of related firms that it owns or with which it has formed strategic partnerships.
- The firm's current *technology*, which must be evaluated to determine if it has proprietary technologies that will allow it to scale with demand and if it has developed the customer relationship, fulfillment, supply chain management, and human resources systems that it will need in order to be viable.
- The *social and legal challenges facing the firm*, which should be examined to determine if the firm has taken into account consumer trust issues such as the privacy and security of personal information and if the firm may be vulnerable to legal challenges.

The key financial factors include:

- *Revenues*, which must be examined to determine if they are growing and at what rate.
- *Cost of sales*, which is the cost of the products sold, including all related costs. The lower the cost of sales compared to revenue, the higher the gross profit.
- *Gross margin*, which is calculated by dividing gross profit by net sales revenue. If the gross margin is improving consistently, the economic outlook for the firm is enhanced.
- *Operating expenses*, which should be evaluated to determine if the firm's needs in the near interim will necessitate increased outlays. Large increases in operating expenses may result in net losses for the firm.
- *Operating margin*, which is calculated by dividing operating income or loss by net sales revenue, and is an indication of a company's ability to turn sales into pre-tax profit after operating expenses are deducted.
- *Net margin,* which is calculated by dividing net income or net loss by net sales revenue. It evaluates the net profit or loss for each dollar of net sales. For example, a net margin of -24% indicates that a firm is losing 24 cents on each dollar of net sales revenue.
- The firm's *balance sheet,* which is a financial snapshot of a company on a given date that displays its financial assets and liabilities. If current assets are less than or not much more than current liabilities, the firm will likely have trouble meeting its short-term obligations.

■ Identify the challenges faced by the different types of online retailers.

There are four major types of online retail business models, and each faces its own particular challenges:

- *Virtual merchants* are single-channel Web firms that generate all of their revenues from online sales. Their challenges include building a business and a brand name quickly, many competitors in the virtual marketplace, substantial costs to build and maintain a Web site, considerable marketing expenses, large customer acquisition costs, a steep learning curve, and the need to quickly achieve operating efficiencies in order to preserve a profit. Amazon is the most well-known example of a virtual merchant.

- *Multi-channel merchants* (bricks-and-clicks) have a network of physical stores as their primary retail channel, but have also begun online operations. Their challenges include high cost of physical buildings, high cost of large sales staffs, the need to coordinate prices across channels, the need to develop methods of handling cross-channel returns from multiple locations, building a credible Web site, hiring new skilled staff, and building rapid-response order entry and fulfillment systems. JCP.com is an example of a bricks-and-clicks company.

- *Catalog merchants* are established companies that have a national offline catalog operation as their largest retail channel, but who have recently developed online capabilities. Their challenges include high costs for printing and mailing, the need to leverage their existing assets and competencies to the new technology environment, the need to develop methods of handling cross-channel returns, building a credible Web site, and hiring new skilled staff. Lands' End is an example of a catalog merchant.

- *Manufacturer-direct merchants* are either single- or multi-channel manufacturers who sell to consumers directly online without the intervention of retailers. They were predicted to play a very large role in e-commerce, but this has not generally happened. Their challenges include channel conflict, which occurs when physical retailers of a manufacturer's products must compete on price and currency of inventory with the manufacturer who does not face the cost of maintaining inventory, physical stores, and a sales staff; quickly developing a fast-response online order and fulfillment system; switching from a supply-push (products are made prior to orders being received based on estimated demand) to a demand-pull model (products are not built until an order is received); and creating sales, service, and support operations online. Dell.com is an example of a manufacturer-direct merchant.

■ Describe the major features of the online service sector.

The service sector is the largest and most rapidly expanding part of the economy of advanced industrial nations. Service industries are companies that provide services (i.e., perform tasks for) consumers, businesses, governments, and other organizations. The major service industry groups are financial services, insurance, real estate, business services, and health services. Within these service industry groups, companies can be further categorized into those that involve transaction brokering and those that involve providing a "hands-on" service. With some exceptions, the service sector is by and large a knowledge- and information-intense industry. For this reason, many services are uniquely suited to e-commerce and the strengths of the Internet.

The rapid expansion of e-commerce services in the areas of finance, including insurance and real estate, travel, and job placement, can be explained by the ability of these firms to:

- collect, store, and disseminate high value information
- provide reliable, fast communication
- personalize and customize service or components of service

E-commerce offers extraordinary opportunities to improve transaction efficiencies and thus productivity in a sector where productivity has so far not been markedly affected by the explosion in information technology.

■ **Discuss the trends taking place in the online financial services industry.**

The online financial services sector is a good example of an e-commerce success story, but the success is somewhat different than what had been predicted in the early days of e-commerce. Today it is the multi-channel established financial firms that are growing the most rapidly and that have the best prospects for long-term viability. Other significant trends include the following:

- Management of financial assets online is growing rapidly.
- In the insurance and real estate industries, consumers still generally utilize the Internet just for research and use a conventional transaction broker to complete the purchase.
- Historically, separate institutions have provided the four generic types of services provided by financial institutions. Today, as a result of the Financial Reform Act of 1998, which permitted banks, brokerage firms, and insurance companies to merge, this is no longer true. This has resulted in two important and related global trends in the financial services industry that have direct consequences for online financial services firms: the move toward industry consolidation and the provision of integrated financial services.

Key features of the online banking and brokerage industries include the following:

- Multi-channel firms that have both physical branches and solid online offerings have assumed market leadership over the pure-online firms that cannot provide customers with many services that still require hands-on interaction.
- Customer acquisition costs are significantly higher for Internet-only banks and brokerages that must invest heavily in marketing versus their established brand-name bricks-and-mortar competitors, which can simply convert existing branch customers to online customers at a much lower cost.
- Financial portals provide comparison shopping services and steer consumers to online providers for independent financial advice and financial planning.
- Account aggregation is another rapidly growing online financial service, which pulls together all of a customer's financial data on a single personalized Web site.
- During the early days of e-commerce, a radically altered online mortgage and lending services market was envisioned in which the mortgage value chain would be simplified and the loan closing process speeded up, with the resulting cost savings passed on to consumers. Affordably building a brand name, the resulting high customer acquisition costs, and instituting these value chain changes proved to be too difficult. Today it is the established banks and lenders who are reaping the benefits of a relatively small but growing market.

- There are three basic types of online mortgage lenders, including established banks, brokerages, and lending organizations; pure-online bankers/brokers; and mortgage brokers.

Key features of the online insurance industry include the following:

- Term life insurance stands out as one product group supporting the early visions of lower search costs, increased price transparency, and the resulting consumer savings. However, in other insurance product lines, the Web offers insurance companies new opportunities for product and service differentiation and price discrimination.
- The insurance industry has several other distinguishing characteristics that make it difficult for it to be completely transferred to the new online channel, such as policies that defy easy comparison and that can only be explained by an experienced sales agent, a traditional reliance on local insurance offices and agents to sell complex products uniquely suited to the circumstances of the insured person and/or property, and a marketplace that is coordinated by state insurance commissions in each state with differing regulations. Although search costs have been dramatically reduced and price comparison shopping is done in an entirely new way, the industry value chain has so far not been significantly impacted.

Key features of the online real estate services industry include the following:

- The early vision that the historically local, complex, and agent-driven real estate industry would be transformed into a disintermediated marketplace where buyers and sellers could transact directly has not been realized. What has happened has been beneficial to buyers, sellers, and real estate agents alike.
- Since it is not possible to complete a property transaction online, the major impact of the online real estate industry is in influencing offline purchases.
- The primary service is a listing of available houses, with secondary links to mortgage lenders, credit reporting agencies, neighborhood information, loan calculators, appraisal reports, sales price histories by neighborhood, school district data, and crime reports.
- The industry value chain, however, has remained unchanged. Home addresses are not available online and users are directed back to the local listing agent for further information about the house.
- Buyers benefit because they can quickly and easily access a wealth of valuable information; sellers benefit because they receive free online advertising for their property; and real estate agents have reported that Internet-informed customers ask to see fewer properties.

■ **Discuss the major trends in the online travel services industry today.**

Online travel services attract the largest single e-commerce audience and the largest slice of B2C revenues. The Internet has become the most common channel used by consumers to research travel options. It is also the most common way for people to search for the best possible prices and book reservations for airline tickets, rental cars, hotel rooms, cruises, and tours. Some of the reasons why online travel services have been so successful include the following:

- Online travel sites offer consumers a one-stop, convenient, leisure and business travel experience where travelers can find content, community, commerce, and customer service. Online sites offer more information and travel options than traditional travel agents, with such services as descriptions of vacations and facilities, chat groups and bulletin boards, and the convenience of purchasing all travel elements at one stop. They also bring consumers and suppliers together in a low transaction cost environment.

- Travel is an information-intensive product as well as an electronic product in the sense that travel requirements can be accomplished for the most part online. Since travel does not require any inventory, suppliers (which are highly fragmented) are always looking for customers to fill excess capacity. Also, travel services do not require an expensive multi-channel physical presence. For these reasons, travel services appear to be particularly well suited for the online marketplace.
- It is important to note that various segments of the travel industry fit this description better than others—for instance, airline reservations, auto rentals, and to a lesser extent, hotels. Cruises and tours are more differentiated with varying quality and a more complex level of information required for the decision-making process. Therefore, cruises, tours, and hotels to some extent will probably not grow as quickly in the online environment.
- In the past five years, corporate travel expenses have mushroomed, leading corporations to seek greater control over employee travel plans. Corporations are outsourcing their travel offices entirely to vendors who can provide Web-based solutions, high-quality service, and lower costs.

The major trends in online travel services include the following:
- The online travel services industry is going through a period of consolidation as stronger offline, established firms purchase weaker and relatively inexpensive online travel agencies in order to build stronger multi-channel travel sites that combine physical presence, television sales outlets, and online sites.
- Suppliers—such as airlines, hotels, and auto rental firms—are attempting to eliminate intermediaries such as GDSs and travel agencies, and develop a direct relationship with consumers. At the same time, successful online travel agencies are attempting to turn themselves into merchants by purchasing large blocks of travel inventory and then reselling it to the public, eliminating the global distributors and earning much higher returns.

■ Identify current trends in the online career services industry.

Next to travel services, job-hunting services have been one of the Internet's most successful online services because they save money for both job hunters and employers. In comparison to online recruiting, traditional recruitment tools have severe limitations:
- Online recruiting provides a more efficient and cost-effective means of linking employers and job hunters and reduces the total time-to-hire.
- Job hunters can easily build, update, and distribute their resumes, conduct job searches, and gather information on employers at their convenience and leisure.
- It is an information-intense business process that the Internet can automate, and thus reduce search time and costs for all parties.

Online recruiting can also serve to establish market prices and terms, thereby identifying both the salary levels for specific jobs and the skill sets required to achieve those salary levels. This should lead to a rationalization of wages, greater labor mobility, and higher efficiency in recruitment and operations as employers are able to more quickly fill positions.

The major trends in the online career services industry are:
- *Consolidation*: The online recruitment industry is going through a period of rapid consolidation led by Monster.
- *Diversification*: There is an explosion of specialty niche employment sites that focus on specific occupations.
- *Localization*: There is a growing focus on local job markets.
- *Job search engines*: New online job search engines that scrape listings from thousands of online job sites pose a threat to established career sites.
- *Social networking*: Many Internet users are beginning to use social networking sites to establish business contacts and find jobs; employers are also using them to identify and find out further information about job candidates.

QUESTIONS

1. Why were so many entrepreneurs drawn to start businesses in the online retail sector initially?
2. What frequently makes the difference between profitable and unprofitable online businesses today?
3. Which segment of the offline retail business is most like online retailing? Why?
4. Name the largest segment of U.S. retail sales. Explain why businesses in this segment have achieved and continue to dominate online retailing.
5. Describe the technological retail revolution that preceded the growth of e-commerce. What were some of the innovations that made later online retailing possible?
6. Name two assumptions e-commerce analysts made early on about consumers and their buying behavior that turned out to be false.
7. Why were customer acquisition costs assumed early on to be lower on the Web? What was supposed to reduce those costs?
8. Explain the distinction between disintermediation and hypermediation as it relates to online retailing.
9. How would you describe the top 10 online retailers as a group? Do they account for a small or a large percent of online business, for example?
10. Name two retail product categories that have been demonstrating greater than 50% annual growth.
11. Compare and contrast virtual merchants and bricks-and-clicks firms. What other type of online retailer is most like the virtual merchant?
12. What is the difference between a supply-push and a demand-pull sales model? Why do most manufacturer-direct firms have difficulty switching to one of these?
13. What are five strategic issues specifically related to a firm's capabilities? How are they different from industry-related strategic issues?
14. Which is a better measure of a firm's financial health: revenues, gross margin, or net margin? Why?
15. What are some of the difficulties in providing services in an online environment? What factors differentiate the services sector from the retail sector, for example?
16. Compare and contrast the two major types of online services industries. What two major features differentiate services from other industries?

17. Name and describe the three types of online mortgage vendors. What are the major advantages of using an online mortgage site? What factors are slowing the growth of such service businesses?

18. What is the biggest deterrent to growth of the online insurance industry nationally?

19. Define channel conflict and explain how it currently applies to the mortgage and insurance industries. Name two online insurance companies or brokers.

20. What is the most common use of real estate Web sites? What do most consumers do when they go there?

21. Name and describe the four types of services provided by financial services firms on the Web.

22. Who are the major players in the financial industry consolidation currently occurring worldwide?

23. Explain the two global trends impacting the structure of the financial services industry and their impact on online operations.

24. How have travel services suppliers benefited from consumer use of travel Web sites?

25. What are the two major segments of travel? Which one is growing the fastest and why?

26. Explain how global distribution systems (GDSs) function.

27. Name and describe the five traditional recruitment tools companies have used to identify and attract employees. What are the disadvantages of such tools in light of new online sites?

28. In addition to matching job applicants with available positions, what larger function do online job sites fill? Explain how such sites can affect salaries and going rates.

29. Given the popularity of online career sites, why are classified ads still the preferred information source for so many job seekers and employers?

PROJECTS

1. Find the Securities and Exchange Commission Web site at Sec.gov, and access the EDGAR archives, where you can review 10-K filings for all public companies. Search for the 10-K report for the most recent completed fiscal year for two online retail companies of your choice (preferably ones operating in the same area, such as Staples Inc. and Office Depot Inc.). Prepare a presentation that compares the financial stability and prospects of the two businesses, focusing specifically on the performance of their respective Internet operations.

2. Examine the financial statements for Amazon and Best Buy Co. Inc. What observations can you make about the two businesses? Which one is stronger financially and why? Which one's business model appears to be weaker and why? If you could identify two major problem areas for each, what would they be? Prepare a presentation that makes your case.

3. Conduct a thorough analysis—strategic and financial—of one of the following companies or another of your own choosing: Bluefly Inc., Drugstore.com, Inc. or 1-800-Flowers.com, Inc. Prepare a presentation that summarizes your observations about the company's Internet operations and future prospects.

4. Find an example not mentioned in the text of each of the four types of online retailing business models. Prepare a short report describing each firm and why it is an example of the particular business model.

5. Drawing on material in the chapter and your own research, prepare a short paper describing your views on the major social and legal issues facing online retailers.

6. Conduct a thorough analysis—strategic and financial—of one of the following Web sites: Progressive.com, Insure.com, or Insweb.com. Prepare a presentation that summarizes your observations about the company's operations and future prospects.

7. Choose a services industry not discussed in the chapter (such as legal services, medical services, accounting services, or another of your choosing). Prepare a 3- to 5-page report discussing recent trends affecting online provision of these services.

8. Together with a teammate, investigate the use of wireless applications (including iPhone apps) in the financial services industries. Prepare a short joint presentation on your findings.

9. Find at least two examples of companies not mentioned in the text that act as transaction brokers and at least two examples of companies that provide a hands-on service. Prepare a short memo describing the services each company offers and explaining why the company should be categorized as a transaction broker or a hands-on service provider.

WEB SITE RESOURCES www.azimuth-interactive.com/ecommerce6e

- Additional projects, exercises, and tutorials
- Careers: Explore career opportunities in e-commerce
- Raising capital and business plans

CHAPTER 10

Online Content and Media

After reading this chapter, you will be able to:

- Identify the major trends in the consumption of media and online content.
- Discuss the concept of media convergence and the challenges it faces.
- Describe the five basic content revenue models.
- Discuss the key challenges facing content producers and owners.
- Understand the key factors affecting the online publishing industry.
- Understand the key factors affecting the online entertainment industry.

Information Wants to Be Expensive

The age of "free news" may be over, victim of a failed online business model. The old Web adage that "information wants to be free" is being replaced by a new realization that "information wants to be expensive," especially if it's high value and exclusive.

In August 2009, Rupert Murdoch, known as the man who owns the news because he owns more newspapers than anyone else, announced that visitors to Web sites of newspapers owned by his firm, News Corp, will have to start paying fees to read the news online. Two years prior, in 2007, upon purchasing Dow Jones Corporation, owner of the *Wall Street Journal*, Murdoch announced that he would shortly eliminate fees for subscriptions to the online edition of the *Wall Street Journal* and grow the paper's online audience to 50 million readers.

What changed in the last two years for Murdoch and owners of newspapers around the world was a rapid decline in advertising revenues (both display and classifieds) of newspapers, in some cases down 50% over two years. News Corp itself posted a loss of $230 million in the second quarter of 2009, as revenues fell 11%. While newspaper readership is falling and advertising is moving to the Web, readers of online newspapers are booming, especially among the young, as more and more people turn to the Internet as their source of news. Unique visitors at newspaper sites are up 12% over 2008, and page views are up 14%. Around 73 million visitors to newspaper sites generate 3.5 billion page views each month, giving online newspapers a 42% reach in the total Web audience. Anyone who thinks newspaper organizations (highly skilled reporters, editors, and managers) are dead just isn't paying attention to the data. Unfortunately, the online ad revenue from display ads has failed to replace the lost revenues from physical newspaper ads. The problem is not getting people to read the paper online. The problem is making money from what newspapers publish online. Declining newspaper revenues pose a strong challenge to the notion that newspapers can survive the Internet by giving away for free their news and editorial content in order to build audience size, page views, and sufficient revenue from display ads to post a profit.

While the news is filled with now passé articles asking the question "Can newspapers survive the Web?", a small group of analysts believe this is the wrong question. A better question is "Can newspapers create valuable online content that people are willing to pay for?" This latter question raises other questions, such as what is "valuable content." Two newspapers in the world stand out as examples of successful online subscription newspapers that are profitable: the *Wall Street Journal* and the *Financial Times of London* (owned by Pearson Ltd.). Let's look at the *Wall Street Journal* to see how it has succeeded online and how it may be a online model for other newspapers to follow.

The *Wall Street Journal* was founded in 1889 by the Dow Jones News Service as a blend of general international and national news, along with in-depth financial reporting. It has a worldwide paid print and online readership of around 2.7 million. In April 1996, the *Journal* launched WSJ.com. In 2009, the *Journal* reached 1 million online paid subscribers, and attracted more than 7 million non-subscribing monthly visitors, and it is the most successful online newspaper in terms of revenue and profits. The *Journal* is one of the very few online newspapers to successfully employ a subscription revenue model. Nearly all other news and magazine publishers have adopted an advertiser supported "free content" model. Currently, subscribers to the *Wall Street Journal* print edition pay $49 a year for access to the online edition; non-subscribers pay $99. Print subscribers pay $119 for the physical newspaper delivered to their door.

But the *Wall Street Journal* is different from most newspapers. Most of the 10,000 online newspapers in the world offer free content. The common view among newspaper publishers is that most online consumers expect information to be free. For instance, when the online magazine *Salon* switched to a subscription fee model, it lost 90% of its readers. Since then, *Salon*'s readership has stabilized and grown, and it has adopted a mixture of free content and premium paid subscriptions, but remains only barely profitable. Online newspapers typically are supported by advertising and sales of classified ads—just as traditional print newspapers have been for centuries—rather than monthly subscription fees. Newspaper publishers seem unable to unlearn the *Salon* experience, and learn a new experience being delivered by content providers such as iTunes.

Why has the *Wall Street Journal* succeeded with a subscription model where others have failed? Brand is certainly one reason. The *Wall Street Journal* has strong brand recognition among American investors. It is well known for its stock quotation services and in-depth reporting on business and general news issues. However, many newspapers such as the *New York Times*, *Los Angeles Times*, and *Washington Post* also have strong national brands, but are fearful of charging subscription fees. The *New York Times* adopted a paid model called Times Select that charged for premium content, and access to the *Times* archives, but dropped that model in 2007 because users were gaining access to the same news from other sites such as Yahoo and Google (some of this news was coming from a hole in the *New York Times* pay-wall). In 2009, the *Times* is re-introducing a premium news service for a fee.

Perhaps one key to the *Wall Street Journal*'s success is that a subscription gives users access to premium content in the form of 25,000 in-depth background reports on companies, an archive of news articles going back to 1996, and access to the Dow Jones Publication Library, which features current and past articles from 7,000 newspapers, magazines, and business-news sources. If you are a stock analyst or an individual investor looking for information on a specific company, this archive of material may be well worth the relatively small annual subscription fee. Coupled with a fine-grained search engine, the *Wall Street Journal*'s archives are unique and differentiated from most other online newspaper offerings. The *Journal* sells access to this premium archival content on a per article basis. The experience of the *Journal* is that you can successfully charge for high-value information that is exclusive to your newspaper, and differentiated. In contrast, no one wants to pay for information that is widely shared.

Readers of the *Journal* are also attracted to its timeliness and Web suitability. Using a structured markup technology provided by OmniMark's Content Engineering system, writers and editors are able to simultaneously author articles for both print and online editions, and then automatically generate Web pages that conform to the *Journal*'s unique print style. This system also permits them to make dynamic changes in news story content, shortening or lengthening stories as needed, without costly page redesign. Writers and editors can post hundreds of up-to-date articles around the clock, and the key page elements—such as size of headlines, space between articles, positioning of navigation buttons, and placement of advertisements—are all generated by the OmniMark system. The same system creates a consistent content archive of news and opinion that can be searched by subscribers. In this sense, Internet distribution technology has led to a convergence in content creation and delivery: news is news, whether it is printed on paper or on a Web page. Like many online newspapers, the *Journal* now also makes extensive use of videos (listed on the home page), and has transformed many of its writers into online interviewers that provide a marvelous personal contact with newsmakers and current topics.

The new technology has transformed the online newspaper experience. Instead of having content trapped on static print pages that are updated daily, the online edition can offer timely breaking news much like a television or radio news show, and like television, provide video access to important news events and newsmakers. WSJ.com uses personalization features to make its content even more compelling. Subscribers can create a personalized WSJ.com home page with user-selected columnists, stock portfolio updates, and company news. In addition, along with other online publishers, users can have news stories on topics and subjects they choose pushed to them using a *Wall Street Journal* RSS feed. The *Journal* also has added major sections available only online: interactive features walk readers through complex stories, and in-depth reports explore topics such as retirement, mutual fund returns, and pension planning. The *Journal* has multiple free Web sites from MarketWatch to the Real Estate and College journals. The *Journal* has been able to leverage this new functionality into higher subscription fees.

SOURCES: "NAA/Nielsen Stats Show Newspapers Own Less Than One Percent of the U.S. Online Audience Page Views, Time Spent," Nieman Journalism Lab, Nieman-lab.org, August 10, 2009; "Ad Slump, Web Charges Hurt News Corp." by Shira Ovide, *Wall Street Journal*, August 8, 2009; "Is Free News a Thing of the Past?" by Clare Davidson, BBC News, August 7, 2009; "News Corp. Plans Fees for Newspaper Sites," by Associated Press, *New York Times*, August 6, 2009; "Looking to Big Screen E-Readers to Help Save the Daily Press," by Brad Stone, *New York Times*, May 4, 2009; "Newspapers' Essential Strengths," by David Carr, *New York Times*, May 4, 2009; "Annual Internet Survey by the Center for the Digital Future Finds Large Increases in Use of Online Newspapers," Center for the Digital Future, USC Annenberg School of Communication, April 28, 2009; "Online Newspaper Audience Climbs 10% in First Quarter," by David Wilkerson, MarketWatch.com, April 23, 2009; "*Wall Street Journal* iPhone App Sets Content Free," by John Abell, *Wall Street Journal*, April 15, 2009; "Media Executives Plan Online Service to Charge for Content," by Richard Perez-Pena, *New York Times*, April 15, 2009; "'Hyperlocal' Web Sites Deliver News Without Newspapers," by Clair Cain Miller and Brad Stone, *New York Times*, April 13, 2009; "They Pay for Cable, Music, and Extra Bags. How About News?," by Richard Perez-Pena, *New York Times*, April 8, 2009; "A.P. Seeks to Rein In Sites Using Its Content," by Richard Perez-Pena, *New York Times*, April 7, 2009; "Information Wants to Be Expensive," by L. Gordon Crovitz, *Wall Street Journal*, February 23, 2009; "Social Networking coming to Wall Journal Website," by Anick Jesdahun, *Time Magazine*, September 15, 2008; "New *Wall Street Journal* Builds on Its Community of Subscribers," by Vindu Goel, *New York Times*, September 15, 2008; "Creative Destruction: An Exploratory Look at News on the Internet," by Thomas Patterson, Joan Shorenstein Center on the Press, Politics, and Public Policy, John F. Kennedy School of Government, Harvard University, August 2007.

In 2008, Murdoch redesigned the look and feel of the print *Journal*. He kept its business focus, but added more general news and a smaller page format, and started a week end magazine to compete more directly with the *New York Times*. In September 2008, Murdoch redesigned the online edition as well.

The new online edition more clearly reflects the capabilities of the Internet and Web 2.0. There are reporter blogs, user comments on all articles, and videos, all updated in real time. The most radical departure is the addition of a social networking capability: the new online *Journal* will allow its 1 million subscribers to comment on any article, pose discussion questions, e-mail one another, and set up profiles that will allow other subscribers to see what they are doing on the site. The goal is to increase reader loyalty, expand the amount of time users spend on the site, and of course increase ad revenues. In April 2009, the *Journal* developed an iPhone app, which makes some of its content available for free, but in the near future a subscription model or advertising model is planned for the iTune's version of the *Journal*. While the *Journal* and the *Financial Times* are successfully charging for their content, whether other newspapers can succeed will depend in part on their ability to produce high-value content available nowhere else, but also, on the culture of the Internet.

Up until iTunes, the prevailing wisdom of the Web glitterati was that Web users expected all information to be free, and users would never pay for content. But the culture of the Internet is changing faster than the experts can change their predictions. iTunes shows us that 50 million Web users are willing to pay for music tracks. Amazon's Kindle is showing us that over a million book readers are willing to pay 9.99 for an e-book. In this new culture of the Web, people are willing to pay for high-quality, high-value, differentiated content served up in a customer friendly experience where it's "cool" to pay.

T he *Wall Street Journal Online* case illustrates how traditional media companies are attempting to adapt to the new opportunities of the Web by developing content experiences for online consumers that would be impossible offline, including video, blogs, interactive features such as games and online crossword puzzles, and more recently, social networking opportunities. It is clear that the future of content—news, music, and video—is online. In the past, online companies had a difficult time becoming profitable. Today, the print industry, including newspapers and magazines, is having a difficult time coping with the movement of their readership to the Web. Broadcast and cable television, along with Hollywood and the music labels, are also wrestling with outdated business models based on physical media. Established media giants are continuing to make extraordinary investments in unique online content, new technology, new digital distribution channels, and entirely new business models. In this chapter, we focus primarily on the publishing and entertainment industries as they attempt to transform their traditional media into Web-deliverable forms and experiences for consumers.

10.1 ONLINE CONTENT

No other sector of the American economy has been so challenged by the Internet and the Web than the content industries. The content industries involve all those businesses that use print, television, and film to communicate, as well as the distribution businesses such as cable, broadcast television, satellite, printers, and retail content stores (like music and video rental stores). As a communications medium, the Web is, by definition, a source of online content. In this chapter, we will look closely at publishing (newspapers, books, and magazines) and entertainment (music, film, games, and television). These industries make up the largest share of the commercial content marketplace, both offline and online. In each of these industries, there are powerful offline brands, significant new pure-play online providers, consumer constraints and opportunities, a variety of legal issues, and technology constraints on rapid deployment of online content.

Table 10.1 describes the most recent trends in online content for 2009–2010.

CONTENT AUDIENCE AND MARKET: WHERE ARE THE EYEBALLS AND THE MONEY?

The average American adult spends almost 3,600 hours each year consuming various media, over one and a half times as as much time spent at work (2,000 hours/year) (see **Figure 10.1**). Media revenues in 2008 were estimated to be $654 billion, and they are expected to grow at a compound rate of 9% (U.S. Census Bureau, 2009).

Media Utilization

The most popular medium is television, followed by radio and the Internet. Together, these three media account for over 80% of the hours spent consuming various media.

TABLE 10.1	TRENDS IN ONLINE CONTENT, 2009–2010

- **Media consumption**: Americans spend almost 3,600 hours a year consuming various types of media, nearly twice as many hours as they work. Internet time exposure grows rapidly, surpassing newspapers, and music, but far behind traditional television and radio.

- **Revenue**: Revenues from Internet media are the fastest-growing media revenues.

- **Eyeballs**: Traditional content audience moves to the Internet, and the annual growth in the Internet audience outpaces all other media.

- **User-generated content**: The Internet inverts the traditional production and business model by having users create much content. Social network sites, video sites like YouTube, personal blogs, and photo sites, show extraordinary growth, threaten traditional entertainment firms, and challenge traditional media for user attention, total audience size, and even legitimacy. User-generated video and TV shows engage more and more users.

- **Technology**: Mobile smartphones and netbook make Web-based music, news, and entertainment available anytime and anywhere.

- **Advertising**: The growing Internet audience causes a rapid expansion in Internet advertising revenues as advertisers move to where the eyeballs are focused.

- **Business models:** Content owners adopt a mixture of business models from advertising supported content, to subscription, and a la carte payment for unbundled products like individual songs, television shows, and movies.

- **Paid content and free content coexist**: The common notion of "Internet means free information" is being replaced by consumer acceptance of paying for premium content, which is growing far faster than other media or than the Internet itself in the United States. At the same time, music, television, and Hollywood studios are making some content free but supported by advertising revenues.

- **Convergence**: Traditional media—newspapers, magazines, and studios—are moving closer to a convergent model based on new technologies and new industry alignments among major media conglomerates. Hollywood and television studios begin video streaming of movies and shows. Internet television divisions of traditional TV studios are formed. Newspapers and magazines add video to their online sites. Internet media firms Yahoo, Google, AOL, MSN, and Apple move into traditional media spaces such as television, telephone, and movie distribution by offering a variety of new online services.

- **Print media**: Newspapers and magazines begin a painful transition to online models buoyed by the growth in online advertising, which is not sufficient to replace lost advertising revenues. Online newspaper readership grows at 12% on average with the top 10 growing at over 25% annually.

- **Entertainment content**: Led by music, an explosion in online video, and the growing interest in online television and feature-length films, the Web emerges as an entertainment powerhouse rivaling broadcast networks, cable, and satellite distribution systems.

- **Consumer taste**: Consumers want to control their own programming. Consumers increasingly support time-shifting and space-shifting in media consumption by demanding to see or hear just about any media wherever and whenever they want using any of several devices like PCs, cell phones, PDAs, or conventional devices.

While the Internet is currently third, Internet utilization has been growing rapidly. (U.S Census Bureau, 2009). In another survey, the Online Publishers Association found that the amount of time people spent online per month had increased from an

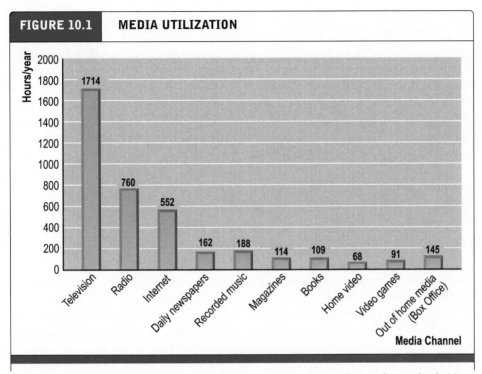

FIGURE 10.1 MEDIA UTILIZATION

Each American spends around 3,600 hours annually, on average, consuming various media, mostly television, radio, and recorded music. However, time spent on the Internet is growing rapidly—it has doubled since 2000, and has overtaken newspapers, music, and magazine.
SOURCE: Based on data from U.S. Census Bureau, 2009; authors' estimates.

average of about 11 hours a month (132 hours a year) in 2003 to over 17 hours a month (205 hours a year) in 2009. Although television rating services like Nielsen do not report a fall in hours of television watching, consumer surveys find that 20% to 30% of media users report using traditional media such as television, radio, and newspapers less, and substitute online entertainment. Over half of television viewers go online using their computers while watching TV (Magid, 2009; Emigh, 2008).

Internet and Traditional Media: Cannibalization versus Complementarity

Most studies reveal that time spent on the Internet reduces consumer time available for other media (Pew Internet & American Life Project, 2006). There has been a massive shift of the general audience to the Web, and once there, an equally massive shift since 2003 towards viewing or listening to content. In 2009, consumers are spending about 42% of their time online (an average of about 7 hours a month) at content sites (news, information, and entertainment), 27% (about 5 hours a month) at communications sites (e-mail and instant messaging), 13% (around 3 hours) at community sites, 13% (about 2 hours and 40 minutes) at commerce sites, and 5% (about 1 hour) at search sites (Online Publishers Association, 2009). In general, Internet users spend 15%–20% less time reading books, newspapers, magazines, and watching television, box office movies, and less time on the phone or listening to the radio. On the other hand, Internet users consume more media of all types than non-Internet users. This reflects the demographics of the Internet user as more literate, wealthier, more technically savvy, and more media aware. In addition, Internet users multitask when using the Internet, frequently listening to music, watching television, and using instant messaging while working on other tasks. Multimedia use reduces the cannibalization impact of the Internet for some visual and aural media, but obviously not for reading books or newspapers. And even for these print media, the Internet is simply an alternative source; Internet users are increasing the time they spend online reading newspapers, magazines, and even books.

Media Revenues

An examination of media revenues reveals somewhat different patterns (see **Figure 10.2**). Entertainment (box office events, home video, video games, and recorded music) garnered 4% of revenues, and 4% of consumer media time.

Television—broadcast, cable, and satellite—remains a major producer of media revenues (37%), while newspapers generate 4% of revenues, down from 10% in previous years.

The Internet constitutes 17% of total media revenues, but this is substantially higher than the 5% of media channel revenues it produced in 2004. Once again, the Internet has grown in a few short years from a zero base to a substantial share of media revenues today. In the next section, we describe the current and emerging online content marketplace.

Figure 10.3 gives some idea of the relative size of the content market, based on per-person spending. Television and home video combined are more than three

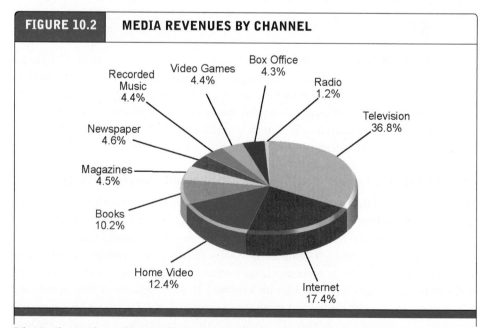

FIGURE 10.2   MEDIA REVENUES BY CHANNEL

Television, home video, and Internet dominate media revenues with 66% of the revenues.
The revenue share for traditional media such as newspapers and magazines has shrunk, while book publishing revenues have remained fairly constant over many years.
SOURCE: Based on data from U.S. Census Bureau, 2009; authors' estimates.

times the size of online (Internet) content, but online content expenditures are rising at twice the rate of home video or TV. At some point in the near future, online revenues will exceed those of broadcast and cable television.

Two Models For Digital Content Delivery: Paid and User-Generated Content

There are two commercial models for delivering content on the Internet: paid versus "free" with advertiser support. There is also completely free user-generated content, which we will discuss later. Contrary to early analysts' projections that "free" would drive "paid" out of business ("information wants to be free"), it turns out that both models are viable now and in the near future. Consumers increasingly choose to pay for high-quality, convenient, and unique content, and they have gladly accepted "free" advertiser-supported content when that content is deemed not worth paying for but entertaining nevertheless. There's nothing contradictory about both models working in tandem, and cooperatively: free content can drive customers to paid content, as the recorded music firms have discovered.

Now let's look at what consumers are buying on the Internet in terms of paid digital content. About 45% of Internet users (80 million users) have downloaded music, and about half of this number have actually paid for music downloads. Around 80% (160 million users) have watched a video online and about 22% (40 million users) have paid for video content at sites such as Hulu and Viacom (comScore, 2009, eMarketer, 2009a, Pew Internet and American Life Project, 2009). The online paid content audience, however, is growing at about 20% a year, faster than the Internet itself. Increasingly, the Internet is changing from primarily a communication medium to an entertainment medium. The growth in the audience size is

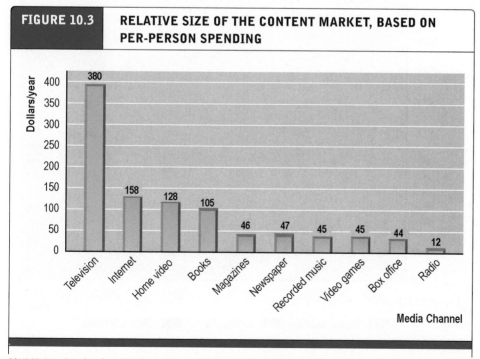

FIGURE 10.3 | **RELATIVE SIZE OF THE CONTENT MARKET, BASED ON PER-PERSON SPENDING**

SOURCE: Based on data from U.S. Census Bureau, 2009; authors' estimates.

largely attributable to the growth in the entertainment segment of music, news, television, and videos.

Figure 10.4 shows the estimated revenues from digital music, online TV, and digital movies.

Now let's look at the user-generated digital content audience. This audience is huge and growing very rapidly. User-generated content—music, videos, and text in the form of blogs—is free and typically advertiser supported. In 2009, about 89 million Internet users (about 45% of all users) have created user-generated content, and about 124 million have viewed it (eMarketer, 2009b). Revenue is generated by advertisers who by 2013 are expected to be spending between $615 million and $870 million advertising around user-generated content. **Table 10.2** shows the top video and user-generated content sites. User-generated content falls into seven primary categories: video, audio, photos, information (news), personal data, reviews, and recommendations (favorites, social bookmarking). By far the largest and potentially most valuable to marketers is the online video audience.

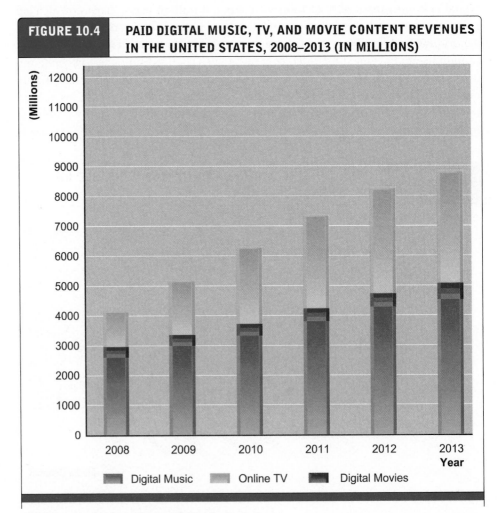

FIGURE 10.4 **PAID DIGITAL MUSIC, TV, AND MOVIE CONTENT REVENUES IN THE UNITED STATES, 2008–2013 (IN MILLIONS)**

Legend: Digital Music, Online TV, Digital Movies

SOURCE: Based on data from eMarketer, 2009a; author's estimates.

TABLE 10.2	TOP 10 U.S. ONLINE VIDEO SITES (JULY 2009 VS JULY 2008)		
SITE	UNIQUE VIEWERS JULY 2009 (in millions)	AVG. VIDEOS PER VIEWER	PERCENT INCREASE/DECREASE IN UNIQUE VIEWERS FROM JULY 2008
Google sites (YouTube)	121	74.1	+24%
Microsoft sites	65	9.8	+97%
Fox Interactive (MySpace)	52	10.8	-6% (decrease)
Yahoo sites	47	7.9	+24%
Viacom Digital	42	19.2	+100%
Hulu	38	12.0	+1,087%
Turner Network	36	11.0	+89%
CBS Interactive	31	4.9	Not available
AOL	24	5.2	+4%
Facebook	20	4.0	Not available

SOURCE: Based on data from comScore, 2009, 2008; Marketingcharts.com, 2009; authors' estimates.

It will come as no surprise that YouTube is the leading advertiser-supported video site, and that the overall size of the online video audience (about 160 million monthly unique viewers as of August 2009) is much larger than traditional television audiences, which numbers in the 10 million range for exceptionally popular shows. In 2009 YouTube will have about 375 million visitors, and, at peak load, 75 million will be online simultaneously. During peak loads, YouTube has to deliver 30 million megabits per second, and spends around $360 million annually just for bandwidth. The social networking sites are just now learning how to monetize this audience through advertising revenues, but so far they have only achieved break-even results.

The simultaneous growth of both paid and free advertiser-supported content on the Internet suggests that these phenomena are complementary in some cases, and can grow together. This may not be true of newspapers and magazines where online content has lessened their readership, and substitution is taking place. But music offers an example of complementarity. Illegal P2P file sharing is just as prevalent as before, involving millions of songs. Yet the parallel growth of paid content sites such as iTunes suggest both models can exist and prosper. "Free" legal music streaming sites like Pandora.com, one of the most popular Internet music sites that builds stations of similar songs for users, work with record label firms to drive customers toward purchase sites.

One question remains: Can the commercial content industries of movies, music, and text that depend on payments or subscriptions make enough money using the advertiser-supported model to make up for losses caused by the decline of their traditional models? In music, the answer is not so far. In high-quality video, the answer is probably yes.

Free or Fee: Attitudes About Paying For Content and the Tolerance for Advertising

In the early years of online content, multiple surveys found that large majorities of the Internet audience expected to pay nothing for online content although equally large majorities were willing to accept advertising as a way to pay for free content. In reality, on the early Web, there wasn't much high-quality content. Until Internet services such as iTunes arrived, few thought the "fee" model could compete with the "free" model, and most Internet aficionados and "experts" just felt that "information [on the Internet] wants to be free." Cable TV systems offer a totally different history: they always charged for service and content, and cable TV "experts" never thought information wanted to be free. Neither did the Hollywood and New York media companies that provided the content to television and movie theaters. Like cable TV, Apple iTunes charges for service and content as well. In a demonstration of just how much quality online content is worth paying for, by 2009, Apple had sold 2.5 billion songs, 50 million TV shows, and over 1.4 million movies. While 33 million Internet users in the United States still download songs from illegal P2P sites, 29 million buy music from legal sites in 2009. Most experts thought free would drive out fee models. As you learned in the opening case, newspapers are now considering charging fees for "premium" content, while offering "free" ad-supported but limited content. These developments were totally unexpected. The culture of the Internet is beginning to change when firms such as YouTube (and its parent Google), which started out with a business model based on amateur videos, and illegally uploaded music videos, begin cooperating closely with Hollywood and New York production studios for premium content. As it turns out, "free" content isn't worth very much and should be free, especially if producers give it away. Premium content is worth a great deal, and should be priced accordingly. As one wag put it, "information wants to be expensive." This witticism was written by Stuart Brand in 1984, the same person who said "information wants to be free." Brand wrote, "On the one hand information wants to be expensive, because it's so valuable. The right information in the right place just changes your life. On the other hand, information wants to be free, because the cost of getting it out is getting lower and lower all the time. So you have these two fighting against each other." (Brand, 1984).

MEDIA INDUSTRY STRUCTURE

The media content industry prior to 1990 was composed of many smaller independent corporations specializing in content creation and distribution in the separate industries of film, television, book and magazine publishing, and newspaper publishing. During the 1990s and into this century, after an extensive period of consolidation, huge entertainment and publishing media conglomerates emerged.

The media industry is still organized largely into three separate vertical stovepipes, with each segment dominated by a few key players. We do not include the delivery platform firms here, such as AT&T, Verizon, Sprint, Dish Network, or Comcast, because in general they do not create content; they just move content across cable, satellite, and telephone lines. Generally, there is very little crossover from one segment to another. Newspapers do not also produce Hollywood films, and publishing firms do not own newspapers or film production studios. Even within media conglomerates that span several different media segments, separate divisions control each media segment. The competition between corporate divisions in mega-sized corporations is often more severe than with marketplace competitors. On the other hand, as the audience moves increasingly to the Internet, even large conglomerates will be forced to follow.

While the commercial media industry is highly concentrated, yet fragmented across media firms, the much larger media ecosystem includes literally millions of individuals and independent entrepreneurs creating content in the form of blogs, YouTube videos, and independent music bands on MySpace. At times, the viewership (or readership) of these much smaller but numerous players exceeds that of the media titans.

MEDIA CONVERGENCE: TECHNOLOGY, CONTENT, AND INDUSTRY STRUCTURE

Media convergence is a much used but poorly defined term. There are at least three dimensions of media where the term convergence has been applied: technology, content (artistic design, production, and distribution), and to the industry's structure as a whole. Ultimately for the consumer, convergence means being able to get any content you want, when you want it, on whatever platform you want it—from an iPod to a wireless PC to a handheld computer.

Technological Convergence

Convergence from a technology perspective (**technological convergence**) has to do with the development of hybrid devices that can combine the functionality of two or more existing media platforms, such as books, newspapers, television, radio, and stereo equipment, into a single device. Examples of technological convergence include the iPhone, BlackBerry, and Palm Pre ("smartphones,") that combine voice, Internet, Wi-Fi, and media services; iPod, which can combine in a handheld computing device music, video, photos, and text; digital interactive television sets that can surf the Web; video game machines that can also surf the Internet; and PCs that play and record music and videos.

technological convergence
development of hybrid devices that can combine the functionality of two or more existing media platforms into a single device

Content Convergence

A second dimension of convergence is **content convergence**. There are three aspects to content convergence: design, production, and distribution.

There is a historical pattern in which content created in an older media technology migrates to the new technology largely intact, with little artistic change. Slowly, the different media are integrated so that consumers can move seamlessly back and forth among them, and artists (and producers) learn more about how to deliver content in the new media. Later, the content itself is transformed by the new media as artists learn how to fully exploit the capabilities in the creation process. At this point, content convergence and transformation has occurred—the art is different because of the new capabilities inherent to new tools. For instance, European master painters of the fifteenth century in Italy, France, and the

content convergence
convergence in the design, production, and distribution of content

Netherlands (such as van Eyck, Caravaggio, Lotto, and Vermeer) quickly adopted new optical devices such as lenses, mirrors, and early projectors called *camera obscura* that could cast near-photographic quality images on canvases, and in the process they developed new theories of perspective and new techniques of painting landscapes and portraits. Suddenly, paintings took on the qualities of precision, detail, and realism found only in photographs (Boxer, 2001). A similar process is occurring today as artists and writers assimilate new digital and Internet tools into their toolkits. For instance, GarageBand from Apple enables low-budget independent bands (literally working in garages) to mix and control eight different digital music tracks to produce professional sounding recordings on a shoestring budget.

On the production side, new tools for digital editing and processing (for film and television) are driving content convergence. Given that the most significant cost of content is its creation, if there is a wide diversity of target delivery platforms, then it is wise to develop and produce only once using technology that can deliver to multiple platforms. Generally, this means creating content on digital devices (hardware and software) so that it can be delivered on multiple digital platforms. Once captured on digital devices, the same content can be archived, sliced into atomistic units, and re-purposed for a wide variety of other platforms and distribution channels.

On the distribution side, it is important that distributors and ultimate consumers have the devices needed to receive, store, and experience the product. While for the most part, technology companies have succeeded in giving consumers portable devices to receive online content, it has been more difficult for the content owners to come up with new, profitable distribution platforms. The music industry has seen its music store model collapse. The feature-length film industry struggles with online digital distribution. Hollywood studios currently deliver copies of new films to thousands of theaters across the country in trucks. A feature-length film can require six large, heavy canisters containing reels of 35mm film. To be able to digitally download the film via satellite, local theaters must be equipped with servers and large hard drives to receive the film, as well as new digital projection equipment. Currently about half of all movie theaters have digital projectors.

Figure 10.5 depicts the process of media convergence and transformation using the example of books. For example, consider this book. The book was designed from the beginning as content to be delivered using both traditional text and the Internet. In that sense, this book is in the media transformation stage. In subsequent years, this same book will be available both as a purely digital work and as a mixed book + Web product. Eventually, it is likely that this book will be available mostly as a purely digital product with substantial visual and aural content that can be displayed on many different digital devices including e-book readers. By that time, the "learning experience" will be transformed. Traditional bound books will probably still be available (books have many advantages), but most likely, print editions will be printed on demand by customers using their own print facilities.

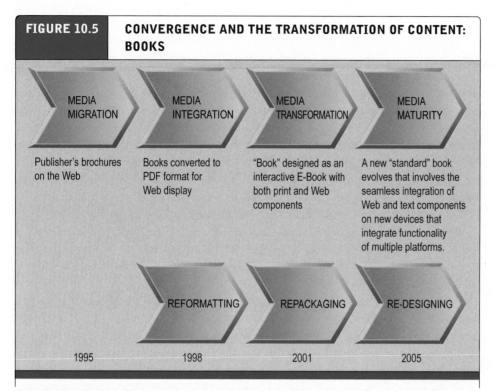

FIGURE 10.5   **CONVERGENCE AND THE TRANSFORMATION OF CONTENT: BOOKS**

The Internet is making it possible for publishers and writers to transform the standard "book" into a new form that integrates features of both text and the Internet, and also transforms the content of the book itself.

Industry Convergence

A third dimension of convergence is the structure of the various media industries. **Industry convergence** refers to the merger of media enterprises into powerful, synergistic combinations that can cross-market content on many different platforms and create new works that use multiple platforms. This can take place either through purchases or through strategic alliances. Traditionally, each type of media—film, text, music, television—had its own separate industry, typically composed of very large players. For instance, the entertainment film industry has been dominated by a few large Hollywood-based production studios, book publication is dominated by a few large book publishers, and music production is dominated by five global record label firms.

However, the Internet has created forces that make the merger of traditionally separate firms in separate media industries a plausible—perhaps necessary—business proposition. Media industry convergence may be necessary to finance the substantial changes in both the technology platform and the content. Traditional media firms by themselves generally do not possess the core competencies, financial heft, content ownership, or channel ownership to bring about Internet media convergence.

The best-known example of media industry convergence is the $100 billion merger of AOL and Time Warner in January 2001. Time Warner was the largest multimedia conglomerate in the United States, but had no Web content per se, and

industry convergence
merger of media enterprises into synergistic combinations that create and cross-market content on different platforms

had experienced an early failure in attempting to build a Web presence. AOL brought to the merger the largest online audience in the United States (nearly 40% of U.S. Internet users at that time), a substantial ISP operation with a monthly billing relationship with the consumer, and a successful track record in providing Internet and Web services and content. The merger plans called for the two companies to provide a single corporate platform for the creation and distribution of high-value content. AOL/Time Warner combined content with distribution. Senior executives at both AOL and Time Warner believed that new content would be created for distribution on both traditional and new media such as the Internet, and the process of transforming media and content to optimize the new Internet technology would begin in earnest with financing provided by successful traditional media such as cable subscriptions and feature film and television production revenue. In this case, convergence did not work well at all, and the merger became known as one of the worst in history. Ten years after the merger, and after several major efforts at revival, Time Warner is selling AOL, which in 2009 produced $3.2 billion in revenue, down 38% in the last two years.

Rupert Murdoch's News Corporation provides a more successful example of convergence. In 2005, News Corp (now a conglomerate with both newspaper and satellite distribution) purchased the Web's most dynamic and fast-growing social network, MySpace. The acquisition has been successful and MySpace is reportedly operating profitably. If traditional media companies have not done well in purchases of Internet platform companies, the technology owners such as Apple, Microsoft, Google, and others have done a bit better in developing content and content distribution channels. Apple created its own online music store and now sells more labeled music than any other retailer; Microsoft created its Xbox 360, and owns other content sources; Google has purchased a social network site, an online video repository, and has created software applications that include entertainment content.

In the end, consumers' demands for content anywhere, anytime, and on any device is pushing all the technology and content companies towards cooperation and convergent behavior.

ONLINE CONTENT REVENUE MODELS AND BUSINESS PROCESSES

We have already discussed the "free" (with ad support) versus paid content models for delivering online content. But the situation is more complex: there are several different "free" revenue models. The basic content revenue models include: marketing, advertising, pay-per-view, subscription, value-added, and mixed, which combines several of the other types (see **Table 10.3**).

In the *marketing revenue model*, media companies give away content for free in the hope that visitors to the site will purchase the product offline or view a show offline. The Web site is intended to generate interest, develop word-of-mouth viral marketing, and deepen the emotional experience for offline product users. Consumer products companies like Procter & Gamble use this model. The revenues produced by this model are difficult to measure directly. Costs of operating the site can be hidden in larger marketing budgets and to some extent recovered through the sale of product-related paraphernalia, such as T-shirts, caps, and toys. This model appears to

TABLE 10.3	ONLINE CONTENT REVENUE MODELS	
TYPE OF REVENUE MODEL	DESCRIPTION	COMMENTS
Marketing: Tide.com	Free content drives offline revenues	May work for strong brands or niche products; used to deepen customer experience
Advertising: Yahoo	Free content is paid for by online advertising	Depends on growth in online ad volume and rates, as well as audience size
Pay-per-view/Pay-for-download: Apple's iTunes Store	Charge for premium content is either a la carte (single tune) or for entire works (e-books)	Opportunities for unbundling digital products; works best with an integrated platform like iTunes Store and iPhones/iPods.
Subscription: Rhapsody	Monthly charges for service	The leading paid content model (more than 80% of online paid content); works for high-value products
Mixed: MSN	Combination of above models	Market segmentation opportunities make this an attractive model, charging for premium service

be effective in deepening the emotional involvement of consumers with the product, thereby engendering loyalty. It has been effective in the marketing of automobiles, personal care and health brands, new films, and media events in general.

In the *advertising revenue model*, content is free to the consumer; advertisers are expected to pay for the cost of the site through placement of ads. In general, the advertising model works exceptionally well for portals, search engines, social networks, and solid niche community sites that can attract either huge general audiences, or committed niche audiences. YouTube, Facebook, and Photobucket rely on this model although each of these "free" sites are adding premium services and content for which users will be charged. Newspapers historically have used this model in combination with premium subscriptions (paid); and as up to half their audience moves to their Internet editions, they will increasingly rely on the same ad model online as they do offline and bring back the concept of subscriptions for Internet reading of their premium content. Small players, like Salon.com, and most blogs, may not have sufficient audience size to make this model work.

In the *pay-per-view/pay-for-download revenue model* (sometimes called "a la carte"), content providers charge for each viewing of premium content such as a video, book, archived newspaper article, or consulting report. Apple's iTunes Music Store, which charges 99 cents to a $1.99 per song download, depending how much music owners believe the market will bear, is the most common example. In general, the online pay-per-view/download model works only for high-perceived-value content that is unique and targeted. Pay-per-view is currently hindered by the difficulty of using the Internet to view sporting events, feature films, and video content, all of which require substantial download times and resources. In other words, if there is little to view, there is no reason to pay for anything. However, in the future, if the Internet can deliver television-quality video or live coverage of sports events, new films, or music concerts, then the pay-per-view revenue model might work for these high-bandwidth media as effectively as it works for cable television.

In the *subscription revenue model*, content providers such as the *Wall Street Journal* and *Consumer Reports* charge a monthly or annual fee for bulk access to online content. Rhapsody and the new Napster music sites use a subscription model of $9.95 to $14.95 (mobile service) per month for access to digital music archives. Both the pay-per-view and subscription models run up against the "free" model offered by P2P networks. Nevertheless, the subscription and pay-per-view models have begun growing at double-digit rates because consumers trust the legitimate firms and are willing to pay for brand-name quality.

The subscription model works very well for valuable, niche content. Hoover's business information services (Hoovers.com) are provided on a subscription basis to company and stock analysts willing to pay the monthly and annual subscription fee. Perhaps one of the most successful "new media" online content firms is RealNetworks. RealNetworks is known mainly for its online media player RealPlayer. But it also operates an online subscription service for streaming video. RealNetworks is a content aggregator bringing together video from CNN, NASCAR auto racing, professional sports teams, and ABC news, and allows the viewer to select content sources. To make things only slightly more complex, most content providers use a variety of revenue models in combination (**Table 10.4**) to maximize revenues, often by offering "premium" services.

This appears to be the model that most online content publishers have adopted. For instance, the online magazine *Salon* receives 40% of its revenue from subscriptions ($29 a year) and 60% from advertising. *Salon* also charges for discussion areas. The company says its Web site has more than 3 million readers a month, of which 74,000 are paying subscribers. Most portals and other Web sites that used to offer free content in the past are now segueing into mixed models to generate revenues and profits in 2009. Free content still abounds, but it is mixed judiciously with pay-for-view, or premium subscription, content options.

Making a Profit with Online Content: From Free to Fee

Despite the resistance of users in the early years of e-commerce, there is broad consensus that many online consumers, perhaps 25%, are increasingly willing to pay for some content, at their discretion, and that sites offering a mix of free and fee content will optimize their revenues.

net value

that portion of perceived customer value that can be attributed to the fact that content is available on the Internet

There appear to be four factors required to charge for online content: focused market, specialized content, sole-source monopoly, and high perceived net value (see **Figure 10.6**). **Net value** refers to that portion of perceived customer value that can be attributed to the fact that content is available on the Internet. Net value derives from the ability of consumers to instantaneously access the information on the Web, search large and deep historical archives, and move the online information to other documents easily. For instance, Hoover's Online, a source of detailed information on businesses and executives worldwide, provides four different subscriptions ranging from $75 a month to $2,995 for a professional subscription. Hoover's content addresses a focused market (business analysts and executive search firms); it has

TABLE 10.4	EXAMPLES OF THE GROWING USE OF MIXED REVENUE MODELS FOR ONLINE CONTENT
COMPANY	**CONTENT**
Salon Media Group	Premium subscription: $36 a year, no banner or pop-up ads, Table Talk login, annual subscribers receive free or discounted additional magazine subscriptions, download Salon to PDA or cell phone
Yahoo	Real-time quotes: $10.95 a month (annual rate), $13.95 a month (monthly rate)
	Yahoo Geocities Plus personal Web pages: $4.95/month basic, $8.95 premium
	Yahoo Mail: MailPlus—19.95/year for no graphical ads and SpamGuard Plus
	Yahoo Games: Allstar—$7.95/month, $59.95/year, no advertisements, special tournaments, access to special games
RealNetworks	Real SuperPass—free 14-day trial, $14.99/month
	Rhapsody Unlimited: $12.99/month, stream unlimited music on PC
	Rhapsody ToGo: $14.99/month, stream unlimited music, transfer a limited number of songs to a portable device
MSN	Windows Live Hotmail: Free; Hotmail Plus $19.95 a year
New York Times	Crossword puzzles: $39.95/annually, $6.95/monthly
Financial Times	Standard online subscription: $181/year, Premium: $299/year

specialized content (data gathered by its own reporters and other sources); it is the sole source for some of this information; and it has high perceived value because it can be quickly accessed, searched, and downloaded into other documents and made a part of business decision making. And the consumers are in a hurry to get the information. In general, the opportunity for paid content varies by the nature of the content and the audience.

KEY CHALLENGES FACING CONTENT PRODUCERS AND OWNERS

While finding a revenue model that works has been the primary business challenge facing online content companies, there are other challenges as well.

Technology

In the past, technology issues (including low bandwidth, poor and unstable desktop and laptop operating systems, low-bandwidth mobile networks offering Internet access, and poor digital production platforms) were the major inhibiting factor in the growth of online content. This is no longer true. The technology platforms to deliver acceptable online content are now available. The only exception is lack of bandwidth for high

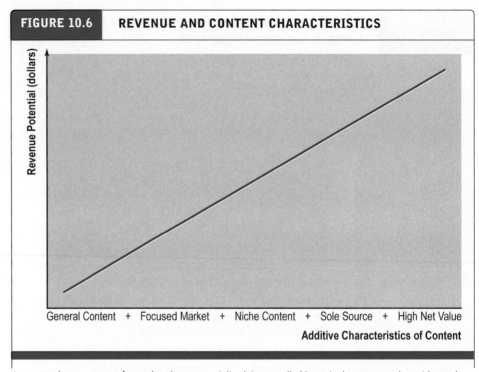

FIGURE 10.6 | **REVENUE AND CONTENT CHARACTERISTICS**

As content becomes more focused and more specialized, is controlled by a single source, and provides real value to consumers for an Internet delivery (i.e., speed, searchability, and portability), the prospects for charging fees for access increases.

definition full-screen video, full-screen standard quality television, and CD-quality music (as opposed to MP3 quality). Yet the streaming quality of video is acceptable and far better than in the past.

Cost

Internet distribution is far more costly than anticipated. Media companies face substantial costs of migrating, repackaging, and ultimately redesigning content for online delivery. The simplest and least-expensive first-step approach is to migrate existing content to the Web. Even this step requires new staff with new skills, a delivery mechanism, Web designers, and technicians. The costs of migrating can only be justified by increasing sales of offline units. Repackaging content requires substantial creative input and management. The most cost and effort occurs in the third level of media transformation—the redesign of content. There, creative costs can explode as artists, writers, producers, directors, and editors spend thousands of hours designing a "new" content product that optimizes Internet technology while still using many traditional writing and video techniques. For instance, the transformation of traditional film-based movie-making into computer-animated graphical experiences such as *X-Men Origins: Wolverine* requires tens of millions of dollars, and many creative individuals. Other rising costs include paying content writers, actors, and musicians for downloaded content at an acceptable rate. For instance, in 2007, the 12,000 members of the Writers Guild of America went on strike against major television and Hollywood production studios because they believed they were not being adequately compensated for video and television downloads or other digital content.

Distribution Channels and Cannibalization

Many traditional media companies stumble when they try to repurpose their content to the Web. Short of merging with companies that have large Web audiences—as in the AOL/Time Warner merger—media companies are often tempted to strike alliances with intermediaries such as portals or redistributors. Such alliances carry the risk that the media company's brand name might be displaced by the portal's or aggregator's brand name; in addition, whatever revenues are generated must be shared with the intermediary. Hollywood studios and most television broadcasters want to own their customers and prefer to handle distribution from their own portals For instance, Disney, distributes television and video through Apple's iTunes Store as do most television and movie content owners. But why should movie and television studios be dependent on YouTube or Apple iTunes for distribution? Why not own the Internet distribution channels as well? For instance, Hulu.com (one of the most successful online movie sites) was established by NBC Universal (GE), Fox Entertainment Group (News Corp) and ABC Inc. (The Walt Disney Company) in 2008 to control the distribution of movies and television shows.

A related and perhaps more vexing challenge is cannibalization of existing channels. What happens to bookstore or music store sales when books and music are available online for half the price—or even lower? What happens to movie theaters when feature films can be downloaded or streamed off the Internet? Here, content producers must be very careful about pricing and value so as to avoid destroying their existing distribution channels.

Digital Rights Management (DRM)

The uncertainties of content protection are clearly one of the reasons why more high-quality content is not available online. This is especially true of commercial video content. **Digital rights management (DRM)** refers to a combination of technical (both hardware and software) and legal means for protecting digital content from unlimited reproduction without permission. For instance, in 2003, Apple and the music industry attempted to control the distribution of songs downloaded from its iTunes Music Store (now known as the "iTunes Store") by using technology to limit the number of times the songs can be copied to five times, prevent play on uncontrolled MP3 players by using a proprietary file format named Advanced Audio Coding (AAC), and prevent more than seven CD burns of the songs. These actions shored up Apple's position in the music download market, where it has a 90% market share. Finally, it relied on the Digital Millennium Copyright Act to discourage hackers from publishing code to break the encryption scheme. In 2009, Apple abandoned the DRM software because of user objections, and because Amazon opened an online music store in 2007 without any DRM protections, with the support of music label firms.

Some firms with subscription services use technologies that limit the time period that a song can be played without re-subscribing. For instance, songs downloaded

digital rights management (DRM)
refers to the combination of technical and legal means for protecting digital content from unlimited reproduction without permission

from Napster and RealOne will simply not play after 30 days unless the user pays the monthly subscription fee. And if you don't pay, you will lose access to all your songs.

While the issue of DRM is often cast as a contest between content owners and hackers bent on distributing and using "free music," the industry titans themselves are divided on digital rights management. Many industries benefit from the illegal and unfettered downloading of music. For instance, Apple Computer, Intel, Sony, and Microsoft all benefit from the explosion in what Apple CEO Steve Jobs calls computers that can "rip, mix, and burn." In other words, sales of computers (and CD burners from Sony) depend heavily on killer applications like P2P networks and the theft of musical rights. Likewise, Verizon, SBC Communications, and Time Warner Cable (and the major Internet trunk line owners) also depend on their networks being kept as busy as possible. Oddly, many of these companies themselves are significant owners of content—like AOL Time Warner and Sony. Typically, it is the technology companies, such as Apple, Microsoft, Google, Yahoo, and others who are delivery pipes for content, that argue for the elimination of DRM techniques. These companies make very little on content per se, but a great deal on the devices and software that carry the content. And it is the content creators and owners who insist on DRM: they make nothing on the delivery devices, and all their revenue comes from the content. Generally, the telecommunications pipeline companies also favor the elimination of DRM because their revenues come from carrying content.

Insight on Business: Who Owns Your Files takes a further look at these issues.

10.2   THE ONLINE PUBLISHING INDUSTRY

Nothing is quite so fundamental to a civilized society as reading text. Text is the way we record our history, current events, thoughts, and aspirations, and transmit them to all others in the civilization who can read. Even videos require scripts. Today, the publishing industry is a $200 billion media sector based originally on print, and now moving rapidly to the Internet (U.S. Census Bureau, 2009). The Internet offers the text publishing industry an opportunity to move toward a new generation of newspapers, magazines, and books that are produced, processed, stored, distributed, and sold over the Web, available anytime, anywhere, and on any device. The same Internet offers the possibility of destroying many existing print-based businesses that may not be able to make this transition and remain profitable.

ONLINE NEWSPAPERS

Newspapers in 2009 are the most troubled segment of the publishing industry, troubles that result almost exclusively from the availability of alternatives to the printed newspaper, as well as a sluggish response by management to the opportunities on the Internet for news, if not newspapers. Also important is the failure of newspaper management to protect its valuable content from being distributed for free by aggregators such as Yahoo, MSN, and Google. As it turns out, there wouldn't be a Google or Yahoo news functionality without traditional reporters and editors who work for newspapers and create the content.

INSIGHT ON BUSINESS

WHO OWNS YOUR FILES?

In George Orwell's novel, *1984*, the fictional dictator called "Big Brother" directs a pervasive surveillance network of telescreens that monitor what citizens of Oceania read, listen to, and say. In a "life imitates art" management action, on July 17, 2009, Amazon reached out to touch its Kindle customers by deleting digital copies of both *1984* and another Orwell novel, *Animal Farm*, from their Kindle readers. Amazon also deleted all the notes that students may have taken on the book using Kindle's note function. Amazon had discovered that a vendor of books to its Kindle operation had uploaded the two Orwell books using an automated self-service facility but did not actually own the copyrights to the two novels. The rights are held by the Orwell estate and other firms. The Kindle operates on a cellular network where users can download digital e-books from Amazon's servers for play exclusively on the Kindle device. Apparently, the network can operate in reverse as well, something Kindle owners never realized. Amazon can reach down into every Kindle user's device and delete or add files without obtaining permission of the Kindle's owner.

After thousands of Kindle users protested and one filed a lawsuit, Amazon apologized to its customers, promised never to delete downloaded files again, and admitted they had made a mistake. But the Amazon affair brought to the forefront of national attention the question: "Who owns digital entertainment files once they are downloaded to your computers, including smartphones?" The answer is changing and also unclear.

It used to be that when you bought a CD, or a book, you owned it and you could pretty much do what you wanted with it. "Ownership" from a legal perspective means that you have the exclusive right to control and dispose of property (both tangible and intangible goods). If you create and/or own content, you have exclusive rights to that content. From a customer perspective, this also applies. Under the "first sale doctrine," consumers who purchase a product can resell it without infringing on the copyright. In the pre-digital world, copyrighted material was fairly safe from rampant, uncontrolled copying and distribution. Not so in the new digital world: uncontrolled copying and distribution is very easy. From the copyright owners' business perspective, the ease of duplication and distribution threatens the future revenue stream from the copyrighted products.

Creators and publishers of content, from musicians and writers to music label firms and book publishers, have sought to deal with the threat of losing control (and therefore revenues) of the content they own in two ways: software called Digital Rights Management (DRM), and hardware-based walled environments where digital content can be read or played but not used or copied to any other hardware device. Let's take a brief look at these two strategies.

DRM software is intended to stop uncontrolled copying and distribution. DRM software ensures you can't do pretty much anything you want, but instead only things the owner of the content wants. As a matter of fact, you don't really own the music but just "license" it under terms and conditions specified somewhere (usually in the fine print or on a back page on a Web site). It's called a EULA: End User License Agreement, and when you open the package and

(continued)

break the seal, you are agreeing to the terms of this license. DRM software is computer code embedded in songs, movies, or e-books that dictate how these files can be used. DRM software is both hated and loved—by different groups of course. For consumers, DRM is generally hated but tolerated in most instances if the bargain is right. DRM places restrictions on how a music track, for instance, can be used, copied, and distributed.

The best known DRM was Apple's FairPlay. FairPlay rigged each song you "bought" for 99 cents so that you could play it on only five computers, and so that you could burn only seven CDs. And just to add a little salt to these wounds, the songs could only be downloaded in the default iPod Apple AAC format and played only on Apple iPod devices and not on competing MP3 devices, which use a marginally inferior sound-compression protocol called MP3. Users could not edit or sample the song, and Apple reserved the right to change the DRM restrictions any time it wanted. Apple didn't "voluntarily" arrive at this arrangement but instead negotiated it with the real owners of the content, the record label companies. Without these restrictions, the record labels refused to license Apple any content.

Apple was very successful with this business model despite user complaints. But in January 2009, Apple abandoned its DRM software, and removed all anti-copying restrictions from all songs on the iTunes site. Purchasers of earlier DRM-protected songs could convert their originals for new Premium songs for .30 cents a song (hardly a bargain when you have 16 gigabytes of songs). The three major labels (Sony, Universal, and TimeWarner) and Apple reached a compromise: no anti-copying restrictions in return for pricing power to the record labels which raised the price on newly release popular songs to $1.29, keeping most songs at .99 cents, and less popular songs at .69 cents. It's called price discrimination, a basic marketing strategy, and the music labels found it in their business interest to allow copying in return for price discrimination. Apple found it in its business interest to allow variable pricing in the hope that more customers would buy more songs, and more iPods and iPhone devices.

Apple was also responding to competition from Amazon. While iTunes commands 80% of the music download business, Amazon has risen from zero to 20% in a single year. At launch in 2007, Amazon offered over 2 million songs from more than 180,000 artists and over 20,000 labels. In 2009, Amazon's library contains over 8 million songs. All of its songs are available as MP3 tracks without any digital rights protection, and at variable prices determined by the record labels, from .89 cents to $1.29, with albums going for $5.99 to $9.99. A year before Apple launched its DRM-free music, the record labels had cut a deal with Amazon reportedly as a means of reducing Apple's market dominance in the music download business where it was a near monopoly for a short period of time. The strategy worked.

In this sense, DRM is dead in the music world although it survives in the Hollywood movie world and is reappearing in the newspaper content world. The Associated Press (AP), an organization owned by major newspapers to share news stories, announced in July 2009 that it will "envelope" its articles, photos, videos, and headlines in a "protective wrapper" to track the use of its information through a news database that keeps track of Internet content. AP chief executive Tom Curley told the *New York Times* "If someone [Google] can build a multibillion-dollar business out of keywords, we can build a multi-hundred-billion business out of headlines, and we're going to do that." DRM is also alive and well on cable TV where pay-per-view movies cannot be recorded, stored, or copied because of encoding software.

(continued)

Paid music downloads are growing rapidly, much more rapidly than illegal downloads. In 2009, legitimate paid music downloads expanded by 30% over 2008, as 50 million people downloaded music (while 17 million fewer people bought CDs). At Atlantic Records, digital sales exceeded CD sales, a first for any record label. But competition to both Apple and Amazon is coming from subscription services and social networks, challenging the entire download-a-tune business model. While everyone has heard of iTunes and Amazon, consumers are turning to streaming sites such as Pandora, which doubled in size in 2008 alone to include 18% of all Internet users! Pandora's online streaming service is free to users and is supported by advertisements for iTunes and Amazon, among others, where listeners can purchase the music being played. Social networks, especially MySpace, YouTube, and Facebook, are growing huge music audiences—20% of online consumers (and half of teenagers) listen to music social networks in 2009. While illegal sites still attract a majority of Internet consumers who are under the age of 25, by the time people are 30 and older, only 4% are still downloading music from illegal sites. Strengthened by the Supreme Court ruling against file-sharing sites, the last commercially viable U.S.-based file-sharing service, BearShare, collapsed under legal assault from the record label industry. BearShare settled allegations of copyright infringement for $30 million in 2006. However, pirate and offshore sites continue to fuel the P2P downloading phenomenon mostly among the under-twenty crowd.

Streaming services do not allow users to record, save, copy, and distribute their music. The question of ownership seems more clear: you pay for access to the streaming library and if you stop paying, you no longer can access the library. While there are some tools that can capture MP3 files, they are generally too sophisticated for the general audience. This is different from the Kindle situation where users downloaded books to a device they owned.

Kindle users thought they "owned" the digital books they downloaded. But the Kindle users who protested Amazon's decision to remove Orwell's books from their Kindles must not have read the Terms of Use agreement that comes with the device and which says: "Digital Content will be deemed licensed to you by Amazon under this Agreement unless otherwise expressly provided by Amazon…you may not sell, rent, lease, distribute, broadcast, sublicense or otherwise assign any rights to the Digital Content…and you will not encourage, assist or authorize any other person to, bypass, modify, defeat or circumvent security features that protect the Digital Content. And "we may terminate a subscription at our discretion without notice, for example, if a Periodical is no longer available; if we terminate a subscription in advance of the end of its term, we will give you a prorated refund."

Up until 2009, it looked as if the ownership interests of consumers and the ownership interests of copyright owners were diametrically opposed. Consumers either expected to download free content and not pay the owners of content, or they expected to pay for and download a book or music track, and just like the traditional physical products, do whatever they wanted to do with the product. Copyright owners expected consumers to pay for every copy of the book or music that was downloaded, just like the physical products. The situation was complicated by the presence of Internet channel owners: companies such as Verizon and AT&T, which own the cellular and Internet networks, and Apple, Microsoft, and Google, all of whom made money by attracting customers to view free content. The more free content, the larger the audience. They have no business interest in protecting the rights of music, movie, writers, artists, musicians, and content owners. The ensuing debate has raged since MP3 music files first became popular on the Internet in 1997. Phrases that termi-

(continued)

nate clear thinking, such as "information wants to be free," and lawsuits by record companies against file-sharers, spurred the debate to new heights of frenzy. A deal seemed impossible.

But a new reality is slowly taking hold in which content owners and Internet distributors are recognizing they need one another. Digital device firms such as Apple, which also runs the world's largest download music service, now recognize that they need the quality content of record labels and Hollywood studios. They can't dictate terms to the music industry. Online con-tent servers such as Google (especially YouTube) also recognize that without the major newspapers, studios, and music firms, they would have little high-quality popular content to sell. What would Google news be without news reporting organizations and newspapers? YouTube without music videos? Along with the players various business interests, there's been a change in consumer culture as well. Largely as the result of Apple's iTunes Store, it's become acceptable, even cool, to pay for content such as music online.

SOURCES: "Blood on the Tracks: DRM Debate Heats Up," by Pat Pilcher, *New Zealand Herald*, August 5, 2009; "Associated Press to Protect News with Digital Rights Management," out-law.com, July 27, 2009; "Amazon Faces a Fight Over Its E-Books," by Brad Stone, *New York Times*, July 27, 2009; A.P. Cracks Down on Unpaid Use of Articles on Web," By Richard Perez-Pena, *New York Times*, July 24, 2009; "Sony Agrees to Provide Its Older Songs to eMusic," by Brad Stone, *New York Times*, June 1, 2009; "Music Labels Cut Friendlier Deals with Start-Ups," by Brad Stone, *New York Times*, May 28, 2009; "Music Consumption Habits Continue to Shift: NPD," by Joseph Palenchar, Twice.com, March 17, 2009; "Want to Copy iTunes Music? Go Ahead, Apple Says," by Brad Stone, *New York Times*, January 7, 2009; "Digital Sales Surpass CDs at Atlantic," by Tim Arango, *New York Times*, November 26, 2008; "Amazon Gains Share of Shrinking Paid Music Market," by Saul Hansell, *New York Times*, April 17, 2008; "Music Industry, Souring on Apple, Embraces Amazon Service," by Jeff Leeds, *New York Times*, January 14, 2008; "Music Service From Amazon Takes on iTunes," by Ethan Smith and Vauhini Vara, *Wall Street Journal*, May 17, 2007; "Amazon to Sell Music Without Copy Protection," by Brad Stone and Jeff Leeds, *New York Times*, May 17, 2007.

Over 60% of newspapers have reduced news staff in the last three years, and 61% report shrinking the size of the newspaper. Readership has been declining for ten years, advertising is down 15% a year, subscriptions are down, and old readers are not being replaced by young readers who get the news online. To make matters worse, in the recession of 2009, online ad revenues, which newspapers increasingly are depending on, are flat (eMarketer, 2009c). Alternative online sources of news such as Yahoo, Google, and even blogs, have became major sources of news for many Americans. Much of this "news" is redistributed content generated by newspapers! Alternatives to newspaper classified ads like Craigslist, have decimated newspaper classified revenues.

But there is good news too. Online readership of newspapers is growing at 17% a year. New reading devices from smartphones to new larger e-screen readers connected to wireless networks offer opportunities for online newspapers to be read everywhere. A new Internet culture is supportive of paying for quality content. Newspaper owners, faced with extinction, are exploring ways to protect their content, and introduce paid "premium" news and views. Pure Internet aggregators of news such as Google and Yahoo are beginning to recognize that if the newspaper industry disappears, there will be little news to aggregate, distribute, and place ads against. Amateur blogs and tweets may be wonderful for expressing opinions, or making instant reports on events as they occur, but they are no substitute for professional reporters and editors, and not a place for brand-conscious advertisers. Therefore, the Internet distributors are recognizing they have a vested interest in keeping the newspaper content industry in working order.

According to the Newspaper Association of America, print newspapers have around 49 million paid subscribers, down from 62 million in 1990. On an average day, 95 million people read a newspaper, and on Sunday there are more than 105 million readers. Even when compared to YouTube (4–6 million unique visitors a day), these are impressive audience sizes. Offline newspaper readership of physical papers has declined at about 2% a year for several years, while online readership is at an all-time high of about 70 million in 2009, growing at 17% a year. The online audience increases the overall footprint of the newspaper media. Total advertising at newspapers in 2008 is $32 billion, and declining at 15% a year. However, online newspaper ad revenues in 2009 are $3.2 billion and were flat year over year. In a nutshell, this is the problem confronting newspapers: how to grow online revenues to offset the losses from print advertising (eMarketer, 2009c; Newspaper Association of America, 2009).

Audience Size and Growth

There are more than 10,000 online newspapers in the world. Online newspaper readership is growing at 17% a year. According to Nielsen Online, the total Web audience for online newspapers in the United States during the first seven months of 2009 was typically between 70 and 75 million (Newspaper Association of America, 2009) (see **Figure 10.7** for a list of the top 10). The average online visitor stayed on the site for 35 to 45 minutes. Online newspapers are the dominant local Web site: 62% of Internet users look for local news on a local newspaper Web site. Given this huge online newspaper audience, it is clear that the future of newspapers lies in the online market even as readership and subscriptions to the traditional print newspapers continues to decline at a steady pace.

Next to social networks, newspapers produce the largest online audiences of any media, and in that sense, contrary to popular opinion, are one of the most successful forms of online content to date. The Internet provides existing branded newspapers the opportunity to extend their brands to a new online audience, and also gives entrepreneurial firms the opportunity to offer services—such as classified job listings—on the Web that were previously delivered by newspapers. Online newspapers are the top choice for local news and information for Internet users in the United States.

While newspapers have done an excellent job at increasing their Web presence and audience, few have reached break-even operations, although some are close. Instead, online classified and advertising revenues have not kept pace with the fall in revenues from their traditional print editions. There are several reasons for this: increased competition from general portal sites moving into the content aggregation business, loss of classified ads to online portals, job sites, and free listing services such as Craigslist. Craigslist is reported to have wiped out $50 million in classified ads for San Francisco Chronicle.

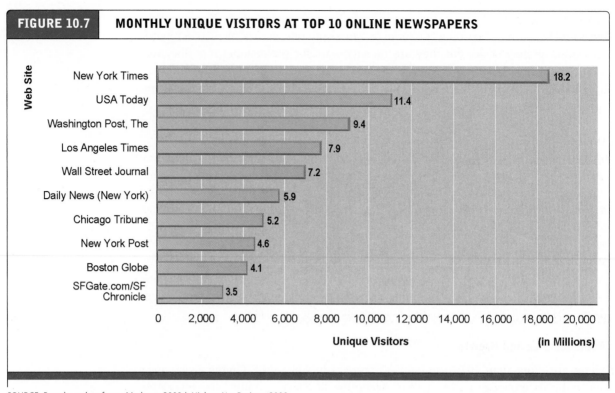

FIGURE 10.7 **MONTHLY UNIQUE VISITORS AT TOP 10 ONLINE NEWSPAPERS**

SOURCE: Based on data from eMarketer, 2009d; Nielsen Net Ratings, 2009.

The Web has provided an opportunity for newspapers to extend their offline brands, but at the same time it has given entrepreneurs the opportunity to take part of the newspapers' content—such as weather, classified ads, or current national and international news (but not local news).

Internet firms have emerged that threaten to take much of the classified ads business away from newspapers. Sites such as Monster, Craigslist, Autobytel, and CNET have moved aggressively to develop online classified ads for jobs, automobiles, and real estate, while others have developed deep and rich content in specialized areas such as automobiles, computers, cameras, and other hobbyist topics. Many of these firms have drained significant readership from newspapers for specialized, deep content; created nationwide marketplaces that did not exist before; and put a significant dent in local newspaper classified revenues. Classified revenues account for approximately 40% of newspaper revenue.

Newspaper Business Models

The online newspaper industry has gone through several business models, from fee, to free, and most recently, struggling to return to a fee-based business model. In the past, a few online newspapers such as the *New York Times*, *Wall Street Journal*, and *Financial Times* (U.K.) charged for some or all online content, especially premium content. In the case of the *Times*, access to the *Times* archives was a paid service. Most newspapers did not charge for online content, and even the *Times* abandoned its Times Select subscription service for archived content. The result was that content generated by newspapers became freely available across the Web, where it could be indexed by search engines that redistributed the headlines and content. Newspaper headlines became the primary content on Google News and Yahoo News. Newspapers benefitted from this because a Google listing brought readers to the newspaper, where readers could be exposed to advertising. In 2009, the threatened destruction of the newspaper industry is causing newspaper management to re-think free content supported by online ads placed at the newspapers' sites. The Associated Press has started negotiations with Google to consider payment schemes for the use of its head-lines, and exploring ways to use DRM software to protect its headlines. The *Wall Street Journal* was prepared to abandon the fee model in 2008, but in 2009, the parent News Corp, the largest owner of newspapers in the world and the owner of MySpace, announced plans to begin charging for all its online content across the world.

Traditional newspapers make money by selling subscriptions for regular delivery and by selling advertising space, both fine-print classified ads as well as traditional ads placed on pages. Newspaper ads typically are paid for by local merchants selling goods and services in the area of a newspaper's circulation. Advertising accounts for 41% of newspaper revenues, up from 30% in 1980, and subscriptions account for 50% of revenue, with other miscellaneous income coming from printing legal notices. As a percentage of overall revenue, online revenues rarely exceed 10%, although online revenues are by far the faster growing. In general, newspapers are finding it difficult to replace offline readers with online readers simply because they cannot derive enough revenue from online readers. Advertisers are willing to pay much higher rates for print ads than online ads. The ratio of print revenue to online revenue per cus-tomer is roughly 3:1. For instance, a single offline subscriber, on average, generates $900 in revenue, while an online customer generates only $300 in revenue. Either the total number of online readers needs to increase dramatically relative to the offline audience, or newspapers need to figure out how to derive more revenue from each customer through increased advertising.

In response to declining or stagnant revenue growth, newspapers have sought alliances with one another and with online technology power houses such as Yahoo and Google in response to the challenge posed by pure-play online classified job sites, and the newspaper industry has sought industry-wide alliances to develop competing sites and to move toward a value-added revenue model for this segment. To compete against Monster.com, the *New York Times*, Times-Mirror Company, the *Tribune*, and the *Washington Post* have created a territorial model called CareerBuilder.com, a job-listing site with 2 million jobs and 25 million monthly visitors. Gannett, McClatchy, and Tribune Co., which collectively own hundreds of local newspapers, formed an alliance called Open Network to offer advertisers one-stop shopping for national (as opposed to local) newspaper advertising. Yahoo and a consortium of seven newspaper chains representing 176 daily papers around the country have formed a partnership to share content, technology, and advertising. The idea is to have newspapers place their ads on Yahoo's classified job site, and use HotJobs tech-nology to run their own online career ads. Yahoo will in turn tag and index the newspapers' content so it can be found easily on the Web. Google has created a system for auctioning ads for many of the largest newspaper companies, including Gannett, Tribune, the New York Times, Hearst, and others.

Many, but not all, efforts by newspapers to adapt to the Internet involve making alliances with Internet titans such as Google and Yahoo, which have huge online audiences. These efforts involve sharing revenue with Internet partners. A different strategy is emerging based on the proliferation of e-reader devices such as smartphones like the iPhone, and dedicated devices like the Kindle, Sony e-reader, and the new IREX e-reader with an 8-inch touchscreen. Sales of the new e-readers are expected to reach well over 5 million units annually in 2009 and 2010—a five-fold growth from 2008. Each of these devices has, or will have, reader apps that present newspaper content in a way that closely matches the offline editions and is familiar to readers. The IREX reader uses an industry-standard ePub format, and is continuously connected to the Barnes & Noble e-bookstore via the Verizon 3G network. Unlike Kindle, which is tied to the U.S. carrier Sprint, IREX will work anywhere in the world.

These new reader devices offer newspapers an opportunity to connect directly with their readers anytime and anywhere. What's missing is a newspaper version of the iTunes Store, a single online store where you can find newspaper content from any newspaper in the U.S. or the world. But not for long. NewspaperDirect.com is an online store that has same day online editions of more than 1,100 newspapers from 87 countries in 41 languages. Unlimited subscriptions are $29.00 a month, economy editions are $9.95 for 31 articles, and most individual articles cost .99 cents. Along with other traditional providers of text products such as Barnes & Noble, sites like NewspaperDirect offer the newspaper industry a way to deliver their content on a contemporary digital platform.

Convergence

In terms of our schema of convergence—technology, content, and industry structure—the newspaper industry is rushing pell mell to a convergent model of news, content, and services. Soon newspapers will be offering social networking sites for local groups.

Technology The movement of published text to the Web was the first step toward technology platform convergence, but obviously this did not take advantage of the interactive features of the Web. The newspaper industry has been slow to invest in Internet technology, although this is changing as video, RSS feeds, blogs, and user feedback forums grow.

Content Online newspapers have transformed themselves into multimedia platforms with a variety of digital content. Four content changes are apparent: premium archived content, fine-grained search, videos reporting, and RSS feeds. **Figure 10.8** summarizes the transformation of online newspapers as digital outlets.

The online environment permits considerable extension to traditional newspaper content. For instance, newspapers can offer access to premium archive content by permitting users to search back issues. The inherent fine-grained search capability of

FIGURE 10.8 **INTERACTIVE FEATURES OFFERED ON THE WEB SITES OF THE TOP 100 U.S. NEWSPAPERS (% OF TOTAL)**

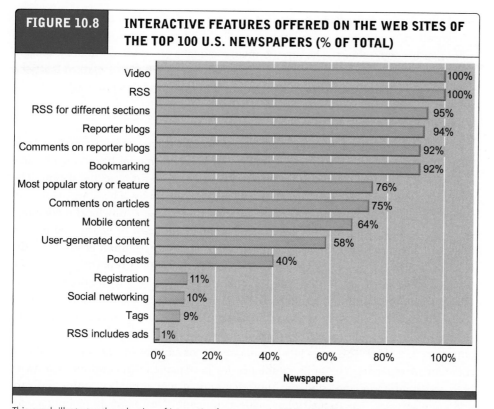

This graph illustrates the adoption of interactive features on the Web sites of the top 100 newspapers as of August 2008.

SOURCES: Based on data from the Bivings Group, 2008; eMarketer, 2009c.

the Internet platform increases ease of access to news and archival information for consumers. The most significant change in content is timeliness. The Internet frees newspapers from the time-bound character of paper and printing presses and allows for instant updates to breaking stories. In this sense, online newspapers can, for the first time, compete directly with television and radio for reporting breaking stories. Visit the online *New York Times* or *Wall Street Journal*, or a local online newspaper today, and you will see breaking news that is just a few minutes old. This is a sea change from traditional newspapers.

Industry Structure The newspaper industry is a mature industry that is ripe for further consolidation and expansion onto the Web. Historically, hundreds of local newspapers have been combined into larger national chains. Now the chains themselves need to be consolidated in order to create truly national advertising markets, and leverage their local readership (something Google, Microsoft, and Yahoo do not have). The problem has been finding deep-pocket media titans to purchase the papers and make hefty technology investments. Generally, the returns on newspaper investments do not meet the hurdle rates for most media titan firms. Instead, newspaper companies tend to buy one another, or are bought as play things for the idle rich. The McClatchy Company purchased the second largest newspaper chain,

Knight Ridder, in June 2006. In April 2007, Sam Zell, Chicago real estate magnate, purchased in the Tribune Company in an $8.2 billion deal, but only put up $315 million of his own money. The new company will take on $8 billion in debt, most of it owned by the employee pension plan. The only exception to this pattern has been the News Corp purchase of Dow Jones, publisher of the *Wall Street Journal*.

Challenges: Disruptive Technologies

The online newspaper industry would appear at first glance to be a classic case of disruptive technology destroying a traditional business model based on physical products and physical distribution. This may turn out to be the case, but it cannot be the final assessment just yet. The industry is changing rapidly. There are significant assets that newspapers have—excellent content and writing, strong local readership, strong local advertising, and a fragmented but huge audience of nearly 100 million readers that rivals Yahoo, Google, and Microsoft's audience. Content is still king: the thousands of blogs in the blogospheres depend on traditional reporting media like television and newspapers to create the content that the blog writers can react to. Without the original content creators in the form of professional reporters and news organizations, the blogosphere would be a dull place. The people who read newspapers are very different from the people who visit YouTube: they are wealthier, more educated, and older. This is an ideal demographic for advertisers and a potential gold mine for newspapers. The online audience for newspapers will continue to grow in both sheer numbers and sophistication, demanding higher-quality online delivery and more services. The industry has made significant investments in technology for Web content creation and delivery. Many national newspapers have slowed down investment in online operations because they did not make a profit at first. The challenge is for newspaper owners and managers to invest heavily in the online editions even if they do not meet investment criteria at first. If the newspaper industry has a future, it will be online. The challenge for newspapers is to create value by focusing on differentiated, timely, and exclusive content available nowhere else. And to make this content available anywhere, anytime, any place, on any device. Oddly, Apple's iTunes may have shown newspapers the future by developing micro-payment systems to sell individual music content files for .99 cents, and to sell bundles of music (albums) for a reasonable price. There's no reason newspapers cannot sell articles, stories, and editorials online for .99 cents or $10 for a monthly bundle. Today, none do.

BOOKS: THE EVOLUTION OF E-BOOKS

In April 2000, Stephen King, one of America's most popular writers, published a novella called *Riding the Bullet*. This novella was only available as an e-book. King was the first major fiction writer to create an e-book-only volume of a new work. King's publisher, Simon & Schuster, arranged for sales online through online retailers such as Amazon. In the first day, there were 400,000 downloads, so many that Amazon's servers nearly crashed several times. More than 500,000 downloads occurred in the first week, for a price of $2.50 for a 66-page novella—about the same price per page as a standard King hardcover novel. While Amazon gave the book away for free in the first two weeks, when it began charging for the book, sales continued to be brisk.

In 2009, Amazon's e-book store contains an estimated 300,000 titles (many titles are classic out of print and copyright books, of copyright but there are many popular copyrighted books as well). There are an estimated 600,000 Kindles being used today, and Amazon is racking up 600,000 sales a week. Kindle users are avid book readers and purchase one book a week. Amazon's founder Jeff Bezos has let slip that when both paper and e-book editions exist for the same book, e-book sales are about 35% of the paperback sales (Rosenthal, 2009).

E-books are surprisingly a very hot topic in 2009 as Google battles the major tech companies, authors, publishing firms, the United States Congress, the Department of Justice, and the European Commission over the future of online digital books. Meanwhile, device makers such as Amazon, Sony, IREX, and Reader Daily Edition are delivering new readers to market seemingly every month. In the wings, Apple is preparing to release its large-screen Internet computer and reader device.

In the Internet age, books are supposed to die off and go away. Who wants to read books when YouTube has over 5.5 billion video streams covering most topics known to man, and Google can provide access to the world's information? Steve Jobs noted in an interview about the Kindle e-book reader, "It doesn't matter how good or bad the product [e-book reader] is, the fact is that people don't read anymore. Forty percent of the people in the U.S. read one book or less last year. The whole conception is flawed at the top because people don't read anymore." Actually, in 2009, over 3 billion books will be sold in the United States, generating around $25 billion in revenue. Americans in fact read 10 books per year per person

The essential questions facing the book publishing industry are: If people are willing to buy physical books, would they also be willing to buy electronic versions of books? What kind of device would readers like to use when reading digital books? The next question is, "How much would they be willing to pay for an e-book?" And finally, "What changes to the concept of the book itself might be necessary to encourage people to buy e-books online?"

The Internet already has brought about significant changes in book sales and distribution, and is beginning to have an impact on the design, creation, and production of books. The book itself, and the reading experience, is starting to slowly morph into a truly different product. E-books, online print-on-demand books, and mixed media books are beginning to appear and are changing the concept of the traditional book from a passive form of entertainment to a more interactive form of engagement.

The modern book is not really very different from the first two-facing page, bound books that began to appear in seventeenth century Europe. The traditional book has a very simple, non-digital operating system: text appears left to right, pages are numbered, there is a hard front and back cover, and text pages are bound together by stitching or glue. In educational and reference books, there is an alphabetical index in the back of the book that permits direct access to the book's content. While these traditional books will be with us for many years given their portability, ease of use, and flexibility, a parallel new world of e-books is expected to emerge in the next five years.

E-books

E-books have had a glorious history of birth, death, rebirth, and death again. In 2009, e-books are back, this time with powerful backers such as Amazon, Sony, Yahoo, Google, and Microsoft, along with start-ups like IREX. The Google Book Search Project is scanning millions of books in large university libraries. When you click on a search result for a book from the Library Project, you will see basic bibliographic information about the book, and in many cases, a few sentences (called "snippets") showing your search term in context. If the book is out of copyright, you will be able to view and download the entire book. In all cases, you'll see links directing you to online bookstores where you can buy the book and libraries where you can borrow it. Google books will, of course, only be searchable with the Google search engine, and none of the scanned books will be compatible with similar efforts by Microsoft or members of the Open Book Alliance (see the case study at the end of Chapter 8).

Electronic books were around for many years before the Internet. In 1971, Michael Hart began Project Gutenberg at the Materials Research Lab at the University of Illinois. Hart began by typing in the Declaration of Independence, and proceeded to put more than 2,000 classic books online at the University's Computer Center. The books are all in ASCII plain text without traditional book fonts or formatting. While not a joy to read, they were free. In 1990, Voyager Company, a New York-based media company, began putting books such as *Jurassic Park* and *Alice in Wonderland* on CDs. However, with the exception of encyclopedias and large reference texts, popular books on CDs never were a commercial success. They were expensive to produce and distribute, and appeared in the marketplace before most PC users had CD-ROM drives.

The development of the Internet and the Web, along with small, powerful handheld devices, have greatly changed the possibilities for e-books. The Web offered publishers much lower distribution costs (each "copy" on the Web can be downloaded for almost no cost), and unlike the early computer-based e-books, all the formatting, fonts, and colors used by publishers in high-quality books could be preserved when Adobe's Portable Document Format (PDF) is used to create the text.

There are many different types of commercial e-books (see **Table 10.5**). The two most common e-books are Web-accessed or Web-downloadable. **Web-accessed e-books** are stored on the publisher's servers and purchasers pay a fee for reading the book on-screen; in some cases these e-books can also be printed by the individual user. The most successful Web-accessed e-books are online encyclopedias such as the abridged edition of the *Encyclopedia Britannica*, and open source encyclopedias like Wikipedia.com. CourseSmart is a new e-textbook service formed by the six largest publishers of textbooks in the world. With CourseSmart, college students can subscribe to online textbooks for half the price of purchasing a physical textbook (including this book!). The book can be accessed from any Internet connected computer, anywhere, anytime. Students can also print chapters.

Web-downloadable e-books are a more user-friendly e-book that can be downloaded from the Web, stored as a file on the client PC, and in many cases printed, although some e-books have security locks that prevent printing. The largest collections of downloadable e-books are held by Google (Google Books

Web-accessed e-book

an e-book stored on a publisher's server that consumers access and read on the Web

Web-downloadable e-book

an e-book that can be downloaded from the Web, stored as a file on the client PC, and perhaps even printed

TABLE 10.5	TYPES OF E-BOOKS
E-BOOK TYPE	DESCRIPTION
Web-accessed e-books	E-book remains on publisher's Web site and is read only on the site. Purchasers pay a subscription fee for access.
Web-downloadable e-books	Contents of e-book can be downloaded to client PC for reading. Printing may or may not be possible. Purchaser pays for initial download and reading, or content is paid for by advertising, such as Google e-books. Subsequent use may be metered or free.
Dedicated e-book reader	Contents of e-book can be downloaded only to dedicated hardware device either directly connected to the Web or through a PC connection. Kindle and Sony readers.
General-purpose PDA reader	Contents of e-book can be downloaded from the Web to a general-purpose handheld smartphone such as an iPhone , Palm Pre, or BlackBerrry.
Print-on-demand books	Contents of a book are stored on a Web server; they can be downloaded on demand for local printing and even binding.

Project, and Google Books Library Project). The Google Books Project involves scanning millions of entire physical books, many of them out of copyright, or "orphaned" by authors and publishers. Google refuses to say how many books it has scanned, but estimates suggest somewhere between 1 and 2 million titles are in the book database. The Google Books Library Project works with many large research and public libraries to scan all their holdings, and make them available to the public as a library resource. Google's plan is to monetize these databases by posting advertisements next to book pages. These plans are currently held in check because of a lawsuit brought by authors and publishers against Google. Other large downloadable e-book collections are held by NetLibrary and Questia.

Dedicated e-book readers are single-purpose devices that have proprietary operating systems that can download from the Web and read proprietary formatted files created for those devices. Each dedicated reader makes available to customers several thousand generally popular titles. Franklin Electronic Publisher's eBook-Man was one of the first dedicated e-book readers. Prices ranged from a low of $129 to a high of $199 retail. The product was discontinued in 2001 after sales failed to reach expectations. Other players have since stepped up to the plate. Amazon, Sony, and IREX have brought back the dedicated e-book reader device from what most considered certain death. The Amazon Kindle is now in its second generation and can hold 1,500 books. The Kindle DX has a larger (8-inch) screen suited for books and newspapers. The IREX uses a larger format screen ideal for newspapers, and comfortable for book readers. The new dedicated readers rely on electronic ink technology, which comes close to the clarity of print, and are continuously connected to 3G networks so new books can be purchased and downloaded.

dedicated e-book reader
a single-purpose device with a proprietary operating system that can download from the Web and read proprietary formatted files created for that device

General-purpose Internet device readers like iPhones and BlackBerrys, and their associated reader apps, are a major comptetitor of dedicated readers. iPhone has an estimated 3.5 million e-book app users, and after games (20% of apps), e-book apps are the second largest category of apps (14%). There are about 10,000 e-book apps in the iTunes Store, over 90% of which are free. By 2009, Apple had sold 16 million iPod Touch devices and over 17 million iPhones. These provide a very large useful platform for e-books.

print-on-demand book
custom-published book

Print-on-demand books are less well known, but arguably are one of the largest form of electronic publishing. Sometimes called "custom publishing," print-on-demand books are usually professional or educational titles that are stored on mainframe storage devices ready for printing in small print runs on demand. For instance, most college publishers have a "custom book" program that allows professors to put together digitally stored chapters from many different books, along with articles from scholarly journals, and to publish a small print run of, say, 400 books for a single class. Generally, these books are no less costly to produce or purchase, but they have the advantage of flexible content that can be changed to meet the specific needs of users. "Print on demand" books is also a euphemism for vanity press books, or self-published books on the Internet. There is a lively market for self-published books on the Internet, although it is difficult to identify the precise size of this market, or who is paying the money for publishing—the writer or the reader.

Book Audience Size and Growth

In 2009, consumers will spend about $25 billion for the purchase of 3.2 billion books: $13 billion on consumer trade books, and $12 billion for professional, scholarly, and higher education textbooks (AAP, 2009). Americans in fact read 10 books per year per person, and many more for people over 17. In a recession when not down much is actually up, the book industry is holding very steady, much better than industrials, consumer products, and of course financials, which tanked, and a little better than the hi-tech Silicon Valley firms. However, book readership is flat, with young people reading fewer books than in the past while an expanding elderly population reads more than in the past.

Publishing the same number of titles and raising prices, publishers have kept revenues about even with inflation. Unlike newspapers, the number of book readers has been constant and is anchored in the large, over-40-years-of-age demographic. Per capita spending for trade books was about $106 in 2009, higher than video games ($44), and in-theater movies and other box office events ($44). In other words, books are a substantial element in the consumer's time and revenue content budgets, and for professional and educational titles, book publishing is growing more than twice as fast as the general U.S. economy (U.S. Census Bureau, 2009).

Unlike reading newspapers, reading books on the Internet (or any electronic device) is not a popular activity. Only 3% of Internet users report reading books online although this number is expected to double by 2010 as dedicated readers sales grow, and Google Books Project comes online. (eMarketer, 2008). Online e-book sales—both reading online and downloading e-books for offline reading—generated over $100 million in 2009. This means that, currently, e-books of any kind are a tiny share of the $25 billion annual consumption of books—less than 1 percent! E-book sales are nevertheless the fastest growing delivery platform for text content: 45% annual growth in revenues since 2004, and 50% annual increases going forward to 2013. Buying physical books online is one of the most popular activities of Internet users. The huge online audience for published books has had a significant impact on the book distribution and sales business, and represents an extraordinary opportunity to introduce new electronic editions of books in the future. It raises a few questions: Will people pay for e-books, and how much will e-book sales grow? Potentially, the market for online e-books could become large if consumers were willing to read electronic editions of books.

Figure 10.9 describes the estimated future growth of e-book sales on the Web. There is no single catalog of e-books, and therefore it is difficult to estimate the total number of new e-book titles each year. However, it is likely that between 2,000 and 3,000 new commercial e-book titles will be published in 2009, not counting several thousand self-published e-books, and not counting Google book and library projects.

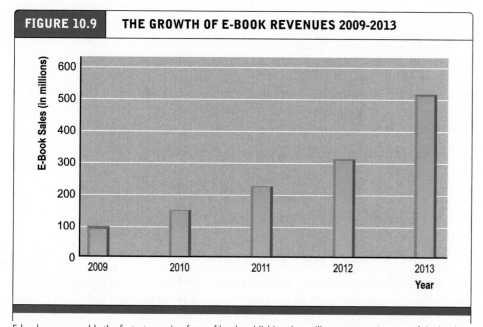

FIGURE 10.9 | **THE GROWTH OF E-BOOK REVENUES 2009-2013**

E-books are arguably the fastest growing form of book publishing, but still represent a tiny part of the book publishing industry.

SOURCE: Based on data from Bookseller.com, 2009; authors' estimates.

Content: Advantages and Disadvantages of E-books

Stephen Riggio, CEO of Barnes & Noble, the world's largest bookseller, when asked about the future of e-books, said, "It's a very tiny, tiny market. The book is a perfect technology. If it were invented today, it would be revolutionary. It's user-friendly; it's portable. Books are relatively inexpensive. They have value as physical objects; they last a lifetime." (Jaworowski, 2006). Nevertheless, e-books offer many advantages compared to traditional published works. Among these are:

- Reduced transaction costs for the user via instant downloads
- Increased accessibility to entire libraries from the home or office
- Searchable text
- Easy integration of e-book text with new text by cutting and pasting
- Modularization of the book's content down to the sentence and word level
- Ease in updating
- Lower production and distribution costs
- Longer lasting
- Increased opportunities for writers to publish
- Increased availability of out-of-print books and increased value of book archives
- Reduced cost of library functions, further democratizing access to books
- Reduced retail costs for the consumer
- Reduced weight for book bags

While this is a formidable list of advantages, e-books also have many disadvantages that have reduced their market acceptance. Among the most important disadvantages of e-books are:

- Require expensive and complex electronic devices to use
- Less portability than print books
- Reduced quality of on-screen print, making them more difficult to read
- Multiple competing standards and formats
- Uncertain business models
- Copyright management and royalty issues with authors

As one commentator noted, reading an e-book is just like reading a regular book except that it requires an expensive machine, it is not portable, and it is difficult to read. Worse, you need to replace batteries, and they are hard to read at the beach. However, the most recent devices from Sony and Amazon have enough battery power to read several books and are easily read at the beach (under an umbrella). Even better, the Kindle and the iPhone can download hundreds of books from the wireless Web even at the beach.

E-book Industry Revenue Models

The e-book industry is composed of intermediary retailers, traditional publishers, technology developers, and vanity presses. Some of the key players in the new e-book industry are listed in **Table 10.6**. Together, these players have pursued a wide variety of business models and developed many alliances in a collective effort to move text onto the computer screen.

TABLE 10.6	EXAMPLE E-BOOK INDUSTRY FIRMS
COMPANY	E-BOOK ACTIVITIES
Distributors	
Amazon	Largest online general retailer of physical and e-books; creator of the Kindle e-book reader
Google	Largest collection of downloadable e-books in the world
Barnesandnoble.com	General audience online retailer of books and publisher of e-books.
NetLibrary	Second largest online e-library, now owned by Online Computer Library Center (200,000 volumes)
Questia	Largest online research library and e-book site by subscription (over 1.5 million titles)
ebrary	Online research library by subscription using proprietary reader for PCs.
Fictionwise	Distributor of multi-platform e-books
Adobe eBook Store	Online sales of e-books demonstrating the Acrobat platform
Technology Developers	
Adobe Systems Inc.	Owners of Acrobat and PDF file format for e-book display on PC, CRT, and LCD screens
InterTrust Technologies	DRM software tools
Microsoft	Microsoft Reader software for e-book display on cell phones and PCs; supporter of Open eBook standard
Palm	Smartphone hardware and operating system; can be used for e-books
Sony	Manufacturer of e-book readers
MobiPocket	French company; creator of universal reader for cell phones and PCs, with DRM software for publishers; secure and encrypted books based on serial number of handheld devices
Amazon	Creator of the most popular e-book reader, the Kindle.
Apple	Creator of the most popular smartphone platform also used as a reader device.
Traditional Publishers	
Pearson PLC	Developing new models of online educational e-books
Thomson Learning	Educational publisher that plans to derive 50% of its revenue from e-materials by 2010
Random House	Largest trade book publisher; has developed a separate division to develop e-book titles
CourseSmart	Consortium of the six largest textbook publishers offering thousands of e-textbooks to college students at half price
Vanity e-Presses (on-demand publishers)	
Xlibris (Random House)	Self-publishing online
Ebooks.com	Online sales and publishing
Authorhouse	Self-publishing online

In the traditional commercial book business model, publishers pay authors advances against earnings to write books. Publishers provide editorial, marketing, and sales expertise, and then sell these works to national distributors or directly to large retail book chains. In the case of noncommercial books, authors pay so-called vanity presses to publish and sell their books, receiving very little if any editorial or marketing assistance. The development of e-books has brought about several changes in this traditional model.

The primary consumer e-book revenue model is pay-for-download, a model that involves traditional publishers and authors creating electronic editions of books, and publishers and distributors selling these works in their entirety through new online bookstore intermediaries such as Barnesandnoble.com and Amazon. E-books have not changed the traditional revenue model significantly. In general, publishers have not begun to sell e-books directly to the online audience simply because they do not have the experience or expertise to do so although in the future they could. Barnesandnoble.com is a special case. It occasionally acts as a publisher by commissioning new e-works; at the same time it is a retailer of those e-works.

A second e-book revenue model involves the licensing of entire e-libraries of content. This market involves major institutional customers like public and academic libraries, and corporate libraries. Licensing is similar to a subscription model; users pay either a monthly subscription fee or a flat fee for annual access to hundreds of titles. The licensing model is exemplified by NetLibrary. NetLibrary was the first large-scale experiment that involved the licensing of entire electronic libraries to universities and colleges. Many public libraries have begun to reach out to their Internet-enabled users, and greatly expand their local reach by offering e-books. For instance, New York City Public Library has over 3,000 electronic titles; the King County Library in Washington has over 8,500 online titles.

A third business model exemplified by Google is an advertising-supported model where the distributor (Google) arranges with publishers for the rights to display a book, and then shares revenue with the publishers (about 70%) generated by ads placed on book pages.

Convergence

The publishing industry is making very uneven progress toward media convergence in terms of technology platform, content, and industry structure. In the past, progress was slowed by poor business models and lack of financial resources. Today, it is slowed by greed and competition among technology firms, each of which is seeking to develop a proprietary solution to the problem of getting books online with a viable business model.

Technology One would think that it would be a simple matter to merge the world of text and books with that of the Internet and the Web, which originally were both text-based media. However, four technology-based difficulties have slowed this aspect of convergence: poor computer screen resolution, the lack of portable reader devices that can compete with the portability of the traditional book, the absence of a powerful DRM technology that can protect the copyrights of digital works, and the lack of standards to define cross-platform e-books.

One solution for the portability of e-books are smartphones like the iPhone and BlackBerry. However, the screens on current smart phones and handheld computers are still too small for comfortable text reading. The printed page has a resolution of 1,200 dots per inch compared to computer displays with resolutions of about 72 to 96 dots per inch. Display of text on standard PC screens also produces eye-strain because of low resolution. Microsoft's ClearType and Adobe's CoolType represent two attempts to remedy this issue. Both are **sub-pixel display technologies** that enhance resolution by dividing the screen into sub-pixels and filling in sub-pixels with grey color to form a more uniform image of each letter. Horizontal resolution is increased by about 30% over traditional display software. ClearType and CoolType can be downloaded for free from Microsoft and Adobe Web sites. In 2009, dedicated e-book readers like Kindle and IREX use electronic ink technology, which approaches print quality and uses far less energy than an LCD screen. Electronic ink looks like paper in appearance but is in fact an ultra-thin plastic film that encapsulates electronically charged particles that change from black to white in response to electronic signals. Electronic Ink Displays (EPDs) give the viewer the experience of reading from paper, while having the power of updatable information. EPDs have very low power consumption, are viewable in sunlight, and are very rugged (they don't break on dropping).

As noted previously, several technology firms have developed **digital rights management (DRM)**, server software that helps prevent illegal distribution of paid content over the Web. Adobe Acrobat comes with limited DRM software that can control printing and copying of downloaded matter. Intertrust is another industry leader in this field. Hackers can break most of these DRM technologies, however, and therefore, many publishing firms have been reluctant to publish works on the Web. MobiPocket has developed DRM software that encrypts content and provides a separate key for each work purchased that is based on the serial number of the PDA. This means the content can be played on only that device, it may not be copied for use on other devices, and it may be restricted in terms of the number of playbacks permitted (Mobipocket.com, 2007).

Table 10.7 describes the current leading standards for e-books. The most widely adopted standard is the Adobe Acrobat PDF file format. Tens of millions of computer users have downloaded this file-formatting software. It preserves fonts, formatting, and graphics information and can be used on almost any computer including Macintosh, Unix-based, and PCs. Open eBook (OEB) is an emerging industry-formatting standard that is supported by publishers and software firms such as Microsoft. OEB provides a specification for representing the content of e-books, and is based on HTML and XML, making it universal across all platforms and types of screens. Currently, OEB supports only minimal formatting and is best for simple text, not complex graphics combined with text.

Online Information Exchange (ONIX) is an industry standard for transmitting information about books, or "meta data." For instance, a book jacket may contain review comments, a description of contents, a picture of the author, and an author biography. Currently, there is no way to communicate this information electronically from the publisher to the online bookstore that wants to display this meta

sub-pixel display technologies
technologies that help enhance resolution of e-book reader display screens

digital rights management (DRM) software
server software that helps prevent illegal distribution of paid content over the Web

TABLE 10.7	STANDARDS FOR E-BOOKS
E-BOOK STANDARD/SOFTWARE	**DESCRIPTION**
Screen Display	
Microsoft Reader Clear-Type	Free software for improving LCD text display through sub-pixel rendering on Microsoft CE PDA devices.
Adobe CoolType	Free software for improving LCD text display through sub-pixel rendering on PDAs.
E-Ink	Electronic ink display for LCDs.
Formats	
Open eBook (OEB and OEB.LIT)	Microsoft-supported industry group to define e-book formatting. OEB.LIT adds DRM capabilities.
Adobe Portable Document Format (PDF)	Adobe's free viewer software for PC and PDA screen display of rich text, complex fonts, and formatting. Works best on PC screens. New versions contain DRM capabilities.
TK3 (NightKitchen)	CRT and LCD display of text, images, sounds, and video.
MobiPocket	Proprietary format that plays on all handheld devices.
Book Industry Product Description	
ONIX	Universal, international industry standard for describing book products and contents based on XML.

data on a Web page. ONIX is an XML-based set of approximately 200 tags (e.g., < PublisherName > Scribner's < /PublisherName >) that can easily be read and communicated to book distributors and retailers (Editeur.org, 2007; Book Industry Study Group, 2007).

Content E-books today have made little progress toward content convergence. Most e-books contain only text and graphics, and often are simply PDF versions of files sent to the printers to run the physical presses. E-books can be placed along a continuum of transformation (and cost). E-books currently are in the media integration stage where text is being reformatted for electronic display. This is a low-cost beginning, allowing publishers to focus their attention and budgets on building their online distribution networks. However, some firms are beginning to experiment with more interactive experiences that will transform e-books into multimedia events containing lectures, speeches, interviews with the authors, online polls and quizzes, online updates of content, and videos to support the experience (see *Insight on Society: The Future of Books*).

Industry Structure Unlike the recorded music industry, the book industry has not been transformed by the Internet. However, it is being challenged by

INSIGHT ON SOCIETY

THE FUTURE OF BOOKS

What do you think of when you think about what a "book" is, or looks like? Chances are you still think of the traditional "book," printed on paper, and bound with a hard or soft cover, with a finite beginning, middle, and end. When most people think of an e-book, they think of a traditional book converted into a page-turner. All e-book readers today are based on the metaphor of "the page." However, in the near future, traditional notions about what constitutes a "book" will change, and "books" will assume a variety of different forms that integrate audio and video with text. The result will not be a "book" in the traditional sense. Perhaps it will be called a "learning experience" or just an "experience." Instead of asking your friends if they've read a book, you'll ask instead "Have you experienced this?"

For instance, you've read in this chapter about different types of e-books. You can read a book on a Kindle, IRex, Sony Reader, on an iPhone, or an iPod. However, these are often traditional books just being delivered on a new format. Taking e-books one step further, say out to 2014, they most likely will evolve into much richer learning environments with substantial audio, video, and community participation than is true of today's text-only e-books. You can see the potential future of the e-book by visiting the Wall Street Journal Web site. There you will find one of the world's most successful business publications integrating text with video, reporter blogs, user commentary, up-to-the-minute reporting, interviews, and podcasts. Social networking has also been added to enable the creation of financial communities of practice. If newspapers can look like this, why can't e-books?

But what about the form of the book itself? Why, for instance, should a book have just a single author or a few authors? Why should books be read alone? Sagas—the ancient lengthy stories of an entire people shared through an oral tradition— had multiple authors. Sagas were read and repeated in groups. It is possible on the Internet to have a community of readers contribute to both the authorship of the online e-book and the experience of reading the book. You can call it "social publishing" or "social writing." Wikipedia, for instance, is a constantly updated online "e-book" encyclopedia written by thousands of contributors. Wikibooks, its less well-known cousin, brings the wiki movement to the creation of textbooks. David Carr, a journalist for the *New York Times,* and Simon and Schuster, have collaborated to create NightoftheGun.com, a Web site that is part and parcel of Carr's memoir, *The Night of the Gun.* When Carr created his work, he developed a database of content, including hundreds of hours of recorded interviews, documents, reports, letters, legal communications, photos, and keepsakes. The Web site offers a fully immersive multimedia experience where the story is in the hands of the reader.

Unigo.com offers another take on the future of "books" by creating online experiences that involve text and media. If you're like most college students, when you began to think about applying to college, probably one of the first places you turned to for information was a traditional college guide book, like those published by *The Princeton Review,* Peterson's Fiske, or *U.S. News and World Report,* or perhaps "The Insider's Guide to Colleges" by the staff of the *Yale Daily News.* But even books hundreds of pages long are limited in terms of the volume and type of information they can provide

(continued)

about the thousands of different colleges across the country. For Jordan Goldman, a 26-year-old recent Wesleyan graduate, this was a problem looking for a solution; and his solution is one that may threaten the publishing industry's stranglehold on the delivery of college information via traditionally published books.

What Goldman envisioned, and launched in September 2008, with the backing of Frank Sica, a former president of Soros Private Funds Management, is Unigo.com, a free, advertising-supported site that offers a student-generated guide to North American colleges. The site features brief editorial overviews of each of the colleges featured, but the real meat is furnished by students in the form of responses to essay-based questionnaires, photos, videos, and uploaded writing samples. When launched, over 30,000 individual bits of content had been submitted. Today, 15,000 students have contributed profiles for 250 colleges, which include text and video. Fifteen editors monitor the quality of the content submitted. At Davidson College, for example, about 230 current students (1/8th of the student body) submitted photos, reviews, and video. As one person noted, its one thing to read in a guidebook that a school sits on a lake, and another to look at a video and see students hanging out in beautiful surroundings.

Every student who joins Unigo has a user profile, and users can search the site for material submitted by those who they believe might be similar to themselves. For instance, a user can search for reviews of Harvard by English majors, and contact students who submitted material with follow-up questions. Users can also search for schools by size, setting, region, selectivity, and tuition. And branching into the social network space, the My Unigo section of the site allows users to organize all of the site's content according to their personal interests, and also add their own content.

As Goldman notes: "That the best resource for a four-year, $200,000 decision are these books—with no photos, no videos, no interactivity, only three-to-five pages per school on average, fully updated usually once every several years—just doesn't make the grade." For many students and parents, spending a few hours on Unigo's site can be just as valuable as spending $3,000 to $5,000 dollars on a college counselor who provides advice on what colleges would be good for you. Goldman and Unigo's financial backers think their "grassroots" movement to wrest control over the dissemination of information about colleges from traditional publishers will revolutionize the way students decide about which school to attend.

As we see throughout this chapter, the Internet is changing the consumer's sense of entertainment and even education. Heightened expectations for participation, involvement, engagement, and self-control are driving consumers toward Web sites and content providers that can provide these kinds of experiences, creating new opportunities for innovative publishers.

■■■ **SOURCES:** "Rethinking College Prep Costs in Tough Times," by Alina Tugend, *New York Times*, February 27, 2009; "Unigo.com Gives Everyone a Say About College Picks," by Walter Mossberg, *Wall Street Journal*, February 19, 2009; "The Unigo Blog," Unigoblog.wordpress.com, September 24, 2008; "About This Site," Nightofthegun.com, September 24, 2008; "The Tell- All Campus Tour," by Jonathan Dee, *New York Times*, September 21, 2008; "Envisioning the Next Chapter for Electronic Books," by Brad Stone, *New York Times*, September 7, 2007; "An Entire Bookshelf, in Your Hands," by Peter Wayner, *New York Times*, August 9, 2007.

Google and Microsoft, who both want to index copyrighted books and make portions ("snippets" determined by Google) available online; by college students, their parents, and Congress, who want lower prices for textbooks; by very large distributors like Barnes & Noble, who want to move into actual publishing with very low-cost books; to a lesser extent by user-generated content in the form of blogs and self-published books; and by slow growth in physical book sales. The book publishing industry and the creation, production, and distribution of e-books is still dominated by a few titans, with the level of industry concentration increasing as large media companies such as Bertelsmann (Random House), and large text publishing companies, such as Pearson, Thomson, and McGraw-Hill, absorb smaller presses. Nevertheless, the Internet has created many new opportunities for authors, publishers, distributors, and specialized book retailers. Entrepreneurial start-up firms such as NetLibrary demonstrated that a market existed for inexpensive digital libraries. Entrepreneurial online book distributors from Amazon and Barnesandnoble.com to much smaller, specialized topic, boutique online distributors have demonstrated a huge marketplace for online distribution of traditional books. Online book distributors such as Barnesandnoble.com have commissioned new e-book titles and moved into publishing. Authors have published works directly to the public without the intervention of publishers in the blogosphere, as well as through online vanity presses that charge authors for the privilege of publishing their works. The open source movement has created online encyclopedias like Wikipedia that offer incredible depth (but also occasional erroneous and misleading entries). Publishers such as Random House have simultaneously moved into direct distribution to the public of selected works (while continuing to utilize online distributors such as Amazon). Technology providers such as Adobe have begun limited distribution of e-books, and Palm has purchased the e-book assets of Peanutpress.com and begun selling e-books directly to the public. In this sense, the industry has become much more diverse than in the past, including hardware and software makers who have an interest in the success of e-books.

10.3 THE ONLINE ENTERTAINMENT INDUSTRY

The entertainment industry is generally considered to be composed of four traditional, commercial players and one new arrival: television, radio broadcasting, Hollywood films, music, and video games (the new arrival). **Figure 10.10** illustrates the estimated relative sizes of these commercial entertainment markets as of 2009. By far, the largest entertainment producer is television (broadcast, satellite, and cable), followed by film, then radio, with music and video games tied for fourth. While PC and console games have grown to be larger than film box office revenues, total Hollywood film revenues dwarf the game industry when DVD sales and rentals, licensing, and ancillary products are added.

Along with the other content industries, the entertainment segment is undergoing a transformation brought about by the Internet. Several forces are at work. Accelerated platform development such as the iPhone/iPod video and music platform, and digital cellular networks, have changed consumer preferences and increased demand for video, television, and game entertainment delivered over Internet devices whether in subscription or a la carte pay-per-view forms. Other social networking platforms are also spurring the delivery of entertainment content to desktop

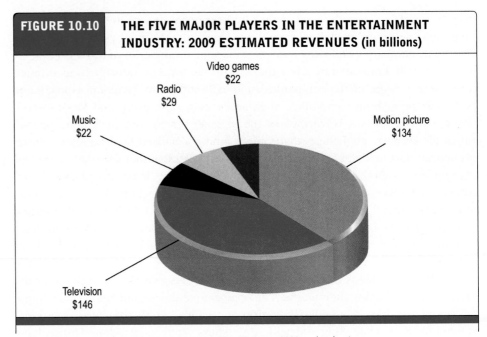

FIGURE 10.10 THE FIVE MAJOR PLAYERS IN THE ENTERTAINMENT INDUSTRY: 2009 ESTIMATED REVENUES (in billions)

Video games $22

Radio $29

Music $22

Motion picture $134

Television $146

SOURCES: Based on data from U.S. Census Bureau, 2009; NPD Group, 2009; authors' estimates.

and laptop PCs, handhelds, and phones. iTunes and other legitimate music subscription services like Rhapsody have also demonstrated a viable business model where millions of consumers are willing to pay reasonable prices for high-quality content, portability, and convenience. The growth in broadband has obviously made possible both wired and wireless delivery of all forms of entertainment over the Internet, potentially displacing cable and broadcast television networks. The development of high-quality customer experiences at online entertainment sites has in many cases eliminated the need for digital rights management restrictions. Closed platforms, like the Kindle, also work to obviate the need for DRM. Subscription services for music and video are inherently protected from copyright protection because the content is never downloaded to a PC (similar to cable TV). All of these forces have combined in 2009 to bring about a transformation in the entertainment industries.

The ideal Internet content e-commerce world would allow consumers to watch any movie, listen to any music, watch any TV show, and play any game, when they wanted, where they wanted, and using whatever Internet device was convenient. Consumers would be billed monthly for these services by a single provider of Internet service. This idealized version of a convergent media world is many years away. But clearly this is the direction of the Internet-enabled entertainment industry in 2009.

When we think of the producers of entertainment in the offline world, we tend to think about television networks such as ABC, NBC, or CBS; Hollywood film studios such as MGM, Disney, Paramount, and Twentieth Century Fox; and music labels such as Sony BMG, Atlantic Records, Columbia Records, and Warner Records. Interestingly, none of these international brand names have a significant entertainment presence on the Internet. Although traditional forms of entertainment such as television shows and Hollywood movies are just now appearing on the Web, neither the television nor film industries have built an industry-wide delivery system. Instead, they are building alliances with portals like Yahoo, Google, AOL, and MSN, and a new player in media distribution, Apple Computer.

While industry titans waver, online consumers are redefining and considerably broadening the concept of entertainment. We refer to this development as "non-traditional" entertainment or what most refer to as user-generated content, which also have entertainment value including user videos uploaded to YouTube, photos uploaded to Photobucket and shared, as well as blogs. User-generated content reflects some of the same shifts in consumer preferences experienced by traditional media: people want to participate in the creation and distribution of content.

ONLINE ENTERTAINMENT AUDIENCE SIZE AND GROWTH

Measuring the size and growth of the Internet content audience is far less precise than measuring a television audience simply because there is no audience measurement service for the Internet. Estimates of audience size are typically based on responses to surveys rather than actual consumer behavior.

Online Traditional Entertainment

Recognizing the difficulties of measuring an Internet audience, let's first examine the use of "traditional" entertainment content, such as films, music, sports, and games; then we will look at non-traditional online entertainment. **Figure 10.11** shows the current and projected growth for commercial online entertainment revenues for the major players: music, Internet radio, online TV, online games, and online video. Music downloads lead the list of commercial entertainment revenues in 2009, followed by online games, TV, radio, and online video.

There are some interesting changes by 2013. Music continues to be the largest form of online entertainment, but video nearly catches up, and online games expands very rapidly from their small base. Online TV and radio remain relatively smaller generators of revenue, declining in significance when compared to music and video. On a media utilization basis, however, more than 49 million people listen to Internet radio in 2009, and if this audience could be monetized, revenues would become much larger than reported here (Audio4cast, 2009).

User-Generated Content: Where Does It Fit?

Whereas traditional commercial entertainment is produced by professional entertainers and producers, user-generated entertainment involves all those other activities that people voluntarily engage in to have fun, such as shooting videos, taking pictures, recording music and sharing it, and writing blogs. We have extensively documented the user-generated phenomenon in previous chapters. The question for this chapter is, "How does this content fit into the overall entertainment picture?"

The answer appears to be that user-generated content is both a substitute as well as a complement to traditional commercial entertainment. As people spend more time consuming user-generated content, they may spend less time consuming commercial content. As advertising revenues grow on social networks and

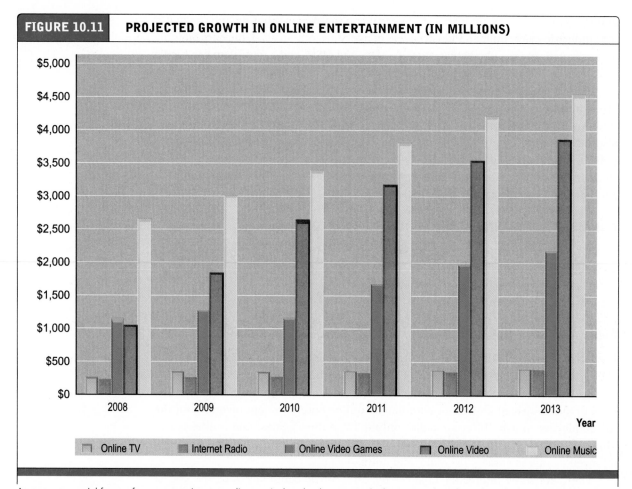

| FIGURE 10.11 | PROJECTED GROWTH IN ONLINE ENTERTAINMENT (IN MILLIONS) |

Legend: Online TV, Internet Radio, Online Video Games, Online Video, Online Music

Year: 2008, 2009, 2010, 2011, 2012, 2013

Among commercial forms of mass entertainment, online music downloads engages the largest number of people and generates the largest revenues on the Web in 2009. However, online video and games will grow dramatically in the next four years, with video approaching music in revenues.

SOURCES: Based on data from eMarketer, Inc., 2009e; Veronis Suhler Stevenson, 2009; author's estimates.

YouTube in order to capture an audience of nearly 90 million people, advertising revenues for commercial media may not grow as fast as they might have otherwise. On the other hand, box office and DVD video sales have not declined in the presence of alternative video formats. Instead people just watched more video of all kinds.

Figure 10.12 characterizes different types of Web entertainment experiences along two dimensions: user focus and user control. Sites that offer nontraditional user-generated forms of entertainment are unique not only because they afford access to large digital archives, promote fine-grained searching, and enable users to create their own archives, but also because they permit users high levels of control over both the program content and the program focus. For example, a social network site like MySpace offers user-generated content that is viewed by others as

FIGURE 10.12 **USER ROLE IN ENTERTAINMENT**

USER CONTROL

	HIGH	LOW
HIGH	Internet programming Music download networks Auction sites	Reality TV shows TV game shows
LOW	Traditional fan clubs MTV music shows	Traditional media programming

USER FOCUS

Popular Internet entertainment sites offer users high levels of control and user focus. Traditional media programming content is determined by programmers and has a celebrity focus. Traditional media has moved to become more participatory and more user-focused, but cannot match Internet levels of interactivity and user contribution to content.

"entertaining." The hypothesis is that sites that offer both high user focus and high user control will have the fastest rates of growth. MySpace is illustrative of this hypothesis. MySpace started out as a independent, music-oriented social networking site where new bands not signed by major record labels could find new listeners, and where people could form networks of friends by creating their own home pages and displaying personal comments, text, photos, and music. By giving users control over their environment and focusing the site on users, the site routinely attracts over 60 million visitors a month in 2009.

CONTENT

The Internet has greatly changed the packaging, distribution, marketing, and sale of traditional entertainment content, with the largest impacts on music. Music may be a precursor to similar changes in the film and television segments. In the case of music, the package is being transformed from a traditional CD album containing 12 to 15 songs, to the download of single songs a la carte. In other words, the impact of the Internet has been to unbundle the traditional music package, permitting customers to buy what they want. The distribution is changing from retail stores selling physical product, to Internet delivery and playback on a wide variety of digital devices from iPods, to PCs, to PDAs. Finally, the marketing and sales have changed as well. New groups have their own Web sites, and can find their own niche audiences on MySpace and other sites, to some extent democratizing the process of establishing a music brand. Established groups can bypass traditional marketing and sales organizations by creating their own Web distribution network. Not many established groups have gone this route entirely, but most such groups use the Web to market themselves.

ONLINE ENTERTAINMENT INDUSTRY REVENUE MODELS

Online entertainment sites have adopted many of the same revenue models as depicted previously in Table 10.3: marketing, advertising, pay-per-view, subscription, value-added, and mixed. Television networks and Hollywood studios are beginning to sell episodes on a pay-per-view basis on iTunes, and entire series online on their own corporate sites.

CONVERGENCE

While there is clearly a movement toward convergence in technology platform, content, and industry structure, this movement has been slow because of both technological and market institutional forces.

Technology In musical entertainment, the technology platform has converged as PCs and handheld devices such as Apple's iPod and iPhone become music listening stations playing MP3 tracks, and general-purpose computing and communication devices. The PC has also become a game station, capable of playing highly interactive rich media games with the same alacrity as dedicated game stations. In turn, many dedicated game stations such as Microsoft's Xbox 360 and Sony's PlayStation Portable (PSP) can be connected to the Web for interactive play and downloading new game software.

For movies and television, technology convergence has been hampered by the unwillingness of the movie industry to make its products available on a wide range of Internet-enabled devices, in large part because of concerns over piracy. Illegal downloading of movies has grown almost as fast as illegal music downloads, although because of the size of movie downloads, and the movie industry's efforts to close down illegal movie-sharing sites, illegal video downloads do not approach the volume of illegal musical downloads. The industry estimates it is losing $3 billion in sales a year from Internet piracy, and $4 billion a year from counterfeit DVDs (out of a total industry revenue of $80 billion in 2009).

While Hollywood and New York film and television network producers are obviously concerned about increasing piracy and the lack of Internet security, they have made several important moves towards legitimate Internet distribution either through downloads from movie sites they control or through alliances with other platform owners like Apple (iTunes Store). There are several independent and industry-sponsored ventures: Hulu, MovieFlix, Movies.com, and Spike.com. MovieFlix offers downloads of out-of-date and even out-of-copyright movies, some for free. It has alliances with Yahoo and other online portal movie distributors. Movies.com is sponsored by Disney and was intended to distribute films from Disney, Miramax, and Twentieth Century Fox using either high-speed Internet or digital cable systems. But these plans never materialized, and today Movies.com only offers trailers, theater reservation information, and general information service. Spike.com (formerly iFilm) is primarily a movie portal site with general information, that intended to provide legal movie downloads, but was purchased by Viacom and is now part of the MTV network where it only provides short film clips for advertisers. The only industry-supported sites currently offering Internet downloads of contemporary feature-length films are Movielink (a joint venture of MGM, Paramount Pictures, Sony Pictures, Universal, and Warner Bros.), CinemaNow, and Hulu. Using a DRM envelope, users can download movies of about 500 megabytes in size for $1.99 to $4.99 per film. The consumer has 30 days to watch the movie, and once activated, 24 hours to view the movie on their PCs. After these time limits, the movie cannot be played. You can also rent movies for as low as 99 cents. CinemaNow holds the Internet distribution rights to the most extensive and comprehensive library of content available on demand via the public Internet and private broadband networks. The CinemaNow library contains approximately 7,500 feature-length films, shorts, music concerts, and television programs from more than 250 film production studios. While these industry consortia may develop significant delivery capabilities, it is also the case that if millions of Americans decide to download movies over the Internet on a Saturday night, more than 50% of the Internet's capacity could be consumed, leading to significant brownouts and server outages in local areas. By 2009, the movie and television studios have began licensing some of their content to Amazon in a move to parry Apple's growing dominance in video and TV streaming and downloads. Amazon currently has several thousand movies and television episodes for sale.

Perhaps the largest movie industry-sponsored, Internet success story is Hulu.com. Hulu is a joint venture of NBC Universal Films, Disney, News Corp, and private investors. Hulu offers free streaming TV shows, trailers, and older movies for free using an advertiser-supported model. Hulu is often among the top 10 destination sites on the Internet.

The standards issue has largely been solved by movie sites, which typically use the Flash media player found in all current browsers.

Content In a convergent world, the creation, production, and distribution of entertainment content would be entirely digital, with few, if any, analog devices or physical products and their physical distribution channels. The Internet increasingly will come into direct competition with cable and satellite distribution channels. However, these physical and analog distribution channels are under increasing challenge from digital and Internet-based distribution. Hence, the content is moving off physical delivery platforms and toward Internet delivery platforms under user control.

In the areas of content creation and production, there has been significant progress for digital tools. Hollywood filmmakers are increasingly using digital cameras for selected movie scenes, and digital effects have come to play a larger role in many movies. Much of the editing of film is currently performed on digital editing computer workstations before the images are returned to analog 35mm film for distribution to theaters. Independent and low-budget filmmakers are creating feature-length films on digital cameras, editing in digital environments, and distributing directly on the Web to niche audiences at independent film sites. In television, digital cameras are now typical while editing and production is almost entirely digital. Likewise, in music, recording is performed on digital devices and mixed using digital mixers before production of digital CDs. Independent bands move their music directly from digital mixers to the Internet, skipping the CD production stage entirely. Composers, arrangers, and music educators have widely adopted two digital notation programs, Finale and Sibelius, to create music scores.

Industry Structure The existing industry value chain is highly inefficient and fractured. For the entertainment industry to move aggressively onto the Web there needs to be a reorganization of the value chain either through corporate mergers, or strategic alliances, or both. In the process of reorganization, traditional distributors (like cable TV and broadcast television) most likely will experience severe disruptions to their business models as the Internet replaces them as a distribution media.

Figure 10.13 illustrates the existing players and industry value chain and three alternative arrangements. The entertainment industry has never been a neat and tidy industry to describe. There are many players and forces—including government regulators and courts—that shape the industry. In the existing model, creators of entertainment such as music labels or television producers sell to distributors, who in turn sell to local retail stores or local television stations, who then sell or rent to consumers. In the film industry, court decisions in the 1930s and 1940s forced production studios to give up ownership of local theaters on antitrust grounds, fearing the large Hollywood production studios would monopolize the film industry. One possible alternative to this fractionated industry is the *content owner direct model*. The Internet offers entertainment content producers (the music labels, Hollywood studios, and television content

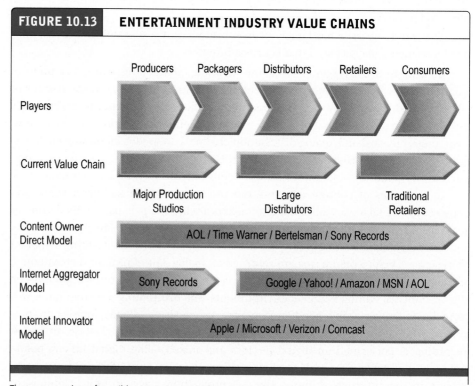

There are a variety of possible entertainment industry value chains in the near-term future.

producers) the opportunity to dominate the industry value chain by eliminating the distributors and retailers and selling directly to the consumer. This has not yet been a successful model to date because the content producers know so little about the Internet and have not been successful on the Internet. A second possibility is the *aggregator model*. In this model, Web-based intermediaries such as Yahoo, Google, Amazon, and MSN that aggregate large audiences enter into strategic alliances with content owners to provide content to the aggregators. Yahoo fits into this model because it has begun hiring its own news reporters, and funding production of independent films that it can distribute on its portal.

A third possible model is the *Internet innovator model* in which successful Internet technology companies that develop the technology platforms (such as Apple and Microsoft, as well as Internet communications platform providers like Verizon and Comcast Cable) move back into the value chain and begin creating their own content for exclusive distribution on their proprietary platform or channels. Good examples are Microsoft's Xbox video game platform, Yahoo's move into content creation in 2009, Apple's iTunes Store, and Verizon's premium service package for DSL broadband.

Insight on Technology: Hollywood Meets the Internet: Round 2 describes how Hollywood studios are struggling with the issues presented by the Internet.

INSIGHT ON TECHNOLOGY

HOLLYWOOD MEETS THE INTERNET: ROUND 2

In tough times, real people go to the movies. All things considered, 2008 was a "not as bad at it could be" year for the motion picture industry. Despite the worst recession since the 1930s, box office receipts in the United States reached $9.79 billion, up 2%. Worldwide box office receipts were $28 billion, up 5%. Overall, there are 64,000 movie screens in the United States, of which 64% have switched to digital (they receive and display movies as digital files as opposed to multiple 35mm cans). Hollywood created 610 movies in 2008, also up 2% over the previous year. The largest-grossing movie in 2008 was *The Dark Knight*, which grossed $1 billion in global box office, and another $230 million in DVD sales so far. Not bad for a movie that cost $185 million to make! If only all movies could produce results like that, Hollywood would be golden.

At the DVD store, in contrast, total sales and rentals were off—down 5% from the previous year to $22 billion (in 2007, they were down 3%). DVD sales started slipping in 2006. This is important because Hollywood makes a huge profit on DVD sales, about $17.62 per DVD, and its sells about 17 billion units a year, producing about $14.5 billion in revenues in the United States alone. Hollywood makes 50% more off from its DVDs than it does from the box office. Overall, movie industry total revenues have been flat, about $60 billion in the United States. In addition to the recession, this is also due in part to slow or static growth in its products, with prices more or less stable, while the costs of producing the average Hollywood film have skyrocketed to about $120 million per title on average.

There are several reasons for the fall off in DVD sales, but chief among them are piracy of DVD products, declining prices in other distribution channels (pay-per-view and cable television), and alternative forms of movie entertainment available on the Internet. Movie pirates have improved their taste in stolen product and prefer to steal production-quality DVDs before the movies are introduced to the box office, and then put them on any of several BitTorrent networks where they can be shared. For example, *X-Men Origins: Wolverine*, the Marvel Comics-based American superhero film was released worldwide on May 1, 2009. Unfortunately, pirates obtained an unfinished production-quality DVD copy of the movie and by March 31, 2009, the movie had been downloaded more than a million times according to TorrentFreak, a blog devoted to BitTorrent file sharing. At least 1 million fewer people paid at the box office. Arguably, many millions of DVDs of *Wolverine* will not be sold as a result. All told, the last survey of movie piracy claimed the loss to Hollywood of piracy worldwide is about $5 billion annually.

Unlike the music industry, which up until recently focused primarily on an aggressive legal assault on pirates with some success, the movie industry has taken both defensive and offensive measures. Hollywood continues to support DRM and other strategies to prevent piracy. In August 2009, the Motion Picture Association of America (MPAA) won an injunction against RealNetwork's sale of RealDVD, a software program that allowed users to remove the DRM protection of Hollywood DVDs and store the files on their hard drives (or anywhere). MPAA argued this was a violation of the "anti-circumvention"

(continued)

provisions of the Digital Millenium Copyright Act (DMCA). These provisions make it illegal to defeat the DRM protections placed on digital products. The MPAA has generally won lawsuits involving the protection of DRM software used to protect DVDs.

But the motion picture industry has also taken a number of steps to develop online delivery mechanisms and new innovative products that customers hopefully will want to buy. The industry has improved the DVD product by introducing Blu-Ray technology, improving the quality of the picture. It has added interactivity to Blu-Ray discs that allow people to chat on the Internet as they watch the same movie. Called BD-Live, it's part movie, part game, and part social network (but it does require both parties to be connected to the Web as they watch). Other innovations include permitting iTunes to download movies to customers' iPhones, in-store kiosks that offer a dozen titles on physical DVDs, and other kiosks offering thousands of titles that are burned to a disc while you wait and are stored digitally in the kiosks. Hollywood is also planning for "cloud movies," movies that you purchase or subscribe to and which are stored on the Internet where you can access them from any device of your choice, at anytime.

Perhaps the most forward-thinking move on the part of Hollywood has been its determination to take control of the Internet digital distribution channel by setting up its own Web sites such as Hulu, CinemaNow, and Movelink (in partnership with Blockbuster). Rather than have YouTube (Google) distribute their movies, Hollywood uses these and other sites to deliver movies to the customer, controlling the price, the form of distribution (download versus streaming) selection, and total revenue stream. Warner has decided to go into retail distribution of its library of older films by establishing its own streaming service. YouTube, Amazon, and Apple have come around to making deals with Hollywood on all these matters in order to gain access to legitimate, high-quality content that their customers wants. In 2009, YouTube, seeking high-quality videos that advertisers would not feel embarrassed about, cut a deal with MGM to distribute MGM's backlist (old films) and full-length episodes of *Star Trek*.

The result is that Hollywood is getting its products to the public, including using the Internet, at a "reasonable" price and in a customer-friendly environment, which demands movies that can be played anytime, on a variety of devices, on demand. Moreover, the Internet culture is changing, becoming more mature about paying for content. Maybe it's a result of the "graying" of America, or an acceptance by all demographic groups on the Web that paying a reasonable fee for a high-quality content experience is "worth it." The alternative (piracy) is costly and often does not result in a great experience. There are search costs to find the movie you want, wait costs for the download, and uncertainty about quality.

SOURCES: "Theatrical Market Statistics," Motion Picture Association of America, MPAA.org, 2009; "Hollywood Wins Key Round Against RealNetworks' RealDVD," by Stephen Wildstrom, BusinessWeek.com, August 11, 2009; "Warner Brothers Launches On Demand DVD Sales," by Thomas Arnold, *USAToday*, July 17, 2009; "In Digital Age Can Movie Piracy Be Stopped?" by Lisa France, CNN.com, May 2, 2009; "Fox's New Plan to Spur DVD Sales: Rip Out the Extras from Rentals," by M.G. Siegler, Digitalventurebeat.com, March 5, 2009; "The Way We'll Watch," by Sarah McBride, *Wall Street Journal*, December 8, 2008; "New Amazon Service Streams TV Shows and Films to PCs," by Walter Mossberg, *Wall Street Journal*, September 11, 2008.

10.4 CASE STUDY

Google and YouTube Together:
Pass the Popcorn While This Ad Plays

Ever since Google bought YouTube in November 2006, some have wondered just exactly how Google was going to make the $1.65 billion purchase price worthwhile. Wall Street, on the other hand, had no doubts that Google would make a killing, and Google's stock price quickly shot up from the unprecedented $500 level for most of 2007 to the super-unprecedented level of $700 in November 2007. This gave Google a price/earnings ratio of 49, just shy of the moon, and a market capitalization of $200 billion, which was over 10 times the market capitalization of General Motors at the time, the largest car company on earth. In 2008, with the world in a recession, advertising in general stalling, and Internet advertising growing more slowly, Google's stock dropped 70% to the $250 range. In 2009, as economic conditions slowly brighten, Google's stock has made a comeback, and is selling at about $430 with a price earnings ratio of 30, up considerably from its lowest levels on the strength of search engine advertising. YouTube has not helped Google's stock price because analysts believe it actually lost $250 million in 2008. Why did the stock market value the Google/YouTube purchase so fondly at first, and then have second thoughts? What are the skeptics saying? Are they just jealous of Google's evident success in purchasing the largest group of eyeballs on the Web, namely, YouTube's audience of 120 million unique visitors?

The answer from Google is that it plans to turn the Web's largest repository of video, and the largest video audience share, into the next big, killer app for advertising, namely, the largest advertising platform in history. Bigger than search, and bigger than television. What it tells investors is that this huge audience can be "monetized" by displaying ads alongside the videos, and displaying banners on opening screens.

Just how much video does YouTube have? This has turned into an amateur sport and estimates vary, but the most recent estimates are that YouTube has somewhere between 84 million and 142 million videos stored on up to or about 1 petabyte of hard drives around the world, representing about 100 billion minutes of video. Analysts estimate that in 2009, YouTube will serve around 95 billion videos streams, up 66% over 2008. If only each of these would pay a penny! YouTube itself is secretive about the number of videos in part because it raises the question of "Why does it have so many videos if it can't make enough money to pay the rent?" And "How can YouTube/Google continue to pay the infrastructure costs of so many videos?"

How many people are attracted to these videos and for how long? comScore estimates that in August 2009, YouTube drew over 120 million unique visitors in the United States, with the average stay about five minutes, viewing on average two videos at a time. As of August 2009, YouTube was streaming around 10 billion video streams a month in the United States. Only 2% of these monthly viewers view daily, compared to Yahoo, for instance, where 40% of visitors visit every day. Yahoo has around 150 million unique visitors, who stay on average about one hour a visit to view all types of content (not just video), generating a whopping 37 billion pages views a month! Each page view is an advertising opportunity. Google (just the search site itself) also has about 150 million unique monthly visitors, who stay less than 24 minutes, generating 10 billion page views a month, on their way to their destination Web site. Over 30% of Google visitors visit daily. So while YouTube has grown explosively, it still has a way to go to catch Yahoo or Google and lacks the retention time (page views) and frequency of visits found at the major portals.

What YouTube needs is not just more content but quality content, content that is really interesting, keeps people on the sites, and draws millions of viewers back every day. Chances are this does not mean user-generated videos, which typically have an average audience of around 10 people, are top listed for one day, then fall into oblivion. Really popular user-generated videos or music videos launched by record label companies that get passed around the Web in a viral network may top off with 2 million viewers, but this is a rare event and usually reserved for celebrities caught in compromising situations, already popular musicians, or popular copyrighted videos illegally posted.

No, what YouTube needs is expertly crafted video that accounts for the lion's share of their visitors' attention. Where can this video be obtained? In the early years, the answer was to have unique visitors upload snippets of Hollywood movies and television shows such as *The Sopranos*, *The Colbert Report*, and Jon Stewart's *The Daily Show*. As you learned in Chapter 8, this situation caused heartburn among copyright owners such as Viacom (a media conglomerate that owns Paramount Pictures, MTV, and BET cable networks), which sued Google in 2008 for $1 billion, a fair chunk of change. The complaint alleges that "YouTube deliberately built up a library of infringing works to draw traffic to the YouTube site, enabling it to gain a commanding market share, earn significant revenues and increase its enterprise value." The lawsuit has resulted in a seemingly endless discovery process involving hundreds of thousands of documents, including a list of all the videos that YouTube's customers have viewed! Google responded that copyright law shields it from liability for clips posted by its users.

Arguably, as much as 25% of all YouTube video involves copyrighted film clips and/or copyrighted music, and possibly more than 80% of total views. How large the number really is remains unknown. But it is large enough to give skeptics of the Google/YouTube venture a reason to crow. A student Web site at Massachusetts Institute of Technology called YouTomb.mit.edu monitors about 400,000 of the most popular YouTube videos and has identified that 15,000 were removed by YouTube as copyright violations, about 3% of the most popular videos. However, this is a tiny sample of a much larger universe of purloined content.

In order to deal with the complaints of the big Hollywood studios and New York television producers, YouTube has restricted advertising to only those pages where the permission of copy right holders has been obtained. Google also developed a software program called YouTube Video Identification that is now used by 300 copyright owners to scan the YouTube video database for their own copyrighted material. These copyright owners have two choices: they can ask YouTube to take the material down, or they can place advertisements for their products right next to the illegal postings! Brilliant. In this manner, Google has reversed the opposition among copyright holders and changed them into rank opportunists. While most large-scale advertisers do not want their ads showing up next to an amateur home video, they are more than willing to place their ads next to high-quality, copyrighted material that they happen to own. Universal Pictures, and other studios, are now using YouTube to plant clips from their movies on YouTube, and seek to take advantage of YouTube's viral marketing platform. Now the copyright owners are saying, "Watch this content, pass it around, and come to our movies!"

In the last two years, under the threat of endless lawsuits for copyright infringement, and the rise of alternative video sources that have the backing of the movie and television industries such as Hulu, EpixHD, CinemaNow, Movielink, and Apple's iTunes Store, YouTube and Google have radically changed their business approach to quality video content. While still taking in millions of videos a day from amateurs, they have begun courting the likes of Hollywood and New York film and television producers. In 2008, YouTube struck deals with CBS, ESPN, HBO, Showtime, C-Span, and MGM, to obtain copyrighted content against which ads can be displayed. YouTube now emphasizes that it's a "great place for premium content." YouTube allows these heavy hitters to establish their own exclusive "channel" on YouTube where they can control the content, and then display ads against that content, sharing the revenue with YouTube. The concept of "channels" where content is reliable, supplied by the advertiser, and under their control, has greatly increased the attractiveness of YouTube as an advertising venue.

In 2009, YouTube has continued to broaden its premium content offerings. The company has cut deals with Sony, Lionsgate, the BBC, Starz, Discovery, and National Geographic to provide full-length movies and TV shows for free on YouTube. Other partners include Anime Network, Cinetic Rights Management, Current TV, Documentary Channel, FirstLook Studios, and IndieFlix. These full-length movies will all be "back list" or older movies that have gone through the traditional movie and television maturation process. For YouTube, these deals provide an opportunity to display ads during commercial breaks, and to provide visitors with a coherent, reliable entertainment menu. Insiders report that YouTube is considering charging for "premium video."

Sony is participating in part because it wants to drive traffic to its own movie site, Crackle.com. Crackle.com offers free films and TV shows and makes money from selling ads before, during, and after the video. Crackle currently has about 60 movies on its site, and will provide only 12 of these movies to YouTube. "It's all about driving traffic to Crackle," said a source close to the deal. Similarly, the other studios in the deals will send viewers to their owners' proprietary video services or split ad revenue with YouTube. In the process of striking deals with the major content owners, Google has finally come to the realization that YouTube will not be the Internet's single source for all the world's video. Google now recognizes it's a pluralistic and diverse world with lots of powerful players that it needs to survive and make a profit. Gone is the in-your-face attitude of earlier years when YouTube claimed that in Silicon Valley, copyrights didn't matter.

YouTube has also developed a "sponsored videos" program (also called "promoted videos") in which it selects amateur videos with unusual appeal, and offers advertisers text ads displayed on the lower portion of the video screen. In this program, advertisers bid for keywords (just like Google's AdSense) and Google uses its search algorithms to match a proper video with the keywords. The sponsored videos have a Flash animation overlaid on the bottom of the video window, starting 10 seconds after the real video rolls, and disappearing in 10 seconds unless the user clicks on the animation, in which case they are taken to the advertiser's site. Google research claims that 10 times more people click on these overlays than standard banner ads (no great achievement given the low rate of banner ad clicks), suggesting a 1% click-through rate, and that fewer than 10% close the banner window. The video is paused while the ad runs its 10 seconds. How annoying is that? On a recent day, for instance, clicking on "Nora Piano Playing Cat" brought up a video of the cat Nora "playing" the piano, with an ad for REI (Receational Equipment Incorporated, a sporting goods firm) displayed in the lower quarter of the screen. With so many people searching on YouTube each day, it's a wonder they did not think of this sooner. However, advertisers are still wary of the program simply because their ads may show up on an embarrassing video. The connection between REI and a cat playing the piano is not clear, suggesting that the algorithm that links the two needs some refining. What Fortune 1000 company would want to place ads next to amateur videos? Analysts estimate that only 4% of YouTube's videos are of sufficient quality and sanity to support advertising.

Setting aside where the page views are coming from, what is Google's formula for making a profit from this investment? The thinking on the Street is that the purchase price of $1.65 billion indicates that Google expected to generate profits of over $150 million a year (assuming a 10% discount rate, an unending stream of revenue, and that people don't get tired of videos and turn elsewhere). The formula Google has come up with is advertising to the 100 million unique visitors. One problem with this is that most users on the Internet expect video to be free and without ads. In fact, the response rate to videos used in display advertising is still nothing to write home about—just .4%, although four times as good as a regular banner ad. The standard pre-roll video that you get every time you want to watch something interesting has turned out to be a big audience killer. Half the viewers just hit the return button and skip the video they wanted to see rather than sit through the video ad, or hit the "Skip this" button if one is offered.

Adding a bit of pressure to Google's efforts to monetize YouTube's audience, Credit Suisse reported in April 2009 that YouTube would lose approximately $470 million in 2009, rather than show a profit of anywhere near $150 million needed to amortize the purchase price. While YouTube remains the leader in online video, with a 41% share of total domestic video streams, "monetization remains challenging," Credit Suisse analysts Spencer Wang and Kenneth Sena wrote. The site is expected to generate about $240 million in revenue in 2009, up about 20% year over year. However, the cost of infrastructure, licensing of content, ad-revenue sharing, and sales and marketing add up to $711 million. Bandwidth alone runs about $1 million a day (51% of expenses), sharing of ad revenues another 36%. The issue for YouTube, the analysts argued, "is to increase the percentage of its videos

SOURCES: "Google to Host Time Warner Content on YouTube, " by John Kell, *Wall Street Journal*, August 19, 2009; "Google to Buy On2 as It Looks To Boost Video," by Jerry Dicolo, *Wall Street Journal*, August 6, 2009; "Google Still Loves YouTube," by Jessi Hempel, Brainstormtech.net, July 31, 2009; "YouTube Logs Film, TV Deals," by Marc Graser, *Variety*, April 16, 2009; "YouTube May Lose $470 Million in 2009: Analysts," by Todd Spangler, Multichannel.com, April 3, 2009; "YouTube is Missing a Golden Opportunity," by Liz Gannes, *Business Week*, March 16, 2009; "No End in Sight for Critical Viacom-YouTube DMCA Case," by Liz Gannes, Newteevee.com, December 9, 2008; "YouTube Refocuses on Premium, and Misses the Point," by Liz Gannes, *Business Week*, December 5, 2008; "Studios Hope YouTube Tie Sells Movie," by Peter Sanders, *Wall Street Journal*, September 18, 2008; "Now Playing on YouTube: Clips With Ads," by Brian Stelter, *New York Times*, August 16, 2008; "Google Push to Sell Ads on YouTube Hits Snags," by Kevin Delaney, *Wall Street Journal*, July 9, 2008.

that can be monetized (likely through more deals with content companies) and to drive more advertiser demand through standardization of ad formats and improved ad effectiveness."

The result of following a legal path—showing ads next to copyrighted material only with the permission of the owners—is that Google will have to make its $150 million a year in profits from legitimate, high-quality content only. Really popular user-generated online stars such as Lonelygirl15 have left YouTube in a huff because her videos will not receive any ad revenue. In other words, if YouTube continues on the branded, legal content path, it could alienate the very users who have made it popular, according to Jupiter Research analyst, Emily Riley. "If people come to the front page of the site and it becomes commercialized," she said, "it's going to be like going to the mall or grocery store rather than talking to your friends." But the YouTube audience is more mature now, Google is more mature now, the venue has become more legitimate as major Fortune 500 companies establish channels (even universities have channels), and many visitors are becoming accustomed to advertiser-supported videos and paying for quality content if necessary. It's too early to tell if Google paid too much. Pass the popcorn while this ad plays.

Case Study Questions

1. In your view, and experience on YouTube, will typical YouTube viewers accept advertising while watching the videos?

2. What responsibility does YouTube have in removing copyrighted material from its site? YouTube claims it is in compliance with the Digital Millenium Copyright Act, which requires owners of content to notify Web sites when their copyrights are infringed. Why is this a good solution for YouTube but a poor solution for copyright owners?

3 Assume you were a manufacturer of sporting goods, and wanted to use YouTube videos as a marketing tool to establish your brand. What concerns would you have about using YouTube? How would you use YouTube's various innovations to promote your firm?

4. When you think of YouTube, what perceptions come to mind? Do you think YouTube can become an outlet for feature-length Hollywood movies?

10.5 REVIEW

KEY CONCEPTS

■ **Identify the major trends in the consumption of media and online content.**

Major trends in the consumption of media and online content include the following:
- The average American adult spends over 3,600 hours per year consuming various media. The most hours are spent viewing television, followed by listening to the radio, and then the Internet.
- Recent studies have suggested that television viewing among Internet users is lower than among non-users and that Internet users spend less time reading books, newspapers, and magazines, and less time on the phone and listening to the radio, supporting the view that Internet usage cannibalizes other media distribution channels. However, Internet users also consume more media of all types than non-Internet users, in large part because they often multitask using multiple media.
- In terms of revenue, television garners the largest share of revenue, followed by home video, and then consumer Internet.
- Total direct paid online content revenues for digital music, television, and movies in the United States in 2007 is over $5 billion.

■ **Discuss the concept of media convergence and the challenges it faces.**

The concept of media convergence has three dimensions:
- *Technological convergence,* which refers to the development of hybrid devices that can combine the functionality of two or more media platforms, such as books, newspapers, television, radio and stereo equipment, into a single device.
- *Content convergence,* with respect to content design, production, and distribution.
- *Media industry convergence,* which refers to the merger of media enterprises into powerful, synergistic combinations that can cross-market content on many different platforms and create works that use multiple platforms.
- In the early years of e-commerce, many believed that media convergence would occur quickly. However, many early efforts failed, and new efforts are just now appearing.

■ **Describe the basic content revenue models.**

In general, most content on the Web is free and most users expect it to remain free. Overcoming this expectation is the major challenge for the online content industry. Thus far, five basic revenue models have been employed in the online content arena:
- *The marketing revenue model.* Content is given away for free in the hope that site visitors will purchase the product or view a show offline. This model is thought to increase brand loyalty while the costs of the site are at least partially recouped through the sales of product-related paraphernalia.
- *The advertising revenue model.* Content is given away for free, and advertisers are expected to pay for the cost of the site through the placement of banner and rich-media ads. This model has become successful and supports sites like Yahoo.

- *The pay-per-view/pay-for-download revenue model.* Each viewing of premium content or downloading is charged to the user. This model—sometimes called "a la carte"—has been successful for music audiences. It works for targeted audiences who are looking for deep, rich, niche content. Pay-per-view is expected to be a more prevalent and successful business model when the bandwidth capability to view sporting events, feature films, and other video content is perfected and becomes more widespread.
- *The subscription revenue model.* A monthly or annual access fee is charged to users for access to content. So far, this model has worked for music sites like Rhapsody and some newspapers. It may work for high-value niche content that is not available anywhere else, such as music tracks that are released to these users before they are released to the general population.
- *The mixed revenue model.* A model that combines several of the other types of revenue models.

For the most part, content firms have decided that there is more to be gained from the advertising model, offering free content to users and in return exposing them to graphical display ads. In order to generate meaningful revenues, firms must do four things:
- Target a focused audience
- Provide specialized content
- Be the sole source monopoly for the content
- Engender high perceived net value so consumers believe that there is value in obtaining the information instantaneously on the Web

■ **Discuss the key challenges facing content producers and owners.**

The key challenges facing content producers and owners are as follows:
- *Bandwidth challenges.* Although there is plenty of long-haul fiber-optic bandwidth available, there are critical bottlenecks in home bandwidth. These limitations restrict both the ability for pay-per-view revenue models to develop for films and video and the development of advanced e-books using video and audio.
- *Platform challenges.* These include the current unsuitability of the PC screen for viewing DVDs and e-books, the unsuitability of PDAs for text display, and the lack of acceptance of wireless cell phones as Web devices in the United States.
- *Cost challenges.* Internet distribution is far more costly than was originally anticipated, and substantial costs are faced by media companies in migrating, repackaging, and redesigning content for online delivery.
- *Consumer attitudes.* Consumers have strongly resisted paying for Web content, although this is changing as media companies learn how to use the Web to deliver high-value, focused, and deep information and content.
- *Cannibalization of existing distribution channels.* Media companies are often tempted to strike alliances with successful portals or redistributors. The risk is that the media firm's brand name will become diluted or displaced and that any revenues generated will have to be shared with the intermediary. There is the risk that existing traditional distribution channels will be destroyed because they are no longer profitable.
- *Pricing and value when redesigning content for the Web.* If the price is set too low, higher-priced and profitable distribution channels could be choked off.
- *Rights management challenges.* These include the ability to protect content from being stolen, duplicated, and distributed for free and the issue of royalties paid to artists and writers.

■ **Understand the key factors affecting the online publishing industry.**

Key factors affecting online newspapers include:

- *Audience size and growth.* There are more than 10,000 online newspapers worldwide, with about 70 million readers in the United States.
  In terms of sheer audience size, this makes online newspapers the most successful online content providers to date.

- *Content.* Online newspapers offer premium archived content, fine-grained searching ability, timeliness, and content with reach and depth.

- *Competition.* New online classified ad firms have challenged newspapers by developing deep, rich content in specialized areas.

- *Revenue models and results.* Online newspapers predominantly rely upon an advertising model. Some also supplement revenues by using a pay-per-view model for premium or archival content. This has not for the most part been a successful business model. The *Wall Street Journal* is one of the few standouts that has successfully used the subscription business model for newspapers.

- *Convergence.* Technology convergence is in its infancy, with only the first step accomplished: the movement of published text to the Web. Wireless mobile news delivery is the next step, and this is currently being invested in by the top 10 newspapers despite overall losses. Content convergence has occurred in a limited way in the areas of production and distribution. Industry structure has seen no movement toward cross-media convergence, although consolidation of the industry has occurred.

- *Challenges.* Technology challenges include developing wireless mobile delivery platforms and micropayment systems to provide a low-cost mechanism for selling single articles. Consumer attitudes have remained intransigent on the issue of paying for news content, and some online newspapers have experienced cannibalization of their main distribution channel. Another challenge is digital leakage, which occurs when a paid for and downloaded article is redistributed via e-mail or posted for free viewing on a Web site.

Key factors affecting e-books include:

- *Audience size and growth.* In 2007, online e-book sales are expected to generate around $100 million in revenue, compared with $25 billion overall for all books. E-book sales are the fastest-growing type of book sale. Reading books online is not a popular activity, but buying books online is one of the most popular activities of Internet users. This huge online audience for published books has had a significant impact on book distribution and sales, and represents an extraordinary opportunity to introduce new electronic editions of books. The future market for e-books is going to depend largely on how rapidly traditional trade and academic book publishers move existing and new works to the e-book format, and on new technology.

- *Content.* E-books have advantages over published books. Instant downloading can reduce transaction costs, and text is searchable and can be easily integrated with new text via cutting and pasting. They can be modularized down to the sentence and word level, and thus can be much more easily updated or changed, resulting in lower production and distribution costs and a longer-lasting work. However, they also have disadvantages. E-books require expensive and complex electronic devices to use, are difficult to read on-screen, have multiple competing standards and uncertain business models, and raise copyright and royalty issues with authors. Although the prices for dedicated e-book readers are falling and the sizes of libraries are increasing, these challenges are formidable.

- *Revenue models and results.* The e-book industry is composed of intermediary retailers, traditional publishers, technology developers, and vanity presses. The primary e-book revenue model is pay-for-download, in which traditional publishers and authors create e-books and publishers sell these works in their entirety through online bookstore intermediaries. The traditional revenue model for the commercial book industry has not been changed much by the introduction of e-books, mainly because most publishers have chosen not to develop online capabilities. A second revenue model involves the licensing of entire e-libraries. This model is similar to the subscription model in that users pay either a monthly or an annual fee for access to hundreds of titles. Neither business model is yet profitable, but a five-year development period is expected.

- *Convergence.* The publishing industry is making steady progress toward media convergence. Technological convergence has been slowed by the poor resolution of computer screens, the lack of portable reader devices that can compete with the portability of a published book, the absence of DRM technology, and the lack of standards to define cross-platform e-books so that they can be viewed on many different devices. A likely solution to the portability problem is the use of PDAs, but the current PDAs are too small for comfortable reading. Several screen enhancement solutions have been developed using sub-pixel display technologies, and the development of electronic ink and electronic paper displays. Several technology firms have also developed DRM software to control printing and copying of downloaded materials; however, hackers have been able to break most DRM technologies, so the hesitancy of publishing firms to publish works on the Web has yet to be overcome. Some cross-platform standards are already available and new ones are beginning to emerge. Adobe Acrobat PDF files are the most commonly used standard to date; other standards include OEB and ONIX. Not much content design convergence has yet occurred. So far, text is simply being integrated into electronic display forms, and experimentations with more interactive formats are just beginning. Content production and distribution convergence have seen more progress. The development of XML and large-scale online text/graphic storage systems have transformed the book production process and made it more efficient. In distribution of book content, the Web has opened up an entirely new distribution channel. Industry structure has not changed much.

Huge publishing behemoths have long dominated the publishing industry, and the 1990s saw even further consolidation of power. Nevertheless, the Internet has created new opportunities for authors, publishers, and distributors. Authors have published works directly to the public; publishers have moved into direct distribution to the public of selected works; large online book distributors have commissioned new e-book titles and moved into publishing; technology providers have begun limited distribution of e-books; and NetLibrary has demonstrated that a market existed for inexpensive digital libraries that could be distributed to colleges, universities, and traditional libraries.

■ **Understand the key factors affecting the online entertainment industry.**

There are five main players in the entertainment sector: television, film, music, video games, and radio broadcasting. The entertainment segment is currently undergoing great change, brought about the Internet. Consumers have begun to accept paying for content, and working with DRM restrictions.

Key factors include the following:

- *Audience size and growth.* Music downloads are the most popular form of entertainment, with online games second, followed by film, and sports. However, the amount of time users spend at music sites is not high because they typically download and store a track for future use. The sites with the highest usage levels are those that allow high levels of user control and participation. In the absence of film and TV on the Web, users are defining new forms of non-traditional entertainment that do not involve the traditional media titans, including blogs and user-generated content on social networking sites.

- *Content.* Packaging, distribution, marketing, and sales of music tracks have greatly changed in the Internet age. Huge online digital searchable music archives with millions of songs now exist from which users can mix and match to create their own personalized library. One main reason for the popularity of these services is that they enable users to become their own music packagers and distributors. This is the unique feature of online entertainment as compared to traditional entertainment. It offers users high levels of control over both program content and program focus.

- *Revenue models and results.* Television and movie sites typically use a marketing model, attempting to extend their brand influence and the audience for their offline product. Apple's a la carte model where users pay for a single music track download has been exceptionally successful. Many film sites use a pay-per-view rental model, or pay-for-download model. Many music entertainment sites are now successful with a monthly subscription model as well.

- *Convergence.* Convergence has been slow due to both technological and market forces. The technology platform for music has converged PCs and handheld devices such as Apple's iPod to become digital music listening systems. A new platform has arrived. The PC has also become a game station, with capabilities rivaling dedicated game stations. In turn, many dedicated game stations can now be connected to the Web for interactive play. Technology convergence for movies and television has been stalled by the lack of standards, the slow acceptance of high-bandwidth connections in the United States, and inadequate Internet backbone capacity. The film industry has moved very slowly in making content available on the Internet for fear of losing control over its content. There are only a few sites supporting legal Internet downloads of feature-length films. Technology standards are not a large issue as most consumers have become used to using one of three standards: Windows Media Player, Apple's QuickTime, or RealNetworks RealOne media player. Content creation and production convergence is occurring, with filmmakers and television studios increasingly using digital cameras and film editing done at digital computer workstations. Music is recorded on digital devices using digital mixers before it is digitally imprinted on CDs. Industry structure convergence in the entertainment industry, as in all content industries, is moving toward the merger of content and distribution. Content owners and producers are largely seeking to own their own distribution channels, cutting out the profits of distributors, resellers, and retailers. The belief appears to be widespread that successful media companies will need to own their entire value chain from content creation to consumer use.

QUESTIONS

1. What are the three dimensions in which the term convergence has been applied? What does each of these areas of convergence entail?
2. Why has media industry convergence not occurred as rapidly as predicted? What are the five basic revenue models for online content, and what is their major challenge? What will have to be done in order to overcome this obstacle to profitability?
3. What is the pay-per-view/pay-per-download revenue model, what type of content is it suitable for, and when is it expected to be successful?
4. What four things must content provider firms do in order to generate meaningful revenues?
5. What are the technological challenges facing content producers and owners?
6. Identify and explain the four other challenges facing content producers and owners.
7. How has the Internet impacted the content that newspapers can offer?
8. What changes have occurred for newspapers in the classified ads department?
9. What are the key challenges facing the online newspaper industry?
10. What are the advantages and disadvantages of e-book content?
11. How has the Internet changed the packaging, distribution, marketing, and sale of traditional music tracks?
12. What are the factors that make nontraditional, distinctly Web entertainment sites so popular with users?
13. What would complete content convergence in the entertainment industry look like? Has it occurred?

PROJECTS

1. Research the issue of media convergence in the newspaper industry. Do you believe that convergence will be good for the practice of journalism? Develop a reasoned argument on either side of the issue and write a 3- to 5-page report on

the topic. Include in your discussion the barriers to convergence and whether these restrictions should be eased.

2. Go to Amazon and explore the different digital products that are available. Prepare a presentation to convey your findings to the class. For example, are there Web-accessed, Web-downloadable, dedicated e-books, or books for smartphones offered? Which are in greater abundance?

3. Go to TBO.com (Tampa Bay Online). Surf the site and sample the offerings. Prepare a presentation to describe and display the efforts you see at technology, content, and industry structure convergence as well as the revenue model being used. Who owns this site?

4. Examine and report on the progress, if any, made with respect to the delivery of movies on demand over the Internet.

5. Has technology platform, content design, or industry structure convergence occurred in the online magazine industry? Prepare a short report discussing this issue.

WEB SITE RESOURCES azimuth-interactive.com/ecommerce6e

- Additional projects, exercises, and tutorials
- Careers: Explore career opportunities in e-commerce
- Raising capital and business plans

CHAPTER 11

Social Networks, Auctions, and Portals

After reading this chapter, you will be able to:

- Explain the difference between a traditional social network and an online social network.
- Understand how a social network differs from a portal.
- Describe the different types of social networks and online communities and their business models.
- Describe the major types of auctions, their benefits and costs, and how they operate.
- Understand when to use auctions in a business.
- Recognize the potential for auction abuse and fraud.
- Describe the major types of Internet portals.
- Understand the business models of portals.

Social Network Fever Spreads to the Professions

When social networks first appeared a few years ago, it was widely believed this phenomenon would be limited to crazed teenagers already incapacitated by excessive time spent on video game machines. Most serious technoratis in Silicon Valley, and Wall Street, felt this was a blip on the horizon, and their full attention was occupied primarily by search engines, search engine marketing, and ad placement. But when the population of social network participants pushed past 50 million, then 75 million, even the technical elite woke up to the fact that these huge audiences were not just a bunch of teenagers, but that instead a wide slice of American society was also participating. Steve Ballmer, CEO of Microsoft, said in September 2007 that "I think these things [social networks] are going to have some legs, and yet there's a faddishness, a faddish nature about anything that basically appeals to younger people." This was a month before Microsoft paid $250 million for a small stake in Facebook, which valued the company at $15 billion. Trying to sound convincing, Eric Schmidt, CEO of Google, declared that "I know a lot of people think this [social networking] is a blip, but it's real, it's serious." He said this just before spending $1.65 billion for YouTube.

The social networking craze obviously has awakened the technology giants, but they focus mostly on the really huge audiences attracted to the general networking sites such as Facebook, MySpace, and YouTube. However, in the background there are a fast-growing collection of social networks that are aimed at communities of practitioners or specific interest groups.

Take LinkedIn, for example, probably the best-known and most popular business networking site. LinkedIn is an online network with more than 47 million worldwide members in over 200 countries, representing 170 different industries. Every 25 days or so, another million people join LinkedIn., and in 2009, the amount of time users spend on the site has doubled from 2008. LinkedIn allows a member to create a profile, including a photo, that summarizes his or her professional accomplishments. Members' networks include their connections, their connections' connections, as well as people they know, potentially linking you to thousands of others. LinkedIn has been valued by its investors at $1 billion and reportedly has annual revenue over $100 million. Many analysts expected LinkedIn to go public sometime in 2010.

Those with a particular interest in the stock market can choose from a whole crop of Web sites aimed at stock investors who want to share their ideas with other investors. These social networks are not just bulletin boards with anonymous comments, but active communities where users are identified and their performance ranked according to the performance of their stock picks. One network is StockTickr, which has about 2,500 members. The first page on the screen is a list of stocks that his friends are investing in, along with their stock picking scores. Like the larger social network sites, the financial sites allow users to connect with other investors, discuss issues focused on the stock market, and sometimes just show off users' investing prowess. Some of the new sites include Duedee, where users are rated against other members on the performance of their "virtual" portfolios, and TradeKing, where users can search for others with similar trading styles and view recent trades. While most of these sites have fewer than 5,000 members, they are relatively new. The Motley Fool, one of the best known online stock investment services, started its CAPS stock-rating social network in 2006 and has around 140,000 members.

You can find similar social networking sites for a variety of specific professional groups such as health care (DailyStrength.org), law (LawLink), physicians (Sermo), wireless industry executives (INmobile.org), and advertising professionals (AdGabber). These social networks encourage members to discuss the realities of their professions and practices, sharing successes and failures. There are also general business social networks designed more to develop a network for career advancement, such as Ecademy, and Ryze. The rapid growth of professional social networks linked to industry and careers shows how widespread and nearly universal the appeal of social networks are. While e-mail remains the Web's most popular activity, it is about to be eclipsed by social networking. What explains the very broad attraction to social networking? E-mail is excellent for communicating with other individuals, or even a small group. But e-mail is not very good at getting a sense of what others in the group are thinking, especially if the group numbers more than a dozen people. The strength of social networking lies in its ability to reveal group attitudes and opinions, values, and practices.

Professionals who join social networks need to be careful about the content they provide, and the distribution of this content. As business social networks have grown, and as the number of participants expands, employers are finding them a great place to discover the "inner" person who applies for a job. A recent Harris survey found that 45% of employers use social networks to screen job candidates, and 35% percent have decided not to offer a job to a candidate based on the content discovered on social networking sites. Provocative photos and references to drinking and drugs, are the most common factors in deciding not to offer a job. For this reason, it is a very wise move to use Facebook's and other sites' maximum privacy settings, and release to the public only the most innocuous content. Likewise, be cautious of social networking sites that do not provide "take down" policies, which allow users to remove embarrassing materials from their pages.

SOURCES: "Influence Marketing With Social Networks," by Lee Oden, Toprankblog.com, September 16, 2009; "Online Social Networks Go to Work," by Xeni Jardan, Msnbc.com, September 16, 2009; "About LinkedIn," Linkedin.com, September 2009; "More Employers Use Social Networks to Check Out Applicants," by Jenna Wortham, *New York Times*, August 20, 2009; "Silicon Valley's Six Hottest Startups," Reuters.com, August 19, 2009; "Social Networking for Business is the Next Big Thing," by Jane Roberts, Commercialappeal.com, June 8, 2008; "Social Networking Goes Professional," by Jessica Vascellaro, *Wall Street Journal*, August 20, 2007; "A New Way to Rate Stock Tips," by Jane Kim, *Wall Street Journal*, January 3, 2007.

I n this chapter, we discuss social networks, auctions, and portals. One might ask, "What do social networks, auctions, and portals have in common?" They are all based on feelings of shared interest and self-identification—in short, a sense of community. Social networks and online communities explicitly attract people with shared affinities, such as ethnicity, gender, religion, and political views, or shared interests, such as hobbies, sports, and vacations. The auction site eBay started as a community of people interested in trading unwanted but functional items for which there was no ready commercial market. That community turned out to be huge—much larger than anyone expected. Portals also contain strong elements of community by providing access to community-fostering technologies such as e-mail, chat groups, bulletin boards, and discussion forums.

11.1 SOCIAL NETWORKS AND ONLINE COMMUNITIES

The Internet was designed originally as a communications medium to connect scientists in computer science departments around the continental United States. From the beginning, the Internet was intended, in part, as a community building technology that would allow scientists to share data, knowledge, and opinions in a real-time online environment (see Chapter 3) (Hiltzik, 1999). The result of this early Internet was the first "virtual communities" (Rheingold, 1993). As the Internet grew in the late 1980s to include scientists from many disciplines and thousands of university campuses, thousands of virtual communities sprang up among small groups of scientists in very different disciplines that communicated regularly using Internet e-mail, listservs, and bulletin boards. The first articles and books on the new electronic communities began appearing in the mid to late 1980s (Kiesler et al. 1984; Kiesler, 1986). One of the earliest online communities, The Well, was formed in San Francisco in 1985 by a small group of people who once shared an 1,800-acre commune in Tennessee. The Well is a online community that now has thousands of members devoted to discussion, debate, advice, and help (Hafner, 1997; Rheingold, 1998). With the development of the Web in the early 1990s, millions of people began obtaining Internet accounts and Web e-mail, and the community-building impact of the Internet strengthened. By the late 1990s, the commercial value of online communities was recognized as a potential new business model (Hagel and Armstrong, 1997).

The early online communities involved a relatively small number of Web aficionados, and users with intense interests in technology, politics, literature, and ideas. The technology was largely limited to posting text messages on bulletin boards sponsored by the community, and one-to-one, or one-to-many e-mails. In addition to The Well, early networks included GeoCities, a Web site hosting service based on neighborhoods. By 2002, however, the nature of online communities had begun to change. Cell phones and mobile Internet devices provided widespread access, making it possible to communicate nearly instantly with friends and relatives, and keep track of one another in a way not possible before. User-created Web sites called blogs became inexpensive and easy to set up without any technical expertise. These technologies also enabled sharing of rich media such as photos and videos made possible by the spreading use of digital cameras, digital video cameras, cell phones with cameras, and portable digital music players. Suddenly there was a much wider audience for sharing interests and activities, and much more to share.

A new culture emerged as well. The broad democratization of the technology and its spread to the larger population meant that online social networking was no longer limited to a small group but instead broadened to include a much wider set of people and tastes, especially pre-teens, teens, and college students who were the fastest to adopt many of these new technologies. The new social networking culture is very personal and "me" centered, displaying photos and broadcasting personal activities, interests, hobbies, and relationships on social network profiles. Today's social networks are as much a sociological phenomenon as they are a technology phenomenon.

Currently, social network participation is one of the most common usages of the Internet. About 44% of all Internet users in the United States—about 88 million Americans—have at one time or another gone online to a social network site. Facebook has 300 million active users, and is now over twice the size of MySpace, which reports 130 million active users. Twitter, a newer entrant in the social network arena, has grown rapidly, with an estimated 18 million unique visitors as of September 2009, a 200% increase over the prior year (eMarketer, 2009a, b).

Worldwide, the social networking phenomena is even stronger. According to a Universal McCann survey, seven other countries (Russia, India, China, Brazil, the United Kingdom, South Korea, and Spain) had even higher percentages of social networking participation than the United States. Worldwide, over 60% of active Internet users ages 16-54 had a social network profile in 2009, and over 70% had visited a friend's profile (Universal McCann, 2009). Users spend an average of 3.7 hours per month on social networks, with Russian users leading the pack at 6.6 hours (U.S. users are 9th, above the average, at 4.2 hours) (comScore, 2009a). Although Facebook and MySpace dominate the global social network marketspace, in some countries, more localized social networks are signficant, such as Orkut (owned by Google) in Brazil, Mixi in Japan, 51 in China, and Werkentwenn in Germany. There is an online social network for you to join almost anywhere you go!

WHAT IS AN ONLINE SOCIAL NETWORK?

So exactly how do we define an online social network, and how is it any different from, say, an offline social network? Sociologists, who frequently criticize modern society for having destroyed traditional communities, unfortunately have not given us very good definitions of social networks and community. One study examined 94 different sociological definitions of community and found four areas of agreement. **Social networks** involve (a) a group of people, (b) shared social interaction, (c) common ties among members, and (d) people who share an area for some period of time (Hillery, 1955). This will be our working definition of a social network. Social networks do not necessarily have shared goals, purposes, or intentions. Indeed, social networks can be places where people just "hang out," share space, and communicate.

Now it's a short step to defining an **online social network** as an area online where people who share common ties can interact with one another. This definition is very

social network
involves a group of people, shared social interaction, common ties among members, and people who share an area for some period of time

close to that of Howard Rheingold's—one of The Well's early participants—who coined the term *virtual communities* as "cultural aggregations that emerge when enough people bump into each other often enough in cyberspace." It is a group of people who may or may not meet one another face to face, and who exchange words and ideas through the mediation of an online social meeting space. The Internet removes the geographic and time limitations of offline social networks. To be in an online network, you don't need to meet face to face, in a common room, at a common time.

online social network
an area online, where people who share common ties can interact with one another

THE DIFFERENCE BETWEEN SOCIAL NETWORKS AND PORTALS

We describe portals in the last section of this chapter. Portals began as search engines and then added content, Internet, and e-commerce services. In order to survive, portals have added many community-building and social networking features including chat groups, bulletin boards, free Web site design and hosting, and other features that encourage visitors to stay on the site and interact with others who share their interests. Yahoo, for instance, uses deep vertical content features to retain its audience on site and maximize revenue opportunities. Portals have begun to measure their success in terms of their social networking features. For instance, Yahoo has purchased several Web properties, such as Flickr (a photo-sharing site) and HotJobs, which have social network features. Portals have moved toward becoming general community meeting places in an effort to enlarge and retain audience share and increase revenues. User-generated content on portals is one way to entice visitors to stay online at the site (and of course view more commercials).

Similarly, sites that began as narrowly focused content or affinity group community sites, such as iVillage, a site devoted to women's issues, have added more general portal-like services including general Web searching, general news, weather, travel information, and a wide variety of e-commerce services, often provided by portals seeking alliances. Browsers such as Mozilla's Firefox and Microsoft's Internet Explorer 7 and 8 are adding social networking features as well. There is no reason why social networking has to be limited to self-proclaimed social network sites such as Facebook. Social networking is a functionality, not a Web site. As a result, social networks and portals have moved closer together and at times are indistinguishable from one another.

THE GROWTH OF SOCIAL NETWORKS AND ONLINE COMMUNITIES

Facebook, MySpace, Twitter, and Classmates.com are all examples of popular online communities. **Figure 11.1** shows the top 10 social network sites , which together account for well over 90% of the Internet's social networking activity.

In 2009, Facebook passed MySpace as the largest social network in terms of total members (over 300 million worldwide in September 2009) and unique visitors (92 million in the United States in August 2009). MySpace has been relegated to second place, with about 130 million members worldwide and around 64 million unique visitors per month in the United States. While social networks originally attracted mostly young Internet users, today social networking is not just about teens and college students, but a much larger social phenomenon. For instance, according to Facebook, users over 34 make up 49% of its user population. And, although in August 2009, male

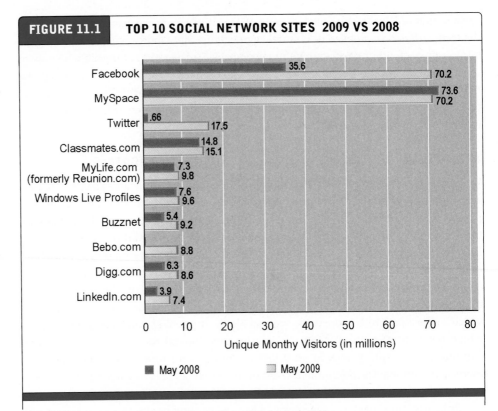

FIGURE 11.1 — TOP 10 SOCIAL NETWORK SITES 2009 VS 2008

SOURCE: Based on data from eMarketer, 2009c; comScore, 2009; Facebook, 2009.

teens 13–17 were still Facebook's fastest growing age group, the second-fastest growing was men ages 45–54, followed by women 45–54, and 55–65 (eMarketer, 2009d).

It is easy to both overestimate and underestimate the significance of social networks. According to comScore, the social networking category has a total unique audience in the United States of about 147 million. In contrast, the top four portal/search engine sites (Google, Yahoo, MSN, and AOL) together have a total unique audience of over 550 million. (Obviously, with 200 million people on the Internet in the United States, users are unique to more than one site.) Although Facebook's 92 million unique visitors seems high, consider that Yahoo's various sites have over 158 million.

The number of unique visitors is just one way to measure the influence of a site. Time on site is another important metric. Interestingly, while Facebook has leapfrogged past MySpace in most metrics, MySpace leads in the average amount of time its users spend on site per month (240 minutes, compared to 180 minutes for Facebook), perhaps due to the fact that it has more entertainment-related content such as music (Ryan, 2009). Although the average length of a visit to one of the big portals such as Yahoo, MSN, and AOL is typically quite short, they have a much higher average number of visits per month (eMarketer, 2009c, e).

The amount of advertising revenue generated by sites is perhaps the ultimate metric. The top four portal/search engines (Google, Yahoo, MSN, and AOL) will generate about $14.5 billion in U.S. advertising revenue in 2009. In contrast, social networking sites in the United States in 2009 are expected to generate about $1.1 billion in advertising revenue. Social networking sites are the fastest growing form of Internet usage, but they are not yet as powerful as traditional search engines/portals in terms of unique visitors, overall reach, and ad dollars generated.

TURNING SOCIAL NETWORKS INTO BUSINESSES

While the early social networks had a difficult time raising capital and revenues, today's top networking sites are now learning how to monetize their huge audiences. Early networking sites relied on subscriptions, but today, social networks rely on advertising. Users of portals and search engines have come to accept advertising as the preferred means of supporting Web experiences rather than paying for it. **Figure 11.2** shows the amount of ad spending on social networks.

The techniques for marketing on social networks are still being worked out. Unlike portals where banner ads are an accepted phenomenon, this is not true on some social network sites such as LinkedIn.

TYPES OF SOCIAL NETWORKS AND THEIR BUSINESS MODELS

There are many types and many ways of classifying social networks and online communities. While the most popular general social networks have adopted an advertising model, other kinds of networks have different revenue sources. Social networks have different types of sponsors, and different kinds of members. For instance, some are created by firms such as IBM for the exclusive use of their sales force or other employees (intra-firm communities or B2E [business-to-employee] communities); others are built for suppliers and resellers (inter-organizational or B2B

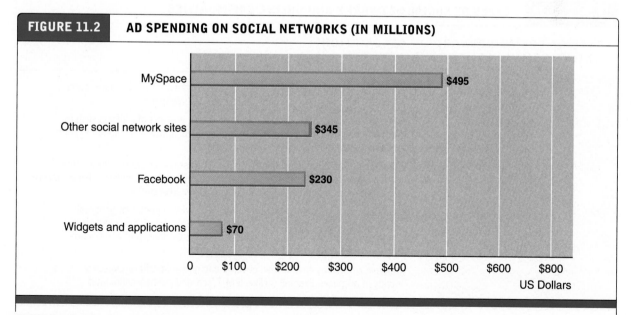

FIGURE 11.2 | **AD SPENDING ON SOCIAL NETWORKS (IN MILLIONS)**

SOURCE: Based on data from eMarketer, 2009c.

communities); and others are built by dedicated individuals for other similar persons with shared interests (P2P [people-to-people] communities). In this chapter, we will discuss B2C communities for the most part, although we also discuss briefly P2P communities of practice.

Table 11.1 describes in greater detail the five generic types of social networks and online communities: general, practice, interest, affinity, and sponsored. Each type of community can have a commercial intent or commercial consequence. We use this schema to explore the business models of commercial communities.

General communities offer members opportunities to interact with a general audience organized into general topics. Within the topics, members can find hundreds of specific discussion groups attended by thousands of like-minded members who share an interest in that topic. The purpose of the general community is to attract enough members to populate a wide range of topics and discussion groups. The business model of general communities is typically advertising supported by selling ad space on pages and videos.

Practice networks offer members focused discussion groups, help, information, and knowledge relating to an area of shared practice. For instance, Linux.org is a non-profit community for the open source movement, a worldwide global effort involving thousands of programmers who develop computer code for the Linux operating system and share the results freely with all. Other online communities involve artists, educators, art dealers, photographers, and nurses. Practice networks can be either profit-based or nonprofit, and support themselves by advertising or user donations.

general communities
offer members opportunities to interact with a general audience organized into general topics

practice networks
offer members focused discussion groups, help, information, and knowledge relating to an area of shared practice

TABLE 11.1	TYPES OF SOCIAL NETWORKS AND ONLINE COMMUNITIES
TYPE OF SOCIAL NETWORK/ ONLINE COMMUNITY	**DESCRIPTION**
General	Online social gathering place to meet and socialize with friends, share content, schedules, and interests. Examples: Facebook and MySpace
Practice	Social network of professionals and practitioners, creators of artifacts such as computer code or music. Examples: Just Plain Folks (musicians community) and LinkedIn (business)
Interest	Community built around a common interest, such as games, sports, music, stock markets, politics, health, finance, foreign affairs, or lifestyle. Examples: E-democracy.org (political discussion group) and SocialPicks (stock market site)
Affinity	Community of members who self-identify with a demographic or geographic category, such as women, African Americans, or Arab Americans. Examples: BlackPlanet (African American community and networking site) and iVillage (focusing on women)
Sponsored	Network created by commercial, government, and nonprofit organizations for a variety of purposes. Examples: Nike, IBM, Cisco, and political candidates

Interest-based social networks offer members focused discussion groups based on a shared interest in some specific subject, such as business careers, boats, horses, health, skiing, and thousands of other topics. Because the audience for interest communities is necessarily much smaller and more targeted, these communities have usually relied on advertising and tenancy/sponsorship deals. Sites such as Spoke.com, Jigsaw.com, Fool.com, Military.com, and Sailing Anarchy all are examples of Web sites that attract people who share a common pursuit. These sites are usually advertising supported.

Affinity communities offer members focused discussions and interaction with other people who share the same affinity. Affinity refers to self- and group identification. For instance, people can self-identify themselves on the basis of religion, ethnicity, gender, sexual orientation, political beliefs, geographical location, and hundreds of other categories. For instance, iVillage, Oxygen, and NaturallyCurly are affinity sites designed to attract women. These sites offer women discussion and services that focus on topics such as babies, beauty, books, diet and fitness, entertainment, health, and home and garden. These sites are supported by advertising along with revenues from sales of products.

Sponsored communities are online communities created by government, nonprofit, or for-profit organizations for the purpose of pursuing organizational goals. These goals can be diverse, from increasing the information available to citizens; for instance, a local county government site such as Westchestergov.com, the Web site for Westchester County (New York) government; to an online auction site such as eBay; to a product site such as Tide.com, which is sponsored by an offline branded product company (Procter & Gamble). Cisco, IBM, HP, and hundreds of other companies have developed their internal corporate social networks as a way of sharing knowledge.

SOCIAL NETWORK FEATURES AND TECHNOLOGIES

Social networks have developed software applications that allow users to engage in a number of activities. Not all sites have the same features, but there is an emerging feature set among the larger communities. Some of these software tools are built into the site, while others can be added by users to their profile pages as widgets (described in earlier chapters). **Table 11.2** describes some of social network functionalities.

THE FUTURE OF SOCIAL NETWORKS

While today's social networking scene is highly concentrated among the top 10 general networking sites, this is unlikely to remain the case. Networks are springing up all over the Internet based on intensely felt interests of smaller groups of people, draining potential members from the general sites. General networking sites are poor places to meet new people, and most online social networks reflect offline friendships and associations.

Today's networks are places you go online, but in the future, browsers, portals, and general Web sites will have social networking functionality built in, making it less necessary that you go to a social network site, and more likely that social networking will come to you (see *Insight on Technology: Social Operating Systems: Facebook vs. Google*). The biggest Web e-mail services (who also happen to be the big portals) are

interest-based social networks
offer members focused discussion groups based on a shared interest in some specific topic

affinity communities
offer members focused discussions and interaction with other people who share the same affinity

sponsored communities
online communities created for the purpose of pursuing organizational (and often commercial) goals

TABLE 11.2	SOCIAL NETWORK FEATURES AND TECHNOLOGIES
FEATURE	DESCRIPTION
Profiles	Users create Web pages that describe themselves on a variety of dimensions.
Friends network	Ability to create a linked group of friends.
Network discovery	Ability to find other networks and find new groups and friends
Favorites	Ability to communicate favorite sites, bookmarks, content, and destinations.
E-mail	Send e-mail within the social network sites to friends.
Storage	Storage space for network members, content.
Instant messaging	Immediate one-to-one contact with friends through the community facility
Message boards	Posting of messages to groups of friends, and other groups' members
Online polling	Polling of member opinion.
Chat	Online immediate group discussion; Internet relay chat (IRC)
Discussion groups	Discussion groups and forums organized by topic.
Experts online	Certified experts in selected areas respond to queries.
Membership management tools	Ability of site managers to edit content, and dialog; remove objectionable material; protect security and privacy.

adding features that allow users to perform sociable functions like tracking friends, creating profiles, and joining other groups. Yahoo's 280 million worldwide e-mail users together are arguably the world's largest inactive and undiscovered network. Network aggregators are also emerging: SocialURL, ProfileFly, and ProfileLinker allow people to aggregate feeds from their different social network profiles, making it less necessary to visit the destination site itself.

11.2   ONLINE AUCTIONS

Online auction sites are among the most popular consumer-to-consumer (C2C) e-commerce sites on the Internet although the popularity of auctions, and their growth rates, have slowed in recent years as customers' preferences for a "buy now" fixed-price model increase. Nevertheless, the online auction industry in the United States grew by over 10% in 2008 despite the recession. The market leader in C2C auctions is eBay, which has 86 million active users in the United States, over 140 million items listed on any given day within 18,000 categories, and in 2008, $5.5 billion in net revenues from its Marketplaces segment. EBay marketplace revenue growth slowed to 2.2% in 2008 in part because of the recession and in part because

INSIGHT ON TECHNOLOGY

SOCIAL OPERATING SYSTEMS: FACEBOOK VS. GOOGLE

In the ongoing battles between hype and substance on the Internet, fantasy and reality, hubris and humility, Silicon Valley takes no prisoners and has no equals. Google wants to organize the world's information, Amazon wants to be the world's store, and now Facebook wants to be the "social operating system" for the Internet, according to founder and CEO Mark Zuckerberg. Facebook wants to connect the world in one big social network (that it owns). He wants Facebook to "connect everyone." Microsoft, owner of the world's desktops with a 95% market share, will just have to move on over while Facebook engineers this feat. Google will have to be satisfied being a search engine where people don't hang around very long. In September 2009, Facebook announced it has over 300 million users worldwide. In the United States, Facebook has about 92 million unique visitors a month, and 65 million people worldwide now actively using Facebook on their mobile devices—a significant increase from 20 million last year.

What can a social operating system possibly be? When we think of an operating system such as Windows, Mac OS or Linux, we think of a software tool that controls the resources of the computer and provides the platform on which applications are built, launched, and operate. How can Facebook replace this? The answer is, it can't. But what Facebook can do is build, or encourage others to build, thousands of software applications.

In 2007, Facebook took its two major assets—its membership base and its technology—and made them available to everyone. It adopted a strategy that involved opening up its technology platform to anyone who wanted to create an application and make it available to Facebook users. Developers could develop widgets and other Java applications to perform thousands of different tasks, and even use the apps to display ads and keep all the revenues. As a result, Facebook has become a kind of Web inside the Web—a platform or area where Web pages created by users (called "profiles") are linked together by the users themselves into networks, and where the applications are supplied by outside developers. The applications range from tools such as iLike, which lets you find friends who share your musical tastes, to PopFly, a tool that lets you create links to Windows applications and Facebook, to the Washington Post's "political compass" application that allows you to calculate your place on a political spectrum of your friends, to games like Red Bull Roshambull, and a program to "poke" people (mostly people of the opposite sex that you would like to know). iLike is now making more money on Facebook selling ads, and getting commissions from selling songs, and concert tickets, than it does from its own Web site, iLike.com.

As of September 2009, Facebook's platform engages more than 1 million developers in180 countries and supports 350,000 active applications. Over 250 applications have more than one million users, and 70% of Facebook users engage with platform apps every month. In contrast, there are about 15,000 Apple's iPhone apps in 2009.

The only problem? Facebook's applications operate in a closed sandbox where only Facebook can play. The rest of the world is shut out, and none of the applications play on other social networks of which there are thousands. As it turns out, Facebook managers want to connect the world as long as everyone plays (and spends time and money) in Facebook's backyard. The same is true of Apple's iPhone apps: they only play on the iPhone operating system.

(continued)

At some point in the future, these applications could include typical Microsoft Office functionality such as word processing and spreadsheets. But probably not, because these applications are already well performed by Microsoft Office and others. Instead, businesses will be turning to Facebook to enhance the productivity of their employees by developing collaboration and meeting tools. Is Microsoft worried? Probably not, because people will still need a Windows or other operating system such as Mac OS to gain access to Facebook. So the social network operating system is not a substitute for a computer operating system. Not yet. Does Microsoft want to play in this new arena? Yes. It invested $250 million in Facebook in October 2007 for a 1.6% stake. This valued Facebook at $15 billion, and was a sign of how desperate Microsoft was to play in this new field. In 2008, CEO Zuckerberg claimed Facebook had revenue of $350 million a year, and analysts estimate revenues for 2009 at about $400 million. Earnings are another matter. While Facebook is claiming it broke even for 2009, as a private company it does not have to publish its results. It's quite a distance to the $15 billion that Microsoft paid for its tiny Facebook share.

Not to be outdone by a mere start-up, Google refuses to give up the top spot in Silicon Valley's pantheon of creative genius. If Facebook promises to connect the world, Google wants to make sure it can play there too. Actually, Google wants to create a social networking world that runs on its standards and that would be universal to all social networks now and in the future. The problem with Facebook's opening to the world is that it's a closed world and creates applications that run only on Facebook. There are thousands of social networks that are more specialized, and are growing at faster rates than the big general social networks like Facebook and MySpace. Instead, Google has created a set of standard programs that enable three generic social network core functions and that would be usable on all social networks. You can see these programs at Opensocial.org. These core functions are profile information (user data), friends information (social graph), and activities (events like news, schedules, reports of friends movements).

OpenSocial already has many friends who will host these applications, such as MySpace, Orkut, LinkedIn, XING, Bebo, hi5, Hyves.net, Ning, and Socialtext, among others. Developers include YzZee, Oxylab, Viadeo, and Oracle, along with thousands of individual small developers. All told, if you add up all the social networks that host OpenSocial applications, as of September 2009, it will reach over 600 million users, somewhat larger than Facebook's platform. The advantage for developers is that they can develop one application and have it run on all social networks. Another advantage is that this functionality can be added to any program, browser, or Office application. For instance, you might be working on a particularly annoying spreadsheet and get help instantly from one of your business pals who's a wiz at spreadsheets. Or be in a Word document and suffer a loss of words. What better time to call in help from your friends? One consequence is that social networking functionality can be added to any program, and you will no longer have to go a social network site such as Facebook in order to network. Social networking is a functionality, not a URL. As a functionality, it can be available to all, and built into any software application.

SOURCES: "Facebook's Private Surprise," by Taylor Buley, *Forbes*, September 16, 2009; "Facebook Platform Statistics," Facebook.com, September 16, 2009; "Business of Social Applications," Shawn Shen, Google Developer Alliance, September 15, 2009; "Bubbling Widget Growth," Alibaba.com, August 31, 2009; "Chattty Zuckerberg Tells All About Facebook Finances," by Kara Swicher, Allthingsd.com, January 31, 2009; "OpenSocial Turns One: My, How You've Grown," by Jason Kincaid, Techcrunch.com, November 13, 2008; "Facebook Opens Its Pages As a Way to Fuel Growth," *Wall Street Journal*, May 21, 2007.

customers moved away from auctions towards a fixed-price model provided by Amazon and other competitors. (eBay Inc., 2009). In the United States alone, there are several hundred auction sites, some specializing in unique collectible products such as stamps and coins, others adopting a more generalist approach in which just about any good can be found for sale. Increasingly, established portals and online retail sites—from Yahoo and MSN to JCPenney and Sam's Club—are adding auctions to their sites. And, as noted in Chapter 12, auctions constitute a significant part of all B2B e-commerce in 2009, and over a third of procurement officers use auctions to procure goods. What explains the extraordinary popularity of auctions? Do consumers always get lower prices at auctions? Why do merchants auction their products if the prices they receive are so low?

DEFINING AND MEASURING THE GROWTH OF AUCTIONS AND DYNAMIC PRICING

Auctions are markets in which prices are variable and based on the competition among participants who are buying or selling products and services. Auctions are one type of **dynamic pricing**, in which the price of the product varies, depending directly on the demand characteristics of the customer and the supply situation of the seller. There is a wide variety of dynamically priced markets, from simple haggling, bartering, and negotiating between one buyer and one seller, to much more sophisticated public auctions in which there may be thousands of sellers and thousands of buyers, as in a single stock market for a bundle of shares.

> **auctions**
> markets in which prices are variable and based on the competition among participants who are buying or selling products and services

In dynamic pricing, merchants change their prices based on both their understanding of how much value the customer attaches to the product and their own desire to make a sale. Likewise, customers change their offers to buy based on both their perceptions of the seller's desire to sell and their own need for the product. If you as a customer really want the product right now, you will be charged a higher price in a dynamic pricing regime, and you will willingly pay a higher price than if you placed less value on the product and were willing to wait several days to buy it. For instance, if you want to travel from New York to San Francisco to attend a last-minute business conference, and then return as soon as possible, you will be charged twice as much as a tourist who agrees to stay over the weekend.

> **dynamic pricing**
> the price of the product varies, depending directly on the demand characteristics of the customer and the supply situation of the seller

In contrast, traditional mass-market merchants generally use **fixed pricing**— one national price, everywhere, for everyone. Fixed pricing first appeared in the nineteenth century with the development of mass national markets and retail stores that could sell to a national audience. Prior to this period, all pricing was dynamic and local, with prices derived through a process of negotiation between the customer and the merchant. Computers and the development of the Internet have contributed to a return of dynamic pricing. The difference is that with the Internet, dynamic pricing can be conducted globally, continuously, and at a very low cost.

> **fixed pricing**
> one national price, everywhere, for everyone

There are many other types of dynamic pricing that preceded the Internet. Airlines have used dynamic pricing since the early 1980s to change the price of airline tickets depending on available unused capacity and the willingness of business travelers to pay a premium for immediate bookings. Airline yield management software programs seek to ensure that a perishable item (an empty airline seat is useless once the plane takes off) is sold before flight time at some price above zero.

The use of coupons sent to selected customers, and even college scholarships given to selected students to encourage their enrollment, are a form of both price discrimination and dynamic pricing. In these examples, the price of the item is adjusted to demand and available supply, and certain consumers are discriminated against by charging them higher prices while others are advantaged by receiving lower prices for the same products, namely, a reduced price for an item or a college education.

Newer forms of dynamic pricing on the Internet include bundling, trigger pricing, utilization pricing, and personalization pricing. As discussed in Chapter 6, bundling of digital goods is the practice of including low-demand products in a bundle "for free" in order to increase total revenues. **Trigger pricing**, used in m-commerce applications, adjusts prices based on the location of the consumer—for example, walking within 400 yards of a restaurant may trigger an immediate 10% dinner coupon on a portable Web device. **Utilization pricing** adjusts prices based on utilization of the product; for example, Progressive Insurance Company adjusts the annual cost of automobile insurance based on mileage driven. **Personalization pricing** adjusts prices based on the merchant's estimate of how much the customer truly values the product; for instance, Web merchants may charge committed fans of a musician higher prices for the privilege of receiving a new DVD before its official release to retail stores. Higher-cost hardbound books sell primarily to committed fans of writers, while less-committed fans wait for cheaper paperback versions to appear.

Auctions—one form of dynamic pricing mechanism—are used throughout the e-commerce landscape. The most widely known auctions are **consumer-to-consumer (C2C) auctions**, in which the auction house is simply an intermediary market maker, providing a forum where consumers—buyers and sellers—can discover prices and trade. Less well known are **business-to-consumer (B2C) auctions** where a business owns or controls assets and uses dynamic pricing to establish the price. Established merchants on occasion use B2C auctions to sell excess goods. This form of auction or dynamic pricing will grow along with C2C auctions. Online auctions are expected to grow in the range of around 5% to 10% annually between 2009 and 2013. In 2009, C2C auction sites in the United States generated about $25 billion in gross revenue, and B2C auction sites generated about $19 billion.

Some leading online auction sites are listed in **Table 11.3**. Auctions are not limited to goods and services. They can also be used to allocate resources, and bundles of resources, among any group of bidders. For instance, if you wanted to establish an optimal schedule for assigned tasks in an office among a group of clerical workers, an auction in which workers bid for assignments would come close to producing a nearly

trigger pricing
adjusts prices based on the location of the consumer

utilization pricing
adjusts prices based on utilization of the product

personalization pricing
adjusts prices based on the merchant's estimate of how much the customer truly values the product

consumer-to-consumer (C2C) auctions
auction house acts as an intermediary market maker, providing a forum where consumers can discover prices and trade

business-to-consumer (B2C) auctions
auction house sells goods it owns, or controls, using various dynamic pricing models

TABLE 11.3	LEADING ONLINE AUCTION SITES
GENERAL	
eBay	The world market leader in auctions: 72 million visitors a month and millions of products.
uBid	Marketplace for excess inventory from pre-approved merchants.
eBid	In business since 1998. Operates in 18 countries, including U.S. Currently, the top competitor to eBay. Offers much lower fees.
Bid4Assets	Liquidation of distressed assets from government and the public sector, corporations, restructurings, and bankruptcies.
Auctions.samsclub	Sam's Club brand merchandise in a variety of categories.
SPECIALIZED	
BidZ	Live auction format for online jewelry.
Racersauction	Specialized site for automobile racing parts.
Philatelicphantasies	Stamp site for professionals, monthly online stamp auction.
Teletrade	America's largest fully automated auction company of certified coins including ancient gold, silver, and copper coins. Also offers sports cards.
Baseball-cards.com	The Internet's first baseball card store. Offers weekly auctions of baseball, football, basketball, hockey, wire photos, and more.
Oldandsold	Online auction service specializing in quality antiques. Dealers pay a 3% commission on merchandise sold.

optimal solution in a short amount of time (Parkes and Ungar, 2000). In short, auctions—like all markets—are ways of allocating resources among independent agents (bidders).

WHY ARE AUCTIONS SO POPULAR? BENEFITS AND COSTS OF AUCTIONS

The Internet is primarily responsible for the resurgence in auctions. Although electronic network-based auctions such as AUCNET in Japan (an electronic automobile auction for used cars) were developed in the late 1980s, these pre-Internet auctions required an expensive telecommunications network to implement. The Internet provides a global environment and very low fixed and operational costs for the aggregation of huge buyer audiences composed of millions of consumers worldwide who can use a universally available technology (Internet browsers) to shop for goods (Bapna, et al., 2001).

Benefits of Auctions

Aside from the sheer game-like fun of participating in auctions, consumers, merchants, and society as a whole derive a number of economic benefits from participating in Internet auctions. These benefits include:

- **Liquidity:** Sellers can find willing buyers, and buyers can find sellers. The Internet enormously increased the liquidity of traditional auctions that usually required all participants to be present in a single room. Now, sellers and buyers can be located anywhere around the globe. Just as important, buyers and sellers can find a global market for rare items that would not have existed before the Internet.

- **Price discovery:** Buyers and sellers can quickly and efficiently develop prices for items that are difficult to assess, where the price depends on demand and supply, and where the product is rare. For instance, how could a merchant (or buyer) price a Greek oil lamp made in 550 B.C. (to use just one example of the rare items that can be found on eBay)? How could a consumer even find a Greek oil lamp without the Internet? It would be difficult and costly for all parties.

- **Price transparency:** Public Internet auctions allow everyone in the world to see the asking and bidding prices for items. It is difficult for merchants to engage in price discrimination (charging some customers more) when the items are available on auctions. However, because even huge auction sites such as eBay do not include all the world's online auction items (there are other auction sites in the world), there still may be more than one world price for a given item (there are inter-market price differences).

- **Market efficiency:** Auctions can, and often do, lead to reduced prices, and hence reduced profits for merchants, leading to an increase in consumer welfare—one measure of market efficiency. Online auctions provide consumers the chance to find real bargains at potentially give-away prices; they also provide access to a very wide selection of goods that would be impossible for consumers to physically access by visiting stores.

- **Lower transaction costs:** Online auctions can lower the cost of selling and purchasing products, benefiting both merchants and consumers. Like other Internet markets, such as retail markets, Internet auctions have very low (but not zero) transaction costs. A sale at an auction can be consummated quickly and with very low transaction costs when compared to the physical world of markets.

- **Consumer aggregation:** Sellers benefit from large auction sites' ability to aggregate a large number of consumers who are motivated to purchase something in one marketspace. Auction-site search engines that lead consumers directly to the products they are seeking make it very likely that consumers who visit a specific auction really are interested and ready to buy at some price.

- **Network effects:** The larger an auction site becomes in terms of visitors and products for sale, the more valuable it becomes as a marketplace for everyone by providing liquidity and several other benefits listed previously, such as lower transaction costs, higher efficiency, and better price transparency. For instance, because eBay is so large—garnering close to 90% of all C2C auction commerce in the United States—it is quite likely you will find what you want to buy at a good price, and highly probable you will find a buyer for just about anything.

Risks and Costs of Auctions for Consumers and Businesses

There are a number of risks and costs involved in participating in auctions. In some cases, auction markets can fail—like all markets at times (we describe auction market failure in more detail later). Some of the more important risks and costs to keep in mind are:

- **Delayed consumption costs:** Internet auctions can go on for days, and shipping will take additional time. If you ordered from a mail-order catalog, you would likely receive the product much faster, or if you went to a physical store, you would be able to obtain the product immediately.

- **Monitoring costs:** Participation in auctions requires your time to monitor bidding.

- **Equipment costs:** Internet auctions require you to purchase a computer system, pay for Internet access, and learn a complex operating system.

- **Trust risks:** Online auctions are the single largest source of Internet fraud. Using auctions increases the risk of experiencing a loss.

- **Fulfillment costs:** Typically, the buyer pays fulfillment costs of packing, shipping, and insurance, whereas at a physical store these costs are included in the retail price.

Auction sites such as eBay have taken a number of steps to reduce consumer participation costs and trust risk. For instance, auction sites attempt to solve the trust problem by providing a rating system in which previous customers rate sellers based on their overall experience with the merchant. Although helpful, this solution does not always work. Auction fraud is the leading source of e-commerce complaints to federal law enforcement officials. One partial solution to high monitoring costs is, ironically, fixed pricing. At eBay, consumers can reduce the cost of monitoring and waiting for auctions to end by simply clicking on the "Buy It Now!" button and paying a premium price. The difference between the "Buy It Now" price and the auction price is the cost of monitoring. Also, most online auctions reduce monitoring costs by providing both a watch list and proxy bidding. **Watch lists** permit the consumer to monitor specific auctions of interest, requiring the consumer to pay close attention only in the last few minutes of bidding. **Proxy bidding** allows the consumer to enter a maximum price, and the auction software automatically bids for the goods up to that maximum price in small increments.

Nevertheless, given the costs of participating in online auctions, the generally lower cost of goods on Internet auctions is in part a compensation for the other additional costs consumers experience. On the other hand, consumers experience lower search costs and transaction costs because there usually are no intermediaries (unless, of course, the seller is an online business operating on an auction site, in which case there is a middleman cost), and usually there are no local or state taxes.

Merchants face considerable risks and costs as well. At auctions, merchants may end up selling goods for prices far below what they might have achieved in conventional markets. Merchants also face risks of nonpayment, false bidding, bid rigging, monitoring, transaction fees charged by the auction site, credit card transaction processing fees, and the administration costs of entering price and product information. We explore the benefits and risks for merchants later in this chapter.

watch lists
permit the consumer to monitor specific auctions of interest

proxy bidding
allows the consumer to enter a maximum price, and the auction software automatically bids for the goods up to that maximum price in small increments

Market-Maker Benefits: Auctions as an E-commerce Business Model

Online auctions have been among the most successful business models in retail and B2B commerce. EBay, the Internet's most lucrative auction site, has been profitable nearly since its inception. The strategy for eBay has been to make money off every stage in the auction cycle. EBay earns revenue in several ways: transaction fees based on the amount of the sale, listing fees for display of goods, financial service fees from payment systems such as PayPal, and advertising or placement fees where sellers pay extra for special services such as particular display or listing services. In addition, eBay purchased Skype, the Internet telephone company, so that buyers and sellers could communicate online with one another during the auction process. In 2006, eBay paid $2.6 billion for Skype, then took a write-down in value to $1.4 billion in 2008. EBay is spinning off Skype as a "bad fit" for the company, and in 2009, and is likely to sell Skype at well below $1 billion.

However, it is on the cost side that online auctions have extraordinary advantages over ordinary retail or catalog sites. Auction sites carry no inventory and do not perform any fulfillment activities—they need no warehouses, shipping, or logistical facilities. Sellers and consumers provide these services and bear these costs. In this sense, online auctions are an ideal digital business because they involve simply the transfer of information.

Even though eBay has been extraordinarily successful, the success of online auctions is qualified by the fact that the marketplace for online auctions is highly concentrated. EBay dominates the online auction market, followed by eBid and uBid. Many of the smaller auction sites are not profitable because they lack sufficient sellers and buyers to achieve liquidity. In auctions, network effects are highly influential, and the tendency is for one or two very large auction sites to dominate, with hundreds of smaller specialty auction sites (sites that sell specialized goods such as stamps) being barely profitable.

TYPES AND EXAMPLES OF AUCTIONS

Auction theory is a well-established area of research, largely in economics (McAfee and McMillan, 1987; Milogram, 1989; Vickrey, 1961). Much of this research is theoretical, and prior to the emergence of public Internet auctions, there was not a great deal of empirical data on auctions or consumer behavior in auctions. Previous literature has identified a wide range of auction types, some of which are seller-biased, and others of which are more buyer-biased. Internet auctions are very different from traditional auctions. Traditional auctions are relatively short-lived (such as a Sotheby's art auction), and have a fixed number of bidders, usually present in the same room. Online Internet auctions, in contrast, can go on much longer (a week), and have a variable number of bidders who come and go from the auction arena.

Internet Auction Basics

Before a business turns to auctions as a marketing channel, its managers need to understand some basic facts about online auctions.

Market Power and Bias in Dynamically Priced Markets Dynamically priced markets are not always "fair" in the sense of distributing market power to influence prices.

Figure 11.3 illustrates four different market bias situations that occur in dynamic markets.

In situations in which the number of buyers and sellers is few or equal in size, markets tend to be neutral, favoring neither the buyer nor the seller. One-on-one negotiations, barter markets, and stock exchanges all have this quality of neutrality, although specialists and market makers exact a commission for matching buy and sell orders. In stock markets, which are sometimes called a "double auction" because bids and offers are made continuously, many sellers and buyers call out prices for bundles of stock (of which there is a very large supply) until a deal is struck. In contrast, auctions such as those run by eBay and reverse auctions offered by companies such as Priceline have built-in biases. Usually on eBay, there is just one seller or a small number of sellers marketing goods that are in limited supply (or even rare goods) to millions of buyers who are competing on price. Priceline offers just the opposite bias and shares many features with a sealed-bid RFQ (request for quote) market. In Priceline's reverse auctions (described in greater detail later in this chapter), buyers post their unique needs for goods and services and a price they are willing to pay, while many sellers compete against one another for the available business. Of course, inherent bias in a marketplace does not mean consumers and merchants cannot find "good deals" and thousands of motivated customers willing to purchase goods at profitable prices.

However, the inherent biases should provide cautions to both merchants and consumers; namely, goods in auctions sometimes sell for far above their fair market value as they get bid too high, and sometimes for far less than their fair market value as merchants become too desperate for business. **Fair market value** could be defined here as the average of prices for that product or service in a variety of dynamic and fixed-price markets around the world. We explore other auction market failures in a later section.

fair market value
the average of prices for a product or service in a variety of dynamic and fixed-price markets around the world

| FIGURE 11.3 | BIAS IN DYNAMICALLY PRICED MARKETS |

BUYERS

	One/Few	Many
One/Few	Market Neutral (Negotiation)	Seller Bias (eBay Auction)
Many	Buyer Bias (Priceline and Sealed Bidding)	Market Neutral (Stock Exchanges)

SELLERS

Dynamically priced markets can be either neutral or biased in favor of buyers or sellers.

Price Allocation Rules: Uniform vs. Discriminatory Pricing There are different rules for establishing the winning bids and prices in auctions where there are multiple units for sale, say, 10 IBM laptop PCs. With a **uniform pricing rule**, there are multiple winners and they all pay the same price (usually the lowest winning bid—sometimes called a market clearing price). Other auctions use **discriminatory pricing** in which winners pay different amounts depending on what they bid. See, for instance, Ubid.com, which typically auctions multiple units from manufacturers. Like so many other auction rules, price allocation can change bidding strategy in auctions. For instance, in a uniform pricing auction for 10 IBM laptops, you may bid a very high price for a few units, knowing that others will not follow, but you will only pay a price equal to the lowest winning bid needed to clear out the units from the market. The person who bid for the tenth unit may have only bid 75% as high as your offer. Nevertheless, that is the price you will actually pay—the price needed to "clear the market" of all units. However, under a discriminatory pricing rule, you would be forced to pay your high bid. Obviously, from a buyer's point of view, uniform pricing is better, but from a merchant's point of view, discriminatory pricing is much better.

Public vs. Private Information in Dynamically Priced Markets In some dynamic markets, the prices being bid are secret, and are known only to one party. For instance, a firm may issue a request for bid to electrical contractors for provision of electrical service on a new building. Bidders are requested to submit sealed bids, and the lowest bidder (subject to qualifications) will be the winner. In this instance, the bidders do not know what others are bidding, and must bid their "best" price. The danger here is **bid rigging**, in which bidders communicate prior to submitting their bids, and rig their bids to ensure that the lowest price is higher than it might otherwise be (which benefits the bidder, who in this instance is receiving the bid price as payment for services to be rendered). This is a common problem in sealed bid markets. However, in auction markets, bid prices are usually public information, available to all. Here the risks are that bidders agree offline to limit their bids, that sellers use shills to submit false bids, or that sellers use the market itself as a signaling device, driving prices up. Open markets permit large players to signal prices or engage in **price matching**, where sellers agree informally or formally to set floor prices on auction items below which they will not sell. Generally such collusion exists on the sell side, where there are just a few sellers or auction houses in a position to fix prices.

uniform pricing rule
there are multiple winners and they all pay the same price

discriminatory pricing
winners pay different amounts depending on what they bid

bid rigging
bidders communicate prior to submitting their bids, and rig their bids to ensure that the lowest price is higher than it might otherwise be

price matching
sellers agree informally or formally to set floor prices on auction items below which they will not sell

Types of Auctions

Now that you have learned some basic auction market rules and practices, it's time to consider some of the major forms of dynamically priced markets and auctions, both online and offline. **Table 11.4** describes the major types of auctions, how they work, and their biases. As you can see in Table 11.4, aside from the different formats and rules, there are many other differences among auctions. As noted above, there are both discriminatory and uniform pricing rules, although the latter seem to be most common. Also, in some auctions, there are multiple units for sale, whereas in others, there is only a single unit for sale. The major types of Internet auctions are English, Dutch-Internet, Name Your Own Price, and Group Buying.

TABLE 11.4	TYPES OF AUCTIONS AND DYNAMIC PRICING MECHANISMS	
AUCTION TYPE	**MECHANISM**	**BIAS**
Sealed bid market (B2B e-procurement— Ariba Sourcing; Elance)	Sealed-bid auction, RFQs. Winner is chosen from lowest bidders at acceptable quality levels.	Buyer bias: Multiple vendors competing against one another.
Elance)Vickrey auction (private auction)	Sealed-bid auction, single unit; highest bidder wins at the second-highest bid price.	Seller bias: Single seller and multiple buyers competing against one another
English auction (eBay)	Public ascending price, single unit; highest bidder wins at a price just above the second highest bid. Buyers can skip bidding at each price, but return at higher prices.	Seller bias: Single seller and multiple buyers competing against one another
Dutch-traditional (Dutch flower market)	Public descending-price auction, single unit; seller lowers price until a buyer takes the product.	Seller bias: Single seller, and multiple buyers competing against one another
Dutch-Internet (eBay Dutch Auction)	Public ascending price, multiple unit. Buyers bid on quantity and price. Final per-unit price is lowest successful bid, which sets a uniform price for all higher bidders as well (uniform price rule).	Seller bias: Small number of sellers and many buyers
Japanese auction (private auction)	Public ascending price, single unit; highest bidder wins at a price just above second-highest bid (reservation price) and buyers must bid at each price to stay in auction.	Seller bias: Single seller and many buyers
Yankee auction-Internet (variation on Dutch auction)	Public ascending price, multiple unit. Buyers bid on quantity and price per unit. Bidders ranked on price per unit, units, and time. Winners pay their actual bid prices (discriminatory rule).	Seller bias: Single seller and multiple buyers competing against one another
Reverse auction	Public reverse English auction, descending prices, single unit. Sellers bid on price to provide products or services; winning bid is the lowest-price provider. Similar to sealed bid markets.	Buyer bias: Multiple sellers competing against one another
Group buying (Groupon)	Public reverse auction, descending prices, multiple units. Buyers bid on price per unit and units. Groups of sellers bid on price; winning bid is lowest-price provider.	Buyer bias: Multiple sellers competing against one another
Name Your Own Price (Priceline)	Similar to a reverse auction except the price the consumer is willing to pay is fixed and the price offered is nonpublic. Requires a commitment to purchase at the first offered price.	Buyer bias: Multiple sellers competing against one another for an individual's business
Double auction (Nasdaq and stock markets)	Public bid-ask negotiation; sellers ask, buyers bid. Sale consummated when participants agree on price and quantity.	Neutral: Multiple buyers and sellers competing against one another. Market bias: trading specialists (matchmakers)

NOTE: "Public" means all participants can observe prices offered.

English auction

most common form of auction; the highest bidder wins

English Auctions The **English auction** is the easiest to understand and the most common form of auction on eBay. Typically, there is a single item up for sale from a single seller. There is a time limit when the auction ends, a reserve price below which the seller will not sell (usually secret), and a minimum incremental bid set. Multiple buyers bid against one another until the auction time limit is reached. The highest bidder wins the item (if the reserve price of the seller has been met or exceeded). English auctions are considered to be seller-biased because multiple buyers compete against one another—usually anonymously.

Traditional Dutch Auctions In the traditional Dutch auction in Aalsmeer, Holland, 5,000 flower growers—who own the auction facility—sell bundles of graded flowers to 2,000 buyers. The Dutch auction uses a clock visible to all that displays the starting price growers want for their flowers. Every few seconds, the clock ticks to a lower price. When buyers want to buy at the displayed price, they push a button to accept the lot of flowers at that price. If buyers fail to bid in a timely fashion, their competitors will win the flowers. The auction is very efficient: on average, Aalsmeer conducts 50,000 transactions daily for 15 million flowers. Dutch flower auctions are now conducted over the Internet. Buyers no longer have to be present at the market to bid, and sellers no longer have to have their flowers present in adjacent warehouses, but can ship directly from their farms (Kambil and vanHeck, 1996).

Dutch Internet auction

public ascending price, multiple unit auction. Final price is lowest successful bid, which sets price for all higher bidders

Dutch Internet Auctions In **Dutch Internet auctions**, such as those on eBay, OnSale, and others, the rules and action are different from the classical Dutch auction. The Dutch Internet auction format is perfect for sellers that have many identical items to sell. Sellers start by listing a minimum price, or a starting bid for one item, and the number of items for sale. Bidders specify both a bid price and the quantity they want to buy. The uniform price reigns. Winning bidders pay the same price per item, which is the lowest successful bid. This market clearing price can be less than some bids. If there are more buyers than items, the earliest successful bids get the goods. In general, high bidders get the quantity they want at the lowest successful price, whereas low successful bidders might not get the quantity they want (but they will get something). The action is usually quite rapid, and proxy bidding is not used. **Table 11.5** shows closing data from a sample Dutch Internet auction for a bundle of laptop computers.

In Table 11.5, the bids are arranged by price and then quantity. Under a uniform pricing rule, the lowest winning bid that clears the market of all 10 laptops is $736 and all winners pay this amount. However, the lowest winning bidder, JB505, will only receive three laptops, not four, because higher bidders are given their full allotments.

Name Your Own Price Auctions Auctions pioneered by Priceline are the second most-popular auction format on the Web. Although Priceline also acts as an intermediary, buying blocks of airline tickets and vacation packages at a discount and selling them at a reduced retail price or matching its inventory to bidders, it is best known for its Name Your Own Price auctions, where users specify what they are willing to pay for goods or services, and multiple providers bid for their business. Prices do not descend and are fixed: the initial consumer offer is a commitment to purchase at that price. In 2009, Priceline has over 10 million unique visitors a month, and almost $2 billion in revenues. It is one of the top-ranked travel sites in the United States. Today,

TABLE 11.5	A MULTI-UNIT DUTCH INTERNET AUCTION

CLOSING AUCTION DATA

Lot number	8740240
Total Number of Units	10
Description	HP Pavilion DV7T Laptop; Win Vista; Intel Core 2 Duo 2.1GHz, 17" widescreen; 4 GB memory; 320 GB hard drive
Reserve Price	None

BIDDER	DATE	TIME	BID	QUANTITY
JDMTKIS	10/25/09	18:35	$750	4
KTTX	10/25/09	18:55	$745	3
JB505	10/25/09	19:05	$736	4
VAMP	10/25/09	19:10	$730	2
DPVS	10/25/09	19:20	$730	1
RSF34	10/25/09	19:24	$725	1
CMCAL	10/25/09	19:25	$725	2

it also arranges for the sale of new cars, hotel accommodations, car rentals, long distance telephone service, and home finance.

Table 11.6 describes the products and services available in Priceline's Name Your Own Price auctions. Clearly, a major attraction of Priceline is that it offers consumers a market biased in their favor and very low prices, up to 40% off. Brand-name suppliers compete with one another to supply services to consumers. However, it is unclear at this time if the Priceline business model can extend to other categories of products. Experiments to sell gasoline and groceries through Priceline failed.

But how can Priceline offer discounts up to 40% off prices for services provided by major name brand providers? There are several answers. First, Priceline "shields the brand" by not publicizing the prices at which major brands sell. This reduces conflict with traditional channels, including direct sales. Second, the services being sold are perishable: if a Priceline consumer did not pay something for the empty airline seat, rental car, or hotel room, sellers would not receive any revenue. Hence, sellers are highly motivated to at least cover the costs of their services by selling in a spot market at very low prices.

The strategy for sellers is to sell as much as possible through more profitable channels and then unload excess capacity on spot markets such as Priceline. This works to the advantage of consumers, sellers, and Priceline, which charges a transaction fee to sellers.

Group Buying Auctions: Demand Aggregators A **demand aggregator** facilitates group buying of products at dynamically adjusted discount prices based on high-volume

demand aggregators
suppliers or market makers who group unrelated buyers into a single purchase in return for offering a lower purchase price. Prices on multiple units fall as the number of buyers increase

TABLE 11.6	PRICELINE NAME YOUR OWN PRICE OFFERINGS
SERVICE/PRODUCT	**DESCRIPTION**
Airline seats	Brand-name carriers bid for individual consumer business—perishable items that airlines are motivated to sell at the last minute.
Hotel rooms	Brand-name hotels bid for consumer business—perishable services that hotels are motivated to sell on a last-minute basis.
Rental cars	Brand-name rental companies bid for consumer business—perishable services that rental companies are motivated to sell on a last-minute basis.
Vacation packages	Brand-name hotels and air carriers bid for consumer business—perishable services that providers are motivated to sell on a last-minute basis.
Cruises	Cruise ship companies bid for consumer business, especially active in off-season periods.

purchases. The originator of demand aggregation was Mercata, formed in 1998, and the Web's largest retail demand aggregator until it ceased operations in January 2001, when needed venture capital financing did not materialize. Mercata holds several patents covering online demand aggregation. The largest supplier today of demand aggregation software is Ewinwin, a B2B demand aggregator. In general, demand aggregation did not work well for retail sales, but it has found a home in B2B commerce as a way of organizing group buying. Trade associations and industry-buying groups have traditionally pursued group buying plans in order to reduce costs from large suppliers.

Online demand aggregation is built on two principles. First, sellers are more likely to offer discounts to buyers purchasing in volume, and, second, buyers increase their purchases as prices fall. Prices are expected to dynamically adjust to the volume of the order and the motivations of the vendors.

Although online sites dedicated to retail group buying were not a commercial success, their software and business practices have been integrated into B2B and business-to-government (B2G) sites as one of many dynamic-pricing mechanisms. For instance, the federal government's Department of Homeland Security is building a centralized purchasing portal that will aggregate the demand for IT commodities (such as PCs, routers, and other equipment) from many different constituent agencies in order to reduce costs. In general, demand aggregation is suitable for MRO products (commodity-like products) that are frequently purchased by a large number of organizations in high volume.

Professional Service Auctions Perhaps one of the more interesting uses for auctions on the Web is eBay's marketplace for professional services, Elance. This auction is a sealed-bid, dynamic-priced market for freelance professional services from legal and marketing services to graphics design and programming. Firms looking for professional services post a project description and request for bid on Elance. Providers of services bid for the work. The buyer can choose from among bidders on the basis of both cost and perceived quality of the providers that can be gauged from the feedback of clients posted on the site. This type of auction is a reverse Vickrey-like auction where sealed bids are submitted and the winner is usually the low-cost provider of services. Another similar site is SoloGig.

Auction Aggregators (Mega Auctions) With thousands of auctions available on the Web, how can you, your customers, or your business find the right auction for products of interest that you want to either buy or sell? **Auction aggregators** (sometimes called mega auctions) offer one solution to this problem of multiple Internet markets and inter-market price differences. Auction aggregators use computer programs to search thousands of Web auction sites, accumulating information on products, bids, auction duration, and bid increments. Consumers search auction aggregator sites for products of interest, and the site returns a list of both fixed-price sales locations and auction locations where the product is for sale. Auction aggregators work by sending Web crawlers to thousands of auction sites every night (and on some sites during the day as well), gathering all information on product listings—just like an ordinary single consumer would. However, the major sites have effectively prevented auction aggregators from searching their sites without a license.

auction aggregators use computer programs to search thousands of Web auction sites, and aggregate information on products, bids, auction duration, and bid increments

WHEN TO USE AUCTIONS (AND FOR WHAT) IN BUSINESS

There are many different situations in which auctions are an appropriate channel for businesses to consider. For much of this chapter, we have looked at auctions from a consumer point of view. The objective of consumers is to receive the greatest value for the lowest cost. Switch perspectives now to that of a business. Remember that the objective for businesses using auctions is to maximize their revenue (their share of consumer surplus) by finding the true market value of products and services, a market value that hopefully is higher in the auction channel than in fixed-price channels. **Table 11.7** provides an overview of factors to consider.

The factors to consider include:

- **Type of product:** Online auctions are most commonly used for rare and unique products for which prices are difficult to discover, and there may have been no market for the goods. However, Priceline has succeeded in developing auctions for perishable commodities (such as airline seats) for which retail prices have already been established, and some B2B auctions involve commodities such as steel (often sold at distress prices). New clothing items, new digital cameras, and new computers are generally not sold at auction because their prices are easy to discover; catalog prices are high, sustainable, and profitable; they are not perishable; and there exists an efficient market channel in the form of retail stores (online and offline).

- **Product life cycle:** For the most part, businesses have traditionally used auctions for goods at the end of their product life cycle and for products where auctions yield a higher price than fixed-price liquidation sales. However, products at the beginning of their life cycle are increasingly being sold at auction. Early releases of music, books, videos, games, and digital appliances can be sold to highly

TABLE 11.7	FACTORS TO CONSIDER WHEN CHOOSING AUCTIONS
CONSIDERATIONS	DESCRIPTION
Type of product	Rare, unique, commodity, perishable
Stage of product life cycle	Early, mature, late
Channel-management issues	Conflict with retail distributors; differentiation
Type of auction	Seller vs. buyer bias
Initial pricing	Low vs. high
Bid increment amounts	Low vs. high
Auction length	Short vs. long
Number of items	Single vs. multiple
Price-allocation rule	Uniform vs. discriminatory
Information sharing	Closed vs. open bidding

motivated early adopters who want to be the first in their neighborhood with new products. Online sales of event tickets from music concerts to sports events now account for upwards of 25% of all event ticket sales in the United States.

- **Channel management:** Established retailers such as JCPenney and Wal-Mart, and manufacturers in general, must be careful not to allow their auction activity to interfere with their existing profitable channels. For this reason, items found on established retail-site auctions tend to be late in their product life cycle, or have quantity purchase requirements.

- **Type of auction:** Sellers obviously should choose auctions where there are many buyers and only a few, or even one, seller. English ascending-price auctions such as those at eBay are best for sellers because as the number of bidders increases the higher the price tends to move.

- **Initial pricing:** Research suggests that auction items should start out with low initial bid prices in order to encourage more bidders to bid (see "Bid increments" below). The lower the price, the larger the number of bidders will appear. The larger the number of bidders, the higher the prices move.

- **Bid increments:** It its generally safest to keep bid increments low so as to increase the number of bidders and the frequency of their bids. If bidders can be convinced that, for just a few more dollars, they can win the auction, then they will tend to make the higher bid and forget about the total amount they are bidding.

- **Auction length:** In general, the longer auctions are scheduled, the larger the number of bidders and the higher the prices can be go. However, once the new bid arrival rate drops off and approaches zero, bid prices stabilize. Most eBay auctions are scheduled for three days.

- **Number of items:** When a business has a number of items to sell, buyers usually expect a "volume discount," and this expectation can cause lower bids in return.

Therefore, sellers should consider breaking up very large bundles into smaller bundles auctioned at different times.

- **Price allocation rule:** Most buyers believe it is "fair" that everyone pay the same price in a multi-unit auction, and a uniform pricing rule is recommended. EBay Dutch Internet auctions encourage this expectation. The idea that some buyers should pay more based on their differential need for the product is not widely supported. Therefore, sellers who want to price discriminate should do so by holding auctions for the same goods on different auction markets, or at different times, to prevent direct price comparison.

- **Closed vs. open bidding:** Closed bidding has many advantages for the seller, and sellers should use this approach whenever possible because it permits price discrimination without offending buyers. However, open bidding carries the advantage of "herd effects" and "winning effects" (described later in the chapter) in which consumers' competitive instincts to "win" drive prices higher than even secret bidding would achieve.

SELLER AND CONSUMER BEHAVIOR AT AUCTIONS

In addition to these structural considerations, you should also consider the behavior of consumers at auction sites. Research on consumer behavior at online auction sites is growing, but is still in its infancy. However, early research has produced some interesting findings.

Seller Profits: Arrival Rate, Auction Length, and Number of Units

The profit to the seller is a function of the arrival rate, auction length, and the number of units for auction. However, each of these relationships suffers a declining return to scale and rapidly falls off after an optimal point is reached (Vakrat and Seidman, 1998, 1999) (see **Figure 11.4**). For this reason, in real-world auctions on eBay, sellers with a large number of units to sell, say, hundreds of PC laptops, usually have multiple concurrent auctions with about 10 units for sale in each auction, with a duration of three days. The auction is just long enough to attract most of the likely bidders, but not so long as to run up the cost of posting the auction beyond a profitable level. The more popular an auction (the more bidders who arrive), the longer an auction should be, up to the point where the costs of maintaining the auction listing outweigh the additional profit brought by the last bidder. These dynamics suggest a kind of bidding frenzy for popular items, in which the prices bid depend on the number of bidders, length of time, and units offered.

Auction Prices: Are They the Lowest?

It is widely assumed that auction prices are lower than prices in other fixed-price markets. Empirical evidence is mixed on this assumption. Vakrat and Seidmann (1999) found auction prices were 25% lower on average than prices for the identical goods found in catalogs produced by the same retailers. Brynjolfsson and (2000) also found that auction prices for CDs were lower than online store prices. Lee found, however, that auction prices for used cars in Japan on the AUCNET auc-

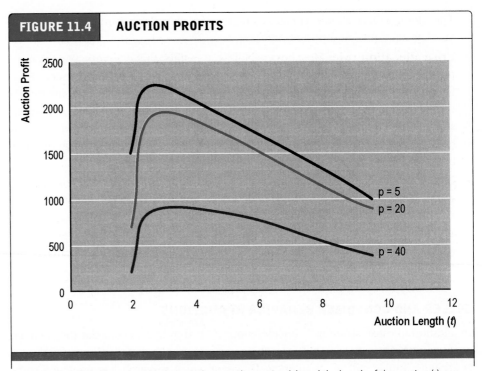

FIGURE 11.4 | **AUCTION PROFITS**

An auction's profit is determined by the arrival rate at the auction (p), and the length of the auction (t). Profitability rises rapidly at first, but then falls off rapidly as costs rise. Profits also rise with the number of units auctioned up to a maximum point, and then fall off rapidly.

SOURCE: Based on data from Vakrat and Seidmann, 1998.

tion site were actually higher than fixed-price markets, in part because the quality of cars on the auction site was higher than cars found in car lots (Lee et al., 1999–2000).

There are many reasons why auction prices might be higher than those in fixed-price markets for items of identical quality, and why auction prices in one auction market may be higher than those in other auction markets. A considerable body of research has shown that consumers are not driven solely by value maximization, but instead are influenced by many situational factors, irrelevant and wrong information, and misperceptions when they make market decisions (Simonson and Tversky, 1992). Auctions are social events—shared social environments, where bidders adjust to one another (Hanson and Putler, 1996). Briefly, bidders base their bids on what others previously bid, and this can lead to an upward cascading effect (Arkes and Hutzel, 2000). In a study of hundreds of eBay auctions for Sony PlayStations, CD players, Mexican pottery, and Italian silk ties, Dholakia and Soltysinski (2001) found that bidders exhibited **herd behavior** (the tendency to gravitate toward, and bid for, auction listings with one or more existing bids) by making multiple bids on some auctions (coveted comparables), and making no bids at auctions for comparable items (overlooked comparables). Herd behavior was lower for products where there was more agreement and more objective clues on the value

herd behavior

the tendency to gravitate toward, and bid for, auction listings with one or more existing bids of the products—Sony PlayStations, for instance, compared to Italian silk ties. Herd behavior resulted in consumers paying higher prices than necessary for reasons having no foundation in economic reality.

The behavioral reality of participating in auctions can produce many unintended results. Winners can suffer **winner's regret**, the feeling after winning an auction that they paid too much for an item, which indicates that their winning bid does not reflect what they thought the item was worth but rather what the second bidder thought the item was worth. Sellers can experience **seller's lament**, reflecting the fact that they sold an item at a price just above the second place bidder, never knowing how much the ultimate winner might have paid or the true value to the final winner. Auction losers can experience **loser's lament**, the feeling of having been too cheap in bidding and failing to win. In summary, auctions can lead to both winners paying too much and sellers receiving too little. Both of these outcomes can be minimized when sellers and buyers have a very clear understanding of the prices for items in a variety of different online and offline markets.

The *Insight on Society* story, *Swoopo: Online Auction or Game of Chance* discusses an online auction site whose business model is designed to exploit some of the behavioral economics associated with online auctions.

winner's regret
the winner's feeling after an auction that he or she paid too much for an item

seller's lament
concern that one will never know how much the ultimate winner might have paid, or the true value to the final winner

loser's lament
the feeling of having been too cheap in bidding and failing to win

Consumer Trust in Auctions

Auction sites have the same difficulties creating a sense of consumer trust as all other e-commerce Web sites, although in the case of auction sites, the operators of the marketplace do not directly control the quality of goods being offered and cannot directly vouch for the integrity of customers. This opens the possibility for criminal actors to appear as either sellers or buyers. EBay is the single largest source of consumer fraud on the Internet. Several studies have found that trust and credibility increase as users gain more experience, if trusted third-party seals are present, and if the site has a wide variety of consumer services for tracking purchases (or fraud), thus giving the user a sense of control (Krishnamurthy, 2001; Stanford-Makovsky, 2002; Nikander and Karnonen, 2002; Bailey, et al., 2002; Kollock, 1999). Because of the powerful role that trust plays in online consumer behavior, eBay and most auction sites make considerable efforts to develop automated trust-enhancing mechanisms such as seller and buyer ratings, escrow services, and authenticity guarantees (see the next section).

WHEN AUCTION MARKETS FAIL: FRAUD AND ABUSE IN AUCTIONS

Markets fail to produce socially desirable outcomes (maximizing consumer welfare) in four situations: information asymmetry, monopoly power, public goods, and externalities.

Online and offline auction markets are particularly prone to fraud, which produces information asymmetries between sellers and buyers and among buyers, which in turn causes auction markets to fail. According to the Internet Crime Complaint Center (IC3), Internet auction fraud was the second most reported offense, generating over 25% of all complaints. (National White Collar Crime Center/FBI, 2009). The median loss was $610 and the most common fraudulent payment mecha-

INSIGHT ON SOCIETY

SWOOPO: ONLINE AUCTION OR GAME OF CHANCE

When reporters, bloggers, and others write about Swoopo, they use words like "addictive" and "insidious." They compare it to crack cocaine. Some question whether it's really an online auction site, or just a gambling site using the auctions as a ruse. And others wonder if it's even legal in the United States to operate a site with Swoopo's rules. Swoopo, founded in Germany in 2005 and originally called Telebid, bills itself as an online auction Web site that, according to its CEO Gunnar Piening, "combines the elements of online auctions, skill games and traditional e-commerce to make shopping fun again." That sounds good. Except that no matter how much "skill" a bidder has, there is no way to influence the outcome of an individual auction. And it costs money to bid—that sounds like betting.

How does the site work? On Swoopo, registered bidders compete to purchase merchandise, primarily but not exclusively electronics, at greatly discounted prices. Unlike eBay, Swoopo uses a B2C model, offering the merchandise directly to consumers, not acting as a middleman for consumers to sell their products to other consumers. Hundreds of items are auctioned simultaneously. Some are localized or U.S. only, others are open to registered bidders anywhere in the world.

In a Swoopo auction, the item is initially offered at a very low price, which goes up in small increments, typically $.12 per bid, but sometimes as little as $.01. Registered bidders pay $.60 for every bid they make. And here's the kicker—every time a bid is made, the auction clock is reset by adding 20 seconds. So unlike eBay, no one can come in at the last second, make a big bid and "swipe" the item.

When bidders register on Swoopo, they purchase BidPacks in increments of 40, 75, 150, 400 or 1,000 at a cost of $.60 each. Then they can start "shopping." Bidders can also use BidButler, an automated tool that allows the bidder to set a minimum bid and a maximum bid and let BidButler take care of the rest. That way the bidder doesn't have to stay on the Swoopo site and follow the live auction.

The Web site's FAQ page offers advice about how to bid and pitfalls to avoid. The language implies that there are "strategies" that will increase the odds of "winning" a particular item. But bidders can do nothing to increase their odds of winning, and at $.60 a bid, the company, like the "house" in Las Vegas or Atlantic City, is the one making the money. In order to further the illusion that users can win many items in a short period of time, Swoopo limits registered users to "winning" a maximum of eight items in a 28-day period.

Here's a concrete example. Recently, a MacBook Pro sold on Swoopo for $35.86. Its suggested retail price is $1,799, so it sounds like a pretty good deal. It's particularly good for Swoopo. In this auction, each bid raised the price by $.01 increments, so there were 3,568 bids made. Before selling the computer, Swoopo took in $2,151 in bid fees. The winner bid more than 750 times, paying $469.80 in fees. So the winner did pretty well, but losers may spend hundreds of dollars in bidding fees before walking away empty-handed. Swoopo does offer bidders the option to "Swoop it Now," or buy the same item offered in an auction for the full price (minus the amount that person has already spent on bids) while the auction is still going on.

As of July 2009, Swoopo had 2.5 million registered users, and offices in six countries. Its revenue has doubled every year since its founding, despite reports that the company loses money on 70% of the auctions. The losses are usually on the

(continued)

smaller-ticket items like DVDs, while the company makes money on bigger-ticket items like the MacBook Pro. In the spring of 2009, Swoopo announced that August Capital, a U.S. venture capital firm, was investing $10 million to help the company expand worldwide.

Swoopo is not the only e-commerce company in this business. The competition includes GoBid and Rockybid, which are currently operational, and Project Fair Bid, a new site which will launch in March 2010 with the help of $4.5 million from three U.S. venture capital firms. And just about every week a new competitor pops up on the Web. Swoopo combines elements of gambling, game theory, behavioral economics and science to create a site that some consumers will find addictive. By adding 20 seconds to the clock every time a bid is made, Swoopo creates the impression that an auction is about to end, although it may go on for hours more. But potential bidders get the sense that time is running out so they keep bidding to make sure they don't lose the item at the last minute. And after making multiple bids, people begin to operate on the theory of "sunk cost," feeling like they've already spent a certain amount of money and all they need to do is spend a little more to win the item. However, that is not the case. As long as the auction is still running, the money a bidder has spent in the past has nothing do with winning the item or even improving the chances of winning. Spending more money gets bidders no closer to their goal. Under this fallacy of the sunk cost, Swoopo efficiently gets people to make bad choices.

Further, there's an urge to believe that there are strategies that will beat the system. But there are none. In fact, the bigger and more popular Swoopo gets, the harder it will be to win because more people will bid for each item. It's like the lottery. You can't win if you don't play, but buying more tickets doesn't increase the chance of winning unless you can control the number of tickets other people buy.

There's also something called the jackpot effect that comes into play on Swoopo. When bidders fixate on the "big prize," they forget the incremental costs of participation. It works like a slot machine, but with Swoopo the other bidders are the random number generators. The home page even looks like a slot machine, with six live auctions counting down all the time. And the site uses all kinds of language to make it sound like users have some control—they do not.

Even the science of how the brain functions comes into play with Swoopo. Research has shown that people don't need to win to get the dopamine boost that comes with winning. They just need to think they're close to winning—that if they keep at it the reward will come. And even when they lose, or have what they perceive as a "near miss" experience, it feels awful, yet it provides the illusion of control. People think a near miss means they are more likely to win the next time, even though the reality is that the odds don't bear this out.

Finally, in addition to the behavioral questions, there are legal questions regarding the Swoopo's payment per bid system. States don't specifically allow this kind of system, but they don't specifically prohibit it either. No lawsuits have been filed yet, so for now, the question of whether bidding on items on Swoopo is really gambling and not participating in an online auction remains an open one.

SOURCES: "Swoopo! Do Penny Auction Sites Run Afoul of California Gambling Laws?" by David Johnson, Digitalmediallawyerblog.com, August 18, 2009; "Sites Ask Users to Spend to Save," by Brad Stone, *New York Times*, August 16, 2009; "This Company is Inside Your Head," by John Rosevear, Fool.com, August 14, 2009; "Online Auctions: Mind the Pennies," *The Economist*, August 13, 2009; "At Swoopo, Shopping's Steep Spiral into Addiction," by Mark Gimein, Washingtonpost.com, July 12, 2009; "Swoopo: The Frontal Cortex," by Jonah Lehrer, Scienceblogs.com, July 10, 2009; "Unique Auction Site Swoopo Expands To Canada, Testing "Buy It Now", by Jason Kincaid, Techcrunch.com, June 26, 2009; "August Capital Helps Fund Online Shopping Site Swoopo," *Silicon Valley/San Jose Business Journal,* April 2, 2009; "Swoopo - eBay's (More) Evil Twin," by Ted Dziuba, *The Register*, January 2, 2009; "Profitable Until Deemed Illegal," by Jeff Atwood, Codinghorror.com, Decemmber 11, 2008; "Swoopo Looks to Set the Record Straight," by Ed Oswald, Technologizer.com, October 9, 2008; "Gadgetell Interview: Swoopo Speaks," by JG Mason, Gadgetell.com, October 3, 2008; "Entertainment Shopping Portal Swoopo Launches US-Site," by Ina Steiner, AuctionBytes.com, September 17, 2008.

nisms were money orders and credit cards. The Federal Trade Commission (FTC), in 2009, had some good news: Internet auction fraud complaints dropped to 13th place in the consumer complaint category—only 17,000 complaints of fraud were reported to the FTC. (The leading complaint was identity theft [314,000 complaints]) (Federal Trade Commission, 2008). However, this data fails to measure the overall extent of auction fraud because many consumers do not report being defrauded to the FTC. **Table 11.8** lists the most common and important frauds.

EBay and many other auction sites have investigation units that receive complaints from consumers and investigate reported abuses. Nevertheless, with millions of visitors per week and hundreds of thousands of auctions to monitor, eBay is highly dependent on the good faith of sellers and consumers to follow the rules.

11.3   E-COMMERCE PORTALS

Port: From the Latin porta, an entrance or gateway to a locality.

Portals are the most frequently visited sites on the Web if only because they typically are the first page to which many users point their browser on startup. The top portals such as Yahoo, MSN, and AOL have hundreds of millions of unique visitors worldwide each month. Web portal sites are gateways to the more than 50 billion Web pages available on the Internet. Perhaps the most important service provided by portals is that of helping people find the information they are looking for on the Web. The original portals in the early days of e-commerce were search engines. Consumers would pass through search engine portals on their way to rich, detailed, in-depth content on the Web. But portals have evolved into much more complex Web sites that provide news, entertainment, maps, images, social networks, in-depth information, and education on a growing variety of topics all contained at the portal site. Portals today seek to be a sticky destination site, not merely a gateway through which visitors pass. In this respect, Web portals are very much like television networks: destination sites for content supported by advertising revenues. Portals today want visitors to stay a long time—the longer the better. For the most part they succeed: portals are places where people linger for a long time.

enterprise portals
help employees navigate to the enterprise's human resource and corporate content

Portals also serve important functions within a business or organization. Most corporations, universities, churches, and other formal organizations have **enterprise portals** that help employees or members navigate to important content, such as human resources information, corporate news, or organizational announcements. For instance, your university has a portal through which you can register for courses, find out classroom assignments, and perform a host of other important student activities. Increasingly, these enterprise portals also provide general-purpose news and financial real-time feeds provided by content providers outside the organization, such as MSNBC News and generalized Web search capabilities. Corporate portals and intranets are the subject of other textbooks focused on the corporate uses of Web technology and are beyond the scope of this book (see Laudon and Laudon, 2009). Our focus here will be on e-commerce portals.

TABLE 11.8	TYPES OF AUCTION FRAUDS
TYPE OF FRAUD	**DESCRIPTION**
Feedback Offenses	
Shill feedback	Using secondary IDs or other auction site members to inflate seller ratings
Feedback abuse	Any abuse of the feedback forum
Feedback extortion	Threatening negative feedback in return for a benefit
Feedback solicitation	Offering to sell, trade, or buy feedback
Buying Offenses	
Transaction interference	E-mailing buyers to warn them away from a seller
Invalid bid retraction	Using the retraction option to make high bids, discovering the maximum bid of current high bidder, then retracting bid
Persistent bidding	Persisting in making bids despite a warning that bids are not welcome
Unwelcome buyer	Buying in violation of seller's terms
Bid shielding	Using secondary user IDs or other members to artificially raise the bidding price of an item
Nonpayment after buying	Blocking legitimate buyers by bidding high, then not paying
Selling Offenses	
Shill bidding	Using secondary user IDs or bidders who have no actual intention to buy to artificially raise the price of an item
Seller nonperformance	Accepting payment and failing to deliver the promised goods, either at all, or delivering goods not as described in auction (counterfeit or poor quality)
Nonselling seller	Refusing payment, failure to deliver after a successful auction
Fee avoidance	Any of a variety of mechanisms for avoiding paying listing fees
Transaction interception	Pretending you are a seller and accepting payment
Contact Information/Identity Offenses	
Misrepresentation of identity	Claiming to be an employee of the auction site; representing oneself as another auction site member
False or missing contact information	Providing false information or leaving information out
Dead/invalid e-mail addresses	Providing false contact information
Underage user	User under 18
Miscellaneous Offenses	
Interference with site	Using any software program that would interfere with auction site operations
Bid siphoning	E-mailing another seller's bidders and offering the same product for less
Sending spam	Sending unsolicited offers to bidders

THE GROWTH AND EVOLUTION OF PORTALS

Web portals have changed a great deal from their initial function and role. As noted above, most of today's well-known portals began as search engines. The initial function provided by portals such as Yahoo, Lycos, Excite, AltaVista, Ask Jeeves, and later Google was to index Web page content and make this content available to users in a convenient form. Early portals expected visitors to stay only a few minutes at the site. As millions of people signed on to the Internet in the late 1990s, the number of visitors to basic search engine sites exploded commensurately. At first, few people understood how a Web search site could make money by passing customers on to other destinations. But search sites attracted huge audiences, and therein lay the foundation for their success as vehicles for marketing and advertising. Search sites, recognizing the potential for commerce, expanded their offerings from simple navigation to include commerce (the sale of items directly from the Web site as well as advertising for other retail sites), content (in the form of news at first, and later in the form of weather, investments, games, health, and other subject matter), and distribution of others' content. These three characteristics have become the basic definition of portal sites since 2006, namely, sites that provide three functions: navigation of the Web, commerce, and content.

Because the value of portals to advertisers and content owners is largely a function of the size of the audience each portal reaches, portals compete with one another on reach and unique visitors. *Reach* is defined as the percentage of the Web audience that visits the site in a month (or some other time period), and *unique visitors* is defined as the number of uniquely identified individuals who visit in a month. Portals are inevitably subject to network effects: The value of the portal to advertisers and consumers increases geometrically as reach increases, which, in turn, attracts still more customers. These effects have resulted in the differentiation of the portal marketspace into three tiers: a few general-purpose mega portal sites that garner 60%–80% of the Web audience, second-tier general-purpose sites that hover around 20%–30% reach, and third-tier specialized vertical market portals that attract 2%–10% of the audience. As described in Chapter 3, the top five portals/search engines (Google, Yahoo, MSN/Bing, AOL, and Ask.com) account for over 90% of online searches. A similar pattern of concentration is observed when considering the audience share of portals/search engines as illustrated in **Figure 11.5** (see page 755). However this picture is changing as large audiences move to social networking sites, and millions of users make these sites their opening or home pages.

For more insight into the nature of the competition and change among the top portals, read *Insight on Business: The Transformation of AOL.*

TYPES OF PORTALS: GENERAL-PURPOSE AND VERTICAL MARKET

general purpose portals
attempt to attract a very large general audience and then retain the audience on-site by providing in-depth vertical content

There are two primary types of portals: general-purpose portals and vertical market portals. **General-purpose portals** attempt to attract a very large general audience and then retain the audience on-site by providing in-depth vertical content channels. Some general purpose portals—such as MSN—also offer limited ISP services usually

INSIGHT ON BUSINESS

THE TRANSFORMATION OF AOL

AOL began its life in the early 1980s as Control Video Corporation, providing an online service called Gameline for the Atari 2600 video game console. For $1 a game, subscribers could temporarily download games, keep track of high scores, and play the downloaded game until they downloaded another one. The company didn't make enough money, and in May 1983 it was reorganized as Quantum Computer Services, providing a dedicated online service for Commodore 64 and 128 computers called Quantum Link. In 1988, the company added online services called Apple Link and PC Link, and in 1989, its name was changed to America Online.

In February 1991, AOL launched an online program for the DOS operating system (the early Microsoft operating system that used text commands) and one for Windows the following year. AOL positioned itself as the online service for people who were not familiar with computers. This was in contrast to CompuServe, which served the technical community. Positioning AOL as the company for those who weren't comfortable with technology was very effective initially, but as broadband connections became widespread, and users more sophisticated, over time AOL suffered because it was perceived as stodgy, slow, and uncool.

AOL provided proprietary software, and enabled communication among users through chat rooms. The company charged users hefty hourly fees, but in 1996, AOL switched over to a subscription-based model, charging $19.99 per month. AOL's user base grew to 10 million people. AOL distributed it program by sending millions of CD-ROMs in the mail to potential adopters. Its popularity was based on its ease of use and brand exposure—AOL was everywhere. Many users got their first exposure to the Web, e-mail, instant messaging, and chat rooms through their AOL memberships. The interface was user-friendly. However, from early on, there were complaints about dropped connections and busy signals, and the company was slow to provide access to the open Internet for its subscribers. But it continued to grow. In 1996, in another boon to its brand, AOL signed a five-year agreement that it would be bundled with Windows on new PCs. The first major Web portal for the general public was on its way.

In 1999, CEO Steve Case said that Windows was in the past, and predicted that AOL would be the next Microsoft. This is not exactly how the story unfolded. While AOL grew to be the number one supplier of dial-up Internet connections for millions of Americans, when the company tried to exploit the tremendous name-recognition and prominence of the brand, they failed over and over again. Its biggest failure, though not its only one, was not anticipating the impact that broadband would have on the way that people would choose to access the Internet. But that's getting ahead of the story.

In 2000, before the company's spectacular fall began, Time Warner bought AOL for $165 billion. Despite the media fanfare, there were problems with the merger from the start. It is now known as perhaps the largest single investment error in the history of the Web. On the announcement of the purchase, high-flying AOL stock dropped sharply due to fears that Time Warner's old media assets would drag AOL down. After all, Time Warner was an "old" media company that supposedly had little to offer the Internet and Web, and had no Web assets or experience. In the

(continued)

first year after the purchase, the merged company already had difficulty reaching growth targets, possibly because AOL had improperly inflated its pre-merger revenue. In 2002, advertising revenue declined sharply. The number of AOL ISP subscribers peaked in the fall of that year, at 26.7 million, and has been declining ever since. Today there are 6.2 million ISP subscribers, and they are dropping off steadily at the rate of 200,000 per month.

There are those who believe it didn't have to turn out that way. The merging of one of the foremost providers of "old fashioned" content with one of the largest distributors of "online" content might have made sense if it had been managed differently. But it wasn't.

With very few people involved in the deal, senior staff at both companies didn't feel like they had a stake in the success of the merged entity. Key players at Time Warner resented the merger, and thought it was a waste of time and money. To make matters worse, corporate leadership did little to persuade brand/division heads that it was their responsibility to make the merged company work. Time Warner executives feared the AOL team would try to take over the company and force them out so they refused to collaborate. Remarkably, Time Warner's top content providers, including CNN, HBO, Fortune, and Sports Illustrated, put their content almost anywhere on the Web except AOL.

Then came broadband. For most of its history, AOL users were forced to stay on the AOL platform because there were few higher bandwidth alternatives. The company unfortunately underestimated how attractive broadband would become. By 2004, people were rapidly embracing broadband. At the same time, Google's search engine advertising took off and banner advertising on the site took off with it. Yahoo was successful with banner display ads, and they added content that drew the broadband audience.

AOL/Time Warner had plenty of content available, including news, text, magazines, and skilled writers and producers, but they were unable to bring it to the Web. Quickly, AOL began to look like a brand that was not sophisticated and not in tune with the times. Even when AOL made its subscriber-only content freely available, it was too little, too late.

By 2006, AOL abandoned marketing its access services to concentrate on free Web sites. The CEO was fired, and replaced by an NBC executive who didn't have an Internet background, ushering in a tumultuous era with three CEOs and five VPs of marketing in a three-year period.

In 2007, AOL began pursuing a new strategy of creating several different brands. In 2008, Time Warner was in ongoing talks to sell AOL to Microsoft or Google. In 2009, Time Warner decided instead to spin off the company. Before doing that, they bought back Google's 5% stake in the company for $283 million. Google had paid $1 billion for that stake in 2005.

The third CEO in three years, Tim Armstrong, came on board in 2009. He has added senior staff members from Google and Yahoo. Armstrong wants to focus on turning the company into the biggest creator of premium content on the Web and the largest seller of online display ads. He describes AOL as "a small little company that has gone through some challenging times that is trying to find a way to come up with ideas that will connect with an audience."

He has his work cut out for him. In 2009, AOL's revenue is projected at $3.2 billion, down 38% in two years. The company's market value is clearly well below the $20 billion valuation in 2005. Current estimates are closer to $5.7 billion, less than 30% of the 2005 number, and a small fraction of the $165 billion purchase price in 2000. In the short term, Armstrong has announced that AOL will not abandon its ISP subscriber business, which, despite its slow

(continued)

contraction, still provides valuable revenue for the company.

You can see AOL's new strategy in place at AOL's corporate headquarters in New York City, where 300 staff members (there are 7,000 staffers worldwide), work full-time producing content. Many of these are new employees recently laid off by "old" media such as magazines and newspapers. They are joined by freelancers and programmers all over the world, who are cranking out copy and editing photos, and posting all of it to more than 80 AOL-owned Web sites, 10 of them ranked in Technorati's top 100. The shrinking newspaper and magazine industries have helped AOL to hire top talent from publications such as the *New York Times*, *Washington Post*, *USA Today*, *Time* and *Newsweek* to write this content. Finally, AOL is focusing on content and digital distribution platforms like Web sites and blogs.

There is some evidence that this model may work. AOL launched the Web site Politics Daily in April 2009, and the site already has 3.6 million unique visitors per month. Politico, a much more established name, has only 1.1 million. In aggregate, the media properties of AOL, sites such as Engadget, TMZ, and Fan-House, have 76 million unique visitors per month. This audience is monetized through display advertising. Many of these sites are not visibly AOL properties. Armstrong says that's just smart business. Disney, he points out, owns ABC and ESPN, but doesn't make that obvious to TV watchers on a daily basis. If sites are to be seen as authentic, they can't be seen as a product of an unimaginative conglomerate. Another part of the strategy involved focusing on local experiences and content, including providing self-service applications for consumers and advertisers. So AOL will build local networks with local services. Armstrong says local advertising is a prime area for innovation and that AOL already has a significant audience. He

adds that local advertising accounts for 39% of all advertising dollars spent annually in the United States.

The company has already put its money where its mouth is in this area. In June 2009, AOL acquired two companies, Patch Media Corporation, a local news and information platform aimed at serving local towns and communities, and Going, Inc., a local platform for people to discover and share information about things to do in a number of leading U.S. cities. To build additional advertising revenue, AOL has implemented a technology called BidPlace, which allows advertisers to bid to buy ads across a large network of AOL-owned sites and those it represents as middleman. BidPlace clients use a Web interface to define an ad budget, manage bids, and have access to analytics. As of May 2009, this network, made up of thousands of sites, reaches 91% of the 200 million Americans online. In September 2009, Google unveiled the DoubleClick Ad Exchange—a similar service in conjunction with DoubleClick, which it had purchased 18 months previously—which will make the market for such services more crowded and thus challenging for AOL. AOL is also strengthening its sales force to sell ads to major marketers on AOL premium Web properties such as the AOL home page and MapQuest.

Some smaller fixes have been put in place too. AOL pulled back the size of ads on a number of its Web sites to make pages look less cluttered, and to show that consumer preferences are a priority. So far this move has helped and audience size has increased where this strategy has been implemented has increased. With only 3.1% of the search market, Armstrong is not focusing there. Instead he expects revenue to come from building out content and building out advertising networks as described above. AOL has signed an exclusive agreement with Google to provide search services through December 2010. The

(continued)

company will "shop" around when that deal expires, possibly shifting to Microsoft/Bing.

AOL's strategy to focus on content and advertising is risky. Content is expensive, and the banner ad supply inventory is huge. The price charged for banner ads is exceptionally low because they don't work well compared to search ads, and they are not considered culturally hip. But then again, neither is Yahoo, and millions of people have Yahoo as their home page, use Yahoo e-mail and read their news and celebrity content.

The large amount of data AOL has on users is an advantage. As an ISP from the beginning of the Web, the company has plenty of individual personal information on subscribers. This can help advertisers create targeted marketing programs to reach their desired customer.

The vertical blogs AOL is creating (70 plus to date including Boombox (hiphop), Wallet Pop (personal finance) and Paw Nation (pets)) attract a committed, dedicated audience that will respond to targeted ads at a much higher rate than generic portal content such as Yahoo's. Create a horse blog and sell horse stuff. Do that a thousand times and you might have a business. How many such vertical markets like that exist? Probably enough to keep AOL blog creators busy and profitable.

Finally, while the spin-off from Time Warner is important, some believe that the recruitment of top Google and Yahoo executives is more important. They bring more educated analysis of consumer behavior, which can lead to better targeted advertising, more revenue and a successful company. Time will tell whether AOL will find its niche this time.

SOURCES: "AOL Blossoms as Print Retreats," by David Carr, *New York Times*, August 17, 2009; "Google Dumps Iinvestment," Venturebeat, *New York Times*, July 27, 2009; "Eleven Years of Ambition and Failure at AOL," by Saul Hansell, *New York Times*, July 24, 2009; "Daring to Dream of a Resurgent AOL," by Saul Hansell, *New York Times*, July 23, 2009; "Before Spin-off, AOL Tries for that Start-up Feeling," *New York Times*, July 20, 2009; "Advertising Overhaul Among Changes at AOL," by Rachel Metz, Thestreet.com, July 20, 2009; "AOL CEO Tim Armstrong: "The Model Is Disney,"" by Greg Sterling, Searchengineland.com, July 20, 2009; "With Ex-Google Exec, AOL Seeks Another Fresh Start," by Rachel Metz, *Associated Press*, May 24, 2009; "Spin-off from Time Warner," *Los Angeles Times*, May 29, 2009; "Acquisition of Local Content Providers Patch and Going," Smartbrief.com, July 11, 2009.

in conjunction with major telecommunications providers, plus Web search engines, free e-mail, personal home pages, chat rooms, community building software, and bulletin boards. Vertical content channels on general-purpose portal sites offer content such as sports scores, stock tickers, health tips, instant messaging, automobile information, and auctions.

Vertical market portals (sometimes also referred to as destination sites or vortals) attempt to attract highly focused, loyal audiences with a deep interest either in community or specialized content—from sports to the weather. In addition to their focused content, vertical market portals have recently begun adding many of the features found in general-purpose portals.

The concentration of audience share in the portal market reflects (in addition to network effects) the limited time budget of consumers. This limited time budget works to the advantage of general-purpose portals. Consumers have a finite amount of time to spend on the Web, and as a result, most consumers visit fewer than 30 unique domains each month. Facing limited time, consumers concentrate their visits at sites that can satisfy a broad range of interests, from weather and travel information, to stocks, sports, and entertainment content.

vertical market portals

attempt to attract highly focused, loyal audiences with a deep interest in either community or specialized content

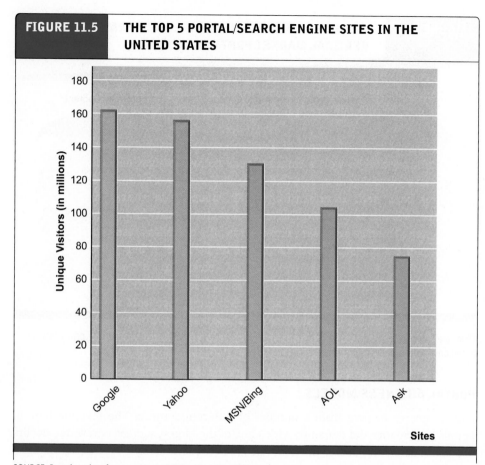

FIGURE 11.5 THE TOP 5 PORTAL/SEARCH ENGINE SITES IN THE UNITED STATES

SOURCE: Based on data from comScore, 2009; eMarketer, 2009e.

General-purpose sites such as Yahoo try to be all things to all people, and attract a broad audience with both generalized navigation services and also in-depth content and community efforts. For instance, Yahoo has become the Web's largest source of news: more people visit Yahoo News than any other news site including online newspapers. Yet recent changes in consumer behavior on the Web show that consumers are spending less time "surfing the Web" and on general browsing, and more time doing focused searches, research, and participating in social networks. These trends will advantage special-purpose, vertical market sites that can provide focused, in-depth community and content.

As a general matter, the general-purpose portals are very well-known brands, while the vertical content and affinity group portals tend to have less well-known brands. **Figure 11.6** lists examples of general-purpose portals and the two main types of vertical market portals.

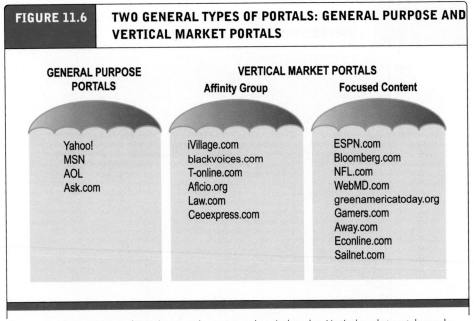

FIGURE 11.6 — TWO GENERAL TYPES OF PORTALS: GENERAL PURPOSE AND VERTICAL MARKET PORTALS

There are two general types of portals: general-purpose and vertical market. Vertical market portals may be based on affinity groups or on focused content.

PORTAL BUSINESS MODELS

Portals receive income from a number of different sources. The revenue base of portals is changing and dynamic, with some of the largest sources of revenue declining. **Table 11.9** summarizes the major portal revenue sources.

ISP services revenue represents a declining part of the revenue base for portal sites, although for AOL, for instance, it still generates a significant amount of revenue. More and more Americans have switched to broadband connections provided by giant telephone and cable companies. The business strategies of both general-purpose and vertical portals have changed greatly because of the rapid

TABLE 11.9	TYPICAL PORTAL REVENUE SOURCES
PORTAL REVENUE SOURCE	DESCRIPTION
ISP services	Providing Web access and e-mail services for a monthly fee
General advertising	Charging for impressions delivered
Tenancy deals	Fixed charge for guaranteed number of impressions, exclusive partnerships, "sole providers"
Commissions on sales	Revenue based on sales at the site by independent providers
Subscription fees	Charging for premium content

growth in search engine advertising and intelligent ad placement networks such as Google's AdSense, which can place ads on thousands of Web sites based on the content of the Web site. General portal sites such as AOL, MSN, and Yahoo did not have well-developed search engines, and hence have not grown as fast as Google, which has a powerful search engine. Portal sites have invested billions of dollars to catch up with Google. On the other hand, general portals have content, which Google did not (originally have, although it is adding to its content by purchasing YouTube, and adding Google sites devoted to news, financial information, images, maps, etc.). Yahoo and MSN visitors stay on-site a long time reading news, content, and sending e-mail. General portals are attempting to provide more premium content focused on sub-communities of their portal audience. Advertisers on portals are especially interested in focused, revenue-producing premium content available on Web portals because it attracts a more committed audience.

For instance, financial service firms pay premium advertising rates to advertise on portal finance service areas such as Yahoo's Finance pages. As noted in Chapters 6 and 7, there is a direct relationship between the revenue derived from a customer and the focus of the customer segment (see **Figure 11.7**).

The survival strategy for general-purpose portals in the future is therefore to develop deep, rich, vertical content in order to reach customers at the site. The strategy for much smaller vertical market portals is to put together a collection of vertical portals to form a vertical portal network, a collection of deep, rich content sites. The strategy for search engine sites such as Google is to obtain more content to attract users for a long time and expose them to more ad pages (or screens).

| FIGURE 11.7 | REVENUE PER CUSTOMER AND MARKET FOCUS |

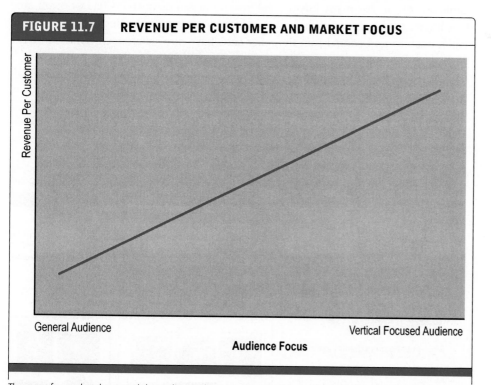

The more focused and targeted the audience, the more revenue that can be derived per customer for an appropriately targeted product or service.

11.4   CASE STUDY

eBay Fine-Tunes its Strategy

Since its inception, eBay has been synonymous with Internet auctions. The company has been the first and by far the most successful Internet auction business, mushrooming into a gigantic electronic marketplace hosting 25 million sellers all over the world. Founded in 1995 by Pierre Omidyar and originally known as AuctionWeb, eBay has come a long way from its first sale, a broken laser pointer. The company now sells a staggeringly diverse array of goods and is one of the world's most easily recognizable and well-known Web sites.

In 1998, eBay had revenues of $4.8 million in the United States. A decade later, in 2008, eBay's Marketplaces segment generated over $5.5 billion in revenue worldwide from selling about $60 billion in merchandise. Hundreds of thousands of people support themselves by selling on eBay, and many millions more use eBay to supplement their income. During the 2008 holiday season, eBay was the most visited site on the Web, with 85.4 million active visitors.

However, in the first quarter of 2009, eBay's revenue shrank for the first time in the company's history. One reason is that consumers appear to be gravitating toward fixed-price retailers, such as Amazon, which has sustained steady growth despite the economic downturn. For many buyers, the novelty of online auctions has worn off, and these buyers have returned to the easier and simpler method of buying fixed-price goods. Search engines and comparison-shopping sites have also taken away some of eBay's auction business by making items easier to find on other Web sites. As it turns out, many do not want to wait for an auction to conclude, and just want to buy the product.

In response, eBay's leadership has begun taking the necessary steps to meet the shift in demand by consumers from auctions to fixed-price goods. The company unveiled a three-year revival plan in which the overall goal was to create a comprehensive array of marketplaces located in one central online location. Bidding on auctions, clicking on ads, scanning classifieds, and making outright purchases will all be possible from the flagship eBay site and its affiliates.

The recently hired CEO John Donahoe wants to focus eBay's business on the "secondary market," which includes overstock and out-of-season items as well as the used and antique items that eBay has been know for. He wants the eBay buying experience to emulate that of a low-price bulk retailer such as Costco, where "the inventory is somewhat fluid, but everything they've got is a great deal." He's also going after Overstock.com, which has done exceptionally well selling overstocked and discontinued items. To that end, Donahoe is trying to move eBay away from auctions toward fixed-price listings. Although this move has appealed to investors, it angered many of the smaller sellers of unique goods that have in the past come to symbolize the company's success. Some longtime sellers chose to move their business elsewhere.

EBay has traditionally derived the bulk of its revenue from fees and commissions associated with its sales transactions. A portion of eBay's revenue comes from direct advertising on the site, and some comes from end-to-end service providers such as PayPal (also owned by eBay) which increase the ease and speed of eBay transactions. The site imposes several types of fees on sellers, including posting fees for listing items as well as a collection fee on sold items. Traditionally, eBay was seen as a favorable proposition for smaller sellers to find markets for rare goods, or goods that are otherwise difficult to value.

In order to provide more incentive for bulk sellers of fixed-price goods to post their items on the site, eBay significantly adjusted its fee structure as part of its revival plan. The company reduced posting fees for adding an item online and increased the collection fee for sold items. For example, the fee to list a $25 auction item dropped to $1.00 from $1.20, but eBay's sales commission on the same item rose from 5.75 percent to 8.75 percent. In August 2008, eBay lowered its listing fees for all sellers offering fixed-priced items under its "Buy It Now" format. EBay's managers apparently believe that sellers are very sensitive to high listing fees, which are highly visible to sellers, and less sensitive to sales commissions. Lowering the fees on the front end, and raising them on the back end, is one way to maximize eBay revenue.

For bulk sellers, this was a boon. Prior to the change, posting large quantities of items was an expensive undertaking, since only a fraction of those posted items actually sold. Paying these posting fees represented the bulk of their expenditures. But for smaller sellers of unique, expensive items, increasing the percentages of collection fees meant that they would make significantly less per sale.

EBay also adjusted its search ordering system so that highly rated merchants appear first and receive more exposure. Previously, the first items to be displayed were those for which an auction was about to end. EBay's new search system uses a complicated formula that takes into account an item's price and how well that item's seller ranks in customer satisfaction. At first glance, this adjustment doesn't benefit any particular group of sellers more than the rest. But eBay also rolled out a rating system that made acquiring a high rating a much more time-consuming undertaking, favoring larger sellers with the time and energy to build a favorable rating. The company also removed the ability of sellers to assign negative ratings to buyers, a feature which many sellers felt protected them against late or non-payment on the part of buyers. The company's reasoning for this change was to stop sellers from rating buyers poorly as revenge for poor customer satisfaction ratings. Smaller sellers were incensed, claiming that the company was unnecessarily mistreating the group that spurred them to market dominance.

Not long ago, eBay's growth strategy focused on expansion in geography and scope and on continuing innovation to enhance the variety and appeal of products on its sites. EBay has always been active in developing and acquiring new products and services that encompass all the activities people perform on the Internet. Earlier this decade, the company fashioned a diversified portfolio of companies with a hand in each of the Internet's big cash pots: shopping, communicating, search, and entertainment. They are now realizing that some of these acquisitions were not good fits with their core business.

PayPal, whose service enables the exchange of money between individuals over the Internet, brings additional transaction-based fee revenue, and has been a significant bright spot for eBay's future prospects. EBay is banking on PayPal becoming the standard payment method for online transactions. The service already receives 40 percent of its business from payment transactions that are not associated with eBay. Management is using PayPal, a high-growth area, to help refocus the business and jump-start stagnant growth.

In 2005, eBay acquired Shopping.com, an online shopping comparison site, and Skype Technologies, which provides a service for free or low-cost voice calls over the Internet. Markets that eBay traditionally had trouble penetrating, such as real estate, travel, new-car sales, and expensive collectibles, require more communication among buyers and sellers than eBay currently offers, and Skype provides voice communication services to help sellers and purchasers reach a price and conclude a transaction.

But in 2009, eBay announced its plans to unload Skype, admitting it was a mistake to acquire the company. EBay assumed that buyers and sellers would use Skype to communicate about transactions, but the feature never caught on as expected. Skype cost eBay $2.6 billion, but eBay stands to recoup only a portion of that initial sum. Investors had urged the company to sell Skype, and channel the funds they receive into new growth initiatives.

EBay contintues to expand through acquisitions. The company acquired the ticket-reselling Web site StubHub, bought a 25-percent stake in classified ad site Craigslist, and purchased Kurant (now ProStores), whose technology helps users set up online stores. Some analysts report that while many of eBay's individual acquisitions appear to have been successful, they haven't created the synergy that was intended, and diversification has detracted from eBay's core business, auctions. These analysts seem to have missed the point. EBay mangers are intentionally jettisoning

SOURCES: "Is John Donahoe Finally Turning eBay Around?" by Kevin Kelleher, www.gigaom.com, June 14, 2009; "EBay Outlines Three-Year Revival Plan," by Peter Burrows, *Business Week*, March 12, 2009; "Auctions Fade in eBay's Bid for Growth," by Geoffrey A. Fowler, *Wall Street Journal*, May 26, 2009; "EBay Retreats in Web Retailing," by Geoffrey A. Fowler, *Wall Street Journal*, March 12, 2009 "EBay to Unload Skype in IPO, Citing Poor Fit," by Geoffrey A. Fowler, *Wall Street Journal*, April 15, 2009; "EBay Looks Abroad for Growth," by Geoffrey A. Fowler and Evan Ramstad, *Wall Street Journal*, April 15, 2009; "EBay's New Leader Moves Swiftly on a Revamping," by Brad Stone, *New York Times*, January 24, 2008.

the auction format despite the oppositions of thousands of eBay merchants. Donahoe regularly appears on lists of "disliked CEOs," and sellers have voiced their discontent via online forums and shareholder meetings. But Donahoe and the rest of eBay's management maintains that hosting fixed-price sales by reliable retailers makes shopping more customer-friendly and predictable. Will cultivating large sellers dilute eBay's brand and reputation as a dynamic flea market? Or will it steer eBay toward a faster-growing segment in retail e-commerce growth? Reports from 2009 appear promising. Despite the unfavorable economic climate, eBay's stock tanked down to $10 in early 2009 but has rallied to $24 in the fall, gaining 71%. However, eBay's site traffic is continuing to slowly erode as consumers gravitate towards Amazon and other similar sites. EBay still has a way to go to recoup its dot-com glory days. Can the Web's most prominent online auction site change course so dramatically from the formula that made it successful?

Case Study Questions

1. Contrast eBay's original business model with its latest proposed business model.

2. What are the problems that eBay is currently facing? How is eBay trying to solve these problems?

3. Are the solutions eBay is seeking to implement good solutions? Why or why not? Are there any other solutions that eBay should consider?

4. Who are eBay's top three competitors online, and how will eBay's new strategy help them compete? Will eBay be providing a differentiated service to customers?

11.5 REVIEW

KEY CONCEPTS

■ Explain the difference between a traditional social network and an online social network, and understand how an online community differs from a portal.

Social networks involve:
- A group of people
- Shared social interaction
- Common ties among members
- A shared area for some period of time

By extension, an online social network is an area online where people who share common ties can interact with one another.

■ Understand how a social network differs from a portal.

The difference between social networks and portals has become blurred. Originally, portals began as search engines. Then they added content and eventually many community-building features such as chat rooms, bulletin boards, and free Web site design and hosting. Social network sites began as content-specific locations and added more general portal services such as Web searching, general news, weather, and travel information, as well as a wide variety of e-commerce services.

- **Describe the different types of social networks and online communities and their business models.**

- *General communities:* Members can interact with a general audience segmented into numerous different groups. The purpose is to attract enough members to populate a wide range of topical discussion groups. Most general communities began as non-commercial subscription-based endeavors, but many have been purchased by larger community portal sites.
- *Practice networks:* Members can participate in discussion groups and get help or simply information relating to an area of shared practice, such as art, education, or medicine. These generally have a nonprofit business model in which they simply attempt to collect enough in subscription fees, sales commissions, and limited advertising to cover the cost of operations.
- *Interest-based communities:* Members can participate in focused discussion groups on a shared interest such as boats, horses, skiing, travel, or health. The advertising business model has worked because the targeted audience is attractive to marketers. Tenancy and sponsorship deals provide another similar revenue stream.
- *Affinity communities:* Members can participate in focused discussions with others who share the same affinity or group identification, such as religion, ethnicity, gender, sexual orientation, or political beliefs. The business model is a mixture of subscription revenue from premium content and services, advertising, tenancy/sponsorships, and distribution agreements.
- *Sponsored communities:* Members can participate in online communities created by government, nonprofit, or for-profit organizations for the purpose of pursuing organizational goals. These types of sites vary widely from local government sites to branded product sites. They use community technologies and techniques to distribute information or extend brand influence. The goal of a branded product site is to increase offline product sales. These sites do not seek to make a profit and in fact are often cost centers.

- **Describe the major types of auctions, their benefits and costs, and how they operate.**

Auctions are markets where prices vary (dynamic pricing) depending on the competition among the participants who are buying or selling products or services. They can be classified broadly as C2C or B2C, although generally the term C2C auction refers to the venue in which the sale takes place, for example, a consumer-oriented Web site such as eBay, which also auctions items from established merchants. A B2C auction refers to an established online merchant that offers its own auctions. There are also numerous B2B online auctions for buyers of industrial parts, raw materials, commodities, and services. Within these three broad categories of auctions are several major auction types classified based upon how the bidding mechanisms work in each system:

- *English auctions:* A single item is up for sale from a single seller. Multiple buyers bid against one another within a specific time frame, with the highest bidder winning the object, as long as the high bid has exceeded the reserve bid set by the seller, below which he or she refuses to sell.
- *Traditional Dutch auctions:* Sellers with many identical items sold in lots list a starting price and time for the opening of bids. As the clock advances, the price for each lot falls until a buyer offers to buy at that price.
- *Internet Dutch auctions:* Sellers with many identical items for sale list a minimum price or starting bid, and buyers indicate both a bid price and a quantity desired. The lowest winning bid that clears the available quantity is paid by all winning bidders. Those with the highest bid are assured of receiving the quantity they desire, but only pay the amount of the lowest successful bid (uniform pricing rule).
- *Name Your Own Price or reverse auctions:* Buyers specify the price they are willing to pay for an item, and multiple sellers bid for their business. This is one example of discriminatory pricing in which winners may pay different amounts for the same product or service depending on how much they have bid.
- *Group buying or demand aggregation auctions:* In the group-buying format, the more users who sign on to buy an item, the lower the price for the item falls. These are generally B2B or B2G sites where small businesses can collectively receive discount prices for items that are purchased in high volumes.

Benefits of auctions include:

- *Liquidity:* Sellers and buyers are connected in a global marketplace.
- *Price discovery:* Even difficult-to price-items can be competitively priced based on supply and demand.
- *Price transparency:* Everyone in the world can see the asking and bidding prices for items, although prices can vary from auction site to auction site.
- *Market efficiency:* Consumers are offered access to a selection of goods that would be impossible to access physically, and consumer welfare is often increased due to reduced prices.
- *Lower transaction costs:* Merchants and consumers alike are benefited by the reduced costs of selling and purchasing goods compared to the physical marketplace.
- *Consumer aggregation:* A large number of consumers who are motivated to buy are amassed in one marketplace—a great convenience to the seller.
- *Network effects:* The larger an auction site becomes in the numbers of both users and products, the greater the benefits become and therefore the more valuable a marketplace it becomes.
- *Market-maker benefits:* Auction sites have no inventory carrying costs or shipping costs, making them perhaps the ideal online business in that their main function is the transfer of information.

Costs of auctions include:

- *Delayed consumption:* Auctions can go on for days, and the product must then be shipped to the buyer. Buyers will typically want to pay less for an item they cannot immediately obtain.
- *Monitoring costs:* Buyers must spend time monitoring the bidding.
- *Equipment costs:* Buyers must purchase, or have already purchased, computer systems and Internet service, and learned how to operate these systems.
- *Trust risks:* Consumers face an increased risk of experiencing a loss as online auctions are the largest source of Internet fraud.
- *Fulfillment costs:* Buyers must pay for packing, shipping, and insurance, and will factor this cost into their bid price.

Auction sites have sought to reduce these risks through various methods including:

- *Rating systems:* Previous customers rate sellers based on their experience with them and post them on the site for other buyers to see.
- *Watch lists:* These allow buyers to monitor specific auctions as they proceed over a number of days and only pay close attention in the last few minutes of bidding.
- *Proxy bidding:* Buyers can enter a maximum price they are willing to pay, and the auction software will automatically place incremental bids as their original bid is surpassed.

■ **Understand when to use auctions in a business.**

Auctions can be an appropriate channel for businesses to sell items in a variety of situations. The factors for businesses to consider include:

- *The type of product:* Rare and unique products are well suited to the auction marketplace as are perishable items such as airline tickets, hotel rooms, car rentals, and tickets to plays, concerts, and sporting events.
- *The product life cycle:* Traditionally, auctions have been used by businesses to generate a higher profit on items at the end of their life cycle than they would receive from product liquidation sales. However, they are now more frequently being used at the beginning of a product's life cycle to generate premium prices from highly motivated early adopters.
- *Channel management:* Businesses must be careful when deciding whether to pursue an auction strategy to ensure that products at auction do not compete with products in their existing profitable channels. This is why most established retail firms tend to use auctions for products at the end of their life cycles or to have quantity purchasing requirements.
- *The type of auction:* Businesses should choose seller-biased auctions where there are many buyers and only one or a few sellers, preferably using the English ascending price system to drive the price up as high as possible.
- *Initial pricing:* Auction items should start with a low initial bid in order to attract more bidders, because the more bidders an item has, the higher the final price will be driven.
- *Bid increments:* When increments are kept low, more bidders are attracted and the frequency of their bidding is increased. This can translate into a higher final price as bidders are prodded onward in small steps.
- *Auction length:* In general, the longer an auction runs, the more bidders will enter the auction, and the higher the final price will be. However, if an auction

continues for too long, the bid prices will stabilize and the cost of posting the auction may outweigh the profit from any further price increases.

- *Number of items:* If a business has a large quantity of items to sell, it should break the lot up into smaller bundles and auction them at different times so that buyers do not expect a volume discount.
- *Price allocation rule:* Since most buyers are biased toward the uniform pricing rule, sellers should use different auction markets, or auction the same goods at different times in order to price discriminate.
- *Closed vs. open bidding:* Closed bidding should be used whenever possible because it benefits a seller by allowing price discrimination. However, open bidding can sometimes be beneficial when herd behavior kicks in, causing multiple bids on highly visited auctions, while overlooked and lightly trafficked auctions for the same or comparable items languish. This generally occurs when there are few objective measures of a product's true value in the marketplace.

■ Recognize the potential for auction abuse and fraud.

Auctions are particularly prone to fraud, which produces information asymmetries between buyers and sellers. Some of the possible abuses and frauds include:

- *Bid rigging:* Agreeing offline to limit bids or using shills to submit false bids that drive prices up.
- *Price matching:* Agreeing informally or formally to set floor prices on auction items below which sellers will not sell in open markets.
- *Shill feedback, defensive:* Using secondary IDs or other auction members to inflate seller ratings.
- *Shill feedback, offensive:* Using secondary IDs or other auction members to deflate ratings for another user (feedback bombs).
- *Feedback extortion:* Threatening negative feedback in return for a benefit.
- *Transaction interference:* E-mailing buyers to warn them away from a seller.
- *Bid manipulation:* Using the retraction option to make high bids, discovering the maximum bid of the current high bidder, and then retracting the bid.
- *Non-payment after winning.*
- *Blocking legitimate buyers by bidding high, then not paying.*
- *Shill bidding:* Using secondary user IDs or other auction members to artificially raise the price of an item.
- *Transaction non-performance:* Accepting payment and failing to deliver.
- *Non-selling seller:* Refusing payment or failing to deliver after a successful auction.
- *Bid siphoning:* E-mailing another seller's bidders and offering the same product for less.

■ Describe the major types of Internet portals.

Web portals are gateways to the more than 50 billion Web pages available on the Internet. Originally, their primary purpose was to help users find information on the Web, but they evolved into destination sites that provided a myriad of content from news to entertainment. Today, portals serve three main purposes: navigation of the Web, content, and commerce. Among the major portal types are:

- *Enterprise portals:* Corporations, universities, churches, and other organizations create these sites to help employees or members navigate to important content such as corporate news or organizational announcements.
- *General-purpose portals:* Examples are AOL, Yahoo, and MSN, which try to attract a very large general audience by providing many in-depth vertical content channels. They also offer ISP services on a subscription basis, search engines, e-mail, chat, bulletin boards, and personal home pages.
- *Vertical market portals:* Also called destination sites, they attempt to attract a highly focused, loyal audience with an intense interest in either a community they belong to or an interest they hold. Recent studies have found that users with limited time resources are interested in concentrating their Web site visiting on focused searches in areas that appeal to them. Vertical market portals can be divided into two main classifications, although hybrids that overlap the two classifications also exist.
- *Affinity groups:* Statistical aggregates of people who identify themselves by their attitudes, values, beliefs, and behavior. Affinity portals exist to serve such broad constituencies as women, African Americans, and gays as well as much more focused constituencies such as union members, religious groups, and even home schooling families.
- *Focused content portals:* These sites contain in-depth information on a particular topic that all members are interested in. They can provide content on such broad topics as sports, news, weather, entertainment, finance, or business, or they can appeal to a much more focused interest group such as boat, horse, or video game enthusiasts.

■ Understand the business models of portals.

Portals receive revenue from a number of different sources. The business model is presently changing and adapting to declines in certain revenue streams, particularly advertising revenues. Revenue sources can include:

- *ISP services:* Providing Web access and e-mail services for a monthly fee
- *General advertising:* Charging for impressions delivered
- *Tenancy deals:* Locking in long-term, multiple-year deals so a company is guaranteed a number of impressions with premium placement on home pages and through exclusive marketing deals
- *Subscription fees:* Charging for premium content
- *Commissions on sales:* Earning revenue based on sales at the site by independent merchants.

The survival strategy for general-purpose portals is to develop deep, rich, vertical content in order to attract advertisers to various niche groups that they can target with focused ads. The strategy for the small vertical market portals is to build a collection of vertical portals, thereby creating a network of deep, rich content sites for the same reason.

QUESTIONS

1. Why did most communities in the early days of e-commerce fail? What factors enable online social networks to prosper today?
2. How does a social network differ from a portal? How are the two similar?

3. What is an affinity community, and what is its business model?

4. What is personalization or personal value pricing, and how can it be used at the beginning of a product's life cycle to increase revenues?

5. List and briefly explain three of the benefits of auction markets.

6. What are the four major costs to consumers of participating in an auction?

7. Under what conditions does a seller bias exist in an auction market? When does a buyer bias exist?

8. What are the two price allocation rules in auction markets? Explain the difference between them.

9. What is an auction aggregator and how does it work?

10. What types of products are well suited for an auction market? At what points in the product life cycle can auction markets prove beneficial for marketers?

11. What three characteristics define a portal site today?

12. What is a vertical market portal, and how might recent trends in consumer behavior prove advantageous to this business model?

13. What are the two main types of vertical market portals, and how are they distinguished from one and other?

14. List and briefly explain the main revenue sources for the portal business model.

PROJECTS

1. Find two examples of an affinity portal and two examples of a focused-content portal. Prepare a presentation explaining why each of your examples should be categorized as an affinity portal or a focused content portal. For each example, surf the site and describe the services each site provides. Try to determine what revenue model each of your examples is using and, if possible, how many members or registered visitors the site has attracted.

2. Examine the use of auctions by businesses. Go to any auction site of your choosing and look for outlet auctions or auctions directly from merchants. Research at least three products up for sale. What stage in the product life cycle do these products fall into? Are there quantity purchasing requirements? What was the opening bid price? What are the bid increments? What is the auction duration? Analyze why these firms have used the auction channel to sell these goods and prepare a short report on your findings.

3. Visit one for-profit-sponsored and one nonprofit-sponsored social network. Create a presentation to describe and demonstrate the offering at each site. What organizational objectives is each pursuing? How is the for-profit company using community building technologies as a customer relations management tool?

WEB SITE RESOURCES www.azimuth-interactive.com/ecommerce6e

- ■ Additional projects, exercises, and tutorials
- ■ Careers: Explore career opportunities in e-commerce
- ■ Raising capital and business plans

CHAPTER 12

B2B E-commerce: Supply Chain Management and Collaborative Commerce

LEARNING OBJECTIVES

After reading this chapter, you will be able to:

- Define B2B commerce and understand its scope and history.
- Understand the procurement process, the supply chain, and collaborative commerce.
- Identify the main types of B2B e-commerce: Net marketplaces and private industrial networks.
- Understand the four types of Net marketplaces.
- Identify the major trends in the development of Net marketplaces.
- Identify the role of private industrial networks in transforming the supply chain.
- Understand the role of private industrial networks in supporting collaborative commerce.

Volkswagen
Builds Its B2B Net Marketplace

Volkswagen AG is Europe's largest car manufacturer, producing 6.3 million cars, trucks, and vans each year. In addition to the Volkswagen brand, the Volkswagen Group also owns luxury carmakers such as Audi, Bentley, Scania Bugatti, and Lamborghini, and family car makers SEAT in Spain and Skoda in the Czech Republic. The company has 370,000 employees and operates plants in Europe, Africa, the Asian/Pacific rim, and the Americas.

The various companies in the Volkswagen Group annually purchase components, automotive parts, and indirect materials worth about 72 billion euros, or about $100 billion (which constitutes about 83% of Volkswagen's annual revenue). Obviously, the procurement process and relationships with suppliers are absolutely critical for Volkswagen's success.

Today, the Volkswagen Group manages almost all of its procurement needs via the Internet. It began building its Internet platform, VWGroupSupply.com, in 2000. The Volkswagen Group was looking for ways to create more efficient relationships with its suppliers and reduce the cost of paper-based procurement processes. However, the company did not want to automate procurement using a public independent exchange or an industry consortium because it would have had fto adapt its own business processes to a common framework that could be used by many different organizations. Volkswagen hoped that by building its own B2B network, it could compete more effectively against other automakers. Volkswagen decided, for instance, not to participate in Covisint, the giant automotive industry consortium backed by major car manufacturers such as Ford, General Motors, and DaimlerChrysler, which provided procurement and other supply chain services for these companies, other automotive manufacturers, and their suppliers.

Instead, Volkswagen opted for a private platform that would allow it to integrate its suppliers more tightly with its own business processes, and where it could control more precisely who was invited to participate. VWGroupSupply now handles over 90% of all global purchasing for the Volkswagen Group, including all automotive and parts components. It is one of the most comprehensive e-procurement systems in the global automotive industry. From an initial seven applications, the platform now offers over 60 different online applications, such as requests for quotations (RFQs), contract negotiations, catalog purchases, purchase order management, engineering change management, vehicle program management, and payments, among others. The Volkswagen Group developed the platform using technology from a number of vendors, including Ariba, IBM, and i2 Technologies.

Suppliers of all sizes can access VWGroupSupply with standard Web browser software. The Web site is limited to suppliers who have done business with one or more companies in the Volkswagen Group and potential new suppliers who go through an authorization process. Currently, over 35,000 suppliers are registered, and there are over 110,000 users. The system maintains a common data repository with details on each supplier concerning procurement, logistics, production, quality, technical design, and finance.

VWSupplyGroup's online catalog currently contains about 2.5 million items from 590 global suppliers. There are 14,200 internal users of the online catalog who have conducted over 1.5 million transactions with a value totaling 380 million euros ($447 million). The catalog uses the eCl@ss standard for classifying its contents. All suppliers who participate in the catalog ordering process classify their products using this standard.

Online negotiations involve multiple bids by suppliers for various purchasing contracts. VWGroupSupply ensures that all participants meet its technical and commercial qualifications. Before an online solicitation begins, the system informs vendors about the data and precise rules governing the negotiations. In 2008, VWSupply conducted around 3,000 online contract negotiations online, with a value of 11.9 billion euros ($16.6 billion).

Shifts in market demand have a drastic impact on Volkswagen's production activities and affect the ability of suppliers to deliver. Production bottlenecks can result if suppliers are unprepared for a sudden upsurge in demand. If suppliers stock too much inventory, they may incur excess costs from running at overcapacity. VWGroupSupply has an application called electronic Capacity Management (eCAP) to alert both Volkswagen and its suppliers to changes in trends in advance.

eCAP enables suppliers to track Volkswagen's continually updated production plans and materials requirements in real time online. This capability captures information about participating suppliers' planned maximum and minimum capacities. If Volkswagen production requirements go beyond these limits, the system sets off an alarm so both parties can react quickly. eCAP maintains information on over 400 suppliers and 4,000 critical parts.

In March 2009, VWGroupSupply unveiled a new Web site intended to provide better navigation, greater clarity, new content, and a simplified registration process for new suppliers.

SOURCES: VWGroupSupply.com, September 2009; "Best Practices: VW Revs Up its B2B Engine," by Martin Hoffman, *Optimize*, March 2004.

The VWGroupSupply case illustrates the exciting potential for B2B e-commerce to lower production costs, speed up new product delivery, and ultimately revolutionize both the manufacturing process inherited from the early twentieth century and the way we purchase industrial products. VWGroupSupply is an example of just one type of B2B e-commerce, but there are many other equally promising efforts to using the Internet to change the relationships among manufacturers and their suppliers. The success of VWGroupSupply and similar networks operated by the major automobile firms in the world stands in contrast to an earlier industry-sponsored Net marketplace called Covisint. Founded in 1999 by five of the world's largest automakers (General Motors, Ford, Chrysler, Nissan, and Peugeot), Covisint hoped to provide an electronic market connecting thousands of suppliers to a few huge buyers using auctions and procurement services. While initially successful, Covisint was dismantled and sold off in June 2004. Its auction business was sold to FreeMarkets, an early B2B auction company which itself was sold to Ariba later in 2004. The rest of Covisint's procurement software and operations were sold to CompuWare, a software services company, which maintains the Covisint brand name and provides software services to the automotive industry using Covisint.

The failure of Covisint and the simultaneous growth in B2B e-commerce efforts such as VWGroupSupply illustrates the difficulties of achieving the broad visions established during the early days of e-commerce. From a high point of 1,500 online B2B exchanges in 2000, the number has dwindled to less than 200 survivors today. Like B2C commerce, the B2B marketplace has consolidated, evolved, and moved on to more attainable visions. In the process, many B2B efforts have experienced extraordinary success. There are many failed efforts to consider as well; these provide important lessons to all managers.

In this chapter, we examine the many different types of Internet-based B2B commerce in detail. In Section 12.1, we define B2B commerce and place it in the context of trends in supply chain management, which, ultimately, is the objective of B2B commerce—to help businesses manage the flow of supplies needed for production. The next two sections describe the two fundamental types of B2B e-commerce: Net marketplaces and private industrial networks. We describe four major types of Net marketplaces, their biases (seller, buyer, and neutral), accessibility (private versus public), and value creation dynamics, and then the emergence of private Internet-based industrial networks that tie a smaller number of organizations into a collaborative commercial system.

Table 12.1 summarizes the leading trends in B2B e-commerce in the 2009–2010 period. Perhaps the most important theme is the growing comfort level that business firms have with the Internet as a viable method of purchase, payment, and collaboration among partners in the supply chain.

TABLE 12.1	MAJOR TRENDS IN B2B E-COMMERCE, 2009–2010

- B2B e-commerce continues to grow , although at a somewhat slower pace than in previous years due to the widespread economic recession, as business firms gain experience and knowledge in exploiting the Internet.
- Business firms increase their comfort level with Internet security and payments, helping to expand their use of B2B channels.
- Growing realization that the most important benefits to B2B commerce are not lower costs of raw materials (although these costs do decline), but rather gains in supply chain efficiency, better spend management, and improved business processes.
- Decline in growth of independent Net marketplace exchanges, but rapid growth in e-procurement firms and private industrial networks.
- Rapid growth in collaborative commerce B2B applications based on private networks.
- Continued consolidation in the B2B Net marketplace and software vendor markets as fewer but stronger firms purchase weaker firms born in early years of B2B e-commerce.
- B2B communities emerge allowing firms in the same industry to collectively work on reducing costs by integrating their enterprise resource planning (ERP) systems.
- B2B systems move to cloud providers like IBM, Amazon, Google, and HP as their core technology.
- More B2B software providers switch to Software as a Service (SaaS) model, providing inexpensive online access to trading platforms.

12.1 B2B E-COMMERCE AND SUPPLY CHAIN MANAGEMENT

The trade between business firms represents a huge marketplace. The total amount of B2B trade in the United States in 2009 is about $11.5 trillion, with B2B e-commerce (online B2B) contributing about $3.36 trillion of that amount (U.S. Census Bureau, 2009a, b; authors' estimates). By 2013, B2B e-commerce should grow to about $4.75 trillion in the United States, assuming an average growth rate of about 9%.

The process of conducting trade among business firms is complex and requires significant human intervention, and therefore, it consumes significant resources. Some firms estimate that each corporate purchase order for support products costs them, on average, at least $100 in administrative overhead. Administrative overhead includes processing paper, approving purchase decisions, spending time using the telephone and fax machines to search for products and arrange for purchases, arranging for shipping, and receiving the goods . Across the economy, this adds up to trillions of dollars annually being spent for procurement processes that could potentially be automated. If even just a portion of inter-firm trade were automated, and parts of the entire procurement process assisted by the Internet, then literally trillions of dollars might be released for more productive uses, consumer prices potentially would fall, productivity would increase, and the economic wealth of the nation would expand. This is the promise of B2B e-commerce. The challenge of B2B e-commerce is changing existing patterns and systems of procurement, and designing and implementing new Internet-based B2B solutions.

DEFINING AND MEASURING THE GROWTH OF B2B COMMERCE

Before the Internet, business-to-business transactions were referred to simply as *trade* or the *procurement process*. The term **total inter-firm trade** refers to the total flow of value among firms. Today, we use the term **B2B commerce** to describe all types of computer-enabled inter-firm trade, such as the use of the Internet and other networking technologies to exchange value across organizational boundaries. This definition of B2B commerce does not include digital transactions that occur within the boundaries of a single firm—for instance, the transfer of goods and value from one subsidiary to another, or the use of corporate intranets to manage the firm. We use the term **Internet-based B2B commerce** (or **B2B e-commerce**) to describe specifically that portion of B2B commerce that is enabled by the Internet.

THE EVOLUTION OF B2B COMMERCE

B2B commerce has evolved over a 35-year period through several technology-driven stages (see **Figure 12.1**). The first step in the development of B2B commerce in the mid-1970s was **automated order entry systems** that involved the use of telephone modems to send digital orders to health care products companies such as Baxter Healthcare. Baxter, a diversified supplier of hospital supplies, placed telephone modems in its customers' procurement offices to automate re-ordering from Baxter's computerized inventory database (and to discourage re-ordering from competitors). This early technology was replaced by personal computers using private networks in the late 1980s, and by Internet workstations accessing electronic online catalogs in the late 1990s. Automated order entry systems are **seller-side solutions**. They are owned by the suppliers and are

total inter-firm trade
the total flow of value among firms

B2B commerce
all types of computer-enabled inter-firm trade

Internet-based B2B commerce
(B2B e-commerce)
that portion of B2B commerce that is enabled by the Internet

automated order entry systems
involve the use of telephone modems to send digital orders

seller-side solutions
seller-biased markets that are owned by, and show only goods from, a single seller

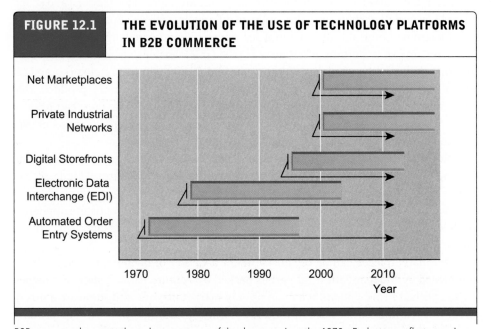

FIGURE 12.1 | **THE EVOLUTION OF THE USE OF TECHNOLOGY PLATFORMS IN B2B COMMERCE**

B2B commerce has gone through many stages of development since the 1970s. Each stage reflects a major change in technology platforms from mainframes to private dedicated networks, and finally to the Internet.

electronic data interchange (EDI)

a communications standard for sharing business documents and settlement information among a small number of firms

buyer-side solutions

buyer-biased markets that are owned by buyers and that aim to reduce the procurement costs of supplies for buyers

hub-and-spoke system

suppliers connected to a central hub of buyers via private dedicated networks

vertical market

one that provides expertise and products for a specific industry

horizontal markets

markets that serve many different industries

B2B electronic storefronts

online catalogs of products made available to the public marketplace by a single supplier

Net marketplace

brings hundreds to thousands of suppliers and buyers into a single Internet-based environment to conduct trade

seller-biased markets—they show only goods from a single seller. Customers benefited from these systems because they reduced the costs of inventory replenishment and were paid for largely by the suppliers. Automated order entry systems continue to play an important role in B2B commerce.

By the late 1970s, a new form of computer-to-computer communication called **electronic data interchange (EDI)** emerged. We describe EDI in greater detail later in this chapter, but at this point, it is necessary only to know that EDI is a communications standard for sharing business documents such as invoices, purchase orders, shipping bills, product stocking numbers (SKUs), and settlement information among a small number of firms. Virtually all large firms have EDI systems, and most industry groups have industry standards for defining documents in that industry. EDI systems are owned by the buyers, and hence they are **buyer-side solutions** and buyer-biased because they aim to reduce the procurement costs of supplies for the buyer. Of course, by automating the transaction, EDI systems also benefit the sellers by reducing costs of serving their customers. The topology of EDI systems is often referred to as a **hub-and-spoke** system, with the buyers in the center and the suppliers connected to the central hub via private dedicated networks.

EDI systems generally serve vertical markets. A **vertical market** is one that provides expertise and products for a specific industry, such as automobiles. In contrast, **horizontal markets** serve many different industries.

Electronic storefronts emerged in the mid-1990s along with the commercialization of the Internet. **B2B electronic storefronts** are perhaps the simplest and easiest to understand form of B2B e-commerce, because they are just online catalogs of products made available to the public marketplace by a single supplier—similar to Amazon for the B2C retail market. Owned by the suppliers, they are seller-side solutions and seller-biased because they show only the products offered by a single supplier.

Electronic storefronts are a natural descendant of automated order entry systems, but there are two important differences: (1) the far less expensive and more universal Internet becomes the communication media and displaces private networks, and (2) electronic storefronts tend to serve horizontal markets—they carry products that serve a wide variety of industries. Although electronic storefronts emerged prior to Net marketplaces (described next), they are usually considered a type of Net marketplace.

Net marketplaces emerged in the late 1990s as a natural extension and scaling-up of the electronic storefronts. There are many different kinds of Net marketplaces , which we describe in detail in Section 12.2, but the essential characteristic of a Net marketplace is that they bring hundreds to thousands of suppliers—each with electronic catalogs and potentially thousands of purchasing firms—into a single Internet-based environment to conduct trade.

Net marketplaces can be organized under a variety of ownership models. Some are owned by independent third parties backed by venture capital, some are owned by established firms who are the main or only market players, and some are a mix of both. Net marketplaces establish the prices of the goods they offer in four primary ways—fixed catalog prices, or more dynamic pricing, such as negotiation, auction, or bid/ask ("exchange" model). Net marketplaces earn revenue in a number of ways, including transaction fees, subscription fees, service fees, software licensing fees, advertising and marketing, and sales of data and information.

Although the primary benefits and biases of Net marketplaces have to be determined on a case-by-case basis depending on ownership and pricing mechanisms, it is often the case that Net marketplaces are biased against suppliers because they can force suppliers to reveal their prices and terms to other suppliers in the marketplace. Net marketplaces can also significantly extend the benefits of simple electronic storefronts by seeking to automate the procurement value chain of both selling and buying firms.

Private industrial networks also emerged in the late 1990s as natural extensions of EDI systems and the existing close relationships that developed between large industrial firms and their suppliers. Described in more detail in Section 12.3, **private industrial networks** (sometimes also referred to as a *private trading exchange*, or *PTX*) are Internet-based communication environments that extend far beyond procurement to encompass truly collaborative commerce. Private industrial networks permit buyer firms and their principal suppliers to share product design and development, marketing, inventory, production scheduling, and unstructured communications. Like EDI, private industrial networks are owned by the buyers and are buyer-side solutions with buyer biases. These systems are directly intended to improve the cost position and flexibility of large industrial firms (Kumaran, 2002).

Naturally, private industrial networks have significant benefits for suppliers as well. Inclusion in the direct supply chain for a major industrial purchasing company can allow a supplier to increase both revenue and margins because the environment is not competitive—only a few suppliers are included in the private industrial network. These networks are the most prevalent form of Internet-based B2B commerce, and this will continue into the foreseeable future.

private industrial networks (private trading exchange, PTX)
Internet-based communication environments that extend far beyond procurement to encompass truly collaborative commerce

THE GROWTH OF B2B E-COMMERCE 2009-2013

In the period 2009–2013, B2B e-commerce is projected to grow from about 30% to 35% of total inter-firm trade in the United States, or from $3.36 trillion in 2009 to $4.7 trillion in 2013 (see **Figure 12.2**).

Several observations are important to note with respect to Figure 12.2. First, it shows that the initial belief that electronic marketplaces would become the dominant form of B2B e-commerce is not supported. Second, private industrial networks play a dominant role in B2B e-commerce, both now and in the future. Third, non-EDI B2B e-commerce is the most rapidly growing type of B2B e-commerce, and EDI is still quite large but will decline over time.

Industry Forecasts

Not all industries will be similarly affected by B2B e-commerce, and not all industries can similarly benefit from B2B. Several factors influence the speed with which industries migrate to B2B e-commerce and the volume of transactions. Those industries in which there is already significant utilization of EDI (indicating

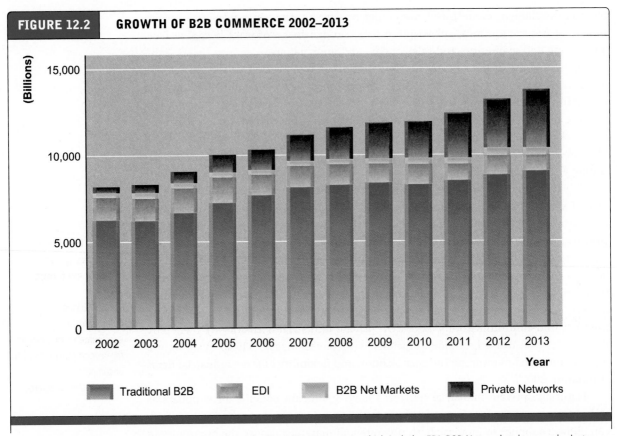

FIGURE 12.2 | **GROWTH OF B2B COMMERCE 2002–2013**

Private industrial networks are the fastest growing form of online B2B e-commerce, which includes EDI, B2B Net marketplaces, and private industrial markets.

SOURCES: Based on data from U.S. Census Bureau, 2009a, b; authors' estimates.

concentration of buyers and suppliers) and large investments in information technology and Internet infrastructure can be expected to move first and fastest to B2B e-commerce utilization. The aerospace and defense, computer, and industrial equipment industries meet these criteria. Where the marketplace is highly concentrated on either the purchasing or selling side, or both, conditions are also ripe for rapid B2B e-commerce growth, as in energy and chemical industries. In the case of health care, the federal government, health care providers (doctors and hospitals), and major insurance companies are moving rapidly towards a national medical record system and the use of Internet for managing medical payments.

POTENTIAL BENEFITS OF B2B E-COMMERCE

Regardless of the specific type of B2B e-commerce, as a whole, Internet-based B2B commerce promises many strategic benefits to participating firms—both buyers and sellers—and impressive gains for the economy as a whole. B2B e-commerce can:

- Lower administrative costs
- Lower search costs for buyers

- Reduce inventory costs by increasing competition among suppliers (increasing price transparency) and reducing inventory to the bare minimum
- Lower transaction costs by eliminating paperwork and automating parts of the procurement process
- Increase production flexibility by ensuring delivery of parts "just in time"
- Improve quality of products by increasing cooperation among buyers and sellers and reducing quality issues
- Decrease product cycle time by sharing designs and production schedules with suppliers
- Increase opportunities for collaborating with suppliers and distributors
- Create greater price transparency—the ability to see the actual buy and sell prices in a market

B2B e-commerce offers potential first-mover strategic benefits for individual firms as well. Firms that move their procurement processes online first will experience impressive gains in productivity, cost reduction, and potentially much faster introduction of new, higher-quality products. While these gains may be imitated by other competing firms, it is also clear from the brief history of B2B e-commerce that firms making sustained investments in information technology and Internet-based B2B commerce can adapt much faster to new technologies as they emerge, creating a string of first-mover advantages.

THE PROCUREMENT PROCESS AND THE SUPPLY CHAIN

The subject of B2B e-commerce can be complex because there are so many ways the Internet can be used to support the exchange of goods and payments among organizations. Ultimately, B2B e-commerce is about changing the **procurement process** (the way business firms purchase the goods they need to produce the goods they will ultimately sell to consumers) of thousands of firms across the United States and the world.

One way to enter this area of Internet-based B2B commerce is to examine the existing procurement process (see **Figure 12.3**). Firms purchase goods from a set of suppliers, and they in turn purchase their inputs from a set of suppliers. This set of firms is linked through a series of transactions referred to as the **supply chain**. The supply chain includes not just the firms themselves, but also the relationships among them and the processes that connect them.

There are seven separate steps in the procurement process. The first three steps involve the decision of who to buy from and what to pay: searching for suppliers of specific products; qualifying both the seller and the products they sell; and negotiating prices, credit terms, escrow requirements, quality, and scheduling of delivery. Once a supplier is identified, purchase orders are issued, the buyer is sent an invoice, the goods are shipped, and the buyer sends a payment. Each of these steps in the procurement process is composed of many separate sub-activities. Each of these activities must be recorded in the information systems of the seller, buyer, and shipper. Often, this data entry is not automatic and involves some manual labor.

procurement process
tthe way firms purchase the goods they need to produce goods for consumers

supply chain
firms that purchase goods, their suppliers, and their suppliers' suppliers. Includes not only the firms themselves, but also the relationships among them, and the processes that connect them

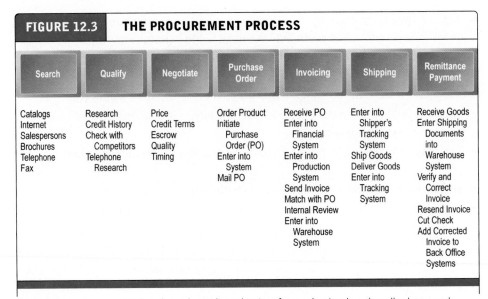

FIGURE 12.3   THE PROCUREMENT PROCESS

Search	Qualify	Negotiate	Purchase Order	Invoicing	Shipping	Remittance Payment
Catalogs	Research	Price	Order Product	Receive PO	Enter into	Receive Goods
Internet	Credit History	Credit Terms	Initiate	Enter into	Shipper's	Enter Shipping
Salespersons	Check with	Escrow	Purchase	Financial	Tracking	Documents
Brochures	Competitors	Quality	Order (PO)	System	System	into
Telephone	Telephone	Timing	Enter into	Enter into	Ship Goods	Warehouse
Fax	Research		System	Production	Deliver Goods	System
			Mail PO	System	Enter into	Verify and
				Send Invoice	Tracking	Correct
				Match with PO	System	Invoice
				Internal Review		Resend Invoice
				Enter into		Cut Check
				Warehouse		Add Corrected
				System		Invoice to
						Back Office
						Systems

The procurement process is a lengthy and complicated series of steps that involves the seller, buyer, and shipping companies in a series of connected transactions.

direct goods
goods directly involved in the production process

indirect goods
all other goods not directly involved in the production process

MRO goods
products for maintenance, repair, and operations

contract purchasing
involves long-term written agreements to purchase specified products, under agreed-upon terms and quality, for an extended period of time

spot purchasing
involves the purchase of goods based on immediate needs in larger marketplaces that involve many suppliers

Types of Procurement

Two distinctions are important for understanding how B2B e-commerce can improve the procurement process. First, firms make purchases of two kinds of goods from suppliers: direct goods and indirect goods. **Direct goods** are goods integrally involved in the production process; for instance, when an automobile manufacturer purchases sheet steel for auto body production. **Indirect goods** are all other goods not directly involved in the production process, such as office supplies and maintenance products. Often these goods are called **MRO goods**—products for maintenance, repair, and operations.

Second, firms use two different methods for purchasing goods: contract purchasing and spot purchasing. **Contract purchasing** involves long-term written agreements to purchase specified products, with agreed-upon terms and quality, for an extended period of time. Generally, firms purchase direct goods using long-term contracts. **Spot purchasing** involves the purchase of goods based on immediate needs in larger marketplaces that involve many suppliers. Generally, firms use spot purchasing for indirect goods, although in some cases, firms also use spot purchasing for direct goods.

According to several estimates, about 80% of inter-firm trade involves contract purchasing of direct goods, and 20% involves spot purchasing of indirect goods (Sodhi, 2001; Kaplan and Sawhney, 2000). This finding is significant for understanding B2B e-commerce, as we see below.

Although the procurement process involves the purchasing of goods, it is extraordinarily information-intense, involving the movement of information among many existing corporate systems. The procurement process today is also very labor-intensive, directly involving over 3.3 million employees in the United States, not including those engaged in transportation, finance, insurance, or general office administration related to the process (U.S. Census Bureau, 2009a).

In the long term, the success or failure of B2B e-commerce depends on changing the day-to-day behavior of these 3.5 million people. The key players in the procurement process are the purchasing managers. They ultimately decide who to buy from, what to buy, and on what terms. Purchasing managers ("procurement managers" in the business press) are also the key decision makers for the adoption of B2B e-commerce solutions.

The Internet could make an important contribution in simplifying the procurement process by bringing buyers and sellers together in a single marketplace and reducing search, research, and negotiating costs. This would appear to be very helpful for spot purchases of indirect goods. Later in the procurement process, the Internet could make an important contribution simply as a powerful communications medium, transferring information among the sellers, buyers, and shippers, and helping managers coordinate the procurement process. This would appear to be very helpful for contract purchases of direct goods. To a large extent, this is the promise of B2B e-commerce. But it is not the whole story.

Although Figure 12.3 captures some of the complexity of the procurement process, it is important to realize that firms purchase thousands of goods from thousands of suppliers. The suppliers, in turn, must purchase their inputs from their suppliers. Large manufacturers such as Ford Motor Company have over 20,000 suppliers of parts, packaging, and technology. The number of secondary and tertiary suppliers is at least as large. Together, this extended **multi-tier supply chain** (the chain of primary, secondary, and tertiary suppliers) constitutes a crucial aspect of the industrial infrastructure of the economy. **Figure 12.4** depicts a firm's multi-tier supply chain.

multi-tier supply chain
the chain of primary, secondary, and tertiary suppliers

The supply chain depicted in Figure 12.4 is a three-tier chain simplified for the sake of illustration. In fact, large Fortune 1000 firms have thousands of suppliers, who in turn have thousands of smaller suppliers. The complexity of the supply chain suggests a combinatorial explosion. Assuming a manufacturer has four primary suppliers and each one has three primary suppliers, and each of these has three primary suppliers, then the total number of suppliers in the chain (including the buying firm) rises to 53. This figure does not include the shippers, insurers, and financiers involved in the transactions.

Immediately, you can see from Figure 12.4 that the procurement process involves a very large number of suppliers, each of whom must be coordinated with the production needs of the ultimate purchaser—the buying firm.

The Role of Existing Legacy Computer Systems

Complicating any efforts to coordinate the many firms in a supply chain is the fact that each firm generally has its own set of legacy computer systems, often homegrown or customized, that cannot easily pass information to other systems. **Legacy computer systems** generally are older mainframe and minicomputer systems used to manage key business processes within a firm in a variety of functional areas from manufacturing, logistics, finance, and human resources. Converting these older systems to new Internet and client/server-based systems is very expensive and takes many years.

legacy computer systems
generally are older mainframe and minicomputer systems used to manage key business processes within a firm in a variety of functional areas

FIGURE 12.4 **THE MULTI-TIER SUPPLY CHAIN**

Tier 3   Tier 2   Tier 1

SELLERS   **BUYER**

The supply chain for every firm is composed of multiple tiers of suppliers.

materials requirements planning (MRP) system

legacy system that enables companies to predict, track, and manage all the constituent parts of complex manufactured goods

One typical legacy system is a **materials requirements planning (MRP) system** that enables companies to predict, track, and manage all the constituent parts of complex manufactured goods such as automobiles, machine tools, and industrial equipment. An MRP system stores and generates a bill of material (BOM) that lists all the parts needed to manufacture a product. The MRP system also generates a production schedule that describes the order in which parts are used and the production time for each step in production. The BOM and production schedule are then used to generate purchase orders to suppliers. The MRP system can be run as often as needed, generating a dynamic production environment.

enterprise resource planning (ERP) system

a more sophisticated MRP system that includes human resource and financial components

Many larger firms have installed **enterprise resource planning (ERP) systems**, which are more sophisticated MRP systems that include human resource and financial components. With an ERP system in place, orders from customers are translated into BOMs, production schedules, and human resource and financial requirements, including notifying the finance department to issue invoices to customers and pay suppliers. ERP systems were not originally designed to coordinate the flow of information among a large set of supplier firms, but most ERP vendors now supply B2B modules that can manage B2B processes.

TRENDS IN SUPPLY CHAIN MANAGEMENT AND COLLABORATIVE COMMERCE

It is impossible to comprehend the actual and potential contribution of Internet-based B2B commerce, or the successes and failures of B2B e-commerce vendors and markets, without understanding ongoing efforts to improve the procurement process through a variety of supply chain management programs that long preceded the development of e-commerce.

Supply chain management (**SCM**) refers to a wide variety of activities that firms and industries use to coordinate the key players in their procurement process. For the most part, today's procurement managers work with telephones, fax machines, face-to-face conversations, and instinct, relying on trusted long-term suppliers for their strategic purchases of goods directly involved in the production process.

There have been four major developments in supply chain management over the two decades that preceded the development of the Internet and set the ground rules for understanding how B2B e-commerce works (or fails to work). These developments are supply chain simplification, electronic data interchange (EDI), supply chain management systems, and collaborative commerce.

Supply Chain Simplification

Many manufacturing firms have spent the past two decades reducing the size of their supply chains and working more closely with a smaller group of "strategic" supplier firms to reduce both product costs and administrative costs, while improving quality. Following the lead of Japanese industry, for instance, the automobile industry has systematically reduced the number of its suppliers by over 50%. Instead of open bidding for orders, large manufacturers have chosen to work with strategic partner supply firms under long-term contracts that guarantee the supplier business, but also establish quality, cost, and timing goals. These strategic partnership programs are essential for just-in-time production models, and often involve joint product development and design, integration of computer systems, and tight coupling of the production processes of two or more companies. **Tight coupling** is a method for ensuring that suppliers precisely deliver the ordered parts at a specific time and to a particular location, to ensure the production process is not interrupted for lack of parts.

Electronic Data Interchange (EDI)

As noted in the previous section, B2B e-commerce did not originate with the Internet, but in fact has its roots in technologies such as EDI that were first developed in the mid-1970s and 1980s. EDI is a broadly defined communications protocol for exchanging documents among computers using technical standards developed by the American National Standards Institute (ANSI X12 standards) and international bodies such as the United Nations (EDIFACT standards).

EDI was developed to reduce the cost, delays, and errors inherent in the manual exchanges of documents such as purchase orders, shipping documents, price lists, payments, and customer data. EDI differs from an unstructured message because its messages are organized with distinct fields for each of the important pieces of information in a commercial transaction such as transaction date, product purchased, amount, sender's name, address, and recipient's name.

Each major industry in the United States and throughout much of the industrial world has EDI industry committees that define the structure and information fields of electronic documents for that industry. EDI communications at first relied on private point-to-point circuit-switched communication networks and private value-added networks that connected key participants in the supply chain (Laudon and Laudon, 2009). Estimates indicate that B2B e-commerce EDI transactions will total about $1 trillion in 2009, about 30% of all B2B e-commerce. (U.S. Census Bureau, 2009a, b; authors' estimates). In this sense, EDI is particularly important in the development of B2B e-commerce.

EDI has evolved significantly since the 1980s (see **Figure 12.5**). Initially, EDI focused on document automation (Stage 1). Procurement agents created purchase orders electronically and sent them to trading partners, who in turn shipped order fulfillment and shipping notices electronically back to the purchaser. Invoices, payments, and other documents followed. These early implementations replaced the postal system for document transmission, and resulted in same-day shipping of orders (rather than a week's delay caused by the postal system), reduced errors, and lower costs.

FIGURE 12.5 **THE EVOLUTION OF EDI AS A B2B MEDIUM**

EDI has evolved from a simple point-to-point digital communications medium to a many-to-one enabling tool for continuous inventory replenishment.

The second stage of EDI development began in the early 1990s, driven largely by the automation of internal industrial processes and movement toward just-in-time production and continuous production. The new methods of production called for greater flexibility in scheduling, shipping, and financing of supplies. EDI evolved to become a system for document elimination. To support the new automated production processes used by manufacturers, EDI was used to eliminate purchase orders and other documents entirely, replacing them with production schedules and inventory balances. Supplier firms were sent monthly statements of production requirements and precise scheduled delivery times, and the orders would be fulfilled continuously, with inventory and payments being adjusted at the end of each month.

In the third stage of EDI, beginning in the mid-1990s, suppliers were given online access to selected parts of the purchasing firm's production and delivery schedules, and, under long-term contracts, were required to meet those schedules on their own without intervention by firm purchasing agents. Movement toward this continuous access model of EDI was spurred in the 1990s by large manufacturing and process firms (such as oil and chemical companies) that were implementing ERP systems. These systems required standardization of business processes and resulted in the automation of production, logistics, and many financial processes. These new processes required much closer relationships with suppliers, who were required to be more precise in delivery scheduling and more flexible in inventory management. This level of supplier precision could never be achieved economically by human purchasing agents. This third stage of EDI introduced the era of continuous replenishment. For instance, Wal-Mart and Toys "R"Us provide their suppliers with access to their store inventories, and the suppliers are expected to keep the stock of items on the shelf within pre-specified targets. Similar developments occurred in the grocery industry.

Today, EDI must be viewed as a general enabling technology that provides for the exchange of critical business information between computer applications supporting a wide variety of business processes. EDI is an important industrial network technology, suited to support communications among a small set of strategic partners in direct, long-term trading relationships. The technical platform of EDI has changed from mainframes to personal computers, and the telecommunications environment is changing from private, dedicated networks to the Internet (referred to as Internet-based EDI, or just Internet EDI). Most industry groups are moving toward XML as the language for expressing EDI commercial documents and communications.

The strength of EDI is its ability to support direct commercial transactions among strategically related firms in an industrial network, but this is its weakness as well. EDI is not well suited for the development of electronic marketplaces, where thousands of suppliers and purchasers meet in a digital arena to negotiate prices. EDI supports direct bilateral communications among a small set of firms and does not permit the multilateral, dynamic relationships of a true marketplace. EDI does not provide for price transparency among a large number of suppliers, does not scale easily to include new participants, and is not a real-time communications environment. EDI does not have a rich communications environment that can simultaneously support e-mail messaging, sharing of graphic documents, network meetings, or user-friendly flexible database creation and management. For these features, Internet-based software has emerged that is described below. EDI is also an expensive proposition, and a staff of dedicated programmers is required to implement it in large firms; in some cases, a considerable amount of time is also needed to reprogram existing enterprise systems to work with EDI protocols. Small firms are typically required to adopt EDI in order to supply large firms, and there are less-expensive, small-firm solutions for implementing EDI.

Supply Chain Management Systems

Supply chain simplification, focusing on strategic partners in the production process, ERP systems, and continuous inventory replenishment, are the foundation for contemporary **supply chain management (SCM) systems**. Supply chain management systems continuously link the activities of buying, making, and moving products from suppliers to purchasing firms, as well as integrating the demand side of the business equation by including the order entry system in the process. With an SCM system and continuous replenishment, inventory is eliminated and production begins only when an order is received (see **Figure 12.6**). This is especially important in industries in which the product is perishable or experiences declining market value rapidly after production. Personal computers fit this description.

Hewlett-Packard (HP) has a Web-based order-driven supply chain management system that begins with either a customer placing an order online or the receipt of

supply chain management (SCM) systems

continuously link the activities of buying, making, and moving products from suppliers to purchasing firms, as well as integrating the demand side of the business equation by including the order entry system in the process

FIGURE 12.6   **SUPPLY CHAIN MANAGEMENT SYTEMS**

SCM systems coordinate the activities of suppliers, shippers, and order entry systems to automate order entry through production, payment, and shipping business processes.

an order from a dealer. The order is forwarded from the order entry system to HP's production and delivery system. From there, the order is routed to one of several HP contractor supplier firms. One such firm is Synnex in Fremont, California. At Synnex, computers verify the order with HP and validate the ordered configuration to ensure the PC can be manufactured (e.g., will not have missing parts or fail a design specification set by HP). The order is then forwarded to a computer-based production control system that issues a bar-coded production ticket to factory assemblers. Simultaneously, a parts order is forwarded to Synnex's warehouse and inventory management system. A worker assembles the computer, and then the computer is boxed, tagged, and shipped to the customer. The delivery is monitored and tracked by HP's supply chain management system, which links directly to one of several overnight delivery systems operated by Airborne Express, Federal Express, and UPS. The elapsed time from order entry to shipping is 48 hours. With this system, Synnex and HP have eliminated the need to hold PCs in inventory, reduced cycle time from one week to 48 hours, and reduced errors. HP has extended this system to become a global B2B order tracking, reporting, and support system for large HP customers. The site now operates in 10 languages, 43 currencies, and more than 200 countries (Synnex Corporation, 2009; Hewlett-Packard, 2009).

Implementing an order-driven, Web-based supply chain management system is not always easy, however, as *Insight on Technology: RFID AutoIdentification: Making Your Supply Chain Visible* illustrates.

Collaborative Commerce

Collaborative commerce is a direct extension of supply chain management systems, as well as supply chain simplification. **Collaborative commerce** is defined as the use of digital technologies to permit organizations to collaboratively design, develop, build, and manage products through their life cycles. This is a much broader mission than EDI or simply managing the flow of information among organizations. Collaborative commerce involves a definitive move from a transaction focus to a relationship focus among the supply chain participants. Rather than having an arm's-length adversarial relationship with suppliers, collaborative commerce fosters sharing of sensitive internal information with suppliers and purchasers. Managing collaborative commerce requires knowing exactly what information to share with whom. Collaborative commerce extends beyond supply chain management activities to include the collaborative development of new products and services by multiple cooperating firms.

collaborative commerce
the use of digital technologies to permit organizations to collaboratively design, develop, build, and manage products through their life cycles

A good example of a collaborative commerce system is provided by Group Dekko. Group Dekko produces a variety of components including wire harnesses, molded plastic parts, and metal stamping for automobiles, appliances, and office furniture. In order to work with its large customers—automobile and appliance manufacturers—Group Dekko had to implement quality-control procedures conforming with international standard ISO 9000. The Group Dekko Services Department implemented a common, shared database of ISO documents using a software package called Lotus Domino to coordinate the efforts of the partner firms in Group Dekko. Lotus Domino is the Internet-based version of Lotus Notes, a collaborative document management

INSIGHT ON TECHNOLOGY

RFID AUTOIDENTIFICATION: MAKING YOUR SUPPLY CHAIN VISIBLE

It's 10 PM. Do you know where your containers are? If you're in business anywhere in the world today, and that business involves physical goods, then chances are quite good that your business depends on the movement of goods in containers. In fact, there are more than 200 million sea cargo containers moving every year among the world's seaports, and nearly 50% of the value of all U.S. imports arrive via sea cargo containers each year. The containers are loaded onto ships, and stacked high on the deck. The containers also fit on the back of trucks and on railway carriages. So when the containers are unloaded from the ship, they continue their journey from the port on the back of trucks or trains. It is a fast and efficient way of moving cargo. A standard container is 20 feet long, 8 feet wide, and 8 feet 6 inches high—big enough to hold several cars.

Prior to the development of containers, all ocean-going cargo was loaded and unloaded onto ships in huge nets by dock workers, one package at a time. While the container revolutionized ocean shipping, vastly increasing productivity and reducing breakage, keeping track of 200 million cargo containers is difficult. While each container has its own permanent ID number painted on the side, as well as a bar code identification tag, this number must be entered manually by dock workers, or scanned up close. Identification of containers is prone to errors and slow. If you had to find one container on a dock containing over 1,000 containers, you would have to read each ID number until you found the one you wanted.

Tracking containers is just one part of the larger B2B product identification problem. Retailers such as Wal-Mart, Target, and Amazon find it difficult and expensive to track millions of annual shipments into and out of their warehouses

and sales floors; the automotive industry finds it costly and difficult to synchronize the flow of parts into its factories; the U.S. Department of Defense logistics system finds it difficult to keep track of the movement of troop supplies; and the airline industry often loses bags in transit.

Thirty years ago, the development of the Uniform Product Code (UPC) and the ubiquitous bar code label was an initial first step towards automating the identification of goods. But the bar code technology of the 1970s still required humans or sometimes machines to scan products. The problem with bar codes is that they don't talk—they are passive labels that must be read or scanned.

Today, a new technology to replace bar codes is being deployed among the largest manufacturing and retailing firms. Radio frequency identification (RFID) involves the use of tags attached to products or product containers that transmit a radio signal in the 850 megahertz to 2.5 gigahertz range that continuously identifies themselves to radio receivers in warehouses, factories, retail floors, or on board ships. RFID labels are really tiny computer chips and a battery that are used to transmit each product's electronic product code to receivers nearby.

RFID has several key advantages over the old bar code scanner technology. RFID eliminates the line-of-sight reading requirement of bar codes and greatly increases the distance from which scanning can be done from a few inches up to 90 feet. RFID systems can be used just about anywhere—from clothing tags to missiles to pet tags to food—anywhere that a unique identification system is needed. The tag can carry information as simple as a pet owner's name and address or the cleaning instruction on a sweater to as complex as instructions on how to assemble a car. Best of all, instead of looking at a warehouse

(continued)

filled with thousands of packages that can't talk, you could be listening to these same thousands of packages each chirping a unique code, identifying themselves to you. Finding the single package you are looking for is much simplified. RFID tags produce a steady stream of data that can be entered into Internet—and intranet-based corporate applications such as SCM and ERP systems.

In 2009, the global RFID market is estimated to be $5.5 billion, with a U.S. market of $3 billion. The RFID market is expanding rapidly because of the growing use of RFIDs by governments, as well as private industry.

The tagging of apparel by companies such as Marks & Spencer and American Apparel is now in the roll-out phase with 200 million RFID labels being used for apparel (including laundry) globally in 2009. In total, 2.35 billion tags will be sold in 2009 compared with 1.97 billion in 2008, 1.74 billion in 2006, and 1.02 billion in 2005. Major computer firms such as Microsoft, IBM, and Hewlett-Packard are investing over several hundred million dollars each over the next five years to develop RFID software that will link RFID data to firms' SCM systems. Wal-Mart, the world's largest retailer, has made RFID an impor-

tant part of its supply chain strategy. It began by mandating that its top 100 suppliers place RFID tags on all cases and pallets headed for the firm's Dallas distribution centers by January 2005. Currently, about 600 of Wal-Mart's U.S. suppliers are tagging cases and pallets of some of the products they ship. About 1,000 Wal-Mart stores are RFID-enabled, with another 400 planned, as well as six of its distribution centers. In January 2008, the RFID program at Sam's Club became mandatory, with suppliers charged $2 per pallet for deliveries without RFID tags. Although Wal-Mart remains committed to the technology and estimates that it could increase sales by $287 million by using RFID technology, its implementation to date has had mixed results. In 2009, Wal-Mart and Sam's Club have slowed down their implementation plan to allow suppliers more time to adjust to Wal-Mart's requirements. At the same, RFID is receiving a powerful boost from the Department of Defense which is requiring suppliers to use RFID.

As adoption of the technology increases, RFID will have a profound impact on B2B e-commerce by reducing the cost of tracking goods through industry supply chains, reducing errors, and increasing the chances that the right product will be sent to the right customer.

SOURCES: "RFID Printers Adapt to Changing Market Needs," by Brian Albright, Integrated Solutions, September 2009; "Bar Code Labelling, RFID, ASNs All Smooth the Flow of Goods," SCDigest.com, September 9, 2009; "IDTechEx Report: Apparel RFID 2008-2018," by Cathryn Hindle, Just-style.com, August 12, 2009; "Global RFID Market to be Worth USD 5.56 Billion in 2009," Report, ThePaypers.com, August 27, 2009; "The Up and Down of Wal-Mart RFID Implementation," by EcoSensa, March 24, 2009; "Apparel RFID 2008-2018" by Cathryn Hindle, IDTechEx Report, August 12, 2008; "Wal-Mart RFID Plan Has Mixed Results," RFID News, April 28, 2008; "Wal-Mart Gets Tough on RFID," by Mary Hayes Weier, *InformationWeek*, January 19, 2008; "Wal-Mart Eyes $287 Million Benefit from RFID," by Dan Nystedt, *Network World*, October 12, 2007; "Wal-Mart, Sam's Club Push RFID Further Along, *RFID Journal*, October 5, 2007.

and communications package. In this way, the separate Dekko companies could share standards, documents, graphics, and experiences in implementing the quality standards. This environment is being extended to share engineering drawings, bills of material, pricing, and routing information for new products. The goal is to involve Group Dekko companies, as well as their suppliers and customers, in the complete flow of design and product information (Group Dekko, 2008; IBM, 2005, 2003).

Although collaborative commerce can involve customers as well as suppliers in the development of products, for the most part, collaborative commerce is concerned with the development of a rich communications environment to enable inter-firm sharing of designs, production plans, inventory levels, delivery schedules, and even the development of shared products (see **Figure 12.7**).

Efforts to develop closer collaboration among suppliers and purchasers originated in the late 1970s at Xerox Parc, Xerox Corporation's research center in Palo Alto. Development of the appropriate software to enable rich communications was furthered by research conducted by Lotus Development Corporation in the early 1990s. The development of the Internet as a rich communications medium has displaced proprietary software tools, and today, collaborative commerce almost always involves the use of Internet technologies to support sharing of graphic designs, documents, messages, and network meetings.

Collaborative commerce is very different from EDI, which is a technology for structured communications among firms. Collaborative commerce is more like an interactive teleconference among members of the supply chain. EDI and collaborative commerce share one characteristic: they are not open, competitive marketplaces, but instead are, technically, private industrial networks that connect strategic partners in a supply chain.

In Section 12.3, we discuss collaborative commerce in greater depth as a technology that enables private industrial networks.

| FIGURE 12.7 | ELEMENTS OF A COLLABORATIVE COMMERCE SYSTEM |

A collaborative commerce application includes a central data repository where employees at several different firms can store engineering drawings and other documents. A workflow engine determines who can see this data and what rules will apply for displaying the data on individual workstations. A viewer can be a browser operating on a workstation.

MAIN TYPES OF INTERNET-BASED B2B COMMERCE

There are two generic types of Internet-based B2B commerce systems: Net marketplaces and private industrial networks (see **Figure 12.8**). Within each of these general categories there are many different subtypes that we discuss in the following sections.

Net marketplaces (also referred to as exchanges) bring together potentially thousands of sellers and buyers into a single digital marketplace operated over the Internet. Net marketplaces are transaction-based, support many-to-many as well as one-to-many relationships, and bear some resemblance to financial markets such as the New York Stock Exchange. There are many different types of Net marketplaces, with different pricing mechanisms, biases, and value propositions that will be explored in Section 12.2 (Kerrigan, et al., 2001). Private industrial networks bring together a small number of strategic business partner firms that collaborate to develop highly efficient supply chains and satisfy customer demand for products. Private industrial networks are relationship-based, support many-to-one or many-to-few relationships, and bear some resemblance to internal collaborative work environments. There are many different types of private industrial networks, as discussed in Section 12.3. Private industrial networks are by far the largest form of B2B e-commerce, and account for over 10 times as much revenue as Net marketplaces.

12.2 NET MARKETPLACES

One of the most compelling visions of B2B e-commerce is that of an electronic marketplace on the Internet that would bring thousands of fragmented suppliers

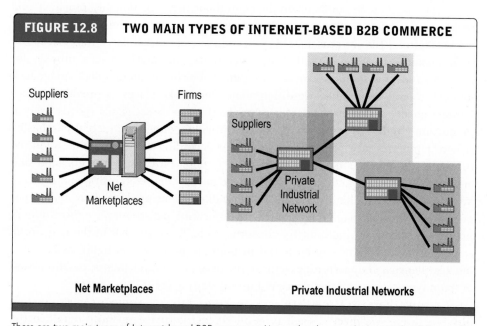

FIGURE 12.8   TWO MAIN TYPES OF INTERNET-BASED B2B COMMERCE

Net Marketplaces   **Private Industrial Networks**

There are two main types of Internet-based B2B commerce: Net marketplaces and private industrial networks.

into contact with hundreds of major purchasers of industrial goods for the purpose of conducting "frictionless" commerce. The hope was that these suppliers would compete with one another on price, transactions would be automated and low cost, and as a result, the price of industrial supplies would fall. By extracting fees from buyers and sellers on each transaction, third-party intermediary market makers could earn significant revenues. These Net marketplaces could scale easily as volume increased by simply adding more computers and communications equipment.

In pursuit of this vision, well over 1,500 Net marketplaces sprang up in the early days of e-commerce. Unfortunately,many of them have since disappeared and the population is expected to stabilize at about 200. Still, many survive, and they are joined by other types of Net marketplaces—some private and some public—based on different assumptions that are quite successful

THE VARIETY AND CHARACTERISTICS OF NET MARKETPLACES

There is a confusing variety of Net marketplaces today, and several different ways to classify them. For instance, some writers classify Net marketplaces on the basis of their pricing mechanisms—auction, bid/ask, negotiated price, and fixed prices—while others classify markets based on characteristics of the markets they serve (vertical versus horizontal, or sell-side versus buy-side), or ownership (industry-owned consortia versus independent third-party intermediaries). **Table 12.2** describes some of the important characteristics of Net marketplaces.

TYPES OF NET MARKETPLACES

Although each of these distinctions helps describe the phenomenon of Net marketplaces, they do not focus on the central business functionality provided, and they are not capable by themselves of describing the variety of Net marketplaces.

In **Figure 12.9**, we present a classification of Net marketplaces that focuses on their business functionality; that is, what these Net marketplaces provide for businesses seeking solutions. We use two dimensions of Net marketplaces to create a four-cell classification table. We differentiate Net marketplaces as providing either indirect goods (goods used to support production) or direct goods (goods used in production), and we distinguish markets as providing either contractual purchasing (where purchases take place over many years according to a contract between the firm and its vendor) or spot purchasing (where purchases are episodic and anonymous—vendors and buyers do not have an ongoing relationship and may not know one another). The intersection of these dimensions produces four main types of Net marketplaces that are relatively straightforward: e-distributors, e-procurement networks, exchanges, and industry consortia. Note, however, that in the real world, some Net marketplaces can be found in multiple parts of this figure as business models change and opportunities appear and disappear. Nevertheless, the discussion of "pure types" of Net marketplaces is a useful starting point.

Each of these Net marketplaces seeks to provide value to customers in different ways. We discuss each type of Net marketplace in more detail in the following sections.

TABLE 12.2	OTHER CHARACTERISTICS OF NET MARKETPLACES: A B2B VOCABULARY
CHARACTERISTIC	**MEANING**
Bias	Sell-side vs. buy-side vs. neutral. Whose interests are advantaged: buyers, sellers, or no bias?
Ownership	Industry vs. third party. Who owns the marketplace?
Pricing mechanism	Fixed-price catalogs, auctions, bid/ask, and RFPs/RFQs.
Scope/Focus	Horizontal vs. vertical markets.
Value creation	What benefits do they offer customers or suppliers?
Access to market	In public markets, any firm can enter, but in private markets, entry is by invitation only.

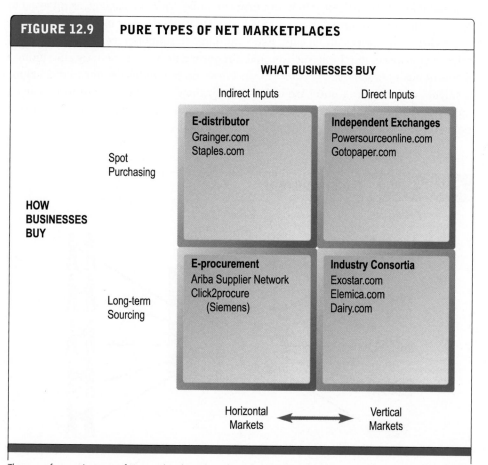

FIGURE 12.9   PURE TYPES OF NET MARKETPLACES

There are four main types of Net marketplaces based on the intersection of two dimensions: how businesses buy and what they buy. A third dimension—horizontal versus vertical markets—also distinguishes the different types of Net marketplaces.

E-distributors

e-distributor

provides electronic catalog
that represents the
products of thousands of
direct manufacturers

E-distributors are the most common and most easily understood type of Net marketplace. An **e-distributor** provides an electronic catalog that represents the products of thousands of direct manufacturers (see **Figure 12.10**). An e-distributor is the equivalent of Amazon.com for industry. E-distributors are independently owned intermediaries that offer industrial customers a single source from which to order indirect goods (often referred to as MRO) on a spot, as-needed basis. Reportedly, about 40% of corporate purchases cannot be satisfied under a company's existing contracts, and must be purchased on a spot basis (Jupiter Media Metrix, 2001a; Devine, et al., 2001). E-distributors make money by charging a markup on products they distribute.

Organizations and firms in all industries require MRO supplies. The MRO function maintains, repairs, and operates commercial buildings and maintains all the machinery of these buildings from heating, ventilating, and air conditioning systems to lighting fixtures.

E-distributors operate in horizontal markets because they serve many different industries with products from many different suppliers. E-distributors usually operate "public" markets in the sense that any firm can order from the catalog, as opposed to "private" markets, where membership is restricted to selected firms.

E-distributor prices are usually fixed, but large customers receive discounts and other incentives to purchase, such as credit, reporting on account activity, and limited forms of business purchasing rules (for instance, no purchases greater than $500 for a single item without a purchase order). The primary benefits offered to industrial customers are lower search costs, lower transaction costs, wide selection, rapid delivery, and low prices.

FIGURE 12.10	E-DISTRIBUTORS

E-distributors are firms that bring the products of thousands of suppliers into a single online electronic catalog for sale to thousands of buyer firms. E-distributors are sometimes referred to as one-to-many markets, one seller serving many firms.

The most frequently cited example of a public e-distribution market is W.W. Grainger. Grainger is involved in both long-term systematic sourcing as well as spot sourcing, but its emphasis is on spot sourcing. Grainger's business model is to become the world's leading source of MRO suppliers, and its revenue model is that of a typical retailer: it owns the products, and takes a markup on the products it sells to customers. At Grainger.com, users get an electronic online version of Grainger's famous seven-pound catalog, plus other parts not available in the catalog (adding up to around 475,000 parts), and complete electronic ordering and payment (W.W. Grainger Inc., 2009).

E-procurement

An **e-procurement Net marketplace** is an independently owned intermediary that connects hundreds of online suppliers offering millions of maintenance and repair parts to business firms who pay fees to join the market (see **Figure 12.11**). E-procurement Net marketplaces are typically used for long-term contractual purchasing of indirect goods (MRO); they create online horizontal markets, but they also provide for members' spot sourcing of MRO supplies. E-procurement companies make money by charging a percentage of each transaction, licensing consulting services and software, and assessing network use fees.

E-procurement companies expand on the business model of simpler e-distributors by including the online catalogs of hundreds of suppliers and offering value chain

e-procurement Net marketplace
independently owned intermediary that connects hundreds of online suppliers offering millions of maintenance and repair parts to business firms who pay fees to join the market

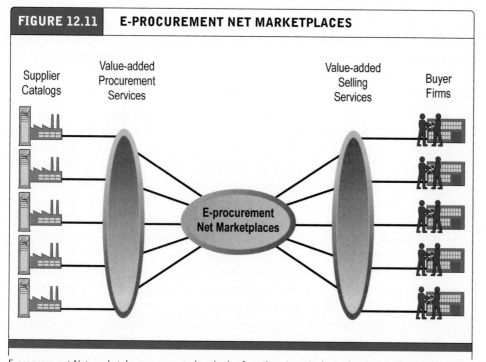

FIGURE 12.11 **E-PROCUREMENT NET MARKETPLACES**

E-procurement Net marketplaces aggregate hundreds of catalogs in a single marketplace and make them available to firms, often on a custom basis that reflects only the suppliers desired by the participating firms.

**value chain
management (VCM)
services**
include automation of a
firm's entire procurement
process on the buyer side
and automation of the
selling business processes
on the seller side

management services to both buyers and sellers. **Value chain management** (VCM) **services** provided by e-procurement companies include automation of a firm's entire procurement process on the buyer side and automation of the selling business processes on the seller side. For purchasers, e-procurement companies automate purchase orders, requisitions, sourcing, business rules enforcement, invoicing, and payment. For suppliers, e-procurement companies provide catalog creation and content management, order management, fulfillment, invoicing, shipment, and settlement.

E-procurement Net marketplaces are sometimes referred to as many-to-many markets. They are mediated by an independent third party that purports to represent both buyers and sellers, and hence claim to be neutral. On the other hand, because they may include the catalogs of both competing suppliers and competing e-distributors, they have a likely bias in favor of the buyers. Nevertheless, by aggregating huge buyer firms into their networks, they provide distinct marketing benefits for suppliers and reduce customer acquisition costs.

Players in this market segment include Ariba (which purchased its primary competitor, FreeMarkets, in 2004), Perfect Commerce, BravoSolution, A.T. Kearney Procurement & Analytic Solutions, and Emptoris. The very large enterprise software firms—Oracle, SAP, i2, and JDA Software Group (which acquired Manugistics in 2006)—now also offer procurement solutions to their customers and compete directly against the early entrants in this market.

General Dynamics, for instance, one of the largest defense contractors, uses Ariba e-sourcing software to spend about $8.3 billion annually. General Dynamics uses Ariba's online e-auctions and automated RFQ software to reduce the cost of direct and indirect goods, and to reduce overall transaction costs with vendors. General Dynamics claims an overall reduction of 10%–15% in the cost of goods purchased through its new systems (Ariba, 2009; Hannon, 2003).

Exchanges

exchange
independently owned
online marketplace that
connects hundreds to
potentially thousands of
suppliers and buyers in a
dynamic, real-time
environment

An **exchange** is an independently owned online marketplace that connects hundreds to potentially thousands of suppliers and buyers in a dynamic, real-time environment (see **Figure 12.12**). Exchanges generally create vertical markets that focus on the spot-purchasing requirements of large firms in a single industry, such as computers and telecommunications, electronics, food, and industrial equipment, although there are exceptions to this generalization as described in this section. Exchanges were the prototype Internet-based marketplace in the early days of e-commerce; as noted above, over 1,000 were created in this period, but most have failed.

Exchanges make money by charging a commission on the transaction. The pricing model can be through an online negotiation, auction, RFQ, or fixed buy-and-sell prices. The benefits offered to customers of exchanges include reduced search cost for parts and spare capacity. Other benefits include lower prices created by a global marketplace driven by competition among suppliers who would, presumably, sell goods at very low profit margins at one world-market price. The benefits offered suppliers are access to a global purchasing environment and the opportunity

FIGURE 12.12   EXCHANGES

Buyer Firms

Electronic Marketplace

Suppliers

Market Maker's Proprietary Software Envelope

Independent exchanges bring potentially thousands of suppliers to a vertical (industry-specific) marketplace to sell their goods to potentially thousands of buyer firms. Exchanges are sometimes referred to as many-to-many markets because they have many suppliers serving many buyer firms.

to unload production overruns (although at very competitive prices and low profit margins). Even though they are private intermediaries, exchanges are public in the sense of permitting any bona fide buyer or seller to participate.

Exchanges tend to be biased toward the buyer even though they are independently owned and presumably neutral. Suppliers are disadvantaged by the fact that exchanges put them in direct price competition with other similar suppliers around the globe, driving profit margins down. Exchanges have failed primarily because suppliers have refused to join them, and hence, the existing markets have very low liquidity, defeating the very purpose and benefits of an exchange. **Liquidity** is typically measured by the number of buyers and sellers in a market, the volume of transactions, and the size of transactions. You know a market is liquid when you can buy or sell just about any size order at just about any time you want. On all of these measures, many exchanges failed, resulting in a very small number of participants, few trades, and small trade value per transaction. The most common reason for not using exchanges is the absence of traditional, trusted suppliers.

While most exchanges tend to be vertical marketplaces offering direct supplies, some exchanges offer indirect inputs as well, such as electricity and power, transportation services (usually to the transportation industry), and professional services. **Table 12.4** lists a few examples of some current independent exchanges.

The following capsule description of several exchanges provides insight into their origins and current functions.

liquidity

typically measured by the number of buyers and sellers in a market, the volume of transactions, and the size of transactions

TABLE 12.4	EXAMPLES OF INDEPENDENT EXCHANGES
EXCHANGE	**FOCUS**
PowerSource Online	Computer parts exchange
Converge	Semiconductors and computer peripherals
Smarterwork	Spare professional services from Web design to legal advice
Active International	Trading in underutilized manufacturing capacity
IntercontinentalExchange	International online marketplace for over 600 commodities

Global Wine & Spirits (GWS) (Globalwinespirits.com) is somewhat unique among independent exchanges, not only as a start-up that has managed to survive, but also as a latecomer to the B2B e-commerce community. GWS opened in 1999, but did not begin to trade products online until May 2001. Based in Montreal, Quebec, GWS is operated by Mediagrif Interactive Technologies Inc., a Canadian company that operates a number of independent exchanges in a variety of industries. GWS offers a spot marketplace for wines, where wine and spirit producers offer wines for sale; a "call for tenders" market, where members make offers to purchase wines and spirits; a trade database with listings of thousands of industry professionals; and a wine and spirits catalog with over 35,000 products. (Global Wine & Spirits, 2008).

Inventory Locator Service (ILS) has its roots as an offline intermediary, serving as a listing service for aftermarket parts in the aerospace industry. Upon opening in 1979, ILS initially provided a telephone and fax-based directory of aftermarket parts to airplane owners and mechanics, along with government procurement professionals. As early as 1984, ILS incorporated e-mail capabilities as part of its RFQ services, and by 1998, it had begun to conduct online auctions for hard-to-find parts. Today, ILS maintains an Internet-accessible database of over 5 billion aerospace and marine industry parts, and has also developed an eRFQ feature that helps users streamline their sourcing processes. The network's 20,000 subscribers in 93 different countries access the site over 60,000 times a day. (Inventory Locator Service, 2009).

Industry Consortia

industry consortium
industry-owned vertical market that enables buyers to purchase direct inputs (both goods and services) from a limited set of invited participants

An **industry consortium** is an industry-owned vertical market that enables buyers to purchase direct inputs (both goods and services) from a limited set of invited participants (see **Figure 12.13**). Industry consortia emphasize long-term contractual purchasing, the development of stable relationships (as opposed to merely an anonymous transaction emphasis), and the creation of industry-wide data standards and synchronization efforts. Industry consortia are more focused on optimizing long-term supply relationships than independent exchanges, which tend to focus more on short-term transactions. The ultimate objective of industry consortia is the unification of supply chains within entire industries, across many tiers, through common data definitions, network standards, and computing platforms. In addition, industry

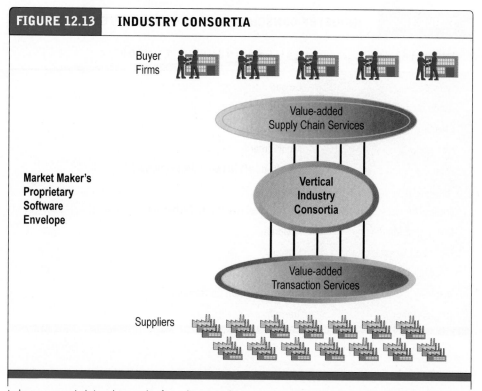

FIGURE 12.13   **INDUSTRY CONSORTIA**

Buyer Firms

Value-added Supply Chain Services

Market Maker's Proprietary Software Envelope

Vertical Industry Consortia

Value-added Transaction Services

Suppliers

Industry consortia bring thousands of suppliers into direct contact with a smaller number of very large buyers. The market makers provide value-added software services for procurement, transaction management, shipping, and payment for both buyers and suppliers. Industry consortia are sometimes referred to as many-to-few markets, where many suppliers (albeit selected by the buyers) serve a few very large buyers, mediated by a variety of value-added services.

consortia, unlike independent exchanges described previously, take their marching orders from the industry and not from venture capitalists or investment bankers. This means any profits from operating industry consortia are returned to industry business firms.

Industry consortia sprang up in 1999 and 2000 in part as a reaction to the earlier development of independently owned exchanges, which were viewed by large industries (such as the automotive and chemical industries) as market interlopers that would not directly serve the interests of large buyers, but would instead line their own pockets and those of their venture capital investors. Rather than "pay-to-play," large firms decided to "pay-to-own" their markets. Another concern of large firms was that Net marketplaces would work only if large suppliers and buyers participated, and only if there was liquidity. Independent exchanges were not attracting enough players to achieve liquidity. In addition, exchanges often failed to provide additional value-added services that would transform the value chain for the entire industry, including linking the new marketplaces to firms' ERP systems. More than 60 industry consortia now exist, with many industries having more than one (see **Table 12.5**).

TABLE 12.5	INDUSTRY CONSORTIA BY INDUSTRY (SEPTEMBER 2009)
INDUSTRY	NAME OF INDUSTRY CONSORTIA
Aerospace	Exostar
Automotive	SupplyOn
Chemical	Elemica
Financial	MuniCenter
Food	Dairy.com, eFSNetwork (iTrade Network)
Hospitality	Avendra
Medical Services, Supplies	GHX (Global Healthcare Exchange)
Metals and Mining	Quadrem
Paper and Forest Products	Liason
Shipping	OceanConnect
Textiles	TheSeam (Cotton Consortium)
Transportation	Transplace

The industries with the most consortia are food, metals, and chemicals, although these are not necessarily the largest consortia in terms of revenue. Many very large Fortune 500 and private firms are investors in several industry consortia. For instance, Cargill—the world's largest private corporation—invested in six consortia that exist at various points in Cargill's and the food industry's tangled value chain.

Industry consortia make money in a number of ways. Industry members usually pay for the creation of the consortia's capabilities and contribute initial operating capital. Then industry consortia charge buyer and seller firms transaction and subscription fees. Industry members—both buyers and sellers—are expected to reap benefits far greater than their contributions through the rationalization of the procurement process, competition among vendors, and closer relationships with vendors.

Industry consortia offer many different pricing mechanisms, ranging from auctions to fixed prices to RFQs, depending on the products and the situation. Prices can also be negotiated, and the environment, while competitive, is nevertheless restricted to a smaller number of buyers—selected, reliable, and long-term suppliers who are often viewed as "strategic industry" partners. The bias of industry consortia is clearly toward the large buyers who control access to this lucrative market channel and can benefit from competitive pricing offered by alternative suppliers. Benefits to suppliers come from access to large buyer firm procurement systems, long-term stable relationships, and large order sizes.

Industry consortia can and often do force suppliers to use the consortia's networks and proprietary software as a condition of selling to the industry's members. Although exchanges failed for a lack of suppliers and liquidity, the market power of consortia members ensures suppliers will participate, so consortia may be able to avoid the fate of voluntary exchanges. Clearly, industry consortia are at an advantage when compared to independent exchanges because, unlike the venture-capital-backed exchanges, they have deep-pocket financial backing from the very start and guaranteed liquidity based on a steady flow of large firm orders. Yet industry consortia are a relatively new phenomenon, and the long-term profitability of these consortia, especially when several consortia exist for a single industry, has yet to be demonstrated.

The following capsule descriptions of two industry consortia illustrate their vitality and growth potential.

Exostar is an aerospace industry consortium. Its founding partners include BAE Systems, Boeing, Lockheed Martin, Raytheon, and Rolls-Royce. Exostar has taken a slow but steady approach to building its technology platform. It has kept its focus on the direct procurement and supply chain needs of its largest members, and taken its time developing a portfolio of technology solutions that meet its needs. Its current products include Supply Pass, an integrated suite of tools that enables suppliers to handle buyer transactions via the Internet; SourcePass, which provides a dynamic bidding environment for buyers and sellers; and ProcurePass, which enables buyers to handle supplier transactions online, among others. As of September 2009, Exostar served a community of more than 40,000 trading partners, (Exostar, 2009).

Serving the mining, minerals, and metals industries, Quadrem initially opened in May 2000 with 14 founding members. Its current shareholders include some of the world's largest natural resource companies, such as Alcoa, DeBeers, and Phelps Dodge, and together represent about $90 billion in annual spending. As of 2009, Quadrem's network includes more than 60,000 suppliers and 1,500 buyers, and handles more than $20 billion in annual orders (Quadrem International Ltd., 2009).

THE LONG-TERM DYNAMICS OF NET MARKETPLACES

Net marketplaces are changing rapidly because of the widespread failures of early exchanges and a growing realization by key participants that real value will derive from B2B e-commerce only when it can change the entire procurement system, the supply chain, and the process of collaboration among firms. Several industry consortia have transformed themselves into industry data standards and synchronization forums. The consolidation of Net marketplaces in 2003 and 2004 has resulted in remaining firms that are much stronger and that are beginning to grow rapidly once again. In fact, B2B online transaction volumes are growing worldwide and within the United States at 20%–30% per year.

Figure 12.14 depicts some of these changes. Pure Net marketplace exchanges are moving away from the simple "electronic marketplace" vision, and toward playing a more central role in changing the procurement process. Independent exchanges are ideal buy-out candidates for industry consortia because they have often developed the technology infrastructure. In any event, consortia and exchanges are beginning to work together in selected markets. Likewise, e-distributors are securing admission to large e-procurement systems and also seeking admission to industry consortia as suppliers of indirect goods.

FIGURE 12.14   NET MARKETPLACE TRENDS

E-distributors and exchanges are migrating their business models toward more sustained, higher value-added relationships with buyer firms by providing e-procurement services and participating in industry consortia.

Other notable trends include the movement from simple transactions involving spot purchasing to longer-term contractual relationships involving both indirect and direct goods (Wise and Morrison, 2000). The complexity and duration of transactions is increasing, and both buyers and suppliers are becoming accustomed to working in a digital environment, and making less use of the fax machine and telephone. To date, Net marketplaces, as well as private industrial networks, have emerged in a political climate friendly to large-scale cooperation among very large firms. However, the possibility exists that Net marketplaces may provide some firms with an ideal platform to collude on pricing, market sharing, and market access, all of which would be anti-competitive and reduce the efficiency of the marketplace. *Insight on Society: Are Net Marketplaces Anti-Competitive Cartels?* considers the anti-competitive possibilities inherent in Net marketplaces.

12.3   PRIVATE INDUSTRIAL NETWORKS

Private industrial networks today form the largest part of B2B e-commerce, both on and off the Internet. Industry analysts estimate that in 2009, about 50% of B2B expenditures by large firms will be for the development of private industrial networks. Private industrial networks can be considered the foundation of the

INSIGHT ON SOCIETY

ARE NET MARKETPLACES ANTI-COMPETITIVE CARTELS?

Although Net marketplaces and private industrial networks often lead to extraordinary gains in efficiency for both firms and industries as a whole, ironically, they also provide some equally powerful tools for reducing competition in the marketplace and driving up prices to consumers, and even reducing variety in the marketplace as well. There are two types of antitrust concerns: the market for goods and the market for B2B marketplaces themselves.

In the market for goods, the primary antitrust concerns are information sharing that permits or encourages price fixing, monopsony (when a cartel or monopoly drives down input prices below the value of goods), and exclusion (preventing new companies from entering a marketplace).

For instance, in a Net marketplace owned by large industry players (such as the chemical exchange Elemica), owner-members could collude with one another on the prices they are willing to pay for inputs. Price collusion does not necessarily involve a formal agreement among colluders, but can take place in highly efficient markets through "parallel pricing," or informal arrangements among suppliers to a market to "agree" on prices through market communication.

Information sharing may also lead to market-sharing agreements in which manufacturers divide the market into segments and agree to produce only enough for their allocated segment. In a monopsony, large buyers have so much power that they can control input prices by buying less of an input. Net marketplaces could be used to exclude rival competitive firms, forcing their rivals to pay higher prices for inputs. For instance, chemical firms that do not pay to

support Elemica might be precluded from obtaining the best prices possible on the market.

The recent brief history of Net marketplaces suggests that they inherently consolidate into one or two Net marketplaces in each industry and therefore become the dominant players; they experience network effects in the sense that the larger Net marketplaces become, the more attractive they are to join; and they experience economies of scale insofar as the larger they become, the more efficient and liquid they become. Together, these factors lead to the surviving Net marketplaces having extraordinary market power. These concerns primarily apply to industry consortia, although they also arise in independent exchanges as well. Researchers have found for instance that industry owned net market places are more likely to survive than third-party networks, and inherently lead to a small number of networks or a single network in an industry.

In the market for Net marketplaces, a very large Net marketplace formed by buyers or sellers could prevent other entrepreneurial market makers from starting up because of the high switching costs involved and the network effects of large markets. Such Net marketplaces may devise rules that specifically proscribe the members from purchasing in any other markets. Moreover, once a Net marketplace attracts, say, 90% of the buyers and sellers in a marketspace, it experiences powerful network effects and resulting high levels of liquidity; it becomes, in essence, the only marketplace with a sufficient number of buyers and sellers to support trading systematically.

Even though B2B Net marketplaces are new, the antitrust issues and concepts are not.

(continued)

Information sharing among competitors, monopsony, and exclusion from necessary facilities are issues that have arisen in the context of airline reservation systems, railroad terminal facilities, and film distribution by the motion picture industry. There are Justice Department rules (Competitor Collaboration Guidelines) that describe permissible information sharing and collaboration among competitors, and a large body of case law and scholarship that has developed principles for determining when collaboration among competing firms becomes illegal. In general, courts and scholars have sought to proscribe any behavior that would harm competition in the marketplace and harm customers by raising prices and/or reducing selection. A wide variety of behaviors are tolerated by courts up until the point where the consequences are harmful to competition, and ultimately to the consumer or buyers who are forced to pay higher prices.

In a report on competition in B2B markets, the Federal Trade Commission (FTC) concluded that no action was needed now to ensure B2B markets remained competitive. The FTC, however, continues to monitor the behavior of large Net marketplaces, as well as the trading that occurs within them, for signs of collusion, monopsony power, and exclusionary behavior that might harm competition.

SOURCES: "The Sustainability of B2B Marketplaces: Ownership Structure, Market Competition, and Prior Buyer-Seller Connections," by Kexin Zhao, et. al., *Decision Support Systems*, May 2009; "Ownership Influences On Vertical B2B E-marketplaces' Survival," by Weijun Zheng, *Issues in Informing Science and Information Technology*, Vol. 9, 2009; "E-Commerce Transaction Mechanisms And Buyer-Supplier Relationships," by Sungmin Ryu, et. al., *Journal of Business and Economics Research*, February 2009; "Clarity is the Missing Link in Supply Chain," by Phred Dvorak, *Wall Street Journal*, May 18, 2009; "Competition Policy Implications of Electronic Business-to-Business Marketplaces: Issues for Marketers," by Andrew Pressey and John Ashton, Centre for Competition Policy Working Paper 07–15, June 2007; "The New Economy and Beyond: Past, Present, and Future," edited by Dennis W. Jansen, Edward Elgar Publishing, 2006; "B2B Companies Face Antitrust Questions," by Quentin Riegel, National Association of Manufacturers, "Would B2B Exchanges Have Antitrust Issues?" by Tair-Rong Sheu, 30th Research Conference on Communication, Information and Internet Policy, September 29, 2002; "An Overview of Federal Trade Commission Antitrust Activities," Prepared statement of the Federal Trade Commission, Committee on the Judiciary, United States Senate, September 19, 2002; "Beyond Covisint: Antitrust Scrutiny of B2B Exchanges," by F. Martin Dajani, *Journal of the Missouri Bar*, July/August 2001; "Case Studies for Federal Trade Commission Public Workshop on Emerging Issues for Competition Policy in the World of E-Commerce," Federal Trade Commission, May 7, 2001; "Evaluating the Antitrust Risks of the Internet Entwined Business," by Shawn Potter, *West Virginia Journal of Law and Technology*, May 4, 2001; "Entering the 21st Century: Competition Policy in the World of B2B Marketplaces," Federal Trade Commission, October 2000.

"extended enterprise," and the notion that firms can extend their boundaries and their business processes to include supply chain and logistics partners.

WHAT ARE PRIVATE INDUSTRIAL NETWORKS?

As noted at the beginning of this chapter, private industrial networks are direct descendants of existing EDI networks, and they are closely tied to existing ERP systems used by large firms. A private industrial network (sometimes referred to as a private trading exchange, or PTX) is a Web-enabled network for the coordination of trans-organizational business processes (sometimes also called collaborative commerce). A **trans-organizational business process** requires at least two independent firms to perform (Laudon and Laudon, 2009). For the most part, these networks originate in and closely involve the manufacturing and related support industries, and therefore we refer to them as "industrial" networks, although in the future they could just as easily apply to some services. These networks can be industry-wide, but often begin and sometimes focus on the voluntary coordination of a

trans-organizational business process
process that requires at least two independent firms to perform

group of supplying firms centered about a single, very large manufacturing firm. Private industrial networks can be viewed as "extended enterprises" in the sense that they often begin as ERP systems in a single firm, and are then expanded to include (often using an extranet) the firm's major suppliers. **Figure 12.15** illustrates a private industrial network originally built by Procter & Gamble (P&G) in the United States to coordinate supply chains among its suppliers, distributors, truckers, and retailers.

In P&G's private industrial network shown in Figure 12.15, customer sales are captured at the cash register, which then initiates a flow of information back to distributors, P&G, and its suppliers. This tells P&G and its suppliers the exact level of demand for thousands of products. This information is then used to initiate production, supply, and transportation to replenish products at the distributors and retailers. This process is called an efficient customer response system (a demand-pull production model), and it relies on an equally efficient supply chain management system to coordinate the supply side.

Not surprisingly, there is not a great deal of detailed information about private industrial networks. Most companies that originate and participate in these networks view them as a competitive advantage, and therefore they are reluctant to release information about how much they cost and how they operate.

GE, Dell Computer, Cisco Systems, Microsoft, IBM, Nike, Coca-Cola, Wal-Mart, Nokia, and Hewlett-Packard are among the firms operating successful private industrial networks.

FIGURE 12.15   PROCTER & GAMBLE'S PRIVATE INDUSTRIAL NETWORK

Procter & Gamble's private industrial network attempts to coordinate the trans-organizational business processes of the many firms it deals with in the consumer products industry.

CHARACTERISTICS OF PRIVATE INDUSTRIAL NETWORKS

The central focus of private industrial networks is to provide an industry-wide global solution to achieve the highest levels of efficiency. The specific objectives of a private industrial network include:

- Developing efficient purchasing and selling business processes industry-wide
- Developing industry-wide resource planning to supplement enterprise-wide resource planning
- Increasing supply chain visibility—knowing the inventory levels of buyers and suppliers
- Achieving closer buyer-supplier relationships, including demand forecasting, communications, and conflict resolution
- Operating on a global scale—globalization
- Reducing industry risk by preventing imbalances of supply and demand, including developing financial derivatives, insurance, and futures markets

Private industrial networks serve different goals from Net marketplaces. Net marketplaces are primarily transaction-oriented, whereas private industrial networks focus on continuous business process coordination between companies. This can include much more than just supply chain management, such as product design, sourcing, demand forecasting, asset management, sales, and marketing. Private industrial networks do support transactions, but that is not their primary focus.

Private industrial networks usually focus on a single sponsoring company that "owns" the network, sets the rules, establishes governance (a structure of authority, rule enforcement, and control), and invites firms to participate at its sole discretion. Therefore, these networks are "private." This sets them apart from industry consortia, which are usually owned by major firms collectively through equity participation. Whereas Net marketplaces have a strong focus on indirect goods and services, private industrial networks focus on strategic, direct goods and services.

For instance, Ace Hardware, a cooperative of 5,100 retail hardware stores, uses a private industrial network to manage inventory levels and collaborate with suppliers by linking 14 Ace distribution centers and nine key suppliers. In the past, a team of 30 Ace procurement managers used faxes, phones, and an older EDI system to buy products for retail members. It took seven to ten days to process an order. Suppliers had no access to inventory levels in retail stores or Ace distribution centers, forcing them to guess their likely production requirements. Manco, one large supplier of Ace, now uses the Internet-based private industrial network to accurately gauge demand for more than 200 products, from duct tape to shelf liners, that it supplies Ace. The more streamlined ordering process has allowed Manco to reduce distribution costs by 28% and freight costs by 18% (VICS, 2004; ADX Corporation, 2004; Gleason, 2003).

Perhaps no single firm better illustrates the benefits of developing private industrial networks than Wal-Mart, described in *Insight on Business: Wal-Mart Develops a Private Industrial Network.*

INSIGHT ON BUSINESS

WAL-MART DEVELOPS A PRIVATE INDUSTRIAL NETWORK

Wal-Mart is a well-known leader in the application of network technology to the coordination of its supply chain. With sales of more than $405 billion for the fiscal year ending January 31, 2009, Wal-Mart has been able to use information technology to achieve a decisive cost advantage over competitors. As you might imagine, the world's largest retailer also has the world's largest supply chain, with more than 60,000 suppliers worldwide. In the next five years, the company plans to expand from around 4,200 retail stores in the United States (including Sam's Clubs) to over 5,000, and increase its selection of goods to include automobiles, pianos, groceries, high-fashion clothing, and personal computers. In other words, Wal-Mart's strategic plan is to be where they are not now. All of this will require an even more capable private industrial network than what is now in place.

In the late 1980s, Wal-Mart developed the beginnings of collaborative commerce using an EDI-based SCM system that required its large suppliers to use Wal-Mart's proprietary EDI network to respond to orders from Wal-Mart purchasing managers. In 1991, Wal-Mart expanded the capabilities of its EDI-based network by introducing Retail Link. This system connected Wal-Mart's largest suppliers to Wal-Mart's own inventory management system, and it required large suppliers to track actual sales by stores and to replenish supplies as dictated by demand and following rules imposed by Wal-Mart. Wal-Mart also introduced financial payment systems that ensure that Wal-Mart does not own the goods until they arrive and are shelved.

In 1997, Wal-Mart moved Retail Link to an extranet that allowed suppliers to directly link over the Internet into Wal-Mart's inventory management system. In 2000, Wal-Mart hired an outside firm to upgrade Retail Link from being a supply chain management tool toward a more collaborative forecasting, planning, and replenishment system. Using demand aggregation software provided by Atlas Metaprise Software, Wal-Mart purchasing agents can now aggregate demand from Wal-Mart's 4,200 separate stores in the United States into a single RFQ from suppliers. This gives Wal-Mart tremendous clout with even the largest suppliers. Wal-Mart and Atlas plan to first build a global sourcing network. Previously, Wal-Mart's foreign location buyers relied on a mix of telephones, fax, and e-mail to communicate their spending forecasts. The new system allows them to submit forecasts via the Internet. Wal-Mart headquarters in turn issues worldwide RFQs for all stores. The Atlas software helps Wal-Mart purchasing agents select a winning bid and negotiate final contracts.

In addition, suppliers can now immediately access information on inventories, purchase orders, invoice status, and sales forecasts, based on 104 weeks of online, real-time, item-level data. The system does not require smaller supplier firms to adopt expensive EDI software solutions. Instead, they can use standard browsers and PCs loaded with free software from Wal-Mart. There are now over 20,000 suppliers—small and large—participating in Wal-Mart's network.

In 2002, Wal-Mart switched to an entirely Internet-based private network. Wal-Mart adopted AS2, a software package from iSoft Corporation, a Dallas-based software company. AS2 implements EDI-INT (an Internet-based standard version of EDI), and the result is a

(continued)

radical reduction in communications costs. Wal-Mart uses Sterling Commerce (the largest single provider of EDI communication systems to industry) and IBM to support this EDI initiative. The AS2 initiative lets suppliers connect, deliver, validate, and reply to data securely over the Internet. IBM uses its expertise to assist Wal-Mart suppliers in selecting and implementing the appropriate AS2-certified solutions that best meet their needs. Sterling Commerce provides interoperability services for EDI-INT AS2 connectivity between Wal-Mart and its suppliers. In 2007, Wal-Mart's rapid growth, especially global operations, forced it go outside for its financial services operation systems. Wal-Mart hired SAP, an enterprise software mangement firm, to build a global financial management system for Wal-Mart. Wal-Mart has finally started to outgrow its homegrown systems.

Despite the recession, in 2009, Wal-Mart's sales are growing slowly while other retailers suffer declining revenues of 10%–20%. In the first quarter of 2009, Wal-Mart's profits of $302 billion were the same as 2008, while revenues fell only .6%. Same-store sales in the U.S. increased by 5.6% in the first quarter. Wal-mart continues to innovate its products and services. In 2009, it announced it would develop a Web site where Wal-Mart suppliers could sell their goods directly to consumers (watch out Amazon), and that it would enter into the medical records business by building a package of hardware, software, and support for small doctor's offices at half the price of competitors.

Wal-Mart's success spurred its competitors in the retail industry to develop industry-wide private industrial networks such as Global NetXchange (now Agentrics) in an effort to duplicate the success of Wal-Mart. Wal-Mart executives have said Wal-Mart would not join these networks, or any industry-sponsored consortium or independent exchange, because doing so would only help its competitors achieve what Wal-Mart has already accomplished with Retail Link. To compete with the efficiencies attained by Wal-Mart, other retailers, such as JCPenney, have implemented their own extensive private industrial networks to link suppliers to their stores' inventories directly over the Internet. JCPenney has even given over some of its inventory control and product selection to its largest apparel provider, TAL Apparel Ltd. of Hong Kong.

SOURCES: "Wal-Mart Stores Web Site Creates New Program That Lets Outside Retailers Offer Products," taragana.com, August 31, 2009; Wal-Mart Stores Inc., Report on Form 10-K for the fiscal year ended January 31, 2009, filed April 4, 2009; "Wal-Mart Says Its Market Share Is Rising," by Stephanie Rosenblum, *New York Times*, May 15, 2009; "Wal-Mart Plans to Market Digital Health Records System," by Steve Lohr, *New York Times*, March 14, 2009; "Wal-Mart Stores Inc.-Requirements," Walmart.com, September 25, 2008; "How Wal-Mart Lost Its Technology Edge," by Thomas Wailgum, *Network World*, October 5, 2007; "Who Gains, Who Loses, from RFID's Growing Presence in the Marketplace?," Knowledge@Wharton, March 23, 2005; "Fruit Vendor Updates Systems to Satisfy Wal-Mart" by Stacy Cowley, *CIO*, August 1, 2004; "Suppliers May Miss Tracking Mandate Set by Wal-Mart," by Ann Zimmerman, *Wall Street Journal*, March 31, 2004.

PRIVATE INDUSTRIAL NETWORKS AND COLLABORATIVE COMMERCE

Private industrial networks can do much more than just serve a supply chain and efficient customer response system. They can also include other activities of a single large manufacturing firm, including design of products and engineering diagrams, as well as marketing plans and demand forecasting. Collaboration among businesses can take many forms and involve a wide range of activities—from simple supply chain management to coordinating market feedback to designers at supply firms (see **Figure 12.16**).

FIGURE 12.16 **PIECES OF THE COLLABORATIVE COMMERCE PUZZLE**

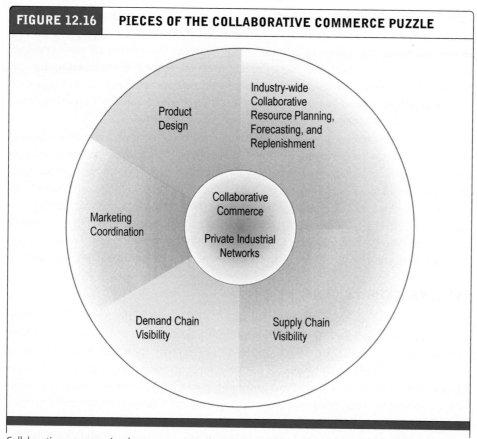

Collaborative commerce involves many cooperative activities among supply and sales firms closely interacting with a single large firm through a private industrial network.

One form of collaboration—and perhaps the most profound—is industry-wide **collaborative resource planning, forecasting, and replenishment (CPFR)**, which involves working with network members to forecast demand, develop production plans, and coordinate shipping, warehousing, and stocking activities to ensure retail and wholesale shelf space is replenished with just the right amount of goods. If this goal is achieved, hundreds of millions of dollars of excess inventory and capacity could be wrung out of an industry. This activity alone is likely to produce the largest benefits and justify the cost of developing private industrial networks.

A second area of collaboration is *demand chain visibility*. In the past, it was impossible to know where excess capacity or supplies existed in the supply and distribution chains. For instance, retailers might have significantly overstocked shelves, but suppliers and manufacturers—not knowing this—might be building excess capacity or supplies for even more production. These excess inventories would raise costs for the entire industry and create extraordinary pressures to discount merchandise, reducing profits for everyone.

A third area of collaboration is *marketing coordination and product design*. Manufacturers that use or produce highly engineered parts use private industrial networks to

collaborative resource planning, forecasting, and replenishment (CPFR)

involves working with network members to forecast demand, develop production plans, and coordinate shipping, warehousing, and stocking activities to ensure that retail and wholesale shelf space is replenished with just the right amount of goods coordinate both their internal design and marketing activities, as well as related activities of their supply and distribution chain partners. By involving their suppliers in product design and marketing initiatives, manufacturing firms can ensure that the parts produced actually fulfill the claims of marketers. On the reverse flow, feedback from customers can be used by marketers to speak directly to product designers at the firm and its suppliers. For the first time, "closed loop marketing"—customer feedback directly impacting design and production—described in Chapter 6—can become a reality.

Chrysler, for instance, developed a collaborative commerce application called the Supply Partner Information Network (SPIN) for its suppliers. SPIN is an extranet-based supply chain management and support system that permits supplier employees at locations around the world to access Chrysler's real-time procurement, inventory, and demand forecasting systems, as well as longer-term strategy applications. Chrysler's Part Quality Supply System operating within SPIN tracks all production parts from supplier to shipper, factory installation, and after-market replacement. Chrysler estimated it has increased productivity of its entire "extended enterprise" family of suppliers by 20% (IBM, undated).

IMPLEMENTATION BARRIERS

Although private industrial networks represent a large part of the future of B2B, there are many barriers to its complete implementation (Watson and Fenner, 2000). Participating firms are required to share sensitive data with their business partners, up and down the supply chain. What in the past was considered proprietary and secret must now be shared. In a digital environment, it can be difficult to control the limits of information sharing. Information a firm gives gladly to its largest customer may end up being shared with its closest competitor.

Integrating private industrial networks into existing ERP systems and EDI networks poses a significant investment of time and money. Most ERP systems were not designed initially to work as extranets, or even to be very Internet-friendly. Most ERP systems are based on models of business processes that are entirely internal to the firm.

Adopting private industrial networks also requires a change in mindset and behavior for employees. Essentially, employees must shift their loyalties from the firm to the wider trans-organizational enterprise and recognize that their fate is intertwined with the fate of their suppliers and distributors. Suppliers in turn are required to change the way they manage and allocate their resources because their own production is tightly coupled with the demands of their private industrial network partners. All participants in the supply and distribution chains, with the exception of the large network owner, lose some of their independence, and must initiate large behavioral change programs in order to participate (Laudon, 2000).

INDUSTRY-WIDE PRIVATE INDUSTRIAL NETWORKS

Single-firm networks can be so successful that they become adopted by the entire industry, and they can be used also to coordinate activities among firms in different industries altogether. For instance, the P&G system described previously was so successful that P&G sold the software to IBM, which then re-sold the system to the entire consumer products industry in the United States. P&G believed that only by changing the entire industry of supply, procurement, and distribution could it achieve its goals of efficiency and effectiveness. Other examples of industry-wide private industrial networks include 1 SYNC and Agentrics. 1SYNC was formed by the merger of UCCnet and Transora in August 2005. 1SYNC offers a collaborative community of trading partners that includes 4,000 leading manufacturers in the alcohol and beverage, automotive, entertainment, grocery, healthcare, and office supplies industry. 1SYNC offers a range of data synchronization services that enable the elimination of costly data errors, increased supply chain efficiencies, and the advancement of next-generation technologies such as its Electronic Product Code (1SYNC, 2009).

Agentrics was established in 2000 under the name GlobalNetXchange (GNX) by eight of the world's largest retailers: Sears, Carrefour, Coles Myer, KarstadtQuelle, Kroger, MetroAG, Pinault-Printemps-Redoute, and Sainsbury. In 2005, GNX merged with WorldWide Retail Exchange, a retail industry consortium, and changed its name to Agentrics. Agentrics focuses on auctions and other services and standards for the retail industry. The combined entity is backed by 45 of the world's largest retailers and suppliers, who represent more than $1 trillion in sales (Agentrics, 2009).

Figure 12.17 illustrates an industry-wide private industrial network.

In the future, barring intervention by antitrust enforcers, we can expect many private industrial networks to expand into much larger industry-wide networks seeking to coordinate all the thousands of key players in vertical industries.

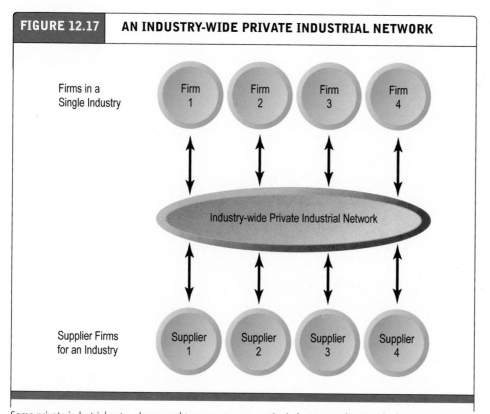

| FIGURE 12.17 | AN INDUSTRY-WIDE PRIVATE INDUSTRIAL NETWORK |

Some private industrial networks expand to encompass an entire industry, coordinating the business processes for suppliers, transporters, production firms, and ultimately distributors and retailers.

THE LONG-TERM DYNAMICS OF PRIVATE INDUSTRIAL NETWORKS

It is apparent that as large firms become more accustomed to working closely with both their supply chain partners and their distributors on the demand side, they will seek to push the boundaries of their networks to extend across the industry as a whole, to other industries, and to elaborate new roles for themselves and others. For instance, the computer manufacturer Hewlett-Packard discovered through its private industrial network that resin manufacturers were charging higher prices for resins they shipped to the molding manufacturers who make the plastic cases for HP computers. The molding manufacturers historically are very slow in paying their bills, and as a result, their resin suppliers raised their prices. HP moved in as a market maker and purchased resins from the suppliers at a market price, then re-sold them at the same price to the molders. HP has more clout to collect from the molders than resin manufacturers (Turek and Gilbert, 2001). In the next five years, we may see that individual large firms will be able to intervene in global supply relationships in order to overcome bottlenecks that otherwise would be hidden from manufacturers.

12.4 CASE STUDY

Elemica:
Cooperation, Collaboration, and Community

I t may seem unusual to refer to an entire industry as a "community," a word reserved typically for collections of people who more or less know one another. Trade associations are one example of an industrial community. Trade associations form in an effort to pursue the interests of all members in the community although usually they do not include customers in the community. Elemica is a B2B industry trading hub aiming to revolutionize the entire supply chain of the chemical industry worldwide by creating a "community of suppliers and customers" who have mutual interests. Elemica's purpose is not just to foster cooperation on a one-to-one inter-firm basis, or just to foster collaboration on multi-firm projects, but instead to lift all boats on an industry tide by making all firms more efficient. Elemica is one of the few survivors of the early B2B e-commerce years.

Elemica is a global e-commerce company founded by 22 leading corporations in the chemical industry (including oil and industrial gases) to provide Web-based order management and supply chain applications and services. Elemica enables one-stop shopping through a single hub so companies can buy and sell chemicals to one another through their ERP systems, or using a Web alternative. It also helps companies automate all of their business processes, creating efficiencies and economies of scale that lead to an improved bottom line.

How does Elemica achieve community among a diverse, global collection of firms where firms are often both customers and vendors to one another? The really unusual aspect of Elemica is that the "social glue" bringing members of the community together is the ability to link together the ERP systems of all participating companies, and use this "super platform" to permit the companies to communicate with one another electronically, and to conduct transactions, handle logistics, and keep the books. It's as if a single, huge industry with hundreds of large players both vendors and customers had a single computer system to facilitate transactions among all parties, or groups of parties. In this sense, Elemica is one of the most sophisticated technology platforms in the B2B space.

Elemica's ERP-to-ERP connectivity enables companies to link their internal IT systems through a neutral platform so that information is moved into each company's database while maintaining confidentiality and security. The chemical and oil industries were among the first users of ERP systems (referred to in the early years as "manufacturing resource planning systems"). These large-scale systems were developed by single firms in order to rationalize and control the manufacturing process. They achieved this objective by identifying the outputs, inputs, and processes involved in manufacturing and automating key elements including inventory control and planning, process control, warehousing and storage, and shipping/logistics. If a company needed to produce 10 tons of polyethylene plastic, its ERP system could tell it precisely how many tons of petrochemical inputs were required, when they should be delivered to manufacturing, the machinery and labor force required to manufacture the product, how long it would take, where it would be stored, and how it would be shipped. The systems can estimate the cost at any stage.

Elemica is the first e-commerce company in the chemical industry to successfully commercialize ERP-to-ERP connectivity. Elemica facilitates transactions of all types including order processing and billing, and logistics management. However, unlike some other companies in the field, Elemica does not buy, sell, or own products. Instead it acts as an intermediary, or hub, linking companies together to automate confidential transactions. Like eBay or a credit card company, Elemica's revenue comes from charging transaction fees on a per-transaction basis. Elemica's network of clients allows a company that signs up for its services to do business with all other linked buyers and sellers who already have contracts in place.

Elemica offers a variety of e-commerce services for suppliers and customers in the chemical industry, so they can automate their business process and their internal purchasing. Elemica provides a modular, hosted solution to simplify sales, procurement, and financial processes; integrate supply chain partners to diminish communication barriers; and reduce overhead and errors.

Elemica integrates information flow among global trading partners using a business process network (BPN). Each client uses a single connection to Elemica for all transactions. Once a company connects to Elemica, it can have access to thousands of other customers. Clients are charged for the service based on volume of usage. This is much more efficient than older EDI solutions to inter-company transactions.

Elemica offers four modules: procurement, logistics, customer replenishment (automated inventory replenishment and ordering), and order management. Using these modules, companies can automate ordering, invoicing, tracking of shipments, and day-to-day business operations. Companies can sign up for one module or multiple modules depending on their needs.

Here's an example of how Elemica works. Let's say you have an order from a customer for 10 tons of polyethylene, but that you are missing a key ingredient, vinyl acetate, although you have plenty of the basic ingredient ethylene on hand. You put a message into your ERP system, which then goes to Elemica's platform requesting availability from Elemica's members for 1 ton of vinyl acetate. At this point, the purchasing firm (your firm) is completely anonymous. Several of Elemica's members respond with quotations for 1 ton of vinyl acetate. The quote responders are anonymous at this point. Based on the prices quoted, your firm decides to purchase from one of the Elemica community members. When shipping is arranged, the identity of the partners is revealed. All of this takes place in a few seconds with little or no human intervention. Once an order is confirmed, Elemica's platform can be leveraged to plan and coordinate delivery, and automatically invoice and pay one another. For small or medium firms that may not have an ERP system, Elemica has a Web portal with online software that allows firms to participate in the community with suppliers and customers.

Unlike the automobile industry, or the airline industry where a few companies dominate, the $1.3 trillion chemical industry is made up of many companies of all sizes. The top 10 companies generate only 10% of the industry's annual revenue total, and the largest player, Dow Chemical, is responsible for 2%. In addition, unlike many other industries, chemical companies often buy the output of other chemical companies and use it as raw materials for products, so they are often each other's competitors and customers.

By the late 1990s, senior leaders at some of the larger chemical companies were aware of changes in technology that made the adaptation of information technology and the tools of e-commerce more appealing. The question was how to best use these advances to benefit their businesses. Leaders from Dow Chemical and DuPont began discussing this subject and determined that a cooperative alliance would be the most efficient way to move forward. They were met with initial skepticism by marketing and sales staff, worried that online procurement would negatively affect customer relationships. Further, senior corporate leadership wasn't sure that e-commerce would have any use in the chemical industry at all. And companies were cautious about the expense of investing in the infrastructure necessary for e-commerce.

However, there were compelling opportunities that were impossible to dismiss, including lowering costs, creating closer connections with customers, and differentiating companies on something other than price. At the same time, new start-ups like e-Chemicals and PlasticsNet were making traditional chemical companies nervous. What would happen if their efforts to use information technology to streamline an inefficient supply chain helped them capture market share? In other words, if the more traditional companies didn't move forward, they might end up losing the revenue race.

When Dow began looking at start-ups that were using e-commerce and talking to their customers, they found that customers were concerned about making an investment to establish online connections with multiple firms. Dow and DuPont decided that the best, and most economically efficient, option was to offer customers the option of a one-to-one link. This would remove the obstacle of multiple connections. And they decided to do this through a strong, third-party site so customers could have one-stop shopping. Concern about lack of control with a third party led the two companies to decide that the answer was to start their own third-party e-commerce company, partnering with other companies to create the critical mass to make it viable.

In 1999, the corporate boards of Dow and DuPont agreed that there were major advantages to online transaction processing and additional online connections among buyers and sellers. Clearly, the customer didn't want to make multiple connections due to cost and time involved so a "hub" concept was the most viable. And a neutral community was the best approach.

In order to encourage buy-in from potential partners, all corporate participants were offered equal ownership positions. Dow and DuPont also reviewed the concept with the relevant regulatory agencies and received up-front approval. Ultimately, 22 global chemical companies were involved in the launch of Elemica.

When Elemica opened its doors in 1999, there were 50 start-up B2B e-commerce companies in the chemical industry. Nearly all of these B2B companies were third-party-owned Net marketplaces suitable at best for short-term sourcing of some direct inputs. By 2009, only a handful of these Net marketplaces for the chemical industry exist. The largest of these competitors is ChemConnect, which was founded in 1995, and has 9,000 customers in 150 countries. While ChemConnect does offer services similar to Elemica, unlike Elemica, it also provides online auctions and private collaborative hubs to facilitate buying or selling of chemicals on a spot basis. And ChemConnect does not connect the ERP systems of participants. Elemica focuses on building longer-term business relationships by creating committed and contractual supply chains. The company acts as a hub only, and does not directly buy and sell chemical products.

Companies who sign on with Elemica have the support of Elemica's Professional Services & Implementation Team to work with staff to ensure a successful on-boarding process and acceptance of the business value with key trading partners. Many of Elemica's staff came from the chemical industry and are integral to the success of this training. Once companies witness that more orders are being delivered and received on time, and that their bills were going out faster and being paid faster, the up-front on-boarding and training became easier.

Today, Elemica, a privately held company, has 150 employees, 2,500 partners in its supply chain network, and $60 billion in annual transactions. Its home base is in Pennsylvania, and it has overseas offices in Amsterdam, Frankfurt, London, Seoul, Shanghai, Singapore, and Tokyo.

In July 2009, Elemica announced a merger with RubberNetwork LLC, a $10 billion global rubber and tire company. Mike McGuigan, president and CEO of Elemica, will run the merged company.

Elemica's business model has been successful primarily because it addresses the e-commerce needs of chemical companies of all sizes. It does this by offering multiple options for connecting to its hub system, multiple products that can be used alone or in combination, and by ensuring that only one connection is needed for all transactions. Customers can use Elemica, and take advantage of technology it offers, without purchasing an additional internal system.

With Elemica modules and technology, companies benefit from improved operational efficiency, reduced costs due to elimination of redundant systems and excess inventory, and a much higher percentage of safe and reliable deliveries. The flexibility of Elemica's modules and connections combines simplification, standardization, and efficiency. And clients have increased their profitability and improved cash flow through faster payment.

Several very large chemical companies use Elemica's platform. In Europe, Shell Oil started using Elemica after recognizing that it had ongoing problems with the coordination of paperwork processing and deliveries. Truck drivers would arrive at delivery sites and wait up to two hours while paperwork was filled out. These delays were costing Shell money. Once Shell began using Elemica, things improved. Today, paperwork is processed 24 hours a day, and truck waiting time has been cut from an average of two hours to an average of 15 minutes. Given this success, Shell continues to expand its relationship with Elemica.

Dow Chemical began to transition to full procurement automation with Elemica in 2007. Three hundred of their MRO suppliers are now linked to Elemica's platform. Errors are down 75%, and Dow has achieved economies of scale that have led to meaningful financial savings. Elemica helped Dow unify multiple, disparate business processes, reduced the cost of getting contracted items from suppliers, and increased efficiency in procurement, operations, IT, and accounts payable.

Rohm and Haas, a specialty materials company and subsidiary of Dow Chemical, decided to automate receipt and payment of its 650,000 annual invoices by moving all related processes online. The company was looking to reduce its error rate through the elimination of manual retyping of data, and to decrease the time between invoice and payment to and from suppliers. They chose Elemica's electronic invoicing solution. The company's management knew that transitioning their suppliers to electronic invoicing would take a significant amount of effort on their part. So Rohm and Haas held a series of seminars for up to 200 suppliers at a time to teach them the new process. The seminars occurred in the United States and Europe. Suppliers were told that they would have to use the tools they were shown if they wanted to continue doing business with Rohm and Haas.

At the end of this conversion process, the vast majority of invoices were processed electronically. In addition to a reduction in errors, the implementation of Elemica's electronic invoicing helped identify internal inconsistencies, and helped standardized units of measure and presentation of taxes and special charges. Rohm and Haas invoices are typically paid in 13 days, half of the 28 days typical for paper invoices.

Air Products & Chemicals, Inc. is a global provider of gases and chemicals with 22,000 employees worldwide, and $10 billion in revenue. A major customer asked them for online ordering, but the initial method proposed would have required considerable additional work for both parties. Since both companies were connected to Elemica, there was a better option—the Elemica Supply Chain Hosted Solution

SOURCES: "Elemica and Rubber-Network Merge," SDCExec.com, August 25, 2009; "Case Study: Elemica," http://www.ebusiness-watch.org/studies, August 25, 2009; "Once Elemica Tackled the Hard Part, the Rest Was Easy," SupplyChainBrain.com August 05, 2009; "Elemica Merger with Rubber Network," Philly.com, August 3, 2009; "Elemica Automates B2B Transactions Between Trading Partners—Speeding Up Orders by 78%," Softwareag.com, January 2009; "Top Chemical Company Selects Elemica's Business Process Network to Automate Global Procurement," Redorbit.com, December 18, 2008; "Elemica: Standards and Business," by Mike McGuigan, CEO, November 6, 2007, www.pidx.org/events/upload/Elemica.ppt; "Elemica: Simplification + Efficiency = Increased Profitability," by Fran Keeth, Elemica Business Leadership Forum, Philadelphia, Pennsylvania, September 13, 2005, www-static.shell.com; "The Journey of Elemica: An e-Commerce Consortium," by Andrew Liveris, Business Group President, Performance Chemicals. Strategic Alliances Conference, April 9, 2002, www.dow.com/ebusiness/news/ecspeech.htm.

(SCHS). With the assistance of Elemica consultants to sort out technical issues with interfaces and existing systems, the project went forward.

Case Study Questions

1. Why is Elemica described as an example of an industry consortia Net marketplace? How does it differ from other types of Net marketplaces like ChemConnect?

2. If you were a small chemical company, what concerns would you have about joining Elemica?

3. Elemica claims to provide a community for participants where they can transact, coordinate, and cooperate to produce products for less. Yet these firms also compete with one another when they sell chemicals to end-user firms in the automobile, airline, and manufacturing industries. How is this possible?

4. Review the concept of "an industry-wide private industrial network," and describe how Elemica illustrates many of the features of such a network.

12.5 REVIEW

KEY CONCEPTS

■ **Define B2B commerce and understand its scope and history.**

Before the Internet, business-to-business transactions were referred to simply as *trade* or the *procurement process*. Today, we use the term *B2B commerce* to describe all types of computer-assisted inter-firm trade, and the term *Internet-based B2B commerce* or *B2B e-commerce* to describe specifically that portion of B2B commerce that uses the Internet to assist firms in buying and selling a variety of goods to each other. The process of conducting trade among businesses consumes many business resources, including the time spent by employees processing orders, making and approving purchasing decisions, searching for products, and arranging for their purchase, shipment, receipt, and payment. Across the economy, this amounts to trillions of dollars spent annually on procurement processes. If a significant portion of this inter-firm trade could be automated and parts of the procurement process assisted by the Internet, millions or even trillions of dollars could be freed up for other uses, resulting in increased productivity and increased national economic wealth.

In order to understand the history of B2B commerce, you must understand several key stages including:

- *Automated order entry systems*, developed in the 1970s, used the telephone to send digital orders to companies. Telephone modems were placed in the offices of the customers for a particular business. This enabled procurement managers to directly access the firm's inventory database to automatically reorder products.

- *EDI* or *electronic data interchange*, developed in the late 1970s, is a communications standard for sharing various procurement documents including invoices, purchase orders, shipping bills, product stocking numbers (SKUs), and settlement information for an industry. It was developed to reduce the costs, delays, and errors inherent in the manual exchange of documents.
- *Electronic storefronts* emerged in the 1990s along with the commercialization of the Internet. They are online catalogs containing the products that are made available to the general public by a single vendor.
- *Net marketplaces* emerged in the late 1990s as a natural extension and scaling-up of the electronic storefront. The essential characteristic of all Net marketplaces is that they bring hundreds of suppliers, each with its own electronic catalog, together with potentially thousands of purchasing firms to form a single Internet-based marketplace.
- *Private industrial networks* also emerged in the late 1990s with the commercialization of the Internet as natural extensions of EDI systems and the existing close relationships that developed between large industrial firms and their suppliers.

Before you can understand each of the different types of Net marketplaces, you must be familiar with several other key concepts:

- *Seller-side solutions* are owned by the suppliers of goods and are seller-biased markets that only display goods from a single seller. Customers benefit because these systems reduce the costs of inventory replenishment and are paid for mainly by the suppliers. Automated order entry systems are seller-side solutions.
- *Buyer-side solutions* are owned by the buyers of goods and are buyer-biased markets because they reduce procurement costs for the buyer. Sellers also benefit because the cost of serving a company's customers is reduced. EDI systems are buyer-side solutions.
- *Vertical markets* provide expertise and products targeted to a specific industry. EDI systems usually serve vertical markets.
- *Horizontal markets* serve a myriad of different industries. Electronic storefronts are an example of a horizontal market in that they tend to carry a wide variety of products that are useful to any number of different industries.

■ Understand the procurement process, the supply chain, and collaborative commerce.

- The *procurement process* refers to the way business firms purchase the goods they need in order to produce the goods they will ultimately sell to consumers. Firms purchase goods from a set of suppliers who in turn purchase their inputs from a set of suppliers. These firms are linked in a series of connected transactions.
- The *supply chain* is the series of transactions that links sets of firms that do business with each other. It includes not only the firms themselves but also the relationships between them and the processes that connect them.

There are seven steps in the procurement process:
- Searching for suppliers for specific products
- Qualifying the sellers and the products they sell
- Negotiating prices, credit terms, escrow requirements, and quality requirements

- Scheduling delivery
- Issuing purchase orders
- Sending invoices
- Shipping the product

Each step is composed of separate sub-steps that must be recorded in the information systems of the buyer, seller, and shipper. There are two different types of procurements and two different methods of purchasing goods:

- *Purchases of direct goods*—goods that are directly involved in the production process.
- *Purchases of indirect goods*—goods needed to carry out the production process but that are not directly involved in creating the end product.
- *Contract purchases*—long-term agreements to buy a specified amount of a product. There are pre-specified quality requirements and pre-specified terms.
- *Spot purchases*—for acquisition of goods that meet the immediate needs of a firm. Indirect purchases are most often made on a spot-purchase basis in a large marketplace that includes many suppliers.

The term *multi-tier supply chain* is used to describe the complex series of transactions that exists between a single firm with multiple primary suppliers, the secondary suppliers who do business with those primary suppliers, and the tertiary suppliers who do business with the secondary suppliers.

Trends in supply chain management (the activities that firms and industries use to coordinate the key players in their procurement process) include:

- *Supply chain simplification,* which refers to the reduction of the size of a firm's supply chain. Firms today generally prefer to work closely with a strategic group of suppliers in order to reduce both product costs and administrative costs. Long-term contract purchases containing pre-specified product quality requirements and pre-specified timing goals have been shown to improve end-product quality and ensure uninterrupted production.
- *Supply chain management systems,* which coordinate and link the activities of suppliers, shippers, and order entry systems to automate the order entry process from start to finish, including the purchase, production, and moving of a product from a supplier to a purchasing firm.
- *Collaborative commerce,* which is a direct extension of supply chain management systems as well as supply chain simplification. It is the use of digital technologies to permit the supplier and the purchaser to share sensitive company information in order to collaboratively design, develop, build, and manage products throughout their life cycles.

■   Identify the main types of B2B commerce: Net marketplaces and private industrial networks.

There are two generic types of B2B commerce and many different subtypes within those two main categories of Internet commerce:

- *Net marketplaces,* which are also referred to as exchanges or hubs, assemble hundreds to thousands of sellers and buyers in a single digital marketplace on the Internet. They can be owned by either the buyer or the seller, or they can operate as independent intermediaries between the buyer and seller.
- *Private industrial networks* bring together a small number of strategic business partners who collaborate with one another to develop highly efficient supply

chains and to satisfy customer demand for product. They are by far the largest form of B2B commerce.

- **Understand the four types of Net marketplaces.**

There are four main types of "pure" Net marketplaces:
- *E-distributors* are independently owned intermediaries that offer industrial customers a single source from which to make spot purchases of indirect or MRO goods. E-distributors operate in a horizontal market that serves many different industries with products from many different suppliers.
- *E-procurement Net marketplaces* are independently owned intermediaries connecting hundreds of online suppliers offering millions of MRO goods to business firms who pay a fee to join the market. E-procurement Net marketplaces operate in a horizontal market in which long-term contractual purchasing agreements are used to buy indirect goods.
- *Exchanges* are independently owned online marketplaces that connect hundreds to thousands of suppliers and buyers in a dynamic real-time environment. They are typically vertical markets in which spot purchases can be made for direct inputs (both goods and services). Exchanges make money by charging a commission on each transaction.
- *Industry consortia* are industry-owned vertical markets where long-term contractual purchases of direct inputs can be made from a limited set of invited participants. Consortia serve to reduce supply chain inefficiencies by unifying the supply chain for an industry through a common network and computing platform.

- **Identify the major trends in the development of Net marketplaces.**

- In the early days of e-commerce, independent exchanges were the prototype Internet-based marketplace and over 1,000 of them were created; however, most of them did not succeed. The main reason independent exchanges failed is that they did not attract enough players to achieve liquidity (measured by the number of buyers and sellers in the market, the transaction volume, and the size of the transactions).
- Industry consortia sprang up partly in reaction to the earlier development of independently owned exchanges that were viewed by large industries as interlopers who would not directly serve their needs. Industry consortia are profitable because they charge the large buyer firms transaction and subscription fees, but the rationalization of the procurement process, the competition among the vendors, and the closer relationship with the vendors are benefits that more than offset the costs of membership to the firms. However, the long-term profitability of consortia has yet to be proven.
- The failure of the early exchanges is one reason Net marketplaces are changing so rapidly. Participants have come to realize that the real value of B2B commerce will only be realized when it succeeds in changing the entire procurement system, the supply chain, and the process of collaboration among firms.

- **Identify the role of private industrial networks in transforming the supply chain.**

- Private industrial networks, which presently dominate B2B commerce, are Web-enabled networks for coordinating trans-organizational business processes (collaborative commerce). These networks range in scope from a single firm to an entire industry.

- Although the central purpose of a private industrial network is to provide industry-wide global solutions to achieve the highest levels of efficiency, they generally start with a single sponsoring company that "owns" the network. This differentiates private industrial networks from industry consortia that are usually owned collectively by major firms through equity participation.
- Private industrial networks are transforming the supply chain by focusing on continuous business process coordination between companies. This coordination includes much more than just transaction support and supply chain management. Product design, demand forecasting, asset management, and sales and marketing plans can all be coordinated among network members.

■ Understand the role of private industrial networks in supporting collaborative commerce.

Collaboration among businesses can take many forms and involve a wide range of activities. Some of the forms of collaboration used by private industrial networks include the following:

- *CPFR* or *industry-wide collaborative resource planning, forecasting, and replenishment* involves working with network members to forecast demand, develop production plans, and coordinate shipping, warehousing, and stocking activities. The goal is to ensure that retail and wholesale shelf space is precisely maintained.
- *Supply-chain and distribution chain visibility* refers to the fact that, in the past, it was impossible to know where excess capacity existed in a supply or distribution chain. Eliminating excess inventories by halting the production of overstocked goods can raise the profit margins for all network members because products will no longer need to be discounted in order to move them off the shelves.
- *Marketing and product design collaboration* can be used to involve a firm's suppliers in product design and marketing activities as well as in the related activities of their supply and distribution chain partners. This can ensure that the parts used to build a product live up to the claims of the marketers. Collaborative commerce applications used in a private industrial network can also make possible closed loop marketing in which customer feedback will directly impact product design.

QUESTIONS

1. Explain the differences among total inter-firm trade, B2B commerce, and B2B e-commerce.
2. What are the key attributes of an electronic storefront? What early technology are they descended from?
3. List at least five potential benefits of B2B e-commerce.
4. Name and define the two distinct types of procurements firms make. Explain the difference between the two.
5. Name and define the two methods of purchasing goods.
6. Define the term supply chain and explain what SCM systems attempt to do. What does supply chain simplification entail?
7. Explain the difference between a horizontal market and a vertical market.

8. How do the value chain management services provided by e-procurement companies benefit buyers? What services do they provide to suppliers?
9. What are the three dimensions that characterize an e-procurement market based on its business functionality? Name two other market characteristics of an e-procurement Net marketplace.
10. Identify and briefly explain the anti-competitive possibilities inherent in Net marketplaces.
11. List three of the objectives of a private industrial network.
12. What is the main reason why many of the independent exchanges developed in the early days of e-commerce failed?
13. Explain the difference between an industry consortium and a private industrial network.
14. What is CPFR, and what benefits could it achieve for the members of a private industrial network?
15. What are the barriers to the complete implementation of private industrial networks?

PROJECTS

1. Choose an industry and a B2B vertical market maker that interests you. Investigate the site and prepare a report that describes the size of the industry served, the type of Net marketplace provided, the benefits promised by the site for both suppliers and purchasers, and the history of the company. You might also investigate the bias (buyer versus seller), ownership (suppliers, buyers, independents), pricing mechanism(s), scope and focus, and access (public versus private) of the Net marketplace.

2. Examine the Web site of one of the e-distributors listed in Figure 12.9, and compare and contrast it to one of the Web sites listed for e-procurement Net marketplaces. If you were a business manager of a medium-sized firm, how would you decide where to purchase your indirect inputs—from an e-distributor or an e-procurement Net marketplace? Write a short report detailing your analysis.

3. Assume you are a procurement officer for an office furniture manufacturer of steel office equipment. You have a single factory located in the Midwest with 2,000 employees. You sell about 40% of your office furniture to retail-oriented catalog outlets such as Quill in response to specific customer orders, and the remainder of your output is sold to resellers under long-term contracts. You have a choice of purchasing raw steel inputs—mostly cold-rolled sheet steel—from an exchange and/or from an industry consortium. Which alternative would you choose and why? Prepare a presentation for management supporting your position.

4. Find a Net marketplace that has failed (possible candidates include Aerospan.com, Chemdex.com, Petrocosm.com, E-steel.com, or another of your choosing). Investigate the reasons behind its failure. Prepare a short report on your findings and your analysis of the lessons that can be learned from its demise.

WEB SITE RESOURCES www.azimuth-interactive.com/ecommerce6e

- Additional projects, exercises, and tutorials
- Careers: Explore career opportunities in e-commerce
- Raising capital and business plans

References

CHAPTER 1

AccuStream iMedia Research, "Subscription and Download Media Stores 2003-2010." (January 27, 2009).

Aguiar, Mark and Erik Hurst. "Life-Cycle Prices and Production." *American Economic Review* 97:5, 1533-1559. (January 1, 2008).

Alessandria, George. "Consumer Search, Price Dispersion, and International Relative Price Fluctuations." *International Economic Review* 50:3, 803-829 (September 1, 2009).

Bailey, Joseph P. *Intermediation and Electronic Markets: Aggregation and Pricing in Internet Commerce.* Ph. D., Technology, Management and Policy, Massachusetts Institute of Technology (1998a).

Bakos, Yannis. "Reducing Buyer Search Costs: Implications for Electronic Marketplaces." *Management Science* (December 1997).

Banerjee, Suman and Chakravarty, Amiya. "Price Setting and Price Discovery Strategies with a Mix of Frequent and Infrequent Internet Users." (April 15, 2005). SSRN: http://ssrn.com/abstract=650706.

Baye, Michael R. "Price Dispersion in the Lab and on the Internet: Theory and Evidence." *Rand Journal of Economics* (2004).

Baye, Michael R., John Morgan, and Patrick Scholten. "Temporal Price Dispersion: Evidence from an Online Consumer Electronics Market." *Journal of Interactive Marketing* (January 2004).

Brynjolfsson, Erik, and Michael Smith. "Frictionless Commerce? A Comparison of Internet and Conventional Retailers." *Management Science* (April 2000).

Compete.com. "Site Profile for Digg.com." (September 29, 2009).

comScore. "Google Sites Surpasses 10 Billion Video Views in August." (September 28, 2009a).

comScore. "comScore Media Metrix Ranks Top 50 U.S. Web Properties for August 2009." (September 21, 2009b)

comScore. "Global Internet Audience Surpasses 1 Billion Visitors, According to comScore." (January 23, 2009c).

eBay, Inc. Report on Form 10-K for the fiscal year ending December 31, 2008 filed with the Securities and Exchange Commission (February 20, 2009).

eMarketer, Inc. (Jeffrey Grau). "Retail E-commerce Forecast: Cautious Optimism." (June 2009a).

eMarketer, Inc. "QuickStats: "Internet Users in the United States, 2007-2013 (in Millions)." (September 2009b).

eMarketer, Inc. (Lisa E. Phillips). "US Internet Users." (February 2009c),

eMarketer, Inc. "QuickStats: "Broadband: Household Penetration (% of total households) in the United States, 2007-2013." (September 2009d)

eMarketer, Inc. "Quick Stats, "Mobile Internet Users in the United States, 2007-2013 (in Millions) (September 2009e)

eMarketer, Inc. "QuickStats, "Mobile Phone Subscribers in the United States, 2007-2013 (in Millions)." (September 2009f).

eMarketer, Inc. "Online Sales of the Top 500 US Retail Websites, by Company Type, 2008 (billions and % share)." (May 1, 2009g).

eMarketer, Inc. "Top 15 Online Retailers, Ranked by Online Sales, 2008 (billions)." (May 1, 2009h)

eMarketer, Inc. (Jeffrey Grau). "U.S. Retail E-commerce: Slower But Still Steady Growth." (May 2008a).

eMarketer, Inc. "What Do Shoppers Research on the Web." (October 13, 2008b).

Evans, Philip, and Thomas S. Wurster. *Blown to Bits: How the New Economics of Information Transforms Strategy.* Cambridge, MA: Harvard Business School Press (2000).

Evans, Philip, and Thomas S. Wurster. "Getting Real About Virtual Commerce." *Harvard Business Review* (November-December 1999).

Evans, Philip, and Thomas S. Wurster. "Strategy and the New Economics of Information." *Harvard Business Review* (September-October 1997).

Fink, Eugene, Josh Johnson, and Jerry Hu. "Exchange Market for Complex Goods: Theory and Experiments." *Communications of the ACM.* (April, 2004).

Google. "More Google Products." Google.com (September 24, 2009)._

Internet Retailer. "Top 500 Guide 2009 Edition." (2009).

Internet Systems Consortium, Inc. "ISC Internet Domain Survey." (January 2009).

Internet World Stats. "Internet Usage Statistics : The Internet Big Picture: -World Internet Users and Population Stats (as of June 30, 2009)."

(September 2009)

Ipoque. "Internet Study 2008/2009 Finds Web and Streaming Outgrows P2P Traffic." Ipogue.com (February 2009).

Kalakota, Ravi, and Marcia Robinson. *e-Business 2.0: Roadmap for Success, 2nd edition.* Reading, MA: Addison Wesley (2003).

Kambil, Ajit. "Doing Business in the Wired World." *IEEE Computer* (May 1997).

Linden Lab. "1 Billion Hours, 1 Billion Dollars Served: Second Life Celebrates Major Milestones for Virtual Worlds." (September 22, 2009).

Mesenbourg, Thomas L. "Measuring Electronic Business: Definitions, Underlying Concepts, and Measurement Plans." U. S. Department of Commerce Bureau of the Census (August 2001).

Nash-equilibrium.com. "Relative Dispersion." (September 24, 2009).

Nielsen Online: "YouTube Maintains Top Ranking by Total Streams and Hulu Grows 490 Percent Year-Over-Year, According to Nielsen Online." (May 14, 2009).

Peterson, Andrew. "WordPress Usage: 202 Million Worldwide 62.8 Million US." Andrewapeterson.com (September 22, 2009).

Pew Internet & American Life Project. "Daily Internet Activities." (July 2009).

Photobucket.com "Photobucket introduces new visual search powered by Microsoft Silverlight." (June 18, 2009).

PricewaterhouseCoopers/National Venture Capital Association. MoneyTree Report, Data: Thomson Financial (2009).

Rayport, Jeffrey F., and Bernard J. Jaworski. *Introduction to E-commerce, 2nd edition.* New York: McGraw-Hill (2003).

Shapiro, Carl, and Hal R. Varian. *Information Rules. A Strategic Guide to the Network Economy.* Cambridge, MA: Harvard Business School Press (1999).

Sinha, Indajit. "Cost Transparency: The Net's Threat to Prices and Brands." *Harvard Business Review* (March-April 2000).

Slatalla, Michelle. "Online Shopper: Price Comparison Sites Do the Legwork." *New York Times* (February 3, 2005).

Smith, Michael; Joseph Bailey; and Erik Brynjolfsson. "Understanding Digital Markets: Review and Assessment." In Erik Brynjolfsson and Brian Kahin (eds.) *Understanding the Digital Economy.* Cambridge MA: MIT Press (2000).

Tversky, A., and D. Kahneman. "The Framing of Decisions and the Psychology of Choice." *Science*

(January 1981).

U.S. Census Bureau. "E-Stats Report 2007 E-commerce Multi-Sector Report." (May 28, 2009a).

U.S. Census Bureau. *Statistical Abstract of the United States: 2009* (2009b).

Varian, Hal R. "5 Habits of Highly Effective Revolution." *Forbes ASAP* (February 21, 2000a).

Varian, Hal R. "When Commerce Moves On, Competition Can Work in Strange Ways." *New York Times* (August 24, 2000b).

Wikipedia.org. "Wikipedia: About." (September 24, 2009).

CHAPTER 2

Agentrics LLC. "Fact Sheet." Agentrics.com (January 2009).

Arthur, W. Brian. "Increasing Returns and the New World of Business." *Harvard Business Review* (July-August 1996).

Bakos, Yannis. "The Emerging Role of Electronic Marketplaces on the Internet." *Communications of the ACM* (August 1998).

Bakos, Yannis; Henry Lucas; Wonseok Oh; Sivakuman Viswanathan; Gary Simon; and Bruce Weber. "The Impact of Electronic Commerce in the Retail Brokerage Industry: Trading Costs of Internet Versus Full Service Firms." Center for Research on Information Systems, Stern School of Business, New York University (July 2000).

Barney, J. B. "Firm Resources and Sustained Competitive Advantage." *Journal of Management* Vol. 17, No. 1 (1991).

Bellman, Steven; Gerland L. Lohse; and Eric J. Johnson. "Predictors of Online Buying Behavior." *Communications of the ACM* (December 1999).

Day, George S.; Adam J. Fein; and Gregg Ruppersberger. "Shakeouts in Digital Markets." *California Management Review* Vol. 45, No. 3 (Winter 2003).

eBay, Inc. eBay Inc. Reports Second Quarter 2009 Results." (July 22, 2009).

eMarketer, Inc. "US Subscription and Download Media Store Revenues, 2007-2009 (billions and % change)." (January 27, 2009a).

eMarketer, Inc. "QuickStats, "Mobile Phone Subscribers in Worldwide, 2007-2013 (in Billions)."(September 24, 2009b).

eMarketer, Inc. (Noah Elkin). "Automotive Industry Online." (May 1, 2004).

Fisher, William W. III. "The Growth of Intellectual Property: A History of the Ownership of Ideas in the United States." Cyber.law.harvard.edu/people/tfisher/iphistory.pdf (1999).

Gebauer, Judith, and Michael Zagler. "Assessing the Status Quo and Future of B2B E-Commerce. *International Federation of Purchasing and Materials Management* (December 2000).

Gerace, Thomas. "Encyclopedia Britannica." Harvard Business School Case Study 396-051 (1999).

Ghosh, Shikhar. "Making Business Sense of the Internet." Harvard Business Review (March-April 1998).

Gulati, Ranjay, and Jason Garino. "Getting the Right Mix of Bricks and Clicks." *Harvard Business Review* (May-June 2000).

JiWire.com. "Wi-Fi Finder." (September 24, 2009).

Kambil, Ajit. "Doing Business in the Wired World." *IEEE Computer* (May 1997).

Kambil, Ajit; Ari Ginsberg; and Michael Bloch. "Reinventing Value Propositions." Working Paper, NYU Center for Research on Information Systems (1998).

Kanter, Elizabeth Ross. "The Ten Deadly Mistakes of Wanna-Dots." *Harvard Business Review* (January 2001).

Kaplan, Steven, and Mohanbir Sawhney. "E-Hubs: The New B2B Marketplaces." *Harvard Business Review* (May-June 2000).

Kim, W. Chan, and Renee Mauborgne. "Knowing a Winning Business Idea When You See One." *Harvard Business Review* (September-October 2000).

Madnick, Stuart and Michael Siegel. "Seizing the Opportunity: Exploiting Web Aggregation." MIT Sloan School of Management, Working Paper 144 (December 2001).

Magretta, Joan. "Why Business Models Matter." *Harvard Business Review* (May 2002).

Nielsen. "Bing Search Increases 22 Percent Month-Over-Month in August, According to Nielsen." (September 14, 2009).

Online Publishers Association. Paid Online Content U.S. Market Spending Report Fiscal Year 2005 (March 14, 2006).

Porter, Michael E. "Strategy and the Internet." *Harvard Business Review* (March 2001).

Porter, Michael E. *Competitive Advantage: Creating and Sustaining Superior Performance.* New York: Free Press (1985).

Rigdon, Joan I. "The Second-Mover Advantage." *Red Herring* (September 1, 2000).

Teece, David J. "Profiting from Technological Innovation: Implications for Integration, Collaboration, Licensing and Public Policy." *Research Policy* 15 (1986).

Timmers, Paul. "Business Models for Electronic Markets" *Electronic Markets* Vol. 8, No. 2 (1998).

Ulfelder, Steve. "B2B Exchange Survivors." *Computerworld* (February 2, 2004).

U.S. Census Bureau Statistical Abstract of the United States: 2009 (2009a).

U.S. Census Bureau. "E-Stats Report 2007 E-commerce Multi-Sector Report." (May 28, 2009b).

CHAPTER 3

Apple, Inc. "Movie Fans Can Buy & Rent in High Definition on the iTunes Store." (March 19, 2009).

Berners-Lee, Tim; Robert Cailliau; Ari Luotonen; Henrik Frystyk Nielsen; and Arthur Secret. "The World Wide Web." *Communications of the ACM* (August 1994).

Bluetooth SIG. "Bluetooth: The Official Bluetooth Website." Bluetooth.com (2005).

Boingo Wireless. "Home Page." (September 24, 2009).

Brandt, Richard. "Net Assets: How Stanford's Computer Science Department Changed the Way We Get Information." *Stanford Magazine* (November/December 2004).

Bush, Vannevar. "As We May Think." *Atlantic Monthly* (July 1945).

Cerf, V., and R. Kahn, "A Protocol for Packet Network Intercommunication." *IEEE Transactions on Communications*, Vol. COM-22, No. 5, pp 637-648 (May 1974).

Cisco Systems, Inc. "IP Multicast Technical Overview." (August 2007).

Computer Science and Telecommunications Board. National Research Council (NRC). Networking Health: Prescriptions for the Internet." Washington DC: National Academy Press (2000).

ComScore. "comScore Releases August 2009 U.S. Search Engine Rankings." (September 22, 2009a).

comScore. "ComScore Media Metrix Ranks Top 50 Web Properties for August 2009." (September 21, 2009b).

comScore. "Google Sites Surpasses 10 Billion Video Views in August." (September 28, 2009c).

eMarketer, Inc. (Lisa E. Phillips). "US Internet Users." (February 2009a).

eMarketer, Inc. "Quick Stats, Mobile Internet Users in the United States, 2007-2013 (in Millions)." (September 24, 2009b).

eMarketer, Inc. "Quick Stats, "Mobile Internet Users in Worldwide, 2007- 2013 (in Millions)." (September 24, 2009c).

eMarketer, Inc. "Smartphones Boost Lagging Mobile Market." (August 10, 2009d).

eMarketer, Inc. "US Unique Mobile IM Users, by

Application, March 2009 (millions)." (July 1, 2009e).

eMarketer, Inc.(David Hallerman). "Search Marketing Trends: Back to Basics." (February 2009f).

eMarketer, Inc. "Changes in Shopping Behavior due to Economic Downturn According to US Internet Users, August 2008 (% of Respondents) (March 1, 2009g).

eMarketer, Inc. (Paul Verna). "The Blogosphere: A-Twitter with Activity." (April 2009h).

eMarketer, Inc. (Paul Verna). "Podcasting: Into the Mainstream." (March 2009i)

eMarketer, Inc. (Debra A. Williamson). "Social Network Ad Spending to Fall." (May 13, 2009j)

eMarketer, Inc. (Ben Macklin). "Broadband Services: VOIP and IPTV Trends," (April 2008a).

Federal Networking Council. "FNC Resolution: Definition of 'Internet.'" (October 24, 1995).

Gartner, Inc. "Forecast, PC Installed Base Worldwide 2004-2012: April 2009 Update" (March 31, 2009).

Geni.net. "Global Environment for Network Innovations." (September 2008).

Google, Inc. "Paving the Road to Apps Adoption in Large Enterprises." (July 7, 2009).

Gross, Grant. "NSF Seeks Ambitious Next-Generation Internet Project." *Computerworld* (August 29, 2005).

Hansell, Saul. "Plugging in $40 Computers." *New York Times* (March 5, 2009).

Internet Corporation for Assigned Names and Numbers (ICANN). "Top-Level Domains (gTLDs)." Icann.org (2009).

Internet Society. "Internet Standards." Internet Society. (September 2008).

Internet Society. "RFC 2616: Hypertext Transfer Protocol-HTTP/1.1." (June 1999).

Internet Society. "RFC 2821: Simple Mail Transfer Protocol" (April 2001).

Internet Society. "RFC 1939: Post Office Protocol-Version 3." (May 1996).

Internet Society. "RFC 3501: Internet Message Access Protocol-Version 4rev1" (March 2003).

Internet Society. "RFC 0959: File Transfer Protocol." (October, 1985).

Internet Society. "RFC 854: Telnet Protocol Specification." (May 1983).

Internet World Stats. "Internet Usage Statistics : The Internet Big Picture-

World Internet Users and Population Stats." As of June 30, 2009 (September 2009)

Kleinrock, Leonard. *1964 Communication Nets: Stochastic Message Flow and Delay.* New York: McGraw-Hill (1964).

Leiner, Barry M.; Vinton G. Cerf; David D. Clark; Robert E. Kahn; Leonard Kleinrock; Daniel C. Lynch; Jon Postel; Larry G. Roberts; and Stephen Wolff. "All About the Internet: A Brief History of the Internet." *Internet Society* (ISOC) (August 2000).

Microsoft "Windows Live Messenger Turns 10." (July 22, 2009).

National Research Council. "The Internet's Coming of Age." Washington DC: National Academy Press (2000).

Net Applications. "Browser Market Share Report." (September 2008).

Netcraft. "September 2009 Web Server Survey." (September 2009).

Nielsen Company. "Bing Search Increases 22 Percent Month-Over-Month in August, According to Nielsen." (September 14, 2009).

NLR.net. "National Lambda Rail." NLR.net. (September 2008).

Point Topic. "Global Broadband Statistics" (June 22, 2009).

Radicatti Group. "The Radicati Group Releases "Email Statistics Report, 2009-2013."" (May 6, 2009).

Robinson, JJ. "Cloud Computing Spending Leaps 21%." *Information Age* (April 14, 2009).

Sha, Agam. "PC Shipments to Recover in 2010, IDC Says." IDC News Service (March 5, 2009).

Sperling, Ed. "Amazon's Golden Cloud." Forbes.com (June 29, 2009).

Stross, Randall. "The PC Doesn't Have to Be an Anchor." *New York Times* (April 18, 2009).

Technorati, Inc. "State of the Blogoshpere/2009" (2009).

U.S. Department of Commerce. "Letter to ICANN Chairman." http://www.ntia.doc.gov/comments/2008/ICANN_080730.html (July 30, 2008)

Visualware, Inc., "VisualRoute Traceroute Server." Visualroute.visualware.com (September 2007).

VoIP.Biz-News.com. "Skype Taking Larger Share of International Voice Traffic." (March 25, 2009).

Wayport, Inc. "AT&T to Acquire Wayport." (November 6, 2008).

Yahoo. "Why Yahoo: Yahoo! Properties/Messenger." http://advertising.yahoo.com/advertisers/whyyahoo#Messenger (September 2009).

Zakon, Robert H. "Hobbes' Internet Timeline v8.1." Zakon.org (2005).

Ziff-Davis Publishing. "Ted Nelson: Hypertext Pioneer." Techtv.com (1998).

ZigBee Alliance. "ZigBee Smart Energy: The Standard for Energy Efficiency." ZigBee.org.

(June 23, 2008)

Zillman, Marcus. "Deep Web Research." LLRX.com (2005).

CHAPTER 4

Banker, Rajiv D., and Chris F. Kemerer. "Scale Economies in New Software Development." *IEEE Transactions on Software Engineering*, Vol. 15, No. 10 (1989).

Bluefly, Inc. Report Form 10-K for the Year Ended December 30, 2008 filed with the Securities & Exchange Commission (March 5, 2009).

CMSWatch.com (2009).

Doyle, Barry and Cristina Videria Lopes. "Survey of Technologies for Web Application Development." ACM, Vol.2., No. 3. (June 2005).

eMarketer, Inc. (Lisa E. Phillips). "US Internet Users" (February 2009).

Google. "Google Analytics Product Tour." (2009).

Hostway. "Hostway Pet Peeves Survey: Top Line Results." Hostway.com, (2007).

IBM (High Volume Web Sites Team). "Best Practices for High-Volume Web Sites." *IBM Redbooks* (December 2002).

IBM (Nigel Trickett, Tatsuhiko Nakagawa, Ravi Mani, Diana Gfroerer). "Understanding IBM eServer pSeries Performance and Sizing." IBM Redbooks (January 24, 2003).

Laudon, Kenneth C. and Jane P. Laudon. *Management Information Systems: Managing the Digital Firm*. 11th edition. Upper Saddle River, NJ: Prentice Hall (2009).

Lientz, Bennet P., and E. Burton Swanson. *Software Maintenance Management*. Reading MA: Addison-Wesley (1980).

WebTrends, Inc. "WebTrends Analytics 9." (2009).

CHAPTER 5

Associated Press. "FBI Ditches Carnivore Surveillance System." Foxnews.com (January 18, 2005).

Boncella, Robert J. "Web Security for E-Commerce." *Communications of the Association for Information Systems*, Vol. 4. (November 2000).

Borden, Anne. "Credit Card Theft: An 'Inside Job'." Lawyersandsettlements.com (May 14, 2007).

Butterfield, Ethan. "Agencies Making Little Progress Against Cybervandalism." *Government Computer News* (September 1, 2005).

Cardline. "Online Payments to Rise by 70% by 2013, Research Shows." (November 14, 2008).

Channelinsider.com. "Network Solutions Suffers Large Data Breach." (July 24, 2009).

Computer Security Institute. "CSI Survey 2008." (2008).

CTIA. "CTIA-The Wireless Association Announces Semi-Annual Wireless Industry Survey Results." (April 1, 2009).

Cybersource, Inc. "Online Fraud Report-2009 Edition." (2009).

Dash, Eric. "Data Breach Could Affect Millions of TJX Shoppers." *New York Times* (January 19, 2007).

Davies, Shaun. "Japan's Wallet Phone Explosion." News.ninemsn.com.au (March 4, 2009).

Denning, Dorothy E., and William E. Baugh. "Hiding Crimes in Cyberspace." *Information, Communication, and Society* Vol. 2, No. 3 (Autumn 1999).

Electronic Privacy Information Center (EPIC). "Cryptography and Liberty 2000. An International Survey of Encryption Policy." Washington D. C. (2000).

Ellison, Carl, and Bruce Schneier. "Ten Risks of PKI: What You're Not Being Told About Public Key Infrastructure." *Computer Security Journal*, Vol. XVI, No. 1 (Winter 2000).

eMarketer, Inc. "M-Commerce Ringing Up (Some) Sales." (June 10, 2009).

Federal Bureau Investigation. "Over 1 Million Potential Victims of Botnet CyberCrime." (June 13, 2007).

Fiserv, Inc. "Fiserv Survey Shows Online Banking Growing, Now Used by Four out of Five Online Households." (July 14, 2009).

Fiserv, Inc. "2007 Consumer Bills Payment Trends Survey: Volume of Electronic Payments." (2007).

Forrester Research, Inc. (Edward Kountz) "US Electronic Bill Payment and Presentment Forecast, 2009 to 2014." (June 15, 2009).

Forrester Research. "State of Enterprise IT Security: 2008-2009." (December 24, 2008).

Gaudin, Sharon. "Three Indicted for Hack Attacks on Heartland, Hannaford." *Computerworld* (August 17, 2009).

Javelin Strategy & Reseach. "2009 Identity Fraud Survey Report." (February 9, 2009).

Javelin Strategy & Research "Online Retail Payments Forecast." (November 10, 2008).

Keizer, Gregg. "Mac, Windows Clipboards Poisoned by URL Attacks." Computerworld.com (August 19, 2008).

Keizer, Gregg. "Monster.com Identity Attack May Claim More Victims." InfoWorld (August 20, 2007).

Kerner, Sean Michael. "Researchers: Conficker Still a Threat." Internetnews.com (July 31, 2009).

MacKie-Mason, K. Jeffrey and Kimberly White. "Evaluating and Selecting Digital Payment Mechansims." Selected Papers from the 1996 Telecommunications Policy Research Conference, Lawrence Erlbaum Associates, Inc, 1996.

Markoff, John. "VeriSign Moves to Address an Internet Security Problem." *New York Times* (February 8, 2007).

Microsoft, Inc. (Malware Protection Center). "Protecting Our Customers from Half a Million New Unique Malicious Files Every Day." (April 30, 2009).

Mullenweg, Matt. "Percentage of Splogs." http://ma.tt/2008/03/percentage-of-splogs (March 3, 2008).

National White Collar Crime Center and the Federal Bureau of Investigation. "Internet Crime Complaint Center 2008 Internet Crime Report." (2009).

Peretti, Kimberly. "Data Breaches: What the Underground World of 'Carding' Reveals," *Santa Clara Computer and High Technology Journal*, Vol. 25 (2008).

Ponemon Institute. "Study on the Uncertainty of Data Breach Detection: Report of IT Practitioners in the United States, UK, France and Germany." (June 2008).

Schwartz, John. "Fighting Crime Online: Who is in Harm's Way?" *New York Times* (February 8, 2001).

Shields, Mike. "Mobile Shopping Poised for Growth." *Adweek* (May 27, 2009).

Steel, Emily. "Web Ad Sales Open Doors to Viruses." *Wall Street Journal* (June 15, 2009).

Stein, Lincoln D. *Web Security: A Step-by-Step Reference Guide.* Reading, MA: Addison-Wesley (1998).

Symantec, Inc. "Internet Security Threat Report Volume XIV: April 2009." (April 2009).

Symantec, Inc. ""Report on the Underground Economy: July 07-June 08." (November 2008).

Symantec, Inc. "Symantec Internet Security Threat Report. Trends for January 2007-June 2007." Volume XII (September 2007).

United States Government Accountability Office. "Critical Infrastructure Protection: Department of Homeland Security Faces Challenges in Fulfilling Cybersecurity Responsibilities." (May 2005).

US-CERT. "Cyber Security Bulletin SB09-236, Vulnerability Summary for the Week of August 17, 2009." (August 2009).

Vijayan, Jaikumar. "Canadian Probe Finds TJX Breach Followed Wireless Hack." *Computerworld* (September 25, 2007).

CHAPTER 6

Adomavicius, Gediminas, and Alexander Tuzhilin. "Expert-Driven Validation of Rule-Based User Models in Personalization Applications." *Data Mining and Knowledge Discovery* (January 2001a).

Adomavicius, Gediminas, and Alexander Tuzhilin. "Using Data Mining Methods to Build Customer Profiles." *IEEE Computer* (February 2001b).

Ailawadi, K.L.; D.R. Lehmann; and S.A. Neslin. "Revenue Premium as an Outcome Measure of Brand Equity." *Journal of Marketing* (October 2003).

Akerlof, G. "The Market for 'Lemons' Quality Under Uncertainty and the Market Mechanism." *Quarterly Journal of Economics* (August 1970).

Awad, Neveen; Michael Smith, and Mayuram Krishnan. "The Consumer Online Purchase Decision: A Model of Consideration Set Formation and Buyer Conversion Rate Across Market Leaders and Market Followers." Working Paper Series, SSRN (September 2007).

Ba, Sulin, and Paul Pavlou. "Evidence on the Effect of Trust Building Technology in Electronic Markets: Price Premiums and Buyer Behavior." *MIS Quarterly* (September 2002).

Bailey, J., and Erik Brynjolfsson. "An Exploratory Study of the Emerging Role of Electronic Intermediaries." *International Journal of Electronic Commerce* (Spring, 1997).

Bakos, J. Y., and Erik Brynjolfsson. "Bundling and Competition on the Internet: Aggregation Strategies for Information Goods." *Marketing Science* (January 2000).

Baye, Michael R.; John Morgan; and Patrick Scholten. "Price Dispersion in the Small and in the Large: Evidence from an Internet Price Comparison Site." Nash-equilibrium. com, (August 2002a).

Baye, Michael R.; John Morgan; and Patrick Scholten. "The Value of Information in an Online Consumer Market." *Journal of Public Policy and Marketing* (August 2002b).

Bell, David R. and Sangyoung Song. "Social Contagion and Trial on the Internet: Evidence from Online Grocery Retailing." Unpublished paper. The Wharton School, University of Pennsylvania (May 12, 2004).

Berg, Julie, John Matthews, and Constance O'Hare, "Measuring Brand Health to Improve Top Line

Performance." (Fall 2007).

BIGresearch and Retail Advertising and Marketing Association. "Simultaneous Media Usage Study." (March 14, 2008).

Briggs, Bill. "Who Puts the "E" in E-commerce." *Internet Retailer* (August 2009).

Brynjolfsson, Erik, and M. D. Smith. "Frictionless Commerce? A Comparison of Internet and Conventional Retailer." *Management Science* (April 2000).

Brynjolfsson, Erik; Michael D. Smith; and Yu Hu. "Consumer Surplus in the Digital Economy: Estimating the Value of Increased Product Variety at Online Booksellers." Working Paper, *Information, Operations, and Management Sciences Research Seminar Series*, Stern School of Business (April 17, 2003).

Carpenter, Phil. *eBrands: Building an Internet Business at Breakneck Speed.* Cambridge MA: Harvard Business School Press (2000).

Chan, P. K. "A Non-Invasive Learning Approach to Building Web User Profiles." In *Proceedings of ACM SIGKDD International Conference* (1999).

Clay, K.; K. Ramayya; and E. Wolff. "Retail Strategies on the Web: Price and Non-Price Competition in the On Line Book Industry." Working Paper, *MIT E-commerce Forum* (1999).

Compaq, Inc. "Compaq White Paper." Compaq.com (November 1998).

Corritore, C.L., B. Kracher, S. Wiedenbeck, "On-line trust: concepts, evolving themes, a model," *International Journal of Human-Computer Studies* (2006).

Cross, Robert. "Launching the Revenue Rocket: How Revenue Management Can Work For Your Business." *Cornell Hotel and Restaurant Administration Quarterly* (April 1997).

Darlin, Damon. "Using Free to Turn a Profit." *New York Times* (August 29. 2009).

Datran Media. "Annual Marketing Survey 2009." (January 2009).

Doolin, Bill; Stuart Dillion, and Fiona Thompson. "Perceived Risk, the Internet Shopping Experience, and Online Purchasing Behvaior." In Annie Becker (editor), Electronic Commerce: Concepts, Methodologies, Tools and Applications. Information Science Reference (2007).

Ellison, Sarah. "Web-Brand Study Says Awareness Isn't Trust." *Wall Street Journal* (June 7, 2000).

eMarketer, Inc. (Lisa E. Phillips). "US Internet Users." (February 2009a).

eMarketer, Inc. (Jeffrey Grau). "Retail E-commerce Forecast: Cautious Optimism." (June 2009b).

eMarketer, Inc. (Paul Verna). "The Blogosphere: A-Twitter with Activity." (April 2009c).

eMarketer, Inc. (Debra A. Williamson). "Social Network Ad Spending: A Brighter Outlook Next Year." (July 2009d).

eMarketer, Inc. "TV, Web Vie for Viewer Attention." (March 5, 2008a).

eMarketer, Inc. (Jeffrey Grau). "US Retail ECommerce." (May 2008b).

eMarketer, Inc. "Media that Influence Online Searchers by US Adult Internet Users, by Age, December 2007." (May 14, 2008c).

eMarketer, Inc. "US Internet Users Who Know How to Delete Cookies Effectively, 2005-2008." (August 7, 2008d).

eMarketer, Inc. "Word-of-Mouth Marketing and the Influence Economy." (October 13, 2008e).

eMarketer, Inc. (Paul Verna). "The Blogosphere: A Mass Movement from Grass Roots." (May 2008f).

eMarketer, Inc. "US Country Overview." (October 2007a).

eMarketer, Inc. (Jeffrey Grau). "US Retail ECommerce: Entering the MultiChannel Era." (May 2007b).

eMarketer, Inc., "Average Number of First-Party and Third-Party Cookies Preserved vs. Reset on US Household Internet Computers." (June 2007c).

Evans, P., and T. S. Wurster. "Getting Real About Virtual Commerce." *Harvard Business Review* (November-December 1999).

Fawcett, Tom, and Foster Provost. "Adaptive Fraud Detection." *Data Mining and Knowledge Discovery* (1997).

Fawcett, Tom, and Foster Provost. "Combining Data Mining and Machine Learning for Effective User Profiling." In *Proceedings of the Second International Conference on Knowledge Discovery and Data Mining* (1996).

Feldwick, Paul. "What Is Brand Equity Anyway, and How Do You Measure It?" *Journal of the Market Research Society* (April 1996).

Forrester Research, Inc. "Designing Transactive Content." (February 1998).

Forrester Research, Inc. "Transactive Content." (October 1997).

Godin, Seth. *Permission Marketing.* New York: Simon & Schuster (1999).

Golder, Peter. "What History Teaches Us About the Endurance of Brands." *Stern Business* (Fall 2000).

Gulati, Ranjay, and Jason Garino. "Getting the Right Mix of Bricks and Clicks." *Harvard Business Review* (May-June 2000).

Giuliani, John. "Dotomis Riding Personalized Media Beyond Behavioral Targeting." AdExchanger.com (September 15, 2009).

Humphreys, Jeffrey M. "The Multicultural Economy 2008." Terry College of Business, University of Georgia (January 2009).

Insight Express. "Study Finds Online Population Increasingly Values Cookies." (August 7, 2008).

Interbrand. "Best Global Brands: 2009 Rankings." (September 2009).

Internet Retailer. "E-retailers Face Tough Challenges in Wooing Store Shoppers, New Study Says." (July 13, 2006).

Internet Retailer. "Top 500 Guide 2009 Edition." (2009a).

Internet Retailer. "Website Design, Content, and Rich Media." (January 2009b)

Kim, D. and I. Benbasat. "The Effects of Trust-Assuring Arguments on Consumer Trust in Internet Stores," *Information Systems Research* (2006).

Kim, D. and I. Benbasat. "Designs for Effective Implementation of Trust Assurances in Internet Stores," *Communications of the ACM* (July 2007).

Kotler, Philip, and Gary Armstrong. *Principles of Marketing, 13th Edition*. Upper Saddle River, NJ: Prentice Hall (2009).

Kraemer, Kenneth L.; Jason Dedrick; and Sandra Yamashiro. "Refining and Extending the Business Model With Information Technology: Dell Computer Corporation." *The Information Society* (January-March 2000).

Leiter, Daniel B. and Thierry Warin. "An Empirical Study of Price Disperson in Homogeneous Goods Markets." Middlebury College Economics Discussion Paper No. 07-10. 2007

Lohse, L. G., G. Bellman, and E. J. Johnson. "Consumer Buying Behavior on the Internet: Findings from Panel Data." *Journal of Interactive Marketing* (Winter 2000).

Mishra, D. P., J. B. Heide, and S. G. Cort. "Information Asymmetry and Levels of Agency Relationships." *Journal of Marketing Research.* (1998).

Mobasher, Bamshad. "Data Mining for Web Personalization." Center for Web Intelligence, School of Computer Science, Telecommunication, and Information Systems, DePaul University, Chicago, Illinois. (2007).

Nash-equilibrium.com. "Relative Dispersion." (September 9, 2009).

Nie, Norman, and Lutz Erbring. "Internet and Society: A Preliminary Report." *Stanford Institute for the Quantitative Study of Society* (February 17, 2000).

Opinion Research Corporation. "Online Consumer Product Reviews Have Big Influence." Opinion Research Corporation (April 16, 2009).

Pavlou, Paul. "Institution-Based Trust in Interorganizational Exchange Relationships: The Role of Online B2B Marketplaces on Trust Formation." *Journal of Strategic Information Systems* (2002).

Pavlou, Paul A. and Angelika Dimoka. "The Nature and Role of Feedback Text Comments in Online Marketplaces: Implications for Trust Building, Price Premiums, and Seller Differentiation." *Information Systems Research* (August 2006).

Pavlou, P. A. and M. Fygenson (2005). "Understanding and Predicting Electronic Commerce Adoption: An Extension of the Theory of Planned Behavior." *MIS Quarterly* (2005).

Pew Internet & American Life Project. "May-June 2005 Tracking Survey." (August 9, 2005a).

Pew Internet & American Life Project (Amanda Lenhart, Mary Madden and Paul Hitlin). "Teens and Technology." (July 27, 2005b).

Pew Internet & American Life Project (John B. Horrigan). "Home Broadband Adoption 2008." (July 2, 2008).

Pew Internet & American Life Project. "Daily Internet Activities." (July 2009a).

Pew Internet & American Life Project. "Demographics of Internet Users." (July 2009b).

Rayport, J. F., and J. J. Sviokla. "Exploiting the Virtual Value Chain." *Harvard Business Review* (November-December 1995).

Reichheld, Frederick F., and Phil Schefter. "ELoyalty: Your Secret Weapon on the Web." *Harvard Business Review* (July-August 2000).

Rodgers, Zachary. "Measuring Blog Marketing." Clickz.com (January 12, 2005).

Saunders, Peter Lee, and Andrea Chester. "Shyness and the Internet: Social Problem or Panacea?" Division of Psychology, School of Health Sciences, RMIT University, City Campus, Melbourne, Victoria, Australia (2008).

Scholten, Patrick, and S. Adam Smith. "Price Dispersion Then and Now: Evidence from Retail and E-tail Markets." Nash-equilibrium.com. (July 2002).

Shapiro, Carl, and Hal Varian. *Information Rules: A Strategic Guide to the Network Economy*. Cambridge, MA: Harvard Business School Press (1999).

Shapiro, Carl, and Hal Varian. "Versioning: The

Smart Way to Sell Information." *Harvard Business Review* (November-December 1998).

Shklovski, Irina; Sara Kiesler, and Robert Kraut. "The Internet and Social Interaction: A Meta-analysis and Critique of Studies, 1995-2003." Carnegie Mellon University (2004).

Sinha, Indrajit. "Cost Transparency: The Net's Real Threat to Prices and Brands." *Harvard Business Review* (March-April 2000).

Smith, M. D.; J. Bailey; and E. Brynjolfsson. "Understanding Digital Markets: Review and Assessment," in E. Brynjolfsson and B. Kahin (eds.), *Understanding the Digital Economy.* Cambridge, MA: MIT Press (1999).

Starbuck, William, and Paul C. Nystrom. "Why Many Firms Run Into Crises, and Why Some Survive." Working Paper. Stern School of Business, Management and Organizational Behavior (1997).

Sterling Commerce and Deloitte Consulting. "What Consumers Want in Their Shopping Experience." (August 2007).

Surowiecki, James. *The Wisdom of Crowds: Why the Many are Smarter than the Few and How Collective Wisdom Shapes Business, Economies, Societies and Nations.* New York: Doubleday, (2004).

Teece, David J. "Profiting from Technological Innovation: Implications for Integration, Collaboration, Licensing and Public Policy." *Research Policy*, 15 (1986).

US Census Bureau. "Annual Estimates of Resident Population by Sex, Race, and Hispanic Origin for the United States." (May 14, 2009).

U.S.C Annenberg School Center for the Digital Future, "The Digital Future Report, Surveying the Digital Future, Year Four, Ten Years, Ten Trends." (September, 2004).

Van den Poel, Dirk and Wouter Buckinx. "Predicting Online Purchasing Behavior." *European Journal of Operations Research*, Vol. 166, Issue 2 (2005).

von Hippel, Eric. *The Sources of Innovation.* New York: Oxford University Press (1994).

von Hippel, Eric. *Democratizing Innovation.* Cambridge : MIT Press, (2005).

Wigand, R. T., and R. I. Benjamin. "Electronic Commerce: Effects on Electronic Markets." *Journal of Computer Mediated Communication* (December 1995).

Williamson, O. E. *The Economic Institutions of Capitalism.* New York: Free Press (1985).

Wolfinbarger, Mary, and Mary Gilly. "Shopping Online for Freedom, Control and Fun."
California Management Review (Winter 2001).

CHAPTER 7

Anderson, Eric; Erik Brynjolfsson, Yu Hu, and Duncan Simester, "Understanding the Impact of Marketing Actions in Traditional Channels on the Internet: Evidence From a Large Field Experiment." (January 2005).

Battelle, John. "Search Blog." Battellemedia.com/archives/000063.php (November 13, 2003).

Beval Saddlery Ltd. "Products." Beval.com (2008).

Briggs, Rex. "How Internet Advertising Works." ESO-MAR "Net Effects" Conference, London. (February 22, 1999).

Cable & Telecommunications Association for Marketing."Tracking Entertainment and Technology: Consumer Value in Media." June/July Pulse Report (August 4, 2009).

Click Forensics. "Industry Click Fraud Rate Drops to 12.7% in Q2." (July 23, 2009).

comScore. "Google Sites Surpasses 10 Billion Video Views in August." (September 28, 2009).

Consumer Reports WebWatch. "Searching for Disclosure: How Search Engines Alert Consumers to the Presence of Advertising in Search Results." Consumerwebwatch.org (November 2004).

Consumer Reports Web Watch. "Still in Search of Disclosure: Re-evaluating How Search Engines Explain the Presence of Advertising in Search Results." (June 9, 2005).

Davern, Michael J.; Dov Te'eni; and Jae Yun Moon. "Information Environments and Human Behavior Over Time: From Initial Preferences to Mature Usage." Department of Information Systems, Stern School of Business, New York University (2001).

Direct Marketing Association (DMA). "State of the Catalog Industry, 2008 Edition." (August 27, 2008).

Doubleclick. "The Brand Value of Rich Media and Video Ads," Doubleclick (Google), (June 2009a).

Doubleclick. "2008 Year in Review Benchmarks." Doubleclick (Google). (June 2009b).

Dynamic Logic. "Video Ads Achieve Greater Branding Impact With Fewer Impressions." *Beyond the Click: Insights from Marketing Effectiveness Research* (December 2004).

Ellison, Nicole, Charles Steinfeld, and Cliff Lampe. "Spatially Bounded Online Social Networks and Social Capital: The Role of Facebook." Department of Telecommunications, Information Studies, and Media, Michigan State

University. Paper presented at the Annual Conference of the International Communication Association, Dresden, Germany (June 2006).

eMarketer, Inc. (David Hallerman). "US Advertising Spending: The New Reality." (April 2009a).

eMarketer, Inc. "Digital Advertising: Where's the Money?" (August 2009b).

eMarketer, Inc. (Debra A.Williamson). "Social Networks: Five Consumer Trends for 2009." (February 2009c).

eMarketer, Inc. (Debra A. Williamson). Social Network Ad Spending: A Brighter Outlook Next Year." (August 2009d).

eMarketer, Inc. "US Next-Generation Video Game Console Sales, January-June 2009 (units)." (July 16, 2009e).

eMarketer, Inc. (Jeffery Grau). "Multichannel Retailing: A Competitive Differentiator." (July 2009f).

eMarketer, Inc. "The Sad Tale of the Abandoned Cart." (June 30, 2009g).

eMarketer, Inc. "How Much Time People Really Spend with Ads." (August 24, 2009h).

eMarketer, Inc. (David Hallerman). "Ad Spending Trends: The Internet and Other Media." (October 2005).

eMarketer, Inc. (David Hallerman). "US Advertising Spending." (November 2007a).

eMarketer, Inc. (David Hallerman). "E-Mail Marketing." (September 2007b).

eMarketer, Inc. (David Hallerman) "Behavioral Targeting: Marketing Trends." (June 2008a).

eMarketer, Inc. (Paul Verna) "The Blogosphere: Mass Movement From the Grass Roots." (May 2008b).

eMarketer, Inc. "Changing Video Gamer Demographics." (July 25, 2008c).

Epsilon. "Epsilon Q1 2009 U.S. Email Trend Results: Performance Remains Stable in 2009." (July 8, 2009)

E-tailing Group. "8th Annual Merchant Survey." (April 2009).

Eyeblaster. " "Trends of Time and Attention in Online Advertising." (July 22, 2009).

Fair Isaac Corporation. "New Fair Isaac Research Indicates Click Fraud is Potentially Large Problem in Parts of Search Engine Advertising." (May 18, 2007).

Flanigan, Andrew, and Miriam J. Metzger. "The Role of Site Features, User Attributes, and Information Verification Behaviors on the Perceived Credibility of Web-based Information." *New Media & Society*, Vol. 9, No. 2 (2007)

Fogg, B.J., Cathey Soohoo, David Danielson, Leslie Marable, Julliane Stanford, and Ellen Tauber.

"How Do Users Evaluate the Credibility of Web Sites? A Study with Over 2,500 Participants." Proceedings of DUX2003, Designing for User Experiences. (2003).

Hotchkiss, Gord , Tracy Sherman, Rick Tobin, Cory Bates and Krista Brown. "Search Engine Results 2010." Enquiroresearch.com (September, 2007).

Interactive Advertising Bureau. "IAB Standards and Guidelines." Iab.net (September 2008).

Interactive Advertising Bureau (IAB)/PricewaterhouseCoopers. "IAB Internet Advertising Revenue Report 2009 Full Year Results" (March 2009).

Jansen, Bernard, and Amanda Spink. "Investigating Customer Click Through Behavior With Integrated Sponsored and Nonsponsored Results." International Journal of Marketing and Advertising. (Vol. 5, 2009).

Lohse, L. G.; G. Bellman; and E. J. Johnson. "Consumer Buying Behavior on the Internet: Findings from Panel Data." *Journal of Interactive Marketing* (Winter 2000).

National Conference of State Legislatures. "State Laws Relating to Unsolicited Commercial of Bulk E-mail (SPAM)." (September 14, 2008).

Nielsen, Jakob. "F-Shaped Pattern For Reading Web Content, Nielsen's Alertbox." (April 17, 2006).

Novak, T. P.; D. L. Hoffman; and Y. F. Yung. "Measuring the Customer Experience in Online Environments: A Structural Modeling Approach." *Marketing Science* (Winter, 2000).

Pew Internet & American Life Project. "Daily Internet Activities." (July 15, 2009).

Pew Internet & American Life Project (Lee Rainie). "Search Engine Use November 2005." (November 2005).

Shrestha, Sav and Kelsi Lenz. "EyeGaze Patterns while Searching vs. Browsing a Website." Software Usability Research Laboratory, Department of Psychology, Wichita State University, Wichita, KS 67260-0034 (September, 2007).

Story, Louise. "It's an Ad, Ad, Ad World." *New York Times* (August 6, 2007).

Sullivan, Danny. "FTC Recommends Disclosure to Search Engines." Searchenginewatch.com (February 13, 2003).

Symantec. "Symantec Global Internet Security Threat Report. Trends for 2008." Volume XIV (April 2009).

Symantec Message Labs. "MessageLabs Intelligence: August 2009

"Cutwail Damaged By ISP Shutdown Whilst Donbot Offers Medical Assistance to Billions." (August,

2009).

Tsai, Janice; S. Egelman, L. Cranor, and A. Acquisti. "The Effect of Online Privacy Information on Purchasing Behavior: An Experimental Study." Paper presented at the Workshop on the Economics of Information Security, June 7-8, 2007, Pittsburgh, PA. (June 2007).

Walker, Marlon A. "Online Service Lags at Big Firms." *Wall Street Journal* (July 1, 2004).

Weber, Thomas. "A 'Sticky' Situation: How a Web Buzzword Spun Out of Control." *Wall Street Journal* (March 5, 2001).

CHAPTER 8

Apple Computer, Inc. v. Microsoft Corp. 709 F. Supp. 925, 926 (N. D. Cal. 1989); 799 F. Supp. 1006, 1017 (N. D. Cal., 1992); 35 F. 3d 1435 (9th Cir.); cert. denied, 63 U. S. L. W. 3518 (U.S., Feb. 21, 1995) (No. 94-1121).

Associated Press. "Google Settles Final Piece of Geico Case." BizReport.com (September 8, 2005).

Audi AG and Volkswagen of America, Inc. v. Bob D'Amato No. 05-2359, 6th Circuit (November 27, 2006).

Bernina of America, Inc. v. Fashion Fabrics Int'l., Inc. 2001 U. S. Dist. LEXIS 1211 (N. D. Ill., Feb. 8, 2001).

Brown Bag vs. Symantec Corp., 960 F. 2d 1465 (9th Cir. 1992).

Chiappetta, Vincent. "Defining the Proper Scope of Internet Patents: If We Don't Know Where We Want to Go, We're Unlikely to Get There." *Michigan Telecommunications Technology Law Review* (May 2001).

Clifford, Stephanie. "Web Privacy on the Radar in Congress." *New York Times* (August 10, 2008).

Diamond v. Chakrabarty, 447 US 303 (1980).

Dueker, Kenneth Sutherlin. "Trademark Law Lost in Cyberspace: Trademark Protection for Internet Addresses." *Harvard Journal of Law and Technology* (Summer 1996).

E. & J. Gallo Winery v. Spider Webs Ltd. 129 F. Supp. 2d 1033 (S.D. Tex., 2001) aff'd 286 F. 3d 270 (5th Cir., 2002).

Elgin, Ben and Bruce Einhorn. "The Great Firewall of China." *BusinessWeek* (January 12, 2006).

eMarketer, Inc. "The Controversy Over Personalized Ads." (June 25, 2009).

eMarketer, Inc. "Some Users Distrust Search Engines." (July 23, 2007a)

eMarketer, Inc. "When Bad Ads Harm Good E-commerce." (July 3, 2007b)

eMarketer, Inc. "Online Buyers Will Pay Extra for Privacy." (June 14, 2007c)

Federal Trade Commission. "FTC Staff Revises Online Behavioral Advertising Principles" (February 12, 2009).

Federal Trade Commission. "Privacy Online: Fair Information Practices in the Electronic Marketplace." (May 2000a).

Federal Trade Commission. "Online Profiling: A Report to Congress." (June 2000b).

Federal Trade Commission. "Privacy Online: A Report to Congress." (June 1998).

Federal Trade Commission. "Individual Reference Services: A Report to Congress." (December 1997).

Field v. Google, Inc. 412 F.Supp. 2nd 1106 (D. Nev., 2006).

Fisher, William W. III. "The Growth of Intellectual Property: A History of the Ownership of Ideas in the United States." Law.harvard.edu/Academic_Affairs/coursepages/tfisher/iphistory.html (1999).

Ford Motor Co. v. Lapertosa 2001 U. S. Dist. LEXIS 253 (E. D. Mich. Jan. 3, 2001).

Frackman, Andrews; Claudia Ray, and Rebecca C. Martin. *Internet and Online Privacy: A Legal and Business Guide.* ALM Publishing (2002).

Google, Inc. v. American Blind & Wallpaper Factory, Inc. Case No. 03-5340 JF (RS) (N.D. Cal., April 18, 2007).

Government Employees Insurance Company v. Google, Inc. Civ. Action No. 1:04cv507 (E.D. VA, December 15, 2004).

Greenhouse, Linda. "20 Year Extension of Existing Copyrights Is Upheld." *New York Times* (January 16, 2003a).

Greenhouse, Linda. "Justices Back Law to Make Libraries Use Internet Filters." *New York Times* (June 24, 2003b).

Greenhouse, Linda. "Supreme Court Upholds Child Pornography Law." *New York Times* (May 20, 2008).

Gross, Grant. "House Panel Votes to Extend Net Tax Ban." *InfoWorld* (October 11, 2007).

Hafner, Katie and Matt Richtel. "Google Resists U.S. Subpoena of Search Data." *New York Times* (January 20, 2006).

Hansell, Saul and Eric Lichtblau. "U.S. Wants Internet Companies to Keep Web-Surfing Records." *New York Times* (June 2006).

Harmon, Amy. "Pondering Value of Copyright vs. Innovation." *New York Times* (March 3, 2003).

Ho, Victoria. "China Accused of Rerouting Search Traffic to Baidu." CNETNews.com (October 22, 2007).

Hoofnagle, Chris Jay. "Privacy Self-Regulation: A Decade of Disappointment." Electronic Privacy Information Center (Epic.org) (March 4, 2005).

Kelly v. ArribaSoft. 336 F3rd 811 (CA 9th, 2003).

Laudon, Kenneth. "Markets and Privacy." *Communications of the ACM* (September 1996).

Liedtke, Michael. "Microsoft, Yahoo Tweak Privacy Policies." *USA Today* (July 23, 2007).

MarkMonitor. "MarkMonitor Year-in-Review Report Finds Online Abuse of Major Brands Was a Growth Industry for Fraudsters in 2008." (March 9, 2009).

Markoff, John. "Control the Internet? A Futile Pursuit, Some Say." *New York Times* (November 14, 2005).

McMillan, Robert. "Porn Typosquatter Fined Again by FTC." *InfoWorld* (October 16, 2007).

Miller, John W. and Christopher Rhoads, "U.S. Fights to Keep Control Of Global Internet Oversight." *Wall Street Journal* (November 16, 2005).

Moore, Matt. "ICANN Rejects Creation of ".XXX" Domain." *USA Today* (March 30, 2007).

Nakashima, Ellen. "NebuAd Halts Plans for Web Tracking." *Washington Post* (September 4, 2008).

Nash, David B. "Orderly Expansion of the International Top-Level Domains: Concurrent Trademark Users Need a Way Out of the Internet Trademark Quagmire." *The John Marshall Journal of Computer and Information Law* Vol. 15, No. 3 (1997).

Nettis Environment Ltd. v. IWI, Inc. 46 F. Supp. 2d 722 (N. D. Ohio 1999).

Network Advertising Initiative. "Participating Networks." (September 2009a).

Network Advertising Initiative. "Highlights from the Federal Trade Commission Staff Report for Online Behavioral Advertising." (February 17, 2009b)

New York Times. "Bailouts Gone Wild. Porn Chiefs Seek $5 Billion." (January 7, 2009).

Nissan Motor Co., Ltd. v. Nissan Computer Corp. 289 F. Supp. 2d 1154 (C. D. Cal.), aff'd, 2000 U. S. App. LEXIS 33937 (9th Cir. Dec. 26, 2000).

PaineWebber Inc. v. Fortuny, Civ. A. No. 99-0456-A (E. D. Va. Apr. 9, 1999).

Perfect 10, Inc. v. Amazon.com, Inc. 487 F3rd 701 (CA 9th, 2007).

Pew Internet & American Life Project. "Daily Internet Activities." (July 15, 2009).

Playboy Enterprises, Inc. v. Global Site Designs, Inc. 1999 WL 311707 (S. D. Fla. May 15, 1999).

Playboy Enterprises, Inc. v. Netscape Communications, Inc. 354 F. 3rd 1020 (9th Cir., 2004).

Reuters. "U.S. Internet Gambling Laws Breach WTO Rules: EU." (March 26, 2009).

Sharma, Amol, and Don Clark. "Tech Guru Riles the Industry By Seeking Huge Patent Fees." *Wall Street Journal* (September 17, 2008).

State Street Bank & Trust Co. v. Signature Financial Group, 149 F. 3d 1368 (1998).

Story, Louise. "F.T.C. Member Vows Tighter Controls of Online Ads." *New York Times* (November 2, 2007).

Takenaka, Toshiko. "International and Comparative Law Perspective on Internet Patents." *Michigan Telecommunications Technology Law Review* (May 15, 2001).

Thurm, Scott. "The Ultimate Weapon: It's the Patent." Wall Street Journal (April 17, 2000a).

Ticketmaster v. Tickets.com. 2000 U.S. Dist. Lexis 4553 (C.D. Cal., August 2000).

United States Copyright Office. "Digital Millennium Copyright Act of 1998: U.S. Copyright Office Summary." (December 1998).

United States Department of Health, Education and Welfare (US-DHEW). Records, Computers and Rights of Citizens. Cambridge, MA: MIT Press (1973).

United States Patent and Trademark Office. "Class 705 Application Filing and Patents Issued Data." (January 2009).

Van Kirk, Andrew. "Platform for Privacy Preferences (P3P): Privacy Without Teeth." (March 10, 2005).

Varian, Hal, "Forget Taxing Internet Sales. In Fact, Just Forget Sales Taxes Altogether." *New York Times* (March 8, 2001).

CHAPTER 9

Amazon.com, Inc. Amazon.com Inc. Form 10-K for the fiscal year ended December 31, 2008, filed with the Securities and Exchange Commission (January 30, 2009).

Brown, Jeffrey, and Austan Goolsbee. "Does the Internet Make Markets More Competitive? Evidence from the Life Insurance Industry." John F. Kennedy School of Government, Harvard University. Research Working Paper RWP00-007 (2000).

Brynjolfsson, Erik; Astrid Andrea Dick and Michael D. Smith. "Search and Product Differentiation at an Internet Shopbot," Center for eBusiness@MIT (December, 2004).

California Association of Realtors. "2008 Survey of California Home Buyers." (September 11, 2008).

Center for Realtor Technology, National Association of Realtors. "2007 Technology Survey." (2007).

Computer Associates. "2008 Security and Privacy

Survey." (July 2008).

comScore,. "comScore State of Online Banking." (April 21, 2009a).]

comScore "U.S. Auto Insurance Policies Purchased Online Up 7 Percent In 2008 Versus Year Ago Despite Soft Consumer Demand." (April 2, 2009b).

comScore. "comScore Media Metrix Ranks Top 50 U.S. Web Properties for June 2009." (July 21, 2009c.)

Curran, Kelly. "Originations Could Fall Below $1.3 Trillion in 2009." Housingwire.com (November 20, 2008).

Dell Inc. Form 10-K for the fiscal year ended January 30, 2009, filed with the Securities and Exchange Commission (March 26, 2009).

eMarketer, Inc. (Jeffrey Grau). "Retail E-commerce Forecast: Cautious Optimism." (June 2009a).

eMarketer, Inc. "Frequency With Which US Internet Users Perform Financial Transactions Online." (April 27, 2009b).

eMarketer, Inc. "US Online Leisure/Unmanaged Business Travel Sales, 2008-2013 (billions and % change). (June 15, 2009c)

eMarketer, Inc. "US Online Leisure Travel Sales, by Sector, 2008-2012 (billions)." (January 20, 2009d).

eMarketer, Inc. "Recruiters Find Prospects on Social Nets." (June 26, 2009e).

eMarketer, Inc. "Bank Marketing Online." (June 2008a).

eMarketer, Inc. "Majority of 2007 Travel Booked Online." (January 15, 2008b).

eMarketer, Inc. (Jeffrey Grau). "U.S. Online Travel: The Threat of Commoditization." (April 2007).

eMarketer, Inc. (Jeffrey Grau). "Career Planning and Job Hunting Online." (December 2006).

eMarketer, Inc. (Jeffrey Grau). "E-commerce in the US: Retail Trends." (May 2005a).

eMarketer, Inc. (Jeffrey Grau). "Online Travel Worldwide." (December 2005b).

Evans, Philip, and Thomas S. Wurster. *Blown to Bits: How the New Economics of Information Transforms Strategy.* Cambridge, MA: Harvard Business School Press (2000).

Finkelstein, Alex. "No Big Surprise: Residential Agents' Total Commissions Down by $12B." (March 11, 2009).

Fiserv. "Fiserv Survey Shows Online Banking Growing, Now Used by Four of Five Online Households." (July 14, 2009).

Forrester Research, Inc. "The State of Retailing Online 2008" (April 2008).

Hitwise. "Top 20 Banking Websites." (October 2009).

Hough, Jack. "Should You Hurry to Buy Life Insurance." SmartMoney (September 18, 2009).

Internet Retailer. "Top 500 Guide 2009 Edition." (2009).

JC Penney Company, Inc. Report on Form 10-K for the fiscal year ended January 31, 2009 filed with the Securities and Exchange Commission (March 31, 2009).

Joyce, Susan P. "Top 50+ Employers Recruiting on Twitter." Job-hunt.org *June 9, 2009).

Lands' End, Inc. "About Lands' End." Landsend.com (2009).

Laudon, Kenneth C., and Jane P. Laudon. *Management Information Systems: Managing the Digital Firm, 11th edition.* Upper Saddle River, NJ: Prentice Hall (2009).

LinkedIn.com. "LinkedIn Launches New Tools to Boost HR Professionals' Efficiency as Responses to Job Posting Double in Challenging Economy." (February 2, 2009).

MarketingCharts.com. "Top 10 Online Trading Sites - July 2009." (July 2009).

Microsoft. "Automakers Should Turn to Technology to Target Millennials, Reports New Microsoft Survey." (January 26, 2009).

Nielsen/NetRatings NetView. "Top 10 Online Trading Destinations - July 2009." (July 2009)

Perkins, Broderick. "Online Mortgage Shopping Today." *Realty Times* (January 23, 2004).

Pew Internet & American Life Project. "Daily Internet Activities." (July 15, 2009a).

Pew Internet & American Life Project. "Generations Online in 2009 Charts." (January 28, 2009b).

Reuters. "Number of U.S. Online Banking Customers Continues to Grow Despite Challenging Financial Times." (April 21, 2009).

U. S. Census Bureau. "Census of Service Industries." (2001).

U.S. Census Bureau. *Statistical Abstract of the United States 2009* (2009).

U.S. Department of Commerce. "E-Stats, 2007 E-commerce Multi-sector Report." (May 28, 2009).

U.S. Department of Labor. Dictionary of Occupational Titles, 4th edition. (1991).

University of Southern California Annenberg School Center for the Digital Future "2009 Digital Future Report." (April 28, 2009).

CHAPTER 10

American Association of Publishers. "Industry Statistics." (March 31, 2009).

Audio4cast. "Internet Radio Audience 2009." Audio4cast.com (April 2009).

Bivings Group. "The Use of the Internet by America's Largest Newspapers." (December 18, 2008).

Book Industry Study Group. "What We Do: ONIX for Books: Downloads andLists." Bisg.org (2009).

Bookseller.com "US Book Sales Could Hit$100M in 2009." (February 2009).

Boxer, Sarah. "Paintings Too Perfect? The Great Optics Debate." *New York Times* (December 4, 2001).

Brand, Stuart. "The First Hackers conference in 1984." Transcript in *The Media Lab: Inventing the Future at MIT*, Viking Penguin, (1987).

comScore. "Coogle Sites Surpasses 10 Billion Views in August." (September 28, 2009).

comScore. "YouTube Draws 5 Billion U.S. Online Video Views in July 2008." (September 10, 2008).

Editeur.org. "ONIX for Books."(2009).

eMarketer, Inc. (Paul Verna). "Video Content: A Premium Opportunity." (August 2009a).

eMarketer, Inc. (Paul Verna) "User-Generated Content: More Popular than Profitable." (January 2009b).

eMarketer, Inc. Newspapers in Crisis (Carol Krol). (January 2009c).

eMarketer, Inc. "Top 10 Online Newspapers in the US, Ranked by Unique Visitors, December 2007 & December 2008 (thousands and % change) (January 26, 2009d).

eMarketer, Inc. (Paul Verna) "Digital Entertainment Meets Social Media." (June 2009e)

eMarketer, Inc. "US E-Book Sales." (April 2008)

Emigh, Jacqueline. "Analysts: Consumers Drop TV, Turn to Internet for Entertainment." Betanews.com (November 25, 2009).

Frank N. Magid Associates. "Magid Media Futures 2009." (June 2009).

Jaworowski, Ken. "Words Printed on Pages Still Sell Well." *New York Times* (April 15, 2006).

Mobipocket.com. "Mobipocket Creator 4.2." (September 2009).

Newspaper Association of America. "Trends and Numbers." (September 2009).

Nielsen Net Ratings. "Web Traffic to Top 10 Online Newspapers." (January 2009).

Online Publishers Association. "Consumers are Spending the Lionshare of their Time Online with Content." (September 17, 2009).

Pew Internet & American Life Project. "Daily Internet Activities." (July 12, 2009)

Pew Internet & American Life Project (John B. Horrigan). "The Internet as a Resource for News and Information About Science." (November 20, 2006).

(Rosenthal, Morris. "How Many Kindle eBooks are Selling Based on Amazon Sales Ranking." Fonerbooks.com (2009).

U.S. Census Bureau. *Statistical Abstract of the United States 2009* (2009).

Veronis Suhler Stevenson. "Communications Industry Forecast, 2009-2013." (August 3, 2009).

Weil, Jonathon. "Securities Rules Help to Close the Earning Reports GAAP." *Wall Street Journal* (April 24, 2003).

Yodlee, Inc. "Yodlee Meets Growing Demand for Online Financial Services." (August 18, 2009).

Washington Post, The, et al. v. TotalNews, Inc., et al. S.D.N.Y, Civil Action Number 97-1190. (February 1997).

Winston, Brian. *Media Technology and Society: A History From the Telegraph to the Internet.* Routledge (1998).

Worthen, Ben. "Red Light Sites Give Green Light to IT Innovation." ITBusiness.ca (August 13, 2009).

W3C Platform for Privacy Preferences Initiative." P3P 1. 0: A New Standard in Online Privacy." Platform for Privacy Preferences Initiative. (June 16, 2003).

Zeller, Tom, Jr. "Your Life As An Open Book." *New York Times* (August 12, 2006).

CHAPTER 11

Arkes, H. R., and L. Hutzel. "The Role of Probability of Success Estimates in the Sunk Cost Effect." *Journal of Behavioral Decisionmaking* (2000).

Bailey, Brian P.; Laura J. Gurak; and Joseph Konstan, "Do You Trust Me? An Examination of Trust in Computer-Mediated Exchange," In *Human Factors and Web Development, 2nd Edition.* Mahwah, NJ: Lawrence Erlbaum (2002).

Bapna, Ravi; Paulo Goes; and Alok Gupta. "Insights and Analyses of Online Auctions." *Communications of the ACM* (November 2001).

Brynjolfsson, Erik, and Michael Smith. "Frictionless Commerce? A Comparison of Internet and Conventional Retailers." *Management Science* (April 2000).

comScore. "comScore Media Metrix Ranks Top 50 U.S. Web Properties for August 2009." (September 21, 2009).

Dholakia, Utpal, and Kerry Soltysinski. "Coveted or Overlooked? The Psychology of Bidding for Comparable Listings in Digital Auctions." *Marketing Letters* (2001).

eBay, Inc. Report on Form 10-K for the fiscal year ended December 31, 2008, filed with the Securities and Exchange Commission (February

20, 2009).

eMarketer, Inc. (Debra A. Williamson), "Social Networks: Five Consumer Trends for 2009." (February 2009a).

eMarketer, Inc. "US Twitter Usage Surpasses Earlier Estimates." (September 14, 2009b).

eMarketer, 2009 (Debra A. Williamson). "Social Network Ad Spending: A Brighter Outlook Next Year." (July 2009c).

eMarketer, Inc. "Demographics of Facebook Growth." (September 17, 2009d).

eMarketer, Inc. (David Hallerman). "US Advertising Spending-the New Reality." (April 2009e)

eMarketer, Inc. "Top 25 Web Properties Among US Internet Users, August 2009 (millions)." [September 22, 2009f).

Facebook. "Statistics." (September 29, 2009).

Federal Trade Commission. "FTC Releases List of Top Consumer Complaints in 2008." (February 26, 2009).

Hafner, Katie. "The Epic Saga of The Well: The World's Most Influential Online Community (and It's Not AOL)." *Wired* (May 1997).

Hagel, John III, and Arthur G. Armstrong. *Net Gain: Expanding Markets Through Virtual Communities.* Cambridge, MA: Harvard Business School Press (1997).

Hanson, Ward, and D. S. Putler. "Hits and Misses: Herd Behavior and Online Product Popularity." *Marketing Letters* (1996).

Hillery, George A. "Definitions of Community: Areas of Agreement." *Rural Sociology* (1955).

Hiltzik, Michael. *Dealers of Lightning: Xerox PARC and the Dawn of the Computer Age.* New York: Harper Collins (1999).

InsideFacebook,com "comScore: Facebook Passed MySpace in the US for the First Time in May." (June 15, 2009a).

InsideFacebook.com. "Social Networks More Than 20 percent of Online Ad Impressions." (September 2, 2009).

Kambil, Ajit, and Eric van Heck. "Competition in the Dutch Flower Market." New York University, Stern School of Business, Center for Information Systems Research (1996).

Kiesler, Sara. "The Hidden Messages in Computer Networks." *Harvard Business Review* (January-February 1986).

Kiesler, Sara; Jane Siegel; and Timothy W. McGuire. "Social Psychological Aspects of Computer-Mediated Communication." *American Psychologist* (October 1984).

Kollock, Peter. "The Production of Trust in Online Markets" In *Advances in Group Processes* (Vol 16) edited by E. J. Lawler, M. Macy, S. Thyne and H. A. Walker. Greenwich, CT: JAI Press (1999).

Krishnamurthy, Sandeep. "An Empirical Study of the Causal Antecedents of Customer Confidence in ETailers." *First Monday* (January 2001).

Laudon, Kenneth C. and Jane P. Laudon. *Management Information Systems: Managing the Digital Firm.* 11th edition. Upper Saddle River, NJ, Prentice Hall (2009).

Lee, H. G.; J. C. Westland; and S. Hong. "The Impact of Electronic Marketplaces on Product Prices: An Empirical Study of Aucnet." *International Journal of Electronic Commerce* (Winter 1999-2000).

McAfee R., and John McMillan. "Auctions and Bidding." *Journal of Economic Literature* (June 1987).

Milogram, Paul R. "Auctions and Bidding: A Primer." *Journal of Economic Perspectives* (Summer 1989).

National White Collar Crime Center and the Federal Bureau of Investigation. "Internet Crime Complaint Center 2008 Internet Crime Report." (2009).

Nikander, Pekka, and Kristina Karvonen. "Users and Trust in Cyberspace." In the *Proceedings of Cambridge Security Protocols Workshop 2000*, April 3-5, 2000, Cambridge University (2002).

Parkes, David C., and Lyle Ungar. "Iterative Combinatorial Auctions: Theory and Practice." Proceedings of the 17th National Conference on Artificial Intelligence (AAAI-00) (2000).

Rheingold, Howard. H*osting Web Communities.* New York: John Wiley and Sons (1998). Also see Rheingold.com for more recent articles by Rheingold.

Rheingold, Howard. *The Virtual Community.* Cambridge MA: MIT Press (1993).

Ryan, Sean. "July 2009 Comscore Engagement Stats-Games, Worlds, Dating and Social Dominate the Charts." Sharkjumping.com. (July 8, 2009).

Stanford Persuasive Technology Lab and Makovsky & Company. "Stanford-Makovsky Web Credibility Study 2002." Stanford Persuasive Technology Lab. (Spring 2002).

Vakrat, Yaniv, and Abraham Seidmann. "Can Online Auctions Beat Online Catalogs?" Proceedings of the 20th Conference on Information Systems (December 1999).

Vakrat, Yaniv, and Abraham Seidmann. "Analysis and Design Models for Online Auctions." Proceedings of the 4th Informs Conference on Information Systems and Technology. (May

1998).

Vickrey, William. "Counterspeculation, Auctions and Competitive Sealed Tenders." *Journal of Finance* (March 1961).

CHAPTER 12

ADX Corporation. "Ace Hardware Expands Relationship with ADX for Improved Supply Chain Integration." (January 12, 2004).

Agentrics. "About Agentrics." (September 2009).

Ariba Inc. Ariba.com. "Ariba Customers: Success Stories." (September 2009)

Devine, Dennis A.; Christopher B. Dugan; Mikolaus D. Semaca; and Kevin J. Speicher. "Building Enduring Consortia." *McKinsey Quarterly* (2001).

Exostar LLC. "Exostar at a Glance." (September 2009).

Fuscaldo, Donna. "Building a Market. The Construction Industry Had Little Interest in Online Exchanges. Collaboration Services May Get Better Results." *Wall Street Journal* (April 15, 2002).

Gleason, Karen. "CPFR At Ace Hardware." (2003).

Global Wine & Spirits. "About Us." Globalwinespirts.com (September 2009).

Group Dekko. "About Us." (September 2009).

Hannon, David. "Bring E-Sourcing to a Decentralized Spend." *Purchasing* (May 15, 2003).

Hewlett-Packard. "HP.com Business to Business." Hp.com (September 2009).

IBM. "Group Dekko Harnesses Greater Efficiency Through Server Consolidation." IBM Case Study. Ibm.com (March 25, 2005).

IBM. "Group Dekko Collaborating With Customers on Product Development." IBM Case Study. Ibm.com (June 2003).

Inventory Locator Service LLC. ILSmart.com Home Page (September 2009).

Jupiter Media Metrix. (Jon Gibs, Lead Analyst). "BtoB Supplier Strategies." (May 22, 2001).

Kaplan, Steven, and Mohanbir Sawhney. "E-Hubs: The New B2B Marketplaces." *Harvard Business Review* (May-June 2000).

Kerrigan, Ryan; Eric Roegner; Dennis Swinford; and Craig Zawada. "B2B Basics." *McKinsey Quarterly* (2001).

Kumaran, S. "A Framework-Based Approach to Building Private Trading Exchanges." *IBM Systems Journal* (July 2002).

Laudon, Kenneth C. and Jane P. Laudon. *Management Information Systems: Managing the Digital Firm.* 11th edition. Upper Saddle River, NJ: Prentice Hall (2009).

Laudon, Kenneth C. "The Promise and Potential of Enterprise Systems and Industrial Networks." The Concours Group (2000).

1Sync. "About Us" 1Sync.org (September 2009).

Quadrem. "About Quadrem" (September 2009).

Sodhi, Manmohan S. "2001: A Cyberspace Odyssey." *OR.MS Today* (February 2001).

Synnex Corporation. Form 10-K for the fiscal year ended November 30, 2008, filed with the Securities and Exchange Commission (January 27, 2009).

Turek, Norbert, and Gilbert, Alorie. "Atlas Shoulders The Private Exchange Load." *InfoWeek* (March 26, 2001).

U.S. Census Bureau. *Statistical Abstract of the United States: 2009.* (2009a).

U.S. Census Bureau. "eStats Report 2007 E-commerce Multi-sector Report." Table 7 (May 28, 2009b).

VICS. (Voluntary Interindustry Commerce Standards). "Collaborative Planning, Forecasting, and Replenishment (CPFR)." (May 2004).

Watson, James K., and Joe Fenner. "So Many Choices, So Little Integration." Informationweek.com (October 16, 2000).

Wise, Richard, and Dave Morrison. "Beyond the Exchange: The Future of B2B." *Harvard Business Review* (November-December 2000).

W.W. Grainger. Inc. Form 10-K for the fiscal year ended December 31, 2008, filed with the Securities and Exchange Commission (February 27, 2009).

Index

O

Credits

CHAPTER 1

p. 3, screenshot of Facebook.com © Facebook, Inc., 2009; Facebook® is a trademark of Facebook, Inc; Used with permission; Figure 1.2, reprinted by permission of Harvard Business School Press. From *Blown to Bits: How the New Economics of Information Transforms Strategy*, by Evans, Philip, and Thomas S. Wurster. Cambridge, MA, 2000. Copyright © 2000 by the Harvard Business School Publishing Corporation; all rights reserved; Figure 1.3, from Internet Systems Consortium, 2009; Figure 1.6, © 2009 eMarketer, Inc. Used with permission; Figure 1.7, data provided by PricewaterhouseCoopers/National Venture Capital Association MoneyTree Report, Data: Thomson Financial; Figure 1.8, © 2009 eMarketer, Inc. Used with permission.

CHAPTER 2

Figure 2.1, screenshot of Ancestry.com subscription page, © Ancestry.com, 2009; p. 82, screenshot of Bing.com, Microsoft product screen shot reprinted with permission from Microsoft Corporation; Figure 2.3, courtesy of Apple; Figure 2.4, reprinted by permission of Harvard Business Review. From "Strategy and the Internet" by Michael E. Porter, March 2001. Copyright © 2001 by the Harvard Business School of Publishing Corporation; all rights reserved; p. 109, screenshot of Priceline.com home page © 2009 Priceline.com Inc.

CHAPTER 3

p. 121, screenshot of Wikitude.me © Mobilizy GmbH, 2009; Figure 3.10, © Visualware, Inc., 2007. Used with permission; Figure 3.11, from National Academy Press, © 2000; Figure 3.14, from Internet2.edu, © 2008; Figure 3.17, adapted from Cisco Systems, 2007, Internet2.edu, 2000; p. 188 screenshot of Akamai.com © 2007 Akamai Technologies, Inc.;

CHAPTER 4

p.199, simulator shot reprinted with permission from International Business Machines Corporation, © 2003; ; p. 215, screenshot of NaturallyCurly.com home page © NaturallyCurly.com, Inc. 2009. Used with permission; Figure 4.10, screenshot of WebTrends Analytics 9, © WebTrends, Inc., 2009. Used with permission;

Figure 4.10, screenshot of Google Analytics © Google Inc, 2009; Figure 4.13, from !BM, 2003; Figure 4.16, based on data from Hostway Corporation's survey, Consumers' Pet Peeves about Commercial Web Sites, 2007.

CHAPTER 5

p. 263, screenshot of VisualDDoS, Sandia National Laboratories: Center for Cyber Defenders Program, 2007; Figure 5.1, based on data from Computer Security Institute, 2009; Table 5.1, based on data from the Symantec Internet Security Threat Report © Symantec Corporation, 2009. Used with permission. Figures 5.3 and 5.3, from Communications of the Association for Information Systems, Vol. 4, Article 11, November 2000; Table 5.6, from MacKie-Mason; K. Jeffrey; and Kimberly White: "Evaluating and Selecting Digital Payment Mechanisms," Selected Papers From the 1996 Telecommunications Policy Research Conference, published by Lawrence Erlbaum Associates, Inc.; p. 326, screenshot of PayPal.com home page: These materials have been reproduced with the permission of PayPal, Inc. Copyright © 2009 PayPal, Inc. All rights reserved.

CHAPTER 6

p. 337, screenshot of Netflix.com home page, reproduced by permission of Netflix, Inc., © 2009 Netflix, Inc. All rights reserved. Photograph on Netflix.com home page "Family on couch" © Remy Haynes Photography; Figures 6.1 and 6.7 adapted from Kotler and Armstrong, *Principles of Marketing*, 13e, 2009. Reprinted by permission of Pearson Education, Inc., Upper Saddle River, NJ; Figure 6.2, from Journal of Interactive Marketing, Winter 2000, Lohse, Bellman, Johnson, "Consumer Buying on the Internet: Findings from Panel Data," © Elsevier 2009; Figure 6.5, © 2009 eMarketer, Inc. Used with permission; Figure 6.9, from nash-equilibrium.com; © 2008 by Michael R. Baye, John Morgan and Patrick Sholten. All rights reserved; Figure 6.10, from Azimuth Interactive, Inc., © 2009; Figure 6.13, from Adomavicius, Gediminas, and Alexander Tuzhilin, "Using Data Mining Methods to Build Customer Profiles," IEEE Computer (February 2001b) © IEEE 2001. Used with permission; p. 398, screenshot from VML SEER ™, © VML, 2007. Used with permission; Figure 6.19, reprinted by permission, Bakos and

Brynjolfsson, "Bundling Information Goods: Pricing, Profits, and Efficiency," Management Science, December, 1999. Copyright 1999, the Institute for Operations Research and the Management Sciences (INFORMS), 7240 Parkway Drive, Suite 310, Hanover, MD 21076 USA; p. 413, screenshot of Liquidation.com home page, © 2009 Liquidity Services, Inc; Table 6.1, from Pew Internet & American Life Project. "Daily Internet Activities," (last updated July 15, 2009) http://www.pewinternet.org/Trend-Data/Online-Activities-Daily.aspx, accessed October 5, 2009; Table 6.2, from Pew Internet & American Life Project, "Demographics of Internet Users," (last updated July 15, 2008), http://www.pewinternet.org/Trend-Data/Whos-Online.aspx, accessed October 5, 2009; Table 6.3, from Horrigan, John A. Home Broadband Adoption Report 2008, Pew Internet & American Life Project, July 2, 2008; http://www.pewinternet.org/pdfs/ PIP_Broadband_2008.pdf, accessed September 15, 2009; p. 26.; Table 6.4 © 2007 eMarketer, Inc. Used with permission; Table 6.5 © 2008 eMarketer, Inc. Used with permission.

CHAPTER 7

p. 425, screenshot of Actiontuners.com home page © Action Marketing, 2008. Used with permission; Figure 7.1,© 2009 eMarketer, Inc. Used with permission; Table 7.2 © 2009 eMarketer, Inc. Used with permission; Figure 7.2, from Interactive Advertising Bureau, 2008; Figure 7.5, screenshot of Yahoo! search results reproduced with permission of Yahoo! Inc. ® 2008; Figure 7.6, from page 8, Symantec's MessageLabs Intelligence: August 2009 report, "Cutwail Damaged By ISP Shutdown Medical Assistance to Billions", © Symantec's MessageLabs Intelligence Report, August 2009; Figure 7.7, based on Data from Symantec Internet Security Threat Report © Symantec Corporation, 2009. Used with permission; Figure 7.8, screenshot from Beval.com © 2006 Beval Saddlery, Ltd.; Figure 7.13, from Fogg, B.J., Cathy Soohoo, David Danielson, Leslie Marable, Julianne Stanford, and Ellen Tauber. "How Do Users Evaluate the Creditability of Web Sites? A Study with Over 2,500 Participants." Consumer Reports WebWatch (www.consumerwebwatch.org) and Stanford University Persuasive Technology Lab. Proceedings of DUX2003, Designing for User Experiences (2003).

CHAPTER 8

p. 491, screenshot of Secondlife.com home page, © Linden Lab, 2007; Figure 8.2(A) from www.w3.org/P3P/brochure.html, © 3/16/2003 World Wide Web Consortium (Massachusetts Institute of Technology, European Research Consortium for Informatics and Mathematics, Keio University). All Rights Reserved; p. 558, screenshot of Google Books © Google Inc, 2009.

CHAPTER 9

p. 571, screenshot of Bluenile.com home page © Blue Nile, Inc., 2007. Used with permission; Figures 9.4, 9.5 © 2009 eMarketer, Inc. Used with permission.

CHAPTER 10

p. 649, screenshot of WSJ.com reprinted with permission of Wall Street Journal Online, Copyright © 2009 Dow Jones & Company, Inc. All Rights Reserved Worldwide; Figure 10.7 © 2009 eMarketer, Inc. Used with permission.

CHAPTER 11

p. 717, screenshot of LinkedIn.com © LinkedIn Corporation, 2009. Used with permission; Figure 11.2, © 2009 eMarketer, Inc. Used with permission; Figure 11.4, reprinted by permission, Vakrat, Yaniv, and Abraham Siedmann, "Analysis and Design Models for Online Auctions." *Proceeds of the 4th Informs Conference on Information Systems and Technology, May 1998.* Copyright 1998, the Institute for Operations Research and the Management Sciences (INFORMS), 7240 Parkway Drive, Suite 310, Hanover, MD 21076 USA; p. 758, Screenshot of eBay.com: "These materials have been reproduced with the permission of eBay Inc." © 2009 eBay Inc. All rights reserved.

CHAPTER 12

p. 769, screenshot of VWGroupSupply.com home page, © Volkswagen Aktiengesellschaft, 2009; p. 811, screenshot of Elemica.com home page © Elemica Inc. 2009.